New England

Kim Grant, Andrew Bender, Alex Hershey,
John Spelman, Mara Vorhees

Contents

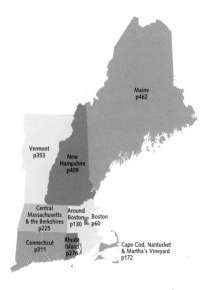

Destination New England

Whether you are an American traveler, or a traveler seeking to understand America, New England's diversity will challenge expectations. By all means, journey with romanticized visions: ivy-covered towers of higher learning bathed in autumn light, prosaic white-clapboard churches on village greens, granite mountain majesty, harsh but compellingly dramatic rocky coastline. Those images won't disappoint. But there are other complexions to these diverse states.

Massachusetts is a powerhouse, with Boston the hub of commerce and culture. America's smallest state, Rhode Island, is enhanced rather than diminished by size, while Connecticut's coastal cities have a cosmopolitan feel thanks to nearby New York City. Vermont has unspoiled peaks and forests, lakes and towns. 'Flatlanders' (non-Vermonters) flock to the Green Mountains to relax outdoors in every season. New Hampshire boasts right-wing, less-government, pro-commerce policies, as well as the nonpartisan majesty of the White Mountain National Forest. And magnificent Maine harbors vast forests and 3500 miles of indented coastline.

Like its European namesake, New England packs a ton of history, culture and character into a small space. From Boston, no point in the six states is more than a day's drive away.

As you plan, include in your mental mise-en-scène the vitality, ethnicity and rich variety of New England. Old mill towns sport fresh faces, and in today's New England the emblematic scents of traditional steamed lobster, cod fish and clam 'chowdah' are augmented with the zest of Puerto Rican and Thai specialties. If you keep your taste buds attuned to today while letting New England's yesteryear simmer in the background, the stew called New England will settle nicely on your palette.

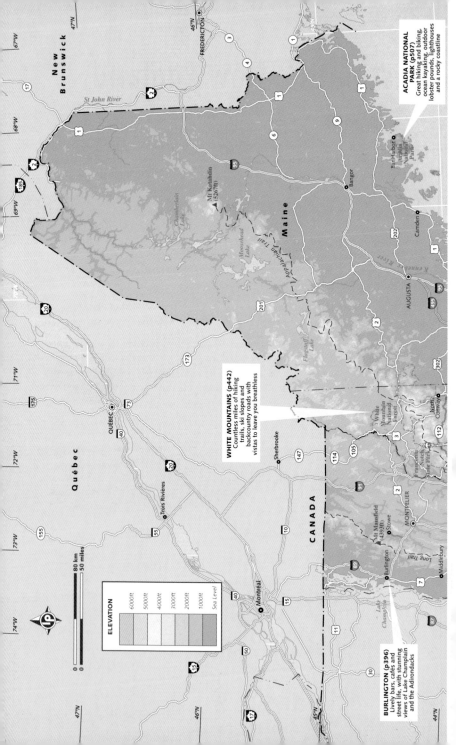

ACADIA NATIONAL PARK (p507)
Great hiking and biking, ocean kayaking, outdoor lobster pounds, lighthouses and a rocky coastline

WHITE MOUNTAINS (p442)
Countless miles of hiking trails, ski slopes and backcountry roads with vistas to leave you breathless

BURLINGTON (p396)
Lively bars, cafés and street life, with stunning views of Lake Champlain and the Adirondacks

ELEVATION

6000ft
5000ft
4000ft
3000ft
2000ft
1000ft
Sea Level

80 km
50 miles

New Brunswick

FREDERICTON

St John River

Québec

CANADA

Maine

Mt Katahdin
(5267ft)

Moosehead Lake

Chamberlain Lake

Appalachian Trail

Bangor

Camden

AUGUSTA

Kennebec River

Flagstaff Lake

White Mountain National Forest

North Conway

Franconia Notch State Park

MONTPELIER

Mt Mansfield
(4393ft)

Stowe

Burlington

Lake Champlain

Long Trail

Middlebury

Sherbrooke

QUÉBEC

Trois Rivières

Montréal

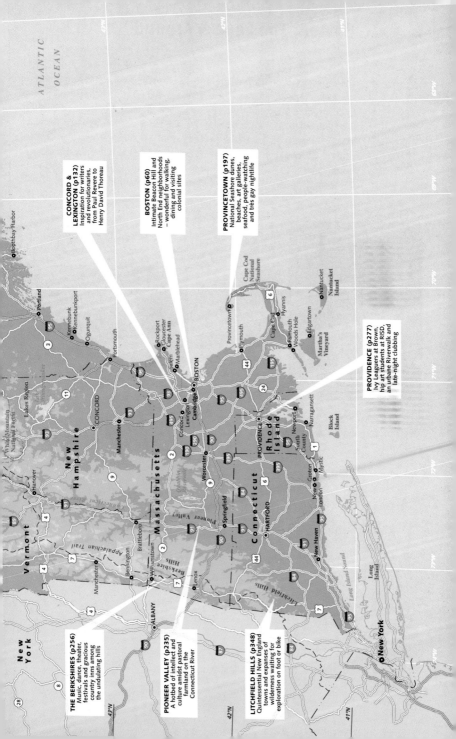

CONCORD & LEXINGTON (p132)
Inspiration for writers and revolutionaries, from Paul Revere to Henry David Thoreau

BOSTON (p60)
Intimate Beacon Hill and North End neighborhoods – wonderful for walking, dining and visiting colonial sites

PROVINCETOWN (p197)
National Seashore dunes, beaches, art galleries, seafood, people-watching and très gay nightlife

PROVIDENCE (p277)
Ivy Leaguers at Brown, hip art students at RISD, an urbane Riverwalk and late-night clubbing

THE BERKSHIRES (p256)
Music, dance, theater, festivals and gracious country inns among the undulating hills

PIONEER VALLEY (p235)
A hotbed of intellect and culture amidst pastoral farmland on the Connecticut River

LITCHFIELD HILLS (p348)
Quintessential New England towns and expanses of wilderness waiting for exploration on foot or bike

Boston, The Cape & Around

The self-proclaimed 'Hub of the Universe,' **Boston** (p60) is the centerpiece of any New England odyssey. Once you've explored the historic **Freedom Trail** (p90), inspired yourself in the city's **museums** (p73) and gastro-hedonized in the **North End** (p79), it's just a hop and a skip to historic **Salem** (p143), **Lexington** (p132), **Concord** (p136) and **Walden Pond** (p138). For the beachy scene, **Cape Cod** (p174) is peachy keen. Among the dunes you'll find the bohemian paradise of **Provincetown** (p197). And if you weren't a li'l tyke in 1950s America, you can live that childhood in idyllic **Nantucket** (p203) or **Martha's Vineyard** (p212).

RICHARD CUMMINS

Fly to the Salem Witch Museum (p146) to learn more about the 1692 trials

Visit Boston's (p60) Financial District – just one of the city's many drawcards

KIM GRANT

Travel far east and dip your toe in the Atlantic on the Cape Cod Seashore (p193)

KIM GRANT

JON DAVISON

Explore the waterfalls, hiking trails, skiing slopes, campgrounds and beaches of New Hampshire's White Mountains National Forest (p442)

IZZET KERIBAR

Revel in leaf-peeping delights during Vermont's glorious fall foliage season

Make a stop at Maine's must-see destination, Acadia National Park (p507)

EDDIE BRADY

HIGHLIGHTS Vermont, New Hampshire & Maine

Placid **Vermont** (p353) boasts unparalleled aesthetic appeal, with the USA's best fall foliage, rolling green hills and alluring country towns. When you're done hiking the **Long Trail** (p366), kick back in a sumptuous B&B and enjoy pancakes with fresh maple syrup. Across the border, New Hampshire's terrain is as rugged as its inhabitants, with the majestic **White Mountains** (p442) its principal draw. Perched on top of both states is taciturn **Maine** (p462), encompassing strings of beautiful fishing villages – think fresh lobster every day – as well as the grandeur of **Acadia National Park** (p507).

Connecticut, Rhode Island & Central Massachusetts

New England's heartland is a perfect hideaway for those in the know. Tourists who think Connecticut is all about industry haven't roamed the **Mystic seaport** (p315) or eaten pizza in **New Haven** (p326), and those who believe that Rhode Island means 'small' haven't gawked at the mansions of **Newport** (p291) or eaten giant clam cakes in **Providence** (p277). The region's best-kept secret is central Massachusetts, where travelers are left in peace to absorb the majesty of the **Berkshires** (p256), revel in the festivities at **Tanglewood** (p266) and be seduced by the ersatz nostalgia of **Old Sturbridge Village** (p233).

BRENT WINEBRENNER

Plunge back in time to the New England of the 1830s at Old Sturbridge Village (p233) in central Massachusetts

Visit Rhode Island for beaches, festivals and mansions

JON DAVISON

Ease your way into holiday mode with a sunset stroll through the Mystic seaport (p315)

RICHARD CUMMINS

Getting Started

Planning a New England adventure requires a 'normal' amount of advance work. Although it's a geographically small region, trying to see and do too much might result in remembering too little and spending too much time in the car. And yes, without a doubt, traveling by car is the preferred method of transportation.

Your biggest decision? Decide what your priorities are before arriving. Are you a gastronomic fanatic who wants to build your trip around seasonal bounty? Or a camper who enjoys waking and sleeping with the rhythms of nature? Are you more interested in meandering back roads than breaking in hiking boots? Is catching a Red Sox game more enlivening to you than catching a trout midstream? On a scale of 1 to 10, how interested are you in searching out colonial history versus modern art? Are you more fond of the quirky or the traditional?

Whatever your answer, New England will oblige. The same is true for costs; travel here can break the bank or be a balm to the budget.

See Climate Charts (p529) for more information.

WHEN TO GO

With four distinct seasons, travel in New England presents four different faces. If you're prepared to roll with abrupt and dramatic weather changes, you can explore New England year-round. Many travelers think of New England primarily as a summer destination. But that would unduly discount the entire catalog of winter sports (see p52) and the peak fall foliage season, when the drama of leaf-peeping reaches its zenith (p17).

If temperate spring weather lasts a while, traveling from late April to early June can be glorious, with apple and cherry trees in bloom and farmers out tapping maple trees for sap (see boxed text p56). If spring is short, as it usually is, it may arrive on a Tuesday, to be followed on Wednesday by the heat and humidity of summer.

In July and August, summer resort areas are very busy, accommodations are fully booked and restaurants are crowded. With the exception of the coast or mountains, summers can be uncomfortably humid. Unless your heart is set on swimming, time your travel between mid-May and mid-June, before local schools close and families hit the road. But avoid Boston at the end of May when the city is packed for college graduations. Another great time is early September – after the big summer rush but

---

DON'T LEAVE HOME WITHOUT ...

- A jacket or sweater and layers if you're lingering on the coast or in northern mountains
- A demure bathing suit (remember, New England is full of Puritans)
- Footwear with good traction for hiking on the rocky coastline
- Lightweight rain gear for spring and fall
- Packing traditional film in your carry-on, as opposed to your checked, luggage (where it will be subject to high radiation)
- Binoculars for whale-watching and bird-watching
- Cold-weather gear for winter, such as a fleece jacket, scarf, hat and gloves
- A Boston Red Sox baseball hat so you look like a local

before the 'leaf-peepers' (foliage tourists) arrive. The weather in these shoulder seasons is generally warm and sunny. Autumn harvest time means fresh cranberries on sale in the markets, 'pick-your-own fruit' days and cider-making at orchards (see p57).

Early November is a serene, almost haunting, time before the snows hit and icy winds blow. Winter can be severe or moderate; it's rarely mild. December to March is ski season in the mountains. Almost all of interior New England, not just the mountains, features harsh weather with lakes 'iced in' until April. When it's not snowing, however, you'll find winter in New England likely to be bright and sunny.

For more details, see the individual regional chapters under Climate.

COSTS & MONEY

Travel costs are highest in the summer, during fall foliage and during ski season in the mountains, but so much depends on your travel preferences. If you camp, share a rental car and have picnics, your daily expenses can be as low as $40 per person per day (a bit higher if you spend more time in big cities). Two people staying in budget motels, eating lunch in fast-food restaurants and taking dinner in moderately priced restaurants can expect to spend between $70 and $85 per person per day.

If you spend ample time in resorts and cities, costs will easily add up to $120 per person per day. Two people touring in a rental car, staying at top-end inns and dining as they wish, will undoubtedly drop $150 to $175 per person per day.

Many discounts are available; see p530. Most state tourism centers publish brochures that include discount coupons for places to eat and stay. Also, look for travel coupons on the Internet. Discounts on car rentals and accommodations are often available to members of auto clubs affiliated with the American Automobile Association (AAA; p530).

Parents should inquire about reduced rates on meals and activities for children. Often museums will have a free family day or family discounts. For more information on traveling with children, see p528.

TRAVEL LITERATURE

It never hurts to bone up on background reading to enrich and deepen your experience of a place. Start with *Walden: Or, Life in the Woods* (1854), by Henry David Thoreau, a quiet and searching story of his 26 months in a small cabin on Walden Pond (p138). It's a testament to all those who yearn to live independently and deliberately. Compare that with *A Walk in the Woods* (1999), by Bill Bryson, who, with his friend, hiked the Appalachian Trail as gloriously middle-aged and out-of-shape explorers.

The Scarlet Letter (1850), a literary classic by Nathaniel Hawthorne, is hailed as one of the best pieces of American imaginative writing. In this tale of sin and seduction, Hester Pryne, a proud heroine, is chastised by her 17th-century village and branded an adulteress.

The Crucible (1952), a play by Arthur Miller, offers a terrifying look into the Salem witch trials (see p145). Maine resident Stephen King (p516) penned *Salem's Lot* (1975), which is set in an unassuming small town in Maine and considered one of the scariest vampire books of all time.

John Irving's *A Prayer for Owen Meany* (1989), probably modeled after the prep-school environment at Exeter, is hilarious and profound. Owen Meany will win your heart.

The Perfect Storm: A True Story of Men Against the Sea (1998), by Sebastian Junger, recounts the 'storm of the century' and the plight of

HOW MUCH?

Campsite fee: $12 to $30

Cup of coffee: $2

Local phone call: 25¢

Bike rental per day: $20

Movie ticket: $8 to $9

LONELY PLANET INDEX

Gallon of gas: $2.20

Liter of bottled water: $2

Pint of Sam Adams beer: $4

Souvenir T-shirt: $15 to $20

Bowl of clam chowder: $5

the Gloucester fishermen (p153) aboard the *Andrea Gail* using collected scraps from radio dialogues, eyewitness accounts and other published material.

For more reading ideas, see p36.

INTERNET RESOURCES

Boston Globe's New England Guide (www.boston.com/travel/newengland/) Vast listings of travel tips and itineraries.

Cape Cod Travel (www.capecodtravel.com) Thorough resource for lodging, food and activities.

Discover Vermont (www.discover-vermont.com) Searchable database for Vermont attractions, dining and accommodations.

Lonely Planet (www.lonelyplanet.com) Succinct summaries on traveling to New England; travel news and the subWWWay section with links to useful web resources.

New England Lighthouses (www.lighthouse.cc) A comprehensive list of lighthouses by state.

Yankee Magazine (www.yankeemagazine.com) An excellent general interest site with classic things to see, great destination profiles and events.

TOP TENS
FESTIVALS & EVENTS

New Englanders know how to celebrate, and there's almost always something interesting going on. For a list of public holidays, see p532.

- Patriots' Day (Lexington and Concord, p134 & p95)
- Harborfest (Boston, p96)
- Head of the Charles (Cambridge, p96)
- Haunted Happenings (Salem, p147)
- Tanglewood Music Festival (Lenox, p266)

- Newport Folk Festival (Newport, p297)
- Pumpkin Festival (Keene, p426)
- Old Port St Festival (Portland, p478)
- Gay Pride Carnival (Provincetown, p199)
- Vermont State Fair (Rutland, p382)

NATURE BREAKS

Whatever the season, New England's natural attractions are beguiling and beckon for exploration. It's hard to choose, but here are our top 10 choices for finding your own Walden Pond. For more ideas, see p47.

- Boston Harbor Islands (p76)
- Minuteman Commuter Biketrail (p134)
- Bartholomew's Cobble (p258)
- Nickerson State Park (p186)
- Block Island (p302)

- Housatonic River (p314)
- Waterville Valley (p442)
- Mt Equinox (p371)
- Lake Champlain Islands (p405)
- Asticou Terraces & Azalea Garden (p510)

FARE FOR FOODIES

The feast isn't confined to Thanksgiving, as New England's bountiful food options make all seasons ripe for culinary exploration.

- New Rivers restaurant (p286)
- Northampton, MA (p245)
- North End, Boston (p105)
- Rockmore Floating Restaurant (p148)
- Portland, ME (p478)
- Arrows restaurant (p469)

- Simon Pearce Restaurant (378)
- Main Street Bar & Grill (p389)
- New Haven pizza (p329)
- New Hampshire diners – Four Aces (p433) to Sunny Day (p446) to Lindy's Diner (p426)

Itineraries
CLASSIC ROUTES

CAPE COD (RTE 6A)   Three Days

Only have three days to spare? Welcome to the club. Bostonians head down to the Cape for long weekends throughout the year. After you've successfully fought the bridge traffic (in summer and on holiday weekends), stop in **Sandwich** (p174) to chill out at the tranquil Shawme Pond, poke around the oldest house on the Cape and visit a renowned glass museum. Slide slowly down Rte 6A, popping into antique shops and turning left toward Cape Cod Bay wherever it suits your fancy. In **Brewster** (p186), stop at the Brewster Store and Nickerson State Park and walk the tidal flats. Have a picnic lunch overlooking Rock Harbor or at Nauset Beach in **Orleans** (p191). Take in a seal watch in **Chatham** (p189) before indulging your fantasies about finding the perfect beach at the **Cape Cod National Seashore** (p193). Bayside or oceanside, the artsy **Wellfleet** (p194) is a charmer. At night there's only one place to be: **Provincetown** (p197). Stay for a whale watch and learn about the painters and authors who continue to summer here.

From salt marshes to seal watches, from hidden antique shops to tranquil duck ponds, Cape Cod offers more diversions than apparent at first glance. Sure, the pristine beaches and lobster shacks are renowned, but so are the art galleries in Wellfleet and flashy nightlife options in Provincetown.

COASTAL NEW ENGLAND   Two Weeks

New England is intrinsically tied to the sea – historically, commercially and emotionally. To understand these mythic and actual bonds, just follow the coastline. There's no more perfect place to begin than in **Mystic** (p315), CT. The unmissable Mystic Seaport Museum boasts a re-created 19th-century maritime village come to life. Nearby, in quaint **Stonington** (p320), the Old Lighthouse Museum is perched on the peninsula's tip.

Bike around **Block Island** (p302), RI, greet some piping plovers and hit the beach. Then head for **Newport** (p289), take the Cliff Walk, explore ye olde downtown and spend the evening on Thames St.

Dip into Cape Cod briefly at **Falmouth** (p176) and **Woods Hole** (p180) to check out a lovely lighthouse, plenty of historic houses surrounding a picture-perfect town green and a world-famous oceanographic institute.

Stop in **Plymouth** (p163), MA, to relive the Pilgrims' trans-Atlantic voyage. Then head north to **Boston** (p60), the region's cultural and intellectual capital. Continue northward to **Salem** (p143), rich in history, and to picturesque **Marblehead** (p149). To glimpse New England's fishing industry at work (and to sample its culinary treats), journey to **Cape Ann** (p151).

The **New Hampshire seacoast** (p412) is scant, but not without merit: frolic among the waves and visit historic **Portsmouth** (p415).

Explore the handsome buildings of **Portland** (p473), ME, as well as the Portland Head Light and the Portland Museum of Art. Venture into the lovely (but crowded) **Boothbay Harbor** (p488) for a harbor cruise. Stop in **Camden** (p494) to take a windjammer cruise and clamber to the top of Camden Hills State Park for fine views. **Bar Harbor** (p503) and **Acadia National Park** (p507) are the Holy Grail of the coast.

Almost half of New England's borders abut the mighty Atlantic Ocean, and as such, she is inextricably tied to seafaring rhythms. This granddaddy of a tour links the most historic and active seaports with the most stunningly beautiful and vibrant coastal communities. Past and present merge here like a sun sinking into a horizon.

THE WHITE MOUNTAINS   Four Days

Drive up I-93 to **Franconia Notch State Park** (p448), where you can hike down the Flume, ride a tramway up Cannon Mountain and see what little remains of the Old Man of the Mountain. Spend the night at one of many welcoming inns in **Franconia** (p450) or **Bethlehem** (p450).

From here, journey east on Rte 3, enjoying spectacular views of the White Mountains all around. Stop at the historic Mount Washington Hotel at **Bretton Woods** (p459), a luxurious resort in the midst of mountain scenery. This is the base for a ride on the **Cog Railway** (p457) to the top of Mt Washington, New England's highest peak.

Or, if you prefer to make the climb on your own two feet, continue on Rte 302 to **Crawford Notch State Park** (p457). This is the trailhead for countless hikes in the area, including several routes to the Mt Washington summit. If you wish to hike for longer than a day, you can spend the night at Crawford Notch or at one of the huts operated by the Appalachian Mountain Club. Otherwise, continue on to the quintessential, quaint New England town of **Jackson** (p455), complete with covered bridge.

On your final day, drive west across the White Mountain National Forest on the spectacular **Kancamagus Highway** (p447). The Kancamagus (also known as Rte 112) offers many opportunities to stop for incredible vistas or – if you have the time and energy – more hiking. It terminates at I-93, which will whisk you back to reality.

From soaring and presidential peaks to rushing waterfalls and swirling flumes, these jagged and rugged mountains offer New England's best in every conceivable outdoor sport. But armchair motorists and quiet campers will also be enthralled by utterly accessible vistas and solitary sojourns.

VT 100   One Week

You could spend a lifetime getting intentionally lost on the hard-packed dirt roads of Vermont or you could spend a week meandering on and off this classic route, which touches major towns and minor attractions with delightful consequences. Begin in **Brattleboro** (p357), a counter-culture town with nearby biking and canoeing possibilities and plenty of in-town eateries and pubs.

Head west along the Molly Stark Trail (VT 9) and stop for a hike before coming into **Wilmington** (p364), a big ski destination and a sweet town with plenty of places to grab lunch. Detour to **Weston** (p362), one of several small villages of southern Vermont and home to the **Vermont Country Store** (p362) and then head off to explore Calvin Coolidge's timeless homestead in **Plymouth** (p379).

Expansive vistas unfold with abandon as you approach **Killington** (p380), great for wintertime skiing and summertime mountain biking. Detour across VT 125 to **Middlebury** (p382), a precious college town with buildings bathed in marble. Head north on VT 116 to Lincoln Gap Rd east; this hooks up to VT 100 in **Warren** (p385), which sports a classic general store.

Waitsfield (p385) is renowned for skiing but it's also great for soaring, kayaking and biking. **Stowe** (p390) and its looming Mt Mansfield might just be the outdoor capital of northern Vermont. After exerting yourself skiing or dogsledding, biking or hiking, you might want to indulge in some Ben & Jerry's ice-cream from the factory in **Waterbury** (p392).

For more about this route, see p356.

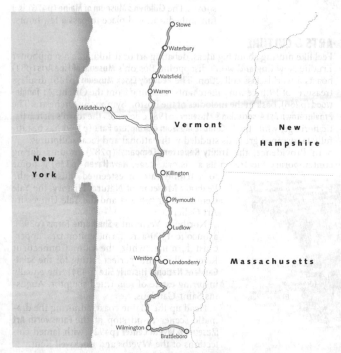

This archetypal artery traverses the stuff of coffee table books: rolling pasture lands and open hillsides, spotted cows and grazing horses, grain silos and dairy barns. Throw in a classic country store, a counter-culture town or two, a vibrant college town and an ice-cream mecca and you've got the makings for one sweet road trip.

TAILORED TRIPS

NEW ENGLAND FOR KIDS

Don't leave home without them! Tykes travel well if you take them to all the right places. In Boston visit the **New England Aquarium** (p77) and take an up-close look at the creatures of the sea. North of Boston, **Salem** (p143) has lots of spooky sights and frightful fun. South of Boston, **Plimoth Plantation** (p164) offers a first-hand look at the life of the Pilgrims.

Heading westward to Massachusetts, the **Eric Carle Museum of Picture Book Art** (p248) celebrates the work of book illustrators, while the **Magic Wings Butterfly Conservatory** (p253) has an 8000-sq-ft glass atrium brimming with

butterflies. On Cape Cod kids love walking way out onto the **Brewster tidal flats** (p187), where they can look for leftover snails.

Roger Williams Park & Zoo (p282) in Rhode Island, a large park of fields and lakes, has an excellent zoo. Connecticut's educational **Trash Museum** (p347) has hands-on exhibits teaching kids about the recycling process.

Heading north, **Ben & Jerry's Ice Cream Factory** (p392) never ceases to delight children – maybe it's the sugar. **Storyland** (p455), a miniature amusement park in New Hampshire, features characters in costume, rides and children's shows. The **Children's Museum of Maine** (p476) is a fun and educational place to pass a few hours.

ARTS & CULTURE

Feel like musing about big ideas, debating art or drinking in a symphony? Erudite New England won't disappoint. Boston's **Museum of Fine Arts** (p84) boasts a world-class collection. The **Peabody Essex Museum** (p146) displays treasures of 19th-century merchants returning from the Orient. At **Tanglewood** (p266), bask in the melodies of the Boston Symphony Orchestra. The **Provincetown Art Association & Museum** (p198) celebrates the town's rich artistic heritage, while the **DeCordova Museum & Sculpture Park** (p139) has beautifully landscaped grounds studded with national and local sculptures.

In Providence, the **Trinity Repertory Company** (p287) mounts daring contemporary theatre on its a historic stage. **New Haven** (p326) is home

to a triumvirate of esteemed museums: the Peabody Museum of Natural History, the Yale Center for British Art and the Yale University Art Gallery.

Northern Vermont's **Shelburne Farms** (p398), a bucolic 1400-acre farm, epitomizes upper-crust farming, while the calm Connecticut River Valley is the perfect setting for the **Saint-Gaudens National Historic Site** (p434), the equally inspiring estate of renowned sculptor, Augustus Saint-Gaudens.

Head up the Maine coast, admiring the dramatic scenery, and stop at the **Farnsworth Art Museum & Wyeth Center** (p492), with famed collections of the Wyeths and Rockwell Kent.

LEAF-PEEPING

It's a major event, one approaching epic proportions in this region: watching leaves turn color. You can do it just about anywhere – all you need is one brilliant tree. But if you're like most people, you want lots and lots of trees. The red-brick buildings and green lawns of **Harvard Yard** (p87) are covered with golden leaves in autumn. For a slightly faster pace, bike the **Minuteman Commuter Bikeway** (p134). At the **Smith College** (p244) and **Mount Holyoke College** (p242) campuses, contemplate the reflection of the trees' fiery crowns in Paradise Pond.

The **Litchfield Hills** (p351) offer a clutch of rolling hills between Cornwall Bridge and Salisbury. **Little Compton** (p296) is a forgotten Rhode Island seaside town of old estates and village greens.

In the **Northeast Kingdom** (p404), take US 91 north from St Johnsbury to the Canadian border for long vistas of dairy farms and sugar maples. Practically anywhere in **central Vermont** (p375) yields blazes of jaw-dropping color.

The **Kancamagus Highway** (p447), a breathtakingly beautiful drive across White Mountains, features spectacular vistas, while the scenic **Connecticut River Valley** (p430) from Keene to Hanover yields fantastic river views.

Inland Maine has myriad possibilities, chief among them the route between **Bethel** (p517) and **Rangeley Lake** (p520).

BEST OUTDOOR RECREATION

No matter the season or sport, brave New England outdoors. Whether you're an Olympic athlete in training or a couch potato in hiding, New England offers all levels of cardio and aerobic pursuits.

In busy Boston Harbor, the **Boston Harbor Islands** (p76) offer surprising hiking, swimming, fishing and even camping opportunities. The North Shore's most inviting beaches include **Crane Beach** (p160) and **Plum Island** (p161), with wide sandy stretches surrounded by dunes and salt marshes.

Thank goodness the **Cape Cod National Seashore** (p193) was protected from rampant development in the 1960s; walking and swimming and sunning are without equal. Nearby, the **Cape Cod Rail Trail** (p184), a flat, off-road track of over 20 miles, is fun for the whole family.

In western Massachusetts, **Mt Greylock** (p273) boasts some 45 miles of hiking trails, several waterfalls and a summit vista overlooking five states. Heading north for the winter, skiing at **Stowe** (p391), whether cross-country or downhill, will get your heart racing, as will rafting the **Kennebec River** (p521). **Waterville Valley** (p442), a planned resort, boasts well-marked trails for hiking, mountain biking, skiing and snowshoeing.

In southern New England, Rhode Island's **Cliff Walk** (p293) makes for a nice stroll along a seaside bluff running through the backyards of Newport's grandest mansions. Kayak or take a ferry to the **Norwalk Islands** (p334), rich with bird life.

For more ideas about how to spend time outdoors, see p47.

The Authors

KIM GRANT Coordinating author, Vermont, Maine

Kim Grant has been wandering around New England since the age of four. She pretended to grow up in the Boston suburbs but really grew up at Mt Holyoke College in western Massachusetts. Since then, she has written Lonely Planet *Boston* and Lonely Planet *Road Trip: New England*, among other Lonely Planet titles. When she resides anywhere it's probably her circa-1900 Victorian house in Dorchester, Boston's most diverse and oldest neighborhood.

My New England

Ironically, after logging about 25,000 miles annually around New England with my car, my tendency after writing guidebooks for 20 years is to sit still. As the Zen poet Ryokan said, 'Living thus, I want for nothing, at peace with all the world.' I find it where the mountain meets the sea at Acadia National Park (p507); where the sea meets the sand in Provincetown (p197); where the white snow of the White Mountain National Forest (p442) softens under foot; where the wide open spaces of the Northeast Kingdom call everything and nothing into question (p404); where all roads East lead to quiet, humble harbors in midcoast Maine (p484); and where home and Mildred's heart resides, in Boston (p60).

ANDREW BENDER Cape Cod, Nantucket & Martha's Vineyard

Yet another Lonely Planet author with an MBA, Andy left the business world to do what every MBA secretly dreams of: travel and write about it. His work has since appeared in *Travel + Leisure*, the *Los Angeles Times*, *Men's Journal* and *Fortune*. After living in Los Angeles for over a decade and covering destinations from Amsterdam to Taiwan for Lonely Planet, this native New Englander was thrilled to finally get an assignment in the place where he vacationed as a child.

ALEX HERSHEY Central Massachusetts & the Berkshires, Connecticut

Alex became enamored with western Massachusetts while attending Smith College in Northampton (Go Pioneers!), and was thankful for this opportunity to become equally entranced with neighboring Connecticut, one of the most overlooked states in the union. She toiled in Lonely Planet's Oakland office for several years before deciding that the open road (basically anything but I-95) suited her better. She currently lives in the Bay Area and is fervently trying to shake her Puritan work ethic.

JOHN SPELMAN
Rhode Island

After an exciting birth in Providence, John got shipped to an unremarkable childhood in the Massachusetts woods. He attended college at Worcester's Clark University, ruining his stomach lining with the grease, coffee and kielbasa of countless diners. He's canoed in Maine, cried on the Appalachian and Long Trails and endorses his grandfather's policy of drinking every cabinet life provides.

John is a PhD student studying architectural history at UVA, and has a Masters of Design Studies from Harvard. He's written several Lonely Planet titles.

MARA VORHEES
Boston, Around Boston, New Hampshire

A freelance travel writer living in Somerville, Mara has contributed pieces to the *Boston Globe Travel*, to *Roll Call's* special edition on the DNC and to Lonely Planet's *Cape Cod, Nantucket & Martha's Vineyard*, among others. Mara is frequently spotted sipping Sam Seasonal in Union Sq and pedaling her road bike along the River Charles.

CONTRIBUTING AUTHOR

Gerald Easter wrote the History chapter. He is a native New Englander with a PhD in political science from Columbia University. He now teaches the same at Boston College.

Snapshot

As far as the ever-widening chasm of the national culture wars go, New England appears true blue. That is to say, in the presidential election of November 2004, each of the six states voted for the national Democratic ticket. Survey an electoral map and you'll find that New England is represented entirely in liberal blue, while regions like the South are wholly cut from conservative red cloth.

This blanket of blue (as seen through a national political prism) might surprise those who feel palpable differences within the relatively tiny region. Pull up a bar stool to converse with locals from six states and those six conversations will be colored with a veritable box of Crayola crayons. At the end of the day, New Englanders are more purple than blue, a jumble of contradictions, shaded by colors at opposite ends of the rainbow, yet connected by the multitude of complementary colors in between.

Bostonians tango in a sea of violet, mauve, lilac, lavender and plum with their neighbors and revel in that nuanced dance. Despite their highly educated ways, though, they forget about the extremes of black and white that exist all around them. They're surprised when the rest of the region (and country) sees them as flaming liberals. Such are the ways of this most provincial region where libertarianism peacefully coexists with tradition.

Outsiders looking in see radical trends taking root in New England. To wit, Massachusetts is the only state in the Union to grant gay couples the right to marry. Around the country this is often interpreted as the beginning of the end for marriage, and yet Massachusetts residents remain faithful to their betrothed far longer than residents of any other state.

Inconsistencies thrive. These six states have increasingly strict public no-smoking policies and yet New Englanders are famous for their libertarian streaks. New Englanders are reserved in their emotions, but when the Boston Red Sox won the World Series in 2004, there was borderline mayhem throughout the region that crossed divisions of class, age and ethnicity.

New England has higher levels of income and education than any other region in the country. But New Hampshire doesn't equitably fund its local school districts, while the entire region is at the bottom of the list when it comes to charitable giving. New England is esteemed around the country as the high priestess of highbrow culture, but surprisingly the state governments do not support the arts in any significant way.

Sit down at that bar stool or a retro diner in northern New England and you're as likely to encounter a vegetarian from an upper-crust Ivy League school as a deer hunter dressed in a flaming orange cap. Sit down at a bar in Ogunquit, ME, and you'll befriend a flaming queen as readily as a crusty lobsterman. Sit down for a microbrew in Vermont and you'll run into a wealthy transplant from Manhattan as easily as an earthy, crunchy lefty. (The industrious family farmers have no time for such revelry but you'll find them engaged at the local country store.) On the surface these scenarios seem to touch the extreme edges of blue and red America, but in New England they read as purple – the color of inclusion, tolerance and free-thinking. At heart, New Englanders respect their neighbor's differences. No matter the nature of their disagreements, New Englanders recognize that the blood that pulses through their veins runs closer to the political color of blue, albeit a purple shade of blue.

History Gerald Easter

WHEN NEW WORLDS COLLIDE

In 1614, English adventurer, Capt John Smith, at the behest of the future King Charles, set sail to assess the commercial opportunities of the New World. Braving the frigid north Atlantic, the plucky explorer reached the rocky coast of present-day Maine and made his way southward to Cape Cod, making contact with the Native Americans, mapping out the coastline and dubbing the region 'New England.'

The land that the first European explorers found was a patchwork of diversity and abundance. Along the shore, tidal flats and salt marshes were rich with shellfish and waterfowl, while the cold waters just offshore teemed with ground fish, especially the mighty cod. In the interior, ice-age glaciers had worn down the mountains, leaving a rolling hilly terrain, dappled with ponds and lakes. The forests of pine, maple, birch and oak were home to moose, deer, bear and beaver. The rivers filled with spawning fish in early spring, while the riverbanks sprouted colorful berries in late summer.

The Europeans also found about 100,000 Native American inhabitants, mostly of the Algonquian nation, organized into small regional tribes. The feisty northern tribes were solely hunter-gatherers, while the more sociable southern tribes hunted and practiced primitive slash-and-burn agriculture. In summer, Native American women tended fields of corn, squash and beans. The Native Americans' subsistence economy involved seasonal migration, following food sources between the coast to the interior, and gift exchange between villages.

Before the wayward Pilgrims arrived, the Native Americans were already acquainted with Portuguese fishermen, French fur traders, English explorers, Dutch merchants and Jesuit missionaries. The Europeans were welcomed as a source of valued manufactured goods, but they were also feared – and for good reason. In the Great Sadness of 1617, a smallpox epidemic devastated the Native American population in the southeast. The Pilgrims were notable as the first Europeans to make a successful settlement in New England. Chief Massasoit of the Wampanoag tribe did not view this scrawny band of settlers as a threat and even hoped that they might be useful allies against his tribal rivals.

But the clash of cultures would soon prove fatal to the Native American way of life. English coastal encampments quickly spread as seemingly unoccupied lands were claimed for the King and commodity export. To the mind of the English, the Native Americans were lazy heathens and undeserving of property rights. According to John Winthrop, the first governor of the Massachusetts Bay Colony, 'God hath hereby cleared our title to this place.' In less than a hundred years, the indigenous population was reduced by 90% by disease, war and forced migration.

In 1675, Wampanoag chief King Philip terrorized the colonists. Twenty-five towns were destroyed and thousands were killed before he was shot, ending King Philip's War.

A SHINING CITY ON A HILL

For some of the earliest settlers, New England held hope of spiritual renewal, while for others, it promised economic enrichment. The colonies

TIMELINE	1000	1497
	The first European explorers – probably the Vikings – arrive in present-day New England	John Cabot claims New England for his patron, King Henry VII of England

long suffered the tensions between community and individualism, piety and profit.

Seventeenth-century England was torn by religious strife. The Protestant Pilgrims were assailed by the Catholic-leaning King James I, who vowed to 'harry them out of the country.' In 1620, the Pilgrims – led by Separatist devotee William Bradford – crossed the Atlantic to establish a community dedicated to religious austerity.

Trouble arose when the badly off-course *Mayflower* weighed anchor in Cape Cod Bay. A group of nonreligious passengers had booked their fares expecting to strike out on their own in Virginia; they threatened a mutiny when they realized they would have to spend the winter with the Separatists. The resulting Mayflower Compact brokered a deal in which both parties would have an equal say in matters of governance. Under Bradford's capable leadership, Plymouth Colony maintained a religious focus and grew modestly over the next decade.

An extensive archive of colonial history, including resources for genealogical research, are at www .mayflowerfamilies.com.

In 1630, the merchant vessel *Arbella* delivered another group of Protestant separatists, the Puritans, 50 miles north of Plymouth. The Puritans were much better prepared: they were well financed, well equipped and 1000 strong, including those of high social rank. At the head of their party, former London court magistrate, John Winthrop, stood atop the Shawmut peninsula of present-day Boston and proclaimed the founding of 'a shining city on a hill.'

The Massachusetts Bay Colony was a product of the ambitions of Puritan gentry, who sought to build a Christian community of personal virtue and industriousness – a community purified of pompous ceremony and official corruption and disdainful of tyranny. Theirs was a kind of legalistic Calvinism, enforced Old Testament style. Anyone missing church without good cause was apt to catch a whipping.

Nathaniel Hawthorne's classic, *The Scarlet Letter*, vividly portrays the austerity of the Massachusetts Bay Colony.

Governor Winthrop constructed centralized institutions to maintain unity among the numerous settlers, who quickly dispersed to choice locations around the harbor and along the rivers. The General Court, an assembly of propertied men, became the principal mechanism of government. Church membership was a prerequisite for political and property rights.

The Puritan theocracy did not go unchallenged in its first decade. In Boston, Anne Hutchinson started a women's Bible circle, where she promoted the idea of salvation through personal revelation. The popularity of this individualist-inspired view was threatening to the colony's patriarchal elders, who arrested the heretic and banished her to an island. One of Hutchinson's arch defenders was her brother-in-law, the Reverend John Wheelwright, who was also forced out of town, leading a group of followers to resettlement in New Hampshire. This was the beginning of a trend in which independent folk, exasperated by encroachments on individual liberty by the Massachusetts state, would flee to the north.

In Salem, Roger Williams chafed under the General Court's meddling in spiritual matters. From his pulpit, he sermonized for religious tolerance, separation of church and state, and respect for Native American rights. Williams and a small group of backers soon found themselves on the road heading south. In 1636, they founded a new settlement, Providence, along Narragansett Bay. The Rhode Island Colony practiced what it preached. It welcomed Anne Hutchinson, declared religious freedom and made peace with the Native Americans.

Meanwhile, Bay Colony officials booted into exile yet another trouble-making parson, Thomas Hooker, whose heresy was to suggest that non-propertied men should not be excluded from political affairs. Hooker relocated to Hartford, amid the growing farm communities of the Connecticut River Valley.

By 1700, the Bay Colony had more than 100,000 settlers. But over time, the Puritan gentry were less able to compel others to embrace their vision of an ideal Christian community. The incessant pull of individual interests and the rise of a secular commercial culture proved to be the undoing of Winthrop's vision of the 'city on the hill.'

CRADLE OF LIBERTY

In 1660, the English Civil War ended and Charles II was restored to the throne. Puritanism was defeated at home and disdained abroad. The Stuart kings were no friends of the Protestant separatists in New England. But their attempt to impose a greater degree of imperial control was fiercely resisted by the free-spirited colonists.

In 1686, King James II reorganized the colonies into a Dominion of New England and appointed Sir Edmund Andros as royal governor. Andros acted quickly to curb colonial independence. He suspended the General Court, levied new taxes, forbade town meetings and Anglicized the church. When he tried to revoke the land-grant charters, the colonists openly defied the King's agent. Andros journeyed to Hartford to confiscate its charter, but during the confrontation the lights suddenly went out in the assembly hall and the charter was whisked outside and hidden in an oak tree.

When King James was deposed and replaced by the Protestant William of Orange in the Glorious Revolution, the colonists rose in rebellion. They seized the obnoxious Andros and shipped him back to England. Although local autonomy was restored, New England from this time was effectively incorporated into the imperial administration.

The demands of empire kept England at war in Europe and in the New World. New Englanders were drawn into the fighting against the French, who controlled Quebec and the Great Lakes regions. The king believed that the colonists should share the costs of empire. In the late 18th century, New England and the British throne clashed over the issue of taxation, exposing the conflicting strains of royal subject and personal liberty.

In 1765, the British Parliament passed the Stamp Act to finance colonial defense. Massachusetts colonists were first to object. Local businessman Sam Adams formed an organization to safeguard colonial autonomy, the Sons of Liberty, which incited a mob to ransack the royal stamp office. The actions were defended in a treatise written by a local lawyer, Sam's cousin John Adams, who cited the Magna Carta's principal of no taxation without consent. Eastern Connecticut and Rhode Island joined the protest. When New England merchants threatened a boycott of British imports, the measure was repealed. The result empowered the colonists.

The British government devised new revenue-raising schemes. Again, they were met with hostile noncompliance, and Boston emerged as the center of conflict. Parliament closed the Massachusetts General Assembly

The Internet Modern History Source Book at www.fordham.edu/halsall /mod/modsbook07 .html is an online archive of colonial documents, including the Mayflower Compact, William Bradford's *History of Plymouth Plantation* and the colonial charters.

The face on the label of Sam Adams beer is actually the mug of Paul Revere.

1686	1692
King James II establishes the Dominion of New England, instituting more rigorous controls over the colonies	Twenty villagers in Salem are killed as a result of witch hysteria

and dispatched two armed regiments to the city. The resented military presence only inflamed local passions. Tensions erupted in the Boston Massacre of March 1770, when a local gang provoked British troops with snowballs until they fired into the crowd and killed five.

Forced underground, the Sons of Liberty set up a covert correspondence system to agitate public sentiment and coordinate strategy with sympathizers. In December 1773, in a daring display of defiance, the Sons of Liberty disguised themselves as Mohawks and dumped a cargo of taxable tea into the harbor. The Boston Tea Party enraged King George, whose retribution was swift and vengeful. The port was blockaded and the city placed under direct military rule.

The conflict tested political loyalties throughout New England. Tory sympathizers included influential merchants, manufacturers and financiers, while the rebels tended to be drawn from lesser merchants, artisans and yeoman farmers. The colonial cause was strongly supported in Rhode Island, Hartford and New Hampshire, where local assemblies voted to provide economic assistance to Boston. Aroused Providence residents even set fire to the British warship *Gaspee*, when it ran aground in Narragansett Bay while chasing suspected smugglers. New Hampshire instigators seized Fort William & Mary when the panicky loyalist governor attempted to enlist more British reinforcements.

> David Hackett Fischer's tome, *Paul Revere's Ride*, provides an in-depth look at the events leading up to the Revolution and the mythical man who made history.

In April 1775, the British again attempted to break colonial resistance, this time by arresting rebel ringleaders Sam Adams and John Hancock and seizing a secret store of gunpowder and arms. As the troops assembled, Paul Revere quietly slipped across the river into Charlestown, where he mounted his famous steed Brown Beauty and galloped off into the night to spread the alarm. By next morning, armed local militias

---

REVOLUTION IN NEW ENGLAND

New England sites figured prominently in the early phase of the War of Independence. Bostonians inflicted a hurtful blow to British morale at the Battle of Bunker Hill in June 1775 (p80). A few weeks later, George Washington assumed command of the Continental Army on Cambridge Common (p86). John Paul Jones sailed his sloop *Ranger* out of Portsmouth (p415) on a bold campaign against the formidable British navy. The coast of Maine (which was still part of Massachusetts) received a pounding from British warships after some locals captured and destroyed a supply ship; while the Maine woods provided a staging area for Benedict Arnold's unsuccessful march on Quebec.

Stirred to action, the Connecticut legislature ordered the expropriation and imprisonment of Tory sympathizers and Connecticut's governor provided valuable provisions to sustain Washington's army at Valley Forge. The British retaliated by assaulting Danbury three different times.

In May 1776, two months before the unveiling of the Declaration of Independence, Rhode Island jumped the gun by being the first colony to declare its outright independence from Great Britain. The British, in turn, occupied Newport and tried to starve Providence into submission.

Ethan Allen and his Green Mountain Boys were essentially a bandit gang, resisting the advances of the New York colony into northwest New England. When war broke out, they sided with the colonial rebellion and used the conflict as an opportunity to declare Vermont independence. Allen ingratiated himself to Washington by capturing Fort Ticonderoga (and its heavy artillery cannon) which was then hauled all the way to Boston and positioned on Dorchester Heights overlooking the harbor. Rather than see their fleet sent to the bottom, the British evacuated the city.

1765	1775
The Stamp Act incites protests among colonists, spurring the formation of the Sons of Liberty	War for Independence breaks out with the Battles of Lexington and Concord

began converging on the area. The incident sparked a skirmish between imperial troops and local farmers on the Old North Bridge in Concord (p136) and the Lexington Green (p132), leaving over a hundred dead. The inevitable had arrived: war for independence.

The other colonies soon joined ranks, heeding the advice of Boston-born Benjamin Franklin, who said 'if we do not hang together, we will surely hang separately.' The war did not go well at first for the feisty, but ill-prepared colonists. The tide turned, however, when the French were finally persuaded to ally with the rebellion. In 1781, the American army and French navy cornered the main British army on the Yorktown peninsula in Virginia and forced their surrender. British rule had come to an end in the American colonies.

OF SAILS & WHALES

New England port cities flourished during the Age of Sail. For the humble fishing villages along the seacoast, breaking into more lucrative markets required cunning and nerve. In the 17th century, the infamous 'triangular trade route' was developed, involving West Indian sugar, New England rum and West African slaves. Merchants who chose not to traffic in human cargo could still make large profits by illicitly undercutting the trade monopolies that the European powers claimed with their West Indian colonies. In the late 17th century, New England in general and Rhode Island in particular provided safe haven for pirates; indeed, Captain Kidd and Black Beard were on a first-name basis with most Newport proprietors.

In the 18th century, Britain's stricter enforcement of trade monopolies and imposition of higher tariffs squeezed the profits of New England merchants – another source of contention between empire and colonies. During the war, New England merchants made small fortunes as privateers and smugglers; when the war ended, they made huge profits opening up trade routes to the Far East.

In his East Boston shipyard, Donald McKay perfected the design of the Clipper ship, whose long V-shaped hull was built for speed. Shipbuilding also thrived in Maine and Connecticut. In the early 19th century, Salem, Newburyport and Portsmouth were among the richest trading cities in the world. The advent of the steam engine in the second half of the 19th century, however, marked the decline of New England seafaring supremacy.

The whaling industry also thrived in New England. Even today, the rich feeding grounds of Stellwagen Banks off Cape Cod attracted whales to the region (p199). In the preindustrial period, whales provided valued commodities such as oil for lamps; teeth and bone for decorative scrimshaw; and other material for hoop skirts, umbrellas and perfume.

New England whalers were strategically placed to pursue the highly sought-after sperm whales along Atlantic migratory routes. Buzzards Bay, Nantucket Island and New Bedford were all prominent whaling centers in their time. In the mid-19th century, New Bedford hosted a whaling fleet of over 300 ships, employing over 10,000 people directly and indirectly, and cashing in at over $12 million in profits.

Whaling was a high-risk occupation. Multinational crews of about 20 sailors, mostly teenagers, cruised the feeding grounds until a suitable

In 1851, Donald McKay's *Flying Cloud* sailed from New York to San Francisco with a damaged mast in just 21 days, shattering all previous records.

The Kendall Institute at the New Bedford Whaling Museum hosts an excellent online research library at www.whalingmuseum.org.

1776	1789
Colonial leaders sign the Declaration of Independence	New Hampshire ratifies the US Constitution, providing the ninth and final vote needed to execute it

In the Heart of the Sea: The Tragedy of the Whaleship Essex, by Nat Philbrik, is the real-life story that inspired *Moby-Dick*.

target was spotted. Smaller teams then scrambled into rowboats to get close enough to harpoon and rope their prey. Once hit, the sailors were off on a 'Nantucket sleigh ride,' as the whales towed the small boats until they finally tired and were killed.

In 1929, the New Bedford–based *Wanderer* returned home for the last time, bringing New England whaling to an end, overtaken by industrial technology and social attitudes.

INDUSTRIAL REVOLUTION

Prior to the 19th century, regional industry remained small-scale, mostly household crafts and artisan shops. Rural areas had small grinding mills or sawmills, while the port cities had industries related to sea trading, ship repairing, fish processing and rum distilling. The disruption of commerce with Britain during the war caused acute shortages of manufactured goods; in response, some New England merchants shifted their investments into industry, with revolutionary results.

New England's industrial revolution began along the banks of the Blackstone River in Rhode Island. Here, in 1790, Quaker merchant Moses Brown contracted English mechanic Samuel Slater to construct a water-powered cotton-spinning factory. Slater had acquired the expertise as a young apprentice in England. However, Britain at the time was so protective of its industrial technology that Parliament prohibited skilled workers from leaving the country, so Slater disguised himself as a farmer to gain passage on a boat heading west. The Brown–Slater partnership was a brilliant success. Their mills sprouted up along the Blackstone, driving a vibrant Rhode Island textile industry. Brown was the founder of Brown University. Slater married Brown's daughter, Hannah, who was one of the first women to file a patent for her invention of a thread spinner.

For extensive information on the mill girls, the labor movement and the history of Lowell, see the National Park Service website at www.nps.gov/lowe.

Thirty miles northwest of Boston, along the Merrimack River, a group of wealthy Massachusetts merchants built one of the wonders of the industrial age: a planned city of five-story red-brick factories, lining the river for nearly a mile, driven by a network of power canals. Named for the project's deceased visionary, Francis Cabot Lowell, the city counted over 40 mills and employed over 10,000 workers; machines hummed 12 hours a day, six days a week.

But this was not the grimy squalor of Manchester; Lowell (p141) was an orderly, planned city. The workforce at first was drawn from the region's young farm women, who lived in dormitories under paternalistic supervision. The 'mill girls' were gradually replaced by cheaper and more compliant Irish immigrant labor.

Paul Revere's copper boilers powered Robert Fulton's first steamboat.

By the middle of the 19th century, steam power and metal machines transformed New England. Railroads crisscrossed the region, hastening industrialization and urbanization. Brawny textile mills arose along rivers in Lawrence, Nashua, Concord and Fall River. Leather works and shoe-making factories appeared near Boston. Springfield and Worcester became centers for tool- and dye-making, southern Connecticut manufactured machinery, and the Maine woods furnished paper mills. Even Paul Revere abandoned his silversmith shop in the North End and set up a rolling copper mill and foundry 15 miles southwest along the Neponset River.

1790	1791
The construction of the Brown–Slater textile mill spurs the Industrial Revolution in New England	Vermont becomes the first new state to join the Union after the original 13

NOT SO SLOW

Boston was for many years a leader in the production and export of rum, made from West Indian sugarcane. By the 20th century, however, most of the distilleries were gone, except one. Near water's edge in the North End a storage tank still stood for the Purity Distilling Company. On a January morning in 1919, the large tank, filled to the brim with brown molasses, suddenly began shuddering and rumbling as its bindings came undone.

The pressure caused the tank to explode like a volcano, spewing two million gallons of molasses into the city. The sweet explosion leveled surrounding tenements, knocked buildings off their foundations and wiped out a loaded freight train. Panic-stricken, man and beast fled the deadly ooze. A molasses wave surged down the streets drowning all in its sticky path. The Great Molasses Flood killed a dozen horses, 21 people and injured more than 100. The cleanup lasted for nearly six months.

NEW ENGLAND MELTING POT

The rapid rise of industry led to sudden social changes as well. The second half of the 19th century brought of wave of immigrant laborers to New England. The world of English-descended Whig Protestants was thrown into turmoil.

The first Irish immigrants arrived to work in the mills in the 1820s. Though their numbers were still modest, their effect on local attitudes was significant. Disparaged by native New Englanders, the Irish were considered an inferior race of moral delinquents, whose spoken brogue was not considered endearing, but rather suggested that one had a shoe in one's mouth. They undercut local workers in the job market. Worse yet, the Irish brought the dreaded religion of pomp and popery that the Puritans had been so anxious to get away from. In 1834, rumors of licentiousness and kidnapping led a Boston mob to torch the Ursuline Convent in present-day Somerville, Massachusetts. In 1837, along Boston's Broad St, an Irish funeral procession met a volunteer fire company and a melee ensued, leaving a row of Irish flats burned to the ground.

A potato famine back home spurred an upsurge in Irish immigration to Boston. Between 1846 and 1856, more than 1000 new immigrants stepped off the boat per month. It was a human floodtide that the city was not prepared to absorb. Anti-immigrant and anti-Catholic sentiments were shrill. The Know Nothing Party sprang up as a political expression of this rabid nativist reaction. Know Nothings swept into office in Massachusetts, Rhode Island and Connecticut, promising to reverse the flow of immigration, to deny the newcomers political rights and to mandate readings from the Protestant Bible in public school.

Subsequent groups of Italian, Portuguese, French Canadian and East European Jewish immigrants suffered similar prejudices and indignities. By the end of the 19th century, the urban landscape of New England resembled a mosaic of clannish ethnic enclaves. Sticking together became an immigrant survival strategy for finding work, housing and like-minded companionship. Neighborhoods took on the feel of the old country with familiar language, cuisine and customs. They provided a base for informal economic activities sustained by codes of local loyalty. They also provided ready-made voting blocs. Control of local government was eventually

Local professor Thomas O'Connor recounts the history of the Irish enclave in *South Boston: My Home Town.*

wrested away from the old English elite and supplanted by ethnic-based political machines.

In the early 20th century, when new Southern and Eastern European immigrants began preaching class solidarity instead of ethnic competition, they were met with renewed fury from New England's ruling elite. Labor unrest in the factories mobilized a harsh political reaction that fed off the twin fears of foreigners and socialism. The 1927 execution on trumped-up murder charges of two Italian anarchists, Sacco and Venzetti, revealed the persistence of class and ethnic animosities. The New England melting pot was more a stew than a puree.

Explore the local history of Boston's ethnic enclaves at www.bostonfamilyhistory.com, featuring walking tours, immigration history and neighborhood development.

REFORM & RACISM

The legacy of race relations in New England is marred by contradictions. Abolitionists and segregationists, reformers and racists have all left their mark.

The first slaves were delivered to Massachusetts Bay Colony from the West Indies in 1638. They became the personal property of wealthy Puritans. By 1700, roughly 400 slaves lived in Boston, with a few free Blacks. In the 18th century, Rhode Island merchants played a leading role in the Atlantic slave trade, financing over 1000 slave ventures and transporting more than 100,000 Africans.

Anthony Hopkins is John Q Adams in *Amistad*, the true story of a runaway slave ship that runs aground off the coast of Connecticut.

A number of New England's black slaves earned their freedom by fighting with the colonists against the British in the revolution. Crispus Attucks, a runaway African Indian slave, became a martyr by falling victim in the Boston Massacre. Salem Poor, an ex-slave who bought his freedom, was distinguished for heroism in the Battle of Bunker Hill.

In the early 19th century, New England became a center of the abolition movement. In Boston, William Lloyd Garrison, a newspaper publisher, Theodore Parker, a Unitarian minister, and Wendell Phillips, an aristocratic lawyer, launched the Anti-Slavery Society to agitate public sentiment.

New England provided numerous stops along the Underground Railroad, a network of safe-houses that helped runaway slaves reach freedom in Canada. In the Civil War, Robert Gould Shaw led the famous 54th Regiment of black troops into battle in South Carolina. Colonel Shaw was killed in action and was buried by the Confederates in a common grave next to the fallen black enlisted men as a mark of disrespect, which was said to please his abolitionist parents.

In the early 20th century, manufacturing jobs in southern Connecticut attracted southern Blacks as part of the Great Migration northward, though European immigrants had already crowded out the labor markets in the rest of New England. For these newcomers, the north promised refuge from racism and poverty. The New England states may have abolished slavery early on, but they still maintained their own informal patterns of racial segregation with African Americans as an underclass.

Although Massachusetts was the first state to elect an African American to the US Senate by popular vote in 1966, race relations were fraught. In the 1970s, Boston was inflamed by racial conflict, when a judge determined that separate was not equal in the public school system. His court order to desegregate the schools through forced busing violated the sanctity of the city's ethnic neighborhoods and exposed underlying racial animosi-

1853	1919
Franklin Pierce becomes US president, the only New Hampshire native to do so	Boston police go out on strike; chaos reigns until the military reserve arrives

ties. The school year was marked by a series of violent incidents involving students and parents alike. In 1990, racial tensions were again aroused when a young white husband murdered his pregnant wife and blamed it on a mysterious black assailant. The mood of the city turned ugly, until the husband's brother finally exposed the story as a lie. The treacherous husband jumped to his death from the Mystic River Bridge, while Boston's white community was left to ponder its fears and prejudices.

TWENTIETH CENTURY TRENDS

The fears of the Yankee old guard were finally realized in the early 20th century, when ethnic-based political machines gained control of city governments in Massachusetts, Rhode Island and Connecticut.

While the Democratic Party was at first associated with rural and radical interests, it became the political instrument of the recently arrived working poor in urban areas. Flamboyant city bosses pursued a populist and activist approach to city politics. Their administrations were steeped in public works, patronage and graft. According to Providence boss Charlie Brayton, 'An honest voter is one who stays bought.'

The Republican Party in New England was cobbled together in the mid-19th century from the Whigs, the Know Nothings and the anti-slavery movement. In the 20th century, it became the political vehicle for the promotion of the values of the old English-descended elite. It envisioned a paternalistic and frugal government, preaching self-help and sobriety.

A lasting strain of independent politics is evident in New England's northern states, sustained by a healthy suspicion of politics, fiscal conservatism and social libertarianism. New England still provides a supportive political climate for social reformers, continuing a legacy that includes 19th-century abolitionists, 20th-century suffragettes, and 21st-century gay rights advocates. While the rest of the American political map is colored red and blue, the 'People's Republic of Cambridge' remains proudly pink.

New England has experienced its share of booms and busts over the past century. The good economic times of the early 20th century came to a crash in the Great Depression. After a brief recovery, the region began to lose its textile industry and manufacturing base to the south. New England industrialists long benefited from war, but defense spending in the region dwindled. With the mills shut down and the seaports quieted, the New England economy languished and its cities fell into disrepair.

But entrepreneurial spirit and technological imagination combined to revive the region. Science, medicine and higher education continued to sustain the economy. Boston, Providence and Hartford were buoyed by banking, finance and insurance. The biggest boost came from the revolution in information technologies, which enabled local companies like Digital, Wang and Lotus to make the 'Massachusetts Miracle,' an economic boom in the 1980s. Even with stock market corrections and bubble bursts, technological developments continue to reinvigorate New England.

As in earlier times, economic change affected social trends. Most notably, the decline of manufacturing in the north and the advent of air-conditioning in the south lured people away from New England, causing a steady decline in population. The recent economic revival has for now

Two influential leaders of the black movement lived in Boston: Martin Luther King studied at Boston University Divinity School and Malcolm X lived in Roxbury as a teenager.

The Last Hurrah is a 1958 film based on the life of James Curley, the corrupt but beloved mayor of Boston.

In 1954, General Dynamics Shipyard in Groton, Connecticut launched the *Nautilus,* the world's first nuclear-powered submarine.

1946	1960
Massachusetts scientist Percy Spenser accidentally melts his chocolate bar and invents the microwave oven	Massachusetts native John F Kennedy is elected president, ushering in the era of Camelot

---

TOP FIVE WHO CHANGED HISTORY

- John Adams – founding father who authored the Massachusetts Constitution (1780), which served as the model for the US Constitution in 1788.
- Alexander Graham Bell – Boston teacher of the deaf who made good with newfangled invention, the telephone.
- Harriet Beecher Stowe – Connecticut crusader who penned a best-selling novel about runaway slaves and started a civil war.
- Ben & Jerry – Vermont hippies noteworthy for popularizing conscientious capitalism and Chunky Monkey (see p392).
- Theo Epstein – boy genius baseball executive who ended 80-plus years of grief by bringing the World Series championship to Boston.

Sarah Messer's youth in the historic Hatch house in Marshfield, Massachusetts inspired her to write *Red House: Being a Mostly Accurate Account of New England's Oldest Continuously Lived-in House* (2004).

stabilized the region's numbers. Meanwhile, new waves of immigrants arrive from East Asia, the Caribbean and Brazil.

In the urban areas, the long-existing ethnic enclaves have begun to break up. Access to higher education has sent second and third generations into prestigious professions and posh suburbs, fostering assimilation and dilution of New England's elite culture. Meanwhile, high real-estate values have meant that property no longer is kept within the family, confirming Cyndi Lauper's astute observation that 'money changes everything.' In a related trend, after several generations of moving away, New Englanders are now moving back into the cities. Downtowns are being revitalized as mills and warehouses are being converted into living spaces, restaurants and retail spaces.

As the 21st century opens, New Englanders are adjusting to changing circumstances and opportunities. The Vermont farmer has gone organic; the Gloucester fisherman is conducting whale-watching tours; the Mohegan Indian is a gaming executive; the Boston Irishman orders chardonnay with sushi; and the New England Yankee is still voting Independent.

1966

Edward Brooke of Massachusetts is the first African American popularly elected to the US Senate

1976

Amid patriotic pageantry and fireworks, New England celebrates its bicentennial

The Culture

Generalizing about regional character is dangerous and reductive. This is particularly true when it comes to New England, which is a diverse assemblage of ethnic and racial communities. But from the outset of European colonialism, New England has been a clannish place, and while the first colonists preached tolerance and respected diversity, dissent and freedom of belief, they preferred to live among their own kind. To some extent this clannishness persists today in New England with people living in Yankee (white Protestant), Irish, Italian, African American, Jewish, Latino, French, Asian or gay enclaves that are side by side, but only modestly integrated, with communities of people of different races, ethnicities or beliefs. Integration occurs in the workplace and schools, but not so much in social venues like restaurants, pubs and clubs.

Good Will Hunting (1997), which catapulted local good guys Ben Affleck and Matt Damon to meteoric fame and fortune, tells the account of a blue-collar kid from South Boston who out-'smahts' the Ivy Leaguers.

REGIONAL IDENTITY

If New Englanders from a multitude of backgrounds share common traits, one of those traits must be a diligent work ethic. A powerful work ethic was at the heart of Puritan beliefs and has been a hallmark of the so-called New England Yankee since the days of the first colonists. It was also an essential quality for surviving New England's challenging climate

VERMONT VS WAL-MART – CAUTION FALLING PRICES

The raging socioeconomic debate about whether Wal-Mart is good for America has acquired a distinctly New England accent in Vermont, with some arguing passionately that the 'low price' way of life will do the state far more harm than good. In a dramatic example of the threat, in May 2004 the National Trust for Historic Preservation put Vermont on its list of the 11 most endangered historic places, in anticipation of a planned Wal-Mart expansion there.

In addition to the now-familiar argument that Wal-Mart and other 'big box' retailers decimate downtowns and run beloved local 'mom-and-pop' merchants out of business, Vermonters quote recent studies supporting the charge that the jobs Wal-Mart trumpets bringing to communities offer inadequate health insurance and few benefits, resulting in strapped local economies being left to pick up the deficit. In 2004 the *New York Times* detailed a study in Georgia that found 10,000 children of Wal-Mart employees were enrolled in the state's welfare healthcare program, costing taxpayers $10 million a year. A similar study in California revealed that the state's taxpayers were stuck with an annual $32 million tab for healthcare expenses of uninsured Wal-Mart employees.

A Wal-Mart spokeswoman told the *Los Angeles Times* that 'Wal-Mart might not be the right job for a family breadwinner.' This is a far cry from the superstore's commercials championing the joy and fulfillment of building and nurturing a family on Wal-Mart wages. It's also a distinct problem for Vermonters hoping for a renaissance for villages past their economic prime.

Still, not all Vermonters are troubled by the arrival of Wal-Mart. In St Albans, where Wal-Mart has announced plans to open a store in 2005, lifelong resident David Giroux observed in the *Burlington Free Press*, 'You can't buy a set of sheets in this town. We've needed this for a while now.'

Wal-Mart has four stores in Vermont, three of which Wal-Mart agreed to downsize from the usual 150,000 to under 80,000 sq ft and retrofit into downtown retail space. The fourth, opened in Williston in 1997, was the first full-sized store in Vermont and was followed by other like retailers – Home Depot, Toy 'R' Us and Bed, Bath and Beyond – to the delight of some and the consternation of others.

Vermont's feisty response to superstore Wal-Mart 'big boxes' signals that 'Always low prices... always' isn't the final word in retailing in every American hamlet, and the time-honored tradition of independent New Englanders questioning economic 'progress' is alive and well.

and rugged geography. Even today, visitors remark at the sense of purpose they feel among New Englanders. 'It's as if everybody thinks they are on important missions,' observed a traveler from France, who noted that pedestrians rarely seem to stroll. By some accounts, Boston's citizens are the fastest walkers of any city population in the world.

Another touchstone of the Yankee character is independence: 'Live Free or Die' is the motto stamped on New Hampshire license plates, and plenty of New Englanders cherish the sentiment. Such rugged individualism cloaks itself in conservative clothing in New England, where women have been voted the worst-dressed females in America by fashion magazines. Except in the boardroom, New England fashion tends toward 'crunchy' chamois shirts, jeans and hiking boots or artsy black sweaters, scarves and dresses worn over purple or orange leggings. Of course, the preppie crowd got their start here: khaki slacks, button-down shirts and loafers are still the uniform du jour for the upper middle class.

Herman Melville's *Moby-Dick* (1851), a major work of Romantic literature, also offers a valuable glimpse into the whaling industry that created fortunes in Nantucket and New Bedford, Massachusetts. Visit Melville's farmhouse, Arrowhead, in Pittsfield, Massachusetts.

LIFESTYLE

So what's to like about New Englanders? Where's the fun? Well, an awful lot of Yankees are culture vultures who love making and consuming art of every variety, from the Boston Symphony to a drag-queen beauty pageant. And many New Englanders are education addicts. In fact, one of the best ways to get to know locals is to enroll in a class. There are thousands of these 'continuing ed' courses, lasting a couple of days or a couple of months, with a class to meet any interest – whether it's belly dancing or astrophysics. After class, check out the pubs, discos and jazz

MASSACHUSETTS GAY MARRIAGE

Massachusetts, the site of the first landing of the Pilgrims, made revolutionary history again by becoming the first state in the Union to end discrimination by allowing same-sex marriage.

In a historic decision in November 2003, the Massachusetts Supreme Judicial Court ruled that excluding same-sex couples from civil marriage is unconstitutional under the Massachusetts Constitution. This landmark ruling was the first of its kind by a United States court and paved the way for gays and lesbians to legally marry in Massachusetts.

The decision, Goodridge v Department of Public Health, brought by New England–based Gay & Lesbian Advocates & Defenders (GLAD), was handed down on November 18, 2003 and six months later, on May 17, 2004, Massachusetts became the first state to grant marriage licenses to same-sex couples. In the six months that followed, more than 4000 same-sex couples were married in Massachusetts.

With pressure from the governor, same-sex couples who are not residents of Massachusetts are currently being denied marriage licenses under an obscure 1913 state law (heretofore not enforced for decades) that was originally intended to restrict interracial marriages. Couples seeking marriage licenses must either be Massachusetts residents or swear that they intend to live in Massachusetts.

Governor Romney and other state officials made every effort to stop same-sex marriage from going forward. In March 2004, the legislature narrowly passed a state constitutional amendment ballot measure that would reverse the Goodridge decision by defining marriage as between a man and a woman. To go into effect, the amendment must be approved a second time by lawmakers during the 2005–2006 legislative session and by voters in November 2006. Stay tuned.

In the meantime, anti-gay advocates tried to have the Goodridge ruling overturned, but in November 2004 the US Supreme Court refused to hear the case, thereby allowing same-sex marriage to continue in Massachusetts (pending the outcome of the state constitutional amendment).

If you are in a same-sex couple and thinking about marrying, gay rights groups strongly urge that you seek legal advice from an attorney about your particular situation. For up-to-the-minute information visit the websites of **GLAD** (www.glad.org) and the **Human Rights Campaign** (www.hrc.org).

clubs. Or experience New England's other addiction: outdoor recreation (see p47). If you like hiking, biking, skiing, sailing, kayaking, jogging or fishing, you'll soon feel right at home.

In a geography so rich with cultures and individuality, there is no such thing as a 'typical' home or family life. The joy here is in the rich tapestry woven by ethnicity, tradition and community. The close-knit and mostly Roman Catholic clans of Irish, Italian and Portuguese must share cultural 'air time' with those New Englanders who claim that the family ethos is liberally defined by a gay couple, both college professors, raising children. While trying to divine the culture and lifestyle of New Englanders, don't generalize, don't assume and get ready to learn – because each clan and lifestyle generally comes equipped with strong opinions and beliefs.

Politically, New England makes for a fascinating stew. Some claim that the influx of immigrants from Asia and Latin America (and a lessening of clear-cut political leanings by traditional New England ethnic groups like Italians and Irish) have transformed the political landscape. But this seems overstated. Urban and rural differences matter more than the ethnic makeups of the locality itself.

One significant concern for New Englanders – and those who would be New Englanders – is the high cost of housing. The monthly payment that would make you landed gentry in Richmond, Virginia, gets you a one-bedroom apartment in downtown Boston. This concerns companies and schools looking to attract talent from elsewhere. Managers in charge of re-cruiting lament the low- to moderate-income family being frozen out of the housing market – and cite numerous cases of recruited talent balking from relocating when they learn how much less house they can afford. Boston and other localities where the issue is most extreme are seeking to address it by expanding the supply of affordable housing with new construction.

POPULATION

New England is home to over 14,000,000 people, or about 5% of the US population. While the region's population has doubled in the 20th century, the total US population has more than quadrupled, so New Englanders now represent a smaller percentage of the US population than they did in 1900. Throughout the last century, Massachusetts and Connecticut represented the largest proportion of New England's population, and in the year 2000 census contained 70% of New England residents. The box below shows New England population by state, as of 2003.

Clint Eastwood's award-winning drama, *Mystic River* (2003), is a gripping tale about three childhood friends from East Boston who are tragically reunited after the daughter of one of them is murdered.

State	Population
Massachusetts	6,433,422
Connecticut	3,483,372
Maine	1,305,728
New Hampshire	1,287,687
Rhode Island	1,076,164
Vermont	619,107

SPORTS

There might as well be a sign on every single New England highway that borders the region: 'Entering Red Sox Nation.' The intensity of area fans has only grown since the Boston Red Sox (p123) broke their agonizing 86-year losing streak and won the 2004 World Series (see p122). This

---

COLLOQUIALISMS

New Englanders, and especially Bostonians, are well known for abbreviating many words. Massachusetts Ave is 'Mass Ave'; the Harvard Business School is 'the B School'; Cape Cod is 'the Cape' and Martha's Vineyard is 'the Vineyard.' Boston's subway system, officially the MBTA Rapid Transit System, becomes 'the T' in local parlance.

But the region is most famous for the broad-voweled English that's commonly called the Boston accent. 'Pahk the cah in Hahvahd Yahd' (park the car in Harvard Yard) is the common joke sentence satirizing the peculiar 'r' that is also common to some dialects in England. During John F Kennedy's presidency, comedians satirized his speech for the 'r's that would disappear in some places ('cah' for car) and pop up in others ('Cuber,' pronounced 'Kyoo-berr,' for Cuba).

To the north, the people of Maine and New Hampshire often punctuate their speech with the meaningless sound 'ayuh' (uh-*yuh*).

See the Glossary (p550) for the meanings of some additional regional colloquialisms.

---

band of scruffy players came to symbolize overcoming adversity for folks around the country. If you're in Boston, consider at least passing by the historic Fenway Park (p84), one of America's oldest parks. Because the Sox have such zealous fans, most games will be sold out. Besides, Sox ticket prices are the highest in the country! Rhode Island hosts the Pawtucket 'PawSox' (www.pawsox.com), a big minor-league Triple-A baseball draw, for which you can usually secure tickets.

Sports fanaticism isn't limited to baseball, though. This simple fact is completely evident when you see broadcast photos of fans with faces painted and beer bellies hanging out in sub-zero temperatures at a football game. The New England Patriots (www.patriots.com), consecutive winners of the Super Bowl in the 2002, 2003 and 2004 seasons, play with a pigskin near Boston (p123) regardless of the weather. Without any of the usual marquee players boasting the best ratings for this or that, this team put individualism aside and pulled together to beat others who looked better on paper. They also took one game at a time. Not a bad philosophy.

Unlike most cities and regions around the country, Boston often fields four competitive teams. Although they haven't really done much for us recently, the storied franchises of hockey's Boston Bruins (p123) and basketball's Boston Celtics (p123) always have potential to make New Englanders proud. The New England Revolution (p123) soccer club is growing by leaps and bounds.

Sports mavens will want to visit the Basketball Hall of Fame (p238), while diehard nostalgics will want to catch a game in the Cape Cod Baseball League (p179), established in 1885.

MULTICULTURALISM

New England landscapes echo with Native American names such as Connecticut, Massachusetts, Narragansett, Pemigewasset, Penobscot and Winnipesaukee, testifying to the peoples who lived here before the arrival of the Europeans. Reporting on his discoveries along the New England coast, Captain John Smith wrote of 'large fields of corn (maize), and great troops of well-proportioned people.' The Native American population at the time might have been somewhere between 25,000 and 75,000, but no one took a census. Scholars believe that about 10 major tribes of the Algonquian linguistic group, often divided into clans, inhabited the present-day New England region when the Pilgrims arrived.

The British and French made the first European claims to this land, and they have left their mark throughout New England. The French presence is

Rhode Island enacted the first laws against slavery in North America on May 18, 1652, more than 100 years before declaring independence from Britain.

TOP FIVE COLLEGE TOWNS

New England is an educational mecca. Her best college towns are notable for their history, heritage, architecture, lively entertainment scene, idyllic settings and cafés. They include:

- Cambridge, Massachusetts (Harvard; p87)
- The Five College Area of the Pioneer Valley in western Massachusetts (Mt Holyoke, Smith, Amherst, Hampshire and UMass; p235)
- Hanover, New Hampshire (Dartmouth College; p431)
- Middlebury, Vermont (Middlebury College; p383)
- New Haven, Connecticut (Yale University; p328)

---

most obvious in northern and eastern Maine and in the northern reaches of Vermont and New Hampshire, where many residents are bilingual. In the mid-19th century, many Africans and Caribbean islanders ended up in New England after fleeing southern slavery via the Underground Railroad.

In the 19th and early 20th centuries, Armenian, Greek, Irish, Italian, Jewish and Portuguese immigrants flooded into the region to provide labor for its factories and fishing boats. Many neighborhoods in the region's cities still hold fast to these century-old European ties.

Recently, immigrants have come from around the world to study at New England's universities, work in its factories or manage its high-tech firms. You can hear Caribbean rhythms in Hartford, Connecticut (CT) and Springfield, Massachusetts (MA); smell Vietnamese and Cambodian cookery in Cambridge and Lowell, MA; and see signs in Brazilian Portuguese in Somerville, MA.

Amistad (1997), an incredibly powerful film, recounts the 1839 revolt and subsequent trial of 55 Africans who commandeered their slave ship and ended up in Connecticut.

MEDIA

As you might imagine, given its colonial heritage, the media began its reign early in New England. The first American newspaper, the quaintly named *Publick Occurrences, Both Foreign and Domestick,* was published in Boston in 1690. The *New England Courant,* published by Benjamin Franklin's older brother James, added news and fiction into the mix 30 years later. Around the same time, the first 'correspondents' were hired to report news from local communities for the *New England Weekly Journal.* In fact, the first printing presses constructed in America were made by Isaac Doolittle of Connecticut around the time of the American Revolution.

Today, the fourth estate is alive and well in New England and busy with the standard newsworthy events. What's the most common topic in the New England media? Corrupt politicians, and the antics of their friends and family. A classic instance was the 2004 story of local Providence TV reporter Jim Taricani, who bravely stood up to heavy fines and contempt citations for refusing to reveal the source of a videotape showing Frank Corrente, a top aid to disgraced Providence mayor Buddy Cianci, accepting a $1000 bribe. Taricani braved the heat, only to accidentally reveal his source to his pal Dennis Aiken, who just happened to be the FBI agent who led the Cianci corruption probe. That's the small world of New England. There's a lot of news to report – and everybody knows somebody involved with making it.

The official website for the *Boston Globe,* www.boston.com, is unparalleled for news and cultural happenings.

RELIGION

New England began its modern history as a haven for religious dissenters, and the tradition of religious freedom and pluralism continues today. The region is home to large numbers of Christian Protestants and

Roman Catholics, and smaller numbers of Jews, Muslims, Hindus and Buddhists. Although relatively few in number (peaking at around 40,000 in the 1930s), Eastern European Jews put their cultural stamp on Boston neighborhoods. Their descendants have created a notable Jewish cultural enclave in the Boston suburb of Brookline and an internationally recognized educational facility, Brandeis University, in Waltham, MA.

The Pilgrims who arrived at Plymouth in 1620 were 'Puritans,' believers in a strict form of Calvinism that sought to 'purify' the church of the 'excesses' of ceremony acquired over the centuries. The Bible was to be interpreted closely, not to be subjected to elaborate theological interpretation.

The Pilgrims disagreed early and often on the details of religious belief and church governance. A common solution to theological disagreements was for the minority group to shove off into the wilderness and establish a new community where they could worship as they wished. Thomas Hooker and his followers abandoned Cambridge, MA to found Hartford, CT; and Roger Williams and his flock split to found Providence, RI. In many cases the new colonial towns, having more recently suffered intolerance, were more tolerant themselves. Newport, RI, although founded by Puritans, soon had a Quaker meetinghouse and a Jewish synagogue.

ARTS

New England looks upon itself as the birthplace of North American culture, and it has a lot of evidence to prove the point. Many of the best known early US architects, painters, silversmiths and other artisans came from New England.

Maybe it's this rich cultural history, maybe it's the scenery, maybe it's the independent smarts, but New Englanders take art and the making of it seriously. You can't toss a lobster tail without hitting a fine arts photographer, a fledgling poet or at least someone running the art league of a small town.

And then there's craft – candles, woodworking, metalwork. From the galleries on Newbury St (p81) in Boston and in every seaside hamlet in Maine to the hand-crafted jewelry in the shops of Newport's Bowen's Wharf there is sumptuous art and fine craft everywhere you look in New England.

Literature

Listen to audio recitations and read interviews and poems by America's favorite poet on www .robertfrost.org.

By the late 19th century, New England's colleges had become magnets for literati of all beliefs and opinions. Some New England towns, most notably Concord, MA, nurtured the seeds of 19th-century America's literary and philosophical flowering. Ralph Waldo Emerson (1803–82) promulgated his teachings from his home in Concord. Emerson's friend and fellow Concordian Henry David Thoreau (1817–62) is best remembered for *Walden, Or, Life in the Woods,* his journal of observations written during his solitary sojourn from 1845–47 in a log cabin at Walden Pond. Louisa May Alcott (1832–88) lived much of her life in Concord, and wrote in order to contribute to the family income. She knew Emerson and Thoreau well. Her largely autobiographical novel *Little Women* is her best-known work.

Prominent writers have deep connections to New England that are plumbed through www .literarytraveler.org.

Few New England authors were more prominent than Mark Twain (born Samuel Clemens, 1835–1910), who reached a worldwide audience. Born in Missouri, Twain settled in Hartford, CT, and there wrote *The Adventures of Tom Sawyer* and *The Adventures of Huckleberry Finn.*

The modern age boasts the same literary tradition. Stephen King, author of horror novels such as *Carrie* and *The Shining,* lives and sets his novels in Maine (see p516). One of the country's finest contemporary voices is Annie Proulx, the award-winning author of *The Shipping News,* who was born and educated in New England. New Hampshire native John Irving wrote *The*

TOP TEN LITERARY LIGHTS

- **Ralph Waldo Emerson** (1803–82) Essayist with a worldwide following and believer in the mystical beauty of all creation; founder of transcendentalism.
- **Henry David Thoreau** (1817–62) Best remembered for *Walden, Or, Life in the Woods*, his journal of observations written during his solitary sojourn from 1845 to 1847 in a log cabin at Walden Pond.
- **Mark Twain** (born Samuel Clemens; 1835–1910) Born in Missouri, Twain settled in Hartford, CT and wrote *The Adventures of Tom Sawyer* and *The Adventures of Huckleberry Finn*.
- **Emily Dickinson** (1830–86) This reclusive 'Belle of Amherst' crafted beautiful poems, mostly published after her death.
- **Edith Wharton** (1862–1937) This Pulitzer Prize–winning novelist's best-known novel, *Ethan Frome*, paints a grim portrayal of emotional attachments on a New England farm.
- **Eugene O'Neill** (1888–1953) From New London, CT; wrote the play *A Long Day's Journey into Night*.
- **Robert Frost** (1874–1963) New England's signature poet, whose many books of poetry use New England themes to explore the depths of human emotions and experience.
- **Stephen King** (born 1947) Maine horror novelist; wrote *Carrie* and *The Shining*.
- **Annie Proulx** (born 1935) New England–born award-winning author of *The Shipping News*.
- **John Irving** (born 1942) New Hampshire native writes novels set in New England, including *The World According to Garp, Hotel New Hampshire* and *A Prayer for Owen Meany*.

World According to Garp, Cider House Rules and others set in New England. Donna Tartt wrote *The Secret History*, in which characters commit murder at a college modeled on her alma mater, Vermont's Bennington College.

Cinema & TV

Films set and shot in New England include *Little Women* (1994), based on Louisa May Alcott's wonderful book about girls growing up in 19th-century Concord, MA. The movie stars Susan Sarandon as Marmie and Winona Ryder as Jo.

Jaws (1975) is an improbable but still terrifying story of a great white shark attacking swimmers on New England beaches; it's set on Martha's Vineyard.

On Golden Pond (1981), the story of two lovers in their declining years, was filmed at New Hampshire's Squam Lake and features fine performances by Henry Fonda and Katharine Hepburn.

The Witches of Eastwick was filmed in Duxbury, MA. *The Crucible*, with Daniel Day-Lewis and Winona Ryder, is a 1996 film adaptation of Arthur Miller's play about the Salem witch trials.

Good Will Hunting, with local-boys-turned-stars Ben Affleck and Matt Damon, is the 1998 hit that tells the story of a blue-collar boy from South Boston who becomes a math/physics savant at the Massachusetts Institute of Technology (MIT).

The Cider House Rules won Michael Caine the Academy Award in 2000 for his role as a doctor in an orphanage in rural Maine.

TV shows produced or set in Boston include *Cheers, Boston Public, The Practice, Spenser for Hire, Ally McBeal* and *St Elsewhere*.

Music

The most famous symphony orchestra in the area is the Boston Symphony Orchestra (BSO; see p119). In summer, the orchestras move outdoors: the

Renowned writers Harriet Beecher Stowe and Mark Twain lived across the street from each other in Hartford, Connecticut.

BSO heads for its season at the Tanglewood estate in Lenox, MA (p266), where it performs along with guest and student artists and ensembles. There are other good chamber music series at Tanglewood as well as in Great Barrington (p257), MA; Stowe (p390) and Marlboro (p361), Vermont (VT); and Blue Hill (p500), Maine (ME), among other venues.

Boston, Burlington, Hartford, New Haven, Newport, Portland, Providence and Worcester are on the circuit for rock, pop and jazz performers year-round. Warm-weather concerts take place outdoors in several cities and resorts, especially in Boston, in Massachusetts' Berkshire Hills, on Cape Cod and in Newport, Rhode Island (RI). Ticket prices vary widely, from a few dollars for standing room to $50 to $100 for the best seats. During the summer many small towns offer evening band or ensemble concerts for free in a central park.

New Hampshire has over 200 registered beekeepers.

Architecture

Though not as eager to break with architectural tradition as are some US regions, New England has its share of dramatic modern structures. These include the glass-sheathed, airfoil skyscrapers of Boston and of Hartford, CT, and the radical IM Pei–designed John F Kennedy Library & Museum (85), just outside of Boston.

During the final decades of the 20th century, historic preservation became a Yankee obsession, and the well-protected and restored historic cores of towns and cities are examples of the many architectural styles that once flourished here. By the 18th century, Yankees were building elaborate Georgian structures inspired by Palladian architecture. Called Georgian after the reigning British monarchs, the style was – and still is – used extensively at Harvard (p86), Dartmouth (p431) and many other New England schools.

Calvin Coolidge, the 30th president of the United States, was sworn in by lamplight at his Vermont home following the death of President Harding.

State capitols built in the 19th century typically featured neoclassical domes, colonnades and arcades. The best example may be the Massachusetts State House (p79), designed by Charles Bulfinch (1763–1844).

New England's fascination with European styles continued into the 20th century, but was diluted by a blossoming of local creativity. While modified Cape Cod cottage styles migrated to the Midwest and California, ranch-style houses started popping up in New England.

In the 1950s and '60s, the international style reigned, producing huge glass and steel towers such as Boston's Prudential Center (p82). Also during this era, preservationists reclaimed the sturdy granite warehouses along Boston's waterfront for apartments, offices, shops and restaurants.

During the prosperity of the 1990s, Boston, Hartford, Providence and Portland reeled under the construction of office towers. But the economic slowdown at the outset of the 21st century has put temporary breaks on development.

Painting, Sculpture & Visual Arts

For all its wealth, 19th-century New England society could not fully nurture its renowned artists, most of whom sought training and artistic fulfillment abroad. These included Henry Sargent (1770–1845), of Gloucester, MA; and James Abbott McNeill Whistler (1834–1903), of Lowell, MA, who challenged the tradition of representational painting by blurring lines and emphasizing the play of light in his work.

An exception was Winslow Homer (1836–1910), who pursued a career as an illustrator for the popular press but later dedicated his talents to painting. Homer is famous for his scenes of the New England coast.

ANTIQUES ROADSHOW

Is it any wonder that *Antiques Roadshow*, the hit PBS TV series, is a smash hit in New England? Yankees are passionate about their antiques, and considering that in the 18th century there wasn't much more to the US than New England – face it – they have a better inventory. New England craftsmen dominated well into the 1800s making beautiful furniture, functional and well-made tools, and goods and artifacts of daily living.

'Our readers are passionate about antiques and collectibles,' says Michael Carlton, editor of *Yankee Magazine*. *Yankee* runs a regular antiques and collectibles column, frequently featuring the work of Skinner, Inc, headquartered in Boston. Skinner is one of the nation's leading auction houses for antiques, and is the premier auction house in New England. Skinner appraisers appear frequently on *Antiques Roadshow*. The company conducts nearly 60 auctions a year, giving art and antiques enthusiasts the opportunity to bid on many rare and desirable objects.

By the 20th century, however, New England was capable of supporting world-class artists. John Singer Sargent (1856–1925) painted his telling portraits of Boston's upper class, and Childe Hassam (1859–1935) used Boston Common and other New England cityscapes and landscapes as subjects for his impressionist works.

Norman Rockwell (1894–1978), perhaps New England's most famous artist, reached his public through his magazine illustrations, particularly the covers for the *Saturday Evening Post*. His pictures cemented US popular culture and helped define the nation's concept of what it meant to be an American. Rockwell lived and worked in Arlington, VT and Stockbridge, MA.

Highly regarded for her 'American primitive' paintings of rural life, Anna Mary Robertson Moses (1860–1961) didn't begin painting until in her late 70s. Work by 'Grandma Moses' resides in Bennington (p366), VT.

New England has produced its share of sculptors. Daniel Chester French (1850–1931) designed the minuteman memorial in Concord, MA, and the seated Lincoln in Washington, DC's Lincoln Memorial. Alexander Calder (1898–1976) made many of his world-famous mobiles and stabiles at his studio in Roxbury, CT.

For a look at what's going on with New England up-and-coming talent, visit the nationally renowned Rhode Island School of Design (RISD; 281) in Providence.

Boston's Black Heritage Trail is thoroughly laid out on www.afroam museum.org, which is also rife with other exhibits and events.

Theater & Dance

It won't come as a surprise that the Puritanical cultural miasma in New England in the 18th century gave church-going Yankees a marked suspicion of plays and show folk. But even then, as now, interest (if not enthusiasm) for the stage abounded, and every ship that arrived from England came with stories of the plays and entertainment in London. In 1750 professional actors from England staged Thomas Otway's tragedy *The Orphan* at a coffee house in State St, Boston. It was such a curiosity that the coffee house was mobbed and a near riot broke out. The ensuing scandal caused the General Court to enforce a law making it a crime to both act or be a spectator of theater of any kind.

Today, New Englanders have great enthusiasm for both viewing and participating in theater and dance. In the larger cities you will find established theater companies and ballet troupes, of course, but nearly every village and hamlet has its own active theater company. A quick visit to www.jacneed.com will yield the community theatrical delights in every New England destination, large and small.

Maine grows 98% of America's blueberries – a whopping 30 million pound annually.

Environment

About 400,000 years ago, a mile-high glacier ground inexorably across New England. Its retreat left the region with a natural playground of clefts and rubble and sheared-off mountainsides. It also left a landscape filled as much with stone as with soil. The soil's richness enabled early, flinty New Englanders to scrape a living out of this rugged countryside, even as the frost-buckled earth exhumed new scatterings of stone into the fields every spring.

Then came the industrial age, which harnessed the big, wide rivers into veins of commerce. By the early 1900s, the Merrimack River in Lowell, Massachusetts (MA), ran bright red or yellow, depending on which color dye the textile mills were using on a particular day. But today, the Merrimack and other watersheds all over New England are in various stages of being nursed back to health, and new threats are being confronted head-on by advocacy groups.

The National Trust for Historic Places (www.nationaltrust.org) recently listed Vermont as one of America's 11 'Most Endangered Historic Places' due to the influx of 'big-box' superstores and the economic and environmental degradation that typically follows (see p31).

Joining urban sprawl as a major concern in New England is the alarming spread of an undersea desert resulting from decades of destructive fishing and waste-dumping practices.

A powerful, prevailing wind pattern known as the 'jet stream' delivers the smog of a nation to New England, elevating the rain's acidity and silencing the birds, frogs and other vulnerable creatures.

An aging nuclear power plant, perched delicately on the edge of the Connecticut River, is attempting to increase its output despite serious management and physical plant issues, and having nowhere to safely store its waste.

Step back from it all, though, and you see that New Englanders get hot under the collar about these things while the sky blazes with impossible beauty, as if straight out of a Maxfield Parrish painting. Who can blame them? Deep forests sigh all around; and the sudden wail of a loon takes your breath away.

The stains of last century's industrial-age polluters are indeed finally beginning to fade. Old brick industrial buildings are now being reclaimed as artists' studios and eclectic shopping districts. People can actually swim and fish in some of the infamously polluted waterways, including parts of the Boston Harbor. We're not home-free, but New Englanders have a fabulous little homeland in which to recharge between battles.

For current information on New England environmental issues, visit the Conservation Law Foundation's website (www.clf.org).

THE LAND

New England's topography may have been sculpted by glaciers, but the region's geological history actually begins several billion years before their appearance. As the earth's crust shrank and wrinkled, massive tectonic plates – million-square-mile swaths of surface area on which our notion of continents serve as icing of sorts – slid and collided. When they pushed up against each other, their unyielding edges rose – such as when you press your fingertips together to make a tepee – and mountain ranges towered into being. Friction and pressure from the clash of rock masses

Dating to 1715, Boston Harbor Light was the country's first lighthouse. In 1998, it also became the last to be automated.

Acadia National Park's 57 miles of hand-constructed carriage roads, built in the early 1930s, are the best broken stone roads in the US.

turned sand to marble (much of which was used to build the nation's capital buildings in Washington, DC) and formed the distinctive gneiss and schist, flecked with shiny mica, seen throughout the region.

Magma (molten rock) from the earth's core crept into crevasses and cracks in the earth's crust and filled huge air bubbles hidden beneath the surface. Rock that cooled slowly deep within the earth became New England's distinctive granite (New Hampshire isn't called the granite state for nothing).

Several hundred million years ago, the earth thrust the bedrock of New England up into a spine of craggy mountains, running roughly northeast to southwest. Over the ages, erosion and the ebb and flow of geologic pressures reduced these early alps to lower heights, so that by eight million years ago they achieved the appearance that they have today.

Just one million years ago, the earth's surface temperature dropped inexplicably. Glaciers ground their way down through New England, blanketing the region with a river of ice a mile thick. Pushed ever southward by the pressure of ice buildup at the North Pole, these glaciers dredged up millions of tons of soil and rock and moved it to the southern New England states. Deposits of soil and rock formed the islands of Nantucket and Martha's Vineyard.

As the earth warmed again some 10,000 to 20,000 years ago, the ice retreated from New England. As it moved away it scooped out holes that became glacial ponds (Thoreau's Walden Pond, p138, for example). Rivers turned into cataracts of raging glacial meltwater, grinding out round potholes and carving huge bowls and contorted shapes out of solid stone. To see some stunning examples, visit New Hampshire's Franconia Notch

> Richly descriptive and leaving you longing for the lush and mossy backwoods, Henry David Thoreau's *The Maine Woods* (1854) is essentially one of the first travelogues published in the USA.

LEAF-PEEPING

One of New England's greatest natural resources is change. No, not the serious kind that requires you to re-examine your life – we mean the kind that causes the lush nimbus of trees to fling off that staid, New England green and deck their boughs with flaming reds, light-bending yellows and ostentatious oranges. We're talking about the changing of the guard from summer to fall, better known as New England's seventh season (after mud season and black-fly season): foliage season.

Peak times vary by latitude and altitude, with the best bets for late September to mid-October. If your holiday is scheduled for a couple of weeks before your destination region's peak foliage moment, bend time back into your favor by traveling north a bit, or even higher in altitude, where the season hits earlier. Even after the party's over, the colorful confetti catches in streams and fades into more hues of rust and brown than could fill a paint chip booklet.

Lest you think that leaf-peeping is only for tourists, you should know that even crusty old Yankees find reasons to take to the back roads during the fall. Weekends bear witness to bumper-to-bumper traffic on the most popular routes. If communing with nature is what you have in mind, head for the wilds on a mid-week morning and find a hiking trail.

Prime driving routes include the Mohawk Trail (MA 2) in the northern Berkshires (p254) and VT 100 (p360) from Wilmington to Stowe. For many more ideas about specific tours, see p17.

The easiest way to pinpoint peak autumn foliage on any given September or October day is to call these numbers:

Connecticut (☎ 800-282-6863)
Maine (☎ 800-533-9595)
Massachusetts (☎ 800-227-6277)
New Hampshire (☎ 800-258-3608)
Rhode Island (☎ 800-556-2484)
Vermont (☎ 802-828-3239)
White Mountain National Forest Service Fall Color Hotline (☎ 800-354-4595)

(p448), which runs by the Pemigewasset River, or visit Lost River Gorge in North Woodstock (p444). The retreating glacier deposited rock and debris in oblong hills called drumlins (for a good example, see Bunker Hill, p80), and left huge granite boulders called erratics in fields and streams.

The resulting landscape has verdant, winding valleys, abundant forests and a rocky coastline sculpted into coves and sprinkled with sandy beaches. To some, the mountains lack the dramatic height of the Rockies, but they are no less rugged and beautiful. Farmers may complain that New England's rock-strewn soil 'grows boulders' (they're actually pushed up by the succession of freezing winters), but outdoors enthusiasts find the New England topography a perfect place for bicycling, hiking, canoeing, kayaking and boating (see p47).

WILDLIFE

An enormous variety of critters make their home, at least temporarily, in New England. A year-round profusion of food fattens them up for the big migration, the long winter's nap or just to survive the harsh winter. You don't have to mount an expedition to the deepest reaches of the forest to see the region's Holy Grail of creatures – the magnificent moose. By the same token, even the rarest blossoms can be found by quiet roadsides as well as deep in the forests, and any open field dazzles with a palette of blooms.

Animals

When people come to New England, they usually want to see a moose. While that's not *always* possible in every corner of the region, knowing where to look can up your odds of encountering the type of wildlife you're hoping to see.

You're more likely to spot a moose the further north you look. The Kancamagus Hwy (p447) in New Hampshire's White Mountains is prime moose-spotting territory, as is the aptly named Moosehead Lake region in Maine (p521). Both places have bogs aplenty, which is where moose like to browse. As with most wildlife, they favor twilight and nighttime. Consider taking a tour with Pemi Valley Excursions (p445) or venture into the Northern Forest Heritage Park (p461), NH.

White-tailed deer are everywhere, as are squirrels (red and grey), chipmunks, raccoons, porcupines and rabbits. Bears tend to keep to areas with large, thick stretches of forest, except where there are backyard birdfeeders or sloppy campsites to raid. For beavers, look for their telltale domed lodges at the edge of a pond (muskrat houses are flatter). Tree stumps chewed to pencil-points are good clues that you're looking in the right place.

Thanks to environmental clean-up efforts, bald eagles are making a comeback in the northeast and can be seen cruising at altitude over large lakes or diving for dinner. Just about any large- to medium-size lake or bog will have a rookery of great blue herons, which roost in May, and Canada geese are everywhere. Find a high point along the Connecticut River Valley (p430) in the fall and watch the annual hawk migration. There's nowhere like Plum Island (p161) or Nantucket (p203), both off the coast of Massachusetts, to take in sea birds, including a healthy population of fish hawks (osprey).

Loons – lonesome wailers, large, buoyant, black-and-white-speckled waterfowl – are usually found on large lakes where the water's edge has not been ransacked by development. Once you hear their yodeling cry, you'll never forget it.

Whales, dolphins and seals play in New England's coastal waters, and ecotourism provides an alternative livelihood for some fishing crews put out of work by the closing of fishing grounds. The whales seem to truly enjoy sporting for the boats; the captains of whale-watching cruises know their 'regulars' by name.

Don't forget the little guys: butterflies (which somehow make the flight from Mexico without arriving in tatters) are always a profligate delight, and gorgeous, green luna moths (as big as your hand) will flap around any light source and plaster themselves against many a lucky windowscreen. Drop a kayak into any lake or pond and you will have a dragonfly battalion riding shotgun.

Last, and most despised, are the black flies. These suckers are after blood, usually yours. They make life miserable from late May to early July and breed in running water, such as streams and rivers. Mosquitoes, which do not have the good grace to leave after couple of months of slapping and swearing, breed in stagnant pools. A repellent containing at least a 20% solution of DEET seems to help, though natives willingly walk around smelling of Avon's citronella-infused Skin-So-Soft.

New England Sea Birds (www.neseabirds.com) devotes itself to birds and animals found off this coastline, and it includes tips on locating rare species and breeding colonies.

Plants

New England – not exactly known for a long growing season, forgiving winters or deep layers of topsoil – requires plants that take root here to really *want* to survive. Still, if a seed falls in the forest, it's bound to take root and strap itself in – with trees sometimes wrapping roots around a boulder like a baseball pitcher preparing a knuckleball. Visit Lost River Gorge (p444) in North Woodstock, New Hampshire for some dramatic examples.

Still, these forests are thick with beech, birch, hemlock, maple, oak, pine and spruce. The hills are alive with wildflowers, whose colors reflect the passing of the season. Springtime's first flower, the dandelion, is spread in exuberant blankets of yellow, the first blossoms available to bees coming out of a long, hive-bound winter. From there, blue and purple blossoms of all kinds signal that summer is around the corner. Blooms warm into reds and yellows as the days lengthen, and the trend skews orange as fall approaches.

Maples are the mascots of the region, yielding not only color in the fall (see p17 for fall foliage routes), but sap in springtime. Balsam sweetens the air in higher-altitude forests, and birches jut out like inverted lightning strikes with greater frequency and thicker trunks the further north you go.

The foraging is good all summer, with a succession of herbs, fruits, roots, shoots, berries and mushrooms. On the cusp of April and May, it's the fiddleheads – young fern shoots – that explain the occasional New Englander bent over on the roadsides, filling plastic bags. After a good, soaking rain, shroomers take to the hills. June brings the strawberries, August the blueberries, and September heralds the cranberry harvests.

Connecticut's Northeast Organic Farms site (www .ctnofa.org) offers farm tours and promotes locally sustainable agriculture and ecologically sound farming and gardening.

ENVIRONMENTAL ISSUES

Pinpointing environmental issues is like pulling a thread on a sweater: any one issue is inextricably connected to the whole. Predictably, battles to protect air, land and water continue to rage, and intangibles, such as aesthetics, sustainability and energy independence, are joining the list of protection-worthy concepts.

New England serves as a spout of sorts through which pollutants from around the country are funneled courtesy of the jet stream weather pattern. Pollution from incinerators, coal- and oil-fired power plants, dirty manufacturing facilities, auto emissions – you name it and here it comes. Consequently, rain and snow contain heavy metals and acidic

Jonathan Harr's *A Civil Action* (1996), made into a popular movie starring John Travolta, follows the true story of a legal case that turned on the connection between industrial polluters and the deaths of children in Woburn, Massachusetts.

compounds, and mercury. Currently, every New England state has issued advisories restricting or condemning consuming fish caught in its waters.

Forest protection butts directly up against an entrenched way of life in northern sections of the region. Venture beyond heavily traveled roads, where loggers leave a buffer of trees shielding horrific, clear-cut sections, and the pretense is dropped, revealing a denuded land. The good news is that more land is falling under environmental easement protection and landowners are requiring more balanced logging practices to reduce the impact of extraction. Conservation groups are lobbying for larger roadless tracts to knit entire ecosystems once divided and conquered by myopic practices dictated by a short-sighted bottom line.

Urban sprawl doesn't just create an ugly blight, consuming rich land that once supported family farms – it is the origin of the latest, major source of pollution in our rivers and streams: stormwater runoff. As more land is paved, rainwater, rich with oils and pollutants picked up from heavy traffic areas, is no longer filtered by the earth before finding its way to New England's water tables and streams.

Not all of the region's magnificent old-growth forests were cleared by settlers in the 1800s and 1900s. The *Sierra Club Guide to Ancient Forest of the Northeast* (2004) leads you to over 130 of these inspiring regional locales.

Too often, environmental protection is ignored by the powers that be until it hits a large enough group in the pocketbook. Hence the dire condition the oceans have reached on every level are only now stimulating large-scale management and reclamation efforts. Dragnet fishing involves literally dragging a weighted net across the ocean floor, devastating everything in its path. Decades of this practice, along with overfishing and increasingly poisonous pollution and dumping, have created something close to a desert on the ocean floor. Now there is a movement toward establishing Marine Protected Areas to restore habitats and create preserves off-limits to fishing. Needless to say, there is strong opposition to this from fishing interests who lack a vision of sustainability – yet again pitching those who make a marginal living against those who would protect the long-term ability for them to do so. But even moderate retooling costs can be enough to sink many small enterprises.

ON WALDEN POND

There is little doubt that Henry David Thoreau would *not* have chosen Walden Pond (138) had he been on the cusp of writing his classic *Walden, Or, Life in the Woods* at the turn of the 21st century. The pond as Thoreau knew it was a secluded cove owned by his close friend Ralph Waldo Emerson. It was there that he lived and contemplated from 1845 to 1847 with studied deliberateness and simplicity, seeking a transcendental truth through an intimate relationship with nature.

Among the most well-known proponents of transcendentalism, Thoreau and Emerson espoused the belief that an understanding of God can be best be achieved through one's own intuitive relationship with the divine spirit that lies within all of nature, including mankind. This, of course, flew in the face of what they saw as the straitjacket of dogma from traditional, spiritually inadequate religions that required blind obedience of the masses. The transcendental movement viewed the industrial revolution as the root of a pervading materialism. Their philosophy embracing social consciousness and an intuitive relationship with the natural world continues to have an effect on our society, from the practice of nonviolent resistance (as practiced by Mahatma Gandhi in India and proponents of the Civil Rights movement in the US) to the environmental movement.

Now the pond's pure tranquility is shattered by a busy road, fee-based parking, a gift shop, a trailer park, and throngs of kayakers, swimmers, fishers and sunbathers. Despair not, however. To find the Walden Pond that *you* seek, perhaps it's best to take a page out of the transcendental playbook and seek your own, intuitive Walden Pond experience. Past the modern trappings and throngs of sun-worshippers, you may still find hints of the tranquil essence shared by Thoreau.

Ocean- and ridgeline-based wind farms promise a step towards energy independence, yet they're still new enough to test the ability to navigate to the truth through anti-wind fear tactics and pro-wind assurances. A proposed farm off the coast of Nantucket (p203) is spiking aesthetic protests as well, with owners of zillion-dollar summer manses foreseeing plunging property values due to a 'diminished view.'

The 'great blackout' of 2003 is being used as rationale for upgrading the transmission power grid. There are strong arguments for funding conservation as well as clean, local energy sources. This would, of course, decrease New Englanders' dependence on big polluters such as oil- and coal-burning plants, and nuclear energy, whose distant smokestacks flavor the sky with their output.

For more information on environmental issues affecting New England, contact the following organizations:

Appalachian Mountain Club (☎ 617-523-0655; www.outdoors.org)
Conservation Law Foundation (☎ 617-350-0990; www.clf.org)
Natural Resources Defense Council (☎ 212-727-2700; www.nrdc.org)
Sierra Club (☎ 415-977-5799; www.sierraclub.org)

Dedicated to land conservation issues and action, the Society for the Protection of New Hampshire Forests (www .forestsociety.org) opens its reservations to visitors.

NATIONAL & STATE PARKS

Whether it's old buildings or open space, preservation is alive and well in New England. Almost a century ago, in 1911, 800,000 acres were set aside in the White Mountain National Forest (p442) of New Hampshire and Maine. Thus New England's first national forest was born. Twenty years later, in 1932, 400,000 acres in Vermont were designated Green Mountain National Forest (p356). Both efforts stemmed from reaction to rapacious logging practices that denuded land and left behind a tinderbox of felled timber, which fueled catastrophic wildfires throughout the region. Now, rising from the ashes, are two extensive swaths of land. They're packed with a playground of natural features and a relatively contiguous ecosystems lending shelter and protection to wildlife. Officials here also have a somewhat more evolved approach to banking natural resources for managed extraction, and for future generations to enjoy.

The Conservation Law Foundation (www.clf.org), New England's leading environmental advocacy organization, reminds us how to keep our natural resources clean and offers plenty of information on climate changes, healthy oceans and fighting urban sprawl.

New England's only national park is sited on the rugged, northeastern coast of Maine; Acadia National Park (p507) contains 7000 acres of granite-domed mountains, 45 miles of carriage roads, 40 miles of sandy beaches, 115 miles of hiking trails, and a sunset view off Cadillac Mountain. It's not to be missed.

The other granddaddy of nationally preserved lands in New England is the Cape Cod National Seashore (p193), a 44,600-acre stretch of rolling dunes and stunning beaches. Laced with salt marshes, pitch-pine and scrub-oak forests and freshwater kettle ponds, it's great for swimming, hiking, cycling, kite-flying and fishing.

State parks are everywhere, even in urban locations, and offer access to some of the area's best natural wonders. Most allow camping, and each offers myriad facilities for its own unique blend of activities. A selection of some of the most interesting parks follows, but you can also consult the New England Outdoors chapter (p47).

The Atlantic coastline of the Cape Cod National Seashore was dubbed an 'ocean graveyard' because so many ships ran afoul of the shoals. Between Truro and Wellfleet alone, almost 1000 ships were lost.

Baxter State Park (p522) The wildest, least-spoiled wilderness area in New England. Hiking, mountaineering, rock and ice climbing and cross-country skiing are available here.
Boston Harbor Islands (p78) There are 34 offshore islands here within minutes of downtown. Activities include swimming, boating, camping and bird-watching.
Camden Hills State Park (p495) One of the prettiest sites in Maine with exquisite views of Penobscot Bay and excellent hiking and cross-country skiing.

Crawford Notch State Park (p458) Here you'll find a steep valley with stunning vistas, with opportunities for hiking and cross-country skiing.

Hammonasset Beach State Park (p332) Forget the world as you stroll the boardwalk and lie on the beach. Camping, swimming, walking and bird-watching are available here.

Monomoy National Wildlife Refuge (p173) This refuge is an important Atlantic seaboard flyway for migrating birds. The bird-watching here is excellent.

Mt Greylock State Reservation (p273) The highest point in Massachusetts, with great mountain views and a lodge. Activities here include hiking, driving and wildlife-watching.

Mt Monadnock State Park (p429) An oft-climbed peak, the area's spiritual vertex, with hiking, cross-country skiing and camping.

October Mountain State Forest (p264) The Appalachian Trail slices through Massachusetts' largest tract of green space. You'll find hiking, fishing and boating here.

Parker River National Wildlife Refuge (Plum Island; p161) Sandy beaches surround acres of wildlife sanctuary in this park that's great for swimming, boating and bird-watching.

Quechee Gorge State Park (p376) Trails wind through fields, forests and alongside a lake. You can enjoy hiking, swimming, camping and cross-country skiing here.

Quoddy Head State Park (p513) The first place in the country to see the sun rise. Hiking, cross-country skiing and whale-watching are on offer.

New England Outdoors

New England holds its own quite nicely in the world of outdoor fun and adventure. From a death-defying plunge down the snow-covered Tuckerman's Ravine in New Hampshire (NH) to kayaking the Connecticut (CT) coastline, there is plenty to keep your heart pounding.

New Hampshire's White Mountains, Vermont's Green Mountains, the Berkshires of Massachusetts and the dense forests of northern Maine offer all types of hiking, rock climbing, camping, canoeing and white-water rafting experiences. Thousands of miles of rugged coastline entice travelers with endless sailing, canoeing, sea kayaking, windsurfing, whale-watching and scuba diving opportunities. You name it, you can probably do it in New England. Swimming, canoeing, boating, fishing and water-skiing are also great on the hundreds of lakes, ponds and rivers here.

Hunting is also a time-honored tradition in New England. Seasons are defined by weapon and/or game and vary by state and locality. Check with a dependable source, such as a hunting shop, the state Fish & Wildlife departments, and tourism bureaus, before setting out.

The unparalleled *AMC White Mountain Guide* (2003) features the most complete trail information for hiking in New Hampshire.

HIKING & WALKING

Freud might say that sometimes a walk is just a walk, but here in New England, we have walks, and then we have *walks*.

The blissfully undisturbed landscape of Rhode Island's Block Island (p302), dubbed 'one of the last great places in the western hemisphere' by the Nature Conservatory, is perfect for gadding about on foot.

If you like edgier walks, try the famed Cliff Walk that runs along the rocky bluffs in Newport (p289), Rhode Island (RI) or, similarly, in Ogunquit (p467), Maine (ME). Either way, the ocean surges on one side and mansions rise in grandeur on the other. For a more transcendental stroll, try circling Thoreau's Walden Pond (p138) in Concord, Massachusetts (MA), without muttering 'simplify, simplify, simplify' somewhere along the way.

During inn-to-inn walking excursions (see p363), you can cover the back roads and teeny towns of central Vermont. Or you can spend the day walking through the White Mountains of New Hampshire alongside swimming holes carved by glacial meltwater, through stands of birch trees and past the cliff where once hung the famed Old Man of the Mountain (p448).

Most of New England's state forests, parks and reservations have walking or hiking trails of varying levels of difficulty (see State & Regional Parks, under the individual state chapters). Many cities and towns also have trail systems like Boston's Emerald Necklace (p88), which meanders through woodlands, parks and city reservations.

For dramatic photos, weather reports and virtual tours of New England's fiercest peak, browse www.mount washington.org.

New England's paths and peaks are detailed at www.mountainwanderer .com, which also has maps and outdoor travel guides.

Mountain Hiking

You won't go wrong deciding which rearing peaks deserve the effort of lugging your knapsack, backpack or climbing gear. Any choice is a good one. The **Appalachian Trail** (☎ 304-535-6331; www.nps.gov/appa; PO Box 807, Harpers Ferry, WV 25425-0807) runs through all the New England states except for Rhode Island, with plenty of access points all along the way.

The White Mountains' (p442) Presidential Range in New Hampshire, while throwing back some of the foulest weather on record, draws everyone from day-hikers to ice and rock climbers to multiday technical mountaineers.

There are 48 peaks in New Hampshire that are over 4,000ft high.

Maine's sublimely remote Mt Katahdin (p522) remains relatively untouched by tourism. Those who make it across the infamous 1.1-mile Knife Edge – 3ft wide in places with a sheer, 1500ft drop on both sides – will remember the experience for life.

Vermont's Green Mountains are seamed with hiking trails, particularly Vermont's own end-to-ender, the Long Trail (p366), with both easy and challenging hikes. Many excellent trails radiate out of the Stowe (p390) area, which also sports world-class ice climbing.

Bunk overnight at the top of Mt Greylock (p273) in the Berkshires of western Massachusetts. It makes an excellent goal for a day's walk from Williamstown.

New Hampshire's utterly accessible Mt Monadnock (p429) is a 'beginners' mountain,' a relatively easy climb up a bald granite batholith.

Mt Jackson in the Presidential Range of the White Mountains was not named after President Jackson; it was named after state geologist Charles T Jackson in 1848.

ORGANIZED HIKES

The **Appalachian Mountain Club** (AMC; ☎ 617-523-0636; www.outdoors.org; 5 Joy St, Boston, MA 02108) offers great outings in every New England state. **AMC Pinkham Notch Camp** (☎ 603-466-2727; www.outdoors.org; Pinkham Notch, NH 16; ☼ 6:30am-10pm) in the White Mountains of New Hampshire is an excellent source of information on gear, courses and outings.

CAMPING & BACKPACKING

Camping in New England is pretty darn safe and pretty darn plentiful. With common-sense precautions, encounters with bears (no grizzlies here), cranky moose and snakes are unusual. It's the nibbling chipmunks, persistent raccoons and tip-toeing deer that are more common. With generous tracts of woodland, New England has plenty of tent sites, yurts, lean-tos and cabins for everyone from car campers to trekkers.

Huts and primitive campsites line the major mountain trail systems, but these can fill quickly during summer, fall and winter weekends. Camping in the White Mountains is a sweet destination, while some cabins and lean-tos in Maine's Baxter State Park (p522) are nice drive-in sites.

Visit practically any spot around the globe and someone will proudly proclaim 'if you don't like the weather here, wait 10 minutes and it'll change.' It's true here as well and campers and backpackers need to be prepared for it. Mt Katahdin (p522) is its own biome, with vastly different weather between the base camp and summit. Mt Washington (p452) is known for thrashing winds and hard-core weather swings. Even in the most civilized of forests, the weather can change swiftly. Bring raingear, plenty of layers of clothing and provisions for more days than you need them in case something happens.

For camping details, see Sleeping under regional chapters, and p526.

CYCLING & MOUNTAIN BIKING

As you bike and hike around New England, you'll see it's laced with graceful stonewalls, the revered subject of *The Granite Kiss* (2001) by Kevin Gardner.

With thousands of miles of back roads and an increased presence of bike lanes in metropolitan areas, it's a lot safer and more pleasurable than ever to cycle through open country and pretty villages, and to explore cities without worrying about parking and the astronomical fees that come with it. Visibility and predictability are the keys to safe city riding, and the more closely you hew to a driver's rules of the road, the better.

Bicycle Touring

Rails-to-Trails (www.railtrails.org) provides a wealth of information on all the nice (mostly) flat railroad beds that have been converted to hiking and biking trails. From Boston to Lexington and Concord, follow part of Paul

Revere's midnight ride to the birthplace of the Revolutionary War on the Minuteman Commuter Bikeway (p90). Use **Rubel BikeMap's** (www.bikemaps .com) *Pocket Rides* to help choose from more than 50 streetwise rides in and around Boston; some feature excellent beach and lighthouse tours.

On Cape Cod in Massachusetts, tool around the Shining Sea Bike Path (p177), the Cape Cod Rail Trail (p184), and the Cape Cod National Seashore bike paths near Provincetown (p193).

In Rhode Island, take a spin on the beautiful 14.5-mile East Bay Bicycle Path (p283), which follows the waterfront out of Providence and weaves past picnic-worthy state parks.

In Burlington (p399), a path several hundred miles long circumnavigates Lake Champlain. A fine ramble close to the city runs 5 miles alongside the lake on a converted railroad bed; check with Local Motion (p399) for information (www.localmotionvt.org).

Islands are particularly well-suited for great biking. Rent wheels for Block Island (p302), Rhode Island; for the carriage roads of Mt Desert Island (p502), Maine; and for Nantucket (p206) and Martha's Vineyard (p214), Massachusetts.

One of the best companies that offers bicycle-touring packages and excursions is Bike Vermont (p377).

> Once chlorophyll (the substance that makes green leaves green) is no longer produced in the autumn, leaves revert to their underlying color.

Mountain Biking

A huge number of fire roads, snowmobile trails and hairy drops at ski areas are fair game for mountain bikers, and New England embraces the sport more and more each year as resorts and private facilities add miles of single-track to their offerings. Foliage season is prime time for gallivanting through psychedelic forests. Springtime thaws in April and early May are recuperative times for the trails, freshly exposed after a long winter's nap. Local bike shops will gladly reveal their favorite haunts.

In Stowe (p393), Vermont, the hills are alive with whoops and hollers as bikers roam the hills on some of the most challenging terrain around. Several shops rent wheels.

The Loon Mountain ski area (p447) of New Hampshire zooms daredevils up the mountain in a handy gondola for a white-knuckle, tooth-rattling trip back down. As usual, ask their bike shop dudes for the lowdown on cool local rides.

Western Maine's Bethel Outdoor Adventure & Campground (p518) will set your wheels in motion in the stunning countryside, home of Sunday River Ski Area.

ROCK CLIMBING

New Hampshire is known as 'the granite state,' a big clue that there's going to be great climbing somewhere nearby, no matter where you are. The same goes for much of the rest of New England, which is crammed with ledges and giant glacial erratics – huge boulders left by receding glaciers, seemingly apropos of nothing. Bring your crash pad, your rack and your climbing buddy and troll the local gear shops and climbing walls, and you'll find someone to deliver the beta on the local climbing scene.

In New Hampshire, Cathedral Ledge (p453) is probably the most famous rock- and ice-climbing spot in New England. Cathedral Ledge soars high above Franconia Notch, and climbers can be seen inching up its face on just about any given day. While beginners are literally learning the ropes, seasoned climbers rope up and climb onward and upward. Two standout climbing schools in North Conway ply these and

> Ropes used in mountain and ice climbing can hold up to 6,000 pounds of weight.

other spots in the White Mountains and beyond. In North Conway the **International Mountain Climbing School** (☎ 603-356-7064; www.ime-usa.com) offers mountaineering and ice- and rock-climbing courses and outings, as does the Eastern Mountain Sports Climbing School (p453).

In Stowe, Vermont, hook up at the Inn at Turner Mill (p394) with inn-keeper and veteran climber Greg Speer for area guidance on the swaths of world-class rock- and ice-climbing pitches.

Acadia National Park (p507) offers dramatic routes on cliffs that rise straight up out of the pitching sea, while remote Mt Katahdin (p522), in the state's interior, offers an alpine feel with long routes. The Acadia Mountain Guides climbing school in Bar Harbor (p509) offers climbing and mountaineering trips, courses and clinics.

SWIMMING, SAILING & SURFING

The ocean never really heats up in New England, but that doesn't stop hoards of hardy Yankees from spilling onto the beaches and into the sea on hot summer days. But it's not just the Atlantic where heels can be cooled. Thanks to a mile-high glacier that covered New England about 30,000 years ago, New England is blessed with a generous scattering of crystal-clear lakes and rivers; surely it's the swimming-hole capital of the world. When the mercury rises just enough, New Englanders head for water, water everywhere, from quiet ponds to raging rivers, open ocean to pounding surf.

Protected from the arctic currents, Rhode Island's beaches tend to be the warmest, particularly at Sakonnet Point, Block Island and Newport. Sweet surfing spots include Town Beach in Narragansett, Point Judith, and First Beach and Second Beach in Newport.

Plum Island (p161), just barely off the coast of Massachusetts, offers a nice combination of dunes, a wide beach and a wildlife sanctuary harboring more than 800 species of plants and wildlife. In Ipswich, Crane Beach (p160) is a wonderful, pristine stretch of sand in the heart of a wildlife refuge, with trails traversing its dunes. Beaches on Cape Cod, Nantucket and Martha's Vineyard are legendary. Bring your surfboard and hang ten at Nantasket Beach in Hull, and Good Harbor (p155) and Long Beach in Gloucester, MA.

New Hampshire's short coastline is hemmed in with condos, but Rye Beach (p413) is an old favorite, drawing crowds from all corners. The Wall in Hampton (p412) attracts surfers.

Maine has a scattering of coastal beaches, including Ogunquit (p467), Old Orchard Beach (p473), Kennebunkport (p469) and Bar Harbor (p503). Old Orchard Beach offers some minor swells to surfers.

For accurate, locally derived information on surfing in New England, visit www.nesurf.com.

Lakes and rivers are great fun for a dip, from the serpentine Saco River that runs alongside the Kancamagus Hwy in New Hampshire to a dozen spots along the Cascade Trail in Franconia Notch State Park (p448). Rangeley Lake (p520) in Maine and New Hampshire's Lake Winnipesaukee (p435) are two of New England's largest inland lakes; the former is quite isolated, but the latter is bursting with resorts, shops and services.

In Vermont, the West River, which runs southeast from Londonderry to Brattleboro, and the Batten Kill, which runs south from Manchester, offer many spots where locals come to frolic.

For maritime sails, options are wonderfully varied: pluck lobster from their traps on a boat out of Wells (p467), Maine; hop aboard a research vessel out of Essex (p337), Connecticut, and learn about the inhabitants

On Golden Pond (1981), starring Henry Fonda and Katharine Hepburn as two lovers in their later years, is set on Squam Lake, New Hampshire.

of the sea. Inherit the wind aboard a windjammer out of Camden (p494), Maine, or a 19th century–style schooner in Mystic (p315), Connecticut. Holler 'thar she blows' from whale-watching boats that depart from Cape Ann (p151), Provincetown (p197), Boston (p60) and Plymouth (p163), all in Massachusetts.

FISHING

In addition to its renown for deep-sea fishing, New England has become a true fly-fishing destination. Why? Because of the famous Orvis (p371) and LL Bean (p481) fly-fishing schools in Vermont and Maine, respectively, and because of an abundance of rivers, lakes and ocean.

Manchester, VT, has become a fly-fishing Mecca because of the trout-sweetened Batten Kill River (p372) and Orvis, the granddaddy of the craft with a retail store, rod-building workshop and the American Museum of Fly-fishing.

Connecticut's Housatonic Meadows State Park (p351) has a two-mile stretch of the Housatonic River set aside exclusively for fly-fishing. Head for the Mountain Goat (p272) in the Berkshires for fly-fishing gear and the best advice on where to use it.

On Block Island, charter a boat and bring back a marlin, or try your luck off Rockport, north of Boston, or Plymouth (p163) to the south of Boston. Opportunities abound in Orleans (p191), where Cape Cod's largest charter fishing fleet is docked.

Maine might as well be fishing heaven with isolated lakes and wild rivers everywhere. It also has a sturdy tradition of excellent guides and pontoon-plane access for some of the most exquisite locations. Sebago Lake (p517) in the southeast corner is a good place to start, but the centrally located Moosehead Lake (p521) region might just be the holy grail. Nearby Greenville is pontoon-central.

At the northern tip of New Hampshire's brief seacoast, find a sweet, hidden spot at Odiorne Point State Park (p413), or head for the high seas out of Hampton Beach (p412). For excellent salmon fishing, head inland to Lake Winnipesaukee (p435).

Check with a local outfitter or at the state's Fish & Wildlife Department for fishing advisories.

CANOEING, KAYAKING & RAFTING

You'll see more kayaks and canoes atop cars speeding down the byways of New England than you can shake a paddle at. Yankees know a good thing when they see it. They know there's always a pond, lake, coastline or river somewhere in the neighborhood, and that they're usually rich with wildlife to boot.

The coast and inland areas are thick with kayaking opportunities for serious sea-kayakers or Sunday-afternoon duffers. Inland lakes for sea kayakers? Yes, some enormous inland lakes such as Vermont's Champlain (p388), New Hampshire's Winnipesauke (p435), and Maine's Moosehead (p521) create their own, swift-moving weather patterns, wild currents and swells that challenge the technique, navigational skills and adrenaline demands of expert sea kayakers. The key is getting the lowdown on local tides, currents and weather prognostications from the locals themselves. Local boat purveyors always have tide charts and advice you would do well to heed.

The Maine islands are great fun to thread through and, when the water is frisky, sea kayakers love playing in the rolling chop. LL Bean (p481) in Freeport will set you up with a boat, tours, lessons and a list

When engaging in cold weather outdoor activities, sprinkle your socks with hot pepper powder to keep your feet warm.

Heading into the remote Maine woods to go canoeing, dogsledding, fishing, ice climbing or kayaking? Locate an expert through www.maineguides.com.

Alpine enthusiasts might consult www.newengland ski.com for snow conditions, current events, special deals, information on gear and links to other shushing sites.

of prime locations for beginners and experts alike. Or ferry out from Casco Bay (p473) to Peaks Island for a frolic. Paddle past ospreys, eagles and bears (oh my!) at Sears Island (p486), just outside of Bath. Wiggle through cranberry bogs or swing with the swells just off Acadia National Park (p507).

The Sakonnet River in Rhode Island feeds into the sea, with estuaries for recreational kayakers and big swells with the big fishies for experts. Meanwhile, you can serenely paddle between interconnected salt ponds on Block Island, communing with the land, sea and sky.

Plum Island (p161), north of Boston, is a sweet spot for all levels, rife with seals and birds galore. Watch the tides, though, or you'll be dragging your yak through sneaker-sucking mud and scootching across sandbars at low tide.

The Norwalk Islands (p334) off the coast of Connecticut are a half-mile out and make for a nice, watery ramble.

For white-water impresarios, check out www.mvpclub.org for dam releases and kayaking events. The Deerfield River (p254) in the Berkshires of Massachusetts is a bronc of a ride. For one of the best floats, with a slow but steady current and some slight riffles, paddle down Vermont's Batten Kill from Manchester to Arlington.

Contoocook River in Hennicker hosts the famous Class III Freight Train run. Even if you're not an expert, it's still thrilling to watch the seeming nonchalance of others in the river's thrashing chaos.

SKIING & SNOWBOARDING

Snowboarding used to be frowned upon by alpine skiers as yet another example of the irritations of youth. Now there's a good chance that the 50-year-old corporate executive next to you on the chairlift will be dangling a board on the trip up. This change is due in part to older folks finally figuring out that boards are easier on the knees (if you survive the steep learning curve). But they've also discovered that shredding actually *is* a blast and not just another symbol of youthful rebellion. Now most ski areas provide ripping half-pipes and special parks where boarders can hurtle and gyrate through the air to their heart's content.

Your next chairlift companion could also be a free-heelin' telemark skier, sporting skis a lot like yours except that their heels aren't locked down. Born in the backcountry and closely related to cross-country skiing, telemark skiing involves a graceful, genuflecting motion to carve a turn. Many bring their sport to downhill areas for the same reason you came: on skis, it's a heck of a lot more fun going down than up. These days, many ski areas throw telemark festivals with free contests, lessons and an excellent chance to try out the gear.

Nordic skiing – whether racing, backcountry or recreational – is popular in this region, and most people have a pair of 15-year-old skis ready to head out the back door. Nearly every town has a cross-country ski trail somewhere, and an inquiry at a local inn or outfitter will most likely yield more trails than you could possibly ski in an entire season.

Whatever your mode for enjoying the gravity of the situation, here are some top locations to savor the snow:

Killington Ski Area (☎ 802-422-3261, 800-621-6867; www.killington.com; 1-day lift ticket $67) Known throughout New England for the earliest and latest runs of the season due to the unbelievably extensive snowmaking apparatuses here. With 200 runs on seven mountains, all manner of lifts (with heated cars) and top-notch facilities, the area works hard to earn the high ticket price. The steepest mogul field in the east, acres of glades and miles of cross-country trails are pure heaven for all kinds of snow sportsters. The nearest town is Killington, VT (p380).

Mad River Glen (☎ 802-496-3551; www.madriverglen.com; 1-day lift ticket $50) The motto here is: 'Ski it if you can.' It's the double-dog-dare-ya of tag lines. Proud of its proletarian roots, this rough-and-ready spot still sports one of the country's last single-chair chairlifts, refuses admittance to boarders and offers some of the most exhilarating, hard-core skiing around. Every year, in March or April, the place explodes with telemark skiers for one of the

SNOWMOBILING

In the rural far north of New England, the main mode of transportation seems to switch from cars to snowmobiles. The four northernmost states in New England have snowmobile trail systems that wind throughout the woods (much on private land and usually with the owner's blessing). Most state parks are open for cruising. Local clubs are sprinkled everywhere and often host group outings and celebrations.

Hot spots include the Northeast Kingdom of Vermont, the north woods of New Hampshire north of the White Mountains, and, of course, snowmobile heaven: the Moosehead Lake region of Maine.

Folks are serious about following 'road' rules and regulations here. Trails are patrolled and fines sting. For information on where to take a training course, how to get a permit, and most of all, where the action is, contact each state's snowmobile association:

Maine Snowmobile Association (☎ 207-622-6983; www.mesnow.com) Oversees 13,000 miles of snow trails and provides information on choice runs.

New Hampshire Snowmobile Association (☎ 603-224-8906; www.nhsa.com) Maintains a whopping 6830 miles of trail.

Snowmobile Association of Massachusetts (www.sledmass.com) The locus for club news, and for finding clubs that can provide information on trails in your destination area.

Vermont Association of Snow Travelers (VAST; ☎ 802-229-0005; www.vtvast.org) With more than 45,000 members and 140 clubs, VAST maintains an incredible network of trails all over Vermont.

> For instruction and tours for sports ranging from rock climbing and mountain biking to fly-fishing and confidence building, consult www.vermont adventuretours.com.

---

oldest and best telemark festivals in the country. You'll be hollering 'Free the heel!' and slapping duct tape over the rips in your ski pants and swapping tall tales by the end of the day. The nearest town is Waitsfield, VT (p385).

Gunstock Ski Area (☎ 802-496-3551, 800-gunstock; www.gunstock.com; 1-day lift ticket $49) This is one of the sweetest, family-style resorts in New England. Most trails are intermediate, though the advanced trails are nice and hair-raising. Tubing trails are a delight, as are the 30 miles of cross-country trails that pass through beautiful forests. Even the clam chowder is made from scratch here, and there's nothing like it for warming up after flying down the mountain all day – and well into the night on the lighted trails. The nearest town is Gilford, NH (p435).

Sunday River Ski Resort (☎ 207-824-3000; www.sundayriver.com; 1-day lift ticket $57) The resort sprawls across eight peaks, and zigzagging across the face of them can take all day. You'll feel the wilderness around you here and from the top you can almost hear its namesake whispering through the valley far below – and yet you'll also be surrounded with every possible luxury in the lodges, spas and condos below. Every sort of winter fun has a place here, where toddlers and Olympians come for some of the finest shooshing in the region. The nearest town is Bethel, ME (p517).

The Maine woods resonate with the call of the wild, and cross-country ski adventures await discovery, from multiday treks in Baxter State Park to family frolics on groomed trails. For the best information, contact the **Maine Nordic Ski Council** (☎ 800-754-9263; www.mnsc.com, Bethel).

Stowe (☎ 800-253-4754, 802-253-3000; www.stowe.com; 1-day lift ticket $65, cross-country $15) This place hosts the largest connected cross-country ski trail network in the East. (Their downhill trails are pretty darn extensive too.) The upper trail system, situated at 2100ft with fabulous views, is great for snowshoeing as well. Families, friends and couples are accommodated in style, whether it be in condos and inns on the mountain or in one of the myriad off-mountain lodges. Stowe (the town) is completely given over to Stowe (the mountain) and to shushers in the winter. It's its raison d'etre.

Craftsbury Outdoor Center (☎ 802-586-7767; www.craftsbury.com; 1-day lift ticket $14) Located in the wooded hills of the Northeast Kingdom, Craftsbury sports 50 miles of groomed trails where families cruise, speedy skate-skiers whoosh and backcountry skiers ply the additional 30 miles of ungroomed trails. This is one of the most renowned cross-country ski centers in the country with a decidedly international draw. The nearest town is Craftsbury, VT (p406).

Blue Hills Reservation (☎ 781-828-5070; www.mass.gov/mdc/blue.htm; lift ticket weekdays/weekends $25/30-33, admission free) Blue Hills offers a nice range of trails quite close to Boston. It's fun for families and experts with easy jaunts and steep, twisty chutes. The nearest town is Milton, MA (p165).

Food & Drink

New England is the home of the first Thanksgiving and of bountiful autumnal harvests. Yes, food is life-sustaining, but it has deep cultural roots in New England. With so much coastline, it's not surprising that seafood plays a prominent role on tables. New England is the undisputed capital of clam chowder and lobster, whether it's served at someone's home, a four-star restaurant, a country inn or a ramshackle seaside lobster shack.

A hundred years ago, Boston was not a dining destination. But it was famous for baked beans (white or navy beans, molasses, salt pork and onions cooked slowly in a crock) and the New England boiled dinner (beef boiled with cabbage, carrots and potatoes). These dishes are not common on menus anymore. Today you'll see the local cuisine shacking up with international influences. Your palate will be titillated with nuance and freshness, especially in and around New England cities and the more-sophisticated resort areas.

Still, some traditions persist. You can buy locally made maple syrup in all the New England states. And Vermont dairy products – milk, cream, yogurt and cheese – are only slightly less famous than that state's most famous edible: Ben & Jerry's ice-cream.

Ben & Jerry's uses 100,000-gallon stainless steel mega-blenders to make its ice-cream.

STAPLES & SPECIALTIES

It's terribly hard to generalize about New England cuisine, but the following will give you a good introduction. Old-time New England cuisine is a blend of Anglo-American, European and Native Indian food traditions. It combined established English recipes with local offerings from the earth, and went easy on spices and herbs – no need to excite the sense palates of those Puritans! (For traditional meals in Boston head to **Durgin Park** (p103) and **Union Oyster House** (p103), also hailed as the oldest bar in America.)

These days, however, the irresistible appeal of New England's cuisine rests on its readiness to update itself. New England food is now a colorful ethnic mix – it's Italian and Irish and Portuguese; it's Thai and it's Chinese.

That rich eclectic fusion means that there's something for everyone, from the discerning foodie to the finicky child. And it's generally healthy. Vegetables, fruits, meat, seafood and dairy products all feature prominently on the local menu and at the greengrocer.

Michael and Jane Stern's *Durgin Park Cookbook* (2003), which features staples of Yankee cooking, includes classic recipes for baked beans, cornbread, chowder and Yankee pot roast.

When they eat breakfast – as opposed to skipping it because they're on the run – locals eat egg dishes, French toast (bread dipped in an egg and cinnamon batter and lightly cooked on a griddle with butter) or stacks of pancakes possibly drenched in blueberries and maple syrup. Lunch often figures around that omnipresent American invention: the sandwich. Whether it's fancy (with multigrain bread, smoked organic turkey and avocado) or simple like a BLT (bacon, lettuce and tomato), they're quick and easy and relatively inexpensive. Dinner is the big meal of the day, whether shared in someone's home or used as a form of entertainment. Inevitably, when a group of friends gets together, it's over a meal. Everyone usually eats their own main dish, but often folks will share appetizers (starters) and desserts.

Seafood & Shellfish

First things first: ask 10 locals for their favorite chowder haunt and you're likely to get 10 different answers. Chowder is chock-full of clams or fish, but the former is far more prevalent. Generally, the meaty insides of giant surf clams are used to make the famous concoction. But clams also come in other varieties, including soft-shelled clams ('steamers' – so-called because they are cooked in steam). Popular types of hard-shelled clams ('quahogs' – pronounced either 'ko-hog' or 'kwa-hog') include littlenecks and cherrystones.

Lobster tourism has reached epic proportions: thousands of travelers make pilgrimages to New England annually to indulge in their favorite lobster delicacies. But lobster devotees may be surprised – if not shocked – to find out that early settlers used lobsters as soil fertilizers and that they initially fed the unsightly crustaceans only to prisoners.

At lobster shacks, you pick your own live lobster and have it steamed or boiled. You can also have it split in two lengthwise and grilled, or you could order a baked stuffed lobster. Be aware, though, that locals frown upon the latter, seeing it as a tourist dish for the uninitiated. For tips on how to eat lobster, see p55.

Mystic Pizza (1988), a celebrated and sappy coming-of-age flick that was primarily shot in Stonington, Connecticut, features Julia Roberts in her breakout role as a waitress at a pizza parlor.

Broiled and fried scrod (defined, really, as any white-fleshed fish) is usually served in fillets, with french fries. The term scrod, by the way, most likely originated in the early stages of the colonization of North America, when sailing captains would pick out the best of the day's catch and store it in a container marked with the initials SCROD. The letters stood for 'Select Catch Remains On Deck.'

Bluefish makes regular menu appearances, as do grilled or smoked swordfish, tuna steaks and striped bass, the latter hunted by weekend fisherpeople on organized boat trips.

Littlenecks and oysters are usually eaten raw with a dollop of cocktail sauce and a few drops of lemon juice. Wellfleet oysters (p194) are the region's choicest oysters. Mussels are less common but no less desirable.

HOW TO EAT A LOBSTER

Eating lobster is a messy affair, so the best place to consume it is outside, in a beachfront lobster 'pound' or 'pool.' That way you won't worry about tearing the critters apart with abandon, using your fingers (which is the only way it can be done).

At lobster pounds, live lobsters are cooked to order. They range in size from 1lb ('chicken lobsters,' or 'chicks') and 1¼lb to 1½lb ('selects') to 'large' lobsters, weighing from 2lb to 20lb. 'Culls,' those missing a claw, are sold at a discount, as the claw meat is considered choice (it's also possible to buy the claws separately). 'Shorts,' smaller than chicks, do not meet the legal minimum size for harvesting.

When you order lobster, you'll be brought a plastic bib, a supply of napkins, a cracker for breaking the claws, a small fork or pick for excavating the tight places, a container of melted butter, a slice of lemon and an alcohol-soaked towelette to wipe your hands after the mess is over.

The lobster may be very hot, with hot water still inside the shell. Start by twisting off the little legs and sucking or chewing out the slender bits of meat inside. Then move on to the claws: twist the claws and knuckles off the body, break them with the cracker and dip the tender meat in butter before eating. Next, pick up the lobster body in one hand and the tail in the other. Twist the tail back and forth to break it off. Tear off each flipper at the end of the tail and suck out the meat. Then use your finger or an implement to push through the hole at the end of the tail where the flippers were, and the big chunk of tail meat will come out.

There is delicious meat in the body as well, though it takes work to get it. Tear off the carapace (back shell), then split the body in two lengthwise. Behind the spot where each small leg was attached is a chunk of meat, best gotten with pick and fingers.

Or, order it off the shell.

Cheese

Vermont is famous for its dairy farms, and it's at the forefront of a movement to return to organic, hormone-free milk. Ben Cohen and Jerry Greenfield, founders of the Ben & Jerry's premium ice-cream company (see p392), established themselves in Vermont because of its good dairy industry.

Cheeses of Vermont (2002), Henry Tewksbury's delightfully passionate guide to artisanal and farmstead cheesemakers, directs explorers to out-of-the-way cheesemaking operations.

Cabot is the big industrial cheese producer in Vermont, but there are dozens of farmsteads tucked away on the back roads that make small batches of goat, cow and sheep cheeses on their family-style farms.

The great variety and high quality of New England cheeses (www .newenglandcheese.com) will thrill the most discriminating gourmet. But the old standby, Vermont Cheddar, is still the most popular New England cheese . And you can watch it, and other types of award-winning cheese, being made at Grafton Village Cheese Company (p363) and at Shelburne Farms (p398), among other places.

Sample a platter of great cheese (the perfect picnic food) in Vermont at Brattleboro Food Co-op (p359), Harvest Market (p394) and Fresh Market (p401).

Fruit & Vegetables

New England grows fruit with abandon and in abundant variety. Arguably, the king of New England fruits is the tiny but oh-so-revered Maine blueberry. Although they're bursting with mega doses of healthful antioxidants, most visitors devour them just because they taste so good. In Maine, they're used in or on everything from pancakes and muffins to pies and ice-cream.

Learn where to pick apples on www.apples -ne.com, which also extols the virtues of varieties grown in New England.

In the fall, bogs in southeastern Massachusetts yield crimson cranberry crops, which are spectacular to look at. With sugar added to sweeten their tartness, cranberries make refreshing juice or are used in the baking of delicious muffins and pies. Thanksgiving dinners today (see the boxed text on p58) are not complete without cranberry sauce.

Apples and strawberries are two other important landmarks on the culinary map of New England. Buy fruit at roadside stands or pick your own at orchards.

LIFE IS SWEET

If you thought March and April were the cruelest months, think again. It's maple-sugaring season in northern New England. Maple-sugar houses offer tours and demonstrations and sometimes have a restaurant attached where travelers can enjoy pancakes in decidedly rustic style. Visit the Robb Family Farm (p358) to watch the process; the Vermont Maple Festival in St Albans (www .vtmaplefestival.org) in late April to revel in all things maple-sugary; or visit New Hampshire on the last Sunday of March, also known as New Hampshire Maple Sunday to indulge in a pancake breakfast. For a list of maple-sugar houses in Massachusetts, visit www.massmaple.org.

Maple sugaring takes place in early spring, when the sharp difference between night- and day-time temperatures induces the maple bush (a grove of maple trees) to ooze its sap. In anticipation of this blessed event, farmers have tapped metal pipes into the trees to collect the sap, hung buckets and laced tubing between the trees. Thanks to this apparatus, the sap flows downhill to the sugar shack with as little effort as possible. Then, they 'sugar the sap off,' boiling it to extract the essence. Thick maple syrup is derived this way. The finest syrup is used on pancakes and waffles, while darker, thicker varieties are good for cooking. If boiling continues, the mixture hardens into maple sugar, which is then made into candy.

Children love maple-sugar candy, but most adults either love or detest the sweetness of maple sugar. There is no middle ground. Nor are maple-sugar devotees daunted by maple sugar's relative costliness compared with white sugar.

Corn, beans and squash – dubbed the life-giving sisters – are staple foods in New England. Boston is even nicknamed Beantown. Boston baked beans (made with pork, maple syrup and, yes, beans) are rare on today's menus, but they were quite common a century ago because they didn't spoil quickly and because they had real energy-boosting qualities.

> Thirty-seven percent of visitors to Vermont buy maple syrup.

Baked Goods

Authentic New England–style meals are sometimes followed by Indian pudding (something akin to soupy gingerbread) or bread pudding. When a contemporary bistro offers a mod version of bread pudding, try it. It'll barely resemble its brethren in the rest of the country.

During the autumn, seasonal pies like pumpkin and apple always feature on menus. Apple cobbler and apple crisp are delicious variations on the theme, especially when topped with homemade ice-cream. From mid-June through July, when strawberry and rhubarb ripen, grab a couple of pieces of strawberry-rhubarb pie.

DRINKS
Alcoholic Drinks

Although the region's northeast is not as fertile as Napa Valley, grape wine is produced in eastern Massachusetts, southeastern Rhode Island and northwestern Connecticut. Even if not great, New England wines are generally drinkable; you may even find a passable blueberry wine in Maine. If you are feeling up for some bacchanalian revelry, tour Haight Vineyards (p358) and Hopkins Vineyard (p349), both in Connecticut.

> The site www.visitnew england.com directs you to New England's vineyards and wineries.

Bostonians take beer seriously and there are plenty of 'microbreweries' in town. Although New England's breweries don't often distribute beyond their local communities, Sam Adams has achieved national and international recognition. You can also tour the Boston Brewing Co (p350).

Outside of Boston, toss back a cold one at Northampton Brewery (p115), Otter Creek Brewing (p247), Long Trail Brewing Company (p383). In Maine, head to Federal Jack's Restaurant & Brew Pub (p376).

The hometown secret in New England is cider and it occupies pride of place on the drink list. Even though it's quite alcoholic, settlers allowed their children to drink it, and clergymen who abstained from harder liquors relished in the sweet-tasting drink.

Nonalcoholic Drinks

If someone asks you what kind of pop you'd like, they're usually not inquiring about your musical preferences. They're referring to soda pop (soft drink). Also, if you don't like ice in your carbonated beverages, let your restaurant server know. Otherwise, you'll get a concoction in which the ratio of soft drink to ice cubes is one to three.

Although tap water is potable almost everywhere in New England, Maine's Poland Spring bottled water is a local favorite.

Unless you like tons of sugar and cream in your coffee, don't order 'regular.' Europeans should order three large mugs (usually served in paper cups) to get their usual fix of caffeine, as coffee in the US is weak by comparison.

CELEBRATIONS

At heart, New England food festivals give thanks for earth's plenty, but they will also give you a feel for local culture. Many shindigs involve hours of volunteer work from people who care about their communities and

---

BE THANKFUL FOR WHAT YOU'VE GOT

Whether you make cranberry sauce from scratch or jiggle a gelatinous mass out from a can; whether you adorn sweet potatoes with marshmallows or roasted pecans; whether your stuffing contains oysters, chestnuts, giblets or fruit...a Thanksgiving meal is always something to behold (p167).

In a time when many Americans have little in common with each other, most celebrate this holiday in a classic way – by overindulging. From penthouses to homeless shelters, folks dive in to mashed potatoes, stuffing, cranberry sauce, gravy and the main event (turkey).

The cooking of turkey has long filled cooks with fear and delight. Young married couples phone home, begging breathlessly for better basting techniques; parents run around in frilly aprons; grandmothers serve as quality control experts. Make no mistake about it: Americans love this meal and this bird. Ben Franklin even preferred the turkey over the eagle as the national bird, and in a long-standing tradition, the US president always pardons one turkey before the mass slaughter.

Thanksgiving can be a stressful time, though. Many people travel long distances to be with their families; airports are crowded and road traffic is terrible. But as Americans gather around the table, something happens. Despite our differences, we give thanks for an overwhelming feeling of unity, happiness and home.

---

want to share it with visitors. New England hosts a number of entertaining summer and fall festivals.

At the **Maine Lobster Festival** (☎ 207-596-0376; www.mainelobsterfestival.com; ☼ early Aug), over 12 tons of lobsters are prepared in the world's largest lobster cooker. The **Oyster Festival** (☎ 203-838-9444; www.seaport.org; ☼ Sep) in Norwalk, Connecticut, celebrates the region's seafaring past. The **Yarmouth Clam Festival** (☎ 207-846-3984; www.clamfestival.com; ☼ Jul) features clam-shucking contests, canoe races and a festival parade. The **Harwich Cranberry Festival** (www.harwich cranberryfestival.com/_harwichcranfest.htm; ☼ mid-Sep) includes bodacious fireworks.

Oddities exist as well, such as the **Zucchini Festival** (☎ 802-228-5830; ☼ late Aug) in Ludlow, Vermont.

WHERE TO EAT & DRINK

It is possible to spend anywhere from $2 to $200 per person for a meal. For the breakdown of our budget categories, see p472.

Except for deep in the forest, you're never far from a place that serves food. Some fast-food restaurants are open 24 hours a day in cities and on highways. (For general opening and closing hours, see p531.) There are variations on this theme, though. Some restaurants serve breakfast all day. Many places open for lunch and dinner continue serving meals right on through the afternoon. Some restaurants serve a lighter, less formal 'bar' or 'tavern' menu until midnight or 1am. Some restaurants close on Monday.

As for costs, breakfast will run $3 to $10, depending on whether you're at a diner or a culinary hot spot. Lunch will be in the $5 to $12 range. You can get a good dinner in a pleasant, though not fancy, restaurant for $15 to $25 per person, not including tax, tip or drinks. In posh big-city restaurants and resorts, it is possible to see a bill of $75 per person. Major cities and more sophisticated country inns serve refined American, continental and international cuisine.

VEGETARIANS & VEGANS

New Englanders like to laud themselves for their liberal attitudes. They take pride in the fact that this is one of the most socially conscious regions of America. Many restaurants will not only provide vegetarian options, but they will do it with panache. Of course, it is easier to find vegetarian options in cosmopolitan areas than tiny towns, but, usually, even at the

The New England Confectionery Company (NECCO), which makes little pastel-colored wafers, was established in 1847 and is the oldest continuously operating candy company in the world.

local diner you can find something healthy and meat-free. So if you're a 'veg-head,' worry not. No one will mind if you ask whether something is prepared with a meat base. Do be careful with chowders, though, because they are usually prepared with fish stock. Armed with this book, vegetarians won't starve in the remote outposts of New England; they'll actually thrive (we frequently list vegetarian dishes offered at restaurants).

Natural food markets and grocery stores are popping up throughout New England faster than weeds in a compost pile.

WHINING & DINING

Traveling with children in New England should be relatively stress-free; it can be both rewarding *and* challenging. No matter what age your child, you can take some steps to make them feel more comfortable on the road.

One of the biggest challenges is dealing with disrupted eating schedules and unfamiliar foods. Ask yourself what special supplies your child will need to make it to the next stop. When entering a restaurant, assess your child's energy level and the noise level of the eatery. If your child is on the verge of exploding and it's a quiet restaurant, consider having a picnic or getting take-out.

If you have spawned picky eaters, stay at a resort or condo so you can stock some of your child's favorite foods, giving them a sense of stability. See also p528.

For gifts, consult www .vermontspecialtyfoods .org, which features local products from pancake mixes to pastas, baked goods to beverages.

HABITS & CUSTOMS

The duration of meals, table manners and etiquette change with different dining situations, but here are a few tips. In fast-food restaurants, you are expected to clear your own tray. Meals at mid-range to upper-end eateries require a 15% to 20% tip for your server (added to the bill; cash preferred). Smoking is usually forbidden in restaurants, but if it is permitted, there should be a smoking section. During a business meal, watch what others order before you order; this is especially true with alcohol. If you are having dinner with an American family, it's polite to bring a bottle of wine or something to share. Be sensitive about when it is time to leave. Depending upon the age of your hosts, it may be earlier than you are used to.

COOKING COURSES

Patron food saint Julia Child, an alumna of Smith College (p244), longtime resident of Cambridge, Massachusetts, and the star of many TV cooking shows, spent four decades teaching people how to cook before she died in 2004. She was active in the Cambridge and Boston community and supported a scholarship program for aspiring culinary arts students. If you want to embody Julia's bon vivant, bon appétit spirit, take a class at the New England Culinary Institute (p389), one of the country's top cooking schools; the Cambridge School of Culinary Arts (p92); or the Rhode Island School of Design (p283), where you can also tour markets and restaurants with reputable chefs.

Join legions of amateur foodies who turn to the mysterious www .phantomgourmet.com, a site based on UPN 38's Phantom Gourmet TV show.

NEW ENGLAND CLAM CHOWDER

There are few things more satisfying than sitting down to a bowl of classic New England clam chowder and a tall glass of beer. Just bringing up the issue, though, of what constitutes the most authentic recipe will instigate a heated row, often involving mention of grandmothers and forefathers. New England clam chowder is a cream-based affair and should never be confused with its counterpart Manhattan clam chowder, which has a tomato base (and is much less satisfying).

Boston

HIGHLIGHTS

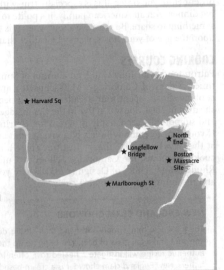

- **Most Spectacular View of the City Skyline** From the Red Line 'T,' as the train crosses the Longfellow Bridge (p81) between Kendall Sq and Charles St/Massachusetts General Hospital

- **Most Dramatic Historic Spot** The cobblestone marker of the site of the Boston Massacre (p73)

- **Loveliest Street** Back Bay's Marlborough St (p81), lined with brownstones and lit with gas lamps

- **Most Worthwhile Wait** For a table at Pomodoro in the North End (p105)

- **Most Talented Buskers** Folk singers in Harvard Sq (p86)

★ Harvard Sq

★ Longfellow Bridge

North End

Boston Massacre Site

★ Marlborough St

■ TELEPHONE CODE: 617	■ POPULATION: 589,000	■ AREA: 48 SQ MILES

'Wicked pisser' is how Bostonians describe their hometown. Wicked, meaning 'extremely'; pisser (pronounced 'pissah') meaning 'supercool.' It is the ultimate compliment. That this crass but colorful phrase so aptly describes this graceful city is a testament to the paradox that is Boston.

Boston's magnetism comes in part from its long history as a prosperous port and regional center of commerce. Calling this quaint city the 'hub of the universe' and the 'Athens of America' might seem a bit of braggadocio now, but these were not empty boasts in the 19th century. The city's glory is retained and radiated by its grand architecture, its population of literati and artists, and its world-renowned academic and cultural institutions. Regardless of inevitable changes, Boston's soul remains grand. Nonetheless, these days she is more complex.

Boston's universities and colleges attract students from all over the world. From September through May, the city overflows with their exuberance. This renewable source of cultural energy supports innumerable sporting events, foreign cinemas, theaters, art galleries, literary cafés, hip bars and music scenes.

Boston is an amalgam of vibrant neighborhoods, from working-class Charlestown to upper-crust Beacon Hill, from the edgy South End to the old-world North End. These worlds come together in an uneasy coexistence, occasionally intermingling and sometimes colliding. Even if you have a sense of historical Boston, she may surprise you. And the country's founding fathers – many of whom walked these same streets – would expect nothing less.

CLIMATE

The climate in Boston is similar to the rest of New England, although it does not enjoy the benefits of the Gulf Stream, as does Cape Cod, nor suffer the winds of the mountains, as do parts of Vermont, New Hampshire and Maine.

Summers are hot and humid, with temperatures ranging from 68°F to 75°F, while winters are cold and wet – average temperatures are between 28° and 38°F. Snowfalls are the norm from December to March.

In spring and fall, temperatures are moderate. These seasons also enjoy the beauty of blooming magnolias and turning leaves, respectively. Unfortunately, these are the seasons when the weather is most unpredictable, especially since the city sits in the midst of colliding weather patterns from the Great Lakes, Canada and the Gulf Stream. Thus, the old saying 'If you don't like the weather, wait a minute' is only a slight exaggeration. Check out the beacon atop the old Hancock building (p83) for an up-to-date weather forecast.

ORIENTATION

For a city of its stature, Boston is geographically small and logistically manageable. The sights and activities of principal interest to travelers are contained within an area that's only about 1 mile wide by 3 miles long. It's bounded on the eastern edge by Boston Harbor and the Atlantic Ocean, on the north by the Charles River and Cambridge. Boston proper has almost 600,000 people; 'greater' Boston has over three million.

Most of Boston's attractions are easily accessed by Massachusetts Bay Transportation Authority (MBTA) subway trains (see p129). To reach Logan International Airport, take the Blue Line to the Airport T-stop, then hop on the fast, free shuttle bus to the terminal. The train stations – North Station and South Station – have dedicated T-stops by the same name (Green/Orange and Red Line respectively).

The Central Artery (also known as I-93 or the John F Fitzgerald Expressway) used to cut right through downtown, separating

MASSACHUSETTS

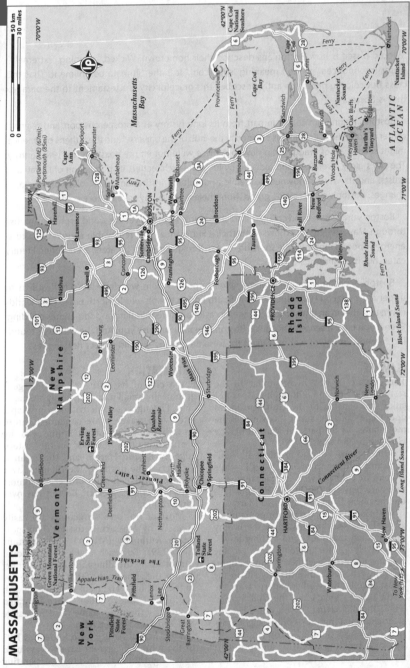

the North End and waterfront from the rest of the city. As a part of the largest public works project in US history, the Central Artery has recently been widened and re-routed underground to alleviate the per-sistent traffic nightmares. (See Dig the Big Dig, p64.) The construction, of course, has created its own set of surface-artery issues, which are only gradually disappearing as the project nears completion. Soon this mess will be replaced with parks and open space known as the Rose Kennedy Green-way. In any case, Boston is much easier to navigate on foot than by car, especially during busy traffic times.

Boston's downtown streets are wind-ing, one way and narrow. Expect to get a bit lost as you wander around Downtown Crossing, the Italian North End, Brahmin Beacon Hill, no-nonsense Government Center, colorful Chinatown and the small Theater District. Abutting downtown, the area of Beacon Hill is bounded by Cam-bridge and Beacon Sts and extends west to the Charles River. Two large parks – the Boston Common and Public Garden – lie adjacent to it to the south.

Back Bay, created thanks to a mid-19th-century landfill project, is more orderly than the rest of the city. Its streets are laid out east to west in alphabetical order: Ar-lington, Berkeley, Clarendon and so on to Hereford. Commonwealth Ave (referred to as 'Comm Ave') is Boston's grandest boulevard, with a grassy promenade run-ning the length of it. The Back Bay ends at Massachusetts Ave (known simply as 'Mass Ave'), which runs northwest across the Charles River and into Cambridge and Harvard Sq.

West of Massachusetts Ave lies Kenmore Sq and the Fenway area. The Fenway in-cludes a 4-mile-long grassy byway that weaves through the city. South of Back Bay is, appropriately, the South End. It lies be-tween Berkeley St to the east and Massa-chusetts Ave to the west, with Huntington and Shawmut Aves defining its northern and southern boundaries.

The Charles River, with a popular grassy esplanade along both its banks, separates Boston and Cambridge, which is home to Harvard University and the Massachusetts Institute of Technology (MIT). The best views of the Boston skyline and Beacon Hill are from the northern banks of the Charles River near the Longfellow Bridge.

Maps

You can get good maps of Boston and New England at just about any bookstore (below). Look for Lonely Planet's manage-able, full-color, laminated map of the city.

If you plan on doing more bicycling than simply along the banks of the Charles River, get *Boston's Bike Map* produced by **Rubel BikeMaps** (☎ 617-776-6567; www.bikemaps.com). It's available from the Globe Corner Bookstore (below) or directly from Rubel ($5). See also p88 for information on its laminated 'Pocket Rides.'

INFORMATION
Bookstores
Brattle Book Shop (Map pp66-8; ☎ 617-542-0210; 9 West St) A treasure trove crammed with out-of-print, rare and first-edition books.

Coop (Harvard Cooperative Society; Map p69; ☎ 617-499-2000; 1400 Massachusetts Ave) Three floors of books, music and every other 'essential' item a student could need. Anyone can buy just about anything emblazoned with the Harvard logo.

Cuttyhunk (Map pp70-1; ☎ 617-574-5000; 1180 Washington St; ✆ 10am-6pm Mon-Sat, noon-6pm Sun) Specializes in gay titles.

Globe Corner Bookstore (Map p69; ☎ 617-497-6277; www.globecorner.com; 49 Palmer St) Specializing in travel literature, guide books and specialty maps, including topographical maps of New England. (For more topos, see also the Appalachian Mountain Club Headquarters, p73.)

Grolier Poetry Bookshop (Map p69; ☎ 617-547-4648; 6 Plympton St) One of the most famous poetry bookstores in the USA.

New Words Women's Bookstore (☎ 617-876-5310; 186 Hampshire St) Devoted to books by, for and about women. Take the Red Line to Central Sq and walk north on Prospect St to Inman Sq.

Out of Town News (Map p69; ☎ 617-354-7777; Harvard Sq) A National Historic Landmark, selling papers from virtually every major US city, as well as from dozens of cities around the world.

Rand McNally Map & Travel Store (Map p69; ☎ 617-720-1125; 84 State St) An excellent choice for travel guides and maps.

Schoenhof's Foreign Books (Map pp66-8; ☎ 617-547-8855; 76a Mt Auburn St) A national center for foreign language materials, books and dictionaries.

Trident Booksellers & Café (Map p70-1; ☎ 617-267-8688; 338 Newbury St; ✆ 9am-midnight) Specializes in New Age titles.

DIG THE BIG DIG

All federal highway projects are local. And few road improvement schemes have been so infamously linked with a locality as the Central Artery/Tunnel project is with the city of Boston. The Big Dig, as it is better known, is now well into its second decade of construction and well past its 15th billion dollar in cost. The project, which is finally nearing completion, has won acclaim and been defamed. Boston motorists have gone from infuriated to confounded to relieved. The Big Dig is an unmatched marvel in terms of civil engineering, urban planning and pork-barrel politics.

The project primarily involved the dismantling of the Central Artery, the perpetually congested raised highway that cut through the downtown. In its place, the Big Dig built more than 40 miles of subterranean superhighway. To undertake a massive public-works project in the heart of the city, according to the former project director, was like 'performing bypass surgery on a patient while he continues to work and play tennis.'

The Big Dig employed the most advanced techniques of urban engineering and environmental science. French-designed slurry walls penetrated 100ft downwards, creating a reinforced underground corridor 200ft wide. Within this precarious swath of city, construction workers carefully excavated around building foundations and subway tunnels, through hazardous landfill and solid bedrock, and under the sludgy harbor floor. The project utilized teams of biologists to prevent a mass out-migration of refugee rats and to assure the seasonal in-migration of spawning herring. The Big Dig even proved a windfall for sifting archeologists, who uncovered the long buried remnants of the colonial American and ancient Indian past (see p86).

And to think the project very nearly never got off the board. Federal funding for the Big Dig was a political present to Boston's Thomas 'Tip' O'Neill, the departing Speaker of the House, which the Democratic Congress included in its 1987 transportation appropriation bill. The proposal was vetoed by Republican President Ronald Reagan, who claimed that he had not seen so much lard since the Iowa State Fair. But the Big Dig would not die. Led by Massachusetts Senator Ted Kennedy, the upper chamber overturned the veto by one vote.

Once ground was broken, the Big Dig quickly grew into an incredible jobs program. At its peak in the 1990s, the project employed over 5000 full-time laborers and an estimated 10,000 more in support staff. The investigations into mismanagement and misappropriation are likely to last longer than the actual construction time.

The Big Dig is more than just a long and winding underground road, it also dramatically changed the face of the city and improved its residents' quality of life. Just north of this high-tech cavern, the highway meets the Charles River. The graceful Leonard Zakim Bridge, named for a local civil rights activist, was designed to span the water crossing. Against the historic backdrop of Bunker Hill, it is the widest cable-stayed bridge in the world. To the south, the Big Dig includes a new harbor tunnel, connecting I-90 with the airport and north shore. The Ted Williams Tunnel, named for a local leftfielder, won the prestigious Outstanding Achievement Award presented by the American Society for Civil Engineering in 1996. Finally, the project will reclaim almost 200 acres of industrial wasteland for parks and recreation. Where the hulking Central Artery once created barriers and shadows, Bostonians will soon enjoy a tree-lined open space, the Rose Kennedy Greenway, named for a local matriarch.

Cultural Centers

French Library (Map pp70-1; ☎ 617-912-0400; www .frenchlib.org; 53 Marlborough St; ⏱ 10am-6pm Mon-Thu, 10am-5pm Fri & Sat) Sponsors regular lectures, films and language classes. Hosts an annual Bastille Day celebration (July 14), during which Marlborough St is closed off.

Goethe Institut (Map pp70-1; ☎ 617-262-6050; www .goethe.de/boston; 170 Beacon St; ⏱ 9:30am-5:30pm Mon-Thu, 9:30am-4:30pm Fri) Sponsors a cultural program of German events and classes; its reference library is also well stocked with books, tapes and periodicals.

New England Irish Cultural Center (☎ 781-821-8291; www.irishculture.org; 200 New Boston Dr, Canton; ⏱ 9am-5pm Mon-Fri) Organizes events to promote Irish culture and community. Based 20 miles south of the city.

Emergency

City of Boston Police Headquarters (Map pp70-1; ☎ 617-343-4200; cnr Ruggles & Tremont Sts)
Road & Traffic Conditions (☎ 617-374-1234)

(Continued on page 72)

WEST GREATER BOSTON

Pier 8

F

Pier 7

Pier 6

Pier 5

Pier 4

Eighth St

Shipyard Park

Charlestown Navy Yard

161

To Constitution Inn; YMCA (0.2mi)

USS Cassin Young

Fifth St

51

E

First Ave

Pier 1

50

Hoosac Pier

Constitution St

Second Ave

Chelsea St

1

Boston Inner Harbor

Constitution Wharf

Battery Wharf

Lincoln Wharf

Union Wharf

Lewis Wharf

Atlantic Ave

166

To East Boston; Logan International Airport (2mi)

Sumner Tunnel (troll)

1A

1A

Commercial St

North St

Hanover Ave

Atlantic Ave

Greenough Ln

Hanover St

Fleet St

Clark St

Richmond St

Fulton St

148

Lincoln St

North Square

138

Charter St

Henchman St

Salem St

Tileston St

Prince St

Bennet St

43

79

71

128

111

74

97

110

89

108

North End

Snowhill St

Sheafe St

Cleveland Pl

Hull St

33

21

19

North End Playground

N Margin St

Prince St

Cooper St

Endicott St

107

Thatcher St

Stillman St

88

18

26

22

Cross St

Blackstone St

Haymarket

Commercial St

MBTA Water Shuttle

D

Constitution Rd

N Washington St

Haverhill St

Congress St

Friend St

Canal St

To Monument Square; Bunker Hill Monument (120yds)

Lomasney Way

Charlestown

Winthrop Square

Tremont St

Park St

Warren St

Soley St

95

101

City Square

John Harvard Mall

Harvard St

Prescott St

134

114

78

107

117

Main St

Devens St

To Paolo's Trattoria (0.3mi)

Old Rutherford Ave

Warren St

Monument Ave

C

Washington St

Lynde St

Rutherford Ave

99

Charlestown Bridge

Paul Revere Park

Leonard Zakim Bridge

1

160

Lovejoy Wharf

Beverly St

North Station

125

61

154

155

53

60

24

O'Neill Federal Building

State Service Center

Stanford St

B

93

Charles River

Nashua St

Suffolk County Jail

Charles St

Martha Rd

Old West End

Hawthorne Pl

Blossom Ct

Blossom St

Parkman St

6

To Community College (0.3mi)

John F Fitzgerald Expwy

Austin St

East St

To Charles River Boat Co; Gondola di Venezia; Cambridge Galleria (0.5mi)

Lechmere Canal

28

Charles River Bridge

Monsignor O'Brien Hwy

Science Park

32

Science Park

Fruit St

Charles St

The Esplanade

Storrow Dr

A

1

2

3

4

Community College

0 — 400 m
0 — 0.3 miles

INFORMATION
Cambridge Visitor Information		
Booth	1	C3
Coop	2	B3
FedEx Kinko's	3	B3
Globe Corner Bookstore	4	C2
Grolier Poetry Bookshop	5	C3

Out of Town News.................(see 1)
Post Office..............................6 B3
Schoenhof's Foreign Books.......7 C3
STA Travel...............................8 C3

SIGHTS & ACTIVITIES (pp74–92)
Arthur M Sackler Museum.........9 D2
Busch-Reisinger Museum.....(see 14)
Cambridge Center for Adult
Education..............................10 B3
Cambridge Common................11 B1
Christ Church.........................12 C2
Dewey, Cheetham & Howe.....13 B3
Fogg Art Museum...................14 D3
John F Kennedy Park...............15 B4
John Harvard Statue...............16 C3
Longfellow National Historic
Site.......................................17 A2
Museum of Natural History......18 D1
Old Burying Ground................19 C2
Radcliffe Yard........................20 B2

SLEEPING (p101)
Charles Hotel.........................21 B3
Irving House..........................22 E2

EATING (pp111–13)
Algiers Coffee House...............23 B3
Bartley's Burger Cottage..........24 D3
Cardullo's...............................25 C3
Cass Mexico...........................26 C3
Craigie St Bistro.....................27 A1
Farmers Market......................28 C3
Garage...................................29 B3
Harvest...................................30 C3
Henrietta's Table................(see 21)
Herrell's..................................31 B2
Hi-Rise Bread Co................(see 21)
Rialto.................................(see 21)
Sabra Grill..............................32 B3
Tanjore..................................33 B3
Toscanini's.............................34 C3
Upstairs on the Square............35 B3

DRINKING (pp115–16)
Hong Kong.............................36 D3
John Harvard's Brew House......37 C3
Shay's....................................38 B3

ENTERTAINMENT (pp117–23)
American Repertory Theater.....39 B2
Brattle Theater.......................40 B3
Club Passim............................41 C3
Harvard Film Archive & Film Study
Library..................................42 D3
Loews Harvard Square.............43 C2
Memorial Hall at Sanders
Theatre............................(see 58)
Nameless Coffeehouse (First Parish
Church)................................44 C2
Regattabar.........................(see 21)

SHOPPING (pp123–5)
Berk's....................................45 C3
Cambridge Artists Cooperative.46 B3
Clothware...............................47 B2
Harvard Collections.................48 C3
J August.................................49 C3
Jasmine/Sola/Sola Men............50 B3
Mudo.....................................51 C3
Oona's Experienced Clothing...52 D3
Second Time Around...............53 B3
Tannery.................................54 B3
Tess.......................................55 C3
Tower Records........................56 C3

TRANSPORT
Thrifty...................................57 B3

OTHER
Harvard Square Hotel...........(see 57)
Harvest Review.......................(see 29)
Holyoke Center.......................58 C3

To Inman Square (0.5mi);
Hotel Marlowe (2mi)

To Chez Henri (0.1mi);
Lizard Lounge (0.2mi);
ABC Cycle (0.2mi);
Best Western
Homestead Inn
Porter Square (0.6mi);
Somerville (1.4mi)

To Cambridge
Historical Society
(0.2mi)

To Elbridge Gerry Estate (0.2mi);
Mt Auburn Cemetery (0.3mi);
Watertown (3mi)

To Charles River
Canoe & Kayak
Center (0.5mi)

To Central Square (.6mi); MIT Museum,
MIT (1mi); Harvard Bridge (1.2mi);
Kendall Square (1.5mi); Longfellow
Bridge (2mi); Hwy 28 (2.5m)

To Boston University/
Bridge (1.2mi);
MIT Museum;
MIT (1.3mi)

To Downtown
Boston (2mi)

Harvard University

Divinity Ave
Oxford St
Cambridge St
Kirkland St
Kirkland Pl
Irving St
Francis Ave
Farrar St
Gund Hall
Science Center
Harvard Yard
Widener Library
Cambridge Common
Radcliffe Yard
Radcliffe College
Law School
Harkness Commons
Massachusetts Ave
Garden St
Brattle St
Mt Auburn St
John F Kennedy St
Charles River
The Esplanade
Anderson Bridge
Memorial Dr
Soldiers Field Rd
Weld Boathouse
Harvard University
Craigie Circle

INFORMATION
Bank of America.................................1 C3
City of Boston Police Headquarters..2 D6
Cuttyhunk Bookstore........................3 H4
FedEx Kinko's...................................4 F2
French Library...................................5 G2
Goethe Institut..................................6 F2
Greater Boston Convention & Visitors
  Bureau (GBCVB)............................7 F3
Post Office..8 F3
Post Office..9 F3
STA Travel......................................10 E3
Tech Superpowers Internet Cafe....11 E3
Trident Booksellers & Café.............12 E3

SIGHTS & ACTIVITIES (pp74–94)
Arlington St Church..........................13 G2
Back Bay Yoga Studio......................14 D3
Baptiste Power Vinyasa Yoga...........15 G3
Beacon Hill Skate.............................16 H3
Boston Bicycle..................................17 B3
Boston Center for Adult
  Education.....................................18 G3
Boston Public Library........................19 F3
Boston University..............................20 B2
Christian Science Church..................21 E4
Community Bicycle Supply................22 G4
Esplanade..23 G1
Fenway Park....................................24 C3
Gibson House Museum.....................25 G2

Institute of Contemporary Art.......26 E3
Isabella Stewart Gardner Museum..27 C5
Jasmine..28 E3
Mapparium.......................(see 29)
Mary Baker Eddy Library................29 E4
Massachusetts College of Art........30 C5
Museum of Fine Arts, Boston.........31 D5
Northeastern University..................32 D5
Old South Church...........................33 F3
Photographic Resource Center.......34 A2
Prudential Center............................35 E3
Prudential Center Skywalk..............36 F3
South End Yoga..............................37 G5
Trinity Church.................................38 G3
Union Park Square...........................39 G4

SLEEPING (pp98–100)
463 Beacon.....................................40 E2
Berkeley Residence YWCA...............41 G3
Boston International Hostel..............42 D3
Buckminster Hotel............................43 C3
Chandler Inn Hotel..........................44 G3
Clarendon Square Inn.......................45 F4
College Club....................................46 G2
Commonwealth Court Guest
  House..47 E3
Copley House..................................48 F4
Copley Inn.......................................49 F3
Copley Square Hotel........................50 F3
Eliot Suite Hotel..............................51 D3
Gryphon House................................52 D3
HI Boston at Fenway........................53 C3
Hotel Commonwealth......................54 C3
Howard Johnson Fenway.................55 C4
Lenox Hotel.....................................56 F3
Midtown Hotel.................................57 E4
Newbury Guest House......................58 E3
YMCA of Greater Boston.................59 E5

EATING (pp107–11)
Ankara Cafe....................................60 C3
Aquitaine...61 G4
Audubon Circle................................62 B3
B&G Oysters Ltd..............................63 G4
Back Bay Summer Shack...................64 E3
Bangkok Cuisine..............................65 E4
Betty's Wok & Noodle Diner............66 E4
Bob the Chef....................................67 E5
Brown Sugar Café............................68 C4
Buteco...69 C4
Café Jaffa..70 E3
Casa Romero...................................71 E3
Charlie's Sandwich Shoppe..............72 F4
Claremont Café................................73 F4
Clio..(see 51)

Croma..74 E3
Dartmouth Café..............................75 F2
Delux Café.......................................76 G3
Elephant Walk..................................77 B3
Emack & Bolio's...............................78 E3
Farmers Market...............................79 F3
Finale Desserterie............................80 H2
Franklin Café....................................81 H4
Garden of Eden Cafe.......................82 E3
Great Bay...83 C3
Hamersley's Bistro...........................84 G4
House of Siam..................................85 F4
Icarus..86 G3
Jae's Café & Grill..............................87 F4

JP Licks..88 E3
L'Espalier...89 E3
Legal Seafoods (Copley Place)........90 F3
Legal Seafoods (Prudential
  Center)...91 F3
Mistral...92 G3
Other Side Cosmic Café...................93 D3
Parish Café & Bar.............................94 G2
Pho Pasteur.....................................95 F2
Red Fez...96 H4
Sonsie...97 E3
Sophia's...98 C4
Tapeo..99 E3
Tim's Tavern....................................100 G3

0 — 500 m
0 — 0.3 miles

DRINKING 🍷🍺 (pp115–16)
Boston Beer Works.................101 C3
Cask 'n Flagon........................102 C3
Clery's Bar & Restaurant........103 G3
Cottonwood Café....................104 G2
Jake Ivory's............................105 C3
Jillian's Billiard Club & Lucky
 Strike.................................106 D3
Modern..................................107 C3
Vox Populi.............................108 F3

ENTERTAINMENT 🎭 (pp117–23)
Avalon...................................109 C3
Axis.......................................110 C3
Berklee Performance Center....111 C3
Bill's Bar...............................112 C3
BosTix...................................113 F3
Boston Center for the Arts......114 G4
Club Café...............................115 G3
Fritz.................................(see 44)
Huntington Theater Company...116 E4
Jacques..................................117 H3
Machine.................................118 C4
New England Conservatory.....119 E4
Ramrod...........................(see 118)
Symphony Hall........................120 E4
Wally's Café...........................121 E5

SHOPPING 🛍 (pp123–5)
Barbara Krakow Gallery...........122 G2
Bromfield Art Gallery..............123 H4
Closet, Inc.......................(see 133)
Copley Place..........................124 F3
Hempfest...............................125 E3
Jasmine/Sola..........................126 E3
John Fluevog.........................127 E3
Looney Tunes........................128 E3
Mudo....................................129 F3
Newbury Comics....................130 E3
Second Time Around...............131 F2
Shops at Prudential Center......132 F2
Society of Arts & Crafts..........133 E3
Tannery.................................134 G2
Virgin Megastore...................135 E3

TRANSPORT (pp126–9)
Enterprise..............................136 F3

OTHER
Bisexual Resource Center.........137 G3
Boston Duck Tours............(see 35)
Fenway Community Health Center
....138 D3
Urban Adventours...............(see 17)

(Continued from page 64)

Internet Access

Wireless access is free at most hotels and many cafés, including Trident Booksellers (p63) and Sonsie (p108). For a list of wifi locations on Newbury St, see www.newbury open.net. Boston Public Library (p73) has free Internet access for 15-minute intervals, or you can get a visitor courtesy card at the circulation desk and sign up for one hour of free terminal time. Arrive first thing in the morning to avoid long waits.

FedEx Kinko's (www.fedexkinkos.com) Harvard Sq (Map p69; ☎ 617-497-0125; 1 Mifflin Pl; ⏰ 24hr); Back Bay (Map pp70-1; ☎ 617-262-6188; 187 Dartmouth St; ⏰ 24hr); Government Center (☎ 617-973-9000; 2 Center Plaza; ⏰ 24hr Mon-Thu, noon-10pm Fri, 7am-10pm Sat, 7am-midnight Sun)

Tech Superpowers Internet Café (Map pp70-1; ☎ 617-267-9716; www.newburyopen.net; 252 Newbury St; per 15 min/hr $3/5; ⏰ 9am-8pm Mon-Fri, noon-7pm Sat & Sun)

Internet Resources

boston.indymedia.org The Boston Independent Media Center, an alternative voice for local news and events.

www.boston.com The online presence of the *Boston Globe*.

www.boston-online.com An offbeat source of local news and information; includes such important resources as a glossary of Bostonese and a guide to public restrooms in the city.

www.bostonphoenix.com The best source of arts, culture and entertainment listings.

www.cityofboston.gov Official website for the city government.

www.sonsofsamhorn.com Dedicated to discussion of all things Red Sox.

Libraries

Boston Public Library (Map pp70-1; ☎ 617-536-5400; www.bpl.org; 700 Boylston St; ⏰ 9am-9pm Mon-Thu, 9am-5pm Fri & Sat year-round, 1-5pm Sun Oct-May) The country's oldest free city library, dating to 1852. See p82 for details on architectural tours.

Media

Bay Windows (www.baywindows.com) Serves the gay and lesbian community.

Boston Globe (www.boston.com) One of two major daily newspapers; publishes an extensive and useful Calendar section every Thursday.

Boston Herald (www.bostonherald.com) The more right-wing daily, competing with the *Boston Globe*; has its own 'Scene' section published every Friday.

Boston Magazine (www.bostonmagazine.com) The city's monthly glossy magazine.

Boston Phoenix (www.bostonphoenix.com) The 'alternative' paper that focuses on arts and entertainment; published weekly.

Improper Bostonian (www.improper.com) A sassy, biweekly distributed free from sidewalk dispenser boxes.

Stuff@Night (www.stuffatnight.com) A free biweekly publication focusing on entertainment events.

Medical Services

In case of a medical emergency, the failsafe response is to go to the emergency room at any local hospital, where staff are required to treat everyone that shows up. Unfortunately, if your life is not threatened, ER

BOSTON IN...

Two Days

Spend your first day reliving Boston's revolutionary history by following the **Freedom Trail** (p90). Take as much time as you need to lounge on the **Boston Common** (p74), peek in the **Old State House** (p75) and visit **Paul Revere's house** (p79). At the end of the walking tour, stroll back into the **North End** (p105) for dinner at one of Boston's best Italian restaurants. On your second day, pack a picnic, rent a bike and ride along the **Charles River** (p81). Go as far as **Harvard Sq** (p86), if you wish, to cruise the campus and browse through the bookstores. Spend the evening in **Cambridge** (p86) hanging out with students and hearing live music.

Four Days

Follow the two-day itinerary, and on your third day escape the city. If revolutionary history is your thing, head to **Lexington** (p132) and **Concord** (p136) to see where it all began. Otherwise, go north to **Salem** (p143) to investigate its maritime culture and the treasures it yielded at the **Peabody Essex Museum** (p146). Spend your last day wandering around Boston's swankiest neighborhood, **Back Bay** (p81): stroll across the **Public Garden** (p79), window shop and gallery hop on **Newbury St** (p81), and go to the top of the **Prudential Center** (p82).

waits can be excruciating long and the cost is exorbitant. Therefore, the ER should be reserved for true emergencies.

CVS (☎ 617-876-5519; Massachusetts Ave, Cambridge; ☼ 24hr) Located in the Porter Sq shopping mall.

Massachusetts General Hospital (MGH; Map pp66-8; ☎ 617-726-2000; 55 Fruit St) Arguably the city's biggest and best; can refer you to smaller clinics and crisis hotlines.

MGH Traveler's Clinic (Map pp66-8; ☎ 617-724-1934; Founder's House, 8th fl, Charles St; ☼ 4:30-7:30pm Mon, 8:30am-5pm Tue, 8:30-11:30am Wed, noon-3pm Thu, 8:30am-12:30pm Fri) Offers immunization services.

Money

There are Cirrus and Plus ATMs all around the city. The following services exchange foreign currency.

Bank of America (☎ 800-841-4000) Downtown (Map pp66-8; 100 Federal St); Government Center (Map ppp66-8; 6 Tremont St); Copley Sq (557 Boylston St); Kenmore Sq (Map pp70-1; 540 Commonwealth Ave); Harvard Sq (Map p69; ☎ 877-353-3939; 1414 Massachusetts Ave, Cambridge)

Travelex America Logan International Airport (☎ 617-567-9881)

Post

Back Bay (Map ppp70-1; ☎ 617-267-8162; 800 Boylston St, Prudential Center)

Beacon Hill (Map pp66-8; ☎ 617-723-1951; 136 Charles St)

Downtown (Map pp66-8; ☎ 617-654-5326; 25 Dorchester Ave; ☼ 24hr) The only recipient for general delivery (poste restante) mail.

Faneuil Hall Marketplace (Map pp66-8; ☎ 617-723-1791) Doesn't accept packages.

Harvard Sq (Map p69; 125 Mt Auburn St)

Tourist Information

Appalachian Mountain Club Headquarters (AMC; Map pp66-8; ☎ 617-523-0636; www.outdoors.org; 5 Joy St; ☼ 8:30am-5pm Mon-Fri) *The* resource for outdoor activities in Boston and throughout New England.

Boston Welcome Center (Map pp66-8; ☎ 617-451-2227; 140 Tremont St; ☼ 9am-6pm) Sells maps, T passes and tickets to local attractions and tours.

Cambridge Visitor Information Booth (Map p69; ☎ 617-441-2884, 800-862-5678; www.cambridge-usa.org; Harvard Sq; ☼ 9am-5pm Mon-Sat, 1-5pm Sun) Detailed information on current Cambridge happenings and self-guided walking tours.

Greater Boston Convention & Visitors Bureau (GBCVB; ☎ 617-536-4100, 800-888-5515; www .bostonusa.com; 2 Copley Pl, Suite 105); Boston Common (Map pp66-8; ☎ 617-426-3115; Tremont & West Sts; ☼ 8:30am-5pm); Prudential Center (Map pp70-1; 800 Boylston St; ☼ 9am-6pm) Write in advance for an information packet, or visit for a subway or bus route map or other information.

Massachusetts Office of Travel & Tourism (Map pp66-8; ☎ 617-973-8500, 800-227-6277; www.massvacation.com; State Transportation Bldg, 10 Park Plaza, Ste 4510; ☼ 9am-5pm Mon-Fri)

National Park Service Visitor Center (NPS; Map pp66-8; ☎ 617-242-5642; 15 State St; ☼ 9am-5pm) Plenty of historical literature, a short slide show and free walking tours of the Freedom Trail.

Travel Agencies

STA Travel (☎ 800-781-4040; www.statravel.com; ☼ 24hr) Back Bay (Map pp70-1; ☎ 617-266-6014; 297 Newbury St; ☼ 10am-6pm Mon-Sat, 10am-5pm Sun); Harvard Sq (Map p69; ☎ 617-576-4623; 65 Mt Auburn St; ☼ 9am-6pm Mon-Fri, 10am-5pm Sat & Sun)

Vacation Outlet (Map pp66-8; ☎ 617-267-8100, 800-527-8646; www.vacationoutlet.com; Filene's Basement, 426 Washington St) Offers lots of last-minute deals that tour consolidators could not sell. Their loss could be your gain.

DANGERS & ANNOYANCES

As with most big US cities, there are run-down sections of Boston where crime is a problem. We haven't listed any sights or activities in these sections. Avoid parks (such as Boston Common) after dark if there are not many other people around. The same goes for unfamiliar, unpeopled streets and subway stations at night. The Back Bay Fens, a gay cruising area, can be dangerous for gays at night. Lastly, you might find a few vestiges of 'skankiness' near the Chinatown subway station, along Washington and Essex Sts, where one or two X-rated shops are hanging on by the thread of a G-string.

SIGHTS
Downtown   Map pp66-8

The pedestrian-only shopping district near the intersection of Washington, Summer and Winter Sts, **Downtown Crossing** bustles with pushcart vendors and street musicians. Just west of here is the focal point of the city, the Boston Common, and a host of historic sights heading north along Tremont St.

The rest of downtown, including the **Financial District**, lies east of Tremont St and stretches all the way to the waterfront. Bounded by State St to the north and Essex St to the south, this area was once the domain of cows. Their well-trodden 17th- and 18th-century paths eventually gave rise to the maze of streets occupied by today's

BOSTON: COLLEGE TOWN

The greater Boston area has many, many college campuses – too many to mention here. The vibrancy of the student population is one of the defining characteristics of this youthful city. Cultural and sporting events aren't restricted to students and are often open to the public (see p122). Following is a list of Boston's major colleges.

■ **Berklee College of Music** (Map pp70-1; ☎ 617-747-2222; www.berklee.edu; 921 Boylston St) One of the country's finest music schools. For performance information, see p117.

■ **Boston University** (BU; Map pp66-8; ☎ 617-353-2000, 617-353-2169; www.bu.edu; 881 Commonwealth Ave) West of Kenmore Sq, enrolls about 30,000 graduate and undergraduate students, and has a huge campus and popular sports teams.

■ **Harvard University** (Map p69; ☎ 617-495-1000, 617-495-1573; www.harvard.edu; Holyoke Center, 1350 Massachusetts Ave) The country's oldest and most prestigious university. See also p86.

■ **Massachusetts College of Art** (Map pp70-1; ☎ 617-879-7333; www.massart.edu; South Bldg, 621 Huntington Ave; ☷ 10am-6pm Mon-Fri, 10am-5pm Sat) Hosts exciting exhibitions of both professional and student work at the Bakalar and Paine Galleries.

■ **Massachusetts Institute of Technology** (MIT; Map p65; ☎ 617-253-4795; www.mit.edu; 77 Massachusetts Ave, Bldg 7) A world-renowned scientific mecca, with a number of excellent museums and an impressive range of public art. See also p88.

■ **Northeastern University** (Map pp70-1; ☎ 617-373-2000; www.northeastern.edu; 360 Huntington Ave) Boasts one of the country's largest work-study co-operative programs.

■ **University of Massachusetts, Boston** (UMass; Map p65; ☎ 617-287-5000; www.umb.edu; 100 Morrissey Blvd) Host to the John F Kennedy Library & Museum (see p85).

Other well-established colleges and universities on the city's fringe:

■ **Boston College** (BC; ☎ 617-552-8000; www.bc.edu; 140 Commonwealth Ave/MA 30, Chestnut Hill) The nation's largest Jesuit community. The large green campus has Gothic towers, stained glass, a good art museum, and excellent Irish and Catholic ephemera collections in the library. Its basketball and football teams are usually high in national rankings. Take the Green 'B' Line to Boston College or the 'C' Line to Cleveland Circle.

■ **Brandeis University** (☎ 781-736-2000; www.brandeis.edu; South St, Waltham) A small campus that includes the Rose Art Museum, specializing in New England art. Take the MBTA commuter rail from North Station to the Brandeis/Roberts stop.

■ **Tufts University** (☎ 617-628-5000; www.tufts.edu; College Ave, Medford) Home to the acclaimed Fletcher School of International Affairs. Take the Red Line to Davis Sq, then a free Tufts shuttle across from the station takes you directly to the campus.

■ **Wellesley College** (☎ 781-283-1000; www.wellesley.edu; 106 Central St, Wellesley) A Seven Sisters women's college that also sports a hilly, wooded campus and the excellent Davis Museum & Cultural Center. Walk from the MBTA commuter rail or drive along MA 16 to MA 135.

high-rises, a distinctive blend of modern and historic architecture.

BOSTON COMMON

Established in 1634, the 50-acre Boston Common is the country's oldest public park. It has served many purposes over the years, including as a campground for British troops during the Revolutionary War and as green grass for cattle grazing up until 1830. Although there is still a grazing ordinance on the books, the Common today serves picnickers, sunbathers and people-watchers.

In winter, the **Frog Pond** attracts crowds of ice skaters (see p90), while July brings in theater lovers for **Free Shakespeare on the Common** (☎ 617-532-1252; www.freeshakespeare.org; admission free), with shows at 8pm Tuesday to Saturday and 7pm Sunday.

PARK STREET CHURCH & OLD GRANARY BURYING GROUND

Noted for its graceful, 200ft steeple, the **Park St Church** (☎ 617-523-3383; www.parkstreet.org; cnr Park & Tremont Sts; ❂ 9:30am-3:30pm Tue-Sat Jul & Aug) has been hosting historic lectures and musical performances from its founding. In 1829 William Lloyd Garrison railed against slavery from the church's pulpit. And on Independence Day in 1831, Samuel Francis Smith's hymn 'America' (My Country 'Tis of Thee) was first sung.

Dating to 1660, the adjacent **Old Granary Burying Ground** (☎ 617-635-4505; Tremont St; admission free; ❂ 9am-5pm) is crammed with expressive headstone carvings. Notable figures buried here include Revolutionary heroes Paul Revere, Samuel Adams and John Hancock; Crispus Attucks, the freed slave, killed in the Boston Massacre in 1770; Benjamin Franklin's parents (he's buried in Philadelphia); and Peter Faneuil of Faneuil Hall fame.

KING'S CHAPEL & BURYING GROUND

Bostonians were not pleased at all when the original Anglican church was erected on this site in 1688. (Remember, it was the Anglicans – the Church of England – whom the Puritans were fleeing.) The granite **chapel** (☎ 617-227-2155; www.kings-chapel.org; 58 Tremont St; admission by donation $2; ❂ 10am-4pm Mon & Thu-Sat Jun-Aug, 10am-4pm Sat rest of year) standing today was built in 1754 around the original wooden structure. Then the wooden church was taken apart and tossed out the windows. If the church seems to be missing something, it is: building funds ran out before a spire could be added. The church houses the largest bell ever made by Paul Revere, as well as a sonorous organ. Services are held at 11am on Sunday, and recitals at 12:15pm Tuesday and 5pm Sunday.

The adjacent **burying ground** contains the grave of John Winthrop, the first governor of the fledgling Massachusetts Bay Colony.

OLD SOUTH MEETING HOUSE

No tax on tea! That was the decision on December 16, 1773, when 5000 angry colonists gathered at the Old South Meeting House to protest British taxes, leading to the Boston Tea Party (p77). These days, the graceful **meeting house** (☎ 617-482-6439; www.oldsouthmeetinghouse.org; 310 Washington St; adult/child/senior & student $5/1/4; ❂ 9:30am-5pm Apr-Oct, 10am-4pm Nov-Mar) is still a gathering place for discussion, although not so much rabble-rousing goes on here anymore. Instead, the meeting house hosts concerts, theater performances and lecture series, as well as walking tours, re-enactments and other historical programs.

OLD STATE HOUSE

Dating to 1713, the **Old State House** (☎ 617-720-3290; 206 Washington St; adult/child/senior & student $3/1/2; ❂ 9am-5pm) is Boston's oldest surviving public building, where the Massachusetts Assembly used to debate the issues of the day. The building is perhaps best known for its balcony, where the Declaration of Independence was first read to Bostonians in 1776. Operated by the Bostonian Society, the museum depicts Boston's role in the Revolutionary War, including videos on the Boston Massacre and the history of the Old State House. The NPS Visitor Center (p73) is across the street on State St.

Encircled by cobblestones, the **Boston Massacre site**, directly in front of the Old State House balcony, marks the spot where, on March 5, 1770, British soldiers fired upon an angry mob of protesting colonists, killing five of them. This incident inflamed anti-British sentiment, which led to the outbreak of the Revolutionary War.

Faneuil Hall Marketplace & Quincy Market & Around   Map pp66-8

The granddaddy of East Coast waterfront revitalizations is **Faneuil Hall Marketplace** (☎ 617-338-2323; cnr Congress & North Sts). The historic hall – the brick building topped with the beloved grasshopper weathervane – was constructed as a market and public meeting place in 1740. Behind Faneuil Hall, three long granite buildings make up the rest of the marketplace, the center of the city's produce and meat industry for almost 150 years. In the 1970s **Quincy Market** was redeveloped into today's touristy, festive shopping and eating center, so it still serves its original purpose, albeit with all the modern trappings. For Faneuil Hall restaurants or shops, see p101 or p123.

The six luminescent glass columns of the **New England Holocaust Memorial** (☎ 617-457-0755; btwn Union & Congress Sts) were constructed in 1995. The towers are engraved with six million numbers, symbolizing the Jews killed in the Holocaust. Each tower – with smoldering coals sending plumes of steam

BOSTON ROGUES GALLERY

Boston folklore is replete with more than patriots, poets and preachers; the city has also produced its fair share of muggers, buggers and thieves. Here is a sample of the most infamous ones.

- **John White Webster** In 1849 this distinguished Harvard chemistry professor committed 'the murder of the century,' when he bashed in the head of Dr George Parkman in the college labora-tory during a quarrel over money. Webster's attempt to conceal the crime by dismembering the corpse and placing it in an incinerator was foiled by a school janitor. The trial attracted scores of spectators seeking a glimpse of the fallen Brahmin. The professor was found guilty and hanged. His story and the evidence are reassembled in Simon Schama's mystery novel, *Dead Certainties*.

- **James Michael Curley** Mayor Curley was the archetype city boss, who once won an election while serving time for cheating on a civil service exam. 'I did it for a friend,' he explained to sympathetic voters. Corruption, graft and blackmail marked his time in the political spotlight. He completed his final term as mayor in 1846 in a jail cell, following a mail fraud conviction. Curley was the model for the protagonist in Frank Skeffington's novel, *The Last Hurrah*, played by Spencer Tracy in the film of the same name.

- **Albert De Salvo** You heard about the Boston Strangler, whose serial murders terrorized the city in the early 1960s. De Salvo raped and killed 13 women, leaving their naked bodies in lewd poses with their stockings tied tightly in a bow under their chin. He gained access to his victims' homes by pretending to be a police detective. De Salvo finally gave himself away when in the middle of an attack he apologized to the intended victim and left. De Salvo was found to be a psychotic schizophrenic and given a life sentence. He was murdered in his cell in 1973. The Boston Strangler was defended by F Lee Bailey in court and portrayed by Tony Curtis on screen.

- **The Brinks Robbers** In 1950, seven armed, masked men entered the Brinks office in the North End and pulled off the richest heist in US history, over $1 million in cash, and $1.5 million more in securities and checks. The sheer audacity of it all caught the public's imagina-tion: so well executed was this 'crime of the century' that police were stumped. Suspicion fi-nally centered on a local gang of petty hoodlums led by Tony Pino. The FBI spent $30 million and six years trying to crack the case. Finally, in 1956, 11 days before the statute of limitations ran out, a confession was extracted from a minor gang member, disgruntled over his share of the loot. Peter Falk depicted likable Tony Pino in the 1978 film *The Brinks Job*.

- **James 'Whitey' Bulger** The volatile bad brother of the former head of the Massachusetts state senate, Whitey has appeared weekly atop the FBI's Most Wanted List since 2000. The Bureau is offering a $1 million reward for information leading to his capture. With Bulger it is personal, since he used his protected status as FBI informant to rise to the top of Boston's criminal underworld as head of the Winter Hill Gang in the 1980s. Wanted for racketeering, drug-trafficking and 18 counts of murder, the 75 year old has been on the lam for nearly a decade. The sordid details are compiled in Dick Lehr and Gerald O'Neil's book *Black Mass*. Whitey's photograph is now showing in a post office near you.

up through the glass corridors – represents a different Nazi death camp. The memorial sits along the Freedom Trail, a sobering re-minder of its larger meaning and value.

Two lifelike bronzes of Boston's former Mayor Curley, a cherished but contro-versial Irish American politician, pose on North St between Union and Congress Sts (see above). To escape Faneuil Hall Mar-ketplace crowds, head to the waterfront **Christopher Columbus Park**, barely northeast of the marketplace.

Waterfront & Seaport District Map pp66-8

With the welcome exception of Christopher Columbus Park (p75), Boston's waterfront is underutilized in terms of public usage. Cruise ships and passenger ferries dominate the wharfs, while luxury hotels and office buildings block public access to the harbor views. The primary draw (albeit a strong one) is the chance to go *under* the sea at one of the country's best indoor aquariums. It is also the jumping-off point to the Harbor Islands (see p78).

For dramatic harbor views with a Boston-skyline backdrop, cross Fort Point Channel (a waterway separating Boston proper from South Boston) to the Seaport District. Here, the stunning Moakley Federal Courthouse is surrounded by landscaped park and waterside walkways. The fast-growing Seaport District is a hodgepodge of old brick warehouses, seafood markets and shipping docks, alongside four-star hotels, convention halls and office buildings. In the middle of it all, the vast, new-in-2004 Boston Convention and Exhibition Center is the driving force behind the district's development.

NEW ENGLAND AQUARIUM

Teeming with sea creatures of all sizes, shapes and colors, the **New England Aquarium** (☎ 617-973-5200; www.neaq.org; Central Wharf, off Old Atlantic Ave; adult/child/senior $16/9/14; ☺ 9am-5pm Mon-Fri, 9am-6pm Sat & Sun, extended hr Jun-Aug) represents Boston's attempt to reconnect the city to the sea. Outdoor harbor seals and sea otters introduce the main indoor attraction: a three-story, cylindrical saltwater tank swirling with over 600 creatures – including turtles, sharks and eels. At the base of the tank, the penguin pool is home to three species of fun-loving penguins. Countless side exhibits explore the lives and habitats of other underwater oddities, including the latest exhibits on ethereal jelly fish and rare, exotic sea dragons. The aquarium also organizes **whale-watching cruises** (adult/senior $29/26, child $20-23; ☺ 9:30am or 10am & 1:30pm or 2pm May-Oct).

The new 3-D **IMAX theater** (adult/child/senior $10/7/7; ☺ 10am-9:30pm) features films with aquatic themes.

CHILDREN'S MUSEUM

The interactive, educational exhibits at this delightful **museum** (☎ 617-426-8855; www.boston kids.org; 300 Congress St; adult/child/senior $9/7/7, Fri evening per person $1; ☺ 10am-5pm Sat-Thu, 10am-9pm Fri) can keep preschoolers to teenagers entertained for hours. Highlights include a bubble exhibit, a two-story climbing maze, a rock-climbing wall, a hands-on construction site, intercultural immersion experiences and a beautiful play space for kids under three years.

BOSTON TEA PARTY SHIP & MUSEUM

On the cold evening of December 16, 1773, a group of fiery colonists disguised as Mohawk Indians burst from the Old South Meeting House (p75) and headed to Griffin's Wharf, where they clamored on board the three ships harbored there. Armed with axes and hatchets, the colonists destroyed 342 crates of British tea, defiantly dumping the precious cargo into the sea. Today the **Boston Tea Party Ship & Museum** (☎ 617-269-7150; www.bostonteaparty ship.com; Congress St Bridge) is testimony to the spirited rebels who refused to pay the levy imposed on their beloved beverage.

At the time of research, the museum was closed for a complete overhaul after suffering extensive fire damage. The new museum, expected to open in late 2005, will include full-size replicas of the historic tall ships, the *Dartmouth* and the *Eleanor*, in addition to the *Brig Beaver*, which existed before. And no doubt visitors will still be invited to drink their fill of tax-free tea.

Government Center   Map pp66-8

Heading north on Congress St brings you smack up against a coldly impersonal mass of concrete buildings dating to the 1960s. Government Center, home to the fortress-like **Boston City Hall**, is widely considered a prime example of poor city planning, especially since its construction destroyed the once lively and ethnically diverse neighborhood known as the West End. What few vestiges remain of the old West End are found in the little byways between Merrimac and Causeway Sts.

MUSEUM OF SCIENCE

With more than 600 interactive exhibits, this **museum** (☎ 617-723-2500; www.mos.org; Science Park, Charles River Dam; adult/child/senior $14/11/12; ☺ 9am-5pm Sat-Thu Sep-Jun, 9am-7pm Sat-Thu Jul-Aug, 9am-9pm Fri year-round) is an educational playground, especially fun for kids. Favorite exhibits include the world's largest lightning-bolt generator, a full-scale space capsule, a World Population Meter and the 20ft-tall Tyrannosaurus rex dinosaur model that stands outside. The museum also houses the **Hayden Planetarium** and **Mugar Omni Theater** (shows adult/child/senior $8.50/6.50/7.50, museum plus one show $18/14/15.50). The Skyline Room Cafeteria offers good food and skyline views.

NEW ENGLAND SPORTS MUSEUM

Nobody can say that Bostonians are not passionate about their sports teams. From the old days of Bobby Orr to Larry Bird to

BOSTON HARBOR ISLANDS   Map p65

Boston Harbor is sprinkled with 34 islands, many of which are open to the public for trail walking, bird-watching, fishing and swimming. The **Boston Harbor Islands** (☎ 617-223-8666; www .bostonislands.org; admission free; ☯ 9am-sunset mid-Apr–mid-Oct) offer a range of ecosystems – sandy beaches, rocky cliffs, fresh and salt-water marsh, and forested trails – only 45 minutes by ferry from downtown Boston. Since the massive, multimillion-dollar clean-up of Boston Harbor in the mid-1990s, the islands are one of the city's most magnificent natural assets.

Georges Island is the transportation hub for the islands and site of Fort Warren, a 19th-century fort and Civil War prison. Guided tours are available. From Georges Island, a free water taxi goes to some of the other islands, including:

- **Bumpkin Island** Enjoy slate beaches and fields overgrown with wildflowers and wild berries.

- **Grape Island** An abundance of wild raspberries, bay berries and elderberries attracts ample bird life. Check out the 'wild edibles' walking tour led by park rangers.

- **Great Brewster** High bluffs offering panoramic vistas of Boston Harbor and Massachusetts Bay. Count four lighthouses from one perch!

- **Little Brewster** Site of Boston Light, the country's oldest lighthouse, which is open for tours by appointment only. The island is accessible to private boaters for pick-up and drop-off only (no docking) on Friday, Saturday and Sunday, from 12:30pm to 3pm.

- **Lovells Island** Picturesque dunes, shady woods and a wide, sandy swimming beach.

- **Peddocks Island** One of the largest Harbor Islands, Peddocks consists of four headlands connected by sandbars (in fact, its area increases from 184 to 288 acres at low tide). Hiking trails wander through marsh, pond and coastal environs.

- **Spectacle Island** Expected to open in 2005 with a new marina, supervised beaches and visitors center. Walking trails will provide access to a 157ft peak overlooking the harbor.

- **Thompson Island** Home of Thompson Island **Outward Bound** (☎ 617-328-3900; www.thompson island.org; adult/child/senior $8/6/7; ☯ 11:30am-5pm Sat Jun-Aug), a non-profit organization that hosts private events. It is open to the public only on Saturdays in summer. The ferry departs at 11:30am from Fan Pier, and returns at 5pm.

- **World's End** Not exactly an island, this 244-acre peninsula is open year-round for hiking, cross-country skiing and horseback riding. It is accessible by car from Hingham, which is 16 miles southeast of Boston.

To get to the islands, **Harbor Express** (☎ 617-222-6999; 1 Long Wharf, off Old Atlantic Ave; ☯ 9am-4pm mid-Apr–mid-Oct) offers regular seasonal ferry service (round-trip adult/child $10/6). Purchase a round-trip ticket to George's Island, where you then catch a free water taxi (another five to 10 minutes) to the smaller islands. For information on camping on the islands, see Urban Adventure, p97.

today's Tom Brady and Manny Ramirez, sports figures and events loom large in the Boston psyche. The **New England Sports Museum** (☎ 617-624-1234; www.sportsmuseum.org; Fleet Center; adult/child $6/4; ☯ 11am-5pm) is proof of that. Exhibits focus on each of the major professional sports, and feature highlights, such as the penalty box from the old Boston Garden and a tribute to the retired numbers of the Boston Celtics. Red Sox Century traces the dramatic history of Boston hometown heroes.

Beacon Hill   Map pp66-8

Beacon Hill is Boston's most handsome and affluent residential neighborhood. Adjacent to Boston Common and the Public Garden, Beacon Hill extends north to Cambridge St and west to the Charles River. Charles St, lined with shops and eateries, divides the flat and hilly parts of the neighborhood. Distinguished 19th-century townhouses, lavender windowpanes, gas lanterns, courtyards, rooftop gardens and picturesque narrow alleyways – this is the stuff of Beacon Hill.

One of Beacon Hill's loveliest spots is the cobblestoned **Acorn St**, the city's oft-photographed narrowest street, and stately **Louisburg Sq**, home to distinguished residents, like author Louisa May Alcott and Senator John Kerry.

PUBLIC GARDEN

Adjacent to the Boston Common, the Public Garden is a 24-acre botanical oasis of cultivated flowerbeds, verdant grass, shading trees and a tranquil lagoon. You can't picnic on the lawn like you can on the Common, but the benches and walkways are lovely for a sit or a stroll. Taking a ride on the **Swan Boats** (☎ 617-522-1966; www.swan boats.com; adult/child/senior $2.50/1/2; ⊕ 10am-4pm mid-Apr–mid-Sep) in the lagoon is a Boston tradition since 1877. And don't miss the famous statue *Make Way for Ducklings,* always a favorite with tiny tots who can climb and sit on the bronze ducks.

MASSACHUSETTS STATE HOUSE

High atop Beacon Hill, Massachusetts leaders and legislators attempt to turn their ideas into concrete policies and practices within the golden-domed **State House** (☎ 617-727-3676; www.sec.state.ma.us; cnr Beacon & Bowdoin Sts; admission free; ⊕ 9am-5pm). Boston's beloved Charles Bulfinch designed the commanding state capitol building, but it was Oliver Wendell Holmes who first dubbed it 'the hub of the solar system' (thus earning Boston the nickname 'the Hub'). A free 40-minute tour includes a discussion of the history, art works, architecture and political personalities as well as a visit to the legislative chambers when it's in session. Tours are held from 10am to 4pm Monday to Friday. Reservations are recommended.

Across the street on the corner of Beacon and Park Sts, the **Robert Gould Shaw Memorial** honors the white Civil War commander of the 54th Massachusetts Regiment, which is the African American unit celebrated in the film *Glory*.

MUSEUM OF AFRO-AMERICAN HISTORY

Beacon Hill was never the exclusive domain of blue-blood Brahmins. Waves of immigrants, and especially African Americans, free from slavery, settled here in the 19th century. The **Museum of Afro-American History** (☎ 617-725-0022; www.afroammuseum.org; 46 Joy St; admission by donation; ⊕ 10am-4pm Mon-Sat) offers permanent exhibits on Boston's African American roots, as well as an extensive library and interactive computer kiosks. The museum occupies two adjacent historic buildings: the **African Meeting House**, the country's oldest African American meeting house, and the **Abiel Smith School**, which housed the country's first primary school for blacks.

The **Black Heritage Trail** (☎ 617-742-5415) is a 1.6-mile walking tour that explores this history further. The NPS (p73) conducts free guided tours in summer (at 10am, noon and 2pm Monday to Saturday), but maps and descriptions for a self-guided tour are available at the museum year-round.

North End   Map pp66-8

Despite the recent demolition of I-93 and the ongoing process of physically reconnecting the North End to the rest of the city, this Old World enclave is still a continent and a century away. Italian immigrants and their descendents have held court in this warren of narrow, winding streets and alleys since the 1920s. Old-timers carry on passionate discussions in Italian and play bocce in the tiny parks. Others complete their ritual Saturday morning shopping at specialty stores selling flowers, freshly made pasta, *cannoli* (sugary pastry filled with ricotta) or *biscotti* (Italian biscuits), and fresh cuts of meat. This slice of southern Europe plays out within a 0.25-mile radius of Boston's oldest colonial buildings. For specialized walking tours of the North End, see p94.

PAUL REVERE HOUSE

On the night of April 18, 1775, silversmith Paul Revere set out from his home on North Sq; he was one of three horseback messengers who carried advance warning on this night of the British march into Concord and Lexington. The small clapboard **house** (☎ 617-523-2338; www.paulreverehouse.org; 19 North Sq; adult/child/senior & student $3/1/2.50; ⊕ 9:30am-5:15pm daily mid-Apr–Oct, 9:30am-4:15pm Tue-Sun Nov–mid-Apr) was built in 1680, which makes it the oldest house in Boston. The house has been restored to its late-17th-century appearance and is open for visitors.

The adjacent **Pierce-Hichborn House**, built in 1710, is a fine example of an English

Renaissance brick house. You can visit it on a guided tour, by appointment only.

OLD NORTH CHURCH

On the same night that Paul Revere rode forth to warn of the onset of British soldiers, the sexton of the Old North Church hung two lanterns in the church steeple to signal that they would come by sea. Today the 1723 **Old North Church** (☎ 617-523-6676; www.old north.com; 193 Salem St; 🕑 9am-6pm Mon-Fri, 9am-5pm Sat & Sun) is still an active Episcopal church – Boston's oldest. Tall white box-pews, many with brass nameplates of early parishioners, occupy the graceful interior. Behind the church, lovely terraces and gardens beautify the exterior. Services are held at 9am, 11am and 5pm on Sunday.

COPP'S HILL

The city's second-oldest cemetery (1660) is **Copp's Hill Burying Ground**, named for the cobbler who owned the land back in the 17th century. Headstones – chipped and pocked by Revolutionary War musket fire – are a poignant reminder of the neighborhood's historic role. Other sections of the cemetery shed light on the little-known black history in the North End.

Across the street is Boston's **narrowest house** (44 Hull St), measuring a tiny 9½ft wide. The c1800 house was reportedly built out of spite to block light from the neighbor's house and to obliterate the view of the house behind it. It is closed to the public.

PAUL REVERE MALL

Often called 'the prado' by locals, shady **Paul Revere Mall** perfectly frames the Old North Church. In addition to being a lively meeting place for North Enders of all generations, it's also one of the few places in the cramped quarter where you can rest as long as you want. Across Hanover St, the 1804 **St Stephen's Church** is Boston's only remaining church designed by renowned architect Charles Bulfinch.

SALEM STREET

The neighborhood's most colorful street is chockablock with specialty markets and restaurants. Stop at the **Bova Italian Bakery** (☎ 617-523-5601; 134 Salem St; 🕑 24hr) for Italian loaves straight from the oven; the aromatic **Polcari's Coffee** (☎ 617-227-0786; 105 Salem St;

🕑 10am-6pm Mon-Sat) for coffee, tea and spices; and **Dairy Fresh Candies** (☎ 617-742-2639; 57 Salem St; 🕑 9am-7pm Mon-Fri, 8am-7pm Sat, 11am-6pm Sun), for an unsurpassed selection of nuts, chocolates, candies and dried fruit. Around the corner to the north is **J Pace & Son** (☎ 617-227-9673; 42 Cross St), a neighborhood Italian grocer serving fresh cheese, olives, bread and prosciutto. See p105 for more suggestions on where to pack your picnic.

Charlestown   Map pp66-8

The Charlestown Navy Yard was a thriving ship-building center from 1800 until the early 1900s. Although it was closed in 1974, the surrounding neighborhood has been making a comeback ever since. The impressive granite buildings have been transformed into shops, condos and offices, which enjoy a panoramic view of Boston. The narrow streets immediately surrounding Monument Sq are lined with restored mid-19th-century Federal and colonial houses. However, a short stroll away from Monument Sq – four or five blocks in any direction – reveals that Charlestown has not strayed too far from its grittier, working-class roots.

USS CONSTITUTION & MUSEUM

Despite its wooden hull, the **USS Constitution** (☎ 617-242-2543; www.ussconstitution.navy.mil; Charlestown Navy Yard; admission free; 🕑 10am-4pm Tue-Sun Apr-Oct, Thu-Sun Nov-Mar) was nicknamed Old Ironsides for never having gone down in a battle. She is still the oldest commissioned US Navy ship (1797), and she is taken out onto Boston Harbor every Fourth of July in order to maintain her commissioned status. Navy personnel give 30-minute guided tours of the top deck, gun deck and cramped quarters. Across from the ship, the **USS Constitution Museum** (☎ 617-426-1812; www.ussconstitutionmuseum .org; admission free; 🕑 9am-6pm May-Oct, 10am-5pm Nov-Apr) has informative hands-on exhibits, historic artifacts, and interactive displays about ship life and the ship's battles.

MONUMENT SQUARE

'Don't fire until you see the whites of their eyes!' came the order from Colonel Prescott to revolutionary troops on June 17, 1775. Considering the ill preparedness of the revolutionary soldiers, the bloody battle that followed resulted in a surprising number of British casualties. Ultimately, however, the Redcoats prevailed (an oft-overlooked fact). The so-called Battle of Bunker Hill is ironically named, as most of the fighting took place on Breed's Hill, where the **Bunker Hill Monument** (☎ 617-242-5641; Monument Sq; admission free; ◯ 9am-4:30pm, 9am-5pm late Jun-early Sep) stands today. The 220ft granite hilltop obelisk rewards physically fit visitors with fine Boston views at the top of its 295 steps. The adjacent lodge contains interesting historical dioramas, and NPS park rangers give summer talks. A re-enactment of the battle takes place every June on Monument Sq.

Back Bay & South End Map pp70-1

During the 1850s, when Boston was experiencing a population and building boom, Back Bay was an uninhabitable tidal flat. To solve the problem, urban planners embarked on an ambitious 40-year project: Fill in the marsh, lay out an orderly grid of streets, erect magnificent Victorian brownstones and design high-minded civic plazas.

Today Back Bay is one of Boston's most cherished treasures. One could easily spend a day strolling down shady Commonwealth Ave, window-shopping on chic Newbury St, taking in the remarkable Victorian architecture and popping into grand churches. Although the neighborhood is home to young professionals and blue-blood Bostonians, Back Bay also has a large student population that keeps it from growing too stodgy.

The area is bounded by the Public Garden and Arlington St to the northeast, Massachusetts Ave to the southwest, the Charles River to the northwest, and Stuart St and Huntington Ave to the southeast. Cross streets are laid out alphabetically from Arlington St to Hereford St. Back Bay is at its most enchanting during May, when magnolia, tulip and dogwood trees are in bloom. Marlborough St is the most tranquil and beautiful of Back Bay's shady, patrician streets.

CHARLES RIVER ESPLANADE

Boston and Cambridge are graced with grassy banks and paved byways along both sides of the curvaceous Charles River. From Beacon St near Arlington St, cross Storrow Dr via the Arthur Fiedler Footbridge to reach the Charles River Esplanade. On warm days, Bostonians migrate here to sunbathe, sail and feed waterfowl gliding along the tranquil riverbank. The **Hatch Memorial Shell**

hosts free outdoor concerts and movies, including the famed July 4 concert by the Boston Pops.

The paths along the river are ideal (though sometimes crowded) for bicycling, jogging or walking. On the Boston side, it's about 2 miles from the Museum of Science at the Esplanade's eastern end to the Anderson Bridge (which turns into John F Kennedy St and leads into Harvard Sq). For a great view of Boston, walk – or take the T Red Line between Charles/MGH and Kendall – across the **Longfellow Bridge**, nicknamed the 'Salt and Pepper' bridge because of its towers' resemblance to the condiment shakers.

NEWBURY STREET

When it comes to shopping, Newbury St is to Boston what Fifth Ave is to New York City. International boutiques and galleries get fancier and pricier the closer you get to the Public Garden. Approaching Massachusetts Ave in the other direction, you'll see more and more nose rings, platform shoes and dyed hair. Newbury St is also fun to wander at night, when shops are closed but the well-lit windows are dressed to the nines. Newbury St is epitomized by its café culture and a worldly, haute-couture crowd. For shopping and eating options, see p123 and p107.

COPLEY SQUARE

Situated between Dartmouth, Clarendon and Boylston Sts, high-minded Copley Sq is surrounded by historic buildings. **Trinity Church** (☎ 617-536-0944; 206 Clarendon St; admission $4; ◯ 8am-6pm) is widely considered a masterpiece of American architecture. Designed by Henry Hobson Richardson from 1872 to 1877, the grand Richardsonian Romanesque building still has an active Episcopal congregation. Tours take place from 9am to 4pm Monday to Saturday and 1pm to 4pm on Sunday; organ recitals are held at 12:15pm on Friday.

Across the street, the 62-story **John Hancock Tower** (200 Clarendon St), constructed with more than 10,000 panels of mirrored glass, stands in stark contrast to Trinity Church. Designed in 1976 by IM Pei, the tower suffered serious initial problems: inferior glass panes were installed, and when the wind whipped up, the panes popped out, falling hundreds of feet to the ground. Fortunately, the panes were replaced and the

THE NEW ICA

In 2004 the Institute of Contemporary Art (ICA) launched construction of a new state-of-the-art museum building on Fan Pier in the Seaport District (p76). The eye-catching building is intended to be the centerpiece of Boston's new waterfront.

The 65,000-sq-ft, four-story building will triple the amount of exhibition space for the ICA. More importantly, it hopes that the striking new space will be a work of art in itself. According to the design, the gallery space is primarily on the upper level, with glass walls facing the harbor. It is 'cantilevered' over a public Harborwalk (also a work in progress). The exterior of this 'gallery box' will be illuminated at night, creating a dramatic effect when seen from water and land.

The new ICA is scheduled to open in 2006.

design problem fixed before anyone was hurt. The observatory on the 60th floor was closed for security reasons in the aftermath of September 11.

BOSTON PUBLIC LIBRARY

This esteemed **library** (BPL; ☎ 617-536-5400; www .bpl.org; 700 Boylston St; admission free; ☺ 9am-9pm Mon-Thu, 9am-5pm Fri & Sat year-round, 1-5pm Sun Oct-May) lends credence to Boston's reputation as the 'Athens of America.' The old building on the square is the McKim building, notable for its magnificent facade and exquisite interior art. Pick up a free brochure and take a self-guided tour, taking note of the murals by Edwin Austin Abbey and John Singer Sargent, and the sculpture by Augustus Saint-Gaudens and Domingo Mora. Alternatively, free one-hour **guided tours** depart from the McKim entrance hall; tours take place at 2pm Sunday, 2:30pm Monday, 6pm Tuesday and Thursday, and 11am Friday and Saturday. An inviting café, Novel, overlooks the enchanting Italianate courtyard.

PRUDENTIAL CENTER

This landmark Boston building is not too much more than a fancy shopping mall, technically called the **Shops at Prudential Center** (☎ 800-SHOP-PRU; www.prudentialcenter.com; 800 Boylston St; ☺ stores 10am-9pm Mon-Sat, 11am-6pm

Sun). For details on its shops and restaurants, see p123 or p107.

For a bird's-eye view of Boston, head to the 50th-floor **Prudential Center Skywalk** (☎ 617-859-0648; adult/child/student/senior $9.50/2/6.50/7; ☺ 10am-10pm), which offers a spectacular 360° view of Boston and Cambridge. The skywalk is completely enclosed by glass. Price of admission includes an entertaining audio tour.

INSTITUTE OF CONTEMPORARY ART

Livening up Boston's often conservative art scene, this **institute** (ICA; ☎ 617-266-5152; www.ica boston.org; 955 Boylston St; adult/child under 12/senior/student $7/free/5/5, free to all 5-9pm Thu; ☺ noon-5pm Tue, Wed & Fri, noon-9pm Thu, 11am-5pm Sat & Sun) exhibits avant-garde art created by well-known national and unknown regional artists. The ICA's galleries are currently housed within a renovated 19th-century firehouse, but a dynamic new state-of-the-art facility on the waterfront is expected to open in 2006; see the boxed text left.

CHRISTIAN SCIENCE CHURCH & MAPPARIUM

Built in 1894, the **Christian Science Church** (☎ 617-450-3790; 175 Huntington Ave; ☺ 10am-4pm Mon-Sat) is the home base for the Church of Christ, Scientist, or Christian Science, founded by Mary Baker Eddy in 1866. Tour the grand basilica, which can seat 3000 worshippers, listen to the 14,000-pipe organ or linger on the expansive plaza with its 670ft-long reflecting pool. Tours (not required) are given on the hour Monday to Saturday.

Right next door, the **Mary Baker Eddy Library** (☎ 617-450-7000; www.marybakereddylibrary.org; 200 Massachusetts Ave; adult/child/senior/student $5/3/3/3; ☺ 10am-5pm Tue-Wed, 10am-9pm Thu-Fri, 10am-5pm Sat & Sun) houses the offices of the internationally regarded daily newspaper, the **Christian Science Monitor** (www.csmonitor.com), as well as one of Boston's hidden treasures, the intriguing **Mapparium**. The Mapparium is a room-size, stained-glass globe that visitors walk through on a glass bridge. It was created in 1935, which is reflected by the globe's geopolitical boundaries. The acoustics, which surprised even the designer, allow everyone in the room to hear even the tiniest whisper. Price of admission into the library allows access to the Mapparium as well as the *Monitor* gallery, from where you can peak into the newspaper production offices.

GIBSON HOUSE MUSEUM

A tour of this jam-packed **museum** (☎ 617-267-6338; www.thegibsonhouse.org; 137 Beacon St; adult/child/senior/student $5/2/4/4), near Arlington St, will give you an idea of what the opulent 19th-century mansions were like. Built by the wealthy widow Catherine Hammond Gibson, it is one of the few remaining single-family homes in Back Bay. Still filled with the Gibson family's furniture and possessions, it offers as much of a history lesson as an architectural tour. Nonetheless, this splendid six-story Victorian brownstone features impressive woodwork and amazing detail. The tour also shows visitors the servants' quarters, a stark contrast to the main part of the house. Tours are held at 1pm, 2pm and 3pm Wednesday to Sunday.

BACK BAY CHURCHES

The **Arlington St Church** (☎ 617-536-7050; www.ascboston.org; 351 Boylston St; ☻ noon-6pm Wed-Sun May-Oct) was the first public building to be erected in Back Bay. The graceful church features extraordinary commissioned Tif-fany windows and 16 bells in its steeple, which was modeled after London's well-known church St Martin-in-the-Fields. The church's Unitarian Universalist ministry is purely progressive. You can attend a service at 11am on Sunday.

The **Old South Church** (☎ 617-536-1970; www.oldsouth.org; 645 Boylston St; ☻ 9am-7pm Mon-Thu, 9am-5pm Fri, 10am-4pm Sat, 9am-4pm Sun), not to be confused with the congregation's previous home at the Old South Meeting House, is a distinctive Italian Gothic structure complete with a campanile and multicolored granite. The congregation boasts many founding fathers among its historic members, including Samuel Adams and Paul Revere. It has existed in its current location since 1875.

SOUTH END

Not to be confused with South Boston ('Southie'), which is still remembered for its residents' violent opposition to integrating the Boston public schools in the 1970s, the South End is a study in ethnic, racial, sexual and economic diversity. The South End doesn't have any sights per se, but it's worth exploring to get a sense of Boston's vibrancy. Huge portions have been claimed by artists, gay men, architects and young professionals, while other parts are less gentrified. Housing projects and halfway houses rub elbows with converted condos.

South End side streets, which boast the country's largest concentration of Victorian row houses, have an almost British temperament. The tiny, elliptical **Union Park Sq**, between Tremont St and Shawmut Ave, and lovely **Rutland Sq**, just north of Tremont St, are quiet, quaint and quintessentially Boston.

Almost 5 miles long, the **Southwest Corridor** is a one-way, paved and landscaped walkway, running between and parallel to Columbus and Huntington Aves. Walk north from Massachusetts Ave for some rewarding views of the Back Bay skyline.

Kenmore Square   Map pp70-1

West of Back Bay, Beacon St and Commonwealth Ave converge at Kenmore Sq, the epicenter of student life in Boston. In addition to the behemoth Boston University, which stretches along Commonwealth Ave, there are more than a half-dozen colleges in the area (see p74). Kenmore Sq has more than its share of clubs (see p116),

---

WEATHER OR NOT

Steady blue, Clear view
Flashing blue, Clouds are due
Steady red, Rain ahead
Flashing red, Snow instead

Since 1950 Bostonians have used this simple rhyme and the weather beacon atop the old Hancock tower (next to the new John Hancock Tower on Copley Sq, p81) to determine if they need to bring their umbrella when they leave the house. And yes, the beacon has been known to flash red in midsummer. But that's not a warning of some extremely inclement New England weather, but rather an indication that the Red Sox game has been cancelled for the night. (Apparently that last line has an asterisk.)

In October 2004, for the first time in Boston history, the weather beacon flashed red and blue simultaneously. And thus a new line was added to the rhyme: 'Flashing blue and flashing red, The Curse of the Bambino is dead!' (see p122).

inexpensive but nondescript eateries, and dormitories disguised as innocuous brownstones. You'll know you're in Kenmore Sq when you spot the 60-sq-ft Citgo sign. This mammoth neon sign has marked the spot since 1965.

PHOTOGRAPHIC RESOURCE CENTER

Located at Boston University, the independent **Photographic Resource Center** (PRC; ☎ 617-975-0600; www.bu.edu/prc; 832 Commonwealth Ave; adult/child/senior/student $3/free/2/2, free to all Thu; 10am-6pm Tue, Wed & Fri, 10am-8pm Thu, noon-5pm Sat & Sun) is one of the few centers in the country devoted exclusively to this art form. The PRC's ever-changing exhibits lean toward the modern and experimental. Other resources include educational programs, a well-stocked library and unique special events.

Fenway   Map pp70-1

The Fenway refers to an urban residential neighborhood, but it is also the name of a highway. Not the least, **Fenway Park** is where the Boston Red Sox play baseball. But when people refer to 'Fenway,' they're generally talking about the **Back Bay Fens**, a tranquil and interconnected park system that extends south from the Charles River Esplanade (at Park Dr or Charlesgate E), along a winding brook to the lush Arnold Arboretum and Franklin Park Zoo. It's part of the **Emerald Necklace**, a series of parks throughout the city, linked in the 1880s and 1890s by landscape architect Frederick Law Olmsted. It's not advisable, however, to linger in the Fenway after dark, especially near the tall reeds.

ARNOLD ARBORETUM

Under a public/private partnership with the city and Harvard University, the 265-acre **Arnold Arboretum** (☎ 617-524-1718; www.arboretum.harvard.edu; 125 Arborway, Jamaica Plain; admission free; sunrise-sunset) is planted with over 13,000 exotic trees, flowering shrubs and other specimens. This gem of a spot is pleasant year-round, but it's particularly beautiful in the spring. Dog walking, Frisbee throwing, bicycling, sledding and general contemplation are encouraged (but picnicking is not allowed). A **visitor center** (9am-4pm Mon-Fri, 10am-4pm Sat, noon-4pm Sun) is located at the main gate, just south of the rotary at US 1 and MA 203. Free one-hour walking tours are offered on alternate Wednesdays and Saturdays from April to November. Take the Orange Line to Forest Hills and walk 0.25 miles northwest to the Forest Hills gate.

FRANKLIN PARK ZOO

While 70-acre Franklin Park is surrounded by one of the city's sketchier neighborhoods, the **zoo** (☎ 617-541-5466; www.zoonewengland.com; 1 Franklin Park Rd; adult/child/senior $9.50/5/8; 10am-5pm Mon-Fri, 10am-6pm Sat & Sun Apr-Sep, 10am-4pm daily Oct-Mar) itself is safe. It boasts a well-designed Tropical Forest pavilion, complete with lush vegetation, waterfalls, lowland gorillas, a panther, warthogs and over 30 species of free-flight birds. The Serengeti Crossing features zebras, wildebeests, ostrich and ibex, and the Australian Outback Trail allows visitors to walk among red kangaroos and wallabies. Don't miss the magical **Butterfly Landing** (admission additional $1; 10am-4:30pm Mon-Fri, 10am-5:30pm Apr-Sep only), where you can stroll among blooming perennials, gushing waterfalls and 1000 fluttering butterflies in free flight. Take the Orange Line to Forest Hills, then ride bus No 16 to the Franklin Park Zoo.

MUSEUM OF FINE ARTS

The collections at the **Museum of Fine Arts, Boston** (MFA; ☎ 617-267-9300; www.mfa.org; 465 Huntington Ave; adult/child/senior/student $15/6.50/13/13, child under 17 free after 3pm Mon-Fri & all day Sat & Sun, reduced admission Wed-Fri after 4:45pm; 10am-4:45pm Sat-Tue, 10am-9:45pm Wed-Fri, West Wing only Thu & Fri evening) are second in this country only to those of New York's Metropolitan Museum of Art. Particularly noteworthy are its holdings of American art, which include major works by John Singleton Copley, Winslow Homer, Edward Hopper and the Hudson River School; American decorative arts are also well represented.

The museum also has an incredible collection of European paintings from the 11th to the 20th centuries, including a huge group of French Impressionists. The recent acquisition of Degas' *Duchessa di Montejasi with Her Daughters* makes the MFA's collection of works by that artist one of the richest in the world. The museum also boasts an excellent collection of Japanese art, including Buddhist and Shinto treasures. When it's time to rest your feet, there are several good cafés and a tranquil Japanese garden.

DETOUR: BROOKLINE

Although it seems to be part of Boston proper, Brookline is a distinct entity with a separate city government. It is a 'streetcar suburb,' a historical term describing its development after electric trolleys were introduced in the late 1800s. Off the beaten tourist path, it combines lovely, tranquil residential areas with lively commercial zones, including Coolidge Corner and Brookline Village. Both have deeply rooted Jewish and Russian populations, as you will notice from the synagogues and kosher delis on every corner. Take the Green 'C' Line to Coolidge Corner or 'D' Line to Brookline Village.

The **John F Kennedy National Memorial Site** (☎ 617-566-7937; www.nps.gov/jofi; 83 Beal St; adult/child $3/free; ☼ 10am-4:30pm Wed-Sun May-Oct) occupies the modest three-story house that was JFK's birthplace and boyhood home. Matriarch Rose Kennedy oversaw its restoration and furnishing in the late 1960s; today her narrative sheds light on the Kennedy's family life. Guided tours allow visitors to see furnishings, photographs and mementos that have been preserved from the time the family lived here. Take the Green 'C' Line to Coolidge Corner and walk north on Harvard St.

ISABELLA STEWART GARDNER MUSEUM

The magnificent Venetian-style palazzo that houses this **museum** (☎ 617-278-5166; www.gardnermuseum.org; 280 The Fenway; adult/child/student/senior $10/free/5/7; ☼ 11am-5pm Tue-Sun) was also home to 'Mrs Jack' Gardner herself until her death in 1924. A monument to one woman's exquisite taste for acquiring unequaled art, the Gardner is filled with almost 2000 priceless objects, primarily European, including outstanding tapestries and Italian Renaissance and 17th-century Dutch paintings.

Since Mrs Jack's will stipulated that her collection remain exactly as it was at the time of her death, nothing in the museum will ever change. That helps explain the few empty spaces on the walls: in 1990 the museum was robbed of nearly $200 million worth of paintings, including a rare and beloved Vermeer. The walls on which they were mounted will remain barren until the paintings are recovered (highly unlikely). The palazzo itself, with a four-story greenhouse courtyard, is a masterpiece, a tranquil oasis alone worth the price of admission. The Gardner's fine café serves lunch.

Columbia Point

This peninsula juts into the harbor south of the city center in Dorchester, one of Boston's edgier neighborhoods. The location is unlikely, but it does offer dramatic views of the city and a pleasant place to stroll. The museums – associated with the University of Massachusetts (UMass) Boston – are a part of ongoing revitalization efforts. Take the Red Line to JFK/UMass and catch a free shuttle bus (departures every 20 minutes) to Columbia Point.

JOHN F KENNEDY LIBRARY & MUSEUM

The legacy of John F Kennedy is ubiquitous in Boston. But the official memorial to the 35th president is the **John F Kennedy Library & Museum** (☎ 617-514-1600; www.jfklibrary.org; Columbia Point, Dorchester; adult/child/senior/student $10/7/8/8; ☼ 9am-5pm). The striking, modern, marble building – designed by IM Pei – was dubbed 'the shining monument by the sea' soon after it opened in 1979. The architectural centerpiece is the magnificent glass pavilion, with soaring 115ft ceilings and floor-to-ceiling windows overlooking Boston Harbor.

The museum is a fitting tribute to JFK's life and legacy. The effective use of video recreates history for visitors who may or may not remember the early 1960s. A highlight is the museum's treatment of the Cuban Missile Crisis: a short film explores the dilemmas and decisions that the president faced, while an archival exhibit displays actual documents and correspondence from these gripping 13 days. Family photographs and private writings – of both John and Jacqueline – add a personal but not overly sentimental dimension to the exhibits.

Interestingly, the library has an archive of writer Ernest Hemingway's manuscripts and papers. About 95% of his works can be accessed if you're interested in research, but there is no exhibit space. What's the connection? Kennedy was key in helping Mary Hemingway, Ernest's fourth wife and widow, get the manuscripts and papers out of Cuba during the first and most intense days of the embargo. When she died, she willed them here, because the library offers the public better access than most archival libraries.

TOP FIVE JFK SITES

Besides the birthplace of the Revolution, Boston is – of course – the birthplace of the Kennedys. Here are our favorite memorial spots.

- **John F Kennedy National Memorial Site** (p85) JFK's birthplace and boyhood home.

- **John F Kennedy Memorial Library & Museum** (p85) An archive of personal and historical documents, films and photographs.

- **John F Kennedy Park** (right) A contemplative spot on the campus of JFK's alma mater.

- **Union Oyster House, Booth No 18** (p103) JFK's favorite place to savor lobster stew on Sunday afternoons.

- **Brattle Bookshop** (p63) A huge (huge!) selection of books about the Kennedy clan, and their legacy in Boston and in the world.

COMMONWEALTH MUSEUM

This **museum** (☎ 617-727-9268; 220 Morrissey Blvd, Columbia Point; admission free; ☉ 9am-5pm Mon-Fri, 9am-3pm alternating Sat) exhibits documents dating back to the first days of colonization. Rotating exhibits showcase various aspects of state history, ranging from the archaeology of the Big Dig to the story of Italian anarchists Sacco and Vanzetti. Exhibits are drawn from the **Massachusetts Archives** (☎ 617-727-2816), a research facility housed on site.

Cambridge   Map p69

Boston's neighbor to the north was home to the country's first college and first printing press. Thus Cambridge established early on its reputation as fertile ground for intellectual and political thought – a reputation that has been upheld over 350 years (and counting). This reputation is due primarily to its hosting of the two academic heavyweights Harvard University and MIT. No less than seven presidents of the USA and countless cabinet members have graduated from Harvard University; 59 MIT faculty, staff and alums have won the Nobel Prize for chemistry, physics, economics, medi-

cine and peace. Most importantly, Cambridge's thousands of student residents ensure the city's continued vibrancy and diversity.

Cambridge is fondly called the 'People's Republic' for its progressive politics. Cantabrigians, as residents are known, vehemently opposed the Vietnam War before others did; they embraced the environmental movement before recycling became profitable; and they were one of the first communities to ban smoking in public buildings.

In this vain, Cambridge has played a historic role in the gay and lesbian rights movement, too. When Irish gays and lesbians were excluded from marching in South Boston's traditional St Patrick's Day parade in the mid-1990s, Cambridge immediately pledged to hold its own inclusive parade. More recently, Cambridge City Hall was the first to issue marriage licenses to gay and lesbian couples, when same-sex marriages became legal in Massachusetts in 2004.

HARVARD SQUARE

Harvard Sq is overflowing with cafés, bookstores, restaurants and street musicians. Although many Cantabrigians rightly complain that the square has lost its edge – once independently owned shops are continually gobbled up by national chains – Harvard Sq is still a vibrant and exciting place to hang out.

Opposite the main entrance to Harvard Yard, **Cambridge Common** is the village green where General Washington took command of the Continental Army on July 3, 1775. **Christ Church** across the street was used as barracks after its loyalist congregation fled. The adjacent **Old Burying Ground** is a tranquil Revolution-era cemetery, where Harvard's first eight presidents are buried.

The tranquil and verdant **Radcliffe Yard** is wedged between Brattle and Garden Sts. Radcliffe College, founded in 1879 as the sister school to the then-all-male Harvard, merged with its behemoth brother in 1975.

Further south along the Charles River, the green lawns of **John F Kennedy Park** pay tribute to Boston's favorite son. A prime spot for picnickers and Frisbee throwers, these are the grounds of Harvard's esteemed Kennedy School of Government.

BOSTON

HARVARD YARD
The geographic heart of **Harvard University** (www.harvard.edu) – where the brick buildings and leaf-covered paths exude academia – is Harvard Yard (through Anderson Gates from Massachusetts Ave). The focal point of the yard is the **John Harvard statue**, where every Harvard hopeful has a photo taken. Daniel Chester French's sculpture, inscribed 'John Harvard, Founder of Harvard College, 1638,' is known as the statue of three lies: (1) it does not actually depict Harvard (since no image of him exists), but a student chosen at random; (2) John Harvard was not the founder of the college, but its first benefactor in 1638; (3) the college was actually founded two years earlier in 1636. The Harvard symbol hardly lives up to the university's motto, *Veritas*, or 'Truth.'

Learn about this and many other fun facts on a free **campus tour** (☎ 617-495-1573; Holyoke Center, 1350 Massachusetts Ave). Tour guides probably won't reveal tidbits like the size of the university's multibillion-dollar endowment, which is the world's second-largest. (Only the endowment of the Catholic Church is bigger.) Tours are held at 10am and 2pm Monday to Friday and 2pm Saturday from September to May, and 10am, 11:15am and 2pm Monday to Friday and 3:15pm Saturday from June to August.

HARVARD MUSEUMS
The combination **Harvard Hot Ticket** (adult/senior/student $10/8/8), on sale at any of the museums mentioned following, provides discounted admission to six university museums and is valid for up to one year.

Several museums operate under the aegis of the **Museum of Natural History** (☎ 617-495-3045; www.hmnh.harvard.edu; 26 Oxford St & 11 Divinity Ave; adult/child/senior/student $7.50/5/6/6, free Wed afternoon & Sun morning; ☷ 9am-5pm), including the Museum of Comparative Zoology, with impressive fossil collections; and the multicultural Peabody Museum of Archaeology and Ethnology, boasting a strong collection of North American Indian artifacts. The highlight is the well-known Botanical Museum, which houses over 800 lifelike pieces of handblown-glass flowers and plants. One ticket is good for all four museums.

Harvard's oldest museum is the **Fogg Art Museum** (☎ 617-495-9400; www.artmuseums.harvard.edu; 32 Quincy St; adult/child/senior/student $6.50/free/5/5, free Sat morning; ☷ 10am-5pm Mon-Sat, 1-5pm Sun). It exhibits Western art from the Middle Ages to the present, including decorative arts.

SHTICK SHIFT
Here's a puzzler. How does a struggling auto repair shop owner parlay a brief spot on local public radio into national fame and fortune? Answer: he is one of the Magliozzi Brothers.

It helped, of course, to be invited back, which Tom Magliozzi was in 1977, when he first accepted the invitation of WBUR in the hope of drumming up some free publicity for his small Cambridge shop, the Good News Garage. It helped even more that Tom brought back with him his wise-cracking mechanic, younger brother Ray, for his next radio gig.

The Magliozzi Brothers were not your typical auto repair guys, nor were they your typical public radio fare. The East Cambridge natives and Massachusetts Institute of Technology (MIT) graduates were adept at leading listeners under the hood and unraveling the mysteries of internal gas combustion, while engaging in nonstop playful banter and sibling rivalry. They also offered insightful and unfiltered opinions of the auto repair profession, the auto industry as a whole, as well as America's car culture.

The audience quickly grew beyond the DIY set, as the *Car Talk* radio guys developed a local cult following. They were no longer the Magliozzi Brothers, humble garage technicians, they were now the Marx Brothers of auto repair, starring in their own weekly version of Grease Monkey Business.

In 1987 Click and Clack, the Tappett Brothers, took their show on the road, via NPR's nationwide network of affiliates. Today *Car Talk* is heard by more than four million listeners on over 500 radios stations each week. The brothers also have a syndicated automotive advice column that runs in 350 newspapers. Their production company, **Dewey, Cheetham and Howe** (cnr Brattle & John F Kennedy Sts, Cambridge), is located in Harvard Sq and their shop, the Good News Garage, still operates in Cambridge.

Don't drive like my brother. Don't drive like *my* brother.

BOSTON

Set around an Italian Renaissance courtyard, the Fogg has one of the country's finest collections of Impressionist and post-Impressionist works. Admission includes entry to the Busch-Reisinger and Arthur M Sackler Museums. Tours are held at 11am Monday to Friday.

Entered through the Fogg, the **Busch-Reisinger Museum** specializes in Central and Northern European art. Tours are conducted at 1pm Monday to Friday. Across the street, the **Arthur M Sackler Museum** (☎ 617-495-9400; 485 Broadway) is devoted to Asian and Islamic art. It boasts the world's most impressive collection of Chinese jade, as well as fine Japanese woodblock prints. It's tours take place at 2pm Monday to Friday.

TORY ROW

Heading west out of Harvard Sq, Brattle St is the epitome of colonial posh. Lined with mansions that were once home to royal sympathizers, the street earned the nickname Tory Row. The Hooper-Lee-Nichols House, a 1685 colonial that is open for architectural tours, is also the address of the **Cambridge Historical Society** (☎ 617-547-4252; www.cambridgehistory.org; 159 Brattle St; adult/senior/student $5/3/3; ☽ 2-4pm Tue-Thu). The urban estate at 33 Elmwood St (between Brattle and Mt Auburn Sts) was the home of Elbridge Gerry, signer of the Declaration of Independence and namesake of the term 'gerrymandering.' Elmwood is now the residence of the president of Harvard University.

Brattle St's most famous resident was Henry Wordsworth Longfellow, whose stately manor is now known as the **Longfellow National Historic Site** (☎ 617-876-4491; www .longfellowhouse.org; 105 Brattle St; ☽ 10am-4:30pm Wed-Sun May-Oct). The poet lived and wrote here from 1837 to 1882, a total of 45 years. Now under the auspices of the NPS, the Georgian mansion contains many of Longfellow's belongings and lush period gardens. After a lengthy restoration, the site now offers poetry readings and historical tours.

MASSACHUSETTS INSTITUTE OF TECHNOLOGY (MIT)

The MIT campus, near Kendall Sq offers a completely novel perspective on Cambridge academia: proudly nerdy, but not quite so tweedy as Harvard. Join an excellent guided **campus tour** (☎ 617-253-4795; www.mit.edu; 77 Massachusetts Ave; ☽ tours 10:45am & 2:45pm Mon-Fri) to best appreciate MIT's amazing contributions to the sciences. Alternatively, get an up-close look at robots, holograms, strobe photography, kinetic sculptures and other scientific wonders at the **MIT Museum** (☎ 617-253-4444; http://web.mit.edu/museum; 265 Massachusetts Ave; adult/child/student/senior $5/2/2/2; ☽ 10am-5pm Tue-Fri, noon-5pm Sat & Sun). See p94 for more details.

A stroll around campus is proof that MIT supports artistic as well as technological innovation. Download a map of the public art that bejewels the East Campus (east of Massachusetts Ave). The nearby **List Visual Arts Center** (☎ 617-253-4680; Weisner Bldg, 20 Ames St; admission free; ☽ noon-6pm Tue-Thu, noon-8pm Fri, noon-6pm Sat & Sun) mounts sophisticated shows of contemporary art across all media. Don't miss the funky **Ray & Maria Stata Center** (32 Vassar St), a new avant-garde building that was designed by architectural legend Frank Gehry. Pick up a map at the information desk for a self-guided tour of the public spaces.

ACTIVITIES
Cycling & Running

More than 50 miles of bicycle trails originate in the Boston area. While riding through the downtown streets can be tricky, these (mostly) off-road trails offer a great opportunity for bikers to avoid traffic and explore

---

DETOUR: MT AUBURN CEMETERY

Brattle St terminates at the Egyptian revival gateway into **Mt Auburn Cemetery** (☎ 617-547-7105; www.mountauburn.org; 580 Mt Auburn St; ☽ 8am-7pm May-Oct, 8am-5pm Nov-Apr). Since 1831 this beautifully landscaped park has been the final resting place for Boston's most influential artistic, literary and philosophic souls. Stroll past the graves of Dorothea Dix, Mary Baker Eddy, Fannie Farmer, Isabella Gardner, Oliver Wendell Holmes Sr, Winslow Homer, Charles Sumner and Henry Wordsworth Longfellow. Flowering with cherry, dogwood and magnolia trees, the cemetery is a welcome respite from the city's turmoil. Hidden among the hills is the exquisite Gothic Revival Bigelow Chapel. At the highest point in the park, Washington Tower offers a panoramic view of Harvard, the Hancock, the Pru and beyond.

A WALK ACROSS THE HARVARD BRIDGE

The Harvard Bridge – from Back Bay in Boston to Massachusetts Institute of Technology (MIT) in Cambridge – is the longest route across the Charles River. It is not too long to walk, but it is long enough to do some wondering while you walk. You might wonder, for example, why the bridge that leads directly into the heart of MIT is named the Harvard Bridge.

According to legend, the state offered to name the bridge after Cambridge's second university. But the brainiac engineers at MIT analyzed the plans for construction and found the bridge was structurally unsound. Not wanting the MIT moniker associated with a faulty feat of engineering, it was suggested that the bridge be better named for the neighboring university up the river. That the bridge was subsequently rebuilt validated the superior brainpower of MIT.

That is only a legend, however (one invented by an MIT student, no doubt). The fact is that the Harvard Bridge was first constructed in 1891, and MIT moved to its current location only in 1916. The bridge was rebuilt in the 1980s to modernize and expand it, but the original name has stuck, at least officially. Most people around Boston actually refer to this bridge as the 'MIT bridge' or the 'Mass Ave bridge' because frankly it makes more sense.

By now, walking across the bridge, perhaps you have reached the halfway point: 'Halfway to Hell' reads the scrawled graffiti. What is all this graffiti anyway? What is a 'smoot?'

A smoot is an obscure unit of measurement that was used to measure the distance of the Harvard Bridge, first in 1958 and every year since. One smoot is approximately 5ft 7in, the height of Oliver R Smoot, who was a pledge of the MIT fraternity Lambda Chi Alpha in '58. He was the shortest pledge that year. And yes, his physical person was actually used for all the measurements. By the end of the exercise, he was so tired his fraternity brothers had to drag him along the bridge.

And now that you have reached the other side of the river, surely you are wondering exactly how long this bridge is. We can't speak for the Harvard students, but certainly every MIT student knows that the Harvard Bridge is 364.4 smoots plus one ear.

---

the city on two wheels. You can take your bike on any of the MBTA subway lines except the Green Line, but you must avoid rush hours (6am to 9am and 4pm to 7pm Monday to Friday) and always ride on the last train car.

Rubel BikeMaps (☎ 617-776-6567; www.bikemaps .com) produces laminated 'Pocket Rides,' 50 different loop rides in greater Boston or from area commuter rail stations. For the metro Boston area, look for the 'BU Bridge Bike Pack,' in which all tours start from the Boston University Bridge, at Essex St near Kenmore Sq. The rides are incredibly detailed and worth every penny.

Try the following outfits for bicycle rental:

Boston Bicycle (Map pp70–1; ☎ 617-236-0752; 842 Beacon St; rental per 24hr $25; ☯ 10am-7pm Mon-Sat, noon-6pm Sun) Also offers customized bike tours through the affiliate Urban Adventours (p94).

Cambridge Bicycle (☎ 617-876-6555; 259 Massachusetts Ave; rental per 24hr $25; ☯ 10am-7pm Mon-Sat, noon-6pm Sun) Near Central Sq.

Community Bicycle Supply (Map pp70–1; ☎ 617-542-8623; 496 Tremont St; rental per day $20; ☯ 10am-7pm Mon-Sat year-round, noon-5pm Sun Apr-Sep)

CHARLES RIVER ROUTE

One of the most popular circuits runs along both sides of the Charles River between the bridge near the Museum of Science and the Mt Auburn St Bridge in Watertown Center (about 5 miles west of Cambridge). The round-trip is 17 miles, but 10 bridges in between offer ample opportunity to turn around and shorten the trip. This trail isn't particularly well maintained (be careful of roots and narrow passes) and is often crowded with pedestrians. On Sunday from mid-April to mid-November, Memorial Dr (Cambridge) is closed to cars between the Eliot Bridge (near Harvard Stadium) and River Rd, which helps to relieve some of the traffic.

EMERALD NECKLACE

This chain of parks runs through the middle of the city, from the Fenway to Jamaica Way to Arnold Arboretum. The packed dirt is fine for mountain bikes and hybrids, but not really suitable for road bikes. This shady path is not as crowded as the Charles River route, but beware of a few dangerous intersections and road crossings.

BOSTON

MINUTEMAN TRAIL

The best of Boston's bicycle trails starts in Arlington (near Alewife T-station) and leads 10 miles to historic Lexington center (p132), then traverses an additional 4 miles of idyllic scenery and terminates in the rural suburb of Bedford. The wide, straight, paved path is in excellent condition, though it also gets crowded on weekends. The Minuteman Trail is also accessible from Davis Sq via the 2-mile Community Path to Arlington.

Boating & Kayaking

The **Charles River Canoe & Kayak Center** (www.ski-paddle.com; canoe/kayak/kids' kayak per hr $13/14/6) has two outlets offering canoe and kayak rental: **Newton** (☎ 617-965-5110; 2401 Commonwealth Ave; ☑ 10am-sunset Mon-Fri, 9am-sunset Sat & Sun Apr-Oct) and **Boston** (☎ 617-462-2513; Soldiers Field Rd; ☑ 4pm-sunset Thu, 1pm-sunset Fri, 10am-sunset Sat & Sun May–mid-Oct). Daily rental rates are also available.

Community Boating (☎ 617-523-1038; www.community-boating.org; Charles River Esplanade; rental per 2 days kayak/sailboat $50/$100; ☑ 1pm-sunset Mon-Fri, 9am-sunset Sat & Sun Apr-Oct) offers experienced sailors unlimited use of sailboats and kayaks, but you'll have to take a test to demonstrate your ability. Between the Hatch Memorial Shell and the Longfellow Bridge; take the Red Line to Charles/MGH.

Skating

The most popular spots for inline skaters are the Charles River Esplanade and – on Sunday – Memorial Dr in Cambridge. You can rent skates from **Beacon Hill Skate** (Map pp70-1; ☎ 617-482-7400; 135 Charles St South; rental per hr/day $10/25; ☑ 11am-5:30pm Mon & Wed-Sat, noon-4pm Sun).

In winter, head to the **Frog Pond** (Map pp66-8; ☎ 617-635-2120; www.cityofboston.gov/parks/FrogPond_winter.asp; adult/child $3/free, skate rental adult/child $7/5; ☑ 10am-9pm Sun-Thu, 10am-10pm Fri & Sat mid-Nov–mid-Mar) on Boston Common, which gets flooded with ice skaters. Skate rental, lockers and restrooms are available at the kiosk next to the pond.

WALKING TOUR: FREEDOM TRAIL

Map p91

The best introduction to revolutionary Boston is the Freedom Trail. The red-brick path winds its way past 16 sites that earned this town its status as the cradle of liberty. The 2.5-mile trail follows the course of the conflict, from the Old State House, where Red-coats killed five men marking the Boston Massacre, to the Old North Church, where the sexton hung two lanterns to warn that British troops would come by sea. Visit the GBCVB tourist information kiosk (p73) at the Boston Common to pick up a free map or to hook up with a 90-minute guided tour led by the **Freedom Trail Foundation** (☎ 617-357-8300; www.thefreedomtrail.org; adult/child $12/6). Tours are held at 11am, noon and 1pm daily.

Start at **Boston Common** (1; p74), America's oldest public park. On the northern side of the park, you can't miss the gold-domed **Massachusetts State House** (2; p79) sitting atop Beacon Hill. On the eastern side of the Common, **Park St Church** (3; p75) stands on the corner of Tremont and Park Sts. Walk north on Tremont St, where you will pass the Egyptian Rival gates of the **Old Granary Burying Ground** (4; p75), the final resting place of many notable patriots.

Continue north to School St, where the stately, columned **King's Chapel** (5; p75) overlooks its adjacent burying ground. If it's open, take a peak at the interior, which is considered one of the finest examples of Georgian architecture. Turn east on School St, and take note of the bronze statue of Benjamin Franklin outside the Old City Hall. A plaque commemorates this spot as the **site of the first public school** (6), Boston Latin School, founded in 1635. Boston Latin continues to operate in the Fenway.

Continue down School St to Washington St, where the little brick building on the corner is known – appropriately – as the **Old Corner Bookstore (7)**. Built in 1718, this building was leased to a bookseller in 1829, when it commenced a 75-year run as a bookstore and literary and intellectual hotspot. It now houses the headquarters of Historic Boston, a nonprofit company that organizes efforts to preserve the city's historic buildings. Diagonally opposite this, the **Old South Meeting House** (8; p75) saw the beginnings of one of the American Revolution's most vociferous protests, the Boston Tea Party.

Further north on Washington St, the **Old State House** (9; p75) was the scene of more historic drama: the first reading of the Declaration of Independence. Outside the Old State House, a ring of cobblestones marks the **Boston Massacre site (10)**, yet another uprising that fueled the revolution. Cross the traffic-filled intersection and head north on

BOSTON

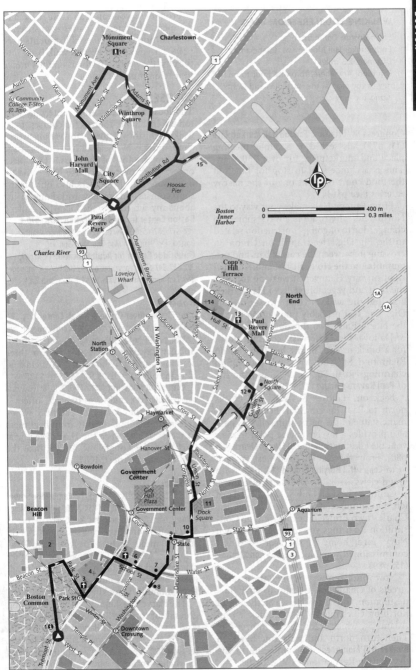

BOSTON

WALKING TOUR: FREEDOM TRAIL

Start: Boston Common
End: Bunker Hill Monument, Charlestown
Distance: 2.5 miles
Duration: Anywhere from one hour to one
day, if you stop at the museums and sights
along the way

Congress St. Historic **Faneuil Hall Marketplace** (**11**; p75) has served as a public meeting place and marketplace for over 250 years. This is a choice spot to stop for lunch at the food court or from one of the nearby eateries (see p101).

From Faneuil Hall, make your way to the North End. The route is always subject to change, due to ongoing construction related to the Big Dig. Head north on Union St, crossing in between the row of bars and restaurants and the Holocaust Memorial. Turn right on tiny Hanover St weaving through the fruit and vegetable stalls of Haymarket, and find the walkway that crosses the Big Dig. You will probably pop out on one of the North End's two thoroughfares, Salem or Hanover Sts. Either way, continue north for a block or two, before heading east on Richmond St. You will find yourself in charming North Sq, which is also the site of **Paul Revere's House** (**12**; p79).

Back on Hanover St, walk two blocks north to Paul Revere Mall. Besides a dramatic statue of the patriot himself, this park also provides a lovely vantage point to view your next destination, the **Old North Church** (**13**; p80). From the church, head west on Hull St to **Copp's Hill Burying Ground** (**14**; p80), with grand views across the river to Charlestown.

Continue west on Hull St to its end. Turn left on Commercial St and walk across the Charlestown Bridge. Turning right on Constitution Rd brings you to the Charlestown Navy Yard, home of the world's oldest commissioned warship, the **USS Constitution** (**15**; p80).

Now wind your way through the historic streets of Charlestown center to your final destination. Cut up to Chelsea St, then head north on Chestnut St. Take a quick left on Adams St, which leads past Winthrop Sq. Then turn north and walk one block to **Bunker Hill Monument** (**16**; p81), site of the devastating Revolutionary War battle.

From here, you can grab a bite to eat and recuperate in one of Charlestown's trendy or traditional eating establishments (see p106). If you're too beat to walk back into the city, the nearest T-stop is on the Orange Line, Community College.

COURSES

The local adult education centers in Boston are incredible sources for courses, from walking historical tours, to writing workshops hosted by local authors, to massage for couples. Most of the classes take place once a week over the course of a semester or season. But the centers also offer many short courses and one-day workshops on just about any subject. Try the following centers:

Boston Center for Adult Education (Map pp70-1; ☎ 617-267-4530; www.bcae.org; 5 Commonwealth Ave, Boston; ✆ 9am-7pm Mon-Thu, 9am-5pm Fri)

Cambridge Center for Adult Education (Map p69; ☎ 617-547-6789; www.ccae.org; 42 Brattle St, Cambridge; ✆ 9am-9pm Mon-Thu, 9am-7pm Fri, 9am-2pm Sat)

Boating

The **Charles River Canoe & Kayak Center** (☎ 617-965-5110; www.ski-paddle.com; 2401 Commonwealth Ave, Newton; per 3/6 hr $75/129; ✆ Apr-Oct) offers introductory kayaking classes for two or three sessions, totaling six hours. It also offers day-long introductory trips for $115 to $125.

Community Boating (☎ 617-523-1038; www.community-boating.org; Charles River Esplanade) offers a wide variety of courses for paddlers, windsurfers and sailors, ranging from beginners to racers. It's between the Hatch Memorial Shell and the Longfellow Bridge; take the Red Line to Charles/MGH.

Cooking

The recreation division of the **Cambridge School of Culinary Arts** (☎ 617-354-2020; www.cambridgeculinary.com; 2020 Massachusetts Ave, Cambridge; courses $60-75) offers one-time courses that focus on seasonal meals, such as 'An American Gathering' or 'A Tuscan Christmas,' or on other crucial cooking skills like 'All you Knead' (basic breads). The most popular course, offered monthly, is cooking for couples.

The Harvest Restaurant has been a training ground for some of Boston's foremost chefs. And once a month, at **Harvest Review** (☎ 617-686-2255; www.the-harvest.com; 44 Brattle St, Cambridge; per event $39) the esteemed restaurant opens its kitchen to the public for food and wine tastings. Each event is hosted by a special guest, from beer brewer to fisherman. Events are held at 6pm (scheduled monthly).

Yoga

For detailed listings of Boston's yoga schools, see www.bostonyoga.com.

The **Back Bay Yoga Studio** (Map pp70-1; ☎ 617-375-0785; www.backbayyoga.com; 1112 Boylston St; yoga adult/senior & student $14/10, massage per 90-min session $75-150 ☒ 6am-9pm Mon-Thu, 6am-7pm Fri, 10am-2pm Sat, 8am-8pm Sun) offers massage to meditation, as well as all forms of yoga.

At **Baptiste Power Vinyasa Yoga** (www.baronbap tiste.com; 90-min class $12) Boston (Map pp70-1; ☎ 617-423-9642; 139 Columbus Ave); Cambridge (☎ 617-661-9642; 2000 Massachusetts Ave, Porter Sq) courses take place in a room where temperatures reach 90°F, allowing for greater flexibility and lots of sweating.

Bikram Yoga (Map pp66-8; ☎ 617-555-9926; www .bikramyoga.com; 108 Lincoln St; 90-min class $16; ☒ 6am-7:30pm Mon-Thu, 9am-5:30pm Fri-Sun) is heat yoga: arrive hydrated and bring a towel.

South End Yoga (Map pp70-1; ☎ 617-247-2716; www .southendyoga.com; 11 W Concord St; per class $12) offers courses in a variety of yoga forms, including ashtanga, mysore and vinyasa. The schedule varies, but usually only offers two classes a day, so check website for details.

BOSTON FOR CHILDREN

Boston is one giant living history museum, the setting for many educational and lively field trips. For the city's most popular spots for kids, see Top Five Kid Spots, right. A handy reference book is *Kidding Around Boston* by Helen Byers. Most importantly, don't forget to think outside the box; many adult-oriented museums and historic sites have special programs geared toward kids. Check the following websites in advance to make the most of your visit with your child.

Boston Public Library (p82; www.bpl.org) BPL offers an incredible Kid's Page, including reading lists, tutorials and homework help for research projects, as well as some other fun and games. A similar site called the Teen Lounge exists for older kids.

Freedom Trail (p90; www.thefreedomtrail.org) Download a scavenger hunt or a reading list for your child before setting out.

Massachusetts State House (p79; www.mass.gov/state house) Check out the Kid's Zone. It features word games, trivia quizzes and the priceless *Ladybug Story*, a tale about

---

TOP FIVE KID SPOTS

- **Museum of Science** (p77) More opportunities to combine fun and learning than anywhere in the city.

- **New England Aquarium** (p77) Explore the most exotic of natural environments… under the sea.

- **Children's Museum** (p77) Hours of fun climbing, constructing and creating. Especially good for kids aged three to eight.

- **Franklin Park Zoo** (p84) Visit the Serengeti Plain, the Australian Outback and the Amazonian Rain Forest all in the course of an afternoon.

- **Boston Tea Party Ship & Museum** (p77) What could be more fun than dumping bales of tea overboard?

---

how a group of kids used the legislative process to make the ladybug the official bug of Massachusetts. Also 'What's under the Gold Dome?' is the kid's guide to the State House.

Museum of Fine Arts (p84; www.mfa.org) Provides information on loads of programs offered by the MFA for kids of all ages. For example, Children's Room (3:30pm to 4:45pm Monday to Friday) allows children aged six to 12 use art, music and poetry to explore the gallery's collections. Teen-to-Teen Art talks (6:30pm to 8:30pm Wednesday) feature teenagers who have been trained at the MFA to engage their peers in creative activities.

Paul Revere House (p79; www.paulreverehouse.org) Features a page 'Just for Kids' that allows children to learn about the Revere family kitchen (including a recipe for a colonial snack: dried apples), play old-fashioned games, read age-specific articles and complete a crossword puzzle about the historic house.

Playgrounds

We're not sure if America's first public park is home to its first playground, but rest assured the Boston Common (p74) has a huge playscape with swings, jungle gyms and all the rest. Across the river, the Cambridge Common (p86) has the same.

Child Care

If you must leave them behind, a few agencies offer temporary babysitting services. Most upscale hotels also offer babysitting services or referral.

Boston Best Babysitter (☎ 617-268-7148; per hr $10-15 plus $35 referral fee)

In Search of Nanny, Inc (☎ 978-777-9891; www
.insearchofnanny.com; per hr $10-18 plus referral fee, 4hr
minimum)

Nanny Poppins (☎ 987-927-1811; www.nannypoppins
.com; per hr $10-18 plus referral fee)

QUIRKY BOSTON
Leave it to the mischievous brainiacs at MIT
to come up with the most bizarre forms
of entertainment in the city. Visit the **MIT
Museum** (☎ 617-253-4444; web.mit.edu/museum; 265
Massachusetts Ave; adult/child/senior/student $5/2/2/2;
☺ 10am-5pm Tue-Fri, noon-5pm Sat & Sun) for an
insider's look at how fun and funky science and technology can be. An exhibit
called Robots and Beyond demonstrates
MIT's ongoing work with artificial intelligence. You can meet humanoid robots,
like observant Cog and personable Kismet,
and decide for yourself if they are smarter
than humans. Sculptor Arthur Ganson
explores the fine line between art and engineering with his display of interactive
sculpture. And the fantastic Light Fantastic
is the world's largest exhibit of holograms –
learn how they are made and how they are
used in fields from art and architecture to
medicine and engineering.

TOURS
TROLLEY TOURS
According to a Duck Tour driver, 'trolleys
can go in the water too... Once.' Nonetheless, trolley tours offer great ease and flexibility because you can hop off at sites along
the route and hop on the next trolley that
comes along. There is little to distinguish
the various companies (besides the color of
the trolley). Tickets for all trolley tours are
available for sale at the Boston Welcome
Center (p73) and online, as well as at the
ticket outlets listed below.

Brush Hill/Gray Line Tours (Map pp66-8; ☎ 781-
986-6100, 800-343-1328; www.brushhilltours.com; 16
Charles St S, State Transportation Bldg; adult/child $26/13;
☺ tour 9:30am May-Nov) Offers a 3½-hour motor-coach
tour of Cambridge, Lexington and Concord. Pick-up is
possible from most hotels in the area.

Discover Boston Trolley Tours (☎ 617-742-1440;
www.discoverbostontours.com; 84 Atlantic Ave; 1-day tour
adult/child/senior $24/15/22, 2-day tour $34/25/32) Offers
audiotapes in Spanish, French, German and Japanese.

Old Town Trolley Tours (☎ 800-868-7482; www
.historictours.com; cnr Central Wharf & Milk St; 1-day tour
adult/child/senior $24/free/22, 2-day tour $34/free/32)

Includes free entry to the multimedia show 'The Whites of their
Eyes' at Beacon Hill Memorial, or a 45-minute harbor cruise.

WALKING TOURS
The NPS offers free guided walking tours of
the Black Heritage Trail (p79). Guides are
also available for the Freedom Trail (p90).
Secret Tour (☎ 617-720-2283; www.northendboston
.com; per person $25; ☺ tours 10am, 1pm & 3pm Fri &
Sat) A two-hour walking tour, beginning at Old North Sq,
that explores the North End's hidden courtyards and
passageways, thus uncovering pieces of the diverse
neighborhood's checkered past.

Little Italy (☎ 617-523-6032; www.micheletopor.com;
per person $45; ☺ tours 10am & 2pm Wed & Sat, 10am
& 3pm Fri) Food and wine consultant Michele Topor leads
this 3½-hour tour around the North End, including shopping in a *salumeria* (corner shop), sampling pastries at the
local *pasticcerias* (pastry shop) and touring an *enoteca* (wine
bar). The sights and smells of the North End provide a great
introduction to Italian cuisine and culture.

Talking Street (☎ 617-262-8687; www.talkingstreet
.com; tour $6) Offers a walking tour called 'Boston: City of
Rebels and Dreamers.' It is unique for several reasons. One,
it is Boston's only cell-phone tour, meaning you call the
designated number for an informative description of each
site. Second, the tour is narrated by Steve Tyler, Boston
native and lead singer of Aerosmith. Other highlights of
the narration include an interview with Red Sox legend
Carl Yastrzremski and instructions on how to eat a *cannoli*
by a North End pastry chef.

CYCLING TOURS
Urban Adventours (Map pp70-1; ☎ 617-233-7595;
www.urbanadventours.com; 842 Beacon St; tour incl bike
$50-75) offers a City View Ride that provides
a great overview of Boston and how to get
around by bike. Rides are held at 10:30am
Monday to Saturday, and 12:30pm Sunday.
Other more specialized tours are for photographers, urban adventurers and couples
(see website for schedule).

BOAT TOURS
Bay State Cruise Company (Map pp66-8; ☎ 617-
748-1428, 866-435-6800; www.baystatecruises.com;
Commonwealth Pier, 200 Seaport Blvd; tickets $16-20;
☺ 8:30-11:30pm Fri & Sat Jun-Sep) Offers a three-hour
evening harbor cruise with music or other entertainment.
Trips depart from the World Trade Center. Guests must be
21 or older.

Boston Duck Tours (☎ 617-723-3825; www.bostonduck
tours.com; adult/child/senior/student $24/15/21/21;
☺ 9am-sunset Apr-Nov) Organizes land and water tours
using modified amphibious vehicles from WWII. They depart

from the Prudential Center (p82) and the Museum of Science (p77). Rain or shine, the narrated tour splashes around the Charles River for about 25 minutes, and then competes with cars on Boston city streets for another 55 minutes. Tours sell out, so it's necessary to buy tickets in advance online or at the point of departure.

Boston Harbor Cruises (Map pp66-8; ☎ 617-227-4320; www.bostonharborcruises.com; 1 Long Wharf; adult/child/senior/student $18/13/16/16) Offers narrated sightseeing trips around the outer harbor at 11am, 1pm and 3pm daily from June to August, and Saturday and Sunday only in September. Other boats go on sunset cruises (prices same) at 7pm daily from June to August, and at 6pm Thursday to Sunday in September, as well as to the USS *Constitution* in Charlestown (adult/senior and student/child $12/11/9) from 10:30am to 4:30pm daily from mid-April to mid-November.

Charles River Boat Co (☎ 617-621-3001; www.charles riverboat.com; Cambridgeside Galleria; adult/child/senior $10/6/9; 🕐 10am-4:15pm daily Jun-Aug, Sat & Sun only Apr, May & Sep) A 75-minute narrated trip of the Charles River Basin between Harvard and the Boston Harbor locks.

Gondola di Venezia (☎ 617-876-2800; www.boston gondolas.com; Community Boating, Charles River Esplanade; per couple 35-min traditional tour $69, 50-min sunset tour $99; 🕐 2-10pm Wed-Sun Jun-Oct) Make no mistake about it – the Charles River is not the Grand Canal, but Gondola di Venezia offers private gondola rides that are still a romantic treat. The gondolier's technique and the craftsmanship of the gondola certainly give the experience a run for the money.

WHALE-WATCHING TOURS
Whale sightings are practically guaranteed at Stellwagen Bank, a fertile feeding ground 25 miles out to sea. The big humpback whales are most impressive while breaching and frolicking; in the spring and fall huge pods of dolphins making their way to and from summers in the Arctic are also impressive. Trips take three to four hours, with onboard commentary provided by naturalists. Dress warmly, even on summer days.

Boston Harbor Cruises (Map pp66-8; ☎ 617-227-4320; www.bostonharborcruises.com; 1 Long Wharf; adult/child/senior $30/24/27) Offers trips from April to November.

New England Aquarium Whale Watch (Map pp66-8; ☎ 617-973-5277; www.neaq.org/visit/wwatch; Central Wharf; adult/senior & student $29/26/26, child $20-23) Has a trip at 10am daily from April to October, with additional cruises May to September. No children under three are permitted on the trip.

OTHER TOURS
The 20-mile **Literary Trail** (☎ 617-350-0358; www .lit-trail.org; adult/child $30/26) tour departs from the Omni Parker House (p97) and visits notable literary sights in Boston, Cambridge and Concord at 9am the second Saturday of every month. Alternatively, buy the excellent book *Literary Trail of Greater Boston* and take a self-guided tour.

FESTIVALS & EVENTS
The *Boston Globe* publishes a Calendar section every Thursday, with up-to-the-minute details on all events. Prior to your arrival, check with the GBCVB (p73) or visit its website www.bostonusa.com. Remember that accommodations are much harder to secure during big events.

January/February
Chinese New Year In late January or early February, climaxes with a colorful parade in Chinatown.

March
St Patrick's Day Parade (☎ 617-268-7955; www.st patricksdayparade.com) In mid-March the large and vocal South Boston Irish community hosts this parade on W Broadway St in Cambridge. Since the mid-1990s the St Patrick's Day Parade has been marred by the council's decision to exclude gay and lesbian Irish groups from marching.

April
Boston Marathon (☎ 617-236-1652; www.boston marathon.org) On the third Monday in April, thousands of runners compete in the 26.2-mile run that has been an annual event for more than a century. Starting in Hopkinton west of the city, the race finishes on Boylston St in front of the Boston Public Library.

Patriot's Day Also on the third Monday in April, this state holiday is celebrated with a re-enactment of Paul Revere's historic ride and the battles at Lexington and Concord (see p132).

May
Lilac Sunday On the third Sunday in May, this event at Arnold Arboretum (p84) celebrates the arrival of spring when more than 400 varieties of fragrant lilacs are in bloom.

Magnolia Trees Mother Nature decides the date that the trees bloom all along Newbury St and Commonwealth Ave in the Back Bay.

June
Bunker Hill Day On June 17, includes a parade and battle re-enactment at Charlestown's Bunker Hill Monument (p80).

Gay Pride Parade (☎ 617-262-9405; www.bostonpride .org) Drawing tens of thousands of participants and spectators, this mid-month parade culminates in a big party on Boston Common (p74).

GAY & LESBIAN BOSTON

Gay men have spiffed up the South End, and lesbians the outlying neighborhoods of Jamaica Plain. Both have thriving communities in Boston, the first city in the first state to legalize same-sex marriage. (In actual fact, it was Cambridge that issued the first marriage license to long-time lesbian couple Susan Shepherd and Marcia Hams at 12:01am on May 17, 2004, the first minute of the first day it was legal to do so.)

Pick up the weekly *Bay Windows* (p72) or the monthly *Sojouner* at Cuttyhunk (p63), Boston's primary gay bookstore. For gay-friendly entertainment venues, see p121.

Other resources:

■ **AIDS Action Hotline** (☎ 800-235-2331)

■ **Bisexual Resource Center** (Map pp70-1; ☎ 617-424-9595; www.biresource.org; 29 Stanhope St)

■ **Fenway Community Health Center** (Map pp70-1; ☎ 617-267-0900; 7 Haviland St)

July

Harborfest (☎ 617-227-1528; www.bostonharborfest .com) This week-long event is an extension of the Fourth of July weekend. One day is always devoted to Children's Day, with face painting, balloons and children's entertainment at venues around the city. On July 4, the Boston Pops gives a free concert on the Esplanade, attended by hundreds of thousands of people. Fireworks cap off the evening.

Chowderfest A very tasty part of Harborfest. Sample dozens of fish and clam chowders prepared by Boston's best restaurants.

July/August

Patron Saints' Feasts (www.northendboston.com) In the North End, Italian festivals honoring patron saints are celebrated with food and music on the weekends.

August

August Moon Festival (☎ 617-542-2574) In mid-August in Chinatown, a Chinese celebration for the end of the harvest season. The feast is capped by dragon and lion dances and eating mooncakes.

Cambridge Carnival (☎ 617-492-2518; www.cambridge carnival.org) The last weekend in August – a fantastic weekend of food and music celebrating Caribbean culture in Central Sq.

September

Boston Blues Festival (www.bluestrust.com) A weekend of free live blues at the Hatch Memorial Shell (p81) on the Charles River Esplanade.

Boston Film Festival (☎ 617-331-9460; www.boston filmfestival.org) Screens a variety of movies at dozens of venues all over the city in mid-September.

Cambridge River Festival (www.cambridgema.gov) A community art festival with a 25-year history. After a hiatus in 2004, the future of this festival is unknown.

October

Head of the Charles (☎ 617-868-6200; www.hocr.org) The world's largest rowing event. The mid-month regatta draws more than 3000 collegiate rowers, while preppy fans line the banks of the river, lounging on blankets and drinking beer (technically illegal).

December

Tree Lighting The huge Prudential Center Christmas tree and trees that ring Boston Common are lit in early December and remain lit throughout the month.

Boston Tea Party Reenactment Every December 16, costumed actors march from downtown to the waterfront and dump bales of tea into the harbor. For details, see p77.

First Night (www.firstnight.org) New Years Eve celebrations begin early on 31 December and continue past midnight, culminating in fireworks over the harbor. Buy a special button from venues around the city that permits entrance into many events. Admission costs $15.

SLEEPING

It's not cheap to sleep in Boston. Despite the opening of many new properties, Boston hotels still enjoy high occupancy rates. So be warned: room rates are among the highest in the country and reservations should be made well in advance.

The majority of hotels are located downtown, in Back Bay, and in Cambridge around Kendall Sq; all of these locations are centrally located, convenient to transport and usually pricey. Remember that city hotels are often less expensive on weekends, when packages are offered to attract nonbusiness travelers.

Hotel prices are usually lowest from mid-November to mid-March, with the exception of major holidays. For this book, price ranges include budget (less than $100), mid-range ($100 to $200) and top end ($200 and up, up, up).

Centralized reservation bureaus can often secure lower rates than you can by yourself, such as **Central Reservation Services of New England** (☎ 617-569-3800, 800-332-3026; www .bostonhotels.net) and **GBCVB** (☎ 617-424-7664; boston usa.worldres.com).

The **B&B Agency of Boston** (☎ 617-720-3540, 800-248-9262, from the UK 0800-895128; www.boston-bnb agency.com; s $70-90, d $100-160) lists about 150 B&Bs and apartments in central locations. It includes everything from elegant Victorian-furnished brownstones to waterfront lofts to a docked wooden sailboat. Fully furnished apartments are also available on a nightly, weekly or monthly basis.

As of 2003 the Boston Public Health Commission passed a regulation restricting smoking in the workplace. While 'smoking rooms' are exempt from this ban, rest assured that all accommodation options will make nonsmoking rooms available to their guests.

Downtown   Map pp66-8
Harborside Inn (☎ 617-723-7500; www.harborsideinn boston.com; 185 State St; r $119-159; P) This urban oasis has 54 rooms in a respectfully renovated 19th-century warehouse. Spacious and light-filled, they feature exposed brick, polished floorboards, and lovely views of the city skyline or atrium. The hotel's delightful restaurant, the Margo Bistro, serves classic New England fare with a modern flair.

Nine Zero (☎ 617-772-5800; www.ninezero.com; 90 Tremont St; r from $249; P 🖳) Rooms are downright sumptuous, from the plush robes to the padded satin hangers to the custom furniture. Fitness center, 24-hour room service and extra special attention for Fido make this classy hotel a wonderful spot for a splurge. Don't miss dinner or drinks at the trendy bar and restaurant Spire.

Omni Parker House (☎ 617-227-8600; www.omni hotels.com; 60 School St; r Apr-Oct $219-239, Nov-Mar $159-199; P 🖳) Dating from 1856, the country's oldest continually operating hotel has over 550 rooms, furnished with cherry furniture and antique heirlooms. But it does not lack for modern amenities either: on-demand movies, high-speed Internet access etc. History buffs might choose one of the individually decorated suites paying tribute to a historic Boston figure. Fitness buffs can request a room with a portable treadmill and healthy snack pack.

Government Center   Map pp66-8
Irish Embassy Hostel (☎ 617-973-4841; 232 Friend St; dm $25) Near the North End and Faneuil Hall, this hostel rents 54 beds (with four to 12 people per room) above its lively eponymous pub. You'll get a tidy place; free sheets and towels; admission to hear live bands in two pubs; an all-you-can-eat barbecue buffet dinner several nights a week; and bargain-price beers. It's unbeatable, but don't get too comfortable; there's a six-night maximum stay. Make reservations as

---

URBAN ADVENTURE

It is a rare opportunity to camp in a major metropolitan area, but you can do it on the Boston Harbor Islands. Of the 34 islands contained within Boston Harbor's State Park, four allow camping: Peddock, Lovell, Grape and Bumpkin. To make reservations, contact the **Department of Environmental Management** (DEM; ☎ 877-422-6762; www.mass.gov/dem/parks/bhis.htm).

Each island has 10 to 12 individual sites and one large group site. Camping is allowed on Saturday from early May to mid-October and nightly between Memorial Day and Labor Day. For more information on the individual islands (and how to get there), see p78.

Keep in mind the following dos and don'ts:

■ Do bring your own water and supplies.

■ Do carry everything in and out.

■ Do hang your food high in the trees out of reach of animals.

■ Don't bring pets or alcohol.

■ Don't make open fires.

■ Don't expect anything more than primitive sites and composting toilets.

far in advance as possible (online at www
.hostels.com).

Beantown Hostel (☎ 617-723-0800; 222 Friend
St; dm $25) Since these 56 beds are operated
by the adjacent Irish Embassy Hostel, the
Beantown offers the same prices and similar facilities.

Shawmut Inn (☎ 617-720-5544, 800-350-7784; www
.shawmutinn.com; 280 Friend St; r $99-139 incl breakfast)
A friendly, small hotel attracting many European guests. The 66 darkish rooms all have
kitchenettes with a microwave, coffeemaker
and refrigerator. Suites with a foldout couch
are available for reduced weekly rentals.

Onyx Hotel (☎ 617-557-9955; www.onyxhotel.com;
155 Portland St; d $229-289, specials d $129; P 🖳)
Since its opening, the Onyx has been in
the news for its Britney Spears Foundation
room, designed by the popstar's mother to
resemble her bedroom ($349 per night, 10%
of revenue goes to the foundation). But this
boutique hotel has much more to offer than
this over-the-top tribute. Done up in jewel
tones and contemporary furniture, the Onyx
exudes warmth and sophistication – two elements that do not always go hand in hand.
Besides the decor, appealing features include
morning car service, passes to a local gym
and an evening wine reception. 'Pet-friendly'
goes to a whole new level, with gourmet
doggy biscuits and a dog-sitting service.

Charlestown

Constitution Inn (☎ 617-241-8400, 800-495-9622;
www.constitutioninn.com; 150 Second Ave, Charlestown
Navy Yard, Charlestown; r $109-129; P 🖳) A short,
scenic boat ride from downtown Boston's
Long Wharf, this excellent choice accommodates active and retired military personnel, as well as civilian guests. You won't see
a disproportionate number of crew cuts,
nor should strident antiwar types be put off.
What you'll find is about 140 tidy twin- and
queen-bed rooms (all with refrigerator, private bath and cable TV), and an excellent
Olympic-class fitness center.

Beacon Hill   Map pp66-8

John Jeffries House (☎ 617-367-1866; www.johnjef
frieshouse.com; 14 David Mugar Way; r $95-125, ste $150-165
Apr-Nov, r $95-110, ste $125-145 Dec-Mar) This four-
story hotel at the base of Beacon Hill has 46
rooms and suites in an early-20th-century
building owned by the Mass Eye and Ear Infirmary. (You don't need any connection to

stay here.) Rooms are nicely decorated with
reproduction furniture, and some still have
original molding and wood floors. Many
rooms also have kitchenettes.

Beacon Hill Hotel & Bistro (☎ 617-723-7575; www
.beaconhillhotel.com; 25 Charles St; r $245-305 incl break-
fast, discounts available Nov-Mar; 🖳) In the heart
of Beacon Hill, 12 individually designed
rooms and one suite make up this exquisite townhouse hotel that manages to combine historic charm with modern comforts.
Most rooms have lovely views of Beacon
Hill or Boston Common, as does the private rooftop terrace. Breakfast is in the cozy
bistro downstairs.

Theater District   Map pp66-8

Milner Hotel (☎ 877-426-6220; www.milner-hotels.com;
78 Charles St S; r Apr-Oct $139, Nov-Mar $109 incl breakfast; P) The Milner's tiny rooms are clean
and fresh, and fully equipped with private
bathroom and TV. This place attracts lots of
Europeans for its friendly atmosphere, excellent value, and great location on the edge of
the South End and the Theater District.

Wyndham Tremont (☎ 617-426-1400, 800-331-
9998; www.wyndham.com; 275 Tremont St; r $249-394
May-Oct, $149-289 Nov-Mar; P 🖳) Built as the na-
tional Elks headquarters, this 1925 hotel retains an ornate and elegant lobby, complete
with chandeliers and a marble stairway and
columns. This hotel has 322 smallish guest
rooms nicely decorated with early American
reproduction furniture and prints from the
Museum of Fine Arts. It is a favorite among
actors and stagehands hanging out in the
surrounding Theater District.

Back Bay   Map pp70-1
MID-RANGE

Newbury Guest House (☎ 617-437-7666; www.newbury
guesthouse.com; 261 Newbury St; r incl breakfast $120-195;
P 🖳) This four-story, c 1882 brownstone is
exquisite, complete with antique furnishings,
ornate moldings and a grand fireplace in the
shared salon. The Newbury St location is also
unbeatable. The 32 rooms offer all the necessary amenities, and the 24-hour concierge
service is also a nice perk for a B&B.

463 Beacon (☎ 617-536-1302; www.463beacon
.com; 463 Beacon St; r $79-149; P) This gracious
brownstone has 20 guest rooms, most with
private bathrooms and kitchenettes. The
rooms have also preserved many of their
architectural features, such as high ceilings,

fireplaces and wood floors. It also has furnished apartments available for daily or weekly rental.

Commonwealth Court Guest House (☎ 617-424-1230, 888-424-1230; www.commonwealthcourt.com; 284 Commonwealth Ave; r Dec-Mar $79-120, Apr-Nov $99-140) Housed in a turn-of-the-century brownstone in the heart of Back Bay, these 20 rooms with kitchenettes, cable TV and free local calls aren't so spiffy, but the price is right for the great location. Inquire about weekly in-season deals, as rates fluctuate.

College Club (☎ 617-536-9510; www.thecollege clubofboston.com; 44 Commonwealth Ave; s without bath/ d with bath incl breakfast $90/150; 🖳) Originally a private club for women college graduates in the 1940s, this place has 11 rooms, now open to both sexes. The rooms have antique furnishings, albeit rather shabby examples; and shared bathrooms are a bit worse for wear. But it offers excellent value, especially for the location just steps from Newbury St.

Copley House (☎ 617-236-8300, 800-331-1318; www.copleyhouse.com; 239 W Newton St; r daily $95-145, weekly $575-875, rates drop about 10-15% Nov-Mar) Copley House maintains accommodations in four locations, each with kitchen facilities, private bathrooms and complete furnishings; check in first at W Newton St Studio. One-bedroom apartments are all in Back Bay. The units are popular with folks looking for an apartment, theater and business people, and tourists.

TOP END

Lenox Hotel (☎ 617-536-5300, 800-225-7676; www .lenox hotel.com; 710 Boylston St; r Apr-Oct $279-329, Nov-Mar $179-229; Ⓟ) One of the classic Back Bay hotels: a fancy old-world lobby (complete with crackling fireplace) gives way to 213 soundproofed guest rooms with classical furnishings, high ceilings, big closets and sitting areas. Many corner rooms feature wood-burning fireplaces – an amenity unique in Boston.

Eliot Suite Hotel (☎ 617-267-1607, 800-443-5468; www.eliothotel.com; 370 Commonwealth Ave; r Apr-Nov $315-415, Dec-Mar $255-365; Ⓟ) This European-style, nine-story hotel has 85 suites and 10 regular rooms in an excellent location between Back Bay and Kenmore Sq. Although the hotel dates to 1925, rooms have been elegantly remodeled with marble tubs, antiques, and French doors separating the living room and bedrooms. The acclaimed restaurant Clio (p109) is on the 1st floor.

Copley Square Hotel (☎ 617-536-9000, 800-225-7062; www.copleysquarehotel.com; 47 Huntington Ave; r Apr-Oct $249-329, Nov-Mar $149-189; Ⓟ) This modest seven-story hostelry was constructed in 1891. It's showing its age a bit in the hallways and bathrooms, but the 143 refurbished rooms are all well equipped and traditionally, comfortably decorated. It's popular with European guests, who appreciate the attentive service and casual atmosphere.

South End   Map pp70-1

Berkeley Residence YWCA (☎ 617-375-2524; www .ywcaboston.org/berkeley; 40 Berkeley St; s/d/tr $56/86/99 incl breakfast; 🖳) Straddling the South End and Back Bay, this Y rents over 200 small rooms (some overlooking the garden) to guests on a nightly and long-term basis. Most are open to women only, although one floor is available for co-ed couples. Bathrooms are shared, as are other useful facilities, such as the telephone, library, TV room and laundry.

Chandler Inn Hotel (☎ 617-482-3450, 800-842-3450; www.chandlerinn.com; 26 Chandler St; r $109-169; 🖳) On a quiet side street in the South End, this pension has a friendly, European atmosphere (thanks in part to its largely European patrons). Also popular with gays, this central hotel has 56 rooms that are simple and clean, if a bit cramped and dark. All have color TVs, and private bathrooms stocked with toiletries. Ask for a room at the back to avoid the noise from the highway.

Midtown Hotel (☎ 617-262-1000, 800-343-1177; 220 Huntington Ave; r Nov-Mar $89-129, Apr-Oct $149-179; Ⓟ 🖳 🖳) Billing itself as 'Boston's affordable alternative,' this comfortable, two-story place on the edge of the South End is a really good deal, especially in the slower seasons. It's not so pretty to look at, but the rooms are comfortable and spacious. And services – such as free (!) parking – add value. Children under 18 stay free with their parents, making this an attractive stop for families.

Copley Inn (☎ 617-232-0300; www.copleyinn.com; 19 Garrison St; r $85-150) In the midst of Back Bay, this brick townhouse has a homey atmosphere and 21 comfortable rooms. They are simply and traditionally decorated, and each has a fully equipped kitchenette.

Clarendon Square Inn (☎ 617-536-2229; www .clarendonsquare.com; 198 W Brookline St; r Nov-Feb $119-209, Mar-Apr $129-249, Sep-Oct $219-289 incl breakfast; 🖳) This stylish brick townhouse, complete with an airy living room and hot tub on the rooftop deck, has only a few rooms, graceful and luxurious though they may be. If you're lucky enough to get one, you'll understand why chichi South End living is all the rage.

Kenmore Square & Fenway   Map pp70–1

BUDGET

Boston International Hostel (☎ 617-536-9455, 800-909-4776; www.bostonhostel.org; 12 Hemenway St; dm members/nonmembers $32/35, d $99 incl breakfast; 🖳) Dorm-style bunk rooms hold four to six people each (same sex), plus there are some rooms for mixed couples. Rates include sheets, towels, soap and shampoo. The 200 beds are almost always full, so reserve as far in advance as possible; book online for a discounted rate ($29/32). Onsite kitchen facilities are decent, but this hostel's best feature is the daily activities arranged by the events coordinator: walking tours, museum visit and comedy clubs, all at discounted (if not free) rates.

Fenway Summer Hostel (☎ 617-267-8599; www .bostonhostel.org; 575 Commonwealth Ave; dm members/nonmembers $35/38, 1–3–person r $89; ☽ Jun–late Aug) This former bi-level hotel now serves as Boston University student dormitories and a summertime hostel that is open to the public. Its 465 beds are all in rooms for three people or less, all with ensuite bathrooms. Other amenities and services include a TV and reading lounge, an information center in the lobby, 24-hour reception, housekeeping, laundry and on-call porters.

YMCA of Greater Boston (☎ 617-536-7800, 617-927-8040; www.ymcaboston.org; 316 Huntington Ave; s/d/tr without bath $45/65/81, s with bath $66 incl breakfast; ☽ Jun-Aug only; 🏊) Clean, comfortable rooms sleep up to four people. Most share a bathroom, but towels, linens and maid service are included in the price. Also included is use of the excellent recreational facility, which has squash courts, a running track, and a sauna and steam room. Book in advance.

MID-RANGE

Buckminster Hotel (☎ 617-236-7050, 800-727-2825; www.bostonhotelbuckminster.com; 645 Beacon St; r $69-139, ste $129-199) This red-brick building in the heart of Kenmore Sq is as close as Boston gets to a pension. Adequate rooms – from economy units to family suites – all have a

TV, microwave, fridge and phone, and each floor has its own laundry and kitchen facilities. Traffic on Beacon St can be noisy.

Howard Johnson Fenway (☎ 617-267-8300, 800-654-2000; www.howardjohnsonboston.com or www.hojo .com; 1271 Boylston St; r Apr-Oct $159-199, Nov-Mar $110-159; 🅿 🏊) This motel is not big on charm, but at least you know exactly what you're getting: comfortable-enough rooms, nondescript dining and reliable service. Its best feature is its location near Fenway Park.

TOP END

Gryphon House (☎ 617-375-9003; www.innboston .com; 9 Bay State Rd; r incl breakfast $189-235 May-Oct, $129-189 Nov-Apr; 🅿) This elegant five-story brownstone B&B features eight suites with in-room gas fireplaces, TV and VCR, CD player and two phone lines. Each room has a different theme, but all have retained late-19th-century period details. Rooms at the back of the house have spectacular views over the river. It's easily one of the nicest places to stay in the city.

Hotel Commonwealth (☎ 617-933-5000, 866-784-4000; www.hotelcommonwealth.com; 500 Commonwealth Ave; 🅿 🖳) Set amid Commonwealth Ave's brownstones and steps from Fenway Park, this independent, luxury hotel enjoys prime real estate. Step off the busy street into an oasis of contemporary calm. Rooms feature dark wood and rich fabrics, lending an old-world feel to the otherwise modern decor. If you came to New England for seafood, don't miss Michael Schlow's latest endeavor, Great Bay (p109), which is located here.

Brookline & Brighton

Bertram Inn (☎ 800-295-3822; www.bertraminn.com; 92 Sewall Ave; r Apr-Oct $129-229, Nov-Mar $109-149 incl breakfast; 🅿 🖳) Brookline's tree-lined streets shelter this authentic turn-of-the-century B&B. Ten rooms and four suites are decorated with antique and reproduction furnishings and Victorian style. The mood is upscale, but welcoming, especially considering the fresh-baked goodies that appear every afternoon. Take the Green Line 'C' train to St Paul St.

Best Western Terrace Inn (☎ 617-566-6260, 800-528-1234; www.bestwestern.com; 1650 Commonwealth Ave, Brighton; r $109-169; 🅿) About 2 miles west of Kenmore Sq (approximately 20 minutes from Boston Common via public transportation), this inn has 72 rooms, some with kitchenettes. It's in the heart of the 'student ghetto,' which means lots of pizza places and beer pubs. Take the Green Line 'B' train to Mt Hood.

Cambridge

Irving House (Map p69; ☎ 617-547-4600, 877-547-4600; www.irvinghouse.com; 24 Irving St, Cambridge; r without bath $105-165 Apr-Oct, $75-115 Nov-Mar, r with bath $135-225 Apr-Oct, $85-155 Nov-Mar, incl breakfast; (P) (💻)) Despite the relatively large size of this place (44 rooms), it still retains a B&B atmosphere thanks to the friendly service and the tranquil residential setting. Steps from Harvard Yard, this family-run joint attracts lots of parents and visiting scholars, so prices increase dramatically during Harvard commencement and other local events. But otherwise, this homey place offers excellent value. If it's full, management will direct you to a nearby sister property, the Harding House.

Best Western Homestead Inn (☎ 617-491-8000, 800-491-4914; www.bestwestern.com; 220 Alewife Brook Parkway, Cambridge; r Apr-Nov $199, Dec-Mar $169 incl breakfast; (P) (🐾)) An easy 10-minute walk to public transportation, this three-story motel has 69 nondescript but comfortable rooms. The neighborhood is not so charming, but it has its advantages: notably, its proximity to the Minuteman Trail (see p90), which runs from Davis Sq in Somerville to Lexington center. A health-food supermarket and movie theater are also nearby. Take the Red Line to Alewife.

Hotel Marlowe (☎ 800-825-7140; www.hotelmarlowe.com; 25 Edwin Land Blvd, Cambridge; d $229-289, specials d $129; (P) (💻)) The Kimpton Group has arrived in the Boston area. This first property, just steps from Cambridgeside Galleria and the Charles River, embodies a chic and unique style, as this organization always tries to do. The rooms are defined by rich colors, playful styles and (some) fantastic river views. Perks include down comforters, Sony Playstations and the *New York Times* delivered to your doorstep – enough to please everyone from creature of comfort to free spirit to intellectual snob. Take the Green Line to Lechmere station.

Charles Hotel (Map p69; ☎ 617-864-1200; www.charleshotel.com; 1 Bennett St; r from $269; (P) (💻)) 'Simple, Stylish, Smart.' Harvard Sq's most illustrious hotel lives up to its motto. Overlooking the Charles River, this institution has hosted the university's most esteemed guests, from Bob Barker to the Dalai Lama.

Design at the Charles – including rooms and restaurants – is surprisingly sparse, but the facilities include the luxuries and amenities one would expect from a highly rated hotel.

EATING

These days you'll have to look hard to find the old standards of New England cuisine: boiled dinner (Irish-style corned beef, potatoes and cabbage); seafood Newburg (fish, shrimp and scallops in a heavy cream sauce); and – of course – Boston baked beans (navy beans and salt pork in molasses). Some chefs might prepare these dishes on a cold winter's day under the trendy label of 'comfort food,' but they no longer define dining in Boston.

Seafood still reigns supreme (and foodies are well advised to take advantage of every opportunity to eat it). It's still frequently fried, but also grilled or pan-seared or prepared in any number of creative ways.

Boston obviously presents some fine opportunities to feast on Italian fare, but other more exotic ethnic cuisines are also well represented, especially Chinese, Japanese, Thai and Indian. In recent years Mediterranean influences have become more pronounced, and Middle Eastern food is becoming mainstream. Whether called tapas or meze, 'small plates' are gaining popularity, as diners recognize the benefit of sampling lots of different menu items.

Eating cheaply does not mean eating badly. But if you want to splurge, you will find some of the country's highest-regarded chefs in Boston. For well-heeled Bostonians, dinner is not a prelude to an evening on the town; it is entertainment in itself. For our purposes, budget classifies restaurants with main dishes under $10; mid-range means $10 to $20; and top end means $20 and higher.

Smoking is not allowed in restaurants or bars in Boston or Cambridge. Restaurants are open daily for lunch between 11:30am and 2:30pm and for dinner from 5:30pm to 10pm or 11pm, unless otherwise specified.

Downtown   Map pp66-8

From cheap street vendors to classy, pricey restaurants, downtown is the epicenter of Boston's culinary culture. Faneuil Hall and its environs are packed with touristy places touting baked beans, live lobsters and other Boston specialties; while further south, the

---

FARMERS MARKETS

Touch the produce at the outdoor **Haymarket Farmers market** (off Blackstone St) and you risk the wrath of the vendors ('They're a friggin' dollar – quit looking at the strawberries and just buy 'em!'). But no one else in the city matches their prices on ripe-and-ready fruits and vegetables. The spectacle takes place every Friday and Saturday, with the best bargains on Saturday afternoon.

Most neighborhoods have a seasonal farmers market from mid-May to late November. In addition to just-picked fruit and local vegetables, you might find Vermont farmstead and artisanal cheese, crusty loaves and tempting fruit tarts, all fresh, fresh, fresh. Locations (☎ 617-626-1700) include:

■ **City Hall Plaza** (Map pp66-8; ☾ 11am-6pm Mon & Wed)

■ **Downtown Crossing** (Map pp66-8; cnr Washington & Summer Sts; ☾ 9am-5pm)

■ **Copley Sq** (Map pp70-1; ☾ 11am-6pm Tue & Fri May-Oct)

■ **Charles Hotel Plaza** (Map pp69; 1 Bennett St, Cambridge; ☾ 10am-3pm Sun)

---

streets east of Boston Common boast some of Boston's finest dining. Downtown is also the workaday world for thousands of bankers, lawyers and office managers, so there is no shortage of sandwich shops and lunch spots.

BUDGET

The cheapest eats in Boston are hawked at Downtown Crossing, on Summer between Washington and Chauncy Sts. Lunch cart vendors offer tasty, inexpensive fast food like burritos (look for Herrera's), sandwiches, sausages, hot dogs and veggie wraps.

Faneuil Hall Marketplace (☎ 617-338-2323; ☾ 10am-9pm Mon-Sat, noon-6pm Sun) Northeast of Congress and State Sts, this food hall offers an impressive variety of eateries under one roof: the place is packed with about 20 restaurants and 40 food stalls. Choose from chowder, bagels, Indian and Greek cuisine, baked goods and ice-cream, and take a seat at one of the tables in the central rotunda.

Chacarero Chilean Cuisine (☎ 617-542-0392; 426 Franklin St; sandwiches $4-6; ☾ 11am-8pm Mon-Fri) A Chacarero is a traditional Chilean sandwich made with tender, grilled chicken or beef, Munster cheese, fresh tomatoes, guacamole and the surprise ingredient, steamed green beans. Stuffed into homemade bread, these sandwiches are the hands-down favorite for lunch in Downtown Crossing. At noon hungry patrons flock here from nearby offices and stores, so be prepared to queue. Seating is at a few sidewalk tables or on the lawn of the Boston Common.

Sultan's Kitchen (☎ 617-570-9009; 116 State St; sandwiches $5-7, mains $7-10; ☾ 11am-5:30pm Mon-

Fri, 11am-3pm Sat) Seasonal vegetables, whole grains, legumes and olive oil are among the ingredients that go into the fresh, healthy and delicious dishes at this Turkish deli. The kebabs are the house specialty, especially *kofta*, made from lean ground lamb. Save room for rice pudding.

Milk Street Cafe Financial District (☎ 617-350-7275; Post Office Sq; ☾ 7am-5pm Mon-Fri); Downtown Crossing (☎ 617-542-3663; 50 Milk St; ☾ 7am-3pm Mon-Fri) The two locations in the heart of the Financial District and near Downtown Crossing are favorite lunchtime spots of the suit crowd. Pasta, salads, soups and sandwiches are filling and inexpensive ($6 to $10), with lots of vegetarian options. The park location at Post Office Sq is pleasant in summer, when café tables are provided outside and diners spill onto the greenery.

MID-RANGE

Mid-range options are extremely limited once you wander away from Faneuil Hall Marketplace. The choices are touristy, but they have their charms.

Bertucci's (☎ 617-227-7889; 22 Merchants Row; mains $12-15, large pizzas $18-20) Despite its nationwide expansion, Bertucci's remains a Boston favorite for brick-oven pizza. The location near Faneuil Hall Marketplace is one of several in the Boston area; others are in the Back Bay and in Harvard Sq. Lunch is a real bargain: all entrées ($8 to $10) come with unlimited salad and fresh, hot rolls.

King Fish Hall (☎ 617-523-8862; South Market, 188 Faneuil Hall Marketplace; lunch $13-16, dinner approx $22; ☾ noon-10pm or 11pm) Chef-entrepreneur Todd English, of Olives (p106) and Figs (p104) fame, has struck again. The imaginative menu offers seafood specialties, like catch-of-the-day roasted on the spit and crispy lobster served 'Cantonese style' (with ginger and scallions). But the real treat is the whimsical under-the-sea decor – tiled tables inlaid with crustacean mosaics, fish mobiles suspended from high ceilings etc. Watch the Faneuil Hall activity from the outdoor terrace, or sit inside and observe the goings-on in the open kitchen.

Durgin Park (☎ 617-227-2038; North Market, 340 Faneuil Hall Marketplace; lunch specials $6-10, mains $15-20; ☺ 11:30am-10pm Mon-Sat, 11:30am-9pm Sun) Known for no-nonsense service and sawdust on the old floorboards underfoot, Durgin Park hasn't changed much since the restaurant was built in 1827. Nor has the menu, which features New England standards, like prime rib, fish chowder, chicken pot pie and Boston baked beans, with strawberry shortcake and Indian pudding for dessert. Be prepared to make friends with the other parties seated at your table.

Union Oyster House (☎ 617-227-2750; 41 Union St; half-dozen oysters $10, mains $16-20; ☺ 11am-9:30pm Sun-Thu, 11am-10pm Fri & Sat) The oldest restaurant in Boston, ye olde Union Oyster House has been serving seafood in this historic red-brick building since 1826. Over the years, countless Boston history makers have propped themselves up at this bar, including Daniel Webster and John F Kennedy. Apparently JFK used to order the lobster bisque, but the raw bar is the real draw. Order a dozen on the half-shell and watch the shucker work his magic.

Sakurabana (☎ 617-542-4311; 57 Broad St; lunch specials $8-12, mains $12-17; ☺ 11am-2:30pm & 5-9pm Mon-Fri, 5-9:30pm Sat) The surroundings aren't too snazzy, but the fish is fresh and tasty at this hole-in-the-wall sushi bar. It gets packed at lunchtime, as white collars descend from the surrounding office buildings to fill up on sashimi, teriyaki and tempura.

Mr Dooley's Boston Tavern (☎ 617-338-5656; 77 Broad St; sandwiches $8, mains $10-15; ☺ noon-10pm Mon-Sat, 11am-10pm Sun) 'A great place for a pint and a chat,' claims the logo of this local Irish pub. It's also not a bad place for a traditional Irish breakfast, complete with imported sausage, bacon, black-and-white pudding, eggs and home fries, available 11am to 4pm Sunday. It's one of the few downtown places open on weekends.

Nightly music, charades, poker and trivia keep regulars entertained throughout the week.

TOP END

Locke-Ober (☎ 617-542-1340; 3 Winter Pl; meals $40-60; ☺ 11:30am-2:30pm & 5:30-10pm Mon-Fri, 5:30-11pm Sat) According to an 1883 guide to Boston: 'The leading French restaurant of the city is Ober's, on Winter Place…This is more than a local fame. It's most patronized by the possessors of long purses.' The description rings true for the successor restaurant, a bastion of Boston Brahmin. Many 19th-century art works and architectural details have survived in the sumptuous dining rooms. Happily, the exclusive men-only policy has not. Chef and owner Lydia Shire has brought Locke-Ober into the 21st century while maintaining a traditional menu and elegant atmosphere. Be sure to dress the part: no sneakers, jeans, shorts or T-shirts.

Mantra (☎ 617-542-8111; 52 Temple Pl; meals $40-60; ☺ 11:30am-2:30pm & 5:30-10pm Mon-Fri, 5:30-11pm Sat) Mantra's vast dining room maintains the elegance of the building's former use as a bank: ornate molding and marble columns still adorn the hall, but the granite counter now serves as a bar, and the trimmings are modern and industrial. It is an ultrachic setting to sample the exotic French-Indian menu items, like wild striped bass with curried mussels or grilled filet mignon with sesame sauce. This place is supercool, and it has the attitude to prove it.

Waterfront   Map pp66-8

Within the grandly renovated South Station, the food court offers a range of fast food, sweets and coffee.

Barking Crab (☎ 617-426-2722; 88 Sleeper St; dishes $12-18; ☺ 11:30am-9:30pm) Everything an indoor clam shack should be, the Barking Crab offers big servings of delicious fried seafood on paper plates at communal picnic tables by the water. The platters, with fries and coleslaw, are worth every penny. It doesn't get more authentic than this.

No Name (☎ 617-338-7539; 15 Fish Pier; dishes $10-15; ☺ 11am-10pm Mon-Sat, 11am-9pm Sun) Another no-frills fish shack, this one on the fish pier itself. The location lends credence to the motto 'Where the fish are so fresh, they jump out of the water and onto your plate.'

It's lost some of its charm since it has been discovered by outsiders, but that doesn't stop dock workers from showing up for fried clams and fish chowder. Cash only.

Intrigue Cafe (☎ 617-856-7744; 70 Rowes Wharf; mains $12-20; ☽ 7am-9pm or 10pm) Within the Boston Harbor Hotel, this is a refined but unpretentious place for a light meal, afternoon tea, or dessert and wine. The food is acceptable if not outstanding. The harbor views are spectacular.

Legal Sea Foods (☎ 617-227-3115; 255 State St, Long Wharf; lunch $8-15, dinner $16-25; ☽ 11am-10pm Mon-Fri, 11am-11pm Sat & Sun) With a reputation and now-national empire built on the motto 'If it's not fresh, it's not Legal,' Legal has few rivals. The menu is simple: every kind of seafood, it seems, broiled, steamed, sautéed, grilled or fried. The clam chowder is considered by some to be New England's best.

Beacon Hill   Map pp66-8
BUDGET

Paramount (☎ 617-720-1152; 44 Charles St; lunch $5-8, dinner $7-15; ☽ 7am-10pm Mon-Thu, 7am-11pm Fri & Sat, 8am-10pm Sun) Not what you'd expect on tony Charles St, this old-fashioned cafeteria is a favorite neighborhood hangout on Beacon Hill. Basic diner fare includes pancakes, steak and eggs, meatloaf and lasagna. The place goes upscale at dinner without losing its down-home charm.

Panificio (☎ 617-227-4340; 144 Charles St; lunch $6-10, dinner $10-20; ☽ 7am-10pm Mon-Fri, 9am-2pm Sat & Sun) This cozy café and bistro is ideal for a mid-week breakfast or a leisurely weekend brunch. Arrive early for frittatas and French toast if you intend to linger over coffee and a newspaper. Pasta is de rigueur for dinner; lunches focus on soups and fancy sandwiches.

Self-caterers might try the gourmet shops at either end of Charles St for gathering picnic supplies to take to Boston Common or the Esplanade. (Remember when assembling a picnic that drinking alcoholic beverages in public is illegal.) **Savenor's** (☎ 617-723-6328; 160 Charles St; ☽ 9am-8pm Mon-Sat, noon-7pm Sun) and **DeLuca's Market** (☎ 617-523-4343; 11 Charles St; ☽ 8am-8pm Mon-Sat, 10am-6pm Sun) both offer fine selections of cheeses, deli items, baked goods and fresh produce.

MID-RANGE
Antonio's Cucina Italiana (☎ 617-367-3310; 288 Cambridge St; mains $10-15; ☽ 11am-3pm & 5-10pm Mon-Fri, 5-10pm Sat & Sun) Antonio offers all the charms of your favorite North End eatery: the cramped quarters and scrumptious southern Italian fare are straight from Hanover St, without the crowds. This neighborhood favorite is little known outside Beacon Hill.

Grotto (☎ 617-227-3434; 37 Bowdoin St; mains $15-22; ☽ 11:30am-3pm & 5-10pm Mon-Fri, 5-10pm Sat & Sun) Tucked into a basement on the backside of Beacon Hill, this cozy, cavelike place lives up to its name. The funky decor might be slightly off-putting, but this relative newcomer has received rave reviews for its mouthwatering pasta, seafood and steaks. Among the Italian innovations, the ricotta and peach ravioli is a favorite.

Charles St offers two options for pizza to die for:

Figs (☎ 617-742-3447; 42 Charles St; mains $11-20; ☽ 5:30-10pm Mon-Fri, 11:30am-10pm Sat & Sun) Celebrity chef Todd English offers creative pizza with whisper-thin crusts.

Upper Crust (☎ 617-723-9600; 20 Charles St; mains $8-15; ☽ 11:30am-10pm) A local favorite for traditional Neapolitan pies.

TOP END
Lalā Rokh (☎ 617-720-5511; 97 Mt Vernon St; mains $18-25; ☽ 5-10pm) Lalā Rokh is the name of a beautiful Persian princess, the protagonist of an epic romance by poet Thomas Moore. The tale epitomizes the exotic East, as does the aromatic, flavorsome food served at this Beacon Hill gem. The ingredients will be familiar to fans of Middle Eastern cuisine, but the subtle innovations – an aromatic spice here or savory herb there – set this cooking apart. Don't be afraid to ask for advice from the knowledgeable waitstaff.

No 9 Park (☎ 617-742-9991; 9 Park St; dinner $60; ☽ 11am-3pm & 6-10pm Mon-Fri, 6-10pm Sat) Set in a 19th-century mansion across from the Massachusetts State House, this swanky place tops many lists for fine dining in Boston. Chef-owner Barbara Lynch has been lauded by food and wine magazines for her delectable French and Italian culinary masterpieces (featured in a daily changing tasting menu, $135 with wine) and her first-rate wine list. The potpourri-scented entry, beaded chandeliers and marble tabletops enhance the experience.

Torch (☎ 617-723-5939; 26 Charles St; dinner $40-60; ☽ 5:30-10:30pm Tue-Sun) This candle-lit corner of Charles St is one of Boston's most romantic affairs. The French fare – featuring seasonal vegetables and lots of local seafood – is invariably excellent. Service, unfortunately, is not so consistent.

North End   Map pp66-8

The streets of the North End are lined with *salumerias* (corner shops) and *pasticcerias* (pastry shops) – and more *ristoranti* (restaurant) per block than anywhere else in Boston.

BUDGET

Pizza rivalries are intense in this neighborhood, where tomato sauce is as thick as blood. Among the contenders for the best slice in the North End are **Galleria Umberto** (☎ 617-227-5709; 289 Hanover St; slices $1; ☖ 11am-2pm or 2:30pm Mon-Sat) and **Ernesto's** (☎ 617-523-1373; 69 Salem St; slices $3; ☖ 11am-9pm Mon-Thu, 11am-10pm Fri & Sat, 11am-5:30pm Sun). Neither has much of a seating area, but that doesn't stop long lines of hungry patrons from queuing up for a slice with the topping of their choice. The grandmother of North End pizzerias is the legendary **Regina Pizzeria** (☎ 617-227-0765; 11½ Thatcher St; large pizzas $12-20; ☖ 11am-11pm), famous for brusque but endearing waitresses and crispy, thin-crust pizza.

To make your own Italian feast, visit one of the North End's authentic *salumerias*, well stocked with fresh bread, pungent cheeses, spicy salamis and oily olives:

Salumeria Italiana (☎ 617-523-8743; 151 Richmond St; ☖ 8am-6pm Mon-Sat)

Salumeria Toscana (☎ 617-720-4243; 272 Hanover St; ☖ 8am-6pm Mon-Sat)

MID-RANGE

Modern Pastry (☎ 617-523-3783; 257 Hanover St; ☖ 8am-10pm Sun-Thu, 8am-11pm Fri & Sat) While crowds of tourists and suburbanites are queuing out the door at Mike's Pastry across the street, pop into the tiny Modern Pastry shop, where the local folk come for dessert. There's no seating area, but the Italian cookies and *cannolis* are divine.

L'Osteria (☎ 617-723-7847; 104 Salem St; mains $14-18) This family-run *ristoranti* typifies the mouth-watering magic and old-world charm of the North End. It's nothing fancy, but the service is friendly and the southern Italian fare is always delicious.

Pomodoro (☎ 617-367-4348; 319 Hanover St; mains $12-20; ☖ 5-10pm) This cozy hole-in-the-wall

on Hanover is one of the North End's most romantic settings for delectable Italian cuisine. The food is simply but perfectly prepared: fresh pasta, spicy tomato sauce, grilled fish and meats, and wine by the glass. Credit cards are not accepted.

Daily Catch (☎ 617-523-8567; 323 Hanover St; mains $16-20; ☖ 11am-10:30pm) Although owner Paul Lombardo long ago added a few tables and an open kitchen, this shoebox fish joint still retains the atmosphere of a retail fish market; fortunately, it also retains the freshness of the fish. There's not much room to maneuver, but you can certainly keep an eye on how your monkfish marsala or lobster *fra diavolo* (spicy tomato sauce) is being prepared. The specialties are calamari, fried to tender perfection, and homemade squid ink pasta.

Fiore (☎ 617-371-1176; 250 Hanover St; mains $18-25, dessert $7-8; ☖ 4-11pm Mon-Fri, noon-11pm Sat & Sun) Come to Fiore – not for anything so special out of the kitchen – but for the fabulous roof deck (the only one in the North End). It's a wonderful place for a drink or dessert on a warm summer evening.

TOP END

Carmen (☎ 617-742-6421; 33 North Sq; mains $22-26) Exposed brick and candlelit tables make this tiny wine bar cozy yet chic. The innovative menu (especially compared to the more traditional North End eateries) offers a selection of small plates providing a fresh take on seasonal vegetables; mains like roast cornish hen and seared tuna sit alongside classic pasta dishes. Be prepared to wait, even with reservations.

Terramia (☎ 617-523-3112; 98 Salem St; mains $22-30; ☖ 5-10pm) Italian impresario Mario Nocera hand selects every mushroom that enters the kitchen at Terramia. The creative menu changes seasonally, and showcases vintage balsamic vinegars, rare Italian cheeses and other delicacies from the motherland.

Restaurant Bricco (☎ 617-248-6800; 241 Hanover St; antipasti $8-10, mains $22-30; ☖ 5-11pm) Brilliantly fused flavors from northern Italy, California, southern France and northern Africa reign in a handsomely Euro-chic dining room. In good weather, casement windows open onto the street. Order antipasti or traditional dishes, but save room for diverse breads and sweet finales.

BOSTON

Charlestown Map pp66-8

Traditionally, Charlestown has not been a major stop for Boston foodies. In recent years, however, the neighborhood's gentrification has attracted the attention of some of the city's top chefs. Now Charlestown's best restaurants draw patrons from all over the city.

Sorelle Bakery Café Monument Ave (☎ 617-242-2125; 1 Monument Ave; ❧ 6:30am-5pm Mon-Fri, 8am-3pm Sat & Sun); City Sq (☎ 617-242-5980; 100 City Sq; ❧ 7:30am-8pm) Now at two locations, Sorelle's has earned a loyal following of regulars who take coffee at the counter, feast on fresh sandwiches ($5 to $8) and scones, and bus their own tables.

Figs (☎ 617-242-2229; 67 Main St; dishes $11-20; ❧ from 5:30pm) This is the second branch of the Beacon Hill pizzeria (see p104).

Tangierino (☎ 617-242-6009; 83 Main St; mains $20-28; ❧ 5:30-11:30pm) This unexpected gem transports guests from a colonial townhouse in historic Charlestown to a sultan's palace in the Moroccan desert. The menu is authentic, featuring North African specialties, like *harira* (lamb and lentil soup), couscous and *tajine* (Moroccan stew), all with a modern flare. But the highlight is the exotic interior, complete with thick, Oriental carpets, plush pillows and rich, jewel-toned tapestries. This is one of the few places in smoke-free Boston where hookah pipes are available in the adjoining casbah lounge.

Olives (☎ 617-242-1999; 10 City Sq; mains $22-25; ❧ 5:30-10pm Mon-Sat) Todd English's first restaurant has long drawn rave reviews for its creative Mediterranean–New American menu, all prepared in the exposed kitchen. You can easily blow $100 for two people here, feasting on the house specialties of spit-roasted meats and savory fish. Expect a high noise level and a wait, unless you arrive very early or very late.

Chef Paul Delios has opened two trendy eateries in Charlestown that showcase his passion for the Mediterranean. His first, **Paolo's Trattoria** (☎ 617-242-7299; 251 Main St; meals $20-30; ❧ 5-9:30pm Sun-Wed, 5-10:30pm Thu-Sat) is casual but quaint, and wildly popular for wood-oven pizza. His success inspired the Greek **Meze Estiatorio** (☎ 617-242-6393; 100 City Sq; meals $20-30; ❧ 5-10pm Sun-Wed, 5-11pm Thu-Sat), a vast space with a huge menu of small plates and incredible views of the Leonard Zakim bridge.

Chinatown & the Leather District Map pp66-8

Adjacent to the eastern edge of the Theater District, the most colorful part of Chinatown is overflowing with authentic restaurants (many open until 4am), bakeries, markets selling live animals, import and textile shops, and phone booths topped with little pagodas. Don't miss the enormous gate that guards Beach and Kingston Sts. In addition to the Chinese, who began arriving in the late 1870s, the community of 8000 also includes Cambodians, Vietnamese and Laotians. The Leather District is the trendy scene unfolding in the streets between Chinatown and South Station.

BUDGET

Chinatown offers some of Boston's best, low-price eating.

Pho Pasteur (☎ 617-482-7467; 682 Washington St; dishes $5-8; ❧ 9am-11pm) This branch of the local chain (p107) serves *pho* (beef noodle soup) and other Vietnamese favorites in the heart of Chinatown.

Buddha's Delight (☎ 617-451-2395; 5 Beach St; mains $7-10; ❧ 11am-9:30pm or 10:30pm) Icicle lights and colorful Buddhas brighten up this local hole-in-the-wall. Vegetarians will be thrilled with noodle soups, tasty tofu dishes and imitation meat dishes, like soybean 'roast pork.'

For excellent seafood specials, try either **Jumbo Seafood** (☎ 617-542-2823; 5-9 Hudson St; lunch specials $5, mains $8-14; ❧ 11am-1am Sun-Thu, 11am-4am Fri & Sat) or **Grand Chau Chow** (☎ 617-292-5166; 45 Beach St; mains lunch $5, dinner $8-10; ❧ 10am-3am Sun-Thu, 10am-4am Fri & Sat), both with plain decor, but well-stocked fish tanks.

MID-RANGE & TOP END

Apollo Grill (☎ 617-423-3888; 84-86 Harrison Ave; mains $10-15; ❧ 11:30am-2:30pm Mon-Fri, 5pm-4am daily) This Japanese-Korean late-night hot spot features tables with built-in hibachi grills for Korean BBQ doused in a secret sauce. Hot soups, tempura and sushi are also popular menu items, keeping this place hopping at all hours of the day and night.

Ginza (☎ 617-338-2261; 16 Hudson St; mains lunch $10, dinner $15-20; ❧ 11:30am-2:30pm Mon-Fri, 5pm-2am Sun-Mon, 5pm-4am Tue-Sat) This traditional Japanese restaurant (complete with servers in kimonos) rates among Boston's best sushi places. The freshest pieces of *nigiri*, sashimi and *maki* are artfully presented, offering a feast for the eyes as well as the palette. The menu also includes a few options for patrons who like their fish cooked.

Penang (☎ 617-451-6373; 685 Washington St; mains average $8-15; ⊗ 11:30am-11:30pm) Some items come with the admonition 'Ask your server for advice before you order!!!' Fortunately, most of Penang's menu items are delightfully different, but not too intimidating. Try one of the house specialties, like mango shrimp, served with sweet and sour sauce in the mango shell.

Shabu-Zen (☎ 617-292-8828; 16 Tyler St; mains $10-15, combos $12-17; ⊗ 11:30am-11pm Sun-Wed, 11:30am-midnight Thu-Sat) For something a bit different, try 'Shabu-Shabu' dining, also known as hot-pot cuisine. Choose from a variety of thinly sliced seafood and meats, a plate of fresh vegetables and an array of homemade broths, then cook it up the way you like it. A divine sensory experience, if only for the enticing aromas of the food cooking all around.

Les Zygomates (☎ 617-542-5108; 129 South St; lunch $10-15, dinner $15-30; ⊗ 11:30am-1am Mon-Fri, 6pm-1am Sat) In the Leather District near South Station, this late-night Parisian bistro serves live jazz alongside classic but contemporary French cuisine. Daily prix fixe menus and Tuesday-night wine tastings ($25; 6pm and 8pm) attract a clientele that is sophisticated but not stuffy.

Theater District   Map pp66-8

Although tiny by New York standards, Boston's Theater District has long served as an important pre-Broadway staging area for shows. Many landmark theaters have recently received long-needed face-lifts, and there is no shortage of restaurants to cater to hungry, theater-going crowds.

blu (☎ 617-375-8550; Sports Club/LA, 4 Avery St; cafeteria $6-10, dining-room lunch $15-20, dinner $24-34; ⊗ 11:30am-2:30pm Mon-Fri, 5:30-10:30pm Mon-Sat, closed Sun) The cafeteria inside the Sports Club/LA attracts a trendy clientele – mostly straight from working out. It's still a mod place to grab a fresh, healthy sandwich or salad. Or head further back to the sophisticated glass-walled dining room, which has spectacular views of the cityscape and a menu to match.

Montien (☎ 617-338-5600; 63 Stuart St; mains lunch $8-10, dinner $10-15) This quiet Thai restaurant and sushi bar is popular with neighborhood residents grabbing a quick bite before

a show. Slide into a cozy booth or enjoy one of the window tables looking out onto the Theater District streets.

Via Matta (☎ 617-422-0008; 79 Park Plaza; enoteca $10-20, mains lunch $16-19, dinner $22-28) Via Matta tries to recreate your finest memories of Italy – the mode, the romance and, of course, the flavors. Sample the chef's whims in the tastefully trendy dining room or better yet in the dark, sexy *enoteca* (wine bar). The latter serves pizza, bruschetta and other small plates late into the night – a perfect place to stop for a bite after the theater.

Troquet (☎ 617-695-9463; 140 Boylston St; bar menu $16-22, mains $26-36) At this delightful wine bar and restaurant, the simply prepared, classic French-American fare is primarily a way to showcase the wine. For every appetizer and main, the menu suggests a selection of wine pairings, all of which are available by the glass. The upstairs dining room offers fabulous views of the Boston Common.

Pigalle (☎ 617-423-4944; 75 Charles St S; mains $32-40; ⊗ 5:30-10pm) The service might be a little snooty – apparently the staff knows that this romantic French bistro is among the hottest dining spots in town. Chef Marc Orfaly has gotten nothing but praise for his seductive culinary creations. The regional tasting menu ($45; available on Sunday) – featuring a three-course dinner paired with wines – offers incredible value.

Back Bay   Map pp70-1

Boston's swankiest neighborhood is certainly also one of its finest dining spots. Newbury St is lined with trendy bars, classy grills and cozy cafés. The abundance of students guarantees that some of these eateries are actually affordable.

BUDGET

Pho Pasteur (☎ 617-262-8200; 119 Newbury St; mains $6-10) One of three branches in the area, this Vietnamese restaurant is almost always packed at meal times. Regulars keep returning for big bowls of spicy stir-fry and delicious vermicelli at prices you can't beat.

Bangkok Cuisine (☎ 617-262-5377; 177a Massachusetts Ave; lunch $6-8, dinner $10-12; ⊗ closed Sun) Near the Boston International Hostel, this was Boston's first Thai restaurant, and it's still one of the best, especially for the price. Come here for reliably tasty, cheap noodles and curry: when the menu says hot, it means it. Don't be surprised by the crowded space and spotty service.

Other Side Cosmic Café (☎ 617-536-9477; 407 Newbury St; dishes $6-8; ⏱ 11am-1am) The 'other side' refers to the other side of Massachusetts Ave, where few strollers crossed before this place opened. 'Cosmic' alludes to its funky, Seattle-inspired style. The 1st floor is done in cast iron, while the 2nd floor is softened by velvet drapes, mismatched couches and low ceilings. Vegetarian chili, sandwiches, fruit and veggie drinks and strong coffee are the order of the day. Some of the 20-something clientele hang out here all day and night.

Café Jaffa (☎ 617-536-0230; 48 Gloucester St; sandwiches $6-8, mains $12-14; ⏱ 11am-10:30pm Mon-Thu, 11am-11pm Fri & Sat, noon-10pm Sun) This storefront eatery is a surprising bargain in the middle of this blue-blood neighborhood. When was the last time you had authentic Turkish coffee, *shwarma* (spicy lamb dish) or falafel in a place with polished wood floors and exposed brick? The open kitchen and painted murals add to the ambiance.

Boston is ground zero for ice-cream wars. Decide for yourself which is best; take the Green Line to Copley and fan out onto Newbury St. **Emack & Bolio's** (☎ 617-536-7127; 290 Newbury St; ⏱ 11am-11:30pm Sun-Thu, 11am-midnight Fri & Sat) takes pride in its status as an old-timer on the Boston gourmet ice-cream scene. **JP Licks** (☎ 617-236-1666; 352 Newbury St) is another local contender. For more on the best ice-cream competition, see p112.

MID-RANGE

Trident Booksellers & Café (☎ 617-267-8688; 338 Newbury St; dishes $10-15; ⏱ 9am-midnight) If you think 'Boston, books and breakfast' go together, head here. The shelves are primarily filled with New Age titles, while the tables are crowded with decidedly down-to-earth salads, soups, sandwiches, pasta dishes and desserts; breakfast is served all day. Vegetarians rejoice over the vegan cashew chili.

Back Bay Summer Shack (☎ 617-867-9955; 50 Dalton St; dishes from $11 according to market prices; ⏱ 11:30am-11pm) Longtime Boston chef Jasper White knows fish and every other type of seafood. He's written cook books about them, and has perfected the art of preparing chowder and lobster dishes. His restaurant is as big and noisy as the lobster is delectable. Traditional lobster rolls, with only a whisper of filler stuffed into hot-dog buns,

are as divine as steamed clams. Portions are large and preparations straightforward. Solo diners aren't shafted here.

Croma (☎ 617-247-3200; 269 Newbury St; pizzas $10-12; ⏱ 11:30am-11pm Sun-Thu, 11:30am-midnight Fri & Sat) The newest place to see and be seen on Newbury St is this stylish pizzeria with a decidedly European feel. The sleek interior and the outdoor patio are both pleasant places to enjoy one of Croma's tasty brick-oven pizzas or a selection from the extensive wine-by-the-glass menu.

Parish Café & Bar (☎ 617-247-4777; 361 Boylston St; sandwiches $10-14; ⏱ noon-2am) Next to the Public Garden, this café is known for creative and hearty sandwiches, each designed by a local celebrity chef. The stylish interior has a long bar backed by TVs and rich red walls, while the outdoor seating is also welcoming. The bar offers 76 different brands of beer, 20 wines by the glass and one spicy sangria.

Betty's Wok & Noodle Diner (☎ 617-424-1950; 250 Huntington Ave; mains $13-16; ⏱ noon-10pm or 11pm Tue-Sun) Although it's adjacent to Symphony Hall, the Huntington Theater Company and Northeastern University, this funky and intentionally retro eatery still feels a bit on the edge. It's worth seeking out for innovative noodle dishes, and spicy and saucy Asian and Latin flavors. Wait until after 8pm on weekends to avoid theater crowds.

Dartmouth Café (☎ 617-266-1122; 160 Commonwealth Ave; sandwiches $8-11, pasta $11-15, mains $12-18; ⏱ 9am-11pm) Unexpected on residential Commonwealth Ave, this trendy bar and grill suffers from a bit of an identity crisis, with its big-screen TV and pool tables alongside the cozy dining room and sidewalk seating. The menu also mixes it up, offering both modern Mediterranean and traditional pub grub. A piano man plays and sings nightly.

Casa Romero (☎ 617-536-4341; 30 Gloucester St; mains $16-22; ⏱ 5-11pm) This unique place serves authentic Mexico City–style cuisine in a lovely courtyard or in an intimate Talavera-tiled dining room. Enchiladas tempt connoisseurs with a spicy green tomatillo sauce (*verde*) or with a milder dark sauce (*poblana*). Another favorite is the *puerco abobado*, which is roasted pork marinated in sweet oranges and smoked chipotle chili.

Sonsie (☎ 617-351-2500; 327 Newbury St; sandwiches $8-10, pasta $15, mains $17-30; ⏱ 7am-1am) This is one of Boston's hippest places to sip a cappuccino. Europeans descend on the place wearing basic black and dark sunglasses. In warm weather, a wall of French doors is flung open, making the indoor tables almost al fresco. During busy mealtimes, café tables are reserved for diners. Pizza, pasta and other light dishes are available. Although full-fledged dining here is pricey (make reservations), the French and Asian fusion menu is worth it.

Tapeo (☎ 617-267-4799; 266 Newbury St; tapas $5-8, mains $23-25; ❧ lunch Sat & Sun, dinner daily) This festive Spanish tapas restaurant has bodega-style dining rooms and, in fine weather, a patio fronting Newbury St. It's the perfect setting for tapas-tasting, sangria-guzzling and sherry-sipping.

Finale Desserterie (☎ 617-423-3184; 1 Columbus Ave; desserts $9-14; ❧ 11:30am-11pm Mon-Wed, 11:30am-midnight Thu-Fri, 6pm-midnight Sat, 4-11pm Sun) Choose from a long list of tempting treats, from crème brulée to chocolate soufflé, and enjoy them with coffee, wine or port. The elegant yet comfortable dining room is set up so that you can watch the pastry chefs perform their magic through mirrors over their workstation. There are also light soups, salads and sandwiches at lunchtime, and appetizer-size dinner dishes so you don't eat sweets on an empty stomach.

For the classic New England dinner, visit one of the Back Bay outlets of Boston's most famous restaurant, Legal Seafood (see p104): **Prudential Center** (☎ 617-266-6800; 800 Boylston St; lunch $8-15, dinner $16-24; ❧ 11am-10:30pm Mon-Thu, 11am-11:30pm Fri & Sat, noon-10pm Sun); **Copley Pl** (☎ 617-266-7775; 100 Huntington Ave; lunch $8-15, dinner $16-24; ❧ 11am-10pm Mon-Sat, noon-9pm Sun).

TOP END

Clio (☎ 617-536-7200; Eliot Suite Hotel, 370 Commonwealth Ave; sushi $12-20, mains $28-36; ❧ 5:30-10pm or 10:30pm Tue-Sun) Art deco posters and leopard-print rugs give this ultrachic boutique restaurant a funky feel. It's an appropriate setting for one of Boston's most innovative chefs: Ken Oringer is masterful when it comes to creative cuisine and pleasing presentation. Look for a French- and Asian-influenced menu that changes frequently according to what's fresh and in season. The on-site sashimi bar, Uni, also gets rave reviews.

L'Espalier (☎ 617-262-3023; 30 Gloucester St; prix fixe without wine $70-88; ❧ 5:30-10:30pm Mon-Sat) The 'crème de la crème' of Boston's culinary scene is this elegant French affair. A variety of prix fixe and tasting menus (with or without wine) offer an exceptional dining experience that tops many short lists. The menus change daily, but usually include a degustation of caviar, a degustation of seasonal vegetables and recommended wine pairings. The 1880 Back Bay townhouse is the perfect setting for such luxury.

South End   Map pp70-1

Much like the neighborhood itself – where the up-and-coming live next door to the down-and-out – the South End boasts an eclectic mix of trendy, high-end eateries and old-school neighborhood cafés.

BUDGET

Charlie's Sandwich Shoppe (☎ 617-536-7669; 429 Columbus Ave; dishes $6-10; ❧ 6am-2:30pm Mon-Fri, 7:30am-1pm Sat) Lawyers in suits and laborers in work boots frequent this classic coffee shop. Charlie has been serving creative omelets, cranberry French toast and other breakfast platters since 1927. For lunch, favorites include turkey hash with two eggs, hot pastrami and homemade pies at a few shared tables or at the counter.

Tim's Tavern (☎ 617-437-6898; 329 Columbus Ave; sandwiches $5-7, mains $8-15; ❧ 11am-midnight Mon-Sat) A great neighborhood joint serving fabulous food but cloaked as a divey bar, Tim's has some of the best (and biggest and cheapest) burgers. Baby back ribs also get raves.

Delux Café (☎ 617-338-5258; 100 Chandler St; mains $8-12; ❧ 5-10pm Mon-Sat) This funky little bar takes a global view of old-fashioned comfort food, such as braised short ribs and Brunswick stew. Try the deluxe grilled cheese – gouda with papaya chutney on homemade peasant bread – not your mother's grilled cheese sandwich! A secret no more, this place is usually packed and particularly popular with the local bike-messenger crowd.

Bob the Chef (☎ 617-536-6204; 604 Columbus Ave; sandwiches $5-7, mains $10-12; ❧ 5-10pm Mon-Thu, 11:30am-midnight Fri & Sat, 10am-10pm Sun) This is Boston's best down-home soul food: barbecue ribs with a hunk of cornbread or fried chicken with collard greens or black-eyed peas. Sit at the long counter or in a booth. The Sunday jazz brunch (adult/child $19/13), served from 10am to 2:30pm, is a local favorite.

MID-RANGE

House of Siam (☎ 617-267-1755; 542 Columbus Ave; lunch $7-8, dinner $10-15) An Asian gem, the House of Siam serves fantastic Thai food in a tasteful, welcoming atmosphere. South End regulars rave about the perfectly spiced curries and fried rice, and the attentive service.

Garden of Eden Cafe (☎ 617-247-8377; 571 Tremont St; sandwiches $8-10, mains $15-20; ☑ 7am-11pm Mon-Fri, 7:30am-11pm Sat & Sun) This neighborhood storefront eatery, with two big communal tables for solo diners, is equally inviting for coffee and dessert or for a full-blown meal. Breakfast dishes, like vegetarian egg soufflé, are available until 2pm. For lunch or dinner, there are hearty specials, creative sandwiches, salads and artisanal cheese platters. Sweet smells from the bakery defy anyone to leave without dessert.

Jae's Café & Grill (☎ 617-421-9405; 520 Columbus Ave; lunch specials $9-10, dinner $15-19) 'Eat at Jae's... Live forever!' is the inviting motto of this popular Pan-Asian restaurant. Enjoy the terrace in fine weather; otherwise, head down to the bar, made cozier by exposed brick walls and colorful fish tanks. The menu of sushi and sashimi is extensive, but the specialty is Korean dishes like *bibim bab* (assorted vegetables, rice and marinated chicken or beef in a hot stone pot).

Franklin Café (☎ 617-350-0010; 278 Shawmut Ave; mains $15-20; ☑ 5:30pm-1:30am) Once the most beloved of all of the neighborhood's restaurants (and that's saying something in this restaurant-rich area), the Franklin has been discovered by outsiders. It's still friendly and hip – a fantastic spot for people-watching, especially if you have your eyes on the beautiful boys of this neighborhood. As for the food, think New American comfort food prepared by a gourmet chef: pan-seared Atlantic cod with oyster mushrooms, scallions and ginger, or roasted turkey meatloaf with spiced fig gravy and chive mashed potatoes.

Claremont Cafe (☎ 617-247-9001; 535 Columbus Ave; lunch $8-12, dinner $20-25; ☑ 7:30am-10pm Tue-Fri, 8am-10:30pm Sat, 9am-10:30pm Sun) This tiny, romantic place offers large portions of its Mediterranean- and South American–inspired cuisine, including Peruvian paella, roasted chicken and pork, grilled seafood and a wide range of tapas. It draws an artsy group of neighborhood residents, especially in the morning for sensational scones.

B&G Oysters Ltd (☎ 617-423-0550; 550 Tremont St; oysters $2 each, mains $19-22; ☑ 11:30am-11pm) This casually cool oyster bar bustles, as patrons flock to the South End to get in on chef Barbara Lynch's latest endeavor. Sit inside at the tiled raw bar or outside on the peaceful terrace, and indulge in a wide selection of the freshest oysters from local waters. An extensive list of wines by the glass or bottle and a modest menu of mains and appetizers (mostly seafood) are ample accompaniment for the oysters.

Red Fez (☎ 617-338-6060; 1222 Washington St; meze $5-12; ☑ 4pm-midnight, 11am-4pm Sun) The brick-walled, light-filled dining room is an inviting setting to feast on Mediterranean and Middle Eastern small plates. A decent wine list, a selection of beers from around the world and the mandatory cocktails (known as 'Fez Tales') round out the menu. This place originally dates to the 1940s, and recently reopened as an exotic destination for hip South End diners.

Aquitaine (☎ 617-424-8577; 569 Tremont St; mains $19-25; ☑ 10am-3pm Sat & Sun, 5-10pm daily) Let this chic French bistro whisk you away to Paris. Sip fine wines at the supercool wine bar up front, then settle into the lively dining room for classics like onion soup, steak *frite* and filet *au poivre*.

TOP END

Hamersley's Bistro (☎ 617-423-2700; 553 Tremont St; mains $25-40; ☑ dinner only) Consistently at the top of every 'best restaurants' list, Hamersley's serves perfectly prepared French/country American cuisine. The seasonal menu might include grilled filet of beef or hot-and-spicy grilled tuna, but the house specialty is a simple, delicious roast chicken with garlic, parsley and lemon ($25). The ambiance is warm and inviting – not at all pretentious for such a classy place. Reservations are highly recommended.

Icarus (☎ 617-426-1790; 3 Appleton St; mains $26-32; ☑ dinner only) This sophisticated restaurant is tucked into the cozy basement of a South End townhouse, providing a warm and inviting atmosphere for a feast. It's classy, not flashy. Dishes on the modern menu are invariably exquisite. A jazz pianist tickles the ivories on Friday night.

Mistral (☎ 617-867-9300; 223 Columbus Ave; mains $34-42; ☑ 6-10pm) This glamorous French place on the border of Back Bay and the

South End attracts the beautiful people from both of these posh neighborhoods. Provençal pottery, patterned textiles and floor-to-ceiling windows provide an elegant atmosphere that conjures up the south of France, while the menu is equally enticing.

Kenmore Square   Map pp70-1

Most places in this neighborhood are targeting the large local student population, meaning there is no shortage of cheap ethnic eats and divey sandwich shops.

Ankara Cafe (☎ 617-437-0404; 472 Commonwealth Ave; dishes $4-6.50; ☺ 8am-midnight) Students flock to this Turkish sandwich joint, where triple-decker sandwiches are named after local colleges. Pizza, salads and frozen yogurt round out the menu for a relatively healthy student diet. Seating is limited.

Elephant Walk (☎ 617-247-1500; 900 Beacon St; mains lunch $8-10, dinner $15-25; ☺ 11:30am-2:30pm Mon-Fri, 5-10pm daily) Highly regarded for its dual menus of classic French and traditional Cambodian cuisine, the Elephant Walk offers a unique – but delectable – dining experience. The large dining room has an exotic decor to match the menu. Make reservations.

Great Bay (☎ 617-532-5300; 500 Commonwealth Ave; mains lunch $14-17, dinner $25-35; ☺ 6-10am & 11:30am-2:30pm Mon-Fri, 7am-noon Sat & Sun, 5-10pm or 11pm daily) Boston's newest favorite seafood restaurant. Grey-orange hues and loungey leather chairs surround a circular bar in the center of the main eating area, while a side dining room is bathed in silkscreen flowers, jewel tones and subdued light. The food is no less delightful – seafood standards like salmon and scallops come alive with fresh herbs, seasonal veggies and spicy island influences.

Fenway   Map pp70-1

Apart from the bars and clubs on Landsdowne St and the museum cafés, the Fenway doesn't attract too many nonresidents for dinner. But the quiet streets between the Back Bay Fens and Fenway Park are home to a few neighborhood favorites that are excellent places to stop if you're in the area. There is also a row of cheap ethnic eateries on Peterborough St.

Buteco (☎ 617-247-9508; 130 Jersey St; mains $8-12; ☺ noon-10pm Mon-Fri, 3-10pm Sat & Sun) Eating at Buteco feels like having dinner in your grandmother's kitchen, if she was Brazilian. The atmosphere is homey and welcoming, and the portions are huge at this Fenway

hole-in-the-wall. It's known for meat dishes, but you can't beat classic rice and beans, especially for vegetarians. The weekend dinner special is usually an amazing *feijoada*, a rich stew of black beans, pork, sausage and dried beef.

Brown Sugar Café (☎ 617-266-2928; 129 Jersey St; mains lunch $6-8, dinner $10-14; ☺ 11am-10pm Mon-Fri, noon-10pm Sat & Sun) This crowded, unassuming neighborhood joint is often lauded for the best Thai food in the city. The delectable dishes are beautifully presented – try the mango curry, with tender chicken simmered in a yellow curry with chunks of ripe mango, tomato, red and green pepper, onion and summer squash. Portions seem even larger when you order takeout.

Audubon Circle (☎ 617-421-1910; 838 Beacon St; sandwiches $7, mains $14-16; ☺ 11:30am-1am daily, brunch 11am-3pm Sun) The long black bar, wood floors and high ceilings lend an industrial feel to this lively pub and restaurant. It exudes a good vibe for catching a bite to eat, watching the game or both. Burgers are highly recommended, or try the unique appetizers, such as spicy beef quesadilla or pork-filled wontons.

Sophia's (☎ 617-351-7001; 1270 Boylston St; small plates $7-14, tasting menu without wine $65; ☺ 6-11pm Tue-Sat) This hot spot for salsa and sangria (see p121) also has an inviting dining room, where executive chef Jeffrey Fournier serves seasonal small plates. Spanish and South American influences are evident in the fish tacos, tuna ceviche and spicy paella. Sophia's unique offering is food and liquor pairings, as Fournier has selected the perfect flavored liqueur or spiced rum to accompany each tasty morsel.

Cambridge: Harvard Square   Map p69

Funky Harvard Sq has coffee houses, sandwich shops, ethnic eateries and upscale restaurants to suit every budget and taste.

BUDGET
Algiers Coffee House (☎ 617-492-1557; 40 Brattle St; dishes $4-12; ☺ 8am-midnight) Although the pace of service can be glacial, the palatial Middle Eastern decor makes this an inviting rest spot. Head to the airy 2nd floor and order a falafel sandwich, a bowl of lentil soup, *merguesa* (lamb sausage) or a lamb kebab. The one good thing about the relaxed service is that you won't be rushed to finish your pot of Arabic coffee or mint tea.

Hi-Rise Bread Co (☎ 617-492-3003; 56 Brattle St; dishes $6-9; 🕑 8:30am-5pm Mon-Fri, 9am-5pm Sat, 10am-4pm Sun) Eating here feels like somebody invited you over for lunch. The cozy dining room upstairs is crowded with mismatched tables, or find a seat on the terrace when weather is fine. You'll be joined by academic types for steaming soups and well-stuffed sandwiches, as well as crusty loaves and irresistible sweets.

Sabra Grill (☎ 617-868-5777; 20 Eliot St; mains $5-10; 🕑 10am-10pm) Sabra served fresh and delicious Middle Eastern takeout long before it was trendy. Vegetarians can't do better than the daily special that never seems to change, a garlicky and delicious roasted veggie sandwich. Others swear by *shwarma* of any kind. Seating is limited, so pick a sandwich and head over to John F Kennedy park for a picnic.

Bartley's Burger Cottage (☎ 617-354-6559; 1246 Massachusetts Ave; burgers $6-8; 🕑 11am-10pm Mon-Sat) Packed with small tables and hungry college students, Bartley's is a primo burger joint, offering at least 40 different burgers. And if none of those suits your fancy, create your own 7oz juicy masterpiece with the toppings of your choice. Sweet potato fries, onion rings, thick frappes and raspberry-lime rickeys complete the classic American meal.

With about a dozen places to eat under one roof, you're bound to find something fast, filling and cheap at the food court in the **Garage** (cnr John F Kennedy & Mt Auburn Sts).

Ice-cream wars continue unabated in Harvard Sq at **Toscanini's** (☎ 617-354-9350; 1310 Massachusetts Ave) and **Herrell's** (☎ 617-497-2179; 15 Dunster St).

Self-caterers should head to the gourmet grocer **Cardullo's** (☎ 617-491-8888; 6 Brattle St; 🕑 8am-8pm Mon-Sat, 11am-7pm Sun), a deli with an impressive assortment of international goods and sandwiches to go. Alternatively, the ritzy Charles Hotel hosts a **Farmers market** (☎ 617-864-2100; 1 Bennett St; 🕑 10am-3pm Sat & Sun Jun-Nov) on its plaza.

MID-RANGE

Tanjore (☎ 617-868-1900; 18 Eliot St; lunch buffet $7; mains $8-15; 🕑 11:30am-11pm) Tanjore's lunchtime buffet has been a favorite of Harvard Sq locals for years. The buffet changes daily, but it always features perfectly fluffy basmati rice, fresh, hot naan bread and subtly delicious *kheer* (rice pudding). This place is

good enough to come for dinner, but the buffet offers superior value.

Café Pamplona (no tel; 12 Bow St; mains $8-12; 🕑 11am-1am Mon-Sat, 2pm-1am Sun) Located in a cozy cellar on a backstreet, this decidedly no-frills, European café is the choice among old-time Cantabrigians. In addition to tea and coffee drinks, Pamplona has light snacks, like gazpacho, sandwiches and *biscotti*. The tiny outdoor terrace is a delight in summer.

Casa Mexico (☎ 617-491-4552; 75 Winthrop St; lunch $6, dinner $10-15; 🕑 noon-2:30pm Mon-Sat, 6-11pm daily) The best place for inexpensive and authentic Mexican on either side of the Charles River, the basement dining room is usually crowded with patrons who come for the *mole poblano* (chicken in rich chocolatey mole sauce), tostadas and enchiladas. It's been around since the 1970s, so it must be doing something right.

Chez Henri (☎ 617-354-8980; 1 Shepard St; mains $14-20, prix fixe $28; 🕑 5:30-10pm Mon-Thu, 5:30-11pm Fri & Sat, 5-9pm Sun) This French-Cuban blend is a dark, romantic bistro offering saffron-soaked mussels, smoked salmon salad and *blanquette de veau* (veal stew). It may sound all French, but the undeniable favorite is the Cubano sandwich off the bar menu.

Henrietta's Table (☎ 617-661-5005; Charles Hotel, 1 Bennett St; mains $13-17; 🕑 7am-10pm) Within the Charles Hotel, this eatery features a New England regional menu highlighting locally grown produce. The creative and 'fresh and honest' preparations, country inn decor and friendly service make it the choice for better-than-home cooking. You'll need an appetite to get your money's worth out of the abundant and deservedly popular brunch (reservations suggested).

TOP END

Craigie St Bistro (☎ 617-497-5511; 5 Craigie Circle; mains $25-31; 🕑 6-10pm Wed-Sun) This romantic Parisian bistro is tucked away in the residential streets north of Harvard Sq. Its charm – besides the interesting French innovations on the menu – lies in the close quarters and superfriendly service.

Rialto (☎ 617-661-5050; 1 Bennett St; mains $25-32; 🕑 5:30-10pm Sun-Thu, 5:30-11pm Fri & Sat) Within the Charles Hotel, you'll pay handsomely for dining in this understated, Euro-chic elegance, but it will be romantic and memorable. Mediterranean-inspired dishes include creamy mussel and saffron stew with leeks, or seared beef tenderloin with cognac sauce and shellfish paella. The vegetarian main course is always equally creative.

Upstairs on the Square (☎ 617-864-1933; 91 Winthrop St; mains $26-36; ⏰ 11am-1am) Pink and gold hues, zebra- and leopard-skin rugs, and lots of glamour and glitz: such is the decor that defines this restaurant, the successor to once-renowned Upstairs at the Pudding. The creative menu and carefully chosen wine list have earned high praise. The downstairs Monday Club Bar is open for lunch, offering a more casual atmosphere, a slightly cheaper menu and a wall of windows overlooking Winthrop Park.

Harvest (☎ 617-868-2255; 44 Brattle St; mains lunch $12-18, dinner $24-34) A Harvard Sq classic, this place is simple but sophisticated, a description that applies to the menu as well as the space. The modern American fare allows for some regional influences, such as the seductive raw bar. Local luminaries, especially Harvard faculty, are often spotted here.

Cambridge: Central, Inman & Kendall Squares

The other squares in Cambridge have a more gritty, neighborhood feel than Harvard Sq. They are home to legions of immigrants from Portugal, Brazil, India and the Caribbean, who provide ample opportunity to sample fare from these countries. They also have the advantage of being off the well-beaten tourist track, but still offer some of the best dining in the city.

BUDGET

Christina's (☎ 617-492-7021; 1255 Cambridge St; ice-cream from $2.50; ⏰ 11:30am-10:30pm or 11:30pm) It's worth the extra trip to Inman Sq to sample this contender in Boston's ice-cream war. The seasonal flavors are tempting, but it's hard to beat the coconut almond on a sugar cone. Take the Red Line to Central Sq and walk north on Prospect St.

1369 Central (☎ 617-576-4600; 757 Massachusetts Ave; ⏰ 7am-11pm Mon-Fri, 8am-11pm Sat, 8am-10pm Sun) Featuring a bohemian atmosphere and attitude, this Central Sq coffee house has good music, serious coffee and a laudable tea selection. The friendly waitstaff can also find you something to snack on if you are hungry.

Emma's (☎ 617-864-8534; 40 Hampshire St; pizza for two $15-18; ⏰ 11:30am-10pm Tue-Sat) This friendly neighborhood pizzeria instills a maniacal devotion in its customers. Make a point of stopping here before or after a flick at the Kendall Square Cinema. Crispy thin crusts and creative topping combinations guarantee that Emma's is consistently rated among the city's best pizza. Slices and salads are sold from the front window. Take the Red Line to Kendall Sq.

Check out the community bulletin board and organic offerings at **Harvest Co-Op Market** (☎ 617-661-1580; 581 Massachusetts Ave). Nearby, two blocks north of Massachusetts Ave, the whole-food supermarket **Bread & Circus** (☎ 617-492-0070; 115 Prospect St) boasts an excellent if pricey selection.

MID-RANGE

Mirade of Science Bar & Grill (☎ 617-868-2866; 321 Massachusetts Ave; mains $8-12; ⏰ 11:30am-1am) With all the decor of your high school science lab, this bar and grill is still pretty hip, and popular among MIT student types. Join them for burgers and other tasty grilled fare. Walk east on Massachusetts Ave from Central Sq.

S&S (☎ 617-354-0777; 1334 Cambridge St; mains lunch $8-10, dinner $10-15; ⏰ 7am-11pm Mon-Wed, 7am-midnight Thu-Fri, 8am-midnight Sat & 8am-10pm Sun) This Jewish deli is an Inman Sq institution, great for homemade soups, hearty sandwiches and breakfast served all day. Enjoy old B&W photos of the neighborhood while you wait for a table, especially if you come for weekend brunch. Take the Red Line to Central Sq and walk north on Prospect St.

Helmand (☎ 617-492-4646; 143 First St; mains $12-18; ⏰ 5-10pm Sun-Thu, 5-11pm Fri & Sat) Fusing flavors and techniques from India and the Middle East, the Helmand shows off the rich, diverse and little-known cuisine of Afghanistan. The active, open kitchen – complete with a bread oven that turns out melt-in-your-mouth flatbread – is entertainment enough in this simple dining room. And the dishes it produces are exotic and enticing. Not to mention that the place is owned by the brother of Afghan President Hamid Karzai. Located across from Cambridgeside Galleria Mall, it's a short walk from Lechmere station on the Green Line.

TOP END

Blue Room (☎ 617-494-9034; 1 Kendall Sq; mains $18-24; ⏰ 5:30-10:30pm daily, brunch 11am-2:30pm Sun) Chef Steve Johnson takes pride in his reliance on organic farms and 'mom-and-pop purveyors' as the source of his produce and meats. He uses them to create a menu that is constantly changing according to what's in season and fresh, but always innovative and delicious. One of Cambridge's top-rated restaurants, the Blue Room still manages to maintain a casual, comfortable atmosphere. Take the Red Line to Kendall Sq.

East Coast Grill (☎ 617-491-6568; 1271 Cambridge St; mains $20-25; ⏰ 5:30-10pm daily, brunch 11am-2:30pm Sun) Seafood with southern spice. Sample appetizers like a chili-crusted tuna taco or buttermilk fried oysters, before diving into fine, fresh seafood. If seafood isn't your thing, there's also a selection of ribs from the oak-smoked pit barbecue. The DIY bloody Mary bar makes this eatery one of the city's top spots for Sunday brunch. Walk north on Prospect St from Central Sq.

DRINKING

Boston is a drinking city, due in no small part to the hordes of Irish immigrants and their descendents who have opened up Erin-themed pubs around the city. Not to mention the staunch sports fans who flock to bars with blaring TVs to watch the Red Sox and the Pats. But this town has something for every palette: microbreweries, swanky martini lounges and stylish wine bars…it all depends on 'what's your poison.'

Note: the drinking age for consuming alcoholic beverages in New England is 21, and in many cases you must be 21 to enter a drinking establishment. Some clubs offer '19-plus' nights; check papers for details. Also, smoking is forbidden in all bars and restaurants in Boston and Cambridge. Bars usually close at 1am, clubs at 2am.

Downtown   Map pp66-8
Black Rose (☎ 617-742-2286; 160 State St; ⏰ 11:30am-2am) The most famous – or perhaps that's infamous – of Boston Irish pubs. Back in the day, rumors ran rampant that a percentage of Black Rose proceeds went to support the IRA. These days the place is not so radical, focusing on hearty food, slow-drawn draughts and boisterous Irish music nightly.

Good Life (☎ 617-451-2622; 28 Kingston St) A nostalgic place that harkens back to the days of Sammy, Frank and Dino. Order from the vast martini menu and groove to live jazz Thursday through Sunday.

Rack Billiard Club (☎ 617-725-1051; 24 Clinton St; ⏰ 4pm-2am) Fourteen pool tables, six plasma TVs and DJs spinning tunes nightly keep this place hopping. The newest thing is 'Exotic Midnight,' which features exotic drinks and – yes – exotic dancers every Thursday. The young professionals who frequent the place are generally still attired in their business duds. For everyone else, the dress code is strictly enforced.

North End & Charlestown   Map pp66-8
Caffè Vittoria (☎ 617-227-7606; 296 Hanover St) An atmospheric, old-world café that has been here since the 1930s; undoubtedly, so have some Italian-speaking patrons. Complete with wrought-iron furniture and old photographs, this is a charming place to have a drink before or after your Italian feast. To get the full effect, wait for a table in the original dining room.

Caffe dello Sport (☎ 617-523-5063; 308 Hanover St) A primo place for watching any sporting event, especially soccer. This place gets packed with old Italian guys cheering on the Boston Red Sox or the Italian football team of their choice.

Warren Tavern (☎ 617-241-8142; 2 Pleasant St; ⏰ 11:15am-1am) One of the oldest pubs in Boston, the Warren Tavern has been pouring pints for its customers since George Washington and Paul Revere drank here. It is named for General Joseph Warren, a fallen hero of the Battle of Bunker Hill (shortly after which – in 1780 – this pub was opened). Food is served nightly until 10:30pm.

Beacon Hill   Map pp66-8
Sevens (☎ 617-523-9074; 77 Charles St; ⏰ 11:30am-1am) This popular Beacon Hill pub is always crowded with friendly folks from the neighborhood. The interior is dark and bare, but the preppy crowd reflects the swankiness of the surrounding streets. Pull up a bar stool or hop in a booth and order a sandwich ($4 to $6) and a beer.

Bull & Finch Pub (☎ 617-227-9605; 84 Beacon St; ⏰ 11am-1:45am) This is an authentic English pub (it was dismantled in England, shipped to Boston and reassembled in this townhouse, the Hampshire House), but that's not why hundreds of tourists descend on the place daily: the pub inspired the TV sitcom *Cheers*. Most visitors are disappointed that the interior bears no resemblance to

BREWPUBS & BREWERY TOURS

Bostonians take beer seriously. In the past decade a number of microbreweries have sprung up in Boston. While all those listed here are recommended for beer and snacks, some serve noteworthy, moderately priced meals.

Boston Beer Co (☎ 617-368-5080; www.samadams.com; 30 Germania St, Jamaica Plain; admission by donation $2) Also known as the Samuel Adams brewery and Boston Beer Museum, Boston Beer Co produces the only local brew that's achieved international fame. Tours take place at 2pm Thursday and Friday, and noon to 2pm on Saturday. In July and August, there's an additional tour at 2pm Wednesday. Take the Orange Line to Stony Brook.

Boston Beer Works Downtown (Map pp66-8; ☎ 617-896-2337; 112 Canal St; ☼ 10:30am-1am); Fenway (Map pp70-1; ☎ 617-536-2337; 61 Brookline Ave; ☼ 10:30am-1am) This brewery has seasonal concoctions brewed in exposed tanks and pipes. About 16 different kinds of beer, including Boston Red, IPA and Buckeye Oatmeal Stout, are usually available and the food isn't bad either. If you don't like sporting crowds, avoid the Fenway branch after a Sox game.

Harpoon Brewery (☎ 617-574-9551; www.harpoonbrewery.com; 306 Northern Ave) This brewery is the largest facility in the state. Complimentary tastings take place in a newly renovated room overlooking the brewery. Tours (including tastings) are held at 3pm Tuesday to Thursday, and 1pm and 3pm Friday and Saturday. Take the Red Line to South Station, then walk (about 20 minutes) over the Northern Ave Bridge to the Marine Industrial Park.

John Harvard's Brew House (Map p69; ☎ 617-868-3585; 33 Dunster St, Cambridge; ☼ 11:30am-12:30am Sun-Thu, 11:30am-1:30am Fri & Sat) This subterranean venue feels like an English pub and has perhaps the best beer among the crowded microbrewery field. You'll find ales and stouts here, plus a sampler rack. Above-average pub grub is available at lunch and dinner, and for Sunday brunch.

Rock Bottom (Map pp66-8; ☎ 617-742-2739; 115 Stuart St) Part of a national brewpub chain, although each outlet brews different beers using ingredients to customize the product. Traditional beer styles are offered alongside more distinctive specialty ales and lagers.

the TV set. More importantly, tourists are the main clientele, so nobody knows your name (or anybody else's).

21st Amendment (☎ 617-221-7100; 150 Bowdoin St; ☼ 11:30am-1am) Across from the Massachusetts State House, this is the favorite watering hole for politicos and staffers. Named for the ever-important amendment repealing Prohibition laws, the place attracts a consistent lunch crowd, as well as regulars who stop by for a pint on their way home from work.

Red Hat (☎ 617-523-2175; 9 Bowdoin St; ☼ 11:30am-2am Mon-Sat, 11:30am-midnight Sun) Another favorite of Boston politicos. Red Hat has a nostalgic air: it is one of the last remaining vestiges of the Old West End. As such, it feels more like *Cheers* than its previously mentioned brethren.

Back Bay & South End   Map pp70-1
Cottonwood Café (☎ 617-247-2225; 222 Berkeley St; ☼ 11am-11pm) Boston's best margaritas. The setting is appropriately southwestern and slightly upscale, while the menu features unexciting versions of various burritos and quesadillas.

Vox Populi (☎ 617-424-8300; 755 Boylston St; ☼ 11:30am-1am) 'Urban chic' is the goal of this bistro and martini bar. The effect is inviting, especially in the 1st-floor fireplace lounge. The eclectic menu represents fusion at its most extreme; if you just come for drinks, you're bound to find something you like on the list of creative martinis and classic cocktails.

Clery's Bar & Restaurant (☎ 617-262-9874; 113 Dartmouth St; ☼ 11am-2am) A spacious bar with big TVs and a cool mosaic floor, this neighborhood place gets pretty boisterous on weekends. Simple pub grub ($9 to $12) complements the drafts and Guinness.

Fenway   Map pp70-1
Behind Fenway Park near Kenmore Sq, clubs are lined up like ducks in a row on Ipswich and Lansdowne Sts.

Jillian's Billiard Club & Lucky Strike (☎ 617-437-0300; 145 Ipswich St; ☼ 11am-2am) Although this three-story club has more than 50 billiard tables, people also come here to play darts, snooker, table tennis and over 250 virtual reality games. The 3rd floor has a sleek, retro bowling alley ($4.50 11am to 5pm, $6 5pm to 2am), completely decked out with a multiscreen video show playing above the lanes. This vast 70,000-sq-ft place has no less than six bars and a full-service restaurant downstairs.

Jake Ivory's (☎ 617-247-1222; www.jakeivorys.com; 9 Lansdowne St; admission Fri & Sat $8; ☽ 7:30pm-2am Thu-Sun) This casual joint features dueling rock and roll pianos. It's rowdy, interactive and fun. Thursday nights are for over 18s, while Saturday and Sunday are for over 21s only. Check the website for discounted entry.

Modern (☎ 617-536-2100; 30 Lansdowne St; admission $10-15; ☽ 10pm-2am Tue & Fri & Sat) With its sleek silver bar and upholstered seats, this is a sophisticated addition to the Lansdowne St scene. Order a martini and take your place among the glamorous crowd checking each other out. This place is connected to the nightclub Embassy next door.

Cask 'n Flagon (☎ 617-536-4840; 62 Brookline Ave; ☽ 11:30am-2am) At the other end of the spectrum, this nostalgic place reflects the real vibe of this neighborhood, which is driven by what's happening at Fenway Park. The pub walls are covered with B&W photos and memorabilia from the greatest moments in Sox history. The place is packed before and after home games, as baseball fans get their buzz on or drown their sorrows. Better to come to watch an away game with the diehards.

Cambridge

Enormous Room (☎ 617-491-5599; 567 Massachusetts Ave; ☽ 5:30pm-midnight) Look for the elephant silhouette marking the entrance to this slick international-themed lounge. Plush Oriental rugs and richly colored pillows create an exotic North African ambience, which is complemented by world music and expensive drinks. Take the Red Line to Central Sq.

Good Life (☎ 617-868-8800; 720 Massachusetts Ave) There is another location of this swinging place in Central Sq. See p114.

Shay's (Map p69; ☎ 617-864-9161; 58 John F Kennedy St; ☽ noon-midnight) Harvard's favorite student bar. It's crowded, cozy and cheap: what's not to love? Shay's also has the advantage of being Harvard Sq's only pub where you can enjoy a beer outside on the tiny terrace.

Hong Kong (Map p69; ☎ 617-864-5311; 1236 Massachusetts Ave) The bar on the 2nd floor is famed for its killer 'scorpion bowls,' which pack a

punch to say the least. This place remains a rite of passage for Harvard freshmen.

Plough & Stars (☎ 617-441-3455; 912 Massachusetts Ave; ☽ 11:30am-1am) A tiny joint with televised English football matches (weekends September to May) and rock bands playing most nights. Take the Red Line to Central Sq.

Field (☎ 617-354-7345; 20 Prospect St; ☽ noon-1am) The funky pulse of Central Sq is still discernible at this unpretentious neighborhood bar.

Somerville

As Cambridge real estate prices skyrocket, many students, artists and musicians have been forced to move to neighboring Somerville. Now working-class Irish mixes with activist do-gooder and up-and-coming bohemian making Somerville, well, the new Cambridge. Davis Sq (a stop on the Red Line) is a particularly hot spot for drinking, music (opposite) and comedy (p120).

Under Bones (☎ 617-628-2200; 55 Chester St; ☽ 5pm-1am) Specializing in rare brews from Belgium to Boston, this amiable bar is in the basement of Redbones barbecue joint. The highlight (besides the beer) is the intriguing, though sometimes disturbing, murals that cover the walls.

Burren (☎ 617-776-6896; 247 Elm St; ☽ noon-1am) An amiable place oozing Irish atmosphere. It features traditional Irish music nightly in the front room and various bands (and an open-mike night) in the back. It's very popular: come early on weekends or expect to wait.

Joshua Tree (☎ 617-623-9910; 256 Elm St; ☽ 11:30am-1am) An Irish pub, but it lacks authenticity. Come instead to watch sports action on the giant-screen TV or to down one of 26 beers on tap. The exception is brunch, which is the real deal, featuring bangers and mash, soda bread, and black-and-white pudding.

Up the road, Union Sq doesn't have its own T-stop, so has yet to undergo the gentrification that Davis Sq has seen. The classic place here is tiny **Tir Na Nog** (☎ 617-628-4300; 366 Somerville Ave), with live music most nights, while **Independent** (☎ 617-440-6021; 75 Union Sq) is more upscale. Take bus No 86 from Harvard Sq or No 87 from Davis Sq.

ENTERTAINMENT

From high culture to low-down blues, Boston's entertainment scene has something for everyone. The vibrant university culture enhances the breadth and depth of cultural offerings on both sides of the river. For up-to-the-minute listings, check out local media publications (p72) and websites (p72).

Live Music

The vibrant music scene in Boston ranges from contemplative folk to lively alternative to snazzy jazz. All of these modes (and more) appear at the city's larger venues.

Orpheum Theater (Map pp66-8; ☎ 617-679-0810; 1 Hamilton Pl) A slightly worn but relatively intimate venue with great acoustics.

Bank of American Pavilion (☎ 617-728-1600; www.fleetbostonpavilion.com; 290 Northern Ave) A white sail-like summertime tent with sweeping harbor views, this place was formerly known as the Fleet Boston Pavilion. Shuttle buses run from South Station.

Memorial Hall at Sanders Theater (☎ 617-496-2222; www.harvard.edu/arts; Holyoke Center, Cambridge) This beautiful, 1166-seat, wood-paneled theater is known for its acoustics. It hosts a wide variety of student performances, as well as visiting speakers and musicians, usually hosted by one part of Harvard or another.

Somerville Theater (☎ 617-625-5700; www.somervilletheatreonline.com; Davis Sq, Somerville) A cinema that also gets used for concerts, especially world music.

ROCK

From legends like Aerosmith and the Cars to modern rockers like the Mighty Mighty Bosstones and the Drop Kick Murphy's, plenty of nationally known bands trace their roots to Boston clubs; in fact, there are more than 5000 bands registered in this city.

Middle East (☎ 617-354-8238; www.mideastclub.com; 472 Massachusetts Ave, Cambridge; admission $8-15) This excellent venue usually has three different gigs going simultaneously, including a free jazz show in the corner. Take the Red Line to Central Sq.

Johnny D's Uptown (☎ 617-776-2004; www.johnnyds.com; 17 Holland St, Somerville; admission $8-12; ⏱ 12:30pm-1am Mon-Fri, 9am-1am Sat & Sun) One of the area's best and most eclectic venues. With a different style of music nightly, it has everything from blues and Cajun to swing and rock and roll. Sunday night blues jams are popular, while weekend jazz brunches are mellow. Take the Red Line to Davis Sq.

TT the Bear's (☎ 617-492-2327; www.ttthebears.com; 10 Brookline St, Cambridge; admission $3-15; ⏱ 6pm or 7pm-midnight or 1am) With live music nightly, this intimate diehard rock joint has been going strong in Central Sq since the 1970s. Lots of popular Boston bands got their start on this tiny stage. Take the Red Line to Central Sq.

Lizard Lounge (☎ 617-547-0759; 1667 Massachusetts Ave, Cambridge; admission varies) Beneath the Cambridge Common Restaurant between Harvard and Porter Sqs, this intimate, basement-level club features live original music nightly. Casual dress is cool. Red Line to Harvard.

Toad (☎ 617-497-4950; 1920 Massachusetts Ave, Cambridge; admission free) Local bands perform funk, R&B, rock and soul nightly at this tiny, ultra-casual place. Red Line to Porter Sq.

Paradise Lounge (☎ 617-562-8800; www.thedise.com; 967 Commonwealth Ave; admission $10-30; ⏱ 6pm-1am) One of Boston's most legendary rock clubs, where you can get up close and personal with some big names. The newly opened lounge has a hip, cozy atmosphere and a limited menu. Take the Green Line 'B' branch past Kenmore Sq to Pleasant St.

BLUES & JAZZ

Wally's Café (Map pp70-1; www.wallyscafe.com; ☎ 617-424-1408; 427 Massachusetts Ave; admission free; ⏱ 9pm-2am daily, 3-7pm Sun) Gritty, smoky and storied, this club is the last survivor of the jazz clubs that once enlivened this neighborhood. Monday is blues, Tuesday funk, Wednesday reggae, Thursday Afro-Cuban, and Friday and Saturday are jazz; the highlight is Sunday's afternoon jam session. There's a one-drink minimum.

Berklee Performance Center (Map pp70-1; www.berkleebpc.com; ☎ concert listings 617-747-8890, box office 617-747-2261; 136 Massachusetts Ave; admission $5-10) This venue hosts jazz concerts given by the Berklee College of Music's renowned faculty members and exceptional students, as well as big-name professional performers.

Cantab Lounge (☎ 617-354-2685; www.cantablounge.com; 738 Massachusetts Ave, Cambridge; admission $5-10) Grungy, dark and laid-back, the Cantab is in keeping with the longtime tradition of pre-rehab Central Sq. It's a well-established bluegrass, blues and oldies venue, where students hang with locals. On Friday and Saturday it features Little Joe Cook, otherwise known as 'the Peanut man.' Take the Red Line to Central Sq.

Ryles (☎ 617-876-9330; www.ryles.com; 212 Hampshire St, Cambridge; admission $10-15; ⏱ 7pm-1am Tue-Thu, 7pm-2am Fri & Sat, 10am-3pm Sun) This great

Inman Sq jazz venue boasts two intimate floors of local and national recording acts. The music is free during the Sunday jazz brunches. Walk north on Prospect St from Central Sq.

Regattabar (Map p69; ☎ 617-661-5500, tickets 617-395-7757; www.regattabarjazz.com; 1 Bennett St, Cambridge; tickets $15-30; ☽ Tue-Sat) Within the Charles Hotel in Harvard Sq, this upscale yacht club–like place books internationally known groups. A limited number of general seating tickets go on sale one hour before show time. Ticket prices vary depending on the fame quotient.

FOLK

Although other clubs occasionally book folk acts, these two places are devoted to giving struggling folk singers a venue.

Club Passim (Map p69; ☎ 617-492-7679; www.clubpassim.com; 47 Palmer St, Cambridge; admission $5-15) This venerable nonprofit club is known nationally for supporting the early careers of singer-songwriters Jackson Browne, Tracy Chapman, Nanci Griffith and Patty Larkin. It's a small club with only 125 seats. Tuesday is open-mike night. It also serves vegetarian meals, but no alcohol.

Nameless Coffeehouse (Map p69; ☎ 617-864-1630; www.namelesscoffeehouse.org; 3 Church St, Cambridge; admission by donation $8) Within the First Parish Church (Unitarian Universalist), this low-key place, run by volunteers, sponsors acoustic singer-songwriters on the first Saturday of each month (at 8pm from September to May).

Theater

Boston is an important 'try-out' city for pre-Broadway shows. The producers get out the kinks here and if the shows has good reviews, off to Broadway it goes. For information on these productions, see www.broadwayinbos ton.com. Several excellent community and university groups stage more adventurous shows, mostly outside the Theater District.

THEATER DISTRICT   Map pp66-8
Charles Playhouse (74 Warrenton St) This two-stage Theater District venue is the setting for **Blue Man Group** (☎ 617-931-9787; www.blueman.com; tickets $43-53), a wildly popular mixed-media performance art group. Since 1996 this team of blue men has been plucking members from the audience and drawing them on stage to

poke fun at the arts community with music and percussion. Another long-running favorite is **Shear Madness** (☎ 617-426-5225; www.shearmadness.com; tickets $37-40), a madcap comedy murder mystery that has a different ending every time. Shear Madness is in the *Guinness Book of World Records* for being the longest-running play of all time.

Colonial Theater (☎ 617-426-9366; 106 Boylston St) The oldest continuously running theater in Boston. Although the lavish Colonial is now enveloped by an office building, it is still resplendent with all the gilded ornamentation, mirrors and frescoes it had in 1900.

Cutler Majestic Theater (☎ 617-824-8000; www.maj.org; 219 Tremont St) Operated by Emerson College, a private performing-arts school, this 1903 beaux-arts building really is majestic. Restored in 2003, the theater now hosts operas, plays, ballet and other top-notch performances.

Opera House (☎ 617-880-2442; 539 Washington St) After more than a decade of neglect, the Opera House reopened its doors in 2004 for a highly acclaimed production of Disney's *Lion King*. The lavish theater has been restored to its 1928 glory, complete with mural-painted ceiling, gold-gilded molding and plush velvet curtains. It's a central part of the ongoing revitalization of Washington St.

Wang Center for the Performing Arts (☎ 617-482-9393, tickets 800-447-7400; www.wangcenter.org; 270 Tremont St) The opulent and enormous Wang Theater, built in 1925, has one of the largest stages in the country. The Boston Ballet performs here, but the Wang also hosts extravagant music and modern dance productions, as well as occasional giant-screen movies (the center was originally built as a movie palace). It also houses the more intimate Shubert theater, known as the 'Little Princess' of the Theater District.

Wilbur Theater (☎ 617-423-4008; 246 Tremont St) Built in 1914 in the Federal Revival style, dramatic in its simplicity (especially in comparison with the more lavish theaters), the theater hosts pre- and post-Broadway touring companies. The lounge is the site of the elegant after-theater club, Aria (p121).

OTHER VENUES

American Repertory Theater (ART; Map p69; ☎ 617-547-8300; www.amrep.org; 64 Brattle St, Cambridge; tickets $25-45) There isn't a bad seat in Harvard University's theater. The prestigious ART stages new plays and experimental interpretations of classics. It also has new, additional performance space at Zero Church St. Student 'rush' tickets for both venues are sold for $12 on the day of the performance.

Huntington Theater Company (Map pp70-1; ☎ 617-266-0800; www.bu.edu/huntington; 264 Huntington Ave; tickets $12-62) This Tony-award-winning theater company performs both modern and classical plays annually in the Greek revival Boston University Theater. Beginning in October 2004, the Huntington will also perform in the new Stanford Calderwood Pavilion at the Boston Center for the Arts (opposite). Call for information about student tickets.

Boston Center for the Arts (BCA; Map pp70-1; ☎ 617-426-7700; www.bostontheaterscene.com; 539 Tremont St; tickets $35-50) There's rarely a dull moment here. Four distinctive performance spaces (as well as the Mills Gallery, a contemporary art space) are well suited to unusual productions. Every October, the BCA hosts the always-provocative Gay, Lesbian, Bisexual and Transgender Theater Festival.

Classical Music & Dance

Boston Ballet (☎ 617-695-6950; www.bostonballet.org; tickets $25-78) This troupe performs both modern and classic works at the Wang Center (opposite). Student 'rush' tickets for $15 are available two hours before the performance; seniors get the same deal, but only for Saturday matinees.

New England Conservatory (Map pp70-1; ☎ concert line 617-585-1122, box office 617-536-2412; www.newenglandconservatory.edu; Jordan Hall, 30 Gainsborough St) Chamber, orchestral, choral and even jazz performances take place in the acoustically superlative Jordan Hall. Most student and faculty concerts are free, but professionals perform here, too.

Symphony Hall (Map pp70-1; ☎ 617-266-1492, tickets 617-266-1200; www.bso.org; 301 Massachusetts Ave; tickets $25-87) Near-perfect acoustics match the ambitious programs of the world-renowned Boston Symphony Orchestra (BSO), which performs from October to April. The Boston Pops plays popular classical music and show tunes from May to mid-July and offers a popular holiday show in December. For same-day discounted 'rush' tickets ($8, one per person – you don't have to be a student), line up at the box office on Tuesday and Thursday at 5pm for the 8pm show, or on Friday at 10am for the 2pm show. (No rush tickets are sold for the Friday or Saturday evening show.) The only other way to beat the high cost of the BSO is to get lucky by catching one of its sporadic (once-monthly) open rehearsals at 7:30pm Wednesday or at 10:30am Thursday. These $16 tickets can be purchased in advance and they usually are.

Cinemas

Films are shown regularly at several venues that you might not expect. Besides the cinemas listed here, check out listings for French films at the French Library and Cultural Center (p64); films followed by panel discussions at the Boston Public Library (p82); arty films in the Remis Auditorium at the Museum of Fine Arts (p84); and free family flicks at the Hatch Memorial Shell (June to August only; p81).

Brattle Theater (Map p69; www.brattlefilm.org; ☎ 617-876-6837; 40 Brattle St, Cambridge) The Brattle is a film lover's 'cinema paradiso.' Film noir, independent films and series that celebrate directors or periods are shown regularly in this renovated 1890 repertory theater. You can often catch a classic double feature.

Coolidge Corner Theater (☎ 617-734-2500; www.coolidge.org; 290 Harvard St, Brookline) The area's only not-for-profit cinema shows documentaries, foreign films and first-run movies on two enormous screens in a grand art deco theater. Cult favorites and kung fu run Friday and Saturday at midnight. Take the Green Line 'C' branch to Coolidge Corner.

Somerville Theatre (☎ 617-625-5700; www.somervilletheatreonline.com; Davis Sq, Somerville) A classic movie house that survived the megaplex invasion, this theater alternates second-run films with live musical performances. Take the Red Line to Davis Sq.

Kendall Square Cinema (☎ 617-494-9800; www.landmarktheaters.com; 1 Kendall Sq, Cambridge) Kendall has nine screens showing foreign films and lesser-known artsy flicks. The concession stand sits alongside a coffee counter that is well equipped with espresso machines and pastries. Take the Red Line to Kendall Sq.

Harvard Film Archive & Film Study Library (Map p69; ☎ 617-495-4700; www.harvardfilmarchive.org; 24 Quincy St, Cambridge) From the offbeat to the classic, at least two films per day are screened at the Carpenter Center for the Visual Arts at Harvard University. Directors and actors are frequently on hand to talk about their work.

Following are some larger mainstream venues:

Loews Boston Common (Map pp66-8; ☎ 617-423-3499; cnr Tremont & Avery Sts) Eighteen big screens and snazzy surroundings.

Loews Harvard Square (p69; ☎ 617-864-4580; 10 Church St, Cambridge) Besides first-run Hollywood standards, this place shows the *Rocky Horror Picture Show* every Saturday at midnight, when costumes and audience participation are required.

Comedy Clubs

Comedy Connection (Map pp66-8; ☎ 617-248-9700; www.comedyconnectionboston.com; Quincy Market, Faneuil Hall Marketplace; tickets $14-40 Fri & Sat, $10-12 Sun-Thu) This 2nd-floor club, above the food court, is the premier comedy spot in Boston, attracting names from Chris Rock to Rosie O'Donnell, as well as local acts.

Nick's Comedy Stop (Map pp66-8; ☎ 617-423-2900; www.nickscomedystop.com; 100 Warrenton St; tickets $10-15) This Theater District venue features both local and national jokesters from Thursday to Saturday. Apparently Massachusetts-native Jay Leno got his start here.

Improv Boston (☎ 617-576-1253; www.improvboston .com; 1253 Cambridge St, Cambridge; tickets $5-12) This witty, long-running ensemble performs at the Back Alley Theater in Inman Sq from Wednesday to Saturday and makes things up as they go along; often audience members throw out ideas and the cast is off and running. The show redefines itself with every fast-paced performance. Sunday shows (7pm) are family oriented. Take the Red Line to Central, then walk north on Prospect St.

Jimmy Tingle's Off Broadway (☎ 617-591-1616; www.jimmytingle.com; 255 Elm St, Somerville; tickets $10-15) Boston's homegrown but nationally known funny man, Jimmy Tingle, performs as well as hosts other comedians at this club in Davis Sq. Like the true Cantabrigian that he is, Jimmy's humor is laced with serious social and political commentary.

Dance Clubs

The thriving club scene is fueled by the constant infusion of thousands of American and international students. Clubs are fairly stable, but the nightly lineup often changes. Check the *Boston Phoenix, Improper Bostonian* or *Stuff@Night* (p72) for up-to-the-minute information. Clubs along Lansdowne St near Kenmore Sq cater to a university crowd, while those in the Theater District are favored by young professionals; Man Ray (opposite), in Cambridge, defies categorization. Cover charges vary widely, from free (if you arrive early) to $20, but the average is usually $10 to $15 on weekends. Most clubs are open 10pm to 2am and require proper dress.

THEATER DISTRICT   Map pp66-8

Felt (☎ 617-350-5555; http://feltclubboston.com; 533 Washington St; ⏰ 4:30pm-2am Tue-Sun) A nightclub, lounge and billiards club all in one. There are only 14 pool tables, so there's usually a wait, but there is plenty of people-watching to do in the meantime. The dance floor is upstairs.

Big Easy (☎ 617-351-7000; www.bigeasyboston.com; 1 Boylston Pl; ⏰ Fri & Sat) The atmosphere here tries to replicate a New Orleans Mardi Gras–style playground. In addition to eclectic cover bands, a DJ spins Latin, international, hip-hop and everything else imaginable. You can just watch from the 2nd-floor balcony if you prefer. The crowd is a bit older here, and the drinks cheaper.

Matrix & Roxy (☎ 617-338-7699, 617-542-4077; www.roxyplex.com; 275-279 Tremont St; admission $12-30; ⏰ Thu-Sat) Within the Wyndham Tremont hotel's stylish, 3rd-floor ballroom, the Roxy is an upscale dance club and performance venue (no jeans, T-shirts or sneakers). Unless live music is scheduled, a DJ spins Latin and salsa, and international and house classics, depending on the night. It's connected to the superchic Caprice Lounge. The same complex houses the ultrahip Matrix, playing high-energy techno, house and disco. Two dance floors, a dozen bars… it's over the top. Pay one admission price for both places.

Venu (☎ 617-338-8061; www.venuboston.com; 100 Warrenton St; ⏰ 11:30pm-2am Tue & Thu-Sun) To signal your insider status at this superchic club, pull out your best designer knockoff and arrive fashionably late for DJ-spun tunes. Fun features include Carnival Sunday with music from Brazil, and the hottest Asian night in town (www.asiannight411.com; reservations recommended) on Saturday.

Aria (☎ 617-338-7080; www.ariaboston.com; 246 Tremont St; ☒ Tue-Sat) Plush and Parisian, Aria attracts a highly stylized, glam set. DJs at this exclusive red-velvet club below the Wilbur Theater spin tunes from hip-hop to R&B to Latin and house. Reservations and proper dress required.

FENWAY & KENMORE SQUARE Map pp70-1

Avalon (☎ 617-262-2424; www.avalonboston.com; 15 Lansdowne St; ☒ Thu-Sun) Boston's premier dance club features international house music, progressive national bands and over-19 nights. The place is huge, especially since its renovation a few years ago. There's little to distinguish Hot & Heavy Thursday from Avaland Friday from Tease Saturday (except the latter, which is an over-21 ladies night). Sunday, however, is gay night.

Axis (☎ 617-262-2437; 13 Lansdowne St; ☒ Thu-Sun) Just next door to Avalon, some might say it's more underground, others just come out and say it's trashier. But most agree that Axis is not as fashionable as its neighbor. Music, when its live, receives rave reviews. The two clubs are connected (and often open for one admission price), so you can make the judgment yourself.

Bill's Bar (☎ 617-421-9678; www.billsbar.com; 5½ Lansdowne St; admission $8-12; ☒ Wed-Sun) The self-mocking 'bastard child of Lansdowne St,' this smaller club, with live music and DJs, is packed with Boston University students who live by alternative music. Specialized nights include Reggae Sunday and Karaoke Wednesday, but otherwise Bill's got live music and DJ's working the wax.

Sophia's (☎ 617-351-7001; www.sangriaandsalsa .com; 1270 Boylston St; ☒ Tue-Sun) Popular with an older international set, this upscale Latin club has wood floors, exposed brick and a rooftop terrace, not to mention a fantastic 'small plates' restaurant downstairs (see p111). In winter a tent keeps the rooftop hot (as if the music doesn't). Check online to reserve your spot at Sangria & Salsa Fridays – $10 for admission including a lesson, or $25 including dinner.

CAMBRIDGE

Man Ray (☎ 617-864-0400; www.manrayclub.com; 21 Brookline St; ☒ 10pm-2am Wed-Sat) Creative attire is encouraged at Central Sq's most 'under-ground' club. As they say, dress to impress, express or distress. (When in doubt wear black; fetishwear is suggested on Friday.) The lineup varies from industrial rock and high-energy dance tunes to campy, classic disco trash and '80s New Wave. Take the Red Line to Central Sq.

Ryles (☎ 617-876-9330; www.ryles.com; 212 Hampshire St; admission $10-12) Weekly world dance parties and salsa lessons turn up the heat on the upstairs dance floor. Walk north on Prospect St from Central Sq.

Gay & Lesbian Venues

Many straight clubs feature gay and lesbian nights. Since schedules and venues change often, check *Bay Windows* (p72) or talk to the folks at Cuttyhunk bookstore (p63).

Chaps (Map pp66-8; ☎ 617-587-0000; www.chapsboston.com; 100 Warrenton St; admission $6; ☒ from 10pm Wed-Thu, from 5pm Sun) One of Boston's most popular gay bars and dance clubs, the lineup at this Theater District club is diverse. Wednesday features Latin house music 'with drag shows and go-go gods to keep it cute'; Sunday tea dances start at 7pm.

Avalon (Map pp70-1; ☎ 617-262-2424; www.avalonboston.com; 15 Lansdowne St) Boston's longest-running gay club night is on Sunday at Avalon. Features world-class DJs and high-class drag.

Club Café (Map pp70-1; ☎ 617-536-0966; 209 Columbus Ave; ☒ 1:30pm-2am Mon-Fri, 2pm-2am Sat, 11am-2am Sun) This popular club is a stalwart of the South End gay scene. The new restaurant up front, 209, serves – to mixed reviews – New England fare with hints of the southwest. Sunday brunch is always packed. But the hotspot is the cool, New-Agey lounge in the back. Thursday to Saturday classic movies and shows run in the Moonshine Video Bar.

Fritz (Map pp70-1; ☎ 617-482-4428; 26 Chandler St) Within the Chandler Inn, this casual watering hole has a nice low-key atmosphere; it's mostly men, but women certainly are welcome.

Jacques (Map pp70-1; ☎ 617-426-8902; 79 Broadway; admission $6-10) Boston's most beautiful ladies put on quite a show at this drag cabaret.

Man Ray (☎ 617-864-0400; 21 Brookline St, Cambridge) Thursday is reserved for the boys here. Cage dancing and creative attire encouraged. Take the Red Line to Central Sq.

Ramrod & Machine (Map pp70-1; ☎ 617-536-1950; www.machineboston.com; 1254 Boylston St) Two clubs in one. Upstairs, Ramrod is a traditional men's leather bar. Downstairs at Machine, you'll find a hot, high-tech dance club. Doors open at 10pm downstairs.

Toast (☎ 617-923-9211; www.toastlounge.com; 70 Union Sq, Somerville; ◷ 8pm-1am Wed-Thu) On Thursday night, this basement martini lounge is Boston's premier club for women, while Wednesday night is gay night. The place has two smallish dance floors, dim lights and a cozy bar. Take bus No 86 from Harvard Sq or No 87 from Lechmere.

Sports

Boston loves its sports teams. And why not, with the three-time world champion New England Patriots and the long-overdue World Series–winning Red Sox? Emotions run high around every sports season, especially for baseball (see the boxed text). There is no better way to strike up a spirited conversation than to inquire about the Sox. For sports talk radio all the time, tune into 850AM.

CURSE? WHAT CURSE?

'And there is pandemonium on the field!' With the final call of baseball's 2004 World Series, the Boston Red Sox had overcome more than just the St Louis Cardinals, but the heavy weight of 86 years of futility and fatalism. Woe is the Fenway Faithful, it was long said, for their team is cursed.

It had all started so well for the Olde Towne team. Then known as the Pilgrims of the upstart American League, Boston captured the first ever World Series in 1903 against the Pittsburgh Pirates of the senior circuit National League. By 1918 Boston, now renamed the Red Sox, had won four more championships. But fortunes soon changed.

On the day after Christmas, 1919, Boston owner Harry Frazee, unwilling to meet the demands of his star player, sold that player's contract to New York owner Colonel Jacob Ruppert for $100,000 cash and $300,000 loan. Ruppert, meanwhile, acquiesced to the player's demand to receive a $20,000 contract and be moved from the pitching mound to the outfield. Now bedecked in Yankee pinstripes, Babe Ruth became baseball's foremost power hitter and, arguably, the greatest player who ever played the game. Led by the Sultan of Swat, the Yankees became perennial contenders, as the Red Sox faded into perpetual also-rans.

Thus, the legend was born of the Curse of the Bambino. Try as they may, success eluded the Red Sox over the years, while the Yankees piled up championship upon championship. Whenever it appeared that a Red Sox season might end in triumph, inexplicable and unnatural forces intervened against them. Bad breaks, botched balls and hanging sliders would suddenly steal defeat from the jaws of victory. The Red Sox–Yankee rivalry was the most intense in all sports, and the most one-sided. As the disappointments accumulated, only one conclusion prevailed – the team was hexed. Sizing up the problem and seizing the initiative, concerned fans even hired a well-known Salem witch to exorcise the angry ghost, to no avail.

The Red Sox were indeed a cursed team for much of the 20th century – cursed by bad management, that is. In 1933 Tom Yawkey turned 30 years old and gained access to a $40 million trust fund. With his birthday allowance, he purchased the Red Sox and Fenway Park. Yawkey was an avid sportsman and a passionate fan, who loved hanging out with and indulging his players. In an era of stinginess, he spent lavishly on his team. The Boston franchise was seen as a country club, where Yawkey employed his drinking buddies in management and his favorite players called the shots.

The Yawkey-led Red Sox were further burdened by the legacy of racism. As society and the game changed, the city and the team did not. Red Sox management passed on the chance to sign Jackie Robinson and Willie Mays. The Red Sox was the last all-white team in the major leagues. The racist reputation of the organization, as well as the city, plagued the franchise well after Yawkey's death in 1976. Not until the 1990s did the team shed this ugly image.

For Red Sox Nation, the past is finally past. On a cold October night in the same House that Ruth Built, the unkempt and unnerved Red Sox thrashed the clean-cut and choked up Yankees in the final game of the American League championship in 2004. Desperate and disbelieving, Yankee fans tried in vain to conjure up the spirit of the Babe, which likely had gone out for more hot dogs and beer. Next up, the Red Sox throttled their old National League nemesis, the St Louis Cardinals, who fell to the hose in four straight. Hell had frozen over. The curse was reversed. The Boston Red Sox were World Series champs.

Boston Red Sox (Map pp70-1; ☎ tickets 617-267-1700; www.redsox.com; 4 Yawkey Way; tickets bleachers $18-20, regular seats $25-55; ☉ season early Apr-late Sep) The Sox play in Fenway Park, the nation's oldest and most storied ballpark, built in 1912. Unfortunately, it is also the most expensive. During sold-out games, there are often first-come, first-served standing-room-only tickets sold at 9am for same-day games; head to the ticket windows on Yawkey Way.

Boston Celtics (Map pp66-8; ☎ info 617-523-3030, tickets 617-931-2000; www.celtics.com; Fleet Center, 150 Causeway St; tickets $10-95; season late Oct-Apr) The Celtics, who've won more basketball championships than any other NBA team, play across from North Station. Tickets start at $10, but you won't be able to see anything from those seats. The Celtics and the Bruins play at the arena formerly known as the Fleet Center, which was undergoing a name change at the time of publication.

Boston Bruins (Map pp66-8; ☎ info 617-624-1900, tickets 617-931-2000; www.bostonbruins.com; Fleet Center, 150 Causeway St; tickets $25-85; season mid-Oct–mid-Apr) The Bruins, under the former star power of Bobby Orr, Phil Esposito and Ray Bourque, play ice hockey. That is, when they are not involved in a labor dispute.

New England Patriots (☎ 508-543-8200, 800-543-1776; www.patriots.com; Gillette Stadium, Foxborough; standing-room tickets $39; season late Aug–late Dec) The three-time Super Bowl champs play football in a new, state-of-the-art stadium that's just 50 minutes south of Boston, but it's hard to get a ticket (most seats are sold to season ticket holders). From I-93, take I-95 south to Rte 1. Otherwise, direct trains go to Foxborough from South Station.

New England Revolution (☎ 877-438-7387; www.revolutionsoccer.net; Gillette Stadium, Foxborough; tickets $20-40; season mid-Apr–early Oct) The local soccer team also plays in Foxborough.

Many colleges also have teams worth watching, and spirited, loyal fans. In April look for the annual Bean Pot Tournament, college hockey's premier event.

Boston University (Map pp70-1; ☎ 617-353-4628; www.agganisarena.com; Agganis Arena, Commonwealth Ave) In January 2005 BU opened a brand-new fancy arena to host its basketball and hockey teams. Take the Green Line 'B' branch to St Paul St.

Boston College (☎ 617-552-3000; www.bceagles.com; Conte Forum, 140 Commonwealth Ave/MA 30, Chestnut Hill) BC is competitive in hockey, football and basketball. Fans are devoted, so tickets are often impossible to get. Take the Green Line 'B' branch to the end.

Harvard University (Map pp69; ☎ 617-495-2211; http://gocrimson.ocsn.com; N Harvard St & Soldiers Field Rd) Harvard's sports teams play across the river in Allston. Staunch Ivy League rivalries bring out alumni and fans.

SHOPPING
Boston may not be alluring for bargain-hunters. But it boasts its fair share of bohemian boutiques, distinctive galleries and offbeat shops. For shopping the old-fashioned way, head to Downtown Crossing. Two large department stores and lots of smaller practical retail outlets cater to every-day Bostonians. For chic boutiques and artsy galleries, you can't beat Newbury St (great for window shopping if not the real deal). Also in the Back Bay, the **Shops at Prudential Center** (Map pp70-1; ☎ 617-267-1002; 800 Boylston St) and **Copley Pl** (Map pp70-1; ☎ 617-369-5000; 100 Huntington Ave) are both vast, light-filled shopping malls filled with pricey shops.

Across the river in Cambridge, Harvard Sq has spirited street life with plenty of musicians and performance artists. Unfortunately, most of the independent stores have been replaced by national chains due to rising rents. Just beyond the Museum of Science, **Cambridgeside Galleria** (☎ 617-621-8666; 100 Cambridgeside Pl, Cambridge) is a three-story mall with 100 shops, including several moderately priced department stores. Take the Green Line to Lechmere.

Antiques
Beacon Hill is a treasure trove for antique hunters. At least a dozen shops are packed onto Charles and River Sts. Don't expect to find any bargains in this tony neighborhood, however.

Boston Antique Co-op (Map pp66-8; ☎ 617-227-9810; 119 Charles St) Dealers specialize in arts and crafts, silver, 17th- and 18th-century textiles, and personal trinkets.

Cambridge Antique Market (☎ 617-868-9655; 201 Monsignor O'Brien Hwy, Cambridge) With five floors of furniture, glass, clothing, pottery and jewelry, you'll probably find a little something to take home. Take the Green Line to Lechmere.

Justin Tyme (☎ 617-491-1088; 91 River St, Cambridge) For a more intimate shopping experience, try this tiny shop specializing in antiques,

BOSTON

TOP FIVE BOSTON SOUVENIRS

■ Yankee Hater (YH) baseball cap from **Out of Left Field** (Map pp66-8; ☎ 617-722-9401; Faneuil Hall)

■ *Make Way for Ducklings*, the famous children's book by Robert McCloskey, from **Coop** (Harvard Cooperative Society; Map p69; ☎ 617-499-2000, 1400 Massachusetts Ave, Cambridge)

■ Antique map of Boston from **Eugene Galleries** (Map pp66-8; ☎ 617-227-3062; 76 Charles St)

■ Complete lobster dinner (packed in dry ice to ship or take home) from **Legal Seafood** (☎ 617-568-2800; www.legalseafoods.com; Logan International Airport)

■ Harvard insignia necktie from **J August** (Map p69; ☎ 617-864-6650; 1320 Massachusetts Ave, Cambridge)

---

collectibles, costume jewelry and vintage clothing. Take the Red Line to Central Sq, then head west on Western Ave for one block until River St forks to the left.

Arts & Crafts

While Newbury St has the most dense concentration of galleries, a few others allow you to support local artists without losing your shirt. There are a number of avant-garde galleries in the Leather District, the area near South Station bounded by South, Lincoln, Essex and Kneeland Sts, and on Harrison Ave in the South End.

Fort Point Arts Community Gallery (Map pp66-8; ☎ 617-423-4299; www.fortpointarts.org; 300 Summer St) The focal point for Boston's cutting edge arts community.

Bromfield Art Gallery (Map pp70-1; ☎ 617-451-3605; 450 Harrison Ave) The city's oldest co-operative, this South End gallery is one of the more accessible, affordable and reputable galleries on the Boston art scene.

Barbara Krakow Gallery (Map pp70-1; ☎ 617-262-4490; 10 Newbury St) This gallery provides an elegant venue for contemporary artists. It's worth a look even if you can't afford to buy anything.

Harvard Collections (Map pp69; ☎ 617-496-0700; 1350 Massachusetts Ave, Cambridge) Fine reproductions and original works inspired by the immense holdings of the Harvard University museums, from African masks and carvings to jewelry crafted from ancient coins.

Society of Arts & Crafts (Map pp70-1; ☎ 617-266-1810; 175 Newbury St) This prestigious, nonprofit gallery was founded in 1897. Within the exhibition and retail space you'll find high-quality weaving, leather, ceramics, furniture and other handcrafted items.

Cambridge Artists' Cooperative (Map pp69; ☎ 617-868-4434; 59a Church St, Cambridge) Craftspeople

double as sales staff at this Harvard Sq co-op that displays over 200 handcrafted objects costing $3 to $1000.

Clothing
NEW

Filene's Basement (Map pp66-8; ☎ 617-542-2011; 426 Washington St) The granddaddy of bargain stores, Filene's Basement carries overstocked and irregular items at everyday low prices in Downtown Crossing. But the deal gets better: items are automatically marked down the longer they remain in the store. With a little bit of luck and lots of determination you could find a $300 designer jacket for $30. But be forewarned: the chances of finding something perfect (ie well made, undamaged, your size and in a color that's not chartreuse) are pretty slim. Patience is a prerequisite, since customers rip through piles of merchandise, turning the place upside down as if a tornado hit it. Even so, it's a sight to see, an experience unique to Boston; don't miss it.

Helen's Leather Shop (Map pp66-8; ☎ 617-742-2077; 110 Charles St) Maybe you didn't come to Boston to buy cowboy boots. But if you did, you'd find an impressive range at this outlet, which also carries gorgeous jackets and bags.

Despite claims that Harvard Sq has turned into an outdoor shopping mall, a few unique boutiques continue to thrive, offering stylish simplicity and casual comfort. A few have branches on Newbury St.

Clothware (Map p69; ☎ 617-661-6441; 52 Brattle St, Cambridge) Innovative clothes by local designers.

Jasmine/Sola Cambridge (Map p69; ☎ 617-354-6043; 36 Brattle St); Back Bay (Map pp70-1; ☎ 617-437-8465; 329 Newbury St) Cambridge has side-by-side stores for men and women, while the store at Back Bay is for women only.

Mudo Cambridge (Map p69; ☎ 617-876-8846; 9 John F Kennedy St); Back Bay (Map pp70-1; ☎ 617-266-7838; 205 Newbury St) Tiny tops and slinky jeans.

Tess (Map p69; ☎ 617-864-8377; 20 Brattle St, Cambridge) High-quality but overpriced.

VINTAGE

Garment District (☎ 617-876-5230; 200 Broadway, Cambridge; ☒ 11am-9pm Sun-Fri, 9am-9pm Sat) If your memories of the fashion-conscious '60s and '70s have faded like an old pair of jeans, entering this store will bring it all back with a vengeance. Downstairs, Dollar-a-Pound has different merchandise and different pricing methods. Like a flea market gone berserk, piles of clothing are dumped on the warehouse floor and folks wade through it looking for their needle in the haystack. Upon checkout, your pile is weighed and you pay 'by the pound.' The price per pound is usually $1.50, but on Friday it's lowered in order to sell the merchandise faster. There are also books, records and cassettes, and kitchen supplies, all priced to move. Take the Red Line to Kendall Sq.

Closet, Inc (Map pp70-1; ☎ 617-536-1919; 175 Newbury St) This second-hand clothing store carries high-quality suits, sweaters, jackets, jeans, gowns and other garb by acclaimed designers. For shoppers with an eye for fashion but without a pocketbook to match. Most items are in perfect condition.

There are other excellent options for vintage clothing:

Second Time Around Harvard Sq (Map p69; ☎ 617-491-7185; 8 Eliot St, Cambridge); Newbury St (Map pp70-1; ☎ 617-247-3504; 176 Newbury St)

Oona's Experienced Clothing (Map p69; ☎ 617-491-2654; 1210 Massachusetts Ave, Cambridge)

SHOES

Berk's (Map p69; ☎ 617-492-9511; 50 John F Kennedy St, Cambridge) A small store with an awesome selection of stylish, comfortable shoes. Great end-of-season sales.

DSW Shoe Warehouse (Map pp66-8; ☎ 617-556-0052; 385 Washington St) A veritable emporium of bargain-priced shoes for all ages and genders. The dizzying array of sneakers, sandals, loafers and boots is enough to wear out even the most dedicated shoe shopper.

John Fluevog (Map pp70-1; ☎ 617-266-1079; 302 Newbury St) Very cool, trendy shoes: they may be more fun to look at than they are comfortable to wear.

Tannery (Map pp70-1; ☎ 617-267-0899; 402 Boylston St) It's not really a place to come for bargains, but this place carries hundreds of the top-name brands in fancy footwear. There's a second branch in **Harvard Sq** (Map p69; ☎ 617-491-0810; 11 Brattle St).

Music

Newbury Comics (Map pp70-1; ☎ 617-236-4930; 332 Newbury St) In addition to namesake comics, it sells new and used alternative rock CDs and records.

Virgin Megastore (Map pp70-1; ☎ 617-896-0950; 360 Newbury St) This music superstore has three floors of CDs and DVDs. Listening stations allow you to sample just about any CD you wish.

Tower Records (Map p69; ☎ 617-876-3377; 95 Mt Auburn St; ☒ until midnight) Harvard's Sq's best-stocked music store.

For used discs and records, try **Cheapo Records** (☎ 617-354-4455; 645 Massachusetts Ave, Cambridge) near Central Sq or **Looney Tunes** (Map pp70-1; ☎ 617-247-2238; 1106 Boylston St).

Novelty Shops

Condom World (Map pp70-1; ☎ 617-267-7233; 332 Newbury St) One size will not fit all.

Hempfest (Map pp70-1; ☎ 617-421-9944; 207 Newbury St) This store sells all manner of products made from hemp, the botanical cousin of marijuana: items to wear, to furnish one's home and even to eat.

Sporting Goods

Hilton's Tent City (Map pp66-8; ☎ 800-362-8368; 272 Friend St) Although it's dusty and musty, Hilton's boasts four floors of tents (set up to test out) and all the camping and backpacking accessories, equipment and clothing you'll ever need – at the lowest prices around.

New Balance Factory Store (☎ 877-623-7867; 40 Life St, Brighton) Factory seconds and overruns of running shoes, fleece jackets and synthetic clothing made by New Balance. You may have to search for your size, but you can easily save 25% to 50% off any given item. Look for the automatic 20% reduction when you trade in an old pair of shoes. This place is not so easy to find: take bus No 64 from Central Sq.

GETTING THERE & AWAY
Air

Logan International Airport (Map p65; ☎ 800-235-6426; MA 1A, East Boston) is served by most major national and international carriers. Its five separate terminals are connected by a frequent shuttle bus (No 11). Logan has been undergoing an expansion for years and the congestion and confusion that it brings come as a shock to travelers. You'll fare better if you assume the worst: don't expect much logic or ease in navigation.

Boat

Boston Harbor Cruises (Map pp66-8; ☎ 617-227-4320) operates boats to George's Island from Long Wharf. See p95 for details.

Bay State Cruise Company (☎ 617-748-1428, 866-435-6800; www.baystatecruises.com) operates boats from Commonwealth Pier in South Boston to Provincetown at the tip of Cape Cod; see p203 for details.

Bus

Boston has a modern, indoor, user-friendly **bus station** (Map pp66-8; no tel; 700 Atlantic Ave), conveniently adjacent to the South Station train station and above a Red Line T stop.

Greyhound (☎ 617-526-1800, 800-231-2222; www .greyhound.com) buses depart for New York City throughout the day. Express buses take only 4½ hours, but others take up to two hours longer. One-way adult fares are $20 for a nonrefundable ticket, $35 for a more flexible ticket. Other sample destinations and adult one-way fares from Boston include the following:

Destination	Fare	Duration
Albany, New York	$32	3½-3¾ hrs
Hartford, Connecticut	$23	2-3 hrs
New Haven, Connecticut	$29	3½ hrs
Newark, New Jersey	$35	6-7 hrs
Providence, Rhode Island	$7.50	1 hr

Inquire about special offers, like buying one round-trip ticket with a three-day advance purchase and getting a companion ticket free. Also, a seven-day advance purchase on one-way tickets often beats all other quoted fares.

Also recommended:

Bonanza (☎ 888-751-8800; www.bonanzabus.com) Serves Falmouth and Woods Hole on Cape Cod, as well as Albany, Hartford, Providence and New York City.

C&J Trailways (☎ 603-430-1100, 800-258-7111; www .cjtrailways.com) Provides daily service to Newburyport, Massachusetts (MA), and Portsmouth, New Hampshire (NH). Kids travel for free.

Concord Trailways (☎ 617-426-8080, 800-639-3317; www.concordtrailways.com) Plies routes from Boston to New Hampshire (Concord, Manchester, and as far up as Conway and Berlin) and Maine (Portland and Bangor). Its partner Dartmouth Coach goes to Hanover, New Hampshire.

Peter Pan Bus Lines (☎ 800-334-6464; www.peterpan bus.com) Serves Northampton and Lenox in western Massachusetts, Hartford, New Haven and New York City.

Plymouth & Brockton Street Railway Co (☎ 508-746-0378; www.p-b.com) Provides frequent service to most towns on Cape Cod, including Hyannis and Provincetown.

Vermont Transit (☎ 800-552-8737; www.vermonttran sit.com) Operates buses to White River Junction and Keene, NH; Portland (year-round) and Bar Harbor (seasonal), Maine (ME). In Vermont (VT), buses go to Burlington, Brattleboro, Bennington and lots of small towns in between.

Car & Motorcycle

From western Massachusetts, the Massachusetts Turnpike ('Mass Pike' or I-90; a toll road) takes you right into downtown. After paying a toll in Newton, drive east 10 more minutes on the pike and pay another 50¢; then the fun begins.

There are three exits for the Boston area: Cambridge, Copley Sq (Prudential Center) and Kneeland St (Chinatown). Then, the turnpike ends abruptly. At that point you can head north or south of the city on the I-93 Expressway (the Central Artery; for details, see p61) or right past South Station, into downtown.

From New York and other southerly points, take I-95 north to MA 128 to I-93, which cuts through the heart of the city. From northerly points, take I-93 south across the Tobin Bridge, which merges into the Central Artery.

A few sample distances from Boston to various points around New England:

Destination	Distance	Duration
Burlington, Vermont	220 miles	4½ hrs
New York, New York	227 miles	4½ hrs
Portland, Maine	108 miles	2¼ hrs
Portsmouth, New Hampshire	57 miles	1 hr
Providence, Rhode Island	45 miles	1 hr

Train

Amtrak (☎ 800-872-7245; www.amtrak.com) trains leave from South Station (Map p66-8), located on the corner of Atlantic Ave and Summer St, but also stop at Back Bay Station (Map pp70-1) on Dartmouth St. Service to New York City's Penn Station costs $64 one way and takes four to 4½ hours. Service to Manhattan on the high-speed Acela train (3½ hours) is a lot more expensive ($99 to $116 one way); reservations are required. Amtrak's online 'Rail Sale' program offers substantial discounts on many reserved tickets.

MBTA commuter rail (☎ 617-222-3200, 800-392-6100; www.mbta.com) trains heading west and north of the city, including to Concord, leave from bustling North Station (Map pp66-8) on Causeway St. Catch the 'beach trains' to Salem, Gloucester and Rockport here. Trains heading south, including to Plymouth, leave from South Station (Map pp66-8).

GETTING AROUND
To/From the Airport

Downtown Boston is just a few miles from Logan International Airport and is accessible by subway (the 'T'), water shuttle, van shuttle, limo, taxi and hire car.

The T, or the **MBTA subway** (☎ 617-222-3200, 800-392-6100; www.mbta.com), is the fastest and cheapest way to reach the city from the airport. From any terminal, take a free, well-marked shuttle bus (No 22 or 33) to the Blue Line T-Station called Airport, purchase a $1.25 token and you'll be downtown within 30 minutes. The subway operates daily from about 5:30am to about 12:30am.

Taxis are plentiful but pricey; traffic snarls can translate into a $20 fare to downtown.

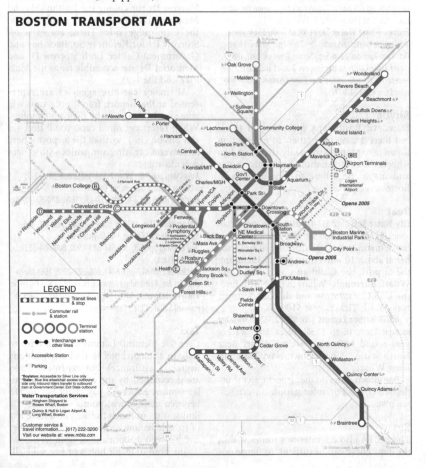

BOSTON TRANSPORT MAP

The regional bus lines (Bonanza, Concord Trailways and Plymouth & Brockton Street Railway Co; p126) operate **Logan Direct** (☎ 800-235-6426), which provides direct bus service ($7) between Logan International Airport and South Station.

Several water shuttles operate between Logan International Airport and the waterfront district in Boston:

MBTA Harbor Express (☎ 617-222-6699; www.harbor express.com; ⏱ 5:45am-11:25pm Mon-Fri, 8am-11:40pm Sat, 8am-10:15pm Sun) Whisks passengers to Long Wharf ($10) in downtown Boston and to South Wharf ($12).

City Water Taxi (☎ 617-422-0392; www.citywatertaxi .com; ⏱ 7am-10pm Mon-Sat, 7am-8pm Sun Apr-Nov) Serves 10 destinations in Boston Harbor, including Long Wharf, the Seaport District and the North End. Use the checkerboard call box at Logan dock to summon the water taxi. Trips cost $10.

Rowes Wharf Water Taxi (☎ 617-406-8584; www .roweswharfwatertaxi.com; ⏱ 7am-7pm Mon-Fri May-Oct, 7am-7pm daily Jun-Sep) Serves Rowes Wharf, the World Trade Center in the Seaport District and the Moakley Federal Courthouse on the Fort Point Channel. A one-way/round trip costs $10/17.

Bicycle

Daredevil Bostonians cycle around town, but there are no bike lanes, so use caution if you take to the Boston city streets on two wheels. For information on biking routes and maps and where to rent bicycles in Boston, see p88.

Boat

City Water Taxi (☎ 617-422-0392; www.citywatertaxi .com; ⏱ 7am-10pm Mon-Sat, 7am-8pm Sun) makes on-demand taxi stops from April to October at about 10 waterfront points, including the airport, the Children's Museum, Long Wharf, Burroughs Wharf in the North End, the USS *Constitution* and the Charlestown Navy Yard. Tickets cost $10.

MBTA Harbor Express (☎ 617-222-3200; www.har borexpress.com; tickets $1.50) plies the waters year-round between Lovejoy Wharf near North Station, Charlestown Navy Yard and Long Wharf.

For information on the airport water shuttle, see p127. For information on cruises, see p94.

Bus

The MBTA also operates bus routes within the city. These can be difficult to figure out for the short-term visitor, but schedules are posted at www.mbta.com and at some bus stops along the routes. Bus fare is 90¢: pay the driver with exact change (you can give him a dollar bill, but you won't get change).

Car & Motorcycle

With any luck you won't have to drive in or around Boston. Not only are the streets a maze of confusion, choked with construction (see the boxed text on p64) and legendary traffic jams, but Boston drivers use their own set of rules. Driving is often considered a sport – in a town that takes its sports very seriously.

Two highways skirt the Charles River: Storrow Dr runs along the Boston side and Memorial Dr (more scenic) parallels it on the Cambridge side. There are exits off Storrow Dr for Kenmore Sq, Back Bay and Government Center. Both Storrow Dr and Memorial Dr are accessible from the Mass Pike and the I-93.

All major car-hire agencies are represented at the airport; free shuttle vans will take you to their nearby pick-up counters. When returning hired cars, you'll find gas stations on US 1 north of the airport. There are several car-hire companies with offices downtown:

Avis (Map pp66-8; ☎ 617-534-1400, 800-331-1212; 3 Center Plaza, Government Center)

Budget (Map pp66-8; ☎ 617-497-1800, 800-527-0700; 24 Park Plaza)

Enterprise (Map pp70-1; ☎ 617-262-8222, 800-736-8222; Prudential Center, 800 Boylston St)

Hertz (Map pp66-8; ☎ 617-338-1500, 800-654-3131; 30 Park Plaza)

National (☎ 617-661-8747, 800-227-7368; 1663 Massa-chusetts Ave, Cambridge) Between Harvard Sq and Porter Sq.

Thrifty (Map p69; ☎ 617-876-2758; 110 Mt Auburn St, Harvard Square Hotel, Cambridge)

Taxi

Cabs are plentiful (although you'll have to walk to a major hotel to find one with any degree of assurance), but expensive. Rates are determined by the meter, which calculates miles. Expect to pay about $10 to $15 between most tourist points within the city limits, without much traffic. You'll have lots of trouble hailing a cab during bad weather and between 3:30pm and 6:30pm weekdays. Again, head to major hotels or Faneuil Hall.

Recommended taxi companies include **Independent** (☎ 617-426-8700) and **Metro Cab** (☎ 617-242-8000).

The T

The **MBTA** (Map p127; ☎ 617-222-3200, 800-392-6100; www.mbta.com) operates the USA's oldest subway, built in 1897. It's known locally as 'the T' and has four lines – the Red, Blue, Green and Orange – that radiate out from the principal downtown stations. These are Park St (which has an information booth), Downtown Crossing, Government Center and State. When traveling away from any of these stations, you are heading outbound.

Tourist passes with unlimited travel (on subway, bus or water shuttle) are available for periods of one week ($35), three days ($18) and one day ($7.50). Kids aged five to 11 pay half-fare. Passes may be purchased at the Boston Welcome Center on Tremont St and at the following T stations: Park St, Government Center, Back Bay, Alewife, Copley, Quincy Adams, Harvard, North Station, South Station, Hynes and Airport. For longer stays, you can buy a monthly pass allowing unlimited use of the subway ($44) or subway-bus combo ($71).

Otherwise, buy tokens at all stations (adult/child $1.25/60¢), except those west of Symphony ('E' branch) and Kenmore ('B,' 'C' and 'D' branches) on the Green Line, which are above ground. You need exact change to board. No fare is collected when heading outbound from an above-ground Green Line station.

The T operates from approximately 5:30am to 12:30am. The last Red Line trains pass through Park St at about 12:30am (depending on the direction), but all T stations and lines are different: check the posting at the station. **Night Owl** (🕑 12:30-2:30am Fri & Sat) is the late-night bus service ($2) that mirrors the sub-way lines on weekends after the subway stops running. Monthly passes are not valid for the Night Owl service.

Around Boston

AROUND BOSTON

HIGHLIGHTS

- **Best Bike Ride**
  Minuteman Commuter Bikeway (p134) from Cambridge to Lexington, and then on to Walden Pond (p138) for a cooling dip

- **Closest-to-City Escape**
  Blue Hills (p165)

- **Sunniest Stretch of Sand**
  Plum Island (p161)

- **Most Delectable Dinner**
  Boiled lobster from Roy Moore's Fish Shack Restaurant (p151) in Rockport

- **Spookiest Stories**
  Witch House in Salem (p146)

- TELEPHONE CODE: 781, 978, 508
- POPULATION: 4.6 MILLION
- AREA: 3000 SQ MILES

Famous village greens, national parks and historic harbors, vividly evoking New England's past, lie within an hour's excursion from Boston. To trace the events leading to the outbreak of the American Revolution in 1775, travelers can follow patriot Paul Revere's famous ride to Lexington's Battle Green, 18 miles northwest of Boston, then continue another six miles along the Battle Rd to Concord. But history and museums are far from the only draws here.

Hiking, whale-watching, canoeing, biking, beaching and picnicking tempt the wild at heart. The entire coast of Massachusetts claims a rich history, but no part offers more recreational, cultural and dining diversions than the North Shore of Boston. Salem was among America's wealthiest ports in the 19th century; Gloucester is the nation's most famous fishing port; and Marblehead remains one of the premier yachting ports in the USA. Trade and fishing have brought wealthy residents, sumptuous houses, and great collections of art and artifacts to the area. Explore the region's rich maritime history and spectacular coastal scenery, and don't miss the opportunity for a seafood feast.

The South Shore is equally blessed with historic sites and natural beauty. Seeing firsthand the challenges faced by the Pilgrims who first landed at Plymouth Rock is a vivid reminder of the value of religious tolerance and stubborn endurance – both at the core of the nation's foundation. And finally, the South Shore offers one of Boston's most accessible retreats just minutes from the city – the inviting Blue Hills.

Information

Massachusetts Tourist Information Center
(☎ 508-746-1150; www.masstourist.com; MA 3 exit 5; ⏱ 6am-5pm Mon-Thu, 6am-8pm Fri, 8am-8pm Sat & Sun) Provides information on many regional destinations in addition to Plymouth.

National & State Parks

The region around Boston includes several diverse sites – significant to the region's revolutionary, mercantile and industrial past – that have been designated as National Historical Parks by the National Park Service (NPS). The Minute Man National Historical Park (p134) incorporates the Battle Rd between Lexington and Concord where the first skirmishes of the revolution developed into full-blown fighting. This area remains much like it was 200 years ago. Other National Historical Parks are less pristine, but still capture a significant piece of the nation's history, including the Lowell National Historic Park (p141), Salem Maritime National Historic Site (p145) and the New Bedford Whaling National Historical Park (p168).

State, county and private efforts have made great strides toward limiting development and preserving ecosystems, especially on the North Shore: much of Cape Ann is protected, as are vast swathes of land further north. Halibut Point (p155) and Sandy Point (p161) are lovely state parks, while Crane Wildlife Refuge (p160) and Parker River National Wildlife Refuge (p161) are managed by the ever-active Trustees of Reservations. Walden Pond (p138) is a wonderful, inspirational natural resource, also managed by Massachusetts, while the acres of undisturbed woods around it are protected by private efforts. Just a few miles south of Boston, the Blue Hills Reservation (p165) is a little-known but much appreciated effort of the Massachusetts Department of Conservation and Recreation.

Getting There & Away

Many of the sights around Boston are accessible by the **Massachusetts Bay Transportation Authority commuter rail** (MBTA; ☎ 617-722-3200, 800-392-6100; www.mbta.com). Trains depart from Boston's North Station to destinations on the North Shore, including a line to Gloucester and Rockport, and another line

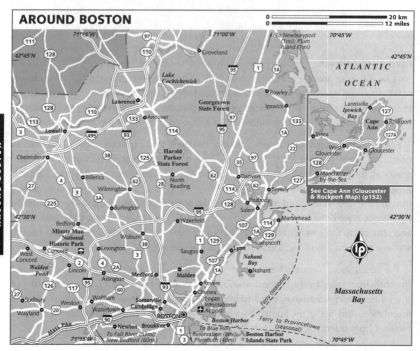

AROUND BOSTON

to Newburyport. Salem is served by both of these train lines. North Station is also the departure point for trains heading west to Concord. Plymouth is served by trains departing from South Station in Boston. Other destinations may be reached by bus, but it's really preferable to use a private vehicle to get the most of a trip out of the city.

WEST OF BOSTON

LEXINGTON
pop 30,355
This upscale suburb, about 18 miles from Boston's center, has a bustling village of white churches, historic taverns and tour buses surrounding the village green. Here, the skirmish between patriots and British troops jumpstarted the War of Independence (p133). While this history is celebrated and preserved, it is stark contrast to the peaceful, even staid, community that is Lexington today. If you stray more than a few blocks from the green, you could be in

Anywhere, USA, with few reminders that this is where it all started. Each year on April 19, however, historians and patriots don their 18th-century costumes and grab their rifles for an elaborate reenactment of the events of 1775 (see p134).

Orientation
MA 4 and MA 225 follow Massachusetts Ave through the center of Lexington. The Battle Green is at the northwestern end of the business district. Minute Man National Historical Park is about two miles west of Lexington center on Route 2A.

Information
Bank of America (1761 Massachusetts Ave; 8:30am-4pm Mon-Fri, 9am-3pm Sat) ATM and exchange facilities.
Lexington Chamber of Commerce Visitor Center (781-862-1450; www.lexingtonchamber.org; 1875 Massachusetts Ave; 9am-5pm Apr-Oct, 10am-4pm Nov-Mar) Opposite Battle Green next to Buckman Tavern.
Lexington Historical Society (781-862-1703; www.lexingtonhistory.org; 1332 Massachusetts Ave)
Post Office (1661 Massachusetts Ave; 8am-6pm Mon-Fri, 8am-2pm Sat)

THE SHOT HEARD AROUND THE WORLD

On April 18, 1775, Paul Revere, William Dawes and Samuel Prescott set out on their midnight ride from Boston to Lexington and Concord. They rode to warn these communities that a British expeditionary force was coming to search for arms rumored to be stockpiled at Concord. The colonial intelligence was so efficient that the local troops of militia, or minutemen, turned out long before the tramp of British boots was heard on the dirt road approaching Lexington.

When 700 Redcoats marched up to Lexington Green just after daybreak on April 19, they found Capt John Parker's company of 77 minutemen lined up in formation to meet them. Clearly outnumbered, Capt Parker ordered his men to disperse peaceably. But the British took this as capitulation and began trying to arrest the 'rebels' who had raised arms against them.

A shot rang out – from which side has never been clear – and then others, and soon eight minutemen lay dead on the green, with 10 others wounded. The skirmish on Lexington Green (now called Battle Green) was the first organized, armed resistance to British rule in a colonial town, and the beginning of the Revolutionary War.

Afterwards, General Gage's expeditionary force of 700 British soldiers marched to nearby Concord and commandeered the Wright Tavern as their headquarters. Their commander sent seven companies off to the north to seize arms reportedly stored at Colonel James Barrett's farm; only three of these companies remained to secure the North Bridge.

The Yankee minutemen, outnumbered, mustered on Punkatasset Hill, northeast of the town center, and awaited reinforcements, which came steadily from surrounding towns. When several hundred had assembled, the minutemen saw smoke rising from the town. The British searchers had found nothing but a few gun carriages, which they burned, but the minutemen assumed the worst.

'Will you let them burn the town down?' shouted their commander. Enraged that the regulars would burn down their homes, the minutemen fired on the now-outnumbered British troops, wounding half of their officers and forcing them back across the North Bridge. Soon the British were on their way out of Concord.

The battle at North Bridge, called 'the shot heard 'round the world' by Ralph Waldo Emerson, was the first successful armed resistance to British rule. But it did not end there.

The British suffered 11 wounded and two dead at North Bridge, but it was only the beginning of the calamity. Minutemen pursued the British troops on their march back to Boston, firing at the Redcoats from behind trees, walls and buildings. Most of this fire did little harm, but occasionally a bullet would find its mark, and in places where the minutemen had defensible positions, British troops fell. They were tired, dispirited and angry when they reached Lexington and encountered 1000 reinforcements.

These guerrilla tactics were unusual for the time, and were looked upon as cowardly and unfair by the British troops. Enraged by the locals' resistance, and by their own ever-mounting casualties, the British rioted and murdered innocent colonials whom they encountered along their line of march. At Menotomy (modern Arlington), 5000 men battled one another. By the time the British regained the safety of Boston, they had suffered 73 dead, 174 wounded and 26 missing. The American losses amounted to 49 dead, 40 wounded and five missing.

The die had been cast. The American colonies stood in armed rebellion against the forces of the British crown.

Sights & Activities

BATTLE GREEN

The Lexington minuteman statue (crafted by Henry Hudson Kitson in 1900) stands guard at the southeast end of Battle Green, honoring the bravery of the 77 minutemen who met the British here in 1775 and the eight who died.

Today the green is tranquil, shaded by tall trees. The **Parker Boulder**, named for the commander of the minutemen, marks the spot where they faced a force almost 10 times their strength. It is inscribed with his instructions to his troops: 'Stand your ground. Don't fire unless fired upon. But if they mean to have a war, let it begin here.' Southeast of the green, history buffs have preserved the **Old Belfry** that sounded the alarm signaling the start of the Revolution.

For a look at the most famous depiction of the battle of Lexington, walk southeast of the green to **Isaac Harris Cary Memorial Hall** (Town Hall; ☎ 781-862-0500; 1625 Massachusetts Ave; admission free; ☼ 8:30am-4:30pm Mon-Fri). Sandham's famous painting *The Dawn of Liberty* hangs flanked by marble statues of patriots John Hancock and Samuel Adams.

BUCKMAN TAVERN

Facing the green next to the visitor center, **Buckman Tavern** (☎ 781-862-5598; 1 Bedford Rd; adult/child/senior $5/3/5; ☼ 10am-5pm Mon-Sat, 1-5pm Sun Apr-Oct), built 1709, was the headquarters of the minutemen. Here, they spent the tense hours between the midnight call to arms and the dawn arrival of the Redcoats. The tavern and inn also served as a field hospital where the wounded were treated after the fight. Today it is a museum of colonial life, with instructive tours given by 'interpreters' in period costume.

HISTORIC HOUSES

The Lexington Historical Society maintains two other historic houses that are open sporadically.

Now serving as the society's headquarters, **Munroe Tavern** (☎ 781-674-9238; 1332 Massachusetts Ave; adult/child/senior $5/3/5), built in 1695, was used by the British as a command post and field infirmary. It is about seven long blocks southeast of the green. The **Hancock-Clarke House** (☎ 781-861-0928; 36 Hancock St; adult/child/senior $5/3/5), built in 1698, was the parsonage of the Reverend Jonas Clarke and the destination of Paul Revere on April 19, 1775.

Combination tickets (two-house adult/child/senior $8/5/7, three-house $12/11/7) are available if you wish to visit more than one site. Tickets can be purchased from 10am to 5pm on Saturday and 1pm to 5pm Sunday from April to October.

MINUTE MAN NATIONAL HISTORICAL PARK

Two miles west of Lexington center, the route that British troops followed to Concord – now called Battle Rd – has been designated a **national park** (☼ dawn-dusk year-round). The excellent **visitors center** (☎ 978-862-7753; www.nps .gov/mima; ☼ 9am-5pm Apr-Oct) at the eastern end of the park shows an informative multimedia presentation depicting Paul Revere's ride and the ensuing battles. Contained

within the park, the **Battle Rd** is a wooded trail that connects the historic sites related to the battles – from Meriam's corner, where gunfire erupted while British soldiers were retreating, to the Paul Revere capture site. Battle Rd is suitable for cycling – slowly – but it is not paved.

CYCLING

The **Minuteman Commuter Bikeway** (p88) follows an old railroad right-of-way from near the Alewife Red Line subway terminus in Cambridge, through Arlington to Lexington and Bedford, a total distance of about 14 miles. From Lexington center, you can also ride along Massachusetts Ave to Rte 2A, which parallels the Battle Rd Trail (left), and eventually leads right into Concord Center.

To reach Walden Pond, turn left off of Rte 2A onto Bedford Rd. A right-hand turn onto Sandy Pond Rd leads past the DeCordova Museum. Fork left onto Baker Bridge Rd, then turn right when it ends at Rte 126, which is Walden St.

MUSEUM OF OUR NATIONAL HERITAGE

More than a mile south of the Battle Green, this **museum** (☎ 781-861-6559; 33 Marrett Rd/MA 2A; admission free; ☼ 10am-5pm Mon-Sat, noon-5pm Sun) was founded by the Scottish Rite Masons in 1975. Four large galleries depict life during the colonial era. One exhibit addresses the age-old question: who fired first? From Lexington center, drive south on Massachusetts Ave and turn right on Marrett Rd (Rte 2A).

Tours

If you prefer to follow in Paul Revere's footsteps in the comfort of an air-conditioned bus, the **Liberty Ride** (☎ 781-862-0500, ext 702; www.libertyride.us; adult/child $20/10; ☼ 10am-5pm) could be for you. The two-hour route starts at the National Heritage Museum and leaves every hour on the hour until 3pm. It covers the major minuteman sites in Lexington and Concord, as well as some of Concord's places of literary importance.

Festivals & Events

At the annual **Patriots Day** festivities (April 19) minuteman companies in colonial dress, bearing colonial matchlock firearms, re-enact the battle on Lexington Green. The British heavies – somewhat fewer than

---

TOP FIVE REVOLUTIONARY WAR SITES

■ **Freedom Trail, Boston** (p90) A 2½ mile trail around Boston's history

■ **Boston Tea Party Ship & Museum, Boston** (p77) Still serving tax-free tea

■ **Battle Green & Buckman Tavern, Lexington** (p133) The fateful site where the minutemen first faced off against the Redcoats

■ **Old North Bridge, Concord** (p136) The retaliation of the minutemen and the site of 'the shot heard around the world'

■ **Minute Man National Historical Park, Lexington** (opposite) Encompassing Battle Rd, the route of the British retreat with minutemen in hot pursuit

---

their original force of 700 – come dressed authentically as well, and the air is again filled with the tramp of hobnailed boots, barked commands, explosions of musket fire and clouds of gun smoke. Authenticity is pursued with some vigor, so the reenactment starts at the same time as the original event: just after dawn.

Sleeping

For a complete list of B&Bs, contact the Lexington visitor center (p132).

Battle Green Inn & Suites (☎ 781-862-6100, 800-343-0235; www.battlegreeninn.com; 1720 Massachusetts Ave; d/tw Apr-Oct $129/149, Nov-Mar $79/99) This is a motel-style lodging right in the center of Lexington's business district. Rooms are set around a light-filled, but airless, enclosed courtyard. Standard rooms are stylish but small, equipped with modern bathrooms and a few comforts, such as coffeemakers. Renovations are ongoing so try to get one of the revamped rooms.

Several chain hotels in the area include:

Holiday Inn Express (☎ 781-861-0850; www.hiexpress .com; 440 Bedford St; r $76-129; ☐ ☐) Take exit 31B off I-95.

Sheraton Lexington Inn (☎ 781-862-8700; www .sheraton.com; 727 Marrett Rd; r Apr-Oct from $109, Nov-Mar $89; ☐) Just west of I-95 exit 30B; follow the signs for Hanscom Field.

Eating & Drinking

More than a dozen eateries lie within a five-minute walk of the Battle Green. Most are open for lunch and dinner daily.

Rancatore's (☎ 781-862-5090; 1752 Massachusetts Ave; ☽ 10am-11pm) Cool off with a scoop of homemade ice-cream or sorbet from this family-run place. The coconut is creamy and irresistible.

Vila Lago Gourmet Foods (☎ 781-861-6174; 1845 Massachusetts Ave; items $4-10) This café has high ceilings, intimate tables, a scent of fresh-roasted coffee and a great deli case. You'll often see cyclists in here kicking back with the daily paper, a cup of exotic java or tea, and a sandwich of roasted turkey, Swiss and sprouts.

Bertucci's (☎ 781-860-9000; 1777 Massachusetts Ave; mains $12-15, pizzas $15-20) Boston's favorite pizza place is equally popular out here. In the very center of town, it serves pizza baked in a wood-fired brick oven, pasta, salads and other light meals. Lunch is a real bargain: unlimited salad and fresh-baked rolls with the purchase of a lunch main.

Mario's Italian Restaurant (☎ 781-861-1182; 1733 Massachusetts Ave; mains $5-9) If chain pizzerias are not your thing, head down the street to this consummate Umbrian bistro. With just 15 tables, all covered in red-and-white check tablecloths, Mario's offers great-value pizza ($8 and up) and carbo loading for cyclists.

Vinny T's (☎ 781-860-5200; 20 Waltham St; mains $15-20) For elaborate Italian fare, Vinny T's serves huge plates of pasta and old-school dishes, like chicken parmigiana and shrimp *fra diavolo* (shrimp in spicy tomato sauce). Dark paneling, Roman murals and Italian torch songs set the tone. The bar is a popular stop for locals and one of the livelier spots in town.

Khushboo (☎ 781-863-2900; 1709 Massachusetts Ave; mains $10-15) If you're in the mood for something exotic, head up the road to this serene Indian affair. If weather is fine, dine on the flower-filled terrace overlooking Massachusetts Ave. Otherwise, enjoy the subdued dining room, decorated in beige tones and centered around a tandoor oven. You might be tempted to fill up on the delectable freshly

baked bread – six kinds of naan and superb
poori – but save room for spicy curries or
tandoori specialties. It's a few blocks south
of Battle Green.

Several recommended options for Asian
fare include:

Dabin (☎ 781-860-0171; 10 Muzzey St; sushi $4-6,
mains $10-15) Fresh sushi or other Japanese and Korean
dishes.

Peking Garden (☎ 781-862-1051; 27-31 Waltham St;
mains $8-14) Eat amid lots of gold paint and birds of paradise.

Yangtze River Restaurant (☎ 781-861-6030; 25 Depot
Sq; dim sum $10, dishes $10-15) Serves spicy Szechuan
cuisine, as well as dim sum (on Saturday and Sunday only).

Getting There & Away

Take MA 2 west from Boston or Cambridge
to exit 54 (Waltham St) or exit 53 (Spring
St). From I-95 (MA 128), take exit 30 or 31.
MBTA (☎ 800-392-6100) bus Nos 62 (Bedford
VA Hospital) and 76 (Hanscom Field) run
from the Red Line Alewife subway terminus
through Lexington center at least hourly on
weekdays, less frequently on Saturday; no
buses on Sunday.

The most enjoyable way to get to Lexington – no contest – is to come by bicycle
via the Minuteman Commuter Bikeway. See
p134 for details. From there you can follow the bikeway another 4 miles west to its
terminus in Bedford, or ride the Battle Rd
Trail to Concord.

CONCORD
pop 16,993

Tall, white church steeples rise above ancient oaks, elms and maples in colonial
Concord, giving the town a stateliness that
belies the Revolutionary War drama that
occurred centuries ago (see p133). Indeed,
it is easy to see how writers, such as Ralph
Waldo Emerson, Nathaniel Hawthorne,
Henry David Thoreau and Louisa May Alcott, found their inspiration here. Concord
was also the home of famed sculptor Daniel
Chester French (who went on to create the
Lincoln Memorial in Washington DC).

These days travelers can retrace history's steps along Battle Rd or experience
Thoreau's Garden of Eden at Walden Pond.
French continues to inspire sculptors and
artists of all types at the DeCordova Sculpture Park. The homes of literary figures,
like Emerson, Hawthorne, and Alcott, are
also open for visitors. For the less-culturally

inclined, the placid Concord River and the
country roads are excellent for canoeing
and cycling.

Orientation

Concord lies about 22 miles northwest of
Boston along MA 2. The center of this
sprawling, mostly rural town is Monument
Sq, marked by its war memorial obelisk.
The Colonial Inn stands on the square's
north side.

Main St runs westward from Monument
Sq through the business district to MA 2.
Walden and Thoreau Sts run southeast from
Main St and out to Walden Pond some 3
miles away. The MBTA commuter rail train
station, Concord Station ('the Depot'), is on
Thoreau St at Sudbury Rd, a mile west of
Monument Sq.

Information

Bank of America (52 Main St; ☒ 8:30am-4pm Mon-Fri,
9am-1pm Sat)

Concord Bookshop (☎ 978-369-2405; 65 Main St)

Concord Chamber of Commerce (☎ 978-369-3120;
www.concordmachamber.org; 100 Main St; ☒ 9:30am-
4:30pm daily Apr-Oct, 9am-2pm Mon-Fri Nov-Mar)

Concord Magazine (www.concordma.com) A quarterly
publication focusing on history and current events of the
town. The associate website is replete with information,
including historical and artistic goings-on.

North Bridge Visitor Center (☎ 978-369-6993;
Liberty St; ☒ 9am-5pm Apr-Oct, 9am-4pm Nov-Mar)

Post Office (34 Walden St; ☒ 9am-5pm Mon-Fri,
9am-noon Sat)

Sights & Activities
MONUMENT SQUARE

The grassy center of Monument Sq is a favorite resting and picnicking spot for cyclists touring Concord's scenic roads. At
the southeastern end of the square is **Wright
Tavern**, one of the first places the British
troops searched in their hunt for arms on
April 19, 1775. It became their headquarters for the operation. At the opposite end
of the square is the **Colonial Inn** (p140), the
center of Concord socializing, now as then.
Old Hill Burying Ground, with graves dating
from colonial times, is on the hillside at
the southeastern end of Monument Sq.

OLD NORTH BRIDGE

The wooden span of Old North Bridge,
now part of Minute Man National His-

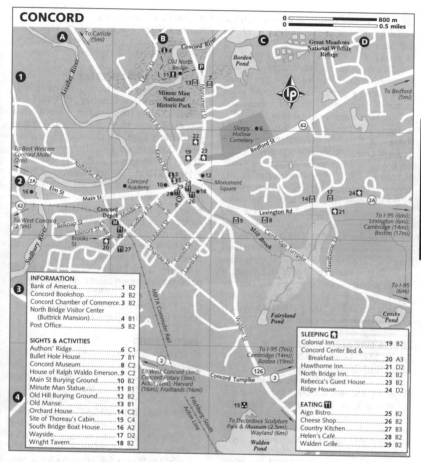

CONCORD

torical Park (p134), has been rebuilt many times, but still gives a good impression of what it must have looked like at the time of the first battle of the Revolution. Daniel French's first statue, the **Minute Man**, presides over the park from the opposite side of the bridge. Up the hill, the Buttrick Mansion houses the park's visitor center (p136).

On your way up here from Monument Sq, keep an eye out for the yellow **Bullet Hole House** on the east side of Monument St. British troops fired at the owner of the house as they retreated from the engagement at North Bridge, and a hole made by one of their bullets can still be seen in the wall of the shed attached to the house.

CONCORD MUSEUM

Southeast of Monument Sq, this **museum** (☎ 978-369-9609; www.concordmuseum.org; 200 Lexington Rd; adult/child/senior/student $8/5/7/7; ☉ 9am-5pm Mon-Sat, noon-5pm Sun Apr-Dec, 11am-4pm Mon-Sat, 1-4pm Sun Jan-Mar) brings together the town's diverse history under one roof. The museum's prized possession is one of the 'two if by sea' lanterns that hung in the steeple of the Old North Church in Boston as a signal to Paul Revere. It also has the world's largest collection of Henry David Thoreau artifacts, including his writing desk from Walden Pond.

EMERSON HOMES

Ralph Waldo Emerson (1803–82) was the paterfamilias of literary Concord, one of

AROUND BOSTON

the great literary figures of his age and the founding thinker of the Transcendentalist movement. He lived in Concord for almost 50 years (1835–82), and his **house** (☎ 978-369-2236; 28 Cambridge Turnpike; adult/child over 7/child under 7 $6/4/free; ⏰ 10am-4:30pm Thu-Sat, 2-4:30pm Sun mid-Apr–Oct) is now a museum. The house often hosted his renowned circle of friends and still contains many original furnishings.

Right next to Old North Bridge, the **Old Manse** (☎ 978-369-3909; www.thetrustees.org; 269 Monument St; adult/child/senior/student $8/5/7/7; ⏰ 10am-5pm Mon-Sat, noon-5pm Sun mid-Apr–Oct) was built in 1769 by Ralph Waldo's grandfather, the Reverend William Emerson, and was owned by the Emerson family for several following generations. It was finally deeded to the NPS in 1938. Today it's a museum filled with mementos of the Emerson family, and also of Nathaniel and Sophia Hawthorne, who lived here from 1842 to 1845 following their marriage. One of the highlights of Old Manse is the gorgeously maintained **grounds** (admission free; ⏰ sunrise-sunset). The fabulous organic garden was planted by Henry David Thoreau as a wedding gift to the Hawthornes.

LOUISA MAY ALCOTT HOMES

Louisa May Alcott (1832–88) was a junior member of Concord's august literary crowd, but her work proved to be durable: *Little Women* (1868–69) is among the most popular young-adult books ever written. The mostly autobiographical novel takes place in Concord; several sequels continued her portrayal of family life in Victorian America with keen perception and affection.

Her childhood home, **Orchard House** (☎ 978-369-4118; www.louisamayalcott.org; 399 Lexington Rd; adult/child/senior/family $7/4/6/16; ⏰ 10am-4:30pm Mon-Sat, 1-4:30pm Sun Apr-Oct, 11am-3pm Mon-Fri, 10am-4:30pm Sat, 1-4:30pm Sun Nov-Mar), is about 1 mile east of Monument Sq. Alcott's father, Bronson, bought the property in 1857 and lived here with his family until his death in 1888. Louisa wrote *Little Women* here in 1868 and died here 20 years later (two days after her father). The house, furnishings and Bronson's Concord School of Philosophy, on the hillside behind the house, are all open to visitors, but only by guided tour. Call in advance or arrive early to confirm a spot in summer.

Another house that Alcott lived in and wrote about is the **Wayside** (☎ 978-369-6975; 455 Lexington Rd; admission $4; ⏰ 10am-6pm mid-Apr–Oct).

At another time it was Nathaniel Hawthorne's home, but most of the remaining furnishings are those of Margaret Sidney, author of *Five Little Peppers*.

SLEEPY HOLLOW CEMETERY

The most famous Concordians rest in spacious **Sleepy Hollow Cemetery** (☎ 978-371-6299; Bedford St). Though the cemetery is only a block east of Monument Sq, the most interesting part, **Authors' Ridge**, is a 15-minute hike along Bedford St (MA 62). Enter the gate from MA 62 and follow signs to Authors' Ridge.

Henry David Thoreau and his family are buried here, as are the Alcotts, and Nathaniel Hawthorne and his wife. Ralph Waldo Emerson's tombstone is a large uncarved rock of New England marble, an appropriate Transcendentalist symbol. Down the hill a bit is the tombstone of Ephraim Bull, developer of the famous Concord grape.

Nearby is the Melvin Memorial, a much photographed monument to the memory of three Concord brothers who died in the Civil War. It is the work of Daniel French, who is buried in Sleepy Hollow also.

WALDEN POND

Henry David Thoreau took the naturalist beliefs of Transcendentalism out of the realm of theory and into practice when he left the comforts of the town and built himself a rustic cabin on the shores of **Walden Pond** (☎ 978-369-3254; www.mass.gov/dem/parks/wldn.htm; 915 Walden St; admission free, parking $5; ⏰ sunrise to sunset). His famous memoir of his time spent there, *Walden, or Life in the Woods* (1854), was full of praise for nature and disapproval of the stresses of civilized life – sentiments that have found an eager audience ever since.

The glacial pond is now a state park, surrounded by acres of forest preserved by the Walden Woods project, a non-profit organization. It lies about 3 miles south of Monument Sq, along Walden St (MA 126) south of MA 2. There's a swimming beach and facilities on the southern side, and a footpath that circles the large pond (about a half-hour stroll). The **site of ruins of Thoreau's cabin** is on the northeast side, marked by a cairn and signs. The beach gets packed in summer, but it's not hard to escape the crowds by following the path along to the other side of the pond.

DECORDOVA MUSEUM & SCULPTURE PARK

The magical **DeCordova Sculpture Park** (☎ 781-259-8355; www.decordova.org; 51 Sandy Pond Rd, Lincoln; admission free when museum closed, adult/child, senior & student $9/6; ☉ sunrise-sunset) encompasses 35 acres of green hills, providing a spectacular natural environment for a constantly changing exhibit of outdoor artwork. As many as 75 pieces are on display at any given time. Inside, the **museum** (adult/child, senior & student $9/6; ☉ 11am-5pm Tue-Sun) hosts rotating exhibits of sculpture, painting, photography and mixed media.

From Concord center, drive east on Rte 2 and turn right on Bedford Rd. From Walden Pond, it is a breathtakingly beautiful and heartachingly hilly drive (or bike ride) from Rte 126 on Baker Bridge Rd. Turn right when the road dead ends at Sandy Pond.

CANOEING

South Bridge Boat House (☎ 978-369-9438; 496 Main St; per hr/day Mon-Fri $10.50/35, per hr/day Sat & Sun $12/45; ☉ Apr-Nov), a mile west of Monument Sq, rents canoes for cruising the Concord and Assabet Rivers. The favorite route is downstream to Old North Bridge, and back past the many fine riverside houses and the campus of prestigious Concord Academy – a paddle of about two hours.

Tours

Concord Walking Tours (☎ 978-287-0897; www.concordguides.com; adult/child/senior/student $19/7-12/15/15; ☉ by appointment) offers a two-hour customized walking tour led by local teachers, authors and historians.

For details on the Liberty Ride, a two-hour tour of the major minuteman sites in Lexington and Concord, as well as some

---

DETOUR: FRUITLANDS

Transcendentalism was a 19th-century social and philosophical movement that flourished from 1836 to 1860 in Boston and Concord. Though small in numbers, the Transcendentalists had a significant effect on American literature and society. Ralph Waldo Emerson, Henry David Thoreau and Margaret Fuller all turned away from their Unitarian tradition to pursue Transcendentalism.

The core of Transcendentalist belief was that each person and element of nature had within them a part of the divine essence, that God 'transcended' all things. The search for divinity was thus not so much in scripture and prayer, nor in perception and reason, but in individual intuition or 'instinct.' By intuition we can know what is right and wrong according to divine law. By intuition we can know the meaning of life. Living in harmony with the natural world was very important to Transcendentalists.

The Transcendentalists founded a periodical, the *Dial*, to disseminate their views, and established the community of Brook Farm (1841–47) based on Transcendentalist doctrines of community life and work, social reform and opposition to slavery. Nathaniel Hawthorne was a resident for a time, and both he and novelist Herman Melville were influenced by Transcendentalist beliefs.

Bronson Alcott (1799–1888), educational and social reformer and father of Louisa May Alcott, joined this group of Concordians in pursuing Transcendental ideals. Toward this end, he founded Fruitlands, an experimental vegetarian community in Harvard, Massachusetts, established in 1843. He lived here with his family (including 10-year-old daughter Louisa) and others for a year before abandoning the project.

Fruitlands Museums (☎ 978-456-3924; 102 Prospect Hill Rd, Harvard; adult/child/senior/student $10/2/8/8; ☉ 11am-4pm Mon-Fri, 10am-5pm Sat & Sun May-Oct) is now open to the public. The original hillside farmhouse, set on spacious grounds with panoramic views of rural hills, dates from the 18th century, and was actually used by Alcott and his utopian 'Con-Sociate' (communal) family.

Other museums have since been moved to the 200-acre estate, including the 1794 Shaker House, an American Indian museum, and a gallery featuring paintings by 19th-century itinerant artists and Hudson River School landscape painters. One of the highlights of a visit is the **Fruitlands Tearoom** (lunch $11-14, brunch buffet $20; ☉ 11am-3pm Wed-Sat, brunch 10am-1pm Sun). Dine alfresco, and soak up the fresh air and fabulous scenery.

Fruitlands is in Harvard, about 30 miles west of Boston. Take Rte 2 to exit 38A, Rte 111. Take the first right onto Old Shirley Rd, which becomes Prospect Hill Rd after 2 miles. The museum entrance is at the top of the hill on the right.

of Concord's places of literary importance, see p134.

Sleeping

While there is a paucity of hotels and motels in Concord, travelers will find more than a dozen B&Bs in the Concord area. Most rooms have private baths, and furnishings from the Federal or Victorian periods. Get a complete list from the Concord Chamber of Commerce (136).

BUDGET & MID-RANGE

Best Western at Historic Concord (☎ 978-369-6100, 800-528-1234; www.bestwestern.com; 740 Elm St; r incl breakfast $99-124; ✕ ✕ ☒) Rooms are the freshly appointed, well-scrubbed units typical of this chain. The brand-new, well-equipped exercise facility is a pleasant surprise. The motel is at MA 2 near the Concord rotary; several restaurants are nearby.

Wayside Inn (☎ 978-443-1776; www.wayside.org; 76 Wayside Rd, Sudbury; s $96-120, d incl breakfast $122-155; ✕) The inn, dating from 1700, was made famous by Longfellow's poems *Tales from a Wayside Inn*, and now boasts that it's the oldest operating inn in the USA. It was restored by Henry Ford in the 1920s, and still operates as a restaurant and hostelry, with 10 period rooms. It's 13 miles south of Concord on US 20.

A few tiny B&Bs near the town center rent out just one or two rooms to guests.

Concord Center B&B (☎ 978-369-8980; www.concordcenterbb.com; 15 Brooks St; r Apr-Nov $125, Dec-Mar $115) An 1876 colonial house owned by a former ballet dancer, with one simple guest room with a gas fireplace.

Ridge House (☎ 978-369-9796; 533 Lexington Rd; r $95-105) A small but welcoming 1850s house, with one double and one twin room that share a bath.

TOP END

Colonial Inn (☎ 978-369-9200, 800-370-9200; www.concordscolonialinn.com; 48 Monument Sq; r $145-325; ✕) Dating from 1716, the Colonial Inn boasts a role in the events of April 19, 1775: a part of the inn was used as a storehouse for colonial arms and provisions. The oldest part of the inn houses 12 of the more expensive guest rooms, a lobby, dining rooms and tavern (featuring afternoon tea). The other less expensive 48 guest rooms are in a modern brick annex. With distinctive dining and nightly entertainment, the inn continues to be a meeting place for townsfolk

and visitors. It also operates **Rebecca's Guest House** (32 Monument St) for longer-term guests.

North Bridge Inn (☎ 978-371-0014; www.northbridgeinn.com; 21 Monument St; r incl breakfast $165-250; ✕) Just next to the Colonial Inn, this inn offers a more intimate experience. Six rooms are decked out with down comforters, plush pillows, tiled bathrooms and kitchenettes. A gourmet breakfast is served in the flower-filled dining room. And the friendly dog Posey greets every guest who walks through the door.

Hawthorne Inn (☎ 978-369-5610; 462 Lexington Rd; r incl breakfast $175-285) Artists Greg Burch and Marilyn Mudry have made this inn their life's work. It has seven rooms, with Oriental carpets, and antique Japanese ukiyo-e prints and sculpture, and private baths. You'll find it about a mile southeast of Monument Sq, across the street from Orchard House.

Eating

Country Kitchen (☎ 978-371-0181; 181 Sudbury Rd; dishes $3-8; ✉ 5am-4pm) The 'Little Yellow House by the Tracks' is the queen of cheap takeout in Concord. The flower boxes, cheery green shutters and picnic-table seating are all part of the warm welcome, as are cheap soups, sandwiches and salads.

Cheese Shop (☎ 978-369-5778; 29 Walden St; sandwiches $4-8; ✉ closed Mon) Stop here for a huge luncheon sandwich, such as the mixed grilled veggie pocket ($6), or for picnic supplies. Wine tasting starts at noon on Saturday.

Helen's Café (☎ 978-369-9885; 17 Main St; mains $5-9; ✉ 7am-9pm) This popular breakfast and lunch spot hums with the sound of silver and plates hitting the Formica table tops. Hungry patrons come looking for homemade soups and grinders, or a thick frappe from the ice-cream counter.

Walden Grille (☎ 978-371-2233; 24 Walden St; lunch $8-12, dinner $18-25) Across from the Cheese Shop, this place, formerly called Walden Station, is a tavern-restaurant with soft lighting, exposed brick walls and lyrical landscape paintings. The New American menu gets mixed reviews, but the setting in a former fire station is welcoming and cool.

Aigo Bistro (☎ 978-371-1333; 84 Thoreau St; mains $23-27; ✉ dinner only) Straight from ultrafancy L'Espalier (p109) in Boston, chef Moncef Meddeb adds North African nuances to his French recipes. The resulting Mediterranean mix is among the more interesting cuisine you will find this far out of the city. Enjoy it in the cool dining room upstairs from the Concord Depot.

Getting There & Away
Driving west on MA 2 from Boston or Cambridge, it's 20-some miles to Concord. Coming from Lexington, follow signs from Lexington Green to Concord and Battle Rd, the route taken by the British troops on April 19, 1775.

MBTA commuter rail (☎ 617-722-3200, 800-392-6100; www.mbta.com; Concord Depot, 90 Thoreau St) trains run between Boston's North Station and Concord Depot eight times a day in either direction on the Fitchburg/South Acton line. The trip takes about 40 minutes ($5).

LOWELL
pop 105,000
Twenty-five miles northwest of Boston, Lowell is a textile mill town located at the confluence of the Concord and Merrimack Rivers. At its heart is a national park that recalls the city's position as the crucible of the Industrial Revolution. In the early 19th century, factories churned out cloth by the mile, driven by the abundant waterpower of Pawtucket Falls. A network of canals and – after 1835 – the Boston & Lowell Railroad shipped raw materials in and finished cloth out. Today a working textile mill, canal boat tours, and trolley rides evoke the birth of America as an industrial giant.

In modern Lowell, high-tech and other industries have diversified the economic base. And an influx of Southeast Asian immigrants has diversified the culture (and cuisine) of this classic New England mill town. Obviously, Lowell is not the city it was 150 years ago, despite the charm of its historic center.

Orientation & Information
From I-495, follow the Lowell Connector to its end at exit 5-C to reach the city center. Trains from Boston terminate at the Gallagher Transportation Terminal on Thorndike St, a 15-minute walk southwest of the city center. A shuttle bus runs every 30 minutes to the Downtown Transit Center in the heart of the city.

Once in the city center, most of the sights are within walking distance. Merrimack St is the main commercial thoroughfare, holding the Downtown Transit Center, the chamber of commerce office and several restaurants.

Greater Merrimack Valley Convention & Visitors Bureau City Center (☎ 978-459-6150, 800-443-3332; www.merrimackvalley.org; 9 Central St; ☽ 8:30am-5pm Mon-Fri); Highway (☎ 978-250-9504; I-495, exit 32; ☽ variable) has two locations that provide the details you'll need.

Sights & Activities
LOWELL NATIONAL HISTORICAL PARK
The historic buildings in the city center – connected by the trolley and canal boats – comprise the **Lowell National Historical Park**

THE TOWN AND THE CITY OF JACK KEROUAC
'Follow along to the center of town, the Square, where at noon everybody knows everybody else.' So Beat Generation author Jack Kerouac described his hometown of Lowell, Massachusetts, in his novel *The Town & The City*.

One of the most influential American authors of the 20th century, Jack Kerouac (1922–69) was born in Lowell at the mill town's industrial peak. He inhabited Lowell's neighborhoods and graduated from Lowell High School. It is not surprising, then, that the author used Lowell as the setting for five of his novels that draw on his youth in the 1920s, '30s and '40s.

Kerouac is remembered annually during the Lowell Celebrates Kerouac (LCK) festival (p142). LCK – in conjunction with the Jack Kerouac Subterranean Information Society – has also compiled a fantastically detailed **walking tour** (http://ecommunity.uml.edu/jklowell) of Lowell, based on places that Kerouac wrote about and experienced.

Of course, Kerouac is most famous for his classic novel *On the Road*. With it, he became a symbol of the spirit of the open road. He eventually went to New York, where he and Allen Ginsberg and William Burroughs formed the core of the Beat Generation of writers. Nonetheless, Kerouac always maintained ties to Lowell, and he is buried in **Edson Cemetery** (cnr Gorham & Saratoga Sts), a pilgrimage site for devotees who were inspired by his free spirit.

(☎ 978-970-5000; www.nps.gov/lowe; 246 Market St, Market Mills; admission free; ⊙ 9am-5pm Mon-Sat, 10am-5pm Sun). It gives a fascinating peak at the workings of a 19th-century industrial town.

The **Boott Cotton Mills Museum** (☎ 978-970-5000; John St; adult/child & student $4/2; ⊙ 9:30am-4:30pm, longer hrs in summer) has exhibits that chronicle the rise and fall of the Industrial Revolution in Lowell, including technological changes, labor movements and immigration. The highlight is a working weave room, with 88 power looms. A special exhibit on **Mill Girls and Immigrants** (☎ 978-970-5000; 40 French St; admission free; ⊙ 1:30-4:30pm) examines the lives of working people.

Dedicated in 1988, the **Jack Kerouac Commemorative** features a landscaped path where excerpts of the writer's work are posted, including opening passages from his five novels set in Lowell. They are thoughtfully displayed with Catholic and Buddhist symbols, representing the belief systems that influenced him. See the boxed text, p141.

WHISTLER HOUSE MUSEUM OF ART

In 1834 Anna Mathilda (McNeill) Whistler, wife of the local agent for the Locks and Canals Corporation, gave birth to future artist James Abbott McNeill Whistler (1834–1903). The coming of the railroad made locks and canals less important, and the Whistlers moved away from Lowell in 1837. Young James went on to become one of America's greatest 19th-century painters.

Whistler's **birthplace** (☎ 978-452-7641; www.whistlerhouse.org; 243 Worthen St; adult/child, senior & student $5/4; ⊙ 11am-4pm Wed-Sun), built in 1823, is now the home of the Lowell Art Association. It contains a permanent collection of the artist's works, and hosts exhibits of works by him, his contemporaries and modern New England artists. Outside, an 8ft bronze statue of the artist, completed by sculptor Mico Kaufman, is at the center of the in-progress Whistler Park and Gardens.

Whistler House is on the west side of the Merrimack Canal, less than two blocks west of the Lowell National Historic Park visitor center.

OTHER MUSEUMS

The **American Textile History Museum** (☎ 978-441-0400; www.athm.org; 491 Dutton St; adult/senior & student $6/4; ⊙ 9am-4pm Mon-Fri, 10am-5pm Sat & Sun) features vintage looms that continue to operate in the weave shed. It's located a block south of the Whistler House.

The **New England Quilt Museum** (☎ 978-452-4207; 18 Shattuck St; adult/senior $5/4; ⊙ 10am-4pm Tue-Sat year-round, noon-4pm Sun May-Dec) has a collection of over 150 antique and contemporary quilts from around New England; it's located a half-block from the Lowell National Historic Park visitor center.

Festivals & Events

Every October, the local non-profit organization **Lowell Celebrates Kerouac** (LCK; ☎ 877-537-6822; lckorg.tripod.com) hosts a weekend of events dedicated to Beat writer Jack Kerouac, featuring tours of many places in his novels, as well as panel discussions, readings, music and poetry. Literature buffs travel from around the world for this unique event.

The **Lowell Folk Festival** (☎ 978-970-5000; www.lowellfolkfestival.org) is three days of food, music (on six stages!), parades and other festivities honoring the diverse multicultural community Lowell has become. It takes place every year at the end of July.

Sleeping

There are not many places to stay in Lowell, nor reasons to stay here. However, if you must spend the night, a few options meet standard needs.

Courtyard Lowell (☎ 978-458-7575; http://marriott.com; 50 Industrial Ave E; r $79-129; ☐ ☎) Although a Marriott Hotel, the Courtyard Lowell manages to maintain a bit of New England charm, with its colonial-style building. Rooms and service are up to snuff, as you would expect.

Doubletree Lowell (☎ 978-452-1200; http://doubletree.hilton.com; 50 Warren St; r from $79) Located in the heart of downtown Lowell overlooking the canals. Some rooms have scenic views of the Merrimac, but all have modern rooms with standard amenities.

Eating & Drinking

Athenian Corner (☎ 978-458-7052; 207 Market St; lunch $7-10, dinner $10-15) Across the street from the Lowell National Historic Park visitor center, this restaurant is a hallmark of Lowell's immigrant Greek community. It offers real-deal Greek specialties, like *faki* (lentil soup), souvlaki and moussaka; finish it off with sticky sweet baklava or creamy rice pudding. Authentic Athens right in Lowell's center.

Quick Pickin's Deli (☎ 978-452-8161; 96 Merrimack St; sandwiches $3-6; ◷ 7am-2pm Mon-Sat) One of the favorite lunch stops for park rangers. With homemade soups and huge sandwiches, it's easy to see why. Walk north on Shattuck St for one long block to Merrimack St and turn right to find this place, opposite John St.

Southeast Asian Restaurant (☎ 978-452-3182; 343 Market St; lunch buffet $7, mains $9-12) Aficionados of Lao, Thai, and Vietnamese cuisines come here from all over New England to feast on truly authentic Asian fare, including the legendary 'bowl of fire' (Lao spicy beef). Southeast Asian vet Joe Antonaccio and his Thai/Lao wife Chanthip have put together one of the most varied collections of delicious recipes from the 'Golden Triangle' west of Chang Mai. The restaurant and associated market are a beacon of culture for Lowell's Southeast Asian immigrants.

Dubliner (☎ 978-458-2120; 197 Market St; mains $5-15) If Lao and Greek are a bit too exotic for your palate, you might prefer a corned beef sandwich and a jar of Guinness from this classic Irish pub. The scene really picks up after 9pm with a local, under-30s crowd.

La Boniche (☎ 978-458-9473; 143 Merrimack St; mains $8-28; ◷ Tue-Sat) This little bistro inspires patrons to rave about the delectable food and attentive service. The two dining rooms in this restored storefront nook fill with scents of French nouvelle cuisine, attracting an upscale crowd for lunch and dinner. The grilled lamb salad rivals the daily quiche for luncheon popularity.

Getting There & Around

Lowell is at the end of the Lowell Connector, a spur road that goes north from MA 3 and I-495.

MBTA commuter rail (☎ 617-722-3200, 800-392-6100) trains depart Boston's North Station for Lowell ($5.25). Trains go in either direction 10 times a day during the week, four times on weekends.

The **Lowell Regional Transit Authority** (☎ 978-452-6161) operates the bus system, including the downtown shuttle buses that link the Gallagher Transportation Terminal and the Downtown Transit Center.

NORTH SHORE

SALEM
pop 40,400

This town's very name conjures up images of diabolical witchcraft and women being burned at the stake. The famous Salem witch trials of 1692 are engrained in the national memory. Indeed, the city of Salem goes all out at Halloween (October 31), when the whole town dresses up for parades and parties, and shops sell all manner of real and ersatz wiccan accessories.

These phenomena obscure Salem's true claim to fame: its glory days as a center for clipper-ship trade with China. The responsible party, Elias Hasket Derby, benefited enormously from his enterprise, eventually becoming America's first millionaire. Derby and his father, Capt Richard Derby, built the 0.5 mile-long Derby Wharf, which is now the center of the Salem Maritime National Historic Site.

Many Salem vessels followed Derby's ship *Grand Turk* around the Cape of Good Hope, and soon the owners founded the East India Marine Society to provide warehousing services for their ships' logs and charts. The new company's charter required the establishment of 'a museum in which to house the natural and artificial curiosities' brought back by members' ships. The collection was the basis for what is now – grown to a half-million artifacts – the world-class Peabody Essex Museum (p146).

Today Salem is a middle-class commuter suburb of Boston with an enviable location on the sea. And its rich history and culture, from witches to ships to art, continue to cast a spell of enchantment on all who visit.

Orientation

Commercial Salem centers around Essex St, a pedestrian mall running east to west from Washington St to the historic Salem Common. One block south, Derby Wharf stretches out into Salem Harbor. The train station is a short walk north of Essex St.

The Heritage Trail is a 1.7-mile route connecting Salem's major historic sites. Follow the red line painted on the sidewalk.

SALEM

AROUND BOSTON

INFORMATION
Bank of America................................1	B4
Central Wharf Visitor Center........2	C3
Destination Salem.........................3	C4
NPS Regional Visitor Center.........4	B3
Post Office.....................................5	B4
Salem Public Library......................6	A3

SIGHTS & ACTIVITIES
Cry Innocent........................(see 9)	
Custom House..............................7	C3
House of the Seven Gables..........8	C3
Old Town Hall...............................9	B3
Peabody Essex Museum...............10	B3
Pickering House...........................11	A4
Salem Trolley Depot....................12	B3
Salem Willows Amusement	
Park..13	E1
Salem Witch Museum..................14	B3
Salem Witch Trials Memorial......15	B3
Stephen Phillips Memorial Trust	
House.....................................16	A3
Waikiki Beach.............................17	F2
West India Goods Store...............18	C3
Witch Dungeon Museum.............19	B3
Witch House...............................20	A3

SLEEPING
Amelia Payson Guest House.......21	B2
Hawthorne Hotel........................22	C3
Inn on Washington Square..........23	A2
Salem Inn....................................24	A3
Salem Waterfront Hotel &	
Suites....................................25	C3

SIGHTS & ACTIVITIES (continued)
Stephen Daniels House...............26	C3
Stepping Stone Inn.....................27	B3
Suzannah Flint House.................28	C3
Winter Island Maritime Park.......29	E2

EATING
Bella Verona...............................30	C3
Brothers.....................................31	B4
Cilantro......................................32	B3
Finz..33	C4
Front Street Coffeehouse............34	B3
Grapevine...................................35	C4
Lyceum Bar & Grill.....................36	B3
Red's Sandwich Shop..................37	B3
Rockmore Floating Restaurant....38	C4
Strega..39	B4
Taste of Cilantro..................(see 32)	

DRINKING
Dodge St....................................40	B4
In a Pig's Eye.............................41	C3
McSwiggin's...............................42	B3
Rockafellas.................................43	B3

TRANSPORT
Shuttle Boat...............................44	C4

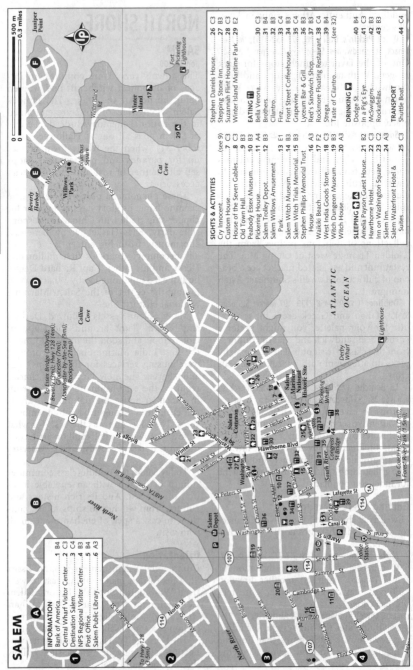

SALEM WITCH TRIALS

In the late 17th century it was widely believed that one could make a pact with the devil in order to gain evil powers to be used against one's enemies. Thousands had been found guilty of witchcraft in Europe in previous centuries. The judges of the Massachusetts Bay Colony had tried 44 persons for witchcraft (hanging three of them) before 1692.

The Reverend Cotton Mather, one of the colony's most fiery preachers, had added his own book on witchcraft to the already considerable literature on the subject. In March 1692 a girl named Betty Parris, who lived in what is now Danvers, and her cousin Abigail began acting strangely. Other children copied their bizarre antics, and their parents came to believe that 'the Devil' had come to their village. (More likely, the girls got hold of a copy of Reverend Mather's book, read how the 'possessed' were thought to behave and acted it out.)

Partly as a prank, the girls accused a slave named Tituba of being a witch. The accused, a half-black, half-Indian woman, 'confessed' under torture and accused two other women of being accomplices, in order to save her own life. Soon the accusations flew thick and fast, as the accused confessed to riding broomsticks, having sex with the devil and participating in witches' sabbaths. They implicated others in attempts to save themselves. The girls, afraid of being discovered as fakes, kept the accusations coming.

Governor Phips appointed a special court to deal with the accusations, but its justices saw fit to accept 'spectral evidence' (evidence of 'spirits' seen only by the witness). With imaginations, superstitions and religious passions enflamed, the situation soon careened out of control.

By September 1692, 156 people stood accused, 55 people had pleaded guilty and implicated others to save their own lives, and 14 women and five men who would not 'confess' to witchcraft had been hanged. Giles Corey, who refused to plead either guilty or not guilty, was pressed to death, and at least four people died in jail of disease.

The frenzy died down when the accusers began pointing at prominent merchants, clergy and even the governor's wife. With the powers-that-be in jeopardy, the trials were called off, the jails were opened and the remaining accused were released. Judges and witnesses confessed to having been misled or having used bad judgment, and the families of many victims were compensated for the injustice.

This cautionary tale of justice gone awry and innocents sacrificed to popular hysteria came powerfully to mind in the 1950s during Senator Joseph R McCarthy's destructive career of ill-considered condemnation and character destruction.

Today the Salem Witch Trials Memorial, a modest monument off Charter St, honors the innocents who died.

Information

Bank of America (193 Washington St; 🕑 9am-4pm Mon-Fri, 9am-2pm Sat)

Central Wharf Visitor Center (☎ 978-740-1660; www.nps.gov/sama; 193 Derby St; admission free; 🕑 9am-5pm)

Destination Salem (☎ 978-744-0004; www.salem .org; 63 Wharf St) The local chamber of commerce visitor center.

Hawthorne in Salem (www.hawthorneinsalem.org) An extensive site with loads of articles about Nathaniel Hawthorne, his life in Salem and his writings about the town.

Historic Salem, Inc (☎ 978-745-0799; www.historic salem.org) A non-profit organization dedicated to architectural preservation in Salem by maintaining a record of 'endangered' architectural resources in the city.

NPS Regional Visitor Center (☎ 978-740-1650; 2 Liberty St; 🕑 9am-5pm)

Post Office (2 Margin St; 🕑 8am-5pm Mon-Fri, 8am-1pm Sat)

Salem Public Library (☎ 978-744-0860; 370 Essex St; 🕑 9am-9pm Mon-Thu, 9am-5pm Fri & Sat year-round, 9am-5pm Sun Jun-Aug) Free Internet access.

Sights & Activities

SALEM MARITIME NATIONAL HISTORIC SITE

This site comprises the custom house, the wharves and the other buildings along Derby St that are remnants of the shipping industry that once thrived along this stretch of Salem. In all, the site comprises 10 different historic locations within a two-block area. Start at the visitor center to pick up a map and to see the informative film *To the Farthest Ports of the Rich East*.

Of the 50 wharves that once lined Salem Harbor, only three remain, the longest of which is **Derby Wharf**. Visitors can stroll out to the end and peek inside the 1871 **lighthouse**. The most prominent building along Derby St is the **Custom House**, where permits and certificates were issued and, of course, taxes paid. Other buildings at the site include warehouses, the scale house, and Elias Hasket Derby's 1762 home. Stop by at the **West India Goods Store**, a working store with spices and other items similar to those sold two centuries ago.

PEABODY ESSEX MUSEUM

All of the art, artifacts and curiosities that Salem merchants brought back from the Far East were the foundation for this **museum** (☎ 866-745-1876, 978-745-1876; www.pem.org; Essex St Mall, New Liberty St; adult/child/senior/student $13/free/11/9; ☻ 10am-5pm). Founded in 1799, it is the country's oldest museum in continuous operation. More importantly, it has recently undergone an extensive $100 million expansion, making it one of the largest museums in New England. The new building itself is impressive, with its light-filled atrium, and is a wonderful setting for the vast collections.

Predictably, the Peabody Essex is particularly strong on Asian art, including pieces from China, Japan, Polynesia, Micronesia and Melanesia. The collection from preindustrial Japan is rated the best in the world. **Yin Yu Tang** is a Chinese house that was shipped to the museum from Huizhou province. Admission to the house is included in your museum entry, but you must obtain a timed ticket for this popular exhibit. The museum also has extensive collections focusing on New England decorative arts and maritime history.

WITCH HOUSE

The tragic events of 1692 have proved a boon to modern operators of Salem witch attractions. The most authentic of more than a score of witchy sites is **Witch House** (☎ 978-744-8815; www.salemweb.com/witchhouse; 310 Essex St; adult/senior/child $7/5/3; ☻ 10am-5pm May-Nov, longer hrs in Oct), operated by the Salem Parks & Recreation Department. This was the home of Jonathan Corwin, a local magistrate who was called on to investigate witchcraft claims. He examined several accused witches, possibly in the 1st-floor rooms of this house.

OTHER WITCHY SITES

The **Salem Witch Museum** (☎ 978-744-1692; www.salemwitchmuseum.com; Washington Sq N; adult/child 6-14/senior $6.50/4.50/6; ☻ 10am-5pm Sep-Jun, 10am-7pm Jul-Aug), housed in a church-like building, has dioramas, exhibits, audiovisual shows and costumed staff who help you to understand the witchcraft scare.

The **Witch Dungeon Museum** (☎ 978-741-3570; 16 Lynde St; adult/child/senior $6/4/5; ☻ 10am-5pm Apr-Nov) stages re-creations of a witch trial based on historical transcripts. **Cry Innocent** (☎ 978-867-4747; www.cryinnocent.com; Old Town Hall; adult/senior & student $8/7; ☻ 11:30am, 1:30pm & 3pm Jun-Aug, Sat & Sun only Sep, 11am & 1pm Oct) is a historical reenactment of the witch trial of Bridget Bishop, in which the audience plays the jury. From the moment you enter Old Town Hall, you are treated like a Puritan living in Salem in 1692.

HOUSE OF SEVEN GABLES

Salem's most famous house is the **House of the Seven Gables** (☎ 978-744-0991; www.7gables.org; 54 Turner St; adult/child/senior $11/7.25/10; ☻ 10am-5pm Nov-Jun, 10am-7pm Jul-Oct), made famous in Nathaniel Hawthorne's 1851 novel of the same name. As he wrote: 'Halfway down a by-street of one of our New England towns stands a rusty wooden house, with seven acutely peaked gables facing towards various points of the compass, and a huge clustered chimney in their midst.' The novel brings to life the gloomy Puritan atmosphere of early New England and its effects on the people's psyches; the house does the same. The admission fee allows entrance to the site's four historic buildings, the Gables Garden Café and luxuriant gardens on the waterfront.

OTHER HISTORIC HOUSES

Lovers of old houses should venture to **Chestnut St**, which is among the most architecturally lovely streets in the country. (Alternatively, follow the McIntire Historic District Walking Trail on p147). One of these stately homes is the **Stephen Phillips Memorial Trust House** (☎ 978-744-0440; www.phillipsmuseum.org; 34 Chestnut St; admission free; ☻ 10am-4pm Mon-Sat Jun-Oct), which displays the family furnishings of Salem sea captains, including a collection of antique carriages and cars.

Furnished in antiques, Salem's **Pickering House** (☎ 978-744-1647; 18 Broad St; admission $4; ☻ 10am-3pm Mon, or by appointment) is said to be the oldest house in the USA continuously occupied by the same family.

The Peabody Essex Museum (p146) also operates three historic houses, which are often rented out for functions but are sometimes open to the public. Contact the museum for information.

PARKS

Less than 2 miles northeast of Salem center is **Salem Willows Amusement Park** (☎ 978-745-0251; 171 Fort Ave; pay per attraction; 10am-11pm Mon-Sat, 11am-11pm Sun Apr-Oct), with beaches, children's rides and games, and harbor cruises. Just south of it is **Winter Island Maritime Park** (☎ 978-745-9430; admission free, parking weekday/weekend $5/10; dawn-dusk), the site of Fort Pickering and its lighthouse. It is now a public park with a campground and the tiny Waikiki Beach (don't get too excited by the name: it's really just wishful thinking). Two miles south of the town center, **Forest River Park** has two beaches, picnic areas and a saltwater swimming pool.

Tours

Pick up a map and description of the following walking tours from any one of the visitors centers. The McIntire Historic District Walking Trail is a 1-mile route that highlights some of Salem's architectural gems, especially the Federal-era homes designed by architect Samuel McIntire.

If you can't get enough of the Salem Maritime National Historic Site, take the self-guided Bowditch's Salem walking tour of the Great Age of Sail. The tour traces the lifelong footsteps of Nathaniel Bowditch, a Salem sailor and author of *The New American Practical Navigator*.

Haunted Footsteps Ghost Tour (☎ 978-745-0666; www.hauntedfootstepsghosttour.com; adult/senior/child $12.50/10/8; dusk May-Nov) Did somebody say murder? This spooky evening – led by lantern light – tells tales of witchcraft and haunted houses. The 90-minute tour departs every evening from the Salem Trolley Depot.

Salem Trolley (☎ 978-744-5469; www.salemtrolley.com; 8 Central St; all-day ticket adult/child 5-14/senior $10/3/9; 10am-5pm daily Apr-Oct, Sat & Sun weather permitting only Mar & Nov) This tour follows a figure-eight route, with a running commentary, past most of the town's places of interest.

Festivals & Events

Everyone in Salem celebrates Halloween, not just the witches. And they celebrate for much of the month of October, when there are special exhibits, parades, concerts, pumpkin carvings, costume parties and trick-or-treating. It all culminates on October 31, with the crowning of the King and Queen of Halloween. Oooh, that's scary. For details, contact **Haunted Happenings** (☎ 877-725-3662; www.hauntedhappenings.org).

Sleeping
BUDGET & MID-RANGE

Salem Waterfront Hotel & Suites (☎ 978-740-8788; www.bwsalem.com; 225 Derby St; r incl breakfast $139-209;) This brand-new Best Western property has a prime location overlooking Pickering Wharf and Salem Harbor. Eighty-six spacious rooms (some of them suites) have graceful decor and all the expected amenities.

Stephen Daniels House (☎ 978-744-5709; 1 Daniels St; r $115) Two blocks north of the waterfront, this must be Salem's oldest lodging, with parts dating from 1667 – before the witch trials. Two walk-in fireplaces grace the common area, and the rooms are filled with period antiques. It is appropriate – in this spooky town – that such an old house be haunted. Rumor has it that a ghost cat roams the ancient halls and has even been known to jump in bed with guests.

Coach House Inn (☎ 978-744-4092, 800-688-8689; www.coachhousesalem.com; 284 Lafayette St; 1-r ste $105-165, 2-r ste $165-205 incl breakfast) This beautiful 1870 Victorian mansion was once the home of a successful sea captain. Now it contains 11 guest rooms, each with a private bath, a four-poster bed and other period details. It's located about a mile south of the town center on MA 1A/MA 114.

Stepping Stone Inn (☎ 978-741-8900; 19 Washington Sq N; r incl breakfast $95-150; closed Dec-Mar) Just off Salem Common, this restored house was built for naval officer Benjamin True in 1846. The eight unique rooms are simply decorated, but they have hardwood floors and some have four-poster beds. Continental breakfast is served in the sunny front room overlooking Washington Sq.

Amelia Payson Guest House (☎ 978-744-8304; www.ameliapaysonhouse.com; 16 Winter St; d with bath incl breakfast $95-125 Apr-Jul, $115-155 Aug-Nov; closed Dec-Mar) This Greek Revival home is decorated with a lot of floral wallpaper, Oriental rugs, rich drapes and ornamental fixtures. It's just steps from Salem Common.

AROUND BOSTON

Winter Island Maritime Park (☎ 978-745-9430; 50 Winter Island Rd; tent/RV sites with electricity $15/30; ☺ May-Oct) Less than 2 miles east of the center of town, this little park has space for 25 tents and 30 RVs. The park is pleasant, but it gets packed in summer.

TOP END

Inn on Washington Square (☎ 978-741-4997; www .washingtonsquareinn.com; 53 Washington Sq N; r incl breakfast $100-200) This tiny place has only three rooms, which are decorated with canopy beds and other period furnishings. The most romantic room is the 'Honeymoon Suite,' fully equipped with a Jacuzzi. Breakfast – which means a basket of homemade muffins – is served in your room.

Hawthorne Hotel (☎ 978-744-4080, 800-729-7829; www.hawthornehotel.com; 18 Washington Sq W; r $104-309) This historic Federalist-style hotel is at the very heart of Salem's center. For years it was the only full-service hotel, with 89 double rooms, a fancy (if staid) restaurant and a cozy pub. Rooms are decked out with reproduction 18th-century furnishings, so you can feel like a wealthy merchant from Salem's glory days. It also operates the Suzannah Flint House, a small B&B in an 1808 Federal House.

Salem Inn (☎ 978-741-0680, 800-446-2995; 7 Summer St; d incl breakfast $119-285) Thirty-three rooms are located in three different historic houses, including the Captain West House, a large brick sea captain's home from 1834. The rooms vary greatly, but they are all individually decorated with antiques, period detail and other charms.

Eating

BUDGET & MID-RANGE

Besides the eateries included here, most of the places listed under Drinking have substantial menus offering pub fare (and more) at mid-range prices.

Brothers (☎ 978-741-4648; 283 Derby St; sandwiches $3-7, mains $6-10; ☺ 6am-9pm Mon-Sat, 6am-8pm Sun) If you are on a tight budget, Brothers is the place for you. Grab a tray and go through the line cafeteria style, choosing breakfast straight off the griddle, a hot dinner, like roast beef or spaghetti and meatballs, or a freshly made sandwich from the deli.

Front Street Coffeehouse (☎ 978-740-6697; 20 Front St) A cool place to sip a caffe latte or munch on a giant sandwich. This is where multipierced urban youth, well-groomed soccer moms and out-of-town visitors all find common ground.

Red's Sandwich Shop (☎ 978-745-3527; 15 Central St; dishes $3-9; ☺ 5am-3pm Mon-Sat, 6am-1pm Sun) This Salem institution has been serving eggs and sandwiches to faithful customers for over 50 years. The food is hearty and basic, but the real attraction is Red's old-school decor, complete with counter service, and friendly faces. It's housed in the old London Coffee House building (1698).

Rockmore Floating Restaurant (☎ 978-740-1001; Pickering Wharf; ☺ 11am-9pm Jun-Aug) That's right: floating. Set on a barge in the middle of Salem Harbor, this clam shack is the ultimate place to refuel on a hot summer day. The food is nothing spectacular, but no place else offers an ocean breeze quite as brisk as this one. Catch the free shuttle boat from the Congress St bridge, but don't forget to tip the captain.

Bella Verona (☎ 978-825-9911; 107 Essex St; mains $8-15; ☺ dinner) This little Italian bistro has only 10 tables, low lights, and walls decorated with the pots and pans of a northern Italian kitchen. It can't be beat for romance, and the pasta is not bad either.

TOP END

Lyceum Bar & Grill (☎ 978-745-7665; 43 Church St; lunch $6-9, dinner $15-25) This historic building has hosted some of America's foremost orators in its lecture halls, from Daniel Webster to Henry David Thoreau. It is most famous, however, as the place where Alexander Graham Bell made his first phone call to his assistant Thomas Watson in 1877. Today the elegant dining room is one of Salem's top dining spots. The New England fare is traditional, but not tired, and service is always excellent.

Finz (☎ 978-774-8485; 76 Wharf St; sandwiches $8, mains $18-25) The highlight is the gracious, spacious dining room with three walls of windows overlooking Salem Harbor. The kitchen keeps customers sated, especially with the char-grilled halibut. The seductive raw bar and carefully chosen wine list are added perks.

Grapevine (☎ 978-745-9335; 26 Congress St; mains $21-27; ☺ 5:30-10pm) Dine alfresco in the lovely flower-filled courtyard or tuck into the romantic dining room. This Mediterranean gem is frequently rated among Boston's best restaurants. The menu changes seasonally, but pasta, seafood and meats are always artfully prepared and presented.

Strega (☎ 978-741-0004; 94 Lafayette St; mains $15-21; ☺ 4pm-12:30am Tue-Sun) Munch on fancy, thin-crust pizza or a sampler of small plates (like white bean puree with warm olives and parmesan crostini) at this elegant Italian affair. The spacious dining room and bar are sumptuous, with low lighting and rich, red drapes – a dark and inviting setting for a romantic dinner or a friendly drink.

Cilantro (☎ 978-745-9436; 282 Derby St; lunch $9-11, dinner $20-22) The North Shore goes south of the border. This is not your mama's Mexican food, though. Cilantro's menu uses inventive dishes like sea bass *al naranjo* (seabass with oranges) or *albondigas al chipotle* (cheese-stuffed meatballs) to draw out the subtle textures and flavors that sometimes get lost in your average taco. For a quicker, less expensive bite, try **A Taste of Cilantro** (☎ 978-745-8928; 282R Derby St; meals $6-10; ☺ 11:30am-2:30pm, 5:30-8pm), located just around the corner.

Drinking

McSwiggins (☎ 978-745-5656; 121 Essex St) If you haven't guessed it yet, every town in Massachusetts (if not the world) has an Irish pub, which guarantees a bowl of beef stew, a pint of Guinness and the ear of a friendly bartender. Salem is no exception, nor is McSwiggins.

In a Pig's Eye (☎ 978-741-4436; 148 Derby St; mains $8-15) This dark, friendly pub boasts an eclectic menu of burgers and beef stroganoff, tasty salads, scallops, ever-popular Mexican fare, and blue plate specials, like mac 'n' cheese. Despite the small space, it has live music (usually acoustic) and even theater performances a few nights a week.

Rockafellas (☎ 978-745-2411; www.rockafellasof salem.com; 231 Essex St; sandwiches $7-11, mains $18-20; ☺ 11:30am-midnight Sun-Wed, 11:30am-1am Thu-Sat) With live entertainment Wednesday through Sunday, this lively restaurant and lounge draws an upscale crowd to kick back and enjoy the semiswanky setting. Music ranges from acoustic to reggae to rock and blues. The menu is all-American, with lots of steaks and sandwiches.

Dodge St (☎ 978-745-0139; 7 Dodge St; ☺ live music 9:30pm) Food is served here, but most people come to suck down a few beers and get their groove on. There's live music, usually rock and blues. If you must eat here, get the ribs.

Getting There & Around

Salem lies 20 miles northeast of Boston, a 35-minute drive on MA 1A (longer during rush hour). Both the Newburyport and Rockport lines of the **MBTA commuter rail** (☎ 617-722-3200, 800-392-6100; www.mbta.com) run from Boston's North Station to Salem Depot ($3.75, 30 minutes). Trains run every 30 minutes during the morning and evening rush hours, hourly during the rest of day, and less on weekends. The MBTA buses No 450 or 455 from Boston's Haymarket Sq (near North Station) take longer than the train and cost no less.

MARBLEHEAD
pop 20,377

First settled in 1629, Marblehead's Old Town is a maritime village with winding streets, brightly painted colonial and Federal houses, and 1000 sailing yachts bobbing at moorings in the harbor. As indicated by the number of boats, this is the Boston area's premier yachting port and one of New England's most prestigious addresses. It has been so for a long time. Incorporated in 1649, citizens of Marblehead boast that their town was the 'birthplace of the navy' because the Marblehead schooner *Hannah* (1775) was the first ship to be commissioned by General George Washington in the Revolutionary War.

Orientation

MA 114 – locally called Pleasant St – passes through modern commercial Marblehead en route to the Marblehead Historic District (Old Town), with its network of narrow, winding, one-way streets. Old Town is difficult to navigate by car and parking can be a challenge. This is definitely a place to explore on foot. Pick up a map from the chamber of commerce information booth (p149). Many restaurants and historic buildings are clustered around the intersection of Pleasant and Washington Sts. From here, State St heads south to the town's main dock and Marblehead Harbor.

Information

Marblehead Chamber of Commerce (www.marble headchamber.org) main office (☎ 781-631-2868; 62 Pleasant St; ☺ 9am-5pm Mon-Fri); information booth (☎ 781-639-8469; cnr Pleasant, Essex & Spring Sts; ☺ noon-5pm Mon-Fri, 10am-5pm Sat & Sun)

Sights & Activities

ABBOTT HALL

Every American is familiar with *The Spirit of '76*, the patriotic painting (c 1876) by Archibald M Willard. It depicts three Revolutionary War figures – a drummer, a fife-player and a flag bearer. The painting hangs in the selectmen's meeting room in **Abbott Hall** (☎ 781-631-0000; Washington Sq, Washington St; admission free; ✆ 9am-4pm, longer hrs in summer), home of the Marblehead Historical Commission. The red-brick building with a lofty clock tower is the seat of Marblehead's town government, and houses artifacts of Marblehead's history, including the original title deed to Marblehead from the Nanapashemet Indians, dated 1684.

HISTORIC HOUSES

The Marblehead Historical Society operates the Georgian **Jeremiah Lee Mansion** (☎ 781-631-1768; 161 Washington St; admission $5; ✆ 10am-4pm Tue-Sat Jun-Oct, gardens open year-round), was built in 1768 on the order of a prominent merchant. It is now a museum with period furnishings, and collections of toys and children's furniture, folk art, and nautical and military artifacts.

Across the street, the **King Hooper Mansion** (☎ 781-631-2608; 8 Hooper St; admission free, donations accepted; ✆ 10am-4pm Mon-Sat, 1-5pm Sun) is the home of the Marblehead Arts Association. The historic 1728 house has four floors of exhibit space, with shows changing monthly.

PARKS

For city dwellers, Marblehead is a lovely, quaint place to come to escape the heat and catch a breeze off the ocean. A myriad of town parks provide an excellent setting for a picnic, stroll or swim.

Steps from State St Landing, hilltop **Crocker Park** provides lovely views of the harbor, not to mention opportunities for swimming and picnicking. Stroll west on Front St from the main town dock.

If instead you walk east on Front St, you will reach **Fort Sewall**, perched on a rocky rise at the mouth of the harbor. The 17th-century fort expanded during the Revolutionary War and is now another pleasant park.

From Pleasant St (MA 114) just south of Marblehead's center, Ocean Ave leads east over a causeway and onto Marblehead Neck, a 2-sq-mile swath of land that juts into the ocean. It is mostly residential and very fancy, with only a few points of public access to the water. On the southeastern side of Marblehead Neck, a short walk takes you to **Castle Rock**, with views of the Boston Ship Channel and Boston's Harbor Islands. At the northern tip of Marblehead Neck, **Chandler Hovey Park**, by Marblehead Light, offers views of Cape Ann and the islands of Salem Bay. The **Audubon Bird Sanctuary** (Ocean Ave; admission free; ✆ sunrise to sunset) is not on the water, but it is a peaceful place for a stroll.

Tours

Participating galleries and historic houses offer a warm welcome to visitors on the **Marblehead Gallery Walk** (☎ 781-639-8469; www.visitmarblehead.com; ✆ 2-4pm May-Oct). Download a map (or pick one up from the chamber of commerce, see p149) before you set out.

Sleeping

Marblehead's dozens of B&Bs cater mostly to weekend visitors (expect higher prices on Saturday and Sunday). None have more than a few rooms, so reservations are essential. You will find a complete list of B&Bs at the chamber of commerce (p149), which will also help with reservations.

A Lady Winette Cottage (☎ 781-631-8579; 3 Corinthian Lane; r $95-115; ✖) This Victorian cottage has two rooms that enjoy private decks, a flower-filled garden and access to a private beach on Marblehead Neck. Turn left at Ocean Ave near the tip of the neck.

Bishops B&B (☎ 781-631-4954; www.bishopsbb.com; 10 Harding Lane; ste $160; ✖) Two spacious suites are decorated with light colors and wicker furniture, resulting in a relaxed beachy atmosphere. Perfect for the prime location on the water. Take Washington St east past the Old Burial Hill and turn right on Harding Lane.

Eagle House B&B (☎ 781-631-1532, 800-572-7335; www.theeaglehouse.com; 96 Front St; r $95-175; ✖) Choose from a two-room suite in this c 1730 house or a one-bedroom guesthouse on the property nearby. One block east of State St Landing, this is the heart of Marblehead's historic district.

Seagull Inn (☎ 781-631-1893; www.seagullinn.com; 106 Harbor Ave; ste incl breakfast $125-250; ✖) This sun-filled inn on Marblehead Neck has three luxury suites, with Shaker furniture, cherry floors, original artwork and ocean views.

Nearby beach access and a glorious garden are added perks. Take Ocean Ave across the Causeway and fork left on Harbor Ave.

Seventeen Chestnut St (☎ 781-631-0941; www.17 chestnutstreet.com; 17 Chestnut St; r with shared bath $80; ⊠) This hospitable house has two tiny guest rooms on the 2nd floor. It's a few blocks from Marblehead center, but not far from the beach. The shared bath facilities make this place relatively cheap by Marblehead standards. Take Essex St to Atlantic Ave and turn left on Chestnut St.

If you are finding there's 'no room at the inn,' **Harbor Light Inn** (☎ 781-631-2186; www.harbor lightinn.com; 58 Washington St; r $125-275; ⊠) and **Marblehead Inn** (☎ 781-630-0000; www.marblehead inn.com; 264 Pleasant St; r $119-219; ⊠) are larger, more modern properties with amenities like fireplaces and Jacuzzis.

Eating & Drinking

Crosby's Market (☎ 781-631-1741; 118 Washington St; deli $2-7; ⏱ 9am-9pm) Visit this large, upscale market in Old Town for all of your picnic needs, including wine and beer. Its extensive deli is rife with the scent of freshly baked pumpernickel, dill pickles and roasted veggie salad.

Driftwood Cafe (☎ 781-631-1145; 63 Front St; dishes $3-7; ⏱ 5:30am-2pm) Right near State St Landing, this inexpensive café in a frame shack is a Marblehead fixture, serving hearty mariners' breakfasts to early risers.

Maddie's Sail Loft (☎ 781-631-9824; 15 State St; lunch $8-12, dinner $12-18) The place to come for local color. Set in a historic house, old-timers pack into this little pub to wolf down fried seafood and swill some beers. It's one block inland from State St Landing.

Barnacle (☎ 781-631-4236; 141 Front St; lunch $5-9, dinner $10-14) Perched on a rocky outcropping at the harbor's edge, the Barnacle is what waterside dining is meant to be. Specialties include steaming hot clam chowder and lobsters straight off the boat. Excellent outdoor seating.

Jack Tar (☎ 781-631-2323; 126 Washington St; sandwiches $8, mains $12-17) Cheery colors and natural light brighten up the basement setting, which is a cozy place to come for a drink or a meal. But in summer you won't want to miss out on the large outdoor patio. This place boasts 'creative takes on traditional dishes,' including reliably tasty brick-oven pizza, homemade pasta and seafood dishes.

Landing (☎ 781-631-1878; 81 Front St; lunch $9-18, dinner $20-40) The atmosphere is staid, but the setting is the draw at this classic seafood restaurant overlooking the harbor. Choose from the full-service restaurant or the pub, which has lighter fare. Either way, don't expect anything too exciting: just sit back and enjoy the view.

Pellino's (☎ 781-631-3344; 261 Washington St; mains $16-25; ⏱ 5-10pm) 'Quaint' is the operative word at this tiny family-run trattoria. The constantly changing menu of regional Italian treats and the excellent wine list make this a North Shore favorite.

Getting There & Away

From Salem, follow MA 114 southeast 4 miles to Marblehead, where it becomes Pleasant St. MBTA bus Nos 441/442 and 448/449 run between Boston's Haymarket Sq (near North Station) and Marblehead. For information on MBTA trains to neighboring Salem, see p149. From Salem's train station, you can take a taxi ($8) to Marblehead.

CAPE ANN

pop 38,000

Lesser known than its sister Cape Cod at the southern end of Massachusetts Bay, Cape Ann is nonetheless a deservedly popular destination for day-trippers, weekend travelers and summer escapists coming from Boston. Cape Ann offers a combination of natural beauty, maritime history and New England charm that is hard to resist.

Founded in 1623 by English fisherfolk, **Gloucester** is among New England's oldest towns. This port on Cape Ann has made its living from fishing for almost 400 years, and inspired books and films like Rudyard Kipling's *Captains Courageous* and Sebastian Junger's *The Perfect Storm*. And despite recent economic diversification, this town still smells of fish. You can't miss the fishing boats, often operated by Italian or Portuguese immigrants, festooned with nets, dredges and winches, tied to the wharves or motoring into the harbor with clouds of hungry seagulls hovering above.

Meanwhile, at the northern tip of Cape Ann, **Rockport** is a quaint contrast to gritty Gloucester. Rockport takes its name from its 19th-century role as a shipping center for granite cut from the local quarries. The stone is still ubiquitous: monuments, building

AROUND BOSTON

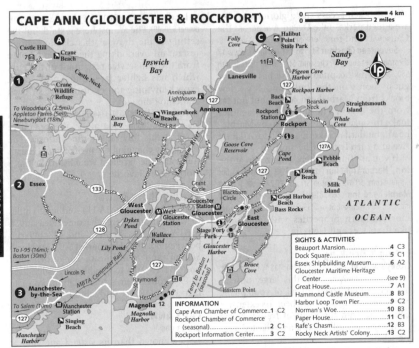

CAPE ANN (GLOUCESTER & ROCKPORT)

SIGHTS & ACTIVITIES
Beauport Mansion.........................**4** C3
Dock Square...............................**5** C1
Essex Shipbuilding Museum..........**6** A2
Gloucester Maritime Heritage
  Center.................................(see **9**)
Great House..............................**7** A1
Hammond Castle Museum...........**8** B3
Harbor Loop Town Pier...............**9** C2
Norman's Woe...........................**10** B3
Paper House.............................**11** C1
Rafe's Chasm...........................**12** B3
Rocky Neck Artists' Colony.........**13** C2

INFORMATION
Cape Ann Chamber of Commerce..**1** C2
Rockport Chamber of Commerce
  (seasonal)..............................**2** C1
Rockport Information Center........**3** C2

foundations, pavements and piers remain as a testament to Rockport's past.

That's about all that remains of this industrial history, however. A century ago, Winslow Homer, Childe Hassam, Fitz Hugh Lane and other acclaimed artists came to Rockport's rugged shores, inspired by the hearty fisherfolk who wrested a hard, but satisfying, living from the sea. The artists started attracting tourists and that's all she wrote. Today Rockport makes its living from tourists who come to look at the artists. The artists have long since given up looking for hearty fishermen because the descendants of the fishers are all running boutiques and B&Bs.

Orientation

Washington St runs from Grant Circle (a rotary out on MA 128) into the center of Gloucester at St Peter's Sq, an irregular brick plaza overlooking the sea. Rogers St, the waterfront road, runs east and west from the plaza; Main St, the business and shopping thoroughfare, is one block inland. East Gloucester, with the Rocky Neck art-

ists' colony, is on the southeastern side of Gloucester Harbor.

Rockport is just up Rte 127 (or Rte 127A if you prefer the scenic route). The center of town is Dock Sq, at the beginning of Bearskin Neck. Parking in Rockport is difficult on summer weekends. Unless you arrive very early, you'd do well to park at one of the lots on MA 127 from Gloucester and take the shuttle bus to Rockport's center.

Information

Cape Ann Chamber of Commerce (☎ 978-283-1601, 800-321-0133; www.capeannvacations.com; 33 Commercial St, Gloucester; ⏲ 8am-5:30pm Mon-Fri, 10am-6pm Sat, 10am-4pm Sun) South of St Peter's Sq.

Gloucester Cooperative Bank (☎ 978-283-8200; 160 Main St, Gloucester; ⏲ 8:30am-3:30pm Mon-Wed, 8:30am-7pm Thu, 8:30am-5pm Fri, 8:30am-1pm Sat)

Post Office (15 Dale Ave, Gloucester; ⏲ 8am-5pm Mon-Fri, 8am-noon Sat)

Rockport Chamber of Commerce (☎ 978-546-6575, 888-726-3922; www.rockportusa.com; 22 Broadway, Rockport; ⏲ 9am-5pm Mon-Sat Apr-Oct, 11am-2pm Mon, Wed & Fri Nov-Mar) On T Wharf just off Mt Pleasant St. A seasonal branch is located 1 mile out of town on Rte 127.

A PERFECT OPPORTUNITY?

In 1991 the fishing boat *Andrea Gail* headed out to sea and immortality, when it encountered the perfect storm. With dawn breaking and George Clooney at the helm, the Gloucester fisherman never looked better, even though disaster loomed just ahead. In a way, this Hollywood image captures more than just the tragic fate of the crew of the *Andrea Gail*, as the proud Gloucester fishing industry itself struggles against seemingly insurmountable forces.

The oldest seaport in the country, Gloucester supported a thriving fishing industry for more than three centuries. Generation after generation of Gloucester fishermen plied the Atlantic Grand Banks for groundfish, such as cod, haddock and flounder. In the days of sail, they used baited lines and salt to preserve the catch. Gloucester boasted one of the largest fleets in the world, with over 400 boats and an extensive processing and support industry along the waterfront.

In the 1900s the industry shifted to steam trawlers with rigged netting. The ships and nets became bigger and bigger, and more and more numerous. Gloucester boats were slow to catch up to the changing technology. As early as 1930 biologists cautioned against over-fishing and warned against the long-term dangers of the new techniques. But it took several decades before the industry began to be regulated.

To protect the industry, the US government extended its claim of coastal waters from 12 to 200 miles. The measure enabled Gloucester to make a brief recovery in the 1980s, but it was not to last. The relentless use of industrial trawling drag nets has now destroyed much of the bottom habitat that sustained the Atlantic groundfish. When the government acted next, it was to curtail the allowable take with the hope of recovery. As the stocks of groundfish dwindled, it was the Gloucester fisherman who was becoming an endangered species.

With the fishing industry in decline, gritty Gloucester is looking to clean itself up as a tourist destination. A part of the old docks is now open to visitors. Whale-watching boats bob in place of the fishing trawlers along the pier. And *The Perfect Storm* has become, perhaps, the perfect opportunity, attracting a stream of film fans who want to have a beer at the Crow's Nest and study the roll call of 'those who have gone to the sea in ships.' Peering out at the quiet harbor, the mystique of the stoic Gloucester fisherman survives.

See Cape Ann (www.seecapeann.com) Cape Ann's online information booth.

Toad Hall Bookstore (☎ 978-546-7323; 51 Main St, Rockport) Socially responsible reading: buy your books here and the shop donates some of its income to environmental projects.

Sights

DOCK SQUARE & BEARSKIN NECK

Dock Sq is the hub of Rockport. Visible from here, the red fishing shack decorated with colorful buoys is known as **Motif No 1**. So many artists of great and minimal talent have been painting and photographing it for so long that it well deserves its tongue-in-cheek name. Actually, it should be called Motif No 1-B, as the original shack vanished during a great storm in 1978 and a brand-new replica was erected in its place. Check out the **gallery** on Bearskin Neck that sells renditions of Motif No 1 as portrayed by an impressionist, expressionist, cubist, Dadaist and just about every other artistic school.

Bearskin Neck is the peninsula that juts into the harbor, lined with galleries, lobster shacks, and souvenir shops. The name 'Bearskin Neck' apparently comes from a historic account of a young boy who was attacked by a bear. In attempt to save the boy, his uncle, Ebenezer Babson, went after the bear with the only weapon he had available at the time – his fish knife. Babson managed to kill the bear and save the child, and then he skinned the bear and laid the pelt on the rocks to dry. The legend lives on in rhyme: 'Babson, Babson, killed a bear, with his knife, I do declare.'

ROCKY NECK ARTISTS COLONY

For more than a century, Cape Ann's rocky coast and fishing fleet have attracted artists like Winslow Homer and Fitz Hugh Lane. This legacy endures, as Gloucester still boasts a vibrant artists community. The narrow peninsula of Rocky Neck, jutting into Gloucester Harbor from East Gloucester, offers inspiring views of the ocean and

AROUND BOSTON

the harbor. Between WWI and WWII, artists began renting little seaside shacks from local fisherfolk, which they used as studios. Today many of these same shanties, considerably gentrified, are **galleries** (☾ 10am-10pm), displaying the work of local artists. One of the galleries is operated by the **North Shore Arts Association** (☎ 978-283-1857; www.northshoreartsassoc .org; 197 East Main St, Pirate's Lane).

Follow Main St east and south around the northeastern end of Gloucester Harbor to East Gloucester. Turn onto Rocky Neck Ave and park in the lot on the right (parking further on in the village proper is nearly impossible in high summer).

GLOUCESTER MARITIME HERITAGE CENTER

Visit Gloucester's **working waterfront** (☎ 978-281-0471; www.gloucestermaritimecenter.org; Harbor Loop, Gloucester; admission by donation, Sea Pocket Lab adult/child/senior $5/2/4; ☾ 10am-5:30pm daily Jun-Aug, Sat & Sun only Sep-Oct) and see the ongoing restoration of wooden boats, watch the operation of a marine railway that hauls ships out of the water, and compare the different kinds of fishing boats that were used over the years. **Sea Pocket Lab** is a hands-on outdoor aquarium with exhibits on local marine habitats. It is a great chance for kids to get down and dirty with sea stars, sea urchins, snails, crabs and seaweed. The **schooner Adventure**, the last dory trawler fishing the Atlantic, is moored here. From the Grant Circle rotary, take Washington St to its terminus. Turn left on Rogers St to Harbor Loop.

Don't leave Gloucester without paying your respects at **St Peter's Sq**. Here stands Leonarde Craske's famous statue, *The Gloucester Fisherman*, often called 'The Man at the Wheel.' The statue is dedicated to 'They That Go Down to the Sea in Ships, 1623–1923.'

CAPE ANN HISTORICAL MUSEUM

This tiny **museum** (☎ 978-283-0455; www.capeann historicalmuseum.org; 27 Pleasant St, Gloucester; adult/student/senior $6.50/4.50/6; ☾ 10am-5pm Tue-Sat Mar-Jan) is a gem – particularly for its impressive collection of paintings by Gloucester native Fitz Hugh Lane. Exhibits also showcase the region's granite quarrying industry and – of course – its maritime history. The museum is in the heart of downtown Gloucester, just north of Main St.

BEAUPORT MANSION

The lavish 'summer cottage' of interior designer Henry Davis Sleeper is known as **Beauport Mansion** (☎ 978-283-0800; www.historic newengland.org; 75 Eastern Point Blvd, Eastern Point, East Gloucester; admission $10; ☾ 10am-4pm Mon-Fri mid-May–mid-Sep, daily mid-Sep–mid-Oct), or the Sleeper-McCann mansion. Sleeper was a prominent interior designer and collector of antiques, and he worked to make his fantasy palace a showplace of American decor. He toured New England in search of houses about to be demolished and bought up selected elements from each: wood paneling, architectural elements and furniture. In place of unity, Sleeper created a wildly eclectic but artistically surprising – and satisfying – place to live. Now in the care of the Society for the Preservation of New England Antiquities, Beauport is open to visitors. Beauport also holds afternoon teas, evening concerts and other special events.

HAMMOND CASTLE MUSEUM

Dr John Hays Hammond, Jr (1888–1965) was an electrical engineer whose inventions were important to the development of radar, sonar and radio remote-control systems, including torpedo guidance. Despite his genius with electrical things, it was not Dr John, but rather Laurens Hammond (unrelated), who invented the electric organ.

Defense contracts filled his bank account, and with this wealth Hammond pursued his passion for collecting European art and architecture. His eccentric home is a castle with four sections, each epitomizing a period in European history: Romanesque, medieval, Gothic and Renaissance. Furnishings, including an 8200-pipe organ in the Romanesque Great Hall, are eclectic, quirky and, at times, beautiful. The **museum** (☎ 978-283-2080; www.hammondcastle.org; 80 Hesperus Ave, Magnolia; admission $7; ☾ 10am-5pm Apr-Oct) offers a 90-minute guided tour as part of the entrance fee.

Hammond Castle overlooks several natural features famous in literature. **Rafe's Chasm** is a cleft in the rocky shoreline that is characterized by turgid and thrashing water. Near it is **Norman's Woe**, the reef on which the ship broke up in Longfellow's poem 'The Wreck of the Hesperus.'

PAPER HOUSE

Inland from Pigeon Cove is the **Paper House** (☎ 978-546-2629; 52 Pigeon Hill St; admission by donation; ⏳ 10am-5pm Apr-Oct), a curiosity begun in 1922 when Elis F Stenman decided something useful should be done with all those daily newspapers lying about. He and his family set to work folding, rolling and pasting the papers into suitable shape as building materials.

Twenty years and 100,000 newspapers later, the house was done. The walls are 215 layers thick, the furnishings – table, chairs, lamps, sofa, even a grandfather clock and a piano – are all made of newspaper. Some pieces even specialize: one desk is made from Christian Science Monitor reports of Charles Lindbergh's flight, and the fireplace mantel is made from rotogravures drawn from the Boston *Sunday Herald* and the New York *Herald Tribune*. On all of the papers in the house, the text is still readable.

BEACHES

Gloucester has several excellent beaches that draw thousands of Boston-area sun-and-sea worshippers on any hot day in July or August. All of these beaches get crowded, especially on weekends, so plan on arriving early.

Perhaps biggest and best of all is **Wingaersheek Beach** (parking Mon-Fri/Sat & Sun $25/15), a wide swath of sand surrounded by Ipswich Bay, the Annisquam River and lots of sand dunes. Facilities include showers, toilets and refreshments. At low tide, a long sandbar stretches for more than 0.5 miles out into the bay, providing a clear view of the Annisquam lighthouse at its tip. Take Rte 128 to Exit 13. Turn left on Concord St and right on Atlantic St.

Good Harbor Beach (parking Mon-Fri/Sat & Sun $25/15) is a spacious, sandy beach east of East Gloucester off MA 127A on the way to Rockport. Parking is very limited here, which has its advantages and disadvantages. Fortunately, the parking lot fills up before the beach does, so if you get here early enough, you will enjoy the minimal crowds all day long. If you are late, you will be turned away at the parking lot.

There are two lovely, small beaches at **Stage Fort Park** (☎ 978-281-8865; parking $10): the picturesque Half-Moon Beach and the more remote Cressy's Beach. The latter is a bit of a trek from the parking lot, but worth it to get away from the other bathing beauties. The park itself is an attractive, well-maintained recreation area with picnic tables, playgrounds and hiking trails.

HALIBUT POINT STATE PARK

Only a few miles north of Dock Sq along MA 127 is **Halibut Point State Park** (☎ 978-546-2997; www.halibutpointstatepark.com; admission per person $2, per car $5; ⏳ sunrise to sunset). A 10-minute walk through the forest brings you to yawning, abandoned granite quarries, huge hills of broken granite rubble, and a granite foreshore of tumbled, smoothed rock perfect for picnicking, sunbathing, reading or painting. The surf can be strong here, making swimming unwise, but natural pools can be good for wading or cooling your feet. Park rangers lead nature walks, explaining the marine life in tidal pools, the working of granite quarries, the local bird life and the area's edible plants.

GOOSE COVE RESERVOIR

Much of the interior of Cape Ann is given over to reservations to preserve the unique ecological habitat of this area. Goose Cove is an Essex County reservation on the eastern side of the Cape. It consists of 26 acres of woodland, rocky shoreline and tidal mudflats. This beautiful area is home to many types of herons, ducks and egrets, not to mention mammals, like fishers and otters. The parking lot is off Washington St (Rte 127) heading north from Gloucester to Lanesville. Trails lead from the parking lot to the water's edge.

Activities
WHALE-WATCHING

Cruises from Gloucester visit Stellwagen Bank Marine Sanctuary, 842 sq miles of open ocean that are rich in marine life. Most companies charge $34/28/20 per adult/senior/child. Whale-watching cruises usually depart several times a day in summer, but only once a day or perhaps only on weekends in April, May, September and October. Reservations are recommended. Try the following outfits:

Cape Ann Whale Watch (☎ 978-283-5110, 800-877-5110; www.caww.com; Rose's Wharf, 415 Main St) Cruises depart from Rose's Wharf, east of Gloucester center (on the way to East Gloucester).

Capt Bill & Sons Whale Watch (☎ 978-283-6995, 800-339-4253; www.captainbillswhalewatch.com; 33 Harbor Loop) The boat leaves from behind Captain Carlo's Seafood Market & Restaurant.

Seven Seas Whale Watch (☎ 978-283-1776, 800-238-1776; www.7seas-whalewatch.com; Rogers St) Seven Seas vessels depart from Rogers St in the center of Gloucester, between St Peter's Sq and the Gloucester House Restaurant.

Yankee Whale Watch (☎ 978-283-0313, 800-942-5464; www.yankeefleet.com; 75 W Essex Ave/MA 133) The Yankee fleet ties up at the dock next door to the Gull Restaurant on MA 133 (MA 128 exit 14).

OTHER WATER ACTIVITIES

Dove's Lobstering & Island Cruises (☎ 978-546-3642; T Wharf; adult/child $10/6, islands $8/5) takes passengers out lobstering for 90 minutes on the 38ft *Dove*, while the afternoons are reserved for hour-long cruises around the islands.

Essex River Adventures (☎ 978-768-3722; www .erba.com; 66R Main St, Essex; tours $25-70) offers basic kayak instruction, as well as paddling tours of the islands and bays.

North Shore Kayak Outdoor Center (☎ 978-546-5050; www.northshorekayak.com; 9 Tuna Wharf; kayaks per day $30-45, bikes per day $16) rents kayaks and bikes, and offers tours.

Rockport Castaway Charters (☎ 978-546-3959; www.rockportcastaways.com) offers full and half-day fishing trips.

Tours

Harbor Tours Inc (☎ 978-283-1979; Harbor Loop; adult/ child $10/5; ☒ 2:30pm Sat & Sun May, 10am & 2:30pm daily Jun-Aug, 10am & 2:30pm Sat & Sun Sep-Oct) Does a complete loop around Cape Ann, Straightsmouth Island, Halibut Point and down the Annisquam River.

Schooner Thomas E Lannon (☎ 978-281-6634; www .schooner.org; Rogers St) This 65ft schooner is the spit and image of the Gloucester fishing schooners. It leaves on two-hour sails from the Seven Seas wharf.

Festivals & Events

The annual **St Peter's Festival** in Gloucester honors the patron saint of fisherfolk on a weekend in late June. The carnival at St Peter's Sq usually features rides, snacks, musical performances and special events, such as a greased pole-climbing competition and boat races. The main event is the procession through the streets of a statue of St Peter. Customarily, the cardinal of the Catholic Archdiocese of Boston attends to bless the fishing fleet. Contact the Cape Ann Chamber of Commerce (p152) for details.

The annual Independence Day **Horribles Parade** takes place every year in Gloucester on the evening of July 3. By tradition, children dress up in fanciful costumes (from horrible to humorous) and compete for prizes. Politicians and local businesses enter floats, and various bands perform.

The **Rockport Chamber Music Festival** (☎ 978-546-7391; www.rcmf.org; 2 Main St) hosts at least 16 concerts by internationally acclaimed performers. Most concerts take place in the Rockport Art Association gallery from mid-June to early July.

Sleeping

BUDGET

Gray Manor (☎ 978-283-5409; 14 Atlantic Rd, East Gloucester; r $70-80; ☒ May-Sep) Just a three-minute walk from popular Good Harbor Beach, this spot has three rooms and six efficiencies. All rooms in this classic summer house have fridge, TV and private bath. They lack the high style or old-fashioned charm of some of the other inns, but they're quite a bargain for the locale.

Tuck Inn (☎ 978-546-7260, 800-789-7260; www.tuck inn.com; 17 High St, Rockport; r $80-125, ste $130-155 incl breakfast; ☒) This inn is a recently renovated 1790s colonial home with nine rooms and a four-person suite offering excellent value. Elegant public rooms feature period decor. Local artwork and homemade quilts are some of the little touches that make the rooms special. The breakfast buffet – complete with fresh, seasonal fruit salads, and fresh-baked muffins and pastries – will be a highlight of your stay.

Lantana House (☎ 978-546-3535, 800-291-3535; 22 Broadway, Rockport; d & tw $89-99) Conveniently located, Lantana House has some of the least-expensive rooms in Rockport. The wide, airy porch and sundeck are wonderful places to have breakfast in the morning or a rest in the afternoon.

Carlson's B&B (☎ 978-546-2770; 43 Broadway, Rockport; d incl breakfast $80-100) Spend the night in the gracious Victorian home of prominent local artist Carol Carlson. Prices include a fabulous gourmet breakfast.

Cape Ann Campsite (☎ 978-283-8683; www.cape anncampsite.com; 80 Atlantic St; per car incl 2 people $20-26, per additional person $8, electricity $8; ☒ May-Oct) If you want to pitch your pup on 50 wooded, hilltop acres, this is your place. Two hundred unique campsites, with lots of shade and privacy.

MID-RANGE

Every year B&Bs open around Cape Ann, bringing a new level of character and value to accommodations. You can search out this emerging market at www.capeannvacations.com or www.innsofrockport.com.

Addison Choate Inn (☎ 978-546-7543, 800-245-7543; www.addisonchoateinn.com; 49 Broadway; r incl breakfast $110-165; ✗ ⌨) This Greek revival residence stands out among Rockport's historic inns. The traditional decor includes canopy beds, wide plank hardwood floors and period wallpaper. The two suites (with kitchenettes) in the carriage house are particularly appealing, with cathedral ceilings and exposed beam ceilings.

Inn on Cove Hill (☎ 978-546-2701; www.innoncovehill.com; 37 Mt Pleasant St, Rockport; r $100-165; ✗) This is a Federal-style house built in 1791 with, so they say, pirates' gold discovered nearby. It has been lovingly restored down to the tiniest detail. Doubles have wide-plank hardwood floors, ornate moldings and canopy beds. The location, a block from Dock Sq, is hard to beat.

Julietta House (☎ 978-281-2300; www.juliettahouse.com; 84 Prospect St, Gloucester; r incl breakfast $95-140; ✗) Steps from Gloucester Harbor, this grand Georgian house has five light-filled rooms with period furnishings and private bathrooms.

White House (☎ 978-525-3642; www.whitehouseofmagnolia.com; 18 Norman Ave, Magnolia; r $105-145) This Victorian Inn has 10 rooms ornately decorated with floral comforters, curtains and wallpapers. If the flower-filled decor gets a little overbearing, step outside onto the shady porch or wander through the lovely gardens.

Bulfinch House (☎ 978-546-9656; www.bulfinchhouse.com; 96 Granite St, Rockport; r $125-160; ✗) This classic Federal-style home was designed by Massachusetts' most famous architect, Charles Bulfinch. The house maintains an old-fashioned feel throughout, with lace curtains and floral linens. All five rooms have private bathroom and water views, while two have access to a grand porch. It's about 1 mile north of Rockport center on Rte 127.

Sally Webster Inn (☎ 978-546-9251, 877-546-9251; www.sallywebster.com; 34 Mt Pleasant St, Rockport; r with bathroom $85-135) This handsome brick colonial, built in 1832, offers eight rooms with early-American decor. Many have working fireplaces, and all have authentic architectural details and period furniture. Well-groomed flowerbeds and cool ocean breezes make the terrace a wonderful respite.

Linden Tree Inn (☎ 978-546-2494, 800-865-2122; 26 King St, Rockport; r incl breakfast $105-130; ✗) Built as a single-family mansion in 1870, this Victorian inn now offers 12 guest rooms with private bathrooms and antique furniture. There are four suites with kitchenette in the carriage house. The owners show off their Anglo roots with scrumptious home-made scones for breakfast. It's just north of Rockport center off Rte 127.

Bearskin Neck Motor Lodge (☎ 978-546-6647; 64 Bear Skin Neck, Rockport; d $99-149; ✗) The only lodging on Bearskin Neck is this motel-style lodge near the end of the strip. Needless to say, every room has a great view – and a balcony from where you can enjoy it. Otherwise, the rooms are fairly simple, but comfortable enough.

Cape Ann Motor Inn (☎ 978-281-2900; www.capeannmotorinn.com; 33 Rockport Rd, Gloucester; $75-145; ✗) A great location halfway between Rockport and Gloucester, and right on Long Beach. All rooms feature glass sliding doors that open onto private balconies with ocean views.

Captain's Bounty Motor Inn (☎ 978-546-9557; 1 Beach St, Rockport; r $100-130; ✗) The draw is the prime location, right on Front Beach and only a few minutes' stroll from Dock Sq. The 24 rooms are simple, but they all have lovely views of the sunrise over the beach and the local lobstermen checking their traps.

Sandy Bay Motor Inn (☎ 978-546-7155, 800-437-7155; www.sandybaymotorinn.com; 183 Main St, Rockport; r $100-150; ✗ ⌨) Rates fluctuate tremendously from season to season, but you can always rely on comfortable, basic rooms and nicely landscaped grounds. Adjoining suites, swimming pool and restaurant make this a convenient place for families. It is less than 2 miles inland along MA 127.

From the terminus of MA 128, take Bass Ave east to Atlantic Rd to find the following sea-view motels.

Ocean View Resort & Inn (☎ 978-283-6200, 800-315-7557; www.oceanviewinnandresort; 171 Atlantic Rd, East Gloucester; r $100-225; ✗ ⌨) An innovative combination of inn and resort. Comfortable rooms and great facilities are housed in lovely Tudor mansions.

Atlantis Motor Inn (☎ 978-283-0014, 800-732-6313; www.atlantismotorinn.com; 125 Atlantic Rd, East Gloucester; r $90-150; ✗ ⌨) A large motel-style facility with standard rooms and a decent café.

Eating & Drinking
GLOUCESTER

Virgilio's Italian Bakery (☎ 978-283-5295; 29 Main St; sandwiches $1-6) Primarily a take-out joint, Virgilio's has excellent sandwiches and other Italian treats. Try the famous St Joseph sandwich – like an Italian sub on a fresh-baked roll. Pick one up and head down to the waterfront for a picnic.

Maria's Pizza (☎ 978-283-7373; 35 Pearl St; pizzas $10-15) Gloucester's favorite pizzeria is across from the train station. Crunchy-crust pizza, fried seafood and thick clam chowder will sate any appetite. Bring your own beer from the 'packy' across the street.

Two Sisters (☎ 978-281-3378; 27 Washington St) This local place is where the fisherfolk go for breakfast when they come in from their catch.

White Rainbow (☎ 978-281-0017; 65 Main St; dinner $35-50; 🕐 5-10:30pm) For elegant dining, this restaurant serves dinner in a cozy brick-lined basement dining room. The menu lists classic main courses – steak, roast duckling, rack of lamb, grilled shrimp. Gloucester gentry come here to see and be seen. Call for reservations.

Franklin Cape Ann (☎ 978-283-7888; 118 Main St; mains $15-20; 🕐 5pm-1am Jun-Sep, 5-11:30pm Sun-Thu, 5pm-1am Fri & Sat Oct-May, kitchen closes 1 hr earlier) The North Shore branch of a South End favorite (see p110), this cool place has an urban atmosphere and an excellent, modern New American menu.

The Rudder (☎ 978-283-7967; 73 Rocky Neck Ave; mains $12-20) Housed in a neat little lobster-man's shack, this is a great date restaurant. Dine in the intimate basement, or on a small waterfront deck with candlelight and jazz on weekends. The food is satisfactory, but the real draw is the atmosphere.

Blackburn Tavern (☎ 978-282-1919; 2 Main St; dishes $5-13; 🕐 11:30am-9:30pm) On the corner of Washington St, this upscale saloon has a cozy bar area and a varied menu. Live music on weekends (Thursday to Saturday) and decent food make this a popular North Shore entertainment spot.

Crow's Nest (☎ 978-281-2965; 334 Main St) The down-and-dirty fisherfolk bar made famous in *The Perfect Storm*. But this is the real McCoy, not the set the movie folks threw up for a few weeks during filming. Come early if you want to drink with the fish crews. It gets crowded with tourists in summer.

You really can't go wrong at any of these local lobster shacks:

The Causeway (☎ 978-281-5256; Essex Ave) Huge portions in a rustic setting.

Lobsta Land (☎ 978-281-0415; 10 Causeway St) Fresh lobster and crispy fried clams.

McT's Lobster House & Tavern (☎ 978-282-0950; 25 Rogers St) Seafood and barbecue right on the waterfront.

ROCKPORT

Dock Sq, at the beginning of Bearskin Neck, has several cafés. And Bearskin Neck is crowded with ice-cream stores, cafés and cozy restaurants. As you walk out the neck, you'll pass several small wharf buildings where you can catch a bowl of chowder, fish-and-chips, and relatively cheap lobster. Many places reduce hours or close completely for the winter. Eateries listed here are open for lunch and dinner unless noted.

Pigeon Cove Lobster Co (☎ 978-546-3000; Granite St) If your lodging includes kitchen facilities, considering the ultimate New England culinary experience: buying your lobsters live and boiling them yourselves. Head to Pigeon Cove for live lobsters straight from the trap and piping-hot, award-winning clam chowder. This is where the fishers are unloading their daily catch from their boats and – if you wish – into your pot.

Helmut's Strudel (☎ 978-546-2824; 69 Bearskin Neck; desserts $2-5) For coffee or tea and dessert, try this bakery, almost near the outer end, serving various strudels, filled croissants, pastries, cider and coffee. Four shaded tables overlook the yacht-filled harbor.

Hula Moon Café (☎ 978-456-5185; 27 Mt Pleasant St; dishes $3-15) This little place has some of the best bargains in the village. The emphasis is on imaginative Hawaiian-style cuisine: think pork and pineapple. Vegetarians can chow down on ultratasty, ultracheap veggie sandwiches.

Top Dog (☎ 978-546-0006; Bearskin Neck; dogs $3-6; 🕐 11am-6pm Mon-Thu, 11am-8pm Fri & Sat) More than a dozen kinds of dogs, from a Shaggy Dog (with fresh coleslaw and barbecue sauce) to a Chihuahua (with jalapenos, salsa and cheese).

Ellen's Harborside (☎ 978-546-2512; 1 Wharf Rd; breakfast $3-6, mains $8-20; 🕐 6am-9pm) By the T-wharf in the center of town, Ellen's has grown famous serving a simple menu of American breakfasts, chicken, ribs and lobster since 1954. You get decent portions, fresh food and low prices. Consider the classic Cubano sandwich, oven-baked with ham, Swiss, pickles and French bread ($6).

Roy Moore Lobster Company (☎ 978-546-6696; 29 Bearskin Neck; dishes $3-16) This takeout kitchen has the cheapest lobster-in-the-rough (around $11) on the Neck. Your beast comes on a tray with melted butter, a fork and a wet wipe for cleanup. You can sit in the back with the fishing boats on a few tables fashioned from lobster traps.

Roy Moore's Fish Shack Restaurant (☎ 978-546-6667; 29 Bearskin Neck; mains $4-18) If you'd like a bit of refinement, go upstairs right next door to Roy Moore's Lobster Company. The prices are still fairly low given its waterview dining room. Don't forget to bring your own beer or wine.

Brackett's (☎ 978-546-2797; 25 Main St; lunch $6-13, dinner $10-18; ⏰ closed Nov-Mar) Locals swear by this cozy little dining nook. The casual pub atmosphere, ocean views and daily specials draw a consistent crowd. The specialty of the house are scrod, shrimp, crab and scallop casseroles, rich in sherry and cream.

My Place by the Sea (☎ 978-546-9667; 68 Bearskin Neck; lunch $8-12, dinner $20-30; ⏰ closed Nov-Apr) Barbara Stavropolos and Kathy Milbury run this romantic spot out at the end of the Neck. The location offers panoramic views of the bay, indoor and outdoor seating, excellent service and imaginative nouvelle cuisine. Lunch is good value: veggies will enjoy the roasted red pepper and grilled portabella topped with mozzarella on a baguette. Innovative seafood specials include Portuguese seafood stew, caramelized sea scallops or lobster tacos. Make reservations for dinner.

Rockport is a dry town, meaning that alcohol is not sold in stores or restaurants, and there are no bars. You can bring your own bottles, and most restaurants will open and serve them for a corkage fee. You can buy liquor outside Rockport at the following places:

Lanesville Package Store (☎ 978-281-0293; 1080 Washington St/MA 127, Lanesville; ⏰ 8am-9pm Mon-Sat, noon-6pm Sun)

Liquor Locker (☎ 978-283-0630; 287 Main St, Gloucester; ⏰ 8am-10pm Mon-Sat, noon-5pm Sun)

Entertainment

Gloucester Stage Company (☎ 978-281-4099; www.gloucesterstage.com; 267 E Main St, Gloucester; tickets $30; ⏰ 8pm Wed-Sun, 5pm Sat & Sun) This company stages excellent small-theater productions of classics and modern works.

Rhumb Line (☎ 978-283-9732; www.therhumbline.com; 40 Railroad Ave, Gloucester) This club across from the train station is the best place on Cape Ann to hear live music, with performances almost nightly. Acts range from mellow acoustic and blues to high-energy rock, with the occasional open-mike night.

Madfish Grille (☎ 978-281-4554; 77 Rocky Neck Ave, East Gloucester; ⏰ closed Nov-Mar) On a wharf at Rocky Neck, the Madfish is a hopping bar that attracts a young, cruisey crowd. Between Memorial Day and Labor Day, it hosts live music Wednesday through Sunday (weekends only in spring and fall). The kitchen turns out excellent, creative dishes.

Getting There & Away

You can reach Cape Ann quickly from Boston or North Shore towns via four-lane Rte 128, but the scenic route on MA 127 follows

---

DETOUR: ESSEX SHIPBUILDING MUSEUM

This unique **museum** (☎ 978-768-7541; www.essexshipbuildingmuseum.org; 66 Main St, Essex; adult/senior & student $5/3; ⏰ noon-4pm Wed-Sun) was established in 1976 as a local repository for all of the shipbuilding artifacts of the local residents. Most of the collections of photos, tools and ship models came from local basements and attics, allowing Essex to truly preserve its local history. Most of the collections are housed in the town's 1835 school house (check out the **Old Burying Ground** behind it). The historical society also operates the **Waterline Center** in the museum shipyard, a section of waterfront property where shipbuilding activities have taken place for hundreds of years. The historic Essex-built schooner, **Evelina M Goulart**, is moored here, as is the **Lewis H Story**, the museum's flagship.

From Rte 128, take exit 15 and turn left on School St (which becomes Southern Ave). Take a left onto Rte 133; the museum and shipyard are on the right-hand side after crossing a causeway and a bridge.

the coastline through the prim villages of Prides Crossing, Manchester-by-the-Sea and Magnolia. MA 127/127A loops around Cape Ann, connecting these towns to Rockport. Driving the entire loop is worth it for the seaside scenery in East Gloucester, Laneville, and Annisquam.

Alternatively, take the Rockport line of the **MBTA commuter rail** (☎ 617-722-3200, 800-392-6100; www.mbta.com) from Boston's North Station ($5.50, one hour). Both Rockport and Gloucester have commuter rail stations.

The **Cape Ann Transportation Authority** (CATA; ☎ 978-283-7916) operates bus routes between the towns of Cape Ann.

IPSWICH & ESSEX
pop 16,254

Heading up the North Shore from Cape Ann, Ipswich and Essex are pretty New England towns surrounded by rocky coast and sandy beaches, extensive marshlands, forested hills and rural farmland.

Ipswich is one of those New England towns that is pretty today because it was poor in the past. With no harbor, and no source of waterpower for factories, commercial and industrial development went elsewhere in the 18th and 19th centuries. As a result, Ipswich's 17th-century houses were not torn down to build grander residences. Today the town is famous for its ample antique shops and succulent clams. Home of novelist John Updike, it is also the setting for some of his novels and short stories like 'A&P,' which is based on the local market.

Sights & Activities
CRANE ESTATE

One of the longest, widest, sandiest beaches in the region is **Crane Beach** (Map p152; ☎ 978-356-4354; www.thetrustees.org; Argilla Rd, Ipswich; [P] Mon-Fri $15, Sat & Sun $20 Jun-Aug, $5 daily Sep-May; ⦿ 8am-sunset), 4 miles of fine-sand barrier beach on Ipswich Bay. It is set in the midst of the Crane Wildlife Refuge, so the entire surrounding area is pristinely beautiful. Five miles of trails traverse the dunes. The only downside is the pesky greenhead flies that buzz around (and bite) in late July and early August.

Above the beach, on Castle Hill, sits the 1920s estate of Chicago plumbing-fixture magnate Richard T Crane. The 59-room Stuart-style **Great House** (☎ 978-356-4351; 290 Argilla Rd; adult/senior $8/6; ⦿ 10am-4pm Wed-Thu

Jun-Sep) is the site of summer concerts and special events. It's open for tours in summer, but only a few days a week. The lovely landscaped grounds, which are open daily, contain several miles of walking trails.

APPLETON FARMS

One of the country's oldest continuously operating farms, **Appleton Farms** (Map p152; ☎ 978-356-5728; 219 County Rd, Ipswich; admission free; ⦿ 8am-sunset) is now maintained and operated by the Trustees of Reservations. Four miles of trails wind along old carriageways, past ancient stonewall property markers and through acres of beautiful grasslands. The store sells fresh, organically grown produce, not to mention tantalizing jams, spreads and sauces made with said produce.

From MA 128, take MA 1A north. Turn left on Cutler Rd and drive 2 miles to the intersection with Highland Rd, where parking is available.

Eating & Sleeping

Inn at Castle Hill (☎ 978-412-2555; http://innatcastlehill.thetrustees.org; 280 Argilla Rd, Ipswich; r $175-385 May-Oct, $115-300 Nov-Apr; ✖) On the grounds of the Crane Estate, this inn is an example of understated luxury. In the midst of acres of beautiful grounds, the inn boasts 10 rooms, each uniquely decorated with subtle elegance. Turndown service, plush robes and afternoon tea are some of the very civilized perks; and who can resist that wrap-around veranda and its magnificent views of the surrounding sand dunes and salt marshes?

Woodman's (☎ 978-768-6057, 800-649-1773; 121 Main St/MA 133, Essex; mains $7-25) This roadhouse is the most famous spot in the area to come for clams, anyway you like 'em. The specialty, of course, is Chubby's original fried clams and crispy onion rings. But this place serves everything from boiled lobsters to homemade clam cakes to a seasonal raw bar. Friendly, family service and tried-and-true seafood make it one of the classic New England eateries. It's on MA 133 on the way to Ipswich from Rockport (exit 14 from MA 128).

Getting There & Away

Ipswich is on the Newburyport line of the **MBTA commuter rail** (☎ 617-222-3200, 800-392-6100; www.mbta.com). Trains leave Boston's North Station for Ipswich ($5.25, 50 minutes)

about 12 times each weekday and five times on Saturday (no trains Sunday).

NEWBURYPORT
pop 17,000

Newburyport's heyday was during the late 18th century, when this town at the mouth of the Merrimack River prospered as a shipping port and silversmith center. Not too much has changed in the last 200 years, as Newburyport's brick buildings and graceful churches still show off the Federal style that was popular back in those days. Today the center of this town is a model of historic preservation and gentrification. Visitors enjoy creative restaurants, pubs, museums and entertainment. Not the least, Newburyport is the gateway to the barrier Plum Island, a national wildlife refuge with some of the best bird-watching in New England.

Orientation & Information

All major roads (MA 113, US 1, and US 1A) lead to the center of the town's commercial and historic district, around the junction of Water and State Sts. The **Greater Newburyport Chamber of Commerce** (☎ 978-462-6680; www.new buryportchamber.org; 38 Merrimac St; ☾ 9am-5pm Mon-Fri, 10am-4pm Sat, noon-4pm Sun) runs a seasonal information booth in Market Sq from June to October.

Sights & Activities

CUSTOM HOUSE MARITIME MUSEUM

The 1835 granite Custom House is an excellent example of Classic Revival architecture built by Robert Mills (of Washington Monument fame). It now houses the **Maritime Museum** (☎ 978-462-8681; www.themaritime society.org; 25 Water St; adult/child & senior $5/4; ☾ Tue-Sat 9am-5pm, noon-4pm Sun Apr-Dec), which exhibits its artifacts from Newburyport's maritime history as a major shipbuilding center and seaport. The Maritime Society also operates **Lowell's Boat Shop** in neighboring Amesbury, the oldest boat shop in America (combo tickets available).

CUSHING HOUSE MUSEUM

This 21-room Federal home houses the **Historical Society of Old Newbury** (☎ 978-462-2681; www .newburyhist.com; 98 High St; adult/child $5/2; ☾ 10am-4pm Tue-Fri, noon-4pm Sat May-Oct). The home is decked out with fine furnishings and decorative pieces from the region. Collections of portraits, silver, needlework, toys and clocks are all on display, not to mention the impressive Oriental collection from Newburyport's early Chinese trade. The society offers guided tours, exhibits, special events and lectures. Last tour begins one hour before closing.

PARKER RIVER NATIONAL WILDLIFE REFUGE

The 4662-acre **sanctuary** (☎ 978-465-5753; www .parkerriver.org; Plum Island; per car or bike/per pedestrian $5/2; ☾ sunrise-sunset) occupies the southern three-quarters of Plum Island. More than 800 species of birds, plants and animals reside in its many ecological habitats, including beaches, sand dunes, salt pans, salt marshes, freshwater impoundments and maritime forests.

The salt pans are excellent for spotting shorebirds during fall migration (July to September), as well as egrets and herons from mid-April to October. The **Hellcat Wildlife Swamp Interpretive Area** has freshwater impoundments, as well as an extensive swamp and forest. Here you'll see waterfowl and shorebirds, including herons. During spring and fall, you can observe migrating songbirds, including magnificent wood-warblers in the woods. In winter the refuge is a good place to see waterfowl, the rough-legged hawk and snowy owl. Several miles of foot trails allow access to much of the area. Observation towers and platforms punctuate the trails at prime bird-watching spots.

PLUM ISLAND BEACHES

A barrier island off the coast of Massachusetts, Plum Island has 9 miles of wide, sandy beaches surrounded by acres of wildlife sanctuary. These are among the nicest beaches on the North Shore, if you head to the furthest points on the island. **Sandy Point** (☎ 978-462-4481; Plum Island; ☾ sunrise-8pm), on the southern tip, is a state park that is popular for swimming, sunning and tidepooling. Parking is available at the Parker River Wildlife Refuge (p161), Sandy Point or in private parking lots. Note: beaches in the refuge are generally closed April to June because of nesting piping plover, but you can go to the public beaches at the north end of the island, where there is a community of vacation homes.

Tours

Newburyport Whale Watch (☎ 800-848-1111; www .newburyportwhalewatch.com; 54 Merrimac St; adult/child/

senior $31/18/26; 10am Mon-Fri, 11am Sat & Sun mid-May–Jun, 8:30am & 1pm Jul-Aug, 11am Sat & Sun Sep–mid-Oct) Whale-watching tours.

Plum Island Kayak (☎ 978-462-5510; www.plumisland kayak.com; 38 Merrimac St; single/tandem per day $52/64; 9am-5pm Mon-Wed, 9am-8pm Thu-Sun Apr-Oct) offers several tours during the day (and night) exploring the islands, mud bars, salt marshes and shorelines. Expect to see lots of birds. Special moonlight paddles and trips to the Isle of Shoals are also popular.

Festivals & Events

For almost 50 years, Newburyport has been hosting the **Yankee Homecoming Festival** (www .yankeehomecoming.com) during the first week in August. The idea is to attract Americans from around the country to return to the region where the nation was born. Festivities include an arts fair and live music on the streets of downtown Newburyport. Sports tournaments (ranging from golf to chess), a boat parade and a popular 10-mile road race are all part of the fun.

Sleeping

Like many historic North Shore towns, Newburyport has become a mecca for B&Bs. Several motels and hotels are located in nearby towns. For a complete list of places to stay and website links, check out www.newbury portchamber.org.

Essex Street Inn (☎ 978-465-3148; www.essexstreet inn.com; 7 Essex St; r incl breakfast $90-175;) This Victorian inn was built as a lodging house in 1880. Today it's an elegant inn: the 17 rooms are all nicely decorated in 19th-century style (some with fireplaces). It's not without modern comforts, however. Several of the more expensive rooms feature whirlpools.

Garrison Inn (☎ 978-499-8500; www.garrisoninn.com; 11 Brown Sq; d incl breakfast $150-230) Once a private mansion, this gracious, red-brick building has been a hostelry for 100 years. It's now a lovely boutique hotel with 24 spacious rooms featuring a variety of architectural charms, including exposed brick walls, cathedral ceilings and spiral staircases. An elevator makes the inn wheelchair accessible. The restaurant on site, David's Tavern, is acclaimed for its menu of eclectic American haute cuisine.

Windsor House (☎ 978-462-3778; 38 Federal St; r incl breakfast $125-165) Guests in this five-room B&B rave about English ambiance, and the personal attention they get from innkeeper Judith and John Harris, otherwise known as Lord and Lady of Penrhyn. Tea is served daily at 4pm in the common room.

Clark Currier Inn (☎ 978-465-8363; www.clarkcurrier inn.com; 45 Green St; r incl breakfast $95-185) Travelers in search of a genteel experience can luxuriate in this 1803 Federal mansion, with its period sitting room, library, fish pond and gazebo. Mary and Bob Nolan have eight rooms for guests, all with private bath. Details like a Franklin stove and canopy beds make this place extra charming.

Newburyport B&B (☎ 978-463-4637; www.newbury portbedandbreakfast.com; 296 High St; r $115-145 May-Oct, $75-110 Nov-Apr;) This grand Georgian colonial has 16 lovely rooms, all graced with a stately elegance. The light-filled sunroom, formal dining room and fancy parlor are all open for guests to enjoy. The grounds include landscaped English gardens surrounding a brick patio.

Eating & Drinking

Angie's Coffee Shop (☎ 978-462-7959; 7 Pleasant St; breakfast & lunch $4-8; 6am-4pm) You gotta love the blue Formica tabletops, as well as the three-egg omelet and sizzling joe in this classic coffee shop, where locals gather for breakfast and gossip.

Rockfish (☎ 978-465-6601; 35 State St; dishes $5-18) The downstairs pub is a great place for people-watching. In warm weather take a table by the large, street-side open windows. Snarf some spicy rockfish cakes, suck on a cold beer, network with the locals, and watch the evening strollers sashay up and down State St. The pub scene is intense on weekend nights with an under-35 crowd. Upstairs, tablecloths and candlelight provide a lovely setting for a fancier menu of inventive fusion dishes (dinner only).

Black Cow Tap & Grill (☎ 978-499-8811; 54 Merrimac St; mains $12-16) You can't beat this upscale pub for burgers and beer. The menu is pretty straightforward (as pub fare should be), but the friendly service and views of the Merrimack River make it a reliable standby for locals and tourists alike.

Grog (☎ 978-465-8008; 13 Middle St; mains $12-17) The Grog has been a Newburyport tradition for over 30 years. Named for the English Navy's traditional ration of rum and water, this place serves its own traditional rations of New England seafood, grilled meats and Mexican favorites. The house specialty is the famous Grog Mixed Grill, featuring chicken, shrimp and steak, grilled to perfection and served over a potato. You will not leave hungry. In the pub downstairs, live music plays Wednesday through Sunday, making this a popular pick-up spot for 20-somethings.

Not Your Average Joe's (☎ 978-462-3808; Firehouse Sq; mains lunch $7-10, dinner $12-16) 'Creative, casual cuisine,' boasts the menu. And Joe does manage to add a twist to traditional comfort foods: Hawaiian steak, for example (flank steak with pineapple salsa), or ground sirloin meatloaf topped with smoked mozzarella and roasted red peppers. The interior is comfortable and cheery – a nice family place.

Mr India Restaurant (☎ 978-465-8600; 114 Merrimack St; mains $8-12) This eatery is perched on the edge of the historic district. The building is Depression-era New England, but the scents and tastes are pure Bombay.

Szechuan Taste, Sushi Yen & Thai Cafe (☎ 978-463-0686; 19 Pleasant St; mains $9-15) If you're in the mood for Asian, but you don't know what, you're bound to figure it out at this Pan-Asian eatery. A sampler of Chinese, Japanese and Thai cuisine, the menu aims to please.

Entertainment

Firehouse Center for the Performing Arts (☎ 978-462-7336; www.firehousecenter.com; 1 Market Sq) There are two art galleries, a 190-seat theater and a restaurant, Not Your Average Joe's (opposite) in this restored 1823 firehouse at Water St. The theater offers year-round concerts, plays and children's theater, with top performers from around New England. Tickets cost $15 to $30.

Getting There & Away

From Boston follow I-95 north. Take exit 57 and follow signs to downtown Newburyport. There are free parking lots on Green and Merrimack Sts. Alternatively, the **MBTA commuter rail** (☎ 800-392-6100; www.mbta.com) runs a line from North Station to Newburyport ($6). There are more than 10 trains daily on weekdays, and there's six on weekends.

C&J Trailways (☎ 800-258-7111; www.cjtrailways.com; Storey Ave) runs about 12 buses daily from Logan International Airport (one way/round-trip $18/19) and Boston's South Station (one way/round-trip $10/16).

SOUTH SHORE

PLYMOUTH

pop 51,700

Historic Plymouth, 'America's Home Town,' is synonymous with Plymouth Rock. Thousands of visitors come here each year to look at this weathered granite ball and to consider what it was like for the Pilgrims, who stepped ashore in this strange land in the winter of 1620, seeking a place where they could practice their religion as they wished without interference from government, and for the Native Americans who were soon wiped out. You can see Plymouth Rock in a mere minute, but the rock is just a symbol of the Pilgrims' struggle, sacrifice and triumph, which are elucidated in many museums and exhibits nearby.

Orientation

'The rock,' on the waterfront, is on Water St at the center of Plymouth, within walking distance of most museums and restaurants. Main St, the main commercial street, is a block inland. Some lodgings are within walking distance, but most require a car.

Information

Destination Plymouth (☎ 508-747-7533; www.visit-plymouth.com; 170 Water St; 🕑 9am-5pm Apr-Nov, 9am-8pm Jun-Aug) Located at the rotary across from Plymouth Harbor; provides assistance with B&B reservations.

Plymouth Guide Online (www.plymouthguide.com) Lots of information about tourist attractions, dining and accommodations in the area.

Plymouth Savings Bank (☎ 508-746-3600; 36 Main St; 🕑 8am-3pm Mon-Wed, 8am-5pm Thu-Fri, 8am-noon Sat)

Post Office (6 Main St; 🕑 8:30am-5pm Mon-Fri, 8:30am-noon Sat)

Yankee Book & Art Gallery (☎ 508-747-2691; 10 North St; 🕑 11am-5pm Mon-Sat, noon-4pm Sun) Offers a selection of books on Pilgrim history.

Sights & Activities

PLYMOUTH ROCK

Plymouth Rock came from Pangaea, the ancient gigantic continent that split in two to form Europe and Africa on the eastern side and North and South America on the western side, leaving the Atlantic Ocean in between. The boulder is of Dedham granite, a rock some 680 million years old. Most of the Dedham granite went to Africa when

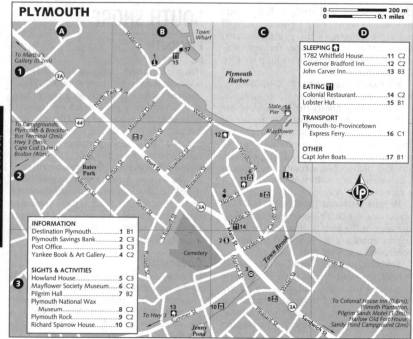

PLYMOUTH

Pangaea split; bits were left in the Atlantica terrain, the geologic area around Boston. About 20,000 years ago, a glacier picked up Plymouth Rock, carried it and dropped it here.

We don't really know that the Pilgrims landed on Plymouth Rock; it's not mentioned in any early written accounts. But the story gained popularity during colonial times. In 1774, 20 yoke of oxen were harnessed to the rock to move it – splitting the rock in the process. Half of the cloven boulder went on display in Pilgrim Hall from 1834 to 1867. The sea and wind lashed at the other half, and innumerable small pieces were chipped off and carried away by souvenir hunters over the centuries.

By the 20th century the rock was an endangered artifact, and steps were taken to protect it. In 1921 the reunited halves were sheltered in the present granite enclosure. In 1989 the rock was repaired and strengthened to withstand weathering. And so it stands today, relatively small, broken and mended, an enduring symbol of the quest for religious freedom.

MAYFLOWER II

If Plymouth Rock tells us little about the Pilgrims, **Mayflower II** (☎ 508-746-1622; State Pier; adult/child/senior $8/6/7, combined ticket to Plimoth Plantation adult/child/senior & student $22/14/20; 🕑 9am-5pm Apr-Nov), a replica of the small ship in which they made the fateful voyage, speaks volumes. Climb aboard and wonder how 102 people – with all the household effects, tools, provisions, animals and seed to establish a colony – could have lived together on this tiny vessel for 66 days, subsisting on hard, moldy biscuits, rancid butter and brackish water as the ship passed through the stormy north Atlantic waters. But they did, landing on this wild, forested shore in the frigid December of 1620 – eloquent testimony to their courage, spirit and the strength of their religious beliefs.

Mayflower II, moored at State Pier, was built in England in 1955 and sailed the Atlantic to Plymouth in 1957.

PLIMOTH PLANTATION

During the winter of 1620–21, half of the Pilgrims died of disease, privation and

---

DETOUR: BLUE HILLS

The Native Americans who lived in this region called themselves 'the people of the great hills.' But when Europeans saw the coastline from their ships, they noticed the blue-grey hue of the slopes in the morning light and dubbed them the Blue Hills – 22 hills in a chain that stretches across the Boston South Shore suburbs.

Blue Hills Reservation (☎ 617-698-1802; www.mass.gov/dcr/parks/metroboston/blue.htm; 695 Hillside St, Milton; ☺ sunrise-sunset) is a state park that encompasses over 7000 acres in the region. A network of 125 miles of trails crosses the hills, including several routes to the summit of Great Blue Hill, the highest peak at 635ft. The rocky summit enjoys fantastic city skyline views – not what you expect in the midst of the wilderness.

The Massachusetts Audubon Society operates a **Trailside Museum** (☎ 617-333-0690; adult/child/senior $3/1.50/2; ☺ 10am-5pm Wed-Sun) that focuses on the flora and fauna of the reservation, including some live animals. **Houghton's Pond** is pleasant for fishing and swimming. Any way you wish to escape the city – rock climbing, cross-country skiing, mountain biking, ice skating – it's all possible.

The Blue Hills Reservation is 8 miles south of Boston in Milton. From Boston, take I-93 south to exit 3, Houghton's Pond. Turn right on Hillside St and take it to Houghton's Pond or reservation headquarters. Alternatively, take the red-line 'T' to Ashmont Station and the high-speed line to Mattapan, from where the Canton & Blue Hills bus goes to the Trailside Museum and Great Blue Hill on Rte 138.

---

exposure to the elements. But new arrivals joined the survivors in 1621; and by 1627, just before an additional influx of Pilgrims founded the colony of Massachusetts Bay, Plymouth Colony was on the road to prosperity.

The **Plimoth Plantation** (☎ 508-746-1622; MA 3A; adult/child/senior $20/12/18, combined ticket to Mayflower II adult/child/senior & student $22/14/20; ☺ 9am-5pm Apr-Nov), a mile or so south of Plymouth Rock, authentically re-creates the Pilgrim's 1627 settlement. Everything in the village – costumes, implements, vocabulary, artistry, recipes and crops – has been painstakingly researched and remade. Even the animals have been bred to be very similar to those that the Pilgrims had. You can see them in **Nye Barn**.

Hobbamock's (Wampanoag) Homesite replicates the life of a Native American community in the same area during that time. The Homesite huts are made of wattle and daub (a framework of woven rods and twigs covered and plastered with clay), and the inhabitants engage in traditional crafts while wearing traditional garb.

Costumed interpreters, acting in character, explain the details of daily life and answer your questions as you watch them work and play. In the crafts center, artisans weave baskets and cloth, throw pottery, and build fine furniture using the techniques and tools of the early 17th century. Exhibits explain how these manufactured goods were shipped across the Atlantic in exchange for colonial necessities. An interactive audio and video exhibit, *Irreconcilable Difference*, illuminates the contrasts between a Native American woman and a Pilgrim woman living between 1627 and 1690.

PILGRIM HALL

Claiming to be the oldest continually operating public museum in the country, **Pilgrim Hall** (☎ 508-746-1620; www.pilgrimhall.org; 75 Court St; adult/child/senior $6/3/5; ☺ 9:30am-4:30pm Feb-Dec) was founded in 1824. Its exhibits are not reproductions, but the real things the Pilgrims and their Wampanoag neighbors used in their daily lives, right down to Miles Standish's sword. Monumental paintings in the museum's collection depict scenes of everyday Pilgrim life.

PLYMOUTH NATIONAL WAX MUSEUM

If you have kids in tow, they will enjoy this **museum** (☎ 508-746-6468; 16 Carver St; adult/child 5-12 $7/2.75; ☺ 9am-5pm Mar-Nov, longer hrs in summer). The life-size wax figures – 180 in 26 scenes – show the progress of the Pilgrims as they left England for Holland, set sail and arrived in America. The museum is set on historic Cole's Hill, the site of the Pilgrim's first burial ground, overlooking Plymouth Rock.

HISTORIC HOUSES

As New England's oldest European community, Plymouth has its share of fine old houses, some very old indeed. The oldest is the **Richard Sparrow House** (☎ 508-747-1240; www.sparrowhouse.com; 42 Summer St; adult/child $2/1; ☒ 10am-5pm Thu-Tue Apr-Dec), built by one of the original Pilgrim settlers in 1640. Today the house contains a gallery that exhibits interesting art by local painters and photographers.

The 1667 **Howland House** (☎ 508-746-9590; 33 Sandwich St; adult/child/senior & student $4/2/3; ☒ 10am-4:30pm late May–mid-Oct) is the only house in Plymouth that was home to a known *Mayflower* passenger.

The **Mayflower Society Museum** (☎ 508-746-2590; www.mayflower.org; 4 Winslow St; ☒ 10am-4pm Jul-Aug, 10am-4pm Sat & Sun only Jun & Sep-Oct) is housed in the magnificent 1754 Winslow House, built by the great-grandson of the third governor of Plymouth Colony. The grandeur of the house shows how wealthy the town became in little more than a century. The architectural details and furnishings in the house are impressive. There is also a library and archives dedicated to genealogical research.

The **Plymouth Antiquarian Society** (☎ 508-746-0012; one house adult/child $4/2, three houses $6/2; ☒ 10am-2pm Mon-Fri Jul-Aug) maintains three historic houses, including the 1677 **Harlow Old Fort House** (119 Sandwich St).

Tours

Capt John Boats (☎ 508-746-2643, 800-242-2469; www.captjohn.com; Town Wharf; ☒ tours Apr-Oct) offers loads of options to get you out on the water: whale-watching cruises (adult/child/senior $29/18/24); all-day fishing trips (adult/child/senior $36/26/31); and harbor cruises (adult/child/senior from $12/8/10). Each option is offered at least once daily in summer.

Sleeping

1782 Whitfield House (☎ 508-747-6735; www.whitfieldhouse.com; 26 North St; r/ste $95/140) This gracious Federal house is in the heart of historic Plymouth. It has only four rooms – each uniquely decorated with the utmost attention to detail. Whether its a working fireplace, a four-poster bed or hand-stenciled wall paintings, you're bound to find something that charms you. An elegant living room and dining room and shady deck are all accessible to guests.

Governor Bradford Inn (☎ 508-746-6200, 800-332-1620; www.governorbradford.com; 98 Water St; d May-Oct $129-189, Nov-Apr $89-159) Named for William Bradford, the second governor of Plymouth Colony and author of the primary historical reference about the Pilgrims, *Of Plimoth Plantation*. This inn does not have much historical value, but it's conveniently located smack dab in the middle of town. Ninety-four rooms are fully equipped with the necessities. The more expensive rooms enjoy harbor views.

Pilgrim Sands Motel (☎ 508-747-0900, 800-729-7263; www.pilgrimsands.com; 150 Warren Ave; d Jun-Oct $130-160, Nov-May $75-125; ☒) This typical beach motel is a good option for families, as it's right on a private beach and directly opposite Plimoth Plantation. Rooms with an ocean view are slightly pricier, but the other rooms look out over Plimoth Plantation, which has its own charm. Some rooms have kitchenettes, but they all have refrigerators.

John Carver Inn (☎ 508-746-7100, 800-274-1620; www.johncarverinn.com; 25 Summer St; d Jun-Oct $139-209, Nov-May $99-169; ☒) This 85-room inn is a boon for families: special packages allow kids to stay for free and include entry to local sights. Best of all, the indoor Pilgrim-theme swimming pool (complete with a *Mayflower* replica!) will keep your little ones entertained for hours. There is also a convenient restaurant onsite.

Colonial House Inn (☎ 508-747-4274; 207 Sandwich St; www.colonialhouseinn.com; d from $125) The sister property to Pilgrim Sands is about a mile south of Plymouth center. Rooms are spacious and comfortable with a hint of elegance. The setting is pleasant for its views of the inner harbor and its location across from the salt marshes.

Myles Standish State Forest (☎ 508-866-2526, reservations mid-May–early Sep 877-422-6762; Cranberry Rd, South Carver; sites $15; ☒ camping Apr-Oct, park year-round) This closest state facility is about 6 miles south of Plymouth. Take MA 3 exit 5 or MA 58 to South Carver and look for Standish signs. Within the 16,000-acre park are 15 miles of biking and hiking trails, nine ponds (two with beaches and one with a bathhouse) and 400 campsites. Campsites right on the water's edge are a little more expensive.

Wompatuck State Park (☎ 781-749-7160, reservations late May–early Sep 877-422-6762; Union St, Hingham; sites without/with electricity $12/15; ☒ camping Apr-Oct, park year-round) From Boston, take MA 3 to exit 14 in Hingham and head 5 miles north on MA 228 to the park. It's about 30 miles north of Plymouth. The 2900-acre park has 262 campsites, 12 miles of paved biking trails, and even more mountain-biking and hiking trails.

Pinewood Lodge Campground (☎ 508-746-3548; www.pinewoodlodge.com; 190 Pinewood Rd; sites without/with electricity $20/24 May, Sep & Oct, $28/32 Jun-Aug; ☺ May-Oct) Off US 44 in Plymouth, this campground offers 250 shady campsites, yet it is among the closest to the town center. It's located on a freshwater lake, which is ideal for fishing and swimming.

Sandy Pond Campground (☎ 508-759-9336; www .sandypond.com; 834 Bourne Rd; sites without/with electricity $26/28; ☺ mid-Apr–Sep) This establishment has 80 campsites with water and electricity, 25 for tents, two sandy beaches and hiking trails. From Boston take MA 3 south to exit 3, bear right, then turn left onto Long Pond Rd and follow signs.

Plymouth Rock KOA Kampground (☎ 508-947-6435; 483 Plymouth St, Middleboro; tent sites $23-30, RV sites $27-44; ☺ Mar-Nov) This developed campground is further away than Sandy Pond or Pinewood, and has upwards of 400 sites. From Boston take I-93 south to MA 24, south to I-495, south to exit 6 (US 44 west) and follow signs.

Eating

Fast-food shops line Water St opposite the *Mayflower II*. For better food at lower prices, walk a block inland to Main St, the attractive thoroughfare of Plymouth's business district, where restaurants are open year-round.

Martha's Galley (☎ 508-747-9200; 179 Court St; mains $12-20; ☺ 4-10pm Tue-Sat) Martha's is the first step toward filling a bit of a dining void in Plymouth. This family-run trattoria is in

---

THE FIRST THANKSGIVING

Plymouth is known for one thing most of all – Pilgrims. And, as all schoolchildren in the US are taught, Pilgrims are known for one thing most of all – Thanksgiving. Maybe two things – Thanksgiving and big-buckled shoes. While footwear styles come and go, Thanksgiving remains a time-honored tradition of feasting and football for American families. But to what extent is today's celebration of Thanksgiving consistent with the Pilgrim forebears?

The first Thanksgiving was held in the early fall of 1621 and lasted for three days. The Pilgrims were thankful, but not for a bountiful harvest. In fact, virtually everything they planted that year failed to come up, except for some native corn. The Pilgrims were thankful simply to be alive. Of the 100 passengers aboard the *Mayflower*, only half survived the first year in the wilderness. There may have been a wild turkey on the table, but the plates more likely featured venison, lobster and squirrel…mmmmm. There was no pumpkin pie, alas, the Pilgrims did not have any ovens.

True to legend, the Indians were on hand for the first feast. Chief Massasoit of the Wampanoags had no problems with the pathetic Pilgrims, since he had set them up on the land of a rival tribe, the Patuxet. The Patuxet certainly would have objected, but they were wiped out by smallpox a year earlier. The Wampanoags, in fact, provided most of the food. The Pilgrims were really not very good hosts.

There were no Lions or Cowboys, but there were games played that weekend. The Pilgrim men folk competed against the natives in shooting, archery and a colonial crude version of croquet.

Thanksgiving with the Pilgrims pretty much ended there. The fall festival was not repeated in subsequent years. The Pilgrims were pious, not partyers. The Wampanoags came to reconsider their stance on the newcomers. Over the years a fall harvest feast was common in some colonies, especially in New England. In 1789 George Washington called for a national Thanksgiving day to honor the new constitution, but again this did not become a widespread annual event.

The Thanksgiving celebrated today has more to do with 19th-century nationalism, than with 17th-century settlers. It is an invented tradition. In 1863, in the midst of civil war, Abraham Lincoln proclaimed the last Thursday in November as a national Thanksgiving holiday. The popular depiction of the Pilgrims in peace and harmony with natives and nature was meant to emphasize the common heritage of a people at war with itself. The Thanksgiving tradition is the celebration of a myth, but a myth that unifies the nation.

Oh, and by the way, the Pilgrims really did not wear big-buckled shoes either.

an unlikely location in a strip mall, which makes it all the more pleasantly surprising when you walk inside. Terracotta walls, exposed brick and tile floors make this place feel cozy. But the emphasis is on the food: pork tenderloin with cranberry and mustard sauce; linguini topped with local littleneck clams in a herb butter sauce; or the signature scallops in ginger sauce. Save room for rich homemade bread pudding.

Colonial Restaurant (☎ 508-746-0838; 39 Main St; dishes $6-12) The atmosphere is pretty staid, but if you're hungry this place will get the job done (and you can't beat the price). The portions are healthy and the seafood fresh. Locals swear by the fish cakes (or anything fried).

Lobster Hut (☎ 508-746-2270; Town Wharf; mains $6-18) Right on the town wharf, five short blocks north of *Mayflower II*, the seaside Lobster Hut has big plates of fried clams, fish-and-chips, and – of course – lobster salad, fried lobster tail, boiled lobsters etc. There is seating inside, but it's much more enjoyable to take a place on the deck and catch a harbor breeze.

Getting There & Away

Plymouth is 41 miles south of Boston via MA 3; it takes an hour with some traffic. From Providence, it's the same distance and time, but you'll want to head west on US 44.

Buses operated by **Plymouth & Brockton** (☎ 508-746-0378, 508-778-9767; www.p-b.com; adult/child/senior $10/5/8) travel hourly to South Station or Logan International Airport in Boston. Heading south, these buses continue as far as Hyannis. The P&B terminal is at the visitor center, exit 5 off MA 3. From there catch a Greater Attleboro Taunton Regional Transit Authority (GATRA) bus to the center of town, about 2 miles away.

You can reach Plymouth from Boston by **MBTA commuter rail** (☎ 617-222-3200, 800-392-6100; www.mbta.com) trains, which depart from South Station three or four times a day ($6). From the station at Cordage Park, GATRA buses connect to Plymouth center.

Operated by the ubiquitous Capt John, the **Plymouth-to-Provincetown Express Ferry** (☎ 508-747-2400, 800-242-2469; State Pier; adult/child/senior/one way $30/20/25/18) deposits you on the tip of the Cape faster than if you drove. From July to August, the 90-minute journey departs Plymouth at 10am and leaves Provincetown

at 4:30pm. It operates Saturday and Sunday only from May to June and September.

NEW BEDFORD

pop 94,000

During its heyday as a whaling port (1765–1860), New Bedford commanded as many as 400 whaling ships. This vast fleet brought home hundreds of thousands of barrels of whale oil for lighting America's lamps. So famous was the town's whaling industry that Herman Melville set his great American novel, *Moby-Dick, or The Whale,* in New Bedford.

When petroleum and electricity supplanted whale oil, New Bedford turned to fishing, scalloping and textile production for its wealth. In recent years the New Bedford economy has floundered as these industries have struggled. The city gets its share of bad press like any city its size. But the city center has its charms: cobblestone streets and gas lanterns recall the romance of the 19th century, while the National Historical Park designation commemorates the whaling heritage.

Orientation

The heart of the old city center is the restored historic district around Melville Mall. The area is about a mile south of I-195 via MA 18 (take the downtown exit 18S). At the first set of lights, take a right and park in the municipal garage on the right. The National Historical Park visitor center is one block away.

Information

New Bedford Office of Tourism (☎ 508-979-1745, 800-508-5353; www.ci.new-bedford.ma.us; Wharfinger Bldg, Pier 3; ☯ 9am-5pm Mon-Fri, 10am-4pm Sat & Sun) Provides general information, including lodging and events. Pick up a self-guided brochure for the 'dock walk,' which orients you to the working harbor.

New Bedford Whaling National Historical Park Visitor Center (☎ 508-996-4095; www.nps.gov/nebe; 33 William St; ☯ 9am-5pm) Offers highly recommended walking tours twice daily in July and August.

Sights & Activities

NEW BEDFORD WHALING NATIONAL HISTORICAL PARK

After a $10 million renovation, the **New Bedford Whaling Museum** (☎ 508-997-0046; www.whaling museum.org; 18 Johnny Cake Hill; adult/child/senior/student $10/6/9/9; ☯ 9am-5pm) occupies seven buildings situated between William and Union Sts. To learn what whaling was all about, you need only tramp the decks of the *Lagoda*, a fully rigged, half-size replica of an actual whaling bark. The onboard tryworks (a brick furnace where try-pots are placed) converted huge chunks of whale blubber into valuable oil. Old photographs and a 22-minute video of an actual whale chase bring this historic period to life. You won't be able to ignore the 66ft blue-whale skeleton and the 100ft-long mural depicting sperm whales. Exhibits of delicate scrimshaw, and the carving of whalebone into jewelry, notions and beautiful household items are also impressive.

The small chapel called **Seamen's Bethel** (☎ 508-992-3295; 15 Johnny Cake Hill; admission free, donations accepted; ☼ 10am-5pm Mon-Fri late May–mid-Oct), across from the Whaling Museum, was a refuge for sailors from the rigors and stresses of maritime life. Melville, who suffered from terrible conditions aboard a whaling ship, immortalized it in *Moby-Dick*.

OTHER MUSEUMS
Antique fire trucks and fire-fighting equipment fill the 1867 firehouse known as Old Station No 4, which houses the **New Bedford Fire Museum** (☎ 508-992-2162; 51 Bedford St; adult/child $4/2; ☼ 9am-4pm Mon-Sat Jul-early Sep). It appeals to children, who love the old trucks, uniforms, pumps and fire poles.

The **New Bedford Art Museum** (☎ 508-961-3071; www.newbedfordartmuseum.org; 608 Pleasant St; adult/senior & student $3/2; ☼ noon-5pm Wed-Sun, noon-7pm Thu Sep-May, 10am-5pm Fri-Wed, 10am-7pm Thu Jun-Aug) is located at City Hall Sq. Rotating exhibits feature regional artists. The space is also used to exhibit whaling artifacts and Quaker pieces from the vast 19th-century collections of the **New Bedford Free Public Library** (☎ 508-991-6275; 613 Main St).

ROTCH-JONES-DUFF HOUSE & GARDEN MUSEUM
New Bedford's grandest **historic house** (☎ 508-997-1401; www.rjdmuseum.org; 396 County St; adult/child/senior/student $5/2/4/4; ☼ 10am-4pm daily Apr-Dec, 10am-4pm Tue-Sun Jan-Mar) was designed in Greek revival style by Richard Upjohn (1802–78), first president of the American Institute of Architects. It was built for whaling merchant William Rotch Jr in 1834 and owned by three prominent families in the following 150 years. The house contains the furniture

and trinkets of these families, tracing the progression of the house's history through the years. The grounds are absolutely lovely landscaped gardens, including the irresistible Wildflower Walk.

Festivals & Events
In 1915, four Madeiran immigrants wanted to recreate the feasts that were celebrated in the country they left behind. Since then, the **Feast of the Blessed Sacrament** (www.portuguesefeast.com) has grown to be the largest Portuguese feast in the country. The four-day feast takes place on the first weekend in August. If you miss the big one, there are many other smaller feasts held throughout the summer.

The weekend **Whaling City Festival** (☎ 508-996-3348; www.whalingcityfestival.com) in early July features amusement-park rides, food vendors, crafts and flea markets, and continuous entertainment. It is a classic civic fair.

Sleeping
Historic New Bedford is not thick with lodging possibilities (save a few – and growing number of – B&Bs). The New Bedford Office of Tourism (opposite) can direct you to places to stay in the surrounding area.

Melville House (☎ 508-990-1566; www.melvillehouse.net; 100 Madison St; d incl breakfast $100-150; ✗) Herman Melville often visited his sister at this 1855 Victorian manse. Of the three guest rooms, the aptly named Herman Melville room evokes the author's memory with a penetrating portrait. A gourmet continental breakfast is served in the solarium.

Captain Haskell's Octagon House (☎ 508-999-3933; 347 Union St; r $110-125 May-Oct, $95-110 Nov-Apr) This architectural oddity was built in 1847, but has undergone extensive renovations in recent years. Three guest rooms feature private baths with claw-foot tubs, walnut and wicker furniture, and lots of antiques. All of the rooms are slightly off in terms of shape, an endearing feature of the octagon construction.

Orchard St Manor (☎ 508-984-3475; 139 Orchard St; r $115, ste $155-230 incl breakfast) Hand-made quilts, antique furniture and private bathrooms grace every room of this elegant Georgian revival home. Besides the formal dining room and parlor, guests can also partake of a billiards room and a 'gathering room' with a circular, cherry bar.

Davenport House (☎ 508-999-1177; 124 Cottage St; r $65-115) Two graceful guest rooms (and one smaller room suitable for a child) are available at this lovely Jacobean inn. Its highlight is the grand, wraparound mahogany porch, which overlooks lovely gardens. Other common areas are also lovely, including a front parlor and family room with working fireplaces, and a formal dining room where breakfast is served.

Eating

Antonio's (☎ 508-990-3636; 267 Cogges-hall St; mains $6-15) Don't miss this hopping taverna, just a block off I-195 in New Bedford's North End, if you want authentic Portuguese cuisine. The house specialty is Antonio's Littlenecks: succulent clams and shrimp in a spicy saffron-tomato sauce.

Freestone's City Grille (☎ 508-993-7477; 41 Williams St; lunch $8-12, dinner $15-20) Freestone's offers 'gay '90s' ambiance in a reclaimed bank building, complete with a stained-glass mirror and a brass monkey. Modern American fare shows hints of Asian influence, especially in the specialty salads. This place is adjacent to the National Historical Park visitor center, so it's easy to find.

Candleworks Restaurant (☎ 508-997-1294; 72 N Water St; lunch $8-15, dinner $20-25; ☽ 11:30am-2pm Mon-Fri, 5:30-10pm daily) In a restored brick candle factory, this chic restaurant is about as good as it gets in New Bedford. You can eat in the cool cellar or under the umbrellas on the patio: either way the setting is luxurious. Italian dishes have a modern, New England flare (lots of seafood). Live piano music fills the air in the evenings.

Getting There & Away

New Bedford is 15 miles from Fall River via I-195. It's another 25 miles via I-195 to Cape Cod's Bourne Bridge.

Bonanza Bus (☎ 888-751-8800; www.bonanzabus .com) offers bus services to Providence ($18) and New York ($48) from the New Bedford ferry dock, while **American Eagle** (☎ 508-993-5040) runs three buses a day to Boston South Station ($11) from the Southeastern Regional Transit Authority (SRTA) station (take a shuttle from the ferry dock).

Ferries run from the New Bedford ferry dock to Vineyard Haven on Martha's Vineyard. A catamaran makes the quick trip in one hour with **New England Fast Ferry Co** (☎ 866-453-6800; www.nefastferry.com) from 6:45am to 7pm (one way adult/child/senior $20/17/17). Four ferries run daily off-season, more in summer. From I-195, take exit 15 to MA 18. Continue south on MA 18 to the fourth set of lights, turn left and follow signs 0.8 miles to Billy Wood's Wharf and the ferry.

FALL RIVER

pop 91,938

Fall River has a good harbor, rivers for water power and a humid climate that's well suited to working woolen thread, so it was natural that it became one of New England's most important textile production centers during the 19th century. Thousands of tons of the local granite were hewn to build the huge textile mills that are still the most prominent feature of Fall River's cityscape. But Fall River was the victim of its own success. Industrial wealth led to inflation and higher costs. After the turn of the 20th century, the textile trade moved to cheaper labor markets in the southern states and then moved overseas, leaving Fall River's great textile mills empty.

Today the great granite buildings are busy again. Fall River has become an off-price shopping mecca, the 'largest factory-outlet shopping center in New England,' as the signs say. Most of the spacious mills are again filled with textiles – goods not made here, but imported from Asia and Latin America.

The **Fall River Area Chamber of Commerce** (☎ 508-676-8226; www.fallriverchamber.com; 200 Pocasset St) can show you the ropes.

Factory-Outlet Stores

The concept of the factory-outlet store began a century ago when flawed, but still usable, products would be sold to locals at very low prices. Today prices often are much the same as in city department stores and specialty shops. But in Fall River, cheap rents in the old mills allow manufacturers to pass on savings to consumers. Over 100 merchants have set up shop in the mills, selling everything from cut-price jeans to designer dresses that are a little out of fashion. You'll find accessories, baskets, books, candy and nuts, carpets, children's clothing, cosmetics, crystal and glass, curtains, furniture, gift wrap and greeting cards, kitchenware, leather goods, linens, lingerie, luggage, toys, raincoats and overcoats, shoes, sweaters, ties, towels and even wallpaper. You can easily reach the outlets via I-195 (they are visible from the road).

Battleship Cove

Take I-195 exit 5 at the Braga Bridge, then follow the signs to **Battleship Cove** (☎ 508-678-1100, 800-533-3194; www.battleshipcove.com; 1 Water St; adult/child/senior $12/7/10; ☼ 9am-5pm), a quiet corner of Mt Hope Bay that holds well-preserved WWII-era vessels that you can visit. The 46,000-ton battleship USS *Massachusetts*, longer than two football fields and taller than a nine-story building, carried a crew of 2300 and was the first and last battleship to fire her 16-inch guns in WWII. The USS *Joseph P Kennedy Jr*, named for President John F Kennedy's older brother, did battle in the Korean and Vietnam Wars and is now a museum. The USS *Lionfish* is a WWII submarine still in full working condition. There are also two Patrol Torpedo (PT) boats, a landing craft, a Japanese attack boat and other craft. Food is available at the site. You can even dine in the Massachusetts' wardroom if you like.

Just past the battleship, the **Marine Museum** (☎ 508-674-3533; www.marinemuseum.org; 70 Water St; adult/child/senior $5/4/4; ☼ 9am-5pm Mon-Sat, 9am-4pm Sun) has an extensive display of intricate ship models, including a scale model of the *Titanic* that was used in the 1950s movie on the subject.

Cape Cod, Nantucket & Martha's Vineyard

CONTENTS

CAPE COD, NANTUCKET & MARTHA'S VINEYARD

HIGHLIGHTS

■ **Best Biking**
Pedaling the exhilarating trails of Martha's Vineyard (p216), Nantucket (p206) or, the granddaddy of them all, the Cape Cod Rail Trail (p184)

■ **Most Dramatic Cliffs**
Gaping at the awesome clay cliffs of Aquinnah (p224), Martha's Vineyard or climbing Provincetown's Pilgrim Monument (p198) for distant views.

■ **Best Whale of a Time**
Learning about whaling history at the Nantucket Whaling Museum (p205) or spotting whales of your own off the coasts of Barnstable (p180) and Provincetown (p199)

■ **Top Tidal Treasures**
Exploring the tidal flats on Cape Cod Bay (p187)

■ **Best Bivalves**
Devouring fresh, deep-fried seafood at clam shacks like Bite (p244), Baxter's Fish 'n' Chips (p182), Cobie's (p187), Sir Cricket's Fish & Chips (p192) or Arnold's Lobster & Clam Bar (p194)

Provincetown ★

Cape Cod Bay

Cape Cod Rail Trail

★ Whale Watching at Barnstable

Bike Trails

★ Clay Cliffs of Aquinnah

Bike Trails

■ TELEPHONE CODE: 508   ■ POPULATION: 255,870   ■ AREA: 548 SQ MILES

If you're like us, in summer your mind goes back to that time in your youth when you were out for a walk or on the beach or alongside a white picket fence, with your best pal at your side, wearing your sundress or your bathing suit, and, ideally, no shoes. In one hand, a softball or swimming goggles, and in the other, the perfect ice-cream cone.

Even if your youth was nothing like that, that's the experience promised by this corner of Massachusetts. Its dunes are covered with beach rose, daylily and eel grass. Sailboats drift off the coast, and even if they're going nowhere it seems far better than whatever else you could be doing with your time.

It's hardly a time warp, though. Nantucket is as modern as it gets, Martha's Vineyard has its share of celebrities, and anybody who thinks that the Cape is all about fried clams and mini-golf has never been to a drag show in Provincetown.

So go out and kayak. Find the perfect lobster roll. See a play. Bike. Spot a whale. Take a step or three back in history, commune with the dunes, explore the tidal flats or marvel at the great clay cliffs.

And don't forget that ice-cream.

Climate

The Cape and Islands are all about summer. The weather's generally warm, though sometimes humid and with rainy patches. Spring and autumn can also be excellent times to travel – you'll miss the summer humidity, though temperatures can be unpredictable. Winter is generally left to locals.

National & State Parks

The Cape Cod National Seashore (CCNS; p198), along the ocean between Eastham and Provincetown, is the largest conservation project in the Cape and Islands. At the Cape's other end, the Cape Cod Canal (p176) offers natural and man-made opportunities for boating, cycling and swimming. The 7600-acre Monomoy National Wildlife Refuge (p189), off Chatham, Cape Cod, is a sanctuary for shore birds and horseshoe crabs.

Nickerson State Park (p186) in Brewster, Cape Cod, is 1900 acres filled with ponds and crisscrossed by forested trails. And the bike path, the Cape Cod Rail Trail (p184), is also a state park and one of the Cape's great assets.

The statewide nonprofit Trustees of Reservations (www.thetrustees.org) oversees some large tracts of land for historic or eco-logical preservation, including Cape Poge Wildlife Refuge and Wasque Reservation on Chappaquiddick Island (p220), Martha's Vineyard, and the Coskata-Coatue Wildlife Refuge on Nantucket (p211).

Getting There & Around

Boston is the most common gateway, but Providence, Rhode Island, is becoming an increasingly important hub. Most visitors travel from these gateways by car.

US 6, also called the Mid-Cape Hwy, is a controlled-access route that runs the length of the Cape. MA 28 is a slower, more commercial road that parallels Buzzards Bay on the west and the Atlantic coast from Falmouth through Orleans. The beautiful MA 6A ('the Old King's Highway') makes an attractive meander, paralleling Cape Cod Bay from Sandwich to Orleans.

Passenger ferries to Martha's Vineyard and Nantucket operate from New Bedford, or the Cape Cod ports of Woods Hole (car ferries also available), Falmouth, Hyannis and Harwich. Provincetown can be reached by passenger ferry from Boston or Plymouth. Many ferries are seasonal, as are air services to Hyannis, Martha's Vineyard, Nantucket and Provincetown.

Services of the **Plymouth & Brockton Bus Company** (☎ 508-746-0378; www.p-b.com) run the length of the Cape from Boston at least four times per day, with more frequent services from Boston to the Cape's transportation hub, Hyannis. Sample one-way fares and travel times from Boston are:

Destination	Price	Duration
Provincetown	$26	3½ hr
Harwich	$21	2½ hr
Hyannis	$16	1½ hr

Within the Cape, sample fares and times are:

Route	Price	Duration
Hyannis-Wellfleet	$8	50 min
Hyannis-Provincetown	$10	80 min
Wellfleet-Provincetown	$4	30 min

There are also local bus services around Hyannis, Yarmouth and Provincetown.

CAPE COD

'The Cape,' as it is universally called by locals, is among New England's favorite summer vacation destinations. Vacationers come in search of fresh seafood and enjoy the beaches that cover much of the Cape's 400 miles of shore. There is beauty in the Cape's dune-studded landscapes cloaked in scrub oak and pine, in its fine stands of tall sea grass and in the grace and dignity of its colonial towns. And on a busy summer day, there's not much wilder than Provincetown.

Locals use a somewhat confusing nomenclature for the Cape's regions. The 'Upper Cape' is nearest to the mainland. 'Mid-Cape' extends from Barnstable and Hyannis eastward toward Orleans. The 'Lower' (or 'Outer') Cape extends north and east from Brewster and Harwich east and north to Provincetown.

SANDWICH
pop 20,136
Sandwich is the Cape's first town (founded in 1637) and the first town of note that you encounter across the Sagamore Bridge from greater Boston. Its village center

couldn't be more sylvan, and there's a renowned horticultural park with Americana collections. The town really came to the fore as a center for glassmaking in the 19th century.

Orientation & Information
Water, Main and Grove Sts converge in the small village center, around Shawme Pond. Tupper Rd, off MA 6A, leads to the marina and town beach.

Sandwich is one of the three communities that make up the Cape Cod Canal region (the other two are Sagamore and Bourne). The **Cape Cod Canal Region Chamber of Commerce** (☎ 508-759-6000; 70 Main St, Buzzards Bay; ☼ 9am-5pm Mon-Fri year-round) occupies a former railroad station in the village of Buzzards Bay, on the mainland side of Bourne Bridge.

In summer, visitors will probably find it more convenient to visit the **seasonal booth** (☎ 508-833-1632; MA 130 N; ☼ 10am-5pm mid-April–late Sep) in Sandwich. It's a short drive from US 6 on your way into town.

Sights & Activities
HERITAGE MUSEUM & GARDEN
About a mile from the center of town, this 76-acre **park** (☎ 508-888-3300; Grove St; 2-day ticket adult/child/child under 5/senior $12/6/free/10; ☼ 9am-6pm Thu-Tue & 9am-8pm Wed May-Oct, 10am-4pm Wed-Sun Nov-Apr) has beautifully landscaped gardens and great collections including vintage automobiles, the Cape Cod Baseball League Hall of Fame, folk art, fine art and miniatures spanning various American periods. Another highlight is a 1912 carousel; you can ride it an no extra charge.

SANDWICH GLASS MUSEUM
Sandwich's famous glassmaking heyday was from 1825 to 1888, and this time is celebrated at the excellent **Sandwich Glass Museum** (☎ 508-888-0251; 129 Main St; adult/child $4.50/1; ☼ 9:30am-5pm Apr-Dec, 9:30am-4pm Wed-Sun Feb-Mar). A multimedia show tells the history of Sandwich and the industry's rise and fall, and you can view examples of molded, blown and etched glass, as well as glass-blowing demonstrations.

DEXTER'S GRIST MILL
On the Edge of Shawme Pond, this **mill** (Water St; adult/child $2.50/1.50, Hoxie House combina-

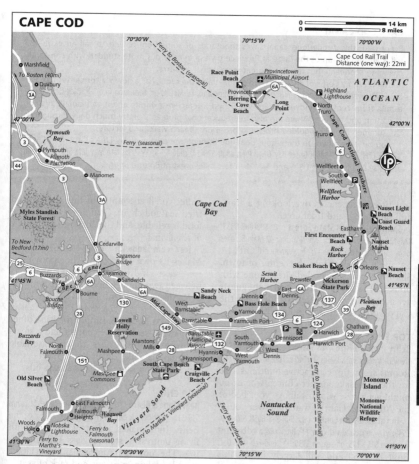

tion ticket $4/2; 🕑 10am-5pm Mon-Sat, 1-5pm Sun mid-Jun–mid-Oct) was originally built in 1654 and rebuilt in 1961. Docents demonstrate the mill's wooden workings and sell cornmeal ground right there.

THORNTON W BURGESS MUSEUM

This tiny **museum** (☎ 508-888-4668; 4 Water St; suggested donation adult/child/family $2/1/5; 🕑 10am-4pm Mon-Sat, 1-4pm Sun mid-Apr–Oct) is dedicated to the children's book author of the same name. Burgess (1874–1965) was a Sandwich native and naturalist, and his 170 titles include *Old Mother West Wind* and the *Peter Cottontail* series. Children enjoy story hours (in season) and playing with puppets on the puppet stage.

HOXIE HOUSE

Built sometime between 1637 and 1670, this restored **house** (☎ 508-888-1173; 18 Water St; adult/child $2.50/1.50; Dexter's Grist Mill combination ticket $4/2; 🕑 10am-5pm Mon-Sat, 1-5pm Sun mid-Jun–mid-Oct) is said to be the oldest 'salt-box'-style house on the Cape. It's also one of the best preserved, since it was inhabited continuously until 1953.

Sleeping
BUDGET & MID-RANGE

Spring Garden Motel (☎ 508-888-0710, 800-303-1751; www.springgarden.com; 578 MA 6A; d incl continental breakfast in season $99-125, off-season $79-99; 🕑 Apr-late Dec; 🖳) About 5 miles east of town, this proudly maintained motel has eight rooms

---

CAPE COD CANAL

Every year, this 7-mile-long canal saves thousands of ships from having to sail an extra 135 miles around the tip of the Cape at Provincetown (a treacherous route studded with constantly changing sandbars), but it's also a great recreational resource.

The US Army Corps of Engineers, which maintains the canal, has a new **visitor center** (☎ 508-833-9678; www.nae.usace.army.mil/recreati/ccc/ccchome.htm; Ed Moffitt Dr; admission free; ❧ May-Oct) about a mile from central Sandwich. Here you'll find interactive exhibits about the canal's history, operation and features. There are also free educational programs pretty much daily throughout the summer, including guided hikes and bike rides, beach walks and lectures.

You can take a two- to three-hour boat ride through the canal with Hy-Line's **Cape Cod Canal Tours** (☎ 508-295-3883; Onset Bay Town Pier; adult $10-14, child $5-8; ❧ trips late May-late Sep, Sat & Sun early May & early Oct), off US 6 and MA 28, a few miles west of Bourne Bridge.

---

and three efficiencies overlooking a tranquil salt marsh and tidal creek.

Shawme-Crowell State Forest (☎ 508-888-0351, 877-422-6762; www.reserveamerica.com; 42 Main St; sites for in-state/out of state $10/12; ❧ year-round) Off MA 6A about 2 miles from the center of town, Shawme has 285 wooded sites (none with hookups) over 3000 acres. Overnight guests get a beach pass. Located 1 mile from the Cape Cod Canal, it's popular with cyclists.

TOP END

Belfry Inne & Bistro (☎ 508-888-8550, 800-844-4542; www.belfryinn.com; 8 Jarves St; r incl full breakfast $110-215) Rooms are in three attractive buildings – go for the namesake former church where you might get a rose window above your bed or the Archangel Gabriel watching over you.

Inn at Sandwich Center (☎ 508-888-6958, 800-249-6949; www.innatsandwich.com; 118 Tupper Rd; d incl breakfast in season $150-175, off-season $130; ❧ mid-Feb–mid-Dec) Built in 1750 and still largely intact, this B&B boasts five fireplaces and some original windows. Up-to-date touches include fancy breakfasts, evening *digestifs* and a hot tub.

Eating

BUDGET & MID-RANGE

Brown Jug (☎ 508-888-4669; 155 Main St) A spiffy new gourmet takeout shop, for when your picnic or romantic evening requires pâté, artisanal breads, cheeses, caviar and the like.

Dunbar Tea Room (☎ 508-833-2485; 1 Water St; dishes $9; ❧ lunch, afternoon tea & dinner) Ever crowded, the Tea Room specializes in ploughman's lunch, quiche, Scottish shortbread and authentic English tea ($11, plus tea) in a countrified setting.

Seafood Sam's (☎ 508-888-4629; Coast Guard Rd; dishes $6-15; ❧ lunch & dinner) This is the first outlet you'll encounter of this Cape-based fried seafood chain. Chain or no chain, the food is reliable, and this location has a view of the Canal.

Ice Cream Sandwich (☎ 508-888-7237; 66 MA 6A) Makes its own ice-cream. The eponymous ice-cream sandwich is a mound of vanilla between two big ol' chocolate chip cookies.

Marshland Restaurant (☎ 508-888-9824; 109 MA 6A; breakfast $2-6, lunch $2-8, dinner $7-13; ❧ breakfast & lunch, dinner Tue-Sun) A simple roadside diner with swivel-seats at the counter and a smattering of booths. Prices are so reasonable (with specials like down-home meatloaf or fancier scallop sauté) that it's always busy.

TOP END

Belfry Inne & Bistro (☎ 508-888-8550; 8 Jarves St; mains $19-31; ❧ dinner Tue-Sun) The ground floor of the Belfry Inne makes a dramatic setting with flying buttresses, stained glass and tall ceilings. The cooking is equally glam: tuna tataki, roast lamb loin in pastry, and rack of veal.

FALMOUTH

pop 32,700

The Cape's second-largest town is a delight. Nothing's more quintessentially New

---

COMING, THIS SUMMER…

Practically every town on the Cape has a summer concert series, held outdoors in a public space such as the town green. Offerings range from jazz, pop or blues by artists of local or national prominence to Sousa marches played by the town band.

Inquire locally at visitor centers for the latest schedules.

England than its village green, or more all-American than its Main St. It's got some 70 miles of coastline, gorgeous woods and excellent summer theater. Falmouth's favorite daughter, Katharine Lee Bates, wrote the words to 'America the Beautiful.'

Orientation

Falmouth sits at the southwest corner of the Cape, bordered by Martha's Vineyard Sound to the south and Buzzard's Bay to the west. From Sandwich, follow MA 28 south to the town center, known as Falmouth Village. Farther east on MA 28, the Falmouth Heights area is known for water views, beachside activities and a ferry to Martha's Vineyard. Ferries also depart from the village of Woods Hole (see the boxed text on p180).

Information

Booksmith (☎ 508-540-6064; 33 Davis Straits), In Falmouth Plaza off MA 28, this independent bookstore is great For grown-ups.

Eight Cousins (☎ 508-548-5548; 189 Main St) A superb children's bookstore.

Falmouth Chamber of Commerce (☎ 508-548-8500, 800-526-8532; www.falmouth-capecod.com; 20 Academy Lane; ❧ 8:30am-5pm Mon-Fri year-round, Sat mid-May–mid-Oct, Sun Jun-early Sep) For in-town tourist information try this place, just off Main St. Web information is also available at www.falmouthvisitor.com.

Falmouth Public Library (☎ 508-457-2555; 123 Katharine Lee Bates Rd; ❧ 9:30am-5:30pm Mon, Thu & Fri, 9:30am-9pm Tue & Wed, 9:30am-5pm Sat) Has Internet access on a first-come first-served basis.

Sights & Activities

MUSEUMS ON THE GREEN

The Falmouth Historical Society's **museums** (☎ 508-548-4857; 55-65 Palmer Ave; adult/child 13 & under $5/free; ❧ 10am-4pm Tue-Sun mid-Jun–Aug, 10am-1pm Sat & Sun early Sep-early Nov) are at the town center. **Julia Wood House** (1790) has an early 19th century doctor's office, while **Conant House** has a room dedicated to Katharine Lee Bates. **Hallett Barn** is full of old tools and farm implements. Docents are usually on hand.

NATURE RESERVES & GARDENS

The tranquil **Ashumet Holly and Wildlife Sanctuary** (☎ 508-362-1426; MA 151, East Falmouth; adult/child $3/2; ❧ sunrise-sunset), a 45-acre Audubon bird sanctuary, has eight nature trails.

East Falmouth's **Waquoit Bay National Estuarine Research Reserve** (☎ 508-457-0495; MA 28;

❧ sunrise-sunset) contains over 2500 acres of barrier beach and a fragile estuary. Great for a walk or a picnic.

BEACHES

Old Silver Beach (P $20), off MA 28A in North Falmouth, is Falmouth's most popular beach and a nice biking destination, with young crowds and long, sandy beaches. Facilities include changing rooms and a snack bar.

There's also **Menauhant Beach** (P $10), Falmouth's best bay beach, off Central Ave from the MA 28 heading east.

Surf Drive Beach (P $10) off Main St, is popular with kayakers and is accessible from the Shining Sea Bike Path (see below).

CYCLING

The Shining Sea Bike Path follows a former railroad bed between Falmouth Village and Woods Hole. Its 7 miles (round-trip) reward cyclists with ocean and lighthouse views. **Corner Cycle** (☎ 508-540-4195; 115 Palmer Av; bike rental half/full day $15/20) rents bikes right near the bike path entrance.

KAYAKING

Waquoit Kayak (☎ 508-548-9722; 1209 E Falmouth Hwy/MA 28, East Falmouth; s/d kayaks $35/45 half day, $49/59 full day, canoes half day/full day $49/59; ❧ Apr-Oct) rents canoes and kayaks; paddling around Waquoit Bay National Estuarine Research Reserve (left) is particularly rewarding.

Festivals & Events

Barnstable County Fair (☎ 508-563-3200; www.barnstablecountyfair.org; County Fairgrounds, MA 151; adult/child $8/free; ❧ late Jul) Over a week of arts and crafts, rides, dog shows, garden and commercial displays and stage performances.

Katharine Lee Bates Poetry Fest & Birthday Party (☯ mid-Aug) The town goes crackers for Katharine, with rhyming games, ice-cream and cake.

Pops Goes the Summer (Barnstable County Fairgrounds; admission free; ☯ early Sep) The annual outdoor pops concert by the Cape Symphony Orchestra.

Christmas Parade (☯ early Dec) The largest of its kind in southern New England. Santa Claus arrives by boat.

Sleeping

BUDGET & MID-RANGE

Elm Arch Inn (☎ 508-548-0133; www.elmarchinn.com; 26 Elm Arch Way; d $90-135; ☯ May-Oct; ☂) Built in the early 19th century, the rambling Elm Arch has 20 colonial-style guest rooms (many with shared bathroom). Some rooms have no air-con, phone or TV, but there's a sun porch for socializing.

Falmouth Heights Motor Lodge (☎ 508-548-3623, 800-468-3623; www.falmouthheightsmotel.com; 146 Falmouth Heights Rd; d incl breakfast in season $105-150, off-season $55; ☂) Within walking distance of the beach and Vineyard ferry, and smarter than your average motel. There are 'wicked clean' rooms, a barbecue and picnic area, and a few studios with kitchenettes.

Seaside Inn (☎ 508-540-4120, 800-827-1976; www.seasideinnfalmouth.com; 263 Grand Ave S; d in season $115-224, off-season $35-149) At this well-kept little colony by the sound, prices are determined by your answers to the following: Balcony? Limited or full ocean view? Kitchenette? Weekend or weekday stay?

Green Harbor Waterfront Lodging (☎ 508-548-4747, 800-548-5556; www.gogreenharbor.com; 134 Acapesket Rd, East Falmouth; d in season $114-166, off-season $44-132; ☯ May-Oct; ☂) Green indeed, on a super-quiet saltwater inlet. There are two pools, boats for loan, and barbecue and laundry facilities, and all 37 rooms have at least fridge and microwave.

Sippewissett Campground & Cabins (☎ 508-548-2542, 800-957-2267; www.sippewissett.com; 836 Palmer Ave; 2-adult sites with off-season discounts & hookups $31-33, without hookups $23-25, cabins in season $350-650, cabins off-season $235-460; ☯ late May–mid-Oct) Off MA 28, about 2 miles north of Falmouth Village, this family-friendly 13-acre place has 100 wooded campsites and 11 camping cabins. Bonuses include a free shuttle to Chapoquoit beach and the Vineyard ferry.

TOP END

Palmer House Inn (☎ 508-548-1230, 800-472-2632; www.palmerhouseinn.com; 81 Palmer Ave; d incl breakfast in season $140-269, off-season $90-199) This early 19th-century house has 17 luxurious rooms decorated with antiques. Extras include lots of snacks, nightly turn-down, triple sheeting and spirited hosts.

Inn on the Sound (☎ 508-457-9666, 800-564-9668; www.innonthesound.com; 313 Grand Ave S; d $150-295; ☯ Apr-Oct) Across from the beach with a clean, contemporary, beach elegance. Many of the 10 rooms have private decks.

Eating

Laureen's (☎ 508-540-9104; 170 Main St; mains lunch $7-13, dinner $18-27; ☯ lunch Mon-Sat year-round, lunch Sun summer, dinner Thu-Sat) From its origins as an upscale deli, Laureen's has grown into a bright and cheery storefront with a constantly changing American menu.

Chapoquoit Grill (☎ 508-540-7794; 410 MA 28A; mains $7-19; ☯ dinner) A few miles north of town, this place has excellent pizzas loaded with garlic and even better nightly seafood and swordfish specials. You'll wait in line in summer, but it's worth it.

La Cucina Sul Mare (☎ 508-548-5600; 237 Main St; mains lunch $6-12, dinner $12-20; ☯ lunch Tue-Sun, dinner daily) You won't leave hungry from this New York–/Boston-style Italian place; think veal or chicken *limone*, Milanese or *picatta*, or fish and pasta dishes.

The Clam Shack (☎ 508-540-7758; 227 Clinton Ave; dishes $3-14; ☯ lunch & dinner May-early Sep) A classic of the genre, right on Falmouth Harbor. It's tiny, with picnic tables on the back deck and lots of fried seafood.

Bangkok Cuisine (☎ 508-495-3760; 809 Main St; specials lunch $7-10, mains dinner $8-17; ☯ lunch Mon-Sat, dinner daily) Comfy, modest place with Thai music on the stereo and embroidered tapestries on the walls; it's one of the best ethnic restaurants we've found on the Cape.

Ben & Bills Chocolate Emporium (☎ 508-548-7878; 209 Main St) This place has been in the same family for generations, with chocolates made in-house, dozens of ice-cream combinations and 24 flavors of saltwater taffy. Adventurous? Try the lobster ice-cream.

Drinking

Coffee Obsession (☎ 508-540-2233; 110 Palmer Ave) The java is strong at the 'Coffee O,' an alternative place a little out of the way. There's communal newspapers, and it's great for hanging out and sipping.

FIELD OF DREAMS

The crack of a wooden bat making contact with a curve ball. The night lights and fireflies. The rudimentary aluminum seats within spitting distance of the third baseman. The free admission. The hopes and dreams of making it big-time.

If you think the major leagues have been sullied by salaries and egos, the Cape Cod Baseball League (CCBL) will give you faith. It's the nation's oldest amateur league (founded in 1885) and remains the country's most competitive summertime proving ground. The league's slogan – 'Where the stars of tomorrow shine tonight' – isn't far from the truth. One-sixth of all players in the major leagues today played here. Some of the best-known names include Hall-of-Famer Red Sox catcher Carlton Fisk and the late Thurman Munson. Barry Zito of the Oakland A's and catcher Jason Varitek are among some 200 CCBL alumni in the majors today.

There are 10 team franchises, located in Bourne, Brewster, Chatham, Cotuit (Barnstable), Falmouth, Harwich, Hyannis, Orleans, Wareham (barely off-Cape) and Yarmouth. The season runs from mid-June to mid-August. Stop into local chambers of commerce for schedules and locations.

Liam Maguire's Irish Pub & Restaurant (☎ 508-548-0285; 273 Main St) Guinness and Harp on draft, Irish waiters, live music nightly and boisterous songfests, including folk, Irish and even karaoke.

Entertainment
THEATER
In summer, Falmouth has one of the Cape's busiest performing arts scenes.

College Light Opera (☎ 508-548-0668; Highfield Theatre, Highfield Dr; tickets $25; ⊙ late Jun-late Aug) A well-regarded summer theater of college-age students from across the country. Expect lots of Broadway and light opera staples.

Cape Cod Theatre Project (☎ 508-457-4242; www.capecodtheatreproject.org; Falmouth Academy, 7 Highfield Dr; tickets $18; ⊙ Jul) The Theatre Project brings actors (occasionally famous ones) together with playwrights to perform staged readings of new works.

NIGHTCLUBS
Boathouse (☎ 508-548-7800; 88 Scranton Ave; ⊙ Apr-Sep) With live music and DJs nightly in summer, and DJs in the spring and fall, this place packs in boisterous 20-somethings.

BARNSTABLE
pop 49,000 (including Hyannis)
Sprawling Barnstable is the Cape's largest town and county seat. It was first settled by English pilgrims in 1639 and is home to the country's oldest Congregational church and library. MA 6A in Barnstable is historic and scenic, and dotted with antique stores, art galleries and craft shops.

Barnstable is made up of seven villages, although only Hyannis gets its own section in this book (p181).

Orientation
Barnstable covers the entire breadth of the Cape, from Cape Cod Bay in the north to Martha's Vineyard Sound in the south.

Most travelers will find themselves in Barnstable Village (along MA 6A) and Cotuit (on MA 28 to the south) – and Hyannis (p181). Locals call MA 6A both Main St and Old King's Hwy, while MA 28 is also called Falmouth Rd.

Information
Hyannis Area Chamber of Commerce (☎ 508-362-5230, 800-449-6647; www.hyannis.com; 1481 MA 132; ⊙ 9am-5pm Mon-Sat year-round, 10am-2pm Sun & holidays in season) Oversees tourism for all of Barnstable.

Sturgis Library (☎ 508-362-6636; 3090 Main St/MA 6A, Barnstable Village; ⊙ 10am-5pm Mon & Wed-Fri, 1-8pm Tue, 10am-4pm Sat) The oldest of its kind in the country, built in 1644. Upstairs is a 1604 bible bought by Barnstable's founding settler, Reverend John Lothrop.

Sights & Activities
CAHOON MUSEUM OF AMERICAN ART
In a house dating from 1775, this intimate **museum** (☎ 508-428-7581; 4676 Falmouth Rd/MA 28, Cotuit; adult/child $4/free; ⊙ 10am-4pm Tue-Sat Feb-Dec) focuses on the works of Martha Cahoon (1905–1999) and Ralph Cahoon (1910–1982), wife and husband painters who lived in this house for 37 years. His work: fanciful images like mermaids fixing dinner; hers: sly observations of American life.

DETOUR: WOODS HOLE

Postage-stamp size Woods Hole, one of the villages in southwest Falmouth, is best known as a seaport and for the Woods Hole Oceanographic Institution (WHOI, pronounced 'hooey'), which undertakes marine research and exploration. With nearly 220 acres of facilities, nearly 60 buildings and laboratories and some 650 employees, it's the largest institution of its kind in the US.

WHOI was founded in 1930 with funding from the Rockefeller Foundation and remains a private institution, although its clients include the US military and local governments. Around 350 different projects are underway at any one time, studying such phenomena as coastal erosion, ocean plant and animal life, and global climate change.

Ninety-minute general guided tours of **WHOI facilities** (☎ 508-289-2252; 93 Water St; admission free but reservation required; 10am & 1:30pm Mon-Fri summer) depart from the WHOI **visitor center** (8am-5pm year-round). WHOI also has an **Exhibition Center** (☎ 508-289-2100; 15 School St; suggested donation adult/child $2/free; 10am-4:30pm Mon-Sat late May-early Sep, hrs vary rest of year).

The **Woods Hole Science Aquarium** (☎ 508-495-2001; cnr Water & Albatross Sts; admission free; 10am-4pm daily mid-Jun–mid-Sep, 10am-4pm Mon-Fri mid-Sep–mid-Jun) has little flash and dazzle, but you'll find unusual sealife specimens, and examples of local fish and the *Homarus americanus* (aka lobster). The big attraction is the twice-daily feedings of seals in front of the building.

SANDY NECK BEACH

Cape Cod Bay's best **beach** (☎ 508-362-8300; P Mon-Fri/Sat & Sun $10/12) is 6 miles long and backed by a network of high dunes. Facilities include a changing room, rest rooms and a snack bar. A 10-mile (round-trip) salt marsh trail begins at the gatehouse parking lot.

WHALE WATCHING

Hyannis Whale Watcher Cruises (☎ 508-362-6088, 888-942-5392; Barnstable Harbor; adult/child/senior $32/18/28; cruises mid-Apr–mid-Oct) offers four-hour narrated trips with an onboard naturalist. On those rare occasions when you don't spot any whales, you get a free pass for your next trip.

Sleeping

Honeysuckle Hill (☎ 508-362-8418, 866-444-5522; www.honeysucklehill.com; 591 MA 6A; d incl breakfast in season $140-170, off-season $120-150) One of the friendliest B&Bs along MA 6A, with four comfortably elegant rooms, generous breakfasts, gardens, snacks and drinks all day, classical music and a genial English innkeeper.

Lamb & Lion Inn (☎ 508-362-6823, 800-909-6923; www.lambandlion.com; 2504 MA 6A; d incl breakfast in season $145-220, off-season $135-155;) The ten rooms at the Lamb & Lion have kitchenettes and surround a pool and hot tub. Some rooms are beachy, others more Colonial in style, but it's all very pleasant and cheery.

Eating

Regatta (☎ 508-428-5715; 4631 Falmouth Ave/MA 28, Cotuit; mains $22-34; dinner in season, with reduced hrs off-season) Frequently said to offer the best dining on the Cape, Regatta serves tapas with world flavors (including those of Italy, Polynesia and Japan) and contemporary American dishes in a candlelit setting. The three-course early-dinner menu ($19 to $21, served from 4:30pm to 5:45pm) is a steal.

Mill Way Fish and Lobster Market (☎ 508-362-2760; 275 Mill Way, Barnstable Harbor; dishes $9-19; lunch & dinner mid-May–mid-Sep) This harborside joint makes great fish sandwiches, fried seafood and fish chowder.

Dolphin (☎ 508-362-6610; 3250 MA 6A; mains lunch $4-13, dinner $18-25; lunch Mon-Sat, dinner daily) It's refreshing: a seafood restaurant without nautical decor or aspirations to be a seaside dive. Instead, it's a low-key place with a long, attractive marble bar, and it's a popular local hangout.

Four Seas (☎ 508-775-1394; 360 S Main St, Centerville) This place has been dispensing homemade ice-cream since 1934! Try the beach plum flavor.

Entertainment

Barnstable Comedy Club (☎ 508-362-6333; www.barnstablecomedyclub.com; 3171 MA 6A; tickets $14-16) Despite its name, it's not a comedy club. Rather, it performs musicals and plays, and is the oldest (1922) nonprofessional theater group in Massachusetts – by some reckonings it's the oldest such group in the entire country.

HYANNIS

pop 14,200

The Cape's commercial and transportation hub has a rejuvenated waterfront and Main St, making it a pleasant (if busy) place to make your next connection. Hyannis also attracts Kennedy fans: it was the summer home of JFK and remains the family compound.

Despite Hyannis' old-line heritage, today Main St has the makings of a mini–United Nations: Brazil, India, Russia and the 'nation' of hip-hop are all represented.

Orientation

Hyannis is the seat of the town of Barnstable. It sits on the south shore of the Cape, facing Martha's Vineyard Sound. The ferry terminals are the Ocean St and South St Docks. From either terminal it's about a five-minute walk to Main St, or another few minutes to Hyannis' brand-new **Transportation Center** (Cnr Main & Center Sts).

Information

Cape Cod Hospital (☎ 508-771-1800; 27 Park St), a few blocks from the center of town, is open 24 hours a day.

Library (☎ 508-775-2280; 401 Main St; ☒ 11am-4pm Mon, Thu & Fri, 11am-8pm Tue & Wed, check for off-season hrs) This large public library has a number of terminals with free Internet access in 30-minute increments.

Sights & Activities

JOHN F KENNEDY HYANNIS MUSEUM

The 35th President of the US summered in Hyannisport (an exclusive section of Hyannis, on the water west of the town center), and this **museum** (☎ 508-790-3077; 397 Main St; adult/child 10-17/child under 10 $5/2.50/free; ☒ 9am-5pm Mon-Sat & noon-5pm Sun mid-Apr–mid-Oct, 10am-4pm Thu-Sat & noon-4pm Sun mid-Oct–Dec & mid-Feb–mid-Apr) celebrates JFK's life here through some 80 heartwarming photographs, a video presentation and artifacts.

A short drive away, a simple **memorial** stands off Ocean St, overlooking the harbor where JFK often sailed.

CAPE COD CHIPS FACTORY

These much-admired chips are of the potato, not the computer, variety, so although they won't work in your Dell, they'll taste good in your gateway. The **factory** (☎ 508-775-3358, 888-881-CHIP; 100 Breed's Hill Rd; admission free; ☒ 9am-5pm Mon-Fri) has a walk-through tour on which you can watch the little buggers march across the production and packaging lines. The whole visit might take you 15 minutes, and you get free samples.

BEACHES

Parking is $10 for all beaches listed.

The **Sea St Beach**, off Sea St from the western end of Main St, is a narrow but decent beach with rest rooms and a bathhouse. **Kalmus Park Beach**, off Ocean St, has a rest room, bathhouse and good windsurfing conditions. **Veteran's Beach**, off Ocean St at the town park, is both park and beach. Families picnic and barbecue (there's a snack bar, too), play paddle ball and swim in shallow waters.

West Hyannisport (technically Centerville) boasts popular **Craigville Beach**, the Cape's largest beach. It has rest rooms and changing rooms.

CAPE COD CENTRAL RAILROAD

A historic **train** (☎ 508-771-3800, 888-797-7245; www.capetrain.com; cnr Center & Main Sts; adult/child/senior $15/11/13; ☒ trips late May-Oct) makes a two-hour scenic run between Hyannis' Transportation Center and the Cape Cod Canal. There are two trips daily except Monday, so you could take the early train, get off in Sandwich, mosey into the village (about a 10-minute walk) and catch the last train back. Inquire about specialized excursions.

CRUISES

Laid-back sailors will enjoy a **catboat ride** (☎ 508-775-0222; www.catboat.com; Ocean St Dock; adult/child/senior $25/10/20; ☒ trips mid-Apr–late Nov), voyages are designed to maximize wind power and minimize motor noise. Trips include nature cruises, port trips, 'blue water' sailing and evening cruises.

The **Hy-Line Company** (☎ 508-790-0696; www.hy-linecruises.com; Ocean St Dock; adult/child 5-12 $12/6; ☒ trips late Apr-late Oct) offers hour-long sightseeing trips of the harbor and bay. Special events include jazz cruises and fishing cruises, as well as an 'ice-cream float,' which is a cruise that allows you to enjoy a sundae with the view.

Festivals & Events

Weekly street fair (☒ 5-10pm Thu late Jun-Aug) Western Main St closes down for this fair, with street performers and amusements for children, and stores and restaurants staying open late.

Pops by the Sea concert (☼ mid-summer) This concert features the Boston Pops Orchestra on the village green, with some 15,000 people turning out for the event.

Sleeping

Anchor-In (☎ 508-775-0357; www.anchorin.com; 1 South St; d incl breakfast in season $139-229, off-season $55-169; ▣ ▦) Sparkly white and practically next door to the Steamship Authority ferries. There's a variety of rooms, but all enjoy a heated pool and harbor-view balconies.

Sea Breeze Inn (☎ 508-771-7213; www.seabreezeinn .com; 270 Ocean Ave; d incl expanded continental breakfast in season $80-140, off-season $60-110) Fourteen clean, pleasant and comfy rooms within a sandal-shuffle of the beach. A few rooms have sea views. There are fancier B&Bs but fewer with more heart.

Captain Gosnold Village (☎ 508-775-9111; www .captaingosnold.com; 230 Gosnold St; d in season/off-season $105/65, studios $90/55, 1-bedroom cottages $170/100; ☼ Apr-Oct; ▦) Named for the explorer who named the region, this complex has 25 small, informal and value-priced units, built in the 1950s and '60s. Air-con costs extra, and beach towels are not provided.

Hyannis Travel Inn (☎ 508-775-8200, 800-352-7190; www.hyannistravelinn.com; 18 North St; d incl breakfast in season $90-140, off-season $39-99; ☼ Feb-Nov; ▦) Although there's nothing distinctive about the 83 rooms here, there are saunas, a hot tub and indoor and outdoor swimming pools, and it has a central location.

Eating

Roadhouse Café (☎ 508-775-2386; 488 South St; mains $8-25; ☼ dinner) Clubby and old-style with spacious booths and white tablecloths. The veal gorgonzola is strong and the linguine *puttanesca* mighty, and we flipped over the house salad dressing.

Naked Oyster (☎ 508-778-6500; 20 Independence Dr; mains $7-25; ☼ lunch Mon-Fri off-season, dinner year-round) Despite the mini-mall location, this place is rather chichi. The oyster menu reads like the Oystertown phone book; other favorites include steak au poivre and roasted seafood.

Brazilian Grill (☎ 508-771-0109; 680 Main St; lunch/ dinner buffet $7/10, with barbecue $13/18; ☼ lunch & din-ner) The amazing buffet includes everything from rice and beans to soups, salads and stewed and marinated fish. However, the star is *churrasco à rodízio* – barbecued meats on skewers.

Egg & I (☎ 508-771-1596; 521 Main St; mains $4-10; ☼ 6am-1pm daily Apr-Oct, Sat & Sun Mar & Nov) It's hard to beat the value, or the imagination: create your own omelette, or go for house specialties like the Italian omelette (with mozzarella, peppers, sausage and marinara), cranberry pancakes or seafood Benedict.

Baxter's Fish 'n' Chips (☎ 508-775-4490; 177 Pleas-ant St; dishes $7-18 or market price; ☼ lunch & dinner) Baxter's serves the requisite fish-and-chips and boasts a raw bar. For many, though, the harborfront location with picnic tables on a floating dock is the real draw.

RooBar City Bistro (☎ 508-778-6515; 586 Main St; mains dinner $18-28, pizzas $10-14; ☼ 4pm-1am). Known for its lively bar scene, this hip place features an exposed kitchen, high ceilings, great people-watching and New American cuisine like littleneck clams with andouille sausage.

Box Lunch (☎ 508-790-5855; 357 Main St; sandwiches around $6; ☼ lunch Mon-Sat) This Cape chain's 'rollwich' (a rolled pita-bread sandwich) is something you need to try once. Many varie-ties have cute names for Pilgrims and ingre-dients like turkey, stuffing and cranberry.

Drinking & Entertainment

Hyport Brewing Company (☎ 508-775-8289; 720 Main St; ☼ 11:30am-1am) The Cape's one and only microbrewery/restaurant brews five of its own; try a sampler of all its varieties for $7. The batter for its fried snacks is made with the house brew.

Prodigal Son (☎ 508-771-1337; 10 Ocean St; dishes $3-7; ☼ 9:30am-6pm Mon & Thu, 9:30am-midnight Wed, Fri & Sat, noon-midnight Sun) A relaxed, borderline-grunge coffeehouse. Its comfortable couches are perfect for listening to live folk, blues and jazz.

Cape Cod Melody Tent (☎ 800-347-0808; www .melodytent.org; 21 W Main St) It's just that – a giant tent, seating 2300 people, but nobody sits more that 50ft from the stage. Between June and August it headlines big-name acts like Mary Chapin Carpenter, Kevin James, the Beach Boys, Tony Bennett, Lyle Lovett, Jimmy Cliff and the Kings (BB and Carole).

Shopping

Main St offers a mishmash of shops, from funky ones geared towards tattooed high schoolers to upscale galleries. Try **Spectrum Gallery** (☎ 508-771-4554; 342 Main St), featuring handmade contemporary American crafts, and **Plush & Plunder** (☎ 508-775-4467; 605 Main St), with retro accessories.

Cape Cod Mall (☎ 508-771-0200; cnr MA 28 & MA 132) is geared to one-stop shopping, with big-box department stores, a large Barnes & Noble and a Regal Cinemas multiplex.

YARMOUTH

pop 25,000

There are basically two Yarmouths, and the one you visit may depend on your needs. The first one, along MA 6A, is called Yarmouth Port – it's green and genteel with shady trees, antique shops and former sea captains' homes. The second Yarmouth is along MA 28 to the south, a flat world of mini-golf and budget motels.

Orientation & Information

Yarmouth stretches from Martha's Vineyard Sound on the south to Cape Cod Bay in the north, with Barnstable to the west and Dennis to the east. US 6A and 6 and MA 28 all run through town.

Staff are friendly and informative at the **Yarmouth Chamber of Commerce** (☎ 508-778-1008, 800-732-1008; www.yarmouthcapecod.com; 424 MA 28, West Yarmouth; ☼ 9am-5pm daily early May–mid-Oct, 9am-5pm Mon-Fri mid-Oct–early May).

Sights & Activities

CAPTAIN BANGS HALLETT HOUSE

Found behind the post office off MA 6A, this **house** (☎ 508-362-3021; 11 Strawberry Lane; adult/child $3/50¢; ☼ tours 1pm, 2pm & 3pm Thu-Sun Jun–mid-Oct) was once home to a prosperous sea captain who made his fortune sailing to China and India. It's furnished with items donated by local citizens.

EDWARD GOREY HOUSE

Across the little square from Capt Bangs Hallett House lived the brilliant and some-

---

WHY THE PINEAPPLE?

Outside the Bangs Hallett House, there's a metal spike sticking out of the hitching post. When sea captains returned from the South Seas, they brought pineapples with them as souvenirs (and presumably as delicacies). A pineapple sticking out of the hitching post was an indication that the captain had returned and was ready to receive visitors.

---

what twisted author and illustrator Edward Gorey. This **house** (☎ 508-362-3909; 8 Strawberry Lane; adult/child/student & senior $5/2/3; ☼ 10am-5pm Wed-Sat, noon-5pm Sun May-Sep, 11am-4pm Thu-Sat, noon-4pm Sun Oct-Apr) has changing exhibits about his life and work, as well as a gift shop featuring Gorey-ana.

HALLETT'S STORE

This historic **store** (☎ 508-362-3362; 139 MA 6A; ☼ Apr-Dec) occupies a revered place in Yarmouth's history, as an apothecary (1889), post office and town meeting hall. It still boasts its original soda fountain. There's a nostalgic little **museum** (☼ generally 11am-3pm) chock-full of items collected over the last 100-plus years.

BEACHES

Grey's Beach (Bass Hole Beach), off Centre St from MA 6A, isn't known for swimming, but it has a long boardwalk onto the tidal marsh and across a creek. It's great for picnics and sunsets, and parking is free.

Seagull Beach (**P** Mon-Fri/Sat, Sun & holidays $10/12), off South Sea Ave from MA 28, is the town's best south-side beach. The approach is actually prettier than for Grey's Beach, alongside a tidal river. There is also a bathhouse.

BOATING

Great Marsh Kayak Tours (☎ 508-775-6447; MA 28, next to Zooquarium; tours $45-70) leads groups on expeditions from exploring local rivers and tides to fly-fishing.

MINI-GOLF

Two South Yarmouth courses set standards. **Bass River Sports World** (☎ 508-398-6070; 934 Main St/MA 28, South Yarmouth; mini-golf $7.50; ☼ Apr-Oct) is a pirate-themed 'adventure golf' course, while **Pirate's Cove** (☎ 508-394-6200; 728 Main St/MA 28, South Yarmouth; adult/child $7.50/6.50; ☼ late Apr-late Oct) has the pedigree to go with its popularity: it was designed by Disney imagineers.

Sleeping

Lane's End Cottage (☎ 508-362-5298; 268 MA 6A, Yarmouthport; d incl full breakfast $120) This c 1740 English-style B&B is tucked right back into the woods and is stuffed with antiques. It has three simple rooms, as well as a marvelous old kitchen and a delightful hostess.

All Seasons Motor Inn (☎ 508-394-7600, 800-527-0359; www.allseasons.com; 1199 MA 28, South Yarmouth;

d in season $129-160, off-season $49-129; □ ⚬) One of the newest and easily the best of Yarmouth's motels, with 114 rooms, two pools (one indoor heated), saunas, Jacuzzi, a games room and a coin laundry.

Village Inn (☎ 508-362-3182; www.thevillageinn capecod.com; 92 MA 6A, Yarmouthport; d incl full breakfast $85-120; ☺ May–mid-Oct) This frou-frou-free, family run hostelry, from the late 18th century, has lots of common space and 10 modest guest rooms of varying sizes; two share a bathroom. There's no air-con or phones in the rooms; the rooms in back are quieter.

Eating
BUDGET & MID-RANGE
Inaho (☎ 508-362-5522; 157 MA 6A, Yarmouth Port; sushi from $3.50, mains $14-25; ☺ dinner Mon-Sat) This Japanese restaurant has excellent sushi and tempura, and more exotic dishes. It's also got one of the most interesting designs in the region, especially the Cape-meets-Kyoto sushi bar.

Captain Parker's Pub (☎ 508-771-4266; 668 MA 28, West Yarmouth; lunch $4-17, dinner $9-22; ☺ lunch & dinner) The Captain has won several 'best chowder' contests and serves better than average pub grub. Expect to find it open even during a hurricane or heavy snow.

Keltic Kitchen (☎ 508-771-4834; 415 MA 28, West Yarmouth; dishes $4-9; ☺ breakfast & lunch) In addition to the usual pancakes and eggs, lots of folks go for the Irish breakfast (eggs, black *and* white pudding, mushrooms, tomatoes etc). Expect a wait Saturday and Sunday.

TOP END
902 Main (☎ 508-398-9902; 902 Main St/MA 28, South Yarmouth; mains $18-29; ☺ dinner Tue-Sun in season, shorter hrs off-season, closed Jan) Proof that beautiful flowers can bloom in the oddest of places. Amid the honky-tonk of MA 28, and you'll find subdued decor and very sophisticated, constantly changing New American cooking.

Abbicci (☎ 508-362-3501; 43 Main St/MA 6A, Yarmouth Port; mains lunch $12-15, dinner $23-34, early dinner specials $17-23; ☺ lunch & dinner) Stylish, contemporary Italian dishes like ravioli stuffed with game are served in a modernized 1775 house. The wine selection is famous.

Entertainment
Movies on the Green (Old Townhouse Park) In summer, movies are projected onto an inflatable screen. Check with the chamber of commerce for schedules.

Shopping
Mermaid Salt Water Taffy (☎ 508-394-7557; 984 MA 28, South Yarmouth; taffy per pound $7.99; ☺ 9am-10pm mid-Apr–mid-Oct) This roadside stand has been making and selling since the 1940s.

DENNIS
pop 16,000
Like Yarmouth, Dennis has a distinctly different character from north to south. The area (known as 'Dennis') along MA 6A has rolling hills, cranberry bogs, salt marshes, old captains' homes, antique stores and artisans' shops. Dennisport, in the south along MA 28, has the expected assortment of motels, casual restaurants and mini-golf.

Dennis is also the beginning of the Cape Cod Rail Trail (p184), the famous bike path through the Cape's backwoods all the way to Wellfleet.

Orientation
MA 134 runs north–south through town, linking MA 6A (in Dennis) to MA 28 (in Dennisport). The Patriot Square shopping center is a useful landmark near the halfway point of MA 134, near the beginning of the Cape Cod Rail Trail. Confusingly, MA 6A and MA 28 are both locally known as Main St.

Scargo Lake and the adjacent landmark Scargo Tower sit near the center of MA 6A. Sesuit Harbor, popular with sport fishermen, is east of Dennis.

Information
Arm Chair Bookstore (☎ 508-385-0900; 619 Main St/ MA 6A; book rental per 4 days/1 week $2/3.50) In Dennis.
Dennis Chamber of Commerce (☎ 508-398-3568, 800-243-9920; www.dennischamber.com; MA 28 at MA 134, West Dennis; ☺ 9am-5pm daily mid-Jun–mid-Oct, 9am-5pm Mon-Fri mid-Oct–mid-Jun) Operates from a little booth behind the Kream 'n' Kone restaurant.
Paperback Cottage (☎ 508-760-2101; 927 Main St/MA 28; book rental per 4 days/1 week $2/3.50) At MA 134 in Dennisport.

Sights & Activities
CAPE COD RAIL TRAIL
The much-loved, 22-mile Cape Cod Rail Trail begins here in Dennis, following the flat Old Colony Railroad bed all the way to Wellfleet. Along the route you'll pass ponds, forests, a country store or three, water vistas, beaches and salt ponds. Even

if some stretches are a tad dull, it's one of the Cape's most pleasant excursions.

Park at the trailhead on MA 134 in South Dennis, just south of US 6. You can rent bikes at **Barbara's Bike and Sports Equipment** (☎ 508-760-4723; 450 MA 134; bike rental per 2 hrs/1 day $10/20; ☺ Apr–mid-Nov, weather permitting).

CAPE MUSEUM OF FINE ARTS

With seven modern, airy galleries on the grounds of the Cape Playhouse (p186), this fine **museum** (☎ 508-385-4477; MA 6A; adult/child under 17 $7/free; ☺ 11am-5pm Tue-Sat, noon-5pm Sun year-round, closes 4pm Jan-early Apr) exhibits Cape artists in many mediums.

SCARGO TOWER

Built on the highest spot in the area – 120ft above sea level – this 38-step, 1902 **tower** (admission free) gives you the best views of the Mid-Cape and, on clear days, to Provincetown. To get here, take MA 6A to Old Bass River Rd and from here turn on to Scargo Hill Rd.

BEACHES

Parking at all of the following beaches is $11.

Wade in on the gently sloping grade at the long, dune-backed **Chapin Memorial Beach**. As with all bayside beaches during low tide, you can walk for a mile out onto the tidal flats.

Corporation Beach is another of the most popular on the bay side, and also one of the best equipped, with picnic space, a boardwalk, and wheelchair facilities.

West Dennis Beach, off MA 28, is a narrow, mile-long beach on Nantucket Sound. It's quite popular; facilities include a snack bar and rest rooms.

Scargo Lake (off MA 6A) is one of the Cape's 365 freshwater lakes, and one of the nicest. Despite its relatively large size, it feels cozy and wooded.

BOATING

Swan River Boat Rentals (☎ 508-398-0080; MA 28, Dennisport; kayak rentals 90 min per single/double $15/25; ☺ May–mid-Oct), near MA 134, allows you to explore the small but interesting Swan River from the vantage point of a canoe, kayak or paddleboat.

Sleeping

Isaiah Hall B&B Inn (☎ 508-385-9928, 800-736-0160; www.isaiahhallinn.com; 152 Whig St, Dennis; d incl breakfast in season $114-255, off-season $105-175) This practically perfect B&B offers 12 unpretentious rooms with TV and VCR in a 19th-century farmhouse, and an attached, renovated barn. There are lovely gardens, an enthusiastic host and plenty of common space.

Scargo Manor (☎ 508-395-5534, 800-595-0034; www.scargomanor.com; 909 Main St/MA 6A, Dennis; d in season $135-235, off-season $105-275) A real winner. The yard abuts pretty Scargo Lake, and the rest of the house is pretty pretty, too. For sports enthusiasts, free hire of boats and bikes is available.

Lighthouse Inn (☎ 508-398-2244; www.lighthouseinn.com; Lighthouse Rd, West Dennis; s incl breakfast $122, d incl breakfast $218-298; ☺ mid-May–mid-Oct; ☐ ☒) Originating as a lighthouse in 1856 and owned by the same family since the 1930s, this place feels like a step back in time. There are nine acres of grassy grounds and a variety of buildings and cottages. Children's programs mean free time for moms and dads. Outdoor activities include kayaking, jet-skiing, volleyball, tennis and shuffleboard.

Huntsman Motor Lodge (☎ 508-394-5415, 800-628-0498; www.thehuntsman.com; 829 Main St/MA 28, West Dennis; d in season $89-98, off-season $49-75; ☐ ☒) This establishment has 18 simple rooms and seven efficiencies, and considering that it's on MA 28 it's actually pretty quiet and wooded.

Eating

Red Pheasant (☎ 508-385-2133, 800-480-2133; 905 Main St/MA 6A, Dennis; mains $19-31; ☺ dinner daily Apr-Dec, Wed-Sun Jan-Mar) This former ship's chandlery is over 200 years old, so you can feel as elegant as your surroundings as you tuck into sole à la meunière, roast duckling, rack of lamb or seasonal creations.

Contrast Bistro and Espresso Bar (☎ 508-385-9100; 605 MA 6A, Dennis; dishes $6-15; ☺ lunch & dinner) This mod bistro serves such disparate dishes as frittata and lasagna, meat loaf, quesadilla, grilled chicken sandwich with sun-dried tomato pesto, and moussaka.

Gina's by the Sea (☎ 508-385-3213; 143 Taunton St, Dennis; mains $10-21; ☺ dinner Thu-Sun Apr-Nov) A short drive north of MA 6A, Gina's is popular, popular, popular, with a way-garlicky northern Italian menu. Arrive early, put your name on the waiting list and go to the beach, a short walk away.

Clancy's of Dennisport (☎ 508-394-6900; 8 Upper County Rd; mains $6-21; ☺ lunch & dinner) Clancy's pondside location makes it a cut above other fried seafood places. It's a natural for families, especially at lunch.

Kream 'n' Kone (☎ 508-394-0808; 961 Main St/MA 28, West Dennis; dishes $3-16; ☹ Mar-Oct) A shrine to fried seafood. The original K 'n' K (established 1953) burned down recently, so it's now in clean new digs with river views.

Sundae School (☎ 508-394-9122; 381 Lower County Rd, Dennisport) Quality in a cone. Enjoy in the homey interior, or order from the outdoor counter.

Entertainment

Cape Playhouse (☎ 508-385-3838, 877-385-3911; www .capeplayhouse.com; 820 MA 6A, Dennis; tickets $25-45) The oldest operating summer theater (1927) in the US and still one of the best. Some of the biggest names in showbiz have appeared on its stage. It hosts a different production each week, and also presents a **Children's Theater** (orchestra/balcony $7/6) with classics, puppetry and more.

Cape Cinema (☎ 508-385-2503; www.capecinema .com; 820 MA 6A, Dennis; adult/concession $8/6) If you visit only one cinema on your trip, make sure you head here. On the grounds of the Cape Playhouse, it shows foreign, art and independent films. The art deco ceiling depicts the heavens.

Christine's (☎ 508-394-7333; 581 MA 28, West Dennis; ☹ year-round, entertainment approx Mar-Sep) Hosts DJ nights as well as live acts ranging from dance bands to comedy, Celtic to cabaret, dinner theater to jazz, and celebrity impersonators.

SPORTS

Cape Cod Crusaders (☎ 508-790-4782; Dennis-Yarmouth Regional High School) The Crusaders, a farm team for the professional New England Revolution soccer team, play from early May to mid-August.

Shopping

Scargo Pottery (☎ 508-385-3894; 30 Dr Lords Rd S, Dennis) Offers a change from the omnipresent antique shops. Barely east of Scargo Lake, off MA 6A, it features playful interpretations of architectural icons; they double as birdhouses.

BREWSTER

pop 10,100

Brewster's backbone, the handsome Old King's Highway/MA 6A, is well known for antique shops and art galleries amid old captains' homes. There's also an excellent natural history museum, an equally exceptional state park, and fine restaurants. Bonus: tidal flats that extend over a mile into the bay at low tide.

Orientation & Information

Everything of interest is on or just off of MA 6A (Main St), which runs the length of the town. Nickerson State Park occupies most of eastern Brewster.

The **Brewster Chamber of Commerce** (☎ 508-896-3500; www.brewstercapecod.org; 2198 Main St/MA 6A; ☹ 9am-3pm daily Jun-Aug, 9am-1pm Mon-Fri May & Sep–mid-Oct) is inside Brewster town hall.

Sights & Activities

CAPE COD MUSEUM OF NATURAL HISTORY

At this large **museum** (☎ 508-896-3867; 869 Main St/ MA 6A; adult/child/child 2 & under $7/3.50/free; ☹ 10am-4pm Wed-Sun Apr-May, 10am-4pm daily Jun-Sep, 10am-4pm Sat & Sun Oct-Dec) you can learn about whales, birds, coastal erosion and snakes. It's set on 80 acres of its own land and adjacent to 300 acres of conservation land: coastal woodlands, salt marshes, and beach dunes.

The museum also sponsors excellent naturalist-led walks, lectures and canoeing and kayaking trips around the Cape.

NEW ENGLAND FIRE & HISTORY MUSEUM

Steer your (inner) three-year-old boy to this **museum** (☎ 508-896-5711; 1439 MA 6A; adult/child under 5/child/senior $7/1/3/6; ☹ 10am-4pm Mon-Sat & noon-4pm Sun late May–mid-Sep, noon-4pm Sat & Sun mid-Sep–mid-Oct). There are over 30 fire engines going back to Colonial times, displays about historic fires and (for your real three-year-olds) a picnic area.

STONY BROOK GRIST MILL

This town-owned **mill** (☎ 508-896-6745; 830 Stony Brook Rd; admission by donation; ☹ 10am-2pm Sat & Sun Jun-Aug) marks one of the Cape's most tranquil, lush spots. The water wheel still turns the machinery.

Try to visit the adjacent open-air **Herring Run** (admission free), in the pond above the mill, when thousands of herring are migrating from the ocean to fresh water in order to spawn (mid-April to mid-May is a good bet).

NICKERSON STATE PARK

With 2000 acres, this park boasts eight ponds (two stocked with trout and bass) and a network of trails for cycling and walking. There are also picnic sites and sandy beaches.

Jack's Boat Rentals (☎ 508-896-8556; Flax Pond; canoe/kayak 1st hr $22/20, per additional hr $14/12) within the park, rents canoes and kayaks. **Barbara's Bike & Sport** (☎ 508-896-7231; Main St/MA 6A) rents bikes by the park entrance for long or short periods.

CYCLING

The Cape Cod Rail Trail (p184) runs through town. **Brewster Bike** (☎ 508-896-8419; 442 Underpass Rd, multispeed bikes per 4/8/24 hrs $15/20/22) has bikes and lots of accessories, while **Rail Trail Bike** (☎ 508-896-8200; 302 Underpass Rd; per 3/24 hrs $15/22; ☾ year-round) is right off MA 6A.

TIDAL FLATS

When the tide goes out on Cape Cod Bay, the flats – basically giant sand bars – offer opportunities to commune with crabs, clams and gulls, and to take in glorious sunsets.

Best access to the tidal flats is via the Point of Rocks or Ellis Landing beaches. You can usually park for free at town beaches when the surge of sunbathers has dissipated (late afternoon and any time between early September and mid-June). Parking stickers may be necessary at other times ($10 per day, $30 per week or $100 per season for non-residents).

Sleeping

Captain Freeman Inn (☎ 508-896-7481, 800-843-4664; www.captainfreemaninn.com; 15 Breakwater Rd; d incl breakfast in season $165-250, off-season $155-200; ☒) The area's most upscale inn offers some rooms with TV and VCR, fireplace, refrigerator, Jacuzzi tub and exceptional low-fat breakfasts.

Isaiah Clark House (☎ 508-896-2223, 800-822-4001; www.isaiahclark.com; 1187 Main St/MA 6A; d incl breakfast in season/off-season $145-150/115-120; ☾ Mar-Dec; ☐) This is a late-18th-century house with seven homey guest rooms, some with fireplace. Your innkeepers are musicians so there's free entertainment, if you're lucky.

Blue Cedar B&B (☎ 508-896-4353, 866-896-4353; www.thebluecedar.com; 699 Main St/MA 6A; d incl breakfast in season $125-150, off-season $110-125; ☾ May-Oct; ☐) This renovated mid-19th-century schoolhouse has three clutter-free rooms, with their original floorboards. There are no phones in the rooms, but there are TVs and VCRs.

Nickerson State Park (☎ 508-896-3491; reservations 877-422-6762; 3488 MA 6A; campsites in-state/out-of-

state $12/15, yurts 4/6 people $25/30; ☾ late May–mid-Oct) The best campsites on the Cape (418 of them), some waterfront. You can reserve up to six months in advance.

Eating

Most Brewster restaurants are open only during the summer and shoulder seasons.

Brewster Fish House (☎ 508-896-7867; 2208 Main St/MA 6A; mains lunch $8-13, dinner $17-29; ☾ lunch & dinner daily in season, shorter hrs off-season, open Apr-Dec) Highly regarded for simple, creatively prepared seafood, eg spicy lobster bisque and scallops with sun-dried tomatoes. Expect a serious wait if you arrive after 6:30pm.

Chillingsworth (☎ 508-896-3640; 2449 Main St/MA 6A; mains lunch $13-17, bistro $17-33, fixed-price dinner $58-68; ☾ lunch Tue-Sun & dinner in season, phone for off-season hrs) The classic here is the seven-course, fixed-price French dinner, but you can have a similar experience without losing your shirt: an à la carte lunch, or the bistro dinner menu in the less formal 'greenhouse.'

Cobie's (☎ 508-896-7021; 3260 Main St/MA 6A; dishes $5-19; ☾ lunch & dinner mid-May–mid-Sep) All-American roadside clam shack just off the Cape Cod Rail Trail.

Entertainment

Woodshed (☎ 508-896-7771; 1993 MA 6A; cover $5) Locals hang out at this rustic bar and restaurant, found just east of the town common within the Brewster Inn. It hosts local bands nightly in summer.

Cape Repertory Theatre (☎ 508-896-1888; www.caperep.org; 3397 MA 6A, East Brewster; adult $18-22, child $10-12; ☾ shows Tue-Sat summer, Thu-Sat spring & autumn) Creative outdoor productions are held in both a 135-seat indoor theater and a natural amphitheater. Productions include musicals and children's fare.

For kids, there are **puppet shows** (☎ 508-896-5577; 1969 Main St/MA 6A; tickets $6; ☾ 9:30am Tue-Thu Jul & Aug) at the First Parish Church. They're a Brewster classic.

Shopping

Brewster has the highest concentration of antique shops on MA 6A. The following non-antique stores are also worth visiting.

Brewster Store (☎ 508-896-3744; cnr MA 6A & MA 124) This old-fashioned country store has managed to stay in operation since 1866, and some of it has barely changed since. Pop upstairs to see town memorabilia.

Sydenstriker Galleries (☎ 508-385-3272; 490 Main St/MA 6A; ☺ galleries daily, workshop Mon-Sat) The craftspeople here employ a locally-developed fusing technique that traps painted shapes (think florals) between two layers of glass.

HARWICH

pop 12,900

Things move a little slower here in Harwich, and that's OK. It has great beaches, one of the Cape's most photographed spots (Wychmere Harbor), some fine restaurants and easy access, including a ferry to Nantucket.

Orientation

Harwich faces Nantucket Sound, with a little stretch reaching around Chatham to poke a toe in Pleasant Bay to the east. Most of what you'll need is along MA 28, through the communities of West Harwich and Harwich Port. Wychmere Harbor sits right off MA 28.

Information

Harwich Chamber of Commerce (☎ 508-432-1165, 800-442-7942; www.harwichcc.com; cnr 1 Schoolhouse Rd & MA 28; ☺ 9am-5pm Mon-Sat, 11am-4pm Sun late May–mid-Oct, reduced hrs rest of year) Next to the Village Center Mall. Has up-to-date lodging info, the comprehensive *Harwich Guide* and the leaflet *A Walk Around Historic Harwich Port*.

Wychmere Book & Coffee (☎ 508-432-7868; 587 MA 28, Harwich Port) Something of a wonder with little reading nooks, and a cozy coffee corner.

Sights & Activities

BROOKS ACADEMY MUSEUM

The Harwich Historical Society's **museum** (☎ 508-432-8089; 80 Parallel St, Harwich; suggested donation $3; ☺ 1-4pm Wed-Fri Jul & Aug, 1-4pm Thu & Fri Sep–mid-Oct) is where to come to learn about the cranberry, first cultivated here in 1846 (previously it had grown wild).

CAPE COD LAVENDER FARM

Acres of planted **lavender fields** (☎ 508-432-8397; Island Pond Trail, Harwich Center; ☺ 10am-5pm) on Harwich's north side blend seamlessly with surrounding conservation land. Stroll alongside the fields, or pick up lavender plants or lavender foods (such as marmalade!).

BEACHES

Harwich Port has great beaches. Park in the center of town (no parking sticker needed) and walk about five minutes down to the water.

Festivals & Events

The 10-day **Harwich Cranberry Festival** (mid-Sep) gets about 40,000 visitors annually.

Sleeping

Wequassett Inn (☎ 508-432-5400, 800-225-7125; www.wequassett.com; Pleasant Bay, East Harwich; d in season/off-season from $400/150; ☺ Apr-Nov; ▣ ▤) The priciest lodging on the Cape offers pretty much anything you could ask of a full-service resort: flower-filled gardens, tennis, fitness, volleyball, private boat launch, fine dining and boat rentals.

Dunscroft by the Sea (☎ 508-432-0810, 800-432-4345, www.dunscroftbythesea.com; 24 Pilgrim Rd, Harwich Port; d in season incl breakfast $195-355, off-season incl breakfast $125-225; ☺ year-round) This 1920s house promises a romantic getaway for couples (rooms are named for famous lovers: Cleo & Anthony, Scarlett & Rhett, Sonny & Cher…). It's 150 yards to a mile-long private beach.

Asa Jones House (☎ 508-430-8399; www.asajoneshouse.com; 44 Oak St, Harwich Center; r incl breakfast $95-150; ▣) This unpretentious, c 1875 home boasts three guest rooms with Victorian and country-style antiques. It's conveniently located for big town events.

Eating

Port (☎ 508-430-5410; 541 MA 28, Harwich Port; mains $16-27; ☺ brunch Sun, dinner daily May-Dec). Port is new and upscale, with a city-contempo vibe and worldly wise flavors: think filet mignon with balsamic-blueberry demi-glace, or Thai-style salmon.

Mason Jar (☎ 508-430-7600; 544 MA 28, Harwich Port; sandwiches around $5.50; ☺ daily in season, Mon-Sat off-season) Harwich's shop of note for fancy sandwiches, cheeses, pâtés, pastries, and lemonade made to order.

Bonatt's Restaurant & Bakery (☎ 508-432-7199; 537 MA 28, Harwich Port; mains breakfast $6-10, lunch $4-17; ☺ breakfast & lunch) In the center of town, this short-order kitchen serves consistent, inexpensive fish-and-chips, melt-a-way fish sandwiches, steak sandwiches and the like.

Seafood Sam's (☎ 508-432-1422; 302 MA 28, Harwich Port; dishes $6-15; ☺ lunch & dinner late Feb-late Nov) Family-style fast-food seafood joint with reliable fryolator standbys and cheap lunch specials.

Schoolhouse Ice Cream & Yogurt (☎ 508-432-7355; 749 MA 28, Harwich Port; ☺ April–mid-Oct) After trying the Harwich mud pie (chocolate ice-cream with chocolate-covered almonds, fudge swirl and bits of chocolate cake), we decided to go back for graduate work.

Entertainment

Harwich Junior Theatre (☎ 508-432-2002; www.hjt capecod.org; cnr Division & Willow Sts, West Harwich; adult/senior/under 21 $16/12/14) Originally a children's summer theater (the country's oldest), in the off-season it also stages fare for grown-ups.

CHATHAM

pop 6650

The patriarch of Cape Cod towns, Chatham has a genteel, refined reserve that is evident along its shady Main St; the shops are upscale and expensive, the lodgings tony. That said, there's something for everyone here – families flock to town for seal-watching.

Orientation

Chatham sits at the 'elbow' of the Cape and is blessed with some 60 miles of shoreline between the ocean, sound and countless coves and inlets. Central Chatham is best explored on foot; it's under 30 minutes' walk from end to end.

Information

Cabbages and Kings (☎ 508-945-1603; Gallery shopping center, 595 Main St) Bookstore in the town center.

Chatham Information Booth (☎ 508-945-5199, 800-715-5567; www.chathaminfo.com; 533 Main St; ☒ 10am-6pm Mon-Sat, noon-6pm Sun late-May–mid-Oct, shorter hrs rest of year) A tiny shed in central Chatham. Another booth is located at the intersection of MA 28 and MA 137 (same opening times and dates as for the main booth).

Eldredge Public Library (☎ 508-945-5170; 564 Main St; ☒ 10am-5pm Mon, Wed, Fri & Sat, 1-9pm Tue & Thu) Has free Internet access in 30-minute increments.

Yellow Umbrella Books (☎ 508-945-0144; 501 Main St) In the town center.

Sights & Activities

CHATHAM LIGHT

For expansive and dramatic vistas of sand and sea, head to this lighthouse viewing area on Shore Rd. The present light dates to 1878 and is visible 15 miles out to sea. Tours are held two to four times per month between May and October.

FISH PIER

In the mid to late afternoon, head to the **Chatham Fish Pier** on the north end of Shore

Rd (near the intersection of Old Harbor Rd) to watch the fishing fleet return with its daily catch. Chatham's boats (which are too small to stay out overnight) haul in some of the freshest fish around.

OLD ATWOOD HOUSE MUSEUM

If you have time for just one historical **museum** (☎ 508-945-2493; 347 Stage Harbor Rd; adult/child under 12/student $5/free/2; ☒ 1-4pm Mon-Fri, 10am-1pm Sat, plus 10am-4pm Mon-Sat when it rains, early Jun-early Oct) on the Cape, make it this one. You'll find the usual items from the China trade, and antique household equipment, plus a rare collection of duck decoys by Chatham resident Anthony Elmer Crowell (1862–1952) – one of his pieces recently sold for almost $1 million. There's also an amazing gallery of WPA-style portraits of locals by Alice Stallknecht (1880–1973).

CHATHAM RAILROAD MUSEUM

The little family-friendly **museum** (www.chatham railroadmuseum.com; 153 Depot Rd; admission by donation; ☒ 10am-4pm Tue-Sat mid-Jun–mid-Sep) is fashioned from an 1887 depot and features a 1910 wooden caboose.

BEACHES

Directly below the lighthouse on Shore Rd, **Chatham Light Beach** is a long, wide sandy beach. Desolate, long **North and South Beaches** are accessible only by shuttle boat. They're worth the journey. **Outermost Harbor Marine** (☎ 508-945-2030), off Morris Island Rd, offers transportation to South Beach (adult/child from $15/7.50 round-trip) and North Monomoy ($20) from late May to mid-October. As it's basically a taxi service, you call when you're ready to depart (don't forget to schedule a return pick-up time).

MONOMOY ISLAND

This 2700-acre wildlife refuge is a haven for offshore birds and seals, and is only accessible by boat. You'll be well rewarded for making the additional effort to reach it. Try to make time for a naturalist-led tour with the **Wellfleet Bay Wildlife Sanctuary** (☎ 508-349-2615) or the **Cape Cod Museum of Natural History** (☎ 508-896-3867); call for reservations.

CYCLING

An extension of the Cape Cod Rail Trail (p184) ends at Chatham, and the town's side streets and shady lanes are well suited to bicycling.

SEAL-WATCHING

Beachcomber (☎ 508-945-5265; adult/child/senior $20/14/18; ☒ tours late May–mid-Oct) takes passengers to desolate stretches of beach or to Monomoy for seal-watching excursions. Tours leave from the Beachcomber office on Crowell Rd.

WATER SPORTS

The waters off Chatham are decent for windsurfing and surfing (although it's not the Banzai Pipeline), and the friendly folks at **Monomoy Sail & Cycle** (☎ 508-945-0811; 275 MA 28, North Chatham; sailboard rental 24 hrs $45) rent sailboards.

Sleeping
BUDGET & MID-RANGE

Moorings (☎ 508-945-0848, 800-320-0848; www.moorings capecod.com; 326 Main St; r incl full breakfast in season $145–235, off-season $80–165; ☒ mid-Feb–Dec) Found in the middle of town, with upgraded accommodations and landscaped grounds. All 16 rooms are comfortably elegant; some have decks and fireplaces.

Bow Roof House (☎ 508-945-1346; 59 Queen Anne Rd; d incl continental breakfast $85-95) It's hard to find places like this anymore. Within walking distance of the town and town beach, this homey, six-room, late-18th-century house is delightfully old-fashioned in price and offerings.

Chatham Highlander (☎ 508-945-9038; www.cape codtravel.com/highlander; 946 MA 28; d Mon-Fri $175-215, Sat & Sun $205-245; ☒) The recently renovated Highlander is within walking distance of town, just beyond the rotary. The 27 rooms are extremely well maintained, each with TV and refrigerator, and there are also two pools.

TOP END

Chatham Bars Inn (☎ 508-945-0096, 800-527-4884; www.chathambarsinn.com; Shore Rd; r in season/off-season from $320/150; ☒) This grande dame resort comprises 205 pricey rooms, and cottages on or near the beach. Its 25 acres include an oceanside heated pool, tennis, golf, private beach, exercise facilities and a free boat shuttle to North Beach. You can always visit just for a drink on the expansive verandah.

Cyrus Kent House (☎ 508-945-9104, 800-338-5368; www.cyruskent.com; 63 Cross St; d incl breakfast in season $155-375, off-season $105-225) On a lazy street but steps from Main St, this B&B has award-winning gardens, Victorian-style rooms with TVs and VCRs, and tea and snacks in the afternoon.

Hawthorne Motel (☎ 508-945-0372; www.thehaw thorne.com; 196 Shore Rd; d in season $215-235, off-season $155-195; ☒ mid-May–mid-Oct; ☐) It's all about location. The 27 rooms and efficiencies here overlook the ocean and a stunning private beach. Despite a four-night minimum-stay policy in summer, some guests have been coming here for over a generation.

Eating
BUDGET & MID-RANGE

Marion's Pie Shop (☎ 508-432-9439; 2022 MA 28; small/large pies sweet $6.50/12.50, savory $9/20; ☒ 8am-6pm Tue-Sat, 8am-4pm Sun, reduced hrs in winter) Wild blueberry and strawberry-rhubarb are among the favorite flavors of sweet pies, and savory pies like chicken, beef or clam will satisfy your hungry crew.

Larry's PX (☎ 508-945-3964; 1591 Main St; mains breakfast $3-8, lunch & dinner $3-16; ☒ breakfast, lunch & dinner) Join families munching around tables for eight, or sidle up to singles reading the paper at the counter. It does a big breakfast business, and you can pick up a foot-long sub to take to the beach.

TOP END

Chatham Bars Inn (☎ 508-945-0096; Shore Rd; buffet breakfast $20, mains breakfast $9-16, dinner $21-37; ☒ breakfast & dinner) A worthy splurge. The breakfast buffet is sumptuous, or try house smoked salmon or a lobster omelette à la carte. Dinner is semiformal; think salmon with lavender butter.

Vining's Bistro (☎ 508-945-5033; 595 Main St; mains $19-29; ☒ dinner) Parents (and others) seeking a quiet night away from the kids can run to this grown-up-style joint. Try the lobster taco as a starter, or pan-roasted scallops with bacon and minced mushrooms.

Impudent Oyster (☎ 508-945-3545; 15 Chatham Bars Ave; mains lunch $7-15, dinner $21-28; ☒ lunch & dinner) This place attracts conservative palates with its seafood menu and fresh-shucked oysters, but adventurers can dabble in flavors as diverse as Italian, Japanese and Portuguese.

Chatham Squire (☎ 508-945-0945; 487 Main St; mains lunch $7-17, dinner $16-20; ☒ lunch & dinner) The town's most popular all-purpose tavern has an easygoing rock and roll atmosphere on one side, family dining on the other, and a long and varied menu of Cape classics. Late at night, it's a popular bar.

Entertainment

Monomoy Theatre (☎ 508-945-1589; 776 Main St/MA 28; tickets $15-25; ☺ late Jun-late Aug) On the way toward Harwich, this well-known playhouse with Ohio University students stages a new production weekly. They've been at it since 1957.

Shopping

Main St is bursting with shops and art galleries that could drain your pockets fast. Here are just a couple:

Munson Gallery (☎ 508-945-2888; 880 Main St) One of the oldest continuously operating galleries in the country (opened in 1860), it represents established and up-and-coming American artists.

Odell's Studio and Gallery (☎ 508-945-3239; 423 Main St) Featuring works by two exceptional artists – a metalsmith (jewelry, sculpture, functional pieces) and a painter.

ORLEANS

pop 6350

To some, Orleans is simply the place where MA 28 and US 6 converge and US 6 heads north to Provincetown. Others know that Nauset Beach is exceptional, that Nauset Marsh has a rich ecosystem worth exploring, and that there are lots of good restaurants in town. It also has an important place in Transatlantic communication history.

Orientation

US 6, MA 6A and MA 28 converge at the rotary at the north edge of town, which marks the border with Eastham. Main St intersects with MA routes 6A and 28 in central Orleans, forming a triangle in the town center. The beautiful Town Cove is just east of the intersection of routes 28 and 6A. The center of Orleans is about 3 miles from Nauset Beach on the ocean side, and about half that distance from picturesque Rock Harbor, on Cape Cod Bay.

Information

Orleans Chamber of Commerce (☎ 508-255-1386; www.capecodorleans.com; Eldredge Park Way; ☺ 10am-6pm Mon-Sat & 11am-3pm Sun late May–mid-Oct, reduced hrs in shoulder season) Maintains an information booth off MA 6A just north of US 6.

Outer Cape Health Services (☎ 508-255-9700; 81 Old Colony Way; ☺ 8am-5pm Mon-Fri with extended summer hrs) The local branch of this medical group.

Snow Library (☎ 508-240-3760; 67 Main St; ☺ 10am-5pm Mon, Thu & Fri, 10am-8pm Tue & Wed, 10am-4pm Sat) Internet access.

Sights & Activities

ROCK HARBOR

This busy fishing pier on the bay side of town is a quiet place when the tides are out, but when the fishing boats are in it's a hub of activity.

Adjacent to the harbor is the **Community of Jesus** (☎ 508-255-1094; www.communityofjesus.org), an ecumenical Christian denomination in the Benedictine monastic tradition, chanting

---

THE ORIGINAL FRENCH CONNECTION

Today's multibillion-dollar telecommunications industry owes a debt of gratitude to Cape Cod's Atlantic Shore. The first cable connection between Europe and the US was established in 1879 by the French Telegraph Company, on a windswept bluff of Eastham near the border with Wellfleet.

When conditions there proved inhospitable, the station was moved to Orleans in 1890, and until the mid-20th century, the French Cable Station transmitted communications via a 3000-mile-long cable between Orleans and Brest, France. Lindbergh's arrival in Paris and Germany's invasion of France were among the messages relayed. The **French Cable Museum** (☎ 508-240-1735; cnr Cove Rd & MA 28; admission free; ☺ 1-4pm Wed-Sat Jul & Aug, 1-4pm Fri & Sat Jun & Sep) in Orleans contains all the original equipment, and staffers help explain everything.

Up the road in South Wellfleet, the Marconi Wireless Station was the first place in the US to transmit messages across the Atlantic Ocean *without* wires and cables. With the technology of the day, however, it took 25,000 volts of electricity to place a long-distance call. In 1903 President Theodore Roosevelt used Guglielmo Marconi's invention to send 'most cordial greetings and good wishes' to King Edward VII in England. Little remains here today except for interpretive plaques and a small model, an expansive vista, a walking trail and a fine beach.

Gregorian chants seven times daily. Visitors can tour the Church of the Transfiguration (under construction until 2010), with tile, fresco and stained-glass works.

BEACHES

One of the Cape's best beaches for walking, sunning or bodysurfing is **Nauset Beach** (P $10), a nine-mile-long barrier beach on the Atlantic. Facilities include rest rooms, changing rooms and a snack bar. Parking is usually free in the off-season.

On the bay side, **Skaket Beach** (P $10) is also popular with families because of its tidal flats and good amenities.

BOATING

The excellent **Goose Hummock Outdoor Center** (☎ 508-255-2620; www.goose.com; canoe & kayak rental per 4 hrs singles $25-35, doubles $35; year-round), found off the MA 6A in Town Cove, rents canoes and kayaks for use on the protected and calm waters of Pleasant Bay and Nauset Marsh. Boating tours include Town Cove ($45, two hours) and Pleasant Bay ($75).

FISHING

Rock Harbor Charter Fleet (☎ 508-255-9757, 800-287-1771; www.rockharborsportfishing.com; Rock Harbor; 4-/8-hr trip per person $115/140; trips timed to tides mid-May–mid-Oct), the Cape's largest charter fishing fleet (with 18 boats), is docked here on Cape Cod Bay. The best way to find a captain is to visit the slips and chat.

Sleeping

Nauset House Inn (☎ 508-255-2195, 800-771-5508; www.nausethouseinn.com; 143 Beach Rd; s incl breakfast $65, d incl breakfast $75-170; Apr-Oct) You'll find friendly innkeepers, 14 comfortable rooms (some with shared bathroom) and plentiful common areas, all about a 10-minute walk to Nauset Beach. However, the rooms don't have air-con or phones.

Parsonage Inn (☎ 508-255-8217, 888-422-8217; www.parsonageinn.com; 202 Main St, East Orleans; d incl breakfast in season $120-155, off-season $95-125; Feb-Dec) This rambling 18th-century residence has eight guest rooms with wide pine floors and canopy beds, and a swell breakfast. Relax in the parlor and enjoy piano played by the hostess. Rooms have TV but no phones.

Ship's Knees Inn (☎ 508-255-1312; 186 Beach Rd, East Orleans; d incl breakfast $75-160;) In a quiet location, with 16 rooms; a few are inn-style, and

even the motel-style rooms have personality if not a lot of space. Two of the rooms share a bathroom, and there's also a tennis court.

Cove (☎ 508-255-1203, 800-343-2233; www.thecove orleans.com; 13 MA 28; r in season $119-179, off-season $62-89;) This motel has 47 pleasantly decorated rooms and suites, with refrigerators, microwaves, cable TV, DVD players and coffeemakers. Your room rate includes a free boat tour of the adjacent Town Cove in summer (subject to availability), and access to a private shoreline, barbecue grills and a heated pool.

Eating

Academy Ocean Grill (☎ 508-240-1585; cnr 2 Academy Pl & MA 28; mains dinner $25-30; lunch Tue-Sun & dinner Wed-Sun Apr–mid-Jan) This outstanding seafood restaurant never disappoints. Look for such creative dishes as swordfish with a basil glaze, sole Française and roasted duck.

Abba (☎ 508-255-8144; cnr West Rd & Old Colony Way; mains $18-32; dinner Tue-Sun) Dishes at this elegant new chef-owned spot meld West, East and Middle East, with dishes such as scallops with eggplant puree, and grilled foie gras with creamy lentils and honey ginger sauce.

Nauset Beach Club (☎ 508-255-8547; 222 Main St, East Orleans; mains $21-32; dinner) Creative Italian cooking for a fashionable crowd – think veal with roasted tomatoes and basil, shaved parmesan and aged balsamic. The room is small, so it can get noisy.

Binnacle Tavern (☎ 508-255-7901; 20 MA 28; mains $12-20; dinner - phone for off-season hrs) This dark and cozy tavern is known for gourmet pizzas, eggplant parmigiana and homemade pasta. The new Arbor restaurant next door has the same owners and a more upscale menu.

Land Ho! (☎ 508-255-5165; 38 MA 6A; lunch $5-9, dinner $7-10, seafood $12-17; lunch & dinner) Locals and visitors alike admire the Ho for inexpensive sandwiches, fried seafood, barbecue ribs, clam pie and burgers. Wood floors, checkered tablecloths and old business signs on the walls create an informal atmosphere.

Sir Cricket's Fish & Chips (☎ 508-255-4453; MA 6A; dishes $10-18; lunch & dinner) A great place for a fish – or an oyster – sandwich or platter. There are just a few tables, and chairs are painted with Orleans scenes.

Jo Mama's New York Bagels (☎ 508-255-0255; 125 MA 6A; breakfast & lunch) It's Brooklyn on the Cape, with bagels (from New York's H&H), smoked whitefish, kosher pastrami, yadda, yadda.

Drinking

Hot Chocolate Sparrow (☎ 508-240-2230; 5 Old Colony Way; ⏱ 6:30am-late night) The Cape's biggest coffee bar has the strongest and most consistent espresso around, or you could try the 'frozen hot chocolate'. Staff also hand-dip chocolates and sell ice-cream.

Mahoney's Atlantic Bar & Grill (☎ 508-255-5505; 28 Main St) A fun place that has live jazz on Thursday and bands on Saturday. There's also satellite TV for watching sports.

Entertainment

THEATER

Academy of Performing Arts Playhouse (☎ 508-255-1963; www.apa1.org; 120 Main St) The Playhouse stages dramas, musicals and comedies in the 1873 former town hall.

EASTHAM

pop 5450

Home to the Cape's oldest windmill, some well-known lighthouses and much of the Cape Cod National Seashore, Eastham is one of the Cape's quietest, most compact towns. It was here in 1620 that the Pilgrims first came across Native Americans at what is now called First Encounter Beach.

Orientation & Information

Eastham is just 3 miles wide from bay to ocean, and 6 miles long. North from the Eastham rotary, US 6 has shops, lodgings and restaurants dotted along its entire length (though, confusingly, many locations do not have building numbers).

Just north of the Fort Hill area, the **chamber of commerce** (☎ 508-255-3444l; www.easthamchamber.com; US 6; ⏱ 10am-5pm late May-Sep, expanded hrs Jul & Aug) maintains the town's information booth.

Sights & Activities

Fort Hill commands a high position above the extensive and fragile Nauset Marsh, and boasts a short but lovely 1.5-mile (round-trip) walking trail that skirts the marsh and goes through a red maple swamp.

Atop Fort Hill, the **Edward Penniman House** (☎ 508-255-3421; admission free; ⏱ 1-4pm Tue-Fri, tours 10am Sat & Mon by reservation), a mid-19th-century sea captain's house, is slowly being restored to its former grandeur. The Salt Pond Visitor Center (below) can tell you the current opening times.

The **Old Schoolhouse Museum** (☎ 508-255-0788; Nauset Rd; admission free; ⏱ 1-4pm Mon-Fri Jul & Aug), marked by a huge set of whale jawbones across from the Salt Pond Visitor Center, features a small exhibit on author Henry Beston's year in a cottage on Coast Guard Beach.

Eastham's landmark **windmill** (cnr US 6 & Samoset Rd; admission free; ⏱ 10am-5pm in summer) is the oldest structure in town, although it was actually built in Plymouth, MA in 1680.

The bike trail from the visitor center to Coast Guard Beach traverses a dramatic salt marsh and a pretty forest. Rent bikes at **Little Capistrano Bike Shop** (☎ 508-255-6515; Salt Pond Rd; 2-8 hr hire adult $10/16, child $8/12; ⏱ Apr–mid-Nov).

CAPE COD NATIONAL SEASHORE

With the backing of President John F Kennedy, Congress established the **Cape Cod National Seashore** (CCNS; www.nps.gov/caco) in 1961. The CCNS includes the whole eastern shoreline of the Outer Cape – more than 42 sq miles of pristine, virtually endless beaches, dunes, nature trails, ponds, salt marshes and forests. Everything of interest is on or just off of US 6.

The **Salt Pond Visitor Center** (☎ 508-255-3421; ⏱ 9am-4:30pm Mar-Dec, to 5pm in season, 9am-4:30pm Sat & Sun Jan & Feb), in Eastham, serves the southern portion of the CCNS. There are excellent exhibits and films about the Cape's geology, history and ever-changing landscape. Check out the daily list of ranger- and naturalist-led walks and talks, which are usually free. There are two short walking trails that lead from the visitor center. The **Province Lands Visitor Center** (☎ 508-487-1256; Race Point Rd; ⏱ 9am-5pm May-Oct), in Provincetown, has similar services and exhibits.

Parking permits at CCNS beaches ($10 per day or $30 per season) are transferable, meaning that you can spend the morning at one CCNS beach and the afternoon at another, and not have to pay the parking fee again.

Beaches

Coast Guard Beach, east of the visitor center, is backed by tall, undulating dune grasses. It's popular with families and surfers. Facilities include rest rooms, showers and changing rooms. In summer, when the beach parking lots fill up, a shuttle bus runs from a parking lot near the visitor center.

Nauset Light Beach, north of Coast Guard Beach, is also the stuff of dreams. Its features and facilities are similar to Coast Guard Beach, but you can park right at the beach. **Nauset Lighthouse**, a picturesque red-and-white striped tower, guards the shoreline. The **Three Sisters Lighthouses** are set back in the woods, up Cable Rd from Nauset Light Beach.

First Encounter Beach (P $12), where Samoset Rd meets Cape Cod Bay and the first skirmish happened between Native Americans and the Pilgrims, is an excellent location to watch the sunset. Parking is $12 daily.

Sleeping

Whalewalk Inn (☎ 508-255-0617, 800-440-1281; www .whalewalkinn.com; 220 Bridge Rd; d incl breakfast in season $195-325, off-season $160-270) This establishment, off the Orleans–Eastham rotary, is the Outer Cape's best B&B, with a mixture of room types. Late in the day: cocktails and cordials!

Over Look Inn (☎ 508-255-1886; www.overlookinn .com; 3085 US 6; d incl breakfast in season $145-240, off-season $115-190; 🖳) Virtually across from the Salt Pond Visitor Center, this historic inn is set back from the road and offers 10 antique-filled guest rooms, plus family suites.

Four Points Hotel – Eastham Cape Cod (☎ 508-255-5000, 800-533-3986; www.capecodfourpoints.com; 3800 US 6; d in season $139-289, off-season $59-169; 🖳) Less than a mile north of Salt Pond Visitor Center, this Sheraton has rooms a cut above Four Points properties we've seen elsewhere. Half the 107 rooms overlook the indoor pool and have decks or balconies.

Midway Motel & Cottages (☎ 508-255-3117, 800-755-3117; www.midwaymotel.com; 5460 US 6, North Eastham; d in season $90-106, off-season $56-65; 🌣 Feb-Oct) The 11 tidy units here are set back from the highway and shaded by oak and pine trees. Some units have full kitchens, others just fridge and microwave.

Hostelling International Eastham (Mid-Cape) (☎ 508-255-2785; www.hiayh.org; 75 Goody Hallett Dr; dm $24; 🌣 mid-May–mid-Sep) With only 50 dorm-style beds in eight cabins, reservations are essential for July and August. From the Orleans rotary, follow Rock Harbor Rd to Bridge Rd, then to Goody Hallett Dr.

Eating

Arnold's Lobster & Clam Bar (☎ 508-255-2575; 3580 US 6; mains $9-30; 🌣 lunch & dinner mid-May–mid-Sep) With the exception of a raw bar and weekday lunch specials as low as $3, you know the menu: fried seafood. People also swear by the chowder and onion rings.

Eastham Lobster Pool (☎ 508-255-9706; 4360 US 6; mains $11-31; 🌣 lunch & dinner Apr-Oct) Despite its simple name, the atmosphere and service here have a bit more polished than other seafood shacks. There's informal indoor and outdoor dining, lots of fish preparations, and steak, chicken and pastas.

Nauset Ice Cream (US 6, North Eastham) is a hole-in-the-wall where the ice-cream is made in house. Adjacent, **Friendly Fisherman** (☎ 508-255-6770; US 6, North Eastham; 🌣 in-season) is a seasonal place with fried seafood and great lobster rolls.

Entertainment

First Encounter Coffee House (☎ 508-255-5438; 220 Samoset Rd; adult $12-15, child free; 🌣 8:30pm 2nd & 4th Sat each month, except Dec & May) The little yellow Chapel of the Pines hosts acoustic and folk performances put on by this long-running organization.

WELLFLEET

pop 2750

Wellfleet's got everything: art galleries, fine beaches, quiet scenic roads, a drive-in movie theater, history and famous oysters. Yet Wellfleet is relatively untouched by rampant development and commercialism; the center of town feels like the Cape as we imagine it may have been the 1920s.

Orientation

Wellfleet is about 6½ miles long from north to south. Like Eastham to the south and Truro to the north, Wellfleet is bisected by US 6 (aka State Hwy), and most of the land east of US 6 is part of the Cape Cod National Seashore.

Information

Oceans of Books (50 Kendrick Ave) An institution (locals know it simply as 'the bookstore') and a marvel. It's been here since the 1930s and is jam-packed with books, magazines and comics, some of which are at least as old as the store.

Outer Cape Health Services (☎ 508-349-3131; 3130 US 6; ☻ 8am-7pm Mon-Fri, 9am-5pm Sat & Sun, additional hrs in mid-summer). For basic medical needs. It's by the flashing light on the north side of town.

Wellfleet Chamber of Commerce (☎ 508-349-2510; www.wellfleetchamber.com; 1410 US 6, South Wellfleet; ☻ 9am-6pm daily late May-early Sep, 10am-4pm Fri-Sun mid-May–mid-Oct) Near the end of the Cape Cod Rail Trail.

Wellfleet Public Library (☎ 508-349-0310; West Main St; ☻ 2-8pm Mon, Wed & Thu, 10am-5pm Tue & Fri, noon-5pm Sat) Has free Internet access.

Sights & Activities

The most remarkable feature of the **First Congregational Church** (200 Main St) is its clock, said to be the only clock in the world to ring 'ship's time': every half-hour, starting with one bell at 12:30pm and adding one bell each half-hour, to a total of eight bells. Thus, if it's 1pm, the clock will ring twice, at 1:30pm three times, at 2pm four times etc, until it reaches 4pm (eight bells). Then the cycle starts all over again, so 4:30pm is one bell, and so on.

Art galleries abound in central Wellfleet – over 20 of them sell both fine art and tour-ist-targeted merchandise. The epicenter is the intersection of Main and Commercial Sts. Many galleries host receptions with free food and drink on Saturday nights in July and August.

BEACHES

Marconi Beach, off US 6, is a narrow Atlantic beach backed by cliffs and high sand dunes. It's part of the Cape Cod National Seashore (p198); facilities include changing rooms, rest rooms and showers. Not much remains

---

CAPE COD'S ATLANTIS

In the early 1800s, 60-acre Billingsgate Island stood in the bay off of Wellfleet, with a fishing community of 30 homes, a whale-oil rendering plant, a school and a lighthouse. But in the mid-1800s the island was split in half by beach erosion, and by 1900 the island was abandoned except for the lighthouse keeper. Billingsgate and its lighthouse completely disappeared in 1942; and now it can be seen only at very low tide as a shoal off northern Wellfleet.

---

of the Marconi Wireless Station (see the boxed text, p191), but a model may remind you of early science fiction movies.

Both **Cahoon Hollow Beach** and **White Crest Beach**, on the Atlantic Ocean, are excellent, but parking is $15 daily. White Crest is popular with surfers and hang gliders.

CYCLING

The Cape Cod Rail Trail (p184) ends at Le-Count Hollow Rd. **Black Duck Sport Shop** (☎ 508-349-9801; 1446 US 6; bikes per day/week adult $20/65, child $10/40) is right at the end of the trail – you can also pick up fishing equipment here.

WILDLIFE REFUGES

Massachusetts' Audubon Society's 1000-acre **Wellfleet Bay Wildlife Sanctuary** (☎ 508-349-2615; 291 State Highway/US 6; adult/child & senior $5/3; ☻ visitor center 8:30am-5pm daily late May–mid-Oct, 8:30am-5pm Tue-Sun mid-Oct-late May) boasts walking trails that cross tidal creeks, salt marshes and a Cape Cod Bay beach. The most popular is the Goose Pond Trail (1.4 miles round-trip) from the Nature Center to a barrier beach. The walking trails are open from 8am to sunset (to 8pm in summer).

Festivals & Events

During the **Wellfleet Oyster Festival** (www.well fleetoysterfest.org; ☻ mid-Oct) the town hall parking lot becomes a food fair, with a beer garden and an oyster shucking contest, and, of course, belly-busters of the blessed bivalves. The festival is so popular that it's hard to believe it started only in 2000.

Sleeping

Inn at Duck Creek (☎ 508-349-9333; www.innatduck creek.com; 70 Main St; r incl breakfast $85-125; ☻ May-Oct) This hospitable inn has a variety of comfort-able rooms – antiquey to contemporary – in three buildings. Some have shared bathroom and claw-foot tubs, and some have air-con.

Stone Lion Inn of Cape Cod (☎ 508-349-9565; www .stonelioncapecod.com; 130 Commercial St; d incl breakfast in season $135-160, off-season $95-105) Built in 1871 and newly opened as an inn, the Stone Li-on's three rooms feel historic without being cloying. Outside, there's a wisteria-shaded gazebo. There aren't any phones or TVs in rooms.

Even'Tide Motel (☎ 508-349-3410, 800-368-0007; www.eventidemotel.com; 650 US 6; d in season $98-155, off-season $65-90, cottages per week $1100; ☻ Apr-Oct;

🖼) This 31-room motel, set back in a grove of trees, also has nine cottages that accommodate up to six people each. Other pluses include in-room fridges, an indoor heated pool, horseshoes and Ping-Pong.

Holden Inn (☎ 508-349-3450; www.theholdeninn .com; 140 Commercial St; s $55, d $75-90; ☷ mid-May–mid-Oct) Originally a captain's house, built in 1840, it's been an inn since the 1920s and not much has changed since. However, it is well-kept, with gardens and picket fences. The 26 guest rooms, many with shared bathroom, are housed in three buildings.

Eating

Finely JP's (☎ 508-349-7500; US 6, South Wellfleet; mains $13-18; ☷ dinner daily in season, Wed-Sun off-season) Although it's got all the charm of a nature lodge, this is a real foodie find. We love the Wellfleet paella, served in a delectable broth. Note: they don't take reservations, but you can call to put your name on the waiting list.

Wicked Oyster (☎ 508-349-3455; 50 Main St; mains lunch $6-12, dinner $6-26; ☷ breakfast & lunch daily, dinner Thu-Tue, closures around Thanksgiving & Christmas holidays) The 'in' crowd hangs out here for fried soft-shell crab, tuna carpaccio, or an Angus tenderloin with Jim Beam caramel sauce, and, of course, oysters.

Aesop's Tables (☎ 508-349-6450; 316 Main St; mains $16-33; ☷ dinner mid-Jun–mid-Sep, reduced hrs May-Oct) Those in the know head here for upscale New American cooking. Downstairs, this old house has received a handsome, sophisticated, contemporary update, while the upstairs bar rocks.

Moby Dick's (☎ 508-349-9795; US 6; dishes $7-20 or market price; ☷ lunch & dinner early May–mid-Oct) Prepare for lines at this professional, self-service place – everyone's after large portions of very fresh seafood. The clam chowder, onion rings and steamers (clams) are particularly good. Bring your own beer or wine.

Lighthouse (☎ 508-349-3681; 317 Main St; breakfast mains $3-9, lunch $4-12, dinner $12-22; ☷ breakfast, lunch & dinner, reduced hrs in off-season) Decent food at good prices: omelettes, sandwiches, big salads and lots of grilled fish, and Guinness on tap.

PJ's (☎ 508-349-2126; US 6; dishes $7-20; ☷ lunch & dinner in season) A roadside clam shack, consistently voted one of the best on the Outer Cape. Order at the counter and eat at long tables or in your car.

Mac's Seafood Market (☎ 508-349-9611; 265 Commercial St) Sushi, fish burritos, ice-cream. And if you can eat all of that in one sitting, you must have a cast iron stomach. Enjoy it at tables with a view of Wellfleet Harbor.

Entertainment

Wellfleet Drive-In (☎ 508-349-7176; US 6; adult/child under 4/child over 4 $7/free/4; ☷ late May–mid-Sep, Sat & Sun mid-Apr–mid-Oct) One of the few remaining drive-in theaters in New England. Both the drive-in and the adjacent Wellfleet Cinema play first-run movies.

Wellfleet Harbor Actors Theater (WHAT; ☎ 508-349-6835, 866-282-WHAT; www.what.org; 1 Kendrick Ave; tickets from $23, $25 Sat night; ☷ mid-May–late Oct) Contemporary, experimental plays staged here are always lively, occasionally bawdy and often the subject of animated conversation.

Beachcomber (☎ 508-349-6055; www.thebeachcomb er.com; Cahoon Hollow Beach; cover varies) The Cape's coolest hangout, this indoor-outdoor, all-in-one restaurant, raw bar, bar and nightclub has live music nightly including reggae, zydeco and blues.

Jim Wolf, Master Storyteller (☎ 508-247-9539; Wellfleet Methodist Church, 250 Main St; adult/child under 5/child $9/free/5; ☷ 7:30pm Wed-Fri, early Jul-early Sep) Entertaining, folksy, a little goofy and thoroughly engaging, Jim Wolf tells stories for kids, and for the kids within us.

Shopping

Wellfleet Flea Market (☎ 508-349-2450; US 6; per car Wed & Sat/Thu/Sun $2/1/3; ☷ Sat & Sun mid-Apr–mid-Oct, Wed & Thu Jul & Aug). On the grounds of the drive-in theater, the Cape's biggest flea market has over 240 dealers covering antique to freshly made, treasures to junk.

TRURO
pop 2100

An odd collection of elements coexist peacefully in Truro: strip motels and cookie-cutter cottage complexes, huge homes in the hills and dales west of US 6, and undeveloped forests and beaches to the east.

Orientation

To reach the bulk of Truro's historic sites on the ocean side, take Highland or South Highland Rds off US 6, or any winding road east or west of US 6. Then let yourself get a little lost, and soak in the distinctive scenery.

Information

Chamber of commerce (☎ 508-487-1288; US 6, North Truro; ☺ 10am-4pm late Jun-early Sep, 10am-4pm Fri-Sun late May-late Jun & early Sep-mid Oct) Information office at Head of the Meadow Beach Rd.

Truro Public Library (☎ 508-487-1125; 5 Library Lane; ☺ 9:30am-8pm Tue & Wed, 9:30am-6pm Thu, 9:30-4pm Fri, 9:30-2pm Sat) Free Internet terminals for public use.

Sights & Activities

The **Cape Cod Light** (Highland Lighthouse; ☎ 508-487-1121; Light House Rd; tours $3; ☺ early May-late Oct) is at the tallest elevation on the Cape (120ft above sea level), and there's been a light visible from here since 1797. Daily tours include a short video, a little exhibit in the Keeper's House and a climb of the 69 steps. Children must be at least 51in tall to make the climb.

The adjacent **Highland House Museum** (☎ 508-487-3397; Light House Rd; adult/child under 12 $3/free; ☺ 10am-4:30pm Jun-Sep) is an excellent local museum dedicated to Truro's farming and maritime past.

The Pilgrim Heights Area, on the north side of town and east of US 6, has two short trails with broad views. One trail leads to the spot where a band of 16 Pilgrims purportedly tasted their first spring water in the New World, in mid-November, 1620.

Part of the Cape Cod National Seashore, **Head of the Meadow Beach**, off US 6, is a wide, dune-backed beach. There are no changing rooms and only porta-potties for rest rooms, but otherwise it's excellent for families. At low tide it's possible to view an 1871 shipwreck. Confusingly, there are two entrances to this beach, each with two parking schemes. The National Seashore beach (parking daily/seasonally $10/30) is to the left, while the town-managed beach (parking daily/weekly/seasonally $10/30/150) is to the right.

Sleeping

Hostelling International, Truro (☎ 508-349-3889, 888-901-2086; www.capecodhostels.org; N Pamet Rd, North Truro; dm Mon-Fri/Sat & Sun $22/24; ☺ late Jun-early Sep) This former Coast Guard station has a dramatic location amid dunes and marshes, just a two-minute walk from the beach. Its 42 beds include some very nice twin rooms, and small private rooms.

Seaside Inn (☎ 508-487-1215; www.seasidevillage .com; 482 Shore Rd/MA 6A, North Truro; d incl extended continental breakfast in season $140-155, off-season $65-125;

☺ mid-May–Nov; 🖳) Rooms are well equipped here, with fridge and microwave, TV and DVD or VCR, beach chairs, and guest-use laundry. It's literally on the beach.

Days' Cottages (☎ 508-487-1062; www.dayscottages .com; 271 Shore Rd/MA 6A, North Truro; cottages in season per night/week $145/990, off-season per night $83, off-season per week $570-600; ☺ May–mid-Oct) The 23 identical cottages here, lined up like ducks between MA 6A and the beach, are an architectural landmark, operating since 1931. That said, they're very basic inside.

North of Highland Camping Area (☎ 508-487-1191; www.capecodcamping.com; 52 Head of the Meadow Rd, North Truro; campsites $22; ☺ mid-May–mid-Sep) The most attractive of the area's campgrounds in terms of its natural setting and its facilities. There are 237 sites sharing 60 forested acres.

Eating

Closing dates vary, so call in advance if you're visiting outside of summer.

Terra Luna (☎ 508-487-1019; 104 Shore Rd/MA 6AR, North Truro; mains $17-21; ☺ dinner mid-May–mid-Oct) Nondescript from the outside, this surprisingly hip bistro exhibits local art on barnboard walls and creative New American and Italian cooking (eg grilled duck breast or shrimp linguine with black olives and feta).

Village Cafe (☎ 508-487-5800; 4 Highland Rd, North Truro; sandwiches $2-7; ☺ breakfast & lunch May-Oct, dinner Jul & Aug) In the center of North Truro, this pleasant little place has outdoor seating, salads, sandwiches, a number of vegetarian offerings, soups, bagels, coffees and slick desserts.

Dutra's Market (☎ 508-487-0711; cnr US 6A & Highland Rd, North Truro; sandwiches $2.50-6) This town landmark carries all the basics including liquors & freshly made sandwiches to go.

PROVINCETOWN

pop 3450

This is it: as far as you can go on the Cape. And more than just geographically.

'P-town' is the region's most lively resort town and New England's gay mecca. Walking down Commercial St through the town center on any given day, you may see crossdressers, leather-clad motorcyclists, barely clad in-line skaters, same-sex couples strolling hand in hand and heterosexual tourists wondering what they've stumbled into on their way to a whale-watch.

CAPE COD, NANTUCKET & MARTHA'S VINEYARD

Orientation

Central Provincetown runs northeast to southwest facing Cape Cod Bay. Outside the town center, it's the dunes of the Cape Cod National Seashore all the way to the Atlantic.

Ferries into Provincetown arrive at either MacMillan Wharf or Fisherman's Wharf, next to each other. If you're driving, you'll most likely enter Provincetown on US 6, parallel to the town center. The airport is 2.5 miles from the town center via Conwell St.

Commercial St is the town's main drag (with shops, lodgings, art and entertainment); it parallels the harbor for the entire length of the town. More car-friendly is Bradford St, a block inland.

MAPS

The basic single-sheet map published by the chamber of commerce should be sufficient for most visitors.

Information

BOOKSTORES

Provincetown Bookshop (☎ 508-487-0964; 246 Commercial St) The city's leading and largest bookseller.

INTERNET ACCESS

Provincetown Public Library (☎ 508-487-7094; 330 Commercial St; ⊙ 10am-5pm Mon & Fri, noon-8pm Tue & Thu, 10am-8pm Wed, 10am-2pm Sat, 1-5pm Sun) Has free Internet access in 30-minute increments.

INTERNET RESOURCES

www.provincetown.com The official website of the chamber of commerce, with most of the information you'll need.

MEDICAL SERVICES

Outer Cape Health Services (☎ 508-487-9395; Harry Kemp Way) Off Conwell St from US 6 – open in summer for walk-ins, and year-round by appointment.

MONEY

Seamen's Bank (☎ 508-487-0035; 221 Commercial St) Has a 24-hour ATM.

POST

Post office (219 Commercial St; ⊙ 8:30am-5pm Mon-Fri & 8am-noon Sat)

TOURIST INFORMATION

Chamber of commerce (☎ 508-487-3424; www.ptown chamber.com; 305 Commercial St, MacMillan Wharf; ⊙ 9am-5pm Jun-Sep, 10am-4pm Mon-Sat Oct-May) General information booth right where the ferries dock; it can answer pretty much any question.

Sights

PILGRIM MONUMENT

You can't miss the 252ft-tall tower of the **Pilgrim Monument & Provincetown Museum** (☎ 508-487-1310; High Pole Rd; adult/child 4-14/senior & student $7/3/5, admission free 9am-noon Sun; ⊙ 9am-7pm Jul & Aug, 9am-5pm Apr-Jun & Sep-Nov, last admission 45min before closing). Completed in 1910, it's the tallest all-granite structure in the USA. Climb the 116 stairs and 60 ramps for a great view of town, the beaches, the spine of the Lower Cape and even Boston in clear weather (30 miles away). At the base of the tower is an old-fashioned museum featuring the struggle of the Pilgrims (p21), and Provincetown history.

EXPEDITION WHYDAH

Of the more than 3000 shipwrecks off the coast of the Cape, the **Whydah** (☎ 508-487-8899; 16 MacMillan Wharf; adult/child 6-12 & senior $8/6; ⊙ 9am-9pm Jun-Aug, 10am-5pm late Apr–mid-Oct) is one of the best documented. Whydah (pronounced *wih*-dah) sank in 1717 and to this day remains the only authenticated pirate ship ever raised. This museum shows coins, jewelry, weapons, the ship's bell and even clothing. The expedition crew, with the aid of the National Geographic Society, has been painstakingly studying and restoring the booty of over 100,000 items.

CAPE COD NATIONAL SEASHORE

The Province Lands Visitor Center (p193) has an amazing 360-degree view, and inside are exhibits and films about the park's topography and ecology.

The **Old Harbor Lifesaving Station** (☎ 508-487-1256; Race Point Beach; admission free; ⊙ 1:30-3pm May–mid-Oct), built in 1898, hosts exhibits about the Cape's fearless 'surfmen' who staged daring rescues of distressed vessels on the treacherous coastline. Try to catch a **reenactment** (adult/child 7-17 & senior $5/2; ⊙ 6pm Thu Jul & Aug).

PROVINCETOWN ART ASSOCIATION & MUSEUM

One of the country's foremost small museums, **Provincetown Art Association & Museum** (PAAM; ☎ 508-487-1750; www.paam.org; 460 Commercial St; ⊙ noon-5pm & 8-10pm daily early Jul-early Sep, noon-4pm Sat & Sun Oct–mid-Apr, noon-4pm Sat & Sun mid-Apr–late May, noon-5pm daily & 8pm-10pm Sat & Sun late May-early Jul & early Sep-end Sep) has a collection of works by some 500 artists who have lived and worked on the Lower Cape, as well as exhibitions by outside artists.

Activities

BEACHES

It's high dunes and pounding surf at **Race Point Beach**, off US 6 in the Cape Cod National Seashore. Lifeguards are on duty, and facilities include rest rooms and showers. It's easily reached via the town shuttle (p203).

The water at **Herring Cove Beach**, at the end of US 6, is calmer at than Race Point and the sunsets more spectacular. Facilities and parking are similar to those at Race Point.

Long Point Beach is reached via the Flyer's Shuttle (p203) or by a two-hour walk (each way) along the stone jetty at the western end of Commercial St.

CYCLING

Seven miles of great paved bike trails crisscross the Cape Cod National Seashore. A loop trail is 5.5 miles, and two spur trails lead to the Herring Cove and Race Point Beaches.

Rent bicycles at **Ptown Bikes** (☎ 508-487-8735; 42 Bradford St; cruiser hire 2/24 hr $7/12, mountain bike hire 2 hr $8-9, 24 hr $17-19), just outside of the town center.

BOATING

Flyer's Boat Rental (☎ 508-487-0898; 131A Commercial St; power boat rental per 2 hr/1 day from $40/100, sailboat rental per 2 hr/1 day from $26/50, kayak rental per 4 hrs/1 day from $24/40; ☺ mid-May–mid-Oct, weather permitting) rents water craft.

Venture Athletics (☎ 508-487-9442; 237 Commercial St, Whaler's Wharf shopping center; 4hr 1-/2-person kayak hire $25/35; ☺ 5am-6pm) rents kayaks and also leads guided kayak tours.

WHALE-WATCHING CRUISES

If you have a choice of launch point for a whale-watch, make it Provincetown. It's closest to the whales – only 6 miles – so you'll spend relatively more time whale-watching than in transit. The following operators guarantee that you'll see whales on the voyage, or you'll receive a certificate for a free cruise.

Dolphin Fleet Whale Watch (☎ 508-349-1900, 800-826-9300; MacMillan Wharf; 3-4 hr trips adult/child

under 5/child 5-12/senior $24/free/20/22; ☺ mid-Apr–Oct, weather permitting) is the leader. There are as many as nine tours daily in peak season. Phone for sailing times.

Boston Harbor Cruises (☎ 617-227-4321, 877-SEE-WHALE; MacMillan Wharf; 2½ hr trips adult/child 4-12/senior $18/10/15; ☺ Mon-Thu late May-late Sep) has cruises by high-speed catamaran. Phone for sailing times.

Tours

TOWN TOURS

Province Lands Visitor Center (☎ 508-487-1310; $5; ☺ 9am Tue in season) This visitor centre has a two-hour town history walking tour. Reservations are required; see p193 for more.

Provincetown Trolley (☎ 508-487-9483; Commercial St; adult/child/senior $9/5/8; ☺ frequent trips May-Oct) For a quick orientation with a 40-minute narrated tour of the major sights, board the trolley in front of town hall.

DUNE TOUR

Art's Dune Tours (☎ 800-894-1951; Standish St; daily tours adult/child $17/10, sunset tours $25/13; ☺ mid-Apr–mid-Nov) On the surface there might not seem to be much ado in the dunes of the Cape Cod National Seashore, but these hour-long narrated van tours are surprisingly informative and scenic. Reservations recommended.

Festivals & Events

Cabaret Fest (May) Several days of performances and workshops for and by cabaret performers.

Fourth of July Weekend P-town's biggest weekend of gay 'circuit' dance parties; the most famous is 'Summer Camp.'

Gay Pride Carnival (mid-Aug) A week-plus of events, parties and fun, with a different theme each year. A highlight is the carnival parade.

Holly Folly (early Dec) Said to be the world's only gay and lesbian holiday festival. Gives new meaning to 'Don we now our gay apparel.'

Sleeping

Reservations are recommended if visiting in summer.

BUDGET

Bill White's Motel (☎ 508-487-1042; www.billwhites motel.com; 29 Bradford St Extension; d in season/off-season $90/72; ☺ early May-late Oct) This 12-unit motel is well maintained by a proud family. Rooms are pretty standard-issue but have Cape touches like quilts and braided rugs.

GAY & LESBIAN PROVINCETOWN

While other cities have their gay districts, in Provincetown the gay district is the entire town. If you don't know what the rainbow flag or the initials LGBT mean, you'll get an education, and if you're remotely homophobic either you'll be uncomfortable in P-town or, better, you'll gain a measure of acceptance.

On 17 May 2004 same-sex marriages became legal in Massachusetts. By November 2004, Provincetown had issued about 925 marriage licenses. Weddings have ranged from intimate ceremonies on the town hall grounds to full-on, catered, flowered, music-filled affairs for 200 (see p32).

As we went to press, there was talk of adding an amendment to the state Constitution to bar same-sex marriage, but the earliest it could be put to a vote is 2007. So for now, party gaily on.

To do just that, try the following places – but remember that even the busiest of places may be deserted if you go at the wrong time. Ask around for the latest. If there's dancing or a theme night, expect to pay up to $10 admission.

Atlantic House (A House; ☎ 508-487-3821; 4 Masonic Place) Eugene O'Neill lived here, Ella Fitzgerald sang here and generations of men have enjoyed its charms. The Little Bar is an intimate pub with a fireplace. There's also the Macho Bar and a dance club and cabaret.

Boatslip Beach Club (☎ 508-487-1669; 161 Commercial St) Known for its wildly popular **afternoon tea dances** (cover $5; �an 4-7pm in season) overlooking the harbor. In summer, it's packed with gorgeous guys.

Chasers (☎ 508-487-7200; 293 Commercial St) A pub with a pool table, Chasers is the women's equivalent of the Atlantic House's Little Bar.

Crown & Anchor (C&A; ☎ 508-487-1430; 247 Commercial St) An entire complex drawing a gay and mixed crowd to its 'leather and Levi's' bar, video bar, disco and drag and cabaret shows.

PiedBar (☎ 508-487-1527; 193A Commercial St) A very popular women's lounge on the water side of Commercial St. Tea dances keep 'em rockin'. Look for any dancing sponsored by GirlPower Events; these chicks rule the roost.

Vixen (☎ 508-487-6424; 336 Commercial St) Popular for its lesbian scene and cabaret shows. Dance club nights include the Wednesday Flashback with '70s and '80s music.

Grand View Inn (☎ 508-487-9193, 888-268-9169; www.grandviewinn.com; 4 Conant St; r incl breakfast in season $80-160, off-season $40-80) It takes its name from the marvelous harbor-view decks, and the gardens are nice, too. Rooms do not have TVs or phones.

Cape Codder (☎ 508-487-0131; 570 Commercial St; s incl breakfast in season/off-season $35/30, d incl breakfast in season $45-70, off season $35-60, apt incl breakfast in season/off-season $150/100; �an Apr-Nov, weather permitting) This very simple place has 15 units, all with shared bathroom. Small rooms are pretty small, there are no TVs or phones in rooms, and there's the occasional wall crack or threadbare bedspread, but for these prices… Nice touch: a private beach.

Dune's Edge Campground (☎ 508-487-9815; www.dunes-edge.com; 386 US 6; campsites in season/off-season $30/25, plus $8 for electrical & water hookups; �an May-Sep) This 100-acre campground has lots of shade trees; it's well kept and quiet.

MID-RANGE

Fairbanks Inn (☎ 508-487-0386, 800-324-7265; www.fairbanksinn.com; 80 Bradford St; d incl breakfast in season $129-299, off-season $65-195; ☐) A gracious and historic 18th-century hostelry, and one of the nicest stays in town. Restored rooms are equipped with mod-cons, the grounds are well kept, and common areas have hearths are popular in the winter.

Beaconlight Guesthouse (☎ 508-487-9603, 800-696-9603; www.beaconlightguesthouse.com; 12 Winthrop St; d incl breakfast in season $145-295, off-season $90-185; ☐) One of the more welcoming and elegant guesthouses in town, with 10 well-equipped, European-style rooms and suites. There's a sherry and port hour, a huge roof deck and a Jacuzzi.

Somerset House (☎ 508-487-0383, 800-575-1850; www.somersethouseinn.com; 378 Commercial St; d incl breakfast in season $130-260, off-season $95-185; ☐ Apr-Oct; ☐) Make your P-town stay a party from the start with barbecues, theme parties and slick guest rooms in styles from safari to classic.

Ampersand Guesthouse (☎ 508-487-0959, 800-574-9645; www.ampersandguesthouse.com; 6 Cottage St; d incl breakfast in season $125-165, off-season $85-115) A nice deal for this quiet location. The Ampersand's two buildings are decorated simply, the better to show off the antique accents.

Masthead (☎ 508-487-0523, 800-395-5095; www.the masthead.com; 31-41 Commercial St; d in season $99-332, off-season $70-190) This funky establishment, a mix of apartments, cottages and motel rooms, sits right on the bay.

TOP END

Crowne Pointe (☎ 508-487-6767, 877-276-9631; www .crownepointe.com; 82 Bradford St; d incl breakfast in season $179-429, off-season $100-379; ☐ ☑) A cluster of restored houses around a central courtyard with Jacuzzis and a small swimming pool. Rooms are all different yet decorated with thought and modern amenities (TV, VCR and DSL). There's quite an extensive breakfast.

Land's End Inn (☎ 508-487-0706, 800-276-7088; www.landsendinn.com; 22 Commercial St; r incl breakfast in season $165-485, off-season $100-385; ☺ Apr-Oct) This 1904 house atop a hill looks like a set of gazebos strung together. Inside, the rooms are an eclectic American aesthetic including handsome woodwork and stained glass.

Eating
BUDGET

Mojo's (☎ 508-487-3140; MacMillan Wharf, 8 Ryder St Extension; dishes $2-14 or market price; ☺ lunch & dinner in season) Provincetown's classic clam shack serves everything from hot dogs and sandwiches to fried seafood, burritos and veggie options.

Karoo Kafe (☎ 508-487-6630; 338 Commercial St; dishes $3-12; ☺ lunch & dinner late May-early Sep, reduced hrs Mar-Dec) A brightly painted, counter-service café featuring home-style cooking from South Africa. *Bobotie* is a mild curry comfort food, or get something *peri-peri* style, for a blast of tomato, garlic, onion and chili.

Portuguese Bakery (☎ 508-487-1803; 299 Commercial St; pastries $1.15-2.29; ☺ Apr-Oct) This simple bakery-lunchroom has been here for a century. Sugar-dusted fried dough is a party on a plate, or try *pastéis de nata* (egg-custard tarts) or something more conventional (éclairs to brownies, cheap breakfasts to sandwiches).

Carriero's Tip for Tops'n (☎ 508-487-1811; 31 Bradford St; breakfast $4-11, lunch $4-10, mains dinner $8-19; ☺ breakfast, lunch & dinner Mar–mid-Nov) This family-run Portuguese place hasn't changed much since the 1960s. Favorites include *caldeirada de peixe*, which is like bouillabaisse with saffron rice.

Lewis Bros (☎ 508-487-1436; 310 Commercial St; ice-cream from $3; ☺ Apr-late Oct) *The* ice-cream spot in town. In addition to traditional flavors, it has some grown-up ones like chocolate Guinness, and mudslide.

Spiritus Pizza (☎ 508-487-2808; 190 Commercial St; whole pizza from $15, slices also available; ☺ Apr-early Nov) This is the place to pick up a late-night slice, or a late-night date if you haven't been lucky at one of the clubs.

MID-RANGE

Café Edwige/Edwige at Night (☎ breakfast 508-487-2008, dinner 508-487-4020; 333 Commercial St; breakfast $5-11, mains dinner $18-29; ☺ breakfast Thu-Tue & dinner daily Jul & Aug, breakfast & dinner Sep-Jun) P-town's most popular breakfast includes choices like broiled sole, fruit pancakes and standards. At dinnertime it's a romantic bistro offering a market-based menu, homemade desserts and the white ginger cosmopolitan.

Ciro & Sal's (☎ 508-487-6444; 4 Kiley Ct; mains $14-30; ☺ dinner) This cellar restaurant is one of the most romantic settings in town. Select from the large menu of pastas, fish and meat (especially veal) dishes.

Napi's (☎ 508-487-1145; 7 Freeman St; lunch $5-13, dinner $15-25; ☺ lunch Sep-Apr, dinner year-round) A lively, welcoming institution around since 1973, this art-filled restaurant has an eclectic, ever-changing menu ranging from organic salads to stir-fry to Portuguese linguica sausage and vegetarian options. Bonus: free parking.

Clem + Ursie's (☎ 508-487-2333; 85 Shank Painter Rd; mains $7-26; ☺ lunch & dinner, phone for off-season hrs) This colorful, counter-service roadhouse with tables decorated by local artists serves traditional New England seafood alongside Jamaican and Portuguese dishes – you'll probably have leftovers.

Bubala's by the Bay (☎ 508-487-0773; 183 Commercial St; mains breakfast $4-10, lunch $6-13, dinner $9-25; ☺ breakfast, lunch & dinner Apr-Oct) Decent food, great people-watching. Keep it simple with omelettes or brioche French toast (breakfast) and burgers (later), and check out the streetside parade.

TOP END

Chester (☎ 508-487-8200; 404 Commercial St; mains $20-38; ☺ dinner late May-early Sep, reduced hrs late Apr-Oct) A special-moment restaurant in a 19th-century Greek Revival captain's house. The American menu changes monthly and concentrates on local ingredients.

Mews Restaurant and Cafe (☎ 508-487-1500; 429 Commercial St; mains $10-30; ☼ dinner year-round, Sun brunch Apr-Oct) Upstairs, this restaurant has a casual dark-lit ambiance, while the downstairs area is right on the sand. Whichever location you choose, the food is exceptional: try the roasted half-duckling with an Asian sweet and spicy glaze. The bar is famous for its martinis.

Martin House (☎ 508-487-1327; 157 Commercial St; mains $24-33; ☼ dinner Thu-Sun Feb-Dec) This rustic 18th-century house has *five* fireplaces, so it's well suited to winter dining. Some dishes on the innovative, changing menu are internationally inspired, some lean towards continental, while others celebrate vegetarians.

Drinking

See the Gay & Lesbian Provincetown boxed text (p200) for more options.

Joe (☎ 508-487-6656; 148A Commercial St) Offers consistently excellent cappuccino. Drink it on the patio out front.

Governor Bradford (☎ 508-487-9618; 312 Commercial St) This local hangout, with big picture windows overlooking Commercial St, has pool tables, chess boards and a large pub menu. It attracts straight night owls with live reggae and rock.

Old Colony (☎ 508-487-2361; 323 Commercial St) This vestige of old Provincetown is a no-frills mariners' haunt where filmmakers shot scenes for *Tough Guys Don't Dance*. It also draws more of a straight crowd.

Entertainment

Tickets for most performances are available through **Ptown Tix** (☎ 508-487-9793, 800-791-7487; www.ptowntix.com; ☼ noon-8pm in season, noon-5pm off-season, extended hrs on show nights; Aquarium Marketplace 209 Commercial St Provincetown Theater 238 Bradford St).

CINEMAS

New Art Cinemas (☎ 508-487-4269; www.newartcinemas.com; 214 Commercial St, Whaler's Wharf shopping center, 2nd fl; adult/child/senior & matinee $8.50/4.50/6.50) Shows art house and more mainstream movies.

LIVE MUSIC

Great Music on Sundays at Five (Unitarian-Universalist Meeting House, 236 Commercial St; tickets $10; ☼ 5pm Sun late May-Oct) A concert series of classical, chamber, folk, Broadway and even gospel music.

LIFE IS A CABARET...

And anyone who thinks otherwise hasn't been to Provincetown.

P-town is full of little theaters featuring drag (and other) performers who would be amazingly good singers, musicians or comedians no matter how they dressed. Expect comediennes/comedians, celebrity impersonators who make lightning-fast costume changes, and innuendo-laden, campy humor. Lesbian-themed acts include comics Lea de Laria, Maggie Cassella and Kate Clinton.

Tickets are generally between $12 and $20, and, depending on the venue, you may be strongly ecouraged to purchase a drink.

In the off-season, Mews Restaurant and Cafe (left) holds a 1960s-style coffee house with open mike on Monday night.

THEATER

Provincetown Theater (2004; ☎ 508-487-9793; 238 Bradford St) This recently opened theater has two companies in residence: the professional theater company Provincetown Rep and the community-based Provincetown Theater Company. The Rep is known for attracting such top names as Wendy Wasserstein and Terrence McNally.

Shopping

Commercial St has the most creative and interesting specialty shops on the Cape. Just a tiny selection:

Ball (☎ 508-487-3000; 134 Commercial St) With clothes that make men look sexy and fabulous, or swimsuits and casual wear for women. It has a proprietary swimsuit design that does for the male lower anatomy what the push-up bra does for the ladies' upper.

Century (☎ 508-487-2332; 205 Commercial St) This has a slick modern design, and barware, eyeglasses and loads of things for the home.

Marine Specialties (☎ 508-487-1730; 235 Commercial St) This cavernous shop sells kitsch and really cool stuff: flip-flops to swimsuits beachwear and surfwear, army/navy surplus, leather, canvas, firemen's coats and...

Shop Therapy (☎ 508-487-9387; 346 Commercial St) Retro and edgy; incense, Rasta clothing, switchblades, jewelry, and greeting cards with naked pictures. Parents, use discretion: your teenagers *will* want to go inside.

Silk & Feathers (☎ 508-487-2057; 377 Commercial St) The wares here are WOW, more like art than women's clothing. There are 'new vintage' looks from all over the world – makers include Lilith and Rozae Nichols.

Womencrafts (☎ 508-487-2501; 376 Commercial St) The name says it all: jewelry, pottery, books and music by female artists from across America.

Getting There & Around

AIR
From Boston, **Cape Air** (☎ 508-487-0241, 800-352-0714; www.flycapeair.com) flies to Provincetown's Municipal Airport (one-way/round-trip $120/199, 25 minutes, daily). Cape Air also runs seasonal services between Provincetown and Nantucket, from early July to early September.

BOAT
From Boston
Bay State Cruise Company (☎ 617-748-1428, 866-435-6800; www.baystatecruises.com) links Provincetown's MacMillan Wharf and Boston's Commonwealth Pier. In Provincetown, it shares an office with the chamber of commerce. There's the fast ferry (per adult/bicycle/child/senior one-way $37/5/27/32, round-trip $58/10/48/53, 1½ hours, three daily late May to late September) or the regular ferry (per adult/bicycle/child/senior one-way $18/5/14/15, round-trip $29/10/19/23, three hours, one daily Friday to Sunday from mid-June to early September).

Boston Harbor Cruises (☎ 617-227-4321; bostonharborcruises.com) also offers a fast ferry service from Long Wharf, Boston (adult/bicycle/child/senior one-way $37/32/27/5, round-trip $58/53/48/10, 1½ hours). There's one service daily from late May to mid-June, and two or three daily from mid-June to mid-October.

From Plymouth
Capt John Boats (☎ 508-747-2400, 800-242-2469; www.captjohn.com) fast ferry departs Plymouth at 10am and returns from Provincetown at 4:30pm (adult/bicycle/child/senior round-trip $30/3/20/25, 1½ hours, daily). There's one trip daily late June to early September, one daily Friday to Sunday from late May to late June, and one daily Tuesday, Wednesday, Saturday and Sunday in September.

To Long Beach
The **Flyer's Shuttle** (☎ 508-487-0898; 131A Commercial St & MacMillan Wharf; one-way/round-trip $8/12; ⊙ 10am-6pm mid-Jun–mid-Sep, weather permitting) ferries sunbathers across the bay to the remote beaches and lighthouse of Long Point.

BUS
The **Plymouth & Brockton** (☎ 508-771-6191) bus stops at the chamber of commerce. Four daily buses (one-way $24, 3½ hours) travel between Provincetown and Boston, with stops in Truro ($2), Wellfleet ($4), Eastham ($5), Orleans ($6), Harwich ($7), Hyannis ($9) and Barnstable ($9). Some buses then continue to Logan Airport in Boston (an extra $5).

From late May to mid-October, the **Shuttle** (☎ 800-352-7155; single trip/day pass $1/3) buses travel up and down Bradford St, to MacMillan Wharf, Herring Cove Beach and North Truro. An additional mid-summer service heads out to the airport, Province Lands Visitor Center and Race Point Beach. Bike racks are available.

CAR
From the Cape Cod Canal via US 6, it takes about 1½ hours to reach Provincetown (65 miles), depending on traffic.

On-street parking is next to impossible, but lot parking costs between $7 and $11 per day. Some visitors park in Truro for free and take the Shuttle (above) into Provincetown.

TAXI
Taxi fares are standardized: $3 per person within town or $5 per person to the airport. Try **Cape Cab** (☎ 508-487-2222), **Mercedes Cab** (☎ 508-487-3333), **PT Cab** (☎ 508-487-9585) or **Queen Cab** (☎ 508-487-5500).

NANTUCKET

One need not be a millionaire to visit Nantucket, but it couldn't hurt. This compact island, thirty miles south of Cape Cod, grew rich from whaling in the 19th century, and recent decades have seen its rebirth as a summer playground for CEOs and society types.

It's easy to see why. Nantucket is New England at its most rose-covered, cobblestoned, cedar-shake, picture-postcard perfect, and even in the peak of summer there's

CAPE COD, NANTUCKET & MARTHA'S VINEYARD

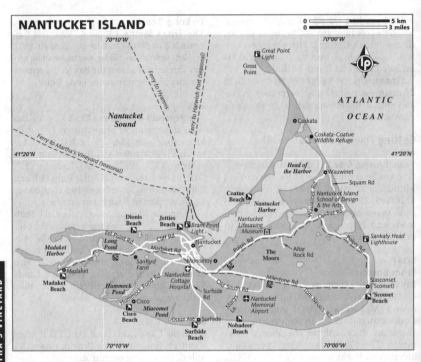

NANTUCKET ISLAND

CAPE COD, NANTUCKET &
MARTHA'S VINEYARD

always a stretch of sandy beach to be found. Outdoor activities abound, and there are fine museums, smart restaurants and fun bars.

Nantucket Town (called 'Town' by the locals) is the island's only real population center. It sits at the western side of Nantucket Harbor. On the Atlantic (east) coast of the island are the communities of Wauwinet and Siasconset (known as ''Sconset'). A small number of residential communities line the south and west coasts.

NANTUCKET TOWN

Nantucket Town boasts streets shaded by towering elms and lined with gracious 19th-century homes. The whole town is a National Historic Landmark, with the country's largest concentration of houses built prior to 1850.

Orientation

There are two ferry terminals: Straight Wharf and Steamboat Wharf. Straight Wharf becomes Main St, the main thoroughfare through the town center, while Steamboat Wharf is just a few short blocks north. The

majority of tourist/visitor facilities are within a 10-minute walk of the wharves. The airport is a few miles southeast of town, via Milestone Rd.

MAPS
The chamber of commerce publishes a detailed map. Bike rental agencies also provide maps for customers.

Information
BOOKSTORES
Mitchell's Book Corner (☎ 508-228-1080; 54 Main St)
Nantucket Bookworks (☎ 508-228-4000; 25 Broad St)

EMERGENCY
Nantucket Police (☎ 508-228-1212; 20 S Water St)

INTERNET ACCESS
A number of locations around town offer high-speed Internet access. Some examples:
Even Keel Café (☎ 508-228-1979; 40 Main St; per 15 min $4)
Nantucket.net (☎ 508-228-6777; 2 Union St; per 30 min $5; ☷ 10am-6pm Mon-Sat) Minimum 30 minutes

INTERNET RESOURCES

www.nantucketchamber.org Chamber of commerce website.

www.nantucket.net Private listings of restaurants, housing, arts and recreation.

LIBRARIES

Nantucket's town library (the Atheneum, right) is also a landmark in its own right.

MEDIA

Inquirer & Mirror (www.ack.net) Newspaper.

WNAN, 91.1FM Public radio station.

MEDICAL SERVICES

Nantucket Cottage Hospital (☎ 508-228-1200; S Prospect St at Vesper Lane; ☒ 24 hrs) The island's only hospital. It's on the edge of town.

MONEY

Pacific National Bank (☎ 508-228-1917; 61 Main St) Also has a 24-hour ATM at the foot of Main St.

POST

Nantucket Post Office (☎ 508-228-1067; 5 Federal St; ☒ 5:30am-5pm Mon-Fri, 8:30am-noon Sat)

TOURIST INFORMATION

Chamber of commerce (☎ 508-228-1700; 48 Main St; ☒ 9am-5pm Mon-Fri) Has information on the island's seasonal activities and special events.

Information kiosk (Straight Wharf; ☒ 10am-5pm late May–mid-Oct)

Visitor Services & Information Bureau (☎ 508-228-0925; 25 Federal St; ☒ 9am-5:30pm daily May-Nov, 9am-5:30pm Mon-Sat Dec-Apr) Has everything you'll need.

Sights

NANTUCKET HISTORICAL ASSOCIATION

For the island's best sightseeing head to the **Nantucket Historical Association** (NHA; ☎ 508-228-1894; www.nha.org; passes historic sites only adult/child $6/3, historic sites & Whaling Museum $18/9; ☒ all sites except Whaling Museum 10am-5pm Mon-Sat & noon-5pm Sun late May-early Sep, limited hrs late Apr-late May & early Sep–mid-Oct). Its nine buildings cover everything from the farming beginnings to prosperous whaling days.

The Historical Association also offers a variety of daily educational programs including lectures on the history of whaling and shipwrecks. Its walking tours (p206) are excellent.

Its most famous property, the **Nantucket Whaling Museum** (☒ 10am-5pm Mon-Wed, Fri & Sat, 10am-9pm Thu, noon-5pm Sun mid-Apr–early Sep, phone for off-season hrs), is in a former whale-oil candle factory. There's a collection of whaling implements, scrimshaw (etchings into whale bones) and excellent whaling history lectures.

Hadwen House (96 Main St), built in 1845, offers an example of privileged life in the 19th century. Working from historical inventories, the NHA restored the house and restocked it with period furniture.

Built in 1686, the **Jethro Coffin House** is called the 'oldest house' because it's the town's oldest building still on its original foundation. It's in the 'salt box' style, with south-facing windows to catch the winter sun and a long, sloping roof to the north to protect from harsh north winds.

The old **mill** is America's oldest working mill (c 1746), as game young docents will demonstrate (conditions permitting).

MARIA MITCHELL ASSOCIATION

Several small **venues** (☎ 508-228-9198; www.mmo .org; 2 Vestal St; combination ticket adult/child & senior $10/7; ☒ mid-Jun–early Sep) are devoted to Maria (pronounced 'Mariah') Mitchell (1818–89), America's first female astronomer. Astronomy was no mere hobby on Nantucket: the nearly 100 whaling ships based here navigated by the stars, and the Mitchell family calibrated ships' instruments. But Maria is revered for discovering a comet in the 1840s, beating some of the world's leading scientists.

At the **Maria Mitchell Birthplace House** (☎ 508-228-2896; adult/child $4/3; 1 Vestal St; ☒ 10am-4pm Tue-Sat), docents tell her inspiring story. The house (1790) is interesting in its own right.

Next door, at **Vestal St Observatory** (☎ 508-228-9273; 3 Vestal St; adult/child $3/1; ☒ tours in season 11am Tue-Sat, off season 11am Sat), student interns demonstrate principles and techniques of astronomy.

On a rolling hill out of town, the **Loines Observatory** (☎ 508-228-9273; Milk St Extension; adult/child $10/6; ☒ 9pm Mon, Wed & Fri Jun-Aug, 8pm Fri Sep-May, weather permitting) opens to the public for nighttime viewings with explanations.

If you're arriving outside of mid-summer, phone ahead to check opening times.

ATHENEUM

More than just a **library** (☎ 508-228-1110; Lower India St; admission free; ☒ 9:30am-8pm Tue & Thu &

9:30am-5pm Wed, Fri & Sat year-round, 9:30am-5pm Mon late May-early Sep), this Greek Revival edifice is one of Nantucket's greatest cultural resources. The Great Hall (on the 2nd floor) has hosted speeches by such notables such as Frederick Douglass and Ralph Waldo Emerson. Opinion-makers continue to speak here.

FIRST CONGREGATIONAL CHURCH
This **church** (☎ 508-228-0950; 62 Centre St; suggested donation adult/child $2.50/50¢; 10am-4pm Mon-Sat mid-Jun–mid-Oct, weather permitting) traces its roots back to the early 1700s. Climb the 94 steps to the steeple for eagle-eye views.

AFRICAN MEETINGHOUSE
In its heyday, Nantucket's Five Corners (where Atlantic Ave meets Pleasant and York Sts) was a prosperous, middle-class African-American neighborhood. This **meetinghouse** (☎ 508-228-9833; cnr Pleasant & York Sts; admission by donation; 11am-3pm Tue-Sat & 1-3pm Sun Jul & Aug, rest of year by appointment) is the nation's second-oldest (1820) surviving structure built by free African Americans.

LIGHTSHIP BASKET MUSEUM
What the lighthouse is to the New England coast, the lightship was to the sea – essentially a floating lighthouse to warn of dangerous shoals or sandbars below. Sailors would stay aboard the lightships for weeks on end, and to combat boredom they created beautiful, intricate baskets that have become emblems of the island. This small **museum** (☎ 508-228-1177; 49 Union St; adult/child & senior $4/2; 10am-4pm Tue-Sat late May–mid-Oct) highlights these craftsmen (and now women).

Activities
BEACHES
You'll have to pedal, hitch or take a bus to the island's prime beaches, but to feel sand between your toes as quickly as possible, head to the small **Children's Beach**, off S Beach St just north of Steamboat Wharf, or **South Beach**, a few blocks south of the wharf.

Jetties Beach, a 20-minute walk or a short bus ride away, is popular because of its location. It's a good walking beach, and well equipped.

CYCLING
Pedaling around Nantucket is a great way to escape summertime crowds and savor the natural beauty. However, if you're male don't ride on the cobblestones of Nantucket Town if you plan to have children!

At least a half-dozen shops rent bikes (between $20 and $25 per day) and provide decent, free island maps with routes highlighted. Try **Young's Bike Shop** (☎ 508-228-1151; 6 Broad St) and **Nantucket Bike Shop** (☎ 508-228-1999; 4 Broad St). Young's delivers, as does **Easy Riders** (☎ 508-325-2722; www.easyriders.com).

Note that every cyclist is required by law to wear a helmet on Nantucket. Bike shops can provide them and the cost is included with rental.

BOATING
Nantucket Community Sailing (☎ 508-228-6600; www.nantucketcommunitysailing.org; 4 Winter St), a nonprofit organization, offers sailing lessons and rentals.

Striped bass and bluefish 'run' off Nantucket's shores. A half-dozen or so charter boats docked at Straight Wharf can take you there.

Tours
TOWN TOURS
The Nantucket Historical Association (p205) and Maria Mitchell Association (p205) offer frequent and very worthwhile historical tours. The Maria Mitchell Association also leads nature-oriented tours. Others include:
Black Heritage Trail (☎ 508-228-9833; tours $10; phone for hrs) This 90-minute tour takes you through some of the town and offers an African-American perspective.
Nantucket Literary Walking Tour (☎ 508-228-9129; phanley@mmo.org; tours $12; 10:30am Fri in season) Follow the footsteps of literary luminaries who visited the island, including Herman Melville, Ernest Hemingway, Rachel Carson and Fred (aka Mr) Rogers. Tours leave from 2 Vestal St.

ISLAND TOURS
The following van tours are a good way to get your bearings around the island in about 90 minutes. Phone for more information and for reservations.
Ara's Tours (☎ 508-228-1951; tours $15, three tours daily year-round, by appointment Nov-Mar) Ara's microbus has huge windows and a raised ceiling for easy viewing. Commentated tour.
Gail's Tours (☎ 508-257-6557; tours $15; tours 10am, 1pm & 3pm) Gail Nickerson Johnson offers the perspective of a sixth-generation islander. She is full of enthusiasm, island trivia and commentary – and she lets you know which famous islanders own which enormous houses.

CRUISES

The **Friendship Sloop Endeavor** (☎ 508-228-5585; Straight Wharf; sails 1 hr $15, 1½ hrs $25-35; May-Oct) runs harbor sails and a sunset cruise.

Festivals & Events

Daffodil Festival (Apr) The island goes yellow in the last full weekend of April with three million blooms, and antique cars that make their way to 'Sconset for a tailgate picnic.

Nantucket Film Festival (mid-Jun) A good time to spot celebrities, but please don't embarrass the rest of us by making a big deal over them.

Independence Day Celebration (Jul) Local firefighters duke it out – the hook and ladder trucks versus the fire pumpers. You *will* get wet.

Christmas Stroll (1st weekend Dec) Nantucket becomes the Christmas town of your fantasies, with locals dressed in 1850s garb, 150 Christmas trees in the town center, the town crier and, of course, Santa Claus.

Sleeping

In July and August advance reservations are a virtual necessity, but between fall and spring you can practically have the run of the place, for a fraction of the cost.

Camping or sleeping under the stars, or even in your car, is prohibited on the island.

BUDGET

Barnacle Inn (☎ 508-228-0332; www.thebarnacleinn .com; 11 Fair St; s/d/tr incl breakfast & private bathroom $85/145/205; late May–mid-Oct) This turn-of-the-19th-century inn is set back from a quiet street. Rooms don't include phones, TVs or air-con, but there are substantial discounts for rooms with shared bathroom.

Nesbitt Inn (☎ 508-228-0156; 21 Broad St; incl breakfast s $55-75, d $65-95, q $95-125) A centrally located 1872 house with 12 rooms (shared bathroom) and two apartments. There are many original Victorian furnishings and a nice deck. There are no phones, TVs or air-con in the rooms.

MID-RANGE

Pineapple Inn (☎ 508-228-9992; www.pineappleinn .com; 10 Hussey St; d incl breakfast in season $195-325, off-season $110-250; late Apr-late Oct) The 12 guest rooms at this 1838 whaling captain's house have been completely renovated with understated elegance. The breakfast has been written up in food magazines.

Century House (☎ 508-228-0150; www.century house.com; 10 Cliff Rd; r $125-295; May-Oct;) The oldest guesthouse on the island has a loyal following. Comfy and unfussy, rooms have

CD and DVD players, and guests can help themselves to snacks and drinks for most of the day.

Martin House Inn (☎ 508-228-0678; www.martin houseinn.net; 61 Centre St; s incl continental breakfast $95-110, d incl continental breakfast in season $180-350, off-season $110-250) Elegantly but unpretentiously furnished with canopy beds, antiques and no phones or TVs in rooms. Many of the 13 rooms have a fireplace, and four rooms have shared bathroom.

Anchor Inn (☎ 508-228-0072; www.anchor-inn.net; 66 Centre St; d incl breakfast in season $175-225, off-season $65-145; Mar-Dec) This former sea captain's house, built in 1806, has 16 nicely appointed rooms with original flooring, queen-size canopy beds, private bathroom, cable TV, phones and famous, fresh-baked muffins for breakfast.

White House (☎ 508-228-4425, 888-577-4425; www .nantucketwhitehouse.com; 48 Centre St; d incl breakfast in season $165-190, off-season $75-160; mid-Apr–Oct) This simple and excellent-value guesthouse has three rooms and a suite.

Harbor Cottages (☎ 508-228-4485; www.nisda.org; 71 Washington St; units in season per night incl breakfast $150-215, per week $945-1225, call for off-season rates) The Nantucket Island School of Design & the Arts (p211) operates these former fishermen's cottages. There are 10 simple studios and one-bedroom cottages, sleeping up to four people.

TOP END

Ship's Inn (☎ 508-228-0040, 888-872-4052; 13 Fair St; s incl continental breakfast $110, d incl continental breakfast $210-235; May-Oct) This 1831 whaling captain's house has 10 large, airy Colonial-style rooms with mod-cons. On a quiet residential street, the house was also the birthplace of abolitionist Lucretia Mott.

Veranda House (☎ 508-228-0695; www.theveranda house.com; 3 Step Ln; r incl breakfast May-Sep $199-349, ask for off-season rates; open mid-Apr–mid-Oct) Probably the most stylish inn on the island, the Veranda House puts contemporary minimalism into an old New England shell, with striking results. There's no air-con (that's what the veranda's for) or TVs in rooms, but you do get bathrobes, Frette linens and portable DVD players. There are less expensive rooms with shared bathroom.

White Elephant (☎ 508-228-2500, 800-455-6574; www.whiteelephanthotel.com; 50 Easton St; r incl breakfast in season/off season from $450/150; May-Oct;   )

The Elephant is one of the town's highest-end lodgings, with touches like leather headboards, a small fitness room, use of a nearby pool, and the beach just outside. Legend has it that the builder was chided for putting up such a large hotel – it was bound to be a white elephant – and the name stuck.

Eating

Nantucket has some exceptional restaurants, but there are also New England lobster houses and inexpensive sandwich shops and bistros.

BUDGET

Fahey & Fromagerie (☎ 508-325-5644; 49 Pleasant St; ❍ mid-Apr–Dec) This gourmet store has packaged, fresh and prepared foods: gazpacho, fresh-made guacamole and nice cheeses and charcuterie.

Sayle's Seafood (☎ 508-228-4599; 99 Washington St Extension; mains $7-20, lobster dinners from $20; ❍ lunch & dinner summer, phone for off-season hrs) For your usual fried and baked seafood, along with seafood sandwiches. Clambakes also available.

Downy Flake (☎ 508-228-4533; 18 Sparks Ave; breakfast $3-9, lunch $3-8; ❍ breakfast daily, lunch Mon-Sat) A no-frills spot on the edge of town, known for blueberry pancakes, Scotch-Irish coffee cake and big breakfasts. Its famous doughnuts (65¢) are among the few foods on the island that aren't oversized.

Something Natural (☎ 508-228-0504; 50 Cliff Rd; dishes $3-9; ❍ breakfast-late afternoon late Apr–mid-Oct) Around since 1970 and grown via word of mouth for sandwiches, breads and snacks.

Island-grown produce is sold at a **farmers market** on Main St, from the backs of trucks during the growing season (daily except Sunday, May through October).

For the really big shopping jobs, visit the supermarkets of **Grand Union** (☎ 508-228-9756; Salem St) near the wharves or **Stop & Shop** (☎ 508-228-2178; Pleasant St) on the way out of town.

MID-RANGE

Black-Eyed Susan's (☎ 508-325-0308; 10 India St; breakfast $6-10, mains dinner $12-28; ❍ breakfast daily, dinner Mon-Sat) It's hard to find anyone who doesn't adore this quietly gourmet place. Snag a seat on the patio or in the hardwood dining room, and try the Pennsylvania Dutch pancakes (with Jarlsberg cheese), Santa Fe hash browns or trout with sauce marinière.

Centre St Bistro (☎ 508-228-8470; 29 Centre St; breakfast $5-10, lunch $5-10, mains dinner $15-22; ❍ breakfast Sat & Sun, lunch Mon-Fri in season, dinner year-round) Poached eggs with pan-fried grits are great for breakfast, and the front patio is excellent for people-watching. The changing dinner menu is hard to pin down, but if we mention warm goat cheese tarts or seared salmon with crispy wontons, do you get the idea?

Sushi by Yoshi (☎ 508-228-1801; 2 E Chestnut St; sushi from $5, mains $7-24; ❍ lunch & dinner) The name says it all: a transplanted Japanese chef and helpers prepare sashimi, sushi and more-exotic creations from a tiny shop. BYOB.

Cambridge St Victuals (☎ 508-228-7109; 12 Cambridge St, mains $9-24; ❍ dinner Apr-Dec) Dim and boisterous C-Street is probably the hippest eatery in town. It specializes in wood-smoked barbecue, but you can also get Middle Eastern flavors, thin-crust pizza and tandoori-style chicken.

Even Keel Café (☎ 508-228-1979; 40 Main St; breakfast $4-13, lunch $6-15, dinner $12-25; ❍ breakfast, lunch & dinner) Popular for coffees, pastries and light meals, this is a great all-purpose stop. There are also more upscale choices like crab cakes and steak with demi-glace. If it's noisy, try the leafy patio out back.

TOP END

American Seasons (☎ 508-228-7111; 80 Centre St; mains $23-30; ❍ dinner in season, Thu-Tue off-season, Apr-Dec). Celebrating the nation's four corners (dishes are themed by region) with an eclectic, thoughtful menu and smart staff. Dine on a folk art table.

21 Federal (☎ 508-228-2121; 21 Federal St; mains $28-38; ❍ in season dinner with reduced off-season hrs, mid-May-Oct) Year-in, year-out, one of the top places in town. It's also one of the handsomest. Expect to see locally grown ingredients prepared New American style.

Pearl (☎ 508-228-9701; 12 Federal St; mains $35-45; ❍ dinner May–mid-Oct) Think of the most chic restaurant in your town and double the chic quotient. Now you've got some idea of the Pearl. If you're lucky enough to get a reservation, try the salt and pepper wok-fried lobster (reserve as early as possible).

Cinco (☎ 508-325-5151; 5 Amelia Dr; tapas $6-13, mains $17-32; ❍ dinner Apr-Dec) Tapas, tapas, tapas. Start with a chili relleno tart, spice-rubbed pork tenderloin, seared fluke over corn puree, or a full-size paella with chicken, chorizo and seafood. It's big-city buzzing when busy.

Boarding House (☎ 508-228-9622; 12 Federal St; mains dinner $24-35; ☺ lunch May-Sep, dinner Apr-Dec) The fashionable Boarding House offers innovative American cuisine. Think grilled salmon with Provencal vegetables, and steak frites with bearnaise aïoli. Scene and be scene in the cozy basement or outdoors.

Drinking
Atlantic Café (AC; ☎ 508-228-0570; 15 S Water St) A casual and fun place that gets louder as the night wears on. It also serves bar snacks and about a dozen beers on tap.

Gazebo (☎ 508-228-1266; Straight Wharf) In good weather, this open-air place gets locals and tourists mixing happily over cocktails.

The restaurants Boarding House (above), Cambridge St Victuals (opposite) and Cinco (opposite) are also known for their bar scenes.

Entertainment
Dreamland Theater (☎ 508-228-5356; 17 S Water St) Shows first-run movies.

Starlight Theatre (☎ 508-228-4435; 1 N Union St) Screens art films and also serves light meals.

Shopping
Nantucket offers dozens of upmarket antique shops, clothing boutiques, jewelry stores and art galleries, and specialty shops that carry the island's signature lightship baskets.

Murray's Toggery Shop (☎ 508-228-0437; www.nantucketreds.com; 62 Main St) Murray's sells all kinds of clothing for you to look your prepped-out best, but the best reason to shop here is the entire section devoted to Nantucket Reds – pale red shirts, shorts, slacks and accessories that trace their origins back to sailcloth.

Four Winds Craft Guild (☎ 508-228-9623; 15 Main St) Has the island's largest selection of lightship baskets. They're not cheap (baskets/purses start at $100/600), but you're assured of quality. The guild is closed in the off-season, which is when you'll have to phone in your order.

Spectrum (☎ 508-228-4606; 26 Main St) Covering the spectrum of American crafts, this store handles about 300 designers and includes glass, ceramics, jewelry and Nantucket baskets.

Sweet Inspirations (☎ 508-228-5814; 26 Centre St) *Darling*, you *must* try the cranberries here. They're covered in orange chocolate, raspberry chocolate or yogurt. *Divine*.

Nantucket Looms (☎ 508-228-1908; www.nantucketlooms.com; 16 Federal St) Blankets, mufflers and baby things in cashmere or mohair are just the start, displayed so beautifully that you'd think you were in an art gallery.

Getting There & Away
AIR
Cape Air & Nantucket Airlines (☎ 800-352-0714; www.flycapeair.com) offer daily flights to and from Boston ($132 each way in summer, 45 minutes, hourly), Hyannis ($49, 20 minutes, hourly), New Bedford ($79.50, 25 minutes, several flights daily), Providence ($120, 40 minutes, mostly hourly in season) and Martha's Vineyard ($125, 35 minutes, several flights most days in season). In recent years Cape Air has also flown a few days per week between Nantucket and Provincetown (25 minutes) in mid-summer. Inquire for latest fares and schedules.

Island Airlines (☎ 508-228-7575, 800-248-7779; www.nantucket.net/trans/islandair) also operates from Hyannis (20 minutes, at least hourly in season) with similar fares to those of Cape Air.

As we went to press, **US Airways Express** (☎ 800-428-4322; www.usairways.com) and **Continental Express** (☎ 800-525-0280; www.continental.com) offered services from New York's LaGuardia and Newark Airports respectively. Check for latest fares and schedules.

BOAT
Nantucket is reached by ferries from Cape Cod and Martha's Vineyard.

From Hyannis
Ferries of the **Steamship Authority** (Cape reservations line ☎ 508-477-8600, Cape day-of-sailing information line ☎ 508-771-4000, Nantucket reservation line ☎ 508-228-3274, Nantucket information line ☎ 508-228-0262; www.steamshipauthority.com; South St Dock, Hyannis to Steamboat Wharf, Nantucket) carry people and autos. Make car reservations months in advance for summer, if you can. There are six ferries per day mid-May to mid-September and three per day the rest of the year (round-trip adult/bicycle/child under 5/child $28/12/free/13.50, 2¼ hrs). Taking your car costs $200 from November to April and $350 from May to October.

If you're not taking a car, the Steamship Authority Fast Ferry Flying Cloud makes five to six round-trips (adult/bicycle/child $55/12/41.50) daily year-round. Somewhat more reliable is the **Hy-Line Grey Lady Catama-ran** (☎ 508-778-0404, 888-778-1132), which also of-fers hour-long journeys (round-trip adult/bicycle/child $61/10/43) between Straight Wharf, Nantucket and Ocean St Dock, Hy-annis. Advance reservations are strongly rec-ommended. The boat makes six trips daily in summer, and five the rest of the year.

Hy-Line (☎ 508-778-2600, advance sales 888-778-1132; www.hy-linecruises.com; ☽ early May-late Oct) also offers a passenger-only ferry service between Ocean Dock, Hyannis and Straight Wharf, Nantucket (round-trip adult/bicy-cle/child $30/10/16, two hours). There are three boats in each direction daily from late May to mid-September, which goes down to one boat during the off-peak season.

Parking in Hyannis starts at around $10 per calendar day.

From Harwich

Avoid Hyannis traffic by traveling from Har-wich. **Freedom Cruise Line** (☎ 508-432-8999; www.nantucketislandferry.com; Route 28 at Saquatucket Harbor, Harwich Port) offers morning, noon and evening passenger-only ferries between late June and early September (adult/bicycle/child $48/10/38, 1½ hours). Outside of that pe-riod, there's one daily morning ferry between late May and mid-October, which leaves you under six hours on the island if you're a day-tripper. Advance reservations are recom-mended. Overnight parking in Harwich is $12 per night; same-day parking is free.

From Martha's Vineyard

Hy-Line (☎ Oak Bluffs 508-693-0112, Nantucket 508-228-3949; www.hy-linecruises.com) operates three daily interisland passenger ferries in each direc-tion from early June to mid-September (one-way adult/bicycle/child $14/5/7, round-trip $28/10/14, 2¼ hours).

Getting Around

BUS

Nantucket Regional Transit Authority (NRTA, 'Nerta'; ☎ 508-228-7025; www.shuttlenantucket.com; 22 Federal St) runs shuttle buses all over the island. Buses have racks for up to two bikes.

Services run from late May to late Sep-tember, but schedules are subject to change. Check with NRTA for the latest.

Individual fares generally cost $1 or $2, but NRTA passes cost $7/12/20 for one/three/seven days. These tickets and passes

may be purchased on board buses. Longer-term passes are available for 30 days/all sea-son ($50/80) from the NRTA office.

CAR

In summer, the center of town is choked with automobiles, so we don't recommend you adding yours. However, the national chains **Budget** (☎ 508-228-5666, 888-228-5666) and **Hertz** (☎ 508-228-9421, 800-654-3131) are at the airport. **Nantucket Island Rent A Car** (☎ 508-228-9989, 800-508-9972) and **Windmill Auto Rental** (☎ 508-228-1227, 800-228-1227) are also at the airport but offer free pick-up.

In town, head to **Young's** (☎ 508-228-1151; www.youngsbicycleshop.com; 6 Broad St) or **Affordable Rentals** (☎ 508-228-3501, 877-235-3500; 6 S Beach St). Prices start at $49/99 per day for a car/4WD but can easily be double in peak times.

TAXI

Taxi rates are fixed. Rides from Nantucket Town cost $18 to 'Sconset, $11 to Cisco Beach and $9 to the airport. A nominal charge is added per additional passenger, and another charge is added between 1am and 6am.

AROUND THE ISLAND

'Sconset (Siasconset)

Although this village is barely 7 miles from Nantucket Town, sometimes it thinks of itself as worlds apart. Nantucket Town may seem uncrowded and unhurried compared with the rest of the US, but 'Sconset takes it to another level – both in refinement and price.

SIGHTS

Some picturesque **old homes** on Broadway are among the island's most photographed, including the Nauticon Lodge (No 4), the Old Gardner House (No 5) and Auld Lang Syne (No 6). They're private homes now, so do your peeking from a respectful distance, please.

The 1899 **Siasconset Casino** (☎ 508-257-6585; 10 New St) has long hosted university glee clubs, children having a candy pull, or la-dies playing dominoes beneath the elaborate woodworked ceiling.

'Sconset Beach is long and narrow (it's suf-fered erosion in recent years), with signifi-cant surf and undertow. **Sankaty Lighthouse** is visible 30 miles out to sea, on the edge of a rapidly eroding 90ft bluff.

SLEEPING

Summer House (☎ 508-257-4577; www.thesummer house.com; r & cottages incl breakfast in season $575-950, off-season $225-575; ☉ Apr-Dec; ☒) A getaway of low-key elegance. Stay in one of 'Sconset's signature rose-covered cottages, relax by the pool or just drink in the ocean view. Some rooms have fireplaces and whirlpool baths. Shuttles available to town.

EATING

Summer House (☎ 508-257-9976; 17 Ocean Ave; mains lunch $16-28, dinner $31-36; ☉ lunch & dinner mid-May– mid-Oct) About the only place on the island where you can lunch poolside – try a fresh-made pizza, *salade niçoise* or a Kobe beef burger. Sophisticated dinners take place in the garden-style dining room, and the Moby Dick Bar has a piano player.

Chanticleer (☎ 508-257-6231; 9 New St; mains lunch $25-30, dinner $33-45; ☉ lunch & dinner Tue-Sun) Presidents and foreign dignitaries hit the Chanticleer regularly for memorable French cuisine. It's in an elegant and romantic setting – in the courtyard of a rose-covered cottage or in intimate dining rooms.

Sconset Café (☎ 508-257-4008; Post Office Sq; mains lunch $9-17, dinner $20-28; ☉ breakfast, lunch & dinner mid-May–early Oct) Pedal out for breakfast of omelettes or pancakes. Lunches are salads and sandwiches, and dinner has a fancier, frequently changing menu. BYOB.

Siasconset Market (☎ 508-257-9915) In the tiny center of town, this place has picnic supplies and sandwich fixings for cyclists and beachgoers.

Wauwinet & Environs

Near the northeast corner of the island, 5 miles from Nantucket Town, Wauwinet tempts travelers in search of a chic getaway.

This exclusive gated community of 20 or so homes is also the departure point for tours of the **Coskata-Coatue Wildlife Refuge** (☎ 508-228-6799; www.thetrustees.org; adult/child/Trustees of Reservations adult member $40/15/30; ☉ tours 9:30am & 1:30pm mid-May–mid-Oct, sunset Tue Jul & Aug). Natural history tours of 2½ hours take you by over-sand vehicle to view the 1100-acre property, Nantucket's northernmost spit and the Great Point lighthouse. Reservations are essential.

On your way out to Wauwinet is the **Nantucket Island School of Design and the Arts** (NISDA; ☎ 508-228-9248; www.nisda.org; 23 Wauwinet Rd; ☉ year-round), which offers classes and workshops lasting from a half-day to three weeks. Just some of the offerings: painting, quilting, dance, yoga, papermaking, ceramics, dyeing and landscape design. There are also kids' classes.

The **Nantucket Lifesaving Museum** (☎ 508-228-1885; 158 Polpis Rd; adult/child $5/2; ☉ 12:30pm-4:30pm Sat & Sun early May-late May, 12:30pm-4:30pm daily late May–mid-Jun, 9:30am-4pm mid-Jun–mid-Oct) documents the lifesaving stations where 'surfmen' saved mariners from wrecks – some 700 off Nantucket alone. Artifacts include lifesaving boats and equipment, photos and the original Fresnel lenses from the Brant Point and Great Point lighthouses.

SLEEPING & EATING

Wauwinet (☎ 508-228-0145, 800-426-8718; www.wau winet.com; 120 Wauwinet Rd; d incl full breakfast in season $500-1020, off-season $260-730, cottages in season $950-1900, off-season $400-1250; ☉ May-Oct; ☐) The kind of place to go if you're a celebrity and want to be left alone. The Wauwinet has 35 luxuriously appointed rooms and cottages, two beaches, clay tennis courts, a fleet of boats, and even croquet.

Topper's (☎ 508-228-8768; 120 Wauwinet Rd; brunch $38, lunch $23/28/33 for 3/4/5 selection tasting menu, prix-fixe dinner from $78; ☉ brunch Sun, lunch & dinner daily May-Oct) Within the Wauwinet inn, Topper's consistently vies for 'best island dining.' Whether in the beachside garden or indoors, you'll enjoy skillful New American cuisine (eg lobster crab cakes with smoked corn and jalapeno olives), gracious service and a stunning wine list. Inquire about the dinner dress code.

The Wauwinet's free jitney service shuttles guests to and from town about a dozen times a day. For more fun, take the inn's complimentary boat from Nantucket's Straight Wharf (one hour).

South Shore

The two communities here, Surfside and Cisco, consist almost entirely of private homes, but visitors come to this side of the island for its long, broad beaches and a feeling of really being away.

Two south shore beaches are among the island's best. **Surfside Beach**, 3 miles from Nantucket Town and accessible by shuttle bus, is popular with the college and 20-something crowd. It's wide with moderate-to-heavy surf. About a mile from Surfside Rd, **Nobadeer Beach** is below the flight path of the airport, and it attracts a rowdy crowd of good-looking young things.

SLEEPING & EATING
Star of the Sea Youth Hostel (☎ 508-228-0433, 888-901-2084; www.usahostels.org; 31 Western Ave, Surfside; dm members $20-24; ☻ mid-Apr–mid-Oct; ☐) This hostel is across the street from Surfside's beach in the island's first lifesaving station (1874). Dorm-style and cottage-style accommodations are also available. Reservations are essential in summer.

On your way, detour to **Bartlett's Farm** (☎ 508-228-4403; 33 Bartlett Farm Rd). From a humble farm stand, it's grown into huge gourmet market with anything you need for the beach or a quiet dinner at home. No party is complete without a Bartlett's pie for dessert.

Madaket
There's not a lot to see in this western outpost, but **Madaket Beach**, at the end of the namesake bike path, is a popular place to watch sunsets.

If you're a clean-cut 20-something, you'll want to hang out at the **West End** (☎ 508-228-5100; 326 Madaket Rd; mains $6-15; ☻ lunch & dinner in season). It has two bars, many windows, and lots of fried seafood, cheesesteaks, burgers and sandwiches. If you've imbibed one too many, NRTA stops right outside.

MARTHA'S VINEYARD

In 1602, mariner Bartholomew Gosnold cruised the New England coast and stopped at this island. It is thought that he found wild grapes when he stopped at the island, and he named it 'Martha's Vineyard' in honor of his daughter.

From those quaint beginnings, the Vineyard has become one of the premier vacation destinations in New England. Its hallmarks are pretty towns and open spaces, lots of beaches, bike paths, fine restaurants and quaint old inns. While there's a general patrician atmosphere, the Vineyard is more economically and ethnically diverse than Nantucket.

Orientation
Martha's Vineyard sits 7 miles off the south coast of Cape Cod. It's the largest island in New England, approximately 100 sq miles with about 125 miles of shoreline. Martha's Vineyard Sound separates the island from Cape Cod, while Nantucket Sound is to the east.

The main towns and ports of entry are Vineyard Haven, Oak Bluffs and Edgartown, along the northeast section of the island. The quiet towns of West Tisbury, Chilmark, and Aquinnah are collectively referred to as 'Up-Island.'

Local towns publish detailed maps, available at tourist offices.

Information
The following information applies islandwide. See local listings for town-specific information.

EMERGENCY
For nonemergencies and police inquiries, dial ☎ 311.

INTERNET RESOURCES
www.mvgazette.com The *Vineyard Gazette* newspaper.
www.mvweb.com Good general info website.
www.mvy.com Martha's Vineyard's chamber of commerce.

LAUNDRY
Airport Laundromat (☎ 508-693-5005; Martha's Vineyard Airport, West Tisbury; washer/5 min drying time $4.75/25¢; ☻ 8am-7:20pm in season, reduced hrs off-season) The island's only public laundry facilities.

MEDIA
The island's two newspapers are the *MV Times* and *Vineyard Gazette*. The local radio station is WMVY (92.7FM) as well as the public radio station WCAI/WNAN 90.1 and 91.1FM.

MEDICAL SERVICES
Martha's Vineyard Hospital (☎ 508-693-0410; www.marthasvineyardhospital.org) Found off the Vineyard Haven–Oak Bluffs Rd. It has a mix of full-time and visiting specialists.

TOURIST INFORMATION
Martha's Vineyard Chamber of Commerce (☎ 508-693-0085, 800-505-4815; Beach Rd, Vineyard Haven; ☻ 9am-5pm Mon-Fri, 10am-2pm Sat year-round, 10am-4pm Sat & 10am-2pm Sun mid-May–mid-Oct) Publishes a guide to attractions and accommodations, distributes maps and offers other practical advice.

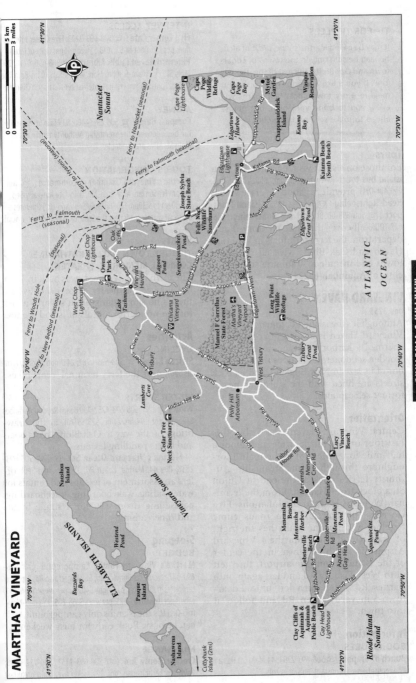

MARTHA'S VINEYARD

0 — 5 km
0 — 3 miles

Nantucket Sound

Ferry to Nantucket (seasonal)

Cape Poge Lighthouse

Cape Poge Wildlife Refuge

Cape Poge Bay

Mytoi Garden

Wasque Reservation

Chappaquiddick Rd

Chappaquiddick Island

Katama Bay

Edgartown Harbor

Edgartown Lighthouse

Edgartown

Katama Rd

Herring Creek Rd

Katama Beach (South Beach)

Edgartown Great Pond

Long Point Wildlife Refuge

Meetinghouse Way

Edgartown–West Tisbury Rd

Felix Neck Wildlife Sanctuary

Joseph Sylvia State Beach

Sengekontacket Pond

Airport Rd

Martha's Vineyard Airport

Manuel F Corellus State Forest

County Rd

Oak Bluffs

East Chop Lighthouse

Owens Park

Vineyard Haven

Lagoon Pond

Main St

Lake Tashmoo

West Chop Lighthouse

Chicama Vineyard

Edgartown–Vineyard Haven Rd

State Rd

Ferry to Falmouth (seasonal)

Ferry to Hyannis (seasonal)

Ferry to Woods Hole

Ferry to New Bedford

Lamberts Cove Rd

Lamberts Cove

Tisbury

Cedar Tree Neck Sanctuary

Indian Hill Rd

West Tisbury

Old County Rd

Polly Hill Arboretum

North Rd

Middle Rd

Panhandle Rd

Tabor House Rd

Menemsha Cross Rd

Chilmark

Lucy Vincent Beach

Tisbury Great Pond

ATLANTIC OCEAN

Vineyard Sound

ELIZABETH ISLANDS

Buzzards Bay

Naushon Island

Westend Pond

Pasque Island

Nashawena Island

Cuttyhunk Island (2mi)

Menemsha Beach

Menemsha Harbor

Menemsha

Menemsha Pond

Lobsterville Beach

Lobsterville Rd

Lobsterville

Aquinnah (Gay Head)

South Rd

Lighthouse Rd

Mioshup Trail

Squibnocket Pond

Clay Cliffs of Aquinnah & Aquinnah Public Beach

Gay Head Lighthouse

Rhode Island Sound

CAPE COD, NANTUCKET & MARTHA'S VINEYARD

41°30'N

41°20'N

41°30'N

41°20'N

70°50'W

70°40'W

70°30'W

TIP FOR TIPPLERS

It may be called Martha's *Vineyard*, but alcohol can be sold only in the towns of Edgartown and Oak Bluffs. The rest of the island is 'dry'. If you'd like a beer or wine with your meal in a dry town, most restaurants will allow you to bring your own, but phone ahead to make sure of their policies.

Tours

For those on a short visit, narrated 2½ hour **island bus tours** (www.mvtour.com; adult/child $19/5; ☒ Apr-Oct) provide a good overview. **Gay Head Sightseeing** (☎ 508-693-1555), **Island Transport** (☎ 508-693-0058) and **MV Sightseeing** (508-627-TOUR) all cover the same territory. Tours depart from the ferry terminals in Vineyard Haven and Oak Bluffs, visit all six island towns and include a 30 minute stop at the cliffs of Aquinnah (p224).

VINEYARD HAVEN

pop 3755

Although it's the island's commercial center, Vineyard Haven is a town of considerable charm. Its harbor boasts more traditional wooden schooners and sloops than any harbor of its size in New England, and its back streets are lined with the sturdy homes of former sea captains.

Orientation

Central Vineyard Haven (aka Tisbury) is just four or five blocks wide and about a half-mile long. Main St is the main thoroughfare through town. Steamship Authority ferries dock at the end of Union St, a block from Main St. From the terminal, Water St leads to the infamous 'Five Corners' intersection: five roads come together and no one really has the right of way. Good luck. Martha's Vineyard Airport is south of town in the center of the island. From the airport, turn left onto West Tisbury Rd and left again onto Barnes Rd. Then turn left onto Edgartown-Vineyard Haven Rd and follow it into town.

Information
BOOKSTORES

Bunch of Grapes (☎ 508-693-2291; 44 Main St) Has a fine reputation and constant 'author events.'

INTERNET ACCESS

Five Corner Café (☎ 508-693-2223; Five Corner Intersection; per 15 min/1 hr $2.50/8; ☒ 6am-6pm daily or later)

Vineyard Haven Public Library (☎ 508-696-4210; 200 Main St; ☒ 10am-5:30pm Mon, Wed & Sat, 10am-8pm Tue & Thu, 1pm-5:30pm Fri) Has Internet terminals (no charge).

MONEY

Compass Bank (☎ 508-696-4400; 91 Main St) Straddles the block between the Steamship Authority terminal and Main St. ATMs are available.

TOURIST INFORMATION

Martha's Vineyard Chamber of Commerce (☒ 8am to 8pm Fri-Sun late May–mid-Jun, daily late Jun–early Sep & 8:30am to 5:30pm Fri-Sun early Sep–mid-Oct) Operates a seasonal visitor center near the Steamship Authority terminal.

Sights
TISBURY TOWN HALL & KATHARINE CORNELL MEMORIAL THEATER

The town hall (Center St) was built in 1844, but it's been a theater since 1971. Even if there's no show going on, it's worth a visit for the wonderful murals of island scenes.

Activities
CYCLING

Strictly Bikes (☎ 508-693-0782; 24 Union St; daily rentals $20), near the ferry terminal, rents bikes.

WATER SPORTS

Wind's Up (☎ 508-693-4252; 199 Beach Rd; double canoes & kayaks per hr/4 hrs/24 hrs $25/55/70), at the drawbridge on the way to Oak Bluffs, rents boats and offers paddling lessons.

Martha's Vineyard Ocean Sports (☎ 508-693-2838; Pier 44, Marina, Beach Rd; ☒ Jun–mid-Sep) offers an assortment of lessons and rentals for water-skiing, wakeboarding, kneeboarding, parasailing (from $90 for a single flight) and inner-tubing.

Sleeping
BUDGET

Martha's Vineyard Family Campground (☎ 508-693-3772; www.campmvfc.com; 569 Edgartown Rd; 2-person campsites/trailer sites per night $40/45, per week $266/301, cabins per night $105-125, per week $665-805; ☒ mid-May–mid-Oct) It's the island's only campground, so it can be busy. Book early for busy weekends.

MID-RANGE

Crocker House Inn (☎ 508-693-1151, 800-772-0206; www.crockerhouseinn.com; 12 Crocker Ave; d incl breakfast

---

THE LIGHTHOUSES OF THE VINEYARD

What's more New England than a lighthouse? And what island has the greatest diversity of lighthouses in America? One guess.

West Chop Lighthouse
The island's last manned lighthouse, on the west side of Vineyard Haven Harbor. An original structure was built in the same spot in 1817, rebuilt in its current brick form in 1838, and moved to its present location at the end of Main St in 1891. It's closed to the public, but there are good walking trails around it.

East Chop Lighthouse
Once the lighthouse in Oak Bluffs was privately owned, but sailing ships refused to pay the fee imposed by the owner. The US government erected the current cast-iron structure in 1871. Until it was painted white in 1988, it was known as the chocolate lighthouse for its reddish-brown color. It's open for limited tours by the **Martha's Vineyard Historical Society** (☎ 508-627-4441; tours adult/child $3/free; ☼ tours around sunset Sun mid-Jun–mid-Sep)

Edgartown Lighthouse
The original lighthouse was built on a man-made island on Edgartown harbor, but the area between the shore and the island has since filled in, a testimony to the ever-shifting sands of the Cape and Islands. The lighthouse is closed to the public.

Cape Poge Lighthouse
In 1801 it cost only $36 to purchase the four acres for the building of this lighthouse on the far corner of Chappaquiddick, and it's a good thing the builders bought so much land. Harsh storms have meant that the lighthouse was destroyed in 1838, then in 1851 and again in 1892. The current structure dates from 1922. Visit via a Cape Poge tour (p220).

Gay Head Lighthouse
It was originally built in 1844, though the current red-brick building replaces a previous wooden one. The current light dates from 1952, when electricity finally came to Aquinnah. The Martha's Vineyard Historical Society runs limited **tours** (☎ 508-645-2111; adult/child under 12 $3/free; ☼ 1½ hrs before sunset for 2 hrs Fri-Sun mid-Jun–mid-Sep).

---

in season $185-365, off-season $115-265) If you have a good arm, this cozy shake-shingled house with eight guest rooms is a stone's throw from the harbor. Rooms have a cheery, summery feel, and the innkeepers offer great advice.

Clark House (☎ 800-696-8633; www.twinoaksinn .com; 20 Edgartown Rd; d incl breakfast in season $129-259, off-season $85-144) Homey and rustic, with antiques. Some rooms don't have bathrooms, but some have sun rooms and/or decks, and there's a relaxing porch. Bike rentals are free.

Kinsman Guest House (☎ 508-693-2311; 278 Main St; d in season/off-season $125/100) A pleasant 10-minute walk from the center of town, this 1880 former captain's house has three guest rooms (two share a bathroom), decorated with care and pride. Note: breakfast not included.

TOP END
Thorncroft Inn (☎ 508-693-3333, 800-332-1236; www .thorncroft.com; 460 Main St; r incl breakfast in season $250-550, off-season $200-425) Caters to couples seeking a getaway. The quiet, wooded setting houses three buildings and is close to two beaches, and in the rooms you'll find specialty bathrobes, antique furniture and nightly turndown service.

Eating
Art Cliff Diner (☎ 508-693-1224; 39 Beach Rd; mains $4-11; ☼ breakfast & lunch Thu-Tue) The Art Cliff

---

RECOMMENDED VINEYARD BIKE ROUTES

Martha's Vineyard is blessed with routes expressly for bikes:

- Oak Bluffs to Edgartown – a causeway takes you between Nantucket Sound and the marshlands.
- The bike path around the state forest in the middle of the island – it's about the only place on the island where you can challenge yourself with moderately steep hills.
- Anywhere on Chappaquiddick.

As attractive as it seems, we recommend against biking on the main streets Up-Island. There are many cars, and the roads are not very wide.

---

does some seriously innovative work courtesy of chef-owner Gina Stanley, formerly of Blair House (the official state guesthouse in Washington). Her blueberry pancakes are famous, as are her frittatas.

Café Moxie (☎ 508-693-1484; 48 Main St; mains lunch $7-13, dinner $19-32; ☽ lunch & dinner in season, phone for off-season hrs) The art on the walls is as interesting as the quietly gourmet cooking in this windowed corner restaurant. Try the mussels with coconut milk, ginger and garlic over udon.

Mediterranean (☎ 508-693-1617, 888-693-1617; 52 Beach Rd; mains lunch $9-14, dinner $23-32; ☽ lunch Mon-Sat, dinner mid-May–mid-Oct) Flavors from across that sea, such as grilled lamb and harissa-rubbed tuna, accompany white-tablecloth service and harbor views.

Black Dog (☎ 508-693-9223; 20 Beach St Extension; mains breakfast $6-9, lunch $8-16, dinner $18-33; ☽ breakfast, lunch & dinner, with occasional closure in off-season) While some complain that this once-humble harborfront tavern with the famous T-shirts has gotten too big for its doghouse, others swear by it. Try the quahog chowder, Delmonico steak or sesame crusted ahi. Expect a wait.

QUICK EATS

John's Fish Market & Sandy's Fish & Chips (☎ 508-693-1220; 5 Martin Rd; dishes $3-18.95; ☽ 9am-7pm Mon-Sat, 9am-6pm Sun) Famous for lobster rolls, Caesar salad, fisherman's stew and Malay-

sian caramelized shrimp. There are also beautiful prepared seafoods and pastas. You'll find this place off State Rd.

Vineyard Gourmet (☎ 508-693-5181; Main St; ☽ 9am-6pm in season, reduced hrs rest of year) Dishes by the pound: pâté, smoked salmon, spiced asparagus spears, flavorful, creative sandwiches and prepared foods.

Drinking

Five Corner Café (☎ 508-693-2223; Five Corner Intersection; ☽ 6am-6pm daily or later) The island's only micro-roaster and Internet café (see p214).

Entertainment

CINEMAS

Capawock Movie House (☎ 508-627-6689; 37 Main St; adult/child $6.50/4.50) Sit in the dark year-round at this old-time 1912 cinema. Discounts available for matinees and seniors.

THEATER

Vineyard Playhouse (☎ 508-696-6300; www.vineyardplayhouse.org; 24 Church St; adult/child & rush tickets/senior & student $35/20/30) The 120-seat Playhouse presents good-quality, challenging shows. In summer, there's a lineup of 'washashores' (Broadway and screen actors). Winter performances feature a mix of community and professional performers.

Shopping

Vineyard Haven, and especially Main St, features a variety of fine art, jewelry, houseware and clothing (especially ladies') shops. Here's a small sample:

Shaw Cramer Gallery (☎ 508-696-7323; 2nd fl 76 Main St) Among the art galleries in town, this one stands out for its wide array of contemporary crafts: framed art, sculpture, furniture and design items.

Midnight Farm (☎ 508-693-1997; 18 Water Cromwell Rd) In the very center of town yet tucked away, owner and singer Carly Simon has laid out an array of gauzy clothing, art books, and rustic yet comfortable housewares.

OAK BLUFFS

pop 3710

This is the island's summer fun center – informal, hip, noisy, downscale, pierced, multiracial…even gaudy.

Other Vineyarders occasionally pooh-pooh Oak Bluffs as 'honky tonk,' but it started out as the opposite of Sin City.

Week-long summer gospel sessions began here in 1835. The pilgrims' tents gradually developed into tent-shaped wooded 'gingerbread houses' that are now the town's signature style. Piety gradually came to co-habitate with pleasure (the town's carousel is one of America's oldest), and nowadays if you're looking for nightlife on the island, this the place to go.

Orientation
Woods Hole and New Bedford ferries dock facing Nantucket Sound, at the intersections of Sea View and Oak Bluffs Aves (seasonal). West along Oak Bluffs Ave is Oak Bluffs Harbor, an inlet where the Island Queen ferry from Falmouth, and Hy-Line ferries to Hyannis and Nantucket dock. The area between the two docks is filled with shops, eateries and bike and car-rental outlets.

Information
MONEY
Compass Bank (☎ 508-693-0095) Across from Steamship Authority.

Martha's Vineyard Cooperative Bank (cnr Lake & Circuit Aves)

TOURIST INFORMATION
Information booth (☎ 508-693-4266; cnr Circuit & Lake Aves; ⚇ 9am to 5pm May–mid-Oct) Behind the Flying Horses Carousel.

Sights
CAMPMEETING ASSOCIATION CAMPGROUND
The religious camp meeting movement started among Presbyterians, Baptists and Methodists in Kentucky in the early 19th century. People would gather around a meadow, sleep in tents and spend a week or so in spiritual communion.

Before long, the practice spread to New England, and in 1835 six Methodist men from Edgartown came across a modest half-acre grove of oaks in what is now Oak Bluffs. A camp meeting was held that year with nine tents and, it's said, 65 conversions and six souls saved.

By the 1860s, this modest meeting had grown to over 570 tents and 16,000 attendees, and soon the tents grew into proper houses. Today these homes around Trinity Park are typified by bold colors and whimsical wood-work, that makes them look like they're dripping with icing. The **Cottage Museum** (☎ 508-693-7784; 1 Trinity Park; adult/child $1.50/50¢; ⚇ 10am-4pm Mon-Sat mid-Jun–mid-Sep) has typical architecture, and it's filled with old furniture and Campmeeting Association artifacts.

Although the camp meetings are no longer week-long extravaganzas drawing tens of thousands, services and other events are still held in the 1879 wrought-iron Trinity Park Tabernacle; services take place on Sundays in July and August, and other events include concerts, community sing-alongs and a flea market.

Head south on the main drag, Circuit Ave, and the Campmeeting Association campground is on your right.

FLYING HORSES CAROUSEL
This national historic **landmark** (☎ 508-693-9481; cnr Lake & Circuit Aves; rides all ages $1.50; ⚇ 11am-4:30pm Sat & Sun late Apr–mid-Oct, 10am-10pm daily late May–early

---

THE AFRICAN-AMERICAN CONNECTION

These days, Oak Bluffs is a prime vacation land for East Coast African-American movers and shak-ers, but African Americans trace their roots on the islands to as early as the late 1600s. African slaves tended farms back then, until a freed slave named Rebecca Amos was willed property by her Wampanoag husband in 1779.

Nantucket and Martha's Vineyard both had small but successful communities of African Ameri-cans, including some noted whaling captains – Martha's Vineyard's first black whaling captain, William Martin, traced his roots back to Rebecca Amos.

It was during the Harlem Renaissance that African-American tourism to Martha's Vineyard really took off. Writer Dorothy West, author of The Wedding, was an early convert to the island's charms. Filmmaker Spike Lee owns a house in 'OB' and Harvard academician Henry Louis 'Skip' Gates Jr frequents the island. Über–lawyer lobbyist Vernon Jordan vacationed here with former president Bill Clinton and family, during Clinton's White House years.

Oak Bluffs' African-American connection was explored in Matty Rich's 1994 movie, The Inkwell.

Sep) claims to be the country's oldest operating merry-go-round (1876). Its 20 horses have manes of real horsehair, and if you stare deep into their glass eyes you'll notice little sterling silver animals inside. Fans of organ music will love the 1929 Wurlitzer.

Activities

BEACHES

Oak Bluffs Town Beach starts by the Steamship Authority pier and heads south toward Edgartown. It is this beach that has a long association with the African-American community.

The narrow, 2-mile-long **Joseph Sylvia State Beach** on Beach Rd (aka the Oak Bluffs-Edgartown Rd) is backed by low dunes. It's also referred to as Bend-in-the-Road Beach as you move toward Edgartown.

CYCLING

Several shops rent bicycles for about $15 to $20 per day, including helmets. In season, they're generally open from 9am to 6pm. Try:

Anderson Bike Rentals (☎ 508-693-9346; Circuit Ave Extension)

De Bettencourt's Bike Shop (☎ 508-693-0011; Circuit Ave Extension)

Ride-On Mopeds (☎ 508-693-2076; 9 Oak Bluffs Ave; moped hire per day $50)

Tours

Two-hour historical walking **tours** (☎ 508-693-0525; adult/child under 12 $10/free; ⏰ 10am Tue & Thu Jul & Aug) of the Campmeeting Association grounds meet at the Trinity Park Tabernacle and include admission to the Cottage Museum.

A number of boats dock at Oak Bluffs Harbor to take you on private expeditions. Typical is **Avalon Harbor Cruises** (☎ 508-524-1445; www.greatharborrental.com; per two hrs & up to 4 adults $120).

Festivals & Events

If you're in Oak Bluffs in mid-August, you won't want to miss the **Grand Illumination Night**, a tradition that dates back to Campmeeting days. Residents gather for a community sing, then the town shuts off all electrical lights and the eldest resident lights a Japanese lantern. Then the rest of the Campmeeting Association follows suit, and an eerie glow of thousands of lanterns fills the neighborhood.

Sleeping

BUDGET

Nashua House (☎ 508-693-0043; www.nashuahouse.com; 30 Kennebec Ave; d in season $99-139, off-season $59-89) Although no-frills (frills being phones, TV, air-con, in-room bathroom or breakfast), this 1873 house received a stem-to-stern renovation in 2000, so it's in pretty nice shape.

MID-RANGE

Narragansett House/Iroquois Cottage (☎ 508-693-3627, 888-693-3627; www.narragansetthouse.com; 46 Narragansett Ave; d incl continental breakfast in season $100-275, off-season $85-225; ⏰ mid-May–mid-Oct) The Victorian-style Narragansett has 13 simple, old-fashioned rooms that are well kept and have new bathrooms. Across the street, Iroquois Cottage is spiffy, renovated and romantic. Note: no air-con.

Oak Bluffs Inn (☎ 508-693-7171, 800-955-6235; www.oakbluffsinn.com; 64 Circuit Ave; d incl breakfast in season $200-280, off-season $135-220; ⏰ May-Oct) The nine rooms and suites all have private bathroom and antiques (early American) or cottage-style furniture (bright and fanciful).

Surfside Motel (☎ 508-693-2500, 800-537-3007; www.mvsurfside.com; 7 Oak Bluffs Ave; d in season $165-295, off-season $65-205) Its location, between the beach and the harborside bar area, means that light sleepers may want to avoid it. Some of the 38 rooms are suites, others have Jacuzzis, and many have water views or refrigerators.

Attleboro House (☎ 508-693-4346; 42 Lake Ave; d $95-115, ste $115-200; ⏰ mid-May–Sep) Guests come here more for the harbor-view location rather than for facilities (no phones, no private bathroom, no breakfast and no air-con). The 11 basic rooms all have sinks, and there's a large attic room for bigger groups.

TOP END

Oak House (☎ 508-693-4187, 800-245-5979; www.vineyardinns.com; 75 Seaview Ave; d incl breakfast & afternoon tea in season $195-315, off-season $160-230; ⏰ May-late Oct) This place is aptly named – handsome rooms have oak furniture, oak walls, even oak ceilings! It faces Nantucket Sound, and most rooms have water views.

Eating

BUDGET

Martha's Vineyard Gourmet Café & Bakery (☎ 508-693-3688; 5 Post Office Sq) It serves coffee, sandwiches, famous apple fritters and cannoli, but *the* time to go is 10pm to 1:30am, when there's a booming business in fresh-made doughnuts sold out the back door.

Slice of Life (☎ 508-693-3838; 50 Circuit Ave; mains $6-12; ☺ breakfast, lunch & dinner) A take-out and casual lunch shop operated by the owners of Sweet Life Café (below). The food is simpler here – breakfast burritos or pancakes, burgers, pizzas, salads, portabello mushroom sandwich – but still well executed.

MID-RANGE

Offshore Ale Co (☎ 508-693-2626; 30 Kennebec Ave; mains lunch $6-12, dinner $11-26, pizzas $13-17; ☺ lunch Tue-Sun May-Sep, dinner year-round) Drink in the scene at this one-time barn, with its cool carpentry and boats suspended from the high ceilings. Offshore brews its own beer and serves it alongside burgers, brick-oven pizzas and seafood.

Giordano's (☎ 508-693-0184; 107 Circuit Ave; mains $8-16; ☺ lunch & dinner late May-early Sep) In business since 1930, Gio's is really three establishments: a family-friendly dining room for pastas, pizzas and home-style Italian-American faves, and counters for pizzas ($11 to $18) and fried seafood ($7.50 to $13).

Zapotec Cafe (☎ 508-693-6800; 14 Kennebec Ave; mains lunch $8-12, dinner $15-20; ☺ lunch Jun-Aug, dinner May–mid-Oct) It's Santa Fe on Nantucket Sound as Mexican and Southwestern dishes like chicken suiza and chimichangas take on Vineyard variations like swordfish fajitas.

TOP END

Sweet Life Café (☎ 508-696-0200; 63 Circuit Ave; mains $26-46; ☺ dinner May-Nov) A chef-owned bistro admired by, well, everybody. Count on roast organic chicken, and sirloin, cod or salmon in various preparations. Plus the setting – indoors or in the garden of this Civil War-era house – makes it a great date place.

Park Corner Bistro (☎ 508-696-9922; 20h Kennebec Ave; mains $13-33; ☺ dinner in season, dinner Wed-Sun off-season) Our favorite new place is both cozy and worldly wise. The menu changes monthly, but we hope they keep the green goddess salad and steak au poivre.

Balance (☎ 508-696-3000; 57 Circuit Ave; mains $19-36; ☺ dinner May-Oct) Big-city experience, with an open kitchen, white tablecloths, pulsing beats and a hopping bar scene. The New American menu features dishes like braised lamb-shank risotto, wild salmon salad and 'big-ass' sea scallops.

Captain's Table (☎ 508-696-0220; 5 Oak Bluffs Ave; mains $20-36; ☺ dinner Thu-Mon) The classic Vineyard steak-and-seafood joint gets an update. The food here is undeniably cosmopolitan (from the signature lobster pan roast to swordfish wasabi), yet the atmosphere stays true to its busy, beachy roots.

Lola's Southern Seafood (☎ 508-693-5007; 15 Beach Rd; brunch $12-15, pub menu $5-14, mains $20-27; ☺ brunch Sun in season, dinner daily, phone for off-season hrs) This hopping joint has authentic barbecue ribs, seafood jambalaya, steaks and other New Orleans–style dishes. Year-round entertainment includes Motown or a cappella during brunch.

Drinking

Mocha Mott's (☎ 508-696-1922; 10 Circuit Ave; breakfast $4, lunch $5; ☺ 6am-8pm) Java junkies follow their noses to this basement hangout.

If you're after something spiked, the restaurants Balance (left), **Nancy's** (☎ 508-693-0007; 29 Lake Ave), Offshore Ale Co (left) and **Tsunami** (☎ 508-696-8900; 8 Circuit Ave Extension) all have bar scenes.

Entertainment

CINEMAS

Visit the historic cinemas, **Island Cinema** (☎ 508-627-MOVY; 1 Circuit Ave; adult/child $7/5) or **Strand Theatre** (☎ 508-627-MOVY(6689); 13 Oak Bluffs Ave; adult/child $7/5).

NIGHTCLUBS

Atlantic Connection (☎ 508-693-7129; www.atlanticconnection.com; 19 Circuit Ave; cover varies) There's usually something rowdy going on here all summer, with everything from reggae, comedy, Brazilian, or hip-hop DJs for 20-somethings.

Lampost/Rare Duck (☎ 508-693-9847; Circuit Ave; ☺ Apr-Oct) The 2nd-floor Lampost features dancing and pool for an under-30 crowd (think Brazilian or Best Male Body nights), while the 1st-floor Rare Duck entertains older patrons more simply with frozen drinks.

EDGARTOWN

pop 3780

Edgartown is classic New England. Its 18th- and 19th-century Greek Revival former whaling captains' houses are perfectly maintained, with clipped lawns, blooming gardens and white picket fences. And since it's not a major transit hub like Vineyard Haven or Oak Bluffs, it doesn't get the same hordes, although summers can still be busy.

Orientation

All roads from the west enter Edgartown via Main St, which extends down to the harbor. Water St runs parallel to the harbor. N Water St leads out to the Edgartown Lighthouse.

Information

BOOKSTORES

Edgartown Books (☎ 508-627-8463; 44 Main St) The place in town for books, as well as occasional readings and signings.

INTERNET ACCESS

Edgartown Public Library (☎ 508-627-4221; 10am-5pm Mon & Wed, noon-8pm Tue & Thu, noon-5pm Fri & Sat) Check your email for free for 15 minutes.

TOURIST INFORMATION

Edgartown Visitors Center (29 Church St; 9am to 5pm Jun-early Sep, with additional summer evening hrs)

Sights

MARTHA'S VINEYARD HISTORICAL SOCIETY

The island's most interesting **museum** (☎ 508-627-4441; www.marthasvineyardhistory.org; 59 School St; adult/child $7/4; 10am-5pm Tue-Sat mid-Jun–mid-Oct, 1-4pm Wed-Fri & 10am-4pm Sat mid-Oct–mid-Jun, 10am-4pm Sat Jan–mid-Mar or by appointment) occupies several buildings. In addition to whaling, sociological and maritime relics, the museum's pride and joy is the huge Fresnel lens that sat in the Gay Head Lighthouse (p215) until electrical power arrived in 1952.

HISTORIC BUILDINGS

At the center of town is a cluster of historic buildings operated by the **Martha's Vineyard Preservation Trust** (☎ 508-627-8619; www.mvpreservation.org). They're open subject to the ability of volunteer docents, so hours are irregular; call for tours and information. Prominent among them are the **Old Whaling Church** (Man St). This former Methodist meetinghouse, built in 1843, combines New England simplicity with the majestic Greek Revival columns. The **Dr Daniel Fisher House** is next door, and behind is the **Vincent House Museum**, said to be the oldest home on the island (1672).

Activities

BEACHES

Lighthouse Beach is easily accessible from the end of N Water St. The lighthouse (p215) is particularly striking at sunset, but it's fun to watch boats put into Edgartown harbor from here any time. Nearby, college students and summer workers hang out on **Fuller St Beach**.

CYCLING

The following agencies all rent bikes at about $20/80 per day/week for adults or $15/65 per day/week for children, and offer bike delivery.

CHAPPAQUIDDICK ISLAND

To most Americans, Chappaquiddick Island, a stone's throw from Edgartown harbor, is known for a tragic accident that has never been conclusively explained: a passenger (Mary Jo Kopechne) drowned in the car of now-US Senator Edward Kennedy when it plunged off a small wooden bridge here in 1969.

That's really too bad, because 'Chappy' should be known for its beauty and unique ecosystem – principally two wildlife refuges. The 516-acre **Cape Poge** is the more interesting of the two topographically, while the 200-acre **Wasque** (pronounced *way*-skwee) is famous for its fishing, beaches and currents.

The sites are administered by the **Trustees of the Reservations** (☎ 508-627-3599; www.thetrustees.org; late May–mid-Oct), which offers a variety of excellent tours. Options include a 2½-hour **natural history tour** (adult/child $30/20, 9am & 2pm) or a 1½-hour **Cape Poge lighthouse tour** (adult/child $20/12; 9am, noon & 2pm), both by over-sand vehicle; and a 2½-hour **canoeing trip** (adult/child $35/18; 9am & 2pm). Adjacent to the Cape Poge parking area is the 14-acre Japanese-inspired **Mytoi Garden**.

The six-car **Chappy Ferry** (On-time Ferry; ☎ 508-627-9427; cnr Daggett & Dock Sts, Edgartown; car & round-trip driver/passenger/bike & rider/motorcycle & rider $8/2/5/6; 7am-midnight end May–mid-Oct, 7am-7:30am, 9pm-10pm & 11pm-11:15pm mid-Oct–end May) is a great no-nonsense service, though during the in season there are often long waits.

Edgartown Bicycles (☎ 508-627-9008; www.edgar
townbicycles.com; 212 Main St)
RW Cutler Bike (☎ 508-627-4052; www.edgartown
bikerentals.com; 1 Main St)
Wheel Happy (☎ 508-627-5928; 8 S Water St & 204
Upper Main St)

Tours
Felix Neck Wildlife Sanctuary (☎ 508-627-4850; www
.massaudubon.org; off Edgartown-Vineyard Haven Rd; trail
access adult/senior & child $4/3; ☺ visitor center 8am-4pm
June-Aug; 8am-4pm Tues-Sat Sep-May) Managed by the
Massachusetts Audubon Society, this sanctuary offers natural
history tours for adults and children; phone for offerings and
prices.
Ghosts, Gossip & Downright Scandal Tour (☎ 508-
627-8619; tours per person $10) Keeps irregular hours but
is well worth it.

Sleeping
BUDGET
Edgartown Commons (☎ 508-627-4671, 800-439-4671;
www.edgartowncommons.com; 20 Pease's Point Way; studio/
2-/3-/4-r apt in season $170/195/245/270, off-season
$90/110/140/160; ☺ May–mid-Oct; ☒) This com-
plex of 1950s-era buildings has 35 studios
and multibed apartments. Guests (mostly
families) can use outdoor barbecues and a
coin-operated laundry. Note: no air-con.

MID-RANGE
Point Way Inn (☎ 508-627-8633, 888-711-6633; www
.pointway.com; 104 Main St; d incl full breakfast & afternoon
tea in season $250-425, off-season $100-300; ☺ Apr-Oct)
This former whaling captain's house has 13
stylish, airy rooms and suites, many with
four-poster canopy beds and fireplaces.
The owners have a car that they loan to
guests (first-come, first-served) for – get
this – free.
Victorian Inn (☎ 508-627-4784; www.thevic.com;
24 S Water St; d incl full breakfast in season $180-385, phone
for off-season rates) And Victorian it is – on the
National Register of Historic Places. Its 14
rooms are filled with antiques and reproductions; many also have decks or balconies. The gregarious innkeeper keeps things
lively.
Edgartown Inn (☎ 508-627-4794; www.edgartown
inn.com; 56 N Water St; d in season $115-250, off-season
$85-180; ☺ mid-Apr-Oct) Edgartown's best bar-
gain – friendly and tidy, and built around
1798. Most rooms have private bathroom
but no phone or TV. Breakfast costs extra
but is worth it.

TOP END
Charlotte Inn (☎ 508-627-4751; 27 S Summer St; d incl
continental breakfast & afternoon tea in season $295-650,
off-season $295-425, ste in season $695-895, off-season
$450-495) This 1860 inn has a well-earned
reputation as one of New England's finest.
Its 23 rooms and two suites are furnished
with practically priceless antiques, and flat-
screen TVs. Children aged 14 and up are
welcome.
Harbor View Hotel (☎ 508-627-7000, 800-225-
6005; www.harbor-view.com; 131 N Water St; r in season
$330-615, off-season $120-410; ☒) On 5.5 acres at
the north edge of town, Edgartown's largest hotel (124 units) dates from 1891; recent additions include cottages and tennis
courts.

Eating
At peak times, waits of 45 minutes to an
hour are not uncommon.
L'Étoile (☎ 508-627-5187; 27 S Summer St; prix-fixe
menus from $72; ☺ dinner in season, phone for off-season
hrs) To woo or just impress, reserve here.
The seasonal menu emphasizes local, organic ingredients, all in a setting worthy of
the Charlotte Inn (above). It's one of the
few places on the island with a dress code.
Chesca's (☎ 508-627-1234; 38 N Water St; dishes
$17-30; ☺ dinner Apr–mid-Oct) Quite pleasant
and very popular. The backbone of Chesca's menu is Italian: think mix-and-match
pastas. But the rest of the menu reflects
an Italian who travels: salmon with a spicy
Thai glaze or seafood paella.
Newes from America (☎ 508-627-4397; 23 Kelley
St; mains $8-11; ☺ lunch & dinner) One of the old-
est buildings in town, this dark, cozy, low-
beamed place serves monstrous portions of
very good pub grub, plus the house draft
beer.
Espresso Love (☎ 508-627-9211; 17 Church St;
mains lunch $6-11, dinner $8-26; ☺ breakfast & lunch
year-round, dinner in season) Serves the richest cup
o' Joe in town, and good muffins. Lunch revolves around sandwiches and soups, while
dinner ranges from Black Angus burgers to
penne pasta.
Among the Flowers Café (☎ 508-627-3233; 17
Mayhew Lane; mains breakfast $2.95-7.95, lunch $4.25-
9.75; ☺ breakfast & lunch May-Oct, dinner Jul & Aug) Join
the locals on the patio for omelettes, soups,
waffles, sandwiches, quiches, even lobster
rolls ($12.95). Although everything's served
on paper or plastic, it's still kinda chichi.

Drinking

Newes from America (☎ 508-627-4397; 23 Kelley St)
The house specialty at this restaurant (see
p221) is a 'rack of beer,' a sampler with five
unusual brews.

Wharf (☎ 508-627-9966; Main St) This year-
round pub is popular with the under-25
preppy set and pick-up scene.

Entertainment

Edgartown Cinema (☎ 508-627-8008; 65 Main St;
adult/child, senior & matinee $8/5.50) Has two screens
and shows recent releases.

Hot Tin Roof (☎ 508-693-1137; www.mvhottinroof
.com; Airport Rd; ⊙ late May–mid-Oct) Its location
near the Martha's Vineyard Airport makes
it feel like it's in West Tisbury, but it is in
Edgartown and that means booze is OK.
Catch live acts a few nights a week, and occasional dance nights. A free shuttle serves
the island's major towns.

Shopping

Christina Gallery (☎ 508-627-8794; 32 N Water St)
Probably Edgartown's best-regarded venue
for framed art and sculpture. There's a great
collection of historical maps.

Edgartown Scrimshaw Gallery (☎ 508-627-9439;
43 Main St) The best place in town, or on the
island for that matter, to pick up scrimshaw.
It also sells framed art.

UP-ISLAND

This pastoral landscape is a patchwork of
rolling fields, lined with stone walls and private dirt roads and dotted with barns and
grazing sheep. Soak up the scenery, take a
hike, pop into a gallery, stop at a farm stand
and munch, lunch and beach.

Unless you plan on staying at the youth
hostel or intend to just hunker down, it's
pretty impractical to stay up-island without
a car.

West Tisbury

pop 2470

The island's agricultural heart has a white
church, mill, ponds and general store, all
evoking an old-time sensibility. Nowadays,
West Tisbury also has artists' studios and
galleries sprinkled throughout.

SIGHTS & ACTIVITIES

Part food shop, part historic landmark, **Alley's General Store** (☎ 508-693-0088; State Rd) is a
favorite local gathering place, and has been
since 1858.

The **Grange Hall** (1859) is a historic meetinghouse, most visited these days for regular
farmer's markets (opposite) and **artisans markets** (⊙ 10am-2pm Sun in season). This post-and-
beam structure is also a venue for concerts,
comedy shows, lectures and other events.

Wildlife Sanctuaries

The **Cedar Tree Neck Sanctuary** (☎ 508-693-5207),
off Indian Hill Rd (off State Rd), has a few
trails crossing its 300 acres of bogs, beaches,
forests and fields. It's a nice place for
birding.

The dense 4400-acre **Manuel F Correllus
State Forest** (☎ 508-693-2540; ⊙ sunrise-sunset),
off the Edgartown–West Tisbury Rd, occupies a huge chunk of the island's mid-
section with walking and biking trails, and
picnic facilities.

Polly Hill Arboretum (☎ 508-693-9426; www.polly
hillarboretum.org; 809 State Rd; adult/child under 12 $5/
free; ⊙ 7am-7pm Thu-Tue late May–mid-Oct, sunrise
to sunset Thu-Tue mid-Oct–late May, visitor center 9am-
4pm Thu-Tue) is a 60-acre celebration of local
woodlands and endangered species.

Art Galleries

This modest-appearing **Craven Gallery** (☎ 508-
693-3535; 495 State Rd) exhibits big-name artists
like Milton Avery and Edward Hopper, and
lesser-known artists who will probably be
famous in due time.

You can't miss the **Field Gallery** (☎ 508-693-
5595, www.fieldgallery.com; 1050 State Rd), a field of
large white sculptures by local artist Thomas Maley (1911–2000), playfully posing
while tourists mill around them. There's an
indoor gallery, too, with works by artists of
local and national renown.

In business since 1954 but hardly old-
school, the **Granary Gallery** (☎ 508-693-0455,
800-472-6279; Old County Rd) manages to stock
everything from photos by Alfred Eisens-
taedt and Margaret Bourke-White to fanciful paintings by local artists.

Master craftspeople turn sand into fragile
and colorful creations at the **Martha's Vineyard
Glass Works** (☎ 508-693-6026; 683 State Rd). If you
can stand the heat, you can watch them.

SLEEPING & EATING

Hosteling International – Martha's Vineyard (☎ 508-
693-2665, 888-901-2087; www.capecodhostels.org; Edgar-

town–West Tisbury Rd; beds $20-27; ⊗ mid-Apr–mid-Oct; 🖳) Constructed in 1955, this 74-bed building was the first custom-built hostel in America. There's a great kitchen, a volleyball court, bike delivery, no curfew, no lockouts, *and* it's right on the bike path. Reserve in summer.

Old Parsonage (☎ 508-696-7745, www.swiftsite.com/oldparsonage; 1005 State Rd; r incl breakfast $100-175; ⊗ late May–mid-Oct) For authentic up-island flavor, this atmospheric hostelry has three rooms (two of which share a bathroom) and one large suite.

Lambert's Cove Country Inn (☎ 508-693-2298; www.lambertscoveinn.com; Lambert's Cove Rd; d incl breakfast in season $185-250, off-season $90-210, mains $21-31; ⊗ accommodation Feb-Dec, restaurant dinner in season, phone for off-season hrs) At the end of a long dirt road, Lambert's 7¼ acres include 15 rooms in three buildings; pine groves; and tennis. The restaurant is one of the island's favorites.

West Tisbury Farmer's Market (State Rd) Head to the Grange Hall (in the center of West Tisbury – you can't miss it) on Saturday from 9am to noon. The market is also open 2:30pm to 5:30pm on Wednesday in July and August.

Chilmark
pop 840

Occupying most of the western side of the island between Martha's Vineyard Sound and the Atlantic, Chilmark is known for rolling hills and an easygoing feeling. Chilmark's chief destination is the 300-plus-year-old fishing port of Menemsha, but there are a few other gathering places around Beetlebung Corner, where South and Middle Rds reconnect after the long journey from West Tisbury.

SIGHTS & ACTIVITIES
If the fishing village of **Menemsha** looks familiar to you, get out your DVD player: it was one of the locations for the movie *Jaws* (Edgartown and Chappaquiddick also figured large). Nowadays, it's a relaxing outpost in which to browse. Basin Rd features fishing boats, lobster pots and fish shacks on one side and dunes on the other, ending at the public **Menemsha Beach**. Sunsets here are pretty spectacular.

A little **bike ferry** (☎ 508-645-3511; one-way/round-trip $4/7; ⊗ mid-Jun–late Sep, phone for hrs) takes people and their bikes to Lobsterville

beach (p224) across the cut, a beach popular with families for its gentle waters.

Lucy Vincent Beach, off South Rd about a half mile before the junction with Middle Rd, is the loveliest stretch of sand on the island, complete with dune-backed cliffs and good, strong surf. It also permits nude bathing. See the beach permits boxed text on p177.

TOURS
The catamaran **Arabella** (☎ 508-645-3511; Menemsha Harbor; daytime/sunset cruise $60/50; ⊗ sailing mid-Jun–late Sep) makes a daily run to nearby Cuttyhunk Island (10am to 4pm) and a two-hour evening sunset trip around the cliffs. Reservations are advised.

SLEEPING & EATING
Chilmark
Captain R Flanders' House (☎ 508-645-3123; www.captainflanders.com; North Rd; s with shared bathroom in season/off-season $80/65, d with private bathroom $195/150, d with shared bathroom $175/115) This 17th-century house enjoys a tranquil setting on 60 acres overlooking a pond, with four modest guest rooms and two snug, romantic cottages. Breakfast is included.

Theo's (☎ 508-645-3322; 74 North Rd, Inn at Blueberry Hill; mains $23-40; ⊗ dinner Jul & Aug, occasional nights May-Oct) Dine on the elegant porch, or, if you're lucky, the lawn. The menu changes nightly, but expect to find upscale dishes like pan-seared scallops with pink grapefruit tarragon beurre blanc, or homemade potato gnocchi.

Beach Plum Inn (☎ 508-645-9454; 50 Beach Plum Lane; mains $32-45; ⊗ dinner in season) Year in, year out, the restaurant at the Beach Plum is one of the highest rated in New England. The menu changes frequently, but favorites include salmon and halibut in various preparations.

Chilmark Store (☎ 508-645-3739; 7 State Rd; dishes $6-8, pizzas $13-24; ⊗ breakfast, lunch & dinner) Combination bourgeois shop, market and local landmark just off of Beetlebung Corner. Salads and sandwiches are enjoyed on rockers on the porch.

Menemsha
Menemsha Inn & Cottages (☎ 508-645-2521; www.menemshainn.com; North Rd; r incl breakfast in season $225-290, off-season $135-180, cottages per week in season $2200-3100, off-season $1400-1900; ⊗ Apr-Nov; 🖳) On a former sheep farm, this secluded place

offers 28 tidy and well-equipped cottages and motel-style rooms.

The following are open only in peak season:

Bite (☎ 508-645-9239; 29 Basin Rd; servings $3-14; ⌚ 11am-sunset in season) It's a fried-food fest, with fried clams, zucchini and the like served piping fresh in brown paper bags. Take it to the beach or eat at picnic tables.

Larsen's Fish Market (☎ 508-645-2680; Basin Rd) Larsen's will sell you a fresh steamed lobster, stuffed quahog or scallops ($2 each) and lots of other choices.

Home Port (☎ 508-645-2679; Menemsha Harbor; mains $26-40 or market price; ⌚ dinner) Famous for lobster prepared eight ways, Home Port is an institution. Prices include appetizer, salad, drink and dessert. Hint: if you order takeout from the back door, you'll get fewer extras but save about 40%.

SHOPPING

Menemsha Blues (☎ 508-645-3800; 2 Basin Rd, Menemsha) An upstart T-shirt shop that's giving the Black Dog (p216) a run for its money.

Chilmark Chocolates (☎ 508-645-3013; State Rd; chocolates per pound $14; ⌚ 11:30am-5:30pm Wed-Sun, closed much of off-season) This shop is worth a visit just for the chocolates, but they'll taste even better knowing that the special needs kids who staff the shop benefit from the proceeds.

If you need a tchotchke, try the **Flea Market in the Meadow** (Middle Rd; ⌚ 8:30am-2pm Wed & Sat late Jun-early Sep). It's 1 mile from Beetlebung Corner.

Aquinnah

pop 340

Apart from its isolation, the chief attraction of Aquinnah is the mile or so of windswept cliffs that form a jagged face down to the Atlantic, astonishing in the colorful variety of sand, gravel, fossils and clay that tell 100,000 centuries of geology.

Aquinnah was also known as Gay Head until the 1990s. That time coincided with an increased consciousness of the native Wampanoag people, and it's here more than anywhere else on the island that you'll notice Wampanoag influence.

SIGHTS & ACTIVITIES

Aquinnah's chief draw, the **Clay Cliffs**, were formed by glaciers more than 100 million years ago. Rising 150ft from the ocean, they're dramatic any time of day. The cliffs are a National Historic Landmark owned by the Wampanoag Native Americans, and it's illegal to bathe in the mud pools that form at the bottom of the cliffs, climb the cliffs, or remove clay from the area.

The 51ft, 1856 brick **Gay Head Lighthouse** (p215) stands precariously at the edge of the bluff.

Aquinnah Public Beach (Ⓟ $15) is a whopping 5 miles long. Access is free, although parking is not. From the parking lot, walk about 700 yards to the beach entrance. Head north for the cliffs (and the nude beach); to the south, the beach is wider, but it's technically restricted to residents only.

Just across from Menemsha Harbor, **Lobsterville Beach** is popular with families because of the gentle surf and shallow water. Without an Aquinnah resident parking pass, take the bike ferry from Menemsha (p215).

SLEEPING & EATING

Duck Inn (☎ 508-645-9018; 10 Duck Pond Way; d incl breakfast in season $115-225, off-season $95-175) Off State Rd, on a bluff a pleasant 25-minute walk from the beach, the rooms here are individually decorated, with perhaps a feather duvet or marble wash basin. Cool!

Outermost Inn (☎ 508-645-3511; www.outermostinn.com; 81 Lighthouse Rd; r incl breakfast in season $280-370, off-season $230-320, prix-fixe meals $72; ⌚ mid-May–mid-Oct) The seven rooms here are contemporary and casual, with lots of windows and sweeping ocean views. Dinner (open to the public) is a prix-fixe extravaganza.

Central Massachusetts & the Berkshires

CONTENTS

HIGHLIGHTS

- **Best Mountaintop Rewards**
  Gazing out over five states from the summit of Mt Greylock (p273) and watching the Connecticut River snake its way through the valley from the top of Mt Holyoke in Skinner State Park (p243)

- **Best Places to Witness Art in Motion**
  Taking in a performance at the Tanglewood Music Festival near Lenox (p264) or at the Jacob's Pillow Dance Festival (p263) in Lee

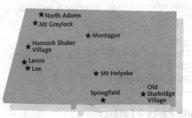

★ North Adams
★ Mt Greylock
★ Montague
★ Hancock Shaker Village
★ Lenox
★ Lee
★ Mt Holyoke
Springfield ★
Old Sturbridge Village ★

- **Most Praiseworthy Recommissions of Old Mills**
  Exploring the enormous Massachusetts Museum of Contemporary Art (p272) in North Adams and the more intimately scaled Montague Bookmill (p255) in Montague

- **Easiest Places to Imagine You're Living in Another Century**
  Letting costumed interpreters fool you into believing it's the mid-1800s in Old Sturbridge Village (p232) and Hancock Shaker Village (p268) near Pittsfield

- **Most Culture Squeezed into the Smallest Area**
  Enveloping yourself in the Springfield Quad (p237) with museums on history, art and science, with a library and a sculpture garden thrown in for good measure

CENTRAL MASSACHUSETTS & THE BERKSHIRES

■ TELEPHONE CODE: 508, 413   ■ POPULATION: 1.6 MILLION   ■ AREA: 4293 SQ MILES

The allure of the Berkshires is well known – few regions can match its wealth of cultural offerings swaddled up in such a harmonious natural setting. One could easily spend an entire summer – or lifetime – hopscotching the patchwork of wilderness areas while taking in a world-class dance festival here, an illustrious musical series there, and excellent summer theater all over the place. And while extreme skiers may head north to Vermont, the kinder, gentler slopes of the Berkshire range promise a ski vacation the whole family can enjoy – and with fewer people fighting over the same patch of land.

On the way west, largely rural Central Massachusetts begs for exploration. The swath from Worcester to Springfield doesn't generally attract the same kind of attention as the Berkshires, with the exception of lovably touristy Old Sturbridge Village. This means that you'll likely be taken for a local while you chow down at a historic Worcester lunch car diner, or for a student as you stroll or bike the streets of the college-rich, cosmopolitan Pioneer Valley. Sprinkled across the rich alluvial farmland flanking the Connecticut and Blackstone Rivers is a blend of colonial, early American and 19th-century villages and towns that evoke simpler times and compel you to linger.

Climate

As with the rest of New England, Massachusetts can be a pleasure to visit any time of year, and its climate does not dramatically differ from that of the rest of the region: winters can be bitterly cold and gloriously snowy, with summers ranging from pleasantly warm to uncomfortably hot. Luckily there's usually a swimming hole close by to jump into.

The peak leaf-peeping window is around the first two weeks of October. Call Massachusetts' **foliage hotline** (☎ 800-227-6277) for specifics.

State Parks & Forests

Dozens of parks and forests pepper Central and Western Massachusetts. In season it will normally cost you $2 per car to park at 'scenic areas' and $5 per car to visit inland swimming beaches. Out of state camping sites run $12 to $15. Check out **MassParks** (www.mass.gov /dem/forparks.htm) for more information about activities and amenities, plus trail maps. You can also call **MassLive** (☎ 413-442-8928, ext 0) for maps to all the region's trails.

Both **Skinner State Park** (p243) on top of Mt Holyoke in Hadley and **Mt Tom State Park** in Holyoke offer incredible views of the Connecticut River Valley, starring the switch-

backing river itself. The parks are popular spots for picnicking and trail walking.

Take in the sweeping vistas of the surrounding five states from atop **Mt Greylock State Park** (p273), the tallest point in the state. You can hike part of the way to the top, or you can drive all the way. The Appalachian Trail passes over its ridge. The **Connecticut River Greenway State Park** runs the length of the state, with eight river access points for pure boating – or simply river lounging – pleasure.

Getting There & Around

AIR

In Connecticut, **Bradley International Airport** (p314) serves Springfield and the Pioneer Valley towns.

BUS

Peter Pan Bus Lines (☎ 617-426-7838, 800-343-9999; www.peterpanbus.com) runs buses daily all over New England and to Washington DC. Several daily buses run between New York City and Sturbridge ($40.50 one-way, 3½ to 4½ hours, 168 miles) and Worcester ($38 one-way, four hours, 178 miles). **Bonanza Bus Lines** (☎ 212-947-1766, 800-556-3815; www.bonanzabus.com) runs buses daily between New York City and Williamstown ($36 one-way, five hours, 198 miles), and between Albany, NY, and Springfield ($26 one-way, 1½ hours, 87 miles), stopping in the major towns along the way.

The **Pioneer Valley Transportation Authority** (PVTA; ☎ 413-586-5806; www.pvta.com) provides bus services to the entire Five College area (the central part of the Pioneer Valley, which encompasses the campuses of Amherst, Smith, Mt Holyoke and Hampshire Colleges, and the University of Massachusetts at Amherst). The Northampton–Amherst route has the most frequent service. **Berkshire Regional Transit Authority** (BRTA; ☎ 413-499-2782) runs buses between all the major Berkshire towns.

CAR
The Massachusetts Turnpike (I-90) and MA 2 are the major east–west roads connecting Boston with central and western Massachusetts. Mass Pike is a toll road between Boston and Springfield.

See p314 for car rental agencies servicing Bradley International Airport.

TRAIN
Amtrak's (☎ 800-872-7245) *Lake Shore Limited* departs from **Boston's South Station** (☎ 617-482-3660), stopping at Framingham, Worcester, Springfield and Pittsfield before reaching Albany, NY.

CENTRAL MASSACHUSETTS

If you have a few days to spend, Central Massachusetts will reward you with driving, cycling and hiking opportunities through a rolling terrain of dairy farms and forests. Along the way you will find engaging museums, hip and historic towns, and an array of both imaginative and 'down-home' restaurants.

WORCESTER
pop 175,000

Blessed with fine museums, one of America's best concert halls, well-preserved 19th-century buildings and respected institutions of higher learning such as Worcester Polytechnic Institute, Worcester (woosta) is starting to emerge as an urban attraction after a half-century of neglect. In spite of a moderate degree of urban renewal, the city has the rough-around-the-edges feel of a place that remains home to a legion of working families, not the gentry.

Worcester is the birthplace of well-known humorist Robert Benchley (1889–1945), whose witticisms – like the oft-quoted 'why don't you get out of that wet coat and into a dry martini?' – are legendary.

Orientation
Commercial St, three blocks west of I-290 and one block east of Main St, is the city's commercial hub. The clock tower on City Hall marks the center of town. The huge DCU Center (formerly the Centrum Center) hulks over the downtown area at the corner of Foster St and Commercial St.

Information
Bank of America (365 Main St at Pearl; ◔ 9am-4pm Mon-Fri) This is a full-service bank right downtown. There are plenty of other banks in town.

Public library (☎ 508-799-1655; 3 Salem Sq; ◔ 9am-9pm Tue-Thu, 9am-5:30pm Fri & Sat) This has free Internet access, but often a long wait.

Tatnuck Bookseller (☎ 508-756-7644; 335 Chandler St; ◔ 8am-9pm Mon-Fri, 9am-10pm Sat, 9am-6pm Sun) The largest independent bookstore in New England, with over 5 miles of books and a busy restaurant. To get there from the center of town, take 122A west about a mile.

Worcester County Convention and Visitors Bureau (☎ 508-753-2920; www.worcester.org; 30 Worcester Center Blvd, Worcester, MA 01608; ◔ 8:30am-5pm Mon-Fri) Staff at this visitor center, across the street from the DCU Center, can help with travelers' questions or problems. Be sure to ask for a 'Great Museum Adventures' pamphlet, which is full of two-for-one discounts for many Worcester attractions. You can also print the coupons out from www.massmuseums.org/coupons.html.

Sights & Activities
WORCESTER ART MUSEUM
During Worcester's golden age, its captains of industry bestowed largesse upon the town and also upon its citizens. The **Worcester Art Museum** (☎ 508-799-4406; www.worcesterart.org; 55 Salisbury St; adult/senior & student/child under 18 $8/6/free, free Sat mornings; ◔ 11am-5pm Wed & Fri, Thu 11am-8pm, Sat 10am-5pm) off Park and Main Sts (follow the signs) is a generous and impressive bequest.

This small museum has a comprehensive collection, ranging from ancient Chinese, Egyptian and Sumerian artifacts to European masterworks and contemporary American pieces, and from the work of

CENTRAL MASSACHUSETTS & THE BERKSHIRES

Japanese *ukiyo-e* (17th- to 19th-century wood-cut) painters to great North American paintings and primitives. Edward Hick's *Peaceable Kingdom* is perhaps the most easily recognizable piece in the collection, but you can also see Paul Gauguin's *Brooding Woman* and Rembrandt's *St Bartholomew*. Several pieces of Paul Revere silver have recently been acquired as well. The museum's collection of more than 2000 photographs spans the history of the medium.

HIGGINS ARMORY MUSEUM

John Woodman Higgins, president of the Worcester Pressed Steel Company, loved good steel. Medieval armorers made good steel, so he collected it: more than 100 full suits of armor for men, women, children and even dogs. His collection got so big (over 8000 pieces) that in 1929 he built a special armory to house it – this art-deco building with interior neogothic accents is the **Higgins Armory Museum** (☎ 508-853-6015; www.higgins.org; 100 Barber Ave; adult/senior/child 6-16 $7.75/7/6.75; ⊙ 10am-4pm Tue-Sat, noon-4pm Sun), off W Boylston St (MA 12). Kids will like the

Quest Gallery, where they can try on 'castle clothing' and replica suits of armor.

AMERICAN SANITARY PLUMBING MUSEUM

Worcester is home to the only known **plumbing museum** (☎ 508-754-9453; 49 Piedmont St; admission free; ⊙ 10am-2pm Tue & Thu, closed Jul & Aug) on the planet, though some others may be in the pipeline. The antique water heaters, bathtubs and sinks hold their own, but it's really the toilets and chamber pots that receive all the lurid attention. Plumber Russell Manoog opened up the museum to display his father's fascinating collection of vintage fixtures, the oldest of which dates back to 1652.

ECOTARIUM

At this **museum** (☎ 508-929-2700; www.ecotarium.org; 222 Harrington Way; adult/child $8/6; ⊙ 10am-5pm Tue-Sat, noon-5pm Sun) and 'center for environmental exploration,' there is an array of exhibits to intrigue young minds. However, the most exciting offerings cost an extra few bucks, like the tree-canopy walks, the planetarium shows, and rides on the one-third size model steam train.

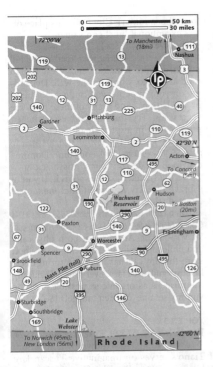

MECHANICS HALL

This **hall** (☎ 508-752-5608, 508-752-0888 box office; www.mechanicshall.org; 321 Main St) took shape in 1857 on the orders of the Worcester County Mechanics Association, a group of artisans and small business owners who typified Worcester's inventive and industrial strength in the mid-19th century. Boasting superb acoustics and housing the historic Hook Organ, Mechanics Hall is regarded as the finest standing pre–Civil War concert hall in the US. Notable speakers have included Henry David Thoreau, Charles Dickens, Mark Twain and Theodore Roosevelt. Restored in 1977, the hall is still used for concerts, lectures and recording sessions. Call for information on visiting hours, or call the box office for tickets to a lecture or performance.

SALISBURY MANSION

Very near the art museum, the **Salisbury Mansion** (☎ 508-753-8278; 40 Highland St; admission $5; ⏰ 1-8:30pm Thu, 1-4pm Fri & Sat), built in 1772, was the Salisbury family home until 1851. It is now preserved as a museum and has been re-created in the style of the early 19th century based on extensive family records.

WORCESTER HISTORICAL MUSEUM

Just around the corner from the art museum, the **Worcester Historical Museum** (☎ 508-753-8278; www.worcesterhistory.org; 30 Elm St; admission $5; ⏰ 10am-4pm Tue-Sat) preserves the record of Worcester's history, particularly its 19th-century golden industrial age.

AMERICAN ANTIQUARIAN SOCIETY

The documents in this **research library** (☎ 508-755-5221; www.americanantiquarian.org; 185 Salisbury St; admission free; ⏰ 9am-5pm Mon-Fri), a few blocks from the art museum, comprise the largest single collection of printed source materials relating to the first 250 years of US history, covering all aspects of colonial and early American culture, history and literature. Free tours run each Wednesday at 3pm.

BLACKSTONE RIVER BIKEWAY

When it is finished in the next three to five years, the **Blackstone River Bikeway** (☎ 401-789-4625; Union Station, 45 Shrewsbury St) will offer a mostly off-road bike trail from Worcester to Providence, RI, 45 miles to the south. The trail laces through historic mill villages and follows remnants of the Blackstone River Canal as well as a railroad right-of-way. Until the bikeway is complete, you can follow the trail on marked roads. Pick up the pamphlet entitled *Driving Tour & Guide to Blackstone Canal Historic Markers* from the visitor center.

Sleeping

Worcester's hotels serve DCU Center arena concertgoers and high-tech firms on the outskirts of the city. This demand has jacked up the rates on most of Worcester's hostelries. You will find more economical tourist lodgings and more charming B&B options about 20 miles southwest, in and around Sturbridge. All the hotels listed below are wheelchair accessible and their rooms offer data ports. The hotel tax rate is 9.7%. Take this into account when figuring lodging costs.

Crowne Plaza (☎ 508-791-1600, 800-227-6963; www.crowneplaza.com; 10 Lincoln Sq; d $100-180; 🅿 Ⓟ) Located between the DCU Center and the art museum, this large hotel stands within walking distance of most of the city's attractions, and offers rooms with fridges and bathrobes. They have both an indoor and an outdoor pool.

Hampton Inn (☎ 508-757-0400, 800-426-7866; www .hamptoninn.com; 110 Summer St/I-290 exit 16; d incl breakfast $108-117; P) Situated right downtown, this place has clean and functionally furnished rooms, with cable TV. Guests get free access to Bally's Gym.

Beechwood Hotel (☎ 508-754-5789, 800-344-2589; www.beechwoodhotel.com; 363 Plantation St; r/ste $149-214/159-234; P) This 73-room hotel is well known to business travelers for its personal service and pastel-toned luxury rooms. It's a cylinder-shaped building east of the city center along MA 9 near the Massachusetts Biotechnology Park.

Best Western Inn & Suites (☎ 508-852-2800, 800-932-3297; www.bestwestern.com; 50 Oriol Dr/I-290 exit 20; r/ste $99-119/139-159; ♿ P) This quiet establishment has 117 comfortable rooms, half of which are condo-style suites. The bedspreads are gaudy, but the grounds are nicely landscaped.

Eating

The core of downtown Worcester is studded with moderately priced lunch spots, many of which offer to-go food you can take to the front of City Hall for an impromptu picnic. The more ethnic and imaginative eateries can be found slightly to the west and south.

A visit to at least one of Worcester's historic **diners** (opposite) should be considered mandatory.

BUDGET & MID-RANGE

Java Hut (☎ 508-752-1678; 1073a Main St at Webster Sq; sandwiches $3-7 ⏰ 11am-1am) This community gathering spot has a humungous menu of coffee drinks, plus tempting veg and nonveg sandwiches and mouth-watering desserts like peanut butter cup pie ($4).

Ivy Kitchen (☎ 508-831-7696; 6 Waldo St; dishes $2-6; ⏰ 6am-2:30pm Mon-Fri) John Keeneway and Sue McFarland do a doubles act in this little short-order place, which is hard to match for friendliness, wit and down-home cooking. An old-school coffee shop, complete with green Formica counters and swiveling stools, the Ivy Kitchen lies just two blocks north of the DCU Center. A three-egg cheese omelette runs just $3.25.

Seoul Leecci (☎ 508-363-0891; 385 Main St; lunch/dinner $6-8/9-15; ⏰ 11am-11pm) A Korean-Japanese restaurant and sushi bar less than a block from the landmark City Hall, this place offers exceptional luncheon values.

One Love Café (☎ 508-753-8663; 800 Main St; dinner mains $9-16; ⏰ noon-8pm Tue, noon-10pm Wed-Sun) Fill up on organic Jamaican and West Indian food at this cozy hole-in-the-wall. Depending on your appetite, you can get 'big tings' or 'likkle tings,' and many of these tings are vegetarian. Try the pungent escoveitched porgies (fish in a spicy vinaigrette).

Maria's Kitchen (☎ 508-797-3380; 826 Main St; mains $5-10; ⏰ 10am-10pm) For some Dominican food made con amor, this black-and-white-tiled cafeteria-style spot is it. If you're a brave one, try the traditional mondongo (stewed tripe).

Living Earth Garden Café (☎ 508-753-1896; 232-4 Chandler St; dishes $6-12; ⏰ 11am-8pm Mon-Fri, 9am-6pm Sat, 11am-5pm Sun) An offshoot both physically and philosophically of the Living Earth food store, this tiny café has a menu featuring über-healthy, guilt-free fare. Everything, including the meat, is as organic as possible. Try the yummy sesame 'chicken' nuggets ($6).

TOP END

Tiano's (☎ 508-752-8901; 55 Pearl St; mains $15-24; ⏰ dinner) In its new downtown location, Tiano's serves up imaginative Tuscan fare like pan-caramelized beef tips and seared fillet of salmon. This is a popular date spot; you will need reservations on Friday and Saturday nights.

Sole Proprietor (☎ 508-798-3474; 118 Highland St; mains lunch/dinner $7-9/16-22; ⏰ lunch & dinner) Overlook the cheesy name and head here for fresh, honest seafood at moderate prices. To keep everyone happy, they've even thrown some sushi rolls and tapas into the mix.

Drinking

Moynagh's Tavern (☎ 508-753-9686; 25 Exchange St) Right next door to the Ivy Kitchen (left), which supplies the pub with food, this authentic Irish-American pub of the first order is the oldest bar in Worcester. Babe Ruth once bowled here when the place was a bowling alley. The crowd is still working folk and the jukebox is overwhelmingly rock and country.

The Irish Times (☎ 508-797-9599; 244 Main St; ⏰ opens 11:30am) Set in a 19th-century three-story building, this place really feels like a Dublin pub, with dark paneling, high ceilings and the scent of Caffrey's. On weekends

WORCESTER DINERS *John Spelman*

Worcester, New England's largest rustbelt city, might look a bit like a black eye, but its occasionally brutal post-industrial landscape has nurtured a great American icon: the diner. Here, you'll find a dozen old relics tucked behind warehouses, underneath old train trestles, or steps from dicey Irish bars. Many of them are the product of the former Worcester Lunch Car Company, which produced 650 pre-fabricated beauties from 1906–1961. Models from the '30s tend to incorporate rich wood-trim and tiling and look like old train cars. Those from the '50s shoot for a sleek 'streamlined' aesthetic, incorporating sheets of gleaming metal into their exteriors.

Following is a list of Worcester's finest. Prepare your stomach for some dirt-cheap coffee.

Boulevard (☎ 508-791-4535; 155 Shrewsbury St; mains $3-8; ⏰ closed 3pm Sun – 10am Mon, otherwise 24hr) Reason enough to live in Worcester, this old dining car looks much like it did in 1936. Experience red formica tables, dark wooden booths, old iceboxes and a big painting of a yellow-jacketed dude who has long stared from the doorway. Food-wise, enjoy eggs, plus a menu of Italian specialties including meatballs, veal and eggplant parmesan. Wistful memories of fabulous grapenut custards haunt college students' dreams decades after leaving Worcester.

Annie's Clark Brunch (☎ 508-756-1550; 934 Main St; breakfast & lunch $2-6; ⏰ 6am-2pm Mon-Sat) On the edge of Clark University's campus, this greasy spoon attracts students, professors, neighborhood Joes and a gravedigger. Nearly everyone is on a first-name basis with Annie, the dirty-mouthed proprietor so connected with the community that Clark recently awarded her an honorary degree. Inside, find dusty pictures of regulars from the last 20 years and an eyebrow-raising number of pigs.

George's Green Island Diner (☎ 508-753-4189; 162 Millbury St; eggs etc $2-5; ⏰ 4:30-11:30am) Inside this spare diner, sit at the counter to behold the world's eighth wonder: a grill in constant use that never dirties. Just how George Army's spatula cooks up all that meat, egg and potato without a stain remains a mystery, but you'll be too distracted by kielbasa and liver and onions to notice. It's in a tough-looking Irish neighborhood. Coffee costs 55¢!

Ralph's Chadwick Square Diner (☎ 508-753-9543; 95 Prescott St; burgers $5; ⏰ 5pm-2am Tue-Sat) Thick burgers draw big crowds to this neon classic lurking behind old warehouses. Attached to one of these warehouse spaces, Ralph's operates as a bar and nightclub and has provided the city with live rock for more then 20 years. There are beer, pool and Husker Du.

Corner Lunch (☎ 508-799-9866; 133 Lamartine St; mains $2.25-6; ⏰ 6am-2pm Mon-Sat, 7am-1pm Sun) Here, you'll find a sweet pre-fab built by DeRaffelle in the 1950s. The exterior contains plenty of silvery metal panels and a big neon sign. Inside, there are fries, club sandwiches, meatloaf and eggs. While the food is bland, the seating is not – it's a patchwork of duct tape and glittery gold Naugahyde. It sits a block from the Miss Worcester Diner, closed at time of research.

Coney Island Hot Dog (☎ 508-753-4362; 158 Southbridge St; hot dog $1.25; ⏰ 10am-8pm Wed-Mon) A giant neon fist grips a wiener dripping yellow neon mustard in the six-story sign outside this Worcester institution from 1918. Inside, eat dogs in an eerily quiet, cavernous space chock-full of wooden booths carved with generations of graffiti. Get the unbeatable Coney Island sauce. It's next to the Greyhound station.

the upstairs is a disco where the DJ spins out techno and dance tunes, and downstairs is pure rock. The dinner patrons are largely urban professionals who come for the fish-and-chips ($11).

Gay & Lesbian Venues

Northampton it ain't, but Worcester does have a growing gay scene.

Vibes (☎ 508-753-9969; 116 Water St; Tue-Sun noon-9pm) It's a coffeehouse…it's a gift shop…it's a gallery space. Swing by and see what's going on.

Both these clubs are found in the south-east part of the city:

MB Lounge (☎ 508-799-4521; 40 Grafton St; cover free-$5) Depending on the night, the lounge runs the gamut from casual neighborhood bar to bass-thumping dance club. Sundays often see appropriately loungey events like crooners on piano.

Rage (☎ 508-756-2227; 104 Water St; cover free-$7). Bigger, badder and more boy-centric than MB Lounge. There's no cover on Retro 80s Sundays and Karaoke Tuesdays, when the crowd is more mixed.

CENTRAL MASSACHUSETTS & THE BERKSHIRES

Entertainment

Pick up the free weeklies *Worcester Magazine* (Womag; www.worcestermag.com), or the more student-targeted *Pulse* for arts and entertainment listings.

Bijou Cinema (☎ 508-757-0900; www.bijou-cinemas.com; cnr Foster St & Worcester Center Blvd; tickets $3-7; ⊙ Wed-Sun) A haven for lovers of independent, art-house and foreign films, Bijou also houses a taqueria, allowing you to chow down while you culture up.

Cinema 320 (☎ 508-793-7477; Jefferson Academic Center, cnr Main & Downing Sts; tickets $5) On the campus of Clark University, they show edgy and relevant contemporary films from all over. The school is about 2 miles south of town center on Main St.

Java Hut (☎ 508-752-1678; 1073a Main St at Webster Sq; ⊙ 11am-1am) As well as serving coffee and food (p230), Java Hut also hosts entertainment like slam poetry and folk singers most nights.

Atrium (☎ 508-363-1392; 1 Exchange Pl) This vast, corporate-feeling complex has among its venues a martini bar, a Hooters-esque sports bar called JJ Juggs and a DJ-based nightclub. Dress to impress.

Mechanics Hall (☎ 508-752-0888; 321 Main St; tickets $18-50) This acoustically superb hall presents classical and jazz events as well as performances by unique troupes like the National Acrobats of Taiwan.

DCU Center (☎ 508-798-8888, 617-931-2000 for tickets; 50 Foster St; tickets $18-150) The arena formerly known as the Centrum, this huge venue attracts nationally known rock groups and other big-crowd acts.

Palladium (☎ 508-797-9696, 800-477-6849; www.the palladium.net; 261 Main St; tickets $10-30) When you're in the mood for metal, hardcore, rap, punk or any combination thereof.

Getting There & Away

Worcester stands at the junction of four interstate highways. About an hour's drive will bring you here from the Boston, Providence, Springfield and Hartford, CT, areas.

Worcester Regional Airport (☎ 888-359-9672; MA 122/Chandler St), several miles due west of the city center, is served by **US Airways Express** (☎ 800-428-4322).

Peter Pan Bus Lines (☎ 508-753-1515; 800-343-9999; 75 Madison St) has direct services between Worcester and Amherst ($20.50 one-way, two hours, 76 miles), Boston ($9 one-way,

---

> **LAKE...ER, WEBSTER**
>
> This pretty lake, popular with boaters, is more famously known by its original Native American name, **Lake Chargoggagoggmanchauggagoggchaubunagungamaugg**. The longest official geographic name in the US roughly translates as 'you fish on your side, I fish on my side, and nobody fishes in the middle.' To get there from Worcester, take I-395 south and get off at Rte 197.

one hour, 39 miles), Hartford ($16.50 one-way, 1½ hours, 69 miles), Lenox ($29 one-way, 2½ hours, 88 miles), Springfield ($17.50 one-way, one hour, 50 miles) and Sturbridge (22 miles, $9 one-way, half-hour) within MA, and to Albany, NY ($28 one-way, 3½ hours, 142 miles), and NYC ($38 on-way, four hours, 178 miles).

Bonanza (☎ 888-751-8800) runs bus services between Worcester and Providence, RI, and departs from the same station as Peter Pan.

Amtrak trains (☎ 508-755-0356, 800-872-7245) stop here en route between Boston and Chicago. **MBTA Commuter Rail** (☎ 617-722-3200, 800-392-6099) runs trains each way from Boston to Worcester several times daily. Trains for both rails leave from Union Station at Washington Sq, one block west of I-290.

STURBRIDGE

pop 8000

Sturbridge can leave a bittersweet taste in the traveler's mouth – here is one of the most visited attractions in New England and one of the rudest examples of how far US culture has traveled in less than 200 years in search of the Yankee dollar.

The town kept much of its colonial character until after WWII. When the Mass Pike (I-90) and I-84 arrived in the late 1950s and joined just north of the town, commerce and change came all at once. To take advantage of the handy highway transportation, the town became host to one of the country's first 'living museums' – Old Sturbridge Village (OSV). The concept of the living museum was new when OSV started. Inevitably, in the community's effort to preserve a working example of a traditional Yankee community within the borders of OSV, it generated a mammoth attraction on whose borders motor inns, fast-food chains, gas stations and roadside shops have sprouted up.

Orientation & Information

There are actually three Sturbridges. The first one you see is the commercial strip along US 20 (Main St) just south of I-90 exit 9, which has most of the town's motels and restaurants. The second is Sturbridge as it used to be, best seen at the town common, backed by the Publick House Historic Inn (p234), on MA 131 half a mile southeast of US 20. The third is Old Sturbridge Village, entered from US 20.

Sturbridge can be outrageously busy with visitors in summer and during the autumn foliage season. Traffic increases exponentially during the three times per year (early May, early July and early September) when the Brimfield Antiques and Collectibles Shows are held in Brimfield, 6 miles west of town along US 20.

The **Sturbridge Area Tourist Association Information Office** (SATA; ☎ 508-347-7594, 800-628-8379; www.sturbridge.org; 380 Main St/US 20; ☑ 9am-5pm) is opposite the entrance to Old Sturbridge Village. The Peter Pan bus stop is here as well.

Sights & Activities

OLD STURBRIDGE VILLAGE

During the first half of the 20th century, two brothers, Albert Wells and J Cheney Wells, lived in Southbridge and carried on a very successful optics business. They were enthusiastic collectors of antiques – so enthusiastic, in fact, that by the end of WWII their collections left no free space in their homes.

They bought 200 acres of forest and meadow in Sturbridge and began to move old buildings from the region to this land. Opened in 1946, **Old Sturbridge Village** (OSV; ☎ 508-347-3362; www.osv.org; US 20; adult/senior/child 3-17 $20/18/5; ☑ 9:30am-5pm daily May-Oct, 9:30am-4pm daily Nov & Dec, Sat & Sun only Jan-Apr) is a re-created New England town of the 1830s, with 40 restored structures filled with the Wells' antiques. Rather than labeling the exhibits, this museum has 'interpreters' – people who dress in costume, ply the trades and occupations of their ancestors and explain to visitors what they are doing. Expect to spend at least three hours here.

Although some historians find the layout of the village less than accurate, attention to detail is high. The country store displays products brought from throughout the world by New England sailing ships. Crafters and artisans ply their trades with authentic tools and materials. The livestock has even been back-bred to approximate the animals – smaller, shaggier, thinner – that lived on New England farms a century and a half ago. The OSV library has more than 20,000 manuscripts and books describing various aspects of early-19th-century life in the region.

Admission is good for two days within a 10-day period. Food services in the village include the tavern, with buffet and à la carte service for full meals, light meals and snacks. There is also a picnic grove with grills and a play area.

HYLAND ORCHARD & BREWERY

This **orchard and brewery** (☎ 508-347-7500; 199 Arnold Rd; admission free; ☑ noon-8pm Tue-Sun, shorter hrs in winter) is a 150-acre family-owned farm and craft brewery that produces its Sturbridge Amber Ale and handful of other beers with well water. Try them all at the tasting bar. Lest you think this is no place for the kids, note that this brewery has a petting farm, pond, playground, ice-cream parlor and café, and bands perform on the weekends. To find Hyland, go west on Main St/US 20 to Arnold Rd, turn right and go 2 miles north on Arnold Rd to the farm. Guided tours are led on Saturdays at 2pm.

ICON EXHIBIT AT SAINT ANNE SHRINE

Since WWII it has been illegal to export icons from Russia, so the collection of 60 rare works preserved at the **icon exhibit** (☎ 508-347-7338; 16 Church St; admission free, donations accepted; ☑ 10am-4pm) at the St Anne Shrine is a treasure. Monsignor Pie Neveu, a Roman Catholic Assumptionist bishop, ministered to a diocese in Russia from 1906 to 1936. While at his post, Bishop Neveu collected valuable Russian icons, a hobby no doubt made easier by the collapse of the old order and the advent of secularist communism. Bishop Neveu's collection was further augmented by acquisitions brought to the USA by the Assumptionist fathers who served as chaplains at the US embassy in Moscow between 1934 and 1941. The collection was installed at the St Anne Shrine in 1971.

Visitors are conveniently steered through the gift shop to get to the icon exhibit. The shrine is just off US 20 at the western end of Sturbridge.

BRIMFIELD ANTIQUE SHOW

Six miles west of Sturbridge along US 20 is the **Brimfield antique show** (www.brimfieldshow.com; US 20 in Brimfield; 6am-sunset), a mecca for collectors of antique furniture, toys and tools. More than 6000 sellers and 130,000 buyers come from all over creation to do business in 23 farmers' fields here, the largest outdoor antiques fair in North America. The town has numerous shops open year-round, but the major antiques and collectibles shows are held in early to mid-May, early July and early September, usually from Tuesday through Sunday. The more 'premium' fields charge an admission fee of around $6, but most are free.

Contact SATA for more details, and be sure to have advance hotel reservations.

Sleeping

Even though Sturbridge is packed with places to stay, many lodgings fill up on Friday and Saturday nights in summer and, especially, in autumn. When the Brimfield Antiques Show (above) is in progress, local lodging prices rise substantially and advance reservations are necessary. If you come in the off season (April or November), the competition keeps the prices low.

Staying in an inn or B&B remote from US 20 and the wheels of commerce is how many travelers preserve that jaunt-in-the-country feeling they get when visiting Sturbridge/Brimfield. In fact, if it's fresh air and tranquility you're seeking, the best option may be to get out of town completely and stay at a farm B&B. The SATA can direct you to its member B&Bs, and it can help you make same-day reservations if you stop in at the information office. If you're looking for more central lodging, look through the motel brochures at SATA – some include coupons that are good for special rates or discounts.

All lodgings listed here offer parking.

BUDGET & MID-RANGE

Sturbridge Coach Motel Lodge (508-347-7327; 408 Main St; www.sturbridgecoach.com; d $59-100;) This quiet, recently renovated motel scored a prime location – within spitting distance of OSV, but set back from US 20 on a small

hill. Rooms are clean and well sized and are equipped with full cable.

Nathan Goodale House (413-245-9228; 11 Warren Rd/MA 19N, Brimfield; d $80;) This lovely white Victorian Italianate house in residential Brimfield lets three rooms, two with private bathroom. The rooms are tastefully decorated.

Commonwealth Cottage B&B (508-347-7708; www.commonwealthcottage.com; 11 Summit Ave, Sturbridge; d $95-145;) Just a few blocks off Main St, the owners of this lovingly tended Queen Anne serve up hearty country breakfasts. In their three cozy rooms a multitude of patterns vie for supremacy.

Lying along a 1-mile stretch of US 20 just off exit 9 is a procession of chain hotels and motels. Rates can vary wildly by season, but doubles generally fall in the range of $70 to $100.

Days Inn (508-347-3391; 66-68 Haynes St;) Off I-84 exit 1 in a quiet, wooded area.

Super 8 (508-347-9000; 358 Main St) Many rooms have views of Cedar Lake.

Econo Lodge (508-347-2324; 682 Main St;)

Best Western American Motor Lodge (508-347-9121; 350 Main St;) Has a playground and game room.

Comfort Inn & Suites (508-347-3313; 215 Charlton Rd;) The suites have fireplaces.

North of I-90 you'll discover **Wells State Park** (508-347-9257; 877-422-6762 reservations; Mountain Rd/MA 49, Sturbridge; tent sites $10-12). This campground offers 60 wooded sites – some lakefront – on its 1470 acres with flush toilets and showers. You can reserve your site in advance with a two-night deposit.

TOP END

Publick House Historic Inn (508-347-3313, 800-782-5425; www.publickhouse.com; MA 131 on the Common;) Sturbridge's most famous historic inn, the 1777 Publick House, faces the village common, half a mile away from the mania of US 20. Three separate buildings make up the property – the Country Motor Lodge ($79 to $125), the Chamberlain House ($140 to $165) with six elegant suites, and the Publick Inn itself ($99 to $165) with canopy beds and 18th-century decor.

Sturbridge Country Inn (508-347-5503; www.sturbridgecountryinn.com; 530 Main St; r/ste $89-149/149-179;) The inn is a stately Greek Revival mansion about a mile west of OSV. Its nine sybaritic, pink-themed rooms all have fireplaces, whirlpool baths and TV. There's a bit of traffic noise in the front rooms.

Eating

US 20 is awash in fast-food outlets, breakfast joints and independent restaurants that offer lunch and dinner.

BUDGET & MID-RANGE

Micknuck's (570 Main St; ⊗ 8am-7pm Mon-Fri, 9am-6pm Sat & Sun) Tucked into the corner of this market is a deli counter that serves up massive gourmet sandwiches, a bag of chips and a superb deli pickle all for under $6. Of course, you can stock up on picnic standards like potato and pasta salads, too. Their cold cuts are strictly top-notch Boar's Head brand.

Annie's Country Kitchen (☎ 508-347-2320; 140 Main St/MA 131; ⊗ 5am-7pm) This is the place for an early breakfast, such as the lumberjack special of ham and three eggs, toast, home fries, juice and coffee for under $6.

Ugly Duckling Loft (☎ 508-347-2321; 520 Main St; mains $8-18; ⊗ 11am-10pm) The less upscale and more fun sister of the downstairs Whistling Swan restaurant, the Ugly Duckling is a popular, boisterous spot with a hefty menu of gourmet sandwiches and salads with mains that run the gamut from Swedish meatballs ($9) to teriyaki stir-fry ($10). There's often live music on weekends. The desserts are outstanding.

Rom's (☎ 508-347-3349; 179 Main St/MA 131; mains lunch/dinner $7-10/11-17; ⊗ lunch & dinner) A Sturbridge roadside institution that seats 500, Rom's serves up big portions of its traditional Italian-American fare (and drinks) for moderate prices. Locals flock to the buffet, and several times a week they hold all-you-can-eat extravaganzas. Across the street from the Sturbridge Plaza shopping center.

TOP END

Cedar Street Restaurant (☎ 508-347-5800; 12 Cedar St; mains $16-25; ⊗ dinner Mon-Sat) A boon for vegetarians and carnivores alike, this white clapboard restaurant just off US 20 changes its menu regularly, but every dish is thoughtfully prepared. Consider the black pepper fettuccini with herbed duck confit or the grilled vegetable kabobs with Greek salad ($15). Try to get a seat on the front patio if the weather's fine.

Publick House (☎ 508-347-3313, 800-782-5425; www.publickhouse.com; MA 131 on the Common; mains $22-33; ⊗ lunch & dinner Mon-Sat, dinner only Sun) This classic country inn features a formal dining room, with traditional New England dishes like apricot-glazed roast chicken; try the pan-seared scallops with fennel ($30). Reservations recommended.

Salem Cross Inn (☎ 508-867-8337; 260 W Main St/MA 9, West Brookfield; mains $18-25; ⊗ lunch & dinner Tue-Fri & Sun, dinner only Sat) If you haven't gotten your fill of colonial reenactment at OSV, head to this inn, built in 1705 and set on 600 lovely acres in West Brookfield. The calf's liver with bacon and caramelized onions is a house specialty ($15). Besides offering traditional New England meals, the inn hosts special events like the 'Fireplace Feast' and 'Herb Sampler.' Their **Hexmark Tavern** (⊗ dinner Tue-Fri) has less fancy fare for less fancy prices. Follow US 20 (2 miles west of OSV) to MA 148 north; 7 miles along, turn left onto MA 9 and go 5 miles.

Getting There & Away

Peter Pan Bus Lines (☎ 508-347-7594, 800-343-9999) runs one-day excursion buses right to OSV from Boston (☎ 617-426-7838) via Worcester, and from New York City (☎ 212-564-8484) via Hartford and Springfield. For other bus routes you must connect at Boston or Springfield. The Peter Pan bus stop is opposite the entrance to OSV, at the SATA information office.

PIONEER VALLEY

It wasn't long after the Pilgrims landed at Plymouth in 1620 that intrepid fur traders and settlers made their way up the Connecticut River deep into the center of New England, and bestowed upon this region the name Pioneer Valley. Folks here seemed to take the name to heart, and by the early 19th century, the patent office could hardly keep up with the inventions that Springfield and other valley towns were churning out. These days it's still known for its intellectual output, though the products now are students: the heart of the valley is often referred to as the Five College Area because it is home to Amherst, Hampshire, Mount Holyoke, and Smith Colleges, and the University of Massachusetts at Amherst, outstanding institutions of higher learning all.

Getting Around

Springfield, the largest city in western Massachusetts, is at the region's transportation nexus. Here the traditional east–west route from Boston to Albany crosses the Connecticut River valley.

The **Pioneer Valley Transportation Authority** (PVTA; ☎ 413-586-5806; www.pvta.com) provides bus services to the entire valley area, with the Northampton to Amherst route having the most frequent service.

Cyclists can enjoy a leisurely ride between Northampton and Amherst on the **Norwottuck Rail Trail**, a 10-mile-long right of way that's been converted to a bike path. It crosses the Connecticut River on a historic 1500ft-long iron bridge. You can rent bikes on Damon Rd in Northampton (☎ 413-545-5353). At any visitor center in the region you can pick up a *Getting Around Clean & Green in the Pioneer Valley* pamphlet published by the **Northeast Sustainable Energy Association** (☎ 413-774-6051; www.nesea.org; 50 Miles St, Greenfield MA 01301) with a map that shows hiking and biking routes and lists parks, swimming areas and area bike shops.

SPRINGFIELD

pop 152,000

Springfield's 19th-century industrial might and a major Civil War armory brought its residents the wealth to build several excellent museums, a library and a grand symphony hall. Basketball players all over the world pay tribute to Springfield with every shot. The game originated here, and now the city has a much-enlarged Basketball Hall of Fame. Springfield is also the birthplace of Theodor Geisel, aka Dr Seuss (p238).

Today Springfield is a city of commuters in suits, and a large immigrant population – mostly from Puerto Rico – who, surprisingly, have brought very little of their culture to the downtown area. The Romanesque buildings around Court Sq and the nearby modern office blocks disgorge an army of workers who flee the city at the conclusion of the working day. Nevertheless, you will find an active night scene downtown doing its patriotic part to increase revenue spending in this financially strapped city.

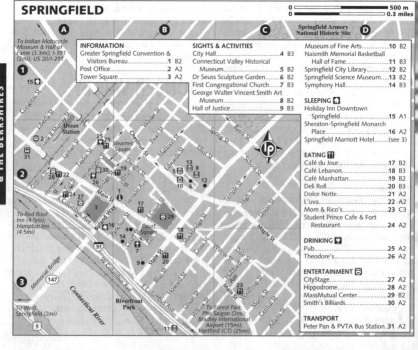

SPRINGFIELD

0 ———— 500 m
0 ———— 0.3 miles

To Indian Motocycle Museum & Hall of Fame (3.3mi); I-391 (2mi); US 20/I-291

INFORMATION
Greater Springfield Convention &
  Visitors Bureau.....................1 B2
Post Office.................................2 A2
Tower Square.........................3 A2

SIGHTS & ACTIVITIES
City Hall......................................4 B3
Connecticut Valley Historical
  Museum..................................5 B2
Dr Seuss Sculpture Garden.......6 B2
First Congregational Church......7 B3
George Walter Vincent Smith Art
  Museum..................................8 B2
Hall of Justice...........................9 B3

Museum of Fine Arts...............10 B2
Naismith Memorial Basketball
  Hall of Fame.........................11 B3
Springfield City Library............12 B2
Springfield Science Museum.....13 B2
Symphony Hall.........................14 B3

SLEEPING
Holiday Inn Downtown
  Springfield...........................15 A1
Sheraton-Springfield Monarch
  Place....................................16 A2
Springfield Marriott Hotel........(see 3)

EATING
Café du Jour...........................17 B2
Café Lebanon..........................18 B3
Café Manhattan......................19 B2
Deli Roll..................................20 B3
Dolce Notte.............................21 A2
L'uva.......................................22 A2
Mom & Rico's..........................23 C3
Student Prince Cafe & Fort
  Restaurant............................24 A2

DRINKING
Pub...25 A2
Theodore's..............................26 A2

ENTERTAINMENT
CityStage.................................27 A2
Hippodrome.............................28 A2
MassMutual Center.................29 B2
Smith's Billiards.......................30 A2

TRANSPORT
Peter Pan & PVTA Bus Station..31 A2

Union Station

Stearnes Square

Springfield Armory National Historic Site

To Red Roof Inn (4.5mi); Hampton Inn (4.5mi)

Court Square

Memorial Bridge

To West Springfield (2mi)

Riverfront Park

Connecticut River

To Forest Park; Pho Saigon (2mi); Bradley International Airport (15mi); Hartford (CT) (25mi)

WHAT'S SPRUNG FROM SPRINGFIELD

In 1794 President George Washington selected Springfield as a location for one of two federal armories that would manufacture muskets for the US Army. The first musket produced here in 1795 was a copy of the French 'Charleville,' popular with US soldiers during the Revolutionary War.

In 1819 Thomas Blanchard invented a wood-turning lathe to produce identical gun stocks quickly and cheaply. Percussion ignition replaced the flintlock, and breech-loaders replaced muzzle-loaders. The Model 1903 Springfield rifle was what American doughboys carried into battle in WWI, and the M-1 Garand, built in Springfield, armed the troops in WWII.

Springfield's impressive list of inventions goes on: the monkey wrench, steel-bladed ice skates, the first planetarium in the USA and the gasoline-powered motorcycle. Another invention was the first practical internal-combustion engine automobile, built in 1894 on the top floor of the building at 41 Taylor St by the Duryea brothers, Charles and Frank. For a short time in the 1930s the world's most elegant auto, the Rolls-Royce, was also assembled in this city.

Orientation

Take I-91 exit 6 northbound or exit 7 southbound, follow it to State St (east) then Main St (north), and you'll be at Court Sq in the heart of Springfield, a good place to start your explorations. Museum Quadrangle is a few blocks northeast, and the Tower Square complex, which includes the Marriott Hotel as well as a clutch of shops and restaurants, is two blocks northwest. The Springfield Armory is a 10-minute walk northeast.

Information

There are many banks clustered around the intersection of Main St, Boland Way and Harrison Ave, near the visitor center. There's free Internet access at the library (below).

Greater Springfield Convention & Visitors Bureau (☎ 413-787-1548, 800-723-1548; www.valleyvisitor.com; 1441 Main St, Springfield, MA 01103; 🕒 9am-5pm Mon-Fri) This is a block-and-a-half north of Court Sq.

Post office (1883 Main St) At the corner of Liberty St, eight blocks north of Court Sq.

Sights & Activities

COURT SQUARE

Fine buildings surround this shady square. You'll see **Symphony Hall** and **City Hall** on its west side. To the south stand the **First Congregational Church** (1819) and the granite **Hall of Justice** (Hampden County Superior Courthouse). William Pynchon, who led the group of Puritans who settled here in 1636, is honored with a statue.

MUSEUM QUADRANGLE

The **Springfield Library & Museums** (☎ 413-263-6800; www.quadrangle.org; 220 State St; adult/senior & student/child 6-17/child under 6 $7/5/3/free; 🕒 noon-4pm Wed-Fri, 11am-4pm Sat & Sun) surround Museum Quadrangle, two blocks northeast of Court Sq. Look for Merrick Park, at the entrance to the quadrangle, and Augustus Saint-Gaudens' statue *The Puritan.*

All four of these museums have the same hours, and one ticket grants entrance to them all, but access to the grounds – and the **Dr Seuss Sculpture Garden** (p238) – is free and open 9am to 8pm daily. Even if your visit to Springfield happens to fall on a Monday or Tuesday when the museums are closed, the quad is well worth a stroll. All the museums have informative plaques posted outside, which explain the history and architecture of the buildings and describe the wealth of offerings housed inside.

The **George Walter Vincent Smith Art Museum** is the gift of a man who amassed a fortune manufacturing carriages and then spent his money on works of art and artifacts. The lovely exterior windows were designed by the Tiffany Studios. Inside there are fine 19th-century American and European paintings, textiles, ceramics and works in several other media. The Japanese armor collection is among the finest outside of Asia.

The art-deco-style **Museum of Fine Arts** has more than 20 galleries filled with lesser paintings of the great European masters and the better works of lesser masters. Among the masterworks here is Erastus Salisbury Field's *The Rise of the American Republic,* hung above the main stairway. In the impressionist and expressionist galleries, look for artworks by Edgar Degas, Gauguin, Camille Pissarro, Pierre-Auguste Renoir and Georges Rouault. In the contemporary gallery there are works by George Bellows,

DR SEUSS NATIONAL MEMORIAL SCULPTURE GARDEN

A childhood that did not include a shelf lined with Dr Seuss books was a deprived one, to be sure. The writer and illustrator responsible for such nonsensically sensible classics as *The Cat in the Hat*, *Norton Hatches an Egg* and *Yertle the Turtle* was born Theodor Seuss Geisel in 1904 in Springfield. Geisel credits his mother for inspiring his signature rhyming style; she would lull him and his sister to sleep by chanting pie lists she remembered from her bakery days back in Germany.

After graduating from Dartmouth College, Geisel made his living primarily as a political cartoonist and ad man. His first children's book, *And to Think That I Saw It on Mulberry Street,* was rejected by dozens of publishers before one bit. Geisel's first major success came with the publication of *The Cat in the Hat,* which he wrote after reading Rudold Flesch's article *Why Can't Johnny Read,* which asserted that children's books of the day were boring and 'antiseptic,' and called upon people like Geisel (and, er, Walt Disney) to raise the standard of primers for young children. By the time he died in 1991, Geisel had published 44 books and his work had been translated into more than 20 languages. His classic *Green Eggs & Ham* is still ranked as one of the top-selling English language books to date.

In 2002 the **Dr Seuss Sculpture Garden** (☎ 800-625-7738; www.catinthehat.org) was completed, featuring bronze pieces made by Geisel's step-daughter, sculptor Lark Grey Dimond-Cates. Among the works in the middle of the Springfield Quad are a 10ft-tall 'book' displaying the entire text of *Oh! The Places You'll Go!* – which has become the archetypal graduation gift – and an impish-looking Geisel sitting at his drawing board, the Cat standing by his shoulder. In the opposite corner of the quad, the squat figure of the Lorax looks beseechingly up at passersby, his famous environmental warning engraved at his feet: 'Unless.'

And to think that it all began in Springfield.

Lyonel Feininger, Georgia O'Keeffe and Picasso. Modern sculptors featured include Leonard Baskin and Richard Stankiewicz. World-renowned Japanese woodblock prints are also found here.

The **Springfield Science Museum** possesses a respectable, if slightly outdated, range of natural history and science exhibits – the Dinosaur Hall has a full-size replica of a Tyrannosaurus rex, the African Hall teaches about the evolution of peoples, animals and ecology, and the aptly named Seymour Planetarium has shows daily (adult/child $3/2).

The **Connecticut Valley Historical Museum** is not as dull as its name may suggest. The rotating exhibits are the highlights – recent installations include one on Dr Seuss and another on the history of the Rolls-Royce in Springfield. The museum's permanent holdings focus on the decorative and domestic arts of the Connecticut River valley from 1636 to the present, with collections of furniture, pewter and glass, and the history of industrial development in the area. The museum's **Genealogy and Local History Library** holds the Ellis Island passenger records and an impressive number of records on French Canadians.

The **Springfield City Library** (413-263-6828; cnr State & Chestnut Sts; ☾ 11am-8pm Mon & Wed, 9am-6pm Tue, Thu & Fri, noon-4pm Sun) has more than a million books, records and videos in its system. Free Internet access can be had here, but the wait can be long.

BASKETBALL HALL OF FAME

Though the emphasis at the **Naismith Memorial Basketball Hall of Fame** (☎ 413-781-6500; www .hoophall.com; 1000 W Columbus Ave; adult/senior/child 5-15/child under 5 $16/13/11/free; ☾ 10am-5pm, open to 6pm Sat) seems to be more hoopla than hoops – an abundance of multiscreened TVs and disembodied cheering – true devotees to the game will be thrilled to shoot baskets, feel the center-court excitement in a wraparound cinema and learn about the sport's history and great players. If hunger strikes, there are plenty of fast-food joints on the premises. At present, exit 7 off I-91 is the way to come, but a new exit is under construction, designed for the sole purpose of spitting visitors off the freeway even closer to the Hall.

SPRINGFIELD ARMORY

The **Springfield Armory National Historic Site** (☎ 413-734-8551; www.nps.gov/spar/home.html; 1 Armory Sq, Federal St; admission free; ☾ 10am-4:30pm Wed-Sun) preserves what remains of the USA's greatest federal armory, built under the command

BIRTH OF BASKETBALL

James Naismith (1861–1939) came to Springfield from Montreal to work as a physical education instructor at the International YMCA Training School (later Springfield College). He wanted to develop a good, fast team sport that could be played indoors during the long New England winters. Sometime in early December of 1891, he had the idea of nailing two wooden peach baskets to opposite walls in the college gymnasium. He wrote down 13 rules for the game (12 of which are still used), and thus basketball was born.

Students at the college took to the new game enthusiastically, and Naismith went on to become basketball coach at the University of Kansas. His successor in that post, Forrest Allen (1885–1974), worked to have basketball included in the Olympic Games, and was successful in 1936.

of General George Washington during the American Revolution. During its heyday in the Civil War, it turned out 1000 muskets a day. Springfield Technical Community College now occupies many of the former firearm factories and officers' quarters, but exhibits in several of the old buildings recall the armory's golden age quite effectively.

On the site, the **Benton Small Arms Museum** holds one of the world's largest collections of firearms, including lots of Remingtons, Colts, Lugers and even weapons from the 1600s. For a truly weird weapon, don't miss the Organ of Rifles.

The Armory is a 10-minute walk northeastward from Court Sq along State St past Museum Quadrangle. If you are driving, take I-291 exit 3 to Armory St and follow it to Federal St.

INDIAN MOTOCYCLE MUSEUM & HALL OF FAME

When Americans hear 'motorcycle,' they are most likely to think 'Harley-Davidson.' But Springfield-based Indian was the first (1901), and was, many say, the best. Up until it disbanded in 1953, the Indian Motocycle Company produced its bikes here in a sprawling factory complex. (The 'r' in motorcycle was dropped as a marketing gimmick.) Through the merger of several bike companies, the Indian Motorcycle Corporation was created in

1999 to jumpstart the manufacture of Indians again, but it's widely accepted that the new bikes don't hold a candle to the originals.

The last of the company's buildings is now the dusty **Indian Motocycle Museum & Hall of Fame** (☎ 413-737-2624; 33 Hendee St; admission $5; ☯ 10am-4pm, 1-4pm Dec & Jan), with the largest, finest collection of Indian bikes and memorabilia in the world. There are other makes as well, and lots of funky period mementos. All of the machines are in working order (note the oil-drip pans underneath), and are taken out and run three times a year. If you like bikes, don't miss this place.

To find the museum, take I-291 exit 4 (St James Ave), then follow the signs north on Page Blvd to Hendee St. You'll find the museum in a low brick building in an industrial area.

FOREST PARK

Two miles south of downtown off Sumner Ave (MA 83) is **Forest Park** (☎ 413-787-6440; off Sumner Ave; in-state car/out-of-state car/walkers & bikers $2-3/4-5/free; ☯ sunrise-sunset), an 800-acre swath of lawns, woods, gardens, ponds, fountains, walking and horse trails, swimming pools and tennis courts. The **Zoo in Forest Park** (413-733-2251; www.forestparkzoo.com; adult/senior & child 5-12/child under 5 $4.50/3.50/2; ☯ 10am-4:30pm Apr-Oct 14, weekends only 10am-3:30pm Oct 15-Nov) has more than 200 animals and a miniature train.

Festivals & Events

In mid-September, sleepy West Springfield explodes into activity with the annual Eastern States Exposition, or the **Big E** (☎ 413-737-2443, 800-334-2443 ticket orders only; www.thebige.com; 1305 Memorial Ave/MA 147; weekend adult/child 6-12 $15/10). The fair goes on for two weeks, with farm exhibits and horse shows, carnival rides and parades, mass consumption of food on sticks, a petting zoo, and performances from the likes of Jessica Simpson and the Peking Acrobats. In addition, each of the six New England states hosts a large pavilion with its own exhibits.

All shows are free once you're in the fairgrounds, but rides cost extra. There's a parking fee, but for about the same price and less hassle you can catch a shuttle that departs from the visitor center. Hotels fill up when the Big E is in session, particularly on Friday and Saturday nights. Admission is a bit cheaper on weekdays.

Sleeping

With the help of **Best B&Bs of Massachusetts** (☎ 413-731-8785, 800-762-2751; www.berkshirebnbhomes .com; 37 George St, Springfield), you can make a reservation at small B&Bs in historic neighborhoods of greater Springfield.

Most of Springfield's more inexpensive motels, including the **Red Roof Inn** (☎ 413-731-1010; 1254 Riverdale St) and the **Hampton Inn** (☎ 413-732-1300; 1011 Riverdale St) are actually in West Springfield off I-91 exit 13, near the intersection with US 5. The hotels in downtown Springfield tend to be luxurious business accommodations. Lodgings mentioned below have parking available.

Holiday Inn Downtown Springfield (☎ 413-781-0900, 800-465-4329; www.ichotelsgroup.com; 117 Dwight St; r/ste $150-170/200; ☒) This hotel at Congress St, just over half a mile north of Court Sq, has 245 rooms, some of which have Internet access. There's an Avis office in the lobby and a fitness room. Kids eat for free at the restaurant.

The city's top two hotels are right in the city center facing one another across Boland Way, at I-91 exit 6 northbound or exit 7 southbound, a block north of Court Sq.

One is the **Springfield Marriott Hotel** (☎ 413-781-7111, 800-228-9290; www.marriott.com; Boland Way at Columbus Ave; d $119-154; ☒). This hotel has a gracious lobby, sauna and fitness room, and 265 sparkling, recently refurbished business-class rooms, most with data ports.

The other is the **Sheraton-Springfield Monarch Place** (☎ 413-781-1010, 800-426-9004; www.sheraton .com; Boland Way at Columbus Ave; d $129-199; ☒). The Sheraton has more than 300 luxury rooms and suites surrounding its central atrium, and you can relax in the whirlpool or sauna after working out in the fitness center. The breakfast buffet is actually pretty decent. Try to snag a room with a river view. Management charge a small parking fee, the sly devils.

Eating

Downtown Springfield has a scarcity of truly noteworthy restaurants. There are, however, lunch places, pubs and bistros in the vicinity of Court Sq and the railroad station that serve up tasty fare.

BUDGET

Mom & Rico's (☎ 413-732-8941; 899 Main St; dishes $3-6; ☺ 8:30am-5:30pm Mon-Fri, 8.30am-3:30pm Sat) Both Rico and his mom will likely be here when you come, bantering in rapid-fire Italian. Gourmet it ain't, but this place is as authentic as they come. Order at the counter, browse the bocce ball paraphernalia (Rico is a fierce advocate – and champion – of the sport) and then sit down at one of the tables to chow down. You won't leave hungry. Try a 'Springfield Pillow,' a variation on the calzone.

Dolce Notte (☎ 413-734-4000; 304 Worthington St; sandwiches $3-6; ☺ 8am-8pm Mon-Wed, 9am-3am Thu-Sat) At the intersection with Dwight St, this small coffeehouse and deli makes a great people-watching perch while you're eating your panini. And thanks to its late weekend hours, it's a logical post-bar-hopping destination.

Café du Jour (☎ 413-732-3900; 1365 Main St; ☺ breakfast & lunch) This café, draped in deep soothing reds, is just northwest of Court St and serves good coffee and snacks of the bagel and pastry variety.

Deli Roll (☎ 413-827-7007; 91 State St; dishes $4-7; ☺ 7am-3pm Mon-Fri) A sandwich shop a block southeast of Court Sq, the Deli Roll has a plethora of meals on bread like the 'tuna-cado,' which is hot tuna plus avocado on a Portuguese roll. The old-timers will park it at a table for hours while the lunch-time businesspeople get their sandwiches to go.

MID-RANGE & TOP END

Student Prince Café & Fort Restaurant (☎ 413-788-6628; 8 Fort St; dinner mains $9-19 ☺ lunch & dinner) The Student Prince has been scratching those schnitzel and sauerkraut itches since 1935 and shows no signs of slowing down. Even if you're not in the mood for heavy starches, come by anyway to take in the stained-glass decor and the impressive bierstein collection (one was owned by a Russian czar). Disappointingly, the beer menu isn't as expansive as one would expect.

Café Lebanon (☎ 413-737-7373; 141 State St; mains lunch/dinner $7-12/12-18; ☺ lunch & dinner Mon-Fri, dinner only Sat & Sun) Here's a cheery Middle Eastern take-out or sit-down eatery with reasonable lunch specials. Several appetizers could make a meal – try the *makanik* (Lebanese sausage and pine nuts sautéed with lemon juice; $7.50). Come for some belly-dancing action on Friday and Saturday nights.

Pho Saigon (☎ 413-781-4488; 398 Dickinson St; dishes $5-13; ☺ lunch & dinner) This local favorite is the spot for fresh, flavorful, moderately priced Vietnamese fare. A full page of the menu is devoted to vegetarian offerings. The service isn't polished or speedy, but who cares? It's on the north side of Forest Park, at Belmont Ave. Cash only.

Café Manhattan (☎ 413-737-7913; 301 Bridge St; lunch/dinner $8-11/13-22; ☷ lunch & dinner Mon-Sat) A dark, saloon-like piano bar and bistro, Café Manhattan serves Italian-American and continental cuisine like chicken marsala. Just eating here makes you feel Italian. It's two blocks northwest of Court Sq.

L'uva (☎ 413-734-1010; 1676 Main St; mains $9-28; ☷ lunch & dinner) Praised equally for their food and the depth and breadth of their wine menu, young L'uva is a welcome bright spot on the city's dining scene. The decor's color scheme reflects its name (Italian for 'the grape'), and the seasonal menu consistently delivers innovative, sumptuous dishes like maple crust scallops with apple-smoked bacon.

Entertainment

You needn't be bored if you make camp in Springfield overnight. The area around Union Station and nearby Worthington St has been an entertainment district for 100 years, and it's brimming with pubs and clubs that draw a large, well-educated crowd of 20- and 30-somethings.

Pick up a copy of the free weekly the **Valley Advocate** (www.valleyadvocate.com), for entertainment listings. It's not exclusive to Springfield, but everything that goes on in town is in there.

DRINKING & LIVE MUSIC

Smith's Billiards (☎ 413-734-9616; 207 Worthington St; ☷ opens at 5pm) This historic pool hall takes billiards seriously, but not too seriously. A vast beer selection ensures that you don't shoot too well. On Mondays it's all-you-can-play for only $5.

Theodore's (☎ 413-736-6000; 201 Worthington St; cover free-$10) Check out this saloon for some of the hottest barbecue and coolest jazz in the Pioneer Valley. Thursday is blues jam night, but Fridays and Saturdays see regional and national blues acts. The kitchen will serve you spicy ribs until midnight on Friday and Saturday.

Café Manhattan (☎ 413-737-7913; 301 Bridge St) Thursday through Saturday you can find live jazz, blues or rock bands going at it here. Some nights are open mike.

Pub (☎ 413-734-8132; 382 Dwight St) On the corner with Worthington, this intimate gay bar offers the standard weekly menu of karaoke, boys' nights etc. Call for details.

Hippodrome (☎ 413-787-0600; www.hdrome.com; 1700 Main St) The Hippodrome began life as the Paramount Theater in 1926 and was reborn as a nightclub in 1999 after years of neglect. Thursday is 18-plus college dance night, and Friday is Latin night. Other evenings may feature a boxing match or an Alice Cooper show.

PERFORMING ARTS

Symphony Hall (☎ 413-788-7033; www.citystage.symphony-hall.com; 34 Court St next to City Hall; tickets $27-52) Recitals and concerts by the members of the **Springfield Symphony Orchestra** (☎ 413-733-2291) occur all year-round in this grand venue.

CityStage (☎ 413-788-7033; www.citystage.symphonyhall.com; 1 Columbus Center; tickets $28-40) For classic hits and contemporary theater, this venue is tops. Shows are Wednesday through Sunday.

MassMutual Center (☎ 413-787-6610; 1277 Main St) When it reopens in late 2005, this building, formerly the Springfield Civic Center, will still be a major venue for conventions, exhibits, big rock concerts and athletic events like Falcons hockey games.

Getting There & Around

Springfield is served by the **Bradley International Airport** (☎ 860-292-2000) in Windsor Locks, CT, 15 miles to the south. For airport transportation, contact **Valley Transporter** (☎ 413-253-1350, 800-872-8752; www.valleytransporter.com). It's around $33 per person one-way between Bradley and downtown Springfield.

Springfield stands at the junction of I-90 and I-91, 26 miles north of Hartford, 100 miles west of Boston, and 145 miles north of New York City.

Springfield is the home of **Peter Pan Bus Lines** (☎ 413-781-2900, 800-343-9999; www.peterpanbus.com; 1776 Main St at Liberty St), which owns Bonanza Bus Lines. Together they serve New England, New York City, Philadelphia, Baltimore and Washington, DC. The bus station is a 10-minute walk northwest of Court Sq. This isn't a complete list, but within Massachusetts, daily Peter Pan buses go from Springfield to Amherst ($6 one-way,

45 minutes, 26 miles), Boston ($21.50 one-way, two hours, 89 miles), Deerfield ($9 one-way, 1¼ hours, 31 miles, one bus daily), Lenox ($16 one-way, 1½ hours, 56 miles, one bus daily), South Hadley, Sturbridge ($12.50 one-way, two hours, 31 miles) and Worcester ($17.50 one-way, one hour, 50 miles). In the rest of New England and slightly beyond, buses go to Albany, NY; Hartford, CT; New Haven, CT; Manchester, NH; New York City; and Newark, New Jersey.

Peter Pan's service connecting the college towns of the Pioneer Valley (Amherst, Holyoke, Northampton and South Hadley) with Springfield and Boston is frequent, with about a dozen buses daily.

Bonanza Bus Lines (☎ 800-556-3815) connects Springfield to Worcester, MA; Boston, MA; Hartford, CT; Providence, RI; Hyannis, MA; Albany, NY; Pittsfield, MA; and Williamstown, MA.

The **Pioneer Valley Transportation Authority** (PVTA; ☎ 413-781-7882; www.pvta.com; 1776 Main St, in the Peter Pan terminal) runs 43 routes to 23 communities in the region. Downtown, the 'Green 3' route connects State St and Liberty St via Main St.

Amtrak's (☎ 800-872-7245) *Lake Shore Limited,* the once-a-day train running between Boston and Chicago, stops at Springfield's **Union Station** (☎ 413-785-4230; 66 Lyman St), a 10-minute walk northwest of Court Sq.

SOUTH HADLEY

pop 18,000

The tiny village of South Hadley, 15 miles north of Springfield at the intersection of MA 116 and MA 47, is the most southerly of the five-college towns, with the country's oldest college for women, Mount Holyoke College, at its physical and cultural center.

For information on the town, visit the **South Hadley Chamber of Commerce** (☎ 413-532-6451; www.southhadleyguide.com; 362 N Main St, South Hadley, MA 01075). Have a look at the **Odyssey Book Shop** (☎ 413-534-7307; 9 College St; ◷ 10am-8pm Mon-Fri, 10am-6pm Sat, noon-5pm Sun) for a sophisticated selection of fiction and nonfiction, new and used books.

Sights & Activities

MOUNT HOLYOKE COLLEGE

Founded in 1837 by teacher Mary Lyon, **Mount Holyoke College** (☎ 413-538-2222; www.mtholyoke.edu; on MA 116 in the center of South Hadley) is the nation's oldest women's college, with a current enrollment of about 2000 students. Call to arrange a campus tour.

The great American landscape architect Frederick Law Olmsted laid out the center of Mount Holyoke's parklike 800-acre campus in the latter part of the 1800s and it ranks as one of the most beautiful college campuses in the country. Among Mt Holyoke's other 19th-century legacies is a hand-crafted organ in the chapel, one

---

METACOMET-MONADNOCK TRAIL

The Metacomet-Monadnock Trail (or M&M Trail in local parlance) is 117 miles of a 200-mile greenway and footpath that traverses some of the most breathtaking scenery in western Massachusetts. It extends from Connecticut along the Connecticut River valley to New Hampshire's Mt Monadnock and beyond.

In Connecticut the trail takes its name from Metacomet (the Indian leader who waged war on the colonists in 1675). It enters Massachusetts near the Agawam/Southwick town line to become Massachusetts' Metacomet-Monadnock Trail. From the state line, the trail proceeds north up the Connecticut River valley through public and private lands, ascends Mt Tom, then heads east along the Holyoke Range, through Skinner State Park and Holyoke Range State Park, before bearing north again.

After entering New Hampshire, the trail ascends Mt Monadnock, where it joins the Monadnock-Sunapee Greenway.

The easiest access to the trail for day hikes is in the state parks, where leaflets and simple local trail maps are available. For longer hikes, it's good to have the *Metacomet-Monadnock Trail Guide* (10th edition, 2004), published by **New England Cartographics** (☎ 888-995-6277; PO Box 9369, North Amherst, MA 01059). Trail excerpts are posted on the website of the **Appalachian Mountain Club Berkshire Chapter** (www.amcberkshire.org/mmtrail; PO Box 9369, North Amherst, MA 01059). The book is also available at local bookshops and outdoors stores.

of the last built by New England's master organ maker, Charles B Fisk.

The campus maintains a half-dozen gardens that are open to strolling from dawn to dusk. The glass **Talcott Greenhouse** (admission free; 9am-4pm Mon-Fri, 1-4pm Sat & Sun) dates back to 1898.

When Albert Bierstadt donated his painting *Hetch Hetchy Canyon* to the college in 1876, the **College Art Museum** (☎ 413-538-2245; Lower Lake Rd; admission free; 11am-5pm Tue-Fri, 1-5pm Sat & Sun) was born. One of the oldest teaching museums in the country, it maintains particular strengths in 19th- and 20th-century American paintings and Asian art.

SKINNER STATE PARK

This mountaintop **park** (☎ 413-586-0350; north of South Hadley off MA 47 in Hadley; admission free, parking fee on weekends $2; sunrise-sunset) is at the summit of Mt Holyoke, at a rather modest-sounding height of 942ft. But that's high enough to earn the visitor panoramic views of the Connecticut River and its oxbow curve, the fertile valley and the distant smudge of Mt Greylock to the west. The **Summit House** (10am-5pm Sat & Sun) used to be the evening drinking spot for 19th-century hunters. There are hiking trails and a picnic area.

HOLYOKE RANGE STATE PARK

This **park** (☎ 413-586-0350; a few miles north of South Hadley on MA 116; admission free; 10am-6pm) has over 30 miles of marked trails, with hikes ranging between 0.75 of a mile and 5.4 miles on the Metacomet-Monadnock Trail (see p242).

Sleeping & Eating

The best sleeps and eats are found in neighboring Amherst (p247) and Northampton (right), respectively.

The Village Commons, designed by the architect Graham Gund, houses stores and eateries, including **Tailgate Picnic Deli & Market** (☎ 413-532-7597; 7 College St; 6:30am-8pm Mon-Sat, 7am-5pm Sun) for gourmet sandwiches and an assortment of coffees. Across the courtyard is the **Thirsty Mind** (☎ 413-538-9303; 19 College St) coffeehouse and used bookstore, where you can settle down with a cappuccino. You may catch some live music, too.

Main Moon (☎ 413-533-8839; 11 College St; mains $4-13; 11am-11:30pm) has tasty, reasonably priced Chinese food.

THE BIRTH OF VOLLEYBALL

Volleyball was invented in nearby Holyoke by William G Morgan, who worked for the Holyoke YMCA. It was intended to be an indoor game for businessmen who found basketball too strenuous. Morgan named his new game 'mintonette,' but a professor at Springfield College thought 'volleyball' more appropriate, because of the back-and-forth movement of the ball.

Entertainment

To sample from the dizzying cultural platter served up by the five colleges, pick up a copy of the *Five College Calendar* in any café or on any campus, or take a look online at http://calendar.fivecolleges.edu. Most of the lectures, plays, and musical and dance performances are free.

The **Tower Theater** (☎ 413-533-3456; 19 College St) shows first-run films and the occasional art-house flick.

Lovers of chamber music shouldn't miss the **Musicorda Summer Festival** (☎ 413-493-1544; Chapel Auditorium on Mt Holyoke campus; tickets $18-22), at which promising young musicians perform alongside the masters in several concert series over a six-week period.

Getting There & Away

PVTA buses can bring you to South Hadley from cities all over New England (see p241).

The PVTA routes of 38, 39 and B43 run between all five colleges. It costs $1.50 per ride, $3 for a one-day pass and $10 for seven days. It's a free ride for students and staff of the colleges.

NORTHAMPTON

pop 30,000

Northampton, home of esteemed Smith College, is where New York's Greenwich Village meets rural New England. The Pioneer Valley's dining and entertainment epicenter with a large selection of moderately priced ethnic restaurants and world-class entertainment, Northampton celebrated its 350th birthday in 2004 and was described by the 'Swedish Nightingale' Jenny Lind in 1850 as the 'Paradise of America.' Unlike so many other century-old claims, this one has stood the test of time admirably.

These days, the presence of college students and their professors gives the town a distinctly liberal political atmosphere. The lesbian community is large and outspoken, such that the college-town lineup of shops, bookstores, cafés and copy shops reflects a strong feminist sensibility. (A popular mug reads 'Northampton: where the coffee is strong and so are the women.')

The famously reticent and conservative Calvin Coolidge served as mayor of Northampton before being elected president in 1923, hence the preponderance of venues in town sporting Cal-based names. Another well-known resident was Sylvester Graham, of Graham Cracker fame. In his day he was considered an eccentric health nut, and his house is now Sylvester's Restaurant (opposite).

You'll still hear dyed-in-the-wool natives shorten Northampton to 'Hamp,' while most students and other recent interlopers use the nickname 'Noho.'

Orientation

The center of town is at the intersection of Main St (aka MA 9) and Pleasant St (MA 5). Main St is where you'll find the core of restaurants, cafés, banks and shops, although most lodgings are on the outskirts. Smith College is on the west end of town, where Main St curves right and turns into Elm St.

Information

Broadside Books (☎ 413-586-4235; 247 Main St; ☺ 9:30am-6pm Mon-Wed, 9:30am-9pm Thu-Sat, noon-6pm Sun) While you're here, pick up a copy of Pulitzer Prize–winning author Tracy Kidder's biography, *Hometown*, which paints a warm, accurate picture of life in Northampton from the perspective of a local policeman.

Greater Northampton Chamber of Commerce (☎ 413-584-1900; www.northamptonuncommon.com; 99 Pleasant St, Northampton, MA 01060; ☺ 9am-5pm Mon-Fri, 10am-2pm Sat & Sun May-Oct)

Sights
SMITH COLLEGE

Founded 'for the education of the intelligent gentlewoman' in 1875 by Sophia Smith, **Smith College** (☎ 413-584-2700; www.smith.edu), at the western end of the downtown area, is the largest women's college in the country, with 2700 students. The verdant 125-acre campus along Elm St holds an eclectic architectural mix of nearly 100 buildings, as well as Paradise Pond. Notable alums of the

college include Sylvia Plath, Julia Child and Gloria Steinem.

Visitors are welcome at the **Lyman Conservatory** (☎ 413-585-2740; ☺ 8:30am-4pm), a collection of Victorian greenhouses that are the venue for the Bulb Show and Chrysanthemum Show (opposite).

You should also set time aside for a visit to the exceptional, newly renovated **Smith College Museum of Art** (☎ 413-585-2760; Elm St at Bedford Tce; adult/senior/student/child 6-12 $5/4/3/2; ☺ 10am-4pm Tue-Sat, noon-4pm Sun) This 25,000-piece collection is strong in 17th-century Dutch and 19th- and 20th-century European and North American paintings, including fine works by Degas, Winslow Homer, Picasso and James Abbott McNeill Whistler. Admission is free to Five College students and staff. Fortunately, **CK's Cafe** (☺ 8am-2am) is more a café in a museum rather than a museum café. Vegans and carnivores are equally well-attended to.

Guided campus tours can be arranged through the **Office of Admissions** (☎ 413-585-2500; on the hr 10am-3pm Mon-Fri, 9-11am Sat), overlooking **Paradise Pond**, or you can guide yourself using the campus map available here.

If you don't take a tour, at least stroll around **Paradise Pond** and take a load off in the Japanese **tea hut**.

THORNES MARKETPLACE

You can't miss this urban mall – it's the green-awninged behemoth taking up a large chunk of Main St. Formerly a department store, it now houses an array of clothing and shoe boutiques, dorm-accessory shops, a music store and a natural foods market.

DINOSAUR FOOTPRINTS

Around 190 million years ago, the Pioneer Valley area was a subtropical swamp, inhabited by carnivorous, two-legged dinosaurs, and a large cluster of their **footprints** (☎ 413-684-0148; Rte 5, Holyoke; admission free; ☺ dawn-dusk) is preserved in situ on the west bank of the Connecticut River. The prints here, some 134 in all, represent three distinct species. In the early 1970s, ichnologist John Ostrom studied the tracks and – based in part on the fact that the majority of the trackways head west – came to the radical conclusion that some species of dinosaurs traveled in packs. Yikes.

From Northampton, go south on Pleasant St/US 5 for about 5 miles. The small parking lot will be on the left-hand side. Look for the sign that says 'Trustees of Reservations.' Park and follow the trail to the left.

Activities

On MA 9 in Florence, **Look Memorial Park** (☎ 413-584-5457; www.lookpark.org) has more than 150 acres of public space to spread out a picnic basket, as well as mini-golf, pedal boats and bumper boats.

The universally accessible **Norwottuck Rail Trail** runs 8.5 miles along MA 9 from Northampton and Hadley and Amherst. Access the trail via the Elwell Recreation Area on Damon Rd where it crosses MA 9. See p249 for details on the Amherst end, including bike rentals.

Festivals & Events

Flower-lovers should check out the renowned annual **Bulb Show** in mid-March and the **Chrysanthemum Show** in November, both held at the Lyman Conservatory at Smith College (opposite).

Springfield has the Big E, but Northampton has the **Tri-County Fair** (☎ 413-584-2237), starting on the Friday of Labor Day weekend. The fair, first held in 1818, features agricultural and livestock exhibits, horse races, food and rides. The Tri-County Fairgrounds, on MA 9 just west of I-91 exit 19 north and US 20 south, is also the site of the **New England Morgan Regional Horse Show** (www .nemha.com), held annually in July.

Sleeping

While the B&B phenomenon is strong in the Pioneer Valley accommodations scene, few are actually in Northampton, although there are many in and around nearby Amherst. Contact the Amherst Area Chamber of Commerce (p248) for a list of area B&Bs.

It's usually easy to find a room during the summer. At other times of year, room price and availability depend on the college's schedule of ceremonies and cultural events. If you're planning a visit during mid-May Commencement Week, book as far in advance as possible. Lodgings mentioned here have parking.

Hotel Northampton (☎ 413-584-3100; www.hotel northampton.com; 36 King St; d $145-215) This grand 99-room hotel right downtown has been receiving Northampton's important guests since 1916. Rooms have all the expected amenities, including wireless access in all rooms. The **Wiggins Tavern** (mains $18-26) serves continental fare every evening but Mondays, and the patio of the casual **Coolidge Park Café** (mains $6-12) offers the perfect vantage point from which to watch the town stroll by.

Autumn Inn (☎ 413-584-7660; 259 Elm St/MA 9; r/ste incl breakfast $90-130/110-150; ☐ ☒) Despite its motel-like layout, this 32-room place just across from Smith College has an inn-like ambience. The comfortable rooms have wireless access.

Lupine House (☎ 413-586-9766, 800-890-9766; www .lupinehouse.com; 185 N Main St, Florence; d $80-90; ☒) Three miles from downtown Northampton, Evelyn and Gil Billings offer three rooms in their home, each with a private bathroom. The attractions here are the big family-style breakfast – they are happy to cater to special dietary needs – and the inn's proximity to Look Park (just up the street) with its hiking and biking trails and tennis courts.

One of the only chain motels in town is the **Best Western** (☎ 413-586-1500, 800-941-3066; 117 Conz St; d $80-130; ☒). Recently renovated, it's right off exit 18 from I-91. Rooms are standard, but if you're feeling frisky, ask for one with a heart-shaped spa bathtub.

Eating

Whatever cuisine or ambience you're in the mood for, Noho's got a restaurant to match. For the scoop on the area's eating scene, check out www.valleydiningguide.com or www.five collegemenu.com.

BUDGET

Sylvester's (☎ 413-586-5343; 111 Pleasant St; mains $5-7; ☒ 7am-2:30pm) Arguably the best breakfast spot in town (and it'll be the Jake's fans arguing), Sylvester's looks like a diner and feels like home. Order the blueberry chocolate-chip pancakes and know happiness. Try to score a seat on the small deck if the weather's nice.

Jake's (☎ 413-584-9613; 17 King St; mains $3-6; ☒ 6:30am-3pm, 11pm-3am Fri & Sat) A no-frills, full-service café with plenty of wooden tables, Jake's is a popular breakfast joint. Thanks to its extended weekend hours, it's also the place to be seen on the flip side of midnight. The kielbasa and sauerkraut lunch is a doozie.

Java Net Café (☎ 413-587-3400; 241 Main St; items $2-5; ☒ 7am-10pm Mon-Fri, 8am-11pm Sat, 8am-9pm Sun) Northampton's only cybercafé serves up coffee, tea, baked goods and the Internet;

it's like a library with large easy chairs and hordes of glossy mags for browsing or buying. You'll pay a steep $2 to log on for 20 minutes. It's also a wireless hot spot.

Haymarket Café (☎ 413-586-9969; 185 Main St; items $4.20-7.25; ☺ 11:30am-9pm) Northampton's coolest hangout spot for bohemians and caffeine addicts now has a small food menu with fancy vegetarian fare like potstickers and Greek artichoke stew. Sit downstairs, where the room is lined with used books.

Miss Florence Diner (☎ 413-584-3137; 99 Main St/MA 9; items $3-9; ☺ 5:30am-9pm Mon-Sat) Appropriately located in Florence, about 3 miles west of Northampton, this picturesque diner has a surprisingly extensive menu. Don't come to be pampered, though – the waitresses are a notoriously cranky bunch.

Herrell's Ice Cream (☎ 413-586-9700; Thornes Marketplace at Old South St; ☺ noon-11:30pm) Steve Herrell has been scooping out gourmet ice cream in flavors both strange and familiar since 1980. Some of the more unexpected concoctions are key lime cardamom, Earl Grey and Twinkie.

MID-RANGE

Paul and Elizabeth's (☎ 413-584-4832; 150 Main St; mains lunch/dinner $6-10/9-14; ☺ lunch & dinner Mon-Sat) Known locally as P&E's, this airy and plant-adorned restaurant sits on the top floor of Thornes Marketplace and is the town's premier natural foods restaurant, serving vegetarian cuisine and seafood, often with an Asian bent. Every dish is a delight and seasonal specials keep the menu fresh. As an appetizer, try the sweet potato risotto cake with dill aioli sauce.

India House (☎ 413-586-6344; 45 State St; mains $14-17; ☺ lunch & dinner) The best Indian food in town. This family-owned restaurant right off Main St gets the atmosphere just right – it makes you feel like you're not in Noho anymore, but doesn't blast the sitar music. Their tandoori dishes are beautiful – try the cilantro-glazed chicken – and their breads are to die for.

¡Cha Cha Cha! (☎ 413-586-7311; 134 Main St; mains $6-12; ☺ 11:30am-10pm) This fast-foodish spot has a hip, order-at-the-counter style. You won't be getting a 100% authentic Mexican experience, but they make some damn good fish tacos, and you can get fun things like cactus in your burrito.

Amanouz (☎ 413-585-9128; 44 Main St; mains $6-11; ☺ 8am-10pm Mon-Thu, 8am-11pm Fri-Sun). This lovable hole-in-the-wall is the place in town for Moroccan and Mediterranean. Try one of their fun specials like Moroccan sardine salad ($7). The falafel sandwich is a disappointment, though.

Teapot (☎ 413-585-9308; 116 Main St; mains $7-16; ☺ 11am-11pm) Teapot pulls off a rare feat by serving high-quality Chinese *and* Japanese cuisine. The airy interior features upscale decor. Chinese lunch specialties are around $5, and Japanese are $7.

TOP END

Mulino's (☎ 413-586-8900; 41 Strong Ave; mains $13-23; ☺ dinner) This family-style trattoria serves big portions of robust Italian mains. It's part of the classy triune that includes the more upscale Brasserie 40-A on the 1st floor and the Bishop's Lounge – with smoking deck – on the 3rd.

Spoleto (☎ 413-586-6313; 50 Main St; mains lunch/dinner $16-21/25-40; ☺ dinner 4-10pm, brunch 11am-2:30pm Sun) This is the quintessential place Smithies bring their visiting parents. The banquet-sized dining room can get a bit loud on a busy night. The classic dishes such as veal scaloppini have Californian accents.

Eastside Grill (☎ 413-586-3347; 19 Strong Ave; mains $11-20; ☺ dinner 4-10pm) A half block south of Main St, this is a steak 'n' seafood kind of place with strong Cajun overtones – its vast menu carries items like Louisiana fried oysters and chicken étouffée. The few nods to vegetarians include butternut ravioli. The chocolate soufflé comes highly recommended. Weekends can be extremely busy, and Eastside Grill doesn't take reservations.

Drinking

Ye Ol' Watering Hole & Beer Can Museum (☎ 413-584-9748; 287 Pleasant St; ☺ opens at 3pm) Hundreds of vintage beer cans line the walls at this old-timers' dive where the Valley's blue-collar crowd rubs elbows with students and scenesters. Cheap drinks, three pool tables and a Golden Tee video game. What more could you ask for?

Tunnel Bar (☎ 413-586-5366; Strong Ave & Pearl St; ☺ opens at 5pm) This bar, housed below Northampton's elegant old railroad station, really *is* a tunnel. Sit in plush chairs and enjoy the fine woodwork at this long, narrow nightspot while you drink somewhat pricey but tasty cocktails and wines.

Northampton Brewery (☎ 413-584-9903; 11 Brewster Ct; mains $7-14; ☺ 11:30am-1am Mon-Sat, noon-1am Sun) This brewpub – the oldest operating brewpub in New England – features excellent beer and nouvelle cuisine mains. Dine in the verdant roof-top beer garden in good weather. The main entrance is actually on Hampton Rd, one long block south of Main St.

Packard's (☎ 413-584-5957; 14 Masonic St) Hit this pub off Main St for the five billiard tables on the 3rd floor, the dartboards or just the numerous nooks and crannies in which to huddle. Plenty of microbrews can keep you company.

Entertainment
Northampton is the center of nightlife for residents, students and faculty in the Five College area. For listings of what's happening throughout the Pioneer Valley, pick up a copy of *The Valley Advocate* (www.valleyadvocate.com), a local free weekly newspaper with lots of listings. For online schedules for the Iron Horse, Calvin Theatre and Pearl Street, go to www.iheg.com. Tickets to any of these can be purchased by calling ☎ 413-586-8686.

LIVE MUSIC
The town's prime venue for folk, jazz and 'other' is the **Iron Horse Music Hall** (☎ 413-584-0610; 20 Center St; tickets $7-25). Call for the current program (artists like Catie Curtis, Nick Lowe and Blackalicious are common fare), then look for the small storefront half a block off Main St with the line of people waiting to get in. They serve food and booze, too.

Calvin Theatre (☎ 413-584-1444; 19 King St; tickets $20-100) Performers from Wilco and Greg Brown to the Alvin Ailey American Dance Theater perform here in the intimate setting of a gorgeously restored movie house.

Pearl Street (☎ 413-584-7771; 10 Pearl St; tickets $10-20). Don't worry, it only looks condemned. At the corner of Strong Ave across the street from the Tunnel Bar, Pearl Street draws in acts like Medeski Martin & Wood and Camper Van Beethoven.

You can usually find live rock or acoustic on Friday and Saturday nights at the **Northampton Brewery** (☎ 413-584-9903; 11 Brewster Ct; ☺ 11:30am-1am Mon-Sat, noon-1am Sun). This pub packs in a mixed gang (both in age and sexual preference) every evening.

THEATER & CINEMA
New Century Theatre (☎ 413-587-3933; www.newcenturytheatre.org; tickets $10-22) One of the best regional theater companies in the US, this troupe stages works by playwrights such as Wendy Wasserstein and Kenneth Lonergan. Performances are held at the Mendenhall Center on the Smith College campus.

Academy of Music Theatre (☎ 413-584-8435; 274 Main St) This gracious, balconied theater is one of the oldest movie houses in the USA (1890), and one of the most beautiful. Shows first-run independent films.

Pleasant St Theater (☎ 413-586-0935; 27 Pleasant St) The setting isn't as glamorous as the Academy's, but the fare runs slightly more alternative.

GAY & LESBIAN VENUES
Northampton itself *is* a gay and lesbian venue, though undeniably more the latter than the former. Most clubs and pubs are a congenial mix of straights and gays.

The main gay-centric dance club is **Diva's** (☎ 413-586-8161; 492 Pleasant St; cover free-$5) which keeps its patrons on a steady diet of thumping house music. There's an outdoor area if it gets to be too much.

Getting There & Around
See p241 for information on air, bus and train services.

If you're driving, you'll find Northampton lies 18 miles north of Springfield on I-91 and 108 miles from Boston.

For information on bicycling, see p249. Buses on PVTA's Northampton–Amherst route provide bike racks.

Pioneer Valley Transit Authority (PVTA; ☎ 413-586-5806; www.pvta.com) provides bus services (with bike racks) to the entire Five College area, with the Northampton–Amherst route having the most frequent service. In Northampton, there's a bus stop in front of John M Green Hall at Smith College on Elm St, and also at several spots on Main St. A single-ride fare is $1; an unlimited one-day pass is $3.

AMHERST
pop 17,000
Best known as the home of prestigious Amherst College, Amherst also hosts the main

campus of the University of Massachusetts and smaller artsy Hampshire College. The town has produced its share of famous people, among whom poet Emily Dickinson, 'the belle of Amherst,' is perhaps the best known. With the influence of almost 30,000 college students, this former farm town rocks!

Orientation

Amherst lies at the intersection of MA 116 and MA 9. At the center of Amherst is the town common, a broad New England green framed by churches and inns.

Information

Amherst Area Chamber of Commerce (☎ 413-253-0700; www.amherstarea.com; 409 Main St at Railroad St, Amherst, MA 01002; ⏱ 9am-5pm Mon- Fri) This is less than half a mile east of Pleasant St. The chamber maintains a summer information booth on the common facing S Pleasant St, directly across from the Peter Pan bus station at 79 S Pleasant St.

Amherst Books (☎ 413-256-1547; 8 Main St; ⏱ 9am-9pm Mon-Sat, noon-5pm Sun) Formerly owned by the Atticus chain, since going independent this small gem of a store has expanded its offerings, especially of poetry and philosophy.

Jeffrey Amherst Bookshop (☎ 413-253-3381; 55 S Pleasant St; ⏱ 8:30am-8pm Mon-Sat, noon-5pm Sun) A full-service bookstore with a remarkable collection of Emily Dickinsonia.

Post office (☎ 413-549-0418; N Pleasant St at Kellogg Ave)

Sights
EMILY DICKINSON MUSEUM

During her lifetime, Emily Dickinson (1830–86) published only seven poems – usually she would just stuff her finely crafted pieces, written on scraps of paper and old envelopes, into her desk. But after her death, more than 1000 of her poems were discovered and published, and her verses on love, death, nature and immortality have made her one of the most important poets in the US.

She was raised in the strict Puritan household of her father, a prominent lawyer. When he was elected to the US Congress, she traveled with him to Washington and Philadelphia, then returned to Amherst and this house to live out the rest of her days in near seclusion. Some say she was in love with the Reverend Charles Wadsworth, a local married clergyman. Unable to show her love, she withdrew from the world into a private realm of pain, passion and poignancy.

This newly realized **museum** (☎ 413-542-8161; 280 Main St; admission adult/senior & student/child 6-18 $8/7/5; ⏱ 1-5pm Wed-Sat, closed mid-Dec–Feb) consists of the museum proper, the Dickinson Homestead and the Evergreens, the house next door where her brother Austin lived with his family. The admission price includes a 75-minute tour of both houses.

Hours vary throughout the year, so call to confirm.

HAMPSHIRE COLLEGE

The region's most innovative center of learning, **Hampshire College** is 3 miles south of Amherst center on MA 116. Students here don't pick a major in the regular sense of the word; rather, the school emphasizes multi-disciplinary, student-initiated courses of study. Contact the **admissions office** (☎ 413-582-5471; www.hampshire.edu) to schedule a tour.

ERIC CARLE MUSEUM OF PICTURE BOOK ART

Co-founded by the author and illustrator of *The Very Hungry Caterpillar*, this superb

A POX UPON YOUR BLANKET

The town of Amherst bears the dubious distinction of deriving its name from one of the first known proponents of biological warfare. Lord Jeffrey Amherst, the commanding general of the British in North America during the French & Indian War (1754–63), cooked up the idea of distributing smallpox-infected blankets to the Native American enemy. In a letter to Colonel Henry Bouquet, Amherst writes: 'Could it not be contrived to send the Small Pox among those disaffected tribes of Indians? We must on this occasion use every stratagem in our power to reduce them.'

Naturally, there is some disagreement as to the extent to which Lord Amherst was personally involved or if perhaps the blanket contamination was unintentional, a goodwill gesture gone awry. But Amherst's letters leave little doubt that he harbored genocidal tendencies, through smallpox and 'Every other method that can serve to Extirpate this Execrable Race.'

No wonder there's no statue of him in town.

museum (☎ 413-658-1100; www.picturebookart.org; 125 W Bay Rd; adult/student/child $4/2/3; ☺ 10am-4pm Tue-Sat, noon-4pm Sun) celebrates book illustrations from around the world with rotating exhibits in three galleries, as well as a solid permanent collection. All visitors (grown-ups included) are encouraged to express their own artistic sentiments in the hands-on art studio. In honor of the aforementioned caterpillar, the café's cookies have holes through their middles.

NATIONAL YIDDISH BOOK CENTER
Right nearby the Eric Carle museum, this **center** (☎ 413-256-4900; www.yiddishbookcenter.org; 1021 West St; admission free; ☺ 10am-3:30pm Mon-Fri, 11am-4pm Sun) got its start when a 23-year-old grad student named Aaron Lansky started realizing that thousands of priceless Yiddish books were being tossed out around the world as a generation passed away and knowledge of the language dwindled. He promptly instigated 'the greatest cultural rescue effort in Jewish history' and now the center houses the largest collection of Yiddish books on the planet.

AMHERST COLLEGE
Founded in 1821, **Amherst** (www.amherst.edu) has retained its character and quality partly by maintaining its small size (1600 students), thus its prestige has grown. The main part of the campus lies just south of the town common. The information booth, on the edge of the town green and closed in winter, has a map and brochure for self-guided walking tours, or you can ask questions at **Converse Hall** (☎ 413-542-2000).

UNIVERSITY OF MASSACHUSETTS AT AMHERST
The **University of Massachusetts at Amherst** (UMass; ☎ 413-545-0111; www.umass.edu), founded in 1863 as the Massachusetts Agricultural College, is now the keystone of the public university system in Massachusetts. About 24,000 students study at the sprawling UMass campus, which is to the northwest of the common. The campus houses the **Fine Arts Center** (☎ 413-545-2511; Haigis Mall; tickets $5-12), a monstrous concrete building that hosts nearly 100 performing arts events per year in its main hall and presents cutting-edge dramatic plays in its New WORLD Theater. A PVTA bus line serves the campus.

ATKINS FARMS COUNTRY MARKET
This **farm produce center** (☎ 413-253-9528; 1150 West St/MA 116 & Bay Rd; admission free; ☺ 7am-8pm) and local institution, about 3 miles south of Amherst, offers maple sugar products in spring, garden produce in summer and apple-picking in autumn. Other activities, such as a scarecrow-making workshop in October, take place throughout the year. A deli/bakery sells picnic supplies. They keep shorter hours in winter.

Activities
See p243 for information on hiking in the Holyoke Range, south of Amherst.

The **Norwottuck Rail Trail** (nor-*wah*-tuk; www.had leyonline.com/railtrail/) is a foot and bike path that follows the former Boston & Maine Railroad right-of-way from Amherst to Hadley to Northampton, a total distance of 8.5 miles. For much of its length, the trail parallels MA 9. Parking and access to the trail can be found on Station Rd in Amherst, at the Mountain Farms Mall on MA 9 in Hadley and at Elwell State Park on Damon Rd in Northampton. Biking the trail is particularly enjoyable. You can rent bikes for the day from **Valley Bicycles** (☎ 413-584-4466; 8 Railroad St). The shop lies right on the Rail Trail in Hadley, southwest of Amherst, just off MA 9.

Two miles north of town, **Puffers Pond** makes for excellent swimming, and has a wooded, secluded beach area that fills with students and locals on a warm day. Nature trails meander through the area as well. To get there, take East Pleasant St to Sand Hill Rd and then right on State St.

Sleeping
Be aware of the college schedules when planning a visit! Visitors are well advised to book as far in advance as possible if planning a trip for late August or mid-May. The Amherst Area Chamber of Commerce (p248) has a list, which includes phone numbers and prices, of more than two dozen member B&Bs. All options listed below have parking available.

BUDGET & MID-RANGE
Amherst B&B (☎ 413-256-6151; 132 Farmington Rd; d incl breakfast $70; ☒ ☖) Across the street from the Emily Dickinson Museum, this private home in a quiet neighborhood has two guest rooms and an in-ground pool.

Campus Center Hotel (☎ 413-549-6000; Campus Ctr, UMass; d incl breakfast $72-109; 🖳) This 116-room hotel is operated by UMass students majoring in Hospitality. Many rooms have views overlooking the campus pond.

Amherst Motel (☎ 413-256-8122; 408 Northampton Rd/MA 9, Hadley; d incl breakfast on weekends $54-68/69-98; 🖳) This motel is on the south side of MA 9, a mile west of the Amherst town common. Rooms are simply furnished but clean. There are some apartments that they rent out monthly.

University Lodge (☎ 413-256-8111; 345 N Pleasant St/MA 116; d $72-99) The attraction of this 20-room motel is the location: only a few blocks north of the town common in the heart of Amherst's restaurant district.

There aren't many campgrounds in this region. One is **White Birch Campground** (☎ 413-665-4941; 214 North St, Whately; tent/RV $23-25/27; 🕑 May-Nov). Follow MA 116 North through North Amherst and Sunderland to South Deerfield, then go southwest to Whately, where you'll find this wooded campground with 60 sites.

TOP END

Lord Jeffrey Inn (☎ 413-253-2576, 800-742-0358; www .lordjefferyinn.com; 30 Boltwood Ave; d $119-169; ☒) A 48-room inn facing the town common, this is the classic college-town inn: colonial, collegiate, cozy and comfortable. The quilts are lovely. If you're an Amherst parent determined to stay here during graduation, make reservations as soon as that acceptance letter arrives. Really.

Allen House Inn (☎ 413-253-5000; www.allenhouse .com; 599 Main St; d incl breakfast $75-175; ☒) This is a prim, faithfully restored Queen Anne–style Victorian cottage with seven rooms, all with private bathroom. It is over half a mile east of Pleasant St. Main St has some traffic noise during the day.

Eating

Being a college town, Amherst is chock-full of places peddling pizza, sandwiches, Chinese takeout, burritos and fresh-brewed coffee. Competition is fierce and quality is high. The fast-food and restaurant zone is on N Pleasant St, north of Main St to Kellogg Ave.

BUDGET

Black Sheep Café (☎ 413-256-1706; 79 Main St; 🕑 6:30am-9pm) Right next door to Lone Wolf, this Amherst mainstay stocks fresh breads, cakes and cookies, and makes gourmet sandwiches ($5 to $6). Expect a long line for coffee in the morning.

Antonio's Pizza by the Slice (☎ 413-253-0808; 31 N Pleasant St; slices $1.50-3; 🕑 10am-1am) Amherst's most popular pizza place features excellent slices as well as cute, jovial dough-tossers. The variety of toppings, flavorings and spices is vast – the black bean with avocado is better than it sounds.

Rao's Coffee Roasting Company (☎ 413-253-9441; 17 Kellogg Ave; prices $2-6; 🕑 7am-11pm Mon-Fri, 8am-11pm Sat & Sun) This cheerful yellow spot is a half-block east of Pleasant St along Boltwood Walk. It serves specialty coffees and appropriate nibbles at its indoor and outdoor café tables. It serves up a slew of delicious specialty coffees and coffee affiliates like muffins, scones, bagels and coffeecakes at its indoor and outdoor tables.

MID-RANGE

Lone Wolf (☎ 413-256-4643; 63 Main St; mains lunch/dinner $4-8/12-18; 🕑 breakfast & lunch daily, dinner Thu-Sat) Thanks to the friendly attentive waitstaff and its use of local, organic ingredients, the Lone Wolf has earned itself a strong fan base, especially among vegetarians and vegans. They kick it up a notch in the evenings, and for the quality of the food – rack of lamb encrusted with Parmesan, mustard seed and rosemary is a signature dish – dinner here is a real value.

La Veracruzana (☎ 413-253-6900; 63 S Pleasant St; mains $3-8; 🕑 10am-9:30pm) This eatery, convenient to the bus station, serves burritos, quesadillas and tacos; the seafood enchiladas with crab, cilantro, onion and tomato are tasty and filling.

Pasta e Basta (☎ 413-256-3550; 26 Main St; mains $7-10; 🕑 11am-11pm Mon-Sat, 1-10pm Sat) What beautiful simplicity – you choose your pasta and then you choose your sauce. There's also a good handful of meat dishes for you Atkins followers, and pizza by the slice. Very kid-friendly.

Amherst Chinese Food (☎ 413-253-7835; 62 Main St; mains lunch/dinner $5-9/7-14; 🕑 lunch & dinner) All the produce at 'AmChi,' as the locals call it, is raised organically by proprietor Tso-Cheng Chang, who also grows the orchids that beautify his restaurant. Flavors are subtle for the most part. The sesame beef gets high praise.

TOP END

The Windowed Hearth (☎ 413-253-2576; 30 Boltwood Ave; mains $19-24; ☺ dinner Wed-Sun) This restaurant is in the Lord Jeffrey Inn, facing the common, and is where folks go when they crave a fancy meal. Pecan-crusted duck breast and tenderloin tips typify the offerings in the formal colonial dining room complete with fireplace. Also in the inn is the more downscale, kid-friendly **Elijah Boltwood's Tavern** (☺ 7am-11pm).

Judie's (☎ 413-253-3491; 51 N Pleasant St; mains lunch/dinner $11-15/16-35; ☺ lunch & dinner Tue-Sun) Both the decor and the menu of this restaurant, in a converted house, could be described as 'eclectic.' One of the more unusual dishes is a chicken 'sandwich' with apple butter, bananas, peanuts, coconut, raisins, cranberry sauce and a curry glaze, served in a popover. There's usually a luncheon special priced around $13.

Drinking & Entertainment

Although a lot of the college crowd head to nearby Northampton to get their party on, you can find plenty of action in Amherst.

Moan & Dove (☎ 413-256-1710; 460 West St; ☺ 3pm-1am Mon-Fri, 1pm-1am Sat & Sun) The folks at this small, dark European-style pub near Hampshire College sure know their beer, and their 150 bottled and 20 draft beers are top notch – try a Belgian lambic, the only

---

THE MYSTERY OF SCOOBY DOO & THE FIVE COLLEGES

Urban legend has it that the lead characters in that wacky and lovable cartoon Scooby Doo represent the five colleges of the Pioneer Valley. Curvaceous redhead Daphne is said to embody Smith, with frumpy but brilliant Velma as Mt Holyoke. Controversy rages over this pairing, however, and you may get the reverse answer based on the partiality of your informant. Chiseled prepster Fred is undeniably Amherst, unintelligible goofball Scooby is UMass, and zoink-prone Shaggy is Hampshire.

It's a fun story, but Scooby Doo creator Fred Silverman has denied its veracity and insists that the show was based on the radio program *I Love a Mystery* and the TV show *The Many Loves of Dobie Gillis*. If there *is* a kernel of truth to the tale, we'll leave it to those meddling kids to find out.

---

type of commercially available beer made with wild yeast. For non-beer snobs, Schlitz and the like are available, but the bartender may smirk at you.

Black Sheep Café (☎ 413-253-3442; 79 Main St; no cover) Welcome to the town's most popular folk club. Live folk music is performed Thursday through Sunday, and not necessarily just at night. On a recent Sunday morning a group fronting a mandolin, upright bass and fiddle was playing to a packed house.

Amherst Brewing Company (☎ 413-253-4400; 24-36 N Pleasant St; no cover). Popular with students, here you can find jazz on Mondays, and blues or rock (or karaoke) on Thursdays and Saturdays. Try their Heather Ale, made with heather flowers in place of hops.

Fine Arts Center (☎ 413-545-2511; UMass campus; tickets $15-45) The university's entertainment auditorium has a full program of classical and world-music concerts, theater, opera and ballet.

Amherst Cinema for Stage & Screen (☎ 413-256-1991; www.amherststagescreen.org; 30 Amity St) As of late 2004, fundraising difficulties had stalled the completion of this new arts venue. When it does, Amherst will boast a veritable nerve center of film, dance, music, theater and the visual arts.

Getting There & Around

Amtrak (☎ 800-872-7245) runs its daily *Vermonter* between New York and Montreal, with a stop at Amherst **depot** (13 Railroad St) just off Main St, half a mile east of the common. The depot is unattended and seating is by reservation only, so you need to call to arrange ticketing at least four days prior to travel.

Peter Pan's Amherst Center Bus Terminal (☎ 413-256-0431; 79 S Pleasant St) is just south of Main St, offering direct or connecting rides throughout New England and as far south as Washington, DC.

Amherst is 80 miles from Boston, 24 miles from Springfield and 7 miles east of Northampton via MA 9.

UMass Transit Service (☎ 413-586-5806) runs free buses along MA 116/Pleasant St between the town center and the UMass campus.

The **PVTA** (☎ 413-586-5806; www.pvta.com) provides bus services to the entire Five College area, with the Northampton–Amherst route having the most frequent service.

DETOUR: LEVERETT PEACE PAGODA

The world could certainly do with a little more peace these days, and a group of monks, nuns and volunteers are doing their part from the top of a hill outside the pea-sized town of Leverett.

There are over 80 so-called peace pagodas all over the globe, and their mission is simple – to spread peace. The **Leverett Peace Pagoda** (☎ 413-367-2202; www.peacepagoda.org; 100 Cave Hill Rd) was the first in the Western Hemisphere, and is run by members of the non-proselytizing Nipponzan Myohoji sect of Buddhism. But no matter what your spiritual inclination, a visit to the pagoda – with its stunning views of the lush valley below – will leave you feeling profoundly serene.

The centerpiece of the area is actually not a pagoda at all, but a stupa – a 100ft-tall white bell-shaped monument to Buddha, meant to be circumambulated, not entered. The grounds' temple was destroyed by fire in 1987, and the dedication of the new temple – built with donated materials and through the sweat of volunteers – will take place in October 2005.

To get to the peace pagoda from Amherst, take MA 9 west until MA 116 north, then turn onto MA 63 north and follow it for about 6.5 miles. Turn right onto Jackson Hill Rd and then another right onto Cave Hill Rd. Park about half a mile up the road. The last half-mile is accessible only by foot. Due to the quiet, introspective nature of the area, visits by young children should be carefully considered.

Buses on this route provide bike racks. Buses stop on main streets of both towns and at Haigis Mall on the UMass campus. A single-ride fare is $1; an unlimited one-day pass is $3.

DEERFIELD

pop 4800

While the modern commercial center is in South Deerfield, it's Historic Deerfield 6 miles to the north that history buffs swarm to, where zoning and preservation keep the rural village looking like a time warp to the 18th century. During the mid-17th century, pioneers settled at Deerfield in the fertile Connecticut River valley 16 miles northwest of what is now Amherst.

Orientation & Information

The main (okay, the only) street of Historic Deerfield is simply called the Street, and it runs parallel to MA 5/10. Follow the signs from I-91.

To get information before you arrive, contact **Historic Deerfield** (☎ 413-774-5581; www .historic-deerfield.org; PO Box 321, Deerfield, MA 01342). In Greenfield is the **Franklin County Chamber of Commerce** (☎ 413-773-5463; www.co.franklin .ma.us; 395 Main St, Greenfield, MA 01302; ⏰ 10am-6pm). When you arrive in town, check in at the **Hall Tavern information Center** (the Street; ⏰ 9:30am-4:30pm) across from the Deerfield Inn. It has maps, brochures and an audiovisual presentation that gives you an overview of Historic Deerfield Village.

Sights & Activities

HISTORIC DEERFIELD VILLAGE

The main street of **Historic Deerfield Village** (☎ 413-774-5581; www.historic-deerfield.org; the Street; adult/child 6-21 $14/5; single house admission $7/5; ⏰ 9:30am-4:30pm) escaped the ravages of time and now presents a noble prospect: a dozen houses dating from the 1700s and 1800s, well preserved and open to the public. It costs nothing to stroll along the Street, or you can take a half-hour tour of each building individually. Guides in the houses provide commentary.

The **Wright House** (1824) has collections of American period paintings, Chippendale and Federal furniture and Chinese export porcelain. There's also the **Henry N Flynt Silver & Metalware Collection** (1814). Furnishings in **Allen House** (1720) were made in the Pioneer Valley and Boston. The **Family Discovery Center**, with hands-on activities for kids and a full-sized house on display showing the construction process step-by-step, should be open by 2007.

The **Stebbins House** (1799–1810) was the home of a rich land-owning family, and is furnished with typical luxury items of the time. In the **Barnard Tavern**, many of the exhibits are touchable, which makes this a favorite with kids. The rooms of the **Wells-Thorn House** (1717–51) are furnished according to period, from colonial times to the Federal period.

The **Dwight House**, built in Springfield in 1725, was moved to Deerfield in 1950. It now holds locally made furniture and, interestingly, an 18th-century doctor's office. **Sheldon House** (1743) was the 18th-century home of the Sheldons, wealthy Deerfield farmers. Contrast its furnishings with those in the Stebbins House, built and furnished a half-century later.

Be sure to visit the **Flynt Center of Early New England Life**; thousands of pieces not on display in the houses are numbered and stored here. Visitors can punch an item's number into a computer and print out its history. Surprisingly absorbing.

MEMORIAL HALL MUSEUM

Here's the **original building** (☎ 413-774-3768; cnr Memorial St, US 5 & MA 10; adult/child under 21 $6/3; ☻ 9:30am-4:30pm May-Oct) of Deerfield Academy (1798), the prestigious preparatory school in town. It's now a museum of Pocumtuck Valley life and history. Puritan and Indian artifacts include carved and painted chests, embroidery, musical instruments and glass-plate photographs (1880–1920).

Don't miss the Indian House Door, a dramatic relic from the French and Indian Wars. In February 1704, Indians attacked the house of the Sheldon family, hacked a hole through the center of the door and did in the inhabitants with musket fire.

MAGIC WINGS BUTTERFLY CONSERVATORY & GARDENS

If you've got young kids in tow, this **butterfly garden** (☎ 413-665-2805; www.magicwings.com; 281 Greenfield Rd/US 5 & MA 10, S Deerfield; adult/senior/student & child $7.50/6.50/4.50; ☻ 9am-6pm summer, closes 5pm rest of year) is sure to be a highlight for them. Everywhere you turn in this 8000-sq-ft, tropically outfitted glass conservatory, you're faced with a fluttering curtain of the friendly things. Despite the numerous signs requesting visitors not to touch the butterflies, the temptation to snap a picture with an Emerald Swallowtail perched on little Jimmy's fingertip is just too strong for some.

CRUISES

For a junket on the Connecticut River, catch a riverboat cruise on the *Quinnetukit II*. A lecturer fills you in on the history, geology and ecology of the river and the region during the 12-mile, 1½-hour ride, and you'll pass under the elegant French King Bridge. Cruises are run by the **Northfield Mountain**

Recreation & Environmental Center (☎ 800-859-2960; on MA 63 north of MA 2; adult/senior/child 14 & under $9/8/5; cruises 11am, 1:15pm & 3pm Wed-Sun). To get to the departure point, take I-91 north to exit 27, then MA 2 east, then MA 63 north. Call for reservations.

Sleeping & Eating

The Franklin County Chamber of Commerce (opposite) can recommend dozens of B&Bs in the region.

Deerfield Inn (☎ 413-774-5587, 800-926-3865; www.deerfieldinn.com; the Street, Deerfield; d incl breakfast $181-248; ✗) This establishment, right at the head of Historic Deerfield's main street, has 23 modernized, spacious rooms each with private bathroom. The inn, built in 1884, was destroyed by fire and rebuilt in 1981. The inn's **dining room** (mains $19-30) uses local, sustainably grown ingredients when possible.

Barton Cove Campground (☎ 413-863-9300; 90 Millers Falls Rd, off MA 2 in Gill; tent site $20-25) Barton Cove has 27 family tent sites on a mile-long wooded peninsula on the Connecticut River, and offer showers and kayak rental as well. The nature trail takes you to dinosaur footprints and nesting bald eagles. Take I-91 exit 27, then MA 2 east for three miles and look for the sign on the right.

There's not a terrible lot for your stomach to get excited about in Deerfield. More enticing fare can be had a bit north in the Shelburne Falls area or back down in the Five College area.

One of the only shining beacons in Deerfield's foggy dining scene is **Sienna** (☎ 413-665-0215; 6-b Elm St; mains $21-26; ☻ dinner Wed-Sun) in South Deerfield. The seasonal menu is not large, freeing up the chefs to focus on the exquisite preparation and presentation. The restaurant's spare lines and persimmon-colored walls contribute to the elegant and romantic atmosphere. To get there from Historic Deerfield, take I-91 south, exit 25. Turn left onto MA 116, cross over I-91 and at the first light make a right onto MA 5 south. At the next set of lights make a left onto Elm St.

Getting There & Away

The air, rail and bus services connect to Springfield (see p241). Deerfield lies off I-91 on MA 5, about 39 miles north of Springfield.

DETOUR: THE MOHAWK TRAIL (MA 2) *Kim Grant*

A sea of color takes hold of the hillsides of northwestern Massachusetts as summer gives way to fall. Head west on MA 2, from Greeenfield to Williamstown on the 63-mile-long road known as the **Mohawk Trail**, and you'll encounter a delectable buffet of cheesy tourist traps, great art, fabulous food and gorgeous scenery. Begun as an American Indian footpath, the byway became a popular trade route among colonial and tribal settlements. It is now recognized as one of the most scenic roads in the US.

The lively **Deerfield River** slides alongside flat, western sections of the route, with roaring, bucking stretches of white-water that turn leaf-peeping into an adrenaline sport for kayakers.

The road winds ever upward. At the **Western Summit**, the landscape sprawls out in a colorful tapestry. To the left, **Mt Greylock** looms as the highest point in Massachusetts. North Adams rests in the seam of the valley along the Hoosic River. To the right is Bald Mountain and views into Vermont.

Ease around the famous, steep **hairpin curve** where horses once strained to haul nitro-glycerine used for blasting the famous railway tunnel. On one brutally cold winter, as a load overturned and an expected explosion never came, a discovery was made: if frozen, the volatile substance could be safely transported.

Nearby **Natural Bridge State Park** is home to some of the most contorted and spectacular results of the eternal battle of water versus stone, resulting in a chasm 60ft deep and 475ft long worn through solid, white marble. And by all means, don't miss stopping in **Shelburne Falls** (below) for lunch, shopping or hanging out at the potholes.

In **North Adams**, fresh new businesses and the sprawling **Mass MoCA** (p272) visual and performing arts center are carving artful niches amid historic buildings and businesses that speak eloquently of other eras.

The road up **Mt Greylock** (p273) is long and steep, with gasp-inducing views. The view from the summit tower stretches well into New Hampshire, Vermont, New York and Massachusetts.

At the end of the day, it's hard to maintain a proper air of aimlessness with so much poking around left undone. But that's the beauty of this region: the more you explore, the more there is left to discover.

SHELBURNE FALLS
pop 2000

The Deerfield River forms the backbone of this cute town, which has become a bastion of artisan craftsmanship. The presence of several excellent restaurants ensures that those who come to shop, view the glacial potholes and stroll the Bridge of Flowers are fed and watered in a gracious manner.

Shelburne Falls is just off MA 2 (the so-called Mohawk Trail)on MA 116. Bridge St is the town's main drag. The **visitor center** (☎ 413-625-2254; www.shelburnefalls.com; 75 Bridge St; ☽ 10am-4pm Mon-Sat, noon-3pm Sun May-Oct) is a great resource for accommodations in the area, especially B&Bs.

Sights & Activities
BRIDGE OF FLOWERS

Shelburne Falls lays on the hype a bit thick, yet one can't deny that its flower-festooned bridge makes for a most photogenic civic centerpiece. One paid gardener and a host of volunteers have been maintaining it since 1929. More than 500 varieties of flowers, scrubs and vines flaunt their colors on the 400ft-long span from early spring through late fall. Access to the bridge is from Water St and there's no charge to walk across.

GLACIAL POTHOLES

The Native Americans called this area Salmon Falls, and the fishing here was so fine that warring tribes made an agreement that they wouldn't fight each other within one day's walk of the falls. These days it's the geologically fascinating glacial potholes that are drawing visitors. Ever since the end of the last Ice Age, stones trapped swirling in the riverbed have been grinding into the rockbed below, creating more than 50 near-perfect circles. The largest known glacial pothole in the world is here, with a diameter of 39ft.

DETOUR: THE MONTAGUE BOOKMILL

You gotta love a place whose motto is 'books you don't need in a place you can't find.' Luckily, both claims are slightly exaggerated. For lovers of both used books and picturesque spots in which to read them, the **Montague Bookmill** (☎ 413-367-9206; www.montaguebookmill.com; 440 Greenfield Rd, Montague; ☯ 10am-6pm) is a cherished spot indeed.

The 1832 building used to be a gristmill, and its westward-facing walls are punctuated by large windows that overlook the roiling water of the Sawmill River. The mill's collection of books is delightfully, academically esoteric – here's where to score a 500-page tome entitled *Transylvanian Cuisine* or a like-new copy of Julia Kristeva's *Semiotic Theory*.

Though the book mill is the biggest draw, several other ventures make it even easier to while away the entire day and night in the vicinity. The **Lady Killigrew Café & Pub** (☯ 10am-10pm Wed-Sun), featuring the same amazing riverside view, offers affordable sandwiches and drinks as well as wireless Internet. The newly opened **Night Kitchen** (☯ dinner Wed-Sun, brunch Sun) sources locally grown ingredients to whip up regional dishes with a creative touch. Several **antique and craft shops** are open Wednesday through Sunday.

To get there from Shelburne Falls (read carefully), take MA 2 east and stay on it until the town of Turners Falls, on the other side of I-91. At the lights by the Turners Falls Bridge, take a right onto Main Rd, over the water. After the bridge, take a left onto 3rd St, which quickly turns into Unity St. When Unity St forks, bear right onto Turners Falls Rd. Follow this road a little more than 4 miles, into Montague. Turn right onto Greenfield Rd.

These days, a hydroelectric dam controls the flow of the Deerfield River over the potholes, so it's possible that on your visit the water will be completely obscuring the holes. Either way it's worth a look – if the flow is a trickle, you see the circles; if it's raging, you'll feel like you're at Niagara Falls. The potholes are at the end of Deerfield Ave.

Sleeping & Eating

Johnson Homestead B&B (☎ 625-6603; 79 E Buckland Rd; d $75-110; ✗) Three rooms are let in this charming Colonial on 80 bucolic acres, a 10-minute drive southwest of town. No credit cards accepted.

High Pocket Farm B&B (☎ 413-624-8988; www.highpocket.com; 38 Adams Place Rd, Colrain; d $90; ✗) Nestled on more than 500 acres about 10 miles north of town is this unique B&B. For horse lovers a stay here is an especial treat. After a phenomenal farm breakfast, guests have the option of taking a guided horseback ride for an additional $50. Three rooms are let, all with private bathroom, and the view from the outdoor hot tub is incredible. Kids will like the game room, complete with ping-pong table. Two night minimum.

A Bottle of Bread (☎ 413-625-6502; 18 Water St; mains $13-17; ☯ dinner Wed-Sun year-round, lunch Fri & Sat spring & summer only) For such an exceptional restaurant, the Bottle is blessedly unpretentious. All its produce is raised by two local

organic farms, and though the meat dishes are flawless, the thrust of the menu is vegetarian and pescetarian. The specials live up to their name. A seat on the deck affords you a view of the bridge.

Tusk 'n' Rattle (☎ 413-625-0200; 10 Bridge St; tapas/mains $5-9/9-17; ☯ lunch & dinner Thu-Mon) This cheerful basement restaurant throws a creative Latin spin on American classics. Order a handful of tapas – like the portobello quesadillas – for the most flavor bang for your buck.

Café Martin (☎ 413-625-2795; 24 Bridge St; dinner mains $12-16; ☯ lunch & dinner Tue-Sat, brunch Sun) Classic continental fare like steak with gorgonzola cozy up on the menu with Latin and Asian-accented dishes such as tuna wasabi, plus plenty of hearty dishes for vegetarians, like the veggie paella ($13).

Shopping

Stop by the visitor center for a complete list of the artisans, from potters to quilters to weavers, that call Shelburne Falls home. Better yet, just take a meander through town.

On your way to the potholes, you won't be able to miss the crowd of people oohing and aahing at the craftspeople shaping molten liquid in the open studio of **North River Glass** (Deerfield Ave; ☯ 10am-5:30pm). Next door you can browse through the gallery of their work in all shapes and colors. If you're a sucker for handmade, strong-smelling candles, keep walking a few more steps to **Mole Hollow Candles** (10am-5:30pm). Bargains are to be had in their 'seconds' section.

Across the river and down Conway St to the left you'll find the **Lamson-Goodnow factory outlet** (10am-5pm Mon-Sat, noon-5pm Sun), with a wide range of finely crafted kitchen knives and barbecue accessories. Established in 1837, the company is the oldest cutlery manufacturer in the country.

THE BERKSHIRES

Few places in America combine culture with rural countryside as deftly as the Berkshire hills in western Massachusetts. Extending from the highest point in the state – Mt Greylock – southward to the Connecticut state line, the Berkshires have been a summer refuge for more than a century, since the rich and famous such as industrialist Andrew Carnegie and author Edith Wharton arrived to build more than 75 summer 'cottages' of grand proportions. Many of these relics survive today as inns or performance venues. Literary giants such as Nathaniel Hawthorne and Herman Melville also set down roots in the area, glorying in the Berkshires' tranquil yet expansive beauty. On summer weekends when the sidewalks are scorching in Boston and New York, crowds of city dwellers jump in their cars and head for the Berkshire breezes.

In the evenings, culture beckons. The Boston Symphony Orchestra's summer concert series at Tanglewood, near Lenox, draws the biggest crowds. The Williamstown Theatre Festival attracts many well-known actors, and the nearby Clark Art Institute's collection of impressionist works rivals any big-city museum.

Most visitors congregate in the southern half of the Berkshires, from Great Barrington to Lenox, where you will find considerable traffic and development along US 7. Williamstown, to the north, is far less crowded, resembling the pastoral setting of Vermont to the north and Connecticut's Litchfield Hills to the south. The Appalachian Trail traverses the hills north to south.

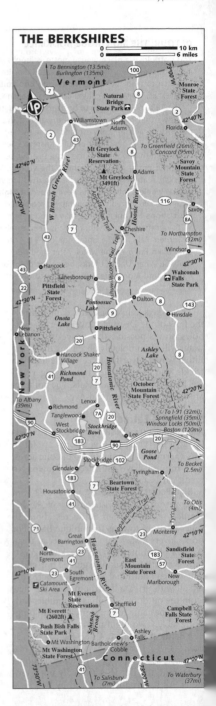

THE BERKSHIRES

BERKSHIRE-GROWN GOODNESS

Undeniably, part of the joy of a drive through the Berkshires – or any part of rural New England, for that matter – is stumbling unexpectedly on a small farm stand and stopping to chat for a while with the farmer who grew those apples or blueberries herself.

But if you don't want to leave it all to chance, or are curious about which restaurants in the region stock their kitchens with farm-fresh vittles, pick up or check out online the **Berkshire Grown** (☎ 413-528-0041; PO Box 983, Great Barrington, MA 01230; www.berkshiregrown.org), a guide to locally grown food, and flowers, as well as other hand-crafted or -raised goodies like cheeses, flowers, maple syrup and meats.

The seasonally published directory lists pick-your-own farms, farmers markets and stands, and member restaurants like **Verdura** (p260) in Great Barrington, **Church St Café** (p268) in Lenox and the **Red Lion Inn** (p262) in Stockbridge. Special events like agricultural fairs, farm dinners and garden tours at places like the **Berkshire Botanical Garden** (p262) in Stockbridge are announced in the guide as well.

Information

Berkshire Chamber of Commerce (☎ 413-499-4000; www.berkshirechamber.com; 75 North St, Suite 360, Pittsfield, MA 01201)

Berkshire Community Radio (WBCR 97.7FM) Broadcasts music, news and commentary to the Southern Berkshire region.

Berkshire Grown (www.berkshiregrown.org) Online or print directory of pick-your-own orchards, farmers markets and restaurants that source organic local ingredients. See p257.

Berkshires Visitors Bureau (☎ 413-743-4500, 800-237-5747; www.berkshires.org; ☺ 8:30am-5pm Mon-Fri); Adams (3 Hoosac St, Adams, MA 01220) Pittsfield (121 South St, Pittsfield, MA 01201) Can help with accommodations (ext 140) and activities planning.

BerkshireWeb (www.berkshireweb.com) Comprehensive yet slightly overcommercial directory of just about everything in the area.

Berkshires Week (www.berkshiresweek.com) The online version of the free newspaper has a calendar of events.

iBerkshires (www.iberkshires.com) Online daily newspaper.

See the Berkshires (www.berkshires.com) Recommendations for dining, lodging, activities, car rental, plus a trip planner.

Southern Berkshire Lodging (☎ 413-528-4006; www.berkshirelodging.com) Emphasis on the higher-end inns. Note that the hotel tax rate is 9.7%. Take this into account when figuring lodging costs.

GREAT BARRINGTON & AROUND
pop 7200

Great Barrington's Main St used to consist of Woolworth's, hardware stores, thrift shops and a run-down diner. They have given way to artsy boutiques, antique shops, coffeehouses and restaurants, so much so that locals are beginning to call their town 'Little SoHo,'

perhaps to appeal to the many city travelers who are now stopping to shop and eat at the best selection of restaurants in the region. But beware: the town's popularity makes for traffic jams on summer weekends.

The town is home to the prestigious and unique Simon's Rock of Bard College, the nation's only liberal arts college designed for students of high school age who crave a more challenging academic environment. Great Barrington also saw the birth of the great African American teacher and civil rights leader William Edward Burghardt DuBois (1868–1963). After receiving a PhD from Harvard, WEB DuBois became a pioneer for civil rights and a cofounder of the NAACP.

Orientation & Information

Great Barrington is 146 miles west of Boston off I-90. Albany, NY, is 50 miles northwest, Springfield is 54 miles east, Boston is 135 miles east, and NYC is 150 miles to the south.

The Housatonic River flows through the center of town just east of Main St/US 7, the central thoroughfare. Most lodgings and restaurants are on Main St or on heavily congested US 7 north, or MA 23/41 southwest of the town. However, the finest accommodations (most of which are B&Bs) are on small roads outside town in the farmlands.

The Southern Berkshire Chamber of Commerce maintains a small **kiosk** (☎ 413-528-1510, 800-269-6062; www.greatbarrington.org; 362 Main St, Great Barrington, MA 01230; ☺ 10am-6pm Tue-Sun), which has maps, brochures, restaurant menus and accommodations lists.

CENTRAL MASSACHUSETTS & THE BERKSHIRES

The public **library**, with 15 minutes of free Internet, and a **Berkshire Bank** with ATM can be found right on the north end of Main St.

Sights & Activities
SEARLES CASTLE
Edward Searles and his wife, Mary Searles, were Great Barrington's most wealthy and prominent citizens in the late 19th century. Mary, the widow of railroad tycoon Mark Hopkins, built an imposing mansion here in 1886. Now called Searles Castle, it stands behind high walls on Main St at the southern end of the town center. Today the great house is the home of John Dewey Academy, a private school, but is unfortunately not open to visitors.

TYRINGHAM
The village of Tyringham, several miles east of Great Barrington and another few miles north of Monterey, is the perfect destination for an excursion deep into the heart of the countryside. Once the home of a Shaker community (1792–1874), the village is now famous for its **Gingerbread House**, an architectural fantasy designed at the beginning of the 20th century by sculptor Henry Hudson Kitson, whose best-known work – a statue of Captain Parker as the minuteman – graces the Lexington Green (p133). The fairytale thatched-roofed cottage, once Kitson's studio, now houses the **Santarella Museum & Gardens** (☎ 413-243-3260; 75 Main Rd; adult/child under 4 $4/free; ☯ 10am-5pm May-Oct). Seeing the exterior of the house and taking a walk through the gardens is probably enough for most people other than fervent art lovers. For places to stay in Tyringham, see p259.

HIKING
Ten miles south of Great Barrington along US 7 and MA 7A toward Ashley Falls is **Bartholomew's Cobble** (☎ 413-229-8600; adult/child 6-12 $5/1; ☯ 9am-5pm mid-Apr–mid-Oct), a 'cobble' being a high, rocky knoll of limestone, marble or quartzite. The highly alkaline soil of this 329-acre reservation supports an unusual variety of trees, flowers, moss and especially ferns. Six miles of hiking trails provide routes for enjoying the cobble and the woods, which are set beneath a flyway used by over 200 species of birds. Try the Ledges Trail that weaves along the Housatonic River. This property belongs to the Trustees of Reservations, a private, statewide conservation and preservation organization.

On US 7, less than 5 miles north of Great Barrington center, **Monument Mountain** (☎ 413-298-3239; admission free) has two trails to the summit of Squaw Peak. Writer Nathaniel Hawthorne wrote that Monument's summit resembled 'a headless sphinx wrapped in a Persian shawl.' On August 5, 1850, Hawthorne climbed the mountain with Oliver Wendell Holmes and Herman Melville. It was the first time Hawthorne and the young Melville met, but they quickly became good friends and kept in touch throughout their lives.

ORCHARDS
About 5 miles north of Great Barrington is **Windy Hill Farm** (☎ 413-298-3217; 686 Stockbridge Rd/ US 7; ☯ 7am-5pm), where more than a score of apple varieties, from pucker-sour to candy-sweet, are yours for the autumn picking. Summer is blueberry season.

Festivals & Events
Aston Magna (☎ 413-528-3595; www.astonmagna .org; tickets about $30) celebrates early classical music with a summer festival and a winter concert series. If you're a devotee of Bach,

---

DETOUR: BASH BISH FALLS

Twelve miles south of South Egremont, right on the New York state line, is **Bash Bish Falls** (☎ 413-528-0330), the largest waterfall in the state. Plunging down a 1000ft gorge, the waterfall's torrent is bifurcated by a massive boulder just above its pool. The falls are a popular spot for landscape painters to set up their easels.

To get there, follow MA 41 south out of Great Barrington and turn right onto Mt Washington Rd and go about eight miles, following signs for the Catamount Ski Area. Then follow signs to the falls, taking East St, then West St and finally bumpy Bash Bish Falls Rd, deep in the Mt Washington State Forest. Stop at the first parking area you come to on your left if you're up to taking the shorter but steeper trail down to the falls. If you (or your young kids) are not, keep going a mile further down the road to the next parking area. This trail takes about 20 minutes but is much more level.

Brahms and Buxtehude, buy your tickets well in advance.

The **Berkshire Opera Company** (☎ 413-644-9988; www.berkshireopera.org; tickets $20-75) stages full-dress productions of classic and modern operas at the Mahaiwe Performing Arts Center in Great Barrington and at other venues in the southern Berkshires.

Sleeping

A good half-hour drive from Lenox and Tanglewood, Great Barrington is nonetheless a popular place for people to stay in the summer. The highest rates listed are for Friday and Saturday nights in the high-peak months of July and August.

There are well over 50 inns and B&Bs within a 10-mile radius of Great Barrington. For links and a full list, log on to www.greatbarrington.org or contact the **Berkshire Lodgings Association** (☎ 413-298-4760, 888-298-4760; www.berkshirelodgings.com). All B&Bs prefer a minimum of two-nights' stay, but it doesn't hurt to ask about single nights.

If you're planning to stay in the area a week or longer it may be worth renting a vacation apartment. Through **Berkshire Pied-à-Terre** (☎ 413-274-6926; www.berkshire-pied-a-terre.com; weekly around $900) you can set yourself up in a lovely, hardwood-floor downtown apartment with fully equipped kitchen.

BUDGET

Briarcliff Inn (☎ 413-528-3000; 506 Stockbridge Rd; d $55-165) Positioned on a far more scenic stretch of US 7 than the motels in town, this one stands directly across from Monument Mountain. Rooms are well maintained and offer TV and king beds.

Lantern House Motel (☎ 413-528-2350; 254 Stockbridge Rd, US 7; d $70-155; 🖵) Just north of the center of town, this motel is set back a bit from the road. Rooms have fridges and cable TV.

Beartown State Forest (☎ 413-528-0904; 69 Blue Hill Rd, Monterey; sites $10-12). It's mostly backpackers who rent sites at this quiet campground, 8 miles out of Great Barrington on MA 23. It has 12 basic sites that overlook 35-acre Benedict Pond. (Site number 11 is the most secluded.) RVs may have trouble getting up the winding road.

Mt Washington State Forest (☎ 413-528-0330; East St, Mt Washington; tent sites $10-12) The forest contains the glorious Bash Bish Falls (op-

posite) as well as 30 miles of trails. Some 15 wilderness camping sites are available for the adventurous.

Tolland State Forest (☎ 413-269-6002; 410 Tolland Rd/MA 8, E Otis; tent sites $10-12) Otis is 16 miles east of Great Barrington along MA 23. This campground has 90 wooded sites set on a peninsula jutting out into the Otis Reservoir.

MID-RANGE

Race Brook Lodge (☎ 413-229-2916; www.rblodge .com; 864 S Undermountain Rd/MA 41, Sheffield; r/ste $80-200/150-270; ✕ 🖵) This 'chintz-free' lodge sits at the base of Mt Race. None of its 33 rooms – spread out over the lodge, cottages and coach house – has a TV or phone, though you can get your techno-fix in the lobby. Take the trail behind the lodge to the mountain's summit, where the Appalachian Trail leads you on a ridge walk.

Baldwin Hill Farm B&B (☎ 413-528-4092, 888-528-4092; www.baldwinhillfarm.com; 121 Baldwin Hill Rd, S Egremont; d $99-150; ✕ 🖵) Baldwin Hill Farm has four rooms of varying amenities and over 300 acres of hilltop land with glorious views of the surrounding mountains. It's off MA 71 in South Egremont.

Sunset Farm B&B (☎ 413-243-3229; www.sunset farminn.com; 74 Tyringham Rd; r/apt $90-110/150; ✕) If you fall in love with Tyringham, you can spend the night here. Situated on a hillside overlooking one of the first Shaker settlements in the Berkshires – and also right across the street from Santarella (see opposite) – this casual B&B commands a view of the Tyringham Valley. All five rooms feature hand-sewn quilts and early American Shaker furniture. No minimum stay required.

Other mid-range options:

Holiday Inn Express (☎ 413-528-1810; 415 Stockbridge Rd; d $96-150; 🖵)

Monument Mountain Motel (☎ 413-528-3272; 249 Stockbridge Rd/MA 7; d $85-135; 🖵) A bit shabby, but clean.

TOP END

Wainwright Inn (☎ 413-528-2062; www.wainwrightinn .com; 518 S Main St; r/ste incl breakfast $100-195/175-275; ✕) This 1766 house with two wrap-around porches has eight impeccably elegant guestrooms, all with private bathroom and most with working fireplaces. Breakfast is a decadent experience. The inn is a short walk from the center of town. Rooms may be less expensive mid-week.

Old Inn on the Green & Gedney Farm (☎ 413-229-3131, 800-286-3139; www.oldinn.com; MA 57, New Marlborough; d $195-365; ⊠) Once a relay stop on the post road from Westfield to Albany, the Old Inn, c 1760, is exactly what most people picture when they think New England country inn. The dining rooms are lit entirely by candlelight, and there are fireplaces and private bathrooms in each of the five rooms. In the summer, dinner is served outside on the garden terrace. A half mile up the road is Gedney Farm, with 16 equally elegant guestrooms in a converted bank barn.

Eating & Drinking

Fare in the restaurants in the town center of Great Barrington ranges from Middle Eastern food to sushi to old-time diner eats, though prices can be a little inflated (welcome to the Berkshires). Railroad St, a tiny crook of a road off Main St, harbors many of the town's excellent eats.

For up-to-date entertainment listings, pick up a copy of the free *Berkshires Week* at most cafés, bars and restaurants.

BUDGET & MID-RANGE

Berkshire Coffee Roasting Company (☎ 413-528-5505; 286 Main St; items $2-7; ⊙ 8am-5pm Mon-Fri, 9am-4pm Sat & Sun) This unpretentious spot is a good place to meet locals in the morning over a cup of joe.

Café Helsinki (☎ 413-528-3394; 284 Main St; mains lunch/dinner $6-12/7-20; ⊙ lunch & dinner Mon & Tue, Thu-Sat, brunch Sun) Plop down on an overstuffed sofa at this café in the back of the Barrington House Atrium and prepare yourself for some Scandinavian and Eastern European comfort food – dishes such as the Mad Russian (potato latkes with gravlax and sour cream) and Sibelius barbecue ribs, named for Finland's most famous composer. In the evenings, outstanding folksy and bluesy musical acts take over the adjoining **Club Helsinki** (tickets $7-35). No cover on Mondays.

Bizen (☎ 413-528-4343; 17 Railroad St; rolls $8-17; ⊙ lunch & dinner) This popular, mostly organic Japanese restaurant features a small sushi bar, sashimi, tempura and a new room for *kaiseki* (the seasonal meal that accompanies a tea ceremony). All meals are served on pottery created by owner Michael Marcus, and rolls sport droll names like Smoke Gets in Your Rice.

Martin's (☎ 413-528-5455; 49 Railroad St; specials $4-10; ⊙ 7am-9pm) Breakfast is served all day at this old-fashioned, black-and-white-tiled diner. There are lots of hearty vegetarian sandwiches, too.

Baba Louie's (☎ 413-528-8100; 284 Main St; mains $6-16; ⊙ 11:30am-9:30pm) Small, cozy Baba's is known for its wood-fired pizza with organic sourdough crust.

La Chosa (☎ 413-528-6380; 284 Main St; burritos $3-6.50; ⊙ 10am-10pm Sun-Thu, noon-10pm Fri & Sat) In the same arcade as Café Helsinki, this is the spot for filling Mexican takeout. Be sure to throw down the extra quarter to have one of their fiery hot sauces added to your burrito. On weekend nights you can often catch live rock here. Cash only.

Uncommon Grounds (☎ 413-528-0858; 103 Stockbridge Rd; sandwiches $5-7; ⊙ 7:30am-5pm) On your left if heading out of town towards Stockbridge, this warm café boasts organic coffee, a juice bar and lots of vegetarian wraps and sandwiches. There's even a kids menu with sandwiches like PB&J and grilled cheese.

Cheesecake Charlie's (☎ 413-528-7790; 271 Main St; lunch $6-11; ⊙ 11:30am-4:30pm, dinner shows at 8pm) As the name suggests, here you'll find 50 varieties of cheesecake as well as an espresso bar. It also offers affordable pastas and sandwiches. Charlie's has an evening cabaret that includes dinner, which will run you around $50.

TOP END

Verdura (☎ 413-528-8969; 44 Railroad St; mains $14-25; ⊙ dinner) Freshness and simplicity is the name of the game at this praiseworthy, golden-walled Tuscan cucina. Chef William Webber fashions rustic yet elegant dishes from organic, local ingredients. The prosciutto-wrapped trout is delectable. Reserve as early as possible. **Dué Enoteca**, the restaurant's fine wine bar next door, serves up Verdura's menu tapas-style.

Union Bar & Grill (☎ 413-528-6228; 293 Main St; mains $18-25; ⊙ dinner Mon, Wed-Sat, brunch Sun, closed Tue, bar open late) This trendy loft is one of the hottest restaurants in the Berkshires. Mains like duck quesadillas and ribs with fennel coleslaw are served on aluminum tables against a backdrop of metallic walls. It's one of the few places in town open late, so you can venture here after going to Tanglewood – and they don't take reservations, so your chances of squeezing in are pretty good. Sunday brunch is accompanied by live jazz.

The Old Mill (☎ 413-528-1421; 53 Main St/MA 23, South Egremont; mains $16-27; ☿ dinner Tue-Sun) This is a 1797 grist mill and blacksmith's shop transformed into a highly praised restaurant serving American and continental cuisine, such as diver scallops and calf liver. Two fireplaces add to its colonial charm.

Castle St Café (☎ 413-528-5244; 10 Castle St; dinner mains $16-28; ☿ dinner Wed-Mon) The piano in the back of this café just off Main St once belonged to Nat King Cole, who owned a summer home in Tyringham. Chef and owner Michael Ballon uses lots of fresh local ingredients, like Pittsfield fettuccine, to create his innovative menu. Pastas and burgers are less expensive. Come for jazz on Friday or Saturday nights.

STOCKBRIDGE

pop 2200

Take a good look down Stockbridge's wide Main St. Notice anything? More specifically, notice anything missing? Not one stoplight stutters the view, not one telephone pole blights the picture-perfect scene – it looks very much the way Norman Rockwell might have seen it.

In fact, Rockwell did see it – he lived and worked in Stockbridge during the last 25 years of his life. Both the town and the artist attract summer and fall visitors en masse, who come to stroll the streets, inspect its shops and sit in the rockers on the porch of the grand old Red Lion Inn. And they come by the busload to visit the Norman Rockwell Museum on the town's outskirts.

Also of interest in this pretty town are Chesterwood, the country home and studio of sculptor Daniel Chester French; Naumkeag, a lavish early-20th-century 'Berkshire cottage'; and the Berkshire Theatre Festival.

Stockbridge makes a convenient Tanglewood home base, with more affordable lodging options than Lenox.

Orientation & Information

Stockbridge is a 7-mile drive from Great Barrington to the south and Lenox to the north. Main St in Stockbridge is MA 102. The central district is only a few blocks long.

In the summertime months, volunteers sometimes staff an information **kiosk** next door to the library on Main St. For accommodations information, you can get in touch with the **Stockbridge Lodging Association** (☎ 413-298-5200; www.stockbridgechamber.org; PO Box 224, Stockbridge, MA 01262; ☿ 9am-5pm Mon, Wed & Fri). **Berkshire Bank** can be found next to the Red Lion Inn.

Sights & Activities

NORMAN ROCKWELL MUSEUM

Norman Rockwell (1894–1978) was born in New York City, and he sold his first magazine cover illustration to the *Saturday Evening Post* in 1916. In the following half-century he did another 321 covers for the *Post,* as well as illustrations for books, posters and many other magazines. His clever, masterful, insightful art made him the best-known and most popular illustrator in US history. His wonderful sense of humor can be seen in his painting *Triple Self Portrait* (1960), where an older Rockwell looks in a mirror, only to paint a much younger version of himself.

The **museum** (☎ 413-298-4100; MA 183; www.nrm.org; adult/student/child $12/7/free; ☿ 10am-5pm) has the largest collection of his original art and also hosts exhibitions of other wholesome, feel-good artists like David Macauley, of *The Way Things Work* fame. The grounds contain Rockwell's studio, too, which was moved here from behind his Stockbridge home. Audio tours are available for an extra fee. The rolling, manicured lawns give way to picturesque views, and there are picnic tables set in a grove near the museum.

To find the museum follow MA 102 west from Stockbridge, turn left (south) on MA 183, and look for the museum on the left side.

CHESTERWOOD

This pastoral 22-acre plot was 'heaven' to its owner Daniel Chester French (1850–1931), the sculptor best known for his statue *The Minute Man* (1875) at the Old North Bridge in Concord and his great seated statue of Abraham Lincoln in the Lincoln Monument in Washington, DC (1922). French lived in New York City but spent most summers after 1897 here at **Chesterwood** (☎ 413-298-3579; 4 Williamsville Rd; family/adult/child $25/10/5; ☿ 10am-5pm May-Oct), his gracious Berkshire estate.

French's more than 100 great public works, mostly monumental, made him a wealthy man. His house and studio are substantially as they were when he lived and worked here, with nearly 500 pieces of sculpture, finished and unfinished, in the barnlike studio. The space and the art have a way of beguiling even those who wouldn't call themselves devoted sculpture enthusiasts.

Tours of the residence and studio leave about every hour. The museum is near the village of Glendale, off MA 183, south of the Norman Rockwell Museum. Follow MA 102 west from Stockbridge and turn left onto Glendale Middle Rd, proceed through Glendale to Williamsville Rd and turn left; the museum is on the right.

BERKSHIRE BOTANICAL GARDEN

Two miles west from the center of Stockbridge, the **Berkshire Botanical Garden** (☎ 413-298-3926; 5 W Stockbridge Rd/MA 102; adult/senior & student/child 12 & under $7/5/free; ☺ 10am-5pm May-Oct) maintains 15 acres of wildflowers, herbs, perennials, water plants and alpine plants. Tours are led on Wednesdays and Saturdays at 10:30am.

NAUMKEAG

This 1885 grand Berkshire 'cottage' on Prospect Hill was the summer house of attorney, diplomat and notable art collector Joseph Hodges Choate; it's crammed with Oriental carpets, Chinese porcelain and other luxury goods. The stunning gardens are the result of 30 years of devoted work on the part of prominent landscape architect Fletcher Steele and the Choate family. The Choates settled on the name Naumkeag mistakenly thinking it meant 'haven of peace' – it's actually Algonquian for 'fishing place.'

You can take a **guided tour** of the house and gardens (☎ 413-298-3239; 5 Prospect St; adult/child 6-12 $10/3, gardens only adult/child $8/3; ☺ 10am-5pm Jun–mid-Oct). Follow Pine St from the Red Lion Inn (right) to Prospect St.

MISSION HOUSE

This 1739 **residence** (☎ 413-298-3239; 19 Main St; adult/child 6-12 $6/3; ☺ 10am-5pm late May-early Sep) was the home of the Reverend John Sergeant, the first missionary to the native peoples in this area, and also for a short time of John Edwards, the fire-and-brimstone Calvinist preacher. It's furnished with 17th- and 18th-century household goods, and features a small museum of Native American artifacts. A guided tour is included in the admission price.

STOCKBRIDGE CEMETERY

Most notable about this pleasant burying ground on the west end of Main St is the so-called **Sedgwick Pie**. When Judge Theodore Sedgwick, the head of the prominent Stockbridge family, died in 1813, he had himself buried in the center of a large plot, around which in concentric circles his and his wife's descendants would be laid to rest as well. Legend goes that the Sedgwicks wanted to see no one but other Sedgwicks when the day of reckoning came, but modern-day family members refute this. Might-as-well-be family members include the servant Mum Bet – whom Judge Sedgwick helped free from slavery – as well as the family dog. The pie lies in the northeast corner.

WEST STOCKBRIDGE

Though not nearly as picturesque as Stockbridge, West Stockbridge still retains its historic charm. Old country stores and the 19th-century train station stand next to new galleries and art studios. This is a great place to stay during Tanglewood season, because Lenox is less than a 15-minute drive away on rarely used backcountry roads.

Charles H Baldwin & Sons Extracts (☎ 413-232-7785; 1 Center St; ☺ 9am-5pm Mon-Sat, noon-3pm Sun) Any baker worth his or her salt knows that the choice of vanilla can mean the difference between so-so cookies and oh-so cookies. The Baldwin family has been making top-quality vanilla extract along with a score of other smellicious extracts and oils since 1888, and they're all made right here. Baldwin's is worth a stop if only for the explosion of nostalgia and novelty gifts that cover every surface of the tiny storefront.

Sleeping

There are numerous inns and B&Bs in and around Stockbridge. The following places deliver a memorable stay at a commensurate price. Rates are for the summer and fall high seasons.

Red Lion Inn (☎ 413-298-5545; www.redlioninn.com; 30 Main St/MA 102; d with/without bathroom $185-225/100-110, ste $275-360; ✕) This huge white frame hotel is at the very heart of Stockbridge. Founded in 1773, it was completely rebuilt after a fire in 1897. Its 108 flowery rooms are dispersed among several buildings, each with unique amenities.

Card Lake Inn (☎ 413-232-0272; www.cardlakeinn .com; 29 Main St/MA 102, West Stockbridge; r/ste incl breakfast $85-165/180-250; ✗) Owned by a young family with twin daughters, this 11-room canary-yellow inn, which used to be stagecoach stop, is a great place for families. Breakfast is hearty and the floors are delightfully unlevel.

Williamsville Inn (☎ 413-274-6118; www.williamsville inn.com; MA 41, West Stockbridge; d $155-195; ✗) This 1797 farmhouse is under new, enthusiastic ownership. Thick wood floors, exposed beams, fireplaces and refreshingly understated decor are de rigueur for the 15 rooms. Renting out the Sarah Hale and Susan B Anthony rooms together is an excellent choice for families – they're within spitting distance of a tree swing and playground. In summer a three-night stay is required. The **dining room** (✆ dinner Fri & Sat; mains $19-26) specializes in German cuisine. The inn is 5 miles south of West Stockbridge towards Great Barrington.

Eating

Elm St Market (☎ 413-298-3654; 4 Elm St; items $3-6; ✆ breakfast & lunch) Just off Main St, this quaint market has a deli counter (where you can order a juicy Rueben sandwich), and a few tables (where you can eat it). Oldies play over the stereo, but the Internet station in the back belies its throwback character.

Caffe Pomo d'Oro (☎ 413-232-4616; 6 Depot St, West Stockbridge; mains lunch/dinner $6-10/18-22; ✆ breakfast & lunch year-round, dinner only in summer) This airy, casual café in the 1838 light-yellow railroad station right next to the post office is where local artisans lunch on omelettes, large sandwiches, freshly made soups and creative mains like smoked trout fillet with horseradish. BYO wine.

Daily Bread Bakery (☎ 413-298-0272; 31 Main St; items $3-8; ✆ breakfast & lunch Mon-Sat) Visit this small, friendly bakery for bagels, bread, cakes, cookies, and rolls that are good for snacks or picnics.

Once Upon a Table (☎ 413-298-3870; 36 Main St; dinner mains $16-22; ✆ lunch & dinner) In the Mews shopping arcade, this bright, yellow spot serves upscale fare on its glass-enclosed porch. Never ones to slack off, the owners change the menu weekly – but expect dishes in the vein of chipotle- and lime-roasted chicken breast and pecan-crusted rainbow trout.

Main St Café (☎ 413-298-3060; 40 Main St; dishes $4-9; ✆ 8am-4pm) Come here for fine sand-wiches and salads. The substantial breakfast burrito is $7.

Red Lion Inn (☎ 413-298-5545; www.redlioninn .com; 30 Main St) The Red Lion is Stockbridge's premier place for dining. Besides the elegant formal **dining room** (mains $22-32; ✆ 7am-10pm), where you can indulge in a roasted native turkey dinner, there's the **Widow Bingham Tavern** (mains $9-21), a rustic colonial pub complete with baskets hanging from the ceiling, serving gourmet sandwiches and many variations on cow. The downstairs **Lion's Den** (☎ 413-298-1654; prices $4-9; ✆ dinner Mon-Thu, lunch & dinner Fri-Sun) is the cocktail lounge, and has a sandwich and salad menu. Folk, jazz or bluegrass music is featured here nearly nightly. In fair weather you can dine in the courtyard out back.

Entertainment

Theater comes in stages at **Berkshire Theatre Festival** (☎ 413-298-5576, 866-811-4111; www .berkshiretheatre.org; PO Box 797, Stockbridge, MA 01262-0797; tickets $40-65). New and innovative plays are staged during this festival, which runs from late June through early September. Recent offerings included *The Misanthrope* and Hermann Hesse's *Siddhartha*. Performances are held at the Main Stage and smaller Unicorn Theatre. The associated **BTF Plays! for Young Audiences** stages works performed by and for children.

LEE
pop 6000

Unless they're heading to the prestigious Jacob's Pillow dance festival or to the outlets, most people go barreling through Lee, forgetting that they're no longer on the turnpike. Though there's nothing wrong with the town, it doesn't hold any must-sees for the tourist – which may be the best reason to exit the highway and explore it for yourself.

Lee is 134 miles from Boston, just off exit 2 of I-90. Great Barrington and Lenox are less than a 10-minute drive away except on busy summer weekends, when the traffic on US 7 can be maddening.

Orientation & Information

The town of Lee is the gateway to Lenox, Stockbridge and Great Barrington. US 20 is Lee's main street, and leads to Lenox.

The **Lee Chamber of Commerce** (☎ 413-243-0852; www.leelodging.org; PO Box 345, Lee, MA 01238-0345; ✆ 10am-4pm Tue-Sat) maintains an information booth on the town green in front of the town hall in summer.

Sights & Activities
JACOB'S PILLOW DANCE FESTIVAL
Founded by Ted Shawn in an old barn in 1932, **Jacob's Pillow** (☎ 413-243-0745; www.jacobs pillow.org; PO Box 287, Lee, MA 01238-0287; shows free-$55; performances mid-Jun–early Sep) is one of the premier summer dance festivals in the USA. Through the years, Alvin Ailey, Merce Cunningham, the Martha Graham Dance Company and other leading interpreters of dance have taken part. A smorgasbord of free shows and talks allows even those on tight budgets to join the fun. The festival theaters are in the village of Becket, 7 miles east of Lee along US 20 and MA 8.

OCTOBER MOUNTAIN STATE FOREST
Most out-of-towners who venture to the Berkshires head to the Mt Greylock State Reservation (see p270) to see the state's highest peak, and thus leave **October Mountain State Forest** (☎ 413-243-1778), a 16,127-acre state park and the largest tract of green space in Massachusetts, to the locals. Hidden amid the hardwoods, Buckley Dunton Reservoir – a small body of water stocked with bass and pickerel – is a great spot for canoeing. For hikers, a 9-mile stretch of the Appalachian Trail pierces the heart of the forest through copses of hemlocks, spruces, birches and oaks. To get there from Lee, follow Rte 20 west for 3 miles and look for signs.

PRIME OUTLETS
If all the cute Berkshire boutiques are getting to you, score some deals at **Prime Outlets** (☎ 413-243-8186; 50 Water St/US 20; ☼ 10am-9pm Mon-Sat, 11am-6pm Sun), with retailers like Timberland, the Gap and London Fog.

Sleeping & Eating
For a comprehensive list of area accommodations visit www.leelodging.org.

Just one of the dozens of B&Bs in the area, **Mill Cottage B&B** (☎ 413-243-4667; www.mill cottage.com; 155 Willow St, South Lee; r/ste $100-145/120-175; ☒) has one large guestroom and one suite available, and overlooks the Housatonic River. A big calico cat resides here.

October Mountain State Forest (☎ 877-422-6762; Center St; sites $10-12) This state forest campground, near the shores of the Housatonic

River, is for campers only and has 47 sites with hot showers. To find the campground, turn east off US 20 onto Center St and follow the signs.

Motels in Lee are clustered around I-90 exit 2, on heavily trafficked Rte 7. They include the following, for which prices range from $68 in low season to $180 in high season:

Super 8 Motel (☎ 413-243-0143; 170 Housatonic St)

Sunset Motel (☎ 413-243-0302; 150 Housatonic St; ☒) Very basic rooms, but quiet.

Pilgrim Motel (☎ 413-243-1328; 165 Housatonic St) Has laundry facilities.

Lee offers a clear dichotomy of lifestyles breakfast:

Juice and Java (☎ 413-243-3131; 60 Main St; items $2-6.50; ☼ breakfast & lunch) Head to this place to stock up on beverages and gourmet sandwiches like grilled eggplant before heading out to hike in October Mountain State Forest. This place stocks the best bagels around, which, granted, isn't saying a whole lot.

Joe's Diner (☎ 413-243-9756; 63 Center St; items $3-10; ☼ 24 hr) There's no better slice of blue-collar Americana in the Berkshires than Joe's Diner, at the north end of Main St. Norman Rockwell's famous painting of a policeman sitting at a counter talking to a young boy, *The Runaway* (1958), was inspired by this diner. Every politician who's ever run for office in Massachusetts has stopped at Joe's to get his or her picture taken and put on the wall. Pancakes or an omelette run $4.

LENOX
pop 5000
This gracious, wealthy town is a historical anomaly: its charm was not destroyed by the Industrial Revolution, and then, prized for its bucolic peace, the town became a summer retreat for wealthy families with surnames like Carnegie, Vanderbilt and Westinghouse, who had made their fortunes by building factories in other towns. Today, Lenox is home to the Tanglewood Music Festival, an incredibly popular summer event. Just past Tanglewood is the Stockbridge Bowl, a supremely cerulean lake.

Originally named Yokuntown after a local Native American leader, Lenox took its current name in honor of Charles Lenox, Duke of Richmond, who had been sympathetic to the American Revolution.

Orientation & Information

It's easy to get around Lenox on foot, though some of its many inns are a mile or two from the center. Tanglewood is 1.5 miles west of Lenox's center along West St/MA 183. Church St is home to the town's best eateries.

The **Lenox Chamber of Commerce & Information Center** (☎ 413-637-3646; www.lenox.org; The Curtis, 5 Walker St, PO Box 646, Lenox, MA 01240; ☙ 10am-4pm Tue-Sat) is a clearinghouse of information.

Simply called the **Bookstore** (☎ 413-637-3390; 9 Housatonic St; ☙ 9am-6pm Mon-Sat, 10am-3pm Sun), this is the place to stop for that map, atlas or summer novel you need.

Sights

THE MOUNT

Almost 50 years after Nathaniel Hawthorne left his home in Lenox (now part of the Tanglewood estate), another writer found inspiration in the Berkshires. Edith Wharton (1862–1937) came to Lenox in 1899 and proceeded to build her palatial estate, the Mount. When not writing, she would entertain friends like Henry James.

Besides such novels as *The Age of Innocence*, Wharton penned *The Decoration of Houses*, which was crucial in legitimizing interior decoration as a profession in the USA. She summered at the Mount for a decade before moving permanently to France.

You can tour the **Mount** (☎ 413-637-1899; 2 Plunkett St; adult/student/child under 12 $16/8/free; ☙ 9am-5pm May-Oct), which is on the outskirts of Lenox at US 7.

BERKSHIRE SCENIC RAILWAY MUSEUM

This **museum** (☎ 413-637-2210; Willow Creek Rd; admission free; ☙ 10am-4pm Sat & Sun May-Oct) of railroad lore is set up in Lenox's 1902 vintage railroad station. Its two elaborate model-railroad displays are favorites with kids. On summer weekends, **rides** (adult/senior/child 4-14 $13/11/8; 2½ hr roundtrip) on a 1950s diesel locomotive connect Lenox and Stockbridge.

The museum is 1.5 miles east of Lenox center, via Housatonic St.

SHAKESPEARE & COMPANY

Another equally enjoyable feature of a Berkshires summer is taking in a performance of one of the Bard's great plays by **Shakespeare & Co** (☎ 413-637-1199; www.shakespeare.org; 70 Kemble St; tickets $15-38; ☙ plays Tue-Sun). The repertoire also includes carefully selected contemporary plays. The summertime **Free Outside Bankside Festival** (☎ 413-637-3353) stages plays, demonstrations and talks that are – you guessed it – held outdoors at the south end of the property and free to all. The company is also in the process of building the world's first historically accurate replica of London's Rose Playhouse, complete with surrounding Elizabethan village.

Activities

Kennedy Park, just north of downtown Lenox on US 7, is popular with mountain bikers in the summer and cross-country skiers in the winter. The **Arcadian Shop** (☎ 413-637-3010; 91 Pittsfield Rd/US 7; ☙ 10am-6pm Mon-Sat, 11am-5pm Sun) rents mountain, road, and children's bikes ($35), kayaks ($35), skis ($11) and snowshoes ($15). Rates are per day.

PLEASANT VALLEY WILDERNESS SANCTUARY

This 1112-acre **wildlife sanctuary** (☎ 413-637-0320; 472 W Mountain Rd; adult/child $4/3; ☙ sunrise-sunset) has 7 miles of pleasant walking trails through forests of maples, oaks, beeches and birches. It's not uncommon to see beavers here if you come at dawn or dusk. A nature center is open daily, and you can arrange canoe trips on the Housatonic from here. To reach the sanctuary, go north on US 7 or MA 7A. Three-quarters of a mile north of the intersection of US 7 and MA 7A, turn left onto W Dugway Rd and go 1.5 miles to the sanctuary.

KRIPALU CENTER

Shadowbrook, the former summer home of Andrew Carnegie, overlooks Stockbridge Bowl and is now one of America's finest **yoga centers** (☎ 413-448-3400; www.kripalu.org; PO Box 793, West St/MA 183, Lenox MA 01240). Kripalu accommodates some 300 students, who come to study yoga, meditation and holistic therapies in a peaceful surrounding. You can't show up for a drop-in class – rather, look into a three-day 'retreat and renewal' program. Family programs are offered as well.

Sleeping

Lenox has no hotels and only a few motels, but does have lots of inns. Because of Tanglewood's weekend concerts, many inns require a two- or three-night minimum

TANGLEWOOD MUSIC FESTIVAL

In 1934 Boston Symphony Orchestra conductor Serge Koussevitzky's dream of a center for serious musical study came true with the acquisition of the 400-acre **Tanglewood Estate** (☎ 413-637-1600; 297 West St/MA 183, Lenox MA) in Lenox. People like Leonard Bernstein and Seiji Ozawa came to Tanglewood as young musicians to study at the side of the great masters.

Today, the Tanglewood Music Festival is among the most esteemed music events in the world. Symphony, pops, chamber music, recitals, jazz and blues are performed from late June through early September. Performance spaces include the 'Shed,' which is anything but – a 6000-seat concert shelter with several sides open to the surrounding lawns – and the Seiji Ozawa Concert Hall.

The Boston Symphony Orchestra concerts on Friday, Saturday and Sunday in July and August are the most popular events. Most casual attendees – up to 8000 of them – arrive three or four hours before concert time, staking out good listening spots on the lawn outside the Shed or the Concert Hall, then relaxing and enjoying elaborate picnics until the music starts.

Contemporary star performers include Midori, Itzhak Perlman, Anne-Sophie Mutter, Yo-Yo Ma and Andre Watts. Popular performers such as James Taylor, Harry Connick Jr, Wynton Marsalis (in jazz mode), the Joshua Redman Quartet and Dave Brubeck have given Tanglewood concerts.

The **visitor center** (☺ 10am-4pm Jul & Aug, Sat & Sun June & Sep-Oct) can help with any questions. The grounds are open year-round for strolling, with free walking tours being offered on Wednesdays at 10:30am and Saturdays at 1:30pm in summer.

Tickets

Tickets range from $16 per person for picnic space on the lawn to more than $90 for the best seats at the most popular concerts. If you hold lawn tickets and it rains, you get wet. There are no refunds or exchanges. At around $175, the Lawn Pass Pack earns you admission to any 11 performances, with a few exceptions. If you arrive about three hours before concert time, you can often get lawn space; Shed and Concert Hall seats should be bought in advance.

For information in fall or winter, call ☎ 617-266-1492 in Boston; otherwise, call Tanglewood directly at ☎ 413-637-1600. Tickets may be purchased at the box office at Tanglewood's main entrance on West St, online (www.bso.org) or through Ticketmaster, which can be reached at ☎ 413-733-2500 in the Berkshires and ☎ 800-347-0808 from other areas.

Children

Lawn tickets for children under 12 are free, thanks to a grant from the TDK company. An adult can score up to four free children's tickets per performance. Adults accompanying kids under five years old are asked to sit with them in the back half of the lawn, and kids this age aren't allowed in the Shed or the Seiji Ozawa Hall during concerts at all.

Eating

Many people pack picnics to eat on the lawn (wine allowed), or buy a prepacked basket available at the gourmet markets in the area.

With a few days' notice you can have a bagged lunch, boxed meal or picnic basket from the **Tanglewood Cafe** (☎ 413-637-5240), but this costs more than (and is not as enjoyable as) picking out your own goodies. The café also serves eat-in lunches. At the grille near the theatre, you'll find hamburger-and-pizza-type fare, and ice-cream and beverage vendors roam the grounds.

Getting There & Parking

Tanglewood is easy to find – just follow the car in front of you! From Lenox center, head west on West St/MA 183 for about a mile, and the main entrance will be on your left. Ample concert parking is available, but remember that parking – and, more importantly, unparking – 6000 cars can take time. It's all organized very well and runs smoothly, but you'll still have to wait a while in your car during the exodus. If your lodging is close, consider walking.

stay on Friday and Saturday nights in summer. That means a Lenox weekend can cost $300 to $500 just for lodging. Many thrifty travelers opt to sleep in lower-priced towns like Great Barrington. But if you can afford them, Lenox's inns provide charming digs and memorable stays. Log on to www.lenox .org for a list and links.

Most inn rooms have a private bath, and include a full breakfast and perhaps afternoon tea. Few Lenox inns accept children under 12, or pets. All lodgings below offer parking.

BUDGET & MIDRANGE

Walker House (☎ 413-637-1271; www.walkerhouse .com; 64 Walker St; d weekday/weekend $90-150/125-200; ✗) This inn, convenient to the town center, boasts the friendliest innkeepers in town, several cats, and an interesting doorstop collection. The eight rooms each have a private bathroom, and some have fireplaces. If the weather's frightful, stay in and watch a movie on their 12ft cinema screen.

Birchwood Inn (☎ 413-637-2600, 800-524-1646; www .birchwood-inn.com; 7 Hubbard St; r/ste $110-250/190-275; ✗) This mansard-roofed house dating from 1767 is now an accommodating inn with glorious views of the town. The 11 spacious rooms all have private bathrooms and about half feature fireplaces.

Village Inn (☎ 413-637-0020, 800-254-0917; www .villageinn-lenox.com; 16 Church St; d $65-265; ✗) This Federal-style inn, under new ownership, was built in 1771. It has 32 rooms of varying amenities and price, and its dining room serves a full breakfast and dinner.

Motel-wise, **Days Inn** (☎ 413-637-3560; 194 Pittsfield Rd; d $60-140) and **County Inn** (☎ 413-637-4244; www.county-inn.com; 130 Pittsfield Rd; d in summer $109-209; ✍) stand on US 7 outside the village to the east.

TOP END

Gateways Inn (☎ 413-637-2532; www.gatewaysinn .com; 51 Walker St; r/ste $100-295/230-450; ✗) This mansion was the home of Harley T Procter (of Procter & Gamble). He supposedly wanted the house to look like a bar of Ivory Soap. (Not even close.) Guestrooms are elegant and unfussy, and the inn owners are unfailingly gracious. Gay-friendly, too.

Stonover Farm B&B (☎ 413-637-9100; www.ston overfarm.com; 169 Undermountain Rd; ste/cottage $275-350/375-485; ✗) Tom and Suky Werman have converted this Berkshire cottage into a three-suite B&B groaning with unsurpassed, yet somehow casual, luxury. The Rock Cottage sits on a hill overlooking the duck pond. The B&B is just 2 miles from Lenox center.

Blantyre (☎ 413-637-3556; www.blantyre.com; Blantyre Rd; r/ste from $375/475; ✍) If money's no object, this is the place for you. This imitation Scottish Tudor mansion sits on 85 acres of grounds dotted with four tennis courts, croquet lawns, hot tub and sauna. Accommodations are available in 25 rooms, suites and cottages; continental breakfast is included. Three miles west of I-90 exit 2 along US 20.

Eating & Drinking

BUDGET

Carol's Restaurant (☎ 413-637-8948; 8 Franklin St; mains $4-8; ✍ 7am-4pm, closed Wed) This is where Old School meets New Age, where you can get a psychic reading with your morning pancakes. James Taylor's favorite omelette – stuffed with tomato, feta and spinach – is physically and spiritually satisfying.

Homer's Variety (☎ 413-637-2564; 35 Housatonic St; dishes $3-8; ✍ 6am-6pm) At this classic diner on Church St, you can sit with the locals at the counter, inhale some coffee and keep your travel budget intact (unless you can't tear yourself away from the huge gumball machine).

Lenox Coffee (☎ 413-637-1606; 52 Main St; ✍ 7am-7pm Mon-Sat, 8am-7pm Sun) The locals linger here over steaming bowls of café au lait.

Señor Chiles (☎ 413-637-2590; 9 Franklin St; mains $11-23; ✍ lunch & dinner) This taqueria-cum-pizzeria wins you over more by virtue of its cheerful decor than for anything resembling haute cuisine, but for reasonably priced – and reasonably good – pies and Mexican dishes (and cerveza to swill concurrently), it can't be beat.

Olde Heritage Tavern (☎ 413-637-0884; 12 Housatonic St; mains $7-13; ✍ 11am-10pm) If you're looking for the saloon in town, this is it. Unlike most of trim Lenox, the Heritage has a natural shagginess about both the interior and exterior of its 1860s-era building. Come for the jalapeño poppers, pool table and cheap drinks.

Nejaime's Wine Cellar (☎ 413-637-2221; 60 Main St; ✍ 9am-9pm Mon-Sat) You can order a Tanglewood picnic basket here ($35 to $40 for two people), or just pick up a few bottles and some gourmet cheeses to get started on your own creation. There's another **shop** (☎ 413-448-2274; 444 Pittsfield Rd/US 7) heading north out of town.

MID-RANGE & TOP END

Napa (☎ 413-637-3204; 30 Church St; dinner mains $13-19; ☽ lunch & dinner) Low-ceilinged and long-barred, Napa exudes a feeling of familiar welcome. Its brand of American cuisine leans heavily on Italy and Mexico, to creative effect. Try to snag a sidewalk seat.

Dish (☎ 413-637-1800; 37 Church St; dinner mains $16-22; ☽ breakfast & lunch, dinner Wed-Mon) When you want something beyond mere grub for breakfast, Dish dishes it out, with apple-stuffed French toast and frittatas bursting with veggies. The execution of the dinner mains at this bistro/café can be slightly uneven, but ask your server what's good that night and you shall be well guided. In the evening, the atmosphere can border on the boisterous.

Church St Café (☎ 413-637-2745; 65 Church St; mains lunch/dinner $11-15/20-29; ☽ lunch & dinner daily in summer, closed Sun & Mon rest of year) This bistro has made customers happy for years with its delicious, locally sourced food served on the deck and in the festive dining rooms hung with local art. Consider the Maine crab cakes with roasted new potatoes ($26). There's always at least one scrumptious, non-token vegetarian main.

Cafe Lucia (☎ 413-637-2640; 80 Church St; pastas/mains $14-26/22-36; ☽ dinner Tue-Sat) This romantic, homey café serves classic, Italian dinners. The osso bucco with risotto is a house specialty.

Bistro Zinc (☎ 413-637-8800; 56 Church St; mains $20-27; ☽ lunch & dinner, bar open late) Très hip. The postmodern decor here is all metal surfaces and light woods, with doors made of French wine crates. The tin ceiling and parquet floors add to the LA feel of this place. The cuisine features tempting New French offerings like lamb loin with baby carrots. Some feel the food is a tad overrated – you can always just slip in after dinner for a glass of wine and get the style points.

Gateways Inn & Restaurant (☎ 413-637-2532; 51 Walker St; dinner mains $24-30; ☽ lunch Sat & Sun, dinner daily, closed Mon in winter) Its elegant, terracotta-toned dining room is known as the place to go in town for an anniversary or birthday dinner. The rack of lamb is the chef's signature dish. Epicurean Tanglewood picnics for two are $50. At their bar and lounge **La Terrazza** you can get cocktails and a lighter meal while absorbing the same refined atmosphere.

Getting There & Away

The nearest airports are in Windsor Locks and in Albany. **Peter Pan Bus Lines** (☎ 800-343-9999) operates between Lenox and Boston ($36.50 one-way, four hours, 145 miles, one bus daily).

Trains stop in nearby Pittsfield. For Amtrak information, see p227. If you're driving, Lenox is 15 miles north of Lee and the same distance from I-90 on US 7.

PITTSFIELD

pop 46,000

Where the northern and southern Berkshires meet, Pittsfield is the service city of the entire region. The thanks it gets for its usefulness and practicality is a low score on the quaintness meter and lame jokes about the appropriateness of its name. This is where the trains stop and where one finds the biggest stores. Travelers pause here for the Hancock Shaker Village and the worthy Berkshire Museum. Opera lovers come to take in a performance of the Berkshire Opera Company.

Information & Orientation

Conveniently, the town is described by the intersection of East and West Sts (which are also US 7) and North and South Sts around Park Sq. The tourist information booth in the square is open daily during the summer, 9am to 5pm.

The **Berkshire Visitors Bureau** (☎ 413-443-9186, 800-237-5747; www.berkshires.org; ☽ 8:30am-5pm Mon-Fri) is inside the Berkshire Common building by the Crowne Plaza Hotel.

Sights

HANCOCK SHAKER VILLAGE

The Shakers were among the earliest of the numerous millennial Christian sects that flourished in the fertile climate of religious freedom in the New World. **Hancock Shaker Village** (☎ 413-443-0188; www.hancockshakervillage .org; US 20; adult/child under 18 $15/free; ☽ 9:30am-5pm), 5 miles west of Pittsfield on US 20, gives you a studied look at the peaceful, prayerful Shaker way of life.

The Hancock Shaker Village was known as the City of Peace and was occupied by

---

SHAKES OF ECSTASY

Adherents of the United Society of Believers in Christ's Second Appearing, founded in 1747, believed that their leader Ann Lee embodied Christ's reappearance on earth. Calling herself Mother Ann, she set sail for New York with eight devotees to set up a community in the New World. When she died, her followers went on to found Shaker communities all over northern New England, one of which, at Sabbathday Lake in Maine, survives to this day.

Followers of the sect strictly observed the principles of communal possessions, pacifism, open confession of sins, and equality – but celibacy – between the sexes. Worship services were characterized by a communal dancelike movement, during which some congregants would be overcome with religious zeal and suffer tremors ('shakes') of ecstasy.

With celibacy as a tenet, Shakerism depended upon conversion for its growth and sustenance. Converts to the church turned over all their worldly possessions to the movement and worked selflessly on its behalf, although members were free to leave at any time. Each community was organized into 'families' of 30 to 90 members, who lived and worked together. Though there was equality of the sexes, there was also a good deal of segregation. For instance, besides remaining celibate, men and women even used separate staircases and ate at opposite ends of the dining room. Communities were largely self-sufficient, trading produce and handicrafts with the rest of the world for the things they could not produce themselves. Work, among Shakers, was considered a consecrated act, an attitude reflected in the high quality of workmanship and design of Shaker furniture and crafts. In effect, every product was a prayer.

Shakers until 1960. At its peak in 1830, the community numbered some 300 souls. Preserved as a historic monument, the village still gives you an insightful look at what the work-focused principles of Shakerism accomplished.

Twenty of the original buildings at Hancock Shaker Village are carefully restored and are open to view. Most famous is the **Round Stone Barn** (1826), but other structures, including the **Brick Dwelling** (1830), the **laundry** and the **machine shop** (1790), the **trustees' office** (1830–95), the **meetinghouse** (1793) and the **sisters'** and **brethren's shops** (1795) are of equal interest.

During the summer, visitors wander around on their own and interpreters in the historic buildings demonstrate the Shaker way of life. The rest of the year, guided tours are given nearly daily between 10am and 3pm. Call for details and reservations.

From Pittsfield center take US 20 southwest. The village is near the intersection with MA 41 (not in the village of Hancock).

BERKSHIRE MUSEUM

Pittsfield's major repository of art, history and natural science is the notable **Berkshire Museum** (☎ 413-443-7171; 39 South St/US 7 just south of Park Sq; adult/senior & student/child 3-18 $7.50/6/4.50; ⏰ 10am-5pm Mon-Sat, noon-5pm Sun). The museum's painting collection holds an impressive number of Hudson River School landscapes and several works by Norman Rockwell, in case you missed his museum in Stockbridge. Children will especially like the Mineral Gallery, where they can try out a Geiger counter, and the aquarium complete with touch tank. The history collections are strong in regional artifacts, tools, firearms, dolls and costumes. A highlight for both young kids and their parents is the collection of Alexander Calder playthings, created by the famous artist when he was earning money as a toy maker. Replicas are set out for all to play with.

MELVILLE'S ARROWHEAD

Novelist Herman Melville (1819–91) lived in Pittsfield from 1850 to 1863. Melville moved to Pittsfield to work on a farm so he could support himself while he wrote. It was here, in the house he called **Arrowhead** (☎ 413-442-1793; 780 Holmes Rd; adult/senior/child 6-16 $10/5/3; ⏰ 9:30am-5pm May-Oct), that he wrote his masterpiece, *Moby-Dick*.

Inspired by the view of Mt Greylock in winter, which supposedly reminded him of a whale, Melville completed the 600-plus pages of *Moby-Dick* in less than a year. The house is now a museum maintained by the Berkshire County Historical Society and is open for visits and guided tours. Call for information on tours in the off-season. To get there from Pittsfield, head south on US 7, and take a left onto Holmes Rd at the Pittsfield/Lenox line.

Sleeping & Eating

Pittsfield has the usual selection of business-oriented hotels and motels for a city of its size. Most visitors prefer to stay in one of the more hip or historical communities such as Lenox (p265), Great Barrington (p259) or Williamstown (p272). If you plan to stop, there are plenty of places to pick up a quick meal on North and South Sts/US 7 as you pass through or around Park Sq.

Elizabeth's (☎ 413-448-8244; 1264 East St; mains $11-18; ☽ dinner Wed-Sun) Not only the best eatery in town, but it's on the short list of the best in the Berkshires. Don't be put off by its location across the street from a vacant General Electric plant, nor by its deceptively casual interior – chefs travel from New York and Boston to sample Tom and Elizabeth Ellis' innovative dishes. Salads are generously sized and bursting with fresh goodness, and the pasta of the day is often something as imaginative as linguine with clam sauce infused with Thai spices (lemongrass and ginger). Elizabeth's is a blue-porched house on the right-hand side, about 2 miles down East St. When the road jogs, stay right (not over the bridge).

Getting There & Away

The nearest airports are **Bradley International** (☎ 860-292-2000) in Windsor Locks and **Albany International** (www.albanyairport.com) in Albany, NY. As of late 2004, there were no public bus lines linking either of these airports with Pittsfield. From Bradley airport, one option is to take the private **Valley Transporter** (☎ 413-253-1350, 800-872-8752; www .valleytransporter .com) to Springfield and then take a **Peter Pan bus** (☎ 800-343-9999) to Pittsfield. From Albany airport, you can take the CDTA's Shutterfly bus into downtown and then catch a **Bonanza bus** (☎ 800-556-3815) for the hour-long ride to Pittsfield.

Pittsfield is 7 miles north of Lenox on US 7 at the intersection with MA 9. It's 57 miles southeast of Albany and 143 miles north of New York City. **Peter Pan** buses operate out of the **Pittsfield Bus Terminal** (☎ 413-442-4451; 57 S Church St) and connect Pittsfield with Albany ($14.50 one-way, one hour, 82 miles, one bus daily); Amherst ($21.50 one-way, three hours, 82 miles, one bus daily); Boston

DETOUR: CRANE MUSEUM OF PAPERMAKING

Since 1879 every single American bill has been printed on paper made by the Crane Company, based in the small mill town of Dalton. This 'Champagne of papers' is made from 100% cotton rag rather than wood, and so is wonderfully strong and creamy as well as environmentally sound. The **museum** (☎ 413-684-6481; Housatonic St, Dalton; admission free; ☽ 2-5pm Mon-Fri Jun-Oct), housed in the original stone mill room built in 1844, traces the history of Zenas Crane's enterprise, which is still family-run after seven generations. The videos – on Crane's papermaking process and on counterfeit detection – are fascinating. Though the museum is free, be sure to bring your wallet in so you can check your bills for authenticity.

To get here from Pittsfield, take MA 9 east for 5 miles. Follow signs for the museum, which will be the small, ivy-covered building furthest to the right from where you park.

($36.50 one-way, 3½ hours, 145 miles, one bus daily); Hartford ($25 one-way, 2½ hours, 84 miles, one bus daily) and New Haven, CT ($36.50 one-way, three hours, 102 miles); Lee ($11 one-way, 30 minutes, 11 miles, one bus daily); Lenox ($9 one-way, 15 minutes, 7 miles, one bus daily); Springfield ($16 one-way, 1½ hours, 56 miles, one bus daily); and Worcester ($29 one-way, 3½ hours, 106 miles, one bus a day), among others.

Bonanza Bus Lines runs daily buses between New York City and Williamstown through Torrington, CT, and Pittsfield. The ride between New York City and Pittsfield takes about four hours.

For **Amtrak** train information, see p227.

WILLIAMSTOWN & NORTH ADAMS
pop 8500

Williamstown lies at the heart of the Purple Valley, so named because the surrounding mountains often seem shrouded in a lavender veil at dusk. Though tucked into the extreme northwestern corner of Massachusetts and thus far from university-strewn Boston or the college-crowded Pioneer Valley, the town qualifies as an academic and artistic enclave par excellence. Williams College is consistently ranked at the tippy-top of the list of the country's best liberal arts schools, and Bennington College is only 30 minutes north in Vermont. Though residents also take pride in their pair of stellar art museums and one of the most respected summer theater festivals in the nation, all this culture hasn't gone to their heads – people really do smile and say hello as you walk down the street.

Orientation & Information

US 7 and MA 2/Main St intersect on the western side of town. The small central commercial district is off Main St on Spring St. Other businesses, including motels, are on US 7 and MA 2 on the outskirts of town. The marble-and-brick buildings of Williams College fill the town center.

In the summer, the **Williamstown Board of Trade** (☎ 413-458-9077; PO Box 357, Williamstown, MA 01267) operates a self-service information booth at the intersection of MA 2 and US 7, a short distance from the Williams Inn.

The **Northern Berkshire Chamber of Commerce** (☎ 413-663-3735; www.nberkshirechamber.com; in the Windsor Mill, Union St/MA 2, North Adams, MA 01247; ⏲ 9am-5pm Mon-Fri) is another information source.

The **Milne Library** (1095 Main St/MA 2; ⏲ 10am-5:30pm Mon-Fri, 10am-4pm Sat), across the street from the Williams Inn, has Internet and wireless access.

Water St Books (☎ 413-458-0249; 26 Water St; ⏲ 9:30am-6pm Mon-Sat, noon-5pm Sun) is the Williams College bookstore, with a friendly staff that know both books and the area.

Sights & Activities

CLARK ART INSTITUTE

The **Sterling & Francine Clark Art Institute** (☎ 413-458-9545; 225 South St; admission Jun-Oct/Nov-May $10/free; ⏲ 10am-5pm Tue-Sun, open Mon Jul & Aug only) is a gem among US art museums. Even if you're not an avid art lover, don't miss it.

Robert Sterling Clark (1877–1956), a Yale engineer whose family had made money in the sewing machine industry, began collecting art in Paris in 1912. He and his wife eventually housed their wonderful collection in Williamstown in a white marble temple built expressly for the purpose. The collections are particularly strong in the Impressionists. Mary Cassatt, Winslow Homer and John Singer Sargent represent contemporary American painting. From earlier centuries, there are excellent works

by Hans Memling, Jean-Honoré Fragonard and Francisco de Goya. One of the most well-known sculptures on display is Degas' famous *Little Dancer of Fourteen Years*.

The institute is less than a mile south of the information booth at the intersection of US 7 and MA 2.

WILLIAMS COLLEGE

When Henry David Thoreau visited the college in 1844, he remarked that 'it would be no small advantage if every college were thus located at the base of a mountain.'

If you take one of the several daily tours leaving from the **admissions office** (☎ 413-597-2211; 333 Stetson Ct), you'll learn why the Williams mascot is a purple cow and how the class of 1887 came to be the first in the nation to wear caps and gowns during commencement.

WILLIAMS COLLEGE MUSEUM OF ART

The Clark Art Institute's sister museum is the excellent **Williams College Museum of Art** (☎ 413-597-2429; www.wcma.org; Main St btwn Water St & Spring St; admission free; ⏲ 10am-5pm Tue-Sat, 1-5pm Sun). Around half of its 12,000 pieces comprise the American Collection, with substantial works by notables such as Edward Hopper (his *Morning in a City* is haunting), Winslow Homer and Grand Wood, to name only a few. The photography collection is equally strong, with representation by Diane Arbus, Man Ray and Alfred Stieglitz. The

---

DETOUR: MASSACHUSETTS MUSEUM OF CONTEMPORARY ART

MASS MoCA (☎ 413-662-2111; www.massmoca.org; 87 Marshall St, North Adams; adult/student/child 6-16 $10/8/4; ☯ 10am-6pm Jul-Aug, 11am-5pm Wed-Mon Sep-Jun) is just an art gallery like Los Angeles is just a city.

The museum's property sprawls over 13 acres of downtown North Adams, or about one-third of the town's entire business district. After the Sprague Electric Company packed up in 1985, more than $31 million was spent to modernize the property into 'the largest gallery in the United States,' which now encompasses 220,000 sq ft over five buildings, including art construction areas, performance centers and 19 galleries. The spaces are huge; one is the size of a football field, large enough to exhibit Robert Rauschenberg's The 1/4 Mile or 2 Furlong Piece, exhibited at the museum's opening in 1999.

In addition to carrying the bread-and-butter rotation of description-defying installation pieces, the museum has evolved into one of the region's key venues for world music, documentary films, lectures and avant-garde dance performances. The very air here seems to drip with creative impulse – someone's even done a photo series of the restrooms.

---

pieces hailing from ancient and medieval cultures are less numerous but equally distinguished. The museum also hosts traveling exhibits and stages its own with works from community and regional artists.

To find the museum, look for the huge bronze eyes embedded in the front lawn on Main St.

CYCLING & HIKING

Williamstown and environs, with rolling farmland and quiet country roads, are excellent for biking. Route 43, along the Green River, is one of the prettier roads. The **Mountain Goat** (☎ 413-458-8445; 130 Water St; bikes per day $25; ☯ 10am-6pm Mon-Sat, noon-5pm Sun) rents bicycles as well as hiking, camping and fly fishing gear. They also sponsor free weekly hikes.

When Boston and Main Railroad gave up on the corridor between Lanesborough and Adams in 1990, citizens agitated to have it recast as a universally accessible walk/bike path, and thus the 11-mile **Ashuwillticook Rail Trail** (☎ 413-442-8928) was born. The trail closely follows the Hoosic River and the Cheshire Reservoir through glorious wetlands, with many benches along the way and a handful of rest facilities. The southern access is by the Berkshire Mall at the intersection of MA 9 and MA 8 between Pittsfield and Dalton, and parking is available at both ends.

Festivals & Events

Shining stars of the theater world descend upon small Williamstown every year from the third week in June to the third week in August. Lest you think that 'summer theater' implies a fluffiness à la 'summer reading,' know that in 2002 the **Williamstown Theatre Festival** (☎ 413-597-3399, tickets 413-597-3400; www.wtfestival.org; PO Box 517, Williamstown, MA 01267) received the Regional Theatre Tony Award, the first summer theater to have ever won it.

The festival mounts the region's major theatrical offerings, and tickets are usually inexpensive. Kevin Kline, Richard Dreyfuss and Gwyneth Paltrow are but a few of the well-known thespians who have performed here. Besides the offerings on the Main Stage and Nikos Stage, there are cabaret performances in area restaurants and a family-oriented free festival runs for two weeks on the campus of the Buxton School.

Sleeping
BUDGET

It's possible to camp in a number of places at **Mt Greylock State Reservation** (☎ 413-499-4262, 877-422-6762; sites $6). The 35 campsites near scenic Stoney Ledge should be your first choice.

If you follow MA 8 north from North Adams, you'll get to **Clarksburg State Park** (☎ 413-664-8345, 877-422-6762; 1199 Middle Rd; sites $12). There are 50 campsites near the lovely and swimmable Mauserts Pond. There are pit toilets but no showers.

South on MA 8 and east on MA 116 is **Savoy Mountain State Forest** (☎ 413-663-8469; Central Shaft Rd/MA 116; campsite/cabin $12/25) This wooded campground has 45 sites, some of which may be reserved in advance, and four very rustic log cabins. There are showers and flush toilets. This is one of the best state parks for mountain biking.

MID-RANGE

River Bend Farm B&B (☎ 413-458-3121; 643 Simmons Rd; d $80-130; ✗) A Georgian tavern since revolutionary times, River Bend Farm owes its careful and authentic restoration to hosts Judy and Dave Looms. Four doubles share two bathrooms here. Just off US 7 on the north side of the little bridge over the Hoosic River, it's a favorite among European travelers. No credit cards accepted, and they're closed October through March.

Steep Acres Farm B&B (☎ 413-458-3774; 520 White Oaks Rd; d $100-160; ✗) The gregarious Gangemi family welcomes travelers to their 30-acre hilltop farm just 2 miles north of Williamstown. From here you get spectacular views of both the Berkshires and the Green Mountains of Vermont. Furnishings and decor feature a 'country' motif (simple elegance), and three of the four rooms have a private bathroom. Kick back at the trout and swimming ponds (complete with beach toys). Reserve *far in advance*.

Williamstown B&B (☎ 413-458-9202; www.williamstownbandb.com; 30 Cold Spring Rd; d with bathroom $100-200; ✗) This meticulously maintained, four-room Victorian B&B has the perfect porch from which to watch the town stroll by. All rooms have a private bathroom, and breakfast is a lovely production. No credit cards accepted – checks are, though.

House on Main St (☎ 413-458-3031; www.houseonmainstreet.com; 1120 W Main St; d incl breakfast $85-150; ✗) This Victorian near the center of town was once owned by the daughter of President Woodrow Wilson. There are six medium-sized rooms (three with private bathrooms and some with TV), and the owners cater to those with food allergies or other dietary restrictions.

You'll find a score of hotels and motels on the outskirts of town on MA 2 East US 7 North.

Northside Motel (☎ 413-458-8107; 45 North St/MA 7; d $75-105; 🖵) This well-run, 30-room motel is very near the information booth, the museums and the center of town.

Maple Terrace Motel (☎ 413-458-9677; www.mapleterrace.com; 555 Main St; d $82-144; 🖵) A small, 15-room place on the outskirts to the east of town, the Maple Terrace is a big old house with motel units behind it. In winter ask about discounted lift tickets to Jiminy Peak ski resort.

MT GREYLOCK STATE RESERVATION

At a modest 3491ft, the state's highest peak can't hold a candle altitude-wise to its western counterparts, but a climb up the 92ft-high War Veterans Memorial Tower at its summit rewards you with a panorama stretching up to 100 verdant miles, across the Taconic, Housatonic and Catskill ranges, and over five states. The mountain sits in an 18-sq-mile forest of fir, beech, birch, maple, oak and spruce that also includes Mt Prospect, Mt Fitch, Mt Williams and Saddle Ball Mt. Wildlife includes bears, bobcats, deer, porcupines, raccoons and birds such as hawks, grouse, thrushes, ravens and wild turkeys. Even if the weather seems drab from the foot, a trip to the summit may well lift you above the gray blanket, and the view with a layer of cloud floating between tree line and sky is simply magical.

The **Mt Greylock State Reservation** (☎ 413-499-4262, 877-422-6762) has some 45 miles of hiking trails, including a portion of the Appalachian Trail. Frequent trail pulloffs on the road up – including some that lead to waterfalls – make it easy to get at least a little hike in before reaching the top. Several state parks have campsites (see opposite). The **Hopper** is a stunning V-shaped wedge of 200-year-old spruce trees that fills a valley between Mts Greylock, Williams and Prospect and Stoney Ledge.

Bascom Lodge (☎ 413-743-1591; 1 Summit Rd; dm/r $36/$98; mid-May–mid-Oct), a truly rustic mountain hostelry, was built as a federal work project in the 1930s at the summit of Mt Greylock. It can provide beds for 34 people, and hearty meals are available, though not included in the price. Reservations are essential.

You can get to Greylock from either Lanesborough (follow the signs 2 miles north of town) or North Adams (from MA 2 west, and again, follow the signs). Either way, it's 10 slow miles to the summit. The Greylock **visitor center** (☎ 413-743-1591; ☉ 9am-4pm) is halfway up via the Lanesborough route. There's a $2 fee to park at the summit.

CENTRAL MASSACHUSETTS & THE BERKSHIRES

TOP END

Most of these have a two-night minimum on Friday and Saturday nights and some require a three-night stay on holidays and during special college events.

Williams Inn (☎ 413-458-9371, 800-828-0133; www .williamsinn.com; 1090 Main St; r/ste $135-220/375-500; ☒ ⬛) Right on the green, this inn is Williamstown's major hotel. Its 125 rooms have luxury-hotel comforts, though more rooms with more charm can be found at area B&Bs. The public areas offer wireless Internet access and the full-service restaurant is quite good.

Guest House at Field Farm (☎ 413-458-3135; www .thetrustees.org; 554 Sloan Rd; r/ste incl breakfast $150-225/250; ☒ ⬛) This was the country estate of Lawrence and Eleanore Bloedel, collectors of 20th-century art. Built in 1948, in spare, clean-lined post-WWII style on 300 wooded acres facing Mt Greylock, the estate was willed to the Trustees of Reservations, which now operates it. All five rooms are done up in modern style and have private bathrooms with plush bathrobes ready and waiting. Some rooms feature fireplaces and private patios. The property also boasts a pond, 4 miles of walking trails and tennis courts.

Harbour House Inn (☎ 413-743-8959; www.harbour houseinn.com; 725 N State Rd/US 8, Cheshire; d incl breakfast $100-165; ☒) This seven-room inn is about 15 miles southeast from Williamstown and 17 miles north from Lenox, but it's worth mentioning because of its spectacular location, on the back side of Mt Greylock. Part of a 200-year-old farm, the Harbor House is now an elegant manor house. The three-room, third-floor Summit View suite ($250) lives up to its name.

Eating & Drinking

For coffee or a light meal, wander along Spring St, the main shopping street. Other areas of town, notably Water St, have restaurants serving more substantial lunches and dinners.

Pappa Charlie's Deli (☎ 413-458-5969; 28 Spring St; dishes $4-6; ☒ 8am-8pm) Here's a welcoming breakfast spot where locals really do ask for 'the usual.' The stars themselves created the lunch sandwiches that bear their names. The Richard Dreyfuss is a thick pastrami and provolone number. Or order a Politician and get anything you want on

it. Downstairs is an organic juice and cof fee bar.

Hot Tomatoes Pizza (☎ 413-458-2722; 100 Water St small/large $7-12/12-19; ☒ lunch & dinner summer, close Sun rest of year) Simply the best pizza in town You won't find any sad-looking salads or second-rate pastas here – these folks stick to what they know best: thin-crust Neapolitan-style pizzas. It's take-out only, but you can head to the riverside picnic tables in the back yard.

Tunnel City Coffee (☎ 413-458-5010; 100 Spring St; ☒ 7am-6pm) A bustling den of cramming students and mentoring professors. Besides liquid caffeine, some seriously delicious desserts like triple-layer mousse cake will get you buzzing. The shop's name is a reference to North Adams, where the beans are roasted.

Lickety Split (☎ 413-458-1818; 69 Spring St; items $3-7; ☒ 11am-6pm) Check out this spot for homemade ice-cream, soups, sandwiches and coffee. Watch the world go by from the front bay window. There's another location at MASS MoCA (p272).

Water St Grill (☎ 413-458-2175; 123 Water St; mains $12-18; ☒ 11:30am-11pm, bar until 1am) Here's a large restaurant that features moderately priced steaks, seafood and a handful of fajitas and tacos. The popular luncheon buffet is only $7. The Grill is open late, so it's a good choice in summer after a play.

Mezze Bistro & Bar (☎ 413-458-0123; 16 Water St; mains $22-25; ☒ dinner) This chic eatery decorated with touches of red velvet is your best bet for glimpsing actors from the Williamstown Theatre after a performance. Roasted red snapper with creamed corn and chanterelles is one of the more American-style mains. Later at night, it's the closest Williamstown gets to having a gay bar.

Hobson's Choice (☎ 413-458-9101; 159 Water St; dinner mains $12-20; ☒ lunch & dinner) Just down the street from the Water St Grill, Hobson's has a down-home feel, complete with country tunes over the stereo system. Soups and sandwiches for lunch are served in cozy booths. Dinner mains include grilled chicken and seafood pasta. The menu warns, 'We cook with wine. Sometimes we even put it in the food.'

Entertainment

During the academic year, call **Concertline** (☎ 413-597-3146) of the Williams College

Department of Music for information on concerts, recitals and performances.

In the summer the **Williamstown Chamber Concerts** (☎ 413-458-8273; tickets $15-22) group stages concerts at the Clark Art Institute.

Images Cinema (☎ 413-458-5612; www.images cinema.org; 50 Spring St; adult/senior & student $8/6) is a single-screen, non-profit arts institution and it's *the* place to catch indie and foreign flicks.

Getting There & Away

Williamstown's bus station is in the lobby of the **Williams Inn** (☎ 413-458-2665), on Main St close to the intersection of US 7 and MA 2.

Bonanza Bus Lines (☎ 800-556-3815) runs two buses daily between Williamstown and NYC ($38.50 one-way), with transfers in Springfield and Pittsfield.

Boston lies 145 miles to the east; Lenox is 29 miles south on US 7.

Rhode Island

HIGHLIGHTS

■ **Most Powerful Ice-Cream**
Heading to Gray's Ice Cream (p296) for goods so delicious that desperate loyalists pay top dollar to have it packed in dry ice and shipped across state lines

■ **Top Café**
Drinking espressos at the Cable Car Cinema (p287), whose pleasant outdoor tables have nurtured many a Providence hipster

■ **Best Summertime Day Trip**
Catching the ferry to Block Island (p302) to be charmed by a pristine, windswept island teeming with birds, beaches and beachgoers

■ **Largest Blue Termite**
Waving at the 2-ton rooftop monolith of Nibbles Woodaway (p277) as you drive south from Providence on I-95

■ **Best Walk**
Strolling along Newport's famed Cliff Walk (p291) and alternatively admiring the looming forms of Vanderbilt-era mansions and a sweeping view of the Atlantic

RHODE ISLAND

■ TELEPHONE CODE: 401 ■ POPULATION: 1.05 MILLION ■ AREA: 1045 SQ MILES

Get ready for clam cakes, quahogs and sand in your sandwiches. Rhode Island and its 400 miles of stellar beaches have attracted desperate citizens from neighboring states since the 19th century. These wayward neighbors come not only for the long, sweeping beaches for which the South County of Rhode Island is correctly famous, but also for the long, sweeping beaches of Sakonnet Point, Block Island and Newport. In its fortuitous position south of Cape Cod's generous arm, Rhode Island is protected from Arctic currents, making the Atlantic here blissfully warmer than at Massachusetts or Maine. Stick that in your Tea Party!

The US's tiniest state features two wonderful cities, both only slightly in from the shore. With its sumptuous Vanderbilt-era mansions and lively summer nightlife, ye olde Newport offers travelers world-renowned summer festivals and scores of 19th-century B&Bs. Those seeking a more cosmopolitan adventure should look to Providence, the region's cultural capital. Here, you'll explore the quiet 18th-century streetscapes of the East Side, catch a play at a top-notch theater, wander through the Italian Federal Hill, bike in solitude along an old rail line or have your shoes stick to the floor in a rock club's bathroom. A large student population afforded by the presence of Brown University and the Rhode Island School of Design enlivens the scene.

Climate

Like Massachusetts (MA) and Connecticut (CT), Rhode Island (RI) experiences muggy, hot summers. The state enjoys a coastal climate, which partially mitigates summertime heat in places adjacent to the ocean. In cooler months, Rhode Island's southern locale makes it much warmer than the northern states. Thus the autumn leaves turn a few weeks later than in Vermont.

State & Regional Parks

As Rhode Island is a tiny state only 30 miles wide, it hasn't the space to contain very many parks, and those parks that exist aren't very large. Contact the **Rhode Island Division of Parks & Recreation** (☎ 401-222-2321; www.riparks.com) for more information.

The Rhode Island Division of Parks & Recreation manages a collection of beaches (see p307) facing the Atlantic Ocean. These are concentrated in South County. The department has also developed a series of scenic bicycle trails that crisscross the state, often following old rail lines. These trails are free of automobile traffic. For route information and maps visit the website of the **Rhode Island Department of Transportation** (www.dot.state.ri.us/WebTran/bikeri.html).

Block Island, dubbed 'one of the last great places in the Western Hemisphere' by the Nature Conservancy, enjoys excellent bird sanctuaries and wildlife preserves. Here, about 25 miles of trails wind past undisturbed brush, wildflowers and nesting birds.

Getting There & Around

Most people arrive by car. I-95 cuts diagonally across the state, providing easy access from coastal Connecticut to the south and Boston to the north. If you're coming from Worcester, you should take Rte 146 to Providence. Distances are not great – it takes less than an hour to drive through Rhode Island on I-95. The state's major airport, TF Green State Airport (see p288) in Warwick, is a 20-minute drive from downtown Providence (if you take I-95 you'll encounter a big-ass blue termite made of wire mesh and fiberglass that's been a state icon since 1980, appearing on lottery tickets and in the movie *Dumb and Dumber*), and a 45-minute drive from Newport.

Providence has excellent bus and train connections to Boston and New York.

PROVIDENCE

pop 176,000

Rhode Island's capital city (and New England's second largest after Boston), Providence presents its visitors with some of the finest urban strolling this side of the

RHODE ISLAND

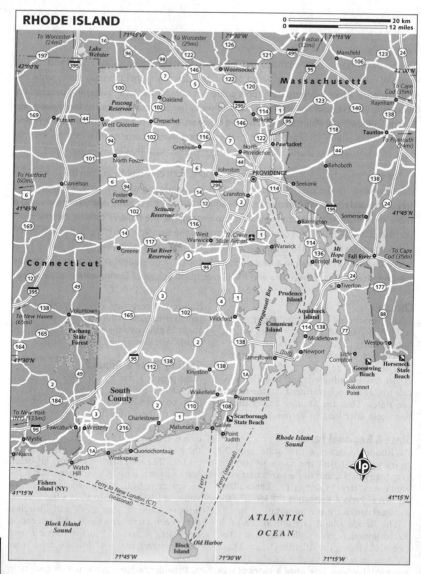

RHODE ISLAND

Connecticut River. In the crisp air and falling leaves of autumn, wander through Brown University's green campus, surrounded by imposing buildings of collegiate Gothic design, explore the 18th-century neighborhood that surrounds it and follow the Riverwalk into downtown. Along the way you'll have opportunities to lounge in the sidewalk café of an art-house theater, dine in some stellar restaurants and knock back a few pints in a red-lit bar favored by Rhode Island School of Design (RISD) students. At night, take in a play at the esteemed Trinity Repertory, pass out in a club or eat some 3am burgers aboard the mobile Haven Bros Diner (p285).

Providence contains a plethora of high-profile universities and colleges, and a correspondingly large student population, helping to keep the city's social and arts scenes lively and current. The most notable of these schools are Brown University and the RISD. The existence of Johnson & Wales University, one of the nation's best culinary arts programs, ensures that you'll always find excellent restaurants in all price ranges throughout the city.

Orientation

Providence is situated at the head of Narragansett Bay astride two rivers, the Moshassuck and the Woonasquatucket, which merge at Waterplace Park to form the Providence River. Surrounding Providence are the populous bedroom suburbs of Warwick, Cranston, Johnston, Pawtucket and East Providence.

I-95 is the primary north–south artery through Providence, with I-195 splitting from it eastward toward Cape Cod. Take exit 22 (Downtown) from I-95 or the Wickenden St exit from I-195 to reach Kennedy Plaza and the Amtrak train station. For the Italian neighborhood and restaurant district of Federal Hill, take exit 21 of I-95 (Atwells Ave/Broadway).

Kennedy Plaza, with the Providence Biltmore hotel and City Hall on its southwestern side, is the center of the city. North of Kennedy Plaza is the Rhode Island state capitol, called the State House, on its hilltop perch.

East of the Providence River is the East Side, marked by College Hill and its wealth of 18th- and 19th-century buildings, plus RISD and Brown University. Federal Hill, the Italian neighborhood to the west, has dozens of good restaurants, pastry shops and taverns along its main axis, Atwells Ave.

The heart of the city is a surprisingly compact area, and you'll get more of the flavor of Providence on foot than you will in a car. Remember to look up! Many of downtown's most architecturally interesting building facades are several stories above street level.

MAPS

For maps and a small selection of guidebooks, try the **Map Center** (☎ 401-421-2184; 671 N Main St; 🕒 9:30am-5:30pm Mon-Fri, 9:30am-1:30pm Sat), just north of downtown.

Information

BOOKSTORES

Brown University Bookstore (☎ 401-863-3168; 244 Thayer St; 🕒 9am-6pm Mon-Fri, 10am-6pm Sat, 11am-5pm Sun) This is the city's most comprehensive bookstore.
Cellar Stories (☎ 401-521-2665; 111 Mathewson St) The tall dusty stacks of this classic are crammed full of used books.

EMERGENCY

Police & Fire Headquarters (☎ emergency 401-272-1111, nonemergency 401-272-3121; 325 Washington St; 🕒 24hr) Should your kitten get stuck, the city's finest will retrieve it.

INTERNET ACCESS

Kinko's (☎ 401-273-2830; 236 Meeting St; 🕒 24hr) Yeah, it's not a charming café, but it also doesn't close.

MEDIA

The daily newspaper for Providence and indeed all of Rhode Island is the **Providence Journal** (www.projo.com). 'Lifebeat,' a daily arts and entertainment section, includes listings of performances and events; the Thursday edition carries an expanded weekend listings section called 'Live.'

The Providence *Phoenix*, which appears Thursday, is the city's free alternative weekly, with nightclub listings and reviews. Find it in record stores, bookstores and cafés on Thayer and Wickenden Sts.

MONEY

Withdrawing money is easy as cake. Fleet maintains an ATM in the Intermodal Transportation Center and a branch office at 100 Washington St. You'll also find ATMs on Atwells Ave and Thayer St.

MEDICAL SERVICES

Rhode Island Hospital (☎ 401-444-4000; 593 Eddy St; 🕒 24hr) South of the center near I-95 exit 19, this is the region's best hospital.

POST

Downtown Post Office (☎ 800-275-8777; 2 Exchange Tce; 🕒 9am-5pm Mon-Fri)
East Side Post Office (☎ 800-275-8777; 306 Thayer St; 🕒 8am-5pm Mon-Fri, 8am-2pm Sat)

TOURIST INFORMATION

Rhode Island Tourism Division (☎ 401-222-2601, 800-556-2484; www.visitrhodeisland.com; 1 W Exchange St, Providence, RI 02903; 🕒 8:30am-4:30pm weekdays)

www.lonelyplanet.com

PROVIDENCE

0 — 500 m
0 — 0.3 miles

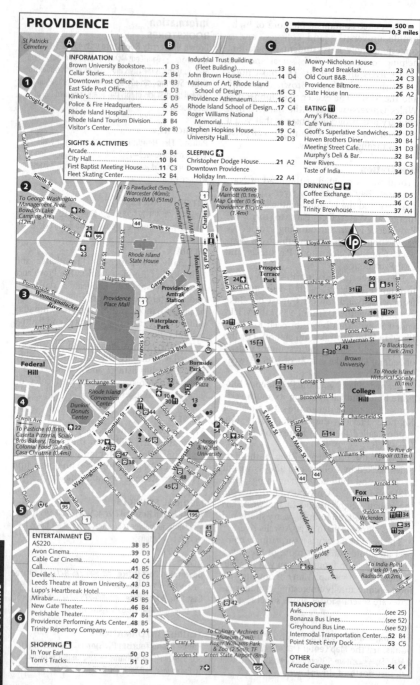

INFORMATION
Brown University Bookstore....................1 D3
Cellar Stories..2 B4
Downtown Post Office.............................3 B3
East Side Post Office................................4 D3
Kinko's...5 D3
Police & Fire Headquarters.......................6 A5
Rhode Island Hospital...............................7 B6
Rhode Island Tourism Division..................8 B4
Visitor's Center.................................(see 8)

SIGHTS & ACTIVITIES
Arcade..9 B4
City Hall..10 B4
First Baptist Meeting House......................11 C3
Fleet Skating Center................................12 B4

Industrial Trust Building
(Fleet Building)..................................13 B4
John Brown House...................................14 D4
Museum of Art, Rhode Island
School of Design................................15 C3
Providence Athenaeum............................16 C4
Rhode Island School of Design...17 C4
Roger Williams National
Memorial...18 B2
Stephen Hopkins House............................19 C4
University Hall...20 D3

SLEEPING
Christopher Dodge House.........................21 A2
Downtown Providence
Holiday Inn..22 A4

Mowry-Nicholson House
Bed and Breakfast..............................23 A3
Old Court B&B..24 C3
Providence Biltmore.................................25 B4
State House Inn.......................................26 A2

EATING
Amy's Place...27 D5
Cafe Yuni..28 D5
Geoff's Superlative Sandwiches...29 D3
Haven Brothers Diner...............................30 B4
Meeting Street Cafe.................................31 D3
Murphy's Deli & Bar.................................32 B4
New Rivers..33 C3
Taste of India..34 D5

DRINKING
Coffee Exchange.....................................35 D5
Red Fez..36 C4
Trinity Brewhouse....................................37 A4

St Patricks
Cemetery

Douglas Ave

Canada St

Smith St

To Pawtucket (5mi);
Worcester (40mi);
Boston (MA) (51mi)

To George Washington
Management Area,
Bowdish Lake
Camping Area
(12mi)

W Park St

Jewett St

Holden St

Park St

Smith St

Francis St

Rhode Island
State House

Canal St

Amtrak/MBTA
Commuter
Rail

N Main St
North Ct

Moshassuck River

Pratt St

Prospect St

To Providence
Marriott (0.1mi);
Map Center (0.5mi);
Providence Bicycle
(1.4mi)

Lloyd Ave

Bowen St

Prospect
Terrace
Park

Cushing St

Meeting St

Olive St

Angell St

Hope St

Brown St

Promenade St

Woonasquatucket
River

Amtrak

Hayes St

Gaspee St

Providence
Amtrak
Station

Providence
Place Mall

Exchange St

Waterplace
Park

Thomas St

Steeple St

Memorial Blvd

Burnside
Park

Exchange Terr

Kennedy
Plaza

Francis St

College St

Fones Alley

Waterman St

To Blackstone
Park (2mi)

Brown
University

To Rhode Island
Historical Society
(0.1mi)

Federal
Hill

W Exchange St

Rhode Island
Convention
Center

Dunkin
Donuts
Center

George St

Benevolent St

College
Hill

Charlesfield St

Brown St

Thayer St

To Rue de
l'Espoir (0.1mi)

Atwells Ave

To Pastiche (0.1mi);
Caserta Pizzeria; Scialo
Bros Bakery; Tony's
Colonial Food (0.3mi);
Casa Christine (0.4mi)

Sabin St

Fountain St

Clemence St

Union St

Dorrance St

Snow St

Westminster

Weybosset St

Johnson
& Wales
University

Peck St

Planet St

Power St

S Main St

Benefit St

Williams St

John St

Washington St

Greene St

Chapel St

Page St

Garnett St

Friendship St

Clifford St

Arnold St

Fox
Point

Transit St

Sheldon St

Wickenden St

Empire St

Dean St

Carpenter St

Franklin St

Broad St

Pine St

Chestnut St

Richmond St

Providence

To India Point
Park (0.1mi);
Radisson (0.2mi)

ENTERTAINMENT
AS220..38 B5
Avon Cinema...39 D3
Cable Car Cinema....................................40 C4
Call..41 B5
Deville's...42 C6
Leeds Theatre at Brown University.............43 D3
Lupo's Heartbreak Hotel............................44 B4
Mirabar..45 B5
New Gate Theater.....................................46 B4
Perishable Theater....................................47 B4
Providence Performing Arts Center............48 B5
Trinity Repertory Company.......................49 A4

SHOPPING
In Your Ear!...50 D3
Tom's Tracks..51 D3

Ship St

Clifford St

Elbow St

Bassett St

Chestnut St

South St

Hospital St

Eddy St

Richmond St

Dyer St

Point St

Point St
Bridge

S Water St

Crary St

Borden St

Elm St

Plain St

Point St

To Culinary Archives &
Museum (2mi);
Roger Williams Park
& Zoo (2.5mi); TF
Green State Airport (8mi)

India St

River

TRANSPORT
Avis..(see 25)
Bonanza Bus Lines............................(see 52)
Greyhound Bus Line..........................(see 52)
Intermodal Transportation Center..............52 B4
Point Street Ferry Dock.............................53 C5

OTHER
Arcade Garage...54 C4

RHODE ISLAND

Will send you booklets and maps on the whole state and update you on special events.

Visitor's Center (☎ 401-751-1177; 1 W Exchange St) For last-minute help after you've arrived in Providence, stop by here for maps and glossy print propaganda.

Sights
THE ARCADE

Designed in 1828, the **Arcade** (☎ 401-598-1199; 65 Weybosset St; ☉ 10am-5pm Mon-Fri, 11am-4pm Sat), America's first enclosed shopping center, uses a form developed in Paris and London. Greek Revival in design, it looks like a temple from the outside. The inside is much like a street – a straight corridor leads to a second entry on Washington St. Bounding the sides of this corridor are ornamented, parallel facades three stories tall, today containing the inexpensive eateries and clothing boutiques that attract a bustling lunchtime crowd from the surrounding business district. Roofed in glass, the interior is awash in natural light. For the best effect, hike up to the galleries on the 2nd or 3rd floor and look over the old cast iron rails at the crowds below, the floor creaking beneath your feet.

RHODE ISLAND STATE HOUSE

Designed by McKim, Mead & White in 1904, the **Rhode Island State House** (☎ 401-222-2357; admission free; ☉ 8:30am-4:30pm Mon-Fri) rises above the Providence skyline, easily visible from the highways that pass through the city. Modeled in part on St Peter's Basilica in Vatican City, this very white building not only has the world's fourth-largest self-supporting marble dome, it also houses Gilbert Stuart's portrait of George Washington, which you might want to compare to a dollar bill from your wallet. Inside the public halls are the battle flags of Rhode Island military units and a curious Civil War cannon, which sat here for a century loaded and ready to shoot until someone thought to check whether it was disarmed.

You might ask yourself, 'who's that giant half-naked guy standing on top of the dome – and what's he doing with that spear?' The golden boy is *The Independent Man*. We don't know what he's doing with his spear, but he should probably put it down – the poor fellow has been struck by lightning almost thirty times.

Visitors are welcome for free guided tours at the Smith St (US 44) entrance. Call a week in advance to arrange one, or drop in for a self-guided version.

BROWN UNIVERSITY

Dominating the crest of the College Hill neighborhood on the East Side, the campus of **Brown University** (☎ 401-863-2378; www.brown.edu) exudes Ivy League charm. University Hall, a 1770 brick edifice used as a barracks during the Revolutionary War, sits at its center. To explore the campus, start at the wrought-iron gates opening from the top of College St and make your way across the green toward Thayer St.

Free tours of the campus leave five times daily on weekdays, and on Saturday morning from mid-September to mid-November, beginning from the **college admission office** (Corliss Brackett House, 45 Prospect St).

MUSEUM OF ART, RHODE ISLAND SCHOOL OF DESIGN

Exhibits in this small but select **museum** (☎ 401-454-6500; www.risd.edu/museum.cfm; 224 Benefit St; adult/child 5-18 yrs/student/senior $8/2/3/5; ☉ 10am-5pm Wed, Thu, Sat & Sun, 10am-8pm Fri) include 19th-century French paintings; classical Greek, Roman and Etruscan art; medieval and Renaissance works; European and Asian decorative arts; and examples of 19th- and 20th-century American painting, furniture and decorative arts. Kids love staring at the mummy, and older-types will be impressed to see the works of Manet, Matisse and Sargent.

The museum stays open until 9pm on the third Thursday of the month; on those days, admission is free after 5pm. It's also free the last Saturday of the month and Sundays from 10am to 1pm.

PROVIDENCE ATHENAEUM

Anyone who has a visceral attraction to books will enjoy a visit to the **Athenaeum** (☎ 401-421-6970; www.providenceathenaeum.org; 251 Benefit St; admission free; ☉ 9am-7pm Mon-Thu, 9am-5pm Fri & Sat, 1-5pm Sun, shorter hrs Jun-Labor Day), a private subscription library. It's one of the oldest libraries in the country (1831). In these stacks poet Edgar Allan Poe carried on his courtship of Providence's Sarah Helen Whitman, who was the inspiration for his poem 'Annabel Lee.'

This is a library of the old school: they store the card catalog in old-fashioned wooden drawers rather than in a computer,

---

PROVIDENCE ARCHITECTURE

Come to Providence and you'll find an urban assemblage of unsurpassable architectural merit – at least within the boundaries of the US. It's the only American city to have its *entire* downtown listed on the National Registry of Historic Places. The beaux-arts City Hall makes an imposing centerpiece to Kennedy Plaza, and the stately white dome of the **Rhode Island State House** (p281) remains visible from many corners of the city. Modeled after Parisian antecedents, the **Arcade** (p281) is an airy, tile-floored passage with shops and cafés on three floors, its marble steps worn into bows by the passage of bygone feet. These impressive buildings, along with the art deco **Industrial Trust building** (Fleet bldg; 55 Exchange Pl) – note the 3rd story friezes of industrial progress on the Westminster St facade – are only a few spoonfuls out of a very big bowl of pudding. The more ordinary 19th-century brick buildings that fill in the majority of the space between their more famously designed neighbors work together to create an extraordinary landscape of harmonious scale, beauty and craftsmanship.

Immediately east of downtown, you'll find College Hill, where you can see the city's colonial history reflected in the multihued 18th-century houses that line **Benefit St** on the East Side. These are, for the most part, private homes, but many are open for tours one weekend in mid-June during the annual **Festival of Historic Homes** (p284). Benefit St is a fitting symbol of the Providence renaissance, rescued by local preservationists in the 1960s from misguided urban-renewal efforts that would have destroyed it. Its treasures range from the 1708 **Stephen Hopkins House** (☎ 401-247-4755; 15 Hopkins St; donations accepted; ☉ 1-4pm Wed & Sat Apr-Nov, otherwise by appt) to the clean Greek Revival lines of William Strickland's 1838 **Providence Athenaeum** (p281). It very intentionally recalls Greek temple forms, thought to be an architectural style which appropriately expressed the democratic ideals of a newly founded nation.

---

and plaster busts and oil paintings on the walls fill in spaces not occupied by books.

JOHN BROWN HOUSE

Called the 'most magnificent and elegant mansion that I have ever seen on this continent' by John Quincy Adams, this brick residence was built in 1786 for Providence merchant John Brown by his brother Joseph. The Rhode Island Historical Society now operates it as a **museum house** (☎ 401-331-8575; 52 Power St; adult/child/senior & student $7/3/5.50; ☉ 10am-5pm Tue-Sat, noon-4pm Sun Apr-Dec, 10am-5pm Fri & Sat, noon-4pm Sun Jan-Mar). A tour takes about one hour.

FIRST BAPTIST MEETING HOUSE

The congregation now resident in the **First Baptist Meeting House** (☎ 401-454-3418; 75 N Main St; admission free; ☉ 10am-4pm Mon-Fri May-Oct) began with Roger Williams and his followers in 1638. Though the congregation consisted of about 50 people when Joseph Brown designed the church in 1774, it was built to hold more than 1000 – at the time nearly a third of the population of Providence. Free guided tours show you the building, or you can use a free pamphlet for a self-guided tour.

CULINARY ARCHIVES & MUSEUM

Johnson & Wales' oddity of a **museum** (☎ 401-598-2805; www.culinary.org; 315 Harborside Blvd; adult/child/student $3/50¢/1; ☉ 9am-5pm Mon-Fri, 10am-5pm Sat) displays about 300,000 objects connected in some way to the culinary arts. Ogle a cookbook collection dating back to the 15th century, resist fingering presidential cutlery and peruse over 4000 menus from around the world.

ROGER WILLIAMS PARK & ZOO

In 1871, Betsey Williams, great-great-great-granddaughter of the founder of Providence, donated her farm to the city as a public park. Today this 430-acre expanse of greenery, only a short drive south of Providence, includes lakes and ponds, forest copses and broad lawns, picnic grounds, the Planetarium and the Museum of Natural History, an operating Victorian Carousel, a boathouse, greenhouses and Williams' cottage.

Perhaps the park's most significant attraction is the **Roger Williams Park & Zoo** (☎ 401-785-3510; www.rogerwilliamsparkzoo.org; 1000 Elmwood Ave; adult/senior & child over 3 yrs $10/6; ☉ 9am-6pm summer weekends, 9am-4pm winter, 9am-5pm other times). The zoo is home to more than 600 animals (polar bears, giraffes, lemurs) and performs some interesting conservation work, such as a study of the endangered American burying beetle. This little guy eats dead animals and needs their carcasses to store his brood in. To reach the park, go south from Providence on I-95 to exit 17 (Elmwood Ave). If you are heading north from Connecticut or from the Rhode Island beaches, take exit 16.

NEIGHBORHOODS

Among the most colorful of Providence's neighborhoods is fervently Italian **Federal Hill** (when Tony Soprano's crew needed a special job done, they came here to enlist the aid of a geriatric, blind hitman. The mobbed-up theme of the neighborhood also rears its head in the 1994 feature film *Federal Hill*). It's a great place to wander, taking in the aromas of sausages, peppers and garlic from neighborhood groceries such as Tony's Colonial Food. Scialo Bakery (p286) is a typical Italian pastry shop, with sweet confections poised atop paper doilies in its glass cases. Many of Providence's best restaurants are on Atwells Ave, a street you can easily identify by looking for a large, floodlit pineapple suspended from a concrete arch spanning the traffic below.

East of the Providence River, **College Hill**, headquarters of Brown University and the RISD, contains a dense and large population of wood-framed houses, largely from the 18th century. Among the (relatively) quiet tree-lined streets of this residential neighborhood, you'll find the two campuses and a lot of folks walking around with blue hair, tweed jackets or thick glasses. The cheap eateries and used record stores that nourish the college-types are located on Thayer St, College Hill's main commercial drag, which is also a second home to teenage loiterers from the suburbs and, in the evenings, a motorcycle gang.

Immediately south of College Hill is **Fox Point**, the waterfront neighborhood where the city's substantial Portuguese population resides. Though gentrification has taken place with influxes of Brown University professors and students and artists from RISD, you can still find an old-world style grocery like the Friends Market on Brook St tucked in among the trendy coffeehouses, salons and galleries. Most of the action in Fox Point centers on Wickenden St, a sedate commercial enterprise with pleasant cafés, good restaurants, an art supply store, a few bars and boutique home-furnishing shops.

PARKS

The landscaped cobblestone paths of the **Riverwalk** lead along the Woonasquatucket River to **Waterplace Park's** central pool and fountain, overlooked by a stepped amphitheater where outdoor performance artists liven up the scene in warm weather. Virtually all of what you see is new, the result of decades of urban renewal. Take a look at the historical maps and photos mounted on the walls of the walkway beneath Memorial Blvd. Waterplace Park also serves as a nucleus for WaterFire (p284).

A great spot from which to get an overview of the city, **Prospect Terrace Park** is a small pocket of green space off Congdon St on the East Side. In warm weather, you'll find students throwing Frisbees, office workers picnicking and kick-ass sunsets. The monumental statue facing the city is that of Providence founder Roger Williams, whose remains were moved to this site in 1939.

Activities
CYCLING

Starting at India Point Park on the Narragansett Bay waterfront in Providence, the scenic **East Bay Bicycle Path** winds its way for 14.5 miles south along a former railroad track. The mostly flat, paved path follows the shoreline to the pretty seaport of Bristol. State parks along the route make good spots for picnics.

Unfortunately there is no central place to rent a bike. The closest place is **Providence Bicycle** (☎ 401-331-6610; 725 Branch Ave; per day $20; ⏰ from 9:30am). Call for directions.

ICE-SKATING

The outdoor **Fleet Skating Center** (☎ 401-331-5544; www.fleetskating.com; 2 Kennedy Plaza; admission/rental $5/5; ⏰ 11am-10pm mid-Nov–mid-Mar) occupies prime downtown real estate. While the Biltmore and Fleet Building provide a nice architectural backdrop, you might have to skate to some seriously loud pop songs.

COOKING

Head over to the culinary arts kitchen studio at the **RISD** (☎ 401-454-6201; www.risd.edu /ce_culinary.cfm; Angell St; single day course $65) where you can take classes that will not only refine your technique, but will also provide plenty of opportunities to shove freshly made delights down your esophagus. These courses are held only a few times each semester, and you should enroll prior to class.

Tours

The **Rhode Island Historical Society** (☎ 401-331-8575; 110 Benevolent St; tours $10 from mid-Jun–mid-Oct) offers daily walking tours of Benefit St and downtown Providence during summer and early fall. The tours don't run very often and start at more than one destination. Call ahead for time and meeting places.

Festivals & Events

Festival of Historic Homes (☎ 401-831-7440; www .ppsri.org) Tour some of the East Side's fabulous 18th-century homes during this annual shindig organized by the Providence Preservation Society. Held in June.

Gallery Night (☎ 401-751-2628; www.gallerynight.info) Held every third Thursday of the month from March to November. Twenty-five galleries around the city open their doors for free viewings.

Rhode Island International Film Festival (☎ 401-861-4445; www.film-festival.org) For six days in mid-August, cool-kids from RISD and beyond screen hundreds of independent shorts and feature-length films.

WaterFire (☎ 401-272-3111; www.waterfire.org) At this exceedingly popular public art installation, scores of flaming braziers anchored into the city's rivers illuminate the water, accompanied by live (and canned) music, outdoor ballroom dancing and ostentatious gondolas drifting by the pyres. WaterFire occurs during the evening about 25 times a year, mostly in summer months.

Sleeping

Rhode Island, devoid of hostels, can be hard on your wallet. The very thrifty might consider staying at a campsite, but as these are always situated outside of urban centers, you'll need a car or heavy-duty interest in cycling to do this.

The rates charged at Providence's hotels vary widely, depending on season and availability. The summer months represent peak season, while the big universities' parents' weekends and graduations fill rooms up to a year in advance.

B&B of Rhode Island (☎ 401-849-1298, 800-828-0000; www.bandbnewport.com; PO Box 3291, Newport, RI 02840) provides listings of B&Bs for the entire state, including Providence.

BUDGET

Camping areas are outside the city, but since Rhode Island is small, they aren't all that far away.

George Washington Management Area (☎ 401-568-2248; US 44; sites residents/out-of-staters $14/20) This area, 2 miles east of the Connecticut state line in West Glocester (and 12 miles west of Providence), has 45 simple tent and RV sites. There are also two shelters ($25 per night) in a wooded area overlooking the Bowdish Reservoir, along with a freshwater beach.

Bowdish Lake Camping Area (☎ 401-568-8890; US Hwy 44; sites $16-45; ☽ May–mid-Oct) If the state-operated campground is full, try this neighboring private campground, which also has a beach providing access to the lake. The 450 sites range in price, depending upon the location and facilities.

As usual, inexpensive motels lurk on the outskirts near interstate exits, about 5 miles from the city center. Head south to Warwick for the **Motel 6** (☎ 401-467-9800; www .motel6.com; 20 Jefferson Blvd; d $55-70; P) as well as the **Extended Stay America** (☎ 401-732-2547; www .extendedstayamerica.com; 245 W Natick Rd; s $85-100; P ⌨), which features humdrum rooms containing kitchenettes.

MID-RANGE

Downtown Providence Holiday Inn (☎ 401-831-3900, 800-465-4329; www.providencehotels.holiday-inn.com; 21 Atwells Ave; r $80-170; P ⌨ ☒) A bleak, gray 12-story tower sandwiched between I-95 (take exit 21) and the large Dunkin' Donuts complex, this 274-room hotel is centrally located between downtown and Federal Hill and has adequate rooms. It runs free shuttles to TF Green State Airport in Warwick.

Radisson (☎ 401-272-5577; www.radisson.com; 220 India St; r $119-139; P ⌨) Hard to find and separated from the rest of the city by I-195, the south side of the hotel affords views over India Point Park and the water. The rooms on the north look directly at the freeway. All rooms are comfortable, though the decorator took a swing and then a miss with the faux-nice patterns explored in their carpet-bedding-chair combination.

Old Court B&B (☎ 401-751-2002; www.oldcourt .com; 144 Benefit St; r $125-165) Well-positioned among the historic buildings of College Hill, this three-story 1863 Italianate home has worn wooden floors, old fireplaces and stacks of charm. Enjoy excellent wallpaper,

---

COFFEE MILK & CABINETS

In 1993, two popular beverages battled each other for the honor of becoming Rhode Island's official state drink: coffee milk and Del's Frozen Lemonade.

Though Del's tastes great, no one really doubted that coffee milk would come out on top. Rhode Island kids have guzzled this mixture of coffee syrup and milk since before the Great Depression. To try it, head to a grocery store, pick up a bottle and go to town.

While we've got your attention, please note this crucially important distinction: in Rhode Island, a milkshake is traditionally syrup and milk blended together without ice cream. Rhode Islanders call the version with ice-cream a 'cabinet' or 'frappe.' (The term 'cabinet' is pretty much specific to Rhode Island, while 'frappe' gets thrown around by folks as far away as Boston.)

---

good jam at breakfast and occasional winter discounts.

State House Inn (☎ 401-351-6111; www.providence -inn.com; 43 Jewett St; r $129-150) A restored 1880s home close to the Rhode Island State House, this B&B's 10 simple rooms, decorated with tasteful colonial and Shaker-style furnishings, have private bathroom, TV and phone. If full, they'll help you book a room at one of two 'sister' inns of similar high quality: **Mowry- Nicholson House B&B** (☎ 401-351-6111; www.providence -suites.com; 57 Brownell St; r $129-250; **P**), a bright blue Victorian with a large wraparound porch, and **Christopher Dodge House** (☎ 401-351- 6111; www.providence-hotel.com; 11 W Park St; r $120-180; **P**), a stately brick Italianate building.

TOP END

Providence Marriott (☎ 401-272-2400, 800-937-7768; www.marriott.com; 1 Orms St; r $129-275; **P** 🖥 📺) Catering primarily to businesspeople, the corporate vibe comes on strong at this Marriott. Rooms feature good beds and pillows, ironing boards and access to a whirlpool, sauna and fitness center. Suites are available.

Providence Biltmore (☎ 401-421-0700, 800-294- 7709; www.providencebiltmore.com; 11 Dorrance St; r $159- 275) Before he shipped off to federal prison, Buddy Cianci, Providence's favorite mayor, spent his days in a lavish suite on the top story of this hotel. The 289 rooms of this beautiful granddaddy from the 1920s offer the finest hotel experience in the city. Ask for a room on a higher floor.

Eating

Both the RISD and Johnson & Wales University have top-notch culinary programs that annually turn out creative new chefs who liven up the city's restaurant scene. The large student population on the East Side assures that plenty of good, inexpensive places

exist around College Hill and Fox Point. To experience old Providence, head over to the restaurant district along Atwells Ave in Federal Hill, long an Italian-American enclave.

In addition to the listings below, check out AS220 (p287), Cable Car Theater (p287) and Trinity Brewhouse (p286).

BUDGET

For a quick, light lunch, don't forget the Arcade (p281).

Haven Brothers Diner (meals $3-7; ☺ 5pm-3am) Parked next to City Hall on Washington St, this diner sits on the back of a truck that has rolled into the same spot every evening for decades. Climb up a rickety ladder to get hamburgers, hot dogs, fries, cabinets (milkshake with ice-cream), lobster salad and little else. Everyone who has lived in Providence for a year or more is likely to have eaten here at least once.

Geoff's Superlative Sandwiches (☎ 401-751-9214; 235 Thayer St; sandwiches $4-6.50; ☺ from 11am) A favorite with students and Attleboro carpenters alike, Geoff's offers a massive menu of creative sandwiches, which includes lots of veggie options. Some kosher meats are available. While you wait, use the big-ass barrel of free pickles to keep your blood sugar up.

Amy's Place (☎ 401-274-9966; 214 Wickenden St; breakfast $2.25-7; ☺ 8am-5pm) For brightly painted furniture, an outdoor patio and smoothies, stop by this new café on Wickenden St. Breakfast options include eggs, French toast and yogurt with granola and a pile of fruit.

Pastiche (☎ 401-861-5190; 92 Spruce St; cake $4- 6; ☺ 8:30am-11pm Tue-Thu, 8:30am-11:30pm Fri & Sat, 10am-10pm Sun) Awash in soothing colors and warmed by a fire in winter, Pastiche offers a seasonal dessert menu. In summer, you might try the apricot almond chiffon cake, a chilled lime mousse tart or maybe an orange chocolate Bavarian cake.

Caserta Pizzeria (☎ 401-621-3618; 121 Spruce St; pizzas $5-15; ⏰ 9:30am-10:30pm Tue-Thu & Sun, 9:30am-11:30pm Fri & Sat) This Federal Hill icon serves some of the best pizza you'll taste. For many, dining at one of its cheap Formica tables is reason enough to visit Rhode Island. It's so popular with local Italian Americans that you need to order several days in advance if you want a pie on Christmas Eve. Cash only.

Scialo Bros Bakery (☎ 401-421-0986; 257 Atwells Ave; sweets $1-3; ⏰ 7:30am-7pm Mon-Thu & Sat, 7:30am-8pm Fri, 7:30am-5pm Sun) Since 1916, the brick ovens at this relic have turned out top-notch butterballs, *torrone* (a nougat and almond combo), amaretti and dozens of other kinds of Italian cookies and pastries. Avoid the *cannoli* (sugary pastry stuffed with sweet ricotta).

Murphy's Deli & Bar (☎ 401-621-8467; 55 Union St; sandwiches $4-7; ⏰ from 10am) For a sandwich and a beer right in the city center, head straight for Murphy's, in the back of the Biltmore parking garage. Besides serving up standard deli sandwiches such as hot pastrami and Swiss cheese ($5.25) since 1929, Murphy's offers a broad selection of instant lottery tickets.

MID-RANGE

Meeting St Café (☎ 401-273-1066; 220 Meeting St; meals $6-14; ⏰ 8am-11pm) For gut-busting sandwiches, as well as lox-oriented breakfasts, head to this delicatessen. Dinner equals vegetarian lasagna ($11), shish kabobs ($10) or good burgers. Enormous oatmeal cookies ($3), voted best in Rhode Island by several polls, measure about 10 inches in diameter.

Taste of India (☎ 401-421-4355; 230 Wickenden St; mains $9-14; ⏰ 11:30am-2:30pm & 5-10pm Mon-Sat, noon-9pm Sun) The bustling lunch crowd at this Indian joint comes for a tasty buffet ($7), curries and a top-notch mango *lassi* (yoghurt drink) made with strong rose water. The room contains cheap carpets, plastic plants and nooks for privacy. BYO alcohol.

Cafe Yuni (☎ 401-272-3585; 10 Traverse St; 2-piece nigiri $3-4; ⏰ noon-10pm Mon-Fri, 12:30-9:30pm Sat; ⊠ ⊠) Serving substantial pieces of fish, Cafe Yuni draws a loyal following with its fresh sushi and polite, charming service. The small restaurant also serves udon noodles ($6.50), stir-fries and *japachae* (stir-fried potato noodles with vegetables). BYO alcohol (no corkage charged).

Casa Christine (☎ 401-453-6255; 145 Spruce St; mains $10-20; ⏰ 11:30am-1:45pm & 5-7:30pm Tue-Fri, 3:45-7:30pm Sat) You'd never stumble across it, but locals in the know find their way to this family-run dining room on a drab backstreet near Caserta (left) to fill up on heaps of home-cooked veal, chicken and fish. Try the artichokes fried with hot peppers, garlic, mozzarella and calamari, served in a small room covered with an odd pastel mural.

TOP END

Rue de l'Espoir (☎ 401-751-8890; 99 Hope St; mains $17-28; ⏰ 7:30am-9pm Tue-Thu, 7:30am-10pm Fri, 8:30am-10:30pm Sat, 8:30am-9pm Sun) The East Side's long-running favorite is not as French as it sounds. The menu is eclectic and ever-changing, with several vegetarian options. The pretty restaurant contains old, wide floorboards, painted wooden booths and flowerboxes.

New Rivers (☎ 401-751-0350; 7 Steeple St; mains $18-30; ⏰ 5:30-10pm) The seasonal menu of this New America bistro features dishes such as grilled bass with locally grown corn, or pork loin wrapped in prosciutto served with stewed white beans and melon relish. The good-looking room combines soft lighting with rich red walls, making it a fine place to peruse a well-conceived wine list. Organic and locally grown produce is used whenever possible.

Drinking

Coffee Exchange (☎ 401-273-1198; 201 Wickenden St; ⏰ 6:30am-11pm) Drink very strong coffee at one of many small tables covering a scratched wooden floor. Nearby, thick layers of flyers are tacked onto boards and a large roaster lurks behind cases displaying the 40 kinds of beans available.

Red Fez (☎ 401-272-1212; 49 Peck St; mains $6-16; ⏰ 4pm-1am Tue & Wed, 4pm-2am Thu-Sat) Packed full of Hasbro copywriters who work on the packaging for Transformers action figures, this dark, spooky bar makes stiff drinks and fantastic grilled cheese sandwiches. What little light exists is red, by which short RISD girls with interesting hair smoke cigarettes. Upstairs is cooler than downstairs.

Trinity Brewhouse (☎ 401-453-2337; 186 Fountain St; dishes $6-15; ⏰ 11:30am-2am) A favorite college hangout in the evenings, this brewhouse serves only its own hop-heavy Irish/British–style beer. There's entertainment most nights, and the kitchen, serving sandwiches (some vegetarian), burgers, shepherd's pie and grilled sausages closes at midnight.

For an old, dirty brown bar, try Murphy's Deli & Bar (opposite).

Entertainment

THEATER

Trinity Repertory Company (☎ 401-351-4242; www .trinityrep.com; 201 Washington St; tickets $30-45) Trinity performs classic and contemporary plays (*The Henriad: Shakespeare's Kings, A Christmas Carol*) in the stunning and historic Lederer Theater downtown. It's a favorite try-out space for Broadway productions, and it's not unusual for well-known stars to turn up in a performance. Over several decades, Trinity Rep has earned a reputation for adventurous productions, but mainstream audiences usually come away satisfied. Student discounts available.

Perishable Theater (☎ 401-331-2695; www.perish able.org; 95 Empire St; tickets from $5) This small theater programs modern plays as well as improv comedy groups. It conducts an annual Women's Playwriting Festival and has recently hosted the phenomenal Pig Iron Theatre Company, whose dark productions combine techniques from shadow puppetry, vaudeville and silent film.

Providence Performing Arts Center (☎ 401-421-2997; www.ppacri.org; 220 Weybosset St; tickets $30-60) This popular venue for touring Broadway musicals is in a former Loew's Theater building dating from 1928. It has a lavish art deco interior, recently restored to its original splendor. See *Oklahoma!, Kenny Roger's Christmas*, Jerry Seinfeld or *Fiddler on the Roof.*

Several smaller theater companies stage contemporary and avant-garde productions. Check local listings in the newspaper or call the following theater companies for upcoming performances at **New Gate Theater** (☎ 401-421-9680; www.newgatetheatre.org; 134 Mathewson St) or **Leeds Theatre at Brown University** (☎ 401-863-2838; www.brown.edu/facilities/theatre; 77 Waterman St), which stages traditional and contemporary productions featuring student actors.

CINEMAS

Cable Car Cinema (☎ 401-272-3970; 204 S Main St; tickets $8; ⊗ 7:30am–end of last show) This theater screens offbeat and foreign films. Inside, patrons sit on couches and sometimes listen to a lovable weirdo sing 'Teddy Bears Picnic' before the show. The attached sidewalk café brews excellent coffee, and serves sandwiches and baked goods. It's a good place to hang out, even if you aren't catching a flick.

Avon Cinema (☎ 401-421-3315; 260 Thayer St; tickets $8.50) On College Hill, Avon's single screen features foreign films, cult classics and experimental movies.

NIGHTCLUBS

The legacy of Six Finger Satellite, Thee Hydrogen Terrors, Les Savy Fav and other notable local bands that have gone on to seminational acclaim is testament to the strength of Providence's live music scene, which remains very active, and the city has more than its fair share of clubs. Refer to the 'Lifebeat' section in the *Providence Journal* or the *Phoenix* for listings of performers, venues and schedules.

Lupo's Heartbreak Hotel (☎ 401-331-5876; www .lupos.com; 79 Washington St; cover $10-20) Providence's legendary music venue, Lupo's recently moved to occupy an old theater. It hosts national acts (They Might Be Giants, Bob Dylan, Ani Difranco) in a relatively small space.

AS220 (☎ 401-831-9327; www.as220.org; 115 Empire St; admission free–$10; ⊗ from 3pm) A longstanding outlet for all forms of Rhode Island art, AS220 (say 'A-S-two-twenty') books experimental bands (Lightning Bolt, tuba and banjo duos), hosts readings and provides gallery space for a very active community. If you need a cup of coffee, vegan cookie, veggie melt with hummus ($3.50) or spinach pie ($1.75), it also operates a café.

Call (☎ 401-751-2255; www.thecallnightclub.com; 15 Elbow St; admission free–$15; ⊗ from 6pm) This smallish blues and rock venue sits in the basement of a turn-of-the-century warehouse. Its well-designed two-tiered floor provides clear views of the stage, and has hosted Kristin Hersh, Jeff Buckley, Taj Mahal, Stereolab and James Cotton. There's a pool table and, best of all, amazingly clean bathrooms.

GAY & LESBIAN VENUES

Mirabar (☎ 401-331-6761; 35 Richmond St; ⊗ 3pm-1am Sun-Thu, 3pm-2am Fri & Sat) This venerable bar attracts devoted regulars, many on a first-name basis with the bartenders. It's got two floors.

The second, a sort of promenade, overlooks the action of the main level's dance floor.

Deville's (☎ 401-751-7166; www.devillesprovidence .com; 150 Point St; ☺ from 7pm Tue-Thu, 4pm-2am Fri & Sun, 8pm-2am Sat) Rhode Island's favorite lesbian club has found itself a new building whose interior details force many to confront memories of watching too much Miami Vice. Though Tubbs is absent, you'll find a dance floor and a good pool table.

SPORTS

Pawtucket Red Sox (☎ 401-724-7300) This Triple-A (minor league) farm team for the Boston Red Sox plays all spring and summer at McCoy Stadium in Pawtucket, just north of Providence. A night here, complete with hot dogs and peanuts, is a favorite way for baseball addicts to get a fix without the hassle and cost of driving to and parking at Fenway Park in Boston. You'll also sit much closer to the field than in a big league park. Take I-95 north to exit 27, 28 or 29 and follow signs to the stadium.

Providence Bruins (☎ 401-331-6700; www.providencebruins.com) Another farm team for Boston, this hockey squad plays a regular schedule at the **Dunkin' Donuts Center** (1 LaSalle Sq) in the fall and winter.

OTHER

Dunkin' Donuts Center (☎ 401-331-6700; 1 LaSalle Sq; ☺ box office 10am-6pm Mon-Fri, 10am-4pm Sat) This arena is the place to see sporting events such as the Harlem Globetrotters and Providence Bruins (above), occasional big-name music groups (Jessica Simpson etc) and boat shows.

Shopping

Tony's Colonial Food (☎ 401-621-8675; 311 Atwells Ave; ☺ 8:30am-6pm Mon-Sat, 8am-5pm Sun) stocks scads of Italian delicacies to keep the Federal Hill natives content. This is the place for imported cheeses, olives, delicacies and white-haired customers with thick accents discussing the replacement organ at their church.

Tom's Tracks (☎ 401-274-0820; 281 Thayer St) Stop by this College Hill old-timer for new and used records. Though the selection isn't huge, you'll find good local and rare stuff. They sell tickets to shows at Lupo's.

In Your Ear! (☎ 401-861-1515; 286 Thayer St) Across the street from Tom's Tracks is Thayer St's other old-school music shop.

Come here for new and used CDs, and to admire concert T-shirts.

In addition to the above, troll Thayer St for vintage clothes and overpriced new items that look vintage.

Getting There & Around

Providence is small, pretty and very walkable, so once you arrive you'll probably want to get around on foot.

AIR

TF Green State Airport (☎ 401-737-8222; www.pvd airport.com) is in Warwick, about 20 minutes south of Providence. Green is served by most major airlines. **Aero-Airport Limousine Service** (☎ 401-737-2868; one way $9) runs a shuttle to most downtown Providence hotels about once an hour. Taxi services include **Airport Taxi** (☎ 401-737-2868) and **Checker Cab** (☎ 401-273-2222). Rhode Island Public Transit Authority (RIPTA) bus Nos 12, 20 and 66 ($1.25, 20 to 30 minutes) run to Kennedy Plaza in Providence. On weekdays, these depart several times an hour from 5am to 8pm followed by infrequent service till 11pm. On Saturday and Sunday, service exists but is significantly reduced.

BOAT

From May through October, RIPTA operates the scenic **Providence/Newport Ferry** (adult/child $7/5, 65 minutes, five to six times daily) from Long Wharf Mall in Newport to the Point St Ferry Dock in Providence.

BUS

All long-distance buses and most local routes stop at the central **Intermodal Transportation Center** (Kennedy Plaza; ☺ 6am-8pm). RIPTA, Greyhound and Bonanza all have ticket counters inside, and there are maps outlining local services. **RIPTA** (☎ 401-781-9400, 800-221-3797; www .ripta.com) links Providence's Kennedy Plaza with the rest of the state for $1.25.

RIPTA bus No 11 (Broad St) takes you from Kennedy Plaza to Broad and Montgomery Sts, from where you can walk to Roger Williams Park & Zoo. Bus No 60 ($1.25, one hour) makes frequent runs from Kennedy Plaza to Newport from 5am to 1am weekdays, 7am to midnight Saturdays, 6am to 10pm Sundays and holidays.

RIPTA also operates two 'trolley' routes ($1, really just a bus that tries to look old).

The Green Line runs from the East Side through downtown to Federal Hill. The Gold Line runs from the Marriott hotel (p285) south to the hospital via Kennedy Plaza, and stops at the Point St Ferry Dock.

Bonanza Bus Lines (☎ 401-751-8800, 888-751-8800; www.bonanzabus.com; Kennedy Plaza) connects Providence and TF Green State Airport with Boston's South Station ($20, 70 minutes, 16 daily) and Boston's Logan International Airport ($20, 75 minutes, 10 daily). Pick it up at Kennedy Plaza or Bonanza's terminal 2 miles north at I-95 exit 25 (Rte 126/Smithfield Ave).

Greyhound (☎ 401-454-0790, 800-231-2222; www.greyhound.com; Kennedy Plaza) buses depart for Boston ($7.50, 70 minutes, eight to nine daily), New York City ($23, four to 5½ hours, eight to 12 daily), New London ($15, 1½ hours, seven daily), New Haven ($21, two hours and 40 minutes, six daily), and Foxwoods Resort Casino, CT ($15, one hour, eight to 12 daily), among other destinations.

CAR & MOTORCYCLE

With hills, two interstates, and two rivers defining its downtown topography, Providence can be a confusing city to find your way around. Expect one-way streets and curving roads. Parking can be difficult downtown and near the train station. For a central lot, park in the huge garage of the Providence Place Mall, a tragedy of massive ugliness inflicted on the hapless city, and get someone at the Gap, Cheesecake Factory or similar to validate your ticket. On the East Side, you can usually find street parking easily.

All of the major car-rental companies have offices at TF Green State Airport in Warwick. **Avis** (☎ 401-521-7900; www.avis.com; Providence Biltmore, 1 Dorrance St; ☽ 8am-6pm Mon-Fri, 8am-4:30pm Sat, 9am-5pm Sun) has an office downtown as well.

TRAIN

Amtrak (☎ 800-872-7245; www.amtrak.com; 100 Gaspee St) trains connect Providence with Boston ($13, 45 minutes, nine daily) and New York ($56 to $60, 3½ hours, four daily). High-speed Acela trains also run to Boston ($30, 40 minutes, five to 10 daily) and New York ($95, 2¾ hours, two to four daily); they shorten your trip and have more comfortable seats but cost more. The Boston run is a rip-off.

The awesome Boston-based **MBTA commuter rail** (☎ 617-222-3200, 800-392-6100; www.mbta.com) runs a considerably cheaper option to Boston ($6, 70 minutes, 12 Monday to Friday and none on weekends) on the same track as Amtrak. It's the Attleboro Line. You'll see the same stuff out the window on a slightly harder seat for half the price.

For information on Amtrak's route between New York and Boston, see p542.

NEWPORT

pop 26,500

Newport's status as a favorite summertime destination stretches back to the 19th century. It was then that America's most fabulously wealthy industrialists erected an unequalled collection of obscenely sumptuous mansions with unimpeded views over the Atlantic. Though Vanderbilt and his pals are long dead, their 'cottages' linger in excellent condition and are the area's premier attraction. Also competing for your attention are a series of music festivals – classical, folk, jazz – which are among the most important in the US.

For those that detest opulent homes and good tunes, the city's crooked colonial streets make for excellent strolling and feature several of New England's most beautiful and oldest religious buildings. The nearby harbor remains one of the most active and important yachting centers in the county. Thames St, the principal commercial drag, teems with restaurants, bars and massive weekend crowds, day and night. Indeed, the town is packed all summer with young day-trippers, older bus tourists, foreign visitors and families whose cars pack the narrow streets, bringing traffic to a standstill.

Orientation

Newport occupies the southwestern end of Aquidneck Island. Adjoining it to the north is Middletown, which holds many of the services, less-expensive residential areas and unsightly commercial strips not allowed in Newport. Most cheap motels and guesthouses are in Middletown, several miles north of the center, while the more expensive inns, B&Bs and hotels are in Newport proper.

Downtown Newport's main north–south commercial streets are America's Cup Ave and Thames (that's 'thaymz,' not 'temz') St, just in from the harbor. There are public

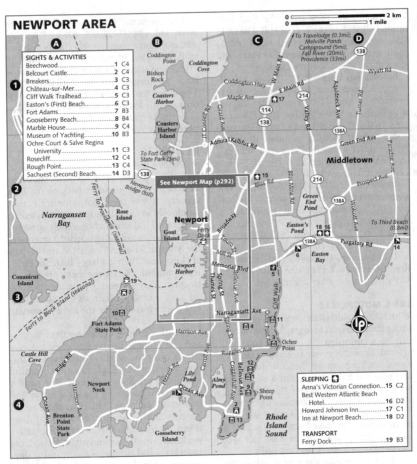

NEWPORT AREA

SIGHTS & ACTIVITIES
Beechwood	1 C4
Belcourt Castle	2 C4
Breakers	3 C3
Château-sur-Mer	4 C3
Cliff Walk Trailhead	5 C3
Easton's (First) Beach	6 C3
Fort Adams	7 B3
Gooseberry Beach	8 B4
Marble House	9 C4
Museum of Yachting	10 B3
Ochre Court & Salve Regina University	11 C3
Rosecliff	12 C4
Rough Point	13 C4
Sachuest (Second) Beach	14 D3

SLEEPING
Anna's Victorian Connection	15 C2
Best Western Atlantic Beach Hotel	16 D2
Howard Johnson Inn	17 C1
Inn at Newport Beach	18 D2

TRANSPORT
Ferry Dock	19 B3

toilets at the entrance to the parking lot at Bowen's Wharf.

Your initial destination in Newport should be the Newport Gateway Transportation & Visitors Center (opposite), which holds the bus station, tourist office and public toilets. Walking or biking around town is probably the best way to go; see p296 for rental information.

In the summer, parking is particularly difficult and expensive. The very lucky might find free parking on the street, though most nonmetered spots are reserved for Newport residents. If you park at a meter (25¢ for 15 minutes, up to two hours), scrupulously observe its time limit or you'll end up with a ticket. The most convenient garage is at the Newport Gateway Transportation & Visitors Center, which gives you the first half-hour for free, the next for $2 and each additional half-hour for $1, up to a maximum of $15.25 per day.

Information

BOOKSTORES

Armchair Sailor Bookstore (Map p292; ☎ 401-847-4252; 543 Thames St; ☺ 10am-6pm Mon-Sat) Come here for books on Newport and Rhode Island and especially the New England coast; also stocks an extensive nautical collection.

EMERGENCY

Police station (Map p292; ☎ 401-847-1212; 120 Broadway; ☺ 24hr)

CLIFF WALK

A narrow footpath that snakes for 3.5 miles along the eastern edge of a peninsula, the Cliff Walk provides one of the finest excuses for exercise you'll encounter. From it's northernmost point, beach traffic and noise will recede behind you as you make your way south. Just steps to your left, a cliff – your faithful companion for the duration of your walk – drops dramatically to a foaming, bubbling Atlantic, which swells against rocky outcroppings. While a short stone wall occasionally protects you from an accidental plunge, often the only barrier is grass, flowers and squat bushes dotted with orange beach plums. For much of the first half mile, a tall hedge will impede your view to the right, with momentary breaks providing glimpses of large estates hinting at what's to come.

It all becomes clear when you arrive at the '40 Steps,' a stone staircase (sometimes used as a casting platform by fishermen) that leads from the top of the cliff to the crashing water below. Here, the hedge drops away, offering a clear view of the walk's first robber-baron-era mansion, Ochre Point (294). Continue south and you'll experience the Breakers (p293), Beechwood (p294), Marble House (p293) and Rough Point (p293). Between these gargantuan monuments to 19th-century excess, you'll see smaller private 'cottages' mysteriously hiding behind protective walls.

The Cliff Walk begins off Memorial Blvd just west of Easton's Beach, and goes south and then west to the intersection of Bellevue and Coggeshall Aves. Strolling its entire length in one direction takes about an hour. The most convenient access point is on Narragansett Ave, which terminates near the Cliff Walk at the 40 Steps. Here, you can park for free from 6am to 9pm (there's a four-hour limit). Many favor this entry point because it shaves the first half-mile off the walk (which is pretty, but lacks mansions).

MEDICAL SERVICES

Newport Hospital (Map p292; ☎ 401-846-6400; 11 Friendship St; ☻ 24hr) Sutures open wounds.

MONEY

There are many ATM machines on Thames St, such as **Citizens Bank** (Map p292; 4 Commercial Wharf), across the street from the post office.

POST

Newport post office (Map p292; ☎ 800-275-8777; 320 Thames St; ☻ 8:30am-5pm Mon-Fri, 9am-1pm Sat)

TOURIST INFORMATION

Newport Gateway Transportation & Visitors Center (Map p292; ☎ 800-976-5122; www.gonewport .com; 23 America's Cup Ave; ☻ 9am-5pm) Operated by the Newport County Convention & Visitors Bureau. Information personnel won't make room reservations, but they post a list of B&Bs, inns and hotels with vacancies, and you can call those for free from a bank of special phones. They've also got free maps.

Sights

NEWPORT MANSIONS

During the 19th century, the wealthiest New York bankers and business families chose Newport as their summer resort. This was pre–income tax America, their fortunes were fabulous and their 'summer cottages' – actually mansions and palaces – were fabu- lous as well. Most mansions are on Bellevue Ave, and they frequently turn up as settings for films like *The Great Gatsby* and PBS series featuring actors with British accents. All visitors to Rhode Island are required to visit at least one of these amazing homes.

Many of the mansions are under the management of the **Preservation Society of Newport County** (Map p292; ☎ 401-847-1000; www .newportmansions.org; 424 Bellevue Ave), which offers combination tickets that save you money if you intend to visit several of its properties. Tickets to all mansions can be purchased at the Newport visitor center (p291). You can also purchase tickets at properties run by the preservation society. A few mansions are still in private hands and aren't open to visitors.

One of the best ways to see the mansions is by bicycle. Cruising along Bellevue Ave at a leisurely place allows you to enjoy the view of the grounds, explore side streets and paths, and ride right up to the mansion entrances without having to worry about parking or holding up traffic. If you can't bring your own bike, you can rent one (see p296).

The following mansions range along or near the Bellevue Ave axis. The only mansions described here not managed by the Preservation Society are Ochre Court, Beechwood, Belcourt Castle and Rough Point.

RHODE ISLAND

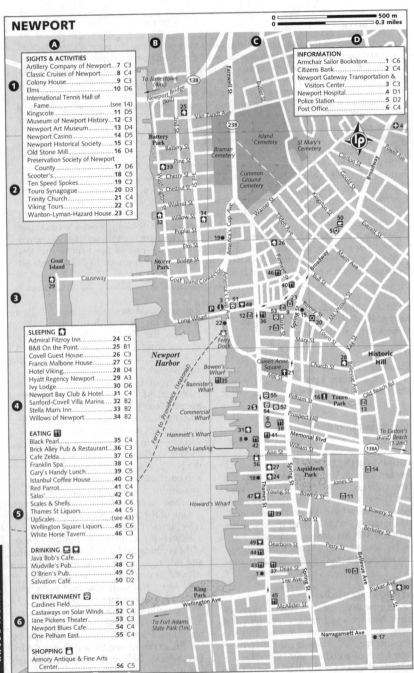

NEWPORT

0 _____ 500 m
0 _____ 0.3 miles

To Jamestown
(4mi)
Newport Bridge
(toll)

Battery
Park

Goat
Island

Causeway

Storer
Park

Bridge St

Goat Island Connector

Long Wharf

Newport
Harbor

Ferry
Dock

Ferry to Providence (seasonal)

Bowen's
Wharf

Bannister's
Wharf

Commercial
Wharf

Hammett's Wharf

Christie's Landing

Howard's Wharf

King
Park

Wellington Ave

To Fort Adams
State Park (1mi)

Van Zandt Ave

Battery St

Pine St

Cherry St

Chestnut St

Walnut St

Willow St

Poplar St

Elm St

Farewell St

Island
Cemetery

Braman
Cemetery

Common
Ground
Cemetery

St Mary's
Cemetery

Clinton St

Gould St

Kingston St

Everett St

Powell Ave

Tilden Ave

Warner St

Farewell St

Broadway

Bull St

Barney St

Mt Vernon St

Mary St

Spring St

Thames St

Touro St

Queen Anne
Square

Mill St

Church St

Pelham St

Prospect Hill

Memorial Blvd

William St

Ann St

Young St

Bowery St

Pope St

Dearborn St

Perry St

Lee Ave

McAlister St

Dean St

Spring St

Historic
Hill

Old Beach Rd

Touro
Park

To Easton's
(First) Beach
(1.2mi)

Aquidneck
Park

Jones St

E Bowery St

Berkeley St

Bellevue Ave

Parker Ave

Clay St

Narragansett Ave

RHODE ISLAND

Your stunning alternative to cycling is to saunter along the famed **Cliff Walk**, a narrow pedestrian path that runs along the edge of a range of steep bluffs. The ocean surges on one side, while the mansions rise in grandeur on the other.

The Breakers

Most magnificent of all the Newport mansions is the **Breakers** (Map p290; ☎ 401-847-1000; adult/child $15/5; 9am-6pm mid-Apr–Jan, 10am-5pm Sat & Sun Jan–mid-Apr), a 70-room Italian Renaissance megapalace inspired by 16th-century Genoese palazzos. Richard Morris Hunt did most of the design, though he imported craftsmen from around the world to perfect the sculptural and decorative programs. The building was completed in 1895 and sits next to Ochre Court at Ochre Point, a prime oceanside site. The furnishings, most made expressly for the Breakers, are all original. Don't miss the Children's Cottage on the grounds.

The Breakers' grand **Stable & Carriage House**, also designed by Hunt, is inland several blocks, on the west side of Bellevue Ave. It is now a museum of Vanderbilt family memorabilia, much of which provides a detailed look at the lifestyle of one of the USA's wealthiest families at the turn of the century.

Rough Point

In 1889, Frederick W Vanderbilt built **Rough Point** (Map p290; ☎ 401-849-7300; www.newportrestoration.com; adult/senior $25/22; 10am-2:40pm Tue-Sat mid-Apr–early-Nov) in the tradition of English manorial estates on a rocky piece of land jutting out into the ocean. Three sides of its hall are nearly transparent with massive windows affording staggering views across the Atlantic. Later purchased by the tobacco baron, James B Duke, the mansion and the rest of his wealth fell into the hands of Duke's only daughter, Doris (aged 13 years). She left the estate to the Newport Restoration Society upon her death.

While the splendor of the grounds is alone worth the steep price of admission, Rough Point also houses much of Doris Duke's impressive art holdings. Displayed in the mansion are works by Renoir, Van Dyck, and craftsmen of the Ming dynasty. You can purchase tickets to Rough Point at Newport's visitor center or online. As parking is virtually nonexistent at Rough Point, most visit the estate using a courtesy shuttle from the visitor center.

The Elms

Nearly identical to the Château d'Asnières built near Paris in 1750, the **Elms** (Map p292; ☎ 401-847-1000; adult/child $10/5; 10am-6pm mid-Apr–Jan, 10am-5pm Sat & Sun Jan–mid-Apr) offers a 'behind-the-scenes' tour (adult/child $15/5) which will have you snaking through the basement operations, servants' quarters and up onto the roof. Along the way you'll learn about the activities of the army of servants and the architectural devices that kept them hidden from the view of those drinking port in the formal rooms.

The graceful summerhouse was designed by Horace Trumbauer in 1901 for Edward J Berwind, a graduate of the US Naval Academy and a Navy officer, who made his fortune by selling coal to the US Navy after his retirement. Threatened with imminent destruction in the early 1960s – incredibly – the mansion was to be replaced with a housing project. However, thanks to the efforts of the Preservation Society, good sense prevailed.

Marble House

Designed by Richard Morris Hunt and built in 1892 for William K Vanderbilt, the younger brother of Cornelius II, **Marble House** (Map p290; ☎ 401-847-1000; adult/child $10/5; 10am-6pm mid-Apr–Jan) receives its inspiration from the palace of Versailles. It comes complete with original Louis XIV–style furnishings – these were custom-made for the mansion. The aptly named Gold Room was created for the Vanderbilts' grand balls. Check out the bright red and green **Chinese Teahouse**, perched on a seaside cliff, which contrasts oddly with the stern gray stone of Marble House, its monumental parent.

Belcourt Castle

Oliver Hazard Perry Belmont, heir to the American Rothschild fortune, had Hunt design **Belcourt Castle** (Map p290; ☎ 401-846-0669; www.belcourtcastle.com; 657 Bellevue Ave; adult/child 6-12 yrs/student 13-17 yrs/senior $10/5/7/8; 9am-5pm late May–mid-Oct), a 60-room monster, according to what he thought were the 17th-century tastes of France's King Louis XIII. Thus the vaulted ceilings and pointy arches. He stocked it with period art, tapestries, furniture, glassware and suits of armor from

32 countries. Staffed by 30 servants, it even had a private menagerie. He and his wife, Alva, the former Mrs William K Vanderbilt, lived here in regal splendor. Tours are offered daily; call for times.

Beechwood

William B Astor built his **Beechwood** (Map p290; ☎ 401-846-3772; www.astorsbeechwood.com; 580 Bellevue Ave; adult/child/senior $15/8/10; ☑ 10am-4pm Feb–mid-May, 10am-4pm mid-May–Nov, call for times Nov-Dec) in 1856. Today, it is occupied by Beechwood Theater Company actors, who bring the house to life by portraying a 'typical' summer house, full of family, staff and guests. While the cast plays croquet most of the year, there are special seasonal events such as evening ghost tours, faux-speakeasy parties and a Christmas Feast.

Kingscote

An Elizabethan fantasy complete with Tiffany glass, **Kingscote** (Map p292; ☎ 401-847-1000; cnr Bellevue Ave & Bowrey St; adult/child $10/5; ☑ 10am-5pm mid-Jun–mid-Sep) was Newport's first 'cottage' strictly for summer use, designed by Richard Upjohn in 1841 for George Noble Jones of Savannah, Georgia. It was later bought by China-trade merchant William H King, who gave the house its name.

Rosecliff

Stanford White designed **Rosecliff** (Map p290; ☎ 401-847-1000; adult/child $10/5; ☑ 10am-6pm mid-Apr–Jan) to look like the Grand Trianon at Versailles, and its palatial ballroom (Newport's largest) and landscaped grounds quickly became the setting for some truly enormous parties. Houdini, the magician, entertained at one. Rosecliff was built for Mrs Hermann Oelrichs, an heiress of the Comstock Lode silver treasure. If the building seems oddly familiar during your visit, that might be because it has appeared in films such as *The Great Gatsby*, *Amistad* and *High Society*.

Château-sur-Mer

Originally designed by Seth Bradford and built of granite for retired banker William S Wetmore in 1852, **Château-sur-Mer** (Map p290; ☎ 401-847-1000; Bellevue Ave; adult/child $10/5; ☑ 10am-6pm mid-Apr–Jan, 10am-5pm Sat & Sun Jan–mid-Apr), a massive Italianate-style villa, was the only home of its scale until the Vanderbilts ponied up the cash for their big-ass homes 40

years later. Richard Morris Hunt remodeled it during the 1870s and '80s to suit the tastes of the original owner's son, who really liked the French Second Empire. Holy mansard!

Ochre Court

Designed by Richard Morris Hunt and built in 1892, **Ochre Court** (Map p290; ☎ 401-847-6650; admission free; ☑ 9am-4pm Mon-Fri) is now the administration building of Salve Regina University. You can visit much of the main floor anytime during opening hours. In summer, there are guided tours.

MUSEUMS & MONUMENTS

The **International Tennis Hall of Fame** (Map p292; ☎ 401-849-3990; www.tennisfame.com; 194 Bellevue Ave; adult/child 16 yrs & under/senior/family $8/4/6/20; ☑ 10am-5pm), just south of Memorial Blvd, is in the historic Newport Casino building (1880). Designed by Stanford White, it exemplifies shingle-style architecture and served as a summer club for Newport's wealthiest residents. The US National Lawn Tennis Championships (forerunner of today's US Open Tennis Tournament) was held here in 1881. Playing on one of its 13 grass courts costs $40 per person per 90 minutes, though the grass courts close for winter.

In Newport's historic Brick Market building, the **Museum of Newport History** (Map p292; ☎ 401-846-0813; Washington Sq; adult/child 5 yrs & older/senior $5/3/4; ☑ 10am-5pm Mon & Wed-Sat, 1-5pm Sun) is run by the Newport Historical Society (p296) and traces the town's eventful history. The museum offers a concise architectural history of the mansions, displays models of yachts, and presents some of the furniture of John Goddard and Job Townsend, two of America's most celebrated craftsmen.

Constructed in 1675, the **Wanton-Lyman-Hazard House** (Map p292; ☎ 401-846-0813; 17 Broadway; admission $4, children under 12 free; ☑ tours 10am, 11am, 1pm, 2pm, 3pm Thu-Sat mid-Jun–Aug, other times by appt) is the oldest surviving house in the city. Used as a residence by colonial governors and well-to-do residents, it's now a museum of colonial Newport history operated by the Newport Historical Society. Tours depart from Colony House.

The **Old Stone Mill** (Map p292; off Bellevue Ave in Touro Park) is a curious stone tower of uncertain provenance. Some people believe it was built by Norse mariners before the voyages of Columbus, making it the oldest-existing structure in the US; others say it's a windmill's base, built by an early governor of the colony.

The Griswold Mansion (1864), a vast Victorian frame summer cottage, houses the **Newport Art Museum** (Map p292; ☎ 401-848-8200; www.newportartmuseum.com; 76 Bellevue Ave; adult/child 5 yrs & under/student/senior $6/free/4/5; ☷ 10am-5pm Mon-Sat, noon-5pm Sun Memorial Day–Columbus Day, 10am-4pm Mon-Sat, noon-4pm Sun Columbus Day–Memorial Day). It has changing exhibits of local paintings, sculpture, metalwork, ceramics, photography etc. Call for current shows. The admission fee depends upon the exhibit, but is usually close to the listed prices.

For decades, Newport was the home port for America's Cup races, which is why it has a **Museum of Yachting** (Map p290; ☎ 401-847-1018; www .moy.org; Fort Adams State Park; adult/senior & child under 12 $4/3; ☷ 10am-5pm mid-May–Oct). Those who dig models of yachts and looking at old life preservers will pee their pants.

As a lantern hanging over the street proclaims, the **Artillery Company of Newport** (Map p292; ☎ 401-846-8488; www.newportartillery.org; 23 Clarke St; adult/child $3/2; ☷ call for hrs) was formed in 1741 under King George II. The present armory, dating from 1836, contains an extensive collection of military uniforms (worn by the likes of Prince Philip, Lord Louis Mountbatten and Colin Powell), paraphernalia and other memorabilia.

HOUSES OF WORSHIP

Touro Synagogue (Map p292; ☎ 401-847-4794; 85 Touro St; ☷ tours 10am-5pm Sun-Fri Jul-Sep, 11am-3pm Sun, 1-3pm Mon-Sat Sep-Oct & May-Jun, 11am-3pm Sun, 1pm Mon-Fri Nov-Apr), designed by Peter Harrison (who did King's Chapel in Boston) and built by the nascent Sephardic Orthodox Congregation Yeshuat Israel in 1763, has the distinction of being North America's oldest Jewish synagogue. Inside, a letter to the congregation from President George Washington, written in 1790, hangs in a prominent spot. There's a historic cemetery just up the street.

The synagogue opens for worship only on Saturday. To visit outside of the listed winter hours, call to make an appointment.

The **Trinity Church** (Map p292; ☎ 401-846-0660; cnr Spring & Church Sts; ☷ 10am-4pm mid-Jun–early Sep, 1-4pm May & mid-Sep–mid-Oct, 10am-1pm rest of year), on Queen Anne Sq, follows the design canon of Sir Christopher Wren's Palladian churches in London. Built in 1725 and 1726, it has a

fine wineglass-shaped pulpit, tall windows to let in light and traditional box pews to keep out drafty air.

STATE PARKS

Fort Adams, built between 1824 and 1857, crowns a rise at the end of the peninsula, which juts northward into Newport Harbor. Like many American coastal fortresses, it had a short, practical life as a deterrent and a long life as a tourist attraction. It's the centerpiece of **Fort Adams State Park** (Map p290; ☎ 401-847-2400; admission free; ☷ 6am-11pm), the venue for the Newport jazz and folk festivals and special events. A beach, picnic and fishing areas and a boat ramp are open daily. You can take a guided tour of the park from mid-May to September (adults/seniors and children aged under 12 $5/4). The Museum of Yachting (left) and the ferry to Block Island are here as well.

At the opposite end of the peninsula, **Brenton Point State Park** (Map p290; ☎ 401-849-4562 summer only; Ocean Dr; ☷ sunrise-sunset), due south of Fort Adams on Ocean Ave, is a prime place for gazing at the ocean and for flying kites.

Activities

BEACHES

Newport's public beaches are on the eastern side of the peninsula along Memorial Blvd. All are open 9am to 6pm in summer and charge a parking fee of $10 per car ($15 on weekends).

Easton's Beach (Map p290; ☎ 401-848-6491), also called First Beach, is the largest, with a pseudo-Victorian pavilion containing bathhouses and showers, a snack bar and a small aquarium where children can see and touch a variety of tide-pool creatures and fish. It's within walking distance of Newport's center.

East of Easton's Beach along Purgatory Rd lies **Sachuest (Second) Beach** (Map p290; ☎ 401-846-6273), named for the nearby wildlife sanctuary. It's prettier and cleaner than Easton's Beach and has showers, a snack bar and a lovely setting, overlooked by the neo-Gothic tower of St George's prep school.

Third Beach (Map p290; ☎ 401-847-1993) is a short distance east of Second Beach. Popular with families because it is protected from the open ocean, Third Beach also appeals to windsurfers because the water is calm and the winds steady.

Other 'pocket' beaches exist along Ocean Ave, but most of these, such as **Bailey's Beach**, are private. An exception is **Gooseberry Beach** (Map p290), open to the public for a fee of $10 per car, $3 for pedestrians and cyclists.

CYCLING

Newport is a fine town for bicycling, with only a few gentle slopes. Observe traffic laws just as you would in a car: ride in the direction of traffic and do not ride on the sidewalk.

Perhaps the most scenic and satisfying ride is the 10-mile loop around Ocean Ave, which includes Bellevue Ave and its many beautiful mansions.

Both the following stores offer free use of helmets and locks:

Scooters (Map p292; ☎ 401-849-4400; 411 Thames St; per hr/day $5/25, each additional day $10; 🕐 9am-7pm Mon-Sat, 9am-6pm Sun) You can rent wheels with a baby seat for $8.50 per hour. Motor scooters cost $30/40/60/89

for one/two/four/eight hours, or $125 for 24 hours (which is about three times what a four-person rental car would cost). **Ten Speed Spokes** (Map p292; ☎ 401-847-5609; 18 Elm St; rental per hr/day $5/25; 🕐 9am-7pm Mon-Sat, 9am-6pm Sun) Really on America's Cup Ave next to the visitor center, rents Specialized brand mountain bikes and hybrids.

Tours

If you'd rather go on your own, the Historical Society has erected 26 self-guided walking-tour signs on the sidewalks of Historic Hill describing many of the prominent and historic buildings found there.

Classic Cruises of Newport (Map p292; ☎ 401-847-0299; Bannister's Wharf; adult/child $17/12; 🕐 mid-May–mid-Oct) Runs excursions on the Rum Runner II, a Prohibition-era bootlegging vessel. The narrated tour will take you past mansions and former speakeasies.

Newport Historical Society (Map p292; ☎ 401-846-0813; 82 Touro St; tours $8; 🕐 10am Thu-Sat May-Sep) Will guide you on a walking tour of Historic Hill, where you'll see austere Georgian mansions, the homes of free

---

DETOUR: LITTLE COMPTON

From Newport, head north on Rte 138 and merge onto Rte 24 north. Cross the Sakonnet River, kiss Aquidneck good-bye, pick up Rte 77 and brace yourself for complete picturesque emersion.

Driving south through the town of Tiverton, you'll follow the course of the wide Sakonnet, with views of distant sailing vessels and Aquidneck Island. After a couple of miles, you'll see gray-shingled **Evelyn's** (☎ 401-624-3100; 2335 Main Rd, Tiverton; fishies $3-12; 🕐 11am-8:30pm Wed-Mon, closed Oct-early April) sitting pleasantly next to a blue inlet with a handful of bobbing dinghies. If hungry, park on the crushed shell driveway for a top-notch open-air lobster roll. Properly fortified, continue south, but be careful not to drive off the road – for now things get tricky, with transfixed out-of-towners veering into ditches, mouths agape. With every rotation of your tires, the landscape gets progressively more beautiful. Rolling fields extend to your left and right. Ramshackle farm stands begin appearing along the road, selling fresh corn and tomatoes. The large, wood-framed homes become older, grayer and statelier. If you survive, you'll arrive at this detour's only traffic light, marking Tiverton's 'Four Corners.' Stop at **Gray's Ice Cream** (16 East Road Tiverton; ice-cream $3-5; 🕐 open year-round) for a coffee cabinet (milkshake with ice-cream), as the locals have been doing for 80 years.

Continue south into Little Compton, where the smell of the sea will meld into your pastoral sensory overload. Turn left at a sign for 'The Common.' When you arrive at this common, you'll probably wet yourself at the classic sight of steeped church, graveyard and nucleated village, such is the cuteness of it all. Turn right after the church, continue to Swamp Rd and make a left. Make a second left onto South Shore Rd, at the end of which you'll find South Shore Beach and, your reward, **Goosewing Beach**. Lovely, remote, ocean-facing Goosewing is the only good public beach in Little Compton, a town on the east shore of Narragansett Bay. Access can be tricky. Due to an ongoing wrangle between the town and the Nature Conservancy over control of the beach, parking and lifeguard coverage are perennially in question. Still, since the dispute began it has been possible to get onto Goosewing by the unusual means of parking at the town beach called South Shore ($10) and walking across a small tidal inlet to the more appealing Goosewing. What makes it so appealing is immediately apparent: the long sand beach with its wide-open ocean view is backed by rolling farmland that's almost a throwback to another era. With no facilities to speak of, Goosewing can't be called convenient, but you won't forget a summer's day spent here.

blacks and slaveholders, and prominent religious landmarks such as Touro Synagogue. Periodically, the society offers African-American and religious heritage tours, where you'll learn why Cotton Mather called Newport 'a sewer of religious contagion.' Tours begin at the Museum of Newport History, on Thames St.

Viking Tours (Map p292; ☎ 401-847-6921; 23 America's Cup Ave; adult/child $11/6; ◷ mid-May–mid-Oct) Offers narrated harbor tours aboard the Viking Queen departing several times daily; among other sights, you'll see Hammersmith Farm, Jacqueline Kennedy's summer home. On Tuesdays and Thursdays, two passengers can ride for the price of one.

Festivals & Events
Newport has a crowded calendar of community celebrations. During your visit, you may find special events involving polo, yachts, flowers and horticulture, yachts, Irish music, clam chowder, yachts, traditional crafts, soapbox racers, tennis, beer and yachts. There's even a **winter festival** (☎ 401-847-7666, 800-976-5122; www.newportevents.com) in mid-February, where you can participate in hokie local events like a citywide scavenger hunt. For the full schedule, see www.gonewport.com.

If you plan to attend any of the major events described below, make sure you reserve accommodations and tickets in advance (tickets usually go on sale in mid-May).

Newport Music Festival (☎ 401-846-1133; www.newportmusic.org; tickets $25-50) In mid-July, this internationally regarded festival offers classical music concerts in many of the great mansions. Order tickets well in advance.

International Tennis Hall of Fame Championships (☎ 401-849-3990; www.tennisfame.org/championship; daily tickets $18-50) For a week in July, the sport's top athletes come to humiliate each other on the famed grass courts.

Newport Folk Festival (☎ 401-847-3700; www.newportfolk.com; adult $25-58, child $5) In early August, big-name stars and up-and-coming groups perform at Fort Adams State Park and other venues around town. Recent acts include Rufus Wainwright, Wilco, and Crosby, Stills & Nash. Zero shade exists at Fort Adams – bring sunscreen.

JVC Jazz Festival/Newport (☎ 401-847-3700; www.festivalproductions.net; adult/child $65/5) Over 50 years old, this classic draws top performers like Dave Brubeck and Ornette Coleman. It usually takes place on a mid-August weekend, with concerts at the Newport Casino (International Tennis Hall of Fame) and Fort Adams State Park. Popular shows can sell out a year in advance.

Newport International Boat Show This boat show (☎ 401-846-1115; www.newportboatshow.com; tickets

$16), held in late September, is the biggest and best known of Newport's many boat and yacht shows.

Sleeping
Newport's lodgings are expensive. The cozy inns and harborside hotels in the center of town generally charge $125 to $200 and up for a double room with breakfast in summer. North of the Newport Gateway Transportation & Visitors Center is the quiet residential district called the Point, with a good collection of small inns and B&Bs. Prices here are generally a bit lower than at lodgings south of the visitor center. The Rhode Island sales tax of 7% and Newport lodging tax of 5% will be added to your bill.

On Friday and Saturday, prices are high; during the music festivals, they're higher still. Sunday through Thursday, rates fall as much as 30%. Many lodgings require a two-night minimum on summer weekends, and a three-night minimum on holidays.

As rooms can be scarce in summer, you might want to use a reservation service. **Anna's Victorian Connection** (Map p290; ☎ 401-849-2489; 5 Fowler Ave, Newport, RI 02840) will make a reservation at any one of 200 hostelries in Rhode Island and southeastern Massachusetts at no cost to you.

B&B of Newport Ltd (☎ 401-846-5408, 800-800-8765; www.bbnewport.com; 33 Russell Ave, Newport, RI 02840) represents 350 establishments in the Newport area. **Taylor-Made Reservations** (☎ 800-848-8848; www.citybythesea.com) represents a full range of lodgings as well.

If you arrive without a reservation, go to the visitor center and ask to see its list of vacancies. Except in summer, you may find handbills in the brochure racks that entitle you to special reduced rates.

Compared to Newport's many wonderful inns, its motels lack character, but they try to make up for this with modern amenities and lower prices. Most are in Middletown on RI 114 (W Main Rd) and RI 138 (E Main Rd). RIPTA bus No 63/Purple Line will take you to downtown Newport, saving you the expense and bother of parking.

BUDGET
Melville Ponds Campground (Map p290; ☎ 401-682-2424; 181 Bradford Ave; tent sites $20, RV sites $26-30; ◷ Apr-Oct) This family-friendly municipal campground has 57 tent sites and 66 RV sites. The tenting spots are wooded, though a bit

small and cramped, and have picnic tables. It's in Portsmouth about 10 miles north of Newport's center. To find it, take RI 114 to Stringham Rd (the turn is not prominent, though there is a small sign), go to Sullivan Rd, then head north to the campground.

Fort Getty State Park (☎ 401-423-7264; tent/RV sites $20/25; ☒ mid-May–Sep) This pleasant park is across the Newport Bridge on Conanicut Island in Jamestown, with 25 tent sites, 100 RV sites and a dock for fishing. From RI 138, go south on North Rd, cross Narragansett Ave and continue on Southwest Ave, then merge into Beaver Tail Rd and turn right onto Fort Getty Rd.

Travelodge (Map p290; ☎ 401-849-4700, 800-862-2006; www.travelodge.com; 1185 W Main Rd/RI 114, Middletown; r $45-120; ☒) If you feel like a supremely generic motel, this chain provides convenient beds about 3 miles north of Newport, unpleasantly situated on a busy state road. If you forgot extra socks, you're in luck – just head to one of many stores in the nearby strip mall. A plus: it often provides the cheapest room in town.

Howard Johnson Inn (Map p290; ☎ 401-849-2000, 800-654-2000; www.hojo.com; 351 W Main Rd/RI 114, Middletown; r $49-149; ☒) Located near an Applebee's and an Ihop, you'll be living the asphalt high-life at this orange-roofed wonder about 3 miles away from downtown Newport. Pets are welcome and there's a tennis court.

MID-RANGE

Ivy Lodge (Map p292; ☎ 401-849-6865, 800-834-6865; www.ivylodge.com; 12 Clay St; r $99-200 with breakfast; P ☐) Though not quite as grand as other Bellevue mansions nearby, the three-story entrance hall of this impressive place packs a wallop, with elaborate oak paneling, a series of interior balconies and a Moorish fireplace. The rooms ain't too shabby either.

Stella Maris Inn (Map p292; ☎ 401-849-2862; www.stellamarisinn.com; 91 Washington St; r $120-200; P) This big, quiet, stone-and-frame inn has numerous fireplaces and heaps of black-walnut furnishings. Rooms with garden views rent for less than those overlooking the water. Good breakfast muffins.

Admiral Fitzroy Inn (Map p292; ☎ 401-848-8000, 866-848-8780; www.admiralfitzroy.com; 398 Thames St; r $75-305; P) Set a bit back from the street, the location of this inn, dating from 1845, provides guests some (but not complete) protection from the noise of Newport's nightlife.

Each of the 17 large rooms has some very tasteful period furnishings, a minirefrigerator and a color TV. Rooms on higher floors have great views over the harbor.

Newport Bay Club & Hotel (Map p292; ☎ 401-849-8600; www.newportbayclub.com; 337 Thames St; r summer $139-319, 1 bedroom ste winter $89-139; P ☐) On the waterfront at the foot of Memorial Blvd, this hotel sits in an old stone wharf building. Its one-bedroom suites range hugely in price, and come with Jacuzzis. Call about the several off-season packages, one of which involves in-room massages.

B&B on the Point (Map p292; ☎ 401-846-8377; www.bandbonthepoint.com; 102 3rd St; r $90-130; P) Between Sycamore and Van Zandt, this plain yellow Victorian home provides comfortable rooms. As it's a bit further from Newport's center than most of its ilk, you can expect a more reasonable rate.

Inn at Newport Beach (Map p290; ☎ 401-846-0310; www.innatnb.com; cnr Memorial Blvd & Wave Ave; d $79-269; P) This imposing, wooden, beachside hotel features excellent views over Eaton's Beach and the distant Cliff Walk, though windows are a bit small. Rooms contain refrigerators, yellow bedspreads, microwaves, and a border of tacky, cheerful sailboats.

Covell Guest House (Map p292; ☎ 401-847-8872; www.web-knowledge.com/covell; 43 Farewell St; r $120-170; P) Red and cute, this five-room guesthouse is several blocks to the east of the Point. It was built in 1805 and renovated in 1982.

Best Western Atlantic Beach Hotel (Map p290; ☎ 401-847-5330; www.bestwestern.com; 34 Wave Ave; r $89-169; P) Nicely situated across the street from Easton's Beach, this place offers a well-used volleyball court. It's located on a lively corner, near several restaurants, bars and surf shops.

TOP END

Sanford-Covell Villa Marina (Map p292; ☎ 401-847-0206; www.sanford-covell.com; 72 Washington St; r $140-275; P ☒) This Victorian 'Stick-style' place was perhaps Newport's most lavish house when a cousin of Ralph W Emerson built it in 1869. Restored by a team of historians from RISD and beyond in the 1980s, every detail enjoys period accuracy. Outside, kick back on the waterfront wraparound veranda or take a dip in a saltwater swimming pool. Rooms vary in size, and some have shared bathrooms. The most expensive provide water views.

One of them contains the oldest bathtub in the States.

Francis Malbone House (Map p292; ☎ 401-846-0392, 800-846-0392; www.malbone.com; 392 Thames St; d May-Oct $245-305, Nov-Apr $150-240; P ⛾) This grand brick mansion was designed by the Touro Synagogue's architect and built in 1760 for a shipping merchant. Now beautifully decorated and immaculately kept, with a lush garden in back, it is one of Newport's finest inns. Some guest rooms have working fireplaces, as do the public rooms. Breakfast and afternoon tea are included.

Hotel Viking (Map p292; ☎ 401-847-3300; www .hotelviking.com; 1 Bellevue Ave; r $119-379; P ⛾) More than 75 years old, this otherwise good-looking brick hotel might want to rethink the faux-Chippendale furnishings that linger in some rooms. The bar on the top floor is the highest point in Newport, offering fine views over the city. It's in a pleasant neighborhood.

Willows of Newport (Map p292; ☎ 401-846-5486; www.thewillowsofnewport.com; 8 Willow St; r $179-278; P) The four rooms of the Willows feature poetry, mints and canopy beds, breakfast in bed included; check out the 'French Victorian secret garden,' full of frog statuary, wooden cartoon bunnies and massive pink bird feeders. Over-the-top icons of romance abound.

Hyatt Regency Newport (Map p292; ☎ 401-851-1234; www.hyatt.com; 1 Goat Island; r winter $129-169, summer $250-385; P ⛾ ⛾) The 264 rooms of this hotel, sandwiched between Goat Island's harbor and a small lighthouse, feature views of the Newport Bridge, downtown and lots of water. It's got a ton of amenities.

Eating

From June through September, reserve your table for dinner in advance, then show up on time or lose your spot. Some restaurants do not take reservations, in which case you must get in line early. Many Newport restaurants don't accept credit cards; ask about payment when you reserve.

The richest selection of restaurants in all price ranges is undoubtedly along lower Thames St, south of America's Cup Ave. Some allow you to BYOB (bring your own bottle of wine or beer), which you can buy at **Thames St Liquors** (Map p292; ☎ 401-847-0017; 517 Thames St; ⛾ 9am-11pm Mon-Sat) or at **Welling-**

ton Square Liquors (Map p292; ☎ 401-846-9463; 580 Thames St; ⛾ 9am-11pm Mon-Sat, noon-6pm Sun).

BUDGET

Franklin Spa (Map p292; ☎ 401-847-3540; 229 Spring St; breakfast & lunch $2-8; ⛾ 6am-2pm Mon-Wed, 6am-3pm Thu-Sat, 7am-1:30pm Sun) This old-school joint slings hash, eggs and grease for cheap. Enjoy your freshly squeezed orange juice, homemade turkey noodle soup ($3.25) or coffee cabinet at a Formica-topped table on a worn white-and-red tiled floor.

Istanbul Coffee House (Map p292; ☎ 401-841-5828; 2 Broadway; specialties $6-13; ⛾ from noon Tue-Sun) For an unforgettable snack, stop by this pleasant coffeehouse for top-notch Middle Eastern black tea and 'cigarette pies' (melted feta with flecks of parsley in crispy Turkish dough). Those suckers are delicious, oily and served with tasty olives.

Gary's Handy Lunch (Map p292; ☎ 401-847-9480; 462 Thames St; breakfast & lunch $2-7; ⛾ 5am-3pm Sun-Fri, 5am-8pm Sat) Locals crowd the booths of this cheap and popular faux 50s–style diner for eggs and ground beef. It's not even close to feeling authentic, but it's still kind of fun. Pass me a gumball.

MID-RANGE

Salas' (Map p292; ☎ 401-846-8772; 345 Thames St; mains $6.50-18; ⛾ from 5pm) Above Percy's Bistro but with a separate entrance, this Newport institution for the hearty, hungry and thrifty serves simple and tasty Italian and seafood dishes, plus a children's menu. Huge plates of pasta in red-clam sauce are sold by weight, and you're likely to be a little sentimental for the place after eating their fantastic clam boil.

Black Pearl (Map p292; ☎ 401-846-5264; Bannister's Wharf; ⛾ noon-1am) This is Newport's 'old reliable,' offering three types of dining. The Tavern's sandwich board and seafood menu ($8 to $18) are long and varied, the atmosphere suitably nautical; have a big bowl of top-notch clam chowder and a beer for less than $10. For traditional swordfish, steaks and rack of lamb ($20 to $40) in fancier surroundings, there's the Commodore's Room. The Hot Dog Annex supplies cheap snacks.

Scales & Shells (Map p292; ☎ 401-846-3474; 527 Thames St; mains $13-22; ⛾ from 5pm) A moderately priced, plainly decorated retro seafood place, Scales & Shells' decor is marked by an open kitchen and a blackboard menu.

Have your squid or lobster mesquite grilled for a change, with a glass of chardonnay from Greenvale, a local Rhode Island vineyard. In summer, a swamped U-shaped bar serves a huge waiting crowd.

Red Parrot (Map p292; ☎ 401-847-3800; 348 Thames St; mains $6-14; ⊗ from noon) A former meatpacking plant, this big three-story restaurant and bar serves burgers, a large menu of buffalo wings, a warm goat cheese mescaline salad and lots of 'Caribbean' frozen drinks.

Brick Alley Pub & Restaurant (Map p292; ☎ 401-849-6334; 140 Thames St; mains $8-20; ⊗ 11:30am-10pm Mon-Fri, 11am-10:30pm Sat & Sun) This centrally located, ever-popular place has a huge menu of snacks, sandwiches, bar food, Mexican specialties and a salad bar, as well as Newport's most elaborate drinks list. A large patio holds many yellow umbrellas and brightly colored Adirondack chairs. The pub is not a chain, but it's beginning to feel like one.

TOP END

Cafe Zelda (Map p292; ☎ 401-849-4002; 528 Thames St; lunch mains $8-13, dinner mains $19-26; ⊗ from 11:30am Thu-Mon, from 3pm Tue & Wed) This bistro, lit by dim, frosted lamps, has a seasonal menu, which might offer chicken, fried lobster, burgers with cheddar and café *frites* ($9.25) or *cappellini* (pasta) and jumbo shrimp with winter squash, walnuts and spinach. The very popular bar is in a separate space next door. Half-price specials on Monday.

White Horse Tavern (Map p292; ☎ 401-849-3600; 26 Marlborough St; lunch $9-15, dinner $28-40; ⊗ from 11:30am) If you'd like to eat at a tavern begun by a 17th-century pirate and that once served as an annual meeting place for the colonial Rhode Island's General Assembly, try this historic, gambrel-roofed beauty. It opened in 1687, and is one of America's oldest taverns. Menus for dinner (at which men should wear a jacket) might include baked escargot, truffle-crusted Atlantic halibut or beef Wellington.

UpScales (Map p292; ☎ 401-847-2000; 527 Thames St; mains $20-40; ⊗ from 5pm) Scales & Shells' more genteel 2nd-floor dining room has higher prices and more gentlemen in pressed pants. Come early or make a reservation; there's often a two-hour wait in summer.

Drinking

Java Bob's Cafe (Map p292; ☎ 401-846-5402; 435 Thames St; ⊗ 7am-10pm) Easy to miss thanks to its 2nd-floor location, this café makes hot chocolate so good that you might be tempted to order it on a sweltering summer day. Otherwise, drink espresso, pet Spock the dog, or eat oatmeal, waffles, and tabbouleh and hummus sandwiches. They've got chess sets and Internet access (per 15 minutes $2.50).

Mudville's Pub (Map p292; ☎ 401-849-1408; 8 W Marlborough St; ⊗ noon-1am) With a back porch sitting about 10ft from the foul line of Cardines Field's outfield (opposite), this bar fills many local sports fans with pub food and beer. It even sponsors a team (the Mudville Nine) that plays in a local league.

O'Brien's Pub (Map p292; ☎ 401-849-6623; 501 Thames St; ⊗ noon-1am) For a beer or a headache-inducing mixed drink, grab a seat under one of the many umbrellas on the patio of this Thames St bar. It's a great place to watch the crowds stream by. Beware of the karaoke that occasionally occurs inside.

Salvation Café (Map p292; ☎ 401-847-2620; www .salvationcafe.com; 140 Broadway; ⊗ from 5-11pm) Combining an outdoor Tiki lounge, corduroy velvet couches, stylish Formica tables and wood-paneled walls, this bar and restaurant is a good place for a hipster drink. It's a bit removed from town, so there are fewer tourists.

Entertainment

This is a resort town, and in July and August it teems with crowds looking for a good time (see p297). For what's going on, check out the Providence *Journal*'s daily 'Lifebeat' section.

Newport Blues Café (Map p292; ☎ 401-841-5510; www.newportblues.com; 286 Thames St; ⊗ dinner 6-10pm, music from 9:30pm) This popular rhythm and blues bar draws quality acts to an old brownstone that was once a bank. Foodwise, you can eat stuffed quahogs ($8), butternut squash ravioli in cream sauce ($14), cod ($15) or pork loin ($15).

Castaways on Solar Winds (Map p292; ☎ 401-849-9928; 28 Prospect Hill St; ⊗ 4pm-1am Wed-Fri, 1pm-1am Sat & Sun) Finally, Newport has opened a gay and lesbian club. The brand new bar sits on a narrow street off Lower Thames.

One Pelham East (Map p292; ☎ 401-847-9460; 1 Pelham St; ⊗ from 6pm) Opposite Bannister's Wharf, this is the place to come for an Irish theme and live music (not all Irish) on many nights. Pelham St, by the way, was the first street in the USA illuminated by gas (1805) and remains lit that way today.

Jane Pickens Theater (Map p292; ☎ 401-846-5252; 49 Touro St; adult/senior $8/6) This nicely restored one-screen art house used to be an Episcopalian church, built around 1834. Simple, pretty and old, the theater contains an organ and balcony.

SPORTS

Cardines Field (Map p292; ☎ 401-845-6832; cnr America's Cup Ave & Marlborough St; tickets $1-4) Likely the third-oldest-standing baseball field in the US (after Wrigley Field in Chicago and Fenway Park in Boston), this relic, home to the **Newport Gulls** (www.newportgulls.com), allows you to see some surprisingly skilled ball for cheap. Because of the seating's close proximity to the field and because the games are sparsely attended, you can easily hear the players trash-talk each other. According to local legend, Babe Ruth once played a game here.

Shopping

Armory Antique & Fine Arts Center (Map p292; ☎ 401-848-2398; 365 Thames St) This shop has more than 125 antique dealers in one building – an ivy-covered, castle-like former armory now stuffed with pottery, porcelain, paintings, estate jewelry and furniture.

Getting There & Around

AIR

Cozy Cab (☎ 401-846-2500, 800-846-1502; www.pvd airport.com/ground_transport/taxi_train.htm) provides shuttle service to TF Green State Airport ($20, 45 minutes) in Warwick. Reservations are recommended.

BICYCLE

For rental information see p296.

BOAT

A RIPTA summer ferry steams to Providence from Long Wharf (adult/child $7/5, 65 minutes, five to six times daily).

From July to early September, **Interstate Navigation** (☎ 401-783-4613; www.blockislandferry.com) runs a ferry from a dock near Fort Adams to Old Harbor in Block Island (one way/round-trip $9/13, two hours, one daily).

BUS

Bonanza Bus Lines (☎ 401-846-1820; 888-751-8800; www.bonanzabus.com), at the Newport Gateway

Transportation & Visitors Center (p291), operates buses to Boston ($19, 1¾ hours, six to seven daily) via Fall River, MA.

The **RIPTA** (☎ 401-781-9400, 800-244-0444; www.ripta.com) runs bus No 60 between Newport (Gateway Center) and Kennedy Plaza in Providence ($1.25, one hour) at least every hour from around 5am to 1am weekdays, 7am to midnight Saturdays, 6am to 10pm Sundays and holidays. RIPTA operates bus No 64 to the Amtrak railroad station in Kingston ($1.25, 90 minutes, five buses Monday to Friday, three on Saturday).

RIPTA runs several bus routes from the Newport Gateway Transportation & Visitors Center every 30 minutes: Bus No 61/Orange Line runs to First and Second Beaches; bus No 62/Red Line runs along Thames St to Fort Adams; bus No 63/Purple Line runs to Middletown and the motels described earlier (p297); and bus No 67/Yellow Line runs along Bellevue Ave to the mansions. Fares are $1.25.

GALILEE & POINT JUDITH
pop few people; 640,000 scallops

Rhode Island's port for car ferries to Block Island is at Galilee State Pier, at the southern end of RI 108 in the village of Galilee, near Point Judith. Galilee – sometimes called Point Judith in ferry schedules – is a real workaday fishing town with docks for fishing craft, a dock for the ferries, Roger W Wheeler Memorial Beach (p308), and Fishermen's Memorial State Park (see p309 for camping information).

All-day parking in Galilee costs $10 to $15 in any of several lots.

The **Portside Restaurant & Chowder House** (☎ 401-783-3821; 321 Great Island Rd; ☼ 8:30am-8pm), the **Top of the Dock Restaurant** (☎ 401-789-7900; 294 Great Island Rd; ☼ 11am-10pm) and other eateries are good for a drink or snack while you're waiting for the boat. (See p306 for ferry details.)

At **Champlin's Seafood** (☎ 401-783-3152; 256 Great Rd; dishes $3-15; ☼ 11am-9pm summer, shorter hrs other times), order a lobster roll, stuffed clams, scallops or one of many sea critters breaded and fried, and hang out on its 2nd-floor deck, which sits inches from the harbor's channel. The swaying masts of rusty fishing vessels keep you company.

Also at the port, **George's of Galilee** (☎ 401-783-2306; cnr Sand Hill Cove & Great Rds; meals $4-20;

RHODE ISLAND

11:30am-11pm summer, shorter hrs other times) has a takeout window where hordes of sandy people line for clam cakes that are crisp on the outside, doughy on the inside and studded with bits of clam. On some summer evenings, a bad two-piece band plays cheesy covers (Natalie Merchant and Bob Marley) out of amps that should be turned down.

BLOCK ISLAND

pop 800

From the deck of the summer ferry, you'll see a cluster of mansard roofs and gingerbread houses rising picturesquely from the commercial village of Old Harbor, where little has changed since about 1895. Yes, they've added lights and toilets, but – especially if you remain after the departure of the masses on the last ferry – the scale and pace of the island will seem distinctly premodern.

The island's attractions are simple. Stretching for several miles to the North of Old Harbor is a lovely beach, long enough to find a quiet spot even on a busy day. Otherwise, bike or hike around the island's rural, rolling farmland, pausing to admire a stately lighthouse or one of the many species of birds that make the island their home. During off-season, the island landscape has the spare, haunted feeling of an Andrew Wyeth painting, with stone walls demarcating centuries-old property lines and few trees to interrupt the ocean views. At this time, the island's population dwindles to a few hundred.

Orientation & Information

It's confusing: all of Block Island is incorporated as the town of New Shoreham, but the main settlement is known as Old Harbor, or just 'the town.' Most of the boating activity is in New Harbor, the island's other main settlement, on the shore of Great Salt Pond.

Block Island doesn't use normal US street addresses. Because the place is so small, each house is assigned a fire number, useful if you're trying to deliver mail or track down a blaze, but not if you're a traveler trying to find your hotel.

For tourist information, contact the **Block Island Chamber of Commerce** (☎ 401-466-2982, 800-383-2474; www.blockislandchamber.com; PO Drawer D, Water St, Block Island, RI 02807; ⏰ 9am-5pm summer, shorter hrs other times). It operates a visitor center near the ferry dock. Juice n' Java (p305) has Internet access.

Sights & Activities

SOUTHEAST LIGHT

You'll likely recognize this red-brick lighthouse building from postcards of the island. Set dramatically atop 200ft red-clay cliffs called **Mohegan Bluffs**, the lighthouse had to be moved back from the eroding cliff edge in 1993. With waves crashing below and sails moving across the Atlantic offshore, it's probably the best place on the island to watch the sunset.

NORTH LIGHT

At **Sandy Point**, the northernmost tip of the island, scenic North Light stands at the end of a long sandy path lined with beach roses. The 1867 lighthouse contains a small maritime museum with information about famous island wrecks. As you travel there along Corn Neck Rd, watch for a cluster of competing lemonade stands. On a hot day, you'll pray that one is open.

BEACHES

The island's east coast, north of Old Harbor, is lined with 2 miles of glorious beach, the **Block Island State Beach**. The southern part, **Benson Town Beach**, sits closest to town; it's got a pavilion for changing and showering. Heading north, you'll next hit **Crescent Beach**, then **Scotch Beach** and finally **Mansion Beach**, named for a mansion of which nothing is left but the foundation. The further up you go, the smaller the crowd gets.

CYCLING

The island is a convenient size for biking, and bicycles as well as mopeds are available for rental at many places in Old Harbor. In fact, many people save money by leaving their cars parked at the ferry dock in Galilee on the mainland and bring only their bikes for a day trip.

Rentals are available from the **Moped Man** (☎ 401-466-5444; Water St; per day $24; ⏰ 9am-6pm), 50 yards from the ferry dock, dealing in Specialized brand hybrids, and **Seacrest Inn** (☎ 401-466-2882; High St; per day $14-19; ⏰ 8am-6pm), which stocks beach cruisers with big handlebars, among many other places. Expect to pay about $20 per day for bikes, $95 per day for mopeds. Most islanders resent the noise and hazards caused by tourists on mopeds, so you'll get friendlier greetings (and exercise) if you opt for a bicycle.

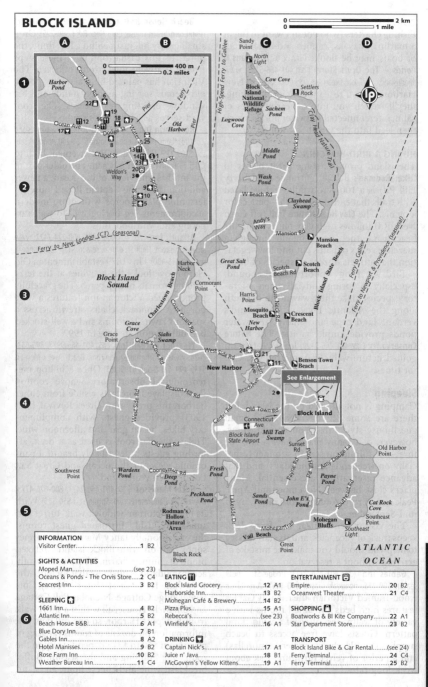

BLOCK ISLAND

RHODE ISLAND

BOATING

Fishing charters (who doesn't want to tug in a marlin?), kayaks, canoes and other types of boats may be booked through **Oceans & Ponds – The Orvis Store** (☎ 401-466-5131; www .blockisland.com/fishbi; Ocean Ave; ◉ from 9am), in New Harbor. If you're canoeing or kayaking, they'll launch you into a nearby series of calm, interconnected saltwater ponds which then lead into the Great Salt Pond.

HIKING & BIRD-WATCHING

The island provides some great places to hike: **Rodman's Hollow** (entrance off Cherry Hill Rd) is a 100-acre wildlife refuge laced with trails that end at the beach – perfect for a picnic. The **Clay Head Nature Trail** (off Corn Neck Rd) follows high clay bluffs along the beachfront, then veers inland through a mazelike series of paths cut into low vegetation that attracts dozens of species of bird.

Bird-watching opportunities abound, especially in spring and fall when migratory species make their way north or south along the Atlantic Flyway. The island's verdant landscape and many freshwater ponds provide ample habitat. The **Nature Conservancy** (☎ 401-466-2129) leads visitors on guided nature walks in some refuges. Call for times.

Sleeping

Camping is not allowed on the island, but there are some 35 cozy B&Bs and small guesthouse-style inns. You should know, however, that many places have a two- or three-day minimum stay in summer (especially on weekends and holidays) and that advance reservations are essential. Many places close between November and April. Peak season runs roughly from mid-May to mid-September.

The visitor center near the ferry dock keeps track of vacancies, and its staff will try to help you should you make the mistake of arriving without a reservation.

Gables Inn (☎ 401-466-2213; Dodge St; r peak season $90-155, nonpeak season $50-145) Another wood-framed Victorian, the friendly Gables features high beds and small rooms with a variety of wallpaper, often of a vivid floral pattern. Guests have free access to beach supplies (towels, chairs, coolers, umbrellas) and a parlor of velvet furniture. Ask about week-long rates.

Beach House B&B (☎ 401-466-2924; www.block island.com/beach-house; Corn Neck Rd; r $90-225) On a small grassy hill just behind a low dune, the porch of this casual option is mere steps from a relatively quiet stretch of beach. The Victorian has painted blue and gray floors, old stereos serving as nightstands and big windows emitting sea breezes. The front yard serves as a sculptor's studio.

Rose Farm Inn (☎ 401-466-2034; www.blockisland .com/rosefarm; High St; r peak season $124-250, nonpeak season $109-215) Rose Farm is convenient both to Old Harbor and the beach. The older part of the inn has fine views of the ocean; a newer addition called the Captain Rose House offers nine plain rooms with more modern accoutrements (eg boring wall-to-wall carpeting and whirlpool tubs).

Atlantic Inn (☎ 401-466-5883, 800-224-7422; www .atlanticinn.com; High St; d peak season $130-230, nonpeak season $115-180) This 1879 establishment in Old Harbor overlooks the activities at the ferry landing from its hilltop perch. The gracefully proportioned Victorian inn features a wide porch, Adirondack chairs strewn across a spacious lawn, 21 rooms and a well-stocked bar. Bill Clinton ate here in 1997.

Weather Bureau Inn (☎ 401-466-9977, 800-633-8624; www.weatherbureauinn.com; Beach Ave; r Mon-Fri $139-199, Sat & Sun $199-265) Once a hilltop meteorological observatory whose rooftop flags displayed forecasts visible from either harbor, this pretty inn (Greek Revival, built 1903) provides guests with complimentary bikes, beach gear and afternoon wine. Today, the flat roof is used as a deck, affording guests indescribably beautiful panoramic views of the ocean and Great Salt Pond. Open year-round.

Hotel Manisses (☎ 401-466-2421, 800-626-4773; www.blockislandresorts.com; Spring St; r $50-315) With its high Victorian 'widow's walk' turret and small but lushly furnished guest rooms, the exceptionally fancy Manisses combines sophistication with Block Island's relaxed brand of country charm. It's part of a family accommodations business that includes the 1661 Inn, 1661 Guest House, Dewey Cottage, Dodge Cottage, Nicholas Ball Cottage and Sheffield House, all within a short walk from Newport Harbor, so one call gets you information on dozens of rooms ranging in price from $50 to $315 depending upon the room, the building and the season. Buffet breakfast, wine and cheese hour, an island tour and service (but not tax) are included. Open year-round.

Blue Dory Inn (☎ 401-466-5891, 800-992-7290; www .blockislandinns.com; Dodge St; d peak season $135-425, nonpeak season $85-225) With 14 small rooms, this cozy place sits at the edge of Old Harbor near the beach. Decorated in Victorian style, it oozes 'romantic' flourishes (fresh flowers and flowery bedding). There's a great porch, and it's open all year. Cookies baked daily.

Eating

Block Island specializes in fish, shellfish and more fish. Generally, cheap food = fried fish; expensive food = nonfried fish. Most places are open for lunch and dinner during the summer; many close off-season.

Block Island Grocery (☎ 401-466-2949; Ocean Ave; 8am-10pm Mon-Sat, 8am-8pm Sun) The biggest grocery store around, it also sells alcohol.

Rebecca's (☎ 401-466-5411; Water St; items $3-9; 7am-2am Thu-Mon, 7am-8pm Tue & Wed) This snack stand serves burgers, chowder, grilled cheese sandwiches, grease and deep-fried sea monster (aka fried clams, fried fish, fried scallops etc) to hungry tourists seated at picnic tables under umbrellas.

Pizza Plus (☎ 401-466-939; Ocean Ave; slice $2; 11am-2pm) It's not the best pizza, but it will do. Especially if you're trying to find something that doesn't have fish in it. The very daring might try their 'breakfast pizza,' which is a pizza crust filled with eggs and topped with lots of meat, peppers and onion.

Mohegan Café & Brewery (☎ 401-466-5911; Water St; burgers & mains $7-23; 11am-10pm) Besides brewing its own beer, this place serves fish-and-chips, veggie wraps and rosemary-rubbed salmon under a pressed-tin roof. It's a dark-wood pub with a few model ships lying around.

Harborside Inn (☎ 401-466-5504; Water St; dinner mains $20-25; 8am-9pm Sun-Thu, 8am-10pm Fri & Sat) A good lunch choice. Sit on a resin chair under a string of umbrellas on a long, raised porch overlooking the passing Water St crowds. It serves American classics such as baked stuffed lobster, prime rib, burgers ($7) and a big menu of salads ($10 to $15).

Winfield's (☎ 401-466-5856; Corn Neck Rd; mains $25-31; from 5:30pm) This upscale room has exposed wooden ceiling beams, white table-cloths, wide floorboards and a menu of items such as salmon roasted on a cedar plank with fresh horseradish, risotto and maple-brined pork.

Hotel Manisses (☎ 401-466-2421; Spring St; mains $20-37; 5:30-9:30pm) Dine in either the Gatsby Room, a tall-ceilinged space with old light fixtures and wicker, or on a fine patio surrounded by flowers and bubbling statuary. The creative menu features local seafood, vegetables from the hotel's garden and sautéed frog legs. Have flaming coffees and outrageous desserts in the parlor.

Drinking

McGovern's Yellow Kittens (☎ 401-466-5855; Corn Neck Rd; from noon) Just north of Old Harbor, McGovern's Yellow Kittens attracts New England–area bands and keeps patrons happy with pool, table tennis and darts. It's been called Yellow Kittens since 1876.

Captain Nick's (☎ 401-466-5670; Ocean Ave; from 5pm) With a patch over one eye, this youngster offers drinks, good times and liquid treasure. It's got live music six days a week, sometimes acoustic, often rock. Please don't forget your bandanna.

Juice n' Java (☎ 401-466-5220; Dodge St; 7am-midnight) This popular coffee shop also serves smoothies – something you'll be very thankful for after last night's encounter with two pounds of lobster and butter. Also on offer are healthy sandwiches, many of them vegetarian. The colorfully painted room provides Internet access ($10 per hour).

Entertainment

Though Block Island quietens down after the last ferry leaves, you can still find some stuff to do at night. Don't forget about drinking (above).

There are two places to catch first-run movies on Block Island: **Oceanwest Theater** (☎ 401-466-2971; New Harbor) and the **Empire** (☎ 401-466-2555; cnr High & Water Sts), which is in a former roller-skating rink in Old Harbor.

Shopping

Opportunities for shopping are limited. Most shops are small, seasonal boutiques along Water and Dodge Sts in Old Harbor. Take a look at the **Boatworks & B.I. Kite Company** (☎ 401-466-2033; Corn Neck Rd; from 9am) if you enjoy running around the beach with strings and diamonds, and the **Star Department Store** (☎ 401-466-554; Water St; 8:30am-10pm), a wood-floored classic that calls itself 'Block Island's general store.' Come here for saltwater taffy and corny island souvenirs.

Getting There & Around
AIR
New England Airlines (☎ 401-800-243-2460) provides air service between Westerly State Airport, on Airport Rd off RI 78, and Block Island State Airport (one way/round-trip $45/76; 12 minutes).

BICYCLE
Biking around the island might be the highlight of your trip, and your best bet for transportation. See p302 for rental information, or bring one on the ferry.

BOAT
Interstate Navigation Co (☎ 401-783-4613; www.block islandferry.com) operates the car-and-passenger ferries from Galilee State Pier, Point Judith, to Old Harbor, Block Island ($15 same day round-trip, one hour, eight times daily mid-June to early September). Cars are carried for $77.80 round-trip; reserve your car space in advance. Bicycles are carried for $2.50 each way. In winter, service is infrequent with perhaps one to three daily departures.

A daily Interstate passenger boat runs in summer (July to mid-September) to Newport's Fort Adams Dock (one way/round-trip $9/13, two hours, one daily) to Old Harbor, Block Island; children pay half the price of adult fares. This boat takes bikes but not cars; finding inexpensive parking in Newport can be difficult.

Island High-Speed Ferry (☎ 401-877-733-9425; www.islandhighspeedferry.com) runs quick catamaran service to New Harbor (round-trip $29; 30 minutes; eight daily) from Point Judith. Its dock is close to Interstate's, and it operates from mid-May to mid-October.

Block Island Ferry Services (☎ 860-444-4624; www .goblockisland.com) offers service from New London, CT, to New Harbor (round-trip $25 to $30, one hour, four daily).

CAR
You don't need a car to get around Block Island and, aside from hotel parking lots, there aren't many places to put one. You'll save a ton of money by leaving it behind, and, besides, you don't really want to screw with the island's pristine ecology.

Block Island Bike & Car Rental (☎ 401-466-2297; Ocean Ave) rents cars, or you can hire a taxi. There are usually several taxis available at the ferry dock in Old Harbor and in New Harbor. See p302 for moped rentals.

WATCH HILL
pop 2000
One of the toniest summer colonies in the Ocean State, Watch Hill occupies a spit of land at the southwesternmost point of Rhode Island, just south of Westerly. Drive into the village along winding RI 1A, and the place grabs you: huge, shingled and Queen Anne summerhouses command the rolling landscape from their perches high on rocky knolls. These houses show the wealth of their owners with subtle good taste; though they were built around the turn of the century, contemporaneously with Newport's mansions, they aren't flashy palaces. Perhaps partly because of that, Watch Hill's houses are still in private hands, while Newport's became white elephants, rescued only as tourist attractions.

Visitors not lucky enough to own a summerhouse here spend their time at the beach and browsing in the shops along Bay St, the main street, a mere two blocks long. If you haven't yet hit puberty or if you've brought children, an ice-cream cone from St Clair's Annex (opposite) and a twirl on the Flying Horses Carousel (below) provide immediate gratification and fodder for fond memories.

Information
Summertime parking in tiny Watch Hill is a real hassle. Most curb parking is vigorously reserved for town residents. If you're lucky, you can snag a free spot (strict three-hour limit) on Bay St. Otherwise, expect to shell out $10 to $15 at one of several lots.

Watch Hill is at the end of Watch Hill Rd, 6 miles south of Westerly and 12 roundabout miles east of Stonington, CT, by car.

Sights & Activities
FLYING HORSES CAROUSEL
The antique merry-go-round at the end of Bay St dates from 1883. Besides being among the few historic carousels still in operation in the country, it boasts a unique design: its horses are suspended on chains so that they really do 'fly' outward as the carousel spins around. Rides cost $1 apiece.

Yes, riders can grab for rings (a brass one equals a free ride).

BEACHES

For a leisurely beach walk, the half-mile stroll to **Napatree Point**, at the westernmost tip of Watch Hill, is unbeatable. With the Atlantic on one side and the yacht-studded Little Narragansett Bay on the other, Napatree is a protected conservation area, so walkers are asked to stay on the trails and off the dunes.

The nearest state beach to Watch Hill is Misquamicut State Beach (p308), 3 miles to the east along RI 1A, but there is a fine free beach right in Watch Hill, in front of the closed Ocean House Hotel. It stretches for several pretty miles from the Watch Hill lighthouse all the way to Misquamicut, with the open ocean crashing on one side and large, gray-shingled homes rising behind grassy dunes on the other. Access to the beach is by a right-of-way off Bluff Ave near Larkin Rd. The closest parking is on Bay St. There are no facilities on the beach and neighboring property owners are vigilant about restricting beachgoers to the public area below the high-tide line. There's also small **Watch Hill Beach** (adult/child $6/4; 🕑 10am-7pm Mon-Fri, 9am-6pm Sat & Sun) behind the Flying Horses Carousel.

Sleeping

Watch Hill Inn (☎ 401-348-6300; www.watchhillinn.com; 38 Bay St; r peak season $165-250, nonpeak season $100-150; 🅿 ✕ 🐾) The wood-floored rooms of this pleasant inn contain Victorian-ish furnishings and overlook the bobbing boats floating in the harbor across the street. It sells out early and hosts a lot of wedding parties.

You could also stay at Grandview B&B (see p309).

Eating

Bay St Deli (☎ 401-596-6606; 112 Bay St; sandwiches $6.50-8; 🕑 8am-8pm) Locals come here for takeout prepared items and specialty sandwiches (roast beef and munster cheese on pumpernickel or a wrap of tabbouleh, cucumber, tomato and sprouts) good for picnics.

St Clair's Annex (☎ 401-348-8407; 41 Bay St; cones from $2; 🕑 7:45am-9pm) This ice-cream shop, across the street from the deli, has been run by the same family for more than a century, and features several dozen flavors of homemade ice-cream. If you don't feel like a frozen treat, they've got breakfast omelettes, hot dogs and lobster salad.

Olympia Tea Room (☎ 401-348-8211; 74 Bay St; lunch $10-15, dinner $14-25; 🕑 from 11am) The most atmospheric restaurant in town, the Olympia is an authentic 1916 soda-fountain-turned-bistro. Varnished wooden booths, pink walls, black-and-white checkered tiles on the floor and the antique marble-topped soda fountain help to ease stuffed flounder and gingerbread down your throat.

In addition to these listings, Bay St has a few other places to grab a snack, including an espresso joint and a pizza place.

SOUTH COUNTY AREA BEACHES

Grab an umbrella, a blanket and four rocks. Not much beats a well-chosen piece of sandy turf on a sunny August day in South County. The sandy shore extends virtually uninterrupted for several dozen miles, and much of it is open to the public. Some beaches teem with thousands of well-oiled young bodies smooshed together like an overstuffed drawer full of hand-knitted sweaters. Others are more subdued, where visitors can thin themselves into relative privacy across a long landscape.

Those afraid of melanomas or disconcerted by the chilly water temperatures in June and early July should take heart that many of the beaches lie near a series of massive salt ponds. These salt ponds are home to multitudes of waterfowl and shellfish, and some (such as Trustom Pond in South Kingstown) have been designated national wildlife refuges. They make for excellent bird-watching. You're likely to see herons, egrets and sandpipers hunting for lunch, and, at low tide, clams squirting from beneath the muddy sand.

Orientation & Information

The stretch of beach that runs from Watch Hill to Point Judith directly faces the Atlantic and has a different kind of geography from the stretch that runs north from Point Judith to Narragansett, which partially faces Narragansett Bay.

The Atlantic-facing stretch is a wide apron of pristine sand separating huge salt ponds such as Quonochontaug and Ninigret from the surfy, generally seaweed-free open ocean. These beaches, which trace the coast like a necklace looped with tidal salt ponds, are similar in nature and, geologically speaking, are all the same beach.

The beaches that front the Narragansett Bay are smaller and divided from one another. Many are in coves surrounded dramatically by huge boulders. These are particularly lovely early and late in the day, when the sun slants on the granite, stage-lighting the scene. They generally have better surf.

For information on the South County area, including beaches and attractions, contact the **South County Tourism Council** (☎ 401-789-4422, 800-548-4662; www.southcountyri.com; 4808 Tower Hill Rd, Wakefield; ☻ 9am-5pm Mon-Fri). For information on the town of Narragansett and its vicinity, hit up the **Narragansett Chamber of Commerce** (☎ 401-783-7121; www.narragansettri.com/chamber; The Towers, RI 1A, PO Box 742, Narragansett, RI 02882; ☻ 9am-4pm). For information on all of Rhode Island's state beaches, call the **Rhode Island Division of Parks & Recreation** (☎ 401-222-2321; www.riparks.com).

Beaches

The following patches of sand (listed from east to west) represent only a partial list of stone-skipping possibilities. At all of them, a parking tariff is imposed from late May to the end of September. At state beaches, Rhode Island residents pay $6 on weekdays and $7 on weekends for each car. Nonresidents pay $12 or $14. Town beaches charge similar rates.

SCARBOROUGH STATE BEACH
Scarborough (sometimes written as 'Scarboro') is the prototypical Rhode Island beach, considered by many the best in the state. A massive, castle-like pavilion, generous boardwalks, a wide and long beachfront, and great, predictable surf make Scarborough special. It tends to attract a lot of teenagers, but it's large enough that other people can take them or leave them. On a hot summer day, expect extra hordes of beachgoers.

NARRAGANSETT TOWN BEACH
Narragansett tends to be crowded because it's an easy walk from the beachy town of Narragansett Pier. It's the only beach in Rhode Island that charges a per-person admission fee ($4) on top of a parking fee ($5). Still, people – surfers in particular – adore it.

ROGER W WHEELER MEMORIAL BEACH
Colloquially known as **Sand Hill Cove**, this beach is the spot for families with small children. Not only does it have a playground and other facilities, it also has an extremely gradual drop-off and little surf because of protection afforded by the rocky arms of a breakwater called the Point Judith Harbor of Refuge. Roger W Wheeler Memorial Beach is just south of Galilee.

SOUTH KINGSTOWN TOWN BEACH
A sandy beach that epitomizes the South County model, the Town Beach provides a small pavilion with restrooms and changing rooms. There's convenient parking in nearby Wakefield.

BLUE SHUTTERS TOWN BEACH
A Charlestown-managed beach, this is also a good choice for families. There are no amusements other than nature's, but there are convenient facilities, a watchful staff of lifeguards, generally mild surf and smaller crowds.

MISQUAMICUT STATE BEACH
With good surf and close proximity to the Connecticut state line, Misquamicut draws huge crowds. It offers families low prices and convenient facilities for changing, showering and eating. Another plus is that it's near an old-fashioned amusement area, Atlantic Beach Park, which ranges between charming and derelict. Here you'll find plenty to enjoy or avoid – water slides, miniature golf, batting cages, kiddie rides, arcade games and, for a lucky few, tetanus shots. Misquamicut is situated just south of Westerly.

Sleeping
For extra listings, contact **B&B Referrals of South Coast Rhode Island** (☎ 800-853-7479; ☻ 11am-7pm), a collective group of 22 quality places in and around the southern coast. The phone is manned by someone familiar with an up-to-date list of vacancies.

BUDGET
Burlingame State Park Campsites (☎ 401-322-7337; www.riparks.com; off US 1 N, Charlestown; tent sites RI residents/nonresidents $14/20; ☻ mid-April–mid-Oct) This lovely campground has more than 750 spacious wooded sites near crystal-clear Watchaug Pond, which provides a good beach for swimming. The park occupies 2100 acres. First-come, first-served is the rule, but you can call ahead to check

on availability. Your stay is limited to two weeks.

Worden's Pond Family Campground (☎ 401-789-9113; 416a Worden's Pond Rd, South Kingstown; tent/RV sites $20/25; ☺ May–mid-Oct) This pleasantly wooded family-owned campground, with 75 tent sites and 125 RV sites, provides access to a calm pond where you can fish and swim. They've got coin-operated showers, a playground and pits for playing the game of horseshoes. From US Hwy 1, follow RI 110, and turn at the second left (Worden's Pond Rd); from there it's less than a mile to the campground.

Fishermen's Memorial State Park (☎ 401-789-8374; www.riparks.com; off RI 108; tent sites RI residents/nonresidents $14/20) In the fishing port of Galilee, this place is so popular that many families return year after year to the same site. There are only 180 campsites at Fishermen's, so it's wise to reserve early by requesting the necessary form from the park management (1011 Point Judith Rd, Narragansett, RI 02882) or the **Division of Parks & Recreation** (☎ 401-222-2632; 2321 Hartford Ave, Johnston, RI 02919).

MID-RANGE

Admiral Dewey Inn (☎ 401-783-2090; 800-457-2090; www.admiraldeweyinn.com; 668 Matunuck Beach Rd, South Kingstown; r $100-150) Near the beachy town of Matunuck, this 1898 National Historic Register building with 10 rooms offers reasonable rates and a two-minute walk to the beach. Most of the rooms in the gray-shingled inn have water views, and there's a broad porch that catches the ocean breeze.

Grandview B&B (☎ 401-596-6384, 800-447-6384; www.grandviewbandb.com; 212 Shore Rd/RI 1A; r peak season $90-120, nonpeak season $85-95) Within the town limits of Westerly, yet close to the beach town of Weekapaug, this modestly furnished guesthouse boasts a stone porch and a knowledgeable proprietor full of friendly tips about the area. In the living room, notice the snowman left behind by the mysterious Apple Valley Quilters.

The Richards (☎ 401-789-7746; therichards144@hotmail.com; 144 Gibson Ave; r $115-175) Built of locally quarried granite, the Gothic English-manor look sets it apart from other B&Bs in Narragansett. Each room contains a working fireplace, and there's a nice garden on the grounds. It's a 10-minute drive to the University of Rhode Island. No kids under 12 are allowed.

TOP END

Weekapaug Inn (☎ 401-322-0301; www.weekapauginn.com; 25 Spray Rock Rd, Weekapaug; lodging per person incl all meals $197-295) A classic with its wraparound porch and lawn sloping down to Quonochontaug Pond (a saltwater tidal pool), this vast shingled inn caters to a rather sedate crowd, many of whom have been regulars for decades. Expect croquet, shuffleboard, tennis and no phones or (gasp!) liquor license. The inn's setting, with its own private ocean beach, is one of the loveliest in New England. Men must wear jackets to dinner.

Eating

Not surprisingly, seafood is the order of the day in South County. Most spots are casual and beachy; shorts and T-shirts are far more common than suits and ties. Nearly every beach has its collection of clam shacks and snack shops good for a quick lunch. For a more elaborate meal, you might just head to Newport, Providence or drop by Point Judith.

Coast Guard House (☎ 401-789-0700; 40 Ocean Dr, Narragansett; mains $13-24; ☺ dinner from 5pm daily, lunch 11:30am-3pm Mon-Fri) For an upscale dinner, this place has long been a Rhode Island favorite, serving pastas, seafood stew and delicious crab cakes. It occupies a dramatic seaside site (waves crash enthusiastically against the building during storms), and practically abuts the stunning Narragansett Towers, two heavy stone towers connected by a bold bridge spanning Ocean Dr, built in the 1880s.

Entertainment

Quiet, seaside South County is not noted for its nightlife, but there are a couple of places in the area where folks can stay up past 9pm.

Theatre-by-the-Sea (☎ 401-782-8587; www.theatrebythesea.com; Cards Pond Rd, South Kingstown; tickets $32) Located in a scenic area close to the beaches of Matunuck, this venue offers a summer schedule of likable musicals and plays in one of the oldest barn theaters in the US.

Ocean Mist (☎ 401-782-3740; 145 Matunuck Beach Rd, South Kingstown; ☺ to 1am) For live music (rock, blues, reggae), try this lively bar. The deck extends over the beach, where you might glimpse a midnight loner casting for blue fish should it get too loud for you inside. They've got pub food and pool tables.

RHODE ISLAND

Shopping

Fantastic Umbrella Factory (☎ 401-364-6616; RI 1A, Charlestown) A sprawling collection of 19th-century farm buildings and elaborate, unkempt gardens, this former commune got its start as one of Rhode Island's strangest stores in 1968. You can find almost anything in the series of sheds filled with a wide variety of gift items: everything from flower bulbs and perennials to greeting cards, toys and handmade jewelry. The organic café (a rarity in Rhode Island) serves quality stuff, and exotic birds and farm animals walk all over the place.

Benny's (☎ 401-783-5170; 688 Kingstown Rd, Wakefield) People in Rhode Island couldn't live without Benny's, an odd chain of small department stores where the strangely service-minded clerks will invariably ask you if need help finding anything. It's hands-down the best place to buy cheap beach supplies (chairs, towels, plastic flip-flops, coolers). While the experience is impossible to describe, those who regularly visit Benny's over a year begin to see it as the living symbol of the state's common culture.

Getting There & Away

Though the Shore Route Amtrak trains between Boston and New York stop in Westerly, you really need a car to efficiently get to the beaches. For those without, RIPTA operate a summer **Beach Bus** (round-trip $3.50, one hour, one daily). From late June to early August, a single bus leaves from Providence, traveling to Galilee State Pier, Roger M Wheeler Memorial Beach and Scarborough State Beach. You'll have about four hours at the shore before the return bus to Providence.

Distances are not great (this is Rhode Island); from Westerly to Wakefield is only about 21 miles. Be warned: traffic to and from the South County beaches can be horrendous on hot summer weekends. Come early, stay late.

Connecticut

HIGHLIGHTS

- **Most Convincing 19th-Century Time Warps**
  Soaking in the atmosphere at the Mystic Seaport Museum (p315), strolling through frozen-in-time colonial Litchfield (p348) and touring Mark Twain's Hartford mansion (p343)

- **Most Likely City in Which to Hobnob With a Future President**
  Immersing yourself in the lively restaurant, museum and theater scene of New Haven (p326)

- **Best Sugar Highs**
  Making your own soda the old-fashioned way at Avery's Beverage Co (p348) in New Britain, and indulging in a few morsels of Belgian chocolate at Belgique Patisserie & Chocolatier (p351) in Kent

- **Best Place to Win – or Lose – Big**
  Trying your luck at the largest casino on earth, (p320)

- **Most Enchanting Drive**
  Whiling away the afternoon on the 12-mile stretch of MA 169 between Woodstock and Brooklyn (p325) picking apples, browsing greenhouses and poking around antique shops

- **TELEPHONE CODE: 860, 203**   - **POPULATION: 3.5 MILLION**   - **AREA: 4845 SQ MILES**

Connecticut

CONNECTICUT

Connecticut isn't one to flaunt her charms. She doesn't so much *suffer* in the shadows of nearby New York City and the more 'New Englandy' northern states as relish in them, reaping the benefits of both associations – like top-notch eateries opened by victims of urban fatigue – minus the attending nuisances that come with overexposure.

To drivers zipping through on I-95, the state may appear as one large industrial zone or bedroom community. But while the coastal region does manufacture everything from helicopters to submarines, and the towns bordering the commuter rails house an army of Manhattan migrants, the harbors of these towns are also home to watermen who still ply the Sound for lobsters and oysters. Exiting the freeway one immediately starts to believe the claim that though it's among the most densely populated states in the country, fully three-quarters of Connecticut is rural.

Though many visitors are drawn to the justifiably popular Mystic Seaport Museum, the re-creation of a 19th-century working coastal town, and to gamble at the largest casino on the planet, such a trip hardly scratches the surface. The Litchfield Hills are awash in forests and vineyards, sparkling lakes and covered bridges. A bizarre-looking castle guards the banks of Mark Twain's beloved Connecticut River, while Twain's house in Hartford is a fanciful reflection of the man himself. New Haven, with Yale University's stately campus and world-class museums, has grown into its name splendidly; Norwalk's SoNo restaurant district is garnering attention; and New London is shaking off decades of torpor with a homegrown arts renaissance.

Information

Connecticut Office of Tourism (☎ 800-282-6863; www.ctbound.org; 505 Hudson St, Hartford) Get a free, comprehensive *Connecticut Vacation Guide*, by mail or at a Welcome Center (at Bradley International Airport Terminals A and B and on major highways entering the state).

CT Now (www.ctnow.com) Online version of the *Hartford Courant*. Free registration required.

Nutmeg B&B Agency (☎ 860-236-6698, 800-727-7592; www.bnb-link.com). For booking of B&Bs. There's a 12% hotel tax levied on all accommodations charges. Figure it in when calculating your lodging costs.

Visit Connecticut (www.visitconnecticut.com) Breaks down the state into regions and offers links to lodging, activities and transportation.

Climate

As with the rest of New England, Connecticut (CT) is truly a four-season destination, and its climate does not dramatically differ from that of the rest of the region; winters are generally cold and snowy, with summers ranging from pleasantly warm to scorching and humid.

In terms of autumnal colors, the Litchfield Hills in the northwest, the northeast Quiet Corner and the state's southwest strip tend to peak over the first two weeks of October. Hartford and its central environs follow a week or so later. Call Connecticut's **foliage hotline** (☎ 800-282-6863) for specifics.

State Parks & Forests

The state has a bevy of wonderful – and some wonderfully undervisited – parks to hike, fish, swim and camp in. (For camping options, including private campgrounds, grab a free copy of the *Connecticut Campground Directory* at any welcome center.) Many sites are designated as parks but are known more for their cultural, historical or simply fun elements, such as the **Essex Steam Train Riverboat Ride** (p337) and the **Dinosaur State Park** (p347), south of Hartford.

Though many Nutmeggers head straight to Watch Hill in Rhode Island when they crave serious ocean action, there are several

CONNECTICUT

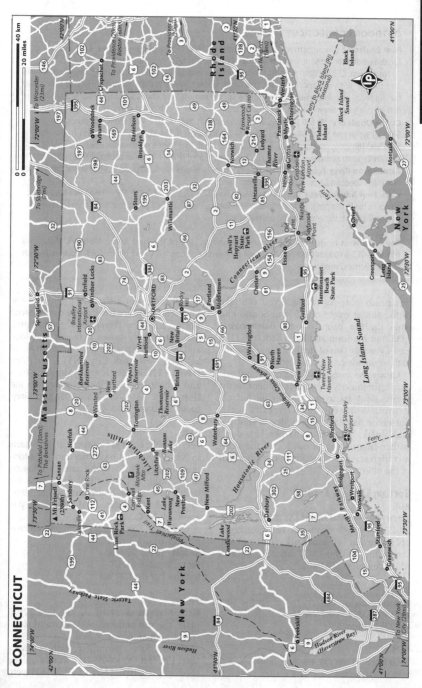

OUTDOOR CONNECTICUT

New England's three northern states – Vermont, New Hampshire and Maine – are justly noted for their outdoor activities, but that doesn't mean that Connecticut can't compete.

Northwest Connecticut's Housatonic River is particularly good for canoeing, kayaking, rafting and tubing. With the spring floods, the white water can reach Class III. Expect to pay about $90 for guided white-water rafting during the spring run-off, and about $25 for unguided rafting the rest of the year. Here is a list of some of the more well-established companies:

Clarke Outdoors (☎ 860-672-6365, www.clarkeoutdoors.com; 163 US 7, West Cornwall; 2-person canoeing $47-52, kayaking per person $40, rafting adult $24-27, child under 16 $14-17; ☿ 10am-5pm Mon-Fri, 9am-6pm Sat & Sun) This group can equip you with a canoe, kayak or raft for a 10-mile run down the Housatonic River. It also leads white-water rafting trips during spring's high water. Guided rafting trips are an additional $80.

Farmington River Tubing (☎ 860-693-6465; www.farmingtonrivertubing.com; CT 44, New Hartford; $18-20 cash only) Tube down 2.5 miles of the Farmington River.

Huck Finn Adventures (☎ 860-693-0385, PO Box 137, Collinsville, CT 06022; $18-20) Huck Finn has a similar service on the Farmington River to Farmington River Tubing. They also offer a guided tour through the Lost Park River, miles of spacious tunnels buried under Hartford.

The Northwest is also home to many ski resorts, one of the best being **Mohawk Mountain** (☎ 860-672-6100, 800-895-5222; www.mohawkmtn.com; 46 Great Hollow Rd, Cornwall) with a 650ft vertical drop.

fine beach state parks where you can take in the sunset over Long Island Sound and frolic in the calm waters. **Hammonasset** (p332) in Madison and **Rocky Neck** (p317) in East Lyme are two of the best, though summer weekends can see big crowds.

Officially, Connecticut's state park authorities are persnickety about your resident versus nonresident status, so displaying out-of-state plates may cost you a few extra bucks. But enforcement of this policy is spotty – many parks, especially the beaches, don't bother charging at all outside of the summer high season, especially in the latter half of the afternoon.

Getting There & Around
AIR
Bradley International Airport (☎ 860-292-2000, 888-624-1533; www.bradleyairport.com), 12 miles north of Hartford in Windsor Locks (I-91 exit 40), serves the Hartford, CT and Springfield, Massachusetts (MA) area.

BOAT
For information on ferry travel, see the New Haven (p332) and New London & Groton (p325) sections.

BUS
Peter Pan Bus Lines (☎ 413-781-3320, 800-343-9999; www.peterpanbus.com) operates routes connect-

ing all the major cities and towns in New England. There are five buses a day between Boston and New Haven ($31, four hours), and three daily buses between Hartford and New Haven ($12.50, one hour) and between New York City (NYC) and New Haven ($21.50, 2½ hours). Similar prices and schedules are offered by **Bonanza Bus Lines** (☎ 401-331-7500, 800-556-3815) and **Greyhound Bus Lines** (☎ 800-231-2222).

CAR
I-95 hugs the coast of Connecticut. I-91 starts in New Haven and heads north. US 7 shimmies up the west side of the state, backboning the Berkshires. Connecticut fuel prices are usually at least 10% higher than in neighboring New England states and increase as you approach NYC.

Car rental companies at Bradley International Airport include:
Budget (☎ 800-527-0700)
Hertz (☎ 800-331-1212)
National (☎ 800-217-7368)

TRAIN
Metro-North trains (☎ 212-532-4900, 800-638-7646) make the run between NYC's Grand Central Station and New Haven.

Connecticut Commuter Rail Service's **Shore Line East** (☎ 800-255-7433) travels up the shore of Long Island Sound. At New Haven, the Shore Line East trains connect with Metro-North and Amtrak routes.

Amtrak (☎ 800-872-7245) trains depart NYC's Penn Station for Connecticut on three lines.

CONNECTICUT COAST

Connecticut's coastline on Long Island Sound is long and varied. Industrial and commercial cities and bedroom communities dominate the western coast. The central coast, from New Haven to the mouth of the Connecticut River, is less urban, with historic towns and villages. The eastern coast includes Mystic, where the Mystic Seaport Museum brings maritime history to life.

MYSTIC

pop 4000

As you round a corner on US 1 heading west into town, your eye is presented with the skyline of masts belonging to the vessels bobbing ever so slightly in the postcard-perfect harbor. There's a sense of self-satisfied calm and composure in the air – until suddenly a heart-stopping steamer whistle blows, followed by the cheerful cling of a drawbridge bell. You know you've arrived in Mystic. And you're not alone.

Mystic was a classic seaport town centuries before the Seaport Museum became such a popular tourist attraction, and the town remains a memorable place to stroll, shop, dine and slurp ice-cream. Less than 10 miles north is the state's official biggest draw, the Foxwoods and Mohegan Sun casinos.

Orientation

Take I-95 exit 90 for the Mystic Seaport Museum and town center. Motels are both north and south of I-95; Mystic Seaport Museum is a mile south of the highway on CT 27 (Greenmanville Ave); the center of the town is less than a mile south further down. Old Mystic is a separate town to the north of I-95.

The Mystic River Bascule Bridge (1922), known locally as 'the drawbridge,' carries US 1 across the Mystic River at the center of the town. It's a familiar ritual in Mystic to wait while the drawbridge is raised for river traffic. There are restaurants situated on both sides of the bridge; most of the ice-cream

shops are on the west side, where you'll also find high-end clothing boutiques and establishments with names like 'Framers of the Lost Art.'

Information

Bank of America (54 W Main St) Has an ATM.

Bank Square Books (☎ 860-536-3795; 53 W Main St; 🕙 10am-6pm Mon & Tue, 10am-9pm Wed-Sat, 11:30am-6pm Sun) This bookstore keeps a good stock of local interest titles, plus the usual suspects. (Note the carving in the shape of a whale on the sidewalk just outside the store.)

Library (☎ 860-536-7721; 40 Library St; 🕙 10am-9pm Mon-Fri, 9am-1pm Sat) This offers Internet access for 25¢ per 20 minutes.

Mystic & Shoreline Visitors Information Center (☎ 860-536-1641; www.mysticinfo.com; 27 Coogan Blvd; 🕙 9am-6pm Mon-Sat, 9am-4:30pm Sun in summer, closes at 4:30pm daily rest of year) The best stop for tourist information in town, located next to the Olde Mystick Village.

Mystic Chamber of Commerce (☎ 860-572-9578; www.mysticchamber.org; 14 Holmes St, Schooner's Wharf) This chamber of commerce is another resource for travelers. There's also a small **information kiosk** (🕙 9am-5pm Mon-Fri) in the train station on Roosevelt St.

Sights & Activities

MYSTIC SEAPORT MUSEUM

From simple beginnings in the 17th century, the village of Mystic grew to become one of the great shipbuilding ports of the East Coast. In the mid-19th century, Mystic's shipyards launched clipper ships, many from the George Greenman & Co Shipyard, which is now the site of **Mystic Seaport Museum** (☎ 860-572-0711; 75 Greenmanville Ave/CT 27; adult/child 6-15/senior $17/9/15; 🕙 9am-5pm). Today, the museum covers 17 acres and includes more than 60 historic buildings, four ships and many smaller vessels. Some buildings in the Seaport are original to the site, but as at Old Sturbridge Village in Massachusetts (p233), many were transported to Mystic from other parts of New England and arranged to re-create the look of the past. Interpreters staff all the buildings and talk about their crafts and trades. Most fun are the demonstrations scattered throughout the day, illuminating such topics as ship-rescue procedures, maritime flag signals and whale-boat launching.

Visitors can board the *Charles W Morgan* (1841), the last surviving American wooden whaling ship; the *LA Dunton,* a three-masted fishing schooner; or the *Joseph*

CONNECTICUT

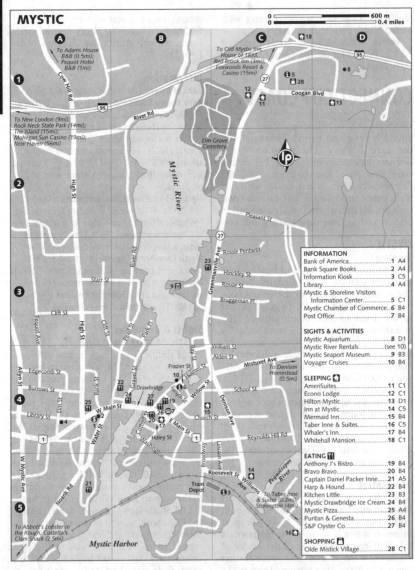

MYSTIC

INFORMATION
Bank of America	1 A4
Bank Square Books	2 A4
Information Kiosk	3 C5
Library	4 A4
Mystic & Shoreline Visitors Information Center	5 C1
Mystic Chamber of Commerce	6 B4
Post Office	7 B4

SIGHTS & ACTIVITIES
Mystic Aquarium	8 D1
Mystic River Rentals	(see 10)
Mystic Seaport Museum	9 B3
Voyager Cruises	10 B4

SLEEPING
AmeriSuites	11 C1
Econo Lodge	12 C1
Hilton Mystic	13 D1
Inn at Mystic	14 C5
Mermaid Inn	15 B4
Taber Inne & Suites	16 C5
Whaler's Inn	17 B4
Whitehall Mansion	18 D1

EATING
Anthony J's Bistro	19 B4
Bravo Bravo	20 B4
Captain Daniel Packer Inne	21 A5
Harp & Hound	22 B4
Kitchen Little	23 B4
Mystic Drawbridge Ice Cream	24 B4
Mystic Pizza	25 A4
Puritan & Genesta	26 B4
S&P Oyster Co.	27 B4

SHOPPING
Olde Mistick Village	28 C1

Conrad, a square-rigged training ship. The museum's exhibits include a replica of the 77ft schooner *Amistad*, the slave ship on which 55 kidnapped Africans cast off their chains and sailed to freedom. In the Steven Spielberg movie *Amistad*, the museum was used to stage many of the scenes that actually took place in colonial New London.

At the Henry B duPont Preservation Shipyard, visitors can watch large wooden boats being restored. Be sure not to miss the Wendell Building, which houses a fascinating collection of ships' figureheads and carvings. Close by is a small 'museum' (more like a playroom) for children aged seven and under. The Seaport also includes a small boat shop, general store, chapel, school, pharmacy, sail loft, shipsmith and ship chandlery – all the sorts of places that you'd expect to find in a real shipbuilding town of 150 years ago.

The **Sabino** (☎ 860-572-5315; adult/child 6-12 $5.25/4.25), a 1908-era steamboat, takes visitors on excursion trips up the Mystic River from May to October. The boat departs from the museum hourly on the half-hour.

MYSTIC AQUARIUM & INSTITUTE FOR EXPLORATION

This state-of-the-art **aquarium** (☎ 860-572-5955; www.mysticaquarium.org; 55 Coogan Blvd; adult/child 3-12/senior $16/11/15; ☉ 9am-6pm Mar-Nov, 10am-4pm Mon-Fri & 9am-6pm Sat & Sun Dec-Feb) boasts more than 6000 species of sea creatures (including a beluga whale), an outdoor viewing area for seals and sea lions, a penguin exhibit, a 1400-seat Marine Theater for dolphin shows, and an 'immersion' theater which involves live underwater web feed of places like the Monterey Bay Marine Sanctuary. The aquarium is also home to the research and exhibition center for the Institute for Exploration, a leader in the field of deep-sea archaeology. Use I-95 exit 90 to get to the museum.

DENISON HOMESTEAD

This **property** (☎ 860-536-9248; 120 Pequotsepos Rd; adult/child under 16/senior & student $4/1/3; ☉ noon-4pm Thu-Mon May-Oct) was home to six generations of the Denison family from 1717 until the 1940s. Each of the rooms is decorated in the style of a different time period: a colonial kitchen, a Revolution-era bedroom, a Federal parlor, a Civil War bedroom and an early-20th-century living room. The last tour starts at 3:30pm.

OLDE MISTICK VILLAGE

Just south of I-95, this pseudocolonial **village green** (☎ 860-536-4941; Coogan Blvd; ☉ 10am-6pm Mon-Sat, noon-5pm Sun) is centered on a Congregational church and surrounded by over 60 shops selling sportswear, gifts, crafts, jewelry and Lladró porcelain.

Mystic's specialty is high-end clothing boutiques. Stroll Main St west of the drawbridge to take it all in.

BOATING, KAYAKING & CYCLING

There's no shortage of outfits ready to whisk you away on a watery adventure. **Voyager**

Cruises (☎ 860-536-0416; www.voyagermystic.com; 15 Holmes St) offers half-day or sunset cruises (adult/child $36/26) or harbor cruises (adult/child $25/15) on the authentic 19th-century replica schooner *Argia*.

You can rent bikes, kayaks and canoes for whole or half days from **Mystic River Rentals** (☎ 860-572-0123; ☉ 8am-6pm summer only), right next door to Voyager Cruises. Kayak lessons are also available.

Sleeping

Mystic offers a multitude of motels and inns, many of which post photographs and links at www.mysticmore.com. In July and August, most lodgings fill up every day. Consider alternatives in nearby communities such as Stonington, New London and Groton. All lodgings offer parking.

BUDGET

Most of Mystic's motels cluster near I-95 exit 90, particularly on CT 27 (Greenmanville Ave/Whitehall Ave) north and south of the interstate. Several other good choices lie east of the center of Mystic along US 1.

Econo Lodge (☎ 860-536-9666; 251 Greenmanville Ave/CT 27; d $89-169; ☑) Across CT 27, this slightly shabby motel has 56 rooms on two floors, all equipped with refrigerators and microwaves.

Though there are several state parks nearer, the closest with camping is **Rocky Neck State Park** (☎ 860-739-5471, 877-668-2267; 244 W Main St, East Lyme; sites $15). South of I-95 off exit 72, this is a well-developed state park with showers, swimming, hiking, horseback riding and a concession stand.

The Island (☎ 860-739-8316; 20 Islanda Ct, East Lyme; tent sites $40-45, RV sites $40-50) Accessible by a land bridge, this year-round campground is set within a lovely 150-acre lake. They take RVs and tent campers in their 35 sites (all but six of the sites are for RVs), some of which are right on the sandy beach. There are also six rustic lakeside **cottages** (☎ 860-739-6644), which are rented out by the week for around $600.

Seaport Campground (☎ 860-536-4044; www.seaportcampground.com; CT 184, Old Mystic; tent sites $33, RV sites without/with hookups $36/38) Seaport has 130 RV sites, a separate tenting area, and services from free hot showers to miniature golf. Open April until mid-September.

MID-RANGE

Whaler's Inn (☎ 800-243-2588, 860-536-1506; www
.whalersinnmystic.com; 20 E Main St; d $89-249) Right in
the center of Mystic, by the drawbridge, this
recently renovated establishment consists
of an 1865 Victorian house, a contempora-
neous inn and a more modern motel structure known as Stonington House. Room
rates vary depending upon the number and
size of beds and the building they're in. Ask
about seasonal packages that include, for
example, admission to the Seaport Museum, dinner for two or a schooner cruise.

Old Mystic Inn (☎ 860-572-9422; www.oldmysticinn
.com; 52 Main St, Old Mystic; d $115-185) Situated in
quiet Old Mystic, north of I-95, this cheerful red B&B has eight guest rooms, six with
working fireplaces (but specify if you want
gas or wood-burning), and two with whirlpool tubs. The rooms, most with four-poster
beds, are named after famous New England
authors.

Mermaid Inn (☎ 860-536-6223; www.mermaidinnof
mystic.com; 2 Broadway Ave; d $175-195) This charming
B&B with a pronounced mermaid theme sits
on a quiet street within walking distance of
the town center. Its three rooms each have
a private bathroom (with bidet), TV and
special touches like fresh flowers and Italian
chocolates. In warm weather, guests enjoy
breakfast on the porch.

Red Brook Inn (☎ 860-572-0349, 800-290-5619; www
.redbrookinn.com; cnr CT 184 & Wells Rd; d $115-165) Three
miles from town, the rural Red Brook Inn
offers guests a choice of two buildings: the
Haley Tavern (1740) with seven guest rooms
and the Crary Homestead (1770) with three.
One can retire to the Gentleman's Parlor
or the Ladies' Parlor in the evening, or the
more inclusive Old Tavern room. Breakfast
is included and it's a hearty one.

Adams House B&B (☎ 860-572-9551; 382 Cow Hill Rd;
d $95-175). Located 1.5 miles from the center of
town, Adams House offers seven cozy rooms
with queen beds and private bathrooms, and
several with a fireplace. The garden cottage
is a good choice for families. Afternoon tea
is included.

Pequot Hotel B&B (☎ 860-572-0390; www.pequot
hotelbandb.com; 711 Cow Hill Rd; d $95-175) This
lovely piece of property was once a stagecoach stop and now has three luxury guest
rooms with bathroom (two with fireplaces).
There are cats and a friendly dog in residence, too.

Taber Inne & Suites (☎ 860-536-4904, 866-466-
6978; www.taberinne.com; 66 Williams Ave; d $85-295,
townhouses $275-375) Popular with families,
Taber offers quite a range of comfortable accommodations, from 28 pleasant motel-type
rooms through to luxurious one- and two-
bedroom townhouses. Guests get full access
to the Mystic Health Club, including the
sauna and indoor pool.

Hilton Mystic (☎ 860-572-0731, 800-445-8667;
www.hiltonmystic.com; 20 Coogan Blvd; d $129-249; 🐾)
This recently renovated Hilton has predictably comfortable accommodations in
a convenient location across from Mystic
Aquarium. Call to ask about special packages, like admission to the Seaport Museum
and the Aquarium. There is a PlayStation in
every room – you have been warned.

AmeriSuites (☎ 860-536-9997, 800-833-1516; 224
Greenmanville Ave/CT 27; ste $129-249; 🐾) Their 80
up-to-date suites, many of which sleep four
or six people, are a good bet for families.
The hotel has a fitness center and all rooms
have data ports and minikitchens.

TOP END

Inn at Mystic (☎ 860-536-9604, 800-237-2415; www.inn
atmystic.com; cnr US 1 & CT 27; d $85-295; 🐾) At this
hilltop Georgian mansion decorated with
colonial-style furniture and antiques, quarters range from simple, clean motel-style
units to luxury chambers, complete with
fireplaces and whirlpool baths. From the
inn's hilltop setting, lawns sweep down to
a boat dock and tennis court, and guests
are free to use the boats, kayaks and putting
greens. Humphrey Bogart and Lauren Bacall
spent their honeymoon here. The **Flood Tide**
(mains $18-24) restaurant is very well regarded.

Whitehall Mansion (☎ 860-572-7280, 800-572-
3993; 40 Whitehall Ave/CT 27; d incl breakfast $89-250)
This grand colonial house dates from 1771.
Each of the five rooms, one of which is
wheelchair accessible, has a fireplace, whirlpool bath and a queen-size canopy bed.
Evening wine and cheese are included.
You'll find the mansion just to the north
of I-95 at the Mystic exit, next to the rather
drab-looking Residence Inn. Whitehall
guests share many of Residence's amenities,
like their health facilities and indoor pool.

House of 1833 B&B (☎ 860-536-6325, 800-367-
1833; 72 N Stonington Rd/CT 201; d summer $99-179, winter
$129-249; 🐾) This Greek Revival mansion has
five luxury guest rooms that are heavy on

the florals and the pink tones. Avail yourself of the tennis court, outdoor pool and bikes. Music from the baby grand piano accompanies your two-course breakfast.

Eating & Drinking

There are several places to grab a snack or sit down to a full meal within Mystic Seaport Museum, but most of Mystic's restaurants are in or near the town center, close to the drawbridge.

BUDGET

Kitchen Little (☎ 860-536-2122; 135 Greenmanville Ave; mains $5-12; ☺ 6:30am-2pm Mon-Fri, 6:30am-1pm Sat & Sun) North of town, this family-run joint is *the* place for breakfast. Grab a seat at one of the tables on the back patio overlooking the water and start trawling through the lengthy, egg-heavy menu. Their ambitious-sounding specials tend to underdeliver – better to stick to their tried-and-trues. No credit cards accepted.

Puritan & Genesta (☎ 860-536-3537; 2 Holmes St; ☺ 8am-7pm Mon-Sat, 10am-6pm Sun) This natural foods store is the place to grab a healthy sandwich or wrap to go and other fast munchies.

Mystic Drawbridge Ice Cream (2 W Main St; ☺ 11am-9pm Sun-Thu, 11am-11pm Fri & Sat) Strolling through town is best done with ice-cream cone in hand, specifically one from here. Some of the more quirky flavors, like pumpkin pie and southern peach are seasonal, but on any given day there will be something innovative to try, like the gooeylicious Sticky Fractured Finger (pieces of butterfingers in caramel ice-cream).

MID-RANGE

Abbott's Lobster in the Rough (☎ 860-536-7719; www.abbotts-lobster.com; 117 Pearl St, Noank; mains $16-30; ☺ lunch & dinner May-Aug, noon-7pm Fri-Sun Sep-Oct) Lobster lovers should check out Abbott's, on the waterfront in neighboring Noank. You order your lobster (or other seafood) at the window, get a number, pick out a picnic table by the water and, when your number is called, pay and dig in. New England doesn't get much better than this on a warm summer night. Just down the road is Abbott's sister business, **Costello's Clam Shack** (www.costellos clamshack.com), open similar hours. To reach both from Mystic, take Water St/Rte 215 west. When you reach a stop sign take a left

(Mosher Ave) and stay right when it divides. Turn left onto Main St and right onto Pearl. BYOB beer or wine.

S&P Oyster Co (☎ 860-536-2674; 1 Holmes St; dinner mains $9-20; ☺ 11:30am-10pm) This place boasts that it has the only bar in town with a water view. The large serving of fish-and-chips is the number one main at lunch and dinner, and serves both New England– and Rhode Island–style clam chowder. There's a children's menu, too. You can dock your boat here while you eat.

Harp & Hound (☎ 860-572-7778; 4 Pearl St; ☺ noon-1am Sun-Thu, noon-2am Fri & Sat) Tucked in a colonial building on the west side of the drawbridge, this local pub offers up a respectable selection of Irish and Scottish malts and ales, and thoughtfully serves some nonliquid sustenance like shepherd's pie to line one's stomach. Stop in for the traditional Irish music if you're in town on a Sunday evening.

Mystic Pizza (☎ 860-536-3737; 56 W Main St; meals $6-18) If the name sounds familiar, it may be because it was the title of one of Julia Roberts' first films. The place might have inspired the movie, but sadly, the pizza, salads and grinders won't likely inspire you.

TOP END

Captain Daniel Packer Inne (☎ 860-536-3555; 32 Water St; mains lunch $8-16, dinner $25-30; ☺ 11am-4pm, 5-10pm) This friendly place occupies a historic house dating from 1754, complete with low-beam ceiling and creaky floorboards. Diners rave about the restaurant's imaginative American cuisine; a favorite is petite filet mignon with gorgonzola sauce and walnut demi-glace. The Inne lies on the west side of the drawbridge, then south on Water St.

Bravo Bravo (☎ 860-536-3228; cnr E Main & Holmes Sts; mains dinner $17-23; ☺ lunch & dinner) This family-friendly eatery serves up nouvelle Italian food – flavorsome and inventive pastas, seafood and beef – in a bright, modern setting. The *zuppa de pescado* (fish soup; $23), seasoned with fennel, leek and saffron, is wonderful.

Anthony J's Bistro (☎ 860-536-0448; 6 Holmes St; mains $9-20; ☺ lunch & dinner) Known locally as AJ's, this slick trattoria serves pizzas for $10 to $12 and carries a full, if not terribly imaginative, menu of Italian specialties, pastas and grills. Half-portions are available.

TAKING A GAMBLE AT FOXWOODS

Rising above the forest canopy of Great Cedar Swamp north of Mystic, the gleaming towers of the mammoth **Foxwoods Resort Casino** (☎ 800-752-9244; www.foxwoods.com) are an alien vision in turquoise and lavender.

Under treaties dating back centuries, native peoples have territorial and legal rights separate from those enjoyed by other citizens of the US. In recent times, these aboriginal nations have used the courts and the Congress to elaborate these treaty rights into a potent vehicle for addressing longstanding discrimination against them and its resulting poverty.

One such group, the 700-member Mashantucket Pequot Tribal Nation, known as 'the fox people,' kept a tenuous hold on a parcel of ancestral land in southeastern Connecticut. The tribe had dwindled to insignificant numbers through assimilation and dispersion, but a few souls refused to abandon the reservation. Living in decrepit trailers dragged onto the land, they fought a dispiriting legal battle against attempts to declare the reservation abandoned.

Their tenacity paid off in 1986 when they reached an agreement with the Connecticut state government that allowed the Pequots to open a high-stakes bingo hall. In 1992, again under an agreement with the state, the tribe borrowed $60 million from a Malaysian casino developer and began to build Foxwoods.

The resort features the world's largest bingo hall, nightclubs with free entertainment, cinemas, rides and video-game and pinball parlors for children. There are about 1400 luxury **guest rooms** (☎ 800-369-9663 for reservations) in three hotels (the Grand Pequot Tower, Great Cedar Hotel and Two Trees Inn).

If you're visiting Foxwoods, it's well worth a few hours of your time to learn a bit about the Mashantucket Pequot tribe. The **Mashantucket Pequot Museum & Research Center** (☎ 860-396-6838, www.pequotmuseum.org; adult/child 6-15/senior $15/10/13; ☺ 9am-5pm) is an ultramodern museum for an ancient people. To truly do it justice, allow several hours for your visit. The free observation tower, which was struck by lightning, should be open again by the time you read this. The last admission to the museum is at 4pm and, conveniently, shuttles run every 20 minutes between the museum and Foxwoods.

To reach Foxwoods, take I-95 to exit 92, then follow CT 2 west; or take I-395 to exit 79A, 80, 81 or 85 and follow the signs for the 'Mashantucket Pequot Reservation.'

Mohegan Sun Casino (☎ 888-226-7711; www.mohegansun.com), at I-395 exit 79A, is a smaller version of Foxwoods operated by the Mohegan tribe on its reservation.

Getting There & Around

Amtrak (☎ 800-872-7245) trains between NYC and Boston on the shore route stop at Mystic's train depot at 12 Roosevelt St, less than a mile south of Mystic Seaport Museum.

Mystic is 9 miles east of New London and Groton. The best route by car is I-95.

STONINGTON

pop 1030

Five miles east of Mystic on US 1, Stonington stands out as one of the most appealing towns on the Connecticut coast. Many of the town's 18th- and 19th-century houses were once sea captains' homes.

It's best to explore this historic town – actually a 'borough,' Connecticut's oldest – on foot. Compactly laid out on a peninsula that juts into Long Island Sound, Stonington is rife with streetscapes of period ar-

chitecture. The short main thoroughfare, Water St, features shops selling high-end antiques, colorful French Quimper porcelain and upscale gifts. There are also a couple of waterfront restaurants and delis. At the southern end of Water St is the 'point' or tip of the peninsula, with a park and tiny beach.

Sights & Activities

Walk down Water St (one-way southbound) to its southern end for a good look at the town, and then back going north on Main St, the other major north–south street, one block east of Water St.

The **Captain Amos Palmer House** (1780; cnr Water & Wall Sts) was the home of the mother and children of artist James McNeill Whistler and later of poet Stephen Vincent Benét. (The house is not open to the public.)

Included in the lighthouse ticket (see below) is admission to the **Capt Nathaniel Palmer House** (☎ 860-535-8445; 40 Palmer St; ☺ 10am-4pm Tue-Sun), one of the finest houses in town and former home of the first American to see the continent of Antarctica (at the tender age of 21, no less).

At the southern end of Water St, close to the point, the houses become plainer and simpler, many dating from the 18th century. These were the residences of ships' carpenters and fishermen.

At the end of the point, near the small duBois Beach, is the **Old Lighthouse Museum** (☎ 860-535-1440; 7 Water St; adult/child 6-12 $5/3; ☺ 10am-5pm Tue-Sun May-Oct). The surprisingly short, octagonal-towered granite lighthouse was moved to its present location in 1840 and deactivated 50 years later. Now it's a museum with exhibits on whaling, Native American artifacts, curios from the China trade, 19th-century oil portraits, wooden boats, weaponry, toys and decoys.

The **Portuguese Holy Ghost Society** building on Main St is a reminder of the contributions made to Stonington by the Azoreans who signed on to Stonington-bound whalers during the 19th century and eventually settled in the village. Today, their descendants still form a significant part of Stonington's population, though the small village's ever-increasing appeal to wealthy New Yorkers seeking summer homes is driving the locals out of the real-estate market.

Sleeping

Stonington is the area's quaintest place to stay; see the Mystic (p317) or New London & Groton (p323) sections for cheaper options.

Inn at Stonington (☎ 860-535-2000; www.innatstonington.com; 60 Water St; d 149-395) Let yourself be pampered at this elegant, modern 18-room inn, complete with evening wine and cheese. Most rooms are equipped with Jacuzzi bath and fireplace, and guests enjoy free use of kayaks, bikes and the town's private beach. It's worth paying a bit more for a seaside room. Children 15 and older are welcome.

Orchard Street Inn (☎ 860-535-2681; www.orchardstreetinn.com; 41 Orchard St; d $125-175) Recently renovated and redecorated, this quiet, unpretentious inn is within easy walking distance of everything in town. The butter-yellow guest cottage houses three rooms, each with a private bathroom and patio and separate entrance. To get there, turn left from Water St at Noah's restaurant and then left onto Orchard. Children 14 and over are welcome.

Randall's Ordinary (☎ 860-599-4540; www.randallsordinary.com; 41 Norwich/Westerly Rd, North Stonington; d $80-400) This is a centuries-old farmhouse that is now an inn and restaurant (see below). As you enter the farm, you're greeted with a sign reading 'Welcome to 1685!' Authenticity of the exterior appearance is a strong point here, even though on the inside the inn has modern conveniences. In the main house there are three guest rooms; nine more are in the barn. All have private bathrooms. The inn's 250 acres sit 8.4 miles northeast of the center of Stonington along CT 2, a third of a mile north of I-95 exit 92.

Budget motels – some of the cheapest accommodations in the area – lie northeast of the center of Stonington along US 1 on the way to Pawcatuck.

Stonington Motel (☎ 860-599-2330; 901 Stonington Rd/US 1, Stonington; d $55-90) This motel's 12 well-used but clean rooms have cable TV, microwaves and fridges, and some are wheelchair accessible. Inquire about weekday discounts.

Cove Ledge Inn & Marina (☎ 860-599-4130; www.coveledgeinn.com; Whewell Circle/US 1, Pawcatuck; d $80-250; ☒) There's a plethora of options here: motel-style rooms ($85 to $95), efficiency rooms ($135 to $145), luxury suites ($165) or guest-house cottages ($200 to $275).

Eating

You will see Stonington's few restaurants as you proceed south on Water St.

Noni's Deli (☎ 860-535-0797; 143 Water St; mains $4-8; ☺ 8am-4pm) This Irish-themed deli is perfect for scoring picnic supplies before heading to the park at the southern end of Water St, or you can eat on their cozy front patio. Try the Galway (crab-cake sandwich) for $4.

Noah's (☎ 860-535-3925; 115 Water St; dinner mains $17-22; ☺ 7am-9pm Tue-Sun) Noah's is a popular, informal place at Church St, with two small rooms topped with original stamped-tin ceilings and oil paintings of Stonington on the walls. Besides Americana standards like asparagus quiche, there are some unexpected dishes like Chinese noodles with chicken.

Water St Café (☎ 860-535-2122; 142 Water St; mains lunch $7-15, dinner $15-25; ☺ lunch & dinner) North of Grand St, this crimson-walled café boasts a menu that is creative and moderately priced –

a rare combination. One recent special was the satisfying Vietnamese fried cod salad with sesame orange dressing.

Skipper's Dock (☎ 860-535-0111; 66 Water St; mains lunch $8-15, dinner $25-35; ⊗ lunch & dinner) This casual, kid-friendly seafood restaurant with a waterside deck is the place to order steamers, lobster or what is locally known as a clam boil – the works, including clams, corn, lobster, fish and sausage. A lunch main will fill you for the day.

Randall's Ordinary (p321; ⊗ closed Jan-Apr) Hearth cooking in the authentic colonial manner is the specialty here. There is just one dinner seating for a fixed-price menu ($39 not including drinks, tax and tip) of slow-simmered soups, beef, fish, chicken or venison, hearth-baked cornbread and colonial-style desserts, served by costumed waitstaff. Reservations are essential.

Shopping

Quimper Faïence (☎ 860-535-1712, 800-470-7339; 141 Water St; ⊗ 10am-5pm Mon-Sat) Stonington is one of only two towns in the country with an official shop for Quimper Faïence. Pronounced 'kamm-*pehr*,' this is the colorfully painted dinnerware handmade in France since the 17th century. Folk-art plates, cups, mugs, platters, figurines and utensils are popular collector's items. Prices are not low, but then again, each Quimper piece is one of a kind by definition.

NEW LONDON & GROTON

pop 66,000

During its golden age in the mid-19th century, New London was home to some 200 whaling vessels. But until recently, the city – stretching along the west bank of the Thames River (that's 'thaymz,' not 'temz') – seemed somewhat exhausted from its trip through the 20th-century industrial wringer. Though there's still a palpable grittiness about the place, the slew of 'vacant' signs are making way for ones reading 'coming soon.' To wit, Pfizer has moved its research and development headquarters to town, and the new Hygienic Arts Park & Amphitheater is bringing the arts into fresh focus in this town where playwright Eugene O'Neill spent his childhood summers.

Over the bridge in Groton is General Dynamics Corporation, a major naval defense contractor, and the US Naval Submarine

Base, the first and the largest in the country. Both are vigorously off-limits to the public, but you can get into the spirit of things with a visit to the Historic Ship Nautilus & Submarine Force Museum (opposite) and the US Coast Guard Academy (opposite; in New London).

Orientation

New London and Groton are 101 miles from Boston and 52 miles from Hartford via interstates. Groton is on the east side of the river.

The bulk of New London's shops, cafés and restaurants line Bank St southwest of the Amtrak train station near the waterfront.

Information

Connecticut East Convention & Visitor's Bureau (☎ 860-444-2206, 800-863-6569; www.mysticmore.com; 470 Bank St, New London; ⊗ 8:30am-4:30pm Mon-Fri)
New London Chamber of Commerce (☎ 860-443-8332; 105 Huntington St, New London; ⊗ 8:30am-4:30pm Mon-Fri)
Visitor Center (☎ 860-444-7264; 228 Eugene O'Neill Dr, New London; ⊗ 10am-4pm summer) Grab maps and brochures even when they're closed.

Sights & Activities
NEW LONDON

A well-laid-out walking tour starts along the restored pedestrian mall called the **Captain's Walk** (State St). The tiny **Nathan Hale Schoolhouse** (☎ 860-443-7949; Union Plaza; admission free; ⊗ noon-4pm Thu-Sat mid-May–mid-Oct) is one of the many Connecticut schoolhouses that bear the name of this peripatetic pedagogue. Hale (1755–76) is famous for his patriotic statement, 'I only regret that I have but one life to lose for my country,' as he was about to be hanged for treason by the British without trial. He taught in this schoolhouse before enlisting in the Connecticut militia.

Nearby is the 1833 **Custom House Maritime Museum** (150 Bank St; adult/child $5/3; ⊗ 1-5pm Tue-Sun), the oldest operating custom house in the country. Its front door is made from the wood of the USS *Constitution*.

On Huntington St right next to the St James' Church, **Whale Oil Row** features four identical white mansions with imposing Doric facades built for whaling merchants in 1830. They're now private businesses and not open to the public, but the exterior view is impressive.

Of the two **Hempsted Houses** (☎ 860-443-7949; 11 Hempstead St; adult/child $5/2; ☑ noon-4pm Thu-Sun May-Oct), the older one (1678) is one of the best-documented 17th-century houses in the country. Maintained by the descendants of the original owners until 1937, it is one of the few 17th-century houses remaining in the area, having survived the burning of New London by Benedict Arnold and the British in 1781. The house is insulated with seaweed, of all things.

Monte Cristo Cottage (☎ 860-443-0051; 325 Pequot Ave; admission $5; ☑ 10am-5pm Tue-Sat, 1-5pm Sun mid-Jun–early Sep) was the boyhood summer home of playwright Eugene O'Neill. Near Ocean Beach Park in the southern districts of the city (follow the signs), the Victorian-style house is now a research library for dramatists. Many of O'Neill's belongings are on display, including his desk. You might recognize the living room: it was the setting for two of O'Neill's most famous plays, *Long Day's Journey into Night* and *Ah, Wilderness!* (Theater buffs should be sure to visit the Eugene O'Neill Theater Center in nearby Waterford, which hosts an annual summer series of readings by young playwrights.) At the time of research, the cottage was undergoing renovations but should be open again by the summer of 2005.

You'll find a lovely strip of more historic houses on Starr St, between Eugene O'Neill Dr and Washington St.

The **Lyman Allyn Art Museum** (☎ 860-443-2545; 625 Williams St; adult/senior & student $5/4; ☑ 10am-5pm Tue-Sat, 1-5pm Sun) is a neoclassical building with exhibits that span the 18th, 19th and 20th centuries, including impressive collections of early American silver and Asian, Greco-Roman and European paintings. There's a self-guided children's art park on the grounds.

From 1931 until 1985, the site that is now the **Hygienic Gardens & Amphitheater Arts Park** (☎ 860-443-8001; www.hygienic.org; 79 Bank St; ☑ gardens & amphitheater daylight hrs, gallery 11am-3pm Thu, 11am-6pm Fri & Sat, noon-3pm Sun) operated as Hygienic Restaurant, named after Hygia the Greek god of cleanliness. It lay fallow as a vacant lot until 2001, when the members of the adjacent Hygienic Art gallery bought up the land with the goal of creating a venue for public art. The project, newly opened in June 2005 and done in Greek Revival style replete with sculptures, mural plaza,

fountains and a large performance area, will endow New London with a vibrant new community gathering spot. There are plans to initiate a free summer film series.

At the southern end of Ocean Ave is **Ocean Beach Park** (☎ 860-510-7263; 1225 Ocean Ave; ⓟ Mon-Fri $9, Sat & Sun $13), a popular beach and amusement area with waterslides, a picnic area, miniature golf, an arcade, a swimming pool and an old-fashioned boardwalk. The parking fee includes admission for everyone in your car, or else it's $5 for adults and $3 for kids. After Labor Day (early September), weekdays are free.

Visitors can stroll the grounds of the **US Coast Guard Academy** (☎ 860-444-8270; 15 Mohegan Ave; admission free; ☑ 11am-5pm), one of the four military academies in the country. Pick up a self-guided walking tour booklet at the museum, which is open year-round from 11am to 5pm.

GROTON

On the Naval Submarine Base, the **Historic Ship Nautilus & Submarine Force Museum** (☎ 860-694-3174, 800-343-0079; 1 Crystal Lake Rd; admission free; ☑ 9am-5pm Wed-Mon, 1-5pm Tue mid-May–Oct; 9am-4pm Wed-Mon Nov–mid-May), is home to *Nautilus*, the world's first nuclear-powered submarine and the first sub to transit the North Pole. The brief audio tour of *Nautilus* is fascinating even to those who aren't military enthusiasts. Other museum exhibits feature working periscopes and sounds of the ocean.

Fort Griswold State Park (☎ 860-445-1729; cnr Monument St & Park Ave; admission free; ☑ 10am-5pm late May-early Sep; 10am-5pm Sat & Sun early Sep–mid-Oct) has a 130ft obelisk that marks the place where colonial troops were defeated and massacred by Benedict Arnold and the British in 1781, in a battle that saw the death of colonial Colonel William Ledyard and the British burning of Groton and New London. Monument House features the Daughters of the American Revolution's collection of Revolutionary and Civil War memorabilia. An excellent spot for a picnic.

Sleeping

For a complete list and links to accommodations in eastern Connecticut, consult www.mysticmore.com. The coming of the Foxwoods and Mohegan Sun casinos (see the boxed text on p320) has spurred motel development around every exit of I-95 in eastern Connecticut. The result is over 60 different motor inns and competitive pricing. All of the major chains are represented. These motels see a lot of clients so don't expect pristine furnishings or meticulous housekeeping.

For camping not far from New London and Groton, see p317.

BUDGET

Thames Inn & Marina (☎ 860-445-8111; 193 Thames St, Groton; d $69-100) Though it prefers guests staying a week or longer, this inn will let rooms, all with fully equipped kitchens, for the night as well. There's a coin-operated laundry.

Motel 6 (☎ 860-739-6991, 800-466-8356; www.motel 6.com; 74 Flanders Rd, Niantic; d $50-70; 🐾) This 93-room motel stands off I-95 at exit 74. There's a coin laundry and a free shuttle to Foxwoods Resort Casino.

MID-RANGE & TOP END

Queen Anne Inn B&B (☎ 860-447-2600, 800-347-8818; www.queen-anne.com; 265 Williams St, New London; d incl breakfast $115-175) All eight rooms at this friendly, antique-laden B&B have their own TV, phone and DSL access. The least expensive room has its bathroom down the hall. Queen Anne isn't quite within walking distance of Bank St but it's convenient from the interstate.

Radisson Hotel New London (☎ 860-443-7000, 800-333-3333; www.radisson.com; 35 Governor Winthrop Blvd, New London; d $99-169; 🐾) Wireless Internet, restaurant, bar, health club and a free shuttle to area casinos are all part of the package at the Radisson. Within walking distance from the train station and ferry terminal.

Holiday Inn (☎ 860-442-0631, 800-465-4329; 380 Bayonet St, New London; d $69-189; 🐾) This newly renovated motel has 133 rooms and three suites, plus a bar, restaurant and fitness center with whirlpool.

Groton Inn & Suites (☎ 860-445-9784, 800-452-2191; www.grotoninn.com; 99 Gold Star Hwy/CT 184, Groton; d $80-200) Groton Inn, at I-95, has apartments, efficiencies and deluxe suites. You also get a restaurant, bar and fitness center.

Lighthouse Inn Resort (☎ 860-443-8411, 888-443-8411; www.lighthouseinn-ct.com; 6 Guthrie Pl, New London; r $99-150, ste $185-369) This sprawling, four-star hotel at the southern end of Montauk Ave offers a variety of deluxe rooms in two buildings – one, the finely restored 1902

mansion, and the other, the Carriage House, whose rooms are the least expensive of the bunch. The resort owns a private beach just for guests.

Eating

New London and Groton are short on fancy restaurants, but you'll find a number of cafés and bars along Bank St in New London. All of the establishments below are in New London unless otherwise noted.

Anastacia's (☎ 860-437-8005; 64 Bank St; mains $4-7; 😊 8am-4pm Mon-Sat, 7:30am-2pm Sun, closed Mon in winter) Reminiscent of grandma's house, Anastacia's is number one for breakfast and brunch. The quiche is tops. In May the huge tree on the back dock is awash with fragrant flowers.

Paul's Pasta Shop (☎ 860-445-5276; 223 Thames St, Groton; 😊 11am-9pm Tue-Sun) When the smell of fresh tomato sauce lulls you into this ultra-casual eatery, you'll most likely find Paul himself standing right behind the counter. All pasta dishes, be it spaghetti and meatballs or linguini primavera, are $7, but for house specialties like Paul's wife Dorothy's five cheese lasagna you'll have to cough up an extra $2. The back dock peers down over the river.

Recovery Room (☎ 860-443-2619; 443 Ocean Ave, New London; mains $7-16; 😊 11:30am-9pm Mon-Sat, 4-9pm Sun) The family-run Recovery Room has New London's best pizza – thin crusted and one-sized – with a variety of interesting topping options. (Sour cream, anyone?) Makes for a good stop en route from a day at Ocean Beach (p323).

Bang Kok City (☎ 860-442-6970; 123 State St, New London; mains $10-15; 😊 lunch & dinner Mon-Sat) The amiable servers here can guide you through the large menu, and the spice level is under your control. Try their memorable *tom yam kong* (spicy shrimp soup). Under the same roof is **Little Tokyo** (☎ 860-447-2388) where a filling yakitori *bento* lunch is $8.

Timothy's (☎ 860-443-8411; mains lunch $10-14, dinner $18-28; 😊 10:30am-3pm & 5-9pm) Blessed with a stunning view of the Sound and decorated with hand-carved chandeliers, this dining room at the Lighthouse Inn Resort (left) promises gracious food in equally gracious surroundings, and excellently named chef Timothy Grills delivers – at dinner try the sautéed salmon medallions with roasted onions served on jasmine rice ($20).

DETOUR: THE QUIET CORNER

Perhaps nowhere else in New England will you find such an undeveloped green valley so close to major urban areas. Dubbed the Quiet Corner, the furthest patch of northeast Connecticut is known (when it's known at all) for farmland, rolling meadows, reasonably priced antiques and most significantly, an air of timelessness. The 12 miles of CT 169 between Brooklyn and Woodstock induces sighs of contentment and frequent pullovers. To get to 169 from New London, take I-395 north for about 32 miles. Here are a few highlights, but off-guidebook exploration is strongly encouraged.

From I-395, take US 6 W to Danielson, where family-run **Logee's Greenhouses** (☎ 860-774-8038; 141 North St off CT 12; ☺ 9am-5pm Mon-Sat, 11am-5pm Sun) has been in the beautifying business since 1893. Stroll through seven greenhouses brimming with over 1000 tropical and subtropical varieties – close your eyes and you're in Bali.

Heading west on US 6 again will bring you to Brooklyn, home of the oldest agricultural fair in the US, held during the third weekend in August.

Dinner at the **Golden Lamb Buttery** (☎ 860-774-4423; 499 Wolf Den Rd, Brooklyn; lunch $20, dinner $65; ☺ lunch Tue-Sat, dinner Fri & Sat) isn't just a meal – it's an experience. Guests mingle over drinks, head off for a hayride and then settle into an award-winning prix-fixe dinner. You'll need to reserve several weeks in advance. Even if you can't squeeze in a visit to the 1000-acre farm, be sure to drive the few miles up Wolf Den Rd and be rewarded with views of pastoral perfection.

Back on CT 169 heading north, stop at the old-fashioned **Woodstock Orchards** (☎ 860-928-2225; 494 CT 169, Woodstock; ☺ 9am-6pm) to pick your own blueberries (late summer) and apples (fall). Or if you're feeling lazy, stock up on all sorts of produce at the farm stand.

For detailed area information, contact **Northeast Connecticut's Quiet Corner** (☎ 860-779-6383; www.ctquietcorner.org).

Drinking

Dutch Tavern (☎ 860-442-3453; 23 Green St) Raise a cold one to Eugene O'Neill at the Dutch, the only surviving bar in town that the playwright frequented (though at the time it was known as the Oak). It's a good honest throwback to an earlier age, from the tin ceiling to the century-old potato salad recipe.

1902 Tavern (☺ 4pm-midnight Mon-Thu, noon-midnight Fri-Sun) Part of the Lighthouse Inn Resort, the Tavern is adorned with sumptuous stained glass and historic photos of the inn and area. It stocks a full bar and a variety of beers on tap. The Tavern's lunch and dinner items come from Timothy's kitchen (p346) but at slighter cheaper prices.

Frank's Place (☎ 860-443-8833; 9 Tilley St) For a quarter-century, Frank's has provided the area's gay community with a comfortable place to eat, drink, play pool and sing karaoke. No matter what the evening's entertainment may turn out to be, there's never a cover charge. Its bird-cage room is not something you see every day.

Getting There & Away

New London's transportation center is the Amtrak train station on Water St at State St; the bus station is in the same building and the ferry terminal (for boats to Long Island, Block Island and Fishers Island) is next door.

AIR

The only commercial flight coming into **Groton-New London Airport** (☎ 860-445-8549) is the **Pan Am Clipper Connection** (☎ 800-359-7262) from Trenton, New Jersey (NJ).

BOAT

Cross Sound Ferry (☎ 860-443-5281, 516-323-2525; www.longislandferry.com; 2 Ferry St, New London) operates car ferries and high-speed passenger ferries year-round between Orient Point, Long Island, NY, and New London, a 1½-hour run on the car ferry, 40 minutes on the high-speed ferry. From late June through Labor Day, ferries depart each port every hour on the hour from 7am to 9pm (last boats at 9:45pm). Off-season, boats tend to run every two hours. For high-speed ferries, the one-way rates are adult/child $16/7.75. The rates for car ferries are adult/child $10.50/5. Cars cost $39, bicycles $2. Call for car reservations.

The **Fishers Island Ferry** (☎ 860-442-0165; www.fiferry.com) runs cars and passengers from New London to the wealthy summer colony at Fishers Island, NY several times a day year-round.

In summer, there are daily boats between New London and Block Island (p302), Rhode Island, and Nantucket (p203) and Martha's Vineyard (p212), MA.

CAR & MOTORCYCLE

For New London, take I-95 exit 84, then go north on CT 32 (Mohegan Ave) for the US Coast Guard Academy, or take I-95 exits 82, 83 or 84 and go south for the city center. The center of the commercial district is just southwest of the Amtrak station along Bank St. Follow Ocean Ave (CT 213) to reach Ocean Beach Park and Harkness Memorial State Park.

For Groton, take I-95 exits 85, 86 or 87.

TRAIN

Amtrak (☎ 800-872-7245) trains between New York and Boston on the shore route stop at New London.

NEW HAVEN

pop 124,500

Much maligned for decades as a stagnant urban seaport, this city has risen from its own ashes to become an arts mecca. As you roll into town along I-91 or I-95, New Haven appears bustling and muscular – it's still an important port, as it has been since the 1630s. Shipping, manufacturing, health care and telecommunications power New Haven's economy. But at the city's center is a tranquil yet dynamic core: New Haven Green, bordered by graceful colonial churches and venerable Yale University and with an impressive fountain at its center. Scores of ethnic restaurants, theaters, museums, pubs and clubs dot the neighborhood and make the Yale University area almost as lively as Cambridge's Harvard Sq, but with better pizza.

Orientation

Entering New Haven along I-95 or I-91 (which joins I-95 right in the city), take I-95 exit 47 for CT 34, the Oak St Connector, to reach New Haven Green, the city center, with Yale to its west. From the Wilbur Cross Parkway, take exit 57, 59 or 60 and follow the signs to the center.

Most hotels and sights are within a few blocks of the green. The bus and train stations are near I-95 in the southeast part of the city. Street parking downtown can be a frustrating proposition. Parking lots are everywhere – strings of them line Crown, George and State Sts. Most lodging options offers parking; exceptions are noted.

Information

BOOKSTORES

Atticus Bookstore Café (☎ 203-776-4040; 1082 Chapel St; ☺ 8am-midnight) A favorite bookstore and café (see p330).

Barnes & Noble Yale Bookstore (☎ 203-777-8440; 77 Broadway; ☺ 9am-9pm Mon-Sat, noon-6pm Sun) Sells not only a rich collection of books, but also Yale sweatshirts and souvenirs.

INTERNET ACCESS

Elm City Java (☎ 203-776-2248; 77 Whitney Ave; ☺ 7am-8pm Mon-Thu, 7am-midnight Fri, 10am-6pm Sat & Sun, shorter hrs in summer) Offers free Internet (with purchase) on four iMacs, and is a wireless hot spot.

Public library (☎ 203-946-8130; 133 Elm St; ☺ noon-8pm Mon, 10am-6pm Tue & Wed, 10am-8pm Thu, 10am-5pm Sat) This has free access; hours fluctuate throughout the year.

MONEY

Scads of ATMs line Church St, especially at the intersections with Elm and Grove Sts.
Bank of America (157 Church St)

POST

Post office (206 Elm St; ☺ 8am-5pm Mon-Fri, 8am-noon Sat) Near the intersection with College St.

TOURIST INFORMATION

Greater New Haven Convention & Visitors Bureau (☎ 203-777-8550, 800-332-7829; www.newhavencvb.org; 59 Elm St; ☺ 8:30am-5pm Mon-Fri) Centrally located downtown.

INFO New Haven (☎ 203-773-9494; 1000 Chapel St; ☺ 10am-9pm Mon-Sat, noon-5pm Sun) Downtown.

Yale University Visitor Center (☎ 203-432-2300; cnr Elm & Temple Sts; ☺ 9am-4:30pm Mon-Fri, 11am-4pm Sat & Sun) Located on the north side of the green. Supplies free campus maps and a self-guided walking-tour pamphlet ($1). For information on guided tours, see p328.

Sights & Activities

NEW HAVEN GREEN

New Haven's spacious town green, the spiritual center of the city, claims three historic churches. The **Trinity Church** (Episcopal), on Chapel St, resembles England's Gothic York

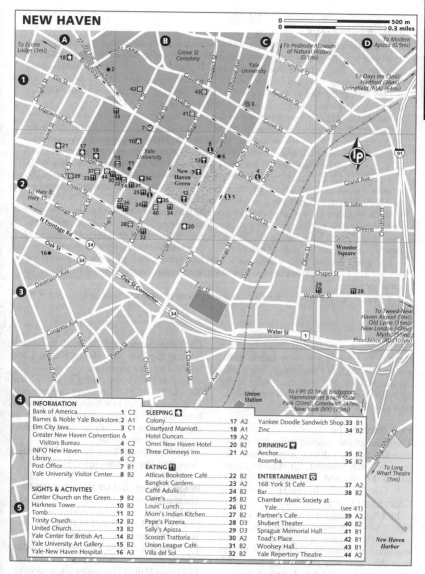

NEW HAVEN

0   500 m
0   0.3 miles

Minster. The Georgian-style **Center Church on the Green** (United Church of Christ, UCC), a good example of New England's interpretation of Palladian architecture, harbors many colonial tombstones in its crypt. **United Church** (UCC), at the northeastern corner of the green, is another Georgian-Palladian work.

GROVE STREET CEMETERY

Three blocks north of the green, this **cemetery** (227 Grove St; ☺ 8am-4pm) holds the graves of several famous New Havenites behind its grand Egyptian Revival gate, including rubber magnate Charles Goodyear, the telegraph inventor Samuel Morse, lexicographer Noah Webster and cotton gin inventor

SKULL & BONES CLUB

Turn north from Chapel St onto High St, and a foreboding, windowless building suddenly looms up on your left. This is the Tomb, home of Yale's most notorious secret society, the Skull & Bones Club. The club attracted more than the usual amount of attention in 2004 when fellow Bonesmen President George W Bush and Senator John Kerry faced off against each other in the presidential election. Despite the media's obsession with the topic, both candidates demurred from discussing the details of their allegiance, in accordance with Bones rules.

Founded in 1832 as a New World version of student societies that were common at the time in Germany, Skull & Bones comprises 15 seniors, tapped at the end of their junior year by the graduating seniors. (Women won eligibility by a wafer-thin voting margin in 1991.) Viewed most innocently, the club is simply an alumni network, a social club, whose members are imbued with a 'mission for moral leadership,' in the words of journalist Ron Rosenbaum. More nefariously, critics claim that it is a hyperelite organization whose goal it is to place its members in the top echelon of power. Indeed, a list of members reads like a 'Who's Who' of high-powered judges, financiers, ambassadors, politicians, publishers and intelligence officers.

No doubt adding to the air of unwholesomeness are the stories of bizarre and diabolical initiation rites – including initiates lying in coffins and spending an evening revealing every sordid detail of their sexual histories with fellow Bonesmen – and claims that the Tomb is full of stolen booty like a set of Hitler's silverware and the skulls of Apache warrior Geronimo and Mexican general Pancho Villa.

Conspiracy theorists don't lack for hypotheses linking the society to pretty much every significant event in the US and beyond over the past 150 years. And who knows? They may be on to something.

If your interest is piqued, check out Yale grad Alexandra Robbins' lurid read *Secrets of the Tomb*.

Eli Whitney. It was the first cemetery in the country to arrange graves by family plots. Around the turn of the century, Yale medical students would sneak in at night to dig up bodies for dissection. Join a free walking tour at 11am on Saturdays.

YALE UNIVERSITY

The third-oldest university in the nation, Yale boasts many distinguished alums, including Noah Webster, Eli Whitney, Samuel FB Morse, and Presidents William H Taft, Gerald Ford, George HW Bush, Bill Clinton and George W Bush.

In 1702, James Pierpont founded a collegiate school in nearby Clinton. In 1717 it went to New Haven in response to a generous grant of funds by Elihu Yale. The next year the name was changed to Yale in his honor, and by 1887 it had expanded its offerings to such an extent that it was time to rename it Yale University. Crowded with old Gothic buildings, Yale's campus dominates the northern and western portions of downtown New Haven. Tallest of its Gothic spires is Harkness Tower, from which a carillon peals at appropriate moments throughout the day. On the south side of the Oak St

Connector is an extensive modern campus holding the Yale-New Haven Hospital and medical science buildings.

Stop at the visitor center at Elm St and Temple St and pick up a free campus map or a walking-tour brochure. For a free one-hour student-guided walking tour, arrive slightly before 10:30am or 2pm weekdays or at 1:30pm weekends.

Yale's museums have outstanding collections, and the art museums are free.

PEABODY MUSEUM OF NATURAL HISTORY

The **museum** (☎ 203-432-5050; 170 Whitney Ave; adult/child 3-15/senior $7/5/6; ☯ 10am-5pm Mon-Sat, noon-5pm Sun), five blocks northeast of the green along Temple St, has a vast collection of animal, vegetable and mineral specimens, including wildlife dioramas, meteorites and minerals. The Great Hall of Dinosaurs illuminates the museum's fossil collection against the backdrop of the Pulitzer Prize–winning mural *The Age of Reptiles*. Parking available.

YALE CENTER FOR BRITISH ART

This **museum** (☎ 203-432-2800; 1080 Chapel St; admission free; ☯ 10am-5pm Tue-Sat, noon-5pm Sun), at the corner of High St holds the most comprehensive collection of British art outside the UK. The permanent collection represents the 16th to mid-19th centuries most significantly, while the work of more modern artists is often on exhibition. Of note is the fact the galleries are not only arranged chronologically, but by 'theme,' such as Ideal Landscape. The museum is housed in the last building designed by American architect Louis Kahn, whose first public commission was the Yale University Art Gallery across the street.

YALE UNIVERSITY ART GALLERY

This outstanding **museum** (☎ 203-432-0600; 1111 Chapel St; admission free; ☯ 10am-5pm Tue-Sat, 1-6pm Sun) is currently undergoing a two-year restoration and renovation, in part to align it with architect Louis Kahn's original vision for the building. Until the Kahn Building reopens in early 2006, the American collection and other selected works can be seen next door at the Gothic-style Swartwout Building, whose entrance is at Chapel and High Sts. The gallery's full collection includes masterworks by Frans Hals, Peter Paul Rubens, Manet, Picasso and van Gogh, plus American silver from the 18th century and art from Africa, Asia, the pre- and post-Columbian Americas and Europe.

Sleeping

BUDGET

Hotel Duncan (☎ 203-787-1273; 1151 Chapel St; s/d/ste $44-50/60/70). Though the shine has rubbed off this fin-de-siècle New Haven gem – with stained carpets, unstable water pressure and exfoliating towels – it's the enduring elements that make a stay here a pleasure still, like the handsome lobby where one can watch New Havenites stroll by and the hand-operated elevator with its uniformed attendant. Today there are 65 rooms let on a long-term basis and 35 for nightly rental. On each floor, the rooms all the way down on the left side have the nicest layouts and tend to be quietest. Check out the wall in the manager's office filled with autographed pictures of celebrity guests like Jodie Foster, Christopher Walken and Kevin Bacon. No parking available.

Days Inn (☎ 203-469-0343, 800-544-8313; www.days inn.com; 270 Foxon Blvd; d $56-64) A few miles north of the city, this inn has 58 rooms, all with data ports and cable TV with HBO. To get there, take I-91 exit 8.

Hammonasset Beach State Park (☎ 860-566-2304, 877-668-2267; I-95 exit 62; sites $15) This campground is on the coast between Madison and Clinton, and despite its 550 sites, is often full in high summer. Reserve early.

MID-RANGE

Colony (☎ 203-776-1234, 800-458-8810; www.colony atyale.com; 1157 Chapel St; s/d $109/119) This modern hotel with 86 luxury rooms, decorated in rich blues or maroons and many with four-poster beds, is within walking distance of everything. If you want a room with a VCR or data port, you'll be charged a small extra fee. Ask about corporate rates.

Courtyard Marriott New Haven (☎ 203-777-6221; www.marriott.com; 30 Whalley Ave; d from $129; ☒) Recently renovated, this hotel has 160 rooms (the higher rooms have good views), all sporting fridges, couches, safes, and high-speed data ports. Make sure to ask about discounts.

Econo Lodge (☎ 203-387-6651; 877-424-6423; www .econolodge.com; 100 Pond Lily Ave; d $69-150; ☒) This inn is just off the Wilbur Cross Parkway (exit 59), several miles to the northeast of town, and has 125 rooms. You get a fitness center and spa along with a well-furnished, recently renovated motel unit.

TOP END

Three Chimneys Inn (☎ 203-777-1201, 800-443-1554; www.threechimneysinn.com; 1201 Chapel St; d incl breakfast $195-215; ☐) A stay in one of the 11 rooms in this sumptuously restored 1870 Victorian 'painted lady' promises to be memorable, with just-so touches at every turn – what with morning coffee over the New York Times, afternoon wine and cheese, and fireside port and sherry in the evening, why even bother venturing into town?

Omni New Haven Hotel (☎ 860-772-6664; www .omnihotels.com; 155 Temple St; d 118-199; ☐) At this enormous, 306-room hotel you get all the smart amenities you'd expect, including a 24-hour fitness center and business center. Ask for a room with a view of either the Sound or the green. Several wheelchair-accessible rooms are available.

Eating & Drinking

Chapel Sq, the area just south of campus roughly between York and Church Sts, constitutes a restaurant and entertainment zone with influences from every part of the globe.

New Haven is known as the pizza capital of New England, if not the entire East Coast.

BUDGET

Yankee Doodle Sandwich & Coffee Shop (☎ 203-865-1074; 258 Elm St; dishes $2-6; ✆ 6am-3:30pm Mon & Tue, 6am-10pm Wed-Fri, 6am-4pm Sat, 7am-3pm Sun) The family-run Doodle is a classic '50s hole-in-the-wall American lunch counter – Formica countertop, chrome and plastic stools, real fountain soda – with prices to match. Despite the name, burgers and breakfast food are the real deals here. The defunct cigarette machine in the corner is kept around for nostalgic reasons – it was installed on the day JFK was shot. When Yale's not in session, Doodle's hours are sharply curtailed.

Claire's (☎ 203-562-3888; 1000 Chapel St; mains $5-8; ✆ 8am-9pm Mon-Fri, 8am-10pm Sat & Sun) Bright, airy and always packed, this is the best vegetarian restaurant in town. The soups, salads and quiches are excellent, though their sandwiches can be a bit anemic. Try one of their creative daily specials like soy chicken Provençal, or for a sweet treat, the Lithuanian coffeecake ($3.60).

Atticus Bookstore Café (☎ 203-776-4040; 1082 Chapel St; dishes $5-8; ✆ 8am-midnight) Named after the first-known publisher, this café has been serving strong coffee and from-scratch soups, sandwiches and pastries amid the stacks for two decades.

Mom's Indian Kitchen (☎ 203-624-8771; 283 Crown St; mains $6-11; ✆ 11am-3pm, 5-10pm) If you like hole-in-the-wall ethnic dining and air that drips with curry, you've got to stop at Mom's. There are only nine tables (with calming green tablecloths) in this storefront operation. Consider the chicken *tikka masala* (spiced and cooked in a yogurt sauce) for $8.25. There are plenty of options to keep nonmeat-eaters happy, especially the weekday veggie lunch specials ($4.25).

Louis' Lunch (☎ 203-562-5507; 261-263 Crown St; original burger $4.50; ✆ 11am-4pm Tue & Wed, noon-2am Thu-Sat) This squat, brick number between College and High Sts claims to be the place where the hamburger was invented – well, almost. Around 1900, when the vertically grilled ground beef sandwich was first introduced at Louis', the restaurant was in a different location. It still uses the historic vertical grills, and serves a few nonburger items as well. Ask for ketchup and feel the disdain rain down upon you.

They close in August and credit cards aren't accepted.

MID-RANGE

Bangkok Gardens (☎ 203-789-8684; 172 York St; mains lunch $5-6, dinner $9-11; ✆ lunch & dinner) Just off Chapel St, this large, white-linened establishment is the center's most popular Thai eatery. The Golden Bay appetizer, fried tofu pouches stuffed with shrimp and veggies, is exquisite. At lunch, big plates of pork, beef and chicken with vegetables are inexpensive.

Villa del Sol (☎ 203-785-9898; 236 Crown St; mains lunch $6-9, dinner $12-20; ✆ 11:30am-11pm) This exuberantly colorful, upscale rendition of a Oaxacan cantina serenades you with mariachi music – recorded – as you tuck into substantial dishes like *cochinita pibil* (shredded white pork with spicy sauce). There are plenty of nonmeat options, like bandera veggie (three enchiladas with three different sauces), and a menu for 'little amigos.'

Pepe's Pizzeria (☎ 203-865-5762; 157 Wooster St; dishes $5-20; ✆ 4-10pm Mon, Wed & Thu, 11:30am-11pm Fri & Sat, 2:30-10pm Sun) Pepe's serves exceptional pizza, just as it has since 1925, in spartan surroundings. Prices vary depending on size and toppings; the large mozzarella pizza runs at $12. No credit cards.

Sally's Apizza (☎ 203-624-5271; 237 Wooster St; pies $7-15; ✆ dinner Tue-Sun) A nearby challenger to Pepe's, the white-clam pie ($10) is legendary for good reason, but all pies share the same thin, crispy crust. Sally's is closed most of September, and doesn't take credit cards.

Modern Apizza (☎ 203-776-5306; 874 State St; pizzas $6-18; ✆ 11am-11pm Tue-Sat, 3-10pm Sun) Lots of locals believe that this place serves up pies as good as, if not better than, the two behemoths mentioned above – and without the throngs of tourists. Despite the name, it's been tossing dough since 1934.

TOP END

Union League Café (☎ 203-562-4299; 1032 Chapel St; mains $20-29; ✆ lunch & dinner) Here's an upscale European bistro in the historic Union League building. Expect a menu featuring continental classics like *cocotte de joues de veau* (organic veal cheeks with sautéed wild mushrooms, $25) along with those of nouvelle cuisine. If your budget won't allow for dinner, slip in for a sinful dessert like *crêpe soufflée au citron* (lemon crepes) washed down with a glass of wine. Date place par excellence.

Caffé Adulis (☎ 203-777-5081; 228 College St; mains $8-22; ⏰ dinner, bar open until 1am) This jewel of a place offers Eritrean-Mediterranean cuisine in a sophisticated but unerringly friendly package. One of the many house special-ties is the shrimp *barka* (pan-seared jumbo shrimp with coconut, tomato and dates over basmati rice, $19). Their wine list is reason enough to linger late into the evening.

Zinc (☎ 203-624-0507; 964 Chapel St; mains lunch $10-12, dinner $19-28; ⏰ dinner Mon, lunch & dinner Tue-Sun) Whenever possible, this trendy bistro's ingredients hail from local organic sources, but the chef draws inspiration from all over, notably Asia and the Southwest. For the most rewarding experience, share several of the small plates for dinner, like their pork and leek dumplings, salmon gravlax rolls or fire-cracker shrimp. It can get noisy in the eve-nings, and reservations are recommended.

Scoozzi Trattoria (☎ 203-776-8268; 1104 Chapel St; mains lunch $9-12, dinner $19-23; ⏰ lunch & dinner) At York St, next to the Yale Repertory Theatre, this basement trattoria serves trendy Ital-ian fare with strong New American cuisine accents. Their little pizzettes and other ap-petizers like the excellent arugula (rocket) salad are favorites with the before- and after-theater crowd, who combine them with wine by the glass to make a light sup-per. More substantial fare includes pasta combinations like ravioli *di basilico* ($21) and new variations on traditional Italian meat courses. Reservations recommended.

Roomba (☎ 203-562-7666; 1044 Chapel St; dinner mains $19-25; ⏰ dinner Tue, lunch & dinner Wed-Sun) Sure, Roomba carries a menu of playful, Nuevo Latino dishes like Caribbean-grilled salmon with lemongrass, but what the place is really known for is sloshing out the best damn mojitos in town. Their desserts ain't bad, either.

Anchor (☎ 203-865-1512; 272 College St; ⏰ 11:30am-1am) You can score the standard pub-grub burgers and what-not here, but you're bet-ter off strolling in later in the evening. The clientele represents a real cross-section of folks. Throw some tunes on the jukebox, get a drink from the full bar and settle into your black-leather banquette booth. No plastic accepted.

Entertainment

As a college town and a city of some size, New Haven has amassed an unusual number of quality theater, dance and musi-cal companies, most of which offer substan-tial discounts to seniors and students – be sure to ask. On any given night you'll be spoilt for choice, from acoustic coffeehouse warblings to symphonic spectacles.

Pick up a copy of the free weeklies *New Haven Advocate* (www.newhavenadvocate .com) and *Play* (www.playnewhaven.com) for up-to-the-minute entertainment listings. The latter is geared more toward the student set.

LIVE MUSIC & NIGHTCLUBS

Toad's Place (☎ recording 203-624-8623, office 203-562-5589; 300 York St; cover free-$25). Toad's is arguably New England's premier music hall – it's where the Rolling Stones chose to kick off their 1989 Steel Wheels tour. These days, an eclectic range of performers work the intimate stage, including They Might Be Gi-ants, Collective Soul and Medeski, Martin & Wood.

Bar (☎ 203-495-1111; 254 Crown St; cover $4-8) This club, facing Louis' Lunch, encom-passes the Brü Rm, the Front Room, the Back Room and various other enclaves. Taken in toto and you're set for brew-pub beer and brick-oven pizza, a free pool table and excellent live music or DJs spinning almost every night of the week. Check the *Advocate* for specifics.

Elm City Java (p326) hosts local acts every Thursday evening, and all the bands you hear over the café's stereo system are New Haven–based. Better yet, their coffee is free-trade organic.

GAY & LESBIAN VENUES

Partner's Café (☎ 203-776-1014; 365 Crown St; cover $3 ⏰ 5pm-1am Fri & Sat) An all-sorts crowd packs it into the three floors at Partner's. There are pool tables, quiet alcoves for conversation, and thumping house music upstairs. Every Sunday is karaoke night and the boys get the run of the place each Tuesday. The poor ladies only get their own night every fourth Saturday. Happy hour, which knocks $1 off cocktails and beer, is 5pm to 8pm.

168 York St Cafe (☎ 203-789-1915; 168 York St; ⏰ 3pm-1am in summer, opens 11am rest of year) This bar/restaurant isn't too far off from its self-billing as a gay Cheers. Sunday and Thursday nights will get you $1 domestic beers.

CONNECTICUT

DETOUR: HAMMONASSET BEACH STATE PARK

Though not off-the-beaten-path by any means, the two full miles of flat, sandy beach at **Hammonasset Beach State Park** (☎ 860-566-2304, 877-668-2267; I-95 exit 62; residents $7-9, out-of-staters $10-14 summer only) handily accommodate summer crowds. This is the ideal beach at which to set up an umbrella-chair, crack open a book and forget about the world. The surf is tame, making swimming superb; restrooms and showering facilities are clean and ample; and a wooden boardwalk runs the length of the park.

Stroll the boardwalk all the way to Meigs Point at the tip of the peninsula and visit the **Nature Center** (☎ 203-245-8743) before heading out on a trail that meanders through saltwater marshes. Excellent bird-watching here.

Hammonasset is an Indian word for 'where we dig holes in the ground,' alluding to agricultural practices. These days it's more likely to refer to the holes of tent stakes. The beach has more than 500 **campsites** (see p329) and in high season they go fast.

PERFORMING ARTS

New Haven Symphony Orchestra (☎ 203-776-1444, 800-292-6476; www.newhavensymphony.org; tickets $10-55) Yale's Woolsey Hall is home to most performances by this orchestra, whose season runs from October through April. Their Pops series performs on Friday evenings.

Chamber Music Society at Yale (☎ 203-432-4158; 470 College St; tickets $25-32) This Yale society sponsors concerts from such eminent ensembles as the Guarneri String Quartet at 8pm Tuesday evenings from September through April in the Morse Recital Hall of Sprague Memorial Hall.

Yale Repertory Theatre (☎ 203-432-1234; 1120 Church St; tickets $38-45). From September to May, a full and varied program of performances is offered. Performing in a converted church, this Tony-winning repertory company has mounted more than 90 world premiers and perform classics and new works featuring graduate students of the Yale School of Drama (Meryl Streep is an alum) as well as professionals.

Long Wharf Theatre (☎ 203-787-4282, 800-782-8497; www.longwharf.org; 222 Sargent Dr; tickets $30-60; ⊙ Oct-Jun) This non-profit regional theater mounts productions from the likes of Tom Stoppard and Eugene O'Neill. It's at I-95 exit 46, on the waterfront.

Shubert Theater (☎ 203-562-5666, 800-228-6622; 247 College St; tickets $18-55; ⊙ Sep-May) Dubbed 'Birthplace of the Nation's Greatest Hits,' since 1914 the Shubert has been hosting ballet and Broadway musicals on their trial runs before heading off to the Big Apple, and have expanded their repertoire to include events such as 'An Evening with David Sedaris.'

New Haven Folk Alliance (www.ctfolk.com) Sponsors September's New Haven Folk Festival (around $24) and various one-off concerts throughout the year.

Other concerts are hosted by the **Yale School of Music** (☎ 203-432-4158), most free of charge, and on occasion by the **Yale Collection of Musical Instruments** (☎ 203-432-0822; tickets $10-20).

Getting There & Around

AIR
Bus G of **Connecticut Transit** (☎ 203-624-0151) gets you to **Tweed-New Haven Airport** (☎ 203-466-8833; I-95 exit 50), from where several commuter airlines can take you to Boston or New York.

BOAT
The **Bridgeport & Port Jefferson Steamboat Company** (☎ 888-443-3779 in CT, 631-473-0286 on Long Island; 102 W Broadway, Port Jefferson, NY) operates its daily car ferries year-round between Bridgeport, 10 miles southwest of New Haven, and Port Jefferson on Long Island about every 1½ hours. The one-way 1½-hour voyage costs $14.50 per adult, $11.50 for a child 12 and under, and $7 for seniors. The fee for a car and driver runs from $38 to $51, depending on the number of passengers. Call to reserve space for your car.

BUS
Peter Pan Bus Lines (☎ 800-343-9999) connects New Haven with NYC ($21.50, 2½ hours, three daily), Hartford ($12.50, one hour, three daily), Springfield ($20.50, two hours, three daily) and Boston ($31, four hours, five daily), as does **Greyhound Bus Lines** (☎ 203-772-2470, 800-221-2222), inside

New Haven's **Union Station** (☎ 203-773-6177; 50 Union Ave).

Connecticut Limousine (☎ 800-472-5466; www .ctlimo.com) runs buses between New Haven and NYC's airports (La Guardia and JFK, plus Newark) for around $50 per person.

CAR & MOTORCYCLE

Avis and Hertz rent cars at Tweed-New Haven Airport. Both can be reached by calling ☎ 203-466-8833. New Haven is 141 miles southwest of Boston, 36 miles south of Hartford, 75 miles from New York and 101 miles from Providence via interstate highways.

TRAIN

Metro-North trains (☎ 212-532-4900, 800-223-6052, 800-638-7646) make the 1½-hour run between NYC's Grand Central Terminal and New Haven's **Union Station** (☎ 203-773-6177, 50 Union Ave), at I-95 exit 47, almost every hour from 7am to midnight on weekdays, with more frequent trains during the morning and evening rush hours. On weekends, trains run about every two hours. Shore Line East runs **Commuter Connection buses** (☎ 203-624-0151) that shuttle passengers from Union Station (in the evenings) and from State St Station (in the mornings) to New Haven Green.

Frequent **Amtrak trains** (☎ 800-872-7245) run from NYC's Penn Station to New Haven's Union Station, but at a higher fare than Metro-North.

Shore Line East (☎ 800-255-7433) travels up the shore of Long Island Sound. At New Haven, the trains connect with Metro-North and Amtrak routes.

NORWALK

pop 84,000

Straddling the Norwalk River and encrusted with the salt spray of the Long Island Sound, Norwalk is a town fiercely proud of its maritime tradition. The area supported a robust oystering industry in the 18th and 19th centuries, but overharvesting in the early 1900s threatened the supply. Thanks to careful regulation, Norwalk is again the state's top oyster producer.

The past decade has brought exciting revitalization to the town. In South Norwalk, the crumbling waterfront has been rebuilt and a clutch of innovative restaurants have set up shop around Washington, Main and Water Sts, earning the area the nickname 'SoNo.' New Yorkers can get from Manhattan to Norwalk in about an hour, and be kayaking around the Norwalk Islands soon after.

Information

Fairfield County's Convention & Visitors Bureau (☎ 203-853-7770, 800-866-7925; www.coastalct.com; Mathews Park, 297 West Ave; ☻ 9am-5pm) Tourist information located in a small stone building.

Sights & Activities
MARITIME AQUARIUM

This **aquarium** (☎ 203-852-0700; www.maritime aquarium.org; 10 N Water St, S Norwalk; adult/child 2-12/ senior $9.75/7.75/9; ☻ 10am-5pm, until 6pm in summer) focuses solely on the marine life of the Long Island Sound, including harbor seals, sand tiger sharks and loggerhead turtles. IMAX movies are also shown throughout the day for an additional fee. For a more hands-on experience, take a 2½-hour cruise on the research vessel *Oceanic* (per person $19.50). Cruises depart at 1pm daily in July and August, and on weekends in April through June and September.

STEPPING STONES MUSEUM FOR CHILDREN

This well-crafted **museum** (☎ 203-899-0606; www .steppingstonesmuseum.org; Mathews Park, 303 West Ave; admission $7; ☻ 10am-5pm summer; closed Tue morning & Mon rest of year) is bursting with interactive, instructive fun, from the weather cycle to gravity to the principles of conservation. The Toddler Terrain is a hit with the under-three crowd. Across the parking lot from the museum is **Devon's Place**, a playground designed with mentally and physically challenged children in mind, but holds appeal for all.

LOCKWOOD-MATHEWS MANSION MUSEUM

This is one of the best surviving Second Empire–style country houses in the nation, so it's no wonder the 62-room **mansion** (☎ 203-838-9799; Mathews Park, 925 West Ave; adult/child under 12 $8/free; ☻ noon-5pm Wed-Sun) was chosen as the set for both the 1975 and 2004 versions of *The Stepford Wives*. The 2nd floor houses the Music Box Society International's permanent collection of music boxes, viewable (and listenable) only if you're on a tour. They leave every hour on the half-hour.

NORWALK ISLANDS

The Norwalk Islands lie a half-mile off the coast of SoNo, and are the playground of a menagerie of gawk-worthy coastal birds. Admission to the historic Sheffield Island Lighthouse is included in the price of the **ferry** (GW Tyler Lighthouse Ferry; ☎ 203-838-9444; adult/child 4-12/child 3 & under $15/12/5, summers only). Or if you want to take matters into your own hands, you can kayak there. The **Small Boat Shop** (☎ 203-854-5223; www.thesmallboatshop.com; 144 Water St; ☺ 10am-5pm Mon-Sat, 10am-3pm Sun) leads two-hour, four-hour and all-day trips to the islands in the summer.

SONO SWITCH TOWER MUSEUM

A bit short on explanatory placards, this modest **museum** (77 Washington St; ☺ noon-5pm Sat & Sun May-Oct; admission free) is a must-see only for the serious railroad buff. But hey, you can't beat the price, and it delivers great views – and accompanying rumblings – of the trains as they go past.

Festivals & Events

The mid-September **Oyster Festival** (☎ 800-866-7925; adult/child/senior $10/3/6) is a big deal, with sky divers, fireworks, bands and, of course, plenty of the slippery guys themselves. The proceeds from the 60,000-plus visitors go to preserving the Sheffield Island Lighthouse.

Sleeping

Silvermine Tavern (☎ 203-847-4558, 888-693-9967; www.silverminetavern.com; 194 Perry Ave; s $80, d $115-150) This inn is about a 15-minute drive – and several centuries away – from downtown Norwalk. All of its antique-laden rooms have a private bathroom. From the center of SoNo, head north on Main St and turn left onto CT 123. Bear right onto Silvermine Ave, and turn right onto Perry Ave.

Main Street Inn (☎ 203-972-2983; 190 Main St, New Canaan; s $90-125, d $115-160) A short drive from Norwalk, this restored Victorian with modern touches lets three spankingly clean rooms. Morning coffee and muffins are included.

Eating

Pasta Nostra (☎ 203-854-9700; 116 Washington St; mains $23-38; ☺ dinner Thu-Sat) You can feel the love at this black-and-white-tiled restaurant, where chef Joe Bruno has been wowing diners since 1984 with his handmade pastas and exquisite attention to detail. Freshness being the paramount principle, even the meat is butchered on site. Meal-wise, you can't go wrong. Reservations required.

Bistro du Soleil (☎ 203-855-9469; 120 Washington St; mains lunch $5-12, dinner $18-35; ☺ lunch & dinner) It's difficult to pigeonhole family-run Soleil's cuisine, and really, there's no need. Stylish yet warm, this bistro deftly executes everything from *langoustine* (shellfish) quesadillas to free-range New Zealand petite lamb chops to fillet of ostrich. The rotating art exhibits ensure a feast for the eyes to rival the one on your plate.

Plum Tree (☎ 203-966-8050; 70 Main St, New Canaan; rolls $5-15; ☺ lunch & dinner Mon-Sat, dinner Sun) If you're dying for some honest Japanese food, you'll be happy to drive the 8 miles north. The service is unfaltering, from the warm washcloth to the complementary tea. The menu carries an impressive array of rolls, like the Serpent – spicy shrimp and asparagus topped with eel ($10). The adventurous among you should order some river crab and watch as the chef plucks the tiny guys from their tank.

Silvermine Tavern (☎ 203-847-4558, 888-693-9967; www.silverminetavern.com; 194 Perry Ave; ☺ lunch & dinner Wed-Sun) Gracious dining is de rigueur here. Warm up on the crisp duck spring rolls ($8) before tackling the pecan-crusted fillet of brook trout ($22). If the weather is fine, be sure to secure seating on the deck overlooking the mill pond. If it's not, try to snag a fireside table.

Jeremiah Donovan's (☎ 203-838-3430; 138 Washington St, S Norwalk; sandwiches $5-10; ☺ 11:30-1am Mon-Sat, noon-6pm Sun) Head to this Victorian-era former saloon if all the SoNo gourmet chic is getting to you (or your kids). Alongside the tuna melts and Reubens on rye, JD dishes out hearty daily specials. Vintage photos of prize fighters festoon the place.

Shacojazz Art Cafe (☎ 203-853-6124; 21 N Main St, S Norwalk; mains $7-15; ☺ 11:30am-9:30pm Tue-Sat, 1-9pm Sun) Had it up to here with clam chowder? Try something a little different at this Afro-Caribbean shop-cum-eatery. A small bowl of the delicious peanut soup is $4, though be warned that its ingredients include fish broth and, er, gizzard.

Getting There & Away

Norwalk is about 32 miles south from New Haven on I-95. There are dozens of weekday

---

DETOUR: UNITED HOUSE WRECKING, INC.

Even if you're one of those folks who reflexively yawns – or gags – at the thought of 'going antiquing,' this extraordinary **antique shop** (☎ 203-348-5371; www.unitedhousewrecking.com; 535 Hope St, Stamford; 9:30am-5:30pm Mon-Sat, noon-5pm Sun) is well worth a visit. Upon pulling into the parking lot you may be greeted with a 15ft-tall Pinocchio standing with a 12ft Statue of Liberty, flanked by dozens of lampposts or scores of cherubic garden sculptures. Inside, the 35,000 sq ft warehouse holds vintage chandeliers, stained glass, furniture and classy knickknacks of all sorts. No room in the car for that one-of-a-kind fireplace mantel? No worries – they ship world-wide. Hyperactive children and accident-prone adults may want to wait outside with Pinocchio.

To get there from I-95 heading south, take exit 9 and turn right at the light onto US 1. Take your first right (Courtland Ave) and left onto Glenbrook Rd. At the light go straight onto Church St and then turn right onto Hope St.

---

trains between NYC's Grand Central Terminal and the South Norwalk Station (and all the stops in between), and a train about every hour on the weekends.

GREENWICH

pop 62,000

For those with money to burn, Greenwich beckons with a main street lined with the likes of Tiffany & Co, Sacks Fifth Avenue and Kate Spade, along with some charming but still pricey nonchain establishments, especially in the home furnishing and kidswear categories. Luckily for the rest of us, Greenwich also holds within its compact downtown a notable museum and an enticing town common (which is a wifi hot spot). Being only 28 miles from Grand Central Terminal, less than an hour by train, makes Greenwich a very doable day trip from NYC, or vice versa.

Information

Norwalk's Fairfield County's Convention & Visitors Bureau (p333) carries information on Greenwich. **Diane's Books** (203-869-1515; 8 Grigg St; 9am-5pm Mon-Sat) boasts the largest selection of family books in the country. It's about equally divided between grown-up and kids books, and they also stock an impressive selection of books on tape.

Bruce Museum

This **museum** (☎ 203-869-0376; www.brucemuseum .org; 1 Museum Dr; adult/student & senior $5/4; 10am-5pm Tue-Sat, 1-5pm Sun) serves up a bit of everything, but there's no suffering from cultural indigestion. Sculpture, photography and Cos Cob Impressionism meld smoothly into exhibits on natural science and anthro-

pology. Recent installations included 'Great Women, Great Science' and the oil sketches of Peter Paul Rubens. The museum is at the south end of Greenwich Ave, just past the train overpass.

Eating

Meli-Melo (362 Greenwich Ave; crepes $3-15; 10am-10pm) For a quick and delicious bite, you can't do better than this place. Meaning 'hodge-podge' in French, Meli-Melo serves salads, soups and sandwiches, but its specialty is undoubtedly buckwheat crepes. Try a wild combination like smoked salmon, chive sauce, lemon and daikon ($9.50). The French onion and French lentil soups are, appropriately, superb.

Restaurant Jean-Louis (☎ 203-622-8450; 61 Lewis St; dinner mains $31-41; lunch & dinner Mon-Fri, dinner Sat) Head here for a meal that neither your tastebuds nor your wallet will forget soon. Jean-Louis and Linda Gerin – chef and manager, respectively – have garnered accolades for their 'nouvelle classique,' with entrees like pan-seared ostrich thigh fillet with polenta and cognac sauce. The five-course *menu dégustation* (tasting menu) is the ideal way to taste a variety of offerings, and the prix-fixe lunch menu is a bargain at $29.

Getting There & Away

To get to the town center from I-95 heading south, take exit 3, then a right onto Arch St and another right onto Greenwich Ave, the main drag in town. If you're driving, avoid heading north from Greenwich anywhere around evening rush hour, or south into town during the morning commute – its proximity to NYC spells traffic nightmare.

The Greenwich train station will drop you off at the south end of Greenwich Ave. There are many daily trains connecting NYC and the rest of the Connecticut seaboard.

LOWER CONNECTICUT RIVER VALLEY

Blessedly, the Connecticut River escaped the bustle of industry and commerce that so often marred the northeast's rivers. The state takes its name from the river, and the fact that it's largely navigable 50 miles inland was one of the reasons the colony, and then the state, prospered in the days before highways. But it's surprisingly shallow near its mouth at the Long Island Sound, and this lack of depth led burgeoning industry to look for better harbors elsewhere, and thus the lower end of the Connecticut has preserved much of its 18th-century appearance.

Historic towns grace the river's banks, including Old Lyme, Essex, Ivoryton, Chester, Hadlyme and East Haddam. Each offers its own charms, and together they enchant visitors with gracious country inns, fine dining, and train rides and river excursions that allow authentic glimpses back into provincial life on the Connecticut.

OLD LYME

pop 7500

Near the mouth of the Connecticut River on the east bank, Old Lyme (I-95 exit 70) was home to some 60 sea captains in the 19th century. Since the early 20th century, however, Old Lyme has been known as the center of the Lyme Art Colony, which embraced and cultivated the American Impressionist movement. Numerous artists, including William Chadwick, Childe Hassam, Willard Metcalfe and Henry Ward came here to paint, staying in the mansion of local art patron Florence Griswold.

Her house (which her artist friends often decorated with murals in lieu of paying rent) is now the **Florence Griswold Museum** (☎ 860-434-5542; 96 Lyme St; adult/child/senior & student $7/4/6; ☼ 10am-5pm Tue-Sat, 1-5pm Sun) and contains a good selection of both Impressionist and Barbizon paintings. The estate consists of the house, the Kreible Museum, the Chadwick studio and Griswold's beloved gardens.

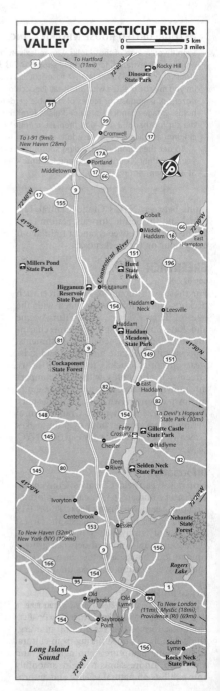

LOWER CONNECTICUT RIVER VALLEY

0 — 5 km
0 — 3 miles

The neighboring **Lyme Academy of Fine Arts** (☎ 860-434-5232; 84 Lyme St; admission free; ☽ 10am-4pm Tue-Sat, 1-4pm Sun) features works by students.

ESSEX
pop 6800

Tree-lined Essex, established in 1635, stands as the chief town of the region and features well-preserved Federal-period houses, legacies of rum and tobacco fortunes made in the 19th century. Essex was also the birthplace of the modern production of witch hazel, a traditional folk medicine. Today, the town has the genteel, aristocratic air of historical handsomeness, and prides itself on the fact that it is the oldest-known continuously operating waterfront in the country.

Coming into the town center from CT 9, you'll eventually find yourself on Main St. The centerpiece of Essex both physically and socially is the 1776 **Griswold Inn**, a hostelry since the time of the Revolutionary War. 'The Gris' is both an inn and a restaurant (see p338), and its taproom is the place to meet the townsfolk.

At the end of Main St is the riverfront and the **Connecticut River Museum** (☎ 860-767-8269; adult/child 6-12/senior $6/3/5; ☽ 10am-5pm Tue-Sun, 10am-4pm Jan-Apr), next to Steamboat Dock. Its meticulous exhibits recount the history of the area. Included among them is a replica of the world's first submarine, the *American Turtle*, a wooden barrel-like vessel built here by Yale student David Bushnell in 1776 and launched at nearby Old Saybrook.

You can lunch at the **Crow's Nest Gourmet Deli** (p339) north of the Gris along Ferry St.

One of the most enjoyable activities here is the **Essex Steam Train & Riverboat Ride** (☎ 860-767-0103, 800-377-3987; www.essexsteamtrain.com; 1 Railroad Ave; train only adult/child $16/8, train & riverboat cruise $24/12). A steam engine powers the train, which rumbles slowly north to the town of Deep River. There you can connect with a riverboat for a cruise up to the Goodspeed Opera House (right) and CT 82 swing bridge before heading back down to Deep River and returning to Essex via train. The roundtrip train ride takes about an hour; with the riverboat ride, the excursion takes 2½ hours. Trains leave the Railroad Ave station five times on weekdays in summer, six times on weekends. Fall foliage runs and dinner trains are scheduled as well. The

depot is on the west side of CT 9 from the main part of Essex. Take CT 9 exit 3A.

A mile west of Essex on the west side of CT 9, is the sleepy town of **Ivoryton**, named for the African elephant tusks imported during the 19th century to make combs and piano keys. Today, the ivory industry is long gone, and most people visit Ivoryton to dine at the **Copper Beech Inn** (p338).

CHESTER
pop 4000

Cupped in the valley of Pattaconk Brook, Chester is another sedate river town. A general store, post office, library and a few shops pretty much account for all the activity in the village. Most visitors come either for fine dining (p339) or to browse in the antique shops and boutiques on the town's charming main street.

From Chester, an eight-car **ferry** (☎ 860-443-3856; car/pedestrian $3/1) crosses the Connecticut River to Hadlyme daily April through November. Crossing eastbound, the ferry drops you at the foot of Gillette Castle in East Haddam.

EAST HADDAM
pop 8700

Two first-rate attractions mark this small town on the east bank of the Connecticut. Looming on one of the Seven Sisters hills above the ferry dock is **Gillette Castle** (☎ 860-526-2336; 67 River Rd; adult/child 6-11 $5/3; ☽ 10am-4:30pm), a turreted, bizarre-looking, 24-room riverstone mansion. Built between 1914 and 1919 by eccentric actor William Gillette, it was modeled on the medieval castles of Germany's Rhineland. Gillette made his name and his considerable fortune on stage in the role of Sherlock Holmes. He created the part himself, based on the famous mystery series by Sir Arthur Conan Doyle and in a sense, he made his castle part of the Holmes role as well: an upstairs room replicates Conan Doyle's description of the sitting room at 221B Baker St, London. Following Gillette's death in 1937, his dream house and its surrounding 117 acres were designated a Connecticut state park.

North of Gillette Castle stands the **Goodspeed Opera House** (☎ 860-873-8668; CT 82 at the bridge; tickets $24-53; ☽ performances Wed-Sun Apr-Dec), an 1876 Victorian music hall renowned as the only theater in the country dedicated

CONNECTICUT

to both the preservation of old and the development of new American musicals. The shows *Man of La Mancha* and *Annie* premiered at the Goodspeed before going on to national fame.

Also in East Haddam is a **Nathan Hale Schoolhouse** (☎ 860-873-9547; Main St; admission free; ☷ by appointment), behind St Stephen's Church in the center of town. He taught in this one-room building from 1773 to 1774.

STATE PARKS & FORESTS

The Lower Connecticut River Valley has several state parks and forests. For more information on any of them, contact the **Bureau of Outdoor Recreation** (☎ 860-424-3200; http://dep.state .ct.us/rec; 79 Elm St, Hartford).

Cockaponset State Forest (☎ 860-663-2030; Haddam) Fishing, hiking and swimming.

Devil's Hopyard State Park (☎ 860-873-8566; off CT 82, East Haddam) With 860 acres for camping and hiking, including the 60ft Chapman Falls.

Haddam Meadows State Park (☎ 860-663-2030; Haddam) Boating, fishing and picnic tables on the riverbank.

Hurd State Park (☎ 860-526-2336; East Hampton) Camping, fishing, hiking and picnicking.

SLEEPING
BUDGET

Saybrook Motor Inn (☎ 860-399-5926; 1575 Boston Post Rd, Old Saybrook; d Sun-Thu $55, Fri & Sat $85) Saybrook offers 24 well-used rooms with refrigerators, TVs and beach passes.

Devil's Hopyard State Park (☎ 860-424-3200, 877-668-2267; off CT 82, East Haddam; sites $11) This 860-acre park has 21 tent sites located near the falls. Water and toilets available.

DEVILS IN THE HOPYARD?

While most historians maintain that the name of the vast, forested Devil's Hopyard State Park derives from a corruption of the name of a one Farmer Dibble who grew hops along the Eight-Mile River, there's no denying that the area has its share of spooky stories. Native Americans believed that the place was home of a *manitou* (god), but the Puritans interpreted the perfectly round potholes underneath Chapman Falls as being the footprints of the Devil himself. As for the legitimacy of the more recent claims of demon sightings, you'll have to decide for yourself.

Wolf's Den (☎ 256 Town St/Rte 82, East Haddam; sites $33; ☷) Offers 205 'mostly grassy' campsites with laundromat, flush toilets and hot showers.

Markham Meadows (☎ 860-267-9738; 7 Markham Rd, East Hampton; sites $30) With 75 sites, this family campground has all the standard amenities. Be prepared to get in the spirit of their summer theme weekends, like Hawaiian Luau.

MID-RANGE

Moderately priced motels stand along US 1 in Old Saybrook, reached via I-95 exit 66. There's another cluster of motels near I-95 exits 67 North and 68 South.

Griswold Inn (☎ 860-767-1776; www.griswoldinn .com; 36 Main St, Essex; r $110-220, ste $160-370) Essex's landmark lodging and dining place. Despite the Gris' antiquity (it has been serving travelers since the Revolution), its 25 guest rooms have modern conveniences. The inn's famous all-you-can-eat Hunt Breakfast (served 11am to 2:30pm Sunday) costs $17. Otherwise, lunch in the dining room is $15 to $25, full dinners $35 to $60. Sunday morning 'Hunt Breakfasts' are a renowned tradition dating to the War of 1812, when British soldiers occupying Essex demanded to be fed well and often.

Bee & Thistle Inn (☎ 860-434-1667, 800-622-4946; www.beeandthistleinn.com; 100 Lyme St, Old Lyme; d incl breakfast $110-194) You'd have to try hard to feel stressed while at this butter-yellow 1756 Dutch Colonial farmhouse overlooking the Lieutenant River. All 11 rooms feature a canopy or four-poster bed, and some share bathrooms. Children over 12 welcome. The romantic, well-regarded dining room features cuisine like butter-roasted lobster tails with fennel and chive couscous.

Super 8 Motel (☎ 860-399-6273, 800-800-8000; www.super8.com; 37 Spencer Plain Rd; d Sun-Thu $70, Fri & Sat $110; ☷) The 44 rooms have cable TV and very basic amenities.

Days Inn (☎ 860-388-3453, 800-329-7466; www .daysinn.com; 1430 Boston Post Rd; d incl breakfast $70-135; ☷) There are 52 standard, fridge-equipped motel rooms here with a two-night minimum stay on weekends in the summer.

TOP END

Copper Beech Inn (☎ 860-767-0330, 888-809-2056; www .copperbeechinn.com; 46 Main St, Ivoryton; d $150-335) Its new owners have upped the game to exquisite result – this place exemplifies 'luxurious getaway.' Each of its 13 rooms – four in the Main House and nine in the Carriage House – is unique, but all are tastefully decorated and brimming with sumptuous touches like extra fluffy white bathrobes. For dinner, place yourself in the able hands of executive chef William Von Ahnen as he conjures up such classic French dishes as grilled breast of duckling ($28). The inn's wine cellar boasts more than 5000 bottles. Reserve well in advance, and contact the inn to find out about weekend package deals, eg lodging plus dinner or an evening at the Goodspeed Opera House. Take CT 9 exit 3 and follow the signs on to Ivoryton and go west 1.6 miles through Centerbrook.

Inn at Chester (☎ 860-526-9541, 800-949-7829; www.innatchester.com; 318 W Main St/CT 148; d $135-300) The original inn at Chester was a farmhouse built in 1776. Several buildings were added during the 20th century to produce a colonial-style inn with modern conveniences in its 44 rooms. The inn's spacious barn dining room serves traditional game dishes (venison, duck) with nouvelle-cuisine touches. The mains cost between $20 and $30. Their popular Sunday brunch is $15 and served from 11am to 2pm. To reach the inn from the center of Chester, follow CT 148 west for 4.4 miles and go past CT 9 exit 6 and Killingworth Reservoir to the inn, which is right on the Chester-Killingworth town line.

EATING

In the Connecticut River Valley, you'll find some of the best restaurants in country inns, such as the Copper Beech (opposite) in Ivoryton, the Griswold (opposite) in Essex, the Bee & Thistle (opposite) in Old Lyme and the Inn at Chester (above).

Olive Oyl's Carry-Out Cuisine (☎ 860-767-4909; 77 Main St, Essex; sandwiches $4-8; ⏲ 7:30am-6pm Tue-Sat, 7:30am-3pm Sun) For good, inexpensive sandwiches and picnic fare like cheese, pâtés and Stewart's soda, head here.

Crow's Nest Gourmet Deli (☎ 860-767-3288; Pratt St, Essex; dishes $3-8; ⏲ breakfast & lunch) This aptly named place overlooks the boatyard and marina from its perch at Brewer's Shipyard. The yachting crowd roosts here after a day on the water. Try the 'fishy swah,' deep-fried fish on a hard roll ($7).

Restaurant du Village (☎ 860-526-5301; 59 Main St, Chester; mains $23-30; ⏲ dinner Wed-Sun) With its wrought-iron gate, lacy white curtains and

flower-filled windowboxes beneath multi-paned windows, this tiny piece of France in Connecticut's countryside has Alsatian-influenced variations like roast duckling with citrus and balsamic vinegar.

SHOPPING

Connecticut River Artisans (☎ 860-526-5575; www.ctartisans.com; 5 W Main St, Chester; ⏲ 11am-6pm Jul-Aug & Nov-Dec, 11am-6pm Wed-Sun Jan-Jun & Sep-Oct) This co-op features one-of-a-kind art and craft pieces including clothing, folk art, furniture, jewelry, paintings, photographs and pottery. The building is also home to the Mill House art gallery.

HARTFORD

pop 124,000

True, it's a rare person who specifically goes to Hartford on vacation – it's a workaday city rather than a tourist destination – but Hartford's fighting hard to change that, with aggressive revitalization projects that are fast changing the shape of the city's skyline.

You'll be surprised at how much Connecticut's capital city has to offer visitors, with particular strengths in history and art. Hartford embodies Connecticut as The Land of Steady Habits; after all, this is where the insurance business was born and where the nation's oldest continuously run newspaper, the *Hartford Courant,* is still published. However, its sizable population makes for a lot of insurance and government office workers ready to blow off some steam at the end of the day and indulge in some readily accessible culture.

ORIENTATION

On its hilltop perch, the pseudo-Gothic Connecticut State Capitol is visible from most of the interstate highways entering the city. The tallest building, with a brilliant laser beacon shining atop it at night, is the Travelers Tower.

The easiest way to take in most of the Hartford attractions – the Wadsworth Atheneum, Old State House and Center Church – is on foot. The houses of literary figures Mark Twain and Harriet Beecher Stowe are a few miles west of the town center off Farmington Ave. There are tons of downtown garages for parking, but for

CONNECTICUT

HARTFORD

0 — 500 m
0 — 0.3 miles

INFORMATION
Bank of America....................................1 C2
Gallow's Hill Bookstore......................2 A6
Greater Hartford Welcome Center....3 C2
Hartford Hospital.................................4 B4
Post Office..5 B2

SIGHTS & ACTIVITIES
Ancient Burying Ground................(see 7)
Bushnell Park Carousel......................6 B3
Center Church.......................................7 C3
Hartford Guides....................................8 C3
Museum of Connecticut History.......9 B3
Old State House..................................10 C3
Pump House Gallery..........................11 C3
State Capitol..12 B3

Travelers Tower..................................13 C3
Wadsworth Atheneum......................14 C3

SLEEPING 🏠
Crowne Plaza Hartford Downtown..15 C2
Goodwin Hotel....................................16 C2
Hilton Hartford...................................17 C2
Holiday Inn Express...........................18 B2
Marriott Residence Inn......................19 C2
Sheraton Hartford..............................20 D3

EATING 🍴
Alchemy Juice Bar & Café.............21 A6
Hot Tomato's......................................22 B2
Pastis..23 B2
Pavilion at State House Square.....24 C2
Peppercorn's Grill..............................25 C3
Pierpont Restaurant....................(see 16)
Tapas..26 B2
Timothy's...27 C2
Trumbull Kitchen...............................28 C2

ENTERTAINMENT 🎭
Black-eyed Sally's BBQ & Blues....29 B2
Brew Ha Ha....................................(see 32)
Bushnell...30 B3
Cinestudio..31 A5
City Steam Brewery Café..................32 C2
Coliseum.......................................(see 33)
Hartford 21...33 C2
Hartford Stage....................................34 C2
Polo Club...35 B6

OTHER
Morgan St Garage..............................36 C2

HARTFORD: CASE STUDY IN URBAN REVIVAL?

Before European colonists arrived, the Saukiog Indians called the Hartford area home. In 1633, the Dutch ventured north from New York and established a trading post called the House of Good Hope on the shore of the Connecticut River. At the same time, a second group of Europeans came west to the Hartford area from the Massachusetts Bay Colony under the leadership of the Reverend Thomas Hooker.

The Hartford Colony became the Colony of Connecticut under the charter granted by King Charles II in 1662. A defining moment in the city's history took place 25 years later when the English governor threatened the charter's provisions. In defiant response, the citizenry hid the charter in the trunk of a large oak tree in Hartford and never surrendered it. A plaque at Charter Oak Place now marks the spot where the tree stood until 1856.

The insurance industry got its start in Hartford as early as the late 18th century: the establishment of the Hartford Fire Insurance Co was a means of guaranteeing the profitability of the shipping trade. By the late 19th century, Hartford was a thriving city, and its location between New York and Boston made it appealing to writers and artists. Samuel Clemens (aka Mark Twain) eventually made Hartford his home. Among the famous author's neighbors were writers Harriet Beecher Stowe and William Dean Howells. Poet Wallace Stevens spent much of the first half of the 20th century as an insurance executive in Hartford while contemplating 'complacencies of the peignoir' (as described in *Sunday Morning*).

Hartford entered a decline in the first half of the 20th century. In the 1960s, an urban planning project gave the city Constitution Plaza, a complex of office buildings in the heart of downtown, and in the '70s, the city opened Civic Center, a venue for concerts and sporting events with associated shops and a hotel. However, the development didn't reap the hoped-for benefits (starting with the roof collapse of the Civic Center Coliseum in 1978), and the fruits of a second ambitious wave of revitalization are just now coming to bear. The 33-acre revitalization project Adriaen's Landing (named for Adriaen Block, the first European to explore the Connecticut River Valley, in 1614) consists of four ambitious elements: a huge convention center is poised to open in June 2005; Marriott Hotel will be showing off its new facelift in July 2005; the retail area of the Civic Center will be demolished to make way for a pedestrian-friendly retail, restaurant and entertainment district, open for business by early 2007; and finally, ground-breaking for a jaw-dropping science center is set for December 2006, with completion slated for early 2008.

Let's hope that Hartford's urban renewal efforts are enough to counteract the commuter syndrome: an excess of people who drive in to work in the insurance towers, but who live – and pay taxes – in smaller towns. Urban renewal will not bring back the prosperous city of Twain's day until the people who work here live here. Time shall soon tell if Hartford's valiant efforts are enough to bring back Hartford's spark.

the most bang for your buck, head to the huge outdoor Morgan St Garage (entrance on Talcott St between Market St and Columbus Blvd).

Continue west on Farmington Ave until it becomes the main street of gentrified West Hartford, a 15-minute drive from downtown Hartford. It's lined with shops and cafés.

INFORMATION
Bookstores
Bookworm (☎ 860-233-2653; 968 Farmington Ave, West Harford; ◷ 9:30am-6pm Mon-Sat, noon-4pm Sun) This is on the shady main street of West Hartford.

Gallows Hill Bookstore (☎ 860-297-2191; 300 Summit St; ◷ 9am-7pm Mon-Fri, 7am-2pm Sat while school is in session) You'll find well-stocked shelves at this bookstore on the campus of Trinity College.

Emergencies
Hartford Hospital (☎ 860-524-2525; 80 Seymour St) South of downtown, this is the city's major medical facility.

Internet access
Cosí Café (☎ 860-521-8495; 970 Farmington Ave, West Harford; ◷ 7am-10pm) This is a wireless hot spot.
Library (☎ 860-695-6300; 500 Main St; ◷ 10am-8pm Mon-Thu, 10am-5pm Sat) The central library is at Arch St and has free Internet access.

CONNECTICUT

Money

ATMs are all over the place.

Bank of America (777 Main St, Central Row) Also has an ATM inside the City Place complex at 185 Asylum St.

Post

Post office (185 Ann St; ⊗ 8:30am-4:30pm Mon-Fri) Between Allyn and Asylum Sts.

Tourist Information

Greater Hartford Welcome Center (☎ 860-244-0253; www.connectthedots.org; 45 Pratt St; ⊗ 9am-5pm Mon-Fri) The bulk of tourist services is at this centrally located center.

SIGHTS & ACTIVITIES

Travelers Tower

Score the best views of the city from the observation deck of the 34-story **Travelers Tower** (☎ 860-277-4208; 740 Main St), named after its tenant, the Travelers Insurance Company. The observation deck is free, but only open from May through October, and you have to climb 70 steps from the elevator to the deck. Keep your eyes peeled for Amelia, a peregrine falcon who since 1997 has made her home on a ledge on the 21st floor. She – along with her mate and their succession of fluffy hatchlings – have inspired peregrine-lovers to establish a **website** (http://falconcam .travelers.com) devoted to the birds.

State Capitol

The **Connecticut State Capitol** (☎ 860-240-0222; cnr Capitol Ave & Trinity St; admission free; ⊗ 8am-5pm Mon-Fri) is an imposing white marble building with Gothic details and a gold-leaf dome. Because of the variety of architectural styles it reflects, it has been dubbed 'the most beautiful ugly building in the world.' Designed by Richard Upjohn in 1879, it's open for free visits. One-hour guided tours, also free, depart hourly from the Legislative Office Building, on Capitol Ave near Broad St, from 9:15am to 1:15pm on weekdays (also 2:15pm in July and August). On Saturday from April to October, they depart hourly from the southwest entrance (Capitol Ave) from 10:15am to 2:15pm.

Museum of Connecticut History

While you're up on Capitol Hill, have a look at this **museum** (☎ 860-757-6535; www.cslib.org/museum .htm; 231 Capitol Ave; admission free; ⊗ 9am-4pm Mon-Fri, 9am-2pm Sat) housed in the State Library and Supreme Court Building just across from the State Capitol. Nationally known for its genealogy library, it also holds Connecticut's royal charter of 1662, a prime collection of Colt firearms (which were manufactured in Hartford), coins and the table at which Abraham Lincoln signed the Emancipation Proclamation.

Wadsworth Atheneum

The nation's oldest continuously operating art museum, the **Wadsworth Atheneum** (☎ 860-278-2670; 600 Main St; adult/child 6-17/senior & student $10/5/8; ⊗ 11am-5pm Wed-Fri, 10am-5pm Sat & Sun) houses more than 40,000 pieces of art in a castlelike Gothic Revival building. On display are paintings by members of the Hudson River School, including some by Hartford resident Frederic Church; 19th-century impressionist works; 18th-century furniture; and the sculptures of the Connecticut artist Alexander Calder. The Amistad Foundation Gallery has an outstanding collection of African American art and historical objects; the Matrix Gallery features works by contemporary artists.

There's a decent café here too, and a free shuttle runs between the museum and the Morgan St Garage (see p339). On Burr Mall between the Atheneum and City Hall stands Alexander Calder's orange Stegosaurus sculpture.

Bushnell Park

Spreading down the hill from Capitol Hill is the 37-acre **Bushnell Park** (☎ 860-522-3668; admission free; ⊗ sunrise-sunset), designed by Jacob Weidenmann in the 1850s. The Tudor-style **Pump House Gallery** (1947) features art exhibits and a summer concert series. If you're a botany buff, take the self-guided tree tour of the park. Pick up a brochure at the Memorial Arch or call ☎ 860-232-6710.

The **Bushnell Park Carousel** (☎ 860-585-5411; rides 50¢; ⊗ 11am-5pm Tue-Sun mid-May–Aug, Sat & Sun only mid-Apr–mid-May & Sep) is a 1914 merry-go-round designed by Stein and Goldstein, with 48 horses and a Wurlitzer band organ. Even if you're not game for a ride, stop by to read the fascinating history placards on display.

The **Gothic Soldiers & Sailors Memorial Arch** which frames the Trinity St entrance commemorates Civil War veterans and offers fine views from its turrets, unfortunately accessible only on a **tour** (☎ 860-232-6710; donations accepted; ⊗ noon Thu May-Oct).

GRABBING THE BRASS RING

In the 12th century, Arabian horsemen played a game called *carosello*, in which teams rode in circles and tossed perfume-filled balls back and forth. The team who dropped the ball would be odoriferously branded by their loss for days. Crusading knights brought the game back to Europe, and the French modified it in order to train nobles and knights for competitions. The men would ride around in a circle on legless wooden horses (powered by the real animals), and try to catch hanging rings on their lances.

Eventually this evolved into the idea of grabbing a brass ring while riding a carousel in order to win a free ride. These days the expression 'grabbing the brass ring' connotes striving to get to the top of one's career. Due to soaring liability insurance rates, only a few carousels in the country let kids (yes, only kids) try for the ring. One is the Flying Horses Carousel (p306) in Watch Hill, RI.

Old State House

Connecticut's **Old State House** (☎ 860-522-6766; www.ctosh.org; 800 Main St; admission free; ◷ 10am-4pm Mon-Sat) is the oldest state capitol in the country. Designed by Charles Bulfinch – who also did the Massachusetts State House in Boston – it was the site of the trial of the Amistad prisoners. Gilbert Stuart's famous portrait of George Washington hangs in the senate chamber. The newly expanded space houses interactive exhibits for kids and adults alike.

Center Church

This **church** (☎ 860-249-5631; 675 Main St; admission free; ◷ by appointment) was established by the Reverend Thomas Hooker when he came to Hartford from the Massachusetts Bay Colony in 1636. The present building dates from 1807 and was modeled on St Martin's-in-the-Fields in London. In the **Ancient Burying Ground** (◷ 10am-4pm) behind the church lie the remains of Hooker and Revolutionary War patriots Joseph and Jeremiah Wadsworth. Some headstones date from the 17th century. Adjacent to the church is Carl Andre's **Stone Field sculpture**, which to some is a powerful minimalist statement. To others, it's exactly what it sounds like – a field of rocks.

Mark Twain House & Museum

For 17 years, encompassing both the best and worst periods of his life, Samuel Langhorne Clemens (1835–1910) and his family lived in this striking orange-and-black brick Victorian **house** (☎ 860-247-0998; 351 Farmington Ave; adult/child 6-12/student/senior $16/8/12/14; ◷ 9:30am-5:30pm, closed Tue Nov-May) which then stood in the pastoral area of the city called Nook Farm. Architect Edward Tuckerman Potter lavishly embellished it with turrets, gables and verandahs, and some of the interiors were done by Louis Comfort Tiffany. Though Twain maintained that it was difficult to write in the house, it was here that he penned some of his most famous works, including *The Adventures of Tom Sawyer*, *The Adventures of Huckleberry Finn* and *A Connecticut Yankee in King Arthur's Court*. A tour is part of the admission fee. The museum center further supplements visitors' appreciation through thoughtfully selected photos, films, artifacts and manuscripts.

Harriet Beecher Stowe House

Next door to the Twain house is this **house** (☎ 860-525-9317; 73 Forest St; adult/child 6-12/senior $6.50/2.75/6; ◷ 9:30am-4pm Mon-Sat, noon-4:30pm Sun) of the woman who wrote the antislavery book *Uncle Tom's Cabin*. Upon meeting Stowe, Abraham Lincoln is alleged to have said, 'So this is the little lady who made this big war.' Built in 1871, the Stowe house reflects the author's strong ideas about decorating and domestic efficiency, as she expressed in her bestseller *American Woman's Home*, which was nearly as popular as the phenomenal *Uncle Tom's Cabin*. The house is light-filled, with big windows draped in plants.

Tickets include admission to the adjoining Katharine S Day House, named for Stowe's grandniece, who sought to preserve the memory of her great-aunt's community spirit and works. The house has 1880s decor as well as changing exhibits.

Elizabeth Park Rose Gardens

Known for its fine collection of 15,000 rose bushes, **Elizabeth Park** (☎ 860-722-6514; Prospect Ave; admission free; ◷ sunrise-sunset daily, greenhouses 8am-3pm Mon-Fri) at Asylum Ave, is a 100-acre – and 100-year-old – preserve on the Hartford–West Hartford town line.

More than 900 varieties such as climbers, American Beauties, ramblers and heavily perfumed damasks cover the grounds. June and July are the months to see the roses in full flower, but they bloom, if less profusely, well into fall. Besides roses, the park tends a tall dahlia display, herb gardens and greenhouses. The landscaped paths make for excellent jogging trails.

HARTFORD & AROUND FOR CHILDREN

They may not yet appreciate the historical significance of the Connecticut Charter or the beauty of the Caravaggio hanging at the Atheneum, but there's plenty in the Hartford area to keep the kids engaged and amused.

Of course, the classic **Bushnell Carousel** (p342) is a must, and a steal at 50¢ a ride. The **Old State House** (p343) has recently developed interactive historical exhibits aimed at kids. The **Hartford Children's Theater** (☎ 860-249-7970; 360 Farmington Ave, Hartford; tickets $12-15) puts on several productions a year, like *Charlotte's Web* and the *Wizard of Oz*. Both children and adults make up the casts.

Lake Compounce Amusement Park (p347) lies 18 miles southwest of Hartford. In New Britain you can all make your own soda at **Avery's Beverage Co** (p348). Ten miles south of Hartford is **Dinosaur State Park** (p347), where the kids can make molds of real dino prints. Just to the east of the city is the wonderful **Trash Museum** (p347).

TOURS

Hartford Guides (☎ 860-522-0855; 523 Main St; suggested donation $5) This organization offers two-hour guided walking tours at 1:30pm on weekdays April through November. Notice of 24 hours is requested.

Heritage Trails Sightseeing Tours (☎ 860-677-8867; www.charteroaktree.com) Heritage Trails lead almost a dozen themed bus tours in the Greater Hartford area, from

---

MUSIC FESTIVALS

The **Greater Hartford Festival of Jazz** (www .jazzhartford.org) is held in Bushnell Park over the third weekend in July. You can also treat yourself to the sweet sounds of the summer-only **Monday Night Jazz Series**, the oldest jazz series in the country. For bluegrass lovers, East Hartford's August **Podunk Music Festival** (☎ 860-291-7350) promises a knee-slappin', foot-stompin' good time.

'Katharine Hepburn's Hartford' to the Black History Freedom Trail in Farmington. Most are $20 per person and no credit cards are accepted.

SLEEPING

There are currently no B&Bs in the city, but there are a number in the surrounding countryside. Call **Nutmeg B&B Agency** (☎ 860-236-6698, 800-727-7592; www.bnb-link.com) for a list and profile of Hartford area B&Bs.

Just outside the center of Hartford are many of the usual chain motels, usually offering the best-value accommodations. Hartford's city-center luxury hotels charge high rates on weekdays and lower rates on weekends. The suburban motels' rates go up on weekends.

Budget

Howard Johnson Express Inn (☎ 860-875-0781; www .hojo.com; 451 Hartford Turnpike, Vernon; d incl breakfast from $65; ☒) This 64-room lodge at I-84 exit 65, is northeast of the city in Vernon, on the way to Boston. Each room has a fridge and microwave, and there's a 24-hour restaurant for your snack-attack pleasure.

Mark Twain Hostel (☎ 860-523-7255, 800-909-4776; www.hiayh.org; 131 Tremont St; dm member/nonmember $18/21, r $45) This rickety place has clean-enough beds, and guests can use the fully equipped kitchen and laundry facilities. It's in the city's West End, off Farmington Ave (I-84 exit 46), a 25-minute walk from downtown and Union Station. Cash preferred. Call for pick-up service.

Motel 6 (☎ 860-563-5900, 800-466-8356; www .motel6.com; 1341 Silas Deane Hwy; d $49-54) The 146 rooms here are both comfortable and clean. There's a coin-operated laundry in the building and a restaurant next door. It is 10 miles south of the city center in Wethersfield at I-91 exit 24.

Mid-Range

Sheraton Hartford (☎ 860-528-9703; www.sheraton .com; 100 E River Dr; d Sun-Thu $149, Fri & Sat $89; ☒) Across the river in East Hartford (I-84 West exit 54, I-84 East exit 53, I-91 North exit 29, I-91 South exit 30, CT 2 exit 4), you find a fitness center, restaurant and lounge. The spacious rooms boast lush ribbed carpets, high-speed data ports and ergonomically designed workstations.

Holiday Inn Express (☎ 860-246-9900; 440 Asylum St; d Sun-Thu $139-149, Fri & Sat $110-129) Smack in the middle of town, this comfortable, 96-room inn has a fitness center, laundry service and fresh cinnamon buns in the morning.

Hilton Hartford (☎ 860-728-5151, 800-325-3535; www.hilton.com; 315 Trumbull St; d Sun-Thu $165, Fri & Sat $85; 🏊) This 22-story hotel just underwent a $22 million face-lift – that's a million per floor. Its 392 rooms and 10 suites all have wireless Internet and well-appointed rooms, some of which overlook the Capitol. Work out in the state-of-the art health facility and then relax in the whirlpool and sauna.

Crowne Plaza Hartford Downtown (☎ 860-549-2400; www.ichotels.com; 50 Morgan St; d Sun-Thu $180, Fri & Sat $130; 🏊) This imposing white block of a building in the city's north side houses 350 luxury guest rooms and is flush with guest services, including shuttle service to Bradley Airport ($15), an outdoor pool and an on-site restaurant. Some rooms are wheelchair accessible.

Top End

Goodwin Hotel (☎ 860-246-7500, 800-922-5006; www.goodwinhotel.com; 1 Haynes St; d Sun-Thu $229, Fri & Sat $299) The fanciest hotel in Hartford, this five-story, 124-room, 1881 red-brick building looks historic on the outside, but inside it has been entirely remodeled to appeal to modern preferences for large, light-filled rooms. Decor is traditional, with antique reproduction furniture. Staff serve afternoon tea in the lobby. Its Pierpont Restaurant, with its deeply burnished walls and continental fare, is well regarded.

Marriott Residence Inn (☎ 860-524-5550, 800-331-3131; www.residenceinn.com; 942 Main St; d Sun-Thu $189, Fri & Sat $149) This 100-unit hotel is housed in the lovely historic Richardson Building. Each room and suite has a full kitchen, data ports, voicemail and cable TV. There's an exercise facility too.

EATING & DRINKING
Budget

Pavilion at State House Square (cnr Main & State Sts; dishes $4-12; ☉ 10am-2pm, hrs may vary) Across from the Old State House on Main St, this vastly popular food court has a dozen vendors selling ethnic and vegetarian lunches in the airy interior courtyard of a high-rise office palace. Try the pad thai ($4.25) at Bangkok or the veggie lasagna at the Natural ($6.25).

Alchemy Juice Bar & Café (☎ 860-246-5700; 203 New Britain Ave; juices $5-9; ☉ 9:30am-8pm Mon-Fri, noon-6pm Sat & Sun) Near the Trinity campus, this is your stop for organic smoothies with names like Planetary Alignment, sandwiches and good vibes (including the wifi ones).

Tapas (☎ 860-525-5988; 126 Ann St; mains $7-11; ☉ 11am-10pm Mon-Fri, 5-11pm Sat) Crowds pack this storefront bistro at lunch and happy hour for good reason. You can sit at high tables or stand at wall counters and rub shoulders with three neighbors while eating blackened chicken tapas ($8) or souvlaki ($7). They brag that their food's so fresh, they don't even have a freezer.

Mid-Range

Timothy's (☎ 860-782-9822; 243 Zion St; mains $6-12; ☉ 7am-8pm Mon- Sat, 9am-3pm Sun) South of downtown heading towards Trinity College, Timothy's helps give natural food restaurants a good name. Hearty, delectable items from all over the globe cuddle up with each other on the menu, like sweet potato enchiladas ($9) and curry chicken salad ($7.50).

Trumbull Kitchen (☎ 860-493-7417; 150 Trumbull St; small dishes/mains $5-12/15-22; ☉ 11:30am-midnight Mon-Fri, 5pm-midnight Sat, 4-10pm Sun) At this slick downtown eatery you can get bites of anything from dim sum, tapas, stone pies or (and?) fondue. The bar stays open later on the weekend, the longer to sample their impressive cocktail list.

Luna Pizza (☎ 860-233-1625; 999 Farmington Ave, West Hartford; pizzas $12-20 ☉ lunch & dinner) The pizzas that come out of the brick oven are divine – crispy and thin-crusted – and the mozzarella is fresh. Luna's space is reminiscent of an upmarket cafeteria, and jazz musicians play on the weekends. Try the salmon, onions and caper pizza. Amazingly, they offer single slices, too.

Peppercorn's Grill (☎ 860-547-1714; 357 Main St; mains $12-20; ☉ lunch & dinner Mon-Sat) Modern American interpretations of traditional Italian dishes are the specialty at this restaurant between Capitol Ave and Buckingham St. In this family-run place, you might find anything from veal saltimbocca ($18) to a zesty dish of ravioli with scallops and lobster ($19).

Hot Tomato's (☎ 860-241-9100; 1 Union Pl; mains lunch $9-14, dinner $15-28; ☉ lunch & dinner Mon-Fri, dinner Sat & Sun) A lot of locals love this place with its café deck overlooking Bushnell Park and the State Capitol. The interior is

CONNECTICUT

postmodern chrome. Try the simple but delicious linguini *vongole* ($19).

Top End

Azul (☎ 860-233-1726; 124 LaSalle Rd, West Hartford; dinner mains $20-28; ⏰ lunch & dinner Mon-Sat, dinner Sun) With its black-clad waiters and slightly relentless sound system, Azul specializes in high-class, presentation-oriented Nuevo Latino dishes like Chilean salmon with ginger chili compote in banana leaf. However, it offers enough Americanized dishes to satisfy the unadventurous. You'll want to spiff up for dinner here.

Pastis (☎ 860-278-8852; 201 Ann St; mains $17-30; ⏰ lunch & dinner Mon-Fri, dinner Sat) A great date place, this French-American bistro wins you over with its intimate tables, candlelight, lace curtains and French acoustic music. The mains, classics like coq au vin, are well done, if not swoon-worthy. Try the seared scallops with saffron rice ($20).

ENTERTAINMENT

Pick up a free copy of the *Hartford Advocate* for up-to-the-minute entertainment listings.

Performing Arts & Cinema

Bushnell (☎ 860-987-5900; www.bushnell.org; 166 Capitol Ave; tickets $20-45) Hosting over 500 events a year, the Bushnell plays a major role in the state's cultural life. Its historic building is where you go for most ballet, symphony, opera and chamber music performances. For current shows contact the **Greater Hartford Arts Council** (☎ 860-525-8629; www.connectthedots.org). For events in Bushnell Park, call ☎ 860-543-8570. **Hartford Symphony** (☎ 860-244-2999; tickets $30-60) stages performances year-round.

Hartford Stage (☎ 860-527-5151; www.hartfordstage .org; 50 Church St; tickets $20-60) Contemporary as well as classic dramas play from September to June. Venturi & Rauch designed the striking theater building of red brick with darker red zigzag details.

Real Art Ways (RAW; ☎ 860-232-1006; www.real artways.org; 56 Arbor St; suggested gallery donation $3; ⏰ 2-10pm Mon-Fri, 2pm-midnight Sat & Sun) Contemporary works in all kinds of media find an outlet at this consistently offbeat and adventurous gallery/cinema/performance space/ lounge. Evening events at RAW usually cost between $5 and $12. You can sip wine or beer while watching the new drag-queen documentary or Vincent Gallo's latest film.

Cinestudio (☎ show times 860-297-2463, office ☎ 860-297-2544; www.cinestudio.org; 300 Summit St) If you want to catch a movie, this gorgeous, velvet-seated cinema at Trinity College shows first-run and art films at lower-than-average prices.

Comedy & Live Music

City Steam Brewery Café (☎ 860-525-1600; 942 Main St; ⏰ 11:30am-1am Mon-Thu, 11:30am-2am Fri & Sat, noon-10pm Sun) This big and boisterous place has plenty of yummy beers on tap. The Naughty Nurse Pale Ale is a bestseller, but be sure to check out their seasonals. The café is also home to the **Brew Ha Ha Comedy Club**, where you can yuk it up with comedians seen on Conan O'Brien and at the Improv. Shows are $15 on Friday and Saturday nights and $5 on Thursdays. You must pay for tickets with your credit card.

Black-eyed Sally's BBQ & Blues (☎ 860-278-7427; 350 Asylum St; cover $4-8, dinner mains $15-18; ⏰ 11:30am-10pm, 5-11pm Sat, 4-9pm Sun) This blues palace drags in local and national acts. The walls are covered with graffiti, some penned by visiting bands. There's live music Wednesday through Saturday, and Sunday and Monday are all-you-can-eat BBQ nights.

Gay & Lesbian Venues

Chez Est (☎ 860-525-3243; 458 Wethersfield Ave; cover free-$5; ⏰ 3pm-1am Sun-Thu, 3pm-2am Fri & Sat) South of Colt Park, Chez Est place has a cozy, mixed crowd. On Mondays, there's no cover and free pool after 8pm; Wednesday means karaoke.

Polo Club (☎ 860-278-3333; 678 Maple Ave; cover $5-8; ⏰ 8pm-2am Thu-Sat) While this place seems to cater more to curious straight couples who come to watch the drag-queen shows than to gays themselves, it's a fun place to lounge around with a martini in hand, feeling fabulous.

GETTING THERE & AROUND

By car, interstates connect Hartford to Boston (102 miles), New Haven (36 miles), New York (117 miles) and Providence (71 miles). The cheapest downtown parking is at the Morgan St Garage on the corner of Morgan and Market Sts.

See p314 for information on air travel via Bradley International Airport in Windsor Locks, and intercity bus service. The city bus service, **Connecticut Transit** (☎ 860-525-9181;

A TRASHY MUSEUM

As a whole, we humans are woefully ignorant of what happens to that juice container once we toss it into the recycling bin. The fascinating (really!) **Trash Museum** (☎ 860-247-4280; www.crra .org; 211 Murphy Rd, Stratford; admission free; ☺ 10am-4pm Tue-Sat July & Aug, noon-4pm Wed-Fri Sep-Jun) educates us on the entire process, from consumption to collection, cleaning, sorting and reselling, with side exhibits on landfills and composting. The best part, however, is standing on the upstairs observation deck to witness the recycling trucks dumping their loads (overwhelmingly milk-carton white with some Tide-red highlights), and watching the monstrous sorting-, cleaning- and crushing-machine do its thing.

Though the museum is geared towards the under-12 set, adults will find it an enlightening visit. To get there from Hartford, take I-91 south and get off at exit 27. Turn left off the ramp onto Airport Rd, and after bearing right at the split, take a left onto Murphy Rd. The museum is housed in the Connecticut Resources Recovery Authority Visitors Center.

www.cttransit.com), can shuttle you from the airport to downtown Hartford for $1.10 on its Bradley Flyer.

By train, **Amtrak** (☎ 800-872-7245) connects Hartford to New York and Boston.

In Hartford, **Union Station** (☎ 860-247-5329; 1 Union Pl) at Spruce St, is the city's transportation center and the place to catch trains, airport shuttles, intercity buses and taxis.

Check the taxi stand outside Union Station, or call **Yellow Cab Co** (☎ 860-666-6666).

AROUND HARTFORD

The environs of Hartford hold many things to see and do. Here are several of the best.

Old Wethersfield

Historic Wethersfield boasts that George Washington stayed here while planning the final victorious campaign of the Revolutionary War. 'Old Wethersfield' (the historic district) has a cache of Revolution-era and colonial houses. Three 18th-century houses comprise the **Webb-Deane-Stevens Museum** (☎ 860-529-0612; 211 Main St; adult/student & child 5 & older/senior $8/4/7; ☺ 10am-4pm Wed-Mon May-Oct, 10am-4pm Sat & Sun Nov-Apr). Exhibits in all the houses bring to life the America of more than two centuries ago. Wethersfield is just 5 miles south of Hartford off I-91 exit 26.

Dinosaur State Park

Two hundred million years ago, dinosaurs traipsed across mudflats near Rocky Hill, 10 miles due south of Hartford along I-91. Their tracks hardened in the mud and remained safely buried until the 20th century, when road-building crews serendipitously uncovered them. Connecticut's answer to

Jurassic Park is **Dinosaur State Park** (☎ 860-529-8423; www.dinosaurstatepark.org; 400 West St; adult/child 6-17 $5/2; ☺ 9am-4:30pm Tue-Sun), where you can view the footprints preserved beneath a geodesic dome and tour an 80ft-long diorama that shows how the tracks were made.

Outside, there are several *in situ* dino prints where visitors can make plaster casts. The casting site is free, open from May through October, and the park provides everything you need but the plaster of paris, 25 pounds of which is recommended to make several decent-sized casts.

The park also has a picnic area and 2 miles of interesting nature trails. Take I-91 exit 23, then go a mile east. No credit cards accepted.

Lake Compounce Theme Park

If the kids are in dire need of a roller coaster and funnel cake infusion but the idea of tackling the huge, unrelentingly commercial Six Flags in Springfield, MA leaves you cold, **Lake Compounce Theme Park** (☎ 860-583-3300; www.lakecompounce.com; 822 Lake Ave, Bristol; adult/child under 52" $31/22; ☺ 11am-8pm mid-Jun–Aug, Sat & Sun only in May & Sep) is the ticket. This 100-acre lakeshore amusement park is in the town of Bristol, 18 miles southwest of Hartford at the junction of CT 61 and CT 132, and boasts two roller coasters (one of which, Boulder Dash, is an excellent wooden specimen), a whitewater raft ride, historic steam train, interactive haunted house and many other amusements. Clipper Cove, with a 300-gallon water bucket, and Splash Harbor Water Park with its pools and waterslides, are perfect for a steaming summer's day. The 180ft free-fall 'swing'

DETOUR: AVERY'S BEVERAGE CO, NEW BRITAIN

It doesn't get much more authentic than **Avery's** (☎ 860-224-0830; www.averysoda.com; 520 Corbin Ave, New Britain; ☼ 8:30am-5:30pm Tue & Wed, 8:30am-7pm Thu, 8:30am-6pm Fri, 8:30am-3pm Sat). Its 30-plus flavors of sodas and seltzers are still made with 1950s technology in the original red barn where it all started back in 1904. The water is pure well and the sugar is pure cane – no high fructose corn syrup here. Stand-bys like Birch Beer and Black Cherry share the stage with concoctions like Half & Half and Pineapple.

If your group is at least four strong, be sure to call ahead to arrange a make-your-own-soda tour ($11.50 per group). You'll go upstairs to the Mixing Room and create three bottles of soda to your exact flavor specifications and then watch the conveyor-belt machine downstairs add the water and CO_2 and affix the cap.

Sodas are sold by the case (within which you can mix and match flavors), but there are some single bottles available for 75¢ a pop.

From Hartford, drive west on I-84 for about 11 miles, and merge onto CT 72 via exit 35. Take exit 7 and turn slightly right onto Corbin Ave.

---

will thrill even the most jaded of extreme sports enthusiasts.

Admission includes unlimited access to most rides and amusements. There's a $5 parking charge.

LITCHFIELD HILLS

The rolling hills in the northwestern corner of Connecticut take their name from the historic town of Litchfield at their heart. Sprinkled with lakes and dotted with forests and state parks rich in waterfalls, this region offers an abundance of tranquility. Only a handful of inns and campgrounds provide for travelers, an intentional curb on development that guarantees the preservation of the area's rural character. Quite a few entertainment industry celebrities keep a low profile on their farms and country estates on the back roads here.

Contact the **Litchfield Hills Visitors Bureau** (☎ 860-567-4506; www.litchfieldhills.com; PO Box 968, Litchfield, CT 06759) for its excellent booklet *Touring by Car, Foot, Boat & Bike*, which includes a map of the area and dozens of detailed itineraries. They also maintain a listing of over 40 hard-to-find inns and B&Bs in the region.

LITCHFIELD

pop 8500

The centerpiece of the region is Litchfield, Connecticut's best-preserved late-18th-century town and the site of the nation's first law school. Surrounding the town are

lush swaths of protected land just aching to be hiked through and picnicked on.

Founded in 1719, Litchfield prospered from 1780 to 1840 on the commerce brought through the town by stagecoaches en route between Hartford and Albany. In the mid-19th century, railroads did away with the coach routes, and industrial water-powered machinery drove Litchfield's artisans out of the markets, leaving the town to retreat into a torpor of faded gentility. This event proved to be Litchfield's salvation, as its grand 18th-century houses were not torn down to build factories, Victorian mansions or malls.

Orientation & Information

The town green is at the intersection of US 202 and CT 63. An 18th-century milestone stands on the green as it has since stagecoach days, when it informed passengers that they had another 33 miles to ride to Hartford, or 102 to NYC.

From June through mid-September, locals staff an **information booth** (☼ 9:30am-4pm) on the town green; it's open only weekends from mid-September through November.

Sights & Activities

A walk around town starts at the information kiosk on the town green, where you should ask for the walking tour sheets. Just north across West St is the town's **historic jail**. Stroll along North St to see the fine houses. More of Litchfield's well-preserved 18th-century houses are along South St. Set well back from the roadway across broad lawns and behind tall trees, the houses take you back visually to Litchfield's golden age.

In 1775, Tapping Reeve established the English-speaking world's first law school at his home, which is now the **Tapping Reeve House & Law School** (☎ 860-567-4501; 82 South St; adult/child under 14/senior & student $5/free/3; 11am-5pm Tue-Sat, 1-5pm Sun mid-May–mid-Nov). When attendance overwhelmed his own house, he built the meticulously preserved one-room schoolhouse in his side yard. John C Calhoun and 130 members of Congress studied here. One of the school's many notable graduates was Aaron Burr, who, while serving as vice president of the US under Jefferson, shot Alexander Hamilton in a duel in 1804. Admission to the history museum included in ticket.

The **Litchfield History Museum** (☎ 860-567-4501; 7 South St; same as Tapping Reeve House) features a small permanent collection, including a dress-up box with colonial clothes for children to try on, plus some local-interest rotating exhibits.

As a boy, Sherman P Haight Jr would go fox hunting on the land where he now makes wines from vinifera and French-American hybrid grapes. **Haight Vineyards** (☎ 860-567-4045, 800-325-5567; 29 Chestnut Hill Rd; admission free; 10:30am-5pm Mon-Sat, noon-5pm Sun), the state's first winery, grows varieties such as chardonnay, Maréchal Foch, Seyval Blanc, Vidal Blanc and Vignoles. Winery tours and free tastings are available. Mr Haight may be retiring soon – when he does, the name may change but the wine won't. The vineyard is 1 mile southeast of Litchfield off CT 118.

The **White Memorial Conservation Center** (☎ 860-567-0857; US 202; admission free; sunrise-sunset) is made up of 400 supremely serene acres. Two dozen trails (0.2 miles to 6 miles long) criss-cross the center, including swamp paths on a raised boardwalk. There's also a **nature museum** (☎ 860-567-0857; adult/child $5/2.50; 9am-5pm Mon-Sat, noon-5pm Sun). For visually impaired visitors, all the information in the museum is presented in braille as well. The center is 2 miles west on 202 from Litchfield.

Topsmead State Forest (☎ 860-567-5694; CT 118, admission free; 8am-sunset), was once the estate of Edith Morton Chase. You can visit her grand Tudor-style summer home (open for free guided tours alternate weekends during summer months, hours vary) complete with its original furnishings. Then spread a blanket on the lawn and have a picnic while enjoying the view at 1230ft. Topsmead is 2 miles east of Litchfield.

You can hike and swim at **Mount Tom State Park** (☎ 860-868-2592; US 202; resident per car $6-7, nonresident per car $7-10 Jun-Aug; 8am-sunset), 3.5 miles west of Bantam. The not-even-1-mile tower trail leads to the stone Mt Tom Tower on the summit.

If your spirit is craving some quiet contemplation, walk the seven-circuit labyrinth at **Wisdom House Retreat Center** (☎ 860-567-3163; 229 E Litchfield Rd; suggested donation $5) Call to arrange a visit, and a volunteer will prepare you for the experience by sharing some background on the labyrinth. Bringing young children isn't recommended.

Sleeping

Litchfield Hills B&B (☎ 860-567-2057; www.litchfield hillsbnb.com; 548 Bantam Rd/Rte 202; d $95-120) One of the oldest houses in Litchfield, this deep-red colonial overlooks the woods of the White Memorial Nature Conservation Center and lets three wicker-centric rooms. A canoe is available for a paddle on the Bantam River across the street, and (well-behaved) children and pets are welcome.

Tollgate Hill Inn (☎ 860-567-1233; 866-567-1233; www.tollgatehill.com; 571 Torrington Rd/Rte 202; r $95-170, ste $160-195) About 2 miles east of town, this 1745 property used to be the main way-station for travelers between Albany and Hartford. All rooms have a private deck and bathroom, data ports and pull-out couch. In the suites you get a wood-burning fireplace, canopy bed, fridge and bar. Suite 10 is a lovely option for families.

Litchfield Inn (☎ 860-567-4503, 800-499-3444; www.litchfieldinnct.com; US 202; d $150-160, theme $240 incl breakfast) Two miles west of Litchfield, set in extensive grounds, this establishment looks like an upscale motel. Its theme rooms, like the masculine-toned Sherlock Holmes and the lavender Lady Agnew (Dennis Hopper slept here) are fun but pricey. The inn's restaurant Bistro East, where Dick Cavett spottings are not unheard of, has an impressive wine selection and stick-to-yer-arteries fare like gorgonzola-crusted steak. Restaurant is closed Mondays.

Hemlock Hill Camp Resort (☎ 860-567-2267; 118 Hemlock Hill Rd; tent sites $22-28, RV sites $32-36; May-late Oct;) This full-service campground with 125 pine-shaded sites, has a stream meandering through it as well as a bocce ball court. From Litchfield, go west along US 202 for a mile, then right on Milton Rd.

Looking Glass Hill Campground (☎ 860-567-2050; 14 Cozy Hill/Rte 202, Bantam; sites around $30; ☽ Apr-early Oct). Five miles west of Litchfield, this simple, appealing place has 50 partially wooded sites, with laundromat, canoeing and room for tents.

Eating & Drinking

Bohemian Pizza & Ditto's Bar (☎ 860-567-3980; 432 Bantam Rd/Rte 202; pizzas $12-19; ☽ 4-9pm Mon, noon-9pm Tue & Wed, noon-10pm Fri & Sat, bar open late) Down the hill, both literally and figuratively, is this wonderful twofer. Head to Boho's for dinner (try the Criss Cross pizza – portobello mushrooms, andouille sausage, grilled chicken and caramelized onions) with its kid-friendly faux-cowskin booths. As the sun sets, the pizza joint and the adjacent dive bar dissolve into one loud, friendly mess. Shoot some free pool while being serenaded by the locals who play (almost) nightly.

Tollgate Hill Restaurant (dinner mains $18-30; ☽ lunch & dinner Wed-Sat, dinner Sun) Listed on the National Register of Historic Places as the Captain William Bull Tavern, this dining room in the Tollgate Hill Inn (p349) has maintained its spare, wide-planked ambience, presenting no unwelcome distraction from the sophistication of its fare. The menu is small but imaginative, with mains like quail in sherry vinegar marinade.

Market Square Café (☎ 860-567-4882; 33 West St; mains lunch $8-18, dinner $22-30; ☽ lunch & dinner) This is the best place in town to pick up deliesque picnic provisions, and it also makes for an unpretentious lunch and dinner spot, focusing on steaks and seafood.

Difranco's Restaurant & Pizzeria (☎ 860-567-8872; 19 West St; dishes $8-16; ☽ 8am-10pm) This local hangout has large booths and a down-home feel. The personal pizza and soup or salad lunch special is a steal at $7. Wine and beer are available.

Aspen Garden (☎ 860-567-9477; 51 West St; dishes $6-16; ☽ 11am-11pm) Aspen Garden serves a good selection of light meals with Greek accents: salads, sandwiches and baklava. They've got a kid's menu for the kids, and a beer menu for you. In good weather, sit at an umbrella-shaded table on the brick terrace.

West St Grill (☎ 860-567-3885; 43 West St; mains lunch $9-18, dinner $19-27; ☽ lunch & dinner Wed-Sun)

The poshest eatery in the town center, this sophisticated city grill and tavern changes its menu seasonally, but always serves creative New American cuisine. There are several sidewalk tables and a pub scene after 9pm.

3W & Blue Bar (☎ 860-567-1742; 3 West St; mains lunch $7-11, dinner $20-26; ☽ lunch & dinner) At this slick new eatery you can stick to standards like top sirloin or submit to the suggestive bamboo and red-lantern decor by ordering an Asian-inspired dish like sesame-crusted tuna. Or just go all the way with some sushi; the Dynamite roll – with shrimp, spicy tuna, salmon and avocado – is dynamite ($12).

Village Restaurant (☎ 860-567-8307; 25 West St; mains lunch $6-9, dinner $17-26; ☽ lunch & dinner) This casual restaurant/pub with a tin ceiling features gourmet sandwiches and more substantial mains as well as beer and wine. Try the ravioli alla vodka ($17).

Getting There & Away

If you're traveling by car, Litchfield lies 34 miles west of Hartford and 36 miles south of Great Barrington, MA, in the Berkshires.

No buses stop in Litchfield proper, but **Bonanza Bus Lines** (☎ 800-556-3815) will get you to Torrington, the closest major town, from NYC ($20, 2½ hours), via Danbury and Waterbury.

LAKE WARAMAUG

Of the dozens of lakes and ponds in the Litchfield Hills, Lake Waramaug, north of New Preston, stands out. Gracious inns dot its shoreline, parts of which are a state park.

As you make your way around the northern shore of the lake on North Shore Rd, you'll come to the **Hopkins Vineyard** (☎ 860-868-7954; 25 Hopkins Rd, New Preston; ☽ 10am-5pm May-Dec, call for hrs rest of the year). The wines, made mostly from French-American hybrid grapes, are eminently drinkable. They host wine tastings, and the view of the lake from the wine bar is worth a little splurge.

Hopkins Inn (☎ 860-868-7295; www.thehopkinsinn .com; 22 Hopkins Rd, New Preston; d $90-190; mains lunch $12-17, dinner $20-26) Next door to the winery, this inn has a variety of lodging options, from rooms with shared bathrooms to lakeview apartments, most decorated in light florals. Its fine restaurant specializes in contemporary Austrian cuisine. In good weather, sit on the terrace with your wienerschnitzel, catch the cooling west wind and vistas overlooking the lake and hills and imagine you're in the Alps. Restaurant is closed January through March.

Lake Waramaug State Park (☎ 860-868-0220, 877-688-2267; 30 Lake Waramaug Rd; sites $13) Around the bend in the lake is this park with 96 campsites, both wooded and open, and many lakeside. The sites usually get booked well in advance. There's a snack bar in the park.

KENT
pop 3000

During the summer and fall, weekenders (often starting on Thursday) throng to Kent's small clutch of art galleries and to its gourmet chocolatier. The small town, about 7 miles west of Warren on CT 341, is also a popular stop for hikers on the Appalachian Trail, which intersects 341 about 2 miles northwest of town.

Pierre and Susan Gilissen have brought to Kent a little slice of Belgium, and for this they are to be commended. In a butter-yellow Victorian they preside over the **Salon de Thé** (☎ 860-927-3681; 1 Bridge St; 😊 lunch Thu & Sun, dinner Fri & Sat), where, after donning your best manners, you can come for lunch, tea or a 'savory dinner' ($30 minimum and reservations strongly recommended). Next door in the carriage house is the **Belgique Patisserie & Chocolatier** (☎ 860-927-3681; 😊 9am-6pm Thu-Sat, 10am-6pm Sun), selling unfathomably rich chocolates, tarts and cocoa.

The rotating exhibits are of consistent high quality at the tiny **Paris-New York-Kent Gallery** (☎ 860-927-4152; 😊 11am-5pm Fri-Sun May-Oct, 11am-5pm Sat & Sun Nov-Dec, closed Jan-Apr), behind the railroad depot in a bright-red train car.

The **Sloane-Stanley Museum** (☎ 860-927-3849; US 7; adult/child/senior & student $4/2/3; 😊 10am-4pm Wed-Sun May-Oct) is a barnful of early American tool and implements – some dating from the 17th century – lovingly collected and arranged by artist and author Eric Sloane. The museum is about 2 miles north of town on the left.

At **Kent Falls State Park**, about 5 miles north of town, the water drops 250ft over a quarter mile before joining up with the Housatonic River. Hike the slightly strenuous trail to the top of the cascade, or just settle into a sunny picnic spot at the bottom.

Just before you reach Kent Falls, you may notice a menagerie of life-sized metal animals grazing off to your right. This is the **studio** (☎ 860-927-3420) of sculptor Denis Curtiss, which is open for browsing most weekends. Call to confirm.

You can rent bikes at **Bicycle Tour Company** (☎ 888-711-5368; 9 Bridge St; per day $25) or they can customize a guided ride for you around the area.

NORTH TO NORFOLK

There's no shortage of postcard-perfect country roads to explore in the Litchfield Hills, but just one delightful stretch is from Cornwall Bridge taking CT 4 west and then CT 41 north to Salisbury.

From May through September, race-car drivers (including celebs like Paul Newman) go at it at **Lime Rock Park** (☎ 860-435-0896; www .limerock.com; 497 Lime Rock Rd, Lakeville; adult/student & senior $6/3). If you've never been to a race, Lime Rock is a picturesque setting for your first time. The speedway is west of US 7 along CT 112.

The lovely, tranquil 14-room historic property at **Cornwall Inn** (☎ 860-672-6884; 800-786-6884; www.cornwallinn.com; 270 Kent Rd/US 7, Cornwall Bridge; r $99-139, ste $129-209 incl breakfast; 🐾) consists of the Inn and the more rustic-flavored Lodge. All the recently refurbished rooms feature down comforters, cable TV and data ports. Fill up on straightforward country cuisine at the **restaurant** (mains $10-29; 😊 dinner Thu-Sun), which features a different fish dish each week.

At first glance the one-story **Inn at Iron Masters** (☎ 860-435-9844; www.innatironmasters .com; 229 Main St/US 44, Lakeville; d incl breakfast $110-175; 🐾) looks suspiciously like a Florida motel, but the rooms are more elegant, the grounds feature gardens and gazebos, and there's a large common fireplace for chilly evenings.

Housatonic Meadows State Park (☎ 860-927-3238; US 7) is famous for its 2-mile-long stretch of water set aside exclusively for fly-fishing. Its **campground** (☎ 860-672-6772, 877-688-2267; sites $13; 😊 mid-Apr–mid-Oct) has 97 sites on the banks of the Housatonic.

Blackberry River Inn (☎ 860-542-5100, 800-414-3636; www.blackberryriverinn.com; 538 Greenwoods Rd/Rte 44, Norfolk; r & ste incl breakfast $85-249; 🐾) has amiable staff, an exceptional breakfast and grounds – complete with open trails – begging to be explored. The inn offers a range of rooms and suites in three buildings; a suite earns you a fireplace, Jacuzzi and sun porch. The least expensive rooms have shared bathroom.

We can't confirm its claim of the 'widest selection of the finest beers in the world,' but the **Norfolk Pub & Restaurant** (☎ 860-542-5716; US 44, Norfolk; mains lunch/dinner $6-9/9-22; ⊙ lunch & dinner Tue-Sun) do indeed serve excellent suds, especially those hailing from Belgium and England. Happily, their solids stand up to their liquids – smart pub grub with some twists. Try the spicy crab cakes

with Thai chili sauce ($15.50). Take note of the chair made of antlers in the corner.

Tea-lovers will want to check out Mary O'Brien's shop **Chaiwalla** (☎ 860-435-9758; 1 Main St/US 44; items $3-10; ⊙ 10am-6pm Wed-Sun) in Salisbury, which serves a variety of tea, especially unblended Darjeelings, as well as traditional accompaniments. Try Mary's famous tomato pie.

While you're in town, check out the oldest public library in the country, too.

Vermont

VERMONT

HIGHLIGHTS

- **Most Rewarding Place to Get Lost**
  The Northeast Kingdom (p404), whose back roads are awash with vast open spaces

- **Cheesiest Way to Pass Time**
  Watching Vermont cheddar curdling at the Grafton Village Cheese Company (p363)

- **Most Mannerly Manor**
  The Inn at Shelburne Farms (p401), an unparalleled manse on the edge of Lake Champlain that has great walking trails

- **Best Place to Go Take a Hike**
  Anywhere along the Long Trail (366), which runs the length of the state

- **Best Bar- & Café-Hopping**
  Downtown Burlington (401), with dozens of watering holes pouring tasty tea and martinis

■ TELEPHONE CODE: 802　　■ POPULATION: 619,107　　■ AREA: 9613 SQ MILES

It's true. The foliage *is* more spectacular here. The mountains are an ecstasy of wild terrain. Even the maple syrup tastes better drawn from these trees, boiled down in springtime by folks in woolly, plaid shirts. Vermont hums with traditions that are alive and well, and that go back hundreds of years: small-scale farmers, artisans and old-style manufacturing endeavors welcome a chance to show off not only their wares, but to reveal the interesting ways in which they go about creating them. Conversely, Vermont is also a place to explore the cutting edge of art and technology, at a surprising profusion of museums, science centers and educational institutions.

There's a well-deserved mystique about the state – a certain soulfulness, if you will, fed in no small part by its half-million fiercely independent inhabitants. Its progressive politicians help fan a dying fire of common sense in the national arena – a trait highly valued by their constituents, who are proud inheritors of the New England traditions of honest work, hard work, good taste and staunch patriotism (on their own terms, of course).

It's easy to experience Vermont on *your* own terms because she'll leave you alone to do so. Arm yourself with a good map, leave the main roads to the masses, and find your own charmed back-way along the capillary network of dirt roads that hug the banks of squiggling rivers, lead through tunnels of trees and lure you to discoveries unexpected.

Information

DeLorme's *Vermont Atlas & Gazetteer* is the best map of the state that modest money can buy.

Vermont Chamber of Commerce (☎ 802-223-3443; www.vtchamber.com) Additional information on hotels, restaurants and other tourist services.

Vermont Department of Tourism and Marketing (☎ 802-828-3236; www.vermontvacation.com; 6 Baldwin St, Montpelier, VT 05633-1301) Producers of a free, detailed road and attractions map and camping guide, this organization also maintains a fabulous Welcome Center on I-91 near the Massachusetts (MA) state line, another on VT 4A near the New York state line and another on I-89 near the Canadian border.

Vermont Ski Areas Association (☎ 802-223-2439; www.skivermont.com) Helpful information on planning ski trips. For daily ski condition reports (in winter only), call ☎ 802-229-0531.

Vermont State Parks (☎ 802-241-3655; www.vtstateparks.com) Complete camping and parks information.

Climate

Because Vermont has such varying elevations and terrains, it's hard to generalize about its climate and how it might impact you. But there are a few things that a traveler can count on. In the winter expect bitter cold and a number of snowstorms that drop at least 5in in one fell swoop. Freezing rain is common. Springtime is fleeting and doesn't really arrive until well into May. Summertime is glorious, and although it can be hazy, the humidity is rarely oppressive. Autumn, when leaves turn ablaze with color, is peak season – with blue-sky days followed by (hopefully) crisp nights.

When climatic conditions may really impact your travel schedule, contact the **highway department** (☎ 802-828-2648) and listen to **An Eye on the Sky** (http://fairbanksmuseum.org/eye.cfm), aired on Vermont Public Radio (at the lower end of your FM dial). These reports provide frequent and utterly entertaining, informative discourses on the wheres and whys of Mother Nature's whims.

National Forests & State Parks

With more than 150,000 acres of protected forest set aside in more than 50 state parks, Vermont ain't called the Green Mountain State for nothing! Finding an exceptional and often under-utilized state park in Vermont is about as easy as breathing. See the various Activities sections (and budget Sleeping options for camping) within each town for

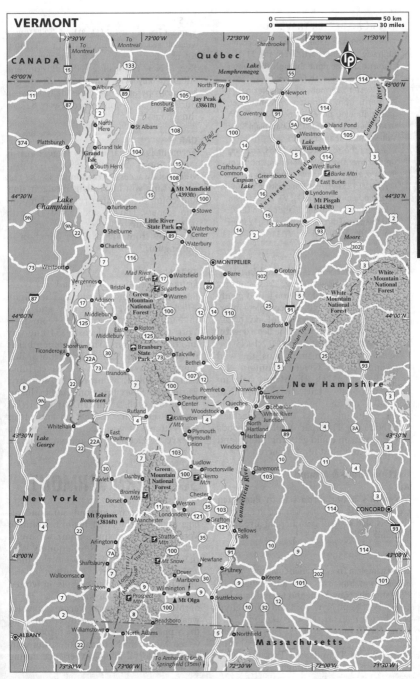

VERMONT

VERMONT

> ### THE ROAD BETTER TRAVELED
>
> The VT 100 (see p360) is the state's scenic highway, snaking north from the Massachusetts border right through the center of Vermont, almost to Québec.
>
> In western Vermont, consider taking VT 7A north from Arlington to Manchester, and continuing on VT 30 north to VT 22A to Middlebury, through the Champlain River Valley, rather than US 7.
>
> Any of the so-called gap roads, crossing up and over the Green Mountains north of Rutland, also offer dramatic mountain scenery. Try VT 125 between Hancock (on VT 100) and Middlebury (on US 7); VT 73 between Talcville (on VT 100) and Brandon (on US 7); and the partial dirt road connecting Warren (on VT 100) to Bristol (on VT 116).

details. Whether you're interested in swimming, hiking, snowshoeing, cross-country skiing, camping or fishing, you'll find plenty of places that fit the bill. For complete information contact the **Vermont State Parks** (☎ 802-241-3655; www.vtstateparks.com) or the **Department of Forests, Parks and Recreation** (☎ 802-241-3665).

Speaking of green mountains, the wild and undeveloped Green Mountain National Forest (p371), which runs right up the center of the state, covers more than 850,000 acres and boasts more than 900 miles of hiking trails. The Appalachian Trail and Long Trail (p366) call these woods home. A person could get delightfully (and metaphorically) lost for days here.

Getting There & Around

AIR
Vermont's major airport is in **Burlington** (☎ 802-863-2874; www.burlingtonintlairport.com), but there is also a small commercial airport in Rutland.

BOAT
Lake Champlain Transportation Company (☎ 802-864-9804; www.ferries.com) runs ferries between Plattsburgh, New York and Grand Isle; between Port Kent, New York and Burlington; and between Essex, New York and Charlotte. **Fort Ti Ferry** (☎ 802-897-7999; www.middlebury.net/tiferry) runs from Larrabees Point in Shoreham to Ticonderoga Landing, New York, from late May through October.

BUS
Vermont Transit (☎ 802-864-6811, 800-552-8737; www.vermonttransit.com) connects major Vermont towns and makes forays to Manchester and Keene, New Hampshire (NH); Boston; and Albany. **Greyhound** (☎ 800-231-2222; www.greyhound.com) operates four buses daily between Burlington and Montreal (one-way $27.50, three hours).

CAR
Vermont is not particularly large, but it is mountainous. Although I-89 and I-91 provide speedy access to certain areas, the rest of the time you must plan to take it slow and enjoy the winding roads and mountain scenery. Having said that, I-91 north of St Johnsbury offers expansive vistas, as does I-89 from White River Junction to Burlington.

TRAIN
Amtrak (☎ 800-872-7245; www.amtrak.com) is relaxing, albeit inconvenient. The *Ethan Allen* departs New York City and stops in Fair Haven and Rutland. From New York City to Rutland costs $54 one-way and takes 5½ hours. The *Vermonter* heads from New York City to Brattleboro, Bellows Falls, Windsor, White River Junction, Randolph, Montpelier, Waterbury, Burlington-Essex Junction and St Albans. If you're a cyclist, you can buy one ticket on the *Vermonter* and get on and off as many times as you like, as long as you reserve a space for you and your bicycle ahead of time.

SOUTHERN VERMONT

Tidy white churches and inns surround village greens throughout historic southern Vermont, a region that's home to several towns that predate the Revolutionary War. In summer, the roads between the three 'cities' of Brattleboro, Bennington and Manchester roll over green hills; in winter, they wind their way toward the ski slopes of Mt Snow, southern Vermont's cold-weather playground. For those on foot, the Appalachian Trail passes through the Green Mountain National Forest here, offering a colorful hiking experience during the fall foliage season.

BRATTLEBORO

pop 11,996

Located at the confluence of the Connecticut and West Rivers, Brattleboro is a little gem that reveals its facets to those who stroll the streets and prowl the dozens of independent shops and eateries. An energetic mix of aging hippies and the latest crop of pierced and tattooed hipsters fuels the town's worldy eclecticism, keeping the downtown scene percolating and skewing its politics decidedly leftward.

The Whetstone Brook runs through the south end of town, where a wooden stockade dubbed Fort Dummer was built to defend Vermont's first Colonial settlement (1724) against Native Americans. The town received its royal charter a year later, named for Colonel William Brattle Jr of the King's Militia, who never set foot in his namesake.

Dr Robert Wesselhoeft developed the Wesselhoeft Water Cure in the mid-1800s, which, at $11, was then America's most expensive treatment. Using the waters of the Whetstone Brook, he treated such luminaries as Harriet Beecher Stowe and Henry Wadsworth Longfellow. At the Old Town Hall (location of the current Main Street Gallery), many celebrated thinkers and entertainers held forth on the concerns of the day, including Oliver Wendell Holmes, Horace Greeley and Will Rogers. Mormon leader Brigham Young was born in Windham County in 1801. Rudyard Kipling married a Brattleboro woman in 1892, and while living here he wrote *The Jungle Book*.

Orientation

Brattleboro proper is east of I-91; West Brattleboro is west of the highway. While most of the action is easily found in the downtown commercial district, the surrounding hillsides are well salted with farms, cheesemakers and artisans, all awaiting discovery on a pleasant back-road ramble.

Information

Brattleboro Books (☎ 802-257-7777; 34-36 Elliot St; ✆ 10am-6pm Mon-Sat, 11am-5pm Sun) One of a trove of bookstores in Brattleboro offering a long list of store-sponsored readings and events. This is a used-book junkie's dream. It has two floors and endless aisles containing more than 75,000 used, out-of-print and even new titles.

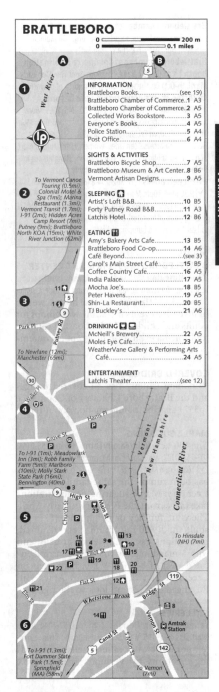

BRATTLEBORO

0 _____ 200 m
0 _____ 0.1 miles

INFORMATION
Brattleboro Books........................(see 19)
Brattleboro Chamber of Commerce..1 A3
Brattleboro Chamber of Commerce..2 A5
Collected Works Bookstore...........3 A5
Everyone's Books...........................4 A5
Police Station................................5 A4
Post Office...................................6 A4

SIGHTS & ACTIVITIES
Brattleboro Bicycle Shop................7 A5
Brattleboro Museum & Art Center..8 B6
Vermont Artisan Designs...............9 A5

SLEEPING 🏠
Artist's Loft B&B..........................10 B5
Forty Putney Road B&B................11 A3
Latchis Hotel...............................12 B6

EATING 🍴
Amy's Bakery Arts Cafe................13 B5
Brattleboro Food Co-op...............14 A6
Café Beyond...............................(see 3)
Carol's Main Street Café..............15 B5
Coffee Country Cafe....................16 A5
India Palace................................17 A5
Mocha Joe's................................18 A5
Peter Havens..............................19 A5
Shin-La Restaurant......................20 B5
TJ Buckley's...............................21 A6

DRINKING 🍷 🍺
McNeill's Brewery.......................22 A5
Moles Eye Cafe..........................23 A5
WeatherVane Gallery & Performing Arts
Café..24 A5

ENTERTAINMENT
Latchis Theater..........................(see 12)

VERMONT

Brattleboro Chamber of Commerce (☎ 802-254-4565; www.brattleborochamber.org; 180 Main St; ☉9am-5pm Mon-Fri, 10am-2pm Sat)

Brattleboro Chamber of Commerce information booth (☎ 802-257-1112; ☉9am-5pm Thu-Mon early-May-late-Oct) On the town green just north of downtown.

Collected Works Bookstore & Café Beyond
(☎ bookstore 802-258-4900, café 802-246-1063; www.collectedworksbooks.com; 29 High St; ☉8am-6pm Mon-Thu, 8am-8:30pm Fri, 9am-6pm Sat, 9am-5:30pm Sun) Here you can browse Zen titles, women's literature and art books, then snuggle into its comfy chairs. Hanging out in its fantastic café is always a prime activity.

Everyone's Books (☎ 802-254-8160; 25 Elliot St; ☉9:30am-5:30pm Mon-Thu, 9:30am-8pm Fri, 9:30am-7pm Sat, 11am-5pm Sun) Sells unusual publications, rabble-rousing political literature and an audacious selection of radical T-shirts and bumper stickers.

Sights

BRATTLEBORO MUSEUM & ART CENTER
This **museum** (☎ 802-257-0124; www.brattleboromuseum.org; 10 Vernon St; adult/child under 6/student/senior $8/free/6/7; ☉11am-5pm Wed-Mon) hosts a wealth of inventive events including workshops for adults and children. It also boasts a rotating multimedia exhibition program of contemporary art.

COVERED BRIDGES
Windham County has 30 covered bridges and the Brattleboro Chamber of Commerce (p357) distributes information about them.

MAPLE SUGARING
The 400-acre **Robb Family Farm** (☎ 802-258-0163, 802-258-0187; www.robbfamilyfarm.com; 827 Ames Hill Rd; ☉10am-5pm Mon, Tue & Thu-Sat & 1-5pm Sun in season) has been run by the same family for about a century. Maple-sugaring demonstrations take place from late February to early April. There are fun hay or sleigh rides ($7/5 per adult/child, $30 minimum spend required, reservations essential), which usually end with a marshmallow roast. The farm is located west of I-91 on VT 9; take a left on Greenleaf St (which becomes Ames Hill Rd), head 3 miles and look to the right.

GALLERIES
Vermont Artisan Designs (☎ 802-257-7044; www.vtartisans.com; 106 Main St; ☉seasonal) This contemporary crafts gallery sells outstanding creations by Vermont artists. Don't miss it.

On the first Friday of each month, join the immensely popular **Gallery Walk** (☎ 802-257-2616; www.gallerywalk.org; ☉5:30-8pm). Since the early 1990s, galleries and businesses have opened their walls to artists from an ever-increasing geographic reach and renown. A free monthly publication, available throughout town and on the website, maps the locations for this self-guided tour.

Activities

CYCLING
Brattleboro Bicycle Shop (☎ 802-254-8644, 800-272-8245; www.bratbike.com; 165 Main St; bike hire daily $20) This shop rents hybrid bicycles and dispenses plenty of advice about where to use them. It doesn't have racks or kids' bikes, though.

CANOEING
Vermont Canoe Touring (☎ 802-257-5008; Veterans Memorial Bridge, 451 Putney Rd; ☉late May–mid-Oct) rents kayaks and canoes. While away an afternoon by bird-watching in the estuaries or visiting an unofficial nude sunbathing spot up the White River.

Festivals & Events
On the first weekend in October, bookworms roam free in the streets at the annual **Literary Festival** (☎ 802-365-4483; www.brattleboroliteraryfestival.org). Events are held in various locations and feature a heady mix of Pulitzer Prize–winners, blockbuster novelists and impressive local talent.

Sleeping
You have the option of cheap camping, moderately priced motels that line Putney Rd (US 5) north of Brattleboro and VT 9 west of town, or more-upscale inns and B&Bs in and around downtown.

BUDGET
Colonial Motel & Spa (☎ 802-254-5040, 800-239-0032; www.colonialmotelspa.com; 889 US 5; r $74-95, ste $140; ▫ ☎) Some of the 73 units here are suites and some also have a kitchen. As for the spa part of the name, it includes Jacuzzis, saunas and steam rooms, and a cramped space with a handful of exercise machines.

Hidden Acres Camp Resort (☎ 802-254-2098, 866-411-2267; www.hiddenacresvt.com; 792 US 5, Dummerston; sites with/without hookups $40/27; ☉May–mid-Nov; ☎) This area has 40 open and wooded sites (12 just for tents), a large recreational vehicle (RV) safari field, a game room, a rec hall and miniature golf. It's about 3 miles north of I-91 exit 3.

Fort Dummer State Park (☎ 802-254-2610; www .vtstateparks.com; 517 Old Guilford Rd; tent/lean-to sites $14/21; ☉ late May-early Sep) This great 217-acre park has 51 sites (10 of them lean-to shelters), hot showers and nature trails. From I-91 exit 1, go north a few hundred yards on US 5. Then go a half-mile east on Fairground Rd, then a mile south on Main St to Old Guilford Rd. There are no RV hookups here.

Brattleboro North KOA (☎ 800-562-5909; www .koa.com; 1238 US 5; sites with/without hookups $28/24; ☉ mid-Apr–late-Oct) Approximately 3 miles north of I-91 exit 3, this KOA is definitely RV territory, with 42 open sites and zero privacy.

MID-RANGE

Latchis Hotel (☎ 802-254-6300; www.latchis.com; 50 Main St; r $65-145) Located in the epicenter of downtown, you can't beat the location of these 30 reasonably priced rooms and suites. The hotel's art deco overtones are refreshing and wonderfully surprising for New England.

Meadowlark Inn (☎ 802-257-4582, 800-616-6359; http://meadowlarkinnvt.com; Orchard St; r $105-160) You'll find exquisite peace here, where you can relax on the porch and watch the landscape unfurl like a living Rembrandt. The innkeepers are culinary-school graduates and serve breakfast and treats just like you wish your mamma used to.

Artist's Loft B&B (☎ 802-257-5181; www.theartists loft.com; 103 Main St; r $118-158) In the heart of downtown, this B&B has only one room, but what a room! Innkeepers (and artists) Patricia Long and William Hays rent a spacious 3rd-floor suite (the size of a large, one-bedroom apartment) that overlooks the Connecticut River and the ever-changing canvas of Wantastiquet Mountain.

TOP END

Forty Putney Road B&B (☎ 802-254-6268, 800-941-2413; www.fortyputneyroad.com; 192 Putney Rd; r incl full breakfast $110-230; ▣) This 70-year-old B&B is a sweet spot just north of town. It has a glorious backyard and a tiny pub, has four rooms plus a cute, separate, self-contained cottage. Overlooking the West River estuary, it also features boat and bike rentals that are just a five-minute walk away.

Eating
BUDGET

Amy's Bakery Arts Cafe (☎ 802-251-1071; 113 Main St; dishes $3-8.50; ☉ 8am-6pm Mon-Sat, 10am-5pm Sun) Of the many bakeries in town that inspire poetic accolades, this one garners the most. Enjoy breakfast breads, pastries and coffee with views of the river and local art. Lunchtime offerings include salads, soups and sandwiches.

Mocha Joe's (☎ 802-257-7794; 82 Main St; ☉ 7am-8pm Mon-Thu, 7am-11pm Fri & Sat, 7:30am-7pm Sun) Before your eyes spy this ultrahip, subterranean space, your nose will locate the exceptionally rich brews.

Coffee Country Cafe (☎ 802-257-0032; 12 Harmony Place; ☉ 7am-6pm Mon-Fri, 8am-6pm Sat, 9am-4pm Sun) This informal place attracts everyone from tongue-studded teenagers to 65-year-old farmers. Drop in for some good java and hot baked goods.

MID-RANGE

Café Beyond (☎ 802-246-1063; 29 High St; breakfast & lunch $6-8, mains dinner $12-18; ☉ 8am-3pm Sun-Wed, 8am-3pm & 5-9pm Thu-Sat, ▣) Head to the Collected Works Bookstore for full meals with international flair. The Thai and Colombian chefs here offer an inspired, world-ranging menu. Additionally, its fabulous bookstore, meeting space and seating designed for lingering draws a wild cross-pollination of, well, lingerers.

Marina Restaurant (☎ 802-257-7563; 28 Springtree Rd; dishes $6-22; ☉ lunch & dinner) This fun, refreshing local favorite blends fantastic food, spirited atmosphere and a sublime location on the banks of the West River. Food is reasonably priced and features all-natural beef filet mignon ($21.95) and daily seafood specials.

Shin-La Restaurant (☎ 802-257-5226; 57 Main St; dishes $3-16; ☉ lunch & dinner Mon-Sat) This low-key local favorite serves excellent Korean and Japanese dishes and sushi.

Brattleboro Food Co-op (☎ 802-257-0236; 2 Main St; ☉ 9am-9pm) This is the perfect place to load up your picnic basket with ready-made eats and treats. It also offers whole-food groceries, organic produce, and an incredible cheese department.

Carol's Main Street Café (☎ 802-254-8380; 73 Main St; ☉ 7am-5pm Mon-Fri, 7am-4pm Sat) This is a great place for picnic fixings – those in the know come for turkey specials on Monday and Friday, tacos on Wednesday, and

VERMONT

VERMONT

THE SPINE OF THE STATE

Vermont has a backbone, and it's called VT 100. Or perhaps we should say Vermont has a heart, and it's called VT 100. Or perhaps we should say Vermont has a soul, and it's writ large along VT 100. Whatever anatomy – tangible or otherwise – you'd like to assign, Vermont has it. And she offers it up with good grace to visitors who have a little time to spare.

The VT 100 snakes north from the Massachusetts border (beginning in Wilmington, p364), along the edge of the Green Mountains and almost to Québec. The landscape, consisting of rolling farmlands as green as billiard felt, is littered with cows and backcountry roads where the only traffic is the local farmer's tractor. We're talking tiny villages (like Weston, p362) with white Congregational churches and white, mid-19th-century clapboard homes that have been converted into inns. We're also talking about the juxtaposition between an ultragourmet stop like the **Village Pantry de Logis** (☎ 802-824-9800; South Londonderry; ⏰ 7am-7pm) and the ever-classic Vermont Country Store (p362).

The heart of central Vermont, north of the massive skiing mountain at Killington (p380), features some of New England's most bucolic countryside. This is where cows begin to outnumber people. Outdoor enthusiasts make frequent pilgrimages to Stowe (p390) to ski and mountain bike, while urban hipsters browse in the antique shops and art galleries of tiny Warren and Waitsfield (p385). For a memorable side trip from Warren village, take Brook Rd to Roxbury Gap Rd and turn left on to E Warren Rd, which deposits you at a covered bridge in Waitsfield Center. Besides, a road trip in Vermont isn't a worthy road trip without at least one covered bridge sighting!

If that little detour whets your appetite, plenty others will keep the juices flowing. From Talcville, take VT 73 across the mountain pass and back; or from Hancock take VT 125. If you need a destination as an excuse, let it be the lovely Texas Falls on VT 125.

For a complete tour of this scenic byway see Lonely Planet's *Road Trip: New England*.

---

hamburgers on Thursday. Or you can explore delectables from an amazing variety of gourmet hot and salad dishes sold by the pound.

India Palace (☎ 802-254-6143; 69 Elliot St; lunch $6-26, dinner $9-36; ⏰ lunch & dinner) This is *the* place for northern Indian cuisine, especially tandoori; lunchtime curries are a bargain.

TOP END

Peter Havens (☎ 802-257-3333; 32 Elliot St; mains $21-27; ⏰ dinner Tue-Sat) This intimate, 10-table local institution features an incredible menu bursting with culinary mastery. Fresh seafood dishes share the roster with venison, duck, tenderloin and pasta dishes (which can be modified for vegetarians). Brimming with intimate and artsy atmosphere, Peter Havens also has a full (eight-seat) bar.

TJ Buckley's (☎ 802-257-4922; 132 Elliot St; mains $30-35; ⏰ dinner Thu-Sun) This upscale but classic and authentic 1927 diner seats just 18 souls, but those lucky 18 are in for an exceptional dinner. The menu of four mains changes nightly, and locals rave that the food here is Brattleboro's best. Reserva-

tions are suggested, and credit cards are not accepted.

Drinking

WeatherVane Gallery & Performing Arts Café (☎ 802-246-2560; 19 Elliot St; dishes $1-10; ⏰ 8am-2am; 🖳) This great hangout is where you'll find the kind of cool, witty guy behind the counter that you always see in movies. Slide into one of the giant booths and enjoy light fare, a full bar and live music. The latter is usually bluesy/folky, but can also be wild and ear-splitting on select nights.

Moles Eye Cafe (☎ 802-257-0771; cnr Main & High Sts; dishes $7-11, cover Fri & Sat nights $5; ⏰ 4pm-midnight Mon-Thu, 11:30am-1am Fri & Sat, meals served until 9pm) This popular, subterranean hangout in an oak-paneled café has live entertainment on Friday and Saturday nights and good meals at moderate prices. Thursday's open mike is usually a blast.

McNeill's Brewery (☎ 802-254-2553; 90 Elliot St; ⏰ 4pm-2am Mon-Thu, 2pm-2am Fri-Sun) This classic pub, inhabited by a lively, friendly local crowd, features 15 beers on tap. The place flows with award-winning suds, including three naturally carbonated, cask-conditioned brews.

Entertainment

Latchis Theater (☎ 802-254-6300; www.latchis.com; 50 Main St) The nicely restored, art deco Latchis Building houses this theater where you can see mainstream and indies on three screens nightly.

You can also catch live music at Weather-Vane Vallery and Performing Arts Café (p359) and Moles Eye Cafe (opposite).

Getting There & Away

Vermont Transit (☎ 800-552-8737; www.vermonttransit .com) runs one daily bus between Brattleboro and Middlebury ($25 to $27, three hours) via Rutland, where there are connecting buses northward. The bus stops behind the **Citgo station** (☎ 802-254-6066) at the intersection of US 5 and I-91.

The **Amtrak** (☎ 800-872-7245; www.amtrak.com) *Vermonter* train stops in Brattleboro. The trip from New York City to Brattleboro costs $52 to $57 one way.

By car, it takes 1¼ hours (40 miles) to traverse scenic VT 9 from Brattleboro to Bennington. From Northampton, MA, it takes less than an hour (40 miles) straight up I-91 to reach Brattleboro.

AROUND BRATTLEBORO

The Lower Connecticut and West River valleys of southern Vermont are home to a warren of pristine villages worth exploring.

Marlboro

pop 981

Upon first sight, this village appears pretty but unremarkable: a white church, a white inn, a white village office building and a few white houses. It lies about 8 miles west of Brattleboro and a short distance off the so-called Molly Stark Trail (VT 9), a road named for the wife of General Stark, the hero of the Revolutionary War's Battle of Bennington (see p366). But scratch a bit beneath the surface and you'll find a real town.

SIGHTS & ACTIVITIES

To chamber-music lovers, Marlboro looms very large as the home of the **Marlboro Music Fest** (☎ 215-569-4690, 802-254-2394 after Jun 15; www .marlboromusic.org; 135 S 18th St, Philadelphia, PA 19103; tickets $5-30; ⌚ Sat & Sun early Jul–mid-Aug). The festival was founded and directed for many years, by the late Rudolf Serkin, and attended by Pablo Casals. The small Marlboro

College comes alive with enthusiastic music students and concertgoers, who consistently pack the small, 700-seat auditorium. Many concerts sell out almost immediately, so it's essential to reserve seats, by phone or mail, in advance. All seating is reserved.

Head west from Marlboro on VT 9 until you get to Augur Hill Rd, where a nice detour awaits. Just for the fun of it, take this side road for about 8 miles to South Newfane. It's a hard-packed spur road that leads past classic farms, alongside little Rock River and through the woods. Take the right split for South Newfane, through a covered bridge dating to 1870 and past the Williamsville General Store. If you're still having fun, backtrack a few miles and take VT 30 north to Newfane proper (see below).

Otherwise, stay on VT 9, which brings you to the top of **Hogback Mountain** (2410ft), where you'll find the **Southern Vermont Natural History Museum** (☎ 802-464-0048; ⌚ 10am-5pm late May-late Oct), an interesting little place that features mounted specimens of more than 500 New England birds and mammals.

At the high point of VT 9, there's a lookout and the family-owned **Skyline Restaurant** (☎ 802-464-3536; dishes $7-10; ⌚ 7:30am-3pm Jan-Oct), where you can dine on homemade soups, a 'monte cristo' (a grilled triple-decker sandwich made with swiss cheese, ham, turkey and drizzled with real maple syrup) and traditional New England comfort foods, all with the backdrop of a marvelous '100-mile' view, and with knotty pine decor.

Newfane

pop 1714

Vermont has dozens of pretty villages, but Newfane is near the top of everyone's list. All the postcard-perfect sights you'd expect in a Vermont town are here: tall old trees, white high-steepled churches, excellent inns and gracious old houses. In spring, Newfane is busy making maple sugar; in summer, yard sales are in full bloom; fall heralds 'leaf peepers'; and winter brings couples seeking cozy rooms in warm hideaways. A short stroll exposes Newfane's core – you'll see the stately Congregational church (1839), the Windham County Courthouse (1825), built in Greek Revival style, and a few antique shops.

Newfane is on VT 30, just 12 miles northwest of Brattleboro, and 19 miles northeast of Wilmington.

VERMONT

VERMONT

EVERYTHING YOU DON'T NEED BUT SOMEHOW WANT TO BUY

Not for nothing does the **Vermont Country Store** (☎ 802-463-2224; www.vermontcountrystore.com; VT 100, Weston) bill itself as a purveyor of practical and hard-to-find items. Here you'll discover taffeta slips, Tangee lipstick, three kinds of shoe stretchers with customizable bunion and corn knobs, gadgets, personal care items and clothing. Some items have survived from past decades and many have become indispensable – once you've been introduced to them.

The Vermont Country Store doesn't just resell or repackage these delightful antiquities. It actively solicits consumers' product memories. It has a team on staff that hunts them down and offers them for sale. Its website proudly lists recent 'finds' requested by their loyal patrons, including:

■ Flicker Shaver

■ Bubble Umbrella

■ Munsingwear Underwear

■ Whip n' Chill Dessert Mix

■ April Violets Eau de Toilette

Lymon Orton, the current proprietor of the Vermont Country Store, has created a time warp, resurrected a simpler era when goods were made to last, and quirky products with appeal (but not a mass market appeal) had a home. In his early years, Orton visited LL Bean in Maine (p481) for retailing advice and has followed it. Bean gave Orton this simple adage: 'Don't oversell your products. Aim for customers to open the package and have the product be better than you said it was.' Orton credits that advice, along with the firm guarantee of satisfaction, with the growth of the business.

This main store (the other one is in Rockingham, VT) is an experience in nostalgia, humor and Yankee ingenuity. You will undoubtedly leave with a handful of charming, eccentric items that you can count on being able to buy for years to come.

SLEEPING & EATING

West River Lodge (☎ 802-365-7745; www.westriver lodge.com; 117 Hill Rd; r incl full breakfast $90-140) Just outside of town, this lodge features English riding workshops (it has its own stables) and eight farmhouse accommodations to fit your family's needs. Some bathrooms are shared.

Four Columns Inn (☎ 802-365-7713, 800-787-6633; www.fourcolumnsinn.com; 21 West St; r incl full breakfast $150-350) Visitors with panache stop in New-fane just long enough for a meal or a night here. The 1830s Greek Revival inn on the common has 16 guest rooms and an excellent dining room serving New American cuisine. Accommodation ranges from elegant, 'simple' country rooms to luxurious suites with fireplaces and Jacuzzis. The steep and wooded property is excellent for hiking or snowshoeing.

Townshend State Park (☎ 802-365-7500; www.vt stateparks.com; VT 30; sites $14; ☙ mid-May–mid-Oct) Tucked deep into the forest about 3 miles north of Newfane, this is one of the state's better places to camp, with 34 tent sites. Hiking trails include the sometimes steep,

challenging path to the summit of Bald Mountain (1680ft), a rocky climb that rises 1100ft in less than a mile. Other trails within Townshend State Park are easier. There's swimming and boating at the nearby Army Corps of Engineers' Recreation Area at Townshend Dam. The West River is good for canoe trips.

Weston
pop 638

On the eastern side of the Green Mountains, Weston is another of Vermont's pristine towns. Its town common is graced with towering maples and a bandstand, and is surrounded by fine summer theater. Weston also draws fans from far and wide to its famed general store (above).

The **Weston Playhouse** (☎ 802-824-5288; tickets $22-26; ☙ performances late Jun–early Sep), Vermont's oldest professional theatre, occupies an old church on the town common and backs onto the West River. It enjoys a good reputation, and if you're in the area, try to obtain tickets. Arrive early for a show or to dine on light fare 'Downstairs at the Playhouse.'

VERMONT

A FOUR-DAY COUNTRYSIDE RAMBLE

In the middle of nowhere in the green hills of Vermont, the roadside rings with the boisterous sounds of silence: the full-throttle chaos of birdsong; the sudden, high whinny of a horse; the animated conversation of a splashing stream.

You're on a four-day, self-guided walking tour, winding on back roads from inn to inn, passing forests and meadows, poking into old general stores and visiting artisans along the way. You're averaging 10 miles daily, after which you collapse into feather beds, Jacuzzis or pond-side Adirondack chairs, your luggage awaiting.

This tour is as much about wandering these peaceful routes as it is about the four inns that link them.

Rowell's Inn in Simonsville is a rambling old stagecoach stop that has boarded travelers for more than 200 years. It is crammed with antique books, games, tools and everyday objects, and is ruled by an emphatic 'please touch' policy. When innkeepers Michael Brengolini and Susan McNulty serve their four-course meals, expect to eat until it hurts because it is impossible to stop.

Eleven miles away lies Inn Victoria, the mansard roof, delicate antiques and confidently flamboyant decor revealing a more-refined side of old Vermont.

The next day's 9-mile stretch leads to the Old Town Farm Inn. Innkeeper Michiko Yoshida-Hunter's family has run a restaurant in Japan near the emperor's summer palace since 1879. Through the 1920s and '30s, they prepared their signature eel dish, *unagi kabayaki*, for Emperor Taisho. That same dish, made from the family's 125-year-old recipe, is, indeed, tender, complex and fit for royalty.

The next day's walk begins high in the hills where the road burrows into trees that are 100 shades of green or red or orange or yellow (depending on the season). Wild turkeys mutter in the underbrush and every breath of air tastes of pure, undiluted sky.

Surrounded by hayfields and forest, and against the backdrop of Okemo Mountain, lies the Combes Family Inn. Ruth Combes joins legions of foragers in the forests in May, gathering fiddlehead ferns and incorporating them into delicious dishes.

The last, 10-mile leg of the tour begins at a small, Benedictine seminary pervaded with a visceral sense of peace. These past four days, when you've wondered 'Are we there yet?,' you have been answered by the sense that you've been 'there' every step of the way.

Vermont Inn-to-Inn Walking Tours (☎ 800-822-8799; www.vermontinntoinnwalking.com; per person, d/s occupancy $499/790, add 15% for Fri/Sat; includes all meals; ☉ May–late Oct) are based in Chester. All inns except Rowell's are BYOB.

Grafton

pop 644

Grafton is right next to Newfane on that shortlist of must-see villages. At the junction of VT 121 and VT 35, it's only about 15 miles north of Newfane. Grafton is graceful, but it's not that way by accident. In the 1960s, the private Windham Foundation established a restoration and preservation program for the entire village, and it has been eminently successful. The town is virtually an open-air museum.

SIGHTS & ACTIVITIES

Grafton Historical Society (☎ 802-843-2584; www .graftonhistory.org; Main St; suggested donation adult/child $3/free; ☉ 10am–noon & 2-4pm late May–mid-Oct) The whole town may be museumlike, but this place is the real museum, with collections of old photographs and objects from everyday life that illuminate rural life in the mid-1800s. It's right near the post office and just south of the Old Tavern.

Grafton Village Cheese Company (☎ 802-843-2221; www.graftonvillagecheese.com; 533 Townshend Rd; admission free; ☉ 8am–4pm Mon-Fri, 10am-4pm Sat & Sun) Head a half-mile south of the village to find mouthwatering, award-winning Covered Bridge Cheddar, which you can sample while watching it be made. Try the four-year-old stuff; it has a distinctive bite.

SLEEPING & EATING

Inn at Woodchuck Hill Farm (☎ 802-843-2398; www .woodchuckhill.com; r with full breakfast with/without bathroom $135/89, ste with full breakfast $155) This 1790s farmhouse, off Middletown Rd, is set up high on 200 acres just outside of Grafton. The innkeepers, Mark and Marilyn Gabriel, provide a welcome to make you feel you're on top of the world. They offer 10 guest rooms and suites filled with lovely antiques; the studio suite with a private deck is particularly coveted. Relax in the sauna in the woods next to the pond – the pond itself is great for swimming, fishing, and canoeing. Or tire yourself by hiking or cross-country skiing the farm's private network of trails.

Old Tavern at Grafton (☎ 802-843-2231, 800-843-1801; www.old-tavern.com; cnr VT 35 & Townshend Rd; r incl full breakfast $115-245, ste $95-450; ☒ May-Mar) The inn's double porch is Grafton's landmark. While the original brick inn is quite formal, many of the 47 guest rooms and suites are less so, scattered around houses within the village. (Some houses can be rented in their entirety, which make them great retreats for families.) As for amenities, the inn has tennis courts, a sand-bottomed swimming pond and cross-country skiing trails. The dining room is New England formal and the cuisine is refined New American, but the café fare is lighter and less formal.

Putney
pop 2679

Where do old hippies go when they grow up? This village answers that question – one look at the general store bulletin board tells you all you need to know about the craftspeople who populate Putney, and their grassroots involvement in local affairs. Pick up a quick bite at the general store in the center of town or at the Putney Food Co-op, just south of the village on US 5. Putney is on US 5, just 10 miles north of Brattleboro via I-91.

Curtis' Barbeque (☎ 802-387-5474; US 5; dishes $4-8; ☒ 10am-dusk Wed-Sun Jun–mid-Oct) This retrofitted school bus dispenses the best ribs and barbecue chicken north of the Mason–Dixon line. The secret's in the sauce.

WILMINGTON
pop 2254

Wilmington is the gateway to Mt Snow, one of New England's best ski resorts and an excellent summertime mountain-biking and golfing spot. Many restaurants and stores cater to families, who are the resort's main clientele.

Orientation & Information

The state's central north–south highway, VT 100, goes north from Wilmington past Haystack and Mt Snow. VT 9, the main route

across southern Vermont, is Wilmington's main street. The **Mt Snow Valley Region Chamber of Commerce** (☎ 802-464-8092; www.visitvermont.com; West Main St, PO Box 3 Wilmington VT 05363; ☒ 10am-5pm) maintains a village office.

Activities

The terrain at **Mt Snow** (☎ 802-464-3333, 800-245-7669; www.mountsnow.com) is diverse, making it popular with families. The resort features 132 trails (20% beginner, 60% intermediate, 20% expert) and 23 lifts, plus a vertical drop of 1700ft and the snowmaking ability to blanket 85% of the trails. Area cross-country routes cover more than 60 miles. As if that weren't enough, you can also undertake snowmobile tours and winter mountain tubing. Come summer, Mt Snow has lots of hiking possibilities, and hosts one of the best mountain-biking schools in the country. All this activity surely warrants a stop at its full-service **Grand Summit Spa** (☎ 802-464-1100, ext 6006), which provides a range of services from sports to Swedish massage, and from energy balancing to reflexology.

To reach Mt Snow/Haystack from Wilmington, travel 10 miles north of town on VT 100. The free bus service, **Moover** (☎ 802-464-8487), transports skiers from Wilmington to the slopes of Mt Snow for free at least every hour between 7am and 5pm.

Sleeping
BUDGET

Vintage Motel (☎ 802-464-8824, 800-899-9660; http ://vintagemotel.net; VT 9; r $65-100; ☒) Found a mile west of the town center, the Vintage Motel has 18 tidy units, each with two full beds, that are a great option for families. The motel sits on 17 acres with direct access to a VAST and a formal network of snowmobile trails, as well as a big 2-acre pond on the premises.

Molly Stark State Park (☎ 802-464-5460; www.vt stateparks.com; VT 9; sites with/without hookups $21/14; ☒ late May–mid-Oct) This 160-acre state park, named for the wife of Revolutionary War general John Stark, is about 3 miles east of Wilmington. From this park's 23 sites and 11 lean-tos, a trail leads to the fire tower on Mt Olga, which affords spectacular views. There are no RV hookups are available here, but other facilities include a playground, picnic pavilion and hot showers. You can also take guided tours of the park.

MID-RANGE

Nutmeg Inn (☎ 802-464-3351, 800-277-5402; www
.nutmeginn.com; VT 9; r incl full breakfast $99-299)
West of Wilmington on VT 9, this 18th-
century farmhouse has been wonderfully
renovated by Gerry and Susan Good-
man. All of its 14 rooms and suites are
furnished with antiques and reproduction
pieces; some rooms even have a Jacuzzi
and fireplace.

Juniper Hill Inn (☎ 802-674-5273; 153 Pembroke
Rd; r $105-215, ☺ May–mid-Oct; ☻) This stately
Colonial revival inn offers 16 guest rooms
(some with fireplaces) and a picturesque
hilltop setting.

TOP END

Trail's End (☎ 802-464-2727, 800-859-2585; www.trails
endvt.com; 5 Trail's End Lane; r incl full breakfast mid-Nov–
mid-Apr $130-370, off-season $120-180; ☻) About 4
miles north of Wilmington and set on 10
acres, Trail's End has a country-home feel.
In addition to 13 cozy rooms and suites
(many with wood-burning fireplaces) and a
game room with a billiard table, it also has
a pond stocked with trout and catfish. Take
VT 100 north from town to E Dover Rd,
which leads to Smith Rd and then Trail's
End Lane.

Snow Goose (☎ 802-464-3984, 888-604-7964; www
.snowgooseinn.com; VT 100, West Dover; r incl full breakfast
Apr-Aug $115-325, Sep-Mar $140-445) Only a mile
from the ski slopes, this elegant, romantic inn has 13 large rooms and suites with
large Jacuzzis, fireplaces and private decks
overlooking the forest. It's like slipping into
a postcard.

Red Shutter Inn (☎ 802-464-3768, 800-845-7548;
www.redshutterinn.com; VT 9; r incl full breakfast $135-
265) Dating from 1894, this grand old house,
restored by innkeepers Lucylee and Gerard
Gingras, has seven rooms and two suites,
each with unique decor. The recently renovated carriage house welcomes guests in its
three rooms or the cozy suite. If you want to
stay in and eat, Chef Gill provides a 'night-
out' in the dining room.

White House of Wilmington (☎ 802-464-2135,
800-541-2135; www.whitehouseinn.com; VT 9; r incl full
breakfast $138-285; ☻) Built as a private home,
this white Federal mansion crowns a hill
on the eastern outskirts of town and boasts
great cross-country trails and 25 luxury
rooms – all adding up to a particularly
romantic stay. Although public rooms are

spacious, they still feel warm thanks to their
large fireplaces. Guest rooms, some with a
balcony and fireplace, are divided between
the main house and the cottage. Other
rooms have a terrace and Jacuzzi.

Eating

BUDGET

Cup N' Saucer (☎ 802-464-5813; VT 100; dishes $2-
6; ☺ 6am-2:30pm) Judging from the muddy
pickups in the parking lot, locals make up
a large percentage of this joint's clientele.
They flock here for burgers and hot, open-
faced turkey sandwiches. Then again, the
pancakes are great and breakfast is served
all day. The circular counter is decidedly
old-fashioned.

Mildred's Fine Foods (☎ 802-464-1224; VT 9;
☺ 11am-5pm) Order excellent deli sandwiches
and wraps and take them away for a picnic,
or eat in.

Dot's (dishes $3-8.50; ☺ 5:30am-8pm) Main St (☎ 802-
464-7284; Main St) Mt Snow (☎ 802-464-6476; VT 100, Mt
Snow) With locations in the village and near
the slopes, Dot's is popular with skiers in
search of cheap sustenance like steak and
eggs for breakfast. Dot's is also known for
quick service and excellent chili.

MID-RANGE & TOP END

Poncho's Wreck (☎ 802-464-9320; 10 S Main St; lunch
$5.50-12, mains dinner $9-26; ☺ lunch Sat & Sun & dinner)
A casual favorite with the après-ski crowd
since 1972, Poncho's menu is extensive,
with plenty of Mexican dishes and steaks.
But don't stray too far from nightly seafood
specials (note the nautical decor). To keep
patrons happy, Poncho's also has an early
bird menu and live entertainment on winter and holiday weekends.

Silo (☎ 802-464-2553; VT 100, West Dover; lunch $4-
10, mains dinner $6-23; ☺ lunch & dinner) This serious
steak house is good for large parties who
all want something different – from stuffed
shrimp to chicken pot pie to Caesar salad to
pastas, pizzas and sandwiches. In the winter,
Silo offers entertainment, DJs, dancing and
10¢ wings (4pm to 6pm).

Alonzo's (☎ 802-464-2355; W Main St; mains $8-22;
☺ dinner) Within the Crafts Inn, Alonzo's
specializes in Italian food, pastas and grilled
dishes. You can also create your own grill
special. May they interest you in something
along the lines of andouille sausage or teriyaki steak?

VERMONT

THE LONG, LONG TRAIL

America's first long-distance hiking trail, Vermont's Long Trail, is a 264-mile mountainous corridor that runs the length of the state from Massachusetts to Canada.

Backpackers have been hiking the south-to-north ridge of the Green Mountains since 1930, when the Green Mountain Club finished clearing the length of the trail. Today, the Green Mountain Club has approximately 6200 members who maintain the trail system, which covers 440 miles when you include the 175 miles of side trails.

And what an impressive network of trails it is. Often only 3ft wide, the Long Trail crosses over streams, skirts every pond from Massachusetts to Canada, and weaves up and down mountains on open ridges to bare summits that offer exceptional vistas of the entire state. Wave after wave of hillside gently rolls back to a sea of green dotted with the occasional pasture or meadow. A little less than half of the trail is located inside the **Green Mountain National Forest** (☎ 802-747-6700).

The trail is best taken from south to north so that you don't have to read the *Guide Book of the Long Trail* backwards. Also recommended is *The Long Trail End-to-Ender's Guide*, packed with nitty-gritty details on equipment sales and repairs, and mail drops and B&Bs that provide trailhead shuttle services. Both guides are published by the Green Mountain Club (see details later in this box).

For shelter, the Green Mountain Club maintains more than 60 lodges and lean-tos along the trail. Hikers can easily walk from one shelter to the next in a day because the rest stops were built at 5- to 7-mile intervals. However, it is imperative that you bring a tent in case a shelter is full. Although the trail is wonderful for a trip of several days, many hikers use it for day hikes.

For more information, contact the **Green Mountain Club** (☎ 802-244-7037; www.greenmountainclub. org; 4711 Waterbury-Stowe Rd, Waterbury Center, VT 05677; ☽ 9am-5pm Mon-Fri Nov-Mar, 9am-5pm Jun-Aug).

Drinking

Maple Leaf Malt & Brewing (☎ 802-464-9900; 3 North Main St; ☽ lunch & dinner) This microbrewery offers weekly entertainment and a full bar.

Getting There & Away

Wilmington is 21 miles west of Brattleboro (a drive of 45 minutes on the winding road) and 20 miles east of Bennington (40 minutes).

BENNINGTON

pop 15637

Bennington, a mix of picture-perfect Vermont village (Old Bennington) and workaday town (Bennington proper), is also home to the famous Bennington Monument that commemorates the crucial Battle of Bennington during the Revolutionary War. Had Colonel Seth Warner and the local 'Green Mountain Boys' not helped weaken British defenses during this battle, the colonies may have been split. Robert Frost, one of the most famous American poets of the 20th century, is buried in Bennington, and a new museum in his old homestead pays eloquent tribute. Located within the bounds of the Green Mountain National Forest, there are many hiking trails nearby, including the granddaddies of them all: the Appalachian and Long Trails.

Orientation

Most businesses, lodgings and restaurants are in downtown Bennington at the convergence of US 7, VT 7A and VT 9, but the Bennington Monument, Bennington Museum and prettiest houses are in Old Bennington, a mile west on VT 9. The actual site of the Battle of Bennington is in Walloomsac, New York, 6 miles west of the monument. The tranquil little village of Arlington is about 10 miles away via VT 7.

Information

Bennington Area Chamber of Commerce (☎ 800-229-0252, 802-447-3311; www.bennington.com; 100 Veterans Memorial Dr/US 7; ☽ 9am-5pm Mon-Fri & 9am-4pm Sat & Sun mid-May–mid-Oct) Offers current and historical information and a self-guided walking tour of historic Old Bennington.

Bennington Bookshop (☎ 802-442-5059; 467 Main St; ☽ 9am-5:30pm Mon-Thu & Sat, 9am-9pm Fri, noon-4pm Sun) At more than 80 years of age, this is one of Vermont's oldest independent bookstores.

Sights

BENNINGTON MUSEUM

Head a mile west from downtown Bennington on VT 9 for this **museum** (☎ 802-447-1571; www.benningtonmuseum.com; W Main St/VT 9; adult/child under 12/student & senior $8/free/7; ☽ 9am-6pm). The

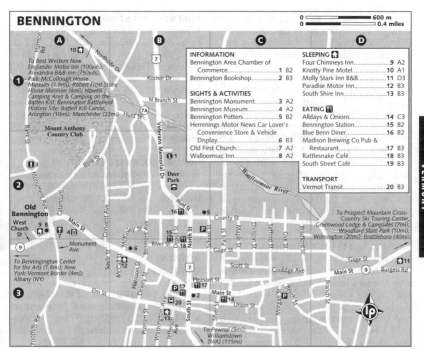

BENNINGTON

INFORMATION	
Bennington Area Chamber of Commerce	1 B2
Bennington Bookshop	2 B3

SIGHTS & ACTIVITIES	
Bennington Monument	3 A2
Bennington Museum	4 A2
Bennington Potters	5 B2
Hemmings Motor News Car Lover's Convenience Store & Vehicle Display	6 B3
Old First Church	7 A2
Walloomsac Inn	8 A2

SLEEPING	
Four Chimneys Inn	9 A2
Knotty Pine Motel	10 A1
Molly Stark Inn B&B	11 D3
Paradise Motor Inn	12 B3
South Shire Inn	13 B3

EATING	
Alldays & Onions	14 C3
Bennington Station	15 B2
Blue Benn Diner	16 B2
Madison Brewing Co Pub & Restaurant	17 B3
Rattlesnake Café	18 B3
South Street Café	19 B3

TRANSPORT	
Vermot Transit	20 B3

museum's outstanding collection of early Americana includes furniture, glassware and pottery (made in Bennington), sculpture, paintings, dolls, toys and military memorabilia. The museum is especially noted for its rich collection of paintings by Anna Mary Moses (1860–1961), better known as 'Grandma Moses.' She painted her lively, natural depictions of farm life from the time she was 70 years of age until she was 100.

OLD BENNINGTON

The charming hilltop site of Colonial Old Bennington is studded with 80 Georgian and Federal houses (dating from 1761 – the year Bennington was founded – to 1830).

The **Old First Church** was built in 1806 in Palladian style. Its churchyard holds the remains of five Vermont governors, numerous Revolutionary War soldiers and poet **Robert Frost** (1874–1963). Frost was born in California of New England stock and lived and wrote in England for a time. However, he is famous for his poems of the New England experience, inspired by his life on several New England farms. Frost became the best-

known, and perhaps best-loved, American poet of the 20th century. In nearby Shaftsbury, visit the new Robert Frost Stone House Museum (p368). One of his farms, Frost Place (p450), is near Franconia, NH, and another is in Ripton, VT, near Middlebury College's Bread Loaf School of English (p385).

Across from the church, the ramshackle 1764 **Walloomsac Inn** (cnr Monument Ave & VT 9) was a working hostelry up until the 1980s, complete with Victorian-era plumbing and spartan appointments. It's now closed.

Up the hill to the north, the **Bennington Monument** (☎ 802-447-0550; www.bennington.com /chamber/walking/monumentdescription.html; 15 Monument Circle; adult/child $2/1; ♥ 9am-5pm Apr-Oct) offers impressive views from the obelisk, which was built between 1887 and 1891. An elevator whisks you 306ft up to the top (purchase tickets at the nearby gift shop).

BENNINGTON BATTLEFIELD HISTORIC SITE

To reach the actual battle site 6 miles away, follow the 'Bennington Battlefield' signs from the monument, along back roads, through a historic covered bridge (there are two others nearby) to North Bennington, then go west on VT 67 to the Bennington Battlefield Historic Site. Admission is free, and picnic tables are provided under welcome shade.

PARK MCCULLOUGH HOUSE MUSEUM

Just off VT 67A in North Bennington, look for the **Park-McCullough House Museum** (☎ 802-442-5441; www.parkmccullough.org; 1 Park St; adult/child under 12/student/senior $8/free/5/7; ⓥ 10am-4pm mid-May–mid-Oct, 10am-4pm Sat & Sun Dec). Built in 1865, this 35-room mansion holds period furnishings and a fine collection of antique dolls, toys and carriages. Tours depart on the hour, with the last one departing at 3pm. The house is also open for Victorian tea and seasonal celebrations.

BENNINGTON CENTER FOR THE ARTS

This **arts center** (☎ 802-442-7158; www.bennington centerforthearts.org; cnr Gypsy Lane & VT 9; adult/child under 12/senior & student $7/free/6; ⓥ 10am-5pm Tue-Sun) has one gallery called the Great Outdoors, which is home to wind sculptures and fanciful metal whirligigs that respond to the breezes. Inside, other galleries feature fine art and Native American art and artifacts. The center's Covered Bridge Museum, the only one of its kind, informs us about how these enduring bridges were made using hand-forged tools.

BENNINGTON POTTERS

The artisans at this **pottery** (☎ 802-447-7531, 800-205-8033; www.benningtonpotters.com; 324 County St; ⓥ 9:30am-6pm Mon-Sat, 10am-5pm Sun) are maintaining a strong tradition of local pottery manufacturing that dates back to the 1700s. Take a self-guided tour through the manufacturing area, which reveals how much handwork still goes into the company's mass-produced items.

HEMMINGS MOTOR NEWS CAR LOVER'S CONVENIENCE STORE & VEHICLE DISPLAY

This stunning **collection** (☎ 802-442-3101, 800-227-4373; www.hemmings.com; 222 Main St; ⓥ 10am-3pm May-Oct) of classic cars, muscle cars, vintage trucks and automobilia dazzles even non-car buffs. Bob, the interpreter, is a walking automobile encyclopedia, and when he's stumped he calls the big man upstairs – the editor of *Hemmings Motor News*, that is.

ROBERT FROST STONE HOUSE MUSEUM

When he moved his family to Shaftsbury (4 miles from Bennington on VT 7A), Robert Frost was 46 years old and at the height of his career. This humble **museum** (☎ 802-447-6200; www.frostfriends.org; 121 VT 7A, Shaftsbury; adult/child under 18 $5/2.50; ⓥ 10am-5pm Tue-Sun) opens a window into the life of the poet, with one entire room dedicated to the creation and criticism of the poem 'Stopping by Woods on a Snowy Evening.'

NORMAL ROCKWELL EXHIBITION

In nearby Arlington, a 10-mile drive north, a Hudson Gothic Church houses this **exhibition** (☎ 802-375-6423; VT 7A, Arlington; nominal admission; ⓥ 10am-4pm May–mid-Oct) of 500 of Rockwell's *Saturday Evening Post* covers and prints. It also shows a short film.

Activities

CANOEING

Head to Arlington for access to some great paddling. **Batten Kill Canoe** (☎ 802-362-2800, 800-421-5268; www.battenkill.com; 6328 VT 7A; tandem canoe or kayak daily $48-60, single $30-35; ⓥ 9am-5:30pm May-Oct) can set you up with single- or multi-day trips on the lovely Batten Kill River.

SKIING

About 7 miles east of Bennington, Prospect Mountain has more than 40km of groomed trails. The **Prospect Mountain Cross-Country Ski Touring Center** (☎ 802-442-2575; www.prospect-mountain.com; VT 9, Woodford) offers ski rentals and lessons as well as snowshoe rentals.

SLEEPING

BUDGET

Knotty Pine Motel (☎ 802-442-5487; www.knotty pinemotel.com; 130 Northside Dr/VT 7A; r $63-95) On VT 7A in a commercial strip just off US 7, this friendly, family run motel has a fairly convenient location and 19 country-style rooms paneled in knotty pine (surprise!).

Paradise Motor Inn (☎ 802-442-8351; www.thepara disemotorinn.com; 141 W Main St; r $75-105; ☒) Paradise is the big, fancy place in town, with 76 rooms and suites, some with private balconies, patios, saunas or spas. It even has tennis courts.

Woodford State Park (☎ 802-447-7169; www.vt stateparks.com; 142 State Park Rd/VT 9; tent/lean-to sites $16/23; ⓥ late May–mid-Oct) Ten miles east of Bennington, this 389-acre park has 83 sites (with 20 lean-tos), a beach, boat and canoe rentals and hiking trails. It's well situated on a mountain plateau. RV hookups are not available.

Camping on the Batten Kill (☎ 802-375-6663, 800-830-6663; www.campvermont.com/battenkill; VT 7A, Arlington; sites with/without hookup $28/20; ☷ mid-Apr–mid-Oct) This campground has more than 100 sites, split between forest, meadow and open areas. Call early to reserve the popular riverside sites. Multiday stays are required during peak periods.

Greenwood Lodge & Campsites (☎ 802-442-2547; www.campvermont.com/greenwood; VT 9, Prospect Mountain; sites with/without hookups $25/20, dm $23, r $45-50; ☷ mid-May–late Oct) Nestled in the Green Mountains in Woodford, this is one of Vermont's best-sited hostels. Accommodations include 17 budget beds and 40 campsites. You'll find it easily, 8 miles east of Bennington on VT 9 at the Prospect Mountain Ski Area. Facilities include hot showers and a game room. Credit cards are not accepted.

MID-RANGE
Alexandra B&B-Inn (☎ 802-442-5619, 888-207-9386; www.alexandrainn.com; Orchard Rd/VT 7A; r $89-165 ▣) About 2 miles north of Bennington, with a view of the monument, this English country-style inn has 12 elegant and spacious rooms, each with a gas fireplace.

Molly Stark Inn B&B (☎ 802-442-9631, 800-356-3076; www.mollystarkinn.com; 1067 E Main St; r $80-125, cottage & ste $150-195) This big 1890 Victorian has six comfy guest rooms, a private honeymoon cottage, and two sugar-house suites with vaulted ceilings, hardwood floors and a double-sided fireplace. Some rooms are not air-conditioned.

South Shire Inn (☎ 802-447-3839; www.southshire .com; 124 Elm St; r $89-190) An extremely posh, antique-filled Victorian inn, South Shire has nine rooms, some of which have fireplaces. For a reasonable price, you can feel like an zillionaire by staying here.

Four Chimneys Inn (☎ 802-447-3500; www.fourchim neys.com; 21 West Rd; r $105-205) The only B&B in Old Bennington, Four Chimneys is a grand white mansion set amid verdant manicured lawns, with 11 conservative rooms.

Eating
BUDGET
South St Café (☎ 802-447-2433; South St; ☷ breakfast, lunch & dinner Mon-Sat, 9am-5pm Sun) Sink into a chair

and sip a cuppa in this pleasant, tin-ceilinged café. Soups, sandwiches or quiche top out at $3.25. Located in Bennington's epicenter, it's an oasis for coffee, tea and bakery treats.

Blue Benn Diner (☎ 802-442-5140; 314 North St; dishes $5-11; ☷ 6am-4pm Mon-Thu, Sat & Sun, 6am-8pm Fri) Can't decide what international cuisine you feel like tonight? If you have a hankering for an atypical menu, crowd into this local favorite. Standard fare is supplemented with Mexican dishes, some Asian dishes, omelettes and lots of vegetarian plates. Breakfast – always a treat – is served all day.

MID-RANGE
Alldays & Onions (☎ 802-447-0043; 519 Main St; dishes $3-9, mains dinner $15-19; ☷ breakfast, lunch & dinner Mon-Sat, brunch Sun) This excellent eatery has creative sandwiches, salads, soups and other light fare by day. By night, try the special 'chicken Alldays' – roasted breast meat with blue cheese. The eclectic wine list is highly complementary.

Madison Brewing Co Pub & Restaurant (☎ 802-442-7397; www.madisonbrewing.com/default.htm; 428 Main St; lunch $6-10, mains dinner $7-20; ☷ lunch & dinner) This pleasant, airy pub features standard fare ranging from sandwiches and burgers to steak and pasta. As an added bonus, it always has six to eight of its own brews on tap. There's nothing like really fresh beer.

Rattlesnake Café (☎ 802-447-7018; 230 North St; mains $6-16; ☷ dinner Tue-Sun) At this artsy, local Mexican joint, a hefty bean and cheese burrito will set you back $8, but it – and the margarita – will be worth every *peso*.

TOP END
Bennington Station (☎ 802-447-1080; 150 Depot St; lunch $7-11, mains dinner $13-25; ☷ lunch & dinner) Set in a beautifully restored 100-year-old train station, this more-conservative restaurant features an extensive menu of prime rib, fish, pasta, salad and children's dishes.

GETTING THERE & AWAY
Vermont Transit (☎ 802-864-6811, 800-552-8737; www .vermonttransit.com), which stops at 126 Washington Ave (☎ 802-442-4808), runs two daily buses from Bennington to Manchester ($10, 30 minutes); the same buses continue on to Middlebury and Burlington.

Bennington is 40 miles west of Brattleboro via VT 9 and 19 miles south of Manchester via US 7.

VERMONT

MANCHESTER

pop 4285

Manchester has been a fashionable resort town for almost two centuries. These days, the draw is mostly winter skiing and up-scale outlet shopping (there are more than 100 shops). But Manchester offers much more, retaining a small-town charm amid the bustle, and boasting fine art, one of Vermont's best trout streams, superb hiking, back-road touring and a beautiful, histori-cal atmosphere. From mid-September to mid-November, one of Vermont's biggest fall festivals, the **Stratton Arts Festival**, takes place at nearby Stratton Mountain.

Two families put Manchester on the map. The first was native son Franklin Orvis (1824–1900), who became a New York businessman but returned to Man-chester to establish the Equinox House Hotel (1849). Orvis did much to beautify Manchester – laying marble sidewalks, constructing public buildings and open-ing forest roads for excursions. Franklin's brother, Charles, founded the Orvis Com-pany, makers of fly-fishing equipment, in 1856. The Manchester-based company now has a worldwide following.

The second family was that of Abra-ham Lincoln (1809–1865), 16th president of the United States. His wife, Mary Todd Lincoln (1818–1882), and their son Robert Todd Lincoln (1843–1926), came here dur-ing the Civil War, and Robert returned to build a mansion – Hildene – a number of years later.

Orientation

US 7 bypasses the town to the east; VT 7A goes right through the town's center.

Manchester has a split personality. When the locals say 'Manchester' or 'Manchester Village,' they're referring to the southern part of the town, a beautiful, dignified, his-toric Vermont village centered on the huge, venerable, posh Equinox hotel.

'Manchester Center,' a few miles north along VT 7A, used to be called Factory Point, but this name didn't fit well with Manchester's resort image, and so it was changed. Manchester Center has several moderately priced inns and inexpensive-to-moderate restaurants, but the area is de-voted mostly to upscale outlet stores – Mark Cross, Giorgio Armani, Polo etc.

Information

Manchester and the Mountains Regional Chamber of Commerce (☎ 800-362-4414, 802-362-2100; www .manchestervermont.net; 5046 Main St, Suite 1, Manchester Center, VT 05255-3451; ⏰ 10am-5pm Mon-Sat year-round, 10am-2pm Sun late May–mid-Oct) Maintains an information office on the village green in Manchester Center. Staff help visitors find rooms and have printouts for hikes of varying difficulty within the Green Mountain National Forest.

Northshire Bookstore (☎ 802-362-2200; www.north shire.com; Main St; ⏰ 10am-7pm; 🖳) An enormous, inde-pendent bookstore with comfy nooks everywhere. It shares a huge hangout space with the attached java-and-munchies joint, **Spiral Café** (☎ 802-362-9944), which offers wireless Internet access and two computers with free usage.

Sights & Activities

HILDENE

The wife and children of Abraham Lincoln, one of the USA's greatest presidents, had tragic lives. His wife went mad, and only one of his four sons lived to adulthood. That son was Robert Todd Lincoln, who served on General Grant's staff during the Civil War. He later became a corporate lawyer in Chi-cago, president of the Pullman Palace Car Company, and secretary of war and minister (ambassador) to Great Britain. Robert Todd Lincoln's 24-room Georgian Revival man-sion, which he named **Hildene** (☎ 802-362-1788; www.hildene.org; VT 7A; adult/child $10/4; ⏰ 9:30am-5pm mid-May–Oct, 11am-3pm Thu-Mon Nov & Dec, free tours every 30 min), is a national treasure. He enjoyed the house until his death, and his great-granddaughter lived in the house until her death in 1975. Soon after, it was converted into a museum, and is filled with many of the Lincoln family's personal effects and furnish-ings. These include the hat Abraham Lincoln probably wore when he delivered the Gettys-burg Address; remarkable brass casts of his hands, the right one swollen from shaking hands while campaigning for presidency; and a 1000-pipe Aeolian organ, played on tours.

Hildene also has a packed concert and lecture series calendar; check its website for up-to-date listings. It also makes a great place to cross-country ski and snowshoe until about mid-March.

ARTS & CONCERTS

In addition to excellent outdoor sculpture gardens, the **Southern Vermont Arts Center** (☎ 802-362-1405; www.svac.org; West Rd; adult/child $6/3; ⏰ galleries 10am-5pm Tue-Sat year-round & noon-5pm

Sun mid-May-Oct) has a full program of concerts from June through August. Its 10 light-filled galleries of classic and contemporary art feature touring shows of sculpture, paintings, prints and photography. Lectures and concerts are held in the 430-seat Arkell Pavilion. After enjoying the museum and surrounding trails, consider staying for a light lunch at its Garden Cafe (p373).

Other summer concerts are organized by **Hildene** (☎ 802-362-1788), the **Manchester Music Festival** (☎ 802-362-1956; www.mmfvt.org) and **Barrows House** (☎ 802-867-4455, 800-639-1620; www.barrowshouse.com), the latter in nearby Dorset.

ALL-WEATHER SPORTS

To reach 3816ft **Mt Equinox** (☎ 802-362-1114; car & driver $8, each additional passenger $2; ☑ 9am-dusk May-Oct as the snow allows), follow VT 7A south out of Manchester and look for Sky Line Dr. It's just 5 miles from Manchester to the summit via this private toll road. It winds seemingly up to the top of the world; it's believed that the mountain's name is a corrupted American Indian phrase meaning 'place where the very top is.' Rather than drive, you could undertake the five-plus-hour hike (2918ft elevation gain) on Burr and Burton, and Lookout Rock Trails, which will take you to the summit and back. Hiking information is available at the Equinox hotel and resort (p373), where the trail begins.

About 5 miles from town, **Bromley Mountain** (☎ 802-824-5522, 800-865-4786; www.bromley.com; VT 11, Peru; rides each $3.50-7.50, book of 10 rides $55) is a small family resort featuring 43 downhill ski runs and 10 chairlifts. In summer, you can try the Alpine Slide (the longest run in North America), a climbing wall, trampolines, a water slide, a children's adventure park and more. Chairlifts whisk hikers and sightseers up to trails. The Long/Appalachian Trail (p371) runs right through Bromley. In mid-August, the UX Open (www.uxopen.com) – a play off for the wildest golf game in the country – takes place on these brush-hogged slopes.

Stratton Mountain (☎ 800-843-6867, 802-297-2200; www.stratton.com; VT 30, Bondville) is an all-season playground about 16 miles east of Manchester. For downhill skiing and snowboarding (mid-November through April, conditions permitting), it has 90 trails and 100 acres of glade and tree skiing terrain, 13 lifts (including a summit gondola) and a vertical drop of more than 2000ft on a 3875ft mountain.

There are also 20 miles of cross-country trails. Summer activities include golf, tennis, squash, swimming, hiking, horseback riding, mountain biking and tons more.

FLY-FISHING

The **American Museum of Fly Fishing** (☎ 802-362-3300; www.amff.com; 4070 VT 7A; adult/child $5/3; ☑ 10am-4pm), next door to Orvis (below), has perhaps the world's best display of fly-fishing equipment. This includes fly collections and rods used by novelists Ernest Hemingway and Zane Grey, and those of several US presidents, including Herbert Hoover. If you can believe it, the latter penned the tome *Flyfishing for Fun & to Wash Your Soul.*

To examine or purchase the new stuff, head across the parking lot to **Orvis** (☎ 802-362-3750; www.orvis.com), on the west side of VT 7A. Try out a rod in the trout ponds on the grounds of this famous fishing, hunting and general outdoor sporting outfitter, or inquire about its fly-fishing schools and free seminars. Across another parking lot is a warehouse filled with sale items, and the rod-building shop (with free tours at 10am Monday to Friday).

HIKING

The **Appalachian Trail** passes just east of Manchester, and in this area it follows the same route as Vermont's **Long Trail** (see p366). Shelters pop up about every 10 miles; some are staffed from June to early October. Good day hikes include one to the summit of Bromley Mountain and another to Stratton Pond. For details and maps, contact the **USFA Green Mountain National Forest** (☎ 802-362-2307; www.fs.fed.us/r9/gmfl; 2538 Depot St/VT 11/30), located about 3 miles east of Manchester Center. The chamber of commerce (opposite) also has detailed printouts.

CYCLING

About a mile from Manchester Center, **Batten Kill Sports Bicycle Shop** (☎ 802-362-2734, 800-340-2734; cnr US 7 & VT 11/30; ☑ 9:30am-5:30pm) rents road, mountain and hybrid bikes for as little as $25 daily, including helmet, lock, trail recommendations and map. It also does repairs.

Tours

For a fun way to wander off the beaten track, try a trip with **Backroad Discovery Tours**

GO FISH...FLY-FISHING IN VERMONT

In essence, fly-fishing boils down to making a fish believe that the colorful bundle of feathers and beads dancing on the end of your line is a nice, juicy bug. Or a shimmering little fish. Or even a delectably gooey leech. As with any culinary endeavor, presentation is everything, and there's no place like the banks of the Batten Kill River to learn how to land one. With the sun glinting through the new buds of spring and the bugs not yet present at maddening levels, the cusp of May and June is one of the best times for neophytes to learn how to make that backlit-by-the-golden-sun cast that ends with a fish in the frying pan.

Or not. Barbless hooks and the catch-and-release ethic rules the rivers nowadays, so it's more likely we'll have a trout fricasseed at a local pub. The idea of hookless fishing appeals to many, where the thrill lies in wooing a fish into striking and hanging on for a second or two, with the unscathed fish spitting out the lure after enduring only a momentary 'What the?'

As with any activity requiring some amount of technical skill, a few lessons can make the difference between a satisfying outing and a frustrating experience fighting with your equipment, tangling lines with your companions and inventing new expletives. Besides the famous **Orvis Fly-Fishing School** (www.orvis.com) in Manchester (p371), **LL Bean** (www.llbean.com) has classes in Freeport, Maine (p481). **Casting for Recovery** (www.castingforrecovery.org) helps women recovering from breast cancer regain a sense of adventure through fly-fishing retreats. Independent instructors and guides also offer instruction, women-only classes and multiday camps.

For these classes, you are issued a whip-thin, 9ft rod. Though it sings as you flick it through the air, it's likely that the line will fall into a limp scribble at your feet.

'You're not going to leave here with a perfect cast,' the instructor will tell you. 'But you're going to get a good start on one. It's up to you to take it from there.' With perfection off the table, you'll begin to relax and enjoy the lesson.

Soon, everything is forgotten but the zing of the line through the air, and you'll focus on how you can approach a tentative grace with subtle shifts in movement. By the end of your three-hour lesson, you will, indeed, be unfurling tidy loops and dropping the line onto the water with a whisper. Occasionally. You'll be hooked.

(☎ 802-362-4997; www.backroaddiscovery.com; 1½ hr sunset tour $15, 3 hr noontime ramble $30; ☼ early Jun–late Oct). You'll get the lowdown on historical and contemporary people and places that make this area unique, and find out where the fall foliage is most outstanding. Weather permitting, a small group rides in an open-air 4WD and travels along some of the prettiest roads in the area. Foul weather nets an enclosed vehicle and is just as much fun. Reservations are strongly recommended, though you can sometimes jump in if there's space.

Sleeping

BUDGET

Aspen Motel (☎ 802-362-2450; 5669 VT 7A; r $65-120; 🖥 🐾) A sprawling place – the Aspen has a social room with a fireplace and 24 rooms, including one cottage suite with a fireplace.

Casa Blanca Motel (☎ 802-362-2145, 800-254-2145; www.casablancamotel.com; 5927 VT 7A; cottages $62-138; 🖥 🐾) This tidy collection of cottages just north of town has 12 units that have been lovingly renovated in different themes.

Camping on the Batten Kill River (p366) is just south of Manchester on VT 7A.

MID-RANGE

Johnny Seesaw's Country Inn & Restaurant (☎ 802-824-5533, 800-424-2729; www.jseesaw.com; 3574 VT 11; r incl full breakfast $80-220) Two hundred yards north of Bromley Mountain, this rustic, laid-back lodge has a huge, circular, stone fireplace in the common/dining room. While the cottage and guest rooms are basic, the tales told around the fire are tall and unforgettable. Just imagine what Charles Lindbergh said when he stayed; he heads the cast of characters who have visited. America's famed 10th Mountain Division was also conceived here in 1940. On a more prosaic note, you can catch live (usually acoustic) music Friday through Sunday, year-round.

Seth Warner Inn (☎ 802-362-3830; www.seth warnerinn1.prodigybiz.com; 2353 VT 7A; r incl full breakfast $120-125) This five-room inn, dating back to 1800, features country decor, antiques, period restoration and an occasional moose in the backyard. It's named after Colonel Seth Warner who, along his Green Mountain Boys, was instrumental in winning the famous Battle of Bennington (see p366). The inn's full breakfasts are legendary.

Barnstead Innstead (☎ 802-362-1619; www.barnsteadinn.com; 349 Bonnet St; r $99-220; ☒) Barely a half-mile from Manchester Center, this hostelry has some charm, a good location and decent prices. The 14 rooms in a renovated 1830s hay barn, complete with exposed beams and homey braided rugs, have all the usual comforts.

TOP END

Inn at Ormsby Hill (☎ 802-362-1163, 800-670-2841; www.ormsbyhill.com; 1842 VT 7A; r incl full breakfast $150-380) Just southwest of Manchester, Ormsby Hill is arguably one of the most welcoming inns in all of New England. Fireplaces, two-person Jacuzzis, antiques, gracious innkeepers and 2.5 acres of lawn are among features that draw repeat guests to its 10 rooms. The inn's absolutely bountiful breakfast offerings are without equal.

Equinox (☎ 802-362-4700, 800-362-4747; www.equinoxresort.com; 3567 Main St/VT 7A; r $229-899; ☐ ☒) One of Vermont's best resorts, this grand property boasts 183 elegant rooms, an 18-hole golf course, two tennis courts, a state-of-the-art fitness center and full-service spa. Other activities include falconry, archery, off-road driving and snowmobiling. Room rates vary with the view and season.

1811 House (☎ 802-362-1811; www.1811house.com; 3654 VT 7A; r $140-280; ☒ pub 5:30-8pm) This refined Federal house, surrounded by 7 acres of lawns and gardens, was built in the 1770s and has served as an inn since 1811. In addition to 14 antique-filled rooms and comfortable, elegant common space, its little pub (open to the public) is straight out of the 1800s, with dark, wood walls and low beams hung with pewter tankards and assorted antique swords and tools. It's the perfect place to linger over a single-malt from its impressive selection of 93 scotches.

Inn at Manchester (☎ 802-362-1793, 800-273-1793; www.innatmanchester.com; 3967 VT 7A; r incl full breakfast $129-299, ste $179-209; ☒) This restored inn and carriage house offers 13 rooms and five suites to a loyal clientele. There's a big front porch, an expansive backyard and comfortable common rooms, one with a wee pub.

Eating

BUDGET

Gourmet Deli (☎ 802-362-1254; 4961 Main St; dishes $7-9; ☒ 7am-3:30pm) Behind the Green Mountain Village Shopping Plaza, this casual place has good value, absolutely delicious sandwiches, soups, salads, chili and the like.

Little Rooster Cafe (☎ 802-362-3496; VT 7A; dishes $5-9; ☒ breakfast & lunch Thu-Tue) This popular, colorful spot serves dishes like Asian vegetables with noodles, and chicken or grilled portobello focaccia.

Mrs Murphy's Donuts & Coffee Shop (☎ 802-362-1874; VT 11/30 East; dishes $3; ☒ 5am-6pm Mon-Sat, 5am-4pm Sun) Manchester's favorite down-home, basic diner serves fresh doughnuts and bacon-and-egg 'tuck-ins' throughout the day – and that's about it, but be sure to order more than one doughnut, or you'll regret it.

MID-RANGE

Garden Cafe (☎ 802-366-8297; West Rd; dishes around $10; ☒ lunch Tue-Sat early Jun–mid-Oct) At the Southern Vermont Arts Center (p370), this indoor and outdoor café pairs very good dishes with the tranquil setting of the sculpture garden.

Up for Breakfast (☎ 802-362-4204; 4935 Main St; dishes $6-14; ☒ 7am-noon) Above Christo's, this artsy nook serves breakfast dishes ranging from *huevos rancheros* (eggs on tortillas) to wild turkey hash (a regional specialty). Sit at the tiny counter to catch the action in the kitchen.

Forty Nine Forty (☎ 802-362-9839; 4940 Main St; all-day menu $5-9, dinner $10-19; ☒ lunch & dinner) In addition to good-noshing appetizers, this pleasant, bright bistro serves veggie burgers, Black Angus burgers and grilled Tuscan cheese sandwiches all day. The evening meals are simple, with grilled chicken, stir-fry or pasta alfredo.

Sirloin Saloon (☎ 802-362-2600; VT 11/30 east; mains $9-22; ☒ dinner) Decked out like a hunting lodge with a Southwest twang, the Sirloin Saloon claims to be Vermont's oldest steak house. The seafood dishes, however, are also well done.

TOP END

Mistral's (☎ 802-362-1779; 10 Toll Gate Rd; mains $27-36; ☒ dinner Wed-Mon) Nestled deep in the woods (off VT 30 and VT 11 east of town) and overlooking Bromley Brook, Mistral's offers fine dining on Norwegian salmon or roast duck in an incredibly intimate setting.

VERMONT

Bistro Henry (☎ 802-362-4982; VT 11/30; mains $21-28; ☽ dinner Tue-Sun) This casual, chef-owned bistro serves creative modern cuisine highlighting fresh seafood, aged meats and fresh vegetables. Its renowned wine selection features eclectic and hard-to-find labels.

Black Swan (☎ 802-362-3807; 4384 VT 7A; mains $17-25; ☽ dinner varies seasonally, but almost daily) This 1834 brick Colonial house is divided into small, charming dining rooms with candlelight and working fireplaces. Continental cuisine is served with a West-Coast influence, and everything at the Black Swan is imaginatively presented and spectacularly delicious.

Getting There & Away

Vermont Transit (☎ 802-864-6811, 800-552-8737; www.vermonttransit.com) runs daily buses (number varies seasonally) from Manchester to Middlebury ($16, two hours) and onward to Burlington and Montreal. The bus stop is at **Village Valet** (☎ 802-362-1226; 4945 Main St).

From Manchester Village, take the back road, West Rd, north to VT 30 to Dorset.

Manchester is 32 miles (one hour with traffic) south of Rutland via US 7, but it's far more scenic to head north on VT 30 through Dorset and onward to Middlebury.

AROUND MANCHESTER

It's hard to get enough of these quintessential Vermont towns, whether they be town-and-country perfect like Dorset or more blue-collar like Pawlet.

Dorset

pop 2051

Six miles northwest of Manchester along VT 30, Dorset is a perfect Vermont village, with its stately inn, lofty church and village green. The difference between this and other Vermont villages, however, is that in Dorset the sidewalks, the church and lots of other buildings are made of creamy marble.

Settled in 1768, Dorset became a farming community with a healthy trade in marble. The **quarry**, about a mile south of the village center, supplied much of the marble for the grand New York Public Library building and numerous other public edifices, but it's now filled with water. It's a lovely place to picnic.

Speaking of marble, stop in at the **Danby Marble Company** (☎ 802-293-5425; VT 7 north of Danby; ☽ May-Oct & mid-Nov–Dec), on the VT 7

north of Danby. The town is the site of what's billed as 'the largest underground marble quarry in the world.' Perhaps you're in need of some marble cut to your specifications? They make everything here from bookends to chessboards to vases.

More than a century ago, the village of Dorset became known as a summer playground for well-to-do city folks. Today, in addition to the village's pristine beauty, the **Dorset Playhouse** (☎ 802-867-5777; www.dorsetplayers.org; Cheney Rd) draws a sophisticated audience. In summer, the actors are professionals; at other times, they're community players.

SLEEPING & EATING

Dovetail Inn (☎ 802-867-5747, 888-867-5747; www.dovetailinn.com; VT 30; r incl continental breakfast $65-195) Innkeepers Jean and Jim Kingston greet travelers at their tidy 1800s inn, which faces the village green. Value-conscious guests will highly approve of the 11 well-kept rooms.

Cornucopia B&B (☎ 802-867-5751, 800-566-5751; www.cornucopiaofdorset.com; VT 30; r incl full breakfast $150-270, cottages $270-300) This refined and elegant B&B has five perfectly kept guest rooms with canopies and four-poster beds. It's easy to appreciate the great attention to detail here – champagne on arrival, being awakened with morning coffee at your door… The cottage suite behind the inn has a loft bedroom, living room with fireplace, kitchen and sundeck.

Dorset Inn (☎ 802-867-5500, 877-367-7389; www.dorsetinn.com; cnr Church & Main Sts; s incl full breakfast $100-145, r $145-225) Vermont's oldest continuously operating inn – in business since 1796 – is still going strong. Just off VT 30, facing the village green, this traditional but updated inn has 31 renovated guest rooms. The front porch rockers provide a nice setting for watching the comings and goings of this sleepy Vermont town. Opt for rates that include dinner, as the chef-owned restaurant is highly regarded.

Emerald Lake State Park (☎ 802-362-1655; www.vtstateparks.com; US 7; sites with/without hookups $23/14; ☽ late May–mid-Oct) Just north of East Dorset, this 430-acre park has 105 sites, including 32 lean-tos. You can swim and canoe on the 80ft-deep lake and hike through the mountains; some trails connect with the Long Trail.

Peltier's (☎ 802-867-4400; VT 30) An institution since 1816, Peltier's sells all manner of edible

Vermont items, especially high-end gourmet goodies and picnic fixings. Staff will even prepare almost any kind of fish, on request.

Pawlet

pop 1412

The alternative route from Manchester to Middlebury is VT 30 north. Along the way you'll pass through the blink-and-you'll-miss-it village of Pawlet. Stop at **Machs' Market** (☎ 802-325-3405; VT 30; ◔ 10am-5pm), a fine old-fashioned general store that generates its electricity from an adjacent stream passing through a gorge. You can see all this from inside the store, thanks to a glass counter.

The village consists of a few little shops and the **Station Restaurant** (☎ 802-325-3041; ◔ 6am-3pm). A former 1905 railroad station in another town, the structure was converted into a classic diner, moved to Pawlet and situated above this babbling brook. Replete with swivel stools and counter, it's also atmospheric thanks to hook-hung cups bearing the names of regulars.

Continuing north, take a quick detour into East Poultney, on VT 140 from VT 30. The classic town green, lined with a fine church and 18th- and 19th-century houses, has a classic old general store.

CENTRAL VERMONT

Vermont's heart features some of New England's most bucolic countryside. Just north of Rutland, Vermont's second-largest city, cows begin to outnumber people. Lovers of the outdoors make frequent pilgrimages to central Vermont, especially to the resort area of Killington, which attracts countless skiers and summer hikers. For those interested in indoor pleasures, antique shops and art galleries dot the back roads between picturesque covered bridges.

WOODSTOCK

pop 3223

Woodstock, Vermont, is the antithesis of that symbol of 1960s hippie living, Woodstock, New York. Vermont's Woodstock, chartered in 1761, has been the highly dignified seat of Windsor County since 1766. It prospered in this role. The townspeople built many grand houses surrounding the town common, and Woodstock's churches boast no fewer than four bells cast by Paul Revere. Senator Jacob Collamer, a friend of President Abraham Lincoln's, once said, 'The good people of Woodstock have less incentive than others to yearn for heaven.' In the 19th century, other New England towns built smoky factories, but the only pollution from Woodstock's main industry, county government, was hot air, and it quickly rose out of sight.

Today, Woodstock is still very beautiful and very wealthy. Spend some time walking around the village green, surrounded by Federal and Greek Revival homes and public buildings. The Rockefellers and the Rothschilds own estates in the surrounding countryside, and the well-to-do come to stay at the grand Woodstock Inn & Resort. Despite its high-tone reputation, the town also offers some reasonably priced lodgings and meal possibilities.

Orientation

Woodstock, off US 4, is part of the Upper Connecticut River Valley community that includes Hanover and Lebanon, in New Hampshire, and Norwich and White River Junction, in Vermont. People think nothing of driving from one of these towns to another to find accommodations, a meal or an amusement.

Information

Woodstock Area Chamber of Commerce (☎ 802-457-3555; www.woodstockvt.com; 18 Central St, Woodstock, VT 05091; ◔ 9:30am-5pm May-Oct) Has a small information booth on the village green that can be quite helpful. Parking places are at a premium in Woodstock, and enforcement is strict, so obey the regulations.
Yankee Bookshop (☎ 802-457-2411; 12 Central St; ◔ 10am-5pm) Great for local guidebooks, maps, and books in general. It's particularly strong in works by local authors and publishers.

Sights

Be sure to look out for Woodstock's three **covered bridges** over the Ottauquechee River.

BILLINGS FARM & MUSEUM

After your walk around town, pay a visit to this **farm museum** (☎ 802-457-2355; www.billings farm.org; VT 12; adult/child/senior $9/4.50/8; ◔ 10am-5pm May-Oct, 10am-4pm Sat & Sun Dec, closed Nov), less than a mile north of the village green, at River Rd. Railroad magnate Frederick

VERMONT

EXPLORING BEYOND THE GORGE

Getting to the middle of nowhere is pretty darn easy in Vermont. While the rumpled, green countryside offers endless miles of solitude, just about any blob of blue on the map will serve as an escape hatch as well – though few as perfectly as North Hartland Lake.

Within minutes of downtown Quechee, you can scoot your boat off the North Hartland Lake Recreation Area ramp. Trees and meadows swallow virtually every shred of evidence that anyone else exists but you and whoever else may be plying these tranquil waters.

You head into the various nooks and rivulets of the 215-acre lake, and just beyond sight of the beach, a noisy great-blue heron rookery occupies the tops of the pines on the north shore. Around the bend an eagle may just be pulling this afternoon's catch out of the water. You'll see an occasional shallow-domed muskrat lodge, and turtles soaking up the sun on floating logs. Keep an eye out for browsing deer on the clearings of the north shore. Follow the left channel as the lake turns swampy, and the channel on either side of a small island leads to the mouth of Quechee Gorge. Park your boat and scramble onto the ledgy outcrop for a rewarding picnic and swimming break. Check out the stunning view up the gorge, with the US 4 bridge appearing delicate and distant. Be aware that the water level can rise quickly during dam releases, so keep an ear cocked for the alarm that sounds the occasional event.

Is it a more intimate experience to bob along the surface of the lake itself, or to explore its shores, meandering through forests and meadows? To find out for yourself, take the walking trail from the VT 4 bridge at the gorge, head away from the dam and keep veering right, or toward the lake, at all the forks (this will make it easier to find your way back, as well.)

From VT 4, head south on Hartland/Quechee Rd for 1.5 miles, left on Clay Hill Rd for just shy of 3 miles to reach the parking area of the **North Hartland Lake Recreation Area** (☎ 802-295-2855; 112 Clay Hill Rd, Hartland; per person/car $1/4; ☷ 8am-8pm Apr-Oct).

With a kiosk just east of the Quechee Gorge bridge, and a main location behind Quechee Inn, Main St (from VT 4, go right after the covered bridge, and the inn is half a mile on the left), **Wilderness Trails** (☎ 802-295-7620; www.wildernesstrailsvt.com) rents boats at $25 per day, from 1 May to 31 October. It also rents bikes. From 1 December to 31 March, it rents cross-country skis & snowshoes – and be sure to ask about its moonlight bonfire trips to the lake. It also offers fly-fishing instruction for $135 per person, plus $30 for each additional person (with a maximum of four people per group). Fishing licenses ($15) are required for this and are supplied by the company. A shuttle service to the North Hartland lake, or the Connecticut or White Rivers, adds $10 per person to the cost.

Billings founded the farm in the late 19th century and ran it on sound 'modern' principles of conservation and animal husbandry. In 1871, he imported cattle directly from the Isle of Jersey in Britain, and the purebred descendants of these early bovine immigrants still give milk on the farm today. Life on the working farm is a mix of 19th- and 20th-century methods, all of which delight curious children. Call for details about the daily demonstrations, audiovisual shows and special programs.

MARSH-BILLINGS-ROCKEFELLER NATIONAL HISTORICAL PARK

This **mansion and park** (☎ 802-457-3368; www.nps.gov/mabi; Elm St; tours adult $9, child $2-7, senior $8; ☷ 10am-4pm late May-Oct, tours every 30min), off VT 12, focuses on the relationship between land stewardship and environmental conserva-

tion. While there is an admission fee to the mansion, the 20 miles of trails and carriage roads are free for exploring. In the winter, they're groomed for cross-country skiing and snowshoeing. Some trails start on the far side of the Ottauquechee River from the village green, along the east edge of the cemetery. When the mansion is closed, the Woodstock Inn & Resort (see p378) has a walking-trail pamphlet.

LONG TRAIL BREWING COMPANY

Halfway between Killington and Woodstock, the **Long Trail Brewing Company** (☎ 802-672-5011; www.longtrail.com; cnr US 4 & VT 100A; admission & tours free; ☷ 10am-6pm Mon-Sat, 1-5pm Sun) brews 'Vermont's No 1 Selling Amber.' Sit down at the visitor center, order a sandwich or burger and wash it down with a cold hearty stout or a fruity blackberry wheat ale.

VERMONT INSTITUTE OF NATURAL SCIENCE
Learn all about raptors and other birds of prey at the **Vermont Institute of Natural Science** (☎ 802-457-2779; www.vinsweb.org; VT 4, Quechee; adult $8, child $1-4, senior $7.20; ☺ 9am-5pm May-Oct, 10am-4pm Nov-Apr), 1½ miles southwest of Woodstock's village green. The two dozen species of raptors living here range from the tiny, 3oz saw-whet owl to the mighty bald eagle. The birds that end up here have sustained permanent injuries that do not allow them to return to life in the wild. Three self-guided nature trails here are delightful for hikes in summer or for snowshoeing in winter.

Activities

Many nearby state parks (see below) offer hiking trails and lakes good for swimming, boating and canoeing.

CYCLING

Bike Vermont (☎ 800-257-2226; www.bikevermont .com; 3-day trip per person $350-395, 6-day $970-1195) operates two- to six-night bike tours, including inn-to-inn tours. The costs fluctuate with the season.

Woodstock Sports (☎ 802-457-1568; 30 Central St; ☺ 8:30am-5:30pm Mon-Sat) and **Cyclery Plus** (☎ 802-457-3377; 490 Woodstock Rd/US 4; ☺ 10am-5pm Mon-Sat) rent bicycles and provide maps of good local routes. Full-day rentals are $25.

SKIING

In 1934, Woodstockers installed the first mechanical ski-tow in the USA, and skiing is still important here. **Suicide Six** (☎ 802-457-6661, 800-448-7900; www.woodstockinn.com; VT 12, Pomfret; ☺ mid-Dec–Mar), 3 miles north of Woodstock, is known for challenging downhill runs. The lower slopes are fine for beginners, though. There are 23 trails (30% beginner, 40% intermediate, 30% expert) and three lifts.

The full-service **Woodstock Ski Touring Center** (☎ 802-457-6674; VT 106), just south of town, rents equipment and has 50 miles of groomed touring trails.

Sleeping

BUDGET

Braeside Motel (☎ 802-457-1366; www.braesidemotel .com; US 4; r $68-108; ☒) East of town, this motel has a nice location and 12 good rooms.

Quechee Gorge State Park (☎ 802-295-2990, 886-2434; www.vtstateparks.com; 190 Dewey Mills Rd, White River Junction; sites with/without hookups $21/14; ☺ mid-May–mid-Oct) Eight miles east of Woodstock and 3 miles west of I-89 along US 4, this 600-acre spot has 54 pine-shaded sites (with six lean-tos) that are a short stroll from Quechee Gorge.

Ascutney State Park (☎ 802-674-2060; www.vt stateparks.com; Black Mountain Rd, Windsor; sites with/without hookups $21/14; ☺ mid-May–mid-Oct) About 22 miles southeast of Woodstock off I-91, these 49 sites (with 10 lean-tos) are at an elevation of 3144ft, and they offer great panoramic views. The 2000-acre park also features a playground, hiking trails and cliffs for hang gliding.

Wilgus State Park (☎ 802-674-5422, 802-886-2434; www.vtstateparks.com; US 5, Windsor; sites with/without hookups $21/14; ☺ mid-May–mid-Oct) The 20 sites and nine lean-tos here, next to the Connecticut River, offer good possibilities for fishing, canoeing and hiking within the park's 100 acres. Two enclosed cabins ($42) are expected to open in 2005. Wilgus is located 2 miles south of I-91 from exit 8.

Silver Lake State Park (☎ 802-234-9451, 886-2434; www.vtstateparks.com; sites with/without hookups $23/16; ☺ mid-May–mid-Oct) This 34-acre park (off VT 12 in Barnard) is 10 miles north of Woodstock and has 47 sites (with seven lean-tos), a beach, boat and canoe rentals and fishing.

Thetford State Park (☎ 802-785-2266; www.vtstate parks.com; Academy Rd, Thetford; sites with/without hookups $21/14; ☺ mid-May–mid-Oct) You'll find 16 sites (two lean-tos), plus hiking trails and a playground here. From I-91 exit 14, go a mile west on VT 113 to Thetford Hill, then a mile south on Academy Rd.

MID-RANGE

Shire Motel (☎ 802-457-2211; www.shiremotel.com; 46 Pleasant St; r $68-228; ☐) Within walking distance of the town center on US 4, this place has 42 comfortable rooms and some luxury suites. It's located on the Ottauquechee River and offers Vermont hospitality with motel convenience.

1830 Shire Town Inn (☎ 802-457-1830, 888-286-1830; www.1830shiretowninn.com; 31 South St; r incl hearty breakfast $85-180; ☺) This cozy B&B has three rooms, all with the seemingly requisite wide period floorboards, thick beams and fireplaces.

Applebutter Inn (☎ 802-457-4158, 800-486-1374; www.applebutterinn.com; 7511 Happy Valley Rd, Taftsville; r incl immense breakfast $85-225) Just 3 miles east of Woodstock and set on 12 extraordinary

acres with one of Vermont's most picturesque barns, the Applebutter is a Federal-
style house (c 1850) with six guest rooms
and a wonderful old kitchen. The house is
furnished with period pieces and Oriental
rugs that partly cover the wide-plank floors.
Credit cards are not accepted.

Woodstocker B&B (☎ 802-457-3896; www.wood
stockervt.com; 61 River St; r incl full breakfast $85-135)
This 1830s hostelry offers nine spacious and
nicely decorated rooms. It's well situated
for exploring central Vermont's history. For
longer stays, ask about the very desirable
suites.

Canterbury House (☎ 802-457-3077, 800-390-3077;
www.thecanterburyhouse.com; 43 Pleasant St; r incl full
breakfast $115-180) These seven charming guest
rooms, filled with antiques, are housed in
a restored 1880s Victorian B&B. The 2nd-
floor bedrooms in the front of the house
are best. For instance, The Monk's Take has
a fireplace and cable TV.

Parker House Inn (☎ 802-295-6077; www.theparker
houseinn.com; 1792 Main St, Quechee; r incl full breakfast
$135-165) A Victorian-style place built in 1857
for former Vermont senator Joseph Parker,
this antique-laden inn features seven large
guest rooms. The downstairs parlors have
been converted into dining rooms, but a
small sitting room remains for your use on
the 2nd floor. A riverside porch just begs to
be part of your day. It's just 100 yards from
one of the Ottauquechee River's covered
bridge and waterfall.

TOP END

Village Inn of Woodstock (☎ 802-457-1255, 800-722-
4571; www.villageinnofwoodstock.com; 41 Pleasant St; r incl
full breakfast $85-240) This lovely Victorian man-
sion, situated on a 40-acre estate, has eight
guest rooms. Most feature feather beds,
down comforters and period details like oak
wainscoting and tin ceilings. Enjoy the cozy
tavern with its stained glass windows and
full bar. Chefs David and Evelyn prepare a
breakfast you're sure to remember fondly.

Woodstock Inn & Resort (☎ 802-457-1100, 800-
448-7900; www.woodstockinn.com; 14 The Green; r $199-
299, ste $454-559; 🏊) One of Vermont's most
luxurious hotels, this resort has extensive
grounds, a formal dining room, an indoor
sports center and 144 guest rooms and suites.
A fire blazes in the huge stone fireplace
from late fall through spring, making this
famous inn even more welcoming. Facilities

include an 18-hole golf course, tennis courts,
cross-country skiing and a fitness center.

Eating
BUDGET

If you have a picnic lunch, take it to the
George Perkins Marsh Man and Nature
Park, a tiny hideaway right next to the river
on Central St, across the street from Pane
e Salute.

Mountain Creamery (☎ 802-457-1715; 33 Central St;
dishes $4-6; 🕑 7am-3pm) In addition to serving
Woodstock's most scrumptious apple pie,
you can also get a sandwich or other yummy
picnic fare here.

MID-RANGE & TOP END

Pane e Salute (☎ 802-457-4882; 61 Central St; breakfast & lunch $4-8, mains dinner $16-20, prix fixe $39;
🕑 breakfast & lunch Thu-Sun year-round, call for winter
dinner times) Specialties include authentic Italian pastries and the best cup of espresso this
side of the Connecticut River. Expect buttery panettone, rolls filled with ricotta, pear
and chocolate, and Florentine coffee cake.
In the evening, you'll be rewarded with classic Italian dishes, from rustic mountainous
ones to aristocratic, citified creations.

Simon Pearce Restaurant (☎ 802-295-1470; The
Mill, Main St, Quechee; lunch $6-15, mains dinner $20-32;
🕑 lunch & dinner) A 10-minute drive from
Woodstock, this creative restaurant enjoys
a dramatic setting in an old brick mill overlooking a waterfall and a covered bridge.
Influenced by New American cuisine, the
menu nevertheless maintains a refreshing
simplicity: try sweet-potato soup, hickory-
smoked coho salmon or grilled leg of lamb
with garlic, rosemary and balsamic vinai-
grette. The restaurant's beautiful stemware
is blown by hand in the Simon Pearce Glass
workshops (p380), also located in the mill;
watch them work while you wait.

Parker House Inn (☎ 802-295-6077; 16 Main St,
Quechee; mains $16-24; 🕑 dinner) Locals concur:
the food here is just as tasty as at Simon
Pearce next door (see above), but the Parker
House prices are lower. Good American
fare is served in the front room or out on
the terrace overlooking the waterfall. The
menu changes often, but look for the likes
of rotisserie-roasted pork finished with a
chimichurri sauce.

Skunk Hollow Tavern (☎ 802-436-2139; Hartland
Four Corners; mains $8-24; 🕑 dinner Wed-Sun) Eight

DETOUR: PLYMOUTH

pop 571

This small farming village, 14 miles southwest of Woodstock, is known for the Calvin Coolidge Homestead.

'If you don't say anything, you won't be called on to repeat it,' said Calvin Coolidge (1872–1933), 30th president of the USA, who was born in Plymouth. He attended nearby Amherst College in Massachusetts, opened a law practice in Northampton, Maine, ran for local office, and then served as state senator, lieutenant governor and governor of Massachusetts. Elected as vice president of the USA on the Warren Harding ticket in 1920, he assumed the presidency upon Harding's sudden death in 1923. Vice President Coolidge was visiting his boyhood home in Plymouth when word came of Harding's death, and his father, Colonel John Coolidge, the local justice of the peace, administered the presidential oath of office by kerosene lamp at 2:47am on August 3, 1923.

Known for his simple, forthright New England style and his personal honesty, Coolidge had the good fortune to preside over a time of great prosperity – the Roaring Twenties. His laissez-faire business policies were well accepted but contributed to the stock market crash of 1929. With wonderful *après-moi-le-déluge* luck, he declined to run for another term as president in 1928, although he probably would have won. Instead, he retired to Northampton to write articles for newspapers and magazines.

Thus, the burden of blame for the Great Depression fell hard on the shoulders of the 31st president, Herbert Hoover, who had engineered many of the Coolidge administration's successes as its Secretary of Commerce. Hoover had only been in office a matter of months when the stock market crashed. In 1931, with many banks failed and a quarter of the nation's workers unemployed, former president Coolidge understatedly reflected, 'The country is not in good shape.'

Coolidge Homestead

The tranquil and perfectly manicured **homestead** (☎ 802-672-3773; www.historicvermont.org/coolidge; VT 100A; adult/child under 14/family $6.50/free/20; ⌚ 9:30am-5pm late May–mid-Oct) is open for tours. You can check out the birthplace, Wilder Barn, a farmers' museum. Wilder House, once the home of Coolidge's mother, has now become a lunchroom. Calvin Coolidge is buried in the local cemetery.

Sleeping

Golden Stage Inn (☎ 802-226-7744, 800-253-8226; www.goldenstageinn.com; Depot St, Proctorsville; r incl full breakfast $79-300; 🏊) One of the coziest overnight stays in the Okemo area, this former 18th-century stagecoach stop off VT 103 is now a nine-room inn with great mountain views. Its 8 acres offer something for everyone, replete as they are with gardens, an orchard and a brook where deer and moose come to drink.

Coolidge State Park (☎ 802-672-3612, 802-886-2434; ww.vtstateparks.com; VT 100A; sites with/without hookups $20/14; ⌚ late May-early Oct) This 165-acre park is 3 miles northeast of Plymouth Union, and even closer to Plymouth itself. The 60 sites (including 35 lean-tos) sit at an elevation of 2100ft in a 25-sq-mile state forest with good hiking and fishing. There's a backcountry camping area where you can pan for gold.

HI-AYH – Trojan Horse Hostel (☎ 802-228-5244, 800-547-7475; www.hiayh.org; 44 Andover St; dm summer/winter $19/25; ⌚ office 8-10am & 5-9pm May-Mar) On VT 100 just south of Ludlow village, 11 miles south of Plymouth, this hostel is a bit more expensive in winter when it's crowded with skiers from the nearby Okemo Mountain ski area. For the months of December through March, you'll need to phone ahead to reserve a room.

miles south of Woodstock, off VT 12, this tiny 200-year-old tavern has worn wooden floors that ooze history. You can have burgers or fish-and-chips ($8) at the bar or head upstairs, where it's more intimate, to enjoy rack of lamb ($24). The same menu is available upstairs and downstairs. It's a treat when there's live music (Wednesday and Friday) and the band takes up half the room.

VERMONT

Jackson House Inn (☎ 802-457-2065; 114-3 Senior Lane/US 4; prix fixe $55; ☽ dinner Jul-Oct, Wed-Sun Nov-Jun) Expect tranquility, exquisite views of Mt Tom and premier cuisine at the Jackson House. The prix-fixe menu might feature scallops and stone crab or duck in phyllo, followed by a main dish of pepper-crusted tuna or a juicy little squab lightly caramelized with maple syrup. The chef also offers a tasting menu at $95, a true treat for your taste buds. End with the pumpkin brulée, steamed lemon pudding or tarte tatin.

Prince & the Pauper (☎ 802-457-1818; 24 Elm St; bistro menu $13-19, mains dinner $21-24, prix fixe $38; ☽ dinner) Woodstock's elegant New American bistro serves a sublime three-course prix-fixe menu. You might order apple-wood-smoked ruby trout with grilled corn cake and crème fraîche from the à la carte menu. Depending on your appetite, lighter bistro fare is always an enticing option as well.

Shopping

Hillbilly Flea Market (☎ 802-672-1331; VT 4, Bridge-water; ☽ 10am-5pm Thu-Sun) The Old Inn Marketplace houses spaces for some 20 local vendors. This flea market is an up-scale treasure trove on the 1st floor of an old mill that dates back to the 1820s.

Simon Pearce Glass (☎ 802-295-2771; www.simon pearce.com; 1760 Main St, Quechee; ☽ store 9am-4pm, glassblowing 9am-9pm) At this exceptional studio and shop (and fine restaurant; see p378), visitors can watch artisans produce distinctive pieces of original glass.

Getting There & Away

Vermont Transit (☎ 802-864-6811, 800-552-8737; www.vermonttransit.com) buses stop at nearby White River Junction (☎ 802-295-3011; Sykes Ave). If you take the bus to White River Junction on your way to Woodstock, you will need to take a taxi (drivers wait at the bus station) from there to Woodstock, a distance of 16 miles.

Amtrak (☎ 800-872-7245; www.amtrak.com) runs the *Vermonter* train, which stops at nearby White River Junction.

It's a straight shot (two hours, 89 miles) via US 4 east to I-89 north to Burlington from Woodstock. It'll take a mere half-hour (20 miles) to reach Killington via US 4 west.

KILLINGTON MOUNTAIN
pop 1102

The largest ski resort in the East is focused on outdoor activities, and it's all centrally located on the mountain. Officially, the mountain town is Sherburne, but there's really not a lot there.

Information

Killington Chamber of Commerce (☎ 802-773-4181; www.killingtonchamber.com; PO Box 114, Killington, Vermont 05751 ☽ 9am-5pm Mon-Fri, occasionally 10am-2pm Sat) Conveniently located on US 4.

Killington Resort (☎ 800-372-2007; www.killington .com) This is basically a central reservation service for the resort, and it's the best source for area services. Sure, staff will send you information prior to your visit, but their main purpose is in helping with accommodations. Since there are well over 100 area places to stay, package deals with sports activities and lodgings can be attractively priced.

Activities
WINTER

Killington (☎ 802-422-3261, 800-621-6867; www.killing ton.com) is Vermont's prime ski resort, and one that also operates the most extensive snowmaking in North America. It offers 200 runs on seven mountains, a vertical drop of more than 3000ft, and 32 lifts, including the Skyeship and K-1 gondola that lifts up to 3000 skiers per hour in heated cars along a 2.5-mile cable. Experienced skiers attempt to ski **Outer Limits**, the steepest mogul run in the East. The area boasts top-notch facilities for every conceivable winter activity, from ice skating to snowboarding. The ski season typically runs from early November through late May.

SUMMER

Killington facilities are also used for other outdoor activities, including excellent hiking and biking.

Mountain Bike & Repair Shop (☎ 802-422-6232; Killington Rd; ☽ Jun–mid-October) rents mountain bikes for $50 daily; helmets and trail maps are included. Serious riders will want to take the 1.25-mile K-1 gondola ride to the 4241ft summit of Killington Mountain, and find their way down along the 45 miles of trails. Mountain-bike trail access costs $8 daily or $30 for trail and gondola access. Inquire about guided tours and packages.

As for hiking, the Mountain Bike & Repair Shop has an excellent (free) map of

KILLINGTON...NEW HAMPSHIRE?

No man (or woman) is an island, but how about a town? Could Killington, Vermont, really end up in the bosom of New Hampshire, albeit from afar? If some townspeople have their way, yes. No one is dumping tea on the ski slopes yet, but the centuries-old Yankee sensitivity to unfair taxation is certainly alive and well in Killington.

At issue is the Act 60 property tax, levied in 1997 to aid the state's public school system. Act 60 assesses towns with higher real estate values – like the wealthy ski resort town of Killington – at a higher rate. In effect, Killington taxes are subsidizing school systems elsewhere in the state. Since 1997, Killington has collected over $20 million a year in taxes and yet it only gets $1 million of that back in provisional state aid.

Hear ye, hear ye: Killington residents march to their own drummer. Rather than leave Vermont, locals are leading a charge to secede to New Hampshire, whose border is 25 miles to the east and where there is no income or sales tax. The crusaders reason that rebirth as a New Hampshire town would save Killington $10 million a year in real estate taxes.

In March 2004 residents voted in an overwhelming majority to make Killington a satellite town of New Hampshire. But, to become reality, approval for the change must be given by both state legislatures. That's not about to happen, but it sure is heartening to know that these Yankee hills are alive with the sound of revolution.

VERMONT

14 self-guided nature hikes. Hikers can ride the gondola to the top (adult/child/senior/family $9/5/5/20) and hike down. If you want to ride up and down, the gondola costs $13/8/8/31 per adult/child/senior/family.

Sleeping

Gifford Woods State Park (☎ 802-775-5354, 886-2434; www.vtstateparks.com; Gifford Woods Rd, Killington; sites with/without hookups $20/14; ☽ late May–early Oct) A half-mile north of US 4 and VT 100, this park has 48 campsites (including 21 lean-tos) set on 114 acres. There are added bonuses of a playground, hiking trails, and fishing in Kent Pond.

For details of condo and house rentals and hotels, the Killington Lodging Resort (see opposite) really finds the best deals.

Eating

The mountain has more than 100 restaurants; you won't go hungry.

Casey's Caboose (☎ 802-422-3795; Killington Rd; dishes $16-27; ☽ lunch Sat & Sun, from 3pm daily) Families should head here, where the atmosphere is great, the buffalo wings are free during happy hour and there's a good children's menu.

Choices Restaurant (☎ 802-422-4030; Glazebrook Center, Killington Rd; dishes $13-22; ☽ lunch & dinner Wed-Sun, brunch Sun) Can't decide what you're in the mood for? Grazers happily munch away on appetizers here, while serious eaters find plenty of satisfying main dishes on

the huge menu. Meals range from soups and salads to pastas and steaks. Chef-owner Claude Blays, a Culinary Institute of America graduate in 1975, prepares winning combinations in this bistro/brassiere/pub.

Casa Bella Inn (☎ 802-746-8943; VT 100; mains $13-21; ☽ dinner) Chef-owner Franco Cacozza, who turned this former stagecoach stop into a pleasant restaurant, offers a traditional menu of authentic Italian dishes. They're complemented by a good cellar filled with Italian wines.

Vermont Inn (☎ 802-775-0708; US 4; mains dinner $13-22; ☽ dinner) Popular with skiers and one of the mountain's best dining values, the inn offers rack of lamb, local veal and variations on the steak theme. The varied menu changes nightly and is served next to a cozy fireplace in winter. A good children's menu is available year-round while early specials are offered until 6:30pm in the summer.

Drinking & Entertainment

With 25 clubs, and lively bars in many restaurants, Killington is where the après-ski scene rages. Many of these nightspots lie along the 4-mile-long Access Rd. Check out these: **Wobbly Barn** (☎ 802-422-3392; ☽ from 3:30pm), with dancing, blues and rock and roll, and the **Pickle Barrel** (☎ 802-422-3035; ☽ from 4pm), with great rock and roll bands. **McGrath's Irish Pub** (☎ 802-775-7181; US 4; ☽ from 11:30 mid-Jun–mid-Apr), at the Inn at Long Trail, has live Irish music on winter weekends.

TOP FIVE SKI RESORTS

Whether it's racing downhill or gliding quietly through the woods, Vermont's mountains and moguls can be mixed and matched to suit your desires. For 24-hour snow reports and trail conditions, call **Vermont Skiing Today Snow Line** (☎ 802-229-0531). For more information on the whole myriad of options, contact the **Vermont Ski Areas Association** (www.skivermont.com). In the meantime, here's our list of the top faves:

Killington (p380) The fantastically long season here runs from early November to late May, making Killington a prime place to shush. The resort offers 200 runs on seven mountains, great lifts and a vertical drop of more than 3000ft.

Mad River Glen (p386) The East's gnarliest lift-served ski area entails navigating rocks, ice and trees.

Mt Snow/Haystack (p364) Families like the diverse terrain here, at Vermont's second-largest ski resort, with 132 trails and 60 miles of cross-country routes.

Stowe/Mt Mansfield (p391) The most highly regarded ski resort in the eastern US, Stowe offers an unparalleled variety of terrain. Let's say you're new to the sport, your partner's an expert and the kids love bopping down the intermediate slopes. Everyone will find their place at Stowe.

Sugarbush (p386) If flying down serpentine trails, around corners and through tight slots, always in the company of trees, amuses then you, then you'll be laughing your head off here.

Getting There & Away

Vermont Transit (☎ 802-864-6811, 800-552-8737; www.vermonttransit.com) buses stop at the **Deli** (☎ 802-775-1599) on US 4 in Killington. The ride from Sherburne to Rutland costs $5.50 one way (30 minutes). Once you're in Rutland, you can catch buses to Burlington, Brattleboro or Bennington.

RUTLAND

pop 17,013

Rutland is Vermont's second-largest city (Burlington is larger – and more charming). US 7 bypasses the center of Rutland, and you should probably do the same. If you need to find a big hardware store, automobile dealership, airport or hospital, Rutland will do. Otherwise, move on.

In the 19th century, Rutland was important as a railroad town. The trains shipped Vermont marble out and the manufactured goods of the world in. But the city's main railroad station was torn down in the 1960s and replaced by a nondescript shopping mall, leaving Rutland without even a visual memory of its heyday.

The **Vermont State Fair** takes place here in early September. It's a fun monster of an old-fashioned country fair, with exhibits, livestock, carnival rides, food booths and lots of priceless local color. The **Rutland Region Chamber of Commerce** (☎ 802-773-2747; www.rutlandvermont.com; 256 N Main St/US 7, Rutland, VT 05701; ☒ 8am-5pm Mon-Fri) can provide you with more information on the fair.

MIDDLEBURY

pop 8190

Prosperity resides at the crossroads, and Middlebury obviously has its share. Aptly named, Middlebury stands at the nexus of eight highways, and as a result the center of town is always busy with traffic.

Middlebury was permanently settled at the end of the 18th century. In 1800, Middlebury College was founded, and it has been synonymous with the town ever since. But the establishment of this renowned liberal arts college was not Middlebury's only educational milestone. In 1814, education pioneer Emma Willard (1787–1870) founded the Middlebury Female Seminary, a college preparatory boarding school designed to prepare women for college admission – a radical idea in early 19th-century America. The school later moved to nearby New York state.

John Deere was an apprentice blacksmith in Middlebury during the 1820s. He soon moved to Illinois, where he discovered that conventional plows had a hard time with the black prairie soils of the Midwest. He fashioned a plow with a one-piece steel plowshare and moldboard, which was a major advance in plow technology. The company was incorporated in 1868 and not only survived the Great Depression but managed to ring up $100 million in gross sales in 1937, 100 years after Deere made his first plow. It's still a multi-million dollar company.

Poet Robert Frost (1874–1963) owned a farm in nearby Ripton, and he cofounded the renowned Bread Loaf School of English at nearby Middlebury College.

Despite Middlebury's history of marble quarrying, most buildings in the town's center are built of brick, wood and schist (a stone). Middlebury College, however, contains many buildings made with white marble and gray limestone.

Orientation

Middlebury stands on hilly ground straddling Otter Creek. Main St/VT 30 crosses the creek just above the Otter Creek Falls. The town green and Middlebury Inn are on the north side of the creek; Frog Hollow (a shopping complex in an old mill) and Middlebury College are to the south.

Information

Addison County Chamber of Commerce (☎ 802-388-7951; www.midvermont.com; 2 Court St, Middlebury, VT 05753; ꙮ 9am-5pm Mon-Fri year-round, noon-4pm Sat late Jun–mid-Oct) On the north side of the creek and facing the town green, this place is ensconced in a grand mansion and dispenses plenty of information.

Vermont Book Shop (☎ 802-388-2061; 38 Main St; ꙮ 8:30am-5:30pm Mon-Sat, 11am-4pm Sun) Features a thorough selection of Vermont and Frost titles.

Sights

MIDDLEBURY COLLEGE

For Middlebury College tours, contact the **admissions office** (☎ 802-443-3000; www.middlebury college.com), in Emma Willard House, on the south side of S Main St/VT 30. Within the Center for the Arts, the **Middlebury College Museum of Art** (☎ 802-443-5007; S Main St/VT 30; admission free; ꙮ 10am-5pm Mon-Fri, noon-5pm Sat & Sun) has good collections of Cypriot pottery, 19th-century European and American sculpture, and modern prints.

FROG HOLLOW CRAFT CENTER

This outstanding Vermont **state craft center** (☎ 802-388-3177; 1 Mill St; ꙮ 10am-5:30pm Mon-Thu, 11am-4pm Fri & Sat, noon-5pm Sun) has an exhibition and sales gallery showing works by many Vermont artisans. It's always worth stopping here.

SHELDON MUSEUM

This 1829 Federal-style brick **mansion-turned-museum** (☎ 802-388-2117; www.henrysheldonmuseum .org; 1 Park St; adult/child under 6/child 6-18/senior $5/ free/3/4.50; ꙮ 10am-5pm Mon-Sat year-round & 11am-

4pm Sun Oct, tours May–Oct) owes its existence to Henry Sheldon, a town clerk, church organist, storekeeper and avid collector of 19th-century Vermontiana. His collection runs the gamut from folk art and furniture to paintings and bric-a-brac.

UNIVERSITY OF VERMONT MORGAN HORSE FARM

In 1789, Justin Morgan and his thoroughbred Arabian colt, Figure, came to Vermont from Springfield, MA. The colt grew to a small bay stallion, and the hardy farmers and loggers of Vermont looked upon him as pretty but not particularly useful. Morgan, however, proved to them the horse's surprising strength, agility, endurance and longevity. Renamed Justin Morgan after his owner, the little horse became the USA's first native breed, useful for heavy work, carriage draft, riding and even war service. Southwestern quarter horses have Morgan blood, as do the American Albino and the Palomino breeds. Pure Morgans are still raised today, with most of the excellent qualities that made them famous two centuries ago.

You can see 70 registered Morgans and tour their stables and the farm grounds at the **University of Vermont's Morgan Horse Farm** (☎ 802-388-2011; Horse Farm Rd; adult/child/teenager $5/2/4; ꙮ 9am-4pm May-Oct), about 3 miles from Middlebury. Drive west on VT 125, then north (right) onto Weybridge St/VT 23 to the farm.

Activities

Undulating with rolling hills and farms, the pastoral countryside around Middlebury makes for great cycling. **Bike Center** (☎ 802-388-6666; www.bikecentermid.com; cnr 74 Main St & Frog Hollow; equipment rental per hr/day/weekend $5/20/35; ꙮ 9:30am-5:30pm Mon-Sat year-round, 1-4pm Sun summer) has plenty of equipment and information on regional biking.

One of New England's best microbreweries, **Otter Creek Brewing** (☎ 802-388-0727, 800-473-0727; 85 Exchange St; ꙮ 10am-6pm Mon-Sat, tours 1pm, 3pm & 5pm Mon-Sat), makes a rich Stovepipe Porter, Copper Ale and other specialty microbrews, some of which are organic. Free samples and guided tours of the brewing process from grain to glass are offered.

The countryside surrounding Middlebury is rife with apple orchards. **Atwood Orchards** (☎ 802-897-5592; Barnum Hill, Shoreham;

VERMONT

⊙ 9am-5:30pm Jul–mid-Oct) has branches ripe for the pickin' in September and October. Pick cherries or enjoy pre-ordered peaches in July. To find this orchard, head west on VT 125, then south on VT 22A; it's located 3 miles south of Shoreham village.

There are lots of good day hikes in the region. Contact the **Green Mountain National Forest District Office** (☎ 802-388-4362; US 7; ⊙ 8am-4:30pm Mon-Fri) for free, detailed printouts of hikes.

Sleeping
BUDGET

There is little camping in or very close to Middlebury, but several places are within an easy drive.

Blue Spruce Motel (☎ 802-388-4091, 800-640-7671; US 7; r $55-135, ste $75-185) A mere 3 miles south of the town center, Blue Spruce has 22 comfortable rooms and suites (which are more like miniapartments that can sleep four).

Sugarhouse Motel (☎ 802-388-2770; US 7; r $50-100) The 14 rooms at this motel, 2 miles north of the town center, all have microwaves and fridges.

Greystone Motel (☎ 802-388-4935; US 7; r $55-95) Just 2 miles south of the town center, this trim motel has 10 rooms with shower only.

DAR State Park (☎ 802-759-2354; www.vtstateparks .com; VT 17; sites with/without hookups $21/14; ⊙ mid-May–early Sep) About 17 miles northwest of Middlebury, DAR enjoys a choice shore location on Lake Champlain between West Addison and Chimney Point. The park has 71 campsites (including 21 lean-tos) as well as boating, fishing and a playground.

Branbury State Park (☎ 802-247-5925; www.vt stateparks.com; VT 53; sites with/without hookups $23/16; ⊙ May–mid-Oct) About 10 miles south of Middlebury on Lake Dunmore, this place has 44 sites (including five lean-tos) on 96 acres. Hiking trails lead to spectacular views.

Ten Acres Campground (☎ 802-759-2662; http ://10acrescampground.com; VT 125, Addison; sites with/ without hookups $28/22; ⊙ May–mid-Oct; ☒) Fifteen miles west of Middlebury and a mile south of the Lake Champlain Bridge to New York, Ten Acres has 90 sites (78 of which have hookups), a large tenting area and lots of amusements.

MID-RANGE

Waybury Inn (☎ 802-388-4015, 800-348-1810; www.way buryinn.com; VT 125, East Middlebury; r incl full breakfast $90-225) This former stagecoach stop has a popular pub and 14 guest rooms, and was a favorite of Robert Frost. The inn's exterior was used as the setting for the 1980s TV show *Newhart*, which popularized innkeeping. In the summer laze away an afternoon in the swimming hole underneath the nearby bridge, and in winter warm yourself in the pub.

Inn on the Green (☎ 802-388-7512, 888-244-7512; www.innonthegreen.com; 19 S Pleasant St; r incl continental breakfast $98-190, ste $150-275) This 1803 Federal-style home offers seven spacious rooms in the house and four more-modern rooms in an adjoining carriage house. It's been lovingly restored to its graceful style of yesteryear.

Middlebury B&B (☎ 802-388-4851; 174 Washington St Extension; d incl buffet breakfast with/without bathroom $125/75) Liz Hunt's B&B, from which you can walk to the center of town, has four rooms (only one of which has a private bathroom). Credit cards are not accepted.

Middlebury Inn (☎ 802-388-4961, 800-842-4666; www.middleburyinn.com; 14 Court House Sq/VT 7; r incl breakfast $88-220) This inn's fine old main building (1827) has beautifully restored formal public rooms with wide hallways, and its charming guest rooms combine past and present. The adjacent Porter Mansion, with 10 Victorian-style rooms, is full of architectural details. The inn is located downtown overlooking the bandstand, but many of the 75 guestrooms are less desirable modern motel units in the back.

TOP END

Swift House Inn (☎ 802-388-9925; www.swifthouseinn .com; cnr Stewart Lane & US 7; r incl continental breakfast $125-275) This grand white Federal house was built in 1814, served as the family estate of philanthropist Jessica Stewart Swift and is surrounded by fine formal lawns and gardens. In addition to 21 luxurious rooms, the inn boasts suites featuring a fireplace, sitting area and Jacuzzi. Other welcome luxuries include a steam room and sauna, a cozy pub, a library, a sunporch and gracious amenities.

Eating
BUDGET

Otter Creek Bakery (☎ 802-388-3371; 14 College St; sandwiches $4-5; ⊙ 7am-6pm Mon-Sat, 7am-3pm Sun) This bakery, with some outdoor seating, is popular for takeout pastries, strong coffee and creative sandwiches. Traveling with a pooch? It'll lick your face if you buy it an Otter Creek dog biscuit.

DETOUR: RIPTON

pop 569

Ten miles southeast of Middlebury on VT 125, Ripton is a beautiful little hamlet set in the Vermont mountains. Two white churches, a few houses, a schoolhouse and a big old country house converted into an inn – that's Ripton. Sit on the lawn in the sun, go down to the river and pitch stones, read, walk, think, talk.

The eight-room **Chipman Inn** (☎ 802-388-2390, 800-890-2390; www.chipmaninn.com; VT 125; r incl full breakfast $105-145; Dec-Mar & May-Oct), a beautiful Federal house built in 1828, is big on Frostiana and also on the peace and quiet that Robert Frost sought. The warming hearth and woodstove are key in wintertime. Since guests dine at communal tables, there is a palpable sense of camaraderie here. Children 12 and older are welcome.

Frost spent 23 years on a nearby farm, and just east of Ripton you'll find the **Robert Frost Wayside Recreation Area**. A forest trail, less than a mile in length, is marked with signs featuring quotations from the poet's works. To get here from Ripton, take VT 125 east for 2 miles, and look for the trail on the right side of the road.

Baba's Market & Deli (☎ 802-388-6408; 54 College St; dishes $5-15; 7am-8pm Tue-Sat) Middlebury students come here for cheap calzones, Middle Eastern specialties and pizzas. Check out the dishes (held in warming trays) before deciding.

Storm Cafe (☎ 802-388-1063; 3 Mill St; lunch $3-8, dinners to go $6-13; 11:30am-6pm Tue-Sat) In the basement of Frog Hollow Mill, this creekside café has soups, salads, sandwiches and the like. The blackboard menu highlights more-substantial dishes like vegetarian lasagna to take away for a late-afternoon picnic or early dinner. In good weather, sit on the terrace overlooking Otter Creek to enjoy what some consider to be the most imaginative menu in town.

Steve's Park Diner (☎ 802-388-3297; 66 Merchants Row; dishes $4-8; 6am-2pm Mon-Sat, 7am-2pm Sun) Perhaps the cheapest place in town, Steve's has small wooden booths, pancakes and sandwiches. It's popular with returning students and young faculty families.

Greenfield's Mercantile (☎ 802-388-8221; 46 Main St; 9am-5pm Mon-Sat, 11am-4pm Sun) Get your smoothies and hemp cookies here. Great combination, eh? And while you're at it, pick up anything else made of hemp.

MID-RANGE

Mister Up's (☎ 802-388-6724; 25 Bakery Lane; dishes $6-14; 11:30am-midnight) Overlooking the creek, Mister Up's is basically a steak, burger and seafood place, with a portobello sandwich or two thrown in for good measure. You can dine outside on the riverside deck or inside the brick and stained-glass greenhouse.

Tully & Marie's (☎ 802-388-4182; 5 Bakery Lane; mains lunch $6-8, dinner $10-20; 11:30am-midnight, closed Tue winter) Overlooking Otter Creek, this small art-deco eatery features lots of delicious vegetarian and vegan dishes. At lunch, try the Indian curry soup with chickpeas or a black-bean burrito. Dinner ranges from pad thai to steak to pan-blackened tuna.

TOP END

Fire & Ice (☎ 802-388-7166; 26 Seymour St; lunch $8-14, mains dinner $15-25; lunch Tue-Sun & dinner) In a setting rich with stained-glass and mahogany, Fire & Ice is known for its prime rib, steaks and salad bar. It's name comes from poem by Robert Frost.

Getting There & Away

Vermont Transit (☎ 802-864-6811, 800-552-8737; www.vermonttransit.com) operates two buses daily on the Burlington–Rutland–Albany route, which stops in Middlebury. It takes an hour to ride from Middlebury to Burlington ($12). You can connect at Albany with buses for NYC and at Burlington with buses for Montreal, Canada. The bus stops at the Middlebury Village Depot. Note: you need a passport to cross into Canada.

By car, it takes about the same amount of time (an hour) to get from Middlebury to either Warren/Waitsfield or Burlington.

WARREN & WAITSFIELD

pop 1697 (Warren); 1686 (Waitsfield)

North of Killington, VT 100 is one of the finest stretches of road in the country – a bucolic mix of rolling hills, covered bridges, ubiquitous white steeples and farmland so fertile you feel like jumping out of the car and digging your hands in the soil. Forty-five miles (or an hour) north of Killington, you'll reach Waitsfield and Warren, towns you may have seen in advertisements for Vermont tourism. They're places where nothing ever changes. This is especially true of Sugarbush and the nearby Mad River ski area, both popular with locals. Mad River still has a chairlift for single skiers, and both mountains feature the New England skiing of yore, a time when trails were cut by hand and weren't much wider than a hiking path.

Orientation & Information

The 'gap roads' that run east to west over the Green Mountains offer some of the most picturesque views of the region. VT 73 crosses the Brandon Gap (2170ft) from Brandon to Rochester and Talcville. VT 125 crosses the Middlebury Gap from East Middlebury (2149ft) to Hancock. A narrow local road crosses Lincoln Gap (2424ft) from Bristol to Warren. (The Lincoln Gap road is closed in wintertime due to heavy snowfall.)

VT 17 crosses the Appalachian Gap (at 2356ft) from Bristol to Irasville and Waitsfield, and this route offers the best views of all.

The **Sugarbush Chamber of Commerce** (☎ 802-496-3409, 800-828-4748; www.madrivervalley.com; PO Box 173 Waitsfield VT 05673, VT 100, Waitsfield; ◷ 9am-5pm Mon-Fri) has additional hours on Saturday (10am to 5pm) during the summer, fall and winter tourism seasons.

Local telephone calls from public phones are free in Warren and Waitsfield, courtesy of the Waitsfield-Fayston Telephone Company. Imagine that.

Activities

SKIING

The nature of New England downhill skiing is flying down serpentine trails, around corners, down quick dips and through tight slots, always in the company of trees. On the best trails, the woods surround you as you whiz by a rolling tapestry of maple, oak, birch, spruce, pine and balsam. That's exactly what happens at **Sugarbush** (☎ 802-583-2381; www.sugarbush.com). Paradise, Castlerock and the backcountry runs in between braid through the forest like a crazed snake.

Subaru wagons with Vermont license plates often have bumper stickers that offer this dare: 'Mad River Glen, Ski It If You Can.' Bumper stickers don't lie. **Mad River Glen** (☎ 802-496-3551; www.madriverglen.com) is the nastiest lift-served ski area in the East, a combination of rocks, ice, trees – and snow, of course. It's truly a place where the ski slope seems little removed from the mountain's gnarled primal state.

Local ski touring centers feature more than 100 miles of groomed cross-country trails. Call the Sugarbush Chamber of Commerce (left) for information. One of the biggest ski touring centers is **Ole's Cross Country Ski Center** (☎ 802-496-3430; www.olesxc.com; 2355 Airport Rd, Warren; ◷ noon-5pm when not snowing, 9am-5pm when snowing).

OTHER ACTIVITIES

Canoeing and kayaking are prime on the Mad River (along VT 100) and White River (along VT 100 near Hancock) in April, May and early June, and on the larger Winooski River (along I-89) in the spring, summer and fall.

Clearwater Sports (☎ 802-496-2708; www.clearwatersports.com; VT 100, Waitsfield; canoe rentals daily $40-60, bike rentals daily $25, 4-hr canoeing & kayaking trips incl lessons per person $58; ◷ 9am-6pm) rents canoes (price depends on whether you need a shuttle service), kayaks, river-floating tubes, in-line skates, bicycles, snowshoes, telemark demo gear and many other types of sports equipment. Clearwater also organizes sea-kayak tours, family overnight tours and one-day guided canoeing and kayaking trips.

Sugarbush Soaring (☎ 802-496-2290; http://sugarbush.org; 20-30 min rides per person $100-115, 2 people $120-160; ◷ May-Oct), off VT 100, offers an unconventional activity. You take off from Warren-Sugarbush Airport in a glider towed by a conventional aircraft. After gaining altitude, you cast off the tow rope and soar quietly through the skies above the mountains and river valleys, kept aloft by updrafts of warm air. A glider can accommodate one or two passengers, but the two-person craft has a weight restriction of 300lb.

Vermont Icelandic Horse Farm (☎ 802-496-7141; N Basin Rd, Waitsfield; rides full-day with lunch/half day without $135/70; ◷ year-round, riding tours by appointment), 1000 yards south of the town common, takes folks on half-day or full-day jaunts year-round. Icelandic horses are fairly easy to ride, even for novice riders.

Sleeping

Because the Sugarbush area is primarily active in the winter ski season, there are no campgrounds nearby. Many accommodations are condos marketed to the ski trade. The largest selection of condos is rented by **Sugarbush Village** (☎ 800-451-4326; www.sugarbush village.com), located right at the ski area. Rentals cost about $90 to $550 per day, depending on condo size and location, and your date of arrival and length of stay.

BUDGET

Hyde Away (☎ 802-496-2322, 800-777-4933; www .hydeawayinn.com; VT 17, Waitsfield; r incl full breakfast $59-169) This 1830 farmhouse, sawmill and barn boasts its own mountain-bike touring center, hiking, and showshoeing trails. The 12 rooms, suites and bunks range from one- and two-person rooms to a suite that sleeps five. Some rooms have private bathrooms, while some are basic bunk rooms with shared bathroom.

MID-RANGE & TOP END

Inn at Round Barn Farm (☎ 802-496-2276, 800-721-8029; www.roundbarninn.com; 1661 E Warren Rd, Waitsfield; r incl huge country breakfast $130-295; ⬆) This premier, elegant inn gets its name from the adjacent 1910 round barn, one of the few authentic and rare round barns remaining in Vermont. The decidedly upscale inn features 12 antique-furnished guest rooms with mountain views, gas fireplaces, canopy beds and antiques. All overlook the meadows and mountains. In winter, guests leave their shoes at the door to preserve the hardwood floors.

Garrison (☎ 802-496-2352, 800-766-7829; VT 17, Waitsfield; r $75-150) Although mainly a condo complex, with one- to four-bedroom units, the motel section at the Garrison rents basic rooms with kitchenettes.

Inn at Mad River Barn (☎ 802-496-3310, 800-631-0466; www.madriverbarn.com; VT 17, Waitsfield; r incl full breakfast $75-150; ⬆) One of the last old-time Vermont lodges. Betsy Kratz operates this 1940s ski lodge and rents 15 rooms, some of which are in the annex with queen-size beds, steam bathrooms and TVs. The charm of the old lodge is preserved with a massive stone fireplace, deep leather chairs and a deck overlooking landscaped gardens.

A pool hidden in a birch grove welcomes guests in summer.

Eating

Skiers' taverns abound in this area. Restaurants are quite busy in the ski season, but a bit sleepy at other times.

BUDGET

Warren Store (☎ 802-496-3864; Main St, Warren; dishes $4-6; ⏱ 8am-6pm or 7pm) This atmospheric country store serves the area's biggest and best sandwiches. Eat on the deck overlooking the waterfall in the summer (except when there are swarms of bees).

MID-RANGE

American Flatbread (☎ 802-496-8856; VT 100, Waitsfield; flatbreads $9-18; ⏱ dinner Fri & Sat) For excellent pizza pies cooked in a primitive wood-fired oven, no one does it better. In fact, the Revolution Flatbread is so good that it's distributed to grocery stores throughout New England and even from Chicago to Florida. Dine in or take out.

John Egan's Big World Pub and Grill (☎ 802-496-3033; VT 100, Waitsfield; dishes $10-17; ⏱ 5pm-closing) Don't let the exterior decor fool you. Extreme skier John Egan has hired a renowned chef from New England Culinary Institute (p389), and the venison and lamb dishes are arguably the finest in the Green Mountain state. That makes foodies happy, but John Egan's is also a brewpub at heart, a hangout for skiers who heartily consume the house brew: Egan's Extreme Ale.

Rositas Mexican (☎ 802-583-3858; Sugarbush Access Rd, Warren; mains $12-18 ⏱ dinner May-Oct, Thu-Tue Nov-Apr) Great burritos, salads, shrimp in tequila and homemade desserts are featured at this fun place, found across from the bridges. Juan Gorilla's cantina and sports bar is located just downstairs.

TOP END

Spotted Cow (☎ 802-496-5151; Bridge St Marketplace, Waitsfield; lunch $9-12, mains dinner $19-28; ⏱ lunch Tue-Sun year-round, dinner Tue-Sun winter) Just off VT 100, locals rave about the Spotted Cow, owned by Bermudian Jay Young. You can't go wrong with a bowl of the Bermudian fish chowder ($6), but then again, the smoked chicken salad at lunch and the pan-fried rainbow trout at dinner are excellent, too. Just because it's small doesn't mean it's not superb.

Common Man (☎ 802-583-2800; 3209 German Flats Rd, Warren; mains $14-27; ☒ dinner Tue-Sun) Despite its proletarian name, this fancy favorite specializes in French, Italian and a smattering of other European cuisines. It's rather like dining around the Continent without leaving Vermont, especially since it's housed in a restored 19th-century barn hung with chandeliers and sporting an open-hearth fire. Menus change often, but the food is always outstanding. Homemade pastas join the signature dishes like Vermont venison with mushrooms and red wine. The wine cellar is impressive.

Getting There & Away

Area bus and train travel is impractical because the nearest Vermont Transit and Amtrak stations are in Waterbury, 14 miles north of Waitsfield (see p396 for details).

From Waitsfield, it's 22 miles (40 minutes) to Stowe via VT 100, about the same if you're taking a detour to Montpelier (via VT 100 north to I-89 south).

NORTHERN VERMONT

Home to the state capital, Montpelier, northern Vermont also contains the state's largest city, Burlington. Never fear, though: this area still features all of the rural charms found elsewhere. Even within Burlington, café-lined streets coexist with scenic paths along Lake Champlain. Further north, the pastoral Northeast Kingdom offers a full range of outdoor activities, from skiing to biking, in the heart of the mountains.

MONTPELIER

pop 7945

Montpelier (pronounced mont-*peel*-yer) would qualify as a large village in some countries. But in sparsely populated Vermont, it is the quaint capital, and perhaps the most charming capital in the country. You may want to visit Montpelier for a good meal or if you are intensely interested in Vermont history and affairs.

Orientation

Montpelier is quite small. It's easy to find the golden dome of the State House and then locate its two other major sights: the museum and the gallery.

Information

Bear Pond Books (☎ 802-229-0774; 77 Main St; ☒ 10am-5:30pm Mon-Fri, 10am-9pm Sat & Sun)
Information kiosk (State St; ☒ summer) Opposite the post office.
Vermont Chamber of Commerce (☎ 802-223-3443, 877-887-3678; www.centralvt.com; ☒ 9am-5pm Mon-Fri) Distributes a wealth of information.

Sights
STATE HOUSE

The front doors of the **State House** (☎ 802-828-2228; www.vtstatehouse.org; State St; admission & tours free; ☒ 8am-4pm Mon-Sat, tours every half-hour 10am-3:30pm Mon-Fri, 11am-2:30pm Sat Jul–mid-Oct) are guarded by a massive statue of Revolutionary War hero Ethan Allen. And the gold dome was built of granite quarried in nearby Barre in 1836. You can wander around the building during weekday business hours, or take one of the free tours.

VERMONT HISTORICAL SOCIETY

Next door to the State House, the Pavilion Building houses this surprisingly excellent **museum** (☎ 802-828-2291; http://vermonthistory.org; State St; adult/student & senior $3/2; ☒ 10am-4:30pm Tue-Fri, 10am-4pm Sat, noon-4pm Sun), devoted to all the considerable things that are fascinating about Vermont.

TW WOOD ART GALLERY

This **gallery** (☎ 802-828-8743; 36 College St; adult/child under 12 $2/free Tue-Sat, admission free Sun; ☒ noon-4pm Tue-Sun), at E State St on the Vermont College campus, was founded in 1895 by Thomas Waterman Wood (1823–1903), a native of Montpelier who gained a regional reputation for his portraits and genre paintings. The museum has a large collection of Wood's art, as well as Depression-era paintings. Changing exhibits, especially of arts created in Vermont, fill the main gallery.

COVERED BRIDGES

Vermont is rife with these classic beauties, but you don't always get two (and almost three) for the price of one. From Montpelier, take VT 12 southwest to Northfield Falls to the intersection of Cox Brook Rd, where two covered bridges straddle a river within walking distance of each other. **Station Bridge** and **Newell Bridge** both span a section of the river that's about 100ft across. **Upper Bridge** is a bit further up Cox Brook Rd. Fittingly, a general store marks the intersection where these timeless icons remain as sentinels.

Festivals & Events

If you enjoy crafts shows, the **Festival of Vermont Crafts** takes place in Montpelier the first weekend of October. The show – as if you needed an excuse – provides an opportunity to enjoy local crafts and good fall foliage simultaneously.

Sleeping

Betsy's Bed & Breakfast (☎ 802-229-0466; www.betsys bnb.com; 74 E State St; r incl full breakfast $65-110) This restored Victorian house, with hosts Jon and Betsy Anderson, is within the historic district and has 12 gracefully appointed rooms and suites decorated with period antiques. Updated amenities include phone and TV; the suites even have kitchens. You'll be just a short walk from the middle of town.

Inn at Montpelier (☎ 802-223-2727; www.innat montpelier.com; 147 Main St; r incl continental breakfast $109-194) This first-rate, 19-room inn, made up of two refurbished Federal houses right in the heart of town, boasts deluxe rooms with fireplaces. Hosts Rita and Rick Rizza have renovated these stately houses and furnished them luxuriously. Hang out for a while with coffee on the wraparound veranda.

Eating

As home to one of the country's finest cooking schools, the **New England Culinary Institute** (NECI; ☎ 802-223-6324; ww.neci.edu), Montpelier is an excellent place to stop for a meal. NECI runs three restaurants in town. Depending on the student chefs of the day, you can either have one of the best meals in New England at an affordable price or a damn good attempt. Be a guinea pig and support someone's learning curve.

La Brioche (☎ 802-229-0443; 89 Main St; sandwiches $5; ☻ 6:30am-7pm Mon-Fri & 7:30am-5pm Sat & Sun) NECI's first restaurant is a casual bakery and café offering soups and sandwiches on homemade bread, among other things. It starts running out of sandwich fixings at about 2pm, so you'd better time it right if you're hungry. Eat in or take out.

Main St Bar & Grill (☎ 802-223-3188; 118 Main St; Sun brunch $17, lunch averages $7, mains dinner $15; ☻ brunch Sun, lunch & dinner daily) NECI's signature restaurant is a multilevel spot boasting an open window to the kitchen – this allows you to watch the student chefs at work. The fare may feature almond-crusted trout and bouillabaisse. Brunch is an all-you-can-eat affair.

Chef's Table (☎ 802-229-9202; 118 Main St; mains dinner $15-29; ☻ dinner Mon-Sat) Since this upstairs, upscale restaurant is run by second-year NECI students, the food is far more innovative than at the Main St Bar & Grill. Specials change nightly but you'll usually find some variant of veal chops, lamb dishes and rosemary seared swordfish.

Sarducci's (☎ 802-223-0229; 3 Main St; lunch $6-8, mains dinner $9-16; ☻ lunch & dinner Mon-Sat, dinner Sun) If you don't feel like tossing the dice and risking a meal made by students, head to Sarducci's, a reliable standby. With tables overlooking the river in an old railroad station, Sarducci's features Italian dishes like pastas, personalized wood-oven pizzas and eggplant parmigiana. The restaurant feels spacious and the lunch portions are very generous.

Getting There & Away

Vermont Transit (☎ 802-864-6811, 800-552-8737; www .vermonttransit.com) runs four buses daily between Boston and Burlington, stopping in Montpelier at the **main terminal** (☎ 802-223-7112; 1 Taylor St). Tickets from Boston to Montpelier cost $43 (four hours); Montpelier to Burlington costs $12 (one hour).

The **Amtrak** (☎ 800-872-7245; www.amtrak.com) *Vermonter* train stops in Montpelier on its way to St Albans. The fare from Brattleboro to Montpelier is $23 to $35, depending on the day of the week.

From Montpelier to Burlington, it's an easy drive on I-89 (38 miles, 45 minutes).

BARRE
pop 9166

Montpelier's smaller neighbor Barre (pronounced *bar*-ee) touts itself as the 'granite capital of the world.'

Sights

ROCK OF AGES QUARRIES

These **quarries** (☎ 802-476-3119; www.rockofages .com; 773 Quarry Hill Rd; ☻ early May-Oct), 4 miles southeast of Barre off I-89 exit 6 off VT 14, are the world's largest granite quarries, covering 50 acres. The granite vein that's mined here is a whopping 6 miles long, 4 miles wide and 10 miles deep. The beautiful, durable, granular stone, formed more than 330 million years ago, is used for

VERMONT

tombstones, building facades, monuments, curbstones and tabletops.

Visit the on-site **Rock of Ages Visitor Center** (admission free, tours per adult/child/senior $4/1.50/3.50; 8:30am-5pm Mon-Sat). The quarry tour includes a short video, and historical exhibits. This 35-minute guided caravan tour of an active quarry heads off-site. At the on-site **Rock of Ages Manufacturing Division** (tours free; 8am-3:30pm Mon-Fri, tours every 45 mins 9:15am-3pm Mon-Sat Jun–mid-Oct), you can watch granite products being made – some with an accuracy that approaches 25-millionths of an inch.

HOPE CEMETERY

Where do old granite carvers go when they die? In Barre, they end up in Hope Cemetery, just a mile north of US 302 on VT 14. To granite carvers, tombstones aren't dreary reminders of mortality but artful celebrations of the carver's life. And what celebrations! A carver and his wife sit up in bed holding hands, smiling for eternity; a granite cube balances precariously on one corner; a carver's favorite armchair is reproduced, larger than life and tellingly empty. If a cemetery can ever be fun, this one is. It's open all the time.

STOWE

pop 4648

In a cozy valley where the West Branch River flows into the Little River and mountains rise up to the sky in all directions, the quintessential Vermont village of Stowe quietly bustles. A high concentration of local artisans share gallery space with those of world renown. A bounty of inns and eateries lines the thoroughfares almost all the way up through stunning Smuggler's Notch, halted at the border of the Green Mountain National Forest where the tallest mountain in Vermont, Mt Mansfield (4393ft), reaches for the stars. More than 200 miles of cross-country ski trails, some of the finest mountain biking and downhill skiing in the East, and world-class rock and ice climbing make this a natural mecca for adrenaline junkies and active families.

Orientation

Stowe is 10 miles north of I-89 on VT 100, and its heart lies at the intersection of VT 100 (Main St) and Mountain Rd (VT 108), which leads up to a dramatic, rocky

---

THE STOWE STORY

Founded in 1794, Stowe was a simple, pretty, backwoods farming town until 1859, when the Summit House was built as a summer resort atop Mt Mansfield. Skiing was introduced around 1912, and in the early 1930s Civilian Conservation Corps (CCC) workers cut the first real ski trails in the mountain's slopes.

In the late 1930s, the Mt Mansfield Corporation was established, and skiing in Stowe really took off after the Corporation installed the longest and highest chairlift in the US. An Austrian ski champion named Sepp Ruschp was hired as the resort's first ski school director, and he eventually rose to become head of the corporation. At the time of Ruschp's death in 1990, Stowe was among the best-regarded ski resorts in the eastern US – a reputation it still maintains.

---

gorge called Smuggler's Notch (the road may be closed in winter, but Smuggler's Notch Resort is open year-round). Many of the village's hotels and restaurants crowd Mountain Rd to the edge of the Green Mountain National Forest.

Information

Bear Pond Books (802-253-8236; Main St, Old Depot Bldg; 9am-6pm Sep-Jun, 9am-9pm Jul & Aug) Here you'll walk the creaky floorboards as you browse its vast offerings of books about Vermont and by Vermonters, as well as those of just about any other subject you'd care to contemplate.

Stowe Area Association (802-253-7321, 800-247-8693; www.gostowe.com; 51 Main St; 9am-8pm Mon-Sat & 9am-5pm Sun Jun–mid-Oct, 10am-6pm Mon-Fri & 9am-5pm Sat & Sun mid-Oct–May) This association is well organized and can help you plan your trip, including making reservations for rental cars and local accommodations.

Sights & Activities

COLD HOLLOW CIDER MILL

Several miles north of Ben & Jerry's on VT 100, you'll want to stop at **Cold Hollow Cider Mill** (802-244-8771, 800-327-7537; www.coldhollow .com; VT 100; 8am-7pm Jul–mid-Oct, 8am-6pm mid-Oct–Jun), and watch them make their famous cider doughnuts (guaranteed love at first bite). The cider itself tastes so crisp and fresh you'd swear there was a spigot coming right out of the tree. The gift shop is packed

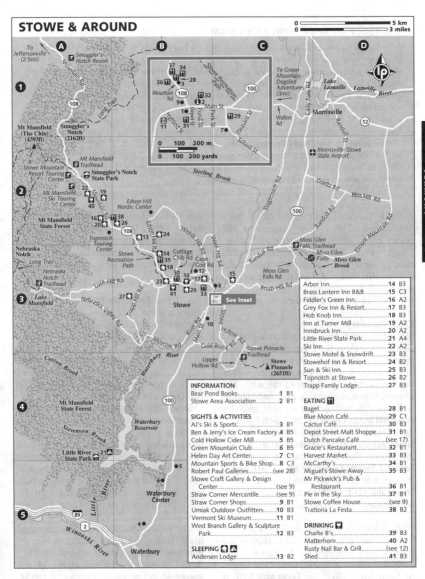

STOWE & AROUND

VERMONT

INFORMATION
Bear Pond Books.....................**1** B1
Stowe Area Association............**2** B1

SIGHTS & ACTIVITIES
AJ's Ski & Sports.....................**3** B1
Ben & Jerry's Ice Cream Factory.**4** B5
Cold Hollow Cider Mill............**5** B5
Green Mountain Club...............**6** B5
Helen Day Art Center...............**7** C1
Mountain Sports & Bike Shop...**8** C3
Robert Paul Galleries.............(see 28)
Stowe Craft Gallery & Design
   Center................................(see 9)
Straw Corner Mercantile.........(see 9)
Straw Corner Shops..................**9** B1
Umiak Outdoor Outfitters.......**10** B3
Vermont Ski Museum...............**11** B1
West Branch Gallery & Sculpture
   Park...................................**12** B3

SLEEPING
Andersen Lodge......................**13** B2

Arbor Inn...............................**14** B3
Brass Lantern Inn B&B.............**15** C3
Fiddler's Green Inn..................**16** A2
Grey Fox Inn & Resort.............**17** B3
Hob Knob Inn.........................**18** B3
Inn at Turner Mill...................**19** A2
Innsbruck Inn.........................**20** A2
Little River State Park.............**21** A4
Ski Inn..................................**22** A2
Stowe Motel & Snowdrift.........**23** B1
Stowehof Inn & Resort.............**24** B2
Sun & Ski Inn.........................**25** B3
Topnotch at Stowe..................**26** B2
Trapp Family Lodge.................**27** B3

EATING
Bagel....................................**28** B1
Blue Moon Café......................**29** C1
Cactus Café............................**30** B3
Depot Street Malt Shoppe........**31** B1
Dutch Pancake Café...............(see 17)
Gracie's Restaurant.................**32** B1
Harvest Market........................**33** B3
McCarthy's.............................**34** B1
Miguel's Stowe Away................**35** B3
Mr Pickwick's Pub &
   Restaurant...........................**36** B1
Pie in the Sky.........................**37** B1
Stowe Coffee House................(see 9)
Trattoria La Festa....................**38** B2

DRINKING
Charlie B's..............................**39** B3
Matterhorn.............................**40** A2
Rusty Nail Bar & Grill.............(see 12)
Shed.....................................**41** B3

with the most inventive gourmet goodies selection in town. Raspberry wasabi dipping mustard, anyone?

SKIING
Downhill
The great **Stowe Mountain Resort Touring Center** (☎ 802-253-7311, 800-253-4754; www.stowe.com; Moun-

tain Rd) offers miles of beautiful trails for beginners, middle-of-the-roadies and hardcore backcountry skiers. Ride the gondola for lunch at the Cliff House, then shush through silent glades.

'The family that skies together, stays together' could be the motto for the **Smuggler's Notch Resort** (☎ 800-451-8752; www.smuggs;

THE SCOOP ON BEN & JERRY'S ICE CREAM

In 1978, Ben Cohen and Jerry Greenfield launched the crazy flavors that forever changed the way ice-cream would be made. While a tour through the factory falls shy of an over-the-top Willie Wonka experience, there is a fun video on the founding fathers. The video follows their long, strange trip from a scoop shop in an abandoned gas station in Burlington, Vermont, to corporate giant – albeit a very nice giant with an inspiring presence of community building and environmental leadership. Call ahead or check its website if you want to take a tour when the factory is running. After chowing your (teeny) 'free' scoops, linger awhile in the final hallway, which is festooned with mementos of the past 25 years of changing the world one scoop at a time.

Ben & Jerry's Ice Cream Factory (☎ 802-882-1240; www.benjerry.com; VT 100N, Waterbury, 1 mile north of I-89; adult/child under 12 & senior $3/2; ☺ 9am-5pm Jun, 9am-8pm Jul-late Aug, 9am-6pm late Aug-late Oct, 10am-5pm late Oct–May) runs tours every 10 minutes from June to August, and the scoop and gift shops remain open one hour past tour times.

VT 108; ☒), located just over the Notch from Stowe. Spread over three mountains, the resort offers incredible alpine and cross-country skiing (14 miles' worth), dogsled rides (reservations strongly recommended), a lit tubing hill, nightly family entertainment, and the only learn-to-ski program for two- to five-year-olds in the country.

Cross-Country

Stowe boasts the second-largest cross-country skiing network in the country (200 miles of groomed and backcountry trails), which links a handful of ski areas, including four of the top ski touring centers in the state. The centers, which connect via groomed trails as well as tough backcountry ski runs, include: **Edson Hill Nordic Center** (☎ 802-253-7371; www.edsonhillmanor.com; 1500 Edson Hill Rd)
Stowe Mountain Resort Touring Center (☎ 802-253-7311, 800-253-4754; www.stowe.com; Mountain Rd)
Topnotch Touring Center (☎ 802-253-6433; www.topnotch-resort.com; 4000 Mountain Rd)
Trapp Family Lodge (☎ 802-253-8511, 800-826-7000; www.trappfamily.com; 700 Trapp Hill Rd)

Within Stowe's wide network of trails that traverse mountains and skirt lakes is the longest cross-country ski trail in the US, a 300-mile-long route that runs the length of Vermont. Called the **Catamount Trail**, it starts in southern Vermont at Readsboro and ends at North Troy on the Canadian border. In between lies some of the finest skiing in the East, from backcountry trails on Mt Mansfield to 11 ski touring centers (some within the Green Mountain National Forest), including **Blueberry Hill** (☎ 802-247-6735, 800-448-0707; www.blueberryhillinn .com; Ripton Rd, Goshen) and **Mountain Top Inn & Resort** (☎ 802-483-2311, 800-445-2100; www.mountaintopinn.com; Mountaintop Rd, Chittenden). Contact the **Catamount Trail Association** (☎ 802-864-5794; www.catamounttrail.org) for more information.

HIKING

The **Stowe Recreation Path** (www.gostowe.com) offers a great in-town escape, as the trail rambles through woods, farms and hillsides. Walk, bike, skate, ski – or swim in one of the classic swimming holes – as you follow the course of the Waterbury River, which weaves alongside Mountain Rd from the village northwest to Stowe Mountain Resort, passing shops and eateries along the way.

Green Mountain Club (☎ 802-244-7037; www.greenmountainclub.org; 4711 Waterbury-Stowe Rd, Waterbury Center, VT 05677), 5 miles south of Stowe, was founded in 1910 to maintain the Long Trail. The club publishes some excellent hikers' materials, available here or by mail. Staff also lead guided hiking, cycling, boating, skiing and snowshoeing day trips. For more information on the Long Trail and trail guidebooks, see p366.

The Green Mountain Club recommends the following day hikes around Stowe:
Moss Glen Falls (Easy, half-mile, half-hour) Follow VT 100 for 3 miles north of Central Stowe and bear right onto Randolph Rd. Go three-tenths of a mile and turn right for the parking area, then walk along the obvious path to reach a deep cascade and waterfalls.
Stowe Pinnacle (Moderate difficulty, 2.8 miles, two hours) Follow VT 100 south of Stowe and turn east onto Gold Brook Rd, proceeding for three-tenths of a mile; cross a bridge and turn left to continue along Gold Brook Rd. About 1.6 miles later, you come to Upper Hollow Rd; turn right and go to the top of the hill, just past Pinnacle Rd, to

find the small parking area on the left. The hike to Stowe Pinnacle, a rocky outcrop offering sweeping mountain views, is short but steep.

Nebraska Notch (Moderate difficulty, 3.2 miles, 2¼ hours) Take VT 100 south of Stowe and turn west onto River Rd, which becomes Moscow Rd. Continue for 5.8 miles to the Lake Mansfield Trout Club. The trail follows an old logging road for a while and then ascends past beaver dams and grand views to join the Long Trail at Taylor Lodge.

Mt Mansfield (Difficult, 7 miles, five hours) Follow VT 108 west from Stowe to the Long Trail parking area, seven-tenths of a mile past Stowe Mountain Resort ski area. Mt Mansfield is thought by some to resemble a man's profile in repose. Follow the Long Trail to the 'chin,' then go south along the summit ridge to Profanity Trail; follow that aptly named route to Taft Lodge, then take the Long Trail back down.

CYCLING & IN-LINE SKATING

Several bike shops can supply you with wheels for light cruising or backwoods exploration. Rent bikes from the **Mountain Sports & Bike Shop** (☎ 802-253-7919; www.mountainsportsvt.com; 580 Mountain Rd; recreation path bikes per 2 hrs/day $11/25, mountain bikes per 4 hrs/day $20/30; ☾ seasonal, phone in advance). There's also **AJ's Ski & Sports** (☎ 802-253-4593, 800-226-6257; www.ajssports.com; Mountain Rd; in-line skate rental per hr/half/full day $7/16/24; ☾ seasonal, phone in advance), which rents in-line skates and bikes.

SNOWSHOEING

Purchase or rent snowshoes at **Umiak Outdoor Outfitters** (☎ 802-253-2317; www.umiak.com; 849 S Main St; ☾ 9am-6pm). Umiak guides also lead popular snowshoeing jaunts, lit by the sun, headlamp or moonlight, for $12 (for a half-hour trip) to $48 (day trip ending with sugar-on-snow, hot cider and Cabot cheese at a remote cabin).

CANOEING & KAYAKING

Umiak Outdoor Outfitters (above) also rents canoes ($34/42 per half/full day) and sport kayaks ($24/32 per half/full day) and will shuttle paddlers and boats to the river and then pick them up at the put-out ($28/38 for a two-/four-hour trip per person, which includes transport and boat rental).

DOGSLEDDING

Learn about the fine art of dogsledding with **Green Mountain Dogsled Adventures** (☎ 802-888-8911, 802-793-6220; www.dogsledvt.com; 535 Bryan Pond Rd, Morrisville; adult/child 3-15 $145/95; ☾ tours by appointment, weather dependent) and meet the dog team that will hurtle you 6 to 8 miles (in 2½

to three hours) over hill and dale through deep woods. These pups are training for the 1000-mile Alaskan Iditerod, so you know they pack some speed. After helping harness the team, you can ride the runners or relax on the sled. Afterwards, warm up in the cabin and head out again for a ski or snowshoe in some of the wildest yet most serene land around. Reservations are required.

VERMONT SKI MUSEUM

Located in an 1818 meeting house that was rolled to its present spot by oxen in the 1860s, this **museum** (☎ 802-253-9911; www.vermontskimuseum.org; 1 S Main St; suggested donation $3-5; ☾ noon-5pm Sun-Thu, noon-8pm Fri-Sat) – a tribute to skiing history – holds much more than an evolution of equipment and a chance to chuckle at what was high, slope-side fashion in the '70s. A huge screen shows ski footage so crazy that you can hardly keep your footing. The most moving exhibit tells the tale of the famous 10th Mountain Division of skiing troops from WWII – it inspires wonder at how they held forth with what was then cutting-edge, canvas- and leather-based gear. Brrrrr.

ART GALLERIES & SHOPS

Stowe has no shortage of galleries and fine craft shops with artists of local and international renown. Within the **Straw Corner Shops** (cnr Main St & Mountain Rd) offerings are surreal, traditional, contemplative, sometimes prankish, and always finely hewn. Look for the **Straw Corner Mercantile** (☎ 802-253-3700; 57 Mountain Rd; ☾ 10am-6pm), featuring primitive folk art, Americana, prints and artsy home accessories; and **Stowe Craft Gallery & Design Center** (☎ 802-253-4693, 877-456-8388; www.stowecraft.com; 55 Mountain Rd; ☾ 10am-6pm), which offers some of the most adventurous, eclectic and surreal works of art and craft.

Don't miss the winding, sculpture-filled paths along the river's edge at the **West Branch Gallery & Sculpture Park** (☎ 802-253-8943; www.christophercurtis.com; ☾ 11am-6pm Tue-Sun). A captivating collection of contemporary sculpture, paintings, photography and fountains fill this gallery and sculptural park, found 1 mile up Mountain Rd from Stowe village.

In the heart of the village, the **Helen Day Art Center** (☎ 802-253-8358; www.helenday.com; School St; ☾ noon-5pm Tue-Sun Jun–mid-Oct & Dec, noon-5pm Tue-Sat mid-Oct–Nov & Jan-May) is a gently provocative community art center with rotating traditional and avant-garde exhibits. It also sponsors 'Exposed,' an annual town-wide outdoor sculptural show that takes place from mid-July to mid-October.

Don't miss **Robert Paul Galleries** (☎ 800-873-3791; www.robertpaulgalleries.com; 394 Mountain Rd; ☻ 10am-6pm Mon-Sat, 10am-5pm Sun), with its absolutely stunning collection of paintings and sculptures.

Sleeping

Stowe has a wide variety of lodging, with dozens of inns, motels and B&Bs; many are along Mountain Rd. The **Stowe Area Association** (☎ 802-253-7321, 800-247-8693; www.gostowe.com) helps with reservations.

BUDGET

Inn at Turner Mill (☎ 802-253-2062, 800-992-0016; www.turnermill.com; 56 Turner Mill Lane; r $60-110) Hidden on 9 acres next to Notch Brook, this inn is just a sweet, 1-mile ski from Stowe's lifts. It's a rustic place with only two rooms, but it makes up for the quantity issue with the innkeepers' encyclopedic knowledge of the area's outdoor activities.

Fiddler's Green Inn (☎ 802-253-8124, 800-882-5346; www.fiddlersgreeninn.com; 4859 Mountain Rd; r $60-90) This 1820s farmhouse has rustic pine walls, a fieldstone fireplace and seven guest rooms geared to outdoor enthusiasts. Not surprisingly, guests congregate around the hearth; it's all quite homey.

Sun & Ski Inn (☎ 802-253-7159, 800-448-5223; www.stowesunandski.com; 1613 Mountain Rd; d $72-112; ☒) A nicely landscaped inn adjacent to the recreation path – the 25-room lodge has a hot tub and sauna.

Andersen Lodge (☎ 802-253-7336, 800-336-7336; www.andersenaustrianinn.com; 3430 Mountain Rd; r incl full breakfast $68-120; ☐ ☒) This Tyrolean-style inn with 17 rooms serves dinner in winter only. Amenities include tennis courts, sauna and Jacuzzi.

Smugglers Notch State Park (☎ 802-253-4014; www.vtstateparks.com; 6443 Mountain Rd; sites $14-21; ☻ late May–mid-Oct) This 35-acre park, 8 miles northwest of Stowe, is perched up on the mountainside. It has 81 tent and trailer sites and 20 lean-tos and walk-in sites. RV hookups are not available.

Little River State Park (☎ 802-244-7103; www.vtstateparks.com; Little River Rd, Waterbury; sites $16-23; ☻ late May–mid-Oct) Just north of I-89, this place has 81 campsites (including 20 lean-tos) next

to Waterbury Reservoir (sorry, there's no beach), on which you can canoe, kayak, fish and swim. Head 1.5 miles west of Waterbury on US 2, then 3.5 miles north on Little River Rd. RV hookups are not available.

MID-RANGE

Ski Inn (☎ 802-253-4050; www.ski-inn.com; 5037 Mountain Rd; r incl full breakfast & dinner in winter $110, incl continental breakfast in summer $55-65) This traditional inn opened in 1941 just after the first chairlift was built in the area. It features 10 clean and simple rooms (some with shared bathroom) and a homey common area. You can cross-country ski, hike and mountain bike right out the back door. Catch the Stowe Mountain shuttle at the end of the driveway and you can alpine and Nordic ski back to the inn at the end of the day. The Catamount Trail (p392) runs right through its 28-acre property.

Brass Lantern Inn B&B (☎ 802-253-2229, 800-729-2980; www.brasslanterninn.com; 71 Maple St/VT 100; r incl full breakfast $95-225) Just north of town, this beautifully renovated inn has nine spacious rooms, six with fireplaces and views of Mt Mansfield.

Hob Knob Inn (☎ 802-253-8549, 800-245-8540; www.hobknobinn.com; 2364 Mountain Rd; r incl breakfast $75-235; ☻ Jun-Aug & Dec-Apr) The 21 large rooms here (some with fireplace, some with efficiency kitchens) are set back from the road. The rustic cabin on a nearby knoll has a huge fieldstone fireplace.

Stowe Motel & Snowdrift (☎ 802-253-7629, 800-829-7629; www.stowemotel.com; 2043 Mountain Rd; r $79-134; ☐ ☒) In addition to 21 efficiencies, suites and houses, this motel's amenities include a tennis court and badminton and lawn games. You can also borrow bicycles to use on the recreation path.

Innsbruck Inn (☎ 802-253-8582, 800-225-8582; www.innsbruckinn.com; 4361 Mountain Rd; r incl breakfast $79-219 winter; ☐) A modern interpretation of a traditional Alpine inn, the 24 rooms and efficiencies here are comfy and well equipped. Inquire about the five-bedroom chalet.

TOP END

Topnotch at Stowe (☎ 802-253-8585, 800-451-8686; www.topnotchresort.com; 4000 Mountain Rd; r $230-345; ☐ ☒) Stowe's most lavish resort, with 92 rooms, really is top-notch. Amenities include a bar, fine dining, indoor and outdoor tennis courts, a skating rink and a touring center.

The spa is legendary, with a waterfall Jacuzzi and luxurious pampering services.

Stowehof Inn & Resort (☎ 802-253-9722, 800-932-7136; www.stowehofinn.com; 434 Edson Hill Rd; r incl full breakfast $103-445; ☒) In addition to a dramatic hillside location, this rustic 46-room inn has a very good dining room, sauna, Jacuzzi, outdoor hot tub, and 30 acres of hiking and cross-country ski trails.

Trapp Family Lodge (☎ 802-253-8511, 800-826-7000; www.trappfamily.com; 700 Trapp Hill Rd; r $198-505; ☐ ☒) Off Luce Hill Rd from Mountain Rd, with wide-open fields and mountain views – this is *the* spot for taking a twirl and pretending you're Julie Andrews. At the Austrian-style chalet, built by Maria von Trapp of *The Sound of Music* fame, there are 96 motel and lodge rooms, and time-share units. The 2700-acre spread offers excellent hiking, snowshoeing and cross-country skiing.

Arbor Inn (☎ 802-253-4772, 800-543-1293; www.arbor innstowe.com; 3214 Mountain Rd; r incl full breakfast $79-295; ☐ ☒) All 12 rooms here (some with full kitchens or Jacuzzis) enjoy excellent views of Mt Mansfield, which is only a 3-mile drive away.

Grey Fox Inn & Resort (☎ 800-544-8454; www .stowegreyfoxinn.com; 990 Mountain Rd; r $80-487; ☐ ☒) The Grey Fox has a good mix of old and new accommodations, the main offerings of which are located in a former ski lodge. Amenities include a fitness room, sauna, Jacuzzi and a bar, and a full breakfast is included at the attached Dutch Pancake Café (right).

Eating

As with any resort area, Stowe food can be expensive and the atmosphere predictable. However, there are some great finds here as well.

BUDGET

Stowe Coffee House (☎ 802-253-2189; 57B Mountain Rd; dishes $5-7; ☒ 8am-6pm) What's art without coffee? After a browse through the nearby art galleries, drop into this coffee house, which serves homemade baked goods specialty lattes. Lunch offerings include wraps, grilled sandwiches, homemade soups, pasta salads and quiches.

Harvest Market (☎ 802-253-3800; 1031 Mountain Rd; ☒ 7am-7pm) This one-stop gourmet purveyor dishes out cold mains by the pound, wonderful Vermont cheeses, wood-fired flatbreads, salads and sandwiches. Don't

even try to leave without something from its dessert section.

Dutch Pancake Café (☎ 802-253-8921; 900 Mountain Rd; dishes $6-10; ☒ 8am-12:30am) Located within the Grey Fox Inn, the Dutch owner here makes more than 75 kinds of *pannekoeken* (Dutch pancakes); some have a Southern American twist with sausage and gravy.

McCarthy's (☎ 802-253-8626; 454 Mountain Rd; dishes $3-7; ☒ 6:30am-2:30pm) Behind the Baggy Knees Shopping Center, McCarthy's draws locals who enjoy hearty breakfasts of French toast, apple pancakes with maple syrup and lots of omelettes.

Bagel (☎ 802-253-9943; 394 Mountain Rd, Baggy Knees Shopping Center; ☒ 6:30am-4:30pm) Grab a bite and a decent caffeine fix here on your way to the slopes.

Depot Street Malt Shoppe (☎ 802-253-4269; 57 Depot St; dishes $3-7; ☒ 11:30am-9pm) Burgers and old-fashioned ice-cream sodas reign at this fun, 1950s-themed restaurant.

MID-RANGE

Miguel's Stowe Away (☎ 800-245-1240, 802-253-7574; 3148 Mountain Rd; dishes $7-20; ☒ dinner) This Mexican farmhouse cantina became so popular that it launched its own line of chips and salsa that's sold around the country. You'll find Tex-Mex, gringo and creative Mexican dishes like salmon with a mango poblano sauce ($19).

Cactus Cafe (☎ 802-253-7770; 2160 Mountain Rd; dishes $12-19; ☒ dinner) If it weren't for the best margaritas in town, the salsa alone would be worth the trip: freshest ingredients, a tease of heat, and some of the most creative Mexican/Southwestern mains on which to slather it.

Pie in the Sky (☎ 802-253-5100; 492 Mountain Rd; dishes $7-17; ☒ lunch & dinner) This affordable eatery is a local favorite for pizza and pasta.

Gracie's Restaurant (☎ 802-253-8741; Main St; mains lunch $5-15, dinner $8-23; ☒ lunch & dinner) Behind Carlson Real Estate, Gracie's has dog-themed specialties, such as a Mexican plate called 'South of the Border Collie.' Or stick to big burgers, hand-cut steaks, Waldorf salad and garlic-laden shrimp scampi. Try its famous 'Doggie Bag' dessert: a white-chocolate bag filled with chocolate mousse and hot fudge.

Trattoria La Festa (☎ 802-253-8480; 4080 Mountain Rd; dishes $9-20; ☒ dinner Mon-Sat) Just north of Topnotch at Stowe, this trattoria has very good Italian fare made by Italian chefs. Check out its spaghetti pescatore, which is

VERMONT

chock-full of mussels, clams and shrimps for $18.50.

TOP END

Blue Moon Café (☎ 802-253-7006; 35 School St; mains $17-29; ☺ dinner daily Dec-Mar & May-Oct, dinner Fri-Sun Nov & Apr) In a converted house with a little sunporch, this intimate bistro is one of New England's top restaurants. Mains change weekly, but they're usually sublime. Look for Maine crabs, salmon dishes, oysters, rabbit and an extensive wine list.

Mr Pickwick's Pub & Restaurant (☎ 802-253-7064; 433 Mountain Rd; breakfast $5-15, lunch $15-25, dinner $17-25; ☺ 8am-midnight) Situated in Ye Olde England Inne, the respectfully teasing bartender at this pub and eatery keeps the crowd on high perk. An old-world feel is fully manifested, and this is the place to try ye olde bangers and mash or ostrich tenderloin. Otherwise, indulge in the Chef's Tasting Dinner (per person $60, reservations required).

Drinking

Charlie B's (☎ 802-253-7355; 1746 Mountain Rd; lunch $8-16, mains dinner $11-22; ☺ lunch & dinner) If you're searching for a standard après-ski scene with a bit more class, check out this place, at the Stoweflake Inn and Resort.

Shed (☎ 802-253-4364; 1859 Mountain Rd; ☺ lunch & dinner) This little microbrewery always has six fresh beers on tap and a crowd of locals tucking into pub fare.

Rusty Nail Bar & Grill (☎ 802-253-6245; www.rusty nailbar.com; 1190 Mountain Rd; lunch $7-8, mains dinner $11-19; ☺ lunch & dinner) You wondered where the wild things are? They're here, hanging around three bars, plenty of pool tables and a dancefloor, where they groove to live bands dishing everything from alt rock to jazz funk to calypso. The martini bar has some local renown. Oh yeah, there's food too, with an inventive menu.

Matterhorn (☎ 802-253-8198; 4969 Mountain Rd; cover free-$15; ☺ late daily Nov–mid-Apr, Thu-Sat mid-Apr-late Nov) At the top of Mountain Rd, this place is always hopping, beginning at 5pm when skiers start to hobble off the slopes. Bands play Friday and Saturday nights.

Getting There & Around

Vermont Transit (☎ 802-864-6811, 800-552-8737; www .vermonttransit.com) buses stop at Waterbury, 10 miles south of Stowe. There is one daily bus from Burlington to Waterbury ($8, 30 min-

utes). From Waterbury, you can call **Peg's Pick Up** (☎ 800-370-9490) for the short drive into Stowe ($20 per person).

The **Amtrak** (☎ 800-872-7245; www.amtrak.com) *Vermonter* train stops daily at Waterbury. Some hotels and inns will arrange to pick up guests at the station.

By car, it's 36 miles (45 minutes) to Burlington from Stowe; head south on VT 100, then north on I-89.

If you don't have your own vehicle, the Stowe Trolley runs every half-hour daily during ski season from Stowe village, along Mountain Rd, to the ski slopes. Pick up a schedule and list of stops at your inn or the Stowe Area Association's information office (p390).

BURLINGTON

pop 39,148

Vermont's largest city would be a small city in most other states, but Burlington's small size is one of its charms. With the University of Vermont (UVM) swelling the city by 13,400 students, and a vibrant cultural and social life, Burlington has a spirited, youthful character. And when it comes to nightlife, Burlington is Vermont's epicenter. Burlington is a smoke-free haven, with an ordinance that forbids smoking in public spaces, including accommodations.

The city's location adds to its charm. Perched on the shore of Lake Champlain, Burlington is less than an hour's drive from Stowe and other Green Mountain towns. In fact, Burlington can be used as a base for exploring much of northwestern Vermont, where each season brings its own festivals and events (see p531).

Orientation

Take I-89 exit 14 to reach the city center; or take exit 13 to I-89 west to head for Shelburne and the motel strip that runs along US 7, south of Burlington. Downtown Burlington is easily negotiated on foot. Parking is usually not a big problem. The heart of the city is the Church St Marketplace and the adjacent pedestrian mall, where an amble is always a pleasure and often a wonderful surprise. Five blocks west along College St is the city's nice Waterfront Park and recreation path.

For information on getting to/from the airport, see p404.

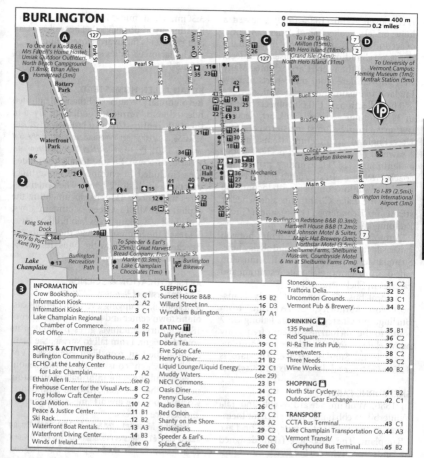

BURLINGTON

Information

Crow Bookshop (☎ 802-862-0848; www.crowbooks
.com; 14 Church St; ☺ 10am-9pm Mon-Wed, 10am-10pm
Thu-Sat, 11am-6pm Sun) A great source of used, new,
remaindered and out-of-print books. It's nicely arranged,
with many temptations.

Information kiosks (802-434-4569; www.bluemap.com;
at the lake end of College St & on Church St; ☺ 10am-5pm
mid-Jun–late Aug, 10am-5pm Sat & Sun mid-May–mid-Jun
& late Aug–mid-Oct)

Lake Champlain Regional Chamber of Commerce
Main St (☎ 802-863-3489; 60 Main St; ☺ 8:30am-5pm
Mon-Fri, 10am-6pm Sat, 10am-5pm Sun late May-early Sep,
longer hrs in summer & fall) Airport (☺ 9am-midnight) Although staff at the Main St branch provide information, they
seem to prefer that you pick up brochures at the rest stop just
north of the Williston exit on I-89, or at its airport location.

Seven Days (www.sevendaysvt.com) One of the best
resources for getting a comprehensive idea of what's going
on in Stowe. This hip, free tabloid is found in stacks just
about everywhere around town.

Sights
SHELBURNE MUSEUM

This extraordinary **museum** (☎ 802-985-3346;
www.shelburnemuseum.org; US 7; adult/child 5 & under/
child 6-14 $18/free/9; ☺ 10am-5pm early May-late Oct), 9
miles south of Burlington off US 7, occupies
45 acres near the former Vanderbilt/Webb
estate. HO and Louisine Havemeyer were patrons of the arts and collectors of European
and old masters paintings. Their daughter
Electra's interests, however, tended toward
the more vernacular and utilitarian. Electra

Havemeyer Webb (1888–1960) amassed a huge, priceless collection of American works of art and craft that she put on display in the numerous buildings of the museum. Indeed, the buildings themselves are exhibits. Many were moved here from other parts of New England to ensure their preservation.

The collections – 150,000 objects housed in 39 buildings – include folk art, decorative arts, Impressionist masterpieces and New England architecture. Items include a sawmill (1786), a covered bridge (1845), a lighthouse (1871), a luxury private rail coach (1890), a classic round barn (1901), a railroad station complete with locomotive (1915), the Lake Champlain side-wheeler steamship *Ticonderoga* (1906), and a Circus Building and 1920s carousel.

A minimal visit takes three hours, but you can easily (and pleasantly) spend all day here. Sustenance is available from the museum café or from a more elaborate restaurant and eateries in Shelburne village.

A local bus (Chittenden County Transportation Authority; CCTA) runs from Burlington's Cherry St terminal along US 7 south to the Shelburne Museum frequently on weekdays and four times on Saturday. There is no Sunday service. The fare is $1/50¢/50¢ per adult/child six to 18/senior.

SHELBURNE FARMS

In 1886, William Seward Webb and Lila Vanderbilt Webb built a little place for themselves in the Vermont countryside on Lake Champlain. The 1400-acre farm, designed by landscape architect Frederick Law Olmsted (who also designed New York's Central Park and Boston's Emerald Necklace), was both a country house for the Webbs and a working farm. The grand, 24-bedroom English-style country manor (completed in 1899), now an inn (p401), is surrounded by working farm buildings inspired by European romanticism.

Today, you can tour **Shelburne Farms** (☎ 802-985-8686, 802-985-8442; www.shelburnefarms.org; off US 7; adult/child 3-17/senior $6/4/5; ⊙ cheesemaking, tours, inn & farmyard 9am-5:30pm mid-May–mid-Oct, walking trails only 10am-5pm mid-Oct–mid-May) and buy some of the cheese, maple syrup, mustard and other items produced here. You can also hike the walking trails and visit the animals in the children's farmyard. The guided 1½-hour tours begin at 9:30am, 11:30am, 1:30pm and 3:30pm from mid-May through October (costing an additional $3). The walking trail and children's farmyard close at 4pm.

The farm is 8 miles south of Burlington, off US 7.

ETHAN ALLEN HOMESTEAD

Revolutionary War hero Ethan Allen, often referred to as 'Vermont's godfather,' lived in this 18th-century Colonial **homestead** (☎ 802-865-4556; www.ethanallenhomestead.org; adult/child/senior/family $5/3/4/15; ⊙ 1-5pm daily May, 10am-5pm Mon-Sat & 1-5pm Sun rest of year). Be sure to take the guided tour (included in entrance fee; tour times vary) into the historic house. The center features multimedia exhibits documenting the exploits of Allen's Green Mountain Boys, and also has walking trails behind the house. To reach the homestead, take the North Ave Beaches exit and follow the signs. It's 1 mile north of Burlington on VT 127.

ARTS, EDUCATION & SCIENCE

The **University of Vermont** (UVM; ☎ 802-656-3131; www.uvm.edu), occupying a verdant campus east of the town center and featuring a number of 18th-century buildings, gives Burlington its youthful vigor. From fall to spring, the main event at the Guterson Field House is UVM hockey, which consistently draws sellout crowds; call ahead for information on getting tickets to these thrillers. Also on campus and worth a look-see are art museums, theaters and science centers.

Fleming Museum (☎ 802-656-2090; www.fleming museum.org; 61 Colchester Ave; adult/child 6 & over & senior $5/3; ⊙ noon-4pm Tue-Fri & 1-5pm Sat & Sun May-Aug, 9am-4pm Tue-Fri & 1-5pm Sat & Sun Sep-Jun), at the UVM, has an collection consisting of more than 17,000 disparate objects, including African masks, Indian drums, samurai armor, an Egyptian mummy and Vermont paintings.

Burlington City Arts (BCA; ☎ 802-865-7166; www.burlingtoncityarts.com), a local arts organization, mounts arts installations and runs classes, workshops, studios and programs.

Under the auspices of BCA, **Firehouse Center for the Visual Arts** (☎ 802-865-7165; 135 Church St; ⊙ noon-5pm Sun-Thu & noon-8pm Fri & Sat May-late Oct, noon-5pm Tue-Sun late Oct-Apr) is an exciting locus for art exhibits, classes and discussions. Ongoing open studios involve the community with an artist in residence. A community darkroom has open studio hours, classes and discussions.

An excellent contemporary and traditional craft center, **Frog Hollow Craft Center** (☎ 802-863-6458; www.froghollow.org; 85 Church St; admission free; ⊗ 10am-6pm Mon-Sat, noon-5pm Sun) feels more like a museum gallery than the retail store that it is. A rigorous jury process screens artisans for acceptance.

The colorful past, present and future of Lake Champlain is explored at the lively **ECHO at the Leahy Center for Lane Champlain** (☎ 802-864-1848; www.echovermont.org; College St; adult/child 3-17/senior $9/6/8; ⊗ 10am-5pm Fri-Wed, 10am-8pm Thu), perched on the edge of the lake. A multitude of aquariums wiggle with life and many exhibits invite inquisitive minds and hands to splash, poke, click, listen and crawl.

SUDS & SWEETS
Learn about the history of microbrews in general, and Magic Hat specifically, on this fun, free, 20-minute **Magic Hat Brewery Artifactory Tour** (☎ 802-658-2739; www.magichat.net; Bartlett Bay Rd; ⊗ tours hourly 3-5pm Wed-Fri, noon-3pm Sat late May-early Sep, no tour Wed Jun-early Sep). Afterwards, you can sample four of 16 beers on tap.

The aroma of rich chocolate is intoxicating as you make your way past the gift shop (if you can) to the glass wall overlooking the small factory of **Lake Champlain Chocolates** (☎ 802-864-1807; www.lakechamplainchocolates.com; 750 Pine St; ⊗ 9am-6pm Mon-Sat, noon-5pm Sun, tours hourly 9am-2pm Mon-Fri). This is where you'll learn all about this company's chocolates. No, you can't run through the chocolate waterfall, but you'll probably savor some samples during one of the tour's several taste tests. The café serves coffee drinks and its own luscious ice-cream.

PEACE & JUSTICE CENTER
Head to Burlington's **Peace & Justice Center** (☎ 802-863-8326; www.pjcvt.org; 21 Church St; ⊗ 10am-6pm Mon-Thu, 10am-8pm Fri & Sat, noon-6pm Sun) for good leftist reading, stickers, products of peace and support. The center is dedicated to community building, inclusion, tolerance and justice.

Activities
See p404 for details of local shops supplying gear for outdoor activities.

WALKING & CYCLING
The **Burlington Recreation Path**, a popular 7.5-mile route for walking, biking, in-line skating and general perambulating, runs along the waterfront through the Waterfront Park and Promenade. Rent bikes at **Ski Rack** (☎ 802-658-3313; www.skirack.com; 85 Main St; bike rental per hr/4 hrs/24 hrs $10/16/22; ⊗ May-Nov). You can also rent in-line skates, roller-skis, tandems, trailer bikes, snowshoes and skis (of course). Catch Tour de France action here on a big-screen TV.

Another spot to rent bikes is **North Star Cyclery** (☎ 802-863-3832; www.northstarsports.net; 100 Main St; bike rental per hr/4 hrs/8 hrs $12/18/24; ⊗ bikes available mid-May–mid-Nov).

Local Motion (☎ 802-652-2453; www.localmotion.org; 1 Steele St; bike rentals per 4/24hrs $18/24; ⊗ 10am-6pm mid-May–mid-Oct), a nonprofit group located at the trailside center, is spearheading an effort to link Burlington to Montreal via Burlington's own Island Line Trail and Canada's Route Verte. Its outpost offers bike rentals, maps, gifts, tours and refreshments. The 13-mile Island Line Trail combines with the waterfront bike path, beginning just south of the Burlington Boathouse and ending on the narrow Colchester causeway that juts 5 miles out into the lake.

BOATING
Approximately 120 miles long and 12 miles wide, **Lake Champlain** is the largest freshwater lake in the country after the Great Lakes. Consistently good wind, sheltered bays, hundreds of islands and scenic anchorages combine to make this immense lake one of the top cruising grounds in the northeast.

You can charter boats of 28ft to 41ft from **Winds of Ireland** (☎ 802-863-5090, 800-458-9301; www.windsofireland.net; Burlington Boathouse, College St; ⊗ late May-early Sept; trips at 11:30, 2:30 and sunset) for anywhere from a half-day to a week. For a two-hour private sail with a captain, for you and five of your closest friends, the price is $210.

Rent all manner of boats at **Waterfront Boat Rentals** (☎ 802-864-4858, 877-964-4858; www.waterfrontboatrentals.com; Perkins Pier; ⊗ 10am-dusk May-Oct) by the one/four/eight hours: canoes cost $15/30/45, kayaks $10/25/35, rowboats $10/25 and whalers $60/150/225. Skiffs ($22 to $225) are priced depending on the size and horsepower as well as the rental duration.

Umiak Outdoor Outfitters (☎ 802-865-6777; www.umiak.com; North Beach, Institute Rd; kayak hire per hr/4 hrs/8 hrs $12/24/32; ⊗ 11am-6pm Jun-late Aug) Interested in river trips, tours, camps and instructional classes? Or how about double kayaks and canoes? These folks can fulfill all these needs; for the rest you're on your own.

Burlington Community Boathouse (☎ 802-865-3377; www.enjoyburlington.com; at the foot of College St; ⊙ mid-May–mid-Oct) Fashioned after Burlington's original 1900's yacht club, this popular hangout is the where hourly and daily boat cruises depart, and where boat rentals set off from. Traveling with your own yacht? Transient dock space is available. The boathouse is easy to spot, located as it is on the waterfront's 8-mile recreational path adjacent to the Waterfront Park and Promenade.

Lake Champlain Paddlers' Trail (☎ 802-658-1414; www.lakechamplaincommittee.org) There's no finer way to enjoy the mammoth Lake Champlain than to set out on a multiday paddling trip. Paddlers are encouraged to join the Lake Champlain Committee ($40 per year), for which they receive an essential guidebook that details the trails, campsites and rules of the nautical road.

DIVING
Ever since the 18th-century French and Indian War, 120-mile-long Lake Champlain has been a major thoroughfare from the St Lawrence Seaway to the Hudson River. During the Revolutionary War and the War of 1812, numerous historic battles were fought on the lake to control this navigational stronghold. In the latter half of the 19th century, commercial vessels replaced gunboats. Many of these military and merchant ships sank to the lake's deep, dark bottom as a result of a cannonball or temperamental weather.

The misfortunes of these vessels make lucky finds for scuba divers. Two hundred wrecks have already been discovered, including the 54ft Revolutionary War boat *Philadelphia*, pulled from the waters in 1935 (and now sitting in the Smithsonian Institution in Washington, DC). Unfortunately, many of the earlier wrecks are far too deep for scuba divers, but six of the commercial vessels that lie on the lake's floor have been preserved by the state of Vermont as an underwater historical site.

All divers must obtain a free permit, available at the Burlington Boathouse (see above) with limited permits available on first-come basis.

Waterfront Diving Center (☎ 802-865-2771, 800-238-7282; www.waterfrontdiving.com; 214 Battery St; ⊙ 9am-6pm Mon-Fri & 9am-5pm Sat mid-Oct–early May,

9am-6:30pm Mon-Fri & 8:30am-5:30pm Sat & Sun early May–mid-Oct) offers rentals, charters, instruction and a full line of snorkeling, swimming, scuba and underwater photography gear.

Tours
In addition to lunch and dinner cruises, the **Spirit of Ethan Allen II** (☎ 802-862-8300; www.soea.com; Burlington Boathouse, College St; ⊙ mid-May–mid-Oct) plies the lake with a 1½-hour, scenic, narrated day cruise (adult/child $12/6), and a 2½-hour sunset cruise (adult/child $17/13) at 6:30pm.

Festivals & Events
On the first Friday of each month, year-round, there's the **First Friday ArtWalk** in town. In early April, nearby St Albans hosts the **Vermont Maple Festival**. In late May, the state's proud dairy heritage is celebrated at the **Vermont Dairy Festival**, held in nearby Enosburg Falls. In late August and early September, the week-long **Champlain Valley Fair** dominates nearby Essex. Early October brings the annual **Applefest** to South Hero.

In Burlington proper, look for the **Discover Jazz Festival** in June; a patriotic civic celebration on the **Fourth of July**; the **Champlain Shakespeare Festival** from July through August; and a very big and festive **First Night** celebration – a winter festival featuring a parade, an ice- and snow-sculpture exhibition, music and more – on December 31. Contact the chamber of commerce (p397) for details.

Sleeping
Burlington's budget and mid-range motels are on the outskirts of town. It's not usually necessary to reserve in advance, but if you call ahead on the day you intend to stay and ask for the 'same-day rate,' you may get a discount. Many of the chain motels lie on Williston Rd east of I-89 exit 14; another cluster is along US 7 north of Burlington in Colchester (take I-89 exit 16). Perhaps the best selection, though, is along Shelburne Rd (US 7) in south Burlington.

BUDGET
Northstar Motel (☎ 802-863-3421; 2427 Shelburne Rd; r incl continental breakfast $30-70) These plain, tidy rooms (32 in all) are neat as a pin and the staff is wonderful. The very nice continental breakfast is served in a comfortable, sunny common area.

Hartwell House B&B (☎ 802-658-9242; www.ver montbedandbreakfast.com; 170 Ferguson Ave; r incl continental breakfast $55-70; 🖳 🖳) In a quiet residential neighborhood just a five-minute drive from the center of town, innkeeper Linda Hartwell offers two clean rooms (with shared bathroom) in her welcoming home. She'll even pick up folks from the bus and train stations, by arrangement.

Countryside Motel (☎ 802-985-2839; 6475 Shelburne Rd; r $55-125; 🖳) This 12-room place is just south of the museum, on spacious grounds. It's nice to eat its free continental breakfast (only available May to October) under the shade trees out back.

Mrs Farrell's Home Hostel (☎ 802-865-3730; www .hiayh.org; dm $17.50, private r $40; 🕑 Apr–Oct) This six-bed hostel is about 3 miles from town and is quiet and tidy. Reservations are essential. Reserve at least 24 hours in advance (calls are taken between 4pm and 6pm) and then arrive by 5pm. Host Nancy Farrell will give you directions to the hostel when you call.

North Beach Campground (☎ 802-862-0942, 800-571-1198; 60 Institute Rd; sites with/without hookups $30/20; 🕑 May–mid-Oct) This great place should be the first choice for tent campers. Right on Lake Champlain, it has 67 tent sites and 69 RV sites with hookups on 45 acres of woods and beach near the city center. To find it, get to Burlington's waterfront, then head north along Battery St and North Ave/VT 127, turning left on Institute Rd.

MID-RANGE

Willard Street Inn (☎ 802-651-8710, 800-577-8712; www.willardstreetinn.com; 349 S Willard St; r incl full breakfast $125-225, ste $225) Perched on a hill within easy walking distance of UVM and the Church St Marketplace, this Queen Anne–style mansion was built in the late 1880s. It has a fine-wood and cut-glass elegance, yet emanates a welcoming warmth. Many of the 14 guest rooms overlook Lake Champlain. The sublime breakfasts might include cranberry-walnut French toast.

Sunset House B&B (☎ 802-864-3790; www.sunset housebb.com; 78 Main St; r $89-129) This nicely restored 1854 Queen Anne–style house is right near the downtown's heart. Almost hostellike with shared bathrooms and a common kitchen, the guest rooms and the continental breakfast are quite lovely.

Burlington Redstone B&B (☎ 802-862-0508; www .burlingtonredstone.com; 497 S Willard St; r incl full breakfast

$145-185) This wonderful old stone house is owned by an avid gardener and you can stroll through her lakeside perennial patches set on a hill. All rooms (actually suites) boast lake views you'll never tire of.

One of a Kind B&B (☎ 802-862-5576, 877-479-2736; www.oneofakindbnb.com; 53 Lakeview Tce; r shared bathroom $90, ste with private bathroom $120) Located in a quiet neighborhood, this sweet, peaceful and creatively renovated 1910 house overlooks Lake Champlain and the Adirondacks. Carry your generous breakfast into the backyard and watch the ever-changing lake. Maggie, the innkeeper, is a font of local information, particularly of the arts scene.

Howard Johnson Motel & Suites (☎ 802-860-6000, 800-874-1554; 1720 Shelburne Rd; r incl continental breakfast $59-149; 🖳) A step up in comfort from other Shelburne Rd motels, this 121-room establishment also has a Jacuzzi, sauna and a free airport shuttle.

TOP END

Inn at Shelburne Farms (☎ 802-985-8498; www.shel burnefarms.org; 1611 Harbor Rd; r with shared bathroom $100-190, with private bathroom $210-385; 🕑 mid-May–mid-Oct) This farm is arguably one of the top 10 places to stay in New England. The inn, 8 miles south of Burlington off US 7, was once the summer mansion of the wealthy Webb family. You can play billiards in its game room or read leather-bound books from its library, or you can just relax in one of the common areas, complete with elegant, original furnishings from this gracious, welcoming country manor. If you're feeling more energetic, the hiking trails (p398) are a not-to-be-missed highlight. The 24 guest rooms vary in size and appointments, which is reflected in the rates.

Wyndham Burlington (☎ 802-658-6500, 800-996-3426; www.wyndham.com; 60 Battery St; r $119-289; 🖳 🖳) This 256-room, business-class hotel offers just what you'd expect for this price: upscale rooms, a workout facility and executive suites with a whole host of other amenities. An on-site café and bistro offer meals throughout the day.

Eating

Most eateries and restaurants are in and near the Church St Marketplace. But if you explore just a little bit further out, your taste buds will be richly rewarded.

BUDGET

Great Harvest Bread Company (☎ 802-660-2733; 382 Pine St; sandwiches $3.50-4.50; ⏰ 7am-6pm Mon-Fri, 8am-5pm Sat) A soft, yeasty scent will surround you and an array of samples will tempt you the minute you enter this sunny, airy, baking paradise. The monthly bread specialties are always imaginative. Great Harvest mills its own flour and offers a delectable variety of grilled paninis.

Radio Bean (☎ 802-660-9346; 8 N Winooski Ave; ⏰ 8am-midnight) This is the social hub for the arts and music scene. A new, low-power FM radio station (105.9) beams over the airwaves from this Dutch-style coffeehouse. Espressos, beer and wine keep things jumping, and grilled sandwiches and baked goods feed the soul ($2 to $6). Live performances nightly include jazz, acoustic music and poetry readings.

Penny Cluse (☎ 802-651-8834; 169 Cherry St; dishes $1-10; ⏰ 6:45am-3pm Mon-Fri, 8am-3pm Sat & Sun) In the original home of Ben & Jerry's ice-cream, Penny Cluse serves one of the best breakfasts in town, including Southwestern selections like breakfast burritos ($6.75). Indeed, local chefs rave about the innovative morning meals served here.

Dobra Tea (☎ 802-951-2424; 80 Church St; dishes $3-7; ⏰ 11am-10pm Mon-Thu, 11am-11pm Fri & Sat, noon-10pm Sun) This Czech-owned tearoom offers about 50 varieties, some seasonal, all hand-selected directly from their regions of origin. The fascinating, sometimes hair-raising, journey of the founder is revealed in the thick menu of teas and light bites. Sit at a table, an up-ended tea box, or on cushions around a small, low pedestal. This quiet, worldly oasis is well worth a visit.

Stonesoup (☎ 802-862-7616; 211 College St; dishes $3-7; ⏰ 7am-7pm Mon & Sat, 7am-9pm Tue-Fri) Stonesoup is a big lunchtime hit with local vegetarians. Homemade soups (about $3), the salad bar and sandwiches with home-baked bread (about $6.50 per pound) are quite popular.

Red Onion (☎ 802-865-2563; 140-1/2 Church St; dishes $3-7; ⏰ 7:30am-8pm Mon-Fri, 10am-8pm Sat, 11am-8pm Sun) Expect lines at lunch, even in the blustery days of winter, at this popular spot offering deeply gorgeous baked goods. Tempting specials include the Red Onion sandwich: turkey, sun-dried tomato mayo, green apples, red onion, smoked Gruyère and bacon.

Muddy Waters (☎ 802-658-0466; 184 Main St; dishes $3-6; ⏰ 7:30am-6pm Mon, 7:30am-midnight Tue-Sat, 10am-10pm Sun) Finally, someone has thought to add beer to the offerings of an earthy java/hangout space. Besides serving all kinds of coffee, Muddy Waters offers juice concoctions, light eats (soup, chili, lasagna, hummus and veggies, and baked goodies), Guinness and a couple of McNeill's brews (from Brattleboro – see p360), so you can enjoy a pint in the cool glow of your laptop (bedecked with a 'Stop bitching, start a revolution' sticker, of course) as you write your novel.

Fresh Market (☎ 802-863-3968; 400 Pine St; sandwiches $5.50; ⏰ 7am-7pm Mon-Sat, 10am-5pm Sun) Come here for an amazing cheese selection, 21 flavors of olives, and beautifully prepared foods such as enormous sandwiches, sushi, pies and salads. The bakery offers all manner of delectables and plenty of tables for relaxing while you're noshing. This mid-sized, bustling health-food grocer offers a tiny produce department and gourmet items, making it the place to stock up for a picnic or a gourmet feast.

Oasis Diner (☎ 802-864-5308; 189 Bank St; dishes $2.50-8; ⏰ 6am-2pm) Just off Church St, this old-time stainless steel diner, where everyone is called 'honey,' has an equally old-time feel and serves cheap meals. When Bill Clinton once ducked through the doorway (literally), he chowed down on a turkey sandwich and a piece of apple pie.

Uncommon Grounds (☎ 802-865-6227; 42 Church St; dishes $2-5; ⏰ 7am-10pm Mon-Thu, 8am-11pm Fri & Sat, 9am-9pm Sun) Take your newspaper, order a cup o' joe and a muffin, grab a sidewalk table and people-watch in good weather. And muse about how good life is.

Liquid Lounge/Liquid Energy (☎ 802-860-7666; 57 Church St; drinks $3-6; ⏰ 9am-6pm; 🖥) By day order wheatgrass concoctions, veggie tonics and other enhanced nutritional drinks, and enjoy them in front of TVs, DSL Internet stations or your own wireless gizmo. Undo all that healthy stuff with beer or wine at night.

Speeder & Earl's (dishes $1-3; ⏰ 8am-5 or 6pm) Church St (☎ 802-860-6630; 104 Church St) Pine St (☎ 802-658-6016; 412 Pine St) Both locations serve up a good cup of coffee, and each is fiercely proud of its own espresso blend – you decide which is better.

Henry's Diner (☎ 802-862-9010; 115 Bank St; dishes under $8; ⏰ 6am-6pm Mon-Fri, 6am-4pm Sat & Sun) A Burlington fixture since 1925, this diner has daily specials for around $5. The food is simple (you can get breakfast all day), the atmosphere homey and pleasant, the prices unbeatable.

MID-RANGE

Vermont Pub & Brewery (☎ 802-865-0500; 144 College St; dishes $5-14; ⏰ 11:30am-2am) This pub's specialty and seasonal brews are made on the premises. Try the Burly Irish Ale, Dogbite Bitter and Vermont Smoked Porter. There's plenty of British pub fare to accompany the pints. Give the cock-a-leekie pie ($6) a try.

Daily Planet (☎ 802-862-9647; 15 Center St; mains $11-20; ⏰ 4-10pm) Popular with locals, Daily Planet serves creative dishes like potato-crusted salmon with Moroccan vegetable sauté, or Thai shrimp salad, in a relaxed and inviting atmosphere.

NECI Commons (☎ 802-862-6324; 25 Church St; lunch $7-11, mains dinner $13-20; ⏰ lunch & dinner daily, brunch Sun) Operated by Montpelier's New England Culinary Institute (p389) students, you can expect dishes such as rotisserie chicken, roasted turkey breast and sea bass. They're all served at a long, welcoming wooden counter, a bar, banquettes, booths and quiet tables. Stop by for gourmet lunchtime picnic fare. A lighter bistro menu is also available (2pm to 4pm weekdays).

Five Spice Cafe (☎ 802-864-4045; 175 Church St; lunch $8-9.50, mains dinner $13-17; ⏰ lunch & dinner) This café is incredibly popular for Sunday dim sum brunches (served Sunday from 11am to 2:30pm, for $2 to $3 per dish), but it'll be worth the wait. The café also serves excellent dishes from China, India, Indonesia, Thailand and Vietnam.

Sweetwaters (☎ 802-864-9800; 120 Church St; mains $7-18; ⏰ lunch & dinner) Drenched in heavily nouveau-Victorian decor, this local watering hole attracts the young and upwardly mobile. In the evening the glass-enclosed patio is loud with chatter and redolent of nachos and chicken wings; the beverage of choice is an exotic beer.

TOP END

Smokejacks (☎ 802-658-1119; 156 Church St; lunch $4-15, mains dinner $15-24; ⏰ lunch & dinner) Known for fresh fish and specialties like smoked Long Island duck breast. The locally famous cheese list features some of America's finest small-farm cheeses.

Shanty on the Shore (☎ 802-864-0238; 181 Battery St; lunch $6-10, mains dinner $11-23; ⏰ lunch & dinner) Facing the car ferry dock and with fine lake views, this combo seafood market and eatery serves lobster, fish and shellfish. The outdoor deck is wonderful in the summer (smoking is permitted here).

Trattoria Delia (☎ 802-864-5253; 152 St Paul St; mains $12-26; ⏰ dinner) Burlington's top Italian restaurant serves homemade pastas and specialties like osso bucco ($17.50) and couples them with an award-winning wine list.

Drinking

The local Burlington Free Press carries a special weekend entertainment section in its Thursday issue, and the free, energetic tabloid Seven Days tells all with a sly dash of attitude. Otherwise, head to the center of Burlington nightlife, Church St Marketplace, thick with restaurants and sidewalk cafés.

Red Square (☎ 802-859-8909; 136 Church St; ⏰ 4pm-2am Mon-Fri, 5pm-2am Sat & Sun) With a stylish Soho-like ambience, Red Square is where knowledgeable Vermonters go to sip martinis or wine, munch on good bar food (including sandwiches) and listen to Burlington's best roadhouse music.

Daily Planet (☎ 802-862-9647; 15 Center St; ⏰ 4-10pm) This welcoming place is where young, hip and alternative-lifestyle types come for a drink. It also serves up creative food (see left).

Wine Works (☎ 802-951-9463; www.wineworks.net; 133 St Paul St; ⏰ from 4:30pm Tue-Sat) You've heard of wines by the glass? Well, these folks also offer wines by the ounce, all the better for teaching your palate a lesson. It's a mod place. Small bites of New England delicacies (like scallops wrapped in bacon, and mini crab cakes) complement its wines.

Three Needs (☎ 802-658-0889; 207 College St; ⏰ 4pm-2am) This pleasant microbrewery wins awards year after year for its brews.

Sweetwaters (☎ 802-864-9800; 120 Church St; ⏰ 11:30am-1am Mon-Sat, 10:30am-11pm Sun) Thirty-somethings who've 'made it' (or hope they have) head here after work, though the action doesn't really pick up until after 9:30pm.

Ri-Ra The Irish Pub (☎ 802-860-9401; 123 Church St; ⏰ 11:30am-2am) This Irish pub was restored in Ireland, dismantled and shipped to the States, so it really does have an authentic feel. Order a pint of Guinness or a dram of uisce beatha (Irish whiskey). Check out folk music on Wednesday and Sunday, a DJ on Friday and bands on Saturday night.

135 Pearl (☎ 802-863-2343; www.135pearl.com; 135 Pearl St; 🕙 7:30pm-2am Mon-Thu, 5pm-2am Fri & Sat) This mixed club has been the hub of Vermont's gay, lesbian, bisexual and transgender scene since the mid-1990s. Not segregated in the least, the club has a cosmopolitan feel because of its proximity to Montreal (only 1¼ hours north). Thursday through Saturday features dancing and a DJ; Wednesday is karaoke night. Otherwise, there's a mixed schedule of cabaret, live music, theater, poetry and art shows. Check it out.

Shopping

Outdoor Gear Exchange (☎ 802-860-0190, 888-547-4327; www.gearx.com; 152 Cherry St) This place rivals major outdoor gear chains for breadth of selection, and definitely trumps them on price for a vast array of used, closeout (clearance), and even new gear and clothing. You name the outdoor pursuit and staff can probably outfit you. Dogs run freely in the aisles, underscoring the fun, relaxed atmosphere, but they must be leashed.

North Star Cyclery (☎ 802-863-3832; www.north starsports.net; 100 Main St; 🕙 10am-6pm Mon-Sat, noon-5pm Sun, slightly longer hrs in the summer) Head to this friendly, laid-back local favorite for an unusually complete selection of clothing, gear and bikes specifically designed for women. Don't worry, guys; there's plenty here for you too. For winter fun, it offers Nordic skis, snowshoes and outerwear.

Getting There & Away

A number of national carriers serve Burlington International Airport, 3 miles east of the city center. You'll find major car-rental companies at the airport.

Vermont Transit (☎ 802-864-6811, 800-552-8737; www.vermonttransit.com), based in Burlington, provides bus service to major Vermont towns, as well as to Manchester and Keene, NH; Albany, New York; and Boston, MA. The **main terminal** (☎ 802-864-6811; 345 Pine St) also serves **Greyhound** (☎ 800-231-2222; www.greyhound.com), which operates buses daily between Burlington and Montreal (one-way $27.50, about 1¼ hours).

The **Amtrak** (☎ 800-872-7245; www.amtrak.com) *Vermonter* train stops in Essex Junction, 5 miles from Burlington. The station is served by local **CCTA buses** (☎ 802-864-2282; www.cctaride.org).

By car, it takes 4½ hours (230 miles) to reach Burlington from Boston; take I-93 to I-89. It's another 1¼ hours (102 miles) from Burlington to Montreal.

Lake Champlain Transportation Co (☎ 802-864-9804; www.ferries.com; King St Dock) runs car ferries connecting Burlington with Port Kent, New York, at least nine times daily from late May to mid-October; there's no service off-season. The one-way voyage takes one hour and 10 minutes and costs $13.25 for a car and driver, and $3.75/1.50 for each additional adult/child aged six to 12.

The company also operates ferries connecting Charlotte, Vermont, with Essex, New York (south of Burlington), for as long as the lake stays unfrozen; and 24-hour, year-round service from Grand Isle, VT (north of Burlington), to Plattsburgh, New York.

Getting Around

Chittenden County Transportation Authority (CCTA; ☎ 802-864-2282; www.cctaride.org) operates buses from its Cherry St terminal to Burlington International Airport. Buses depart Cherry St every half-hour or so, less often on Sunday. There are no services on major holidays. Fares to the airport and around town are $1/50¢ adult/senior and child ages six to 18.

A free College St shuttle bus runs a loop route from the Waterfront Park near the Burlington Boathouse, stopping at Battery St, St Paul St, Church St Marketplace, Winooski Ave, Union St and Willard St, ending at the UVM campus. In summer, shuttle buses run every 10 minutes from 11am to 6pm.

NORTHEAST KINGDOM

Speaking to a small group of constituents in Lyndonville, VT, in 1949, Senator George Aiken noted that 'this is such beautiful country up here. It ought to be called the Northeast Kingdom of Vermont.' The locals took the wise senator's advice. The Northeast Kingdom now consists of a large tract of land wedged between the Québec and NH borders. In a state known for its rural setting (only Wyoming and Alaska contain fewer people), the Kingdom is Vermont's equivalent to putting on its finest pastoral dress, with a few holes here and there. Wave after wave of unspoiled hillside form a vast sea of green, and small villages and farms spread out in the distance under a few soaring summits. Here, inconspicuous inns and

DETOUR: LAKE CHAMPLAIN ISLANDS

For a nice day trip from Burlington, head north on I-89 to US 2 to North and South Hero Islands, connected to the mainland via a causeway road. These unspoiled rural islands, with sweeping water views, are populated year-round by a mere 6500 hearty souls. The flat, relatively untrafficked lanes of the islands are perfect for cycling, and the lake is great for swimming and boating.

The **Champlain Islands Chamber of Commerce** (☎ 802-372-5683, 800-262-5226; www.champlain islands.com; VT 2, North Hero; ✆ 8am-5pm Mon-Fri & 10am-2pm Sat & Sun Jun-Aug, 9am-4pm Mon-Fri Sep-May) maintains an office next to Hero's Welcome General Store and has detailed information. For overnights, the chamber can direct you to a dozen secluded area B&Bs and cabins, each with only a couple of rooms to rent.

Sights & Activities

Hero's Welcome General Store (☎ 802-372-4161; www.heroswelcome.com; US 2, North Hero; ✆ 6:30am-8pm May–mid-Oct, 6:30am-6pm mid-Oct–Apr) rents bikes, kayaks and canoes (late May–mid-Oct), while the **North Hero Marina** (☎ 802-372-5953; www.northhero.com; ✆ seasonal) rents power boats, canoes, kayaks and sailboats, and **South Hero's Apple Island Resort** (☎ 802-372-3922; www.appleisland resort.com; ✆ seasonal) rents sailboats.

Alburg Dunes State Park (☎ 802-796-4170; www.vtstateparks.com; Alburg) has a sandy beach that's great for sunning and swimming (day use only).

Knight Point State Park (☎ 802-372-8389; US 2), on the southern tip of North Hero, offers the best swimming for families, and is also the summer home (July and August) of Herrmann's Royal Lipizzan Stallions. You can visit these gorgeous dancers here from 10am to dusk.

While you're in the area, check out the **Isle La Motte Reef** (☎ 802-928-3364; Fisk Quarry, West Shore Rd), 4 miles south of the shrine. At 480 million years of age, it's the oldest known fossil reef in the world.

St Anne's Shrine (☎ 802-928-3362, 802-928-3385; www.sse.org; 92 St Anne's Rd; ✆ 9am-4pm daily mid-May–mid-Oct, 9am-4pm Mon-Fri mid-Oct–mid-May), established in the 1600s, celebrated the first Mass held in Vermont. Grounds include grottoes, statues, chapels, food service and a small camping area (with/without electrical hookup $15/10; no reservations).

Sleeping & Eating

Grand Isle State Park (☎ 802-372-4300; www.vtstateparks.com; US 2, South Hero; tent/lean-to sites $16/23; ✆ mid-May–mid-Oct) This 226-acre park has 120 tent and RV sites and 36 lean-tos. Although it's the most-visited campground in the state park system, it doesn't have any RV hookups.

Burton Island State Park (☎ 802-524-6353; www.vtstateparks.com; Burton Island; tent/lean-to sites $16/23; ✆ late May-early Sep) Offering a unique lakeside perspective, this 253-acre island can be reached only by boat from the tip of Hathaway Point at Killkare State Park on the eastern shore of the lake. (From St Albans, take VT 36 west.) After you disembark the boat, the park service will transport your camping gear to your site. A marina offers dockside water and electrical service.

Allenholm Farm (☎ 802-372-5566; www.allenholm.com; 111 South St, South Hero; ✆ 9am-5pm Jul-Dec) This is orchard country, but area farms offer more than sublime apples. Come here for local cheese, maple syrup, ice-cream, excellent pies, cider and – of course – crispy, tart and juicy apples.

Hero's Welcome General Store (☎ 802-372-4161; sandwiches $4-6) Do you get the impression that island life revolves around this place? It does; and the café and bakery have the best sandwiches, too.

North Hero House Inn & Restaurant (☎ 802-372-4732, 888-525-3644; www.northherohouse.com; US 2, North Hero; r incl full breakfast $95-295, breakfast buffet $9, dinner $15-28; ✆ Apr-Oct) This landmark 26-room inn, built in the early 1900s, has lakeside rooms as well as rooms in the main inn across the street from the lake. The lakeside rooms have been renovated recently, so grab one if you can. The inn also serves a breakfast buffet and dinner to the public. Friday suppers feature lobsters, served down on the water's edge.

VERMONT

dairy cows contrast with the slick resorts and Morgan horses found in the southern part of the state, and the white steeples are chipped, not freshly painted. It's a region that doesn't put on any airs about attracting tourists.

Orientation & Information

While St Johnsbury is easily reached by I-91 or I-93 (a three-hour drive from Boston through NH), the rest of the Northeast Kingdom is incredibly spread out. Use I-91 as your north–south thoroughfare, and then use smaller routes like VT 5A to find dramatically sited Lake Willoughby, or VT 14 to find Craftsbury Common, a town of white clapboard houses perfectly set around a village green. Other favorite villages include Greensboro, nestled upon the shores of Caspian Lake, and Barton, near pristine Crystal Lake.

The **Northeast Kingdom Chamber of Commerce** (☎ 802-748-3678; www.vermontnekchamber.org; 357 Western Ave, St Johnsbury, VT 05819; ☉ 8:30am-5pm mid-Jun–mid-Oct) runs a convenient information booth at Courthouse Park on Main St, as well as the St Johnsbury location, with plentiful regional information.

Sights

ST JOHNSBURY ATHENAEUM

The **athenaeum** (☎ 802-748-8291; www.stjathenaeum .org; 1171 Main St; admission free; ☉ 10am-8pm Mon & Wed, 10am-5:30pm Tue, Thu & Fri, 9:30am-4pm Sat), founded in 1871 when Horace Fairbanks gave the town a library, was built around some 8000 finely bound copies of the world's classic literature. Fairbanks then added an art gallery and installed works by such noted Hudson River School painters as Asher B Durand, Worthington Whittredge and Jasper Cropsey. His crowning achievement was the purchase of Albert Bierstadt's 10ft-by-15ft *Domes of the Yosemite*. Bierstadt is said to have returned to the gallery every summer until his death to touch up his masterpiece. Today, the Athenaeum's art collection is the USA's oldest art gallery still in its original form.

FAIRBANKS MUSEUM & PLANETARIUM

In 1891, when Franklin Fairbanks' collection of stuffed animals and cultural artifacts from across the globe grew too large for his home, he built the **Fairbanks Museum of Natural Science** (☎ 802-748-2372; www.fairbanks museum.org; 1302 Main St; adult/child/senior/family

$5/3/4/12; ☉ 9am-5pm Mon-Sat, 1-5pm Sun, closed Mon mid-Oct–mid-Apr). This massive stone building with a 30ft-high barrel-vaulted ceiling still displays more than half of Franklin's original collection. Over 3000 preserved animals in glass cases can be seen, including a 1200lb moose shot in Nova Scotia in 1898, an American bison from 1902 and a Bengal tiger. There are planetarium shows at 1:30pm ($3 per person), and also in July and August at 11am.

Activities

Not surprisingly, this sylvan countryside is the perfect playground for New England outdoor activities. Almost any such pursuit is at its best in the Northeast Kingdom.

SKIING

When it's balmy in Boston in winter, you can still expect a blizzard at Vermont's northernmost ski resort, **Jay Peak** (☎ 802-988-2611; www.jaypeakresort.com; VT 242), 8 miles north of Montgomery Center. Bordering Québec, Jay gets more snow than any other ski area in New England (about 350 inches of powder). Being so far north, Jay also sees far more Quebeckers than New Yorkers. Black-diamond lovers enjoy the steeper tree runs off the tram, while novices find the trails in Bonaventure Basin to their liking. Add the natural off-trail terrain, and you have some of the most challenging backcountry snowboarding and skiing runs in America.

Burke Mountain (☎ 802-626-3305; www.skiburke .com), off US 5 in East Burke, is relatively unknown to anyone outside the Northeast Kingdom. Locals enjoy the challenging trails and empty lift lines. Burke has 33 trails (30% beginner, 40% intermediate, 30% expert) and four lifts, including one quad chair and one lift with a vertical drop of 2000ft.

Cross-country skiers are bound to end up at the full-service **Craftsbury Outdoor Center** (☎ 802-586-7767; www.craftsbury.com; Lost Nation Rd), 3 miles from Craftsbury Common. The 80 miles of trails – 50 of them groomed – roll over meadows and weave through forests of maples and firs, offering an ideal experience for all levels. Even if you don't plan on skiing, you should take a drive over to Craftsbury Common, where you'll find what may be Vermont's most spectacular village green. White clapboard buildings surround a rectangular lawn that hasn't changed one iota from the mid-19th century.

Nearby, **Highland Lodge** (☎ 802-533-2647; www .highlandlodge.com; Craftsbury Rd, Greensboro) has 40 miles of trails that slope down to the shores of Caspian Lake.

MOUNTAIN BIKING

On VT 114 off I-91, **East Burke** is a terrific place to start a mountain bike ride. In the summer of 1997, John Worth, co-owner of East Burke Sports, and several other dedicated locals linked together more than 200 miles of single and double tracks and dirt roads to form a network they call the **Kingdom Trails**. Riding on a soft forest floor dusted with pine needles and through century-old farms makes for one of the best mountain-biking experiences in New England. **East Burke Sports** (☎ 802-626-3215; www .eastburkesports.com; VT 114; bike rental daily $20-30) rents bikes and supplies maps.

HIKING

Hiking through **Lake Willoughby**'s stunning beauty will leave even a jaded visitor in awe. Sandwiched between Mt Hor and Mt Pisgah, cliffs plummet more than 1000ft to the glacial waters below and create, in essence, a landlocked fjord. The scenery is best appreciated on the hike (three hours) to the summit of **Mt Pisgah**. From West Burke, take VT 5A for 6 miles to a parking area on the left-hand side of the road, just south of Lake Willoughby. The 2-mile (one-way) **South Trail** begins across the highway. It's about a 30-minute drive from St Johnsbury to Mt Pisgah.

Sleeping

The Northeast Kingdom offers some of the most affordable lodgings in the state. The best accommodations are at small inns on family-run farms or by the shores of a hidden lake.

BUDGET

Craftsbury Bed & Breakfast (☎ 802-586-2206; 414 Wiley Hill Rd, Craftsbury Common; d incl full breakfast $60-80) Set in a farmhouse atop Wylie Hill, this B&B with shared bathrooms offers expansive views of rolling farmland. It's just down the road from the historic village green and close to the Craftsbury Outdoor Center for mountain biking and cross-country skiing. Innkeeper Margy Ramsdell's cinnamon

apple pancakes send guests out ready to tackle their day. Reservations are required.

Rodgers Country Inn (☎ 802-525-6677, 800-729-1704; 582 Rodgers Rd, West Glover; r per person incl breakfast & dinner per day/week $45/250) Not far from the shores of Shadow Lake, Jim and Nancy Rodgers offer five guest rooms in their 1840s farmhouse. Hang out on the front porch and read, or take a stroll on this 350-acre former dairy farm. This inn appeals to people who really want to feel what it's like to live in rural Vermont.

Village Inn of East Burke (☎ 802-626-3161; www .villageinnofeastburke.com; VT 114, East Burke; r incl full breakfast $75-85) Innkeepers Lorraine and George Willy treat guests like family in this good-value B&B at the base of Burke Mountain's ski area. The inn has six very clean rooms, an outdoor Jacuzzi, a guest kitchen and a living room fireplace. From the wonderful 5-acre garden out back, you can follow a trail that leads to a waterfall. (If only life could always be this simple.)

Inn on Trout River (☎ 802-326-4391, 800-338-7049; www.troutinn.com; 241 Main St, Montgomery Center; r per person incl full breakfast $69-96) One of the better places to stay if you plan on skiing Jay Peak. This village house was built by a lumber baron over a century ago, and features 10 guest rooms, one suite and two restaurants (one fancy and one a pub).

Stillwater State Park (☎ 802-584-3822; www.vt stateparks.com; Groton; sites with/without hookups $21/14; ☙ mid-May–mid-Oct) Near to Ricker Pond State Park, off VT 232, Stillwater has 107 sites and a prime swimming spot on the northwestern shores of Lake Groton.

MID-RANGE

Willoughvale Inn (☎ 802-525-4123, 800-594-9102; www.willoughvale.com; VT 5A, Westmore; r incl continental breakfast $69-199, ste $135-245, cottages $139-245) Overlooking the majestic granite cliffs of Mt Hor and Mt Pisgah, this inn sits on the northern shores of Lake Willoughby. It features eight spacious rooms, two suites and four cottages. In summer, cast off from the small beach and kayak (rented for a small fee) on the cool waters of the lake. In winter, rent snowmobiles and head up into the hills.

TOP END

Wildflower Inn (☎ 802-626-8310, 800-627-8310; www .wildflowerinn.com; 2059 Darling Hill Rd, Lyndonville; r incl full breakfast $99-199, ste $169-499; ⊗ Dec-Mar & May-Oct; ☕) This is a perennial favorite with families. Maybe it's because owners Jim and Mary O'Reilly have eight children and their home is littered with toys. Or perhaps it's the hayrides, mountain-bike trails, petting zoo with sheep and goats, playground, tennis courts and heaps of other onsite activities. Besides the cozy sitting rooms with fireplaces, the inn has 10 rooms and 11 suites.

Highland Lodge (☎ 802-533-2647; www.highland lodge.com; Greensboro; r incl breakfast & dinner $120-280; ⊗ late Dec–mid-Mar & Jun–mid-Oct) This 11-room lodge (with additional cottages) is perched on a hill over Caspian Lake, off VT 16, and all guest rooms have a view of the lake. It's also down the road from one of Vermont's best country stores, Willey's. A trail leads to a private beach and canoe rental shop. Wintertime guests can enjoy an extensive cross-country skiing network.

Inn at Mountain View Farm (☎ 802-626-9924, 800-572-4509; www.innmtnview.com; 3383 Darling Hill Rd, East Burke; r incl full breakfast $155-255) Built in 1883 as a gentleman's farm, this splendid place now houses a 14-room inn. Rooms reflect the charm of a spacious, comfortable farmhouse with details like hand-held European shower, spool beds, fainting couch (what's that you say?) and chintz touches. The farm's 440 acres are ideal for mountain biking, cross-country skiing or simply taking a long stroll on the hillside.

Eating

You may be surprised at the region's good cuisine and inexpensive tabs.

BUDGET

Bagel Depot (☎ 802-748-1600; 1216 Railroad St, St Johnsbury; bagels $3-9; ⊗ breakfast & lunch) This Creamery Building eatery serves the freshest bagels in the Northeast Kingdom. Add a cup of Green Mountain Coffee to kick-start your morning or come back for daily lunch specials.

Miss Lyndonville Diner (☎ 802-626-9890; US 5, Lyndonville; dishes $2-11; ⊗ breakfast, lunch & dinner) Five miles north of St Johnsbury and popular with locals, this place also enjoys friendly and prompt service. Large breakfasts are cheap; sandwiches cost a bit more, but the tasty dinners (like roast turkey with all the fixings) are a real steal.

MID-RANGE

River Garden Café (☎ 802-626-3514; VT 114, East Burke; lunch $8, mains dinner $16-22; ⊗ lunch & dinner Tue-Sun, brunch Sun) True to its name, you'll enjoy the back porch (open year-round) and summer patio within earshot of the river. This local favorite offers salads, pastas, filet mignon and stir-fried dishes served in a casually elegant atmosphere. For lunch, try the Green Mountain pizza ($7), topped with Vermont goat cheese, mozzarella, pesto and tomato sauce. As you might have guessed, breads and desserts are homemade.

Anthony's Diner (☎ 802-748-3613; 50 Railroad St, St Johnsbury; dishes $3-15; ⊗ breakfast, lunch & dinner Mon-Sat, breakfast & lunch Sun) While hanging around the large counter, try the mountain-size Vermont woodsman burger. The homemade soups, chowders and desserts are a deserved source of pride.

Willoughvale Inn (☎ 802-525-3234; VT 5A, Westmore; mains $15-24; ⊗ lunch & dinner) If you don't stay here, at least have a meal in its glass-enclosed dining room overlooking Lake Willoughby. Hearty American fare, including prime rib and turkey, prevails, as does the house specialty of stuffed chicken Willoughvale. Then again there's always a giant burger or lasagna.

Cucina di Gerardo (☎ 802-748-6772; 213 Railroad St, St Johnsbury; lunch $7-10, mains dinner $12-22; ⊗ lunch & dinner seasonally) This Creamery Building place serves hearty Italian fare like mussels marinara and fancy gourmet pizzas.

TOP END

Elements (☎ 802-748-8400; 98 Mill Street; dishes $7-23; ⊗ lunch Tue-Fri, dinner Tue-Sat) The setting surely complements Chef Ryan O'Malley's novel menu, which uses local ingredients whenever possible. Try the polenta lasagna with eggplant over roasted vegetables, or trout cakes with tomato jam, wasabi and crème fraîche. The meat loaf is made from local beef. Try to share so that you sample several dishes. Dried cranberries go into the corn bread pudding for dessert – a unique treat. Almost everything is made on the premises.

Getting There & Away

By car, St Johnsbury is 39 miles (45 minutes) from Montpelier via US 2 east, or 76 miles (1½ hours) if you're coming directly from Burlington.

New Hampshire

CONTENTS

NEW HAMPSHIRE

HIGHLIGHTS

- **Most Picturesque Village**
  Jackson (p455), with a quaint covered bridge and dramatic mountain backdrop

- **Loveliest Country Inn**
  Bungay Jar (p451), in Franconia, with exceptional style, warm service and glorious gardens

- **Neatest Kids' Museum**
  Mariposa Museum (p427), in Peterborough, filled with folklore from around the world

- **Most Honky-tonk Fun**
  A tie between the boardwalk at Weirs Beach (p437) and Hampton Beach (p412)

- **Most Exhilarating Moment**
  Reaching the summit, any summit, in the White Mountain Range (p442)

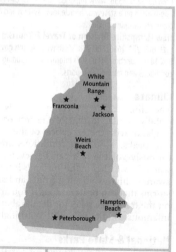

- **TELEPHONE CODE:** 603　　■ **POPULATION:** 1.3 MILLION　　■ **AREA:** 8968 SQ MILES

Ruggedly handsome and fiercely independent, the 'Great Stone Face' that nature carved out of the granite cliff in Franconia Notch really is the perfect symbol of the Granite State. The profile graces license plates, coins and postcards – a testament to the natural beauty and proud resistance that characterize this state. That the forces of nature proved to be too strong for the so-called Old Man of the Mountain to endure (see p448) doesn't diminish the significance of the image New Hampshire continues to embrace.

Geology defines the area, from the rushing rivers and quarry-mined granite that were once its main economic assets, to the White Mountains and glacial lakes that grace its landscape. Even now, with industry and farming in decline, tourists arrive in hordes to hike the peaks, cruise the lakes and marvel at the foliage.

The dramatic White Mountain Range, starring Mt Washington (6288ft), is traversed by trails making it accessible to day hikers. Lake Winnipesaukee is the largest of New Hampshire's lakes, and there are more than 1000 other glacial pools where you can take a dip. And although most visitors don't go to New Hampshire for its cultural attractions, artists have long sought out beautiful places like Monadnock and the Connecticut River Valley for inspiration.

The most politically conservative of the New England states, New Hampshire natives suffer the barbs and insults of their liberal neighbors, but they wouldn't have it any other way. They abide by the famous words of General John Stark, victor at the crucial Battle of Bennington (1777): 'Live free or die.'

Information

New Hampshire Division of Parks & Recreation

(☎ 603-271-3556; www.nhparks.state.nh.us) Offers information on a statewide bicycle route system and a very complete camping guide.

New Hampshire Division of Travel & Tourism

(☎ 603-271-2666, 800-258-3608; www.visitnh.gov; PO Box 1856, Concord, NH 03302) Information including ski conditions and fall foliage reports.

Climate

The climate of New Hampshire (NH) is usually similar to that of the rest of New England, with the exception of the mountain peaks. Mountain conditions are notoriously volatile and can be severe, even when the weather in the lowlands is fine. Be aware of high winds, fog fronts and snowstorms that can be hazardous if you are out on the trails. See p459 for details about the infamous conditions on Mt Washington.

National & State Parks

Prior to the establishment of a national forest in New England, much of the land in this region was decimated by uncontrolled logging and forest fires. The public outcry against this destruction led to the passage of the Weeks Act, federal legislation that allowed the National Park Service (NPS) to purchase land east of the Mississippi River. The White Mountain National Forest (WMNF) was established in 1911 with the first purchase of 7000 acres of land under the Act.

The WMNF (p447) has since expanded to cover 80,000 acres in New Hampshire and Maine. Hiking trails, skiing slopes, campgrounds and swimming beaches – not to mention a few carefully controlled auto roads – provide access to this gigantic natural playground.

Other preservation efforts pale in comparison to the WMNF, but the state of New Hampshire works closely with NPS in the management of an extensive network of state parks, including Franconia Notch, Crawford Notch and Echo Lake, not to mention the entire New Hampshire seacoast.

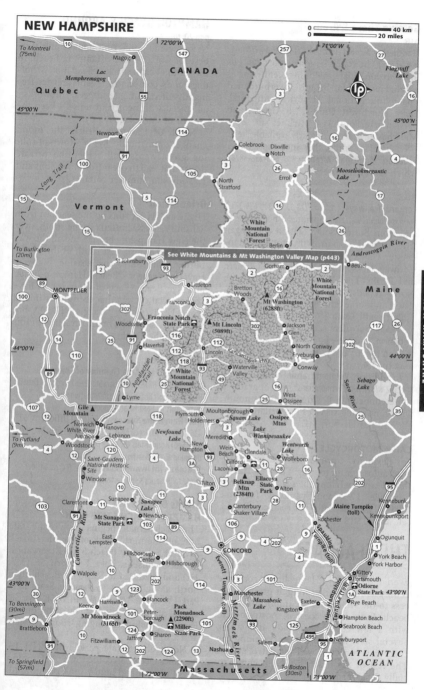

NEW HAMPSHIRE

See White Mountains & Mt Washington Valley Map (p443)

Getting There & Around

AIR
Manchester Airport (☎ 603-624-6539; www.flyman chester.com), the state's largest airport, has enjoyed exponential growth in recent years as a 'relief airport' for Boston's overburdened Logan International Airport. Continental, Delta, Northwest, United, US Airways and particularly Southwest Airlines all serve Manchester. Car rentals are available here. US Airways Express flies into the smaller **Lebanon Municipal Airport** (☎ 603-298-8878), which serves Hanover.

BUS
Concord Trailways (☎ 603-228-3300, 800-639-3317; www.concordtrailways.com) operates a bus route to and from Boston South Station and Logan International Airport, with stops in Manchester, Concord, Meredith, Conway, North Conway, Jackson, Pinkham Notch, Gorham and Berlin. There's another route through North Woodstock/Lincoln, Franconia, Littleton and some other points along the way. **Dartmouth Coach** (☎ 508-448-2800; www.dart mouthcoach.com) offers services from Hanover, Lebanon, and New London to Boston South Station (p126) and Logan International Airport (p125).

In addition, **Vermont Transit** (☎ 603-436-0163, 800-552-8737; www.vermonttransit.com) operates a route connecting Boston and Portsmouth, with continuing services to Portland, Bangor and Bar Harbor, ME.

CAR & MOTORCYCLE
For flexibility, convenience and independence, autos rule for touring. The New Hampshire Turnpike (along the seacoast), Everett Turnpike (I-93) and Spaulding Turnpike (NH 16) are toll roads. For road conditions, call ☎ 800-918-9993.

THE SEACOAST

Even though New Hampshire's coastline is only about 18 miles long, it provides access to the sea and, more importantly, the beach. Indeed, the coast is mostly beach, with a few rocky headlands and coves. Several state beaches and parks along the coast have orderly, well-regulated access. The rest of the beach has been commercially developed.

HAMPTON BEACH & AROUND
pop 20,200

New England beachfront honky-tonk at its best (or worst) – that's Hampton Beach. In the summer clam shacks, cheap motels, hotdog stands, coin-machine game arcades, free nightly entertainment and weekly fireworks – all spiced with neon and noise – keep the crowds of sunseekers happy.

North of Hampton Beach, the mood changes dramatically. **Rye** is a town of rolling greenswards and serpentine private drives that lead to oceanfront mansions and 12-bedroom 'summer cottages.'

Orientation
Highway NH 1A runs up the seacoast from Salisbury, Massachusetts in the south, over the New Hampshire border and all the way up to Portsmouth, just south of the Maine border. En route, the seaside highway traverses Seabrook Beach, Hampton Beach and Rye Beach. Each of these towns have commercial centers that are further inland along US 1 (which parallels NH 1A), but for most visitors the main attraction of this region is the beach.

Information
Hampton Beach Area Chamber of Commerce (☎ 603-926-8718; www.hamptonbeach.org; 169 Ocean Blvd, Hampton Beach) Offers information on hotels, restaurants and tourist attractions.
New Hampshire Seacoast Regional Office (☎ 603-436-1552; 1730 Ocean Blvd, Rye; ☷ 10am-5pm Mon-Fri May-Sep) Administers the state parks in the region – meaning all the beaches.
Seacoast, NH (www.seacoastnh.com) A great insider's guide to 'America's smallest seacoast.'

Sights & Activities
HAMPTON BEACH STATE PARK
The beach actually begins south of the state line, on the north bank of the Merrimack River at Salisbury Beach State Reservation in Massachusetts. Take I-95 exit 56 (MA 1A) and head east to Salisbury Beach, then north along NH 1A to **Hampton Beach State Park** (☎ 603-926-3784; P Mon-Fri $5, Sat & Sun $8) a long stretch of sand shielded by dunes. Facilities include changing rooms, toilets and a snack bar.

North of the state park, where NH 1A becomes Ocean Blvd, the town of Hampton is both beach and honky-tonk playground.

In summer this vast, main beach is crowded with all of humanity: the young, tanned and beautiful – and everyone else. At the center of the strip, the **Hampton Seashell** (☎ 603-926-8717, 603-926-5000) is a bandshell with an amphitheater, as well as public toilets, a first aid station and the chamber of commerce information center (see opposite). Across the boulevard, the Hampton Beach casino (p415) has live entertainment, video games, fast-food stands and souvenir shops. Beach admission is free, but you'll have to feed quarters to the parking meters ($1.50 per hour).

In the residential neighborhoods north of Hampton Beach you'll find a few less crowded and less spectacular beaches. Ten minutes north of Hampton Beach, **North Hampton State Beach** (☎ 603-436-1552) is not nearly as wide but is quieter than its grand southern neighbors. It has all the same facilities, including metered parking.

RYE BEACHES
As NH 1A enters Rye, parking along the road is restricted to vehicles with town parking stickers, but **Jenness State Beach** (☎ 603-436-1552) has a small metered parking lot that's open to the general public. Further north near **Rye Harbor** you're allowed to park along the roadway. Climb over the seawall of rubble and rocks to get to the gravel beach. It lacks facilities, but it is much less crowded than anything further south. Continuing northward, **Wallis Sands State Beach** (☎ 603-436-9404; P Mon-Fri $5, Sat & Sun $8) has a wide sandy beach with views of the Isles of Shoals. Besides the bathhouses, there are verdant grass lawns for children's games and a large parking lot, making this the top spot for families with smaller kids.

ODIORNE POINT STATE PARK
At the northern tip of the seacoast, just before NH 1A turns westward to Portsmouth, lies the underutilized **Odiorne Point State Park** (☎ 603-436-1552; admission free). It lacks a beach, but instead offers seaside strolls and forested trails, as well as sweet, hidden spots for picnicking and fishing. It is also the site of the **Seacoast Science Center** (☎ 603-436-8043; www.seacentre.org; 570 Ocean Blvd, Rye; adult/child $3/1; ۞ 10am-5pm). Undersea videos, huge aquariums and a hands-on 'touch tank' are the highlights of this family favorite. The center hosts lots of special activities such as trail walks, lighthouse tours and concerts.

SURFING
Diehard surfers ride the waves at Hampton Beach from June to October. The **Cinnamon Rainbows Surf Co** (☎ 603-929-7467; www.cinnamon rainbows.com; North Beach, Hampton; lesson per hr with equipment $50, surfboard & wetsuit rental per day $35) offers lessons and equipment rental.

FISHING, WHALE-WATCHING & CRUISING
A variety of fishing trips is offered by **Al Gauron Deep Sea Fishing** (☎ 603-926-2469; www.algauron .com; State Pier, Hampton Beach; adult/child/senior 2hr trips $12/8/10, day trips $36/23/29). These range from daily two-hour trips (at 6:30pm, from July to August) to full-day trips (from 8:30am to 4:30pm, July to August). They are offered less frequently between September and May. Whale watches and other cruise packages are also available.

Daily whale-watching cruises, as well as relaxing cruises to the Isles of Shoals and a Sunset Fireworks cruise are hosted by **Granite State Whale Watch** (☎ 603-964-5545, 800-964-5545; www.granitestatewhalewatch.com; Ocean Blvd, Rye; adult/child/senior whale-watching $22/15/20, other cruises $15/12/13).

Sleeping
Hampton Beach and – to a lesser degree – Rye have no shortage of roadside motels within walking distance of the beach. In fact NH 1A is lined with these places. Many offer ocean views, if you can see past the vast parking lots and the sea of humanity that pack into the waterfront. Whether you're tenting it or dropping big bills in hotels, you'll need reservations during summer months.

There are loads of rental rooms and apartments that also need to be booked well in advance – people start calling in mid-February and March. Contact **Preston Real Estate** (☎ 603-926-2604; 63 Ocean Blvd) in Hampton Beach for week-long rentals. Weekly rates range from $800 to $1000 for a decent but small two-bedroom apartment to as much as $1600 for a three-bedroom place with ocean views. As for hotels, during beach season it's very difficult, if not impossible, to find a room for one night.

BUDGET & MID-RANGE
Hampton Harbor Motel (☎ 603-926-4432; www.hamp tonharbormotel.com; 210 Ashworth Ave, Hampton; d Nov-May $49-69, Jun-Sep $99-109; 🏊) Who needs the beach when your motel has a heated, rooftop

swimming pool? This place is just one block inland from the casino and beach. The four efficiency apartments and 18 rooms have the typical amenities – some have shared balconies. Weekly and monthly rental rates are available.

Atlantic Four Winds Efficiencies (☎ 603-436-5140; www.atlanticfourwinds.com; 1215 Ocean Blvd, Rye; d/ste Jun-Aug $90/125, Sep-Oct $75/95; ☒ ☎) This typical beach motel features 13 rustic cottages located directly opposite Wallis Sands beach. Kitchenettes and extra sleeper sofas offer good value for families, who might also appreciate the distance from the excesses of Hampton Beach.

Lamie's Inn & Tavern (☎ 603-926-0330; www .lamiesinn.com; 490 Lafayette Rd, Hampton; r Nov-Apr $95, May-Oct $115-125; ☒ ☐) If you wish to escape the din and tack of Hampton Beach, head inland to this colonial manor in downtown Hampton. Thirty-two graceful rooms have details like exposed brick walls, four-poster beds and lace curtains. The inn's restaurant, the Old Salt, has a cozy dining room and a fantastic selection of fresh seafood.

Tidewater Campground (☎ 603-926-5474; 160 Lafayette Rd, Hampton; sites without/with hookups $25/32; ☺ mid-May–mid-Oct; ☎) This private 40-acre campground is near the intersection of US 1 and NH 101. It offers 100 sites for tents and recreation vehicles (RVs), including prime shaded spots near the ocean. Top spot for families.

Hampton Beach State Park Campground (☎ 603-926-8990, 603-371-3628; sites $35; ☺ mid-May–mid-Oct) Twenty-eight oceanfront RV sites with little shade or privacy, off NH 1A. This place absolutely requires reservations.

If you don't have your heart set on staying near the ocean, a few inland campgrounds offer attractive, woodsy sites with lots of amenities:

Exeter Elms (☎ 603-778-7631; www.exeterelms.com; 188 Court St, Exeter; tent/RV $24/34 plus adult/child $10/5) Sites are set along the beautiful Exeter River, with access for fishing and canoeing.

Wakeda Campground (☎ 603-772-5274; www.wakeda campground.com; NH 88, Hampton Falls; tent/RV $23/29) Over 400 secluded sites set amidst 180 acres of towering pine trees.

TOP END
Ashworth By the Sea (☎ 603-926-6762, 800-345-6736; www.ashworthhotel.com; 295 Ocean Blvd, Hampton; d Jun-Sep $130-235, Oct-May $75-185; ☒ ☎) This conference- and family-friendly hotel preserves an element of elegance that the rest of Hampton Beach lacks. Its 105 rooms have a contemporary decor and small perks like in-room coffeemakers; many have private balconies and ocean views. Three onsite restaurants provide a nice alternative to fried dough and pizza.

Seaside Village Resort (☎ 603-964-8204; www.sea sidevillageresort.com; 1 Ocean Blvd, North Hampton; r per week $600-750, ste per week $800-1200; ☒) A rarity in New Hampshire, this little resort has cabanas and townhouses that sit right on a private beach. Most have kitchenettes. Unfortunately, July and August are often booked out way in advance.

Eating
You'll have no trouble feeding your face with pizza and cotton candy, which are sold from snack shops up and down NH 1A. Slightly more appealing are the lobster pounds and clam shacks specializing in fried, fried, fried. Besides the places listed here, Lamie's Inn & Tavern (opposite) and the Ashworth By the Sea (below) both have restaurants that are recommended.

Galley Hatch (☎ 603-926-6152; 325 Lafayette Rd/ US 1, Hampton; sandwiches $8, mains $15-22; ☺ lunch & dinner) This popular restaurant serves everything from the requisite fish and sandwiches to steaks, pastas, pizzas and veggie dishes. It also has a couple of lounges with entertainment. If you're hungry, it'll do just fine. It's in Hampton rather than Hampton Beach.

Brown's Seabrook Lobster Pound (☎ 603-474-3331; NH 286; mains $8-20; ☺ daily mid-Apr–mid-Nov, Fri-Sun mid-Apr–mid-Nov) Seasonal lobster pounds line the seacoast along US 1 and NH 1A. Make a slight detour to Seabrook, just south of Hampton Beach, for this year-round pound that overlooks a marsh and serves freshly boiled crustaceans. Bring your own beer and wine and take a seat at one of the picnic tables on the deck.

Carriage House (☎ 603-964-8251; 2263 Ocean Blvd, Rye; mains $20-30; ☺ 5-10pm) The Italian focus does not limit the menu at this upscale eatery, where dishes range from Madras curries to steak *au poivre vert* (steak with green peppercorn sauce). It's all set in a tastefully decorated Cape Cod house – which is somewhat out-of-place on the commercialized New Hampshire coast.

DETOUR: EXETER

Founded in 1638, the town of Exeter gained prominence in New Hampshire early on because it was one of the few towns to build a specially designated meetinghouse, as opposed to holding meetings in a tavern or a church. The meetinghouse would play a crucial role a century later when – in 1774 – Governor John Wentworth dissolved the provincial assembly that met in Portsmouth in an attempt to prevent the election of a continental congress. A series of provincial congresses began to congregate at the meetinghouse in Exeter, which effectively became the seat of government. Exeter served as the capital of New Hampshire during 14 crucial years, when the first New Hampshire constitution was adopted and the US Constitution was ratified.

This early history is still celebrated in Exeter, thanks in part to the **American Independence Museum** (☎ 603-772-2622; www.independencemuseum.org; 1 Governor's Lane) which maintains the town's collections and hosts thematic tours and events.

The collections are housed in the historic **Ladd-Gilman House** (adult/child $5/3; ☯ 10am-4pm Wed-Sat May-Oct), which is preserved as a National Landmark Property. It contains the furnishings and possessions of the Gilman family, who lived here from 1720 to 1820, providing some insights into their lifestyle. But the highlight is the document archive, including two original drafts of the US Constitution and personal correspondence of George Washington, Pierre L'Enfant and other notables. The museum also maintains Fulsome Tavern, which is undergoing extensive renovation.

Every year on a Saturday in July, Exeter hosts the spirited **Revolutionary War Festival**, when the whole town (seemingly) gets up in colonial garb. The procession led by George Washington and the reading of the Declaration of Independence take center stage. But there are loads of other events, from colonial cooking to militia drills to gunpowder races. And an annual charity road race and a night of rock and roll music are reminders that re-enactments are fun, but this is, after all, the 21st century.

To reach Exeter, take I-95 to exit 2, then NH 101 west. Turn left on Portsmouth Ave (NH 108) and right on Water St.

Entertainment

With so many people coming to relax and recreate, it's no surprise that this beach scene boasts a happening night life.

Casino Ballroom (☎ 603-929-4100; www.casinoballroom.com; Ocean Blvd, Hampton Beach) Besides all the arcade rides and miniature golf, the casino has a large theater that draws real names in rock and roll in summer. Back in the day, Led Zeppelin, The Who and Janis Joplin all played here.

La Bec Rouge (☎ 603-926-5050; www.labecrouge.com; 73 Ocean Blvd, Hampton Beach) Calling itself an 'underground pub' (because it is located in the basement), this place has live music ranging from rock to blues to reggae. This is much more of a local place – that goes for the bands as well as the clientele.

Getting There & Around

There is no public transportation servicing the Hampton Beach area. Once you arrive, however, you ditch your car and utilize the **Beach Trolley** (☯ noon-9:30pm Jun-Aug), which circles the beach. Convenient stops include

the chamber of commerce, the Ashworth Hotel and Le Bec Rouge.

PORTSMOUTH

pop 23,000

The New England coast is dotted with graceful old cities that grew to importance during the great days of New England's maritime ascendancy, when local merchants made fortunes trading with the world. Portsmouth is New Hampshire's only such city, but it's one of the region's most visually attractive and historically significant.

Portsmouth's checkered history has left it with a particularly impressive and eclectic array of historic buildings from all periods. It is neither a prissy, perfectly preserved 'museum town,' nor a modernized city, but more of an architectural museum of real life as lived on the New Hampshire seacoast from 1623 to the present day.

Orientation

Historic Portsmouth is surrounded on three sides by water. To the northwest is the North

NEW HAMPSHIRE

Mill Pond, to the northeast is the Piscataqua River and to the southeast is the South Mill Pond. Market St, reached via I-95 exit 7, is the main commercial street and has shops, restaurants and two information centers. Motels are clustered around I-95 exits 5 and 6.

Information

Bank of America (3 Pleasant St, Market Sq; ☉ 9am-4pm Mon-Fri)

Greater Portsmouth Chamber of Commerce (☎ 603-436-1118; www.portsmouthchamber.org; 500 Market St/I-95 exit 7) Also operates an information kiosk in the city center at Market Sq.

Gulliver's (☎ 603-431-5556; 7 Commercial Alley; ☉ 10am-5pm Mon-Sat, noon-5pm Sun) A large selection of maps and travel guidebooks, including an excellent section on New England.

Post office (80 Daniel St; ☉ 7:30am-5pm Mon-Fri, 8am-12:30pm Sat)

River Run Bookstore (☎ 603-431-2100; 7 Commercial Alley; ☉ 10am-5pm Mon-Sat, noon-5pm Sun) An independent bookstore above Gulliver's.

Sights
STRAWBERY BANKE MUSEUM

Unlike other New England historic recreations – Mystic Seaport, Old Sturbridge Village, Plimoth Plantation – **Strawbery Banke Museum** (☎ 603-433-1100; www.strawberybanke.org; 64 Marcy St; adult/child/senior/family May-Oct $15/10/14/35, Nov-Apr $10/5/9/25; ☉ 10am-5pm Mon-Sat & noon-5pm Sun May-Oct, 10am-2pm Thu-Sat & noon-2pm Sun Nov-Apr) does not limit itself to one historical period. Like Portsmouth itself, the museum is an eclectic mix and its 35 buildings span the town's history. Set on a 10-acre site in the Puddle Dock section, Strawbery Banke includes Pitt Tavern (1766), a hotbed of American revolutionary sentiment, Goodwin Mansion (and other grand 19th-century houses from Portsmouth's most prosperous time) and Abbott's Little Corner Store (1943). The admission ticket is good for two consecutive days.

ALBACORE PARK

This park serves as maritime museum and host to the **USS Albacore** (☎ 603-436-3680; 600 Market St; adult/child/senior/family $5/2/4/10; ☉ 9:30am-5pm daily Jun-Oct, 9:30am-4pm Thu-Mon Nov-May), a 205ft-long US Navy submarine. The Albacore was launched from the Portsmouth Naval Shipyard in 1953, and with a crew of 55 men it was piloted around the world for

19 years without firing a shot. When the sub was retired to Portsmouth, it opened to the public and became the centerpiece of the maritime museum.

CHILDREN'S MUSEUM OF PORTSMOUTH

Ensconced in an old meeting house, this exciting **museum** (☎ 603-436-3853; www.childrens-museum.org; 280 Marcy St; adult/senior/child $5/4/5; ☉ 10am-5pm Tue-Sat & 1-5pm Sun, plus 10am-5pm Mon Jun-Aug) has changing exhibits, toys and experiments for children aged between one and 10 years old. As you might expect, many displays elucidate the region's maritime history in an engaging way.

HISTORIC HOUSES

Several of Portsmouth's grand old houses have been beautifully preserved. If you visit, don't miss the lovely landscaped grounds, most of which are bursting with blooming gardens.

John Paul Jones (1747–92) was America's first great naval commander and coined the phrase, 'I have not yet begun to fight!' The 1758 **John Paul Jones House** (☎ 603-436-8420; www.portsmouthhistory.org; 43 Middle St; adult/child $6/2.50; ☉ 11am-5pm Thu-Tue May-Oct) was a boardinghouse when the naval hero lodged here during the outfitting of the Ranger (1777) and the America (1781). It's now the headquarters of the **Portsmouth Historical Society**.

The 1760 **Wentworth Gardner House** (☎ 603-436-4406; 50 Mechanic St; adult/child $5/2; ☉ 1-4pm Tue-Sun Jun-Oct) is one of the finest Georgian houses in the USA. Elizabeth and Mark Hunking Wentworth were among Portsmouth's wealthiest and most prominent citizens, so no expense was spared in building this home, which was a wedding gift for their son. Next door, the **Tobias Lear House** (☉ 1-4pm Wed) is a hip-roofed colonial residence that was home to the family of George Washington's private secretary. The opening hours and admission costs are the same here as at Wentworth Gardner next door.

Originally owned by an influential ship captain, the Georgian **Moffatt-Ladd House** (☎ 603-436-8221; 154 Market St; adult/child $6/2.50; ☉ 11am-5pm Mon-Sat & 1-5pm Sun Jun-Oct) was later the home of General William Whipple, a signer of the Declaration of Independence. The 18th-century chestnut tree and the old-fashioned **gardens** (admission $2) behind the house are delightful.

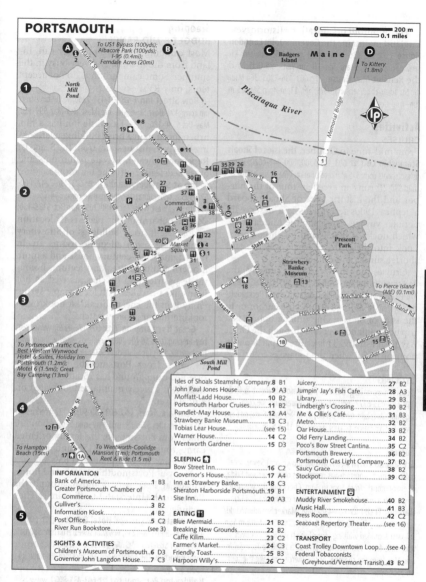

PORTSMOUTH

Isles of Shoals Steamship Company.**8** B1	Juicery.....................................**27** B2
John Paul Jones House..................**9** A3	Jumpin' Jay's Fish Cafe...........**28** A3
Moffatt-Ladd House.....................**10** B2	Library......................................**29** B3
Portsmouth Harbor Cruises.......**11** B2	Lindbergh's Crossing................**30** B2
Rundlet-May House......................**12** A4	Me & Ollie's Café......................**31** B3
Strawbery Banke Museum..........**13** C3	Metro.......................................**32** B2
Tobias Lear House.................(see 15)	Oar House................................**33** B2
Warner House.............................**14** C2	Old Ferry Landing....................**34** B2
Wentworth Gardner....................**15** D3	Poco's Bow Street Cantina......**35** C2
	Portsmouth Brewery.................**36** B2
SLEEPING	Portsmouth Gas Light Company.**37** B2
Bow Street Inn............................**16** C2	Saucy Grace.............................**38** B2
Governor's House........................**17** A4	Stockpot...................................**39** C2
Inn at Strawbery Banke.............**18** C3	
Sheraton Harborside Portsmouth.**19** B1	**ENTERTAINMENT**
Sise Inn.....................................**20** A3	Muddy River Smokehouse........**40** B2
	Music Hall.................................**41** B3
EATING	Press Room...............................**42** C2
Blue Mermaid.............................**21** B2	Seacoast Repertory Theater.......(see 16)
Breaking New Grounds...............**22** B2	
Caffe Kilim.................................**23** C2	**TRANSPORT**
Farmer's Market.........................**24** C3	Coast Trolley Downtown Loop.....(see 4)
Friendly Toast............................**25** B3	Federal Tobacconists
Harpoon Willy's..........................**26** C2	(Greyhound/Vermont Transit).**43** B2

INFORMATION
Bank of America...........................**1** B3	
Greater Portsmouth Chamber of	
Commerce..................................**2** A1	
Gulliver's....................................**3** B2	
Information Kiosk..........................**4** B2	
Post Office..................................**5** C2	
River Run Bookstore...............(see 3)	

SIGHTS & ACTIVITIES
Children's Museum of Portsmouth..**6** D3	
Governor John Langdon House.....**7** C3	

The 1716 **Warner House** (☎ 603-436-5909; www
.warnerhouse.org; cnr Daniel & Chapel Sts; adult/child
$5/2.50; ☺ 11am-4pm Mon-Sat & noon-4pm Sun Jun-Oct)
is a fine brick residence with rich paneling
and lush murals.

The 42-room **Wentworth-Coolidge Man-
sion** (☎ 603-436-6607; 375 Little Harbor Rd; adult/child
$3/free; ☺ 10am-3pm Sat & Sun May-Jun, daily Jul-

Aug), south of the town center, was home
to New Hampshire's first royal governor
and served as the colony's government
center from 1741 to 1767. The lilacs on its
grounds are descendants of the first lilacs
planted in America, which were brought
over from England by Governor Benning
Wentworth.

The nonprofit organization Historic New England maintains the **Governor John Langdon House** (☎ 603-436-3205; 143 Pleasant St; adult/child/senior $6/3/5; ☑ 11am-4pm Fri-Sun Jun–mid-Oct) and the **Rundlet-May House** (☎ 603-436-3205; 364 Middle St; adult/child/senior $6/3/5; ☑ 11am-4pm Sat & Sun Jun–mid-Oct).

Activities

CRUISES

From mid-June to October, the **Isles of Shoals Steamship Co** (☎ 603-431-5500, 800-441-4620; www.islesofshoals.com; 315 Market St, Barker Wharf; adult $16-31, child $10-21) runs an excellent tour of the harbor and the historic Isles of Shoals aboard a replica 1900s ferry. This is a deservedly popular voyage, especially the midday trip, which docks at Star Island for three hours. Look into their all-day whale watches and shorter sunset and dinner cruises.

Cruises on the *Heritage*, run by the **Portsmouth Harbor Cruises** (☎ 603-436-8084, 800-776-0915; www.portsmouthharbor.com; Ceres St Dock; adult/child/senior $18/10/17) go around the harbor or to the Isles of Shoals. One unique option is a trip up an inland river and through the Great Bay tidal estuary. This cruise is particularly popular in fall when the foliage is colorful.

CYCLING

Besides renting bikes, **Portsmouth Rent & Ride** (☎ 603-433-6777; www.portsmouthrentandride.com; 958 Sagamore Ave; bike rental per day $25; ☑ 9am-5pm) offers two-hour bike tours around the Seacoast.

Tours

Art 'Round Town (www.artroundtown.org) Seven local galleries host simultaneous receptions on the second Friday of every month, from 5pm to 8pm. Check out the website or pick up a map from the chamber of commerce (p412).
Harbour Trail (☎ 603-436-3988; Market Sq; adult/child/senior $8/5/7; ☑ 10:30am & 5:30pm Thu-Sat, 1:30pm Sun Jul-Oct) A guided walking tour of the historic downtown and waterfront. Alternatively, pick up a *Walking Tour Guide and Map* from the chamber of commerce and take the tour on your own.

Festivals & Events

Throughout the summer, Portsmouth hosts music, dance, theater and storytelling at the lovely **Prescott Park Arts Festival** (☎ 603-436-2848; www.artfest.org) on the banks of the Piscataqua River. Highlights include a one-day jazz festival, a one-day folk festival and a 'hotly' competitive chili cook-off.

Sleeping

BUDGET & MID-RANGE

Most camping areas are privately run, inland from the seacoast and very busy in the summer. Some campgrounds do not accept tents, only RVs.

Bow Street Inn (☎ 603-431-7760; www.bowstreetinn.com; 121 Bow St; r with breakfast Nov-Mar $99-120, May-Oct $140-180; ☒) This little inn has a hip, urban location in a brick building overlooking the river, just upstairs from the Seacoast Repertory Theater. Private bathrooms and brass bedsteads outfit the ten rooms.

Inn at Strawbery Banke (☎ 603-436-7242, 800-428-3933; www.innatstrawberybanke.com; 314 Court St; d with breakfast Nov-Mar $100-105, Apr-Oct $135-150; ☒) The charm of this place is its location amidst the historic buildings of Strawbery Banke. The seven adequate rooms are in the original 19th-century house and a more modern addition. Breakfast features homemade pastries and quiches, as well as hot items like pancakes with local maple syrup; enjoy it in the cheery breakfast nook overlooking the strawberry patch.

Great Bay Camping (☎ 603-778-0226; www.greatbaycamping.com; 56 NH 108, Newfields; sites without/with hookups $22/26 plus adult/child $6/4; ☑ May-Sep) About 13 miles from Portsmouth, this family-oriented campground has 95 sites best suited to RVs. It's nicely maintained and sited on a tidal river.

Ferndale Acres (☎ 603-659-5082; 132 Wednesday Hill Rd, Lee; sites $28; ☑ mid-May–mid-Sep) About 20 miles from Portsmouth, this family-oriented campground is off NH 155 and has 150 shaded sites for both tents and RVs.

Many of Portsmouth's motels and hotels cluster at I-95 exits 5 and 6, around the Portsmouth (Interstate) traffic circle. They include:
Best Western Wynwood Hotel & Suites (☎ 603-436-7600, 800-528-1234; www.bestwestern.com; 580 US 1 bypass; r $89-189; ☒ ☑) In case you get the late-night munchies, the hotel restaurant Bickford's is open 24 hours a day.
Holiday Inn Portsmouth (☎ 603-431-8000; www.hiportsmouth.com; 300 Woodbury Ave; r $90-150; ☒ ☑) Kids will appreciate the game room and in-room Nintendo.
Motel 6 (☎ 603-334-6606; I-95 at Spaulding TPK; r $69-109; ☒)

TOP END

Sheraton Harborside Portsmouth (☎ 603-431-2300, 800-235-3535; www.sheratonportsmouth.com; 250 Market

St; d Nov-Mar $89-150, Apr-Jun $120-200, Jul-Oct $190-230; 🗙 💻 🐾) The city's grandest accommodations is this hotel and conference center, conveniently located across from the Isles of Shoals Steamship docks, only a three-block stroll from Market Sq. Tasteful is the operative word, from the decor of the 200 rooms to the cozy lounge overlooking the harbor.

Sise Inn (☎ 603-433-1200, 877-747-3466; www.sise inn.com; 40 Court St; d with breakfast Nov-Apr $119-189, May-Oct $189-269; 🗙 💻) A short walk from the city center, this elegant, Queen Anne–style inn dates from 1881. It has 28 rooms and six suites with period furnishings. The rooms do not lack modern comforts, however. Hotel-style accoutrements like CD players and telephones are standard, while some of the larger suites feature Jacuzzis.

Governor's House (☎ 603-427-5140; www.governors -house.com; 32 Miller Ave; r Nov-Mar $165-215, Apr-Oct $195-245; 🗙 💻) This stately Georgian is named for New Hampshire governor Charles Dale, who lived here in the mid-20th century. It has only four guest rooms, but each is exquisite, with unique period furnishings, a private bath with hand-painted tiles and elegant decor. Little luxuries like down comforters, terry bathrobes and an outdoor hot tub make this place ideal for special occasions.

Eating
BUDGET
Breaking New Grounds (☎ 603-436-9555; Market Sq; 🕒 6:30am-10:30pm) The aroma of coffee draws in tourists and locals alike for a cup o' joe. This bright, sunny café is a pleasant place to get lost in the newspaper or converse with your companion.

Me & Ollie's Cafe (☎ 603-436-7777; 10 Pleasant St; mains $5-7; 🕒 7am-6:30pm Mon-Sat, 8am-5pm Sun) Ollie and his partner have figured out that fresh, homemade bread guarantees a delicious sandwich. Take your pick from honey wheat, honest white or triple seed, and add the fillings of your choice. If you prefer, order the soup of the day served in a French boule.

Saucy Grace (☎ 603-431-1178; Penhallow St; sandwiches $6-8; 🕒 7am-10pm Mon & Wed-Sat, 9am-9pm Sun, closed Tue) This eclectic eatery features all kinds of avante garde art – paintings, sculpture and a giant pickle mobile hanging in the corner. The menu is mainly soups, salads, burgers and sandwiches. Come for Sunday brunch with delectable homemade breads and pastries.

Friendly Toast (☎ 603-430-2154; 121 Congress St; mains $4.25-7.75; 🕒 7am-11pm Mon-Thu, 24hr 7am Fri-9pm Sun) The primary appeal of this retro diner is that it is open nonstop from Friday morning through Sunday night. The breakfast menu is huge and it is served around the clock.

Caffe Kilim (☎ 603-436-7730; 79 Daniel St; 🕒 7am-9pm Mon-Sat, 7am-8pm Sun May-Oct, shorter hr Nov-Apr) This little Turkish hole-in-the-wall is a funky addition to New Hampshire's espresso scene. You can haggle over rugs while you sip hot tea, just like in Istanbul.

Juicery (☎ 603-431-0693; 51 Hanover St; 🕒 9am-8pm Mon-Sat, 10am-6pm Sun May-Oct, shorter hr Nov-Apr) Refuel with fresh-squeezed organic juices and all-natural nondairy smoothies. Organic wraps, salads and chili are also available for take-out. This is a vegetarian's delight.

Farmers Market (Parrot Ave; 🕒 8am-1pm Sat May-Oct) Look for fresh produce at this market, two blocks from Market Sq.

MID-RANGE
Blue Mermaid (☎ 603-427-2583; 409 The Hill; lunch $8-16, dinner $13-20) Portsmouth's hippest restaurant is in an odd location a few blocks from the center. A dark-wood floor, jewel-toned tiles and a turquoise-textured ceiling give this place a fun and funky decor. The menu is no less creative. Wood-grilled seafood, burgers and pizzas are specialties, particularly enlivened by a margarita or martini. Ethnic dishes from Asian seared pork to Caribbean pan-seared cod, from Bimini chicken to chicken Santa Fe, also rule the roost.

Jumpin' Jay's Fish Cafe (☎ 603-766-3474; 150 Congress St; mains $15-20; 🕒 5:30-9:30pm Mon-Thu, 5-10pm Fri & Sat, 5-9pm Sun) A sleek industrial decor – complete with funky lighting and chrome bar – characterizes this creative seafood shack. The menu changes daily depending on the catch of the day. But it always features the freshest fish, pan-seared or grilled, as well as a few pasta dishes and the mandatory raw bar. Jay's specialty is his *puttanesca*, linguine sautéed in marinara sauce, olives, capers and the shellfish of your choice.

Portsmouth Gas Light Company (☎ 603-430-9122; 64 Market St; pizzas around $10, mains $9-17; 🕒 11:30am-10pm) Named for the utility company that previously occupied the building, this place is two restaurants in one. Both are pleasant enough, but the basement Downtown Pizza & Pub is dark and cozy – definitely more inviting in cooler weather. In summer, enjoy a traditional menu and live music on the shady terrace.

Harpoon Willy's (☎ 603-433-4441; 67 Bow St; mains $16-22; ☺ lunch & dinner spring-fall) Beneath Porto Bello and open in warm weather only (no one can predict when it will open or close), this open-air harborside eatery specializes in 'lobster in the rough' (simple steamed lobster), large plates of fish-and-chips, fried clams and the like.

Stockpot (☎ 603-431-1851; 53 Bow St; sandwiches $4-8, dinner $15-18; ☺ 11am-10:30pm) Advertising 'good food cheap,' the Stockpot delivers. There are no surprises on the menu, just pub fare with New England influences. Specialties include fish-and-chips ($11) and paella ($15). If you want a tugboat view accompanying your clam chowder and sandwich specials, this is the place.

Old Ferry Landing (☎ 603-431-5510; 10 Ceres St; lunch $6-10, dinner $13-20; ☺ 11:30am-8pm mid-Apr–mid-Sep) This moderately priced seafood restaurant in the former ferry terminal has traditional New England seafood like lobster rolls and haddock sandwiches. Enjoy your feast in a truly nautical setting right next to the tugboats.

Portsmouth Brewery (☎ 603-431-1115; 56 Market St; sandwiches $8-10, pizzas $11, mains $13-20; ☺ 11:30am-11pm) This airy brewpub has a long menu to accompany the homegrown pilsners, porters and ales. Nothing stands out, but this is a pleasant place to get a bite or a pint. Exposed brick and duct work and the brew tanks in the back lend a modern, industrial atmosphere to the reconverted building.

Poco's Bow Street Cantina (☎ 603-431-5967; 37 Bow St; mains $9-19) This cantina serves Southwestern dishes with a New England flair to a fun crowd. While tempted by lobster tacos or seafood chimichangas, keep in mind that no-nonsense steak and seafood dishes are more popular. The waterside dining area is pleasant in good weather, but there are nice harbor views inside, too.

TOP END

Oar House (☎ 603-436-4025; 55 Ceres St; lunch $8-15, dinner $22-34) This place features a dark cozy interior with an inviting wine bar, as well as an outdoor deck (across the street) overlooking the harbor. The menu is diverse, ranging from pizzas and sandwiches at lunch, to serious dinner mains like broiled haddock and roast duck. If you love seafood, try the Oar House delight: broiled shrimp,

scallops and haddock finished with lobster cream sauce.

Lindbergh's Crossing (☎ 603-431-0887; 29 Ceres St; tapas $3-6, mains $18-27; ☺ 5:30-10pm Mon-Fri, wine bar from 4pm Sat & Sun) Down the street, this cozy restaurant and wine bar offers classic Mediterranean fare – seafood paella and the like – as well as innovative tapas and seafood dishes.

Library (☎ 603-431-5202; 401 State St; lunch $10-18, dinner $18-28) Within a palatial and opulent home built by a prominent judge in 1785, the Library features traditional, classic dishes like prime rib, lobster thermadore and rack of lamb. In addition to the wood-paneled dining room, there's an English pub where you can get burgers and salads.

Metro (☎ 603-436-0521; 20 High St; lunch $8-15, dinner $19-29; ☺ 11:30am-2:30pm & 5:30pm-9:30pm Mon-Sat) Dark paneling, wall sconces and white linen tablecloths lend this place a romantic, Parisian feel. Steak frite, bouillabaisse and other classic dishes are served in high style. Look for live jazz on Friday and Saturday evenings.

Entertainment
THEATER

Music Hall (☎ 603-436-2400; www.themusichall.org; 28 Chestnut St; tickets $16-60) For a small town theater, this venue hosts a surprising array of performances, including dance, theater, opera and other music. Musicians, comedians and theater companies from around the country make appearances here.

Seacoast Repertory Theater (☎ 603-433-4472; www.seacoastrep.org; 125 Bow St; tickets $22-30) This theater is housed in a cool, reconverted building on Portsmouth's industrial riverfront. A range of shows is performed here, including lots of musicals.

LIVE MUSIC

Portsmouth is a local mecca for music as well as dining. Several clubs feature ever-changing schedules of local and national acts playing rock, folk, jazz, R&B and so on.

Press Room (☎ 603-431-5186; 77 Daniel St; bar food $5-10; ☺ 4pm-midnight Mon-Fri, noon-midnight Sat) Nightly live music ranges from jazz to blues to folk. There is a long menu of bar food in case the jamming makes you hungry.

Muddy River Smokehouse (☎ 603-430-9582; 21 Congress St) Barbecue and bands (at 8pm from Tuesday to Saturday) compete at this lively Market Sq venue. With swamp-theme murals and rustic wood furniture, the dining room tries to recreate the bayou.

Getting There & Around

Portsmouth is equidistant from Boston and Portland, Maine. It takes about 1¼ hours to travel the 57 miles via I-95 in either direction.

Greyhound/Vermont Transit (☎ 800-552-8737; www.vermonttransit.com) runs several daily buses on a route connecting Boston and Portsmouth with Portland, Bangor and Bar Harbor, Maine. Portsmouth to Boston costs $15 one way. The bus station is located at **Federal Tobacconists** (☎ 603-436-0163, 10 Ladd St), just off Market Sq.

Once in Portsmouth, the **Coast Trolley Downtown Loop** (☎ 603-743-5777; per ride $1, 3-day pass $5; ☼ 8:45am-8:45pm Mon-Sat, 11:45am-8:45pm Sun Jun-Sep) provides shuttle service between public parking lots, Market Sq and the major historic sights around town. Pick up a schedule and route map at the Market Sq information kiosk (p416).

MERRIMACK VALLEY

Although New Hampshire is noted more for mountains than cities, the state does have some urban charms. Manchester, a historic mill city, and Concord, the state's tidy capital, are pleasant – if not overly exotic – places to spend a day. Both are located along the mighty Merrimack River, which has dominated their economies since their founding.

MANCHESTER

pop 106,000

Exploiting the abundant water power of the Merrimack River, Manchester became the state's manufacturing and commercial center in the early 19th century. It is now more of a financial and high-tech hub. Students crowd the campuses of New Hampshire Technical College, Notre Dame College and the University of New Hampshire. And visitors wander the reconverted Amoskeag Mills and ponder the life of a mill worker during the Industrial Revolution.

Orientation

Manchester stretches along the east bank of the Merrimack River; West Manchester is on the river's west side. If you enter Manchester from I-93, you miss the view that defines the city's history: the redbrick swath of the great Amoskeag textile mills stretching along the east bank of the river for over a mile. To get the view, follow I-293 along the west bank of the river. After you've passed the mills, exit via the Amoskeag Bridge or the Queen City Bridge to enter the town. The heart of Manchester lies along Elm St (US 3), running north–south through the business and commercial district. Many hotels and motels are clustered at the interstate exits.

Information

Bank of America Bridge St (cnr Elm & Bridge Sts; ☼ 9am-5pm Mon-Fri); Granite St (cnr Elm & Granite Sts; ☼ 9am-5pm Mon-Fri)
Greater Manchester Chamber of Commerce (☎ 603-666-6600; www.manchester-chamber.org; 889 Elm St, Manchester, NH 03101)
Post office (1000 Elm St)

Sights & Activities

CURRIER MUSEUM OF ART

The state's premier **fine-arts museum** (☎ 603-669-6144; www.currier.org; 201 Myrtle Way; adult/child/senior $5/free/4, admission free 10am-1pm Sat; ☼ 11am-5pm Sun-Mon & Wed & Fri, 11am-8pm Thu, 10am-5pm Sat) has an excellent collection of 19th- and 20th-century European and American art, including painting, decorative arts, photography and sculpture. The **Currier Gallery of Art** is six blocks east of Elm St along Beech St (follow the signs).

The Currier also operates the Frank Lloyd Wright **Zimmerman House** (tours adult/child $9/6), the only house in New England designed by the acclaimed architect that is open to the public (reservations required). Tours depart via shuttlebus from the museum at 2pm Monday, Thursday and Friday, and 1pm and 2:30pm on weekends. The house is closed from January to March.

AMOSKEAG MILLS

These former textile mills, impressive brick buildings with hundreds and hundreds of tall windows, stretch along Commercial St on the Merrimack riverbank for almost 1½ miles. Other mills face the buildings from across the river in West Manchester. For almost a century (1838–1920), the Amoskeag Manufacturing Company was the world's largest textile manufacturer. The mills employed up to 17,000 people a year (out of a city

NEW HAMPSHIRE

population of 70,000). Many mill employees lived in the trim brick tenements stretching up the hillside eastward from the mills. The restored tenements are still used as housing.

Today, Mill No 3 houses the **Millyard Museum** (☎ 603-622-7531; www.manchesterhistoric.org; cnr Commercial & Pleasant Sts; adult/child/senior/student $6/2/5/5; ☽ 10am-4pm Tue-Sat). The museum hosts exhibits, walking tours and other programs that trace the history of Manchester, from the Amoskeag Indians who dwelled in this region, to the Amoskeag Mills that developed it.

Upstairs in the same building, the **SEE Science Center** (☎ 603-669-0400; www.see-sciencecenter .org; 200 Bedford St; admission $5; ☽ 10am-3pm Mon-Fri, noon-5pm Sat & Sun) has hands-on science exhibits to educate and entertain kids from toddlers to teens.

ANHEUSER-BUSCH BREWERY

Beer-lovers will appreciate a tour of the **Anheuser-Busch Brewery** (☎ 603-595-1202; 221 Daniel Webster Hwy, Merrimack; admission free; ☽ 10am-4pm daily May-Dec, Thu-Mon only Jan-Apr), which brews Budweiser and Michelob. The world's largest beer brewer makes 86 million barrels annually at a dozen breweries around the country. You can tour the plant, watch the foamy stuff fermenting, then lift a sample glass yourself. Animal lovers should not miss the **Clydesdale Hamlet**, home of the majestic draft horses that are Anheuser-Busch's trademark. To reach the brewery, go south on I-293 to the Everett Turnpike (US 3) and then take exit 10 (Industrial Drive).

Sleeping

Most lodging here is for business travelers, so prices are often lower on weekends. There are many hotels near the airport.

Ash Street Inn (☎ 603-668-9908; www.ashstreetinn .com; 118 Ash St; r with breakfast $139; ☒) Steps from the Currier, this fantastic Victorian home has five comfortable and cozy rooms. They feature ornamental fireplaces and stained-glass windows – originals from the house's construction in 1885. Plush robes and afternoon tea are some of the luxuries you'll enjoy.

Center of New Hampshire Radisson (☎ 603-625-1000; www.radisson.com; 700 Elm St; d $119-169; ☒ ▣ ▣) This huge conference facility – the largest north of Boston – is right in the middle of the business district, near Veter-

ans' Park. It offers 250 standard rooms and an excellent fitness center.

Comfort Inn (☎ 603-668-2600, 800-228-5150; www .comfortinn.com; 298 Queen City Ave; d $79-99; ☒ ▣) While it is in a commercial district west of the highway and river, this 103-room hotel is still convenient to the Queen City Bridge. Take exit 4 off I-293.

Ramada Inn Manchester (☎ 603-669-2660, 800-272-6232; www.ramada.com; 21 Front St; d $75-100; ☒) The Ramada has 120 comfortable rooms off I-293 exit 6, on the west side of the river. The on-site restaurant is Hooters, for whatever that's worth.

Bear Brook State Park (☎ 603-485-9869, reservations 603-271-3628; NH 28, Allenstown; sites $15; ☽ mid-May–mid-Oct) Although there are no camping places in greater Manchester, southern New Hampshire has a number of nice state parks, including Bear Brook. Halfway to Concord, this 10,000-acre park has 98 sites, which are remotely located on the shore of Beaver Pond. The park has opportunities for hiking and swimming. There are no hookups for RVs. Follow US 3 north, turn right onto NH 28 and follow the signs.

Eating

Most restaurants are on Elm St (US 3) in the center of the business district (take I-293 exit 5 and cross the Granite St Bridge).

Cotton (☎ 603-622-5488; 75 Arms Park Dr; lunch $7-10, dinner $13-20; ☽ lunch Mon-Fri, dinner daily) For artfully prepared food in sophisticated surroundings, this hip restaurant near the river and the Amoskeag mills wins hands down. In warm weather, the vine-shaded terrace is romantic and secluded. Expect organic field greens, thin-crust pizzas and other upscale bistro fare.

Starfish Grill (☎ 603-296-0706; 33 S Commercial St; mains $12-20) Driven by his success at Cotton, chef Jeffrey Paige opened this seafood restaurant at the opposite end of Commercial St. It is equally arty, with colorful fish suspended from the high ceiling. The menu, obviously, is seafood, although the specifics change according to what's fresh. The constant is the high quality and creative presentation. The signature drink is a tropical treat served in a fish bowl.

Lala's Hungarian Pastry (☎ 603-647-7100; 836 Elm St; mains $6-10; ☽ 7am-5pm Mon-Tue, 7am-8pm Wed-Sat) No-nonsense Lala's serves wondrous Hungarian pastries, as well as savory

ethnic luncheon specials like chicken gou-
lash and schnitzel. With wood paneling,
embroidered tapestries and Hungarian
pottery bedecking the tiny café, you might
be fooled into thinking you are back in the
motherland.

Merrimack Restaurant (☎ 603-669-5222; 786 Elm
St; sandwiches $4-6, mains $12-18; ⏰ 7am-9pm Mon-Sat,
7am-2pm Sun) This old-fashioned restaurant
with Naugahyde booths and swivel stools
has familiar American fare – salads, sandwiches, seafood, chicken and steaks – at low
prices. You can't go wrong ordering one
of the daily specials, which usually feature
good old-fashioned comfort food like mac
'n' cheese or meatloaf.

Vetro (☎ 603-627-8464; 815 Elm St) Better for
drinking than eating, Vetro is a superchic
martini bar where Manchester's swinging
singles go to check each other out.

Entertainment
OPERA
Opera New Hampshire (☎ 603-668-5588; www.opera
nh.org; Palace Theatre, 80 Hanover St; tickets $35-55, student
$20-32) Don't be surprised that Manchester
offers a full season of operas at the downtown Palace Theatre.

LIVE MUSIC
Strange Brew Tavern (☎ 603-666-4292; 88 Market St)
This welcoming pub boasts 48 beers on tap,
the largest selection in the state (it claims)!
More importantly, it offers live music seven
nights a week and no cover charge. The
mixed local crowd is friendly and fun.

SPORTS
New Hampshire Fishercats (☎ 603-641-2005; www
.nhfishercats.com; 1000 Elm St; tickets $4-12) New Hamp-
shire's minor-league baseball team is the farm
team for the Toronto Blue Jays, but they attract their own loyal fans. Especially since
they won the Eastern League championship
in 2004 (it must be something in the New
England water). Starting in 2005, the team
play in a brand new stadium on the waterfront west of Granite St.

Getting There & Away
Fast growing but still not too large, **Manchester Airport** (☎ 603-624-6539; www.flymanchester
.com), off US 3 south of Manchester, is a
civilized alternative to Boston's Logan International Airport.

Concord Trailways (www.concordtrailways.com) runs
frequent daily buses to Logan International
Airport ($15, 1½ hours) and South Station
($11, one hour) in Boston, as well as north
to Concord ($11, 30 minutes). Buses de-
part from the **Manchester Transportation Center**
(☎ 603-228-3300, 800-639-3317; 119 Canal St).

Driving from Boston to Manchester via I-
93 and the Everett Turnpike takes an hour.
It's another 30 minutes from Manchester to
Concord via I-93.

CONCORD
pop 38,000
The New Hampshire state capital is a well-
rounded town. Its citizens work in government, light manufacturing, crafts, education
and retail sales, as you'll see immediately
when you approach the gigantic shopping
mall beside I-93. They also quarry granite,
a suitable occupation in the Granite State.
The facades of the State House and many
of the buildings in the historic center were
fashioned from stone quarried nearby.
Concord may not grip you, but with its
modest charms it is a pleasant place to pass
through.

Orientation & Information
I-93 passes just east of the city center, and
US 3 is Main St, where you'll find everything worth visiting. Take I-93 exit 14 or 15
for Main St. The **Greater Concord Chamber of
Commerce** (☎ 603-224-2508; www.concordnhchamber
.com; 40 Commercial St; ⏰ noon-6pm Fri, 10am-4pm Sat &
noon-4pm Sun late May–mid-Oct) maintains a small,
seasonal information kiosk in front of the
State House on N Main St.

Sights
STATE CAPITOL
The state legislature still meets in the original chambers of the handsome 1819 **State
House** (☎ 603-271-2154; 107 N Main St; admission free;
⏰ 8am-4pm Mon-Fri). It's the longest such tenure in the USA. A self-guided tour brochure
is available to point out the building's highlights, including the **Memorial Arch** and the
various monuments around the grounds.
The **Hall of Flags** holds the standards that
state military units carried into battle.
Portraits and statues of New Hampshire
leaders, including the great orator Daniel
Webster, line its corridors and stand in its
lofty halls.

MUSEUM OF NEW HAMPSHIRE HISTORY

The New Hampshire Historical Society operates this intriguing two-story warehouse **museum** (☎ 603-228-6688; www.nhhistory.org; 7 Eagle Sq/N Main St; adult/child/senior/family $5.50/3/4.50/17; ☺ 9:30am-5pm Tue-Sat & noon-5pm Sun year-round, 9:30am-5pm Mon Jul-Oct & Dec). The chronological displays here illuminate such arcane subjects as the milk delivery in New England. One of the most compelling exhibits considers the state's famous residents, from Shaker 'eldresses' to Robert Frost to President Franklin Pierce. The museum also has beautiful 19th-century landscape paintings of the White Mountains. The handsome building itself – granite again – and the small park outside are interesting examples of urban reconversion.

PIERCE MANSE

Franklin Pierce (1804–69), 14th president of the US, is the only man from New Hampshire to be elected into this office. His Concord home, known as the **Pierce Manse** (☎ 603-225-2068, 224-7668; 14 Penacook St; adult/child $3/1; ☺ 11am-3pm Mon-Fri mid-Jun–mid-Sep), is now a museum. It was completed in 1839 and served as his family home from 1842 to 1848, between his Senate and presidential terms. Pierce was the son of a two-term New Hampshire governor, a member and later speaker of the New Hampshire General Court (legislature) and a representative and senator in Congress. He retired from the US Senate to practice law in Concord, maintaining an interest in politics but having little desire to engage in further public service. During the Democratic Party's convention of 1852, however, there were so many strong candidates for the presidency that none could achieve a majority vote. On the 49th ballot, Pierce, a compromise candidate, became the party's nominee, and he went on to win the presidential election.

CHRISTA MCAULIFFE PLANETARIUM

This **planetarium** (☎ 603-271-7827; www.starhop .com; 2 Institute Dr; adult/concession $8/5; ☺ 10am-5pm Mon-Sat, noon-5pm Sun) honors the New Hampshire schoolteacher chosen to be America's first teacher-astronaut. McAuliffe and her fellow astronauts died in the tragic explosion of the Challenger spacecraft on January 28, 1986. Hour-long shows examine topics like space travel to Mars and the power of the sun. 'Tonight's Sky' takes visitors on a tour of the constellations and planets visible that month.

CANTERBURY SHAKER VILLAGE

Members of the United Society of Believers in Christ's Second Appearing were called 'Shakers' because of the religious ecstasies they experienced during worship (see p269). This particular Shaker community was founded in 1792 and was actively occupied for two centuries. Sister Ethel Hudson, last member of the Shaker colony here, died in 1992 at the age of 96.

The **Canterbury Shaker Village** (☎ 603-783-9511, 800-982-9511; www.shakers.org; 288 Shaker Rd; adult/child 6-12/family $10/5/25; ☺ 10am-5pm daily May-Oct, 10am-4pm Sat & Sun Nov-Dec, closed Jan-Apr) is now preserved as a nonprofit trust to present Shaker history. The lone surviving Shaker community, at Sabbathday Lake, ME, still accepts new members.

Canterbury Shaker Village has 'interpreters' in period garb who perform the tasks and labors of community daily life: fashioning Shaker furniture and crafts (for sale in the gift shop) and growing herbs and producing herbal medicines. The guided tour takes you to a herb garden, meetinghouse (1792), apiary (bee house), ministry, 'Sisters' shop (a crafts shop run by Shaker women), laundry, horse barn, infirmary and schoolhouse (1826).

The **Shaker Table** (lunch $9-14, dinner $18-28; ☺ 11:30am-3pm & 5-8:30pm) serves a lovely lunch and a sumptuous candlelight dinner. The menu changes seasonally, but it usually features regional specialties and organic produce from the garden on-site, not to mention sinful desserts. Dinner reservations are recommended. The Canterbury Shaker Village is 15 miles north of Concord on MA 106. Take I-93 to exit 18.

Sleeping

Several highway hotels and motels attract government business, but most tourists rocket through to the mountains or lakes.

Centennial Inn (☎ 603-225-7102, 800-360-4839; 96 Pleasant St; r with breakfast $149-169; ✗) This turn-of-the-20th-century turreted manse has 32 luxurious rooms and suites. Each features warm colors, period furnishings and modern amenities. Common areas are named for famous New Hampshire natives. This place is about 1 mile west of Main St.

DETOUR: LAKE SUNAPEE

Lake Sunapee is a worthwhile detour any time of year. In summer, head to **Lake Sunapee State Park** (☎ 603-763-5561; Newbury; adult/child $3/free; ☑ dawn-dusk Sat-Sun mid-May–mid-Jun & Mon-Fri mid-Jun–mid-Oct), off NH 103, for hiking, picnicking, swimming and fishing. The wide sandy beach has a pleasant grassy sitting area. Canoes and kayaks are available for rental. From I-89 take exit 9, NH 103 to Newbury. In winter, alpine skiing is the attraction at **Mt Sunapee Resort** (☎ 603 763-2356; www.mtsunapee.com; Newbury; adult/child/senior/teen $52/41/41/32 Mon-Fri, $56/36/48/48 Sat-Sun; ☑ 9am-4pm). Mt Sunapee boasts a vertical drop of 1510ft – the biggest in southern New Hampshire. It's not much to compete with Cannon or Loon Mountain, but offers some challenging skiing all the same. Other facilities like rental, lessons and childcare are available.

Coming from Hanover or Concord, take exit 12A off I-89 and turn right on Rte 11. In the town of Sunapee, turn left onto Route 103B. Coming from the south, take exit 9 and follow NH 103 through Bradford and Newbury to Mt Sunapee.

Courtyard Concord (☎ 603-225-0303; http://marriott.com; 70 Constitution Ave; r $94-129; ☒ ☐ ☒) The spacious guest rooms here have a comfortable sitting area and a large work desk, reflecting the business focus of the majority of the clientele. The shuttle bus to Manchester Airport is convenient. The hotel is located near the chamber of commerce, just off Main St at its northern end.

Holiday Inn (☎ 603-224-9534, 800-465-4329; www.concordhi.com; 172 N Main St; d $100-140; ☒ ☐ ☒) The only full-service hotel in the heart of Concord's historic downtown, this comfortable 122-room hotel has all of the expected amenities, including a fitness center, a restaurant and a business center. Check the website for Internet specials.

Eating

Most restaurants catch the legislative lunch crowd across from the State House on N Main St at Park St.

Capitol Grille (☎ 603-228-6608; 1 Eagle Sq; sandwiches $6-8, mains $12-18; ☑ 11am-1am Tue-Fri & Sat, 10am-midnight Sun) This warm, inviting restaurant and bar has a typical pub menu, but the kitchen is willing to make just about anything you have a hankering for. In the evening, the lounge often hosts karaoke or other live music; otherwise something will likely be on the TVs behind the bar.

Bread & Chocolate (☎ 603-228-3330; 20 S Main St; sandwiches $5; ☑ 7:30am-6pm Mon-Fri, 8am-4pm Sat) This exceptional European-style bakery could hold its own in the French or German countryside. And it's not just for dessert – its café also makes a mean sandwich. Standards like ham-and-cheese and tuna salad are served on homemade croissants or bread.

In a Pinch Cafe (☎ 603-226-2272; 146 Pleasant St; mains $4-6; ☑ 7am-3pm Mon-Sat) Located east of the center near the Centennial Inn, this popular joint serves good sandwiches, soups and salads. Grab some picnic fare or relax on the sun porch.

Common Man (☎ 603-228-3463; 25 Water St; lunch $6-10, dinner $12-22) Oven-baked sandwiches constitute the lunch specialties, but dinner is more serious with scrod, baked stuffed shrimp and house specialties including chicken Kiev and prime rib.

Hermanos Cocina Mexicana (☎ 603-224-5669; 11 Hills Ave; mains $5-18; ☑ lunch & dinner) Just off Main St in an unlikely, historic brick building, Hermanos serves authentic and creative Mexican dishes, from pork *taquitos* (mini-tacos) to chimichangas. Head to the upstairs bar for excellent margaritas and catch some live jazz.

Getting There & Away

Driving from Concord to Lincoln via I-93 takes 1¼ hours. It's about 45 minutes from Concord to Weirs Beach via I-93 to US 3 North. **Concord Trailways** (www.concordtrailways.com) has a frequent daily service from the **Trailways Transportation Center** (☎ 603-228-3300, 800-639-3317; 30 Stickney Ave, I-93 exit 14) to Manchester ($5, 30 minutes) and Boston ($12.50, 1½ hours).

MONADNOCK REGION

In the southwestern corner of the state, the pristine villages of Peterborough and Jaffrey Center (2 miles due west of Jaffrey) anchor Mt Monadnock (3165ft). Monadnock – Mountain That Stands Alone' in

Algonquian – is relatively isolated from other peaks, which means hikers to the summit are rewarded with fantastic views of the surrounding countryside. Monadnock has long had the distinction of hosting more hikers than any other mountain in the world, except Mt Fuji. If anybody is counting, Monadnock has probably overtaken the top spot on this list since Fuji now has transportation options, so more hikers are catching a lift. Not so at Monadnock.

KEENE

pop 23,000

At the junction of commercial NH 12 and NH 10, Keene is the region's largest town, where residents run errands and conduct daily business. In town, NH 12 becomes Main St, a busy, bustling town center with lots of shops and restaurants. The **Greater Keene Chamber of Commerce** (☎ 603-352-1303; 48 Central Sq; ☽ 9am-5pm Mon-Fri) dishes up information, while **Toadstool Bookshops** (☎ 603-352-8815; Colony Mill Marketplace; ☽ 10am-9pm Mon-Sat, 11am-6pm Sun) offers new and used books, music and magazines.

Sights

The well-kept, red-brick campus of **Keene State College** (☎ 603-358-2276; www.keene.edu; 229 Main St) is at the west end of Main St, accounting for almost one-quarter of the town's population. The **Thorne Sagendorph Art Gallery** (☎ 603-358-2720; www.keene.edu/tsag; Wyman Way; admission free; ☽ noon-4pm daily, closed Mon Jun-Aug) housed at Keene State College plays a crucial role in supporting the arts in this rural region. Its spacious, skylit halls are a wonderful venue for rotating exhibits of regional and national artists. It hosts an annual exhibit focusing on New Hampshire native artists. The small permanent collection includes pieces by the many national artists that have been drawn to the Monadnock region since the 19th century (see the boxed text opposite).

Festivals & Events

This town comes alive in autumn, especially for the record-breaking **Pumpkin Festival** (www .pumpkinfestival.org). Keene holds the world record for the most jack-o-lanterns lit in the same place at the same time (28,952 in case you were wondering). Every year on the weekend before Halloween, the vil-

lage combines their resources in attempt to break their own record (set in 2003). Pumpkins are posed on a giant scaffolding on Central Sq. A craft fair, costume parade and live music take place in the surrounding streets.

Sleeping & Eating

Carriage Barn Guest House (☎ 603-357-3812; www .carriagebarn.com; 358 Main St; s/d Nov-Apr $65-75, May-Aug $79/89, Sep-Oct $100/110) Four frilly guest rooms in a welcoming house opposite Keene State College. Each comes with a private bathroom, plush terry robes and continental breakfast.

Goose Pond Guest House (☎ 603-357-4787; www .goosepondguesthouse.com; 144 E Surry Rd; r $90-140) Each spacious suite has a private bath and a private entrance, not to mention a fireplace, wainscoting and wide-plank pine floors. Guests can also take advantage of orchard-covered grounds, or the nearby forest preserve or golf course. From Central Sq, take Court St past the hospital. Fork right at the sign for Bretwood Golf Course.

Margaritas (☎ 603-357-4492; 77-81 Main St; $12-17) Fun and festive Margaritas never fails to please with its nine different kinds of fajitas, huge vegetarian selection and namesake icy, limey cocktails. Besides pleasing the palette, this place engages the community by hosting fundraising parties, cultural field trips, and arts and crafts exhibitions.

Lindy's Diner (☎ 603-352-4273; 19 Gilbo Ave; sandwiches $2-4, mains $6-10) It's not hard to believe Lindy's claim that she pours 'the best cup of coffee in town.' Students flock here for daily specials like steak sandwiches ($9) and country fried chicken ($7.50). Sit at the counter, where you can entertain yourself by attempting to answer Trivial Pursuit card questions, or settle back into a booth and peruse the choices on your private juke box.

Entertainment

Colonial Theater (☎ 603-352-2033; www.thecolonial .org; 95 Main St) After 80 years, this classic Main St theater is still going strong. From August to May, the Colonial hosts acts ranging from Dr John to Ken Burns to the St Petersburg Ballet. Every month there is at least one family-oriented show, such as children's theater or acrobatics.

CREATIVE COLONIALISM

The awe-inspiring Mt Monadnock and the serene beauty of the surrounding countryside have long attracted artists and writers to this region. In fact, Monadnock is home to one of the country's oldest artist colonies: MacDowell Colony in Peterborough.

In 1896, the composer Edward MacDowell and his wife Marian bought a farm in Peterborough, where they would retreat in summer to work. There, Edward said, he produced more and better music.

Edward and Marian knew that being surrounded by creative people enhanced one's own creativity. They worked to turn their farm into a place where artists, writers and musicians would come to interact, share their work and foster new creation and collaboration. The colony received its first guests in 1907, but Edward died the following year. It was his wife who oversaw the fundraising, the building of studios and the blossoming of the colony in the years to come.

MacDowell Colony has had remarkable endurance, but it was hardly unique at the time. Around this period, Augustus Saint-Gaudens welcomed myriad friends, acquaintances and apprentices at his estate in Cornish (see p434). And the nearby Dublin Art Colony hosted painters such as Abbott Handerson Thayer, George de Forest Brush, Joseph Lindon Smith and Frank Weston Benson. The Dublin artists also invited friends working in other disciplines. Mark Twain wrote of the Dublin Colony: 'Any place that is good for an artist in paint is good for an artist in morals and ink...'

After her husband's death, Marian MacDowell worked tirelessly to support the MacDowell Colony, and she succeeded in attracting a diverse and dynamic group of colonists ranging from poets to painters and playwrights. Aaron Copland composed parts of *Appalachian Spring* at the colony; Thornton Wilder wrote *Our Town;* Virgil Thomson worked on *Mother of Us All;* and Leonard Bernstein completed his Mass. Milton Avery, James Baldwin, Barbara Tuchman and Alice Walker are but a few of the luminaries that have passed this way.

More than 200 poets, composers, playwrights, architects, filmmakers, painters and photographers still come to Peterborough each year. They come for inspiration from Monadnock, from each other, and from the MacDowells' legacy of creative collaboration that endures to this day.

Getting There & Around

If you are stuck without wheels, **Vermont Transit** (☎ 603-436-0163, 800-552-8737; www.vermont transit.com) serves **Keene bus terminal** (☎ 603-352-1331; 6 Gilbo Ave) from Boston ($25, 2 hours 20 minutes) and Brattleboro ($11, 30 minutes).

PETERBOROUGH & AROUND

pop 6000

The delightful town of Peterborough is a perfect place to recover after spending the day on Mt Monadnock. The growing number of galleries and restaurants do not diminish the small-town charm. Peterborough's claim to fame is that it was the inspiration for *Our Town,* the classic play by Thornton Wilder, who wrote his masterpiece during his time at the MacDowell Colony (see above). Peterborough is unavoidably located just north of the intersection of NH 101 and NH 123/US 202. The heart of town is Depot Sq.

Unless otherwise stated, items in this section are in Peterborough proper.

Information

Greater Peterborough Chamber of Commerce (☎ 603-924-7234; www.peterboroughchamber.com; ☉ 9am-5pm Mon-Fri year-round, 10am-3pm Sat Jun-Oct) Prominent location at the highway intersection.

Toadstool Bookshop (☎ 603-924-3543; 12 Depot St; ☉ 10am-6pm Mon-Fri, 10am-5pm Sat, 10am-4pm Sun)

Sights & Activities

MARIPOSA MUSEUM

'Please touch!' implores this **museum** (☎ 603-924-4555; www.mariposamuseum.org; 26 Main St; adult/child $5/3; ☉ noon-4pm Jun-Aug, 3-5pm Mon-Fri, noon-4pm Sat & Sun Sep-May), which exhibits folk art and folklore from around the world. This is a wonderful place for kids, who are invited to dive into the collections: to try on costumes, experiment with musical instruments, play with toys and make their own art. 'Community Sundays' feature musicians and storytellers who lead interactive performances.

SHARON ARTS CENTER

Based in Sharon, about 8 miles south of Peterborough on NH 123, this **arts center**

NEW HAMPSHIRE

(☎ 603-924-2787; 20-40 Depot St; admission free) also has an annex gallery in Depot Sq. It displays fine arts and crafts by some of the region's many artists.

MILLER STATE PARK

New Hampshire's oldest state park is **Miller State Park** (☎ 603-924-3672; NH 101; admission $3; ⊙ dawn-dusk daily Jun-Oct, Sat & Sun only May & Nov-Dec). Miller is the site of Pack Monadnock, a 2290ft peak (not to be confused with its better-known neighbor, Mt Monadnock). Besides 21 miles of hiking trails, the park also has an auto road to the summit.

Sleeping

For a complete list of smaller places to stay, surf www.monadnocklodging.com or www .nhlodging.com.

Hannah Davis House (☎ 603-585-3344; 186 Depot Rd; d with breakfast $80-165; ✗) This excellent B&B features six rooms and suites decorated with great attention and flair. Fluffy down comforters, canopy beds, shiny hardwood floors and clawfoot tubs are de rigueur, while a few rooms also feature working fireplaces. Breakfast – served on formal china – features homemade goodies like pastries, granola and applesauce, in addition to eggs.

Three Maples (☎ 603-924-3503; www.threemaples .com; cnr NH 123 & Mountain Rd, Sharon; r $80-105; ✗) You'll recognize this colonial inn by the three 100-year-old maple trees dominating the front. The inn's grounds border hundreds of acres of protected land, guaranteeing its peaceful atmosphere. Each of three bedrooms has its own charms, whether it be fireplace, canopy bed or Jacuzzi. This place is 4 miles south of Peterborough in the tiny town of Sharon.

Apple Gate B&B (☎ 603-924-6543; 199 Upland Farm Rd; s $65-80, d $70-85 with breakfast; ✗) This charming 1832 colonial is nestled amongst apple orchards. It has an incredible parlor with crackling fireplace, and a reading room warmed by a wood stove. Breakfast is a romantic treat, served by candlelight. The four guest rooms are each named for a type of apple.

Peterborough Manor B&B (☎ 603-924-9832; www.peterboroughmanor.com; 50 Summer St; d with breakfast $65-75; ✗) This late-19th-century manse offers simple and affordable rooms in a family-friendly environment. Two of the eight guest rooms are suitable for families,

with an extra twin-bed en suite, and there is also a communal kitchen. It is a fantastic bargain located near the town center.

Jack Daniels Motor Inn (☎ 603-924-7548; www .jackdanielsinn.com; 80 Concord St; r $92) This friendly, family-run lodging is right on the Contoocook River, about 1 mile east of town on US 202. Rooms are spacious and comfortable. Discounts are available for single travelers during the week, and kids stay for free all the time.

Greenfield State Park (☎ 603-547-3497; sites $16; ⊙ mid-May–mid-Oct) Twelve miles northeast of Peterborough, off NH 136, this 400-acre park has fine swimming and hiking, as well as canoe and kayak rental. Campers can choose from 257 lakeside tent sites.

Eating

Twelve Pine (☎ 603-924-6140; Depot St; sandwiches $8, pizzas $20; ⊙ 8am-7pm Mon-Fri, 9am-5pm Sat, 9am-4pm Sun) Housed in a former train station, this sweet-smelling café has a good deli selection and specialty foods, as well as a nice coffee-and-juice bar. The little seating area seems to be the place to meet in Peterborough.

Peterborough Diner (☎ 603-924-6202; 10 Depot St; lunch specials $6, dinner $10-12; ⊙ 6am-9pm) This 1950s diner has typical fare served at the counter or in booths. The friendly staff seem to know everyone who walks through the door.

Aesop's Tables (☎ 603-924-1612; 12 Depot St; mains $3-6; ⊙ 7:30am-4pm Mon-Sat) Within the Toadstool Bookstore, which in turn occupies a cavernous former grocery store, this café serves good blackboard specials, sweet treats and coffee. In summer the ice-cream window and patio are popular.

RA Gatto's (☎ 603-924-5000; School St; mains $12-18; ⊙ 11:30am-2:30pm & 4:30-9pm Tue-Sat) For something a bit more formal, check out this classy restaurant serving seafood and pasta. The house specialty is flaky salmon combined with capers, horseradish, dill and breadcrumbs into a salmon cake, then pan fried and served with a lemon dill cream sauce. The vegetarian lasagna – made from an age-old family recipe – is also recommended.

Entertainment

Peterborough Folk Music Society (☎ 603-827-2905; www.acousticmusic.com/pfms; Peterborough Players, Hadley Rd; tickets $15-30, student discount $5) This active group attracts nationally known folk musicians to perform in a wonderful barn-style theater about 3½ miles from Peterborough center. Recent shows have included Greg Brown, Eddie from Ohio and Le Vent de Nord.

Harlow's Pub (☎ 603-924-6365; 3 School St) This local pub features a good selection of draught beers, including a rotating menu of New England brews. There is live music six or seven nights a week. Harlow's has a small selection of sandwiches and Mexican favorites, but the real reason to come here is to sit at the wooden bar.

JAFFREY
pop 5500

The town proper is less interesting than picture-perfect Jaffrey Center, which is 2 miles due west of Jaffrey. Stop at the chamber of commerce and pick up a walking-tour brochure, detailing the historical and architectural highlights of this village. The old **textile mills** along the river now house offices and shops. Other interesting sites include the **Little Red School House** and the **Melville Academy**, which now houses a local museum. Both are open on weekends in summer. For a deeper look at local history, spend some time in the **Old Burying Ground** behind the meetinghouse. Jaffrey Town Green often hosts free concerts on Wednesday nights in summer. Try to catch the Temple Band, the oldest town band in the country.

Information
Jaffrey Chamber of Commerce (☎ 603-532-4549; www.jaffreychamber.com; Main St, cnr NH 124 & NH 202; ☺ 10am-4pm Mon-Fri)

Sleeping & Eating
Inn at Jaffrey Center (☎ 603-532-7800, 877-510-7019; www.theinnatjaffreycenter.com; 379 Main St; r $50-150; ☒) This family affair features 11 unique guest rooms, each with its own color scheme and decorative style. Beautifully maintained grounds and wide porches grace the exterior of the home, while the interior has a warm and welcoming dining room. The bistro is open for all three meals, offering hearty, homemade country fare and an extensive wine list.

Benjamin Prescott Inn (☎ 603-532-6637, 888-950-6637; www.benjaminprescottinn.com; NH 124; d with breakfast $80-160; ☒) In East Jaffrey, this classic mid-19th-century farmhouse has 10 country-style guest rooms that have been meticulously restored. Expansive views of the surrounding 500-acre dairy farm and fields are icing on the cake.

Grand View (☎ 603-532-9880; www.thegrandviewinn.com; 580 Mountain Rd; d $125-175, tw $100; ☒ ☒) This 19th-century country mansion is located at the base of Mt Monadnock and has trailheads to the summit. When you finish your hike, indulge in a massage or soak in the Jacuzzi at the Grand View's spa; then fall into your kingsize bed in one of nine luxurious rooms.

Woodbound Inn (☎ 603-532-8341; www.woodbound.com; 62 Woodbound Rd, Rindge; r $99-109, cabins $145-215; ☒) A family resort on the shores of Lake Contoocook. The lodge here has 44 rooms with a rustic feel but modern conveniences (and breathtaking views of Mt Monadnock). Six lakeside cabins have fireplaces and room for families. Golf, tennis, cross-country ski trails and a private beach are all available for guests to enjoy. The Woodbound is southeast of Jaffrey in Rindge.

Emerald Acres Campground (☎ 603-532-8838; 39 Ridgecrest Rd; sites $20-28; ☺ May-mid-Oct) Off NH 124, these 52 sites sit amidst the pine trees adjacent to Cheshire Pond. The campground is ideal for families who enjoy fishing, swimming and boating.

Aylmer's Grille (☎ 603-532-4949; 21 Main St; lunch $8-12, dinner $18-22) This little restaurant exemplifies casual chic. The dining room is comfortable and welcoming, but just upscale enough to offer a special martini menu. The cuisine is creative American with Mediterranean influences – think chicken *fattoush* (toasted bread and tomato salad) or prawns and pasta.

Kimball Farm (☎ 603-532-5765; NH 124; ☺ 11am-10pm May-Oct) This dairy has achieved more than local fame for its sinfully creamy ice-cream that comes in 40 flavors and unbelievable portion sizes. If you have room for a meal before dessert, the café also serves sandwiches and simple seafood specials.

Getting There & Away
Jaffrey is located at the intersection of US 202 and NH 124, while quaint Jaffrey Center is 2 miles west on NH 124. No public transportation is available.

MT MONADNOCK STATE PARK
This commanding **peak** (☎ 603-532-8862; Dublin Rd; adult/child under 12 $3/free), off NH 124, which

you can see from 50 miles away in any direction, is the area's spiritual vertex. Complete with a visitor center (where you can get good hiking information), 12 miles of ungroomed cross-country ski trails and over 40 miles of hiking trails (6 miles of which reach the summit), this state park is an outdoor wonderland. The White Dot Trail (which turns into the White Cross Trail) from the visitor center to the bare-topped peak is about a 3½-hour hike roundtrip.

Primitive is the operative word if you are thinking of spending the night in the **Monadnock State Park campground** (☎ 603-532-8862, reservations 603-271-3628; NH 124; sites $12-16; ☾ year-round). This 1000-acre park has 21 sites. From November until mid-May there is no water. Since they don't plow the road, you must carry in supplies 1 mile to the campground.

AREA VILLAGES

The region is a web of narrow, indirect roads connecting vintage towns. One could easily spend a couple days hopping from one village to another. There isn't much to do in any one, but they'll linger in your mind long after departing. If you're driving around, stop for a short spell in **Fitzwilliam**, with its town green surrounded by lovely old houses and a graceful town hall (with a stunning steeple). Fitzwilliam is on NH 119, 13 miles southwest of Jaffrey.

Harrisville, northwest of Peterborough via NH 101 and Dublin, is a former mill village that looks much as it did in the late 1700s, when textile mills flourished. But this is no living museum; today, the brick and granite mill buildings have been renovated into functionally aesthetic commercial spaces.

Hancock, north of Peterborough on NH 123, is another quintessential New England village. The town's showpiece is one of the oldest continuously operating inns in New England: **Hancock Inn** (☎ 603-525-3318, 800-525-1789; www.hancockinn.com; 33 Main St, Hancock; d with breakfast $215-250). New Hampshire's oldest inn has 15 rooms, each with its own unique charms. Dome ceilings (in rooms that used to be part of a ballroom), fireplaces and private patios are some of the features. The cozy dining room is open for breakfast and dinner.

Hillsborough Center, 14 miles north of Hancock on NH 123, is another classic, not to be confused with Hillsborough Lower Village and Upper Village. Steeped in the late 18th and early 19th century, the trim little town boasts a number of art studios. Stop into **Caron's Restaurant** (☎ 603-464-3575; 85 Henniker St) to get the local lowdown and a piece of meatloaf.

Walpole, northwest of Keene along NH 12, is another gem. Locals descend from surrounding villages to dine at **Burdick Chocolate** (☎ 603-756-9058; 47 Main St, Walpole; lunch $8-12, dinner $15-22; ☾ noon-2:30pm Mon-Sat, 5:30-9pm Tue-Sat, 10am-3pm Sun). Originally a New York City chocolatier, Burdick moved the operation to this tiny New Hampshire village and opened a sophisticated café to showcase its desserts. Besides rich, chocolatey indulgences, the lively bistro has a full menu of creative new American dishes.

Getting There & Around

It really requires a private vehicle to do any justice to exploring this region. To reach Peterborough and Jaffrey from Manchester, head south then east on NH 101. Expect the 40-mile trip to take about 1½ hours. It also makes sense to visit the region on the way to or from Brattleboro, Vermont.

UPPER CONNECTICUT RIVER VALLEY

The Connecticut River, New England's longest, is the decisive boundary between New Hampshire and Vermont. The Upper Connecticut River Valley extends roughly from Brattleboro, VT (see p357) in the south to Woodsville, New Hampshire in the north, and includes towns on both banks (although only New Hampshire destinations are covered in this section). The river has long been an important byway for explorers and traders. Today, it is an adventure destination for boaters and bird-watchers, canoers and kayakers. The region's largest population center is Lebanon, while the cultural focal point is prestigious Dartmouth College in Hanover.

HANOVER & AROUND
pop 10,850

Dartmouth College was chartered in 1769 primarily 'for the education and instruction of Youth of the Indian Tribes.' The school was located deep in the forests where its prospective students lived. Although teaching

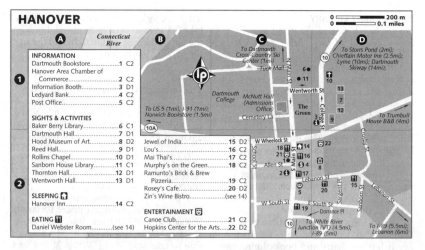

'English Youth and others' was only its secondary purpose, in fact, Dartmouth College graduated few Indian youths and was soon attended almost exclusively by colonists. The college's most illustrious alumnus is Danel Webster (1782–1852), who graduated in 1801 and went on to become a prominent lawyer, US senator, secretary of state and perhaps the USA's most esteemed orator.

Today, Hanover is the quintessential New England college town: graceful Georgian buildings covered in ivy, wide lawns where students toss footballs or stroll to class, streets lined with trees that turn bright shades of orange and gold every fall. The town revolves around Dartmouth College, but that institution offers plenty to keep it lively and fresh.

Hanover is part of a larger community which includes Lebanon, in New Hampshire, as well as Norwich and White River Junction, in Vermont. When looking for services (especially accommodations), consider all of these places, not just Hanover. Unless otherwise stated, items in this section are in Hanover proper.

Orientation

To visit Hanover is to visit Dartmouth College, for the college dominates the town. The central reference for everything is the green, the broad lawn bounded by Wheelock, N Main, Wentworth and College Sts. Many services are along Main St, which runs for several blocks south from the green.

Information

Dartmouth Bookstore (☎ 603-643-3616; 33 S Main St; ⏰ 8am-9pm Mon-Thu, 8am-10pm Fri, 9am-10pm Sat, noon-6pm Sun) An excellent selection of fiction, nonfiction and local reference books, as well as text books and magazines.

Hanover Area Chamber of Commerce (☎ 603-643-3115; www.hanoverchamber.org; 216 Nugget Bldg, Main St) The chamber also maintains an information booth on the village green, staffed from July to mid-September.

Ledyard Bank (☎ 603-643-2244; 38 Main St; ⏰ 9am-5pm Mon-Fri, 9am-noon Sat)

Norwich Bookstore (☎ 802-649-1114; Main St, Norwich) An unusually good bookstore, especially for a small town.

Sights

DARTMOUTH COLLEGE GREEN

The green is the focal point of the campus, both physically and historically. Along the east side of the green, picturesque **Dartmouth Row** (College St) consists of four harmonious Georgian buildings: Wentworth, Dartmouth, Thornton and Reed. Dartmouth Hall was the original college building, constructed in 1791. Just north of Dartmouth Row, **Rollins Chapel** (College St) is a fine example of Richardsonian architecture and a peaceful place to collect your thoughts.

Throughout the year, undergraduate students lead free guided **walking tours** (☎ 603-646-2875; www.dartmouth.edu; 2nd fl, McNutt Hall; ⏰ 10am & 3pm Mon-Fri, 10am & noon Sat) of the Dartmouth campus. Reservations are not required, but you may wish to confirm the schedule in advance.

NEW HAMPSHIRE

BAKER BERRY LIBRARY

On the north side of the green is the college's central library, **Baker Berry Library** (☎ 603-646-2560; ☼ 8am-midnight Mon-Thu, 8am-10pm Fri, 10am-10pm Sat, 10am-midnight Sun). The reserve corridor on the lower level houses an impressive mural called *Epic of American Civilization*, painted by José Clemente Orozco (1883–1949). The renowned Mexican muralist taught and painted at Dartmouth from 1932 to 1934. The mural follows the course of civilization in North America from the time of the Aztecs to the present.

Go upstairs and enjoy the view of the campus from the **Tower Room** on the 2nd floor. This collegiate, wood-paneled room is one of the library's loveliest.

The adjacent **Sanborn House Library** (☎ 603-646-2312) also features ornate woodwork, plush leather chairs and books lining the walls, floor to ceiling, on two levels. It is named for Professor Edwin Sanborn, who taught for almost 50 years in the Department of English. This is where students (and you!) can enjoy a **traditional teatime** (☼ 4pm Mon-Fri) each afternoon.

HOOD MUSEUM OF ART

Shortly after the university's founding in 1769, Dartmouth began to acquire artifacts of artistic or historical interest. Since that time, the collection has expanded to include nearly 60,000 items, which are housed at the **Hood Museum of Art** (☎ 603-646-2808; admission free; ☼ 10am-5pm Tue & Thu-Sat, 10am-9pm Wed, noon-5pm Sun). The collection is particularly strong in American art, including Native American art. One of the highlights is a set of Assyrian reliefs from the Palace of Ashurnasirpal that date to the ninth century BC. Special exhibits often feature contemporary artists.

Activities

HIKING

Just over the river in Norwich, about 7 miles from Hanover, **Gile Mountain** is a popular destination for Dartmouth students looking for a quick escape from the grind. A half-hour hike – and a quick climb up the **fire tower** – rewards adventurers with an incredible view of the Connecticut River Valley and the White Mountains beyond.

Cross the river into Norwich and take Main St through town to Turnpike Rd. Stay left at the fork and straight on Lower Turnpike Rd, even as it turns to gravel. Look for the old farmhouse on the right and the sign for parking on the left.

SKIING

The **Dartmouth Cross Country Ski Center** (☎ 603-643-6534; Occum Pond; day pass $7, ski rental adult/child per day $13/9, snowshoe rental per day $10/7; ☼ 9am-7pm Mon-Fri, 9am-5pm Sat & Sun) maintains over 25km of groomed trails in the immediate vicinity of Dartmouth campus for wintertime fun. Head northeast on Lyme Rd to reach the center. Trails are on the golf course and at Storrs Pond.

With two challenging mountains, minimal crowds and reasonable prices, **Dartmouth Skiway** (☎ 603-795-2143; http://skiway.dartmouth.edu; 39 Grafton Turnpike, Lyme; one-day lift ticket adult/child under 14/student/senior Mon-Fri $26/18/20/20, Sat & Sun & holidays $38/25/25/20) is one of New Hampshire's best skiing value areas. Take NH 10 north to Lyme. Fork right at the white church and continue 3 miles to the Skiway.

Festivals & Events

Each February, Dartmouth celebrates the weeklong **Winter Carnival** (☎ 603-646-3399; www.dartmouth.edu/~sao), featuring special art shows, drama productions, concerts, an ice sculpture contest and other amusements. It is organized by the Student Activities Office in conjunction with the Hopkins Center and other campus groups.

Sleeping

Hanover's economy has a split personality: eating places are designed and priced for students, while lodgings are designed for the well-heeled parents and academic types who come to visit. Thus, meals are cheap, but beds are not. Regional accommodations (in Hanover, Lebanon and White River Junction) are in greatest demand during the fall foliage season, when virtually all the rooms are reserved. Any special event at the college will also create demand.

BUDGET

Chieftain Motor Inn (☎ 603-643-2550, 800-845-3557; www.chieftaininn.com; 84 Lyme Rd; d with breakfast $10-150; ☒ ☑) This 22-room inn has large, clean, comfortable rooms. The pine-paneled rooms are a bit dark, but they are brightened by handmade quilts. The country setting along NH 10 North allows for lovely views of the Connecticut River.

Airport Economy Inn (☎ 603-298-8888, 800-433-3466; 45 Airport Rd, West Lebanon; d Jul-Oct $75-105, d Nov-Jun $55-85) The staff is helpful and the 56 rooms are clean. What more can you ask for at this price?

Storrs Pond Recreation Area (☎ 603-643-2134; NH 10; sites without/with hookups $20/24; ☿ mid-May–mid-Oct; ♨) In addition to 37 woodsy sites on a 15-acre pond, this private campground has tennis courts and two sandy beaches for swimming. From I-89 exit 13, take NH 10 north and look for signs.

Mascoma Lake Camping Area (☎ 603-448-5076; www.mascomalake.com; NH 4A; sites without/with hookups $22/29; ☿ mid-May–mid-Oct) These 90 sites, in nearby Lebanon, are mostly shaded and overlook a lake. This place has lots of recreational facilities like basketball courts, boat rental and kids' play areas.

MID-RANGE & TOP END

Norwich Inn (☎ 802-649-1143; www.norwichinn.com; 325 Main St, Norwich VT; d/ste Dec-Apr $69/129, May-Nov $79/149; ✗) Just across the Connecticut River in Norwich, Vermont, this well-run establishment has 16 attractive inn rooms, seven motel rooms, four vestry apartments and a good traditional dining room. They are all decorated with Victorian antiques and traditional country furniture. The brewpub, Jasper Murdock's Alehouse, will whet your whistle while you are here.

Alden Country Inn (☎ 603-795-2222; www.aldencountryinn.com; 1 Market St, Lyme; d $90-130 Dec-Apr, $140-185 May-Nov; ✗) Ten miles north of Hanover via NH 10 and facing the Lyme Town Common, this 1809 inn has 15 colonial guest rooms with modern facilities. Prices include a full country breakfast with freshly baked scones, eggs, and pancakes topped with local maple syrup. Other equally enticing meals are available in the dining room and tavern.

Trumbull House B&B (☎ 603-643-2370, 800-651-5141; www.trumbullhouse.com; 40 Etna Rd; d $125-175, ste $200-250 with breakfast; ✗) Four miles east of Dartmouth, this B&B is a wonderful alternative to staying in town. It's a family-friendly colonial house, built in 1919, with five luxurious guest rooms and a tranquil pond. A hiking trail links it to the Appalachian Trail (p523).

Hanover Inn (☎ 603-643-4300, 800-443-7024; www.hanoverinn.com; cnr Wheelock & Main Sts; d $257-297;

✗) Hanover's most prominent lodging is, not surprisingly, owned by Dartmouth College. It is located at the heart of Hanover, directly opposite the green. The decor is colonial reproduction and the ambience upscale, with prices to match.

Eating & Drinking
BUDGET & MID-RANGE

Lou's (☎ 603-643-3321; 30 S Main St; mains $5-8; ☿ breakfast & lunch) A Dartmouth institution since 1947, this is Hanover's oldest establishment. The place is always packed with students meeting for a coffee or perusing their books. From the retro tables or the Formica-topped counter, order typical diner food like eggs, sandwiches and burgers. The bakery items are also highly recommended.

Rosey's Cafe (☎ 603-643-5282; 15 Lebanon St; sandwiches $6; ☿ 8:30am-6pm Mon-Sat, 10am-5pm Sun) Rosey's serves up excellent panini sandwiches with ingredients such as eggplant, feta, pesto, tomato and basil. This artsy space is also a cool place to hang out with a cup of robust espresso, especially if you snag a spot on the patio.

Ramunto's Brick & Brew Pizzeria (☎ 603-643-9500; 68 S Main St; sandwiches $4-6, pizzas $10-20; ☿ 11am-midnight) Every college town has one, and this is it: the favorite pizza joint. The specialty here is the famous 'Garlic Knot' pizza topped with tomato and basil. It will stick with you for hours.

Four Aces Diner (☎ 603-298-6827; 23 Bridge St, West Lebanon; mains $5-10; ☿ 5am-8pm Tue-Sat, 7am-3pm Sun, 5am-3pm Mon) Down the road in West Lebanon, smack-talking waitresses serve up stacks of pancakes, steak and eggs, and the daily special omelet, any time of day. With individual juke boxes in every booth and a constantly brewing pot of coffee, this is the classic country diner.

Mai Thai's (☎ 603-643-9980; 44 S Main St; lunch buffet $8.50, mains $6-12; ☿ 11:30am-10pm Mon-Sat) This popular 2nd-floor place has an excellent value lunch buffet and pleasantly upscale environs. Six kinds of curry and five different versions of *pad thai* (Thai noodles) make this a spicy delight.

Jewel of India (☎ 603-643-2217; 27 Lebanon St; lunch $7, mains $6-11; ☿ 11:30am-3pm & 4:30pm-10pm) Exotic music and enticing aromas waft out to the street from this classic New England house. The setting is perhaps incongruous,

NEW HAMPSHIRE

but it's still inviting, especially considering the bargain takeout lunch specials. Sunday brunch features lots of curry and 10 kinds of bread.

Murphy's on the Green (☎ 603-643-4075; 11 S Main St; mains $8-15; ☺ food 11am-10pm, drinks till 12:30am) This is classic collegiate tavern, where students and faculty meet over pints of ale and big, satisfying plates of hearty pub food. Stained-glass windows and church-pew seating enhance the cozy, Irish-pub atmosphere.

TOP END

Zin's Wine Bistro (☎ 603-643-4300; Hanover Inn, cnr Main & Wheelock Sts; mains $7-18; ☺ 11:30am-10pm Mon-Sat, 5:30-10pm Sun) Sophisticated yet comfortable, this bistro in the Hanover Inn is a warm, inviting place for a meal or a drink. The menu features creative presentations of seafood, meats and pastas, and – of course – a wide selection of wines by the glass.

Daniel Webster Room (☎ 603-643-4300; Hanover Inn; mains $23-30; ☺ 7-10:30am daily, 11:30am-1:30pm Mon-Fri & 6-9pm Tue-Sat, 11am-1:30pm Sun) Hanover's most elegant dining place is this refined restaurant in the Hanover Inn. The atmosphere is a little stuffy, but the classic American menu and the ultra-attentive service score highly with diners. The lunch menu is significantly less expensive, but without the high prices and candlelit tables, this place does not seem so out-of-the-ordinary.

Entertainment

Hopkins Center for the Arts (☎ 603-646-2422; www .hop.dartmouth.edu) Dartmouth's outstanding venue for the performing arts. A long way from such cosmopolitan centers as Boston, New York and Montreal, the college makes its own entertainment to fill the long winter nights. Look for playbills promoting everything from movies to live performances by international companies.

Canoe Club (☎ 603-643-9660; www.canoeclub .us; 27 S Main St; mains $15-24) Not your typical college music club. This upscale pub features live music seven nights a week – usually jazz, folk and a little bit of bluegrass. While you are enjoying the tunes, you can sample the sophisticated menu; try hearty mains such as New England shellfish stew or spice-rubbed lamb served on couscous with curried vegetables. The menu changes seasonally but everything is organic.

Getting There & Around

Short-haul 'commuter' subsidiaries of some major airlines link **Lebanon Municipal Airport** (☎ 603-298-8878), 6 miles south of Hanover, with Boston, New York and Philadelphia.

Overland, it takes three hours to reach Hanover from Boston; take I-93 to I-89 to I-91. From Hanover to Burlington, Vermont (VT), it's an additional 2½ hours north via I-89. **Vermont Transit** (☎ 802-864-6811, 800-552-8737; www.vermonttransit.com) has direct buses from Hanover to Logan International Airport ($38.50, three hours) and Manchester

---

DETOUR: SAINT-GAUDENS NATIONAL HISTORIC SITE

In the summer of 1885, the sculptor Augustus Saint-Gaudens rented an old inn near the town of Cornish and came to this beautiful spot in the Connecticut River Valley to work. He returned summer after summer, and eventually bought the place in 1892. The estate, where he lived until his death in 1907, is now open to the public as the **Saint-Gaudens National Historic Site** (☎ 603-675-2175; www.nps.gov/saga; 139 St Gaudens Rd, Cornish; adult/child $5/free; ☺ bldgs 9am-4:30pm May-Oct, grounds 9am-dusk year-round).

Saint-Gaudens is best known for his public monuments, such as the Sherman Monument in New York's Central Park and the Adams Memorial in Rock Creek Park in Washington DC. Perhaps his greatest achievement was the Robert Gold Shaw Memorial across from the State House (p79) in Boston. Recasts of all of these sculptures are scattered around the beautiful grounds of the estates.

In addition to seeing Saint-Gaudens' work, the National Historic Site allows visitors to tour his home and wander the grounds and studios, where artists-in-residence sculpt. The visitors center shows a short film about the artist's life and work. The site is just off NH 12A in Cornish. From I-89, take exit 20 (West Lebanon) and go south on NH 12A. From I-91, take exit 8 (Ascutney) and go east to 12A, heading north.

International Airport ($21, three hours). There is also a service to Burlington, Vermont (two hours) and Montreal (four hours).

Dartmouth Coach (☎ 603-448-2800; www.dart mouthcoach.com) operates five daily shuttles from Hanover to Logan International Airport and South Station in Boston (adult/child one way $35/25, three hours).

Advance Transit (☎ 802-295-1824; www.advance transit.com) travels to White River Junction, Lebanon, West Lebanon and Norwich for free. Bus stops are indicated by a blue-and-yellow AT symbol.

LAKES REGION

Centered on vast Lake Winnipesaukee, the Lakes Region is an odd mix of wondrous natural beauty and commercial tawdriness. The forest-shrouded lakes have beautiful, sinuous coastlines stretching for hundreds of miles. The roads skirting the shores and connecting the lakeside towns, however, are a riotous festival of mindless popular culture, lined with a hodgepodge of shopping malls, amusement arcades, auto dealerships, go-cart tracks, clam shacks, tourist cottages, junk-food outlets and boat docks.

Lake Winnipesaukee, New Hampshire's largest lake, has 183 miles of coastline, more than 300 islands and excellent salmon fishing. No wonder the American Indians named it 'Smile of the Great Spirit.' The prettiest stretches are in the southwest corner between Glendale and Alton (on the shoreline Belknap Point Rd), and in the northeast corner between Wolfeboro and Moultonborough (on NH 109). Stop for a swim, a lakeside picnic or a cruise. If you have children, don't miss a chance to prowl the video arcades, bowl-a-dromes and junkfood cafés of Weirs Beach.

LACONIA & AROUND
pop 16,400

The largest town of the Lakes Region, Laconia is the population center, with a hospital, an auto-parts store and other services. Neighboring Gilford, in the shadow of Belknap Mountain (2384ft), is joined at the hip to, and indistinguishable from, Laconia. Most visitors stay in the towns near the lake, like Glendale and Alton, with their small hotels, motels and cottages shaded by pines.

Orientation & Information
Greater Laconia–Weirs Beach Chamber of Commerce (☎ 603-524-5531; www.laconia-weirs. org; 11 Veterans Sq, Laconia; ☺ 8:30am-5pm Mon-Fri, noon-4pm Sat) Maintains an information office in the old railroad station in the center of town.
Lakes Region Association (☎ 603-744-8664, 800-605-2537; www.lakesregion.org; NH 104, New Hampton) An online business directory with information about skiing, hiking trails, scenic drives, covered bridges and leaf-peeping, as well as local service providers.
Lake Winnipesaukee Home Page (www.winnipesaukee .com) A great independent site with lots of resources, web cams and news.

Sights & Activities
ELLACOYA STATE BEACH PARK
Many lakeshore lodgings have water access, but if your place does not, head for **Ellacoya State Beach Park** (☎ 603-293-7821; admission $3; ☺ late May–mid-Oct), which has a 600ft-wide beach, bathhouse facilities, a picnic area and a campground (see p436). The Sandwich and Ossipee mountains are visible in the distance. This is an excellent place for swimming, fishing and canoeing.

HIKING
Mt Belknap (2384ft) is the highest peak in the Belknap Range, which has many interconnected hiking trails. The most direct route to the summit is from the Belknap Carriage Rd in Gilford. From NH 11A, take Cherry Valley Rd and follow the signs for the Belknap Fire Tower. Three marked trails lead from the parking lot to the summit of Belknap, a one-hour trek. The white-blazed trail leads to the summit of nearby Piper Mountain (2030ft).

Within the Belknap Mountain State Forest, the **Mt Major Summit Trail** is a good 2-mile trek up that 1780ft peak. The summit offers spectacular views of all corners of Lake Winnipesaukee. The trail head is a few miles south of West Alton on NH 11; park just off the road.

SKIING
When the snow covers the ground, Mt Belknap becomes **Gunstock** (☎ 800-486-7862; www.gunstock.com; NH 11A, Gilford; lift tickets adult/child/senior/teen Fri-Sun $49/29/39/39, Tue-Thu $39/19/19/29; ☺ 1-4pm Tue-Fri, 9am-4pm Sat & Sun), a ski area with 45 downhill runs on a vertical drop of 1400ft. There are seven lifts, as well as a ski school, day-care facilities and night skiing (adult/

NEW HAMPSHIRE

child/senior/teen $25/18/18/22) between 4pm and 9pm Tuesday to Thursday, and 4pm and 10pm Friday and Saturday. Most mountain trails are intermediate, with more advanced than beginner trails. A few hills are dedicated to tubing (two/four hours $14/20) – no equipment and no skill required! Over 30 miles of cross-country trails follow the wooded paths around Gilford; this carries a charge of $11 from Tuesday to Thursday, and $13 Friday to Sunday. Rental skis are available, as are snowboards and snowshoes.

Festivals & Events

In early to mid-June, the raucous **Motorcycle Week** (www.laconiamcweek.com) draws two-wheeled crowds to the **New Hampshire International Speedway** (☎ 603-783-4931; www.nhis.com; NH 106, Loudon), south of Laconia. Races, shows and other spectacles create quite a scene. Bikers are everywhere.

Sleeping

Belknap Point Motel (☎ 603-293-7511, 888-454-2537; www.bpmotel.com; 107 Belknap Point Rd, Gilford; r $72-100, ste $82-110) Along Belknap Point Rd, just northwest of Ellacoya State Park, these 16 lakeside motel rooms and apartments with cooking facilities are an excellent choice. The waterfront location yields views of the Ossipees to the east, the foothills of the White Mountains to the north, and Mt Washington in the distance on clear days.

Bay Side Inn (☎ 603-875-5005; www.bayside-inn.com; NH 11D, Alton Bay; ☒) Eighteen attractive guest rooms right on the Winnipesaukee waterfront. Guests enjoy a private beach that is an excellent setting for fishing and swimming. Motorboats (with skis) and kayaks are available for rental. Two-bedroom efficiency suites (and weekly rates) are available for longer-term guests.

Inn at Smith Cove (☎ 603-293-1111; www.innatsmithcove.com; 19 Roberts Rd, Gilford; r with breakfast $90-170; ☒) This elegant Victorian inn has nine uniquely appointed rooms with wonderful lake views and three quaint cottages with a garden setting. A spacious piazza and landscaped grounds lead down to a private beach and boat docks on Lake Winnipesaukee.

Greystone Inn & Motel (☎ 603-293-7377; www.greystoneinn-nh.com; 132 Scenic Dr, Gilford; r $90-120, ste $120-140; ☒) This old farmhouse was undergoing extensive renovation at the time of research, in hopes of restoring its turn-

of-the-century charm. The grounds here include a private beach with a boat dock; paddleboats are available for rental.

Gunstock (☎ 603-293-4341, 800-486-7862; www.gunstock.com; NH 11A, Gilford; sites without/with hookups $25/35; ☺ year-round) The ski area has a large campground that is open when the slopes are closed. It is a woodsy setting in the midst of mountains and lakes. Water hookups are not available in winter, but there are heated bathrooms and drinking water nearby. Gunstock also has some cabins ($70) that sleep five people.

Ellacoya State RV Park (☎ 603-293-7821; reservations 603-436-1552; Gilford; sites $35; ☺ mid-May–mid-Oct) There are 35 unshaded sites with full RV hookups here. The campground, off NH 11, does not have much to offer, but it is right next to the lovely state park grounds.

Eating

Nadia's Trattoria (☎ 603-524-8688; 1402 Lakeshore Rd, Gilford; mains $15-20; ☺ 4:30-9pm May-Aug, Tue-Sun Sep-Apr) One of New Hampshire's finest Italian restaurants. The menu features delectable antipasti, homemade pasta and fresh seafood. Save room for a sweet treat crafted by Bindi, the master Italian pastry chef.

Water St Café (☎ 603-524-4144; 141 Water St, Laconia; breakfast $3-5, sandwiches $5-8; ☺ 5:30am-2pm Mon-Thu & Sat, 5:30am-8pm Fri, 7am-1pm Sun) This friendly, family-run diner specializes in hearty breakfasts for early-risers. Even if you are not up with the sun, you can enjoy daily breakfast specials and omelettes made to order. Lunch focuses on sandwiches.

Getting There & Around

Driving from Laconia to North Conway, take US 3 to NH 25 to NH 16 (1½ hours, 50 miles). **Concord Trailways** (☎ 603-228-3300, 800-639-3317; www.concordtrailways.com) runs a route between Boston and Berlin. Pick it up at the Evans Expressmart/Exxon gas station in Tilton or the Munce's Konvenience/Citgo gas station in New Hampton. Buses go south to Concord ($6.50, one hour), Manchester ($9.50, 1½ hours), Boston ($18.50, 2½ hours) or Logan International Airport ($24, 2½ hours). Heading north, you can go to North Conway (1½ hours), Jackson (1½ hours), Pinkham Notch (two hours) or all the way up to Gorham and Berlin.

The **Greater Laconia Transit Agency** (☎ 603-528-2496, 800-294-2496; all-day pass adult/child $2/1; ☺ July-early September) runs shuttle trolleys through town to Weirs Beach and Meredith.

WEIRS BEACH

Called 'Aquedoctan' by its Native American settlers, Weirs Beach takes its English name from the Indian weirs (enclosures for catching fish) that the first white settlers found along the small sand beach. Today Weirs Beach is the honky-tonk heart of Lake Winnipesaukee's childhood amusements, famous for video-game arcades and fried dough. The vacation scene is completed by a lakefront promenade, a small public beach and a dock for small cruising ships. A water park and drive-in theater are also in the vicinity. Away from the din on the waterfront, you will notice evocative, Victorian-era architecture – somehow out of place in this capital of kitsch.

Weirs Beach is just north of Laconia at the convergence of US 3 and NH 11.

Information

Greater Laconia–Weirs Beach Chamber of Commerce (☎ 603-524-5531; www.laconia-weirs.org; US3) Useful for same-day accommodations; located south of Weirs Beach.

Weirs Beach, NH On-line Guidebook (www.weirsbeach .com) An excellent website with many links to area information.

Sights & Activities

WINNIPESAUKEE SCENIC RAILROAD

The touristy **scenic railroad** (☎ 603-745-2135; www .hoborr.com; adult/child 1hr $9/8, 2hr $10/9; ⏱ 11am-5pm daily Jun-Aug, Sat & Sun only May & Sep-Oct) departs Weirs Beach and Meredith (see p438) for a one- or two-hour lakeside ride aboard '20s and '30s train cars. The train travels to Lake Winnipesaukee's southern tip at Alton Bay before making a U-turn. Kids might wish to ride in the ice-cream parlor car.

MS MOUNT WASHINGTON

This classic **cruising ship** (☎ 603-366-5531; www .cruisenh.com; adult/child $19/9) steams out of Weirs Beach on relaxing 2½-hour scenic lake cruises at 10am and 12:30pm from mid-May to mid-October, with an extra cruise at 3.15pm July to August. Special events include the Sunday champagne brunch cruise and 'Family Fun Fridays,' not to mention the frequent dinner dance cruises ($34 to $42) throughout the summer.

The same company also operates the MV *Sophie C*, a veritable floating **post office** (adult/child $16/8). This US Mail boat delivers packages and letters to quaint ports and otherwise inaccessible island residents on 1½-hour runs at 11am and 2pm. The MV *Doris E* offers **cruises** (adult/child $10/5) of Meredith Bay and northern Lake Winnipesaukee from 10:30am to 7:30pm late June to August. Both leave from Weirs Beach and the *Doris E* also stops at Meredith.

Sleeping

Some of the nicer moderately priced area motels lie on US 3 (Weirs Blvd) between Gilford and Weirs Beach.

Birch Knoll Motel (☎ 603-366-4958; www.birchknoll motel.com; 867 Weirs Blvd; d Jun-early Sep $89-129, late Sep-Oct & May-Jun $59-99; ⏱ May–mid-Oct; ✕ ⛵) This 24-room motel is 1 mile south of Weirs Beach and overlooking Paugus Bay. It is one of the nicer motels in the area, with a private beach, a sunny deck overlooking the lake and a recreation room. Rooms are standard but comfortable and some have lake views.

Baytop Motel (☎ 603-366-2225; www.baytop.com; 1025 Weirs Blvd; d $55-84 Sep-May, $79-109 Jun-early Sep; ✕ ⛵) Just a half-mile south of Weirs Beach, these eight traditional motel rooms and four efficiencies overlook the lake. Rooms are nicely decorated and well equipped with refrigerators, microwaves and coffee-makers. Extra perks include a Jacuzzi and a pingpong table.

Cozy Inn & Lakeview House (☎ 603-366-4310; www.cozyinn-nh.com; 12 Maple St; r $60-90, ste $115-200; cottages $120-175; ✕ ⛵) These two places are side by side, a few steps from the Weirs Beach boardwalk. They offer any type of accommodation you desire: single rooms, larger suites and housekeeping cottages. Management also offers boat trips and skiing lessons.

Hack-Ma-Tack Campground (☎ 603-366-5977; www.hackmatackcampground.com; 713 Endicott St; sites without/with hookups $23/26; ⏱ mid-May–mid-Oct; ⛵) This 17-acre, family-friendly campground is 1½ miles north of Weirs Beach. Its 80 sites are spacious and woodsy. Recreation facilities include a basketball court and playground.

Paugus Bay Campground (☎ 603-366-4757; 96 Hilliard Rd; sites without/with hookups $32/36; ⏱ mid-May–mid-Oct) Off US 3, Paugus has 170 wooded sites overlooking the lake. The campground has a private beach, as well as other recreation facilities.

Eating

Weirs Beach is all about lobsters and fast food: burgers, hot dogs, fried dough, ice-cream, doughnuts, etc. Cruise Lakeside Dr for the snack shops.

Weirs Beach Lobster Pound (☎ 603-366-2255; US 3; mains $5-10; ☉ mid-May–mid-Oct) This is one Weirs Beach institution. Across from the water slide, this restaurant's been here forever. It serves local seafood and steaks and has a children's menu.

Getting There & Around

Weirs Beach is located on the west side of Lake Winnipesaukee. From I-93 take exit 20 (from the south) or 24 (from the north) to US 3. See p436 for information on transportation around the Lakes Region.

MEREDITH & AROUND

pop 6000

More upscale than Weirs Beach, Meredith is still a real Lakes Region town, with a long lakeside commercial strip. Fancy cigar-shaped motorboats cruise past the town dock and check each other out: this is boating culture at its best. US 3, NH 25 and NH 104 converge in Meredith, which is spread along the lakeshore on its west side.

The MS *Mount Washington* (Monday only), the MV *Judge Sewall* and the Winnipesaukee Scenic Railroad all stop at Meredith Town Docks (see p437 for details). **Meredith Chamber of Commerce** (☎ 603-279-6121; www.meredithcc.org; US 3 at Mill St, Meredith; ☉ 9am-5pm Mon-Fri year-round, 9am-5pm Sat, 9am-2pm Sun May-Oct) can answer other questions.

Unless otherwise stated, items in the following section are in Meredith proper.

Sleeping

Tuckernuck Inn (☎ 603-279-5521, 888-858-5521; www.thetuckernuckinn.com; 25 Red Gate Lane; d with breakfast $105-145; ☒) Tuckernuck has five cozy, quiet rooms (one has a fireplace) with stenciled walls and hand-made quilts. From Main St, head inland along Water St, then turn right (uphill) onto Red Gate Lane.

Meredith Inn B&B (☎ 603-279-0000; www.meredithinn.com; Main St; d with breakfast $125-175; ☒) This delightful Victorian inn recently received a complete overhaul, including a new two-story turret and walkout bay windows. Now this elegant gothic rose mansion looks wonderful. Antique furnishings and luxurious bedding outfit the rooms; several rooms also have Jacuzzis and gas fireplaces.

Inns at Mill Falls (☎ 603-279-7006, 800-622-6455; www.millfalls.com; 312 Daniel Webster Way; r Nov-Apr $139-179, Dec-May $169-259; ☒ ☒) Four different properties front Lake Winnipesaukee at different points around Meredith Bay, all offering designer-decorated rooms with lovely water views. Although the management is the same for the entire complex, each property has between 23 and 58 rooms, allowing for a more intimate, innlike atmosphere. Chase House is particularly appealing, as every room has a fireplace. Rooms in Mill Falls ($99 to $169) are less expensive, as this property is not directly on the water, but across busy Daniel Webster Way.

Clearwater Campground (☎ 603-279-7761; www.clearwatercampground.com; NH 104; sites without/with hookups $37/40; ☉ mid-May–mid-Oct) Lots of family facilities accompany these 151 sites on 35 acres on the shores of Lake Pemigewasset. You can rent rowboats, canoes and paddleboats; play horseshoes; or use the beach, playground and game room. When Clearwater closes for the winter, its sister campground across the street, Meredith Woods, remains open year-round.

Harbor Hill Camping Area (☎ 603-279-6910; www.hhcamp.com; NH 25; sites without/with hookups $24/30; ☉ late May–mid-Oct; ☒) This area has 140 sites on 55 wooded acres. This is another family-friendly place, with playgrounds and athletic courts.

Long Island Bridge Campground (☎ 603-253-6053; Moultonboro Neck Rd; sites without/with hookups $22/25; ☉ mid-May–mid-Oct) Thirteen miles northeast of Meredith near Center Harbor, this camping area overlooking the lake has popular tent sites and a private beach. Waterfront sites are more expensive. In July and August, there is a three-day minimum stay. Follow NH 25 east for 1½ miles from Center Harbor, then go south on Moultonboro Neck Rd for 6.5 miles.

White Lake State Park (☎ 603-323-7350; West Ossipee; sites without/with water views $16/22; ☉ mid-May–mid-Oct) White Lake, 22 miles northeast of Meredith off NH 16, has 200 tent sites on over 600 acres, plus swimming and hiking trails. This state park boasts some of New Hampshire's finest swimming in the pristine glacial lake.

Eating

Meredith Bay Bakery & Cafe (☎ 603-279-2279; 7 Main St; mains $5-6; ⊗ breakfast & lunch) Facing the big Mill Falls Marketplace, just inland from the main intersection in town, this bakery draws locals with its huge sandwiches made with fresh-baked bread. The traditional breakfast menu includes steak and hash, eggs Benedict and pancakes.

Lakehouse (☎ 603-279-2253; cnr US 3 & NH 25, Church Landing; mains $15-21; ⊗ 5:30-9:30pm) Within the Inn at Church Landing, this classy restaurant is part of the statewide 'Common Man' family of restaurants. The wide-ranging menu focuses on seafood and steaks, usually prepared with some creative international twist. Enjoy your dinner on the breezy lakeside deck.

Town Docks (☎ 603-279-3445; cnr US 3 & NH 25, Town Docks; sandwich $7-10, mains $8-15) Order your fried clams or crab cake then take a seat on the sunny deck and wait for your number to be called. (Make yourself comfortable, because you might wait a while.) The food is nothing special, but you can't go wrong ordering something fried. And you can't beat the lakeside seating. Don't feed the ducks!

Getting There & Away

Concord Trailways (☎ 603-228-3300, 800-639-3317; www .concordtrailways.com) stops in Meredith (at a Mobil gas station on NH 25; ☎ 603-279-5129) on a route between Boston and Berlin. You can take it to Concord ($10, one hour), Manchester ($12.50, 1½ hours), Boston South Station ($21.50, 2½ hours), and Logan International Airport ($27, 2½ hours).

WOLFEBORO
pop 6100

Named for General Wolfe, who died vanquishing Montcalm on the Plains of Abraham in Quebec, Wolfeboro (founded in 1770) claims to be 'the oldest summer resort in America.' Whether that's true or not, it is the most pleasant lakeside resort town. It's not overly commercialized, but maintains an agreeable bustle.

Wolfeboro is on the eastern shore of Lake Winnipesaukee, at the intersection of NH 28 with the lakeside NH 109. The **Wolfeboro Chamber of Commerce information booth** (☎ 603-569-2200; www.wolfeborochamber.com; 32 Central Ave; ⊗ 10am-5pm Mon-Sat, 11am-3pm Sun Jul–mid-Oct, 10am-3pm Mon-Fri, 9am-noon mid-Oct–Jun) is located inside the old train station.

Sights & Activities

WENTWORTH STATE BEACH

If your lodging or campsite does not have access to the lake, head to this small **beach** (☎ 603-569-3699; NH 109; admission $3; ⊗ dawn-dusk daily Jun-Aug, Sat & Sun only May) on the serene Wentworth Lake. Much smaller but much less developed than Winnipesaukee, Wentworth Lake offers all the same opportunities for swimming, picnicking, hiking and fishing.

LIBBY MUSEUM

At the age of 40, Dr Henry Forrest Libby, a local dentist, began collecting things. In 1912 he built a home for his collections, the **Libby Museum** (☎ 603-569-1035; www .wolfeboro.com/libby; NH 109, Winter Harbor; tickets $3; ⊗ 10am-4pm Tue-Sat, noon-4pm Sun Jun-Sep), which is 3 miles north of Wolfeboro. Starting with butterflies and moths, the amateur naturalist built up a private natural history collection. Other collections followed, including Abenaki relics and early-American farm and home implements.

OTHER MUSEUMS

The **Clark House Museum Complex** (☎ 603-569-4997; 233 S Main St; adult/child under 12 $4/free; ⊗ 11am-3:30pm Mon-Fri, 10am-1:30pm Sat Jul-early Sep) is Wolfeboro's eclectic historical museum, comprising three historic buildings: the 1778 Clark family farmhouse, an 1805 one-room school house, and a replica of an old firehouse. The buildings contain relevant artifacts (such as fire engines!), furniture and the like.

Wolfeboro is an appropriate place for the **New Hampshire Boat Museum** (☎ 603-569-4554; www.nhbm.org; 397 Center St; ⊗ 10am-4pm Mon-Sat, noon-4pm Sun). Nautical types will appreciate the collection of vintage water craft, motors, photographs and other memorabilia.

WALKING TOURS

Wolfeboro is a pretty town with some good examples of New England's architectural styles, from Georgian through Federal, Greek Revival and Second Empire. The information office has several walking-tour pamphlets, including the half-mile-long **Bridge Falls Path**, which runs along the southern shore of Back Bay and the 10-minute walk to **Abenaki Tower**. More intrepid walkers might explore the **Wolfeboro-Sanbornville Recreational Trail**, which follows an abandoned railroad bed for 12 miles.

CRUISES & KAYAKING

The **MS Mount Washington** stops in Wolfeboro as part of its 2½ hour cruise around Lake Winnipesaukee, at 11:15am on Tuesday, Wednesday, Friday and Saturday. See p437 for details.

Helpful staff at the **Winnipesaukee Kayak Co** (☎ 603-569-9926; www.winnikayak.com; 17 Bay St; single/tandem per hr $15/20, per half-day $35/45) organizes kayaking trips and lessons.

Sleeping

Tuc' Me Inn B&B (☎ 603-569-5702; www.tucmeinn.com; 118 N Main St; d with breakfast Nov–mid-Apr $95-105, mid-Apr–Oct $105-125) Just north of Wolfeboro Inn, this unfortunately named B&B has seven lovely rooms. Their various charms include handmade quilts, four-poster beds, cathedral ceilings and private porches. Breakfast is a delight here: a plate of seasonal fresh fruit is followed by homemade goodies like cranberry pancakes or orange-glazed waffles.

Wolfeboro Inn (☎ 603-569-3016, 800-451-2389; www.wolfeboroinn.com; 90 N Main St; d with breakfast Nov-Apr $90-135, May-Oct $135-175) The town's best-known lodging is right on the lake with a private beach. One of the region's most prestigious resorts since 1812, it has 44 very comfortable, individually decorated, country-style rooms in the main inn and in a modern annex. Facilities include a restaurant and pub, Wolfe's Tavern (opposite).

Lakeview Inn (☎ 603-569-1335; www.lakeviewinn.net; 200 N Main St; d Nov-Apr $60, May-Oct $80-100) Part colonial inn, part traditional motor lodge, this place has a total of 17 rooms and efficiencies. They are all comfortable and clean, some with balconies or kitchenettes. The dining room is a local favorite for continental cuisine such as scampi, veal and venison. It's less than a mile north of Wolfeboro's center.

Wolfeboro Campground (☎ 603-569-9881; www.wolfeborocampground.com; 61 Haines Hill Rd; sites without/with hookups $20/22; ⊙ mid-May–mid-Oct) Off NH 28, and about 4.5 miles north of Wolfeboro, this campground has 50 private, wooded sites. It is right on the lake, offering access to well-maintained beaches.

Eating

Yum Yum Shop (☎ 603-569-1919; 16 N Main St; mains $1-4; ⊙ 6am-2pm) From bagels to croissants to doughnuts, the Yum Yum Shop serves all sorts of yummy baked goods. This family-run bakery has been in business for over 50 years so they must be doing something right.

Bailey's (☎ 603-569-3612; Railroad Ave; ice-cream $2-3) This old-time fave has scooped ice cream for generations of families. When it is time to cool off, you will have to choose from more than twenty traditional and not-so-traditional flavors.

Strawberry Patch (☎ 603-569-5523; 50 N Main St; mains $3-8; ⊙ 7am-3pm Mar-Oct) The extensive menu here includes a litany of entirely homemade items: Belgian waffles, eggs with hollandaise sauce, crab omelets and lots of concoctions with strawberries.

Wolfe's Tavern (☎ 603-569-3016; 90 N Main St; mains $14-18) The bar menu at the rustically colonial Wolfeboro Inn (opposite) ranges from burgers to substantial pasta and grilled meats. Terrace tables are set outside in good weather. The Wolfeboro Inn's main dining area, known as the 1812 Steakhouse, is formal and serves conservative American and continental fare.

Cider Press (☎ 603-569-2028; 30 Middleton Rd; mains $12-18; ⊙ 5:30-9:30pm) Off NH 28 south of town, this cozy spot is deservedly popular, with rustic barn board walls, fireplaces and antiques. As for the cuisine, it roams from baby back ribs to grilled salmon. Don't overlook the creative blackboard specials.

Love's Quay (☎ 603-569-3303; 51 Mill St; lunch $7-10, dinner $10-25; ⊙ 11:30am-9pm Sun-Thu, 11:30am-10pm Fri & Sat) In addition to everyday pasta dishes, this lakeside eatery has a dozen nightly specials highlighting fish and lamb. The lounge is open until 1am and often features live music.

Entertainment

Wolfeboro Folk (☎ 603-569-0997; www.wolfeborofolk.com; 90 N Main St; tickets $15-20) This local organization attracts some of the country's top folk musicians, who perform at the ballroom in the Wolfeboro Inn.

Getting There & Around

Wolfeboro is located on the east side of Lake Winnipesaukee. From I-93, take US 3 to its intersection with NH 11. Follow this road south as it skirts the lake. Pick up NH 28 in Alton and head north.

The turn-of-the-century **Molly the Trolley** (☎ 603-569-5257; adult/child $5/2; ⊙ 10am-5pm Jul-

Aug) trundles along Main St, providing narration for the sights along the way.

SQUAM LAKE

Northwest of Lake Winnipesaukee, Squam Lake is more tranquil, more tasteful and more pristine than its big brother. It is also less accessible, lacking any public beaches. Nonetheless, if you choose your lodging carefully, you can enjoy Squam Lake's natural wonders, just like Katherine Hepburn and Henry Fonda did in *On Golden Pond*. With 67 miles of shoreline and 67 islands, there are plenty of opportunities for fishing, kayaking and swimming.

Orientation & Information

Squam Lake's main town is Holderness, at the southwest corner of the lake. Little Squam Lake is a much smaller branch further southwest. US 3 follows the south shore of Squam Lake to Holderness. The road then turns west, skirting the north shore of Little Squam Lake before rejoining I-93 at Ashland. For information query the **Squam Lakes Area Chamber of Commerce** (☎ 603-968-4494; www.squamlakeschamber.com).

Sights & Activities

SQUAM LAKES NATURAL SCIENCE CENTER

To get up close and personal with the wildlife that lives in the Lakes Region, visit the **Squam Lakes Natural Science Center** (☎ 603-968-7194; www.nhnature.org; NH 113, Holderness; adult/child/senior $12/9/11; 🕑 9:30am-4:30pm May-Nov). Four different nature paths weave through the woods and around the marsh. The highlight is the **Gephart Trail**, leading past trailside enclosures that are home to bobcats, fishercats, mountain lions, a great horned owl and a bald eagle, amongst other animals. The nearby **Kirkwood Gardens**, featuring many species of New England native shrubs and flowers, are specially designed to attract birds and butterflies. The center also organizes **nature cruises** (combination tickets adult/child/senior $24/15/20) around Squam Lake.

CRUISES

Squam Lake Tours (☎ 603-968-7577; www.squamlake tours.com; US 3, Holderness; 🕑 tours 10am, 2pm & 4pm May-Oct) visits the singing loons and wondrous Church Island and allows visitors to see the famed sights from *On Golden Pond,* including Thayer Cottage and Purgatory Cove.

Squam Lakes Natural Science Center Tours (☎ 603-968-7194; www.nhnature.org; NH 113, Holderness; adult/child/senior $16/12/14) offers pontoon-boat cruises that observe the loons and eagles, visit sites from *On Golden Pond* or watch the sun set over the lake. Combination tickets are available; see opposite.

Squam Lakes Camp Resort (☎ 603-968-7227; www.squamlakesresort.com) rents out pontoon boats.

Sleeping & Eating

Cottage Place on Squam Lake (☎ 603-968-7116; www.cottageplaceonsquam.com; US 3, Holderness; r $95, cottages $85-120) The cozy, comfortable Cottage Place fronts Squam Lake, offering a private beach, a swimming raft and docking space for boats. There is a wide variety of accommodation, including lakefront cottages and motel suites. Weekly rentals are encouraged in summer.

Little Holland Court (☎ 603-968-4434; www.littlehollandcourt.com; 1121 US 3, Holderness; cottages $95-175; 🕑 May-Oct) This classic New England resort has 18 little cottages – each with kitchenette and screen porches – fronting Little Squam Lake. The sandy beach is suitable for swimming and fishing, while canoes, rowboats and motorboats are available for rental.

Manor on Golden Pond (☎ 603-968-3348; www.manorongoldenpond.com; US 3, Holderness; r $190-235, ste $450 ⊠ 🖳) This luxurious B&B is perched up on Shepard Hill, overlooking serene Squam Lake. Elegant rooms (some with fireplaces and Jacuzzis), gourmet breakfasts and a lovely private beach make this one of the lake region's finest retreats. Extra perks include clay tennis courts, a full service spa and an excellent dining room.

Squam Lake Inn (☎ 603-968-4417; www.squamlakeinn.com; cnr Shepard Hill Rd & US 3 Holderness; r $130-140, ste $160-165; ⊠) This century-old Victorian farmhouse has eight rooms, all decorated in vintage New England style with quilts on the beds, antique furnishings and a local 'Lakes' theme. A mahogany deck and wraparound porch overlook woodsy grounds.

Walter's Basin (☎ 603-968-4412; US 3, Holderness; mains $12-20) Local boaters are encouraged to dock their boats and come in to enjoy a meal at this casual, lakeside spot. Located on Little Squam Lake near the bridge, the friendly restaurant features grilled rainbow trout straight from the lake! Other menu favorites include roast duck and pepper-crusted sirloin steak.

NEW HAMPSHIRE

Getting There & Away

Concord Trailways (☎ 603-228-3300, 800-639-3317; www.concordtrailways.com) stops in Center Harbor, on the east side of Squam Lake, en route from Boston to Berlin. The bus stop is at Fred Fuller Oil/Citgo gas station, on US 25. You can take it to Concord ($10, one hour), Manchester ($12.50, 1½ hours), Boston South Station ($21.50, 2½ hours), and Logan International Airport ($27, 2½ hours). Heading north, this bus goes to North Conway, Pinkham Notch, Gorham and Berlin.

WHITE MOUNTAIN REGION

The White Mountains are New England's most spectacular mountain range and outdoor playground. Hiking, rustic and backwoods camping, canoeing, kayaking and skiing are only some of the outdoor fun you can have here. Much of the region is designated as the White Mountain National Forest (WMNF), thus protecting it from overdevelopment and guaranteeing its wondrous natural beauty for years to come.

Daily/weekly/seasonal parking at National Forest trailheads costs $3/5/20. Purchase parking permits at any of the visitor center ranger stations mentioned above.

WATERVILLE VALLEY & AROUND

pop 260

This beautiful mountain valley was developed as a complete mountain resort community. Condominiums and golf courses are carefully set on picture-perfect Corcoran's Pond, surrounded by miles of downhill and cross-country ski trails, hiking trails, bike routes and in-line skating paths. As early as 1829 there was an incorporated town here in the shadow of Mt Tecumseh, on the banks of the Mad River. But the valley took its present shape during the last decades of the 20th century, when hotels, condominiums, vacation villas, golf courses, ski runs, roads and services were all laid out according to plan by the Waterville Company. The result is a harmonious, although somewhat sterile, resort with lots of organized sports activities.

Orientation

Town Sq is the valley's main service facility, with a post office, bank, information office, laundry, restaurants and shops. This is also the locale of the main accommodation office, where you will check in to your condo.

Information

Connection Corner (☎ 603-236-8175; 6 Village Rd, Town Sq; per 15 min $4; 🕑 8am-5pm Mon-Thu, 8am-7pm Fri & Sat, 8am-5pm Sun) High-speed Internet access is available at the main accommodations office at Town Sq.

Waterville Valley (☎ 800-468-2553; www.waterville.com) All the information you need about snow conditions and skiing facilities.

Waterville Valley Region Chamber of Commerce (☎ 603-726-3804, 800-237-2307; www.watervillevalleyregion.com; 12 Vintinner Rd, Campton; 🕑 9am-5pm) Easily visible on NH 49.

Sleeping & Eating

There is no cheap lodging in Waterville Valley resort, although there are economical lodgings in Campton, 13 miles southwest. Valley reservations are made through a **central service** (☎ 800-468-2553; www.waterville.com). If you call a hotel directly, they may ask if you've ever stayed there before. A 'yes' answer (regardless of your previous lodging history) will probably get you a 'previous-guest' discount of up to 10%. Don't be bashful. For valley condominium rentals, call **Waterville Lodging** (☎ 800-556-6522).

All of the accommodation options in Waterville Valley have restaurants on site. Town Sq also offers a variety of cafés, sandwich shops and restaurants.

Black Bear Lodge (☎ 603-236-4501, 800-349-2327; www.black-bear-lodge.com; 3 Village Rd; ste Apr-June & Nov-Dec $135-190, ste Jan-Mar & June-Oct $160-215; ⊠ 🅿) This all-suite lodge has 107 one- and two-bedroom suites that can sleep up to six people. Kitchens are fully equipped. Prices include access to the excellent athletic center.

Snowy Owl Inn (☎ 603-236-8383, 800-766-9969; www.snowyowlinn.com; 4 Village Rd; r with breakfast $102-148, ste $140-194; ⊠ 🅿) This handsome resort was built to look like a country inn, albeit a large one, with 85 rooms and suites in a range of styles. This place is among the more cozy, thanks in part to the three-story hearth in the main lobby where afternoon wine and cheese are served. If you can lure yourself in from the slopes, the indoor octagonal pool and accompanying spas are supercool.

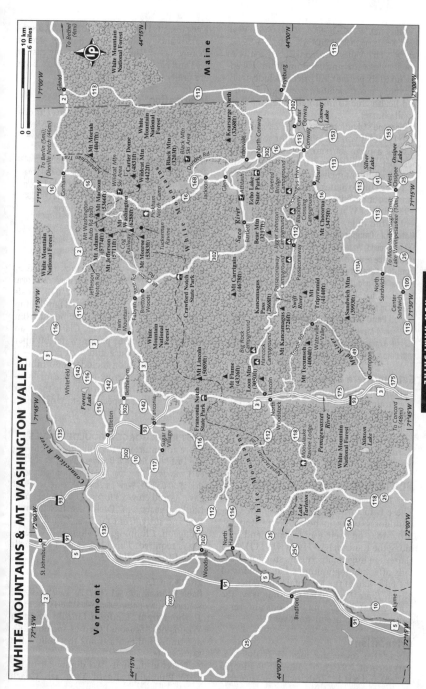

NEW HAMPSHIRE

WHITE MOUNTAINS & MT WASHINGTON VALLEY

Valley Inn (☎ 603-236-8336, 800-343-0969; www.valleyinn.com; Tecumseh Rd; d $64-136 Nov-May, $75-169 Jun-Oct; ✖) The Valley Inn consists of a mix of hotel-style rooms and condominiums (sleeping up to six people). All prices include use of the many resort facilities, from tennis courts and health club to mountain-bike trails and a golf course.

Diamond's Edge North (☎ 603-236-2006; mains $15-25; ☽ 4-9pm) If you are looking for something besides a pizza, burrito or sandwich, your best bet is this place. The diverse, mostly American menu includes options for kids.

Three United States Forest Service (USFS) campgrounds (sites $16), in Campton on I-93 south of Waterville Valley, are convenient to the valley.

Waterville Campground (☎ 603-536-1310; I-93; ☽ year-round) Waterville has 27 very basic sites, some of which can be reserved in advance.

Campton Campground (☎ 603-536-1310; I-93; ☽ mid-Apr–mid-Oct) Campton, with pay showers and flush toilets, has 58 sites near the Mad River; some can be reserved in advance.

Russell Pond Campground (☎ 888-226-7764; Tripoli Rd; ☽ mid-May–mid-Oct) Four miles off I-93, this beautifully sited campground has 86 campsites, many pondside, with flush toilets and pay showers.

Getting There & Around

Driving from Boston to Waterville Valley is a straight three-hour shot via I-93. Take exit 28 (Campton) off I-93 and continue 13 miles northeast on NH 49. Scenic Tripoli Rd (unpaved, closed in winter) pushes northward 27 miles from the valley to Lincoln, which takes another 45 minutes via I-93.

NORTH WOODSTOCK & LINCOLN

pop 1140 (Woodstock), 1270 (Lincoln)

These twin towns serve a diverse clientele. Outdoorsy types in heavy boots stop for provisions on their way to camp and hike along the Kancamagus Hwy (NH 112). And retirees in huge road cruisers stop for cocktails after photographing what remains of the Old Man of the Mountain in Franconia Notch State Park (p448). Either way, the wide variety of accommodations and services make for a useful stopover.

Orientation

These two towns are located at the convergence of I-93 (just south of Franconia Notch) and NH 112 (otherwise known as the Kancamagus Hwy). Each is located on a separate branch of the shallow, boulder-strewn Pemigewasset River – Lincoln to the east of I-93 and North Woodstock to the west. Both are pretty much one-street towns.

Information

Lincoln/Woodstock Chamber of Commerce (☎ 603-745-6621; www.lincolnwoodstock.com; Kancamagus Hwy, Lincoln, NH 03251; ☽ 9am-5pm Mon-Fri) Located above the Laconia Savings Bank.

White Mountains Attractions Association (☎ 603-745-8720; www.visitwhitemountains.com; 200 Kancamagus Hwy; ☽ 8:30am-5pm Apr-Oct) Operates the Lincoln information center, just east of I-93 exit 32. You can pick up detailed hiking brochures for area trails here.

Sights & Activities

CLARK'S TRADING POST & THE WHALE'S TALE

Just north of North Woodstock on US 3, Clark's (☎ 603-745-8913; www.clarkstradingpost.com; US 3, Lincoln; adult/child 3-5/senior $12/3/11; ☽ late May–mid-Oct) has been a traditional family stop since 1928. If the children are bored from too much time in the car, Clark's has an old-fashioned photo parlor, water-bumper boats, a magic house and – of course – a gift shop. Admission includes a 30-minute excursion on a narrow-gauge steam locomotive. The featured attraction is the Bear Show, a rather sad spectacle starring a team of North American black bears.

LOST RIVER GORGE & BOULDER CAVES

More adventurous kids will enjoy exploring the Lost River Gorge & Boulder Caves (☎ 603-745-8031; www.findlostriver.com; NH 112, Kinsman Notch; adult/child $9.50/6.50; ☽ 9am-5pm May-Oct), a network of caverns and crevices formed by glaciers millions of years ago. Each cave has its own title and story, from the Bear Crawl, to the Dungeon. Climbing, crawling and squeezing is required. This place is west of North Woodstock on NH 112.

TRAIN RIDES

Hobo Railroad (☎ 603-745-2135; www.hoborr.com; Kancamagus Hwy, Lincoln; adult/child $10/8) is a scenic, 1½-hour train ride from Lincoln south to Woodstock. Seasonal themes include foliage trains and Santa trains that follow the same route.

Travel in the first-class dining car of the 1924 Pullman-Standard Victorian Coach

Cafe Lafayette (☎ 603-745-3500; www.nhdinnertrain.com; NH 112; adult/child from $60/40). The dining car has been completely and beautifully restored and decorated with dark wood, stained glass and brass fixtures. The train rides along a spur of the Boston and Maine railroad for two hours, while you indulge in a five-course meal.

Tours

All Seasons Adventures (☎ 603-745-8600; www.adventuresnh.com; 134 Main St, Linwood Plaza, Lincoln; transport only $12, transport & bike rental $27) Offers a self-guided bike tour at 10am and 1pm daily, and provides equipment and transportation to the north end of Franconia Notch for a downhill bike ride on the Recreation Trail (see p449).

Outback Kayak (☎ 603-745-2002; www.outbackkayak.com; Main St/US 3, North Woodstock) Provides kayak and snowmobile rental and tour packages.

Pemi Valley Excursions (☎ 603-745-2744; NH 112, Lincoln) Located across from McDonald's, tours include a twilight Moose Tour (adult/child $20/14) which runs from June to October and tracks moose and other wildlife with a 95% success rate, albeit in a 33-passenger bus. A variety of Horseback Trail Rides (one hour $39 to $49, two hours $79) along the banks of the Pemigewasset River are also offered.

Sleeping

BUDGET & MID-RANGE

For the USFS campgrounds along the Kancamagus Hwy east of Lincoln, see p448.

Franconia Notch Motel (☎ 603-745-2229, 800-323-7829; www.franconianotch.com; 572 US 3; d $55-80; ☒) A tidy place with 18 attractive rooms and cottages facing the Pemigewasset River. It's a friendly, family-run place that caters to a lot of international visitors.

Drummer Boy Motor Inn (☎ 603-745-3661; 800-762-7275; www.drummerboymotorinn.com; US 3; d $99-109, ste $159-179; ☒) A semiluxurious place catering to skiers and snowmobilers, who appreciate the sauna, Jacuzzi and spa. Fifty-three rooms – many with kitchenettes – offer decent value any time of year.

Kancamagus Motor Lodge (☎ 603-745-3365, 800-346-4205; www.kancmotorlodge.com; NH 112; d from $79; ☒ ☒) This lodge is on the edge of town on the Kancamagus Hwy. Its 34 modern rooms have all the expected amenities, and a few unexpected ones like steam baths – welcome after a day on the slopes – and private balconies with mountain views. Golf and ski packages are available.

Three Rivers House (☎ 603-745-2711; www.threerivershouse.com; 19 Main St/US 3, North Woodstock; r with

breakfast $65-95, ste $95-135; ☒) One of the oldest houses in the area, this inn was one of several carriage stops that catered to visitors in the 19th century. This hospitality continues today, with a full, hot breakfast every morning. Rooms are comfortable – though not overly stylish – and the lovely grounds overlook a gurgling brook.

Woodward's Resort (☎ 603-745-8141, 800-635-8968; www.woodwardsresort.com; US 3; d $69-119; ☒ ☒) Just north of North Woodstock, this place is a class act. Woodward's has lovely landscaped grounds and lots of facilities, including a sauna, hot tub, racquetball court, tennis court and game room. Rooms are spacious, modern and attractive.

Country Bumpkins Campground (☎ 603-745-8837; www.countrybumpkins.com; US 3; sites without/with hookups $19/25; ☒ Apr-Oct) Near the Pemigewasset River and Bog Brook, this campground has 46 sites which are well maintained but not very private. The camp store specializes in New England kitsch. Take I-93 exit 33 and head south on US 3.

Lost River Valley Campground (☎ 603-745-8321, 800-370-5678; www.lostriver.com; NH 112; tents $23-27, RVs $27-33, cabins from $45; ☒ mid-May–mid-Oct) This excellent, 200-acre campground is on the site of a turn-of-the-century lumber mill, and the water wheel still churns. Many of the 125 sites are on the river, which also offers fishing and hiking possibilities.

TOP END

Wilderness Inn (☎ 603-745-3890, 800-200-9453; www.thewildernessinn.com; cnr US 3 & NH 112; d with breakfast $60-160; ☒) Just south of the junction, this former lumbermill owner's house offers seven guest rooms, ranging from small to suite size, as well as a family-size 'Caribbean Cottage' overlooking Lost River. Each is individually decorated with stenciled walls and international themes. A highlight is the huge breakfast, cooked from scratch and ordered from a menu. Your congenial hosts will be more than happy to suggest restaurants, travel routes and sights in the area.

Woodstock Inn (☎ 603-745-3951, 800-321-3985; www.woodstockinnnh.com; US 3, North Woodstock; r with shared bathroom $65-105, r with private bathroom $89-132, ste $114-229; ☒) This Victorian country inn is in the heart of North Woodstock; indeed it is the town's centerpiece. It features 24 individually appointed rooms, each with modern amenities but old-fashioned style. For dinner, you have your choice of a microbrewery (below) and an upscale restaurant, with outdoor seating on the lovely flower-filled patio. Breakfast is included in the price.

Eating
BUDGET

Peg's Restaurant (☎ 603-745-2740; Main St, North Woodstock, Lincoln; mains $3-7; ☺ 5:30am-4pm Jul-Oct, 5:30am-2pm Nov-Jun) Locals flock to this no-frills eatery for hearty, early breakfasts and late-lunch sandwiches such as roast turkey and meat loaf with gravy. Lunch specials, kids' specials and the infamous 'Hungry Man's Special' make everyone feel pretty special.

Sunny Day Diner (☎ 603-745-4833; US 3, Lincoln; mains $3-15; ☺ 7am-2pm Thu-Mon, dinner Fri & Sat) North of town, this authentic diner serves classic fare such as pork chops with applesauce, fried chicken and cranberry sauce, or New England beans and franks. Breakfast here is divine; try the banana bread French toast.

Elvio's Pizzeria (☎ 603-745-8817; Lincoln Plaza; mains $7-10) Not just for pizza, this strip-mall joint has subs, salads and plates of pasta. When you're in a hurry to hit the highway or trails, Elvio's will hit the spot.

Pig's Ear (☎ 603-745-3330; 112 Main St, North Woodstock; mains $7-12; ☺ noon-8pm Thu-Sun) It's all pork all the time at this little hole-in-the-wall BBQ shack. If you like pulled pork, ribs or sausage, you will love the Pig's Ear. Chicken and cow-lovers might find a few items that suit their fancy too. Veggies will likely go hungry.

MID-RANGE

Gypsy Cafe (☎ 603-745-4395; NH 112, Main St, Lincoln; sandwiches $6-9, mains $12-16; ☺ 11am-9pm Tue-Sun) Catherine and Peter Johnson earned the nickname 'the Gypsies' from their friends because of their love of travel, so they opened this charming little café to share some of their favorite foods from around the world. Menu items range from a Middle Eastern meze plate to cilantro lime pesto pasta to enchiladas *rojas* (red sauce). In the midst of a relative culinary void, this place is a gem.

Fratello's (☎ 603-745-2022; Kancamagus Hwy, Lincoln; lunch $10, dinner $12-16) This classic Italian restaurant features a lengthy menu of brick-oven pizzas, traditional pasta dishes and chicken, veal and fish meals. The dining room is bright and welcoming, thanks to the wall of windows. The upstairs lounge has entertainment on weekends.

Common Man (☎ 603-745-3463; Kancamagus Hwy, Lincoln; mains $12-23) Near the Kancamagus Motor Inn, this successful local chain serves a simple menu of pasta, prime rib and lobster dishes near a massive hearth and warm bar. It is deservedly popular with tourists and locals alike.

Woodstock Station & Brewery (☎ 603-745-3951; Main St, North Woodstock; mains $10-16) Formerly a railroad station, this eatery tries to be everything to everyone. In the end, with more than 150 items, it can probably satisfy just about any food craving, but pasta, sandwiches and burgers are the safest orders. The beer-sodden rear tavern here is one of the most happening places in this neck of the woods.

Entertainment

Papermill Theatre (☎ 603-745-2141; www.papermill theatre.org; NH 112, Inn Season Resorts, Lincoln; adult/child/senior $22/15/17) This local theater shows a wide range of musicals and plays, as well as regular performances of children's theater throughout the summer.

DETOUR: MOOSILAUKE RAVINE LODGE

About 50 miles north of Hanover and 15 miles west of North Woodstock, the **Moosilauke Ravine Lodge** (☎ 603-764-5858; moosilauke.ravine.lodge@dartmouth.edu; dm $20-24, linens $6; meal $7-12; ☺ May-Oct) is a rustic lodging owned and maintained by the Dartmouth Outing Club, but open to the public. The lodge is set in the midst of wooded hills and pristine countryside. Thirty miles of hiking trails connect the lodge to the summit of Mt Moosilauke and other trailheads. The mountain offers fantastic views and uncrowded trails, as it is as yet undiscovered (except by Dartmouth students). Accommodation at Moosilauke is basic bunks and shared baths, but the price is right. Delicious, hearty meals are served family-style in the dining hall.

To reach Moosilauke, take NH 118 west from Woodstock. From Hanover, take NH 10A north to NH 25. Head north on NH 25 and turn right at the junction with NH 118. Moosilauke Ravine Lodge is north of NH 118; follow the signs from the turn-off.

Truant's Taverne & Restaurant (☎ 603-745-2239; Main St; mains $10-14) Live music, pool tables, shuffleboard and darts keep this cozy pub hopping year-round.

Getting There & Away

From Lincoln it takes just over one hour to reach North Conway (42 miles) on the Kancamagus Hwy. It's about 3¼ hours (140 miles) from Boston via I-93. **Concord Trailways** (☎ 603-228-3300, 800-639-3317; www.concordtrailways .com) runs buses between Boston and Littleton that stop at **Munce's Konvenience/Shell gas station** (☎ 603-745-3195; Main St, Lincoln). Catch one to Concord ($13.50, 1½ hours), Manchester ($16, two hours), Boston South Station ($25, three hours) or Logan International Airport ($30, three hours).

KANCAMAGUS HIGHWAY

The winding Kancamagus Hwy (NH 112) between Lincoln and Conway runs right through the WMNF and over Kancamagus Pass (2868ft). Unspoiled by commercial development, the paved road offers easy access to USFS campgrounds, hiking trails and fantastic scenery.

Though the Kancamagus Hwy was paved only in 1964, its name dates to the 17th century. The route is named for Chief Kancamagus, or 'The Fearless One.' In about 1684, Kancamagus assumed the powers of *sagamon* (leader) of the Penacook Indian tribe. He was the third and the final sagamon, succeeding his grandfather, the great Passaconaway, and his uncle Wonalancet. Kancamagus tried to maintain peace between the indigenous peoples and European explorers and settlers, but the newcomers pushed his patience past the breaking point. He finally resorted to battle to rid the region of Europeans. The tide of history was against him, and by 1691 he and his followers were forced to escape northward.

Activities

HIKING

The WMNF is laced with excellent hiking trails of varying difficulty. For detailed trail-by-trail information, stop at any of the WMNF ranger stations (see p452) or the White Mountains Attractions Association (p444). Alternatively, pick up the *AMC White Mountain Guide* from the **Appalachian Mountain Club** (AMC; ☎ 617-523-0636; www

.outdoors.org; 5 Joy St, Boston, MA 02108) or from a local bookshop.

The trailhead for the 2.9-mile **Lincoln Woods Trail** (elevation 1157ft) is located on the Kancamagus Hwy, 5 miles east of I-93. Among the easiest and most popular in the forest, the trail ends at the Pemigewasset Wilderness Boundary (elevation 1450ft).

The easy **Wilderness Trail** begins where the Lincoln Woods Trail ends, and it continues for 6 miles to Stillwater Junction (elevation 2060ft). You can follow the Cedar Brook and Hancock Notch Trails to return to the Kancamagus Hwy, which is some miles east of the Lincoln Woods trailhead parking lot.

LOON MOUNTAIN

For winter fun, skiers should head to **Loon Mountain** (☎ 603-745-8111; www.loonmtn.com; adult/ child/teen Mon-Fri $52/32/42, Sat & Sun $59/37/49; ☾ 9am-3:45pm Mon-Fri, 8am-3:45pm Sat & Sun). Almost 20 miles of trails crisscross this 3050ft mountain, which boasts a 2100ft vertical drop. Skis, snowboards etc are available for rental. At night, the trails open up for **tubing** (walk-up/lift $7/12; ☾ 6-9:40pm Wed-Sun).

Loon Mountain offers its fair share of summer fun as well. A **gondola** (adult/child/ senior $9.50/5.50/8; ☾ 9:30am-5:30pm late Jun–mid-Oct) allows guests to soar to the summit. The facility also offers mountain-bike rentals (adult/child per day $33/29), a climbing wall (single/double climb $6/10) and horseback riding trips (from $39 to $79).

Sleeping

Village of Loon Mountain (☎ 603-745-3401, 800-228-2968; www.vrivacations.com; Kancamagus Hwy; r $135-160, ste $150-185; ☒) This resort includes a lodge with basic suites that sleep at least four people, as well as condos right on the mountainside, so you can ski out the door to the chair lift. Recreational facilities are unlimited here, with tennis courts, horseback riding, hiking and biking on offer.

The heavily wooded USFS campgrounds east of Lincoln along the Kancamagus Hwy are primitive sites (mostly with pit toilets only). The sites are in high demand in the warm months. It is not possible at every campground, but **advance reservations** (☎ 877-444-6777; www.reserveusa.com) are highly recommended where they are accepted (as indicated). Otherwise, arrive early, especially on weekends.

NEW HAMPSHIRE

NEW HAMPSHIRE

DEATH OF AN OLD MAN

The Old Man of the Mountain really was very, very old. Geologists estimate that the 'Great Stone Face' gazed out over Profile Lake for more than 12,000 years. That's why it was such a shock when, on May 3, 2003, the Old Man crumbled.

The collapse of the Old Man of the Mountain was no surprise to those in the know. In fact, the Appalachian Mountain Club had reported on the Old Man's precarious state as early as 1872. Everybody recognized that it wouldn't do to have the stoic symbol of New Hampshire drop off the side of the mountain, and the first repair was made in 1916. Geologists attempted to secure a slipping boulder, which seemed to do the trick, and no further repairs were needed more than 40 years.

Still, it was not permanent. Not in the big scheme.

Scientists have demonstrated how the Old Man's facial structure was made up of five slabs of granite, balanced one on top of another. The problem was that the lower block – the one that was supporting the weight of four others – was balancing precariously on the edge of a cliff. What had started as a crack had over the centuries become a cavern, and now the lower block was completely detached from the side of the mountain. In fact, it was anchored in place only by the weight of the granite blocks above it. And that's how the old man stayed for centuries, carefully balancing on his chin. It's amazing that he lasted as long as he did.

Attempts were made to somehow secure or support the teetering boulder, but to no avail. You can't stop Mother Nature. Every year snow and rain were driven into the cracks and caverns. As temperatures dropped – as they are wont to do in New Hampshire – the water expanded, exacerbating the cracks. Furthermore, minerals in the granite reacted chemically with water, causing the blocks to further corrode.

The gradual process of wear and tear finally upset the balance. The lower slab of granite tumbled off its perch. With no support beneath them, the remaining slabs could not hold and followed suit. The Old Man crumbled.

It seems a tragedy, in some ways. Yet it is somehow a reassuring reminder that time marches on. The earth evolves. Nothing is permanent. Even a 12,000-year-old man must pass.

The following campgrounds are listed from west to east (Lincoln to Conway):

Hancock Campground (☎ 603-744-9165; sites $18; ☻ year-round) Four miles east of Lincoln, this place has 56 sites near the Pemigewasset River and the Wilderness Trail. Reservations accepted December to April only.

Big Rock Campground (☎ 603-744-9165; sites $16; ☻ May-Oct) Big Rock has 28 sites near the Wilderness Trail and is 6 miles east of Lincoln.

Passaconaway Campground (☎ 603-477-5448; sites $16; ☻ mid-May–Oct) This campground is 12 miles west of Conway, and has 33 sites on the Swift River, which is good for fishing.

Jigger Johnson Campground (☎ 603-477-5448; sites $18; ☻ late-May–Oct) Jigger's is 10 miles west of Conway, has 75 sites, flush toilets and pay hot showers. There are nature lectures on summer weekends.

Blackberry Crossing Campground (☎ 603-477-5448; sites $16; ☻ year-round) Six miles west of Conway, this former Civilian Conservation Corps (CCC) camp has 26 sites. In winter, access is walk-in only.

Covered Bridge Campground (sites $16; ☻ mid-May–Oct) Six miles west of Conway, this place has 49 sites, some of which can be reserved. And yes, you do cross the Albany Covered Bridge to reach the campground.

FRANCONIA NOTCH STATE PARK

Franconia Notch, a narrow gorge shaped over the eons by a wild stream cutting through craggy granite, is a dramatic mountain pass. This was long the residence of the infamous Old Man of the Mountain, a natural rock formation that became the symbol of the Granite State. Tragically, the Old Man collapsed in 2003 (see above), which does not stop hordes of tourists from coming here to see the featureless cliff that remains. Despite the Old Man's absence, the attractions of Franconia Notch are many, from the dramatic hike down the Flume gorge to the fantastic views of the Presidentials.

Orientation

The most scenic parts of the notch are protected by the narrow Franconia Notch State Park. Reduced to two lanes, I-93 (renamed the Franconia Notch Parkway) squeezes through the gorge. Services are available in Lincoln and North Woodstock to the south and in Franconia and Littleton further north. Both branches of the **Franconia Notch**

Visitor Center Flume Gorge (☎ 603-745-8391; www
.flumegorge.com; I-93 exit 34A) Lafayette Place (☎ 603-823-9513) have lots of information about the state park and surrounding area. The Flume also has a cafeteria and gift shop.

Sights & Activities
FLUME GORGE & THE BASIN
To see this natural wonder, take the 2-mile self-guided nature walk that includes the 800ft boardwalk through the **Flume** (☎ 603-745-8391; www.flumegorge.com; I-93 exit 34A; adult/child 6-12 $8/5; ☉ 9am-5pm mid-May–mid-Oct), a natural cleft (12ft to 20ft wide) in the granite bedrock. The granite walls tower 70ft to 90ft above you, with moss and plants growing from precarious niches and crevices. Signs along the way explain how nature formed this natural phenomenon. A nearby covered bridge is thought to be one of the oldest in the state, perhaps erected as early as the 1820s.

The **Basin** is a huge glacial pothole, 20ft in diameter, that was carved deep into the granite 15,000 years ago by the action of falling water and swirling stones. The Basin offers a nice (short) walk and a cool spot to ponder a minor wonder of nature.

OLD MAN HISTORIC SITE
In the wake of the Old Man's collapse in 2003 (see the boxed text above), the state of New Hampshire is struggling over the future of this **historic site** (I-93 exit 34B) that once held the symbol of the state. Proposals ranging from interactive museums to statewide sculpture contests are being debated at all levels. In the meantime, the Old Man Historic Site has a small **museum** (admission free; ☉ 9am-5pm) with exhibits on the history of the profile and the attempts to save it from its fate. And you can still pull off at the viewing platform (follow signs for 'Old Man Viewing') and use your imagination.

CANNON MOUNTAIN AERIAL TRAMWAY
Just north of the Old Man Historic Site, a **tramway** (☎ 603-823-8800; www.cannonmt.com; adult/child roundtrip $10/6, one-way $8; ☉ 9am-5pm late May–mid-Oct) shoots up the side of Cannon Mountain, offering a breathtaking view of Franconia Notch and the surrounding mountains. In 1938, the first passenger aerial tramway in North America was installed on this slope. Thankfully, it was replaced in 1980 by the current, larger cable car, capable of carrying

80 passengers up to the summit of Cannon Mountain in five minutes – a 2022ft, 1-mile ride. Alternatively, visitors can hike up the mountain and take the tramway down. Look for the New England Ski Museum in the base station.

ECHO LAKE
Despite the proximity to the highway, this little **lake** (adult/child $3/free, ☉ 10am-5:30pm Jun-Aug) at the foot of Cannon Mountain is a pleasant place to pass an afternoon – swimming, kayaking or canoeing (rentals per hour $10) in the crystal clear waters. And many people do. The small beach gets packed, especially on weekends.

HIKING & CYCLING
The park has good hiking trails; most are relatively short, but some may be steep. For a casual walk or bike ride, you can't do better than the 8-mile paved **Recreation Trail** that wends its way along the Pemigewasset River and through the notch. Bikes are available for rental at the Franconia Sports Shop (p450) or in Lincoln (see p445). Pick up the trail in front of the Flume Gorge Visitor Center.

Other recommended hikes:

Bald Mountain and Artists Bluff Trail Just north of Echo Lake, off NH 18, this 1.5-mile loop skirts the summit of Bald Mountain (2320ft) and Artists Bluff (2368ft), with short spur trails to the summits.

Kinsman Falls On the Cascade Brook, these falls are a short, half-mile hike from the Basin via the Basin Cascade Trail.

Lonesome Lake Trail Departing from Lafayette Place and its campground, this trail climbs 1000ft in 1.5 miles to Lonesome Lake. Various spur trails lead further up to several summits on the Cannon Balls and Cannon Mountain (3700ft to 4180ft) and south to the Basin.

Mt Pemigewasset Trail This trail begins at the Flume Visitor Center and climbs for 1.4 miles to the 2557ft summit of Mt Pemigewasset (Indian Head), offering excellent views. Return by the same trail or the Indian Head Trail, which joins US 3 after 1 mile. From there, it's a 1-mile walk north to the Flume Visitor Center.

SKIING
The slopes at **Cannon Mountain Ski Area** (☎ 603-823-7771; www.cannonmt.com; I-93 exit 2; adult/child/senior/teen Mon-Fri $34/23/23/23, Sat & Sun $45/29/29/37) are positioned so they naturally receive and retain more than the average amount of white stuff. Just in case, the ski area also makes its own snow. The vertical drop is 2146ft, and the slopes Cannon have an aerial tramway,

NEW HAMPSHIRE

three triple and two quad chairlifts, two rope tows and a wonder carpet (a moving walkway for beginners) for accessing its 26 miles of trails and slopes. Other facilities include three cafeterias, a nursery, a ski school, and a ski shop with rental equipment.

Sleeping

Lafayette Place Campground (☎ 603-271-3628; sites $16; ☼ year-round) This popular campground has 97 wooded tent sites that are in heavy demand in summer. Reservations are accepted from January to October; otherwise, arrive early in the day to claim a site. Many of the state park's hiking trails start here.

FRANCONIA & AROUND

pop 924 (Franconia), 2200 (Bethlehem)
A few miles north of the notch via I-93, Franconia is a tranquil town with splendid mountain views and a poetic attraction: Robert Frost's farm. As a rule, the further the distance from the highway, the more picturesque and pristine the destination. Accordingly, the little town of **Bethlehem** and the tiny village of **Sugar Hill** are delightful. One could easily while away an afternoon driving down country roads, poking into antique shops, browsing farm stands and chatting up the locals at divey diners.

Orientation

NH 18, NH 116 and NH 117 meet at the center of Franconia, marked by a prominent, local prep school, Dow Academy. NH 18 is Main St. Sugar Hill is a few miles west along tranquil NH 117. Bethlehem is north along NH 118.

Information

Bethlehem Chamber of Commerce (☎ 888-845-1957; www.bethlehemwhitemtns.com; 2182 Main St, Bethlehem; ☼ 11am-4pm Jun-Oct, variable Nov-Feb, closed Mar-May)
Franconia Notch Chamber of Commerce (☎ 603-823-5661, 800-237-9007; www.franconianotch.org; Main St, Franconia; ☼ 11am-5pm Tue-Sun mid-May–mid-Oct) Southeast of the town center.

Sights & Activities

Robert Frost (1874–1963) was America's most renowned and best-loved poet in the mid-20th century. For several years he lived with his wife and children on a farm near Franconia, now known as the **Frost Place** (☎ 603-823-5510; Ridge Rd; adult/child/senior $3/1.25/2;

☼ 1-5pm Sat & Sun late May-Jun, 1-5pm Wed-Mon Jul-mid-Oct). The years spent here were some of the most productive and inspired of his life. Many of his best and most famous poems describe life on this farm and the scenery surrounding it, including 'The Road Not Taken' and 'Stopping by Woods on a Snowy Evening.'

The farmhouse has been kept as faithful to the period as possible, with numerous exhibits of Frost memorabilia. In the forest behind the house, there is a half-mile-long **nature trail**. Frost's poems are mounted on plaques in sites appropriate to the things the poems describe, and in several places the plaques have been erected at the exact spots where Frost composed the poems. To find Frost's farm, follow NH 116 south from Franconia. After exactly a mile, turn right onto Bickford Hill Rd, then left onto unpaved Ridge Rd. It's a short distance along on the right.

The **Sugar Hill Sampler** (☎ 603-823-8478; NH 117, Sugar Hill; admission free; ☼ 9:30am-5pm May-Oct, 10am-4pm Nov-Jan, closed Feb-Apr) was originally a collection of heirlooms amassed by the Aldrich family over the many years they have lived in Sugar Hill. The collection has expanded to include all sorts of local memorabilia dating from 1780, all housed in an old barn built by the Aldrich ancestors themselves. This place also has a store, selling homemade arts and crafts and edibles.

Franconia Sports Shop (☎ 603-823-5241; www.franconiasports.com; Main St, Franconia; bike rental per day $19) offers bike rental. **Northern Land Guide Service** (☎ 603-869-2634; www.northernguideservices.com; 134 Maple St, Bethlehem) provides services for birding, hiking and wildlife photography.

Festivals & Events

Every year in June, hillsides and valleys in the Franconia region are carpeted with blues and purples, as this spring-blooming wildflower blossoms. It is a spectacular sight, rivaling – locals claim – the fall foliage. The **Fields of Lupine Festival** (www.franconianotch.org) celebrates the annual bloom with garden tours, art exhibits and concerts throughout the month.

Sleeping

BUDGET

Pinestead Farm Lodge (☎ 603-823-8121; 2059 Easton Rd/NH 116; d $36-50) Among the possible accommodations in Franconia is a rarity: a working farm. The family rents 11 clean, simple rooms with shared bath and communal kitchen/sitting rooms. Hosts Bob and Kathleen Sherburn (whose family has been renting rooms since 1899) have an assortment of cattle, chickens, ducks and horses. If you come in March or April, you can watch maple sugaring.

Kinsman Lodge (☎ 603-823-5686; www.kinsman lodge.com; 2165 Easton Rd/NH 116, Franconia; s/d $45/75; ☒) This lodge – built in the 1860s – has nine rooms (with shared bathroom) that are comfortable but not pretentious. They are all on the 2nd floor, while the 1st floor consists of cozy common areas and an inviting porch.

Stonybrook Motel & Lodge (☎ 603-823-5800, 800-722-3552; www.stonybrookmotel.com; NH 18, Franconia; d $75-100; ☒ ☲) A mile south of town, this mountain motel has 23 tidy, comfortable rooms that vary greatly in size. The riverside location is a lovely setting, and the trout pond and surrounding mountain views add to it.

Gale River Motel & Cottages (☎ 603-823-5655, 800-255-7989; www.galerivermotel.com; 1 Main St, Franconia; r $75-95 May-Sep, $95-105 Oct, $55-65 Nov-Apr; ☲) This classic roadside motel has 10 rooms and two cottages, fully equipped and immaculately maintained. Besides the nice views, this place offers a playground, as well as indoor and outdoor Jacuzzis.

Fransted Family Campground (☎ 603-823-5675; NH 18; sites without/with hookups $18/24; ☺ May-Oct) Two miles northwest of Franconia Notch State Park, this wooded campground caters more to tenters (91 sites) than RVers (26 sites). Many sites are along a stream.

MID-RANGE & TOP END

Sugar Hill Inn (☎ 603-823-5621, 800-548-4748; www .sugarhillinn.com, NH 117, Sugar Hill; r with breakfast $100-290, ste $175-380, cottages $155-320; ☒) This restored 1789 farmhouse sits atop a hill lined with sugar maples ablaze in autumn and offering panoramic views any time of year. Sixteen acres of lawns and gardens and 15 romantic guest rooms, not to mention the delectable country breakfast, make this a top choice.

Franconia Inn (☎ 603-823-5542, 800-473-5299; www.franconiainn.com; NH 116, Franconia; d with breakfast $91-185, ste $146-310; ☒) This excellent 34-room inn, just 2 miles south of Franconia, is set on a broad, fertile, pine-fringed river valley. You'll find plenty of common space and well-maintained, traditional guest rooms. The 107-acre estate has prime cross-

country ski possibilities and summertime hiking and horseback riding.

Bungay Jar (☎ 603-823-7775; www.bungayjar.com; 791 Easton Valley Rd, Franconia; r $100-150, ste $135-195; ☒) The Bungay Jar – according to local lore – is a powerful wind that blows through the Easton Valley creating a distinctive melodic sound. If you hear it anywhere, it will be in the magical grounds and gardens of this whimsical B&B. The restored post-and-beam barn now has six gracious guest rooms. The decor is sophisticated instead of old fashioned, but utterly comfortable.

Sunset Hill House (☎ 603-823-5522; www.sunsethill house.com; 231 Sunset Hill Rd, Sugar Hill; r with breakfast $100-150, plus $50 Oct; ☒) This 'Grand Inn,' as it is called, lives up to its moniker. All 28 rooms have lovely views of either the mountains or the adjacent golf course. The pricier rooms feature Jacuzzis, fireplaces and private decks, but all the rooms are lovely. The dining room is a formal affair, but there is also a more casual tavern.

Foxglove (☎ 603-823-8840; www.foxgloveinnh.com; cnr NH 117 & Lovers Lane, Sugar Hill; r with breakfast $145-175; ☒) Any inn located on Lovers Lane must be romantic, and this elegant country inn fits the bill. Newly renovated rooms and suites are cozy – some warmed by a crackling fire. The grounds are graced by lovely terraces, gurgling fountains and – of course – breathtaking mountain vistas. Breakfast is a formal affair with crystal and china.

Franconia Village Hotel (☎ 603-823-7422, 888-669-6777; www.franconiahotel.com; 87 Wallace Hill Rd; d $69-129; ☒ ☲) Franconia's most prominent lodging place (exit 38 off I-93) has 61 modern rooms, plus a lone apartment with a kitchen. It is somewhat of a contrast to all the historic inns around here, but comfortable just the same. In case you are not getting enough exercise hiking up and down the mountains, there is a health club and spa.

Eating

Many of Franconia's inns offer fine dining, including the Franconia Inn (left), Sunset Hill House (above) and Sugar Hill Inn (left).

Polly's Pancake Parlor (☎ 603-823-5575; NH 117, Sugar Hill; mains $5-15; ☺ 7am-3pm May–mid-Oct) Attached to a 19th-century farmhouse 2 miles west of Franconia, this local institution offers pancakes, pancakes and more pancakes. They're excellent, made with home-ground flour and topped with the farm's own maple syrup, eggs and sausages. Polly's cob-smoked bacon is tasty enough to convert a vegetarian. In case someone in your party doesn't like fluffy griddlecakes (blasphemy!), sandwiches and quiches are also available.

Cold Mountain Cafe & Gallery (☎ 603-869-2500; 2015 Main St, Bethlehem; sandwiches $5-7, mains $10-16; ☽ closed Sun) One of the best restaurants in the region, this casual café and gallery has an eclectic menu, from simple sandwiches and salads to substantial dinners like bouillabaisse or rack of lamb. Everything is prepared with the utmost care and presented exquisitely, but the atmosphere is very relaxed. Be prepared to wait for your table (outside, since the place is cozy).

Harman's Cheese & Country Store (☎ 603-823-8000; 1400 NH 117, Sugar Hill) If you need to pack a picnic for your hike – or if you simply wish to stock up on New England goodies before heading home – don't miss this country store, boasting 'the world's greatest cheddar cheese.' It is arguably true. They also have maple syrup, classic New England–style oyster crackers, apple cider (in season) and addictive spicy dill pickles.

Entertainment

Colonial Theater (☎ 603-869-3422; www.bethlehem colonial.org; Main St, Bethlehem; live shows $15-25) This classic theater in downtown Bethlehem needs some renovation, but the auditorium is a cool, historic place to hear the jazz, blues and folk musicians that pass through this little town (more than you would guess). Recent performers have included Aztec Two Step and George Winston. This place also serves as a cinema showing independent and foreign films.

Getting There & Away

From Franconia you can head west to St Johnsbury, Vermont (25 miles, 40 minutes) via I-93, or head east through Crawford Notch to North Conway (45 miles, 1¼ hours) via US 3 to US 302.

Concord Trailways buses (☎ 603-228-3300, 800-639-3317; www.concordtrailways.com) stop at **Kelly's Foodtown** (☎ 603-823-7795) in the center of Franconia. They go south to Lincoln (25 minutes), Concord ($33, two hours), Manchester ($28, 2½ hours), Boston South Station ($19, 3½ hours) and Logan International Airport ($16, 3½ hours).

MT WASHINGTON VALLEY

The Mt Washington Valley stretches north from Conway, at the eastern end of the Kancamagus Hwy. The valley's hub is North Conway, but any of these towns along NH 16/US 302 (also called the White Mountain Hwy) can serve as a gateway to the eastern side of the White Mountains. The valley's namesake is – of course – Mt Washington, New England's highest peak (6288ft), which towers over the valley in the northwest.

NORTH CONWAY & AROUND
pop 2070

The Kancamagus Hwy's eastern terminus is Conway, at the intersection of NH 16, NH 113, NH 153 and US 302. But the region's capital is North Conway, the local hub for trailblazers and outdoor adventurers.

North Conway is not much more than a one-street town. The street is NH 16/US 302, the White Mountain Hwy, also known as Main St, a seemingly endless strip of motor inns, shopping outlets and just about every service a traveler needs. Most of the time, auto traffic on Main St moves at a glacial pace. If your aim is to get around North Conway, not into it, take West Side Rd, which follows the Saco River between Conway and Glen.

Unless otherwise stated, items in the following section are in North Conway proper.

Information

Met (☎ 603-356-2332; Schouler Park, Main St; per hr $8, wireless free) A coffee house offering high-speed Internet connections.

Mt Washington Valley Chamber of Commerce (☎ 603-356-3171; www.mtwashingtonvalley.org; Main St) Just south of the town center.

North Conway Village Map & Guide (www.northcon wayvillage.net) Useful, complimentary maps that are distributed around town.

New Hampshire State Information Office (cnr NH 10 & US 302, Intervale; ☽ 10am-5:30pm Mon-Thu, 7am-11pm Fri-Sun) Two miles north of North Conway center.

Sights & Activities
CONWAY SCENIC RAILROAD
The **Notch Train** (☎ 603-356-5251, 800-232-5251; www.conwayscenic.com; adult/infant/child $38/6/22 mid-

Jun–mid-Sep, $43/6/26 mid-Sep–mid-Oct) was built in 1874 and restored in 1974, and now offers New England's most scenic journey. The spectacular five-hour trip passes through Crawford Notch and terminates at Fabyan Station near Bretton Woods. Accompanying live commentary recounts the railroad's history and folklore. Reservations required.

Alternatively, the same company operates the antique steam **Valley Train**, which makes a shorter journey south through the Mt Washington Valley, stopping in Conway (adult/child $11.50/8) and Bartlett (adult/child $18.50/12.50). Sunset trains, dining trains and other special events are all available.

ECHO LAKE STATE PARK

Two miles west of North Conway via River Rd, this placid **mountain lake** (☎ 603-356-2672; River Rd; admission $3; ☼ dawn-dusk Sat & Sun May, daily Jun-Aug) lies at the foot of White Horse Ledge, a sheer rock wall. A scenic trail circles the lake. There is also a mile-long auto road and hiking trail leading to the 700ft-high Cathedral Ledge, with panoramic White Mountains views. This is a great spot for swimming, picnicking, and rock climbing, but there's no camping.

SKIING

Mt Cranmore Resort (☎ lodging 603-356-5543, snow report 800-786-6754), on the outskirts of North Conway, has a vertical drop of 1200ft, 39 slopes and trails (40% beginner, 40% intermediate and 20% expert), nine lifts and 100% snowmaking ability.

CLIMBING & KAYAKING

Eastern Mountain Sports Climbing School (EMS Climbing School; ☎ 603-356-5433, 800-310-4504; www .emsclimb.com; Main St, Eastern Slope Inn) sells maps and guides to the WMNF, and rents camping equipment, cross-country skis and snowshoes. Year-round, the climbing school offers classes and tours.

Saco Bound Inc (☎ 603-447-2177; www.sacobound .com; US 302, Center Conway; rental per day $25.50) rents out canoes and kayaks and organizes guided trips, including the introductory trip to Weston's Bridge ($16). Also renting kayaks is **Kayak Jack Fun Yak Rentals** (☎ 603-447-5571; NH 16, Conway; rental per day incl transport $25-30), located next to Eastern Slope Campground.

Festivals & Events

Just over the state border in Maine, the annual county **Fryeburg Fair** (☎ 207-935-3268; www .fryeburgfair.com) is one of New England's – if not the country's – largest and best-known agricultural events. Held every year in early October, the week-long fair features harness racing, ox pulling, wreathe making, and judging of just about every kind of farm animal you can imagine. There is also plenty of music, food and other fun.

Sleeping

BUDGET

Albert B Lester Memorial HI-AYH Hostel (☎ 603-447-1001; www.conwayhostel.com; 36 Washington St, Conway; dm $20-23, d $48-54 with breakfast; ☒ ▣) New Hampshire's only youth hostel is in Conway (not North Conway!). This 43-bed place off Main St (NH 16) is a 'sustainable living center' focused on environmentally friendly practices and conservation. The hostel is big on recycling and gives out information on how to apply 'green' technologies to your daily life. More importantly, the facility offers five bedrooms with bunk beds and four family-size rooms. Prices include linens and breakfast. Excellent hiking and bicycling opportunities are just outside the door, and canoeists can easily portage to two nearby rivers. Reservations are accepted with a credit card.

Eastern Inns (☎ 603-356-5447, 800-628-3750; www .easterninns.com; NH 16; s $55-65, d $81-121; ☒ ▣) This tidy place with 56 units (including a few suites) is great for families. Rooms are good value, and facilities include a playground, basketball hoop and game room. Miles of trails – good for hiking, biking and cross-country skiing – are right outside the door.

Cranmore Inn (☎ 603-356-5502, 800-526-5502; www.cranmoreinn.com; 80 Kearsarge St; d with breakfast, shared bathroom $59-89, private bathroom $64-109, ste $79-139; ☒ ▣) The Cranmore has been operating as a country inn since 1863, and it has been known as reliably good value for much of that time. Traditional country decor predominates, meaning lots of floral and frills.

Conway, North Conway and Glen are riddled with commercial campgrounds: **Eastern Slope Camping Area** (☎ 603-447-5092; www.easternslopecamping.com; NH 16, Conway; sites $26-38; ☼ late May–mid-Oct; ▣) Eastern Slope has mountain views, 260 well-kept sites, long beaches on the Saco River and lots of facilities.

NEW HAMPSHIRE

Saco River Camping Area (☎ 603-356-3360; NH 16, North Conway; sites without/with hookups $21/30; ☾ May–mid-Oct; ☒) A riverside campground, away from the highway, with 140 wooded and open sites.

Beach Camping Area (☎ 603-447-2723; www.ucampnh.com/thebeach; 98 Eastern Slope Tce/NH 16, Conway; sites without/with hookups $22/32; ☾ mid-May–mid-Oct) Many of these 124 forested sites are on the Saco River.

Cove Camping Area (☎ 603-447-6734; www.cove camping.com; Conway; tent/lakeside sites $22/48; ☾ late May–mid-Oct) These 95 forested sites are right on Conway Lake, off Stark Rd.

MID-RANGE & TOP END

There are dozens of regional inns and affordable B&Bs, several of which have formed an organization called **Country Inns in the White Mountains** (reservations ☎ 603-356-9460). Rates vary wildly between seasons. Expect the lower end of the range in winter and spring, and higher rates in summer and during foliage season. If money is no object, most places also offer extra-special rooms and suites at higher rates.

Kearsarge Inn (☎ 603-356-8700; www.kearsargeinn .com; 42 Seavey St; r $109-229; ☒) Just off Main St in the heart of North Conway, this lovely inn is the perfect setting if you want an intimate experience near the center of town. The inn is a 'modern rendition' of the historic Kearsarge House, one of the region's first and grandest hotels. Each of the Inn's 15 rooms and suites offers a choice of king- or queen-size beds, gas fireplaces, Jacuzzis and beautiful period furnishings. The innkeepers also operate the fun restaurant next door, Decades.

Victorian Harvest Inn (☎ 603-356-3548; www.vic torianharvestinn.com; 28 Locust Lane; r Nov-Aug $110-150, Sep-Oct $160-240; ☒) Set on a quiet street behind the Red Jacket Mountain View Inn (right), this lovely Victorian is a hidden gem. Eight rooms and a warm, welcoming library are individually decorated, incorporating a southwest theme from the owners' native Texas. A full breakfast – with homemade seasonal fruit, homemade bread and specialty egg dishes – is served in the antique-filled dining room.

1785 Inn (☎ 603-356-9025, 800-421-1785; www.the 1785inn.com; NH 16, Intervale; d with breakfast, shared bathroom $69-139, private bathroom $89-179; ☒ ☒) This colonial hostelry has a deservedly renowned dining room, 17 individually decorated guest rooms and lovely Victorian-style common areas with two fireplaces. Six acres of beautiful grounds include opportunities for hiking and cross-country skiing. It is two miles north of the center of North Conway near the New Hampshire state information center.

1768 Inn (☎ 603-356-3836; www.1768countryinn .com; cnr NH 16 & Artist Falls Rd; d $60-150; ☒) Not to be confused with its (younger) neighbor with a similar name, this is actually the oldest building in North Conway. It is now a fully restored colonial country inn. Rooms are all uniquely decorated with antiques and quilts; some have shared bathrooms. There are also suites with private bathrooms and fireplaces. Breakfast is in the cheery sunroom or in front of the vast fireplace.

Cabernet Inn (☎ 603-356-4704, 800-866-4704; www .cabernetinn.com; NH 16; d with breakfast $90-150; ☒) This 1842 Victorian cottage is north of North Conway center, near Intervale. Each of the 11 guest rooms has antiques and queen beds, while pricier rooms also have fireplaces or Jacuzzis. Two living rooms with fireplaces and a shady deck are open for guests to enjoy and relax in. The large gourmet kitchen is the source of a decadent country breakfast.

Eastern Slope Inn Resort (☎ 603-356-6321, 800-862-1600; www.easternslopeinn.com; NH 16; d $89-139, ste $159-279; ☒ ☒) This posh place has a huge variety of rooms (over 200!) and loads of facilities, including tennis courts, playgrounds and a theater. A fancy resort atmosphere presides. You can't miss the grand building just north of the central business district.

Wyatt House Country Inn (☎ 603-356-7977, 800-527-7978; www.wyatthouseinn.com; NH 16; d with breakfast $89-199; ☒) You'll be pampered with fresh-baked breakfast goods (served by candlelight), afternoon tea and evening sherry. Rooms are uniquely decorated with lots of lace, ruffles and flowers, and furnished with antiques; some have private decks overlooking the serene Saco River.

Stonehurst Manor (☎ 603-356-3113, 800-525-9100; www.stonehurstmanor.com; NH 16; d from $110; ☒ ☒) Spacious, gracious Stonehurst has 25 luxury rooms (many with fireplaces) in a manor house filled with stained glass and oak paneling. The motel annex is less interesting. All rooms have access to 33 acres of landscaped grounds, including tennis courts and beautiful gardens.

Red Jacket Mountain View Inn (☎ 603-356-5411, 800-752-2538; www.redjacketmountainview.com; NH 16; d $99-219; ☒) This 164-room motel has resort-style facilities: saunas, Jacuzzis and tennis courts. Meals are not included, but the Champney's dining room puts out a bountiful breakfast buffet. A similar option is the nearby sister property, **Fox Ridge Resort** (☎ 603-356-3151, 800 343-1804), which has beautifully landscaped grounds and fantastic views in all directions.

Briarcliff Motel (☎ 603-356-5584, 800-338-4291; www.briarcliffmotel.com; NH 16; d $100-125; ✗ ♨) Try to get one of the rooms with a panoramic mountain view or a screen porch overlooking the property. Otherwise, all of the rooms are comfortable and tasteful, with coffeemakers and minirefrigerators.

School House Motel (☎ 603-356-6829; www.school housemotel.com; NH 16; r $110; ♨) This motel is indeed housed in one of North Conway's original schoolhouses, and it has the old bell to prove it. Twenty simple units have your basic motel amenities.

Eating

Many inns – especially those north of the town center and in Jackson (see p456) – have elegant dining rooms with excellent, traditional menus.

Peach's (☎ 603-356-5860; 2506 White Mountain Hwy, Main St; meals $6; ☼ 6am-2:30pm) Away from the in-town bustle, this little house is an excellent option for soups, sandwiches and breakfast. Who can resist fruit-smothered waffles and pancakes and fresh-brewed coffee, served in somebody's cozy living room?

Moat Mountain Smokehouse and Brewing Co (☎ 603-356-6381; 3378 White Mountain Hwy; sandwiches $6-8, mains $12-20) Come here for a plate of BBQ ribs, a bowl of beefy chili or a juicy burger. Wash it down with one of eight brews made on site. The friendly bar also has a pool table and dart boards, so it's a fun place to hang around.

Shalimar (☎ 603-356-0123; 27 Seavey St; lunch $5-7, dinner $9-13; ☼ 11am-2:30pm Tue-Sun & 5pm-10pm daily) This popular and friendly Indian restaurant has tasteful decor and tasty dishes. The place features a children's menu, which significantly broadens the definition of Indian cuisine.

Cafe Noche (☎ 603-447-5050; 147 Main St, Conway; mains $8-10; ☼ 11:30am-9pm) This festive café has some of the best Mexican food north of the Massachusetts border. The bar features a huge selection of tequilas and over 25 types of margaritas!

Horsefeathers (☎ 603-356-2687; Main St; mains $10-20; ☼ 11:30am-10:30pm or 11:30pm) The most popular gathering place in town, Horsefeathers has an encyclopedic menu featuring pasta, salads, sandwiches, burgers, bar snacks and main-course platters.

Bellini's (☎ 603-356-7000; NH 16, Willow Pl mall; mains $13-24; ☼ 5pm-10pm Wed-Sun) Come here for Italian cuisine served in huge portions at moderate prices. The menu includes all the classics, from eggplant parmigiana to a 13-ounce sirloin steak. Bellini's now has a new location in a shopping mall south of the center on Rte 16.

Getting There & Away

Concord Trailways (☎ 603-228-3300, 800-639-3317; www.concordtrailways.com) runs a daily route between Boston and Berlin, which stops in North Conway at the Eastern Slope Inn. The bus stops in Concord ($16.50, 2½ hours) and Manchester ($19.50, three hours) before heading south to Boston ($28, four hours).

JACKSON & AROUND

pop 835

This quintessential New England village is 7 miles north of North Conway. Take NH 16 and then cross the Ellis River via the historic red covered bridge. In addition to being a picture-perfect postcard destination, Jackson village is Mt Washington Valley's premier cross-country ski center. NH 16A circles from NH 16 through the center of Jackson and back to NH 16, and NH 16B heads into the hills.

Glen is 5 miles south of Jackson; unless otherwise stated, items in the following section are in Jackson proper.

Jackson Area Chamber of Commerce (☎ 603-383-9356, 800-866-3334; www.jacksonnh.com; Jackson Falls Marketplace; ☼ 9am-4pm Mon-Fri year-round, 9am-1pm Sat Jul-Feb) can answer your questions.

Sights & Activities
STORYLAND & HERITAGE NEW HAMPSHIRE

In nearby Glen, **Storyland** (☎ 603-383-4186; www .storylandnh.com; NH 16; adult/child under 4 $20/free; ☼ 9am-5pm daily mid-Jun–early Sep, Sat & Sun late May–mid-Jun & early Sep–mid-Oct) is a delightful 30-acre theme and amusement park for children from three to nine years old. The rides, activities and shows are small-scale and well done – a refreshing break from the mega-amusements in other places. For the best value, pay and enter after 3pm, and you'll receive a pass good for the next day as well.

New Hampshire's version of Universal Studios is **Heritage New Hampshire** (☎ 603-383-4186; www.heritagenh.com; NH 16, Glen). It comprises 25 movie sets where visitors can actually walk through, experience the special effects, and interact with costumed actors. Admission and opening hours are the same as Storyland's.

SKIING

Jackson is famous for its 93 miles of cross-country trails. Stop at the **Jackson Ski Touring Foundation Center** (☎ 603-383-9355; www.jacksonxc .org; 153 Main St; day passes adult/child/senior $15/8/12) for passes and to inquire about lessons, rentals and groomed trails.

Black Mountain Ski Area (☎ 603-383-4490, snow report 800-475-4669, lodging reservations 800-698-4490; www.blackmt.com; NH 16B, Jackson; adult/senior/teen/ student Sat & Sun $32/20/20/25, Mon-Fri $20/15/15/20) is a smaller ski area with a vertical drop of 1100ft. Forty trails – equally divided between beginner, intermediate and expert slopes – are served by four lifts. This a good place for beginners and families with small children.

West of Glen, you can play and stay at **Attitash** (☎ 603-374-2368, snow report 877-677-7669, lodging reservations 800-223-7669; www.attitash.com; US 302; adult/child/senior/teen Sun-Fri $49/19/19/39, Sat & holidays $55/35/35/45; 🕙 8am-4pm). The resort includes two mountains, Attitash and Bear Peak, which offer a vertical drop of 1750ft, 12 lifts and 70 ski trails. Half the trails are intermediate level, while the other half are equally divided between expert and beginner level.

From mid-June to mid-October, the chairlifts at Attitash whisk you to the top of the **Alpine Slide** (single ride $13, one-day pass adult/child $29/12), a long track that you schuss down on a little cart. It's an exhilarating ride safe for all ages. There is also **mountain-bike rental and trails** (adult/child $40/20) and **guided horseback riding** (per person $45, children must be over 8 yrs) from mid-June to mid-October.

Sleeping

Inn at Jackson (☎ 603-383-4321; www.innatjackson.com; cnr Main St & Thornhill Rd; d $99-199; 🗙) Enter this charming red farmhouse through the grand foyer where you'll be greeted by enticing aromas wafting from the kitchen. Romantic rooms feature fireplaces and four-poster beds, and an outdoor Jacuzzi is open to all

guests. Breakfast is served on the sun porch or in the dining room next to the fire.

Village House (☎ 603-383-6666, 800-972-8343; www.villagehouse.com; NH 16A; d $75-105; 🕙 💰) This large village house and renovated barn have nine comfy rooms, all furnished simply and stylishly. Rooms have private bathrooms and kitchenettes. Management is 'hands-off' – guests take care of themselves, but they don't lack for privacy.

Covered Bridge Motor Lodge (☎ 603-383-6630, 800-634-2911; www.jacksoncoveredbridge.com; NH 16; d with breakfast $59-99; 🗙 💰) Appropriately, this comfortable 32-room motel is located just south of Jackson's covered bridge. Rooms have – variously – kitchenettes, private balconies and views of a lovely gurgling brook.

Wildcat Inn & Tavern (☎ 603-383-4245, 800-228-4245; www.wildcattavern.com; 3 Main St; d with breakfast $109-129) This centrally located village lodge has a dozen cozy rooms with private bathrooms and antique furnishings. The cottage ($359) – known as the 'Igloo' – sleeps up to six.

Whitney's Inn (☎ 603-383-8916, 800-677-5737; www.whitneysinn.com; NH 16A; d with breakfast $119-179; 🗙) This longtime institution appeals to skiers since there are slopes right out the back door, but it's also a great summertime family destination. The 30 rooms range from family suites to pleasant inn-style rooms and cottages. The renovated barn hosts a recreational room for kids and a lunch room during the winter.

Wentworth (☎ 603-383-9700; www.thewentworth .com; NH 16B; r Nov- Sep $185-215, Oct $215-245; 🗙 💰) This grand country inn is on the edge of Jackson Village and on the edge of a gorgeous public golf course. It is an elegant affair, with 51 spacious rooms, a gracious lobby and dining room and outdoor facilities such as tennis courts.

Eating & Drinking

Many of Jackson's inns have excellent (and expensive) dining rooms.

Thompson House Eatery (☎ 603-383-9341; NH 16B; mains $18-25) Casual but cool, the Thompson House is a local favorite for creative, new American cuisine. The seasonal menu is big on organic, locally grown produce, which is also for sale at the farm stand outside. Eat on the porch, with light filtering through the stained-glass windows, or at the friendly bar.

Wildcat Inn & Tavern (☎ 603-383-4245; 3 Main S; breakfast & lunch $8-12, dinner $15-25) This popular tavern serves hearty fare like lobster Benedict for breakfast, creative sandwiches for lunch, and pasta and steaks for dinner.

White Mountain Cider Co (☎ 603-383-9061; US 302, Glen) If you are packing a picnic for your day hike, stop at this country store. Besides cider, you'll find gourmet coffee, cider doughnuts, apple pie and a whole range of specialty New England products.

Two little cafés with sandwiches and breakfast foods are **As You Like It** (☎ 603-383-6425; NH 16B; mains $3-6; ☺ 7am-6pm Wed-Mon) in the Jackson Falls Marketplace and **Madeline's** (☎ 603-383-8084; NH 16A; sandwich $5) across from the golf shop.

Getting There & Away

Concord Trailways (☎ 603-228-3300, 800-639-3317) runs a daily bus between Boston ($29, four hours) and Berlin, making a stop in Jackson at the **Ellis River Grocery Store** (☎ 603-383-9041, NH 16).

CRAWFORD NOTCH & BRETTON WOODS

US 302 travels west from Glen, then north to Crawford Notch (1773ft), and on to Bretton Woods. Before 1944, the area was known only to locals and wealthy summer visitors who patronized the grand Mt Washington Hotel. When President Roosevelt chose the hotel as the site of the conference to establish a new global economic order after WWII, the whole world learned about Bretton Woods.

The mountainous countryside is still as stunning now as it was during those historic times, the hotel is almost as grand and the name still rings with history. At the very least, stop to admire the view of the great hotel set against the mountains. Ascending Mt Washington on a cog railway powered by a steam locomotive is dramatic fun for all, and a must for railroad buffs.

Information

Complete information about hiking, biking and camping in the area is available from **AMC Highland Center** (☎ 603-466-2727; www .outdoors.org; Crawford Notch; ☺ 9am-5pm Mon-Sat), including maps and trail guides. Daily activities and guided hikes are offered.

Sights & Activities
MT WASHINGTON COG RAILWAY

Purists walk, the lazy drive, but certainly the quaintest way to reach the summit of Mt Washington is to take this **cog railway** (☎ 603-846-5404, 800-922-8825; www.thecog.com; adult/child under 6/child/senior $49/free/35/45; ☺ 9am-4pm daily early Jun-late Oct, variable May & Nov). Since 1869, coal-fired, steam-powered locomotives have followed a 3.5-mile track up a steep mountainside trestle for a three-hour, roundtrip scenic ride. Reservations are highly recommended.

Instead of having drive wheels, a cog locomotive applies power to a cogwheel, or gear wheel, on its undercarriage. The gears engage pins mounted between the rails to pull the locomotive and a single passenger car up the mountainside, burning a ton of coal and blowing a thousand gallons of water into steam along the way. Up to seven locomotives may be huffing and puffing at

BRETTON WOODS MAKES HISTORY

WWII devastated both Europe and Asia, causing the world economy to go into a tailspin. World leaders realized that rebuilding war-torn areas and restoring the world economy would be a principal concern once the fighting stopped.

For three weeks in July 1944, world leaders and financial experts gathered in Bretton Woods for the UN Monetary and Financial Conference. Their purpose was to develop a model for the world's postwar economy. The conference's results included the creation of the International Monetary Fund and the World Bank. The experts also formulated plans for stable currency-exchange rates and temporary assistance to member nations with balance-of-payments problems.

The Bretton Woods conference paved the way for the conference at Dumbarton Oaks in Washington, DC, in September and October 1944, at which time a prototype for the UN charter was written. At Yalta, in February 1945, the shape of the new organization was refined, setting the stage for the UN founding conference, held in San Francisco from April to June 1945. Though some elements of the economic world order that emerged at Bretton Woods – such as the gold standard – have been superseded, much of the conference's work has proven remarkably durable.

NEW HAMPSHIRE

one time here, all with boilers tilted to accommodate the grade, which at the 'Jacob's Ladder' trestle is a 37% grade – the second-steepest railway track in the world.

The base station is 6 miles east of US 302. Turn east in Fabyan, just northwest of the Mt Washington Hotel (between Bretton Woods and Twin Mountain). Also, remember that the average temperature at the summit is 40°F in summer and the wind is always blowing, so bring a sweater and windbreaker.

CRAWFORD NOTCH STATE PARK

In 1826, torrential rains in this steep valley caused massive mud slides that descended on the home of the Willey family. The house was spared, but the family was not – they were outside at the fatal moment and were swept away by the mud. The dramatic incident made the newspapers and fired the imaginations of painter Thomas Cole and author Nathaniel Hawthorne. Both men used the incident for inspiration, thus unwittingly putting Crawford Notch on the tourist maps. Soon, visitors arrived to visit the tragic spot, and they stayed for the bracing mountain air and healthy exercise.

In 1859 the Crawford family opened the Crawford House hotel and began cutting mountain trails so their guests could penetrate the previously trackless wilderness. Their work was the basis for today's excellent system of trails. (The hotel was razed in 1977.) Crawford Notch State Park now occupies this beautiful, historic valley.

From the Willey House site, now used as a **state park visitor center** (☎ 603-374-2272; ☽ dawn-dusk mid-May–mid-Oct), you can walk the easy half-mile Pond Loop Trail, the 1-mile Sam Willey Trail and the Ripley Falls Trail, a 1-mile hike from US 302 via the Ethan Pond Trail. The trailhead for Arethusa Falls, a 1.3-mile hike, is a half-mile south of the Dry River Campground on US 302.

SKIING

Mt Washington Resort at Bretton Woods includes a **ski station** (☎ 603-278-3320; www.bretton woods.com; adult/child/teen/senior Mon-Fri $52/31/41/15 Sat & Sun $59/36/48/59; ☽ 8:30am-4pm) with a vertical drop of 1500ft. Seven different chair lifts serve 88 different trails, most of which are intermediate. The convenient **Family Center** (☎ 603-278-3345; half/full-day lessons $69/89, childcare hourly/half-day/full-day $12/45/69; ☽ 8am-4:30pm) offers childcare and ski lessons for kids. All equipment is available for rental.

The resort also maintains a 62-mile network of trails for **cross-country skiing** (day-pass adult/child $17/12). The trails traverse the resort grounds, crossing open fields, wooded paths and mountain streams. Ski rental and lessons are also available.

Sleeping & Eating

In addition to being recommended lodgings, the Mt Washington Hotel offers extensive breakfast buffets and dress-up dinners, and there are eateries at both the Bretton Arms Inn and the Lodge.

BUDGET & MID-RANGE

AMC Highland Center (☎ 603-466-2727; www.outdoors .org; Crawford Notch; dm adult/child $66/37, s/d with breakfast, dinner & private bathroom per person $143/109; ☒) The newest AMC lodge is set amidst the splendor of Crawford Notch, an ideal base for hiking Mt Washington and many other trails in the area. The grounds are beautiful, rooms are basic but comfortable, meals are hearty and guests are all outdoor enthusiasts. Discounts are available for AMC members. The center also has loads of information about hiking in the region.

Lodge at Bretton Woods (☎ 603-278-1000, 800-258-0330; www.mtwashington.com; US 302; d $99-149; ☒ ☒) Operated by the Mt Washington Resort, this modern place (with 50 spacious rooms) actually enjoys the best view of the Mt Washington Hotel and its mountain backdrop. It has a motor-inn layout and an inexpensive diner, Darby's, on site.

Above the Notch (☎ 603-846-5156; www.above thenotch.com; NH 302; d $68-83) You have to go a little further away from the Mt Washington Hotel if your budget is a little tighter. This classic drive-up motel is a simple, friendly place, conveniently located next to Bretton Woods ski resort and the Cog Railway.

Lakes of the Clouds Hut (☎ 603-466-2727, 800-262-4455; dm adult/child $85/52; ☽ Jun–mid-Sep) Advance reservations are essential for this AMC hut located near the summit of Mt Washington.

Dry River Campground (☎ 603-374-2272; US 302; sites $15; ☽ late May–mid-Oct) Near the southern end of Crawford Notch State Park, this quiet state-run campground has 31 tent sites with a spanking new bathhouse, showers and even laundry facilities.

THESE LEGS CLIMBED MT WASHINGTON!

Mt Washington's summit is at 6288ft, making it the tallest mountain in New England. The **mountain** (www.mountwashington.com) is renowned for its frighteningly bad weather – the average temperature on the summit is 26.5°F. The mercury has fallen as low as -47°F, but only risen as high as 72°F. About 256in (more than 21ft) of snow fall each year. (One year, it was 47ft.) At times the climate can mimic Antarctica's, and hurricane-force winds blow every three days or so, on average. In fact, the highest wind ever recorded was here during a storm in 1934, when gusts reached 231 mph.

If you attempt the summit, pack warm, windproof clothes and shoes, even in high summer, and always consult with AMC hut personnel. Don't be reluctant to turn back if the weather changes for the worse. Dozens of hikers who ignored such warnings and died are commemorated by trailside monuments and crosses.

In good weather, the hike is exhilarating. The only disappointment is exerting hours of effort, exploring remote paths, following caroms and finally reaching the summit, only to discover a parking lot full of cars that motored up. Don't feel bad – just treat yourself to a 'This car climbed Mt Washington' bumper sticker.

Tuckerman Ravine Trail

The Tuckerman Ravine Trail starts at the Pinkham Notch Camp (p460) and continues for 4.2 thigh-burning, knee-scrambling miles to the summit. It takes most relatively fit hikers just over four hours to get to what feels like the top of the world, a bit less time for the trip down. To Tuckerman Ravine itself, the trail is fairly protected, but the steep, rocky headwall and barren cone are exposed to the dependably moody weather. It's a brute of a hike, but what a prize. If your knees can't take the descent, AMC offers a shuttle bus ($24) back to Pinkham Notch Camp.

Ammonoosuc Ravine Trail

This trail, via the AMC's Lakes of the Clouds Hut (elevation 5000ft), is one of the shortest hiking routes to the summit. It's also one of the best routes during inclement weather because it is protected from the worst winds, and, if the weather turns very nasty, you can take shelter in the AMC hut. For overnight lodging and meals, see opposite.

The trail starts at a parking lot on Base Station Rd, near the entrance to the Mt Washington Cog Railway (elevation 2560ft), and climbs easily for 2 miles up the dramatic ravine to Gem Pool. From Gem Pool, however, the climb is far more strenuous and demanding, with a sharp vertical rise to the AMC hut.

Jewell Trail

This trail is more exposed than the Ammonoosuc Ravine Trail and should be used only in good conditions. The last 0.7 mile is above the tree line and very windy. The Jewell Trail starts at the same parking lot as the Ammonoosuc Ravine Trail but follows a more northeasterly course up a ridge. At 2.8 miles, the trail rises above the timberline and climbs 3.5 miles by a series of switchbacks to meet the Gulfside Trail. The Gulfside continues to the summit.

NEW HAMPSHIRE

Crawford Notch General Store & Campground

(☎ 603-374-2779; www.crawfordnotchcamping.com; US 302; sites $18-24; ✌ May–mid-Oct) This handy all-purpose place sells camping supplies and groceries to use at its lovely wooded sites. You'll probably welcome the hot showers.

TOP END

Mt Washington Hotel (☎ 603-278-1000, 800-258-0330; www.mtwashington.com; US 302; d with breakfast & din-
ner $130-270, superior $185-340, ste from $305; ✗ 🞕) Arguably the grande dame of New England lodging, this 200-room hotel has imposing public rooms, 27 holes of golf, 12 clay tennis courts, an equestrian center and other amenities, all on thousands of acres. It is steeped in history, and you can feel it as you wander the elegant halls. Daily tours are available.

Bretton Arms Inn (☎ 603-278-1000, 800-258-0330; www.mtwashington.com; US 302; r with breakfast $65-149, ste $99-199; ⊠) People have been staying here for almost a century. On the same estate as the Mt Washington Hotel, this 34-room manse was built as a grand 'summer cottage' in 1896, but it has been an inn since 1907. It offers a more intimate and more folksy atmosphere.

PINKHAM NOTCH

In the 1820s, a settler named Daniel Pinkham attempted to build a road north from Jackson through the narrow notch on the eastern slope of Mt Washington. Torrential rains in 1826 caused mud slides that buried his best efforts, but not his name. The place is still called Pinkham Notch. It was almost a century later before an auto road was built in the narrow mountain gap and Pinkham's dream of easy transit was finally realized.

Today, the area is still known for its wild beauty even though useful facilities for campers and hikers make it one of the most popular activity centers in the White Mountains. Wildcat Mountain and Tuckerman's Ravine offer good skiing, and an excellent system of trails provides access to natural beauties of the Presidential Range, especially Mt Washington. For the less athletically inclined, the Mt Washington Auto Rd provides easy access to the summit.

Orientation & Information

NH 16 goes north 11 miles from North Conway and Jackson to Pinkham Notch (2032ft), then past the Wildcat Mountain ski area and Tuckerman's Ravine, through the small settlement of Glen House and past the Dolly Copp Campground to Gorham and Berlin.

The nerve center for hiking in the Whites, the **AMC Pinkham Notch Camp** (☎ 603-466-2727; www.outdoors.org; Pinkham Notch, NH 16; ◷ 6:30am-10pm) provides extensive information, maps, lectures and guided hikes, as well as a cafeteria and lodging (see opposite).

Sights & Activities

MT WASHINGTON AUTO ROAD

The **Mt Washington Summit Road Company** (☎ 603-466-3988; www.mt-washington.com/autoroad; $18 per car; $4-7 per passenger; ◷ 8am-4pm May-Oct, longer hr summer, closed Nov-Apr) operates an 8-mile-long alpine toll road from Pinkham Notch to the summit of Mt Washington. The entrance is off NH 16, 2.5 miles north of Pinkham Notch Camp. The toll includes

an audio-cassette tour. If you'd rather not drive, you can take a 1½-hour **guided tour** (adult/child/senior $24/11/22; ◷ 8:30am-5pm). In severe weather, the road may be closed (even in summer).

PINKHAM NOTCH CAMP

Guided nature walks, canoe trips, cross-country ski and snowshoe treks and other outdoor adventures out of Pinkham Notch Camp are organized by the **AMC** (☎ 603-466-2727, 800-262-4455; www.outdoors.org). They also operate a summer hiker's shuttle that stops at many trailheads along US 302 in Pinkham Notch.

The *AMC White Mountain Guide,* on sale here, includes detailed maps and the vital statistics of each trail: how long and how difficult it is, the vertical rise, the average walking time, reference points along the way and information on what to look at as you walk. Individual trail maps and guides are also available. You can also purchase the guide online from the main AMC website.

The AMC maintains hikers' 'high huts' providing meals and lodging. Carter Notch Hut is located on Nineteen-Mile Brook Trail, and Lakes of the Clouds Hut (p458) is sited on Crawford Path. For those hiking the Appalachian Trail (p523), the Zealand and Carter huts are open year-round. For lodging and meals at the camp, see opposite.

SKIING

With a vertical drop of 2112ft, **Wildcat Mountain** (☎ 603-466-3326, 800-255-6439, snow report 800-754-9453; www.skiwildcat.com; NH 16, Pinkham Notch; adult/child/senior/teen $55/25/25/42) tops off at 4415ft. Just north of Jackson, Wildcat's downhill skiing facilities include 44 ski trails (30% beginner, 40% intermediate, 30% expert), four lifts and 90% snowmaking capacity.

The cirque at **Tuckerman Ravine** has several ski trails for ski purists. What's pure about it? No lifts. You climb up the mountain, then ski down. Purists posit that if you climb up, you will have strong legs that won't break easily in a fall on the way down. Tuckerman is perhaps best in spring, when most ski resorts are struggling to keep their snow cover, since nature conspires to keep the ravine in shadow much of the time. Park in the Wildcat Mountain lot for the climb up the ravine.

DETOUR: GREAT NORTH WOODS

Not too many people make it all the way up here, north of Berlin. There are two scenic routes north of the Notches and Bretton Woods. If you've been feeling like you can't see the forest for the trees, nothing beats US 2 from the Vermont/New Hampshire state line to the Maine/New Hampshire state line. The expansive but looming mountain views are unparalleled. Alternatively, if you really want to get remote, or are heading to the outposts of Maine, take NH 16 north from Gorham to Erol. This route runs parallel to the birch-lined Androscoggin River.

You should not come all the way up here without catching a glimpse of a moose in the **Northern Forest Heritage Park** (☎ 603-752-7202; www.northernforestheritage.org; 961 Main St/NH 16, Berlin). If you must, sign up for a Moose Tour and go with professionals in search of huge land-roaming behemoths frolicking in their natural habitat, muddy marshes at the edge of thick forests. From late May to mid-October, the 2½-hour van tours depart daily at about dusk from the information center on the corner of NH 16 and US 2 in the middle of town.

Nestled in a dramatic and narrow valley, the elegant, 15,000-acre resort **Balsams** (☎ 603-255-3400, in New Hampshire 800-255-0800, in the rest of US & Canada 800-255-0600; www.thebalsams.com; NH 26, Dixville Notch; d Nov-Mar $175-195, Apr-May $149-179, Jun-Oct $189-229; ☒), with 212 rooms, has been hosting guests since 1866. The all-inclusive price gives unlimited use of two golf courses, putting greens, tennis courts, a lake, boats, hiking and mountain-biking trails and all other resort services. Other activities include shuffleboard, badminton, croquet, horseshoes, table tennis and billiards. Even if you don't stay, it's worth a drive to check out this rare bird.

WILDCAT SKYRIDE

Wildcat Mountain's summertime **Gondola Skyride** (adult/child $9.50/4.50; ☼ 10am-5pm mid-May–mid-Oct) was the first of its kind in the USA. It operates in summer just for the fun of the ride and the view.

Sleeping & Eating

Joe Dodge Lodge (☎ 603-466-2727, 800-262-4455; NH 16; dm $31/21, dm with meals adult/child $66/37; ☼ year-round) The AMC camp at Pinkham Notch incorporates this lodge, with dorms housing more than 100 beds. Reserve bunks in advance. The camp also has a few private doubles and triples (adult/child $66/37 per person). Discounts are available for AMC members.

Dolly Copp Campground (☎ 603-466-3984; NH 16; sites $18; ☼ mid-May–mid-Oct) This USFS campground is 6 miles north of the AMC camp and has 176 primitive sites. Reservations are accepted.

Getting There & Away

Concord Trailways (☎ 603-228-3300, 800-639-3317; www.concordtrailways.com) runs a daily route between Boston ($31 to $36, four hours) and Berlin, stopping at Pinkham Notch Camp.

Maine

HIGHLIGHTS

- **Best Place for Crusty Crustaceans**
  An outdoor lobster pound anywhere on the coast,
  but especially at Trenton Bridge Lobster Pound (p506)

- **Best Watering Holes**
  Portland's Old Port area (p479) – not for port, but for
  local microbrews

- **Best Lighthouse**
  Pemaquid Point (p492), where jagged rocks jut
  dramatically into the sea

- **Best Place where Land Meets the Sea**
  Acadia National Park (p507), where afternoon tea at
  the Jordan Pond House (p510) is a tradition

- **Best End of the Road Drive** To Stonington (p501), a
  real fishing village that's not gussied up for tourists

Trenton Bridge
★Acadia National Park
Stonington ★
Pemaquid Point
Portland ★

■ TELEPHONE CODE: 207	■ POPULATION: 1.3 MILLION	■ AREA: 35,387 SQ MILES

MAINE

Maine is a paradox for those who try to categorize it and a paradise for those who seek its wildly varying offerings. Most people come here for its dramatic, rockbound coastline and for lobster – and not just any lobster: they come for *Maine* lobster.

The coastline is about 228 miles long as the crow flies. Most travelers venture no further than the southern coast, which is thickly settled with beautifully preserved historic towns, genteel summer resorts and honky-tonk beach towns.

Venture east of Bar Harbor, though, and the coast turns wilder and more isolated. Off Maine's shore, a multitude of islands holds tiny villages, some of which weave sublime magic with staunch tradition. Head north into the mountains for vast (for New England) areas of trackless forest and thousands of glacial lakes and ponds, where loon and moose sightings become blissfully commonplace. Here, rip-snorting rivers are natural roller coasters for rafters. Ski areas offer endless miles of downhill whooshing and cross-country solitude. In Baxter State Park, cloud-piercing Mt Katahdin (5267ft) is the northern terminus of the Appalachian Trail. The Moosehead Lake region is wonderfully isolated yet rich with resorts, cabins and guides, and braided with snowmobile paths and hiking and cross-country ski trails.

While you're here, go ahead and fantasize about chucking it all in and staying put. By the end of your stay, if you're pronouncing your favorite seafood 'lobstah' and weathering the salty winds as gracefully as the gray, cedar shingles on your rental cottage, you'll know your inner Mainiac has found its home.

Information

DeLorme's Maine Atlas & Gazetteer The best map of the state that modest money can buy.

Maine Office of Tourism (☎ 207-287-5711, 888-624-6345; www.visitmaine.com; 59 State House Station, Augusta, ME 04330) These folks maintain information centers on the principal routes into the state – Calais, Fryeburg, Hampden, Houlton, Kittery and Yarmouth. Each facility is open 9am to 5pm, with extended hours in the summer.

Maine Tourism Association (www.mainetourism.com) Links all Chamber of Commerce offices in Maine.

Maine Website (www.maine.gov) The state's official website.

Portland Press Herald (www.pressherald.maine today.com)

Climate

The Inuit have hundreds of names for snowflakes, so you'd think Mainers might have hundreds of names for fog. They don't. But coastal fog in Maine is different from fog any place else. It sticks around longer; it's thicker and more mysterious; it's gentler. It can be as cold as ice or as damp as a washcloth.

In summer coastal Maine tends to be more temperate and less humid than inland Maine because of ocean breezes, but in the winter those same winds can turn mighty bitter. The interior receives its share of snow and arctic blasts. Spring is fleeting and arrives late, and as such, the tourist season on the coast doesn't really open for business in earnest until May. In the fall, blue-sky days tend to be crisp, providing the prefect backdrop for watching the leaves change color. (Consult www.maine foliage.com to track when and where the leaves are peaking.)

National & State Parks

Maine is New England's biggest state, with more open space than the other five. It has parks galore – parks big and small, suitable for every conceivable outdoor activity. From kayaking in lakes and hiking in wilderness, to biking byways and camping with views, Maine has it all. It also boasts New England's only national park, **Acadia National Park** (p507), a deservedly and extremely popular getaway in the summer.

MAINE

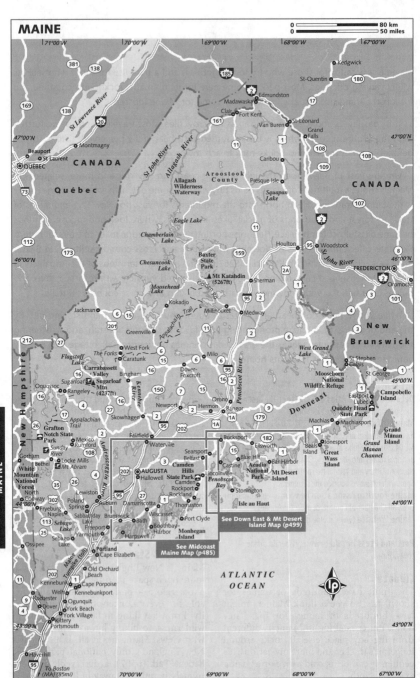

The state's 32 parks are overseen by the **Bureau of Parks & Lands** (☎ 207-287-3821; www.state .me.us/doc/parks) and staff will send you an information packet that describes each in detail. For camping at these parks, call the central **reservation hotline** (☎ 207-287-3824, 800-332-1501 within Maine).

About 275 miles of the 2150-mile **Appalachian Trail** (p523) runs through Maine, and it is perhaps most easily accessible via **Grafton Notch State Park** (p518), although the hiking is tough here. It's northern terminus is **Baxter State Park** (p522) and the summit of **Mt Katahdin**. The **White Mountain National Forest** (p518) also has dramatic sections of protected land in northern Maine, although most people tend to think that the forest stops at the New Hampshire border.

Getting There & Around

AIR
Portland International Jetport (☎ 207-874-8877; www.portlandjetport.org) is the state's main airport, but a number of airlines serve **Bangor International Airport** (☎ 866-359-2264; www.flybangor.com).

BOAT
Maine State Ferry Service (☎ 207-596-2202; www .state.me.us/mdot/opt/ferry/ferry.htm) operates boats to several larger islands. **Bay Ferries** (☎ 207-288-3395; www.catferry.com) offers service from Bar Harbor (p504) to Yarmouth in Nova Scotia (Canada), and **Scotia Prince Cruises** (☎ 800-845-4073; www.scotiaprince.com) has cruises from Portland (p480).

BUS
Concord Trailways (☎ 800-639-3317; www.concordtrail ways.com) operates daily buses between Boston and many Maine towns (including Bangor, Bar Harbor, Bath, Belfast, Brunswick, Camden/Rockport, Damariscotta, Ellsworth, Lincolnville, Portland, Rockland, Searsport, Waldoboro and Wiscasset). Some of these connect with the Maine State Ferry Service to islands off the coast.

SMT/Acadian (☎ 207-945-3000; www.smtbus.com) and **Cyr Bus Lines** (☎ 800-244-2335; www.cyrbustours .com) run buses in various directions from Bangor.

CAR & MOTORCYCLE
Except for the Maine Turnpike (I-95 and I-495) and part of I-295, Maine has no fast, limited-access highways. Roads along the coast flood with traffic during the summer tourist season. As a result, you must plan for more driving time when traveling in Maine.

Note: moose are a particular danger to drivers in Maine, even as far south as Portland – they've been known to cripple a bus and walk away. Be especially watchful in spring and fall and around dusk and dawn, when the moose are most active.

TRAIN
Amtrak's (☎ 800-872-7245; www.amtrak.com) *Downeaster* makes four or five trips daily between Boston, Massachusetts (MA), and Portland, Maine (ME).

THE SEACOAST

Many people associate the Maine coast with the works of the American artist Winslow Homer, who spent his summers in Prout's Neck. His powerful watercolors depict the boulder-strewn coastline, the battering surf of the North Atlantic and the merciless Maine climate, complete with dense fog and forceful gales. That Maine coast does exist – to the north of Prout's Neck (just south of Portland) – but you'll have to slog through some of this most southerly coast before getting to it.

South of Prout's Neck are long stretches of beach inundated with tourists, taffy and T-shirt shops. This is especially true in towns like the Yorks, Ogunquit, Wells and Old Orchard Beach, where the commercialism can be daunting. Kennebunkport, former president George Bush's hideaway, is far more serene.

KITTERY
pop 9543
Entering Kittery from New Hampshire via US 1 or I-95 can be less than thrilling – unless you're going shopping. Kittery is famous for its shopping malls and outlet stores, all of which offer discounts on everything from apparel to china to camping gear.

If shopping is not your bag, you can head straight past Kittery. Move quickly on I-95, or much more slowly on US 1. Keep in mind that US 1 from Kittery to Portland is the Maine coast's commercial artery. And as such, it's lined with motels, campgrounds, gas stations, restaurants and shops. If you need a room, tent site, meal or any other service or product, just get on US 1 and cruise until you find it.

Sleeping & Eating

Portsmouth Harbor Inn & Spa (☎ 207-439-4040; www.innatportsmouth.com; 6 Water St; r incl breakfast in season/off-season $170-220/110-200) Easily the best place to stay in Kittery, this brick B&B is just across the street from the Piscataqua River and within walking distance of Portsmouth, New Hampshire (NH). It has five rooms, decorated with care but on the small side. No matter: the private bathrooms, TVs and phones make up for it. The small spa provides requisite services.

Bob's Clam Hut (☎ 207-439-4233; US 1; dishes $3-6; ☺ lunch & dinner) As the name implies, clams rule the fryolator here, and they have since 1956. Devotees declare that Bob's are best on the entire Maine coast. But just in case you're not fond of these little nuggets (with or without bellies), Bob's also offers all sorts of seafood and sandwiches. Order at the take-out window and grab a covered picnic table.

Shopping

OUTLET SHOPPING

In the space of just 1.3 miles there are upwards of 120 **outlet shops** (☎ 207-439-4367, 888-548-8379; www.thekitteryoutlets.com) lining US 1 in Kittery. Shoppers come to Kittery from far and wide to spend money in order to save money. And save they can: all factory outlets advertise serious discounts off retail prices (up to 70%). Although many savings are no better than you'd find at a sale anywhere, every day is 'sale' day in Kittery. If you're not venturing as far north as Freeport (p481), do some one-stop shopping here for everything from kitchenware to designer jeans to luggage.

Of all the stores, the **Kittery Trading Post** (☎ 207-439-2700) deserves your time and attention. Opened in 1926, it was the original outpost and still sells all number of outdoorsy clothes and gear.

Getting There & Away

From Portsmouth, NH, it's a mere 3 miles to Kittery via US 1 or I-95, crossing the Piscataqua River to get there.

THE YORKS

pop 16,175

York Village, York Harbor and York Beach collectively make up the Yorks. **York Village**, the first city chartered in English North America, has a long and interesting history and well-preserved Colonial buildings in the village center. **York Harbor** was developed more than a century ago as a posh summer resort, and it maintains some of that feeling today. **York Beach** was where the masses came in summer, and its mass-culture roots still show in its large number of recreational vehicle (RV) parks and humdrum commercial development.

For visitor information, drop in to **Jefferds' Tavern Visitor Center** (Lindsay Rd, York Village; ☺ seasonally), off US 1A.

Sights

Historic York was called Agamenticus by pre-Colonial Native American inhabitants. British colonials settled York in 1624, and it was chartered as a city in 1641. The **Old York Historical Society** (☎ 207-363-4974; www.oldyork .com; 207 York St, York Village; adult 1 bldg/all bldgs $5/10, child $3/5; ☺ 10am-5pm Mon-Sat Feb-Dec) is proud of the town's historic buildings and has preserved several of them as a museum of the town's history. Tickets are sold at Jefferds' Tavern Visitor Center.

The historic buildings include the **School House**, a mid-18th-century school building. The **Old Gaol** (jail) gives a vivid impression of crime and punishment two centuries ago. The **Emerson-Wilcox House** is a museum of New England decorative arts and the **Elizabeth Perkins House** was a wealthy family's summer home. The **John Hancock** warehouse preserves the town's industrial and commercial history, while the **George Marshall Store** now houses a research library.

If you have children, you may want to visit **York's Wild Kingdom** (☎ 207-363-4911, 800-456-4911; www.yorkzoo.com; US 1, York Beach; adult/child 3 & under/child 4-10 $16.25/3.50/12.75; ☺ late May–mid-Sep), the state's largest zoo.

Sleeping & Eating

Dockside Guest Quarters (☎ 207-363-2868, 888-860-7428; www.docksidegq.com; Harris Island Rd, York; r summer/off-season $114-192/85-120; ☺ May-Dec, Sat & Sun only Feb-Apr) This quintessential guesthouse has the best views of any accommodations in York and the surrounding towns. In all, there are 26 rooms dispersed between the main 19th-century inn and the more modern cottages. The friendly inn offers bikes, fishing poles and a boat or two. It also has a glassed-in dining room overlooking the harbor, and serves traditional seafood dishes at dinner (mains $15 to $26). At lunchtime, order the local crab cakes ($8).

Inn at Tanglewood Hall (☎ 207-351-1075; www .tanglewoodhall.com; 611 York St, York Harbor; r incl breakfast Jul & Aug/off-season $165-250/125-195; ☺ Apr-Nov) This lovely B&B boasts six rooms with feather beds and private bathrooms. Three of the rooms have private porches. The wraparound porch is a quiet vantage point from which to take in the gardens.

Carla's Bakery & Café (☎ 207-363-4637; 241 York St, York Village; ☺ 6am-3pm Mon-Fri & 8am-1pm Sat) For fantastic salads (like chicken salad with mango chutney), soups, pastries (the scones are great) and fancy sandwiches made with co-op fresh items, Carla's has no equal in the area.

York Beach Fish Market (☎ 207-363-2763; Railroad St, York Beach; ☺ seasonally) When nothing but the absolute best crab rolls or lobster will do, this fish market is your place.

Getting There & Away

From Kittery, it's another 6 miles up US 1 or I-95 to York. York Harbor is about 1 mile due east of York via US 1A; York Beach is 3 miles north of York via US 1A.

OGUNQUIT & WELLS

pop 1226 (Ogunquit); 9400 (Wells)

Famous for its 3-mile-long sand beach that affords swimmers the choice of chilly, pounding surf or warm, peaceful back-cove waters, **Ogunquit** is a small town whose name means 'beautiful place by the sea' in the language of the Algonquin Indians. The beach is special enough to draw hordes of visitors from as far away as New York City, Montreal and Québec City, increasing the town's population exponentially in summer. It is also the US's northeasternmost gay and lesbian mecca, adding a touch of open San Francisco culture to a more conservative Maine one. For more information, have a look at www .gayogunquit.com.

Neighboring **Wells** to the northeast, is more like the eastward continuation of

Ogunquit Beach, with several camping areas and some serious commercial strip development. Wells has good beaches, though, and many useful and relatively inexpensive motels and campgrounds.

Orientation

The center of Ogunquit, called Ogunquit Sq, is the intersection of Main St (US 1), Shore Rd and Beach St. The town, which comprises mostly tourist services, stretches southeast down Shore Rd to Perkins Cove, and northeast to the neighboring town of Wells. Parking in town lots costs $6 per day during the busy summer months.

Information

Ogunquit Chamber of Commerce (☎ 207-646-5533; www.ogunquit.org; PO Box 2289, Ogunquit, MA 03907; ☺ 9am-5pm Mon-Fri & Sun, 10am-6pm Sat) Located on US 1, near the Ogunquit Playhouse and just south of the town's center.

Sights & Activities

MARGINAL WAY

Ogunquit's well-known coastline footpath starts southeast of Beach St at Shore Rd and ends near Perkins Cove. Named because it follows the 'margin' of the sea, the path and right-of-way were ceded to the town in the 1920s after its owner, Josiah Chase, sold off his valuable sea-view property. The scenic walk is slightly more than a mile. If you don't want to walk back, you can hop on the summertime trolley.

WELLS AUTO MUSEUM

In 1946, a Wells resident was given a Stanley Steamer that his uncle found in his Vermont barn. The new owner restored the early-20th-century car, and before he knew it, had a burgeoning collection of restored classic cars powered by steam, electricity and gasoline. Now ensconced in this **museum** (☎ 207-646-9064; Post Rd/US 1, Wells; adult/child under 6/child 6-12 $5/free/2; ☺ 10am-5pm late May–mid-Oct), the collection has 70 cars representing 45 different makes, including Rolls-Royce, Stutz, Cadillac, Packard, Pierce Arrow and Knox.

OGUNQUIT PLAYHOUSE

This 1933 **theater** (☎ 207-646-5511; www.ogun quitplayhouse.org; 10 Main St, Ogunquit; ☺ performances May-Sep) hosts three musicals and two plays annually in the 750-seat theater. You'll

MAINE

occasionally be rewarded by well-known performers in the cast, although it's high caliber without them. Call the box office for exact schedules and ticket prices.

BEACHES

Maine is known for rocky coastline rather than long sublime stretches of unadulterated sands, so these choices are quite popular. They're also family-friendly. **Ogunquit Beach** (or Main Beach to the locals) is only a five-minute walk along aptly named Beach St, east of US 1. Walking to the beach is a good idea in the summer, because the lot fills up early (and it costs $4 per hour to park). The 3-mile-long beach fronts Ogunquit Bay to the south; on the west side of the beach are the warmer waters of the tidal Ogunquit River. Facilities include toilets, changing rooms, restaurants and snack shops.

Footbridge Beach, 2 miles to the north near Wells, is actually the northern extension of Ogunquit Beach. It's reached from US 1 by Ocean St and a footbridge across the Ogunquit River. Another way to access the beach is via Eldridge Rd in Wells – follow the sign for Moody Beach.

Little Beach, near the lighthouse on Marginal Way, is best reached on foot.

Tours
CRUISES

Finestkind (☎ 207-646-5227; www.finestkindcruises .com; Perkins Cove, Ogunquit; adult/child $11-25/$7-25; ☺ 9:30am-3pm May-Oct) This lobster boat takes passengers on a 50-minute voyage where everyone pulls up the contraptions that have snared the crustaceans. Trips leave every hour on the hour. There are also 1½-hour cruises in the late afternoon and evening.

Silverlining (☎ 207-646-9800; Perkins Cove, Ogunquit; adult $35; ☺ 4 trips daily May-Oct) Take a two-hour sail on this 42ft Hinckley sloop (single-masted sailboat), cruising the tranquil and rocky shoreline near Ogunquit. This tour brings you closer to seals, lighthouses and the ways of lobstermen. It's a peaceful way to be on the water.

Sleeping

Many accommodations require minimum two- or three-night stays in summer, particularly on weekends. But many visitors stay for a week or more in efficiency units. Room rates tend to double in July and August and on holiday weekends (see p532).

BUDGET

Campgrounds fill up early in the day in July and August. Travelers are advised to book ahead if possible.

Pinederosa Camping Area (☎ 207-646-2492; www .pinederosa.com; Captain Thomas Rd, Wells; sites $21; ☺ mid-May–mid-Sep; ☒) This secluded campground has 162 sites, most of which are heavily wooded. Because it's a bit of a haul from Ogunquit, a shuttle fortunately runs to and from the beach from 9am to 5pm daily in the summer. To reach the campground, take US 1 for a mile northwest of Ogunquit center and turn just south of the Falls at Ogunquit Motel onto Captain Thomas Rd.

Bourne's Motel (☎ 207-646-2823, 207-646-9093; www.bournesmotel.com; 676 Main St/US 1, Ogunquit; r incl breakfast $75-115; ☺ May-Oct; ☒) North of the town's center, Bourne's has 38 bland rooms but it sure is close to Footbridge Beach.

MID-RANGE & TOP END

Ogunquit has a handful of inns and B&Bs near the beach.

Cape Neddick House B&B (☎ 207-363-2500; www .capeneddickhouse.com; 1300 US 1, Cape Neddick; r incl breakfast $105-175) This late-19th-century Victorian has five rooms. The host also provides cooking classes. (Hint: you'll enjoy breakfast here.)

Ogunquit Beach Inn (☎ 207-646-1112, 888-976-2463; www.ogunquitbeachinn.com; 67 School St, Ogunquit; r incl breakfast Jun & Jul/off-season $89-129/79-89; ☺ Mar-Jan) This gay- and lesbian-friendly B&B has nice rooms equipped with a refrigerator and TV.

Above Tide Inn (☎ 207-646-7454; www.abovetide inn.com; 66 Beach St, Ogunquit; r incl breakfast mid-Jun–Sep/off-season $165-225/95-160; ☺ mid-May–mid-Oct) This aptly named 10-room inn, perched on piles above the Ogunquit River and literally a stone's throw from Ogunquit Beach, boasts very good views from its guest rooms.

Puffin Inn (☎ 207-646-5496; www.puffininn.com; 433 Main St, Ogunquit; r incl breakfast mid-Jun–mid-Sep/off-season $90-160/80-125; ☺ May-Oct) Just north of the center of town, this big Victorian has cheesy decor but a convenient location and 10 rooms.

West Highland Inn (☎ 207-646-2181; www.west highlandinn.com; 38 Shore Rd, Ogunquit; r incl breakfast $80-195; ☺ May-Oct) This centrally located Victorian summer house has 14 warm and charming rooms that are obviously attended to with great pride.

Moon Over Maine (☎ 207-646-6666, 800-851-6837; www.moonovermaine.com; 22 Berwick Rd, Ogunquit; r incl breakfast $79-149) Up the hill from Key Bank, Moon Over Maine is an 1839 Cape-style house with nine rooms and an outdoor hot tub.

Eating

BUDGET & MID-RANGE

Fancy That... (☎ 207-646-4118; Ogunquit Sq, Ogunquit; dishes $3-6; ☯ lunch & dinner May-Oct) Located smack in the middle of Ogunquit Sq, this is a prime place to people-watch. And this eatery serves just the right food for this pastime: pastries, sandwiches and decadently delicious ice-cream. Eat on the terrace at umbrella-shaded tables right next to the busy intersection.

Village Food Market (☎ 207-646-2122; Ogunquit Sq, Ogunquit; sandwiches $3-6; ☯ lunch & dinner) Abutting Fancy That…, this is also a good bet for sandwiches, especially if you want to take them to the beach.

Lobster Shack (☎ 207-646-2941; 110 Perkins Cove Rd, Ogunquit; mains $6-18; ☯ lunch & dinner seasonally) For Ogunquit's cheapest lobster ($15) and steamers ($8), head to this shack, which has been in business since 1947 for good reason.

TOP END

98 Provence (☎ 207-646-9898; 104 Shore Rd; mains $21-28; ☯ dinner May-Oct, Fri-Sun only off-season) For authentic French cuisine and rustic candlelit surroundings, visit this gem of a restaurant. Chef Pierre whips up mouth-watering miracles like roasted boar rib chop with chestnut and dried fruit crust or Vermont pheasant with figs. Collared shirts are required.

Arrows (☎ 207-361-1100; Berwick Rd, Ogunquit; mains $40-44; ☯ dinner Wed-Sun, Sat & Sun only Apr-May & Nov-Dec) One of the two best restaurants in this part of Maine (the other being White Barn Inn in Kennebunkport, see p473), Arrows is located in a wonderfully restored 18th-century farmhouse. The two chef-owners, who hail from San Francisco (where they picked up Asian culinary influences), are known for signature dishes like grilled lobster stewed in Thai-style curry sauce. You can expect to spend more than $100 per couple, but it'll be worth it. Arrows is 4 miles west of Ogunquit; reservations and jackets for men are recommended.

Hurricane Restaurant (☎ 207-646-6348; 111 Perkins Cove Rd; mains $12-28; ☯ lunch & dinner) If gorgeous views sway you, this place will knock you over. Mains feature Maine lobster chowder ($10) and lobster rolls ($15), and you can always make a party of it with fun drinks like chocolate martinis.

Entertainment

Front Porch (☎ 207-646-4005; Ogunquit Sq, Ogunquit; ☯ mid-May–mid-Oct) This classic piano bar, known for its many off-key sing-alongs, is a relaxing place to nurse a Cosmopolitan.

Maine St (☎ 207-646-5101; 195 Main St, Ogunquit; ☯ 5pm-1am Mon-Fri, noon-1am Sat & Sun) If you want to boogie, Ogunquit's hoppin' gay dance club will get you moving.

Getting There & Around

Ogunquit lies 70 miles northeast of Boston off I-95 on US 1. Portsmouth, NH, is just 17 miles southwest of Ogunquit along the coast. Portland is 35 miles to the northeast.

'Trolleys' (more like buses disguised as trolleys) circulate through Ogunquit every 10 minutes, from 8am to 11pm. They only run in the summer months. Leave the driving to them in this congested town; they'll take you from the center of town to the beach or Perkins Cove.

THE KENNEBUNKS

pop 14,196

Together, the towns of Kennebunk, Kennebunkport and Kennebunk Beach make up the Kennebunks. **Kennebunkport**, the most famous of the three towns, is beautiful, historical and absolutely packed in summer. Walk anywhere in the town to see the pristine 100- and 200-year-old houses and mansions, manicured lawns and sea views. Even in the fall, when beach resorts such as Old Orchard Beach have closed down, visitors converge on Kennebunkport to shop in its boutiques, stay in its gracious inns and drive along the ocean to admire the view. Ocean Ave presents the most dramatic vistas, but the back streets, inland from the Kennebunk River and the sea, are less busy.

Orientation

The epicenter of Kennebunkport activity is Dock Sq, just over the bridge on the east side of the Kennebunk River. South of Dock Sq is the historic district, with many fine old mansions, some of which are now inns. Ocean Ave heads south from Dock Sq to the sea, then northeast to Walkers Point and

MAINE

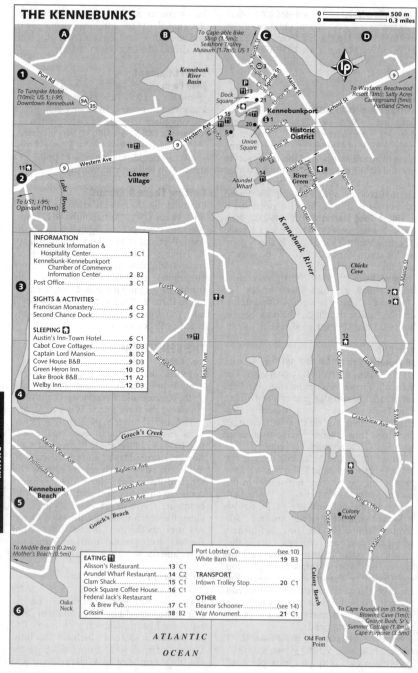

THE KENNEBUNKS

0 _____ 500 m
0 _____ 0.3 miles

To Cape-able Bike Shop (1.5mi); Seashore Trolley Museum (1.7mi); US 1

Port Rd

To Turnpike Motel (10mi); US 1; Downtown Kennebunk

Kennebunk River Basin

Dock Square

Kennebunkport

To Wayfarer, Beachwood Resort (3mi); Salty Acres Campground (5mi); Portland (25mi)

Historic District

Western Ave

Lower Village

Union Square

Arundel Wharf

Lake Brook

To US1; I-95; Ogunquit (10mi)

River Green

Kennebunk River

Chicks Cove

Forest Hill La

Fairfield Dr

Beach Ave

Ocean Ave

Grandview Ave

Gooch's Creek

Marsh View Ave

Peninsula Dr

Bayberry Ave

Gooch Ave

Beach Ave

Kennebunk Beach

Gooch's Beach

King's Hwy

Colony Hotel

To Middle Beach (0.2mi); Mother's Beach (0.5mi)

Oaks Neck

Colony Beach

To Cape Arundel Inn (0.5mi); Blowing Cave (1mi); George Bush, Sr's, Summer Cottage (1.8mi); Cape Porpoise (3.5mi)

Old Fort Point

ATLANTIC OCEAN

MAINE

INFORMATION
Kennebunk Information & Hospitality Center.....................1 C1
Kennebunk-Kennebunkport Chamber of Commerce Information Center..............2 B2
Post Office.................................3 C1

SIGHTS & ACTIVITIES
Franciscan Monastery..................4 C3
Second Chance Dock...................5 C2

SLEEPING
Austin's Inn-Town Hotel................6 C1
Cabot Cove Cottages...................7 D3
Captain Lord Mansion.................8 D2
Cove House B&B.........................9 D3
Green Heron Inn.........................10 D5
Lake Brook B&B.........................11 A2
Welby Inn.................................12 D3

EATING
Alisson's Restaurant..................13 C1
Arundel Wharf Restaurant.......14 C2
Clam Shack...............................15 C1
Dock Square Coffee House......16 C1
Federal Jack's Restaurant & Brew Pub.........................17 C1
Grissini....................................18 B2

Port Lobster Co.....................(see 10)
White Barn Inn.........................19 B3

TRANSPORT
Intown Trolley Stop...................20 C1

OTHER
Eleanor Schooner................(see 14)
War Monument.........................21 C1

the Bush compound (the vacation residence of the elder former president George Bush). It's not all that exciting, but every visitor to Kennebunkport makes the drive to stare at black Secret Service vehicles. Continue northeast on Ocean Ave to reach Cape Porpoise, a charming hamlet.

Kennebunk Lower Village lies on the west side of the Kennebunk River Bridge.

Information

Kennebunkport Information & Hospitality Center
(☎ 207-967-8600; www.visitthekennebunks.com; Union Sq; ☉ 9am-9pm Sat & Sun mid-May–mid-Oct & 10am-9pm Mon-Fri Jun-Sep) This has toilets, brochures, maps and helpful staff who might be able to find you accommodations for the night.

Kennebunk-Kennebunkport Chamber of Commerce Information Center (☎ 207-967-0857; www.visitthekennebunks.com; 17 Western Ave/ME 9, Kennebunk Lower Village; ☉ 9am-5pm Mon-Fri & 11am-3pm Sat & Sun Jun-Aug; 9am-5pm Mon-Sat Sep & Oct, 9am-5pm Mon-Fri Nov-May) This center occupies the yellow building adjacent to the Sunoco station.

Sights & Activities

SEASHORE TROLLEY MUSEUM

Trolleys, the light-rail systems that provided most urban transport a century ago, are the focus of this **museum** (☎ 207-967-2800; www.trolley museum.org; Log Cabin Rd; adult/child 6-16 $7.50/5; ☉ 10am-5pm May-Oct). Founded as the Seashore Electric Railway, the museum now holds 250 streetcars (including one named Desire), as well as antique buses and public transit paraphernalia. Head north on North St from Dock Sq to reach Log Cabin Rd.

BEACHES

Kennebunkport proper has only one beach, **Colony Beach**, which is dominated by the Colony Hotel. But Beach St and Sea Rd (west of Kennebunk River and then south of Kennebunk Lower Village) lead to three good public beaches: **Gooch's Beach**, **Middle Beach** and **Mother's Beach**, known collectively as **Kennebunk Beach**. Beach parking permits cost $10 daily, $20 weekly and $50 seasonally.

CYCLING

A good way to get around Kennebunkport is by bike. **Cape-able Bike Shop** (☎ 207-967-4382, 800-220-0907; www.capeablebikes.com; 83 Arundel Rd, Kennebunkport; ☉ 9am-6pm Mon-Sat & 8am-3pm Sun Apr-Oct) very ably rents these two-wheeled, peddle-

powered vehicles. It charges $8 daily for a three-speed or child's bike, $20 for a hybrid, and $35 for a mountain bike. To find the shop, follow North St from Dock Sq.

Tours

CRUISES

Eleanor (☎ 207-967-8809; Arundel Wharf, Kennebunkport; cruises $38; ☉ seasonal & weather-dependent) This passenger-carrying schooner makes its customers very happy with two-hour sailing cruises off Kennebunkport. Call Capt Rich Woodman or stop by Arundel Wharf for schedules and reservations.

Second Chance (207-967-5507, 800-767-2628; www.first chancewhalewatch.com; 4 Western Ave, Kennebunk; cruises adult/child 6-12 $15/10; ☉ May-Oct) Offers a 1½-hour lobster-boat cruise departing every two hours from 10am to 6pm as well as a four-hour whale-watching voyage that departs at 9am and 2:30pm (adult/child $32/$20). Board the vessels in Kennebunk Lower Village, next to the Kennebunk River Bridge.

Sleeping

Accommodations in Kennebunkport are not cheap, but there are many beautiful inns.

BUDGET

Beachwood Resort (☎ 207-967-2483; www.beach woodmotel.com; 272 Mills Rd/ME 9, Kennebunkport; r $64-125; ☉ mid-May–mid-Oct; ⚠) Facing Salty Acres Campground, this motel has 112 rooms and efficiencies, not all of which have air-con. However, they all have the benefit of shuffleboard and a tennis court.

Turnpike Motel (☎ 207-985-4404; 77 Old Alewife Rd, Kennebunk Beach; r $45-70) This simple and cheap 25-room motel lies just off I-95 precisely at exit 3 in Kennebunk.

Salty Acres Campground (☎ 207-967-2483; ME 9, Kennebunkport; sites $22-30; ☉ mid-May–mid-Oct) This campground, 5 miles northeast of Kennebunkport near Cape Porpoise, has 225 tent and trailer sites, many with electricity and water hook-ups.

MID-RANGE

Cove House B&B (☎ 207-967-3704; www.covehouse .com; S Maine St, Kennebunkport; r incl breakfast $125) A small but comfortable inn overlooking Chick's Cove on the Kennebunk River, this B&B has spacious main house rooms that are strewn with antiques. The secluded cottage, which rents for $135 nightly ($750 weekly), sleeps three and has a three-night minimum.

MAINE

Lake Brook B&B (☎ 207-967-4069; www.lakebrookbb.com; 57 Western Ave, Kennebunk; r incl breakfast May-Oct/off-season $110-150/80-95) On the edge of a salt marsh and tidal brook, this unpretentious, early-20th-century farmhouse has three rooms and one suite.

Green Heron Inn (☎ 207-967-3315; www.greenheroninn.com; 126 Ocean Ave, Kennebunkport; r incl breakfast May-Oct/off-season $125-175/105-125; ☐) This is a great little motel-like lodging, cozy and informal, with fireplaces in some rooms. It also offers a two-bedroom cottage ($175 to $250).

Austin's Inn-Town Hotel (☎ 207-967-2621, 800-468-2621; 28 Dock Sq, Kennebunkport; r $99-175) Just steps from Dock Sq, this place couldn't be more centrally located. It's a modern building, but it's done in traditional style.

Cabot Cove Cottages (☎ 207-967-5424, 800-962-5424; www.cabotcovecottages.com, Kennebunkport; 7 S Maine St; r $95-190; ☉ late May–mid-Oct) Abutting the Kennebunk River, these 15 so-called cottages more closely resemble rustic cabin-efficiencies. Weekly rental is also available.

TOP END

Welby Inn (☎ 207-967-4655; 92 Ocean Ave, Kennebunkport; r incl breakfast $199-279; ☉ mid-May–Dec) This inn ups the ante with many personal touches including fresh flowers in your room and plush terry-cloth bathrobes. The Minnie Watson, Cottage and Grantham rooms overlook the Kennebunk River.

Cape Arundel Inn (☎ 207-967-2125; www.capearundelinn.com; 208 Ocean Ave; r incl breakfast $175-250; ☉ Mar-Jan) Built in 1895, this inn boasts 'very bold ocean views' for all of its 14 rooms, most of which have porches. Rooms are bright and sunny. The inn's restaurant, by the way, is one of the finest in the Kennebunks.

Captain Lord Mansion (☎ 207-967-3141; www.captainlord.com; 6 Pleasant St, Kennebunkport; r incl breakfast Jun-Dec/off-season $257-475/116-375) If cost is no object, this is the place for you. This sea captain's house has been meticulously restored and is, if anything, more plush and beautiful than when lived in by its original occupants. For this price, you'll appreciate the free use of bicycles, fireplaces in all the rooms and (wonder of wonders!) heated bathroom tiles.

Eating

Seafood rules Kennebunk's lunch and dinner menus, but the town has some lower-priced exceptions.

BUDGET

Dock Sq Coffee House (☎ 207-967-4422; 18 Dock Sq, Kennebunkport; pastries $2-4; ☉ 7:30am-5pm Apr, May & Sep-Dec, 7:30am-10pm Jul & Aug) This tiny place – a purveyor of coffee, tea and pastries – is usually packed, and with good reason.

Clam Shack (☎ 207-967-2560; 2 Western Ave, Kennebunk Lower Village, Kennebunkport; dishes $3-13; ☉ lunch & dinner May-Oct) Next to the bridge, this little shack churns out pounds and pounds of short-order hamburgers, and fried-clam and fish plates. You can eat standing up on its deck over the water, which is quite atmospheric, but beware of aggressive and hungry seagulls that will snatch your food.

Port Lobster Co (☎ 207-967-5411; 122 Ocean Ave, Kennebunkport; ☉ 9am-5pm Apr-Dec, closed Sun & Mon in the fall) This simple lobster pound and fish market sells lobster rolls ($8), as well as boiled lobster (market price). However, there's nowhere to sit.

MID-RANGE

Alisson's Restaurant (☎ 207-967-4841; 5 Dock Sq, Kennebunkport; lunch $6-12; ☉ lunch & dinner) Centrally located, Alisson's is crowded throughout the day because of what it offers: decent pub food at good prices. Lunch selections include fried shrimp baskets and crab cakes.

Wayfarer (☎ 207-967-8961; 1 Pier Rd, Cape Porpoise; lunch $5-10, dinner $10-20; ☉ breakfast, lunch & dinner Mon-Sat & brunch Sun Jun-Aug, Wed-Sat Mar-May & Sep-Dec) If casual and affordable are your top priorities, make a beeline for this place and order yourself a large bowl of haddock chowder for $5.25 (lunchtime only).

Federal Jack's Restaurant & Brew Pub (☎ 207-967-4322; 8 Western Ave, Kennebunkport; mains $7-18; ☉ lunch & dinner) Federal Jack's, within the Shipyard complex in Kennebunk Lower Village and above the Kennebunkport Brewing Co, has a good menu of pub grub, salads, sandwiches and pizzas. Head downstairs for some heartier main courses that go handily with a selection of 'hand-crafted' ales on draft. The microbrews here are excellent. Free brewery tours are offered by appointment through the coffee shop downstairs.

Grissini (☎ 207-967-2211; 27 Western Ave; mains $8-14; ☉ dinner) Serves Northern Italian fare in an informal and very airy room. The tastiest dishes include fresh fish, homemade pastas and pizza.

MAINE

TOP END
Arundel Wharf Restaurant (☎ 207-967-3444; Arundel Wharf, Kennebunkport; lunch $4-24, mains dinner $14-30; ☺ lunch & dinner May-Nov) Just south of Dock Sq, this moderately priced lunch place is pleasantly situated, overlooking the Kennebunk River. The full dinners are much more pricey and after dark you don't get to drink in the views.

White Barn Inn (☎ 207-967-2321; www.whitebarn inn.com; 37 Beach Ave, Kennebunkport; 4-course meal $88; chef's tasting menu $108; ☺ dinner) Kennebunkport's most renowned restaurant boasts a country-elegant decor and ambience. The fantastic New American menu changes weekly and features local seafood complemented by locally grown herbs, fruits and vegetables and California greens. Make reservations, and ensure you dress up!

Getting There & Around

The Kennebunks lie halfway between Portsmouth, NH, and Portland, ME (28 miles from each city), just off I-95 on ME 9. Ogunquit is 11 miles to the southwest.

The **Intown Trolley** (☎ 207-967-3686; www.intown trolley.com; Ocean Ave; adult/child $10/5; ☺ 10am-5pm Jul & Aug; 10am-4pm spring & fall) circulates through Kennebunkport all day. You can stay aboard for the entire route for a 45-minute narrated tour, or you can hop on and off at the designated stops, including along Ocean Ave. Tours leave the trolley stops hourly.

OLD ORCHARD BEACH

pop 8856
This quintessential New England beach playground is saturated with lights, music and noise. Skimpily clad crowds of fun-loving sun worshippers make the rounds of fast-food emporiums, mechanical amusements and gimcrack shops selling trinkets. Palace Playland, on the beach at the very center of town, is a fitting symbol, with its carousel, Ferris wheel, children's rides, fried-clam and pizza stands, and T-shirt and souvenir shops.

Old Orchard Beach has long been a favorite summer resort of Québecois, who flock south in July and August. Many signs are in French as well as English, to accommodate the Canadians.

Dozens of little motels and guesthouses line the beaches to the north and south of the town center, and all are full from late June to early September. Before and after that, Old Orchard Beach slumbers.

PORTLAND

pop 64,249
Maine's largest city, port and commercial center is also small, manageable, safe, prosperous and tidy. Much like London, Portland offers many surprising urban perspectives: turn a corner, look down a street and a grand building or view is framed neatly at the end of it. Walk down the old cobblestones of narrow Wharf St at twilight and you'll feel as if a tough fisherman might pop out of nowhere to shanghai somebody.

The city center's architectural unity stems in part from tragedy. The city was ravaged by fire several times in its history, the latest and worst being the conflagration of 1866. Many of the port area's buildings – made mostly of wood – were reduced to ashes.

Portlanders resolved not to let it happen again, so they rebuilt their city in the style of the time, using redbrick and stone. A providential lack of prosperity kept its old buildings from being torn down and replaced by sterile modern structures. Today, the Old Port section of Portland begs for exploration. You'd do well to spend some time here.

Orientation

Portland is set on a ridge of hills along a peninsula surrounded by Fore River, Casco Bay and Back Cove. Portland Harbor, where Fore River empties into Casco Bay, is its historical heart, and it's where you'll spend the majority of your time. Known as the Old Port, it holds most of the city's good restaurants, bars, galleries and shops. Atop the hills at the southwestern end of the peninsula, the Western Promenade is basically a long stretch of green park framing a neighborhood of grand redbrick houses. At the opposite end of the peninsula, the Eastern Promenade, which rings Munjoy Hill, serves the same function, with much finer views of Casco Bay and its islands, though the neighborhood is not nearly as posh.

Downtown Portland, with its business district, museums, shops and galleries, rises between the promenades. Congress St is the main thoroughfare along the top of the ridge, passing Portland's most imposing buildings: city hall, banks, churches and hotels. Commercial St, where many

MAINE

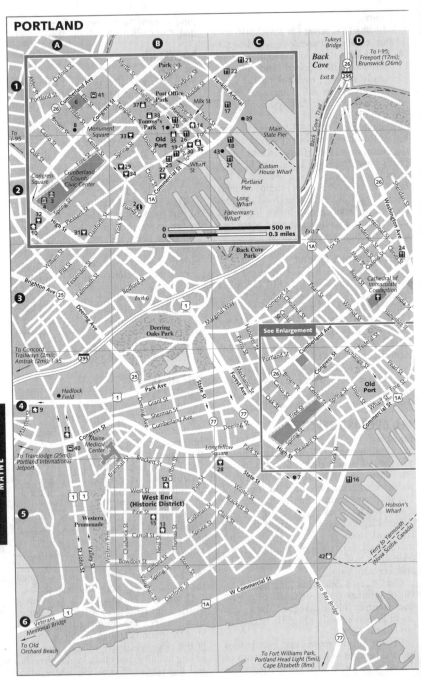

PORTLAND

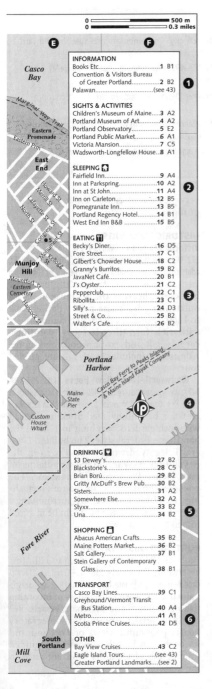

INFORMATION
Books Etc.................................1 B1
Convention & Visitors Bureau
  of Greater Portland..............2 B2
Palawan..............................(see 43)

SIGHTS & ACTIVITIES
Children's Museum of Maine.....3 A2
Portland Museum of Art...........4 A2
Portland Observatory................5 E2
Portland Public Market.............6 A1
Victoria Mansion.....................7 C5
Wadsworth-Longfellow House...8 A1

SLEEPING
Fairfield Inn...........................9 A4
Inn at Parkspring..................10 A2
Inn at St John.......................11 A4
Inn on Carleton.....................12 B5
Pomegranate Inn...................13 B5
Portland Regency Hotel..........14 B1
West End Inn B&B.................15 B5

EATING
Becky's Diner........................16 D5
Fore Street...........................17 C1
Gilbert's Chowder House.........18 C2
Granny's Burritos..................19 B2
JavaNet Café........................20 B1
J's Oyster............................21 C2
Pepperclub..........................22 C1
Ribollita..............................23 C1
Silly's..................................24 D3
Street & Co..........................25 B2
Walter's Cafe........................26 B2

DRINKING
$3 Dewey's..........................27 B2
Blackstone's.........................28 C5
Brian Ború...........................29 B2
Gritty McDuff's Brew Pub........30 B2
Sisters.................................31 A2
Somewhere Else....................32 A2
Styxx..................................33 B2
Una....................................34 B2

SHOPPING
Abacus American Crafts..........35 B2
Maine Potters Market.............36 B2
Salt Gallery..........................37 B1
Stein Gallery of Contemporary
  Glass................................38 B1

TRANSPORT
Casco Bay Lines....................39 C1
Greyhound/Vermont Transit
  Bus Station.......................40 A4
Metro..................................41 A1
Scotia Prince Cruises.............42 D5

OTHER
Bay View Cruises..................43 C2
Eagle Island Tours................(see 43)
Greater Portland Landmarks...(see 2)

businesses are located, runs the length of the peninsula.

I-95 skirts the city to the west, while I-295 makes a detour into the city and hooks back up with I-95 north of Back Cove. Approaching Portland from the south, follow I-95 to exit 6A; take I-295 to exit 4; take US 1 to US 1A heading north (aka Commercial St). Stay on Commercial St right into the Old Port.

From the north, follow I-295 to exit 7, then take the Franklin Arterial (US 1A south).

Information

BOOKSTORES
Books Etc (☎ 207-774-0626; 38 Exchange St) An inviting store for browsing.

EMERGENCY
Maine State Police (☎ 207-624-7076)
Portland police (☎ 207-874-8300)

INTERNET ACCESS
Internet access is free at Portland Public Library (below), but you have to sign up for a guest pass. The good news: it's a wireless hot spot. **JavaNet Café** (☎ 207-773-2469; 37 Exchange St; dishes $1-3; ⊙ 7am-10pm) is another option.

LIBRARIES
Portland Public Library (☎ 207-766-5540; 5 Monument Sq; ⊙ 9am-6pm Mon, Wed & Fri, noon-9pm Tue & Thu, 9am-5pm Sat; 💻)

MEDICAL SERVICES
The following are the city's major medical facilities and both have emergency rooms that are open 24/7.
Maine Medical Center (☎ 207-662-0111; 22 Bramhall St)
Mercy Hospital (☎ 207-879-3000; 144 State St)

POST
Post office (☎ 800-275-8777; 125 Forest Ave; ⊙ 7:30am-7pm Mon-Fri, 7:30am-5pm Sat) The city's most central and convenient post office.

TOURIST INFORMATION
Convention & Visitors Bureau of Greater Portland (☎ 207-772-5800; www.visitportland.com; 245 Commercial St, Portland, ME 04101; ⊙ 8am-5pm Mon-Fri & 10am-3pm Sat mid-Oct–mid-May, 8am-5pm Mon-Fri & 10am-5pm Sat mid-May–mid-Oct) Also has a helpful information office on the south side of the Old Port.

MAINE

PORTLAND ARTS SCENE

Arts aren't limited to museums in this culturally rich city. Contemporary arts rule the Old Port galleries and shops. Among the best are:

- **Stein Gallery of Contemporary Glass** (☎ 207-772-9072; www.steinglass.com; 195 Middle St), with stunningly colorful, abstract and useful art glass.

- **Maine Potters Market** (☎ 207-774-1633; www.mainepottersmarket.com; 376 Fore St), which represents about 15 different ceramicists.

- **Salt Gallery** (☎ 207-761-0660; www.salt.edu; 110 Exchange St), the arm of a documentary institute that exhibits photographs, radio recordings and writing.

- **Abacus American Crafts** (☎ 207-772-4880; 44 Exchange St), displaying a diverse selection of jewelry, ceramics and weavings.

Sights

PORTLAND MUSEUM OF ART

The city's first-rate fine-arts **museum** (☎ 207-775-6148; www.portlandmuseum.org; 7 Congress Sq; adult/child 6-17 $8/2, admission free 5-9pm Fri; ☯ 10am-5pm Tue-Sun, 10am-9pm Fri) has an outstanding collection that's especially rich in the works of Maine painters like Winslow Homer, Edward Hopper, Rockwell Kent and Andrew Wyeth. You'll also find works by European masters, including Degas, Picasso and Renoir. More often than not, there are very good special shows (call, or check the website for current offerings).

CHILDREN'S MUSEUM OF MAINE

Near Congress and High Sts, the **Children's Museum of Maine** (☎ 207-828-1234; www.childrensmuseumofme.org; 142 Free St; adult/child under 1 $5/free, admission free 5-8pm Fri; ☯ 10am-5pm Tue-Sat & Sun noon-5pm Sep-May, 10am-5pm Mon-Sat, noon-5pm Sun Jun-Aug, closed Mon Sep-May) gives children the place and space to try climbing inside an oak tree's hollow trunk in a squirrel suit or to try floating a boat down a model Maine stream. If you have kids in tow, you'd do well to head for the Children's Museum (even on a sunny day). If it's rainy, you'll be in good company. Call for winter hours since they vary.

OLD PORT DISTRICT

About five square blocks in size, and bisected by Fore and Spring Sts, the **Old Port** is chock full of handsome brick buildings that date from the mid- to late 1800s. The majority of Portland's most enticing shops, pubs and restaurants are located within this warren of streets that are lit romantically by gas lanterns in the evening. It's a very pleasant place to wander around, day or night.

HISTORIC BUILDINGS

Victoria Mansion (Morse-Libby House; ☎ 207-772-4841; www.victoriamansion.org; 109 Danforth St; adult/child under 6/child 6-17 $10/free/3; ☯ 10am-4pm Tue-Sat & 1-5pm Sun late May-early Oct), just a few blocks southeast of the art museum, is an outstanding Italianate palace dating back to 1860. Inside, it's decorated sumptuously with rich furniture, frescoes, paintings, carpets, gilt and exotic woods and stone. Admission includes a 45-minute guided tour.

Wadsworth-Longfellow House (☎ 207-879-0427; www.mainehistory.com; 489 Congress St; adult/child $7/3; ☯ 10am-5pm Mon-Sat & noon-5pm Sun late May-late Oct), a beautifully sited brick homestead with lush gardens, was built in 1788 in the handsome Federal style. The builder, General Peleg Wadsworth, was a hero in the Revolutionary War and the grandfather of poet Henry Wadsworth Longfellow. The poet grew up here, and the house's furnishings recall his 19th-century surroundings. Pause for a while and you might be inspired to pen a verse or two.

PORTLAND OBSERVATORY

Built in 1807 on top of Munjoy Hill, this **observatory** (☎ 207-774-5561; 138 Congress St; adult/child 6-16 $5/2; ☯ late May-early Oct) was originally used to warn Portlanders of incoming fishing, military and merchant vessels. Recently restored, the seven-story observatory boasts panoramic views of Portland and its harbor. Admission includes a guided tour of the observatory, and entrance to the museum.

FORT WILLIAMS PARK

Head 4 miles southeast from Portland across the bay via the Casco Bay Bridge to Cape Elizabeth, where you'll find **Fort Williams Park**. It's worth a visit simply for its panoramas and picnic possibilities. Fortification of Portland Head began in 1873, but the installation was not dubbed Fort Williams until 1899. These days, WWII bunkers and gun emplacements (a German U-boat was spotted in Casco Bay in 1942) still dot the rolling lawns of the park. Strange as it may seem, the fort actively guarded the entrance to Casco Bay until 1964.

PORTLAND HEAD LIGHT

Right next to the park stands **Portland Head Light**, the oldest of Maine's 52 functioning lighthouses. It was commissioned by President George Washington in 1791 and staffed until 1989, when machines took over. The keeper's house has been passed into service as the **Museum at Portland Head Light** (☎ 207-799-2661; www.portlandheadlight.com; 1000 Shore Rd; adult/child 6-18 $2/1; ◯ 10am-4pm Jun-Oct, 10am-4pm Sat & Sun Apr-May & Nov–mid-Dec), which traces the maritime and military history of the region. It makes for an interesting visit.

PORTLAND PUBLIC MARKET

Although it only dates from 1998, the **Portland Public Market** (☎ 207-228-2000; www.portlandmarket.com; 25 Preble St; ◯ 9am-7pm Mon-Sat, 10am-5pm Sun) feels like it's been around forever. The 37,000-sq-ft open food hall features 22 locally owned businesses and is a great place to stock up on picnic food. Check out the freshly baked bread, local produce, Maine cheeses and regional wines. Several vendors also serve lunch, and there are numerous tables at which to sit and eat. Don't miss The Pantry, which sells a wide assortment of Maine salsas, salad dressings, honey, jam and granola; or Stone Soup, which features a variety of hot and cold soups.

Activities
JOGGING

Back Cove, northwest of the city's center on the other side of I-295, is surrounded by a 4-mile gravel jogging trail that extends 3 miles further around the **Eastern Promenade**. Take I-295 exit 6 and follow US 1 north, or take bus No 2 to Forest Ave Plaza, bus No 6 to Payson Park or bus No 8 to the Shop 'n Save and you'll be near Back Cove.

SEA KAYAKING

The islands within Casco Bay are ideal for sea kayaking. **Casco Bay Lines** (☎ 207-774-7871; www.cascobaylines.com; 56 Commercial St; adult/child $3/1.50) has boats that depart hourly in the summer for a 15-minute cruise to Peaks Island. Once there, you can hook up with **Maine Island Kayak Company** (☎ 207-766-2373, 800-796-2373; www.maineislandkayak.com; 70 Luther St, Peaks Island; kayak tours $60-110; ◯ May-Nov), a reputable outfitter that offers daily instruction and fine area tours.

Tours
BUS RIDES

While not exactly a tour, a ride on the Metro bus No 1 ($1) is a good and inexpensive way to see the Eastern and Western Promenades, Congress St and the heart of downtown Portland. You can ride until you've had enough. Catch the bus on Congress St.

CRUISES

Bay View Cruises (☎ 207-761-0496; www.bayviewcruisesme.com; Fisherman's Wharf, 184 Commercial St; adult/child $10/7; ◯ daily mid-Jun–Sep, Sat & Sun only May–mid-Jun) Offers four different narrated harbor trips six times daily. Of those the seal cruise is deliciously fun and popular.

Casco Bay Lines (☎ 207-774-7871; www.cascobaylines.com; 56 Commercial St; adult/child 5-9 $3-9.25/$1.50-4.60) This company's ferries cruise the Casco Bay islands delivering mail, freight and visitors. Hop aboard one of these working boats (which are comfortably outfitted) for an idea of what it must be like to live out here. The cruises vary: there's a round-trip cruise to the Diamond Islands (1¾ hours) that costs $11.50/5/9.50 (adult/child aged five to nine/senior); a round-trip naturalist narrated cruise to Bailey Island (5¾ hours) that costs $18/8/16; or a moonlight tour of the bay that costs $11/5/9. All cruises depart from the Casco Bay Lines ferry terminal on Maine State Pier. It's great to get a perspective of Portland from the water.

Eagle Island Tours (☎ 207-774-6498; www.eagleislandtours.com; Long Wharf, 170 Commercial St; adult/child $10/8; ◯ summer only) Runs boat trips around Casco Bay, including sightseeing trips out to Eagle Island and Portland Head Light.

Palawan (☎ 207-773-2163; www.sailpalawan.us; Long Wharf, Commercial St; tours adult/child $10-24/7-13; ◯ May-Oct) This 58ft ocean-racing yacht, designed by Sparkman & Stevens, cruises Casco Bay under sail. Choose your cruise based on price and time: morning trips cost $20 for two hours, afternoon trips $40 for three hours and evening trips $30 for two hours. If you want to sail

MAINE

privately as a couple in July and August, you'll need to reserve ahead of time.

WALKING TOURS

Greater Portland Landmarks (☎ 207-774-5561; adult/child under 16 $8/free; ☼ Mon-Sat Jun–mid-Oct) offers 1½-hour walking tours of the city. It's a fun trip that'll provide you an interesting overview of the city's history as you make your way around the Old Port, Eastern and Western Promenades, and the Portland Head Light. Trips depart at 10:30am in front of the Convention & Visitors Bureau of Greater Portland, 245 Commercial St.

Festivals & Events

The **Old Port Street Festival**, begun in the 1970s, is held the first Sunday in June; it's marked by outdoor performances, a parade and street vendors. As a testimony to the Old Port's continued vibrancy, an Art Walk is held the first Friday of each month at galleries.

Sleeping

BUDGET

Travelodge (☎ 207-774-6101, 800-578-7878; www .travelodge.com; 1200 Brighton Ave; r Jun-Oct/off-season $69-109/49-99) This motel, off I-95 exit 8, has rooms that can accommodate up to four people. This makes them a great bargain for families, and friends traveling together.

MID-RANGE

Most of Portland's hotels are near the bus station and in the Old Port district.

Inn on Carleton (☎ 207-775-1910, 800-639-1779; www.innoncarleton.com; 46 Carleton St; r incl breakfast May-Oct/off-season $129-219/99-179) A restored 1869 Victorian house, this inn has six grandiose rooms, all with massive antique headboards and period furniture.

Inn at Parkspring (☎ 207-774-1059; 800-437-8511; www.innatparkspring.com; 135 Spring St; r incl breakfast $95-145; ☐) This pleasant and hospitable B&B, which was built of wood in 1835, is very centrally located.

Fairfield Inn (☎ 207-871-0611, 800-228-2880; www.marriott.com; 340 Park Ave; r $100-120; ☐ ☒) The simple rooms here are mostly outfitted with two double beds, so that they can accommodate up to four comfortably. From I-95, take exit 6A to I-295 exit 5A (Congress St); at the end of the ramp turn right, then left at the signs for Stroudwater/Westbrook.

Inn at St John (☎ 207-773-6481, 800-636-9127; www.innatstjohn.com; 939 Congress St; r Jun-Aug/off-season $100-184/61-91; ☐) Built in 1897 to house passengers arriving at Union Station, this inn bills itself as Portland's 'low-fat' hotel. It's somewhat noisy, but that's to be expected since its labyrinth of 39 rooms is right across the street from the Greyhound/Vermont Transit bus station, and on the route of city bus Nos 1 and 3.

TOP END

Portland's West End, near the Western Promenade, is a quiet, mostly redbrick residential neighborhood with many grand Victorian houses, some of which have been converted to inns.

Pomegranate Inn (☎ 207-772-1006, 800-356-0408; www.pomegranateinn.com; 49 Neal St; r incl breakfast May-Oct/off-season $175-255/95-155; ☐) Few innkeepers can mix modern art with antiques as skillfully as Isabel Smiles has done here. An antiques dealer and interior designer, Smiles' eclectic taste runs the gamut from faux marble columns in the living room to hand-painted walls and century-old dressers in the eight guest rooms. Large contemporary sculptures and collages are displayed in the hallways. Remarkably, they all seem to fit together.

West End Inn B&B (☎ 207-772-1377, 800-338-1377; www.westendbb.com; 146 Pine St; r incl breakfast mid-May-Oct/off-season $159-209/109-159) Built in 1871, this inn has six rooms, all with TV. It's a very good choice.

Portland Regency Hotel (☎ 207-774-4200, 800-727-3436; www.theregency.com; 20 Milk St; r Jul-Oct/off-season $249-269/159-249; ☐) Portland's most upscale hotel is well located, smack in the middle of the Old Port, a block from the waterfront. This first-rate hotel, ensconced in the Port's substantial redbrick armory, has 95 very comfortable rooms and a fitness center, and offers great added value. Weekend packages are quite attractive.

Eating

Bostonians think little of making the two-hour drive to Portland for an exceptional meal. Why? Because many of these fine dining establishments focus on Maine's abundant goodies – treasures from the sea, as well as locally farmed chickens, venison and organically grown produce. Most of the best restaurants are along Middle St and in the Old Port section of town on Wharf, Exchange and Fore Sts.

BUDGET

JavaNet Café (☎ 207-773-2469; 37 Exchange St; dishes $1-3; ☺ 7am-10pm) This is a great Old Port hangout for surfing the Net while nursing a hot mug of chai. In case you need a sugar chaser with your caffeine fix, staff serve a selection of cookies and pastries as well. There are a handful of Macs (per hour $8), and wireless (per hour $6) and ethernet connections (per hour $6) for you to plug into.

Becky's Diner (☎ 207-773-7070; 390 Commercial St; dishes $3-12; ☺ 4am-9pm) If you want to meet working fisherfolk, opt for breakfast or lunch at this waterfront diner. Sit at the counter and hobnob with the salty dogs and order one of the cheapest meals in town. The diner offers fresh muffins in the morning and sandwiches ($5) in the afternoon.

Granny's Burritos (☎ 207-761-0751; 420 Fore St; burritos $4.50-7; ☺ lunch & dinner) Stop here for a quick, healthful fill-up of protein and carbs. Aiming for customer satisfaction, Granny offers your choice of wrap and whatever fillers you like.

Silly's (☎ 207-772-0360; 40 Washington Ave; mains $3-9; ☺ lunch & dinner Tue-Sun) Away from the Old Port area, this funky little place is worth the walk or short drive. Locals know enough to travel across town to gobble one of the tasty lunchtime *abdullahs* (sandwiches rolled in bakery-fresh tortillas). Dinners, like jerk chicken ($9.50) or fish and chips ($5.75), are as good as they are cheap.

MID-RANGE

Pepperclub (☎ 207-772-0531; 78 Middle St; mains $9-15; ☺ dinner) For the best selection of veggie fare, head here, just northeast of Franklin Arterial. Try to get here early since it's usually packed shortly after 6pm. The reason? The eclectic menu is superb – a Middle Eastern meze plate for starters, then Thai lime vegetables with sesame tofu and udon, or mushroom and fresh basil lasagna. Most main courses are under $13, making probable an excellent, interesting dinner, with wine, for about $20 per person. Service is friendly and good.

Gilbert's Chowder House (☎ 207-871-5636; 92 Commercial St; lunch $10-14, dinner $8-28; ☺ lunch & dinner) This simple diner with a lunch counter and tables on a pier is a great spot for a load of fish and chips ($9) or a big bowl of its renowned thick clam chowder ($5 to $11).

J's Oyster (☎ 207-772-4828; 5 Portland Pier; dishes $6-20; ☺ lunch & dinner) Although it's a total dive, J's Oyster has the cheapest raw bar in town, with a baker's dozen of oysters that costs about $10. It's also the only place in Portland that serves meals until midnight.

TOP END

Ribollita (☎ 207-774-2972; 41 Middle St; mains $11-16; ☺ dinner) This local favorite is one of Portland's best-kept secrets. The tiny restaurant serves fabulous Northern Italian cuisine and prides itself on its handmade pastas. Start with the caramelized onion tart and then move on to shrimp carbonara. Make sure to reserve a table in advance, as this place fills up quickly.

Fore Street (☎ 207-775-2717; 288 Fore St; mains $17-28; ☺ dinner) If you have just one night in Portland to dine, have it here. The airy, exposed-brick and pine-panel room features an open kitchen; chefs busily sauté food and finish plates on three long tables, but the real spectacle is the food. Owner and chef Sam Hayward has made applewood grilling and roasting his forte. The menu changes nightly, but you should try staples such as roasted rope-cultured mussels ($9), which is served in a broth that will leave you craving more.

Street & Co (☎ 207-775-0887; 33 Wharf St; mains $17-22; ☺ dinner) The menu here might be simple, but the seafood is the freshest in town. You'll find grilled, broiled or Cajun-style fish (tuna, salmon, swordfish), plus steamed or sautéed mussels, clams and calamari. Have it served over pasta or in a broth that's destined to be dunked with a hunk of fresh bread. The cramped but congenial dining rooms are usually packed for dinner, so reserve in advance.

Walter's Café (☎ 207-871-9258; 15 Exchange St; lunch $8-12, dinner $15-24; ☺ lunch Mon-Sat, dinner) This is one of Portland's best-loved bistros; a narrow storefront dining room with a high ceiling and even higher culinary aspirations. It's also a really good place for a hot lunch.

Drinking

Fore St, between Union and Exchange Sts, is lined with restaurants and bars. You'll find plenty of places to sample fresh brews made on the premises.

MAINE

$3 Dewey's (☎ 207-772-3310; 241 Commercial St) Typical of most bars around Union St, $3 Dewy's has live music Tuesday through Thursday and beer specials from 4pm to 8pm.

Gritty McDuff's Brew Pub (☎ 207-772-2739; www .grittys.com; 396 Fore St) Portland's most popular spot for a pint of award-winning beer pours a half-dozen ales, porters and stouts. They're are all brewed downstairs.

Brian Ború (☎ 207-780-1506; 57 Center St) This happening Irish pub, between Spring and Fore Sts, is a favorite hangout for the under-30 crowd.

Una (☎ 207-828-0300; 505 Fore St) If you want to sip martinis and act like an urban hipster without going to Boston, head to Una. It's Portland's version of hip.

Entertainment
GAY & LESBIAN VENUES
Somewhere Else (☎ 207-871-9169; www.somewhere elseportland.com; 117 Spring St) If you're in a singing mood, head 'somewhere else.' If you're an exhibitionist, the piano bar here also features karaoke on Tuesday and Thursday nights.

Sisters (☎ 207-774-1505; 45 Danforth St; ☸ Fri-Sun) The most popular lesbian bar in Maine offers DJs, dancing, pool tables, darts and also occasional live music, poetry readings and plays. There's a $3 cover charge on Saturday.

Blackstone's (☎ 207-775-2885; 6 Pine St) This place might well have been named Brothers, since it's Sisters' other half – it's a hot spot for gay men.

Styxx (☎ 207-773-3315; www.styxxportland.com; 3 Spring St; ☸ from 7pm) With a huge dance floor, Styxx is Portland's largest gay bar.

Getting There & Away
AIR
Portland International Jetport (☎ 207-774-7301; www.portlandjetport.org) is Maine's largest and busiest air terminal. The 'International' in the airport's name refers only to flights to and from Canada. For long-distance international flights, you must connect through Boston or NYC. Airlines serving the airport include Continental, Delta, Northwest KLM, United and US Airways (see p539). Metro buses take you from Continental Airlines' doors to the center of town for $1 (see p480). Take bus No 5 and transfer to bus No 8 to get to the Old Port.

BOAT
For passenger ferry cruises between Portland and Bailey Island, see p477.

Scotia Prince Cruises (☎ 207-775-5616, 800-845-4073; www.scotiaprince.com; 468 Commercial St) departs Portland for Yarmouth, Nova Scotia (Canada) each evening at 8pm. Eleven hours later it arrives in Canada at breakfast time. The return trip departs Yarmouth at 9am for Portland, arriving after dinner. You must have proof of citizenship to enter Canada at Yarmouth (US citizens may use their passport or US citizen's birth certificate; non-US citizens need their passport or alien registration (green) card).

The cruises operate daily (with some exceptions) from early May through late October. The one-way Portland-to-Yarmouth overnight fare costs $65 to $90 per adult; a cabin costs $45 to $190 extra. Children cost $38 to $45 (free for those under the age of five); cars cost $85-95. Prices do not include meals (bring your own food, if you can) and port taxes ($3).

On certain days (mostly Tuesday and Wednesday), the car fare is half the normal price; call for details. If you plan your trip well, you can save money. For example: for a couple with two children ages five to 14, with a car, traveling in season in two moderately priced cabins (at night, Portland to Yarmouth), the round-trip fare will reach about $900, with meals, taxes and tips included. Off-season, the same family, staying in the least expensive cabin, sailing at night and bringing their own food, can go round-trip for about $400 minimum.

BUS
Vermont Transit (☎ 207-772-6587, 800-231-2222; www .vermonttransit.com; 950 Congress St), in the Greyhound terminal, runs five to six buses daily to and from Boston (two hours), connecting with buses to Hartford, Connecticut (3¼ hours more) and NYC (4½ hours more).

Vermont Transit also runs three buses northeastward to Brunswick, and four up the Maine Turnpike to Lewiston, Augusta, Waterville and Bangor (3¼ hours), with one bus continuing to Bar Harbor (four hours from Portland).

Concord Trailways (☎ 207-828-1151, 800-639-3317; www.concordtrailways.com) has its terminal on Thompson Point Connector Rd at exit 5A off I-295. It runs 13 nonstop buses daily between Portland and Boston. From Portland, two Concord Trailways buses provide local service to towns northeast as far as Bangor (four hours); one bus connects at Bangor with a Cyr bus headed north to Medway, Sherman, Houlton, Presque Isle and Caribou. This local service goes to Brunswick, Bath, Wiscasset, Damariscotta, Waldoboro, Rockland, Camden/Rockport, Lincolnville, Belfast, Searsport and Bangor.

TRAIN
The **Amtrak** (☎ 800-872-7245; www.amtrak.com) *Downeaster*, making tracks between Boston and Portland, runs four to five trains daily in each direction. The trip takes about 2½ hours, making brief stops in NH in Dover and Durham.

Getting Around
Portland's **Metro** (☎ 207-774-0351; www.gpmetrobus .com) is the local bus company, with its main terminus, 'Metro Pulse,' housed near Monument Sq. The buses line up at the parking

garage on Elm St. Make sure you have exact change of $1 (tickets are purchased on the bus). There are a number of useful routes serving the city center.

Destination	Bus routes
Airport	No 5
Back Cove	Nos 2, 3, 6
Casco Bay Municipal Ferry Terminal	No 8
Concord Trailways Bus Terminal	No 8
Eastern Promenade/Munjoy Hill	No 1
International Ferry Terminal	No 8
Old Port	No 8
Portland Museum of Art	Nos 1, 3, 8
Greyhound/Vermont Transit Bus Station	Nos 1, 3, 5
Western Promenade	Nos 1, 8

FREEPORT
pop 7800
Here, nestled amid the natural beauty of Maine's rockbound coast, is a town devoted almost entirely to city-style shopping. Tony luggage, expensive china, trendy

---

WHAT'S 90 YEARS OLD AND STAYS UP ALL NIGHT? (ANSWER: LL BEAN)

In 1911 Leon Leonwood Bean invented the Maine Hunting Shoe, now known as the 'Bean Boot.' In addition to the quality and practicality of the boot's construction, it was accompanied by a lifetime offer of replacement or repair if outdoorsmen found the item in any way unsatisfactory during the life of the boot. Bean began his successful mail order sales business with a four-page flyer describing the boots and the guarantee sent to out-of-state sportsmen. Other items for the outdoors were added, notably the often-imitated LL Bean Field Coat in 1924, popular for its rugged quality and craftsmanship. These days Bean sells over one billion dollars' worth of clothing, outdoor gear and home furnishings. And the guarantee of no questions asked and 100% satisfaction is still honored.

While the merchant's successful start began through mail order, an additional delight – and must of any visit to Maine – is a visit to the **LL Bean store** (☎ 800-341-4341; www.llbean.com; Main St at Elm St; ☾ 24hrs). For close to 90 years, the store has sold Bean merchandise to the hardy, the sports-minded and the merely curious. In 1951, Bean himself removed the locks from the store doors and made the decision to stay open 24 hours a day, 365 days a year. Since then the store has only closed twice – once in 1963 when President John F Kennedy was assassinated and once in 1967 for LL Bean's funeral.

Popular with locals as well as those 'from away' (ie not from Maine), the store is easily the most popular tourist attraction in Maine. How popular? Maine's entire population is about 1.3 million people – every year, three times that many visit the LL Bean store in Freeport.

Late night shopping at the 24-hour venue is a popular sport for locals and tourists alike, who stock up on the proffered free coffee and candy before admiring huge tents, trying on the blaze-orange hunting gear or enjoying a midnight dip in the trout pond. After-dark celebrity spottings abound – particularly of John Travolta, who owns a home in nearby Islesboro.

Reflecting small town camaraderie, locals often treat LL Bean's as a community center during storms and power outages. Also, nearly all shoppers report the joys of late-night Christmas shopping without crowds. Sportsmen whose companions 'from away' need outfitting before their departures appreciate being able to procure fishing licenses at 4am. On so many levels and in so many ways, no place matches it.

MAINE

clothes and perfumed soaps are all available at more than 100 shops that are backed by a maze of parking lots. The town's mile-long Main St (US 1) is a perpetual traffic jam of cars from all over the country, and Canada. In summer, most of Freeport's shops are busy with shoppers all day and into the night.

Freeport's fame and fortune began a century ago when Leon Leonwood Bean opened a shop to sell equipment and provisions to hunters and fishermen heading north into the Maine woods (see p481).

Orientation

Take I-95 exit 19 or 20 to reach central Freeport. The downtown shopping district along Main St/US 1 is easily negotiated on foot, but you might have to drive a short distance to your lodgings if you plan to stay the night. The epicenter of Freeport shopping is the big LL Bean store (p481) on Main St that made Freeport what it is today. South Freeport, south along US 1, is a sleepy residential community, but its town dock has a good local eatery and bay cruises.

Information

The State of Maine has a large information center facing the DeLorme Mapping Co at I-95 exit 17. It dispenses mountains of information on Freeport and all of Maine. The **Freeport Merchants Marketing Association** (☎ 207-865-1212; www.freeportusa.com; ☼ 9am-5pm Mon-Fri) maintains information kiosks on Main St at Mallet St, and on Mill St a block south of Main St.

Don't miss a visit to **DeLorme Mapping Co** (☎ 207-846-7100; www.delorme.com) and its giant 5300-sq-ft rotating globe, Eartha, in nearby Yarmouth at exit 17 off I-95. Maker of the essential Maine Atlas and Gazetteer, DeLorme also creates maps and software for every destination in the United States.

In summer, this shop – and indeed most of Freeport's shops – are busy with shoppers all day and into the night.

Sights & Activities
DESERT OF MAINE
William Tuttle came to Freeport in 1797 to farm potatoes, but his deadly combination of overgrazing and not rotating crops caused enough erosion to create Maine's only **desert** (☎ 207-865-6962; www.desertofmaine.com; 95 Desert Rd;

adult/child 6-12/child 13-16 $7.75/4.25/5.25; ☼ 9am-dusk May-Oct). The shifting dunes, which are 70ft deep in some areas, cover entire trees and the old farm's buildings. To get to the farm, take I-95 exit 19 and head west of the highway for 2 miles.

HIKING
Bradbury Mountain State Park (528 Hallowell Rd/ME 9, Pownal), 6 miles west of Freeport in northern Pownal, has several miles of forested hiking trails. For some instant gratification, take a little 10-minute hike from the picnic area uphill to the summit. It yields a spectacular view that reaches all the way to the ocean. There's camping as well (see opposite). Surprisingly, one sees very few Freeport shoppers testing their new outdoor gear in this pretty park. To reach it, take ME 125 and ME 136 north from Freeport, and turn left just after crossing I-95; from there, follow the state park signs.

Tours
CRUISES
In South Freeport, a few miles from the frenzy of shopping, you'll find the Freeport Town Wharf, which is the departure point for several boats offering cruises around Casco Bay. To get here, follow US 1 to the 40ft-high statue of a Native American, and follow the unmarked road in front of it (South Freeport Rd) until you get to the four-way stop sign. Hang a right onto Main St and follow to the end.

Atlantic Seal Cruises (☎ 207-865-6112; Freeport Town Wharf; adult/child $20/15; ☼ May-Oct) offers three-hour trips where the captain hauls in lobster traps, and you go in search of wild osprey and adorable seals. Remember to pack a picnic lunch or ask about catered picnics when you make reservations.

Sleeping
BUDGET
A handful of campgrounds are located within a 6-mile radius of Freeport.

Winslow Memorial Park (☎ 207-865-4198; sites with/without water views $23/20; ☼ late May-early Sep) This choice pick (without hookups, which will dissuade RVers) is hard to beat as it's right on the ocean. Head south from Freeport along US 1, take a left at the towering Native American statue, head toward South Freeport and then turn right onto Staples

Point Rd (there's a park sign) and follow it for about 2 miles.

Cedar Haven Campground (☎ 207-865-6254; www.campmaine.com/cedarhaven; 39 Baker Rd/ME 125; sites $20-32; ☺ early May-late Oct) Only about 2.5 miles from Freeport's center, this place has 58 mostly wooded sites.

MID-RANGE

Several B&Bs are on Main St just north of the big Harraseeket Inn. Others are within an easy walk of the city center.

Bagley House Inn (☎ 207-865-6566, 800-765-1772; www.bagleyhouse.com; 1290 Royalsborough Rd, Durham; r incl breakfast Jun-Sep/off-season $95-150/75-150) Only a 10-minute drive from downtown Freeport, in rural Durham, the Bagley House dates from pre-Revolutionary War times. The owners definitely know how to cater to the whims of tired shoppers, with the latter often found lounging in the acres of open fields and gardens. It's a lovely place away from the maddening crowds, offering a glimpse of Maine and the way life should be.

Captain Briggs House Inn (☎ 207-865-1868, 800-217-2477; www.captainbriggs.com; 8 Maple Ave; r/ste incl breakfast $95-145/175-215) This mid-19th century house has five bedrooms, a two-room suite and friendly owners who serve a spectacular breakfast that includes homemade baked goods.

James Place Inn (☎ 207-865-4486, 800-964-8086; www.jamesplaceinn.com; 11 Holbrook St; r incl breakfast May-Nov/Dec-Apr $135-155/110-145) Built in 1880, this B&B has seven guest rooms (three of which boast spas) and a young owner who is a fifth-generation Freeport resident and who knows the area well.

Atlantic Seal B&B (☎ 207-865-6112; 25 Main St, South Freeport; r incl breakfast $125-200) Situated near South Freeport's town dock, this quiet B&B features three rooms with harbor views; it offers boat cruises, as well.

Casco Bay Inn (☎ 207-865-4925; www.cascobayinn.com; 107 US 1; r incl breakfast $60-121) Many chains are south of the town center along US 1 near I-95 exit 19, but the best of the lot is this renovated place, a few minutes' drive south of the town center.

TOP END

Harraseeket Inn (☎ 207-865-9377, 800-342-6423; www.stayfreeport.com; 162 Main St; r incl breakfast May-Oct/off-season $145-279/115-219; ☐ ☒) After an all-day shop until you drop, it's wonderful to know

that it's only a block back from the center of town to Harraseeket Inn with its 84 elegant rooms. You can relax with afternoon tea and cakes and then soak your weary bones in an oversized spa or take a swim in its indoor pool. As an aside: when owner Nancy Gray was 12 years old, her father bought her a gun just in case she got caught on the way home from school between a mother bear and her cub. So, take heed of the bears.

Eating

Freeport's Main St/US 1 has a dozen places to eat, including mobile sausage stands. But, unfortunately, most restaurants serve standard tourist fare. You won't go wrong with the following places.

BUDGET & MID-RANGE

Lobster Cooker (☎ 207-865-4349; 39 Main St, South Freeport; mains $5-20; ☺ lunch & dinner May-Dec, lunch & dinner Wed-Sun Mar & Apr, closed Jan & Feb) This fast-food place abutting LL Bean has excellent clam chowder ($5), good coleslaw and decent steamed lobster lunches (small/large $15/22). Dine inside or on the deck.

Harraseeket Lunch & Lobster Co (☎ 207-865-4888; 36 Main St, South Freeport; mains lunch & dinner $8-18; ☺ lunch & dinner May-Oct) On the town dock, this place serves a full menu of lunch items that are best eaten at shaded picnic tables overlooking the bay. Indulge with a clam-bake or keep it simple with the excellent fish and chips. Live and cooked lobsters are sold for takeout as well.

Village Store (☎ 207-865-4230; 97 South Freeport Rd, South Freeport; sandwiches $4-7; ☺ 7am-5pm Tue-Fri, 7am-3pm Sat & Sun) Hidden away from throngs of shoppers, this nondescript storefront deli is popular with area workers who come for large lunchtime sandwiches. There are several tables if you want to eat here.

TOP END

Broad Arrow Tavern (☎ 800-342-6423; 162 Main St; mains $12-25; ☺ lunch & dinner) Situated within the Harraseeket Inn (left), this tavern has a good selection of microbrews and moderately priced brick-oven specialties. A bowl of hearty lobster stew will set you back $12 but it really constitutes a meal.

Maine Dining Room (☎ 207-865-1085; 162 Main St; mains $25-34; ☺ dinner, brunch Sun) This up-scale dining room, also in the Harraseeket Inn (left), features dishes like fresh tuna with Asian pear and baby bok choy ($29), chateaubriand with truffled asparagus for two prepared at your table ($75) and filet mignon ($34). Tempting dessert crêpes, prepared at the table, provide the perfect ending. The restaurant is also popular for an extravagant Sunday brunch buffet.

Drinking

Gritty McDuff's (☎ 207-865-4321; 187 Lower Main St; mains $7.50-15; ☼ lunch & dinner) Two miles south of LL Bean, McDuff's is deservedly popular for its pub grub and beers. Seasonal brews come and go with the weather. When 'small batch ales' are on tap, order whatever they've made; it doesn't get any fresher than this folks.

Getting There & Away

Freeport, 15 miles north of Portland via I-295, is a mile off the interstate on US 1. For the nearest bus transport, see p480; buses do not stop in Freeport.

MIDCOAST

Midcoast Maine is celebrated for its exceptional natural beauty and down-to-earth residents. You will find a dramatic coastline dotted with friendly seaside villages, thick pine forests and numerous opportunities for biking, hiking, sailing, kayaking and other adventures. You'll also find world famous ports for yachting: Camden, Rockport and Rockland, from which windjammers (multi-masted sailing ships) take passengers on cruises of the jagged coast.

The English first settled this region in 1607, which coincided with the Jamestown settlement in Virginia. Unlike their southerly compatriots, though, these early settlers returned to England within a year. British colonization resumed in 1620. After suffering through the long years of the French and Indian wars, the area became home to a thriving shipbuilding industry, which continues today.

BRUNSWICK

pop 21,172

Brunswick is most famous these days as the home of highly regarded Bowdoin College (founded in 1794), but the town was settled as early as 1628 and incorporated in 1738.

A short drive through the city center reveals stately Federal and Greek mansions built by wealthy sea captains. At 63 Federal St, Harriet Beecher Stowe wrote *Uncle Tom's Cabin*. This story of a runaway slave, published in 1852, was hugely popular. The poignant story fired the imagination of people in the northern states, who saw the book as a powerful indictment against slavery. It was translated into many languages.

Brunswick's green, called the Town Mall, is along Maine St. Farmers markets are set up Tuesday and Friday and there are band concerts Wednesday evening in summer.

Orientation

To someone driving along US 1, the commercial center of Brunswick does not present a very attractive prospect. But, in fact, as the home of Bowdoin College, the town is the cultural center for this part of the state. Turn off US 1 onto aptly named Pleasant St for a completely different view of Brunswick, an attractive, tree-lined street with grand old houses and magnificent gardens.

Information

Midcoast Chamber of Commerce (☎ 207-725-8797; www.midcoastmaine.com; 59 Pleasant St, Brunswick, ME 04011; ☼ 8:30am-5pm Mon-Fri) The folks here can provide you with a map and help you with a room reservation.

Sights
BOWDOIN COLLEGE

One of the oldest colleges in the US, Bowdoin is the alma mater of Henry Wadsworth Longfellow, Nathaniel Hawthorne and US president Franklin Pierce. For general campus information, call ☎ 207-725-3375. For a campus tour, follow the signs from Maine St to Moulton Union. Smith Union is the student center, with an information desk on the mezzanine level, as well as a café, pub, small convenience store, lounge and small art gallery. There's also the requisite bookstore, a mailroom where you can get stamps and send letters, and a bulletin board with information on local events and concerts.

Among the campus sites to visit is the **Bowdoin College Museum of Art** (☎ 207-725-3275; www.bowdoin.edu/artmuseum; admission free; ☼ 10am-5pm Tue-Sat, 2-5pm Sun), located in the quadrangle, which is strong in the works of 19th- and 20th-century European and

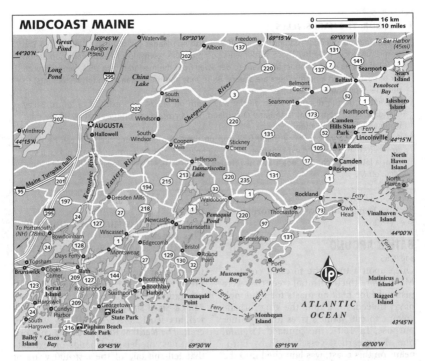

MIDCOAST MAINE

American painters, including Mary Cassatt, Andrew Wyeth and Rockwell Kent.

The **Peary-MacMillan Arctic Museum** (☎ 207-725-3416; Hubbard Hall; admission free; ⏱ 10am-5pm Tue-Sat, 2-5pm Sun) holds memorabilia from the expeditions of Robert Edwin Peary and Donald Baxter MacMillan, Bowdoin alumni who were among the first explorers to reach the North Pole.

PEJEPSCOT MUSEUMS

Local history is preserved in the museums of the Pejepscot Historical Society on the Bowdoin campus.

The **Pejepscot Museum** (☎ 207-729-6606; 159 Park Row; admission free; ⏱ 9am-5pm Tue, Wed & Fri, 9am-8pm Thu, 9am-4pm Sat) displays great old photographs of Brunswick, Topsham and Harpswell. The **Skolfield-Whittier House** (☎ 207-729-6606; 161 Park Row; tours $5; ⏱ for tours only, mid-May–mid-Oct), an adjacent 17-room brick mansion, is a virtual time capsule, closed as it was from 1925 to 1982. Even the receipts for the building's construction and the spices in the kitchen racks are authentic. The **Joshua L Chamberlain Museum** (☎ 207-725-6958; 226 Main St; admission $5;

⏱ 10am-4pm Tue-Sun mid-May–mid-Oct) exhibits artifacts from the late owner's eventful life as college professor, Civil War hero, president of Bowdoin College and four-term governor of Maine. Tours are included with the admission fee.

Festivals & Events

In early August, the four-day **Maine Arts Festival** is held a short distance east of Brunswick in Cooks Corner at Thomas Point Beach.

Entertainment

Bowdoin's Pickard Theater (☎ 207-725-3000; cnr Park Row & Bath Rd, Bowdoin campus) During the summer months this theater hosts the Maine State Music Theater series, a summer musical comedy series that runs eight performances a week, June through August.

Getting There & Away

Brunswick, off I-95 exit 22, is the point at which I-95 heads north and inland toward Augusta, Waterville and Bangor, and US 1 heads northeast along the coast. It's about 9 miles away from Freeport, and

---

DETOUR: THE HARPSWELLS

Several narrow, wooded peninsulas dotted with fishing villages jut southward into Casco Bay from Brunswick. Together these settlements comprise the township of **Harpswell** (population 5239). If you have a few hours and want to get away from the mad traffic on US 1, venture south for a meal or even a night. There are several B&Bs, inns and motels (and enough restaurants) to provide dependable sustenance.

Want to go the distance? Head all the way south on ME 24 (I-95 exits 22 or 24) to Bailey Island, reached from Great Island and Orrs Island. You'll cross three bridges that allow the tides to flow right through them.

The village dock on Bailey Island is a stop on the Casco Bay cruise circuit. It can be more crowded than one would expect when the cruise boats tie up here for their lobster bakes. If you want a lobster lunch, try **Cook's Lobster House** (☎ 207-833-2818; 68 Garrison Cove Rd; ☽ 11:30am-8pm), off ME 24.

---

8 miles from Bath. For bus information, see p480.

BATH & AROUND
pop 9266

Once upon a time, the forested coasts of Maine were thick with tall trees that were just right for making masts for the king's navy. Indeed, for a time the king forbade anyone to cut Maine's trees for any other purpose. In 1607, the pinnace *Virginia*, one of the earliest vessels built by Europeans on this coast, was launched into the Kennebec River at Phippsburg, south of Bath. Later, the shipyards on the Kennebec turned to building coastal freighters, then tall clipper ships and grand multimasted schooners.

Today, Bath continues the tradition by building steel frigates, cruisers and other navy craft at Bath Iron Works (BIW), one of the largest and most active shipyards in the US. The Maine Maritime Museum, south of the shipyard, is Bath's biggest attraction. The other half of town is the picturesque Historic District, with long stretches of 19th-century Victorian homes.

Orientation & Information
Bath has an attractive, small commercial district north of US 1, centered on Front St. The famous ironworks sprawls to the south of US 1. At 3:30pm on weekdays, when the work shift changes at the ironworks, US 1 chokes with cars, and traffic throughout the town comes to a virtual halt. You'd best be through Bath by 3:15pm, or be parked downtown and walking around.

Sights
MAINE MARITIME MUSEUM & SHIPYARD
This **museum** (☎ 207-443-1316; www.bathmaine .com; 243 Washington St; adult/child 6-17 $9.75/8.75; ☽ 9:30am-5pm), south of the ironworks on the western bank of the Kennebec River, preserves the Kennebec's long shipbuilding tradition. In summer, the 19th-century **Percy & Small Shipyard** here still has boatwrights hard at work building wooden craft. The **Maritime History Building** contains paintings, models and hands-on exhibits that tell the tale of the last 400 years of seafaring. In the apprentice shop of the Percy & Small Shipyard, boat builders restore and construct wooden boats using traditional tools and methods. It's all quite fascinating, allowing visitors to fully appreciate the connection between the past and present.

In summer, the cruise boat **Schoodic II** takes visitors for a 50-minute ride on the Kennebec, although this is not included in the museum entry price.

For kids, there's a play ship and picnic area, as well as the working fishing schooner **Sherman Zwicker**, which is docked here July through August.

Sleeping
BUDGET
In addition to one campground, Bath has a number of reasonably priced B&Bs set in nice, converted 19th-century houses.

Benjamin F Packard House (☎ 207-443-6069, 800-516-4578; www.mainecoast.com/packardhouse; 45 Pearl St; r/ste $90/130) This Georgian house (1830) has eight rooms and one suite with private bathroom.

Ocean View Park Campground (☎ 207-389-2564; 817 Popham Rd/ME 209, Popham Beach; RV sites $35-37; ❤ mid-May–mid-Sep) This beachfront RV park is south of Bath at the end of the peninsula, near Popham Beach State Park.

MID-RANGE
Inn at Bath (☎ 207-443-4294, 800-423-0964; www.inn atbath.com; 969 Washington St, Bath; r incl breakfast Jun-Oct/ off-season $125-175/90-185) Bath's most splendid B&B, an early-19th-century Greek home in the heart of the Historic District, has nine elegant rooms and common spaces. The more expensive rooms have spas.

Popham Beach B&B (☎ 207-389-2409; www.pop hambeachbandb.com; 4 Riverview Ave, Phippsburg; r incl breakfast $100-185) Formerly a US Coast Guard station, this upscale B&B has five bright rooms directly on the sands of Popham Beach.

Fairhaven Inn (☎ 207-443-4391, 888-443-4391; www .mainecoast.com/fairhaveninn/; 118 North Bath Rd; r incl breakfast $80-140) Near the Bath Country Club, this early-1800s inn is a few miles north of the city center and set on spacious grounds. Guest rooms are the model of quiet comfort and simplicity, all while providing impressive detailings like fluffy comforters and perhaps an antique bedstead here or there.

1774 Inn (☎ 207-389-1774; www.1774inn.com; 44 Parker Head Rd, Phippsburg; r May-Sep/off-season $105-175/95-150) Overlooking the ocean, and 4 miles south of town, this gorgeous Federal-style house dates to 1774 and was the home of Maine's first US congressman.

Eating
Beale St BBQ & Grill (☎ 207-442-9514; 215 Water St; lunch $6-9, dinner $10-18; ❤ lunch & dinner) Gnaw on some St Louis–style ribs ($12) and sip a Maine microbrew at this restaurant in downtown Bath.

Mae's Cafe & Bakery (☎ 207-442-8577; 160 Centre St; breakfast $4-8, lunch $5-8, dinner $12-17; ❤ breakfast, lunch & dinner) Once known simply for astonishing baked goods and desserts, Mae's has expanded to offer reasonably priced seafood and steak dishes. In particular, don't miss the crab cakes. This is also a popular destination for Sunday brunch.

Cabin (☎ 207-443-6224; 522 Washington St; mains $3-18; ❤ lunch & dinner) Facing BIW, this longtime favorite of navy personnel offers pizzas, pastas and good value subs ($3 to $5). Sit down in one of the small wooden booths or outdoors at picnic tables during the summer.

Getting There & Away
Bath is 8 miles east of Brunswick and 10 miles southwest of Wiscasset on US 1. For bus information, see p480.

WISCASSET
pop 3603

As the sign says, 'Welcome to Wiscasset, the Prettiest Village in Maine.' Other villages may dispute this claim, but Wiscasset's history as a major shipbuilding port in the 19th century has left it with a legacy of exceptionally grand and beautiful houses.

Any town with lots of old houses is also bound to have a thriving antiques trade, and Wiscasset does. You can admire the houses and shops as you pass through along US 1, or better, stop for a meal or the night.

Like Bath, Wiscasset was a shipbuilding and maritime trading center. Great four-masted schooners sailed down the Sheepscot River bound for England and the West Indies – a route known as the Triangle Trade. They carried items such as timber, molasses, rum, salt and salt fish. Two relics of Wiscasset's vanished maritime importance are the wrecked and weather-beaten hulks of the schooners *Hesper* and *Luther Little*. Built to haul lumber to Boston and bring coal back to Wiscasset, they ran aground in 1932 and have been slowly dissolving in the mud along the Sheepscot's west bank ever since.

Orientation & Information
Situated on the wide Sheepscot River, Wiscasset straddles Main St/US 1 and most of it is easily accessible on foot.

Sights
OLD JAIL MUSEUM
About a half-mile north of US 1, this **museum** (☎ 207-882-6817; 133 Federal St/ME 218; adult/child $4/2; ❤ 11am-4pm Tue-Sat Jul & Aug), a hilltop structure of granite, brick and wood, dates back to 1811 when it housed Wiscasset's rowdier citizens.

CASTLE TUCKER
Wiscasset's grandest and best-situated mansion is the 1807 **Castle Tucker** (☎ 207-882-7364; cnr High & Lee Sts; adult/child 6-12/senior $5/2.50/4; ❤ 11am-5pm Tue-Sun Jun–mid-Oct), which commands beautiful views that you can enjoy even if you not decide to tour the castle. (It's reached by a five-minute uphill walk.)

MAINE

Judge Silas Lee built it to resemble a mansion in Dunbar, Scotland, but he only lived here for seven years before dying. Acquired by Capt Richard Tucker in 1858 and owned by his descendants before being acquired by Historic New England, the castle has new owners intent on preserving its past.

MUSICAL WONDER HOUSE
On the way to Castle Tucker, don't overlook this sweet **museum** (☎ 207-882-7163; www.musical wonderhouse.com; 18 High St; half tour/full tour $10/20; ☺ 10am-5pm late May–mid-Oct). Its outstanding collection of antique music boxes, player pianos and early talking machines (gramophones) are displayed in period rooms.

NICKELS-SORTWELL HOUSE
This **historical mansion** (☎ 207-882-6218; www.spnea .org; cnr US 1 & Federal St/ME 218; admission $5; ☺ 11am-5pm Tue-Sun Jun–mid-Oct), just downhill from Bailey Inn, is one of the town's finest Federal houses (built in 1807). Tours begin on the hour and run from 11am to 4pm.

FORT EDGECOMB
An octagonal wooden blockhouse, this **fort** (☎ 207-882-7777; 66 Fort Rd, North Edgecomb; ☺ late May-Sep) was built in 1808 to protect the valuable Wiscasset shipbuilding trade. It sits a half-mile south of the eastern end of the bridge that spans the Sheepscot River. Commanding the riverine approach to the town, the fort is now the area's prime picnic site.

Sleeping
BUDGET
Wiscasset Motor Lodge (☎ 207-882-7137, 800-732-8168; www.wiscassetmotorlodge.com; 596 Bath Rd/US 1; r incl breakfast Jun–mid-Sep/off-season $58-105/50-86; ☺ Apr-Nov) Southwest of the city center, this motel's comfy knotty pine-paneled rooms and cottages are excellent value.

Highnote B&B (☎ 207-882-9628; www.wiscasset .net/highnote; 26 Lee St; r incl breakfast $80) At the Highnote (owned by an opera singer – hence the name), you'll get a spacious room in a Victorian home (1876), a shared bathroom and a European-style breakfast (with fruits, meats, bread and homemade scones). It's within walking distance of all the major sites, antique shops and restaurants in Wiscasset.

Marston House (☎ 207-882-6010, 800-852-4157; www .marstonhouse.com; 101 Main St; r incl breakfast $90; ☺ May-Oct) This B&B has two classy rooms in a late-

19th-century carriage house that are styled with a hint of New England simplicity. It's a romantic setting; the hosts will even set up your room's fireplace. A luscious breakfast – brought to your room in a wicker basket and antique jars – includes fruit, homemade granola and freshly squeezed orange juice. The proprietors also hold antique shows and have beautiful rustic furniture for sale.

MID-RANGE
Sheepscot River Inn (☎ 207-882-6343, 800-427-5503; www.sheepscotriverinn.com; 306 Eddy Rd, Edgecomb; r/cottage/ste incl breakfast $80-120/90-120/89-150; ☺) You can choose here between inn rooms, motor lodge suites and tidy little frame cottages in a pine grove overlooking the river. Pets are welcome for $10 per night.

Eating
Red's Eats (☎ 207-882-6128; Main St; mains $1-13; ☺ lunch & dinner May-Oct) Since the '40s, this red shack at Water St has been a simple take-out stand serving some of the tastiest clam dishes ($8) and whole-lobster rolls ($12.50) in Maine.

Treat's (☎ 207-882-6192; 80 Main St; dishes $3-12; ☺ lunch, closed Sun off-season) Offers homemade pastries, fresh bread, tasty soups and cheeses. If you're tired of tourist fare like lobster and chowder, this is a great place.

Sarah's Café (☎ 207-882-7504; 45 Water St; mains $5-18; ☺ lunch & dinner, breakfast Sat & Sun) This family-oriented place offers mostly Tex-Mex food and is renowned for large sandwiches, soups and burritos.

Le Garage (☎ 207-882-5409; 15 Water St; lunch $6-18, dinner $10-22; ☺ lunch & dinner Jul & Aug, Tue-Sun Sep-Dec & Feb-Jun) Overlooking the wrecks of the wooden schooners *Hesper* and *Luther Little*, Le Garage is the best place for a filling, reasonably priced bona fide meal. Try the sautéed Maine shrimp with herbs and garlic or the 'finnan haddie' (smoked haddock).

Getting There & Away
Wiscasset is 10 miles northeast of Bath, 7 miles west of Damariscotta, 13 miles north of Boothbay Harbor and 23 miles south of Augusta. For bus transportation, see p480.

BOOTHBAY HARBOR
pop 2334
Once a beautiful little seafarers' village on a broad ford-like harbor, Boothbay Harbor is

now fully commercialized and, frankly, overrun by tourists in the summer. Because it's a small town built on and around two hills, its narrow and winding streets become choked with cars. Its sidewalks are thronged with visitors boarding boats for coastal cruises or browsing Boothbay's boutiques. Still, there's good reason for them to be here. The setting couldn't be more picturesque. Try to visit in June or September, when the summer swells have subsided a bit.

Large, well-kept Victorian houses crown the town's many knolls, and a wooden footbridge ambles across the harbor. It's definitely a walking town. After you've strolled the waterfront along Commercial St and the business district along Todd and Townsend Aves, walk along McKown St to the top of McKown Hill for a fine view. Then, take the footbridge across the harbor to the town's East Side, where there are several huge, dockside seafood restaurants.

Orientation

First things first: Boothbay and East Boothbay are separate from Boothbay Harbor, the largest, busiest and prettiest of the three towns. Follow ME 27 south to the town, which you will enter along Oak St (one way) – this runs into Commercial St, the main street.

Dealing with narrow, often one-way roads and scarce parking isn't any fun. It's best to park further out and take the free shuttle into the city center rather than get caught in the slow-moving river of cars. Catch the shuttle at the small mall on Townsend Ave. Once in town, hop aboard the trolley ($1) that tools around.

Information

There's no shortage of helpful and plentiful information around here.

Boothbay Harbor Region Chamber of Commerce (☎ 207-633-2353; www.boothbayharbor.com; 192 Townsend Ave, Boothbay Harbor, ME 04538; ☻ 8am-5pm Jul & Aug, Mon-Fri May, Jun, Sep & Oct)

Boothbay Information Center (☎ 207-633-4743; www.boothbayharbor.com; ME 27, Boothbay, ME 04537; ☻ 8am-5pm May-Oct) Maintains an information office on ME 27.

Sights & Activities
BOOTHBAY RAILWAY VILLAGE

This endearing **village** (☎ 207-633-4727; www.railwayvillage.org; ME 27; adult/child 3-16 $8/4; ☻ 9:30am-

5pm mid-Jun–mid-Oct), a historical replica of a New England town, has 27 buildings and a narrow-gauge steam-train line running through it. It's basically a nonprofit educational park, and has a collection of more than 55 antique steam- and gasoline-powered motor vehicles.

Tours
CRUISES

Boothbay's busy natural harbor features many possibilities for maritime excursions.

Balmy Days Cruises (☎ 207-633-2284, 800-298-2284; www.balmydayscruises.com; Pier 8, Boothbay Harbor; adult/child 3-11 $30/18; ☻ May-Oct) This outfit takes passengers over to Monhegan Island (p493) on day trips, departing Boothbay Harbor after breakfast and returning before supper. Balmy Days also offers relaxing one-hour harbor and nighttime lights tours (adult/child $10/5).

Bay Lady (☎ 207-633-2284; www.balmydayscruises.com; Pier 8, Boothbay Harbor; tours $18; ☻ 5 trips daily May-Oct) This 31ft friendship sloop is the kind of small sailboat that was once favored by lobstermen.

Cap'n Fish's Boat Trips (☎ 207-633-3244, 800-636-3244; www.mainewhales.com; Pier 1, Boothbay Harbor; ☻ May-Oct) These tours travel many routes along the coast and among the islands in search of whales (adult/child $28/15), puffins (adult/child $20/10) and seals (adult/child $14/7). Voyages last from one to three hours. And yes, the owner's name really is Cap'n Fish.

Eastwind (☎ 207-633-6598; www.fishermanswharfinn.com; Fisherman's Wharf, Boothbay Harbor; tours $22; ☻ 4 trips daily May-Oct) This company takes 2½-hour sail-powered cruises around the harbor. From this stately 64ft windjammer you'll see lighthouses, remote islands, and lobstermen hauling traps.

Sleeping

The Boothbays offer campgrounds, motels, inns and B&Bs for every taste and budget. In general, motels on Townsend Ave/ME 27 north of Boothbay Harbor are less expensive than the elaborate places on Atlantic Ave on the harbor's east side. If you don't mind staying outside of town, there are several good choices. The surrounding villages of East Boothbay and West Boothbay Harbor (on Southport Island) are not as touristy or commercial as Boothbay Harbor. In other words, they're a lot more like the real Maine.

BUDGET

Several large campgrounds are north of Boothbay Harbor along ME 27. Most places cater to gigantic land yachts (ie RVs) in need of 30-amp electricity and metered LP gas hookups, but all accept tent campers as well. Tenters may just feel like a fish out of water, that's all.

Little Ponderosa Campground (☎ 207-633-2700; www.littleponderosa.com; ME 27, Boothbay; sites $16-31; ☺ Jun–mid-Oct) Six miles north of Boothbay Harbor, this campground has big open fields for games, and 96 campsites among tall pine trees. With a little luck you'll get one of the 36 sites on the tidal inlet. There's also a shuttle bus ($1) from the campground into Boothbay Harbor.

Gray Homestead (☎ 207-633-4612; www.graysocean camping.com; 21 Homestead Rd, West Boothbay Harbor; sites $21-29; ☺ mid-May–Oct) South of Boothbay Harbor on Southport Island, Gray Homestead has 40 wooded, oceanfront sites. They call this roughing it? You can launch a kayak from your tent or cook a lobster at your site. Not bad, eh?

Topside (☎ 207-633-5404, 877-486-7466; http://home .gwi.net/topside; 60 McKown Hill, Boothbay Harbor; r incl breakfast $70-110; ☺ May-Oct) Atop McKown Hill, Topside has unparalleled views of the town and the harbor. Its 22 rooms are located in the original sea captain's house (preferred) or in the adjoining motel; all have refrigerators.

Pond House (☎ 207-633-5842; www.pondhousemaine .com; 7 Bay St, Boothbay Harbor; r $75-90; ☺ Mar-Jan) A breath of fresh air in this heavily touristed town. It's an artists' retreat that has a studio in a detached barn. As for the five guest rooms, they're simple and spacious, the kind of place that lets you think and renew your spirit.

Howard House Lodge (☎ 207-633-3933, 800-466-6697; www.howardhouselodge.com; 347 Townsend Ave, Boothbay Harbor; r incl breakfast $76-96; ☺ May-Oct) This modern, attractive, comfortable and reasonably priced motel is about a mile north of the city center.

Captain Sawyer's Place (☎ 207-633-2290, 800-434-9657; 55 Commercial St, Boothbay Harbor; r/ste $65-95/115) Look for the big yellow house overlooking the harbor, right in the midst of everything. As you might imagine, rooms in the back here, without a sea view, cost less than those in front. If you feel like a little splurge, the captain's suite has its own deck.

MID-RANGE

Boothbay Harbor has dozens of small inns and B&Bs. From mid-July through early September, reservations are a must.

Five Gables Inn (☎ 207-633-4551, 800-451-5048; www.fivegablesinn.com; Murray Hill Rd, Boothbay Harbor; r incl breakfast $130-200; ☺ mid-May–Oct) This grand 125-year-old hotel with wraparound porch is set on a hill and has a large common living room and 16 guest rooms, most of which offer wonderful views of Linekin Bay. Hosts De and Mike Kennedy (Mike was trained at the Culinary Institute of America) serve a sumptuous breakfast.

Linekin Bay B&B (☎ 207-633-9900, 800-596-7420; www.linekinbaybb.com; 531 Ocean Point Rd/ME 96, Boothbay Harbor; r $105-175) This waterside B&B has four spacious rooms and an extremely amiable host, a retired police officer who enjoys cooking and baking for guests.

Greenleaf Inn (☎ 207-633-7346, 888-950-5524; www .greenleafinn.com; 65 Commercial St, Boothbay Harbor; r incl breakfast May-Oct/off-season $185-195/125-165) This breezy inn has five well-lit rooms, an outdoor hot tub and good breakfasts.

Lawnmere Inn (☎ 207-633-2544, 800-633-7645; www.lawnmereinn.com; 65 Hendricks Hill Rd/ME 27, Boothbay Harbor; r $100-230; ☺ mid-May–Oct) On Southport Island, southwest of Boothbay Harbor, Lawnmere is a nice old 31-room inn. It's set on spacious lawns at the water's edge, far away from the hustle and bustle of town. Prices vary according to view.

Welch House Inn (☎ 207-633-3431, 800-279-7313; www.welchhouse.com; 56 McKown St, Boothbay Harbor; r incl breakfast $85-165; ☺ Apr-Dec) Despite its tacky wallpaper and decorations, this hilltop inn offers great harbor views and superb breakfasts.

Eating

BUDGET

MacNab's Tea Room (☎ 207-633-7222; 5 Lu Yu Tea Lane, Boothbay; dishes $3.50-10; ☺ lunch Tue-Sat) This will be the first spot, but not the last, to tempt you on the road into town. Luckily, MacNab's is also a great place to stop for a bite and a quick pot of tea ($2.50). How about some Scottish soup, a sandwich or dessert?

Upper Deck Cafe (☎ 207-633-7447;, Boothbay Harbor; mains $6-10; ☺ breakfast & lunch May-Oct) For water views and something lighter, this café has an extensive sandwich and salad menu.

MID-RANGE

Harborside Restaurant (☎ 207-633-4074; 12 Bridge St, Boothbay Harbor; mains breakfast/lunch & dinner $5-10/9-22; ☺ breakfast, lunch & dinner May-Oct) Andrew's serves award-winning seafood chowder, lobster pie and lots of sandwiches. And since it's down toward the footbridge with lots of pedestrian traffic, there's also great people-watching.

Lobster Dock (☎ 207-633-7120; 49 Atlantic Ave, Boothbay Harbor; mains $12-20; ☼ lunch & dinner May-Oct) Of all the lobster joints in Boothbay Harbor, this is one of the best and cheapest. It serves traditional shore dinners (steamed clams, boiled lobster and corn on the cob) as well as other seafood. Prices fluctuate with availability and the season.

Lobsterman's Wharf (☎ 207-633-3443; ME 96, East Boothbay; mains dinner $14-22; ☼ lunch & dinner mid-May–mid-Oct) If you're in the mood for a full sit-down restaurant, dining indoors or outdoors, Lobsterman's Wharf is a good choice for seafood.

TOP END
Cabbage Island Clambakes (☎ 207-633-7200; www .cabbageislandclambakes.com; Pier 6, Fisherman's Wharf, Boothbay Harbor; prix fixe $45; ☼ late Jun-early Sep) For a real Maine experience, consider this tour, which sails out of Boothbay Harbor aboard the motor vessel *Argo*. Upon arrival at Cabbage Island, the captain and crew prepare a traditional clambake with seaweed-baked clams, steamed lobsters, clam chowder, corn on the cob and Maine potatoes and onions, followed by Maine blueberry cake and coffee. The two- and four-hour voyages depart at 12:30pm Monday to Friday, 12:30pm and 5pm Saturday, and 11:30am and 2:45pm Sunday.

Getting There & Away
From Wiscasset, continue on US 1 for 2 miles, and then head south on ME 27 for 12 miles through Boothbay to Boothbay Harbor.

DAMARISCOTTA & PEMAQUID
pop 2041
Damariscotta, a pretty Maine town with numerous churches and an attractive commercial district, serves the smaller communities of the Pemaquid Peninsula to the south.

ME 130 goes from Damariscotta through the heart of the Pemaquid Peninsula to **Pemaquid Neck**, the southernmost part of the peninsula. Pemaquid – Abenaki for 'Longest Finger' – is the longest peninsula on the Maine coast and you'll be richly rewarded by driving to its end. Pemaquid Point is one of the most picturesque locales in Maine and artists from all over the world flock here

to capture its beauty in drawings, paintings and photographs.

Although it's bypassed by the masses today, the area was well explored in the early 17th century. English explorers set foot on the Pemaquid Peninsula in the early 1600s, but France claimed the land as well: the great Samuel de Champlain came here in 1605. By the 1620s, the area had a thriving settlement with a customhouse.

Information
Follow US 1B ('Business') to reach the center of town.
Damariscotta Region Chamber of Commerce (☎ 207-563-8340; www.drcc.org; PO Box 13, Damariscotta, ME 04543; ☼ 9am-5pm Mon-Fri) The information office is located in the town center, just beyond where ME 129/130 veers off to the right.
Damariscotta Region Information Bureau (☎ 207-563-3175; www.damariscottaregion.com; ☼ 10am-4pm Tue-Fri & 10am-1pm Mon & Sat Jun-Aug) For tourist information; located west of the town center on US 1.
Maine Coast Book Shop & Café (☎ 207-563-3207; 158 Main St; ☼ daily) Go here for additional area information and a little café with coffee, muffins and sandwiches.

Sights
PEMAQUID BEACH & TRAIL
Believe it or not, there are a few stretches of sandy beach along this rockbound coast, and **Pemaquid Beach** is one of them. As ME 130 approaches Pemaquid Neck, watch for signs on the right (west) for Pemaquid Beach and make a right onto Huddle Rd (which turns into Snowball Hill Rd). The Pemaquid Trail, a paved dead-end road, heads south from Snowball Hill Rd just east of the Pemaquid Beach access road. The beach is set in a park, and both are open in summer for a small fee. The water is usually very cold for swimming. (Remember, this is Maine!)

FORT WILLIAM HENRY
A quarter-mile south of Pemaquid Beach lies the remains of **Fort William Henry** (☎ 207-677-2423, 207-624-6080; adult $2, child under 12 yrs & senior free; ☼ 9am-5pm late May-early Sep). This reconstructed circular stone fort boasts commanding views, old foundations, a burial ground with interesting tombstones, an archaeological dig and a small museum.

This area has a long history with forts and fortification. The first fortress built here, Fort Pemaquid, was overcome and

MAINE

DETOUR: PEMAQUID POINT

Along a 3500-mile coastline famed for its natural beauty, Pemaquid Point stands out because of its tortuous, grainy, igneous rock formations pounded by restless, treacherous seas.

Perched on top of the rocks in **Lighthouse Park** (☼ dawn-dusk) is the 11,000-candlepower **Pemaquid Light**, built in 1827. It's one of the 61 surviving lighthouses along the Maine coast, 52 of which are still in operation. The keeper's house now serves as the **Fishermen's Museum Lighthouse** (Pemaquid Point; admission by donation; ☼ 10am-5pm Mon-Sat, 11am-5pm Sun), displaying fishing paraphernalia and photos, as well as a nautical chart of the entire Maine coast with all the lighthouses marked.

Make sure you take some photographs here at Pemaquid Point. But also take a few minutes to fix the view in your mind, because no photograph can do justice to this wild vista. If you clamber over the rocks beneath the light, do so with great care. Big waves sweep in unexpectedly, and periodically, tourists are swept back out with them, ending their Maine vacations in a sudden, dramatic and fearfully permanent manner.

---

looted by pirates in 1632. In 1689, its replacement, Fort Charles, fell to the allied French and Indians. The fort was later restored and renamed Fort Frederick (1729), but during the Revolutionary War it was torn down. In 1908, it was partially rebuilt as a historic site and called Fort William Henry. The nearby Old Fort House was built about this time and still stands. Got all that?

Sleeping & Eating

Pemaquid Point Campground (☎ 207-677-2267; www.midcoast.com/~ed; 9 Pemaquid Point Campground Rd, New Harbor; sites $23-27; ☼ late Jun-early Sep) Toward Pemaquid Point off ME 130, this basic campground has 20 tent and 30 RV sites.

Bradley Inn (☎ 207-677-2105, 800-942-5560; www .bradleyinn.com; 3063 Bristol Rd, New Harbor; r incl breakfast $155-195; ☼ Apr-Oct) A few hundred yards inland, this upscale place has 16 luxe rooms decorated with Victorian and nautical antiques. The restaurant is relaxed and pricey, but superb.

Hotel Pemaquid (☎ 207-677-2312; www.hotel pemaquid.com; 3098 Bristol Rd/ME 130, New Harbor; r & cottages $80-230) On Pemaquid Point and just 100 yards from the lighthouse park, this wood-frame hotel has a grand front porch with 37 period guest rooms and housekeeping cottages. Although built in the late 1800s, the decor gives it a 1920s feel.

Sea Gull Shop (☎ 207-677-2374; 3119 Bristol Rd; breakfast $7.50, lunch $7-12, dinner $15-20; ☼ breakfast, lunch & dinner May-Oct) If you need refreshments, this place abuts Lighthouse Park and offers those same beautiful views. BYOB.

Getting There & Away

From Wiscasset, continue on US 1 for 7 miles, and head southeast on ME 129 for 2 miles to Damariscotta. Take ME 130 south for 12 miles through New Harbor to Pemaquid Point. To get back to US 1 heading north, take ME 3 for 22 miles north through Round Pond until you reach US 1.

ROCKLAND

pop 7609

Today, Rockland is, along with Camden, the center of Maine's very busy windjammer sailing business. In the summer, windjammers, the tall-masted sailing ships descended from those long built on these shores, cruise up and down the Maine coast, to the delight of their passengers. Rockland is also the birthplace of poet Edna St Vincent Millay (1892–1950), who grew up in neighboring Camden. For information on windjammer cruises and places to stay in the area, see p494.

Sights

FARNSWORTH ART MUSEUM & WYETH CENTER

Rockland is also famous for its **Farnsworth Art Museum & Wyeth Center** (☎ 207-596-6457; www .farnsworthmuseum.org; 16 Museum St; adult/child under 18/student/senior $9/free/5/8; ☼ 9am-5pm late Sep–mid-Oct, 10am-5pm Tue-Sat, 1-5pm Sun mid-Oct–late Sep), one of the country's best small regional museums. Its collection of 5000 works is especially strong in landscape and marine artists who have worked in Maine, such as Andrew, NC and Jamie Wyeth; Louise Nevelson; Rockwell Kent; John Marin and others.

MAINE

OWLS HEAD TRANSPORTATION MUSEUM

Two miles south of Rockland, this **museum** (☎ 207-594-4418; www.ohtm.org; ME 73, Owls Head; adult/child 5-11/family $7/5/18; ☽ 10am-5pm Apr-Oct, 10am-4pm Nov-Mar) collects, preserves (yes, everything works!) and exhibits pre-1920s aircraft, vehicles and engines that were instrumental in the evolution of transportation as we know it today. Besides its year-round exhibits, the museum also has WWI air shows and specialty vehicle shows.

Sleeping & Eating

LimeRock Inn (☎ 207-594-2257, 800-546-3762; www .limerockinn.com; 96 Limerock St; r incl breakfast $100-185) This eight-room mansion, built in 1890 for a local congressman, is decorated with the finest mahogany furniture, rugs and king-size beds that the owners could find.

Primo (☎ 207-596-0770; 2 S Main St/ME 73; mains $15-25; ☽ dinner Thu-Mon) Look what happens when an award-winning chef (Melissa Kelly) marries an award-winning baker and pastry chef (Price Kushner). Set in a Victorian home, this bistro is one of the top restaurants in the Northeast – we're talking from Washington, DC, up to Maine. It features creative veal, lamb and seafood dishes, and the dessert pastries are simply stupendous. Casual dress is fine, but make reservations a month ahead.

Getting There & Away

US Airways Express, operated by **Colgan Air** (☎ 800-428-4322; www.colganair.com), serves Rockland via its route from Boston to Bar Harbor.

Concord Trailways (☎ 800-639-3317; www.concord trailways.com; 517A Main St) runs buses from Boston and Logan Airport to Rockland, via Portland (terminating at the Maine State Ferry Terminal for boats to Vinalhaven). The trip from Boston to Rockland takes 4½ hours.

The **Maine State Ferry Service** (☎ 207-596-2202; www.state.me.us/mdot/opt/ferry/ferry.htm) takes passengers from Rockland to the islands of Vinalhaven and North Haven. Ferries depart Rockland three times daily year-round for the 70-minute trip to North Haven. For Vinalhaven, boats depart four to six times daily year-round.

MONHEGAN ISLAND

pop 75

This rocky outcrop is a deservedly popular summertime destination. The small island (just 1.5 miles long by a half-mile wide) was known to Basque and Portuguese fishers and mariners before the English cruised these waters, but it came into its own as a summer resort in the early 19th century. When the cities of the eastern seaboard were sweltering in summer's heat, cool sea breezes bathed Monhegan and those fortunate enough to have taken refuge here. (Be sure to bring a sweater and windbreaker, as the voyage and the coast can be chilly even in August.)

Early in its history as a resort, Monhegan became popular with artists who admired its dramatic views and agreeable isolation. To this day, the island village remains small and very limited in its services. Residents and visitors are drawn to plain living, deep thinking and traditional village life. The few unpaved roads are lined with stacks of lobster traps.

With few motor vehicles on tiny Monhegan (the ones it has are for essential jobs), Monhegan is laid out for walking. In fact, there are 17 miles of trails. Children, in particular, enjoy the southern tip of the island, with its wrecked ship rusting away, lots of rocks to climb, and cairn-art (stacks of stones and driftwood made into fantasy sculptures). The views from the lighthouse are excellent, and its little museum ($2) is an amusing diversion.

The island's environments – natural, social and commercial – are fragile and thus subject to strict rules: smoking and fires are prohibited outside the village and mountain biking is not allowed. In addition, all telephones require credit cards (there are no coin phones).

Unless you've made reservations well in advance at one of the island's few lodgings, don't plan on finding a room upon arrival. Make sure you take a day excursion from Port Clyde or Boothbay Harbor, and allow yourself at least a half-day to walk the trails over the rocks and around the shore. Stop at the 1824 **lighthouse museum** for a look at the keeper's former house.

Browse www.monhegan.com for more information.

Sleeping

Accommodations are simple and basic on the island; few rooms have private bathrooms. To reserve by mail, send your letter to the lodging in question, Monhegan, ME 04852, and it'll get there.

BUDGET & MID-RANGE

Shining Sails (☎ 207-596-0041; www.shiningsails.com; PO Box 346; r/apt incl breakfast in summer $95-135/$100-160) Shining Sails has fine ocean views from several of its seven rooms and kitchen-equipped apartments.

Monhegan House (☎ 207-594-7983; www.monheganhouse.com; r $75-125; ☉ May-Sep) A guesthouse since 1870, this place has 32 rooms with shared bathroom facilities on the 2nd floor. The café serves three meals and features baked goods made fresh in the inn's kitchen. Meals are not included in the rates.

Trailing Yew (☎ 207-596-0440; per person incl breakfast & dinner $83; ☉ mid-May–mid-Oct) This place has been hosting guests in pretty much the same manner since 1926: 40 spartan guest rooms are illuminated by kerosene lamps, and simple but nutritious meals are served family style. Credit cards are not accepted.

Hitchcock House (☎ 207-594-8137; www.midcoast.com/~hhouse; r & efficiency $80-130) On Horn's Hill, the secluded Hitchcock House has four old-fashioned rooms and two efficiency units (with a kitchen) that provide basic comforts (no more) after a long day outdoors.

Tribler Cottage (☎ 207-594-2445; r $75-135; ☉ mid-May–mid-Oct) Taking in guests since the 1920s, Tribler has one room with a private bathroom, and four efficiency apartments. Meals are not served.

TOP END

Island Inn (☎ 207-596-0371; www.islandinnmonhegan.com; r incl breakfast Jul-Sep/off-season $145-305/$85-260; ☉ May-Oct) A typical Victorian mansard-roofed summer hotel with a big front porch, this hostelry offers marvelous views and 45 small and simple rooms (only eight of which have a private bathroom). All three meals are available in the dining room. Reserve early in the spring for July and August.

Eating

Monhegan House Café (☎ 207-594-7983; lunch $10-15, dinner $20-25; ☉ breakfast, lunch & dinner late May–mid-Oct) This very popular café features a daily blue plate special with coffee and dessert for $15 and huge sandwiches like a half-pound burger.

Barnacle Café & Bakery (☎ 207-594-7995; mains $3-7; ☉ 8am-5pm May-Oct) Right by the wharf, this café has very good pasta and veggie salads, as well as pies and pastries.

North End Market (☎ 207-594-5546; dishes $5-6) Monhegan's only year-round convenience store also sells good homemade soups, salads and sandwiches in the summer.

Island Inn Dining Room (☎ 207-596-0371; mains $15-22; ☉ dinner May-Oct) If you're in the mood for fancy, this is it. Seafood is your best bet.

Getting There & Away

Monhegan-Thomaston Boat Line (☎ 207-372-8848; www.monheganboat.com) operates vessels to Monhegan Island from Port Clyde year-round. Schedules and fares vary according to the season; advance reservations are always a must.

In high summer, boats depart Port Clyde at 7am, 10:30am and 3pm. Return trips depart Monhegan at 9am, 12:30pm and 4:30pm. The first voyage of the day, in the *Laura B*, takes 70 minutes; the later ones, aboard the *Elizabeth Ann*, take 50 minutes. The round-trip fare is $27 for adults and $14 for children aged 12 and under. Parking in Port Clyde costs $4 per day.

Departing New Harbor from Shaw's Fish & Lobster Wharf on ME 32, **Hardy Boat Cruise** (☎ 207-677-2026; www.hardyboat.com; ☉ mid-May–mid-Oct) runs *Hardy III* at 9am and 2pm for Monhegan. It returns to New Harbor at 10:15am and 3:15pm. The round-trip fare is $27 for adults and $15 for children aged under 12; parking is free.

You can also visit Monhegan on a day excursion from Boothbay Harbor (p489) aboard one of the boats run by **Balmy Days Cruises** (☎ 207-633-2284, 800-298-2284; www.balmydayscruises.com; ☉ May-Oct).

CAMDEN

pop 5254

Camden and its picture-perfect harbor, shadowed by the mountains of Camden Hills State Park, is one of the prettiest sites in the state. Home to Maine's large and justly famed fleet of windjammers, Camden continues its historic close links with the sea. Most vacationers come to sail on their boats (or on somebody else's boats) or just to look at boats. But Camden is popular with landlubbers, too, who come into town to shop and dine at seafood restaurants. The adjoining state park offers hiking, picnicking and camping.

Like many communities along the Maine coast, Camden has a long history of shipbuilding. The mammoth six-masted schooner *George W Wells* was built here, setting the world record for the most masts on a sailing ship.

Alas, beauty comes at a price. The cost of Camden's lodgings and food during the summer is higher than those of many other Maine communities.

Orientation

US 1 snakes its way through Camden, and is the town's main street, named Elm St to the south, Main St in the center and High St to the north. Though the downtown section is easily covered on foot, it is several miles from one end of town to the other. Some accommodations are up to a 15-minute walk from the center of town.

Information

Owl & Turtle Bookshop (☎ 207-236-4769; 32 Washington St; ☉ 9am-5:30pm) This is a long-lived place to stop for books.

Rockport, Camden & Lincolnville Chamber of Commerce (☎ 207-236-4404; www.visitcamden.com; PO Box 919, Camden, ME 04843; ☉ 9am-5pm Mon-Fri, 10am-5pm Sat year-round & noon-4pm Sun mid-May–mid-Oct) Has an information office on the waterfront at the public landing in Camden, behind Cappy's.

Sights & Activities

CAMDEN HILLS STATE PARK

Far less crowded than Acadia National Park (p507), the mountaintop at **Camden Hills State Park** (☎ 207-236-3109; adult/child 5-11 $3/1 May-Oct, admission free off-season; ☉ dawn-dusk) offers some exquisite views of Penobscot Bay. The park also boasts an extensive system of well-marked hiking trails – from a half-mile, 45-minute climb up Mt Battie to the 3-mile, two-hour Ski Shelter Trail. Simple trail maps are available at the park entrance, just over 1.5 miles northeast of Camden center on US 1. The picnic area, on the south side of US 1, has short trails down to the shore.

SEA KAYAKING

To cruise the coast at your own speed, contact **Maine Sport Outfitters** (☎ 800-722-0826; www .mainesport.com; Harbor Park, Camden; per day per single/ tandem $50/65; ☉ Mar-Oct). In addition to kayak rentals, this outfit (off US 1) offers two-hour tours of Camden Harbor ($35 per person).

Ducktrap Sea Kayak Tours (☎ 207-236-8608; US 1, Lincolnville; 2hr/half-day tours $25-35/65; ☉ Jun-Aug)

takes folks on coastal tours and has custom-tailored full-day trips.

CYCLING

From Camden, it's a five-minute drive to Lincolnville Beach from where you can take a 20-minute ferry ride to the island of **Islesboro** (for the Islesboro ferry schedule, call ☎ 207-789-5611), one of the finest places to ride in Maine. Rentals are available from Camden's **Ragged Mountain Sports** (☎ 207-236-6664; 46b Elm St; per day $17; ☉ May-Oct).

The island is relatively flat, yet hilly enough to offer majestic vistas of Penobscot Bay and long enough to feature a 28-mile bike loop. Picnic at Pendleton Point, where harbor seals and loons often lounge on the long, striated rocks.

Tours

CRUISES

Camden is at the center of windjammer cruise country, but many boats dock at Rockport and Rockland as well. Cruise itineraries vary with the ship, the weather and the length of the trip, but day-sailers take passengers out for two- to four-hour cruises in Penobscot Bay. Usually you can book your place on a day-sailer the same day, even the same hour. The following boats depart from Camden's Town Landing or adjoining Sharp's Wharf (across from the chamber of commerce):

Appledore (☎ 207-236-8353; www.appledore2.com; 2hr cruise adult $25; ☉ Jan-Oct)

Lively Lady Too (☎ 207-236-6672; tours adult/child under 15 $20/5; ☉ May-Oct) This powerboat, takes visitors on fun two-hour lobstering trips.

Olad (☎ 207-236-2323; www.maineschooners.com; 2hr sail adult/child under 12 $27/15; ☉ May–mid-Oct)

Surprise (☎ 207-236-4687; www.camdenmainesailing. com; 2hr cruise incl snacks adult $28; ☉ May–mid-Oct) Children under 12 are not accepted.

Aboard the schooner **Wendameen** (☎ 207-594-1751; www.schooneryacht.com; per person incl all meals$180; ☉ May-Oct), which takes passengers cruising for a day and overnight, you'll get a good taste of life aboard a windjammer.

Overnight cruises require reservations. For information on various vessels available, contact:

Maine Windjammer Association (☎ 800-807-9463; www.midcoast.com/~sailmwa; PO Box 1144, Blue Hill, ME 04614)

MAINE

North End Shipyard Schooners (☎ 207-594-8007, 800-648-4844; www.midcoast.com/~schooner; PO Box 482, Rockland, ME 04841)

Sleeping

Camden has more than 100 places to stay, most of them small inns or B&Bs, with room prices ranging from $75 to over $300.

BUDGET

In addition to a couple of good, scenic camping options, Camden's other budget accommodations are motels along US 1. Look for a large concentration of them in Lincolnville, just north of Camden.

Birchwood Motel & Cottages (☎ 207-236-4204; www.birchwoodmotel.com; Belfast Rd/US 1; r incl breakfast $65-85; ☺ May-Oct) Just north of Camden, this simple place has 17 motel rooms, all with water views. The 'deluxe king' rooms ($85) are well worth the extra dough. They're newly renovated and fresh feeling.

Camden Hills State Park (☎ 207-236-3109; US 1; sites $15-20; ☺ mid-May–mid-Oct) This popular camping place has hot showers, flush toilets and 107 forested tent and RV sites (none with hookups). Reservations are advised for high summer (July and August). A few sites are held on a first-come, first-served basis, but be sure to arrive by noon to claim one.

Megunticook Campground by the Sea (☎ 207-594-2428, 800-884-2428; www.campgroundbythesea.com; 620 Commercial St/US 1, Rockport; sites $32-41; ☺ mid-May–mid-Oct) This quiet and wooded campground, 3 miles south of Camden, has good sites on the coast.

Towne Motel (☎ 207-236-3377, 800-656-4999; www.camdenmotel.com; 68 Elm St; r Jun-Oct/off-season $99-125/$59-90) Towne Motel has 19 basic rooms right in the center of town.

MID-RANGE

Both the Elm St and High St stretches of US 1 have a number of nice B&Bs.

Nathaniel Hosmer Inn (☎ 207-236-4012, 800-423-4012; www.nathanielhosmerinn.com; 4 Pleasant St; r incl breakfast with bathroom Jun-Aug/off-season $125-165/95-135) Since US 1 runs right through town, quiet accommodations are difficult to come by in Camden. That's where this place stands out from the crowd. With just seven rooms, this simple Federal house sits a block off Elm St in a peaceful residential neighborhood. You'll sleep soundly here.

High Tide Inn (☎ 207-236-3724, 800-778-7068; www.hightideinn.com; US 1; r incl breakfast $85-160; ☺ May-Oct) Situated between Camden and Lincolnville, High Tide has an assortment of basic accommodations from cottages to hotel units to a house. Here's a big plus: it has a beach.

Blackberry Inn (☎ 207-236-6060; www.blackberryinn.com; 82 Elm St; r incl breakfast $95-165) A gorgeous Victorian with high ceilings even on the 2nd floor, the Blackberry offers eight fully restored guest rooms and a spacious efficiency for families. Rooms even boast vintage tin ceilings and fireplaces.

Camden Maine Stay Inn (☎ 207-236-9636; www.camdenmainestay.com; 22 High St/US 1; r incl breakfast $115-165) This fine Greek house (1802) sits at the base of Mt Battie. The owners are some of the most friendly and knowledgeable in town, and they offer eight nicely appointed guest rooms (six with private bathroom).

Captain Swift Inn (☎ 207-236-8113, 800-251-0865; www.swiftinn.com; 72 Elm St; r incl breakfast $85-159; ☐) This 1810 Federal house offers four guest rooms and lots of period details like an early-19th-century fireplace and beehive oven.

Blue Harbor House (☎ 207-236-3196, 800-248-3196; www.blueharborhouse.com; 67 Elm St; r incl breakfast with bathroom $95-205) This cozy New England Cape Cod–style house (1810) has 10 guest rooms and amiable owners.

Strawberry Hill Seaside Inn (☎ 207-594-5462, 800-589-4009; www.strawberryhillseasideinn.com; US 1, Rockport; r $80-180; ☎) Three miles north of Rockland, this place has 21 rooms set on a hillside overlooking the sea. Each of the large rooms has a private porch facing the cove, but you might prefer to walk down to the water's edge to hear the shoreline lap against the rocks.

Whitehall Inn (☎ 207-236-3391, 800-789-6565; www.whitehall-inn.com; 52 High St; r incl breakfast Jul–mid-Oct/off-season $110-170/65-125; ☺ late May–mid-Oct) You can expect traditional, proper New England ambience behind the Ionic columns on the broad front porch here. Most of the 50 rooms in the main inn, the Maine House and the Wicker House have private bathrooms. If you're up for some elegant cuisine at dinnertime, it's served to the public in the equally elegant **dining room** (mains $15-30).

TOP END

Norumbega (☎ 207-236-4646, 877-363-4646; www.norumbegainn.com; 63 High St; r/ste incl breakfast $160-340/295-475) A review of Camden lodgings wouldn't be complete without mentioning Norumbega, a fantastic, castle-like stone Victorian mansion with 13 rooms. Throwing around adjectives like 'exceptional,' 'sumptuous' and 'magnificent' isn't commonplace but neither is this place. Few places in New England can match it for over-the-top qualities.

Eating

As is it with Camden's lodgings, so it is with restaurants: prices tend to be higher here than in most other towns.

BUDGET & MID-RANGE

Frogwater Cafe & Bakery (☎ 207-236-8998; 31 Elm St; mains $5-18; ☻ daily) This place specializes in great vegetarian fare and desserts. Feel righteous by ordering the vegetarian shepherd's pie ($14) and then move to decadence with a cinnamon bread pudding ($5.25).

Cappy's (☎ 207-236-2254; 1 Main St; dishes $5-15) Many places in Maine bill themselves as 'the place for chowder,' but this one, smack in the middle of town, is probably telling the truth. Come here for a huge mug of thick, creamy chowder – chock-full of clams and potatoes, and served with a buttermilk biscuit. You'll leave a happy person. Although the long menu roams from sandwiches and light meals to hearty tuck-ins, stick with the chowder.

Camden Deli (☎ 207-236-8343; 37 Main St; sandwiches $4-10) Feel like a picnic down by the water or on top of Mt Battie? Pick up a substantial sandwich here – there are several vegetarian choices and a wide range of wines from which to choose.

TOP END

Lobster Pound Restaurant (☎ 207-789-5550; US 1, Lincolnville; mains $15-35; ☻ May-Oct) For lobster served and cooked in every imaginable way, few things in life compare with this place, which stands alone on Lincolnville's beach. The restaurant also offers plenty of steamers, shrimp and fish, including a particularly good blackened swordfish ($18).

Atlantica (☎ 207-236-6011; Bay View Landing; lunch $7-14, dinner $18-28; ☻ lunch & dinner Apr-Dec) With the best seafood preparations in town, this chef-owned place serves great dishes like pan-seared peppered tuna ($22) or sautéed gingered scallops ($21). The good bay views complement the cuisine quite nicely.

Waterfront Restaurant (☎ 207-236-3747; Bay View Landing; lunch $7-17, dinner $15-25; ☻ lunch & dinner) This truly waterfront restaurant offers atmospheric dining rooms and a spacious deck right next to the boats. Try a summertime salad with blueberry cake ($8), or eat more seriously at dinnertime. Bursting with clam chowder, steamers, mussels and lobster, the shore dinner is a bargain at $25. If you prefer your food raw and unadorned, a raw bar serves clams and oysters.

Getting There & Away

South of Bangor (53 miles) on US 1, Camden is 85 miles north of Portland and 77 miles southwest of Bar Harbor.

BELFAST & SEARSPORT

pop 6381 (Belfast); 2641 (Searsport)

Just north of Camden on US 1 the roadside is lined with motels, campgrounds, restaurants, antique shops and flea markets. Pass right through or you'll keep pulling over again and again. You'll encounter travelers living at both extremes in Belfast and Searsport. The establishments along here are considerably cheaper than those of Camden, Blue Hill and Bar Harbor, and are more likely to have vacancies in the summer high season.

You can also explore Sears Island from here. It happens to be the largest uninhabited island on the US's eastern seaboard. Paddle here by kayak from Searsport Shores Camping Resort (below; rentals are available for $25/40 for a half/full day) or walk the pedestrian causeway. Then hike around the island and appreciate ospreys, bald eagles and bears (be careful!) in their natural habitat.

Searsport Shores Camping Resort (☎ 207-548-6059; www.campocean.com; 216 W Main St/US 1, Searsport; sites $30-45; ☻ mid-May–mid-Oct) This prime campground, a mile south of Searsport, has 35 tent and 65 RV sites set in a pine-forested waterfront location.

Darby's (☎ 207-338-2339; 155 High St, Belfast; lunch $6-10, dinner $9-15; ☻ lunch & dinner) If you're looking for a bite to eat in Belfast, Darby's won't disappoint. It has an eclectic, reasonably priced menu featuring everything from pad Thai to fish and chips to Moroccan lamb. Rinse it all down with a local microbrew beer.

MAINE

DOWN EAST

Without question, this is quintessential Maine: as you head further and further up the coast toward Canada, the peninsulas seem to become more and more narrow, jutting further into the sea. The fishing villages seem to get smaller, and the lobster pounds closer and closer to the water.

'Down east' starts around Penobscot Bay. If you make time to drive to the edge of the shore, south off US 1, let it be here.

Officially, 'down east' also includes Blue Hill Bay and Frenchman Bay, which frame Mt Desert Island (p502). The region continues 'further down east' (p511) from Acadia all the way to where the US meets the province of New Brunswick, Canada.

BUCKSPORT
pop 4908

A crossroads for highways and rail lines, Bucksport is a workaday town with light industry and a big Champion paper mill. Look a little closer, though, and you'll also find an artsy community, somewhat similar to that of Brattleboro (p357) in Vermont. There are numerous motels, restaurants and other services. The centrally located Bucksport Chamber of Commerce has an **information office** (☎ 207-469-6818; www.buck sportbaychamber.com; 52 Main St, Bucksport, ME 04416; ☒ 10am-5pm Mon-Fri) next to the municipal offices.

Just out of town and north of the bridge on ME 174, the **Fort Knox State Historic Site** (☎ 207-469-7719; 711 Fort Knox Rd, ME 174; adult/toddler/senior/child 5-11 $3/free/free/1; ☒ 9am-sunset), a huge granite fortress, dominates the Penobscot River Narrows. A fortress comes as a surprise in peaceable rural Maine, but only until you learn the spot's history. This part of the Penobscot River Valley was the riverine gateway to Bangor, the commercial heart of Maine's rich timber industry. The area was held by the British in the Revolutionary War and the War of 1812.

In 1839, it appeared that the US and the UK might once again go to war over the disputed boundary between Maine and New Brunswick, and the US government feared that Bangor might once again fall into British hands. To protect the river approach to the city, construction was begun

on Fort Knox in July 1844. Work continued for almost a decade.

The elaborate fortress mounted 64 cannons, with an additional 69 guns defending the outer perimeter. Though it was garrisoned from 1863 to 1866 during the Civil War, and again in 1898 during the Spanish-American War, it never saw any action. Fort Knox was either a great waste of money or an effective military deterrent, depending on your point of view.

Like so many of the world's elaborate military constructions, it is now a tourist attraction. Bring a flashlight if you plan a close examination, as the fort's granite chambers are unlit. There's a nice picnic area outside the admissions gate.

CASTINE
pop 1343

From Orland, a few miles east of Bucksport along US 1, ME 175/166 heads south to the dignified and historic village of Castine. Following an eventful history, today's Castine is charming, quiet and refreshingly off the beaten track. Almost all of its houses were built before 1900, so it's easy to get a feel for how this seaside town would have been back then. It's also the home of the Maine Maritime Academy and its big training ship, the *State of Maine* (1952), which you can visit.

In 1613, seven years before the Pilgrims landed at Plymouth, the French founded Fort Pentagöet – which later became Castine – to serve as a trading post. It was the site of battle after battle through the American Revolution, the War of 1812 and the French and Indian Wars. The French, English, Dutch and Americans all fought for a niche on this bulge of land that extends into Penobscot Bay.

Both Castine and Blue Hill are good places to appreciate pre-tourist boom Maine. These are gorgeous villages with none of the kitsch you'd stumble across in Boothbay Harbor, Bar Harbor or Camden. Castine tends to attract a Washington, DC, bigwig crowd.

Castine is small enough to be easily traversed on foot. Pick up the free map entitled *A Walking Tour of Castine*, readily available at establishments in town.

Sights
FORTS

After such an embattled history, you might expect Castine to have a big old fort or two,

DOWN EAST & MT DESERT ISLAND

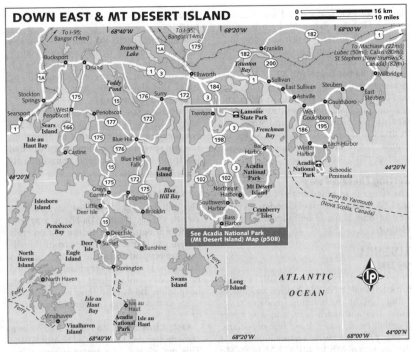

like the great stone citadel of Fort Knox at Bucksport. But no. The forts in Castine are low earthworks, now parklike and grass-covered. Close to the Maine Maritime Academy campus, **Fort George** is near the upper (northern) end of Main St where it meets Battle Ave and Wadsworth Cove Rd. Look for **Fort Pentagöet** on Perkins Rd at Tarratine St. The American **Fort Madison** (earlier called Fort Porter and dating to 1808) is further west along Perkins St, opposite Madockawando St.

WILSON MUSEUM

Stop for a look at the **Wilson Museum** (☎ 207-326-9247; www.wilsonmuseum.org; 107 Perkins St; admission free; ☻ 2-5pm Tue-Sun Jul-Sep) near Fort Pentagöet. It holds a good collection of Native American artifacts, historic tools, farm equipment and other relics from Maine's past.

Sleeping & Eating

There are only a few places to stay in little Castine and most have excellent restaurants.

Castine Inn (☎ 207-326-4365; www.castineinn.com; Main St; r incl breakfast $90-225; ☻ May-Oct) This late-19th-century summer hotel has 19 rooms, all with private bathrooms, but not all of them have been brought into the 21st century like the harborfront rooms have. Common rooms include a lovely living room and little pub, both with a fireplace, and a nice porch overlooking formal gardens. But the inn is best known (nationwide) for its gustatory delights prepared by chef-owners Tom and Amy Gutow. The sublime tasting menu is well worth its price ($75), but there's also a sophisticated à la carte menu ($25 to $35) featuring New American dishes. The wine list matches the menu impeccably.

Pentagöet Inn (☎ 207-326-8616, 800-845-1701; www.pentagoet.com; 26 Main St; r $75-215; ☻ May-Oct) This classy Queen-Anne Victorian, Castine's oldest summer hotel, has a tranquil wrap-around porch overlooking the village and harbor. It's easy to spend a few hours here doing absolutely nothing. But you probably came to eat and sleep, right? In that case, you'll be interested to know that the inn has 16 guest rooms filled with antiques and period details. And you can dine in the intimate and classy restaurant that serves artful

MAINE

platefuls of local seafood and fish. Caution: their bouillabaisse may cause French visitors to weep with envy. For drinking, the inn's striking, old world pub is covered with rare photos of eccentric world leaders.

Castine Harbor Lodge (☎ 207-326-4335; www .castinemaine.com; 147 Perkins St; r $85-245) They sure don't build them like they did in 1893. This gracious and spacious oceanfront house has plenty of places on the porch and broad lawn to drink in classic coastal views. As for the rooms, they're filled with requisite antiques and top notch furnishings.

Getting There & Away

The village is 18 miles south of US 1 at Orland, 56 miles northeast of Camden, 23 miles west of Blue Hill and 56 miles west of Bar Harbor.

BLUE HILL

pop 2390

This dignified, small, Maine coastal town is thick with tall trees, old houses and lots of culture. Many outstanding handicrafts artisans live and work here, and a summer chamber music series draws fine musicians.

Many roads converge on tiny Blue Hill. At the junction of ME 15, ME 172/Main St, ME 175, ME 176 and ME 177, the town of Blue Hill is small enough for easy walking since it has just a few inns, restaurants and antique stores. It's a very pleasant place to while away 1½ or two hours.

The **Blue Hill Chamber of Commerce** (☎ 207-374-3232; www.bluehillme.com; 28 Water St, Blue Hill, ME 04614; ⏰ 10am-4pm Mon-Fri & 9am-1pm Sat Jun-Sep) produces a free map that's available at establishments throughout town.

Festivals & Events

From early July to mid-August, the annual **Kneisel Hall Chamber Music Festival** (☎ 207-374-2811; www.kneisel.org; Pleasant St/ME 15) attracts visitors from Portland, Bar Harbor and beyond. Concerts are held on Friday evenings and Sunday afternoons. The **Blue Hill Fair** (held the first week in September at the fairgrounds northeast of the town center on ME 172), has oxen and horse pulls, sheepdog trials, livestock shows, fireworks, auto-thrill shows, a petting zoo and other countrylike things to do. It's great old-fashioned fun if you're in the area, but it's not worth organizing a trip around if you're not.

Sleeping

BUDGET

Blue Hill Farm Country Inn (☎ 207-374-5166; www .bluehillfarminn.com; ME 15; r incl breakfast Jun-Oct/off-season $75-99/65-85) Two miles north of the village and set on 48 acres of land with hiking trails, this classic 1903 farmhouse has 14 simple and lovely rooms.

Gatherings Family Campground (☎ 207-667-8826; ME 172; tent/RV sites $15-40/35-45; ⏰ Jun-Sep) Northeast of Blue Hill, this campground has tent sites and RV hookups on a wooded lakefront. You can also rent cabins and cottages by the week.

MID-RANGE

Blue Hill Inn (☎ 207-374-2844; www.bluehillinn .com; ME 177; r incl breakfast $138-195) A longtime favorite lodging place in the region, this c 1840 inn is just a few steps from the village center and faces the George Stevens Academy. It offers 10 very nicely appointed rooms, two suites, great morning meals, hospitable hosts and enough common space to make things comfortable on a cold or rainy day.

Captain Isaac Merrill Inn (☎ 207-374-2555; www .captainmerrillinn.com; 1 Union St; r incl breakfast $95-175) This inn, right in the center of things, has only been in business since 1994, but it has the feel of a 19th-century hostelry.

Eating

Blue Hill Co-op (☎ 207-374-2165; Greene's Hill Pl, cnr ME 172 & ME 176; dishes $2-10; ⏰ 8am-3pm) A great place to pick up organic produce and various soy proteins, this co-op also has a little café serving sandwiches and salads. It's a groovy kind of place, where the bulletin board is bursting with yoga classes and articles railing against genetically engineered food. Long live the co-ops!

Arborvine (☎ 207-374-2119; 33 Main St; mains $16-22; ⏰ dinner Wed-Sun, call for the off-season schedule) Out of a sweet 1823 Cape-style house, this place to see and be seen and fine, fine restaurant serves meat and fish endemic to the area. Chef John Hikade manages to incorporate various fruits into almost all of his exquisite dishes. Start with Damariscotta River oysters ($11) and try either the tournedos ($26) or a shellfish specialty such as Maine crab cakes ($22). Blue Hill's top restaurants are very busy at dinner and this is no exception; make reservations.

Getting There & Away

Blue Hill is 23 miles east of Castine, 13 miles southwest of Ellsworth and 18 miles southeast of Bucksport.

DEER ISLE & STONINGTON

pop 1876 (Deer Isle); 1151 (Stonington)

You should definitely go out of your way to travel south along ME 15, where you will encounter views of pristine farms and stretches of rocky Maine coast with sailboats moored offshore. Deer Isle is actually a collection of islands joined by causeways and connected to the mainland by a picturesque, tall and narrow suspension bridge near Sargentville.

The **Deer Isle-Stonington Chamber of Commerce** (☎ 207-348-6124; www.deerislemaine.com; PO Box 490, Deer Isle, ME 04627; ⊗ 10am-4pm mid-Jun–early Sep) maintains an information booth a quarter-mile south of the suspension bridge.

Deer Isle and Stonington are just about 5 miles apart. Stonington is 23 miles south of Blue Hill, 36 miles southwest of Ellsworth and 78 miles east of Camden.

Boats depart Stonington for Isle au Haut (p502).

Deer Isle Village

This small village is simply a collection of shops and services near the famed but low-key Pilgrim's Inn (p502). Seven miles to the east, hidden at the end of Sunshine Rd, look for the exceptional and prestigious **Haystack Mountain School of Crafts** (☎ 207-348-2306; www.hay stack-mtn.org; 89 Haystack School Dr, Sunrise; tours $5; ⊗ tours 1pm Wed Jun-Aug), founded in 1950 and now open for one public tour per week. There are several galleries in Deer Isle and neighboring Stonington worth seeking out, testament to the fascination this beautiful seaside area holds for fine artists. Drop in to any little studio that's marked and you'll be pleasantly impressed and surprised.

Stonington

At the southern tip of Deer Isle, Stonington is at once a granite-quarrying, fishing and tourist town. The three industries have long thrived closely, but separately. Signs warn tourists not to park on the town dock because it is reserved for pickups hauling lobster traps and refrigerated trucks laden with fish. On the main street, art galleries and other shops alternate with auto parts stores and ship chandleries.

Stonington got its name and its early prosperity from the pink granite quarried here. The rocky islets in the harbor attest to the color of the stone, and small-scale quarrying continues today. Stonington calls itself 'the ideal coastal Maine village,' and is proud that it is 'a real place, with a real working harbor,' rather than a fantasy tourist village.

There's not much to do in Stonington, per se, but you'll enjoy it for what it is: a real town situated at the end of a finger-like peninsula. It's particularly beautiful at dusk and dawn, so you might consider staying here overnight. If dramatic light isn't enough to make you change your travel plans, a short walk around town should do it.

Sleeping

BUDGET

Sunshine Campground (☎ 207-348-2663; www.sunshine campground.com; 1181 Sunshine Rd, Sunrise; sites $22-26; ⊗ May-Oct) This heavily wooded campground with 21 sites, rental kayaks and water access is nearly 6 miles east of Deer Isle off ME 15.

Boyce's Motel (☎ 207-367-2421, 800-224-2421; www .boycesmotel.com; Main St, Stonington; r $60-115; ⊗ summer only) A cedar shake–covered hostelry that looks more like an inn, Boyce's rents simple but suitable rooms by the night and cottages by the week ($600 to $800).

Près du Port (☎ 207-367-5007; W Main St; r incl breakfast $80-100; ⊗ May-Oct) Just up the hill at the west end of Main St, this B&B has three harbor-view rooms, two with shared bathroom.

MID-RANGE & TOP END

Goose Cove Lodge (☎ 207-348-2508; www.goosecove lodge.com; Goose Cove Rd, Sunset; r incl breakfast $140-230; ⊗ mid-May–mid-Oct) Well off the beaten path, on a spruce-clad, granite-ledge cliff, Goose Cove is a tranquil hideaway where the sea rolls in over the ledges and the sounds of foghorns wake you up in the morning. Rooms are spread out over 20 acres so the property never feels overrun with guests. Rates include guided nature walks as well as bike and kayak usage. You never have to leave the property since the lodge also serves lunch on the outdoor deck (which has great water views) and fine dinners ($18 to $28 per main), such as pan-seared duck with a side of wild rice and orzo and drizzled with a raspberry demi-glace. Although it's not stuffy, you'll want to dress nicely here.

MAINE

Inn on the Harbor (☎ 207-367-2420, 800-942-2420; www.innontheharbor.com; Main St; r incl breakfast $110-130) Smack in the center of Stonington, this inn has 13 rooms, the least expensive of which face the street. (Waterside views are definitely worth the extra money.) The inn's seaside terrace, which serves breakfast, coffee and snacks, has the best harbor view in town – no question.

Eating

Pilgrim's Inn (☎ 207-348-6615; Main St, Deer Isle; prix fixe $37; ☺ dinner mid-May–mid-Oct) This inn's barn, converted to a rustic dining room, sets the stage for a lovely five-course event by candlelight. Non-inn guests are welcome for dinner but reservations are required.

Lily's Café (☎ 207-367-5936; cnr ME 15 & Airport Rd, Deer Isle; dishes $6-11; ☺ breakfast & lunch) Need to assemble a picnic? Lily's is a fine place to grab a quick sandwich, salad and homemade soup.

Harbor Café (☎ 207-367-5099; Main St, Stonington; mains $3-10; ☺ lunch & dinner) This humble diner, many a local fishermen's favorite, features a welcome list of sandwiches.

Fisherman's Friend Restaurant (☎ 207-367-2442; School St, Stonington; mains $10-18; ☺ 11am-9pm Tue-Sun late May–mid-Oct) Up the hill (away from the water) from Stonington village, Fisherman's Friend serves good, basic Maine seafood like chowder and fried or broiled fish.

Getting There & Away

From Blue Hill, take ME 176 west for 4 miles and then head south on ME 175/15 for 9 miles to Little Deer Isle. Continue through the village on ME 15 south to Deer Isle and keep going until you come to the end of the road in Stonington (about 10 miles from Little Deer Isle.) If you're eventually continuing north on US 1, from Stonington take ME 15 north to ME 172 north to US 1 (about 38 miles).

ISLE AU HAUT

pop 79

Much of Isle au Haut (that's pronounced aisle-a-ho), a rocky island 6 miles long, is under the auspices of Acadia National Park (p507). More remote than the parklands near Bar Harbor, it is not flooded with visitors in summer. Serious hikers can tramp the island's miles of trails and camp for the night in one of the five shelters maintained by the National Park Service (NPS).

For information on hiking and camping on Isle au Haut, contact **Acadia National Park** (☎ 207-288-3338; www.nps.gov/acad; PO Box 177, Bar Harbor, ME 04609; ☺ 8am-4:30pm). Reservations for shelters must be accompanied by payment; reservations for the summer season are not accepted before 1 April.

The **Isle au Haut Boat Company** (☎ 207-367-5193, 207-367-6516; www.isleauhaut.com; adult/child under 12 $16/8) operates daily (year-round) mail-boat trips from Stonington's Atlantic Ave Hardware Dock to the village of Isle au Haut. In summer, except on Sunday, at least three boats a day make the 45-minute crossing. On Sunday and major holidays, service is limited to one boat a day. Bicycles, motorcycles, boats and canoes (no cars) can be carried to the village of Isle au Haut for a fee. Parking in Stonington costs $9 to $11 per day.

MT DESERT ISLAND

From a traveler's point of view, Mt Desert Island is the holy grail of the 'down east' region. It's home to Bar Harbor – Maine's oldest summer resort – and most of Acadia National Park, the only national park in New England (p509). Because of its dramatic Maine scenery and outdoor sports possibilities, the national park is one of the state's most popular and busiest summer resorts. In fact, Acadia is among the most heavily visited national parks in the country.

Visitors come to the island, first and foremost, for the coastal vistas and spruce forests. They hike its 120 miles of trails, bike the 58 miles of unpaved carriage roads, and camp in the park's 500-plus campsites or stay in country inns. They also seek out the 200 species of plants, 80 species of mammals and 273 kinds of birds that live here.

Samuel de Champlain, the intrepid French explorer, sailed along this coast in the early 17th century. Seeing the bare, windswept granite summit of Cadillac Mountain, he called the island on which it stood l'Île des Monts Déserts. The name is still pronounced day-*zehr* almost 400 years later.

Orientation

The resort area of Bar Harbor and Acadia National Park extends from the town of Ellsworth, on US 1, to the southern tip of Mt Desert. The island's major town, Bar

Harbor, is situated on its northeast side, 20 miles southeast of Ellsworth. Acadia National Park covers the majority (but not all) of the island. It also includes tracts of land on the Schoodic Peninsula south of Winter Harbor, across the water to the east and on Isle au Haut, far to the southwest. You can reach Winter Harbor by ferry from Bar Harbor in summer (below); however, the Isle au Haut portion of the park is not easily accessible from Mt Desert Island.

Information

Acadia Area Association (55 West St, Bar Harbor; 10am-6pm Mon-Fri mid-May–mid-Oct) Has an official lodging office.

Acadia Information Center (207-667-8550, 800-358-8550; www.acadiainfo.com; early May–mid-Oct) This is your best bet for information and staff can also make lodging arrangements for you. It's located on your right (ME 3) just before you cross the bridge to Mt Desert Island.

Acadia National Park Information Office (Firefly Lane, Bar Harbor) This offers strictly walk-in service and is run by park rangers. It faces the town green.

Bar Harbor Chamber of Commerce (207-288-5103, 888-540-9990; www.barharbormaine.com; 93 Cottage St, Bar Harbor 04609; 8am-5pm Mon-Fri Jun-Sep, 8am-4pm off-season) Offers maps, guidebooks and general information about the entire region; It also maintains a small information office at 1 Harbor Pl by the Town Pier (which is open 9am to 5pm from mid-May to mid-October).

Hulls Cove Visitor Center (207-288-3338; www.nps .gov/acad; May-Oct) Sixteen miles south of Ellsworth and 3 miles north of Bar Harbor, this is Acadia National Park's visitor center. Off-season, head to Park Headquarters for information, which is 3 miles west of Bar Harbor on ME 233.

Nova Scotia Visitor Information Center (Bar Harbor) For information regarding Nova Scotia (Canada), stop here. It's next to the Criterion Theatre. For getting to Nova Scotia, see p504.

Port in a Storm (207-244-4114; www.portinastorm bookstore.com; 1112 Main St) In Somesville, west of Bar Harbor, you can browse for books in this tranquil setting.

BAR HARBOR

pop 4820

Bar Harbor is Maine's most popular summer resort. It's a very pleasant town of big old houses, some of which have been converted into inns and restaurants, creating a relaxed, but purposeful, way of life.

Bar Harbor was chartered as a town in 1796, while Maine was part of the Commonwealth of Massachusetts. In 1844, landscape painters Thomas Cole and Frederick Church came to Mt Desert and liked what they saw. They sketched the landscape and later returned with their art students. Naturally enough, the wealthy families who purchased their paintings asked Cole and Church about the beautiful land depicted in their paintings, and soon the families began to spend summers on Mt Desert. In a short time, Bar Harbor rivaled Newport, Rhode Island (RI), for the stature of its summer-colony guests. A rail line from Boston and regular steamboat service brought even more visitors. By the end of the 19th century, Bar Harbor was one of the eastern seaboard's most desirable summer resorts.

WWII damaged the tourist trade, but worse damage was to come. In 1947, a vast forest fire torched 17,000 acres of parkland, along with 60 palatial 'summer cottages' of wealthy summer residents, putting an end to Bar Harbor's gilded age. But the town recovered as a destination for the new mobile middle-class of the postwar years.

Although Mt Desert Island still has a number of wealthy summer residents, they are far outnumbered by common folk. There is an especially large contingent of outdoor-sports lovers.

Bar Harbor's busiest season is late June through August. There's a bit of a lull just before and just after Labor Day (early September), but then it gets busy again from foliage season through mid-October.

Orientation & Information

ME 3 approaches Bar Harbor from the north and the west, and it passes right through the town. Main St is the town's principal commercial thoroughfare, along with Cottage St. Mt Desert St has many of the town's inns, just a few minutes' walk from the Town Green.

See p503 for tourist information relating to Bar Harbor.

Activities
ROCK CLIMBING

With all that granite, Acadia National Park is a mecca for rock climbers.

If you're like to learn the sport, the **Atlantic Climbing School** (207-288-2521; www.acadiaclimb ing.com; 67 Main St; half/full day trips $100/180; May-Nov) offer guided trips and instruction.

Not to be outdone, **Acadia Mountain Guides** (207-288-8186; www.acadiamountainguides.com; 198 Main St; half/full day trips $100/190-250; May-Oct)

MAINE

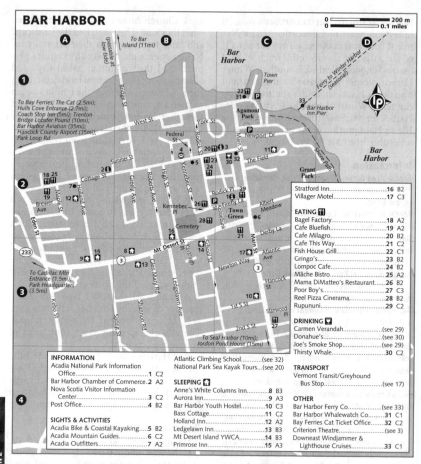

BAR HARBOR

give instruction and can take you to the best climbs.

Both companies have lower prices for groups of two or more.

GLIDING
Bar Harbor Aviation (☎ 207-667-7627; Hancock County-Bar Harbor Airport, ME 3; per couple $130-230; ☼ May-Oct) North of the Trenton Bridge, let your body and spirit take flight in a glider. You'll long remember soaring above Mt Desert Island. Call for reservations.

Tours
CRUISES
Without a doubt, Acadia National Park is the primary lure for visitors to the Bar Har-

bor area, but there are several other worthwhile things to do outside the park. A cruise on Frenchman Bay is one of them. Remember, it is often 20°F cooler on the water than on land, so bring a jacket, or sweater and windbreaker when you go cruisin'.

Bar Harbor Ferry (☎ 207-288-2984; www.down eastwindjammer.com; Bar Harbor Inn Pier; adult/child under 12 $24/15; ☼ mid-May-mid-Oct) Makes frequent one-hour trips to Winter Harbor. It's a nice place to bike, so consider taking your bike along; they cost only an additional $5 to transport.

Bar Harbor Whale Watch Co (☎ 207-288-2386, 800-508-1499; www.whalesrus.com; 1 West St; adult/child under 5/child 5-15 $39/8/25; ☼ Jun-Oct) Runs *Friendship V*, a 116ft steel vessel with three main engines, designed for whale-watching. The company also operates the *Acadian* (adult/child under five/child aged five to 15 $22/5/15), a steel-hulled, motor-driven sightseeing vessel that explores the islands on two-hour cruises with a naturalist.

Bay Ferries (☎ 207-288-3395; www.catferry.com; one-way tickets $45-55, autos $85-95, surcharge per car $15; ☯ Jun-Oct) Operates an ultrafast car ferry, *The Cat*, providing a maritime link between Bar Harbor and Yarmouth, Nova Scotia (Canada). On board, there are buffets, bars, duty-free shops and gambling devices such as slot machines. The voyage between Bar Harbor and Yarmouth takes just 2½ hours, so in a long day, you can cruise there and back, though an overnight stay makes more sense. You can purchase tickets at either the Cat ferry terminal west of Bar Harbor or at the Cat ticket office at the corner of Cottage and Main Sts.

Downeast Windjammer & Lighthouse Cruises (☎ 207-288-4585, 207-288-2373; www.downeastwind jammer.com;; adult/child under 12 $29.50/19.50; ☯ May-Oct) Has three two-hour cruises on the majestic 151ft, four-masted schooner *Margaret Todd*. They sure don't make ships like this anymore. Buy your tickets on the pier.

Sleeping

Bar Harbor has some 2500 guest rooms in dozens of motels and hotels. But the nicest places to stay are the rustic campgrounds of Acadia National Park and the snug Victorian B&Bs of Bar Harbor. The former is cheap, the latter expensive. In July and August, if you haven't made reservations in advance, finding a place in either type of accommodation can be difficult.

BUDGET
For camping in the Park, see p509. Commercial campgrounds are also located along ME 3 near Ellsworth and clustered near the entrances to the park. Numerous inexpensive motels, some charging as little as $60 a room in summer, also line ME 3 from Ellsworth to Bar Harbor. If everything in Bar Harbor is full, which often happens on weekends in the summer, you should be able to locate a motel room along ME 3 without a prior reservation. If you find yourself in this position, however, start your search by noon.

Mt Desert Island YWCA (☎ 207-288-5008; 36 Mt Desert St; s/d $30/35; ☯ year-round) This Y offers simple and safe lodging to women only, and also offers reductions for longer stays. To help folks stay in touch, the Y offers email on weekdays for $2 for a 15-minute session. It's an invaluable resource.

Villager Motel (☎ 207-288-3211, 888-383-3211; www.barharborvillager.com; 207 Main St; r $59-138; ☯ mid-May–Oct) Run by a 10th-generation Bar Harbor family, this spick-and-span motel is a block south of the Town Green and within walking distance of everything. Rates drop in late August.

Bar Harbor Youth Hostel (☎ 207-288-5587; www .barharborhostel.com; 321 Main St; d student/nonstudent $21/24; ☯ from 5pm mid-Jun–Aug) In a highly trafficked tourist town filled with relatively pricey beds, this hostel is much appreciated for its prices. Heck, just the fact that it exists at all, in such a prime location, is cause for celebration.

MID-RANGE
Holland Inn (☎ 207-288-4804; www.hollandinn.com; 35 Holland Ave; r incl breakfast $65-155) This restored 1895 farmhouse, within walking distance of town, is run by young and extremely personable innkeepers who offer five rooms and a great morning repast.

Stratford Inn (☎ 207-288-5189; www.stratfordinn .com; 45 Mt Desert St; r incl breakfast $75-175) An aptly named inn and built by a wealthy Boston publisher in 1900, the Stratford is a Tudor fantasy in the midst of Bar Harbor. It boasts big, airy rooms – you can't go wrong here.

Aurora Inn (☎ 207-288-3771, 800-841-8925; www .aurorainn.com; 51 Holland Ave; r Jun-Oct/off-season $109-149/59-99) Close to the Primrose Inn, this basic place is small, simple and well located.

Primrose Inn (☎ 207-288-4031, 877-846-3424; www.primroseinn.com; 73 Mt Desert St; r incl breakfast $85-215, per week efficiency $600-1150) This 1878 inn, with 11 rooms and four efficiencies, is particularly well kept.

Anne's White Columns Inn (☎ 207-288-5357, 800-321-6379; www.anneswhitecolumns.com; 57 Mt Desert St; r incl breakfast $100-150) This Georgian house with Greek-style columns has 10 tasteful rooms. As an added bonus, afternoon wine and cheese are offered.

TOP END
Most of the huge old 'summer cottages' in Bar Harbor along Mt Desert St have been converted to inns. They're pricey but lovely.

Bass Cottage (☎ 207-288-3705, 866-782-9224; www.basscottage.com; 14 The Field; r incl breakfast mid-Jun–mid-Oct/off-season $225-325/185-250; ☯ May-Oct) Hidden from the throngs but perfectly situated in the center of town, the c 1885

Bass Cottage has recently received a new lease of life. The 10 renovated rooms are awash with antiques, luxurious linens and soothing tones. They're fresh and inviting, without being weighed down by frilly Victorian decor found in many other period guesthouses.

Ledgelawn Inn (☎ 207-288-4596; 800-274-5334; www.barharborvacations.com; 66 Mt Desert St; r incl breakfast $95-295) Bar Harbor's most magnificent downtown inn is this vast Colonial-Revival 'summer cottage,' built in 1904 for a Boston shoe magnate. Well kept to this day, it exudes charm and grandeur and is yours for a price (which varies depending on the day and the room). Rates include afternoon tea.

Eating

Bar Harbor certainly has its fair share of places serving typical tourist fare; however, some local restaurants serve cuisine paralleling that served in Portland. Bar Harbor's most interesting dining possibilities are along Rodick, Kennebec and Cottage Sts.

BUDGET

Cafe Milagro (☎ 207-288-2882; 37½ Cottage St; dishes $1-5; ☒ May-Oct) Next to the Criterion Theatre, Cafe Milagro is good for a cappuccino, latte or mocha and pastries.

Gringo's (☎ 207-288-2326; 30 Rodick St; burritos $5-7, smoothies $4; ☒ lunch & dinner Jun-Oct, lunch daily & dinner Sat & Sun Nov-May) If you're in the mood for a quick, healthful burrito, there's no better place in town. It also serves a tantalizing array of refreshing smoothies.

LOBSTER, LOBSTER EVERYWHERE

The best place for a lobster picnic is one of the lobster pounds clustered north of Trenton Bridge on ME 3, about 6.5 miles south of Ellsworth on the road to Bar Harbor. At these places, a lobster dinner with steamed clams and corn or coleslaw should cost only $12 or so. Prices are usually posted on highway signboards.

The **Trenton Bridge Lobster Pound** (☎ 207-667-2977; ME 3, Ellsworth; dishes $9-20; ☒ lunch & dinner Mon-Sat May–mid-Oct) is the oldest and best of the lobster pounds, and has a pretty water-view picnic area at the north end of the causeway that leads to Mt Desert Island.

Bagel Factory (☎ 207-288-3903; 3 Cadillac Ave; bagels $2-7; ☒ 7am-2pm Tue-Sun) This hole-in-the-wall is the place to finagle a bagel in Bar Harbor. Several kinds of homemade bagels are served with interesting toppings.

MID-RANGE

Rupununi (☎ 207-288-2886; 119 Main St; dishes $5-16; ☒ lunch & dinner Apr-Jan) This place is well suited to families early in the evening because it offers good value standard American fare like burgers and pasta. Perhaps surprisingly, it also has the hottest bar in town upstairs, a cigar den downstairs, pool tables, and dancing with live music (see opposite).

Reel Pizza Cinerama (☎ 207-288-3828; 33B Kennebec St; pizza $9-15; ☒ films at 6 & 8:30pm almost nightly year-round) This place caters to the indulgent among us who like munching on good pizza, drinking local beer and lounging on couches while watching a nightly flick ($5) on the silver screen. Nice combination.

Lompoc Cafe (☎ 207-288-9392; 36 Rodick St; dishes $6-13; ☒ lunch & dinner) South of Cottage, this café has a short but eclectic, international menu – look for dishes like Indonesian peanut chicken, shrimp étouffée ($10 to $13) and ingenious pizzas (Greek, goats cheese etc, $6 to $8). You can also have a glass of Bar Harbor Real Ale. Blueberry ale may satisfy the intrepid. On most evenings, there's live entertainment (see opposite).

Mâche Bistro (☎ 207-288-0447; 135 Cottage St; mains $16-21; ☒ dinner Tue-Sat) Bar Harbor's premier restaurant, Mâche Bistro, serves cuisine that can best be described as New England–eclectic. Chef Chris Jelbert, a veteran line cook of Portland's Fore St (see p479), has been dazzling palates with an ever-changing menu. Start with appetizers like chilled sweet potato bisque ($6) but whatever you do, don't miss Chris' signature dish, luscious breast of duck with orange and ginger ($21).

Cafe Bluefish (☎ 207-288-3696; 122 Cottage St; mains $14-21; ☒ lunch & dinner May-Oct) This intimate storefront bistro offers tasty seafood creations like pecan-crusted salmon ($18) and Cajun-crusted swordfish ($10). Strangely, bluefish isn't on the menu.

Poor Boy's (☎ 207-288-4148; 300 Main St; mains $12-16; ☒ dinner) If you're really not sure what you want to eat, head here (there are 65 mains from which to choose!). But don't let the prices fool you: you can get huge servings of tasty dishes such as chicken marsala, or a five-course lobster dinner. It also has an extensive early-bird menu (4:30pm to 6pm).

TOP END

Cafe This Way (☎ 207-288-4483; 14 Mt Desert St; mains dinner $14-30; breakfast & dinner May-Oct) This casual, quirky eatery is *the* place for breakfast. Really. Try the Maine blueberry pancakes or eggs Benedict with smoked trout. Sit back, listen to smooth jazz, peruse one of the many books and chow down. It also serves fairly sophisticated dinners like seafood spring rolls and baked asiago cheese to start, followed perhaps by Maine crab cakes and cashew-crusted chicken.

Fish House Grill (☎ 207-288-3070; 1 West St; mains $7-25; lunch & dinner May-Jan) Down by the harbor, this seafood restaurant is usually busy because of its peerless pier location, which commands spectacular sunset views of the ocean and the pine-fringed coast. A pound of steamed mussels, or salmon oscar (grilled salmon with crabmeat and asparagus), are just two of many, many good choices.

Mama DiMatteo's Restaurant (☎ 207-288-3666; 34 Kennebec Pl; mains $14-29; dinner) This restaurant serves nouvelle Italian cuisine: sausage mushroom lasagne; shrimp sautéed with prosciutto, capers and olives and the like. If you're in the mood for a pre-dinner cocktail, one of its signature drinks is a Black Widow, which contains Blovod (black vodka) and cranberry juice.

Entertainment

Carmen Verandah (☎ 207-288-2886; 119 Main St; 11am-1am) The 2nd-floor terrace of Rupununi (opposite), with its festive atmosphere, is the place to dance and down a drink in Bar Harbor. It has pool tables, darts and a large dance floor on which to groove to the live music. Downstairs, there's Joe's Smoke Shop, an upscale cigar bar that often can be just as crowded as Carmen Verandah.

Lompoc Cafe (☎ 207-288-9392; www.lompoccafe .com; 36 Rodick St; May-Nov) This homey place hosts a variety of performers playing jazz, blues and folk on the patio. Check the signboard at the corner of Rodick and Cottage Sts for who's on and when. Cover charges vary.

Other good choices for a pint and live music include the **Thirsty Whale** (☎ 207-288-9335; 40 Cottage St) and **Donahue's** (☎ 207-288-3030; 30 Cottage St; May-Oct).

Getting There & Away

US Airways Express, operated by **Colgan Air** (☎ 800-428-4322; www.colganair.com), connects Bar Harbor and Boston with daily flights year-round. The Hancock County Airport is in Trenton, off ME 3, just north of the Trenton Bridge.

Vermont Transit/Greyhound (☎ 207-772-6587, 800-231-2222; www.vermonttransit.com; May-Oct) runs an early morning bus daily from Bar Harbor to Boston and NYC via Bangor and Portland. (Buses stop at the Villager Motel, 207 Main St.) Likewise, a bus starts out from NYC at breakfast time, reaches Boston by lunchtime and arrives in Bar Harbor by dinnertime.

For details on the ferries to Yarmouth, Nova Scotia, see p504.

ACADIA NATIONAL PARK

Acadia National Park, the only national park in all of New England, covers more than 62 sq miles and offers activities for everyone from the couch potato to the hyperactive sports enthusiast.

Orientation & Information

The park's main Hulls Cove entrance, which is northwest of Bar Harbor via ME 3, has a **visitor center** (☎ 207-288-3338; www.nps .gov/acad; 8am-4:30pm in summer), from where the 20-mile-long **Park Loop Rd** circumnavigates the northeastern section of Mt Desert island. It is a one-way road for much of its length.

The admission fee to the park costs $20 ($10 off-season) per vehicle and is good for seven consecutive days. The fee is collected at a booth on the Park Loop Rd, just north of Sand Beach. If you enter the park by bike or on foot, the fee is $10 ($5 off-season) per person.

You'll find other entrances to the park and the Park Loop Rd at the **Cadillac Mountain entrance** just west of Bar Harbor; the **Overlook entrance** south of Bar Harbor; and the **Stanley Brook entrance** east of Northeast Harbor.

Cadillac Mountain (1530ft), the highest point in the park, is a few miles southwest of Bar Harbor, and can be reached by auto road. Most of the carriage roads (closed to motor vehicles) are between Bubble Pond and Somes Sound, to the west of Cadillac Mountain.

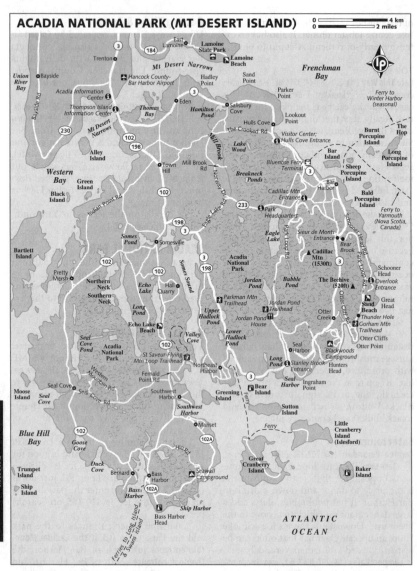

ACADIA NATIONAL PARK (MT DESERT ISLAND)

Call the visitor center for camping, road and weather information. For park emergencies, call ☎ 207-288-3369.

MAPS & GUIDES

Free NPS maps of the park are available at the information and visitor centers. Try and get a copy of the out-of-print *AMC Guide to* *Mt Desert Island & Acadia National Park* by the Appalachian Mountain Club, which has descriptions of all the trails, and a good trail map. *Acadia Revealed*, by Jay Kaiser, is perhaps the most comprehensive guidebook to the park on the market. You can pick up guides and maps at the visitor center (p507) and at bookshops in Bar Harbor.

Activities

TOURING HIGHLIGHTS

Start your tour with an orienting drive along the Park Loop Rd. On the portion called **Ocean Dr**, stop at **Thunder Hole**, south of the **Overlook entrance**, for a look at the surf crashing into a cleft in the granite. (The effect is most dramatic with a strong incoming tide.) **Otter Cliffs**, not far south of Thunder Hole, is basically a wall of pink granite rising right from the sea.

At **Jordan Pond**, there's a nice self-guided nature trail that runs right through middle of the trail and carriage road systems. Stop for tea and popovers (a puffy, hollow muffin-like creation) at **Jordan Pond House** (p510).

For a nice, easy hike, consider making the quick (20-minute) ascent of **The Beehive** near the Overlook entrance. For a slightly longer walk on the more-secluded 'backside' of the island, try the **St Saveur-Flying Mountain Loop Trail**, off Fernald Point Rd, just north of Southwest Harbor. Make sure you wear proper hiking boots (not sandals!) to avoid an injury.

For swimming, try either **Sand Beach** or **Seal Harbor** for chilly salt water, or **Echo Lake** for fresh water. Cyclists should park near Eagle Lake, off ME 233, and pedal on the **carriage paths** around the lake. Finish exploring atop the windy summit of **Cadillac Mountain**, which is quite popular with bands of hardy souls at sunrise.

OUTFITTERS

Acadia is great for all sorts of outdoor activities, including hiking, rock climbing, mountain biking, canoeing and sea kayaking. Numerous outfitters in Bar Harbor (most of which are located at the western end of Cottage street near ME 3) provide guide service, equipment for rent or sale and sports lessons. They include:

Acadia Bike & Coastal Kayaking (Map p504; ☎ 207-288-9605, 800-526-8615; www.acadiafun.com; 48 Cottage St; ☯ May-Nov for kayak and bike rentals, year-round for bike sales)

Acadia Mountain Guides (Map p504; ☎ 207-288-8186; www.acadiamountainguides.com; 198 Main St; ☯ May-Oct)

Acadia Outfitters (Map p504; ☎ 207-288-8118; 106 Cottage St; ☯ May-Oct)

National Park Sea Kayak Tours (Map p504; ☎ 207-288-0342; www.acadiakayak.com; 39 Cottage St; ☯ May-Oct)

Sleeping & Eating

There are three great and rustic campgrounds in the park: **Blackwoods Campground** (☎ 207-288-3338, 800-365-2267), open year-round, requires reservations in summer; **Seawall Campground**, open May through September, rents sites on a first-come, first-served basis; and **Duck Harbor**, on Isle au Haut, requires a special permit and is open mid-May to mid-October. No backcountry camping is allowed. There are also private campgrounds outside the park (see p505).

Coach Stop Inn (☎ 207-288-9886; www.coach stopinn.com; ME 3, Salisbury Cove; r $79-139) Five miles outside of Bar Harbor and just 2 miles from the main entrance to Acadia National Park, this is the oldest surviving area hostelry. It's a five-room inn, built in 1804 and set on 3 acres of gardens.

HOW IT ALL BEGAN

Mt Desert Island was already a booming summer resort for the wealthy by the late 19th century, but it was industrial development, ironically, that caused the creation of **Acadia National Park**. What? The invention of the 'portable sawmill' meant that the forests of the region could be stripped of trees for cheap lumber. In 1901, as a result of this threat, summer residents, led by Harvard University president Charles W Eliot, formed a land trust. Wealthy landowners donated land to the trust, and Acadia's extents grew. By 1916, the trust was a national monument, and in 1919, it became a national park.

John D Rockefeller also donated 10,000 acres of land toward the park. Alarmed at the prospect of the island being overrun with automobiles (as it now is on the regular roads), he ordered construction of 58 miles of one-lane, gravel-topped carriage roads throughout the park. The carriage roads, laid between 1918 and 1940, were to provide access to the park's more remote areas by horse-drawn carriage rather than automobile. Today, they're popular with hikers and mountain bikers.

MAINE

Jordan Pond House (☎ 207-276-3316; www.jordanpond.com; Park Loop Rd, Seal Harbor; mains $8-18; ❧ lunch, tea & dinner mid-May–mid-Oct) The only restaurant within Acadia National Park carries on the long tradition of fine and refined teahouses. It serves tea and delectable popovers with strawberry jam…outdoors, with tables set on a broad lawn, with mountain and water views. The memory will live on long after the popovers leave you. Jackets are suggested at dinner.

Getting There & Around

For information on getting to the island, see p507. A free shuttle system – the 'Island Explorer' – features eight routes that link hotels, inns and campgrounds to destinations within Acadia National Park. Route maps are available at local establishments and www.exploreacadia.com.

AROUND MT DESERT ISLAND

To really get the feel of this island, get out of Bar Harbor and slip into the quieter side, the side that lives closer to the sea. You'll long remember the faces of lobstermen, the smell of seaweed washed ashore, the fog rolling into yacht-laced harbors, the drama of Somes Sound. Armed with rented kayaks, canoes and mountain bikes (see p503), you'll undoubtedly end up here playing most of your time.

Do stop at little Bass Harbor, a classic fishing harbor that couldn't be more quaint precisely because it's so real. And while you're at it, stop for the freshest lobster you'll find anywhere at **Thurston's Lobster Pound** (☎ 207-244-7600; Steamboat Wharf; ❧ late May-Sep) – the lobster comes whole, in rolls, and in seafood stew. It's overlooking Bass Harbor in Bernard.

NORTHEAST HARBOR

One of Mt Desert Island's prime vacation villages, simply called 'Northeast,' has a marina chock-full of yachts. It also features a tiny main street populated with art galleries and boutiques and back streets dotted with mansions, and comfortable summer hideaways that are good for a short stay. It's a tranquil spot.

Information (☎ 207-276-5040; ❧ May-Oct) is available on the hill facing the marina.

Asticou Terraces & Azalea Garden (ME 3; admission by donation; ❧ 7am-7pm Jul-early Sep), designed in 1900, is simply lovely. This 200-acre garden is laced with paths, little shelters and ornamental Japanese-style bridges. Azaleas and rhododendrons bloom profusely from mid-May to mid-June. Don't neglect to wander up the garden's **Thula Lodge** (❧ 10am-5pm late Jun-early Sep), the depository of botanical books, where there's a reflecting pool and well-tended perennial gardens. The terraces zig-zag through the woods and down to the water.

SLEEPING & EATING

Asticou Inn (☎ 207-276-3344, 800-258-3373; www.asticou.com; ME 3; Jul-Aug s/d incl breakfast $150-250/225-285, d off-season $130-215; ❧ mid-May–mid-Oct; ☎) This famed summer hotel has been taking in guests since the late 1880s. It offers elegant common spaces, upwards of 50 rooms and suites, and tennis courts. It's the kind of place where patrons gather for afternoon cocktails rather than merely drinks.

Harbourside Inn (☎ 207-276-3272; www.harboursideinn.com; ME 3; r $125-225; ❧ mid-Jun–mid-Sep) They don't make 'em like this anymore: a shingle-style summer cottage dating from the 1880s with 14 rooms and suites, delightfully surrounded by woods. Most guest rooms have a fireplace; all are outfitted with comfortable antiques. But the real draw is the hospitality of the Sweets, longtime residents of the area who'll happily share their insiders' knowledge with you.

Docksider (☎ 207-276-3965; 14 Sea St; mains $11-20; ❧ 11am-9pm May-Oct) This beloved lobster shack is especially known for its crab cakes and crab sandwiches.

151 Main St (☎ 207-276-9898; 151 Main St; mains $14-21; ❧ dinner Tue-Sun May-Oct) This bistro, serving some of the island's best food outside of Bar Harbor, has an excellent white-clam pizza as well as a griddled beef and pork meatloaf. Whatever else you do, don't skip dessert!

SOUTHWEST HARBOR

pop 1966

More laid-back and less affluent than Northeast Harbor, 'Southwest' is also quite tranquil. But that's a bit deceiving: it's also a major boat-building center and a commercial fishing harbor.

From the Upper Town Dock – a quarter-mile along Clark Point Rd from the flashing light in the center of town – boats venture out into Frenchman Bay to the Cranberry Isles (see p511) and on whale-watching expeditions.

MAINE

SLEEPING & EATING

Claremont (☎ 207-244-5036, 800-244-5036; www .theclaremonthotel.com; Claremont Rd; r mid-Jun–mid-Sep/off-season $180-250/135-185; ☷ late May–mid-Oct) You may want to spend a bit more to stay here and gain access to the most stunning views from any hostelry in the area, where a wraparound porch and sloping broad lawns give way to boats bobbing in the ocean. This, the island's oldest and most graceful hotel, dates from 1884 and has 24 guest rooms decorated in period cottage-style furnishings. It's all lovingly maintained.

Penury Hall (☎ 207-244-7102, 866-473-6425; www.penuryhall.com; 374 Main St; r incl breakfast $75-100) This snug and longtime B&B, the first on Mt Desert Island, rents three rooms (all with private bathroom) in an 1865 schoolhouse. If you want a real taste of old-time Maine, not to mention a really filling breakfast, this is your place. The hosts are incredibly knowledgeable about area activities and lesser-known spots.

Beal's Lobster Pound (☎ 207-244-3202; 1 Clark Point Rd; mains $15-30; ☷ lunch & dinner mid-May–mid-Oct) For serious seafood sustenance and local atmosphere, everyone heads to Beal's. Grab a picnic table and dine on chowder, crabmeat rolls and – what else – lobster.

Restaurant XYZ (☎ 207-244-5221; Shore Rd, Manset; mains $10-17; ☷ lunch & dinner May-Oct) Across from the town dock, this eatery serves authentic Mexican dinners in a fabulous waterfront setting. Order dishes like chicken in a mole sauce and Yucatan-style pork, wash it down with margaritas and consider yourself lucky. You may not be south of the border physically, but you sure will be gastronomically.

FURTHER DOWN EAST

The 'Sunrise Coast' is the moniker given by Maine's tourism promoters for the area that lies east of Ellsworth, all the way to Lubec and Eastport. But to Mainers, this is far 'down east' Maine, the area downwind and east of the rest of the state. It's far, far less traveled, but more scenic and unspoiled. It's much more sparsely populated, slower-paced and more traditional than southcoast and mid-coast Maine. It also has denser coastal fog that creeps in for longer periods of time.

If you seek quiet walks away from the tourist throngs, coastal villages with little impact from tourism, and lower travel prices, explore the 900-plus miles of coastline east of Bar Harbor. But be mindful of the weather.

The best time to visit is July and August because of more dependable weather, but it's hauntingly beautiful in the late spring and early fall, too.

SCHOODIC PENINSULA

Thrusting itself deep into the Atlantic Ocean, the southern tip of this peninsula contains a quiet portion of Acadia National Park. It includes a 7.2-mile shore drive called Schoodic Point Loop Rd, which offers splendid views of Mt Desert Island and Cadillac Mountain. The one-way loop road is excellent for biking since it has a smooth surface and relatively gentle hills. The Fraser's Point park entrance also has a nice picnic area. Further along the loop, reached by a short walk from the road, you'll find Schoodic Head, a 400ft-high promontory with fine ocean views.

MAINE

DETOUR: ISLANDS OFF THE COAST OF THE ISLAND

Cranberry Isles (www.cranberryisles.com) is delightful primarily because it's so off the beaten path. The 400-acre Little Cranberry, more commonly known as **Islesford**, is about 20 minutes offshore from Southwest Harbor. Diversions include a few galleries, a couple of B&Bs and the **Islesford Market** (☎ 207-244-7667; ☷ Mon-Sat mid-Jun–early Sep), where the 80-some year-rounders and 400-some summer folk gather around like it's their own kitchen. Great Cranberry Island is even more low-key; stop in at the **Seawich Café & Cranberry Store** (☎ 207-244-5336) to see who's around and what's up.

Cranberry Cove Boating Co (☎ 207-244-5882; adult/child 3-12 $16/10; ☷ May-Oct) carries passengers to and from the Cranberry Isles aboard the 47-passenger *Island Queen*, which cruises six times daily in summer.

DETOUR: JONESPORT & GREAT WASS ISLAND

At the southern tip of the Schoodic peninsula, just over 4 miles from **Jonesport** (pop 1408), **Great Wass Island** is a standout, a 1540-acre nature reserve under the control of the **Nature Conservancy** (☎ 207-729-5181; www.tnc.org). In order to maintain the integrity of the reserve for those who most appreciate it, the way to it is not well marked. Parking at the trailhead is also limited, but the cars parked there bear license plates from many different states. This is a bird-watching reserve for the cognoscenti.

The reserve's attraction is its rocky coastal scenery, peat bogs, a large stand of jack pines, and bird life, including the amusing puffins. Try to make time for the 2-mile hike to Little Cape Point; it takes about 1½ to two hours, round-trip.

Jonesport and **Beals Island** are traditional Maine fishing and lobstering villages. Even the street signs show it: each one is topped with a carving of a Maine lobster boat. The towns get a smattering of the more discerning tourists during the summer season, most of whom come to take photographs, paint pictures and walk on Great Wass Island. Follow ME 187 to find most of these towns' services, including restaurants and lodgings.

Sleeping & Eating

Henry Point Campground (☎ 207-497-5926; Kelly Point; sites $15-18; ☻ Apr-Nov) On the point in Jonesport, this simple campground has only portable toilets, picnic tables and one big stone fireplace. But it's surrounded by water, and the semishaded sites have fine Maine coast views. To reach it from ME 187, head southeast on Kelley Point Rd, and thereafter, when in doubt, bear right.

Jonesport By the Sea Inn (☎ 207-497-2590, 888-315-4954; www.jonesportbythesea.bigstep.com; 200 Main St/ME 187; r $60-75) Across from the post office, this B&B has five homey, comfortable rooms, some of which have private bathrooms.

Harbor House on Sawyer Cove (☎ 207-497-5417; www.harborhs.com; Sawyer Sq, Jonesport; r $95-110) This old-time Maine B&B and antique shop has two rooms overlooking the harbor. You want a real glimpse of yesteryear Maine? Stay here.

Getting There & Away

To reach Great Wass Island, follow ME 187 into Jonesport. Look for the Union Trust Bank on the left and Tall Barney's Restaurant on the right. Turn left here onto Bridge St, cross the bridge and turn left. A little more than a mile further on, cross the small, inconspicuous bridge that connects Beals Island to Great Wass Island and turn right. A small 'Nature Conservancy' sign points the way. A mile later, the paved road ends, and after another 1½ miles on an unpaved road, you'll come to the Great Wass Island parking lot. It holds about a dozen cars. If the parking lot is full, please don't park on the road; the Conservancy sign suggests that you go away and come back some other time.

North of the peninsula, the little towns of Gouldsboro and Winter Harbor host tourist services like stores and restaurants. Yup, this is definitely the quieter part of Acadia, with fewer crowds – but also fewer activities. For information on local businesses, contact the **Schoodic Peninsula Chamber of Commerce** (☎ 207-963-7658; www.acadia-schoodic.org).

Ocean Wood Campground (☎ 207-963-7194; Schoodic Point Loop Rd; sites $20-30; ☻ seasonally), a pine-filled place that's more akin to a nature preserve than campground, is south of Birch Harbor and ME 186 and has ocean access.

THE MACHIASES
pop 4811

Although Machias proper hosts a branch of the University of Maine, it's not a place to spend any time. However, its beautiful neighbors, East Machias and Machiasport, are worthy of some attention. Machiasport, in fact, is where the first naval engagement of the Revolutionary War took place. After the king of England received the Declaration of Independence from the colonies, he sent a frigate to Machiasport to monitor the timely collection and transportation of lumber to Portland to build his ships. But a few drunken American colonists at **Burnham Tavern** (☎ 207-255-4432; Main St, East Machias; ⊗ 9am-5pm Mon-Fri Jul–mid-Sep) decided to pay the frigate a visit before they could reach shore. After killing the English captain with a single shot to the head, they emptied the ship and burned it on the shores of Jonesport. The king's reaction to this act of rebellion? He ordered his troops to torch Portland.

Don't miss **Jasper Beach**, a bizarre mile-long beach consisting entirely of polished red jasper stones. Listen to their strange song as the tide comes in. It's one of two such beaches in the world (the other is in Japan). To reach it, head down Machias Rd toward the village of Starboard.

The **Machias Bay Area Chamber of Commerce** (☎ 207-255-4402; www.machiaschamber.org; US 1, Machias, ME 04654; ⊗ 10am-4pm Mon-Fri Jun-Aug), next to Moore's Restaurant on the edge of town, provides lots of useful information.

Sleeping & Eating

Plenty of basic motels line US 1 in Machias. But the more serene East Machias and Machiasport have some nice B&Bs.

Machias Motor Inn (☎ 207-255-4861; 26 E Maine St/US 1; r $58-66; ⚛) Next to the landmark Helen's Restaurant, this place has 35 rooms overlooking the Machias River and has an indoor heated pool.

Captain Cates B&B (☎ 207-255-8812; www.captaincates.com; 309 Port Rd/ME 92, Machiasport; r incl breakfast $60-95) Overlooking Machias Bay, this 1850s B&B is furnished with period antiques and has six comfortable rooms with shared bathroom.

Riverside Inn & Restaurant (☎ 207-255-4134; www.riversideinn-maine.com; US 1, East Machias; r incl breakfast May-Oct/off-season $95-130/85-115) About 5 miles east of Machias' center, this large inn has only four guest rooms but it also has a restaurant with a good dinner menu (mains cost $17 to $22; BYOB).

Getting There & Away

From Ellsworth (the gateway to Bar Harbor), Machias is 64 miles north via US 1. From Gouldsboro (the gateway to the Schoodic Peninsula), it's 4 miles. East Machias is 4 miles further north on US 1; Machiasport is 3 miles east of Machias on ME 92.

LUBEC

pop 1652

Perched upon a hill overlooking four light-houses and Canada, this small fishing village makes its living off the trans-border traffic and a bit of tourism. Away from the crowds and traffic of Acadia National Park and surrounds, this is the real Downeast Maine. There's an informal information office in the foyer of the Eastland Motel, on the left-hand side of ME 189 as you roll into town.

Off US 1 at the end of ME 189, Lubec is sited on the US's easternmost border with Canada, 60 miles south of Calais and 88 miles northeast of Mt Desert Island. If you're continuing deep into Canada, pick up Lonely Planet's *Canada* guide.

Sights

QUODDY HEAD STATE PARK

Lubec is about as far east as you can go and still be in the US. People like to watch the sun rise at **Quoddy Head State Park** so they can say they were the first in the country to see it. The 531-acre park's trademark red-and-white-banded West Quoddy Light (1858) is its most photographed feature, but the volcanic bedrock, the subarctic bogland and the extreme tides – almost 16ft in six hours – are really more interesting. The park sports four hiking trails that vary in length from a few hundred feet to 4 miles. Also, you can usually spot finback, minke, humpback and right whales when they migrate here in summer.

OLD SARDINE VILLAGE MUSEUM

In the 1930s, Lubec was the fish-canning capital of the eastern US. The canneries are now long gone, but to see how it was done, drop by the **Old Sardine Village Museum** (adult/child $5/4; ⊗ 1-5pm Tue-Fri, 1-4pm Sun Jul & Aug).

CAMPOBELLO INTERNATIONAL PARK

Once beyond Lubec, you're in Canada, specifically on Campobello Island, home to **Roosevelt Campobello International Park** (☎ 506-752-2922; www.fdr.net; admission free; ⊗ cottage 9am-5pm, last tour at 4:45pm mid-May–mid-Oct, park open year-round). Franklin Roosevelt's father, James, bought land here in 1883 and built a palatial summer 'cottage.' The future US president spent many boyhood summers here, and he was later given the 34-room cottage. Franklin and Eleanor made brief, but well-publicized, visits during his long tenure as president.

MAINE

The park hours, by the way, are given in Eastern Standard Time (which is 10am to 6pm Atlantic Standard Time). Border formalities (p541) are quick and easy for American citizens in cars with US license plates who are crossing into Canada just to visit the park. Travelers from other countries should have their passports (and may need visas) to cross into Canada. The **Campobello Island Chamber of Commerce** (☎ 506-752-2233; ☒ 9am-6pm May-Oct) provides information on local services.

Sleeping & Eating

Home Port Inn (☎ 207-733-2077, 800-457-2077; www.homeportinn.com; 45 Main St; r incl breakfast $75-95; ☒ May-Oct) This hilltop inn, constructed in 1880 and converted to take in guests a century later, offers seven excellent rooms. Fortunately (as eating options are somewhat limited around here), the dining room serves fine dinners ($20 to $30).

Peacock House (☎ 207-733-2403, www.peacockhouse.com; 27 Summer St.; r incl breakfast $75-125; ☒ May-Oct) This house was built in 1860 by an English sea captain and completely restored in 1989. The fine B&B now offers five guest rooms.

South Bay Campground (☎ 207-733-1037; ME 189; sites $20-30; ☒ May-Oct) Just 7½ miles off US 1, this campground has 80 wooded and open field sites as well as a sea-kayak landing.

Murphy's (☎ 207-733-4440; ME 189; dishes $3-10; ☒ 6am-9pm) If you're up early, this local favorite is *the* place for breakfast, which is served all day. For lunch and dinner there's a range of vegetarian specials and a mix of America, Italian and Mexican dishes.

Eastland Motel (☎ 207-733-5501; ME 189; r $55-65) A mile west of Lubec on ME 189, this motel has simple but serviceable rooms with two double beds or a queen bed.

Getting There & Away

From Machias, head 17 miles north on US 1 then take ME 189 northeast for 11 miles to reach Lubec.

CALAIS

pop 3447

Further north of Lubec along US 1, Calais (pronounced cal-us) is a twin town to St Stephen, New Brunswick (Canada). During the War of 1812, when the US and Britain (including Canada) were at war, these two remote outposts of nationalism ignored the distant battles. Their citizens were so closely linked by strong family ties that politics – even war – was ignored.

The town has some interesting houses – some of them constructed in a 'gingerbread' style – strung along US 1, which itself is awash in the local pink granite that was mined in Calais. If you need to stay here for some reason, the tourist **information office** (☎ 207-454-2211; www.visitcalais.com; PO Box 368, Calais, ME 04619-0368, 15 Union St; ☒ 9am-5:30pm) can help.

Southwest of Calais, **Moosehorn National Wildlife Refuge** (☎ 207-454-7161; http://moosehorn.fws.gov; US 1, Baring; admission free; ☒ dawn-dusk) is America's easternmost breeding ground for migratory fowl. With binoculars you can spot numerous nests of America's national white-headed bird of prey, the bald eagle.

St Stephen is the gateway to Atlantic Canada, which is covered in Lonely Planet's *Canada* guide.

From Lubec, head southwest on ME 189 for 11 miles to US 1 at East Machias. Head north on US 1 for 55 miles to Calais; St Stephen is 3 miles across the Canadian border. The inland route from Lubec to Calais is shorter (39 miles) but less scenic. From East Machias take ME 191 north to ME 9 north to Calais.

INLAND MAINE

BANGOR

pop 31,473

Though Bangor figures prominently in present-day Maine, it's off the normal tourist routes. A boomtown during Maine's 19th-century lumbering heyday, Bangor was largely destroyed by a fire in 1911. Today, it's mostly a modern, working-class town, famous as the hometown of best-selling novelist Stephen King (see p516). Look for his appropriately spooky mansion – complete with a bat-and-cobweb fence – among the grand houses along W Broadway.

Information

Bangor Convention & Visitors Bureau (☎ 207-947-5205; www.bangorcvb.org; 1 Cumberland Pl; ☒ 8am-5pm Mon-Fri)

Bangor Region Chamber of Commerce (☎ 207-947-0307; www.bangorregion.com; 519 Main St, Bangor, ME 04402; ☒ 8am-5pm Mon-Fri)

Sights

The **Bangor Museum and Center for History** (☎ 207-942-5766; www.bangormuseum.org) has a Civil War museum in the **Thomas A Hill House** (159 Union St; adult/child under 18 $5/free; ✸ 10am-4pm Tue-Sat). The **Cole Land Transportation Museum** (☎ 207-990-3600; www.colemuseum.org; 405 Perry Rd; adult/child under 19/senior $6/free/4; ✸ 9am-5pm early-May–mid-Nov) has exhibits of antique vehicles and photographs.

Sleeping

BUDGET

Bangor Motor Inn (☎ 207-947-0355, 800-244-0355 in Maine & Canada; www.bangormotorinn.com; 701 Hogan Rd; r incl breakfast May-Oct/off-season $68-88/58-78) Lots of motels are located off I-95, close to the Maine Mall, but you'll save money if you drive beyond the obvious places adjacent to the exit. Having said that, of all the places near the highway, this one (with 103 rooms) offers the best value. It'll even grant discounts if business is slow.

Country Inn (☎ 207-941-0200, 800-244-3961; 936 Stillwater Ave; r $60-80) The fanciest modern hotel in town, up on the hill above Crossroads Plaza, offers reasonable prices and a convenient, yet quietish location.

Paul Bunyan Campground (☎ 207-941-1177; www.paulbunyancampground.com; 1862 Union St, Bangor; sites $15-27; ✸ Apr-Nov) On the outskirts of Bangor, this basic campground has 52 sites.

MID-RANGE

Charles Inn (☎ 207-992-2820; www.thecharlesinn .com; 20 Broad St; r incl buffet breakfast Jun-Aug/off-season $89-139/65-119) This inn offers 35 charming, tidy and renovated rooms. It's located in the central West Market Sq Historic District, which is an area of buildings dating from 1873 when Bangor was Maine's lumber capital. Look for the little park with a fountain and stainless steel sculpture at the intersection of Maine St at Broad and Hammond Sts and you will have found the hotel.

Eating & Drinking

Options are limited to national chain restaurants near I-95 (exit 49) and a few family-owned places in the center.

Sea Dog Brewing Co (☎ 207-947-8009; 26 Front St; dishes $6-20; ✸ 11:30am-1am) This spacious restaurant/pub/nightspot serves sophisticated pub food ($6 to $12) as well as traditional dishes, but stick to the sandwiches, burgers and snacking. As for its fresh, award-winning homemade brews, the fruity wheat ale and Old Gollywobbler brown ale are well worth a try. It's a relaxing place to hang out.

Cafe Nouveau (☎ 207-942-3338; 86 Hammond St; dishes $8-15; ✸ lunch & dinner Tue-Sat) Mostly a wine bar, this place serves excellent tapas-style dishes like lime and cilantro salmon ($10) or duck breast with honey, ginger and lavender ($12). It also has a retail component, the Bangor Wine & Cheese Co.

Whig & Courier (☎ 207-947-4095; 18 Broad St; mains $5-11; ✸ lunch & dinner) This restaurant serves good, cheap pub grub and good pints.

Getting There & Away

Bangor International Airport (☎ 207-947-0384; www.flybangor.com) is served by regional carriers associated with Continental, Delta and US Airways.

Vermont Transit (☎ 207-945-3000, 800-231-2222; www.vermonttransit.com; 158 Main St), at the Bangor Bus Terminal, runs four direct buses daily between Bangor and Boston via Portland and Portsmouth, New Hampshire. **Concord Trailways** (☎ 800-639-3317; www.concordtrailways.com; Trailways Transportation Center, 1039 Union St) has three more, as well as service along the Maine coast to Portland. For more detailed bus routes, see p480.

AUGUSTA

pop 18,560

Maine's capital city is small: there's no doubt about that. Founded as a trading post in 1628, it was later abandoned, then resettled in 1724 at Fort Western (later Hallowell). Lumber, shingles, furs and fish were its early exports to the world, sent down the Kennebec River in sloops built right here. Augusta became Maine's capital in 1827, but was only chartered as a city in 1849. Aside from its museum and some monumental public buildings, there aren't many reasons to venture here. If you happen to be passing by, stop at the Maine State Museum, admire the capitol and browse the antique shops in neighboring, rustic **Hallowell**.

Orientation

Memorial Circle, near the state capitol, is this city's traffic nexus. (US 202, US 201,

MAINE

STEPHEN KING – A REGULAR MAINE-IAC

Master of the macabre and recipient of the 2003 National Book Foundation Medal, Stephen King is a remarkably normal husband and father. He is also a native and lifelong resident of Maine. Born in Portland in 1947, he was the second son of Donald and Nellie King. When his father abandoned the family, his mother took the boys to live temporarily in other states. Eventually they returned to Maine, where King began his fledgling writing career by producing, along with his brother David (now an appliance repairman in New Hampshire), a Mimeographed newspaper called *Dave's Rag*. They sold it for 5¢ a copy. His mother kept the family together by working at Pineland, a residential facility for the mentally challenged in Durham, Vermont.

King graduated from Lisbon Falls High School in 1966, after what he termed an undistinguished academic career. It was marked in 1965 by his first publication, a story called *I was a Teenage Grave Robber*. Let the strangeness begin. He attended the University of Maine, Orono, on scholarship and there enjoyed his first paid publication – $35 for *The Glass Floor*.

King graduated from the University of Maine in 1970 with a BA in English and a teaching certificate. He then proceeded to write while performing a variety of jobs, including pumping gas and being a janitor. He looked for teaching work and avoided the draft – thanks to high blood pressure, poor vision and flat feet – and occasionally sold short stories, mostly to men's magazines.

In 1971, he married college girlfriend Tabitha Spruce and they moved to Hermon, west of Bangor, so Stephen could teach at Hampden Academy. His grand salary of $6400 annually provided a subsistence lifestyle but not much more. Tabitha steadfastly aided King's ambition to write, even famously fishing a manuscript of *Carrie* out of the trash and encouraging him to keep working on it. Her rumored reward when King netted $200,000 from the sale of the paperback rights? He bought her a hairdryer.

Although he now splits his time between Maine and Florida, King's Maine roots run deep and he and his wife provide scholarships for local high school students, as well as contributing to many local charities. Many of King's books and stories are based in Maine, although frequently in fictional towns. In fact, his official website, www.stephenking.com, boasts a rendering of what Maine would look like, if mapped as in King's fiction.

ME 8, ME 11, ME 17, ME 27 and ME 100 all intersect at this large traffic circle.)

Augusta's traditional commercial district sits on the eastern bank of the Kennebec River. Western Ave runs from Memorial Circle due west 1.5 miles to I-95 exit 30; most of Augusta's motels are here. Three miles northwest of town, at I-95 exit 31, you'll find the University of Maine at Augusta, the Augusta Civic Center, the Mall at Augusta, the Kennebec Valley Chamber of Commerce and more chain motels. Water St (US 201/ME 27) runs south from Memorial Circle, past the capitol, to Hallowell. With attractive shops, cafés and restaurants, Hallowell is the pretty appendage of Augusta.

Information

Kennebec Valley Chamber of Commerce (☎ 207-623-4559; www.augustamaine.com; University Dr, Augusta, ME 04332-0676; ☺ 8:30am-5pm Mon-Fri) At I-95 exit 31.

Sights
STATE HOUSE
Built in 1832 and enlarged in 1909, the granite **State House** (☎ 207-287-2301; www.maine.gov; cnr State & Capitol Sts; admission free; ☺ 9am-5pm Mon-Fri) was designed by the famed Boston architect Charles Bulfinch. You can pick up a leaflet for a self-guided tour, or pick up a red courtesy phone and request a free guided tour. Park in the lot on the southwest side of the building, near the Department of Education and Maine State Museum, and enter the capitol through the southwest door.

MAINE STATE MUSEUM
By all means, take a gander within the **Maine State Museum** (☎ 207-287-2301; www.mainestatemuseum.com; 83 State St; adult/child under 6/child 6-18 $2/free/1; ☺ 9am-5pm Tue-Fri, 10am-4pm Sat), ensconced in the Maine State Library and Archives adjacent to the State House. The museum traces Maine's history through an astounding 12,000 years and includes pre-

historic arrowheads and tools, as well as artifacts from more recent centuries.

OLD FORT WESTERN
Located in its own riverside park, **Old Fort Western** (☎ 207-626-2385; www.oldfortwestern.org; 16 Cony St; adult/child 6-16 $5/3; 🕑 10am-4pm Mon-Fri, 1-4pm Sat & Sun Jul-early Sep, call for off-season hrs) was originally built as a frontier outpost in 1754. The restored 16-room structure, now a museum, is New England's oldest surviving wooden fort.

BLAINE HOUSE
The centrally located **Blaine House** (☎ 207-287-2121; 192 State St; admission free; 🕑 2-4pm Tue-Thu), once the family home of US presidential candidate James G Blaine, is now Maine's governors' mansion, and worth a looksee.

Sleeping
Lodging prices are wonderfully low in this nontouristy town.

BUDGET
Motel 6 (☎ 207-622-0000; www.motel6.com; 18 Edison Dr; r $40-55) This chain motel offers the best value in town; children aged 17 and under stay for free with their parents.

MID-RANGE
Maple Hill Farm B&B (☎ 207-622-2708, 800-622-2708; www.maplebb.com; Outlet Rd, Hallowell; r incl breakfast Jun-Sep/off-season $95-185/80-170) For more attractive surroundings, take I-95 exit 30 for US 202 West, then immediately turn left onto Whitten Rd and follow the signs. Hosted by Maine (state) Senator Scott Cowger, this late-Victorian B&B is set on 130 acres of rolling hayfields and marked by trails ripe for exploration. Many guest rooms have whirlpool tubs and fireplaces.

Best Western Senator Inn & Conference Center (☎ 207-622-5804, 877-772-2224; www.bestwestern.com; 284 Western Ave; r $120-150) This classy, business-oriented place has big, comfortable and luxurious rooms.

Eating
A cluster of fast-food chain restaurants is located at I-95 exit 30, but for more interesting food, cruise Water St/US 201/ME 27, south of the capitol in Hallowell.

Thai Riverview Restaurant (☎ 207-622-2638; 272 Water St, Hallowell; mains $8-12; 🕑 lunch & dinner)

This very decent Thai restaurant has nice views overlooking the Kennebec River.

CJ's Pizza (☎ 207-626-2906; 339 Water St, Hallowell; dishes $5-16; 🕑 lunch & dinner) Serves the cheapest sandwiches, pasta plates and pizzas in town.

Getting There & Away
Augusta is 23 miles north of Wiscasset. **Greyhound** (☎ 207-622-1601; www.greyhound.com) buses stop at Augusta State Airport.

WESTERN LAKES & MOUNTAINS

Western Maine receives far fewer visitors than coastal Maine, which thrills the outdoorsy types who love western Maine the way it is. The fine old town of Bethel and the outdoor pleasures of the Rangeley Lakes are relatively accessible to city-dwellers in Boston, Providence and New York. Bethel is also very close to the White Mountain National Forest in New Hampshire and Maine.

Perhaps surprisingly, the mountains of western Maine yield an abundance of gemstones, such as amethyst, aquamarine and tourmaline. Keep your eyes open for gem shops.

SEBAGO LAKE
pop 1433
Sebago, a mere 15 miles northwest of Portland, is one of Maine's largest and most accessible lakes. Small settlements dot the eastern shore, which is best reached by US 302 from Portland. The town of Sebago Lake, at the lake's southern end, is small and sleepy. East Sebago (on the lake's western shore!) has a few inns and cabins for rent.

Sebago Lake State Park (☎ 207-693-6613; 🕑 May-Oct), on the northern tip of the lake, offers camping, picnicking, swimming, boating and fishing.

From Portland take US 302 west to South Casco (28 miles) and Naples (which is 7 miles further).

BETHEL
pop 2411
For a small farm town surrounded by Maine woods, Bethel, 63 miles northwest of Portland via ME 26, is surprisingly beautiful

MAINE

DETOUR: THE LAST SHAKERS

Take I-495 exit 11, then ME 26 to reach the town of **Sabbathday Lake** (30 miles north of Portland), near the lake of the same name. Sabbathday has the nation's only active **Shaker community** (☎ 207-926-4597; www.shaker.lib.me.us; adult/child $6.50/2; ☽ 2hr guided tours 10am-4:30pm Mon-Sat late May–mid-Oct). It was founded in the 18th century, and a small number of devotees (perhaps four or five) keep the Shaker tradition of prayer, simple living, hard work and fine artistry alive (for more on the Shaker sect and its beginnings, see the boxed text on p269).

Among the plain white, well-kept buildings of the community are a welcome center, museum, and shop selling the community's crafts. Most other buildings, including the impressive Brick Dwelling House, are not open to visitors.

A few miles to the north is the village of **Poland Spring** that's famous for its mineral water, which is now sold throughout the US. In the early 19th century, a visitor was miraculously cured by drinking water from Poland Spring. Not known to miss a good thing, the locals opened hotels to cater to those wanting to take the waters.

---

and refined. It's a prime spot to be during Maine's colorful fall foliage season and during the winter ski season. Part of its backwoods sophistication comes from being the home of Gould Academy, a well-regarded prep school founded in 1836.

The town is small enough that you can find your way around easily. Just in case, though, the **Bethel Area Chamber of Commerce** (☎ 207-824-2282; www.bethelmaine.com; 8 Station Pl, PO Box 1247, Bethel, ME 04217; ☽ 9am-6pm Mon-Fri year-round, 10am-6pm Sat & Sun Nov-Apr) maintains an information office in the Bethel Station building. The Evans Notch Ranger Station of the **White Mountain National Forest** (☎ 207-824-2134; 18 Mayville Rd/US 2; ☽ daily in summer, weekends in winter) is loaded with good information about hiking, camping and every conceivable kind of area recreation.

Sights & Activities
DR MOSES MASON HOUSE
Stop by this historic **house** (☎ 207-824-2908, 800-824-2910; www.bethelhistorical.org; 10-14 Broad St; adult/child 6-12 $3/1.50; ☽ 1-4pm Tue-Sun Jul & Aug), now the research library of the Bethel Historical Society, to glimpse how a prominent local physician and state representative lived during the mid-1800s.

SUMMER SPORTS
You can **golf** at the Bethel Inn & Country Club (see opposite), take scenic drives, and hike in the nearby forests. The **Mt Will Trail** starts from US 2, east of Bethel, and ascends to mountain ledges with fine views of the Androscoggin Valley. **Grafton Notch State Park**, north of Bethel via ME 26, of-fers hiking trails and pretty waterfalls, but no camping. Try the park's 1.5-mile trail up to Table Rock Overlook, or the walk to Eyebrow Loop and Cascade Falls, with excellent picnicking possibilities right by the falls.

If you head west on US 2 toward New Hampshire, be sure to admire the **Shelburne birches**, a high concentration of the white-barked trees that grow between Gilead and Shelburne.

Bethel Outdoor Adventure & Campground (☎ 207-824-4224, 800-533-3607; www.betheloutdoor adventure.com; 121 Mayville Rd/US 2; ☽ May-Oct) rents canoes, kayaks and bicycles, and it arranges lessons, guided trips and shuttles to and from the Androscoggin River. **Wild River Adventures** (☎ 207-824-2608; 288 Vernon St; ☽ May-Oct) offers similar services.

Mahoosuc Mountain Sports (☎ 207-875-3786; ME 26, Locke Mills) rents mountain and road bikes for seasonal excursions into the nearby countryside. It also sells ski equipment year-round.

WINTER SPORTS
The mountains near Bethel are home to several major New England ski resorts.

Sunday River Ski Resort (☎ 207-824-3000; www .sundayriver.com; Sunday River Rd, Bethel), 6 miles north of Bethel along ME 5/26, boasts eight mountain peaks and 128 trails. It's regarded as one of the region's best family ski destinations.

Mt Abram (☎ 207-875-5003; www.skimtabram.com; Howe Hill Rd, Locke Mills) is a small, very family-friendly and reasonably priced ski area with 42 trails just southeast of Bethel.

MAINE

Sleeping

For its small size, Bethel has a surprising number of places to stay. This is because it's a crossroads town at the junction of routes between the Maine coast, northern Maine and New Hampshire. Bethel has only one motel in the town center, but most others are located along US 2 to the north. Prices listed below are for the summer, but during the ski season, prices are higher; ask about ski and meal packages when making winter reservations.

The Bethel Chamber of Commerce operates the **Bethel Area Reservations Service** (☎ 800-442-5826; www.bethelmaine.com), which can help with rooms.

BUDGET

There are five simple public campgrounds, with well water and toilets, in the Maine portion of the White Mountain National Forest: Basin Pond, Cold River, Crocker Pond, Hastings and Wild River. For more information, contact the **Evans Notch Visitor Center** (☎ 207-824-2134; 18 Mayville Rd/US 2; www .fs.fed.us/r9/white/; ☑ 8am-4:30pm Mon-Fri).

Chapman Inn (☎ 207-824-2657, 877-359-1498; www.chapmaninn.com; 1 Mill Hill Rd; dm/r $33/69-109) Among the nicest, most economical and best-located lodgings, Chapman Inn has a 24-bed dorm and nine rooms for singles, couples and families; the cheaper rooms have shared bathrooms.

Holidae House B&B (☎ 207-824-3400, 800-882-3306; 85 Main St; r $40) This Victorian has two intimate rooms with private bathrooms; a studio apartment; and a three-bedroom apartment.

Stony Brook Recreation (☎ 207-824-2836; www .stonybrookrec.com; US 2, Hanover; sites $16-22) With 100 acres of forest along the Androscoggin River, this great site is east of Bethel. Most sites offer lean-tos to provide shelter from wet weather.

MID-RANGE

Sudbury Inn & Suds Pub (☎ 207-824-2174, 800-395-7837; www.sudburyinn.com; 151 Main St; r/apt $74-134/275-350) The town's unofficial social center has 18 guest rooms, a restaurant and pub. Within the late-19th-century Victorian house and adjacent carriage house, you'll find simple but attractive rooms. The apartments sleep up to eight people each.

Norseman Inn & Motel (☎ 207-824-2002, 800-824-0722; www.norsemaninn.com; 134 Mayville Rd/US 2; motel r $58-138, inn r $78-148) Choose between rooms in a 200-year-old inn, a renovated century-old barn, or the more modern (and air-con) motel.

Briar Lea Inn & Restaurant (☎ 207-824-4717, 877-311-1299; www.briarleainn.com; 150 Mayville Rd/US 2; r incl breakfast $79-129) This 150-year-old Georgian farmhouse has a variety of unpretentious and well-cared-for rooms.

TOP END

Bethel Inn & Country Club (☎ 207-824-2175, 800-654-0125; www.bethelinn.com; Broad St; r $258-458; ☒) Dominating the town common, this establishment boasts fully fledged resort facilities like an 18-hole golf course designed by Geoffrey Cornish, a golf school, tennis, an outdoor heated swimming pool, saunas, workout and game rooms and a lake boathouse. They're all set on manicured grounds. Rates depend on when you come, how long you stay and which of the several degrees of luxury you choose, but all rates include breakfast and dinner.

River View Resort (☎ 207-824-2808; www.river viewresort.com; 357 Mayville Rd; ste $100-255; ☒) Geared toward families who might settle in for a long weekend and for couples, this place has 32 very comfortable, modern, two-bedroom suites with fully equipped kitchens. As for the so-called resort amenities, look for a tennis court, spa, sauna and game room. Suites sleep up to five people.

Eating & Drinking

Bethel doesn't have a lot of restaurants from which to choose, but a surprising number of them have good vegetarian dishes.

MID-RANGE & TOP END

Cafe DiCocoa (☎ 207-824-5282; 125 Main St; lunch $7-11; ☑ breakfast & lunch) This café features good coffee (and espresso), wholegrain baked goods and vegetarian lunches that are also available to go.

Sunday River Brewing Company (☎ 207-824-4253; cnr US 2 & Sunday River Rd; lunch $8-12, dinner $14-25; ☑ lunch & dinner) Bethel's brewpub features a half-dozen of its own brews (from a light golden lager to a black porter), as well as a variety of sandwiches, steaks, barbecued meats and vegetarian plates for lunch and dinner.

MAINE

Sudbury Inn (☎ 207-824-2174; 151 Main St; mains $18-30; ☺ inn dinner Thu-Sat, pub dinner nightly) This inn (see p519) has a cozy dining room upstairs with an excellent menu. But the downstairs Suds Pub is more fun and features a tavern menu (with great pizzas!), a huge selection of draft and bottled beers – many from Maine microbreweries – and, on some nights, live entertainment.

Briar Lea Inn & Restaurant (☎ 207-824-4717; 150 Mayville Rd/US 2; breakfast $4-10, dinner $15-30; ☺ breakfast & dinner) Attention skiers: when you want or need breakfast to be the main event of the day, Briar Lea delivers with bounty and choice.

SS Milton (☎ 207-824-2589; 43 Main St; lunch $6-11, dinner $12-24; ☺ lunch May-Oct, dinner) A local favorite, this place has an innovative menu, decent prices and nice outdoor seating in good weather.

Getting There & Away
From Naples (on Lake Sebago), take US 302 east for 2 miles to ME 11 north. Head 14 miles north to ME 26 west and continue another 36 miles to Bethel. If you're heading into the White Mountains of New Hampshire (see p442), take US 2 east from Bethel towards Gorham (22 miles) and head south to North Conway (p452).

RANGELEY LAKE & AROUND
pop 1200

From Bethel to Rangeley Lake, along the 67-mile route via US 2 and ME 17, the road climbs through country that's exceptionally beautiful – even for Maine. During the early 20th century, the lakes in this region were dotted with vast frame hotels and peopled with vacationers from Boston, New York and Philadelphia. Though most of the great hotels are gone – victims of changed economics and vacation preferences – the reasons for spending time here remain.

The **Rangeley Lakes Chamber of Commerce** (☎ 207-864-5364, 800-685-2537; www.rangeleymaine .com; Main St, Rangeley, PO Box 317, Rangeley, ME 04970; ☺ 9am-5pm Mon-Sat) can answer questions.

Activities
SKIING
The mountains around Rangeley offer a few skiing and snowboarding options.

Sugarloaf (☎ 207-237-2000, 800-843-5623; www .sugarloaf.com; ME 16, Kingfield) is good for down-hill skiing and snowboarding; its lifts whisk you above the tree line in no time.

Sugarloaf Outdoor Center (☎ 207-237-6830; www.sugarloaf.com/nordic; ME 27/ME 16, Carrabassett Valley), near Sugarloaf, has 136 miles of groomed cross-country trails.

Saddleback Ski Area (☎ 207-864-5671; www .saddlebackmaine.com; Rangeley), at 4120ft, has 40 alpine ski trails with seven lifts and three T-bars. Call for lodging information.

Sleeping
In the village of Rangeley proper, a few vestiges of the region's early-20th-century heyday remain.

North Country Inn B&B (☎ 207-864-2440; www .northcountrybb.com; Main St; r incl breakfast $96-106) Constructed by Rangeley's first multimillionaire, this gorgeous 1912 house – which faces the town park and lake – was a speakeasy during America's Prohibition days.

Rangeley Inn & Motor Lodge (☎ 207-864-3341, 800-666-3687; www.rangeleyinn.com; 51 Main St; r $84-129) Built in 1907, this spacious motel still hosts guests in 35 inn rooms and 15 motel rooms.

Country Club Inn (☎ 207-864-3831; www.range leyme.com/ccinn; 1 Country Club Dr; d incl breakfast $114) Off ME 4, this inn has 20 rooms with views of Rangeley Lake and is next to the public golf course.

NORTH WOODS

On a map, it appears as if the further north you go in Maine, the fewer roads there are. You'd think this is trackless wilderness. In fact, this vast area is owned by large paper companies that harvest timber for their paper mills. The land is crisscrossed by a series of rough logging roads. Logs used to be floated down the region's many rivers, but this practice increased the tannin levels in the rivers and threatened the ecological balance. Roads came with the advent of the internal combustion engine.

Now that logs are out of the rivers, white-water rafters are in them. The **Kennebec River**, below the Harris Hydroelectric Station, passes through a dramatic 12-mile gorge that's one of the US's prime rafting locations (see p521). Outflow from the hydroelectric station is controlled, which means that there is always water, and the

KENNEBEC RIVER RAFTING TRIPS

The villages of **Caratunk** and **The Forks**, south of Jackman via US 201, are both at the center of the Kennebec rafting area. White-water rafting trips down the Kennebec and nearby rivers are wonderful adventures. Trips cost from $80 to $115 per person and are suitable for everyone from children (ages eight and older) to seniors in their 70s. No experience is necessary for many trips.

Reserve your rafting trip in advance and bring a bathing suit, wool or polar fleece sweater, windbreaker or rain suit. Avoid cotton clothing (such as T-shirts and jeans), because cotton dries slowly and will make you feel cold; synthetics are better. Wear more clothing than you think you'll need, and bring a towel to dry off with and a dry change of clothes for the end of the trip. Sneakers or other soft-soled footwear are required in the inflatable rafts. Before 30 June and after 1 September, a wetsuit may be required because of cold water temperature. (Rafting companies often rent the suits and booties.)

Numerous companies run organized rafting trips, which includes lodgings on the Kennebec, Dead or Penobscot Rivers. Rafting companies supply the raft, paddles, life vest, helmet, life preserver and first-aid kit. There will be a pre-trip orientation meeting with instruction about rafting and white-water safety. Your rafting company usually provides lunch (often grilled on the riverbank) as well. Trips range in difficulty from Class II (easy enough for children aged eight and older) to Class V (intense, difficult rapids, with a minimum age of 15).

Most rafting companies have agreements with local lodgings (inns, dorms and campgrounds) for your accommodations. Ask about their inclusive rafting packages.

A reliable area standby if you don't book through a rafting company is the **Inn by the River** (☎ 207-663-2181; www.innbytheriver.com; US 201, HCR 63, Box 24, West Forks, ME 04985; r incl breakfast $75-160), a modern lodge overlooking the river, which has very comfortable rooms.

Rafting companies we recommend:

- **Crab Apple Whitewater** (☎ 207-663-4491, 800-553-7238; www.crabapplewhitewater.com; HCR 63, Box 25, The Forks, ME 04985), which also runs trips on rivers in western Massachusetts.
- **Maine Whitewater** (☎ 800-345-6246; www.mainewhitewater.com; PO Box 633, Bingham, ME 04920)
- **New England Outdoor Center** (☎ 207-723-5438, 800-766-7238; www.neoc.com; PO Box 669, Millinocket, ME 04462), which also runs canoe trips on the Allagash Wilderness Waterway.
- **Northern Outdoors** (☎ 207-663-4466, 888-770-7533; www.northernoutdoors.com; Old Canada Rd, National Service Byway, Rte 201, PO Box 100, The Forks, ME 04985), which runs rafting, mountain-biking, fishing and sea-kayaking trips in Maine.
- **Professional River Runners of Maine** (☎ 207-663-2229, 800-325-3911; www.proriverrunners.com; PO Box 92, West Forks, ME 04985), which also runs rafting trips on other rivers in the eastern US.
- **Three Rivers Whitewater, Inc** (☎ 800-786-6878; www.threeriverswhitewater.com; PO Box 10, West Forks, ME 04985), which also runs rafting trips on the Rapid River.

periodic big releases make for more exciting rafting.

The **Kennebec Valley Tourism Council** (☎ 800-393-8629; www.kennebecvalley.org; 21 University Dr, Augusta, ME 04901; ☽ 8:30am-5pm Mon-Fri) will help with information.

Maine sporting camps – those remote forest outposts for hunters, fishers and other deep-woods types – still flourish in the most remote regions. For information, contact the **Maine Sporting Camp Association** (☎ 207-723-6622; www.mainesportingcamps.com; PO Box 119, Millinocket, ME 04462).

MOOSEHEAD LAKE

pop 1623 (Greenville)

North of Greenville, Moosehead Lake is huge. In fact, it is the largest lake completely contained within any one New England state. (Lake Champlain is bigger, but it's split between Vermont, New York and Canada). This is lumber and backwoods country, which is why **Greenville** is the region's largest seaplane station. Pontoon planes will take you even deeper into the Maine woods for fishing trips. Though once a bustling summer resort, Greenville has

MAINE

reverted to a backwoods outpost. A few of the old summer hotels survive, but most of the visitors today are camping or heading through on their way to Baxter State Park and Mt Katahdin.

For more regional information, contact the **Moosehead Lake Region Chamber of Commerce** (☎ 207-695-2702; www.mooseheadlake.org; ME 15, Greenville, PO Box 581, Greenville, ME 04441; ☯ 9am-5pm summer, 10am-4pm Tue-Sat winter).

Owned and maintained by the Moosehead Marine Museum, the **SS Katahdin** (☎ 207-695-2716; www.katahdincruises.com; adult/child $30-40/15-25; ☯ May-Oct) is a 115ft steamboat built in 1914. It still makes the rounds – more like three- to eight-hour cruises – on Moosehead Lake from Greenville's center, just like it did in Greenville's heyday. The lake's colorful history is preserved in the museum right in the center of town.

From Bangor, head south on I-95 for 23 miles, then north on ME 11/7/23 for 26 miles, then 2 miles west on ME 16/6 and then 22 miles north on ME 15/6 to Greenville, the gateway to Moosehead Lake.

BAXTER STATE PARK

Mt Katahdin (5267ft), Maine's tallest mountain and the northern end of the over-2000-mile-long **Appalachian Trail**, is the centerpiece of Baxter State Park, which boasts 46 other mountain peaks, 1200 campsites and 180 miles of hiking trails. Mt Katahdin offers the wildest, most unspoiled wilderness adventures in New England. Katahdin has a reputation for being a real rock climber's mountain.

Despite its relative inaccessibility – deep in the Maine woods over unpaved roads – Baxter hosts over 100,000 visitors every year, mostly from mid-May through mid-October. It's also open December through March for winter activities.

To fully enjoy Baxter State Park ($8 per day per person), you must arrive at the park entrance early in the day – only so many visitors are allowed in on any given day. You should also be well equipped for camping and perhaps for hiking and canoeing. Campsites in the park cost $9 per person ($18 minimum) and must be reserved well in advance by contacting **Baxter State Park** (☎ 207-723-5140; www.baxterstateparkauthority.com; 64 Balsam Dr, Millinocket, ME 04462). You may also want more information from the **Maine Ap-**

palachian Trail Club (www.matc.org; PO Box 283, Augusta, ME 04330) and the **Katahdin Area Chamber of Commerce** (☎ 207-723-4443; www.katahdinmaine .com; 1029 Central St, Millinocket, ME 04462).

If you are unable to secure a reservation at one of the park's campsites, you can usually find a private campground just outside the Togue Ponds and Matagamon gates into the park. There are several in Medway (just off I-95 exit 56), in Millinocket and in Greenville.

From Bangor, head north on I-95 for 61 miles to Medway, then head 10 miles northwest on ME 11 to Millinocket and then continue another 10 miles beyond Millinocket to the southern entrance of the park. From Greenville, if you have a 4WD, take Lily Bay Rd to Kokadjo, where the road becomes a dirt logging road (Sias Hill Rd). Take this until you get to the end and make a right on paved Golden Rd. This is a gorgeous drive, and you're likely to see moose in streams if you're on Golden Rd toward dusk. However, be careful: these are logging roads! Those humongous trucks can be dangerous when coming around the bends.

From the turnoff at Medway on I-95, it's another 106 miles via ME 11 to Fort Kent and Clair on the Canadian border. This is not a convenient or direct route to Quebec, but if it's your chosen path here's the route. From the US-Canada border, head northeast on Canadian Hwy 120 to Edmunston and then northwest on Hwy 2/185 to Rivière-du-Loup and south along the St Lawrence River to Quebec. Expect the trip to take about 3 ½ hours (360 kilometers).

ONWARD TO QUEBEC

From West Fork, take US 201 north for 42 miles toward St Georges in Canada. From the border it's about two hours (150 kilometers) – a straight shot up Hwy 173 and Hwy 73 to Quebec.

Caratunk and West Forks, both on US 201 (50 and 60 miles north of Waterville respectively), serve as the base for outfitter-led rafting trips down the Allagash River.

ALLAGASH RIVER & AROUND

Home to the original Acadians, for whom the national park was named, **Aroostook County** is huge, covering more than 6400 sq miles (making it larger than the states of

THRU-HIKERS & THE APPALACHIAN TRAIL   *John Spelman*

One of America's greatest (and most protracted) adventures, the Appalachian Trail, snakes for more than 2100 scenic miles from Springer Mountain in Georgia to Mt Katahdin in Maine. It's America's oldest and most famous long-distance hiking trail, and many of its most interesting bits lie within New England. This stretch of trail (690 miles long) passes through the states of Connecticut, Massachusetts, Vermont, New Hampshire and Maine, missing only Rhode Island. From south to north, it winds through the rolling hills and farmland of the Berkshires, runs through several small villages, navigates the pastoral splendor of the Green Mountains and, for 13 breathtaking miles, traverses along the alpine crest of the Presidential Range in the White Mountains. Here, you'll walk along a rocky ridge well above tree-line, climb the tallest mountain in the Northeast (Washington, 6288ft) and have the option of staying in some of the plushest accommodation available in the American Wilderness: a series of meal-providing mountain-top cabins spaced no more then a day's hike apart. After the White Mountains, you'll hit Maine, the '100-mile wilderness,' difficult river fords, Baxter State Park, and, if you timed things correctly, not too many black flies.

Each year, several thousand thru-hikers attempt to walk the entire trail in one go, with only a few hundred succeeding. Populated by nature enthusiasts, oddballs and adventurers, this crew generally begins in the south and, very, very slowly, works its way north. Because the walk takes between five and seven months to complete and because early winters make much of Maine impassable by October's end, most northbound hikers begin their journey from Springer Mountain in April or May. The simultaneous rush of hikers helps to create a sense of camaraderie among the group, and reinforces the cult-like culture that has developed among thru-hikers. The creation of a strong community between thru-hikers is not surprising – after all, they spend night after smelly night sleeping together in communal shelters, provide a support network for one another in case of equipment or medical emergency, and are driven by the same singular, fanatical purpose. It is common for thru-hikers to give one another trail names (eg Mud Elephant, Bluejay and Mail Drop), names that reference traits exhibited by a particular hiker during their grueling march.

Planning a thru hike – or a long sectional hike – requires a lot of planning. Consult www .appalachiantrail.org for excellent info on regulations, advice on when to avoid Vermont's mud season, how to access the trail, and other practical concerns, such as where to order maps and guidebooks. If you don't, you'll risk repeating my mistakes, which involved heaps of physical pain, tear-stained cheeks, an embarrassing phone call to mother and a hitch-hiking ordeal featuring a cigar-chewing freak who frisked me for weapons. Don't forget sunscreen!

Connecticut and Rhode Island combined). 'The county,' as it's called, has more than 2000 lakes, ponds, streams and rivers. The western half of the county is mostly deep forest owned by the timber and paper companies; it's also home to the **Allagash Wilderness Waterway** (☎ 207-941-4014), a protected natural area with 92 miles of ponds, lakes and north-flowing rivers, which makes it a prime site for canoe trips. However, the long eastern half is good farming country, though the growing season is short – it's perfect for raising potatoes. The farmers of Aroostook County take advantage of this fact by producing 1.5 million tons of potatoes every year.

If you're into potatoes or forests, Aroostook is heaven. Sit down at a restaurant in Houlton, Presque Isle or Madawaska and you'll find potatoes on the menu in all sorts of original ways. The names of the many varieties of the noble spud – Kennebec, Katahdin, Norchip, Superior, Ontario, Russet Burbank, Norgold Russet – are bandied about by the locals over breakfast.

Unless you're in the business, the fascination provided by tubers fades fast, though. You may well find Aroostook to be a pretty place to pass through on your way elsewhere.

I-95 ends at Houlton, on the border with the Canadian province of New Brunswick. Hwy 95 continues on the other side of the border and links you to Hwy 2, the Trans-Canada Hwy.

MAINE

From Houlton, US 1 goes north to Presque Isle, Caribou and Van Buren before crossing into New Brunswick. You can continue on Hwy 17 to Campbellton and Québec's beautiful Gaspé Peninsula, or head northwest on Hwy 185 (the Trans-Canada), to Rivière-du-Loup, Québec, then southwest up the St Lawrence to Québec City. The fastest route from Maine to Québec City is I-95 to Fairfield, just north of Winslow, then US 201 north via Skowhegan, Bingham, the Kennebec Valley and Jackman. But this way you don't get to see several thousand square miles of potatoes.

Various local information offices in the area include:

Caribou (☎ 207-498-6156; http://cariboumaine.org)

Houlton (☎ 207-532-4216; www.houlton.com)

Presque Isle (☎ 207-764-6561; www.presqueisle.net)

Van Buren (☎ 207-868-5059; www.vanburenmaine.com)

Directory

ACCOMMODATIONS

New England provides an array of accommodations from simple campsites and B&Bs to mid-range inns and top-end hotels. But truly inexpensive accommodations are rare. The most comfortable accommodations for the lowest price are usually found in that great American invention, the roadside motel.

For last-minute deals, check www.expedia.com, www.travelocity.com, www.orbitz.com, www.priceline.com, www.hotwire.com and www.hotels.com.

If you're traveling with children, be sure to ask about children-related policies before making reservations (see p528).

Our reviews indicate rates for single occupancy (s), double (d) or simply the room (r), when there's no appreciable difference in the rate for one or two people. Unless otherwise noted, breakfast is not included, bathrooms are private and all lodging is open year-round; rates generally don't include taxes of a whopping 5.2% to 12%, depending on the state (see p535).

A double room in our budget category costs $100 or less; mid-range doubles cost $100 to $200; top-end rooms start at $200.

As for icons (see inside cover), a parking icon is only employed in cities where free parking is not readily available. The air-conditioning icon only appears in locations where the weather might warrant it (like Cape Cod and other shoreline areas). The Internet icon appears where establishments provide a computer terminal; the pool icon appears when there is swimming on premises. When there is an additional fee for parking or Internet usage, a fee follows the icon. Smoking is not permitted indoors for most of the destinations in this book, although restaurants in New Hampshire do provide a no-smoking section. It's safest to assume it is not permitted.

PRACTICALITIES

Electricity Voltage is 110/120V, 60 cycles.
Laundry Most accommodations have inexpensive coin-operated washers and dryers.
Newspapers The *Boston Globe,* the largest area newspaper, is available throughout New England.
Radio National Public Radio (NPR) features a level-headed approach to news and talk radio and is found between 89 and 92 on your FM dial.
TV All the major US TV networks are represented, but look for New England Cable News for the best regional coverage.
Video Video systems use the NTSC color TV standard, not compatible with the PAL system.
Weights & Measures Distances are measured in feet, yards and miles; weights are tallied in ounces, pounds and tons.

A reservation guarantees your room, but most reservations require a deposit, after which, if you change your mind, the establishment will only refund your money if they're able to re-book your room within a certain period. Note the cancellation policies and other restrictions before making a deposit.

High season varies slightly depending on the region within New England. In general, the peak travel season to New England is summer and fall. For example, high season on Cape Cod and the Maine Coast is late May to early September, but in the mountains of New Hampshire, it's during fall (mid-September to mid-October). In some Vermont regions, though, high season equates with ski season (late December to late March). We have broken out high and low periods within each accommodation write-up to be as clear as possible.

Holidays (p532) and school vacations always command premium prices. When demand peaks (and during special events no matter the time of year, see p531), book lodgings well in advance.

B&Bs, Inns & Guesthouses

Accommodations in New England vary from small B&Bs to rambling old inns that have sheltered travelers for several centuries.

In smaller towns, guesthouses with simple rooms may charge $60 to $85 for rooms with shared bathroom, breakfast included. Others are relentlessly charming, with frilly decor and doting hosts. These fancier B&Bs charge $100 to $150 per night with private bathroom. Historic inns converted from wealthy summer homes, decorated with antique furnishings and equipped with every conceivable modern amenity easily cost $200 a night and up. Most inns require a minimum stay of two or three days on weekends, advance reservations and bills paid in advance by check or in cash (not by credit card).

Many B&Bs are booked through agencies, including the following:

Destinnations (☎ 207-563-2506, 800-333-4667; www .destinnations.com; 16 East Pond Rd, Nobleboro, ME 04555) A reservation and itinerary-planning service for visitors staying in New England more than a few nights.

Central Reservation Service of New England (☎ 617-569-3800, 800-332-3026; www.bostonhotels .net; 300 Terminal C, Logan Airport, Boston, MA 02128) Knowledgeable advice and discounted rates.

Bed & Breakfast Reservations (☎ 617-964-1606, 800-832-2632; www.bbreserve.com; 11A Beach Rd, Gloucester, MA 01930) Books B&B, historic inns, and apartments in Massachusetts and northern New England.

Camping

You can buy camping equipment at many places like **Hilton's Tent City** (Map pp66-8; p125) in Boston and LL Bean (p481) in Freeport, Maine.

With few exceptions, you'll have to camp in established campgrounds (there's no bivouacking on the side of the road). Make reservations well in advance (especially in July and August) for the best chance of getting a site. Private campgrounds are always more expensive ($18 to $40) and less spacious than state parks, and they often boast recreational facilities like playgrounds, swimming, game rooms and miniature golf.

Rough camping is occasionally permitted in the Green Mountain National Forest (p371) or the White Mountain National Forest (p442), but often it must be at established sites; it's usually free. Drive-up sites in national forests with basic services generally cost about $10. State and national park sites usually offer a few more services (like flush toilets, hot showers and dump station for RVs). Tent sites at these places cost between $10 and $20; most campgrounds are open from mid-May to mid-October.

For complete camping information, contact the following:

Connecticut Bureau of Outdoor Recreation (☎ 860-424-3200; http://dep.state.ct.us/stateparks)

Maine Bureau of Parks & Lands (☎ 207-287-3821; www.state.me.us/doc/parks)

Massachusetts Department of Conservation & Recreation (☎ 617-626-1250; www.mass.gov/dcr)

New Hampshire Division of Parks & Recreation (☎ 603-271-3556; www.nhparks.state.nh.us)

Rhode Island Division of Parks & Recreation (☎ 401-222-2321; www.riparks.com)

Vermont State Parks (☎ 802-241-3655; www.vtstate parks.com)

Cottages, Cabins & Condos

Renting a cottage or condominium is not particularly easy for those who don't live in the region. But your best bet is to contact local chambers of commerce (see Information under each town) and ask for listings of available properties.

Cottages and cabins are generally found on Cape Cod, Nantucket, Martha's Vineyard and in New England's woods. They are two- or three-room vacation bungalows with basic furnishings, bathroom and kitchen. Condos are usually capable of accommodating more people than an efficiency unit (below) – some condos can sleep six, eight or even 10 people in a small multi-room apartment with kitchen and dining facilities. Rates vary greatly, from $70 to $700 per night, depending upon the location, season and size. Mountainside condos are especially popular with skiers, but they're much cheaper during the warmer months.

Efficiencies

An 'efficiency,' in New England parlance, is a hotel, motel or inn room, or one-room cabin, with cooking and dining facilities: stove, sink, refrigerator, dining table and chairs, cooking utensils and tableware. Efficiency units, which physically resemble their brethren in all but their interior amenities, are located throughout New England in all but the most upscale communities. They usually cost slightly more than standard rooms.

Hotels & Resorts

New England hotels, mostly found in cities, are generally large and lavish, except for a few small, inexpensive 'boutique' hotels (which are small and understatedly lavish). Resorts often offer a wide variety of guest activities, such as golf, horseback riding, skiing or water sports. Prices range from $100 to $200 and up per night; ask about discounts and special packages when you make reservations. Virtually all large hotels have toll-free numbers for making reservations, but you may find better discounts by calling the hotel directly.

Hostels

Hosteling isn't as well developed in New England as it is in Europe. But some prime destinations – including Boston (p96), Cape Cod (p174), Bar Harbor (p503), Martha's Vineyard (p212) and Nantucket (p203) – have hostels that allow you to stay in $150-per-night destinations for $20 to $25. Needless to say, advance reservations are essential.

US citizens/residents can join **Hostelling International-American Youth Hostels** (HI-AYH; ☎ 301-495-1240; www.hiayh.org; 8401 Colesville Rd, ste 600, Silver Spring, MD 20910) by calling and requesting a membership form or by downloading a form from the website and mailing or faxing it. Membership can also be purchased at regional council offices and at many (but not all) youth hostels. Non-US residents should buy a HI-AYH membership in their home countries. If you are not a member, you can still stay in US hostels by purchasing 'Welcome Stamps' for each night. When you have six stamps, your stamp card becomes a one-year HI-AYH membership card which is valid throughout the world.

HI-AYH has its own toll- and surcharge-free reservations service (☎ 800-909-4776), but not all hostels participate in the service. The HI-AYH card may be used to receive discounts at some local merchants and services, including some intercity bus companies.

Two hosteling councils cover New England. **HI-AYH Eastern New England Council** (☎ 617-779-0900; www.usahostels.org; 1105 Commonwealth Ave, Boston, MA 02215) covers Eastern Massachusetts, Maine as well as New Hampshire. The **HI-AYH Yankee Council** (☎ 860-683-2847; www.yankeehostels.org; PO Box 87, Windsor, CT 06095) covers Connecticut, Vermont and Western Massachusetts.

New England hostels are located in the following towns:

Connecticut Hartford
Maine Bar Harbor
Massachusetts Boston, Eastham and Truro (Cape Cod), Martha's Vineyard, Nantucket
New Hampshire Conway
Vermont Bennington, Burlington, Woodford (near Bennington)

Motels

Motels, located on the highway or on the outskirts of most cities, range from 10-room places in need of paint to resort-style facilities. Prices range from $50 to $100 and up. Motels offer standard accommodations: a room entered from the outside, with private bathroom, color cable TV, heat and air con. Some motels have small refrigerators, and many provide a simple breakfast, often at no extra charge. Most also provide toll-free reservations lines.

DIRECTORY

ACTIVITIES

For a complete discussion of the wealth, depth and breadth of ways to have fun in New England, see the New England Outdoors chapter (p47). Two activities specific to New England bear mentioning here, though. Consider cruising for a few days along the gorgeous Maine coast, among the world's finest sail-cruising areas. Traditional wooden schooners (or windjammers) use Camden (p495), Rockport and Rockland as their home ports. The other activity is whale-watching. Once known for their prowess in seeking out whales for slaughter, New England's sea captains now follow the whales with boatloads of camera-carrying summer tourists. Cruises depart from Barnstable (p180), Provincetown (p199), Boston (p77), Plymouth (p166), Gloucester and Newburyport (p161), MA; Portsmouth (p418), NH; and Kennebunkport (p471), Boothbay Harbor (p489) and Bar Harbor (p504), ME, among other coastal towns.

BUSINESS HOURS

Unless there are variances of more than a half-hour in either direction, the following serve as 'normal' opening hours for entries in this book:

Banks 8:30am to 4pm Monday to Friday; some banks open until 6pm Friday and 9am to noon Saturday.

Bars & Clubs Until midnight daily; some clubs till 2am Thursday to Saturday.

Businesses 9am to 5pm Monday to Friday; some post offices open 9am to noon Saturday.

Restaurants Breakfast 6am to 10am, lunch 11:30am to 2pm, dinner 5pm to 9:30pm.

Shops 9am to 5pm Monday to Saturday; some also open noon to 5pm Sunday; major shopping areas and malls keep extended hours.

CHILDREN

Traveling within New England with children presents no destination-specific problems. Successful travel with young children does, though, require planning and effort. Try not to overdo things; even for adults, packing too much into the time available can cause problems. Include children in the trip planning; if they've helped to work out where you will be going, they will be much more interested when they get there.

Consult Lonely Planet's *Travel with Children*, which has lots of valuable tips and interesting anecdotal stories.

Practicalities

How welcome are children? At many smaller B&Bs and inns (p526), they're not. But since establishments are not allowed by law to discriminate, proprietors won't usually say 'no' outright. They'll try to dissuade you gently, so listen carefully to their answers. But in motels and hotels, children under age 17 or 18 are usually free when sharing a room with their parents and using existing bedding. Cots and roll-away beds are usually available (for an additional fee) in hotels and resorts. When places are particularly family friendly, we say so.

Some resorts, like the Chatham Bars Inn on Cape Cod (p190), offer camp-style programs for children three to 15 (see the Sleeping section in the relevant chapters).

Because children are seen as well as heard in New England, many restaurants have children's menus with significantly lower prices. High chairs are usually available, but it pays to inquire ahead of time.

Most car rental companies (see p544) lease child-safety seats, but they don't always have them on hand; reserve in advance if you can.

Sights & Activities

Family-friendly sights abound in New England and we have peppered suggestions throughout the regional chapters where we have ferreted out activities worth your time even when it's not raining and Junior is driving you up the wall. For more suggestions, see New England for Kids (p16).

As for specifics, Massachusetts has more than its fair share of things to do with the kids. Try the Basketball Hall of Fame (p238), the Dr Seuss National Memorial Sculpture Garden (p237) or visit the Magic Wings Butterfly Conservatory (p253), an 8000-sq-ft glass atrium brimming with butterflies and educational exhibits about them.

In Boston, among the dozens of things to do, consider visiting the Science Museum (p77), with fun, fascinating, educational exhibits and hands-on experiments for kids of all ages. For plenty more ideas, see Boston for Children (p93) and Top Five Kid Spots (p93).

In New Hampshire, Hampton Beach (p412) has miles of beaches, video game arcades and miniature golf. In Rhode Island, spend a day at the beach in Watch Hill (p307), where you can take a spin on a flying carousel and have some ice-cream. In Connecticut, the Essex Steam Train & Riverboat Ride (p337) takes families on a 2½-hour jaunt on an old-time steam engine and riverboat.

Don't forget: many activities require that children be of a certain height in order to participate; unless Junior is 6ft tall and six years old, it's always best to inquire.

CLIMATE CHARTS

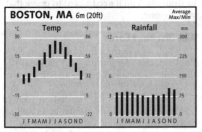

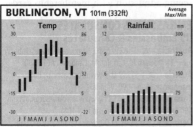

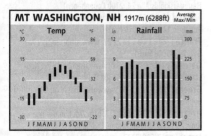

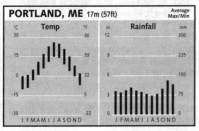

COURSES

Opportunities abound across erudite New England to educate yourself while on vacation. In Boston you can take sailing classes at Community Boating (p90), cooking classes at Cambridge School of Culinary Arts (p92) and yoga classes at Baptiste Power Vinyasa Yoga (p93). For more on Cooking Courses, see p59.

You can also take fly-fishing classes at the famous Orvis Fly-Fishing School (p371) in Manchester or at LL Bean (p481) in Freeport, ME. For the artistically minded, art classes are offered at Burlington City Arts (p398) in Vermont.

For information on Elderhostel, see p530.

CUSTOMS

Each visitor is allowed to bring 1 liter of liquor and 200 cigarettes duty free into the US, but you must be at least 21 years old to possess the former and 18 years old to possess the latter. In addition, each traveler is permitted to bring up to $100-worth of gift merchandise into the US without incurring any duty.

DANGERS & ANNOYANCES

New England's cities are among the safer US cities, but you should observe the following standard urban safety guidelines:
- Lock valuables in your hotel room or put them in the hotel safe.
- Lock your car doors and don't leave any valuables visible.
- Avoid walking alone on empty streets or in parks at night.
- Try to use ATMs only in well-trafficked areas.
- Street people and panhandlers may approach visitors; nearly all of them are harmless.

As for rural dangers, be aware of hunters during the November hunting season. 'No Hunting' signs are widely ignored and are not a guarantee of safety.

For health concerns, see the Health chapter (p546).

DISABLED TRAVELERS

Travel within New England is becoming less difficult for people with disabilities, but it's still not easy. Public buildings are now required by law to be wheelchair accessible and also to have appropriate restroom facilities. Public transportation services must be made accessible to all, and telephone companies are required to provide relay operators for the hearing impaired. Many banks provide ATM instructions in braille, curb ramps are common, many busy intersections have audible crossing signals, and most chain hotels have suites for disabled guests. Even so, it's best to call ahead to see what's available.

A number of organizations specialize in the needs of disabled travelers:

Mobility International USA (☎ 541-343-1284; www .miusa.org; PO Box 10767, Eugene, OR 97440) Advises disabled travelers on mobility issues, but primarily runs an educational exchange program.

Society for the Advancement of Travel for the Handicapped (SATH; ☎ 212-447-7284; www.sath .org; 347 Fifth Ave, ste 610, New York, NY 10016) Publishes a quarterly magazine; has various information sheets on travel for the disabled.

Twin Peaks Press (☎ 360-694-2462, 800-637-2256; http://home.pacifier.com/~twinpeak; PO Box 129, Vancouver, WA 98666) Publishes a quarterly newsletter, directories and access guides.

DISCOUNT CARDS

Yankee frugality is not a myth; it's alive and well in New England. Plenty of discounts are available; you just have to know when, where and whom to ask for them.

Senior Cards

Travelers aged 50 years and older can receive rate cuts and benefits at many places. Inquire about discounts at hotels, museums and restaurants *before* you make your reservation. With the Golden Age Passport, US citizens aged 62 or over receive free admission to national parks nationwide and a 50% reduction on camping fees. Apply in person at Acadia National Park (p502), or call ☎ 877-444-6777.

Some national advocacy groups:

American Association of Retired Persons (AARP; ☎ 888-687-2277; www.aarp.org; 601 E St NW, Washington, DC 20049) Advocacy group for Americans 50 years old and older; a good resource for travel bargains. US residents can get one-year/three-year memberships for US$12.50/29.50.

Elderhostel (☎ 877-426-8056; www.elderhostel.org; 11 Ave de Lafayette, Boston, MA 02111) Nonprofit organization offering seniors the opportunity to attend academic college courses throughout the US and Canada.

Student & Youth Cards

Most hostels in the US are members of Hostelling International-American Youth Hostels (HI-AYH; see p527), which offer low-cost accommodations to card carrying members. In college towns such as Amherst (p247), Boston (p60), Cambridge (p86), Hanover (p430) or New Haven (p326), your student ID card sometimes can get you discounts. Museums and attractions outside these cities may also give small discounts to students. You'll need a card to prove that you are one.

AAA Discount Cards

If you plan on doing a lot of driving in New England, consider joining your national automobile association before arriving in the US. Members of clubs affiliated with the American Automobile Association (AAA; p544) can get roadside assistance as well as discounts on lodging, car rental and sightseeing admission with membership cards.

EMBASSIES & CONSULATES
US Embassies & Consulates

Australia (☎ 02-6214 5600; http://canberra.usembassy .gov; 21 Moonah Pl, Yarralumla, Canberra, ACT 2600)

Austria (☎ 1-31339-0; www.usembassy.at; Boltzmanngasse 16, A-1090, Vienna)

Canada (☎ 613-238 5335; www.usembassycanada.gov; 490 Sussex Dr, Ottawa, Ontario K1N 1G8)

Denmark (☎ 33 41 71 00; www.usembassy.dk; Dag Hammarskjölds Allé 24, 2100 Copenhagen)

Finland (☎ 9-616-250; www.usembassy.fi; Itäinen Puistotie 14 B, 00140 Helsinki)

France (☎ 33 1 43 12 22 22; www.amb-usa.fr; 2 Av Gabriel, 75008 Paris)

Germany (☎ 030-8305 0; www.usembassy.de; Neustädtische Kirchstrasse 4-5, 10117 Berlin)

Greece (☎ 1-721-2951; www.usembassy.gr; 91 Vasilissis Sophias Blvd, 10160 Athens)

Ireland (☎ 353 1 668 8777; http://dublin.usembassy .gov; 42 Elgin Rd, Ballsbridge, Dublin 4)

Israel (☎ 3-519-7327; www.usembassy-israel.org.il; 71 Hayarkon St, Tel Aviv 63903)

Italy (☎ 39 06 46741; www.usembassy.it; Via Veneto 119/A, 00187 Rome)

Japan (☎ 03-3224 5000; http://tokyo.usembassy.gov; 10-5, Akasaka 1-chome, Minato-ku, Tokyo)

Mexico (☎ 5-209-9100; www.usembassy-mexico.gov; Paseo de la Reforma 305, Colonia Cuauhtémoc, 06500 México, DF)

Netherlands (☎ 070-310 9209; www.usemb.nl; Lange Voorhout 102, 2514 EJ The Hague)

New Zealand (☎ 04-462 6000; www.usembassy.org.nz;
29 Fitzherbert Tce, PO Box 1190, Thorndon, Wellington)
Spain (☎ 807-488-472 from Spain only, US passport
holders in Spain call ☎ 91587-2240; http://madrid
.usembassy.gov; Calle Serrano 75, 28006 Madrid)
Sweden (☎ 08 783 53 00; http://stockholm.usembassy
.gov; Dag Hammarskjölds Väg 31, SE-115 89 Stockholm)
Switzerland (☎ 031-357-7011; www.us-embassy.ch;
Jubiläumsstrasse 93, CH-3005 Bern)
UK (☎ 020-7499 9000; www.usembassy.org.uk; 24/31
Grosvenor Sq, London W1A 1AE)

Embassies & Consulates in New England

Embassies are in Washington, DC. Some
countries maintain consulates, honorary
consuls or consular agents in Boston. To
get the telephone number of an embassy or
consulate not listed below, call directory assistance for the city in which you hope to find
a diplomatic office (Boston ☎ 617-555-1212;
Washington ☎ 202-555-1212).

Australia Embassy (☎ 202-797-3000; www.austemb
.org; 1601 Massachusetts Ave NW, Washington, DC 20036)
Canada Consulate (☎ 617-262-3760; www.canadian
embassy.org; 3 Copley Pl, ste 400, Boston, MA 02116)
France Consulate (☎ 617-542-7374; www.consulfrance
-boston.org; 31 St James Ave, ste 750, Boston, MA 02116)
Germany Consulate (☎ 617-536-4414; www.germany
info.org; 3 Copley Pl, ste 500, Boston, MA 02116)
Ireland Consulate (☎ 617-267-9330; www.ireland
emb.org; Chase Bldg, 535 Boylston St, Boston, MA 02116)
Israel Embassy (☎ 202-364-5500; www.embassyofisrael
.org; 3514 International Dr NW, Washington, DC 20008)
Italy Consulate (☎ 617-542-0483; www.italianconsulate
boston.org; 100 Boylston St, ste 900, Boston, MA 02116)
Japan Embassy (☎ 202-238-6700; www.us.emb-japan
.go.jp; 2520 Massachusetts Ave NW, DC 20008)
Mexico Embassy (☎ 202-736-1002; www.embassy
ofmexico.org; 2827 16th St NW, Washington, DC 20009)
Netherlands Consulate (☎ 617-542-8452; www.cgny
.org; 20 Park Plaza, ste 524, Boston, MA 02116)
New Zealand Embassy (☎ 202-328-4800; www.nz
embassy.com/usa; 37 Observatory Circle NW, Washington,
DC 20008)
UK Consulate (☎ 617-625-4500; www.britainusa.com
/boston; 1 Memorial Dr, 15th fl, Cambridge, MA 02142)

FESTIVALS & EVENTS

Special events never cease in New England,
including holiday celebrations, harvest celebrations and craft fairs. Tourist information offices and websites have complete
information; see the regional chapters for
more details. Also see our Top 10 Festivals
(p11) and holidays (p532).

FOOD

The Eating section for each destination is
broken down into three price categories:
budget (for meals costing $10 or less), mid-
range (where most main dishes cost $10 to
$20) and top end (where most dinner mains
cost more than $20). These price estimates
do not include taxes, tips or beverages.

For details about New England specialties
and delicacies, see Food & Drink (p54).

GAY & LESBIAN TRAVELERS

Out and active gay communities are visible across New England, especially in cities
such as Boston (p60), New Haven (p326)
and Burlington (p396), which have substantial gay populations, and where it is
easier for gay men and women to live their
lives with a certain amount of openness.
(Boston's South End neighborhood (p81)
rules the roost on this front.) When you
travel outside large cities, it is a bit harder to
be open about your sexual preferences. Gay
travelers should be careful – holding hands
in public might get you bashed.

Provincetown (p197) and Ogunquit (p467)
are gay meccas during the summer. College
and university towns like Northampton
(p243) and Burlington (p396) also have lively
lesbian communities year-round. Most cities
have a gay or alternative newspaper like *Bay
Windows*, a Boston-based publication that
lists current events and local contacts.

Good national guidebooks include *Damron Women's Traveller*, providing listings
for lesbians; *Damron Men's Travel Guide*,
for men; and *Damron Accommodations*,
with listings of gay-owned or gay-friendly
accommodations nationwide. All three are
published by the **Damron Company** (☎ 415-255-
0404, 800-462-6654; www.damron.com).

Another good resource is the **Gay Yellow
Pages** (☎ 212-674-0120; www.gayyellowpages.com),
which has national and regional editions.

National resources include the following:
Lambda Legal Defense Fund (☎ 212-809-8585 NYC
office, 213-382-7600 LA office; www.lambdalegal.org)
National AIDS/HIV Hotline (☎ 800-342-2437; www
.ashastd.org)
National Gay/Lesbian Task Force (☎ 202-332-6483;
www.ngltf.org; 1325 Massachusetts Ave NW,
Suite 600, Washington, DC)

For more information about gays and being
gay in New England, see p32 and p32; for

legal matters see right. The boxed text on p96 has information on gay and lesbian Boston.

HOLIDAYS

Also see p531 and p9.

New Year's Day January 1
Martin Luther King Jr Day third Monday of January
Presidents' Day third Monday of February
Easter in March or April
Memorial Day last Monday of May
Independence Day July 4
Labor Day first Monday of September
Columbus Day second Monday of October
Veterans Day November 11
Thanksgiving fourth Thursday of November
Christmas Day December 25

INSURANCE

It's expensive to get sick, crash a car or have things stolen from you in the US. For rental car insurance see p544 and for health insurance see p546. To protect yourself from items that may be stolen from your car, consult your homeowner's (or renter's) insurance policy before leaving home.

INTERNET ACCESS

If you usually access your email through your office or school, you'll find it easier to open a free account with Yahoo! (www.yahoo.com) or Hotmail (www.hotmail.com).

If you bring a laptop with you from outside the US, it's worth investing in a universal AC and plug adapter. Also, your PC-card modem may not work once you leave your home country – but you won't know until you try. The safest option? Buy a reputable 'global' modem before leaving home. Ensure that you have at least a US RJ-11 telephone adapter that works with your modem. For more technical help, visit www.teleadapt.com.

Cybercafés and business centers like Kinkos offer inexpensive online computer access. When hostels or other lodgings provide access, this is noted with an 🖳 . See the relevant Internet Access sections (under Information) in individual chapters.

If your hotel room does not have a modem port on its phone, you can plug into the main line – as long as you remember to set your machine to dial for an outside line first.

For more information, also see Internet Resources p11.

LEGAL MATTERS

If you are arrested for a serious offence, you are allowed to remain silent, entitled to have an attorney present during any interrogation and presumed innocent until proven guilty. You have the right to an attorney from the very first moment you are arrested. If you can't afford one, the state must provide one for free. All persons who are arrested have the right to make one phone call. If you don't have a lawyer or family member to help you, call your embassy or consulate.

The minimum age for drinking alcoholic beverages is 21. You'll need a government-issued photo ID (such as a passport or US driver's license). Stiff fines, jail time and penalties can be incurred if you are caught driving under the influence of alcohol or providing alcohol to minors.

LEGAL AGES

The legal age for certain activities around New England varies by state. Ages below are listed in this order: Massachusetts, Connecticut, Rhode Island, Vermont, New Hampshire, Maine.

Driving 18/16/18/16/17/16
Voting 18 in every state
Drinking 21 in every state
Heterosexual sex 16 in every state
Homosexual sex 18/no age/no age/no age/18/no age

MAPS

Local chambers of commerce usually hand out simple maps of their towns.

The most detailed state highway maps are those distributed free by state governments. You can call or write state tourism offices in advance (see p536) and have the maps sent to you, or you can pick up the maps at highway tourism information offices ('welcome centers') when you enter a state on a major highway.

If you plan to do a lot of hiking or biking in a particular state, buy a map from the **Delorme Mapping Company** (☎ 207-846-7100; www.delorme.com), which publishes individual state maps (about $20). Nothing compares to these atlas-style books if you're delving into the heart of New England's backcountry roads. The Massachusetts map is done at an impressive 1:80,000 scale.

US Dept of the Interior Geological Survey (USGS; www.usgs.gov) topographical maps are superb close-up maps for hiking. For fast and easy service, you may order maps from Boston's **Globe Corner Bookstore** (☎ 617-497-6277, 800-358-6013; www.globecorner.com).

Hiking trail maps are available from outdoors organizations, such as the Appalachian Mountain Club (see p48).

MONEY

The dollar (commonly called a buck) is divided into 100 cents. Coins come in denominations of one cent (penny), five cents (nickel), 10 cents (dime), 25 cents (quarter) and the rare 50-cent piece (half dollar). Notes come in one-, five-, 10-, 20-, 50- and 100-dollar denominations.

See the Quick Reference inside the front cover for exchange rates and Getting Started (p10) for information on costs.

ATMs, Cash

Automatic teller machines (ATMs) are great for quick cash influxes and can negate the need for traveler's checks entirely, but watch out for ATM surcharges. Most banks in New England charge around $1.50 per withdrawal.

The Cirrus and Plus systems both have extensive ATM networks that will give cash advances on major credit cards and allow cash withdrawals with affiliated ATM cards. Look for ATMs outside banks, and in large grocery stores, shopping centers, convenience stores and gas stations.

If you're carrying foreign currency, it can be exchanged for US dollars at Logan International Airport in Boston. Even some larger banks in Boston can't change currency.

Some banks in small vacation towns frequented by Canadian tourists will buy and sell Canadian currency; some businesses near the border will offer to accept Canadian dollars 'at par,' meaning that they will accept Canadian dollars as though they were US dollars, in effect giving you a substantial discount on your purchase.

Credit Cards

Major credit cards are widely accepted throughout New England, including at car rental agencies and at most hotels, restaurants, gas stations, grocery stores and tour operators. Many B&Bs and some condominiums – particularly those handled through rental agencies – do not accept credit cards, however. We have noted that in our reviews when it is the case.

American Express (☎ 800-528-4800)
Diners Club (☎ 800-234-6377)
Discover (☎ 800-347-2683)
MasterCard (☎ 800-826-2181)
Visa (☎ 800-336-8472)

Tipping

Taxi drivers and baggage carriers expect tips (15% and $1 per bag, respectively). Waiters and bartenders rely on tips for their livelihoods. Tip 15% unless the service is terrible (in which case a complaint to the manager is warranted), or about 20% if the service is great. Never tip in fast-food, takeout or buffet-style restaurants where you serve yourself. Baggage carriers in airports and hotels get US$1 for the first bag and 75¢ for each additional bag. In hotels with daily housekeeping, leave a few dollars in the room for the staff when you check out. In budget hotels, tips are not expected, but always appreciated.

Traveler's Checks

Traveler's checks provide protection from theft and loss. For refunds on lost or stolen traveler's checks, call **American Express** (☎ 800-992-3404) or **Thomas Cook** (☎ 800-287-7362). Keeping a record of the check numbers and those you have used is vital for replacing lost checks, so keep this information separate from the checks themselves.

Foreign visitors carrying traveler's checks will find things easier if they are in US dollars. Most mid-range and upscale restaurants, hotels and shops accept US dollar traveler's checks and treat them just like cash.

PHOTOGRAPHY & VIDEO

There are virtually no restrictions on photography in except within museums and at some musical and artistic performances.

For the traditionalists out there, both print and slide film are readily available in New England. Furthermore, every town of any size has a photo shop that stocks cameras and accessories. With little effort you should be able to find a shop to develop your color print film in one hour, or at least on the same day. Expect to pay about $7 to process a roll of 24 color prints. If you're in

---

TOP 5 PHOTO TIPS

For the very complete short course on photographic ins and outs, dos and don'ts, consult Lonely Planet's *Travel Photography*. In the meantime, try these tips:

- Shoot at dusk and dawn – sure it's hard to wake up and be in the right place at the right time, but the light is more angular and dramatic.

- Include people for perspective – when you get home, your friends won't ask 'How big was that?'

- Shoot street life – shots of one building after another will test your friends' patience.

- Change perspective – get low and shoot up; get high and look down.

- Move in closer – whether it's people or places, there's almost no such thing as too close (and when there, it's called an abstraction!).

New England for any length of time, have your film developed here, as summertime heat and humidity greatly accelerate the deterioration of exposed film.

With high-powered X-ray machines now at many airports, don't pack film into checked luggage or carry-on bags. Instead carry your film in a baggie to show separately to airport security officials (known as a hand check). Remember to finish off the roll in your camera and take it out, too, or those photos may end up foggy.

For video information, see p525. For more specific photographic tips, see above.

POST

No matter how much people like to complain, the **US postal service** (☎ 800-275-8777; www.usps.gov) provides great service for the price. For 1st-class mail sent and delivered within the US, postage rates are 37¢ for letters up to 1oz (23¢ for each additional ounce) and 23¢ for standard-sized postcards. If you have the correct postage, drop your mail into any blue mailbox. However, to send a package weighing 16oz or more, you must bring it to a post office. Post office locations are listed in the Information sections for major towns.

International airmail rates for letters up to 1oz are 60¢ to Canada or Mexico, 80¢ to other countries. Postcards cost 50¢ to Canada or Mexico and 70¢ to other countries.

You can have mail sent to you c/o General Delivery at most big post offices in New England. When you pick up your mail, bring some photo identification. General delivery mail is usually held for up to 30 days. Most hotels will also hold mail for incoming guests.

Call private shippers like **United Parcel Service** (UPS; ☎ 800-742-5877) and **Federal Express** (FedEx; ☎ 800-463-3339) for more important or larger items.

SHOPPING

New England has a lot of fine craftspeople, and quality handicrafts can be readily found in each state. Save some money so you can spend it here.

In Connecticut, home to crafty Martha Stewart, don't miss Connecticut River Artisans (p339) in East Haddam or Quimper Faïence (p332) in Stonington, one of the few official shops that sells these one-of-a-kind folk-art plates, cups and figurines.

If you want to bypass Maine's outlet scene, head to Blue Hill (p500), a small town with many outstanding artisans. Or visit the Haystack Mountain School of Crafts (p501) in Deer Isle Village.

Boston has a few craft cooperatives, which are goldmines for craft-seekers. Seek out the Cambridge Artists' Cooperative (p124) and the Society of Arts & Crafts (p124) located on fashionable Newbury Street. In Western Massachusetts don't miss the colorful and fragile North River Glass (p255) in Shelburne Falls.

New Hampshire offers intrepid shoppers a curious mix of mall mania and quality artisan shops. The main drag in North Conway (p452) is lined with an endless strip of outlets, while the Canterbury Shaker Village (p424) offers a quiet glimpse of old New England life, where you can watch employees fashion Shaker furniture (and then consider a purchase).

When in Rhode Island, visit the Arcade (p281), America's first enclosed shopping center and the Armory Antique & Fine Arts Center (p301), which houses over 125 antique dealers in a provocative old military armory.

Vermont crafts are more akin to fine arts than you might think, and you can spend a fortune on one-of-a-kind pieces. Great shopping towns include Brattleboro (stop at the Vermont Artisan Designs, p358); Middlebury (don't miss the Frog Hollow Craft Center, p383) and Burlington (p396). Manchester (p370) is famed for upscale outlet shops, while Simon Pearce Glass (p380) in Quechee has one-of-a-kind creations and the Vermont Country Store (p362) sells things you'll find nowhere else.

Shopaholics love searching for discounted clothing, shoes, china and jewelry at Boston's Filene's Basement (p124) and at factory outlet stores in Fall River (p170) and New Bedford (p168), MA. North Conway (p452), NH, and Freeport (p481) and Kittery (p465), ME, also have massive factory-outlet malls.

SOLO TRAVELERS

Travel, including solo travel, is generally safe and easy. In general, women need to exercise more vigilance in large cities than in rural areas. Everyone, though, should avoid hiking, cycling long distances or camping alone, especially in unfamiliar places. For more safety advice see Women Travelers (537) and Dangers & Annoyances (p529).

TAXES

State	Meal	Lodging	Sales
Connecticut	6%	12%	6%
Maine	7%	7%	5%
Massachusetts	5%	5.2%	5%
New Hampshire	8%	8%	n/a
Rhode Island	8%	12%	7%
Vermont	9%	9%	6%

TELEPHONE

Always dial '1' before toll-free (800, 888 etc) and domestic long-distance numbers. Remember that some toll-free numbers may only work within the region or from the US mainland, for instance. But you'll only know if it works by making the call.

All phone numbers in the US consist of a three-digit area code followed by a seven-digit local number. Because of the exponential growth of telephone numbers in New England, you now must dial ☎ 1 + area code + the seven-digit number for local as well as long-distance calls in many areas, particularly in eastern Massachusetts.

Pay phones aren't as readily found at shopping centers, gas stations and other public places now that cell phones are more prevalent, but keep your eyes peeled and you'll find them. Calls made within town are local and cost 25¢ or 50¢.

To make international calls direct, dial ☎ 011 + country code + area code + number. (An exception is calls made to Canada, where you dial ☎ 1 + area code + number. International rates apply to Canada.)

For international operator assistance, dial ☎ 0. The operator can provide specific rate information and tell you which time periods are the cheapest for calling.

If you're calling New England from abroad, the international country code for the US is ☎ 1. All calls to New England are then followed by the area code and the seven-digit local number.

Cellular Phones

The US uses a variety of cell-phone systems, 99% of which are incompatible with the GSM 900/1800 standard used throughout Europe and Asia. Check with your cellular service provider before departure about using your phone in New England. Verizon has the most extensive cellular network in New England, but Cingular and Sprint also have decent coverage. Once you get up into the mountains and off the main interstates in Vermont, New Hampshire and Maine, cell-phone reception is often downright non-existent. Forget about using it on hiking trails.

Phone Codes

See the Quick Facts Boxed Text for each state.

Phone Cards

These private prepaid cards are available from convenience stores, supermarkets and pharmacies. Cards sold by major telecommunications companies like AT&T may offer better deals than upstart companies.

TIME

New England observes daylight saving time, which involves setting clocks ahead one hour on the first Sunday in April and back one hour on the last Sunday in October. The US (excluding Alaska and Hawaii) spans four time zones. New England is on US Eastern Time.

When it's noon in New England, it's:

11am in Chicago (same day)
9am in San Francisco (same day)
noon in Montreal (same day)
9am in Vancouver (same day)
2am in Tokyo (next day)
4am in Melbourne (next day)
5pm in London (same day)
6pm in Amsterdam (same day)
6pm in Paris (same day)
6pm in Rome (same day)

TOILETS

Americans have many names for public toilet facilities, but the most common names are 'restroom,' 'bathroom,' or 'ladies'/men's room.' Of course, you can just ask for the 'toilet.'

Restrooms can be difficult to find in the larger cities of New England. There is no public mandate stating that restaurants, hotels or public sites must open their doors to those in need, but you can usually find relief at information centers and larger hotels. The city of Boston has a few coin-operated toilets placed at key tourist destinations (that cost 25¢ for 15 minutes).

TOURIST INFORMATION

State and regional tourist offices include the following:

Cape Cod Canal Region Chamber of Commerce
(☎ 508-759-6000; www.capecodcanalchamber.org; 70 Main St, Buzzards Bay, MA 02532)
Connecticut Office of Tourism (☎ 800-282-6863; www.ctbound.org; 505 Hudson St, Hartford, CT 06106-7106)
Greater Boston Convention & Visitors Bureau
(☎ 536-4100, 800-888-5515; www.bostonusa.com; 2 Copley Pl, ste 195, Boston, MA 0216)
Maine Office of Tourism (☎ 207-287-5711, 888-624-6345; www.visitmaine.com; 59 State House Station, Augusta, ME 04330)
Massachusetts Office of Travel & Tourism (☎ 617-973-8500, 800-227-6277; www.massvacation.com; State Transportation Bldg, 10 Park Plaza, ste 4510, Boston, MA 02116)
New Hampshire Division of Travel & Tourism
(☎ 603-271-2666, 800-258-3608; www.visitnh.gov; PO Box 1856, Concord, NH 03302)
Rhode Island Tourism Division (☎ 401-222-2601, 800-556-2484; www.visitrhodeisland.com; 1 W Exchange St, Providence, RI 02903)
Vermont Dept of Tourism and Marketing (☎ 802-828-3236; www.vermontvacation.com; 6 Baldwin St, Montpelier, VT 05633-1301)

Chambers of Commerce

Often associated with convention and visitors' bureaus (CVBs), these are membership organizations for local businesses including hotels, restaurants and shops. Although they often provide maps and other useful information, they usually don't tell you about establishments that are not chamber members, and these nonmembers are often the cheapest or most independent establishments.

A local chamber of commerce usually maintains an information booth at the entrance to the town or in the town center, often open only during tourist seasons (summer, foliage season, ski season).

TOURS

For those with limited time, package tours can sometimes be the cheapest way to go. Basic ones cover airfare and accommodation, while deluxe packages include car rental, island-hopping and all sorts of activities. Alternative tours include Bike Vermont (p377), which operates two- to six-night bike tours; Vermont Inn-to-Inn Walking Tours (p363), which offers the same but for those interested in getting around on two feet rather than two wheels; and Elderhostel (p530), which offers educational programs for seniors.

Throughout New England you'll find many towns with a historical society that offers walking tours. They're usually very good and rather inexpensive. Kayaking tours, which are always fun for families and the inner-child, are plentiful on inland lakes and along the coast. Always keep an eye out for quirky tours like Moose Tours in Northern Forest Heritage Park (p461) or nature tours like Art's Dune Tours (p199).

VISAS

Since the establishment of the Department of Homeland Security following the events of September 11, 2001, immigration now falls under the purview of the **Bureau of Citizenship and Immigration Service** (BCIS; www.bcis.gov).

Getting into the United States can be a bureaucratic nightmare, depending on your country of origin. To make matters worse, the rules are rapidly changing. For up-to-date information about visas and immigration, check with the **US State Department** (www.travel.his.com/visa/).

Most foreign visitors to the US need a visa. However, there is a Visa Waiver Program in which citizens of certain countries may enter the US for stays of 90 days or less without first obtaining a US visa. This list is subject to continual re-examination and bureaucratic rejiggering. Currently these countries include Andorra, Australia, Austria, Belgium, Brunei, Denmark, Finland, France, Germany, Iceland, Ireland, Italy, Japan, Liechtenstein, Luxembourg, Monaco, the Netherlands, New Zealand, Norway, Portugal, San Marino, Singapore, Slovenia, Spain, Sweden, Switzerland, and the UK. Under this program you must have a round-trip ticket (or onward ticket to any foreign destination) that is non-refundable in the US and you will not be allowed to extend your stay beyond 90 days.

Because the Department of Homeland Security is continually modifying its entry requirements, even those with visa waivers may be subject to enrolment in the US-Visit program. This program may require that visa recipients have a machine-readable passport and/or a digital scan of their fingerprints. Contact the **Department of Homeland Security** (www.dhs.gov) for current requirements.

Nonetheless, your passport should be valid for at least six months longer than your intended stay and you'll need to submit a recent photo (50.8mm x 50.8mm) with the visa application. Documents of financial stability and/or guarantees from a US resident are sometimes required, particularly for those from developing countries. Visa applicants may be required to 'demonstrate binding obligations' that will ensure their return home. Because of this requirement, those planning to travel through other countries before arriving in the US are generally better off applying for their US visa while they are still in their home country rather than while on the road.

The validity period for a US visitor visa depends on your home country. The actual length of time you'll be allowed to stay in the US is determined by the BCIS at the port of entry.

WOMEN TRAVELERS

Contemporary women in New England can take some comfort in knowing that generations of the region's women have won respect and equality for females in business, arts, science, politics, education, religion and community service. In fact, in some communities like Nantucket, which developed as a matriarchy run by the Quaker 'gray ladies' (while the men were at sea, whaling), women still dominate commercial and community affairs.

Nevertheless, women travelers everywhere, including in New England, do face challenges particular to their gender. Avoiding vulnerable situations and conducting yourself in a common-sense manner will help you to avoid most problems. You're more vulnerable if you've been drinking or using drugs than if you're sober, and you're more vulnerable alone than if you're with company. If you don't want company, most men will respect a firm but polite 'no thank you.'

If despite all your precautions you are assaulted, call the police (☎ 911). Many cities have rape crisis centers to aid victims of rape. For the telephone number of the nearest center, call directory information (☎ 411 or 1 + area code + 555-1212).

The **National Organization for Women** (NOW; ☎ 202-331-0066; www.now.org; 1000 16th St NW, ste 700, Washington, DC 20036) is a good resource for a variety of information and can refer you to state and local chapters. **Planned Parenthood** (☎ 212-541-7800; www.plannedparenthood.org; 26 Bleecker St, New York, NY 10019) can refer you to clinics throughout the country and offer advice on medical issues.

WORK

You will find lots of summer jobs at New England seaside and mountain resorts. These are usually low-paying service jobs filled by young people (often college students) who are happy to work part of the day so they can play the rest. If you want such a job, contact the local chambers of commerce or businesses well in advance. You can't depend on finding a job just by arriving in May or June and looking around.

In winter, contact New England's ski resorts, where full- and part-time help is often welcome.

Foreigners entering the US to work must have a visa that permits it. Apply for a work visa from the US embassy in your home country before you leave. The type of visa varies, depending on how long you're staying and the kind of work you plan to do. Generally, you need either a J-1 visa, which you can obtain by joining a visitor-exchange program (issued mostly to students for work in summer camps), or an H-2B visa, when you are sponsored by a US employer.

The latter can be difficult to procure unless you can show that you already have a job

offer from an employer who considers your qualifications to be unique and not readily available in the US. There are, of course, many foreigners working illegally in the country. Controversial laws prescribe punishments for employers employing 'aliens' (foreigners) who do not have the proper visas. Bureau of Citizenship and Immigration Service officers can be persistent and insistent in their enforcement of the laws.

Transportation

CONTENTS

THINGS CHANGE...

The information in this chapter is particularly vulnerable to change. Check directly with the airline or a travel agent to make sure you understand how a fare (and ticket you may buy) works and be aware of the security requirements for international travel. Shop carefully. The details given in this chapter should be regarded as pointers and are not a substitute for your own careful, up-to-date research.

GETTING THERE & AWAY

While the two most common ways to reach New England are by air and car, you can also get here easily by train and bus. Boston (p127) is the region's hub for air travel, but some international travelers fly into New York City to do some sightseeing before heading up to New England.

ENTERING THE COUNTRY

Despite the fact that Boston's Logan International Airport was intimately connected to the disaster on September 11, 2001, entering the country here is no different than entering any major US city. Be patient and pleasant and you will have no problems. As for border crossings from Canada, the worst problems you will encounter are long lines waiting in your car (see p541).

AIR

Because of New England's location on the densely populated US Atlantic seaboard between New York and eastern Canada, air travelers have a number of ways to approach the region.

Airports & Airlines
NEW ENGLAND

The major gateway to the region is Boston's **Logan International Airport** (BOS; ☎ 800-235-6426; www.massport.com), which offers many direct, nonstop flights from major airports in the US and abroad.

Depending on where you will be doing the bulk of your exploring, several other airports in the region receive national and international flights:

Bangor (BGR; ☎ 866-359-2264; www.flybangor.com) Serving central Maine.

Bradley International (BDL; ☎ 888-624-1533; www.bradleyairport.com) Serving Hartford, CT, and Springfield, MA.

Burlington (BTV; ☎ 802-863-1889; www.burlington intlairport.com) Serving northern Vermont.

Manchester (MHT; ☎ 603-624-6539; www.flymanchester.com) Serving southern and central New Hampshire.

Portland Jetport (PWM; ☎ 207-874-8877; www.portlandjetport.org) Serving coastal Maine.

TF Green (PVD; ☎ 888-268-7222; www.pvdairport.com) Serving Providence, RI.

NEW YORK CITY

Flights into metro New York may be more convenient for some travelers, who have three airports from which to choose:

JFK International (JFK; ☎ 718-244-4444; www.panynj.gov/aviation/lgaframe)

LaGuardia (LGA; ☎ 718-244-4444; www.panynj.gov)

Newark International (EWR; ☎ 973-961-6000; www.newarkairport.com)

Tickets

Airfares to the US and New England range from incredibly low to obscenely high. The best deals are often found on the Internet.

TRANSPORTATION

TRANSPORTATION

AIRLINES FLYING TO AND FROM NEW ENGLAND

Aer Lingus (EI; ☎ 800-474-7424; www
.aerlingus.com)

AeroMexico (AM; ☎ 800-237-6639; www.aero
mexico.com)

Air Canada (AC; ☎ 888-247-2262; www
.aircanada.ca)

Air France (AF; ☎ 800-237-2747; www
.airfrance.com)

Air New Zealand (NZ; ☎ 800-262-1234; www
.airnz.co.nz)

Air Tran (FL; ☎ 800-247-8726; www.airtran.com)

Alaska Airlines (AS; ☎ 800-252-7522; www
.alaskaair.com)

Alitalia (AZ; ☎ 800-223-5730; www.alitaliausa
.com)

America West (HP; ☎ 800-235-9292; www
.americawest.com)

American (AA; ☎ 800-223-5436; www.aa.com)

ATA (TZ; ☎ 800-225-2995; www.ata.com)

British Airways (BA; ☎ 800-247-9297; www
.britishairways.com)

Continental (CO; ☎ 800-523-3273; www
.continental.com)

Delta (DL; ☎ 800-221-1212; www.delta.com)

Icelandair (FI; ☎ 800-223-5500; www.iceland
air.com)

Japan Airlines (NQ; ☎ 800-525-3663; www
.japanair.com)

Jet Blue (JB; ☎ 800-538-2583; www.jetblue.com)

Lufthansa (LH; ☎ 800-645-3880; www
.lufthansa.com)

Northwest-KLM (NW; ☎ 800-225-2525; www
.nwa.com)

Qantas (QF; ☎ 800-227-4500; www.quantasusa
.com)

Song (SQ; ☎ 800-359-7664; www.flysong.com)

Southwest (SW; ☎ 800-435-9792; www
.southwest.com)

Swiss (LX; ☎ 877-359-7947; www.swiss.com)

United (UA; ☎ 800-241-6522; www.united.com)

US Airways (US; ☎ 800-428-4322; www
.usairways.com)

Virgin Atlantic (VS; ☎ 800-862-8621; www
.virginatlantic.com)

Start searching at www.travelocity.com, www.expedia.com or www.orbitz.com. Then head to **STA Travel** (☎ 800-777-0112; www.statravel.com), which might be offering good fares online and which has offices in major cities nation- and worldwide.

Many domestic carriers offer special fares to visitors who are not US citizens. Typically, you must purchase a booklet of coupons in conjunction with a flight into the US from a foreign country other than Canada or Mexico. In addition to other restrictions, these coupons typically must be used within a limited period of time.

Round-the-world (RTW) tickets can be a great deal if you want to visit other regions on your way to New England. Often they are the same price – or not much more expensive – than a simple round-trip ticket to the USA. RTW itineraries that include stops in South America or Africa, though, can be substantially more expensive. **British Airways** (☎ 800-247-9297; www.britishairways.com) and **Qantas** (☎ 800-227-4500; www.qantasusa.com) offer the best plans through programs called oneworld Explorer and Global Explorer, respectively.

Most airlines require a 14-day advance purchase. But if you're flying standby, call the airline a day or two before the flight and make a standby reservation so that you'll get priority.

Australia

Qantas flies to Los Angeles from Sydney, Melbourne and Brisbane. United flies from Sydney to San Francisco and Los Angeles, where connector flights are available to the East Coast. In the summertime, fares are generally around A$2700 to A$3200 (US$2000 to US$2500) for a round-trip from Melbourne or Sydney to Boston.

From Australia, a Qantas RTW ticket permits six stops in North America and the Caribbean, four stops in Europe and four stops in Asia for A$3539 (US$2735).

Canada

Boston receives daily direct and nonstop flights from most major Canadian cities on many major carriers, including Air Canada, American, Delta, Northwest and United. Canadian fares to Boston in the summertime are reasonable: you can expect to find round-trips from Halifax for C$350 (US$290), from Montreal for C$290 (US$230) and from Toronto for C$290 (US$230).

The Canadian Federation of Students' **Travel CUTS** (www.travelcuts.com) travel agency offers low fares and has offices in major cities throughout Canada.

Continental Europe

Many carriers offer direct services to Boston, but prices can vary substantially depending on the season and directness of routing. In Paris, **STA** (☎ 01-44-41-89-80; www.sta.com) is a popular place to start for well-priced tickets. From Frankfurt to Boston, expect a round-trip ticket to cost €490 (US$650) in the winter, €750 (US$1000) in the summer; from Amsterdam the prices are about €560 ($750) and €1130 ($1500), respectively.

Virgin Atlantic flights from Paris to New York with seven-day advance purchase range from €750 to €1500 (US$1000 to US$2000). When calculating costs, don't forget to add the cost of getting from New York to Boston or New England via some other mode of transportation.

New Zealand

United and Air New Zealand both fly to San Francisco and Los Angeles from Auckland (via Sydney). Fares are generally around NZ$2200 (US$1500). Connector flights are readily available to the East Coast.

From New Zealand, a RTW ticket via North America, Europe and Asia with Air New Zealand and other airlines costs NZ$3100 and up.

UK & Ireland

London is arguably the world's headquarters for bucket shops specializing in discount tickets, and they are well advertised. Two good, reliable agents for cheap tickets in the UK are **Trailfinders** (☎ 020-7628-7628; www.trailfinders.co.uk; 1 Threadneedle St, London) and **STA Travel** (☎ 020-240-9821; www.statravel.co.uk; 33 Bedford St, Covent Garden, London).

British Airways flies (round-trip) nonstop between London and Boston for about £500 (US$1000) in summer, £250 (US$500) in winter. Virgin Atlantic has round-trip summertime fares from London to Boston for £450 (US$1000), or to New York for £384 (US$618), allowing a one-month maximum stay and requiring a 21-day advance

---

TRAVEL AGENTS & ONLINE TICKET SITES

You have a choice: talk to a live agent or tap the computer keys. Frankly, your odds are better doing it yourself if you can make the time. The following agents and websites are recommended:

STA Travel (☎ 800-777-0112; www.statravel.com)
Travelocity (www.travelocity.com)
Expedia.com (www.expedia.com)
Orbitz (www.orbitz.com)
CheapTickets (www.cheaptickets.com)
Atevo (www.atevo.com)
Best Fares (www.bestfares.com)

---

purchase. Wintertime flights from London can be as low as £230 (US$450) to Boston or £190 (US$375) to New York.

Aer Lingus offers direct flights from Shannon and Dublin to Boston for about £270 (US$360) in summer.

USA

Competition is high among airlines flying to Boston from major US cities. With a bit of luck and flexibility, you can usually get a flight from the West Coast to Boston for about $400 round-trip. From Washington, DC, fares are in the $200 round-trip range. From Chicago, expect to spend about $300 round-trip. Savvy Internet browsers can cut the cost of coast-to-coast airfares in half with a bit of flexibility. At last look, for instance, Jet Blue flew from San Francisco to Boston twice daily (nonstop) for $200 plus taxes. That almost makes a bi-coastal life possible!

LAND

Almost every New Englander knows the story about the British coming to Boston in 1776 'one if by land, two if by sea' (see p80). Well in this case, most visitors, unlike the British, arrive by land.

Border Crossings

Generally, crossing the US/Canadian border is pretty straightforward. The biggest hassle is usually the length of the lines. Citizens of the US can cross with a valid passport or birth certificate, while visitors from other countries are required to have a passport. You may also be asked to show a return plane ticket or proof of sufficient funds, but this is rare.

TRANSPORTATION

TRANSPORTATION

Bus

You can get to New England by bus from all parts of the US and Canada, but the trip will be long and may not be much less expensive than a discounted flight. Bus companies usually offer special promotional fares; ask about them when you call the bus company.

For travel between San Francisco and New England, **Green Tortoise** (☎ 415-956-7500, 800-867-8647; www.greentortoise.com) buses are relaxing and entertaining. You'll spend 12 to 14 days winding across the country via state and national parks, monuments, forests and anywhere else your fellow passengers agree to stop; flexibility is key. Fares are $649, plus a food fund payment of $171 per person.

Bonanza Bus Lines (☎ 888-751-8800; www.bonanzabus.com) operates routes from New York City to the Berkshires, and from New York City to Cape Cod via Providence. Bonanza also operates buses to Newport and New Bedford.

Greyhound (☎ 800-231-2222; www.greyhound.com) operates buses from New York City to Hartford, Springfield, Worcester, New Haven, New London, Providence and Cape Cod.

Vermont Transit (☎ 802-864-6811, 800-552-8737; www.vermonttransit.com) serves Montreal, Vermont, Boston, Maine and several points in New Hampshire in conjunction with Greyhound.

Fung Wah (www.fungwahbus.com) provides service between New York City's Chinatown and Boston's Chinatown one-way for $15.

Car & Motorcycle

Interstate highways crisscross New England, and offer forest, farm and mountain scenery once you are clear of urban areas and the I-95 corridor between Boston and New York. These interstate highways connect the region to New York, Washington, DC, Montreal and points south and west. See opposite for more on car and motorcycle travel in New England.

Train

Rail passenger service in the US is operated primarily by **Amtrak** (☎ 800-872-7245; www.amtrak.com). Service along the 'Northeast Corridor' (connecting Boston, Providence, Hartford and New Haven with New York and Washington, DC) is some of the most frequent in Amtrak's system.

Amtrak's high-speed 'Acela' trains make the trip from New York City to Boston in three hours. One-way weekend special fares aboard Acela trains cost $99 from New York and $176 from Washington, DC. About 10 trains depart New York City daily for Boston's South Station (p126).

Amtrak has a few different routes to and through New England. The *Vermonter* runs through New Haven and Hartford, CT, Springfield and Amherst, MA, and then on to St Albans in Vermont.

The *Montrealer* runs to northern Vermont along the Connecticut River Valley, with stops in New Haven, CT, Amherst, MA and Essex Junction (for Burlington), White River Junction and Brattleboro, VT.

The *Lake Shore Limited* departs Chicago each evening for Boston, making stops in Springfield, Worcester and Boston.

Amtrak offers excursion fares, seasonal discounts and rail passes good for unlimited travel during a certain period of time. Children receive discounts as well. The fares listed below are unreserved, coach class, one-way fares to Boston.

From	Fare (one-way peak/non-peak)	Duration
New York, NY	$64/99	4 hrs
Chicago, IL	$70/91	23 hrs
Washington, DC	$91/176	9 hrs
San Francisco, CA	$137/216	72 hrs

GETTING AROUND

Simply put, the best way to get around New England is by car. The region is relatively small, the highways are good and public transportation is not as frequent or as widespread as in some other countries. Still, there are the alternatives of air, train and bus.

AIR

Regional and commuter airlines connect New England's cities and resorts with Boston and New York City. The following airports receive scheduled flights:

Barnstable Municipal Airport (☎ 508-775-2020) Serves Cape Cod.

Bradley International Airport (☎ 888-624-1533) Serves Connecticut and the Berkshires and Central Massachusetts.

Burlington Airport (☎ 802-863-1889) Vermont's major airport.
Groton/New London Airport (☎ 860-445-8549) Serves the southeastern Connecticut coast.
Manchester Airport (☎ 603-624-6539) Serves south-central New Hampshire and metropolitan Boston.
Martha's Vineyard Airport (☎ 508-693-7022) Serves the Vineyard.
Nantucket Airport (☎ 508-325-5300) Serves Nantucket Island.
TF Green State Airport (☎ 888-268-7222) Serves Providence with several major and regional carriers.
Worcester Municipal Airport (☎ 508-799-1741) Serves central Massachusetts.

Regular flights reach Maine's regional airports in Bangor, Bar Harbor/Hancock County and Portland. For more on these airports, see the Getting There & Away sections under each town.

Airlines in New England
Cape Air (☎ 800-352-0714; www.flycapeair.com) Flights to Cape Cod, Martha's Vineyard and Nantucket.
Delta (☎ 800-221-1212; www.delta.com) Largest NE carrier.
Nantucket Air (☎ 800-635-8787; www.nantuketair lines.com) Flights from Cape Cod to Nantucket.
New England Airlines (☎ 800-243-2460; www.block -island.com/nea/) Flights to Block Island from Westerly.
US Airways Express (☎ 800-428-4322; www.usair ways.com) Flights to ME, NH and Cape Cod.

BICYCLE
Bicycling is a popular New England sport and means of transport on both city streets and country roads. Several of the larger cities have systems of bike paths that make bike travel much easier and more pleasant. Disused railroad rights-of-way have also been turned into bike trails. The Cape Cod Rail Trail (p184) between Dennis and Wellfleet is a prominent example.

Bicycle rentals are available in most New England cities, towns and resorts at reasonable prices (often $15 to $20 per day). Many rental shops are mentioned in this guide.

For more on bicycling, see p48 .

BOAT
Boat service in New England is more accurately called ferry service and it tends to be more for pleasure excursions than transportation. There are a couple of exceptions though.

In Massachusetts, you can take a ferry between Boston and Provincetown on Cape Cod (p203). Ferries leave for Martha's Vineyard from Falmouth, Woods Hole, New Bedford and Hyannis. You can reach Nantucket (p209) from Woods Hole and Hyannis.

In Connecticut, ferries travel between Bridgeport and Port Jefferson (Long Island, New York, see p332); New London and Block Island (p306); New London and Orient Point (Long Island, see p325); and New London and Fisher's Island (New York, see p325).

In Vermont, there's a ferry running from Burlington to New York state, traversing Lake Champlain (p404).

In Maine, you can travel by ferry between Bar Harbor (p505) and Portland (p480) and Yarmouth, Nova Scotia; local ferries also service island communities like Monhegan, North Haven and Vinalhaven.

BUS
Buses go to more places than airplanes or trains, but the routes still miss a lot, bypassing some prime destinations, and service is often very infrequent. Individual route prices are covered under the Getting There & Away sections of regional chapters.

Bonanza Bus Lines (☎ 888-751-8800; www.bon anzabus.com) has a hub in Providence.
Greyhound (☎ 800-231-2222; www.greyhound .com) operates buses connecting Boston with New York City, Hartford and New Haven, CT, as well as the Berkshires, Springfield and Worcester, MA.
Peter Pan Bus Lines (☎ 413-781-3320, 800-343-9999; www.peterpanbus.com) is based in Springfield and offers good service in Central Massachusetts and the Berkshires.
Vermont Transit Lines (☎ 802-864-6811, 800-552-8737; www.vermonttransit.com), based in White River Junction, has routes connecting major Vermont towns with Boston; Manchester and Portsmouth, NH; and Bangor, Bar Harbor, Brunswick and Portland, ME.
Plymouth & Brockton (☎ 508-778-9767; www.p-b .com) serves Plymouth on Boston's South Shore as well as Sagamore, Barnstable, Hyannis, Chatham and Provincetown (all on Cape Cod).
Concord Trailways (☎ 800-639-3317; www.con cordtrailways.com), based in Concord, NH, provides most of the bus service in the state and serves Maine, New Hampshire and Boston.

C&J Trailways (☎ 800-258-7111; www.cjtrailways .com) serves Boston's Logan International Airport and South Station from Newburyport, MA, and Portsmouth, NH.

Bus Passes & Reservations
Some companies offer special deals if you purchase more than one ticket at a time. For instance, if you purchase four roundtrip tickets with the same departure and arrival cities from Peter Pan and Bonanza, the price is $14 per ticket plus tax. Vermont Transit offers a pass for 10 consecutive days of travel that can be used anywhere in the US for $269.

Bus reservations are not usually necessary, except around holidays.

CAR & MOTORCYCLE
Yes, driving is the best way to see New England. But heads up: New England drivers, particularly around Boston and other cities, are aggressive, speedy and unpredictable. Traffic jams are common in urban areas.

As for parking, municipalities control parking by signs on the street stating explicitly what may or may not be done. Meters require multiple feedings with quarters. A yellow line or yellow-painted curb means that no parking is allowed there.

Automobile Associations
The **American Automobile Association** (AAA; ☎ 800-564-6222) provides members with maps and other information. Members also get discounts on car rentals, air tickets, some hotels, some sightseeing attractions, as well as emergency road service and towing (☎ 800-222-4357). AAA has reciprocal agreements with automobile associations in other countries. Be sure to bring your membership card from your country of origin.

Driver's License
An international driving license, obtained before you leave home, is only necessary if your country of origin is a non–English speaking one.

Fuel
Gas stations are ubiquitous and many are open 24 hours a day. Small-town stations may be open only from 7am to 8pm or 9pm. Plan on spending $2.00 to $2.50 per US gallon.

At some stations, you must pay before you pump; at others, you may pump before you pay. The more modern pumps have credit/debit card terminals built into them, so you can pay with plastic right at the pump. At more expensive, 'full service' stations, an attendant will pump your gas for you; no tip is expected.

Hire
Rental cars are readily available. With advance reservations for a small car, the daily rate with unlimited mileage is about $50, while typical weekly rates are $250 to $300. (Rates for mid-size cars are often only a tad higher.) Dropping off the car at a different location from where you picked it up usually incurs an additional fee. It always pays to shop around between rental companies. You can often snag great last-minute deals via the Internet.

Having a major credit card greatly simplifies the rental process. Without one, some agents simply will not rent vehicles, while others require prepayment, a deposit of $200 per week, pay stubs, proof of round-trip airfare and more.

The following companies operate in New England:

Alamo (☎ 800-327-9633; www.goalamo.com)
Avis (☎ 800-321-3712; www.avis.com)
Budget (☎ 800-527-0700; www.budget.com)
Dollar (☎ 800-800-4000; www.dollarcar.com)
Enterprise (☎ 800-736-8222; www.enterprise.com)
Hertz (☎ 800-654-3131; www.hertz.com)
National (☎ 800-227-7368; www.nationalcar.com)
Thrifty (☎ 800-367-2277; www.thrifty.com)

There are a handful of smaller agencies as well, but for the most part, big companies offer newer, more reliable cars and fewer hassles. That said, the best smaller agency is **Rent-A-Wreck** (☎ 800-535-1391; www.rentawreck.com).

Insurance
Liability insurance covers people and property that you might hit. For damage to the actual rental vehicle, a collision damage waiver (CDW) is available for about $15 a day. If you have collision coverage on your vehicle at home, it might cover damages to car rentals; inquire before departing. Additionally, some credit cards offer reimbursement coverage for collision damages if you rent the car with that credit card; again,

check before departing. Most credit card coverage isn't valid for rentals of more than 15 days or for exotic models, jeeps, vans and 4WD vehicles. Car rental companies offer insurance.

Road Conditions & Hazards

New England roads – even the warren of hard-packed dirt roads that crisscross Vermont – are very good. Some roads across northern mountain passes in Vermont, New Hampshire and Maine are closed during the winter, but good signage gives you plenty of warning.

Road Rules

Driving laws are different in each of the New England states, but most require the use of safety belts. In every state, children under four years of age must be placed in a child safety seat secured by a seat belt. Most states require motorcycle riders to wear helmets whenever they ride. In any case, use of a helmet is highly recommended.

The maximum speed limit on most New England interstates is 65mph, but some have a limit of 55mph. On undivided highways, the speed limit will vary from 30mph to 55mph. Police enforce speed limits by patrolling in police cruisers and in unmarked cars. Fines can cost upwards of $350 in Connecticut, and it's similarly expensive in other states.

LOCAL TRANSPORTATION

City buses, and the T (the subway/underground system) in Boston, provide useful transportation within the larger cities and to some suburbs. Resort areas also tend to have regional bus lines. See Getting Around under the relevant regional sections for more information.

Taxis are common in the largest cities, but in smaller cities and towns, you will probably have to telephone a cab to pick you up. Shuttles may take travelers from their hotel to the airport.

TRAIN

Shore Line East (☎ 203-777-7433; www.rideworks .com/rwsl.htm) trains connect the coastal towns between the New York border and New Haven. **Metro-North** (☎ 212-532-4900, 800-638-7646; www.mta.info) trains run between New York City and New Haven. In Boston, **MBTA Commuter Rail** trains (☎ 800-392-6100; www.mbta.com) travel to the west and north, making stops at Concord, Rockport, Gloucester and Manchester; see p127 for more information.

TRANSPORTATION

Health

CONTENTS

The North American continent encompasses an extraordinary range of climates and terrains, many of which may be encountered in New England. Because of the high level of hygiene here, infectious diseases will not be a significant concern for most travelers, who will most likely experience nothing worse than a little diarrhea or a mild respiratory infection.

BEFORE YOU GO

HEALTH INSURANCE

The United States offers possibly the finest health care in the world. The problem is that, unless you have good insurance, it can be prohibitively expensive. It's essential to purchase travel health insurance if your regular policy doesn't cover you when you're abroad.

Bring any medications you may need in their original containers, clearly labeled. A signed, dated letter from your physician that describes all medical conditions and medications, including generic names, is also a good idea.

If your health insurance does not cover you for medical expenses abroad, consider getting supplemental insurance. Check the Subwwway section of the Lonely Planet website (www.lonelyplanet.com/subwwway) for more information. Make sure you find out in advance if your insurance plan will make payments directly to providers or reimburse you later for overseas health expenditures.

RECOMMENDED VACCINATIONS

No special vaccines are required or recommended for travel to New England. All travelers should be up-to-date on routine immunizations.

INTERNET RESOURCES

There is a large amount of travel health advice on the Internet. The World Health Organization (WHO) publishes a superb book, called *International Travel and Health*, which is revised annually and is available online at no cost from its website at www.who.int/ith/. Another website of general interest is MD Travel Health at www.mdtravelhealth.com, which provides complete travel health recommendations for every country; it's updated daily, also at no cost.

It's usually a good idea to consult your government's travel health website before departure, if one is available:

Australia (www.dfat.gov.au/travel/)
Canada (www.hc-sc.gc.ca/english/index.html)
UK (www.doh.gov.uk/traveladvice/index.htm)
US (www.cdc.gov/travel/)

IN THE USA

AVAILABILITY & COST OF HEALTH CARE

In general, if you have a medical emergency, the best bet is to find the nearest hospital and go to its emergency room. If the problem isn't urgent, you can call a nearby hospital and ask for a referral to a local physician, which is usually cheaper than a trip to the emergency room. You should avoid stand-alone, for-profit urgent care centers, which tend to perform large numbers of expensive tests, even for minor illnesses.

Pharmacies are abundantly supplied throughout the USA, but you could find that some medications that are available over-the-counter in your home country require a prescription here, and, as always, if you don't have insurance to cover the cost of these prescriptions, they can be shockingly expensive.

INFECTIOUS DISEASES

In addition to more common ailments, there are several infectious diseases that are unknown or uncommon outside North America. Most are acquired by mosquito or tick bites.

West Nile Virus

These infections were unknown in the United States until a few years ago, but have now been reported in almost all 50 states. The virus is transmitted by culex mosquitoes, which are active in late summer and early fall and generally bite after dusk. Most infections are mild or asymptomatic, but the virus may infect the central nervous system, leading to fever, headache, confusion, lethargy, coma and sometimes death. There is no treatment for West Nile virus. For the latest update on the areas affected by West Nile, go to the US Geological Survey website (http://westnilemaps.usgs.gov/).

Lyme Disease

This disease has been reported from many states, but most documented cases occur in the northeastern part of the country, especially in New York, New Jersey, Connecticut and Massachusetts. Lyme disease is transmitted by deer ticks, which are only 1mm to 2mm long. Most cases occur in the late spring and summer. The CDC has an informative, if slightly scary, web page on Lyme disease at www.cdc.gov/ncidod/dvbid/lyme/.

The first symptom is usually an expanding red rash that is often pale in the center, known as a bull's eye rash. However, in many cases, no rash is observed. Flu-like symptoms are common, including fever, headache, joint pains, body aches and malaise. When the infection is treated promptly with an appropriate antibiotic, usually doxycycline or amoxicillin, the cure rate is high. Luckily, since the tick must be attached for 36 hours or more to transmit Lyme disease, most cases can be prevented by performing a thorough tick check after you've been outdoors, as described on p548.

Rabies

Rabies is a viral infection of the brain and spinal cord that is almost always fatal. The rabies virus is carried in the saliva of infected animals and is typically transmitted through an animal bite, though contamination of any break in the skin with infected saliva may result in rabies. In the US, most cases of human rabies are related to exposure to bats. Rabies may also be contracted from raccoons, skunks, foxes and unvaccinated cats and dogs.

If there is any possibility, however small, that you have been exposed to rabies, you should seek preventative treatment, which consists of rabies immune globulin and rabies vaccine and is quite safe. In particular, any contact with a bat should be discussed with health authorities, because bats have small teeth and may not leave obvious bite marks. If you wake up to find a bat in your room, or discover a bat in a room with small children, rabies prophylaxis may be necessary.

Giardiasis

This parasitic infection of the small intestine occurs throughout North America and the world. Symptoms may include nausea, bloating, cramps, and diarrhea, and may last for weeks. To protect yourself from giardia, you should avoid drinking directly from lakes, ponds, streams and rivers, which may be contaminated by animal or human feces. The infection can also be transmitted from person-to-person if proper hand washing is not performed. Giardiasis is easily diagnosed by a stool test and readily treated with antibiotics.

HIV/AIDS

As with most parts of the world, HIV infection occurs throughout the United States. You should never assume, on the basis of someone's background or appearance, that they're free of this or any other sexually transmitted disease. Be sure to use a condom for all sexual encounters.

ENVIRONMENTAL HAZARDS
Bites & Stings

Common sense approaches to these concerns are the most effective: wear boots when hiking to protect from snakes, wear long sleeves and pants to protect from ticks and mosquitoes. If you're bitten, don't overreact. Stay calm and follow the recommended treatment.

HEALTH

HEALTH

MOSQUITO BITES

When traveling in areas where West Nile or other mosquito-borne illnesses have been reported, keep yourself covered (wear long sleeves, long pants, hats and shoes rather than sandals) and apply a good insect repellent, preferably one containing DEET, to exposed skin and clothing. In general, adults and children over 12 should use preparations containing 25% to 35% DEET, which usually lasts about six hours. Children between two and 12 years of age should use preparations containing no more than 10% DEET, applied sparingly, which will usually last about three hours. Neurologic toxicity has been reported from DEET, especially in children, but appears to be extremely uncommon and generally related to overuse. DEET-containing compounds should not be used on children under age two.

Insect repellents containing certain botanical products, including eucalyptus oil and soybean oil, are effective but last only 1½ to two hours. Products based on citronella are not effective.

Visit the website of the **Center for Disease Control's website** (CDC; www.cdc.gov/ncidod/dvbid/westnile/prevention_info.htm) for information about preventing mosquito bites.

TICK BITES

Ticks are parasitic arachnids that may be present in brush, forest and grasslands, where hikers often get them on their legs or in their boots. Adult ticks suck blood from hosts by burrowing into the skin and can carry infections such as Lyme disease.

Always check your body for ticks after walking through high grass or thickly forested areas. If ticks are found unattached, they can simply be brushed off. If a tick is found attached, press down around the tick's head with tweezers, grab the head and gently pull upwards – do not twist it. (If no tweezers are available, use your fingers, but protect them from contamination with a piece of tissue or paper.) Do not rub oil, alcohol or petroleum jelly on it. If you get sick in the following couple of weeks, consult a doctor.

ANIMAL BITES

Do not attempt to pet, handle, or feed any animal, with the exception of domestic animals known to be free of any infectious disease. Most animal injuries are directly related to a person's attempt to touch or feed the animal.

Any bite or scratch by a mammal, including bats, should be promptly and thoroughly cleansed with large amounts of soap and water, followed by application of an antiseptic such as iodine or alcohol. The local health authorities should be contacted immediately for possible postexposure rabies treatment, whether or not you've been immunized against rabies. It may also be advisable to start an antibiotic, since wounds caused by animal bites and scratches frequently become infected.

SNAKE BITES

There are several varieties of venomous snakes in the US, but unlike those in other countries they do not cause instantaneous death, and antivenins are available. First aid is to place a light constricting bandage over the bite, keep the wounded part below the level of the heart and move it as little as possible. Stay calm and get to a medical facility as soon as possible. Bring the dead snake for identification if you can, but don't risk being bitten again. Do not use the mythic 'cut an X and suck out the venom' trick; this causes more damage to snakebite victims than the bites themselves.

SPIDER & SCORPION BITES

Although there are many species of spiders in New England, the only ones that cause significant human illness are the black widow, brown recluse and hobo spiders. The black widow is black or brown in color, measuring about 15mm in body length, with a shiny top, fat body, and distinctive red or orange hourglass figure on its underside. It's found throughout the US, usually in barns, woodpiles, sheds, harvested crops and bowls of outdoor toilets. The brown recluse spider is brown in color, usually 10mm in body length, with a dark violin-shaped mark on the top of the upper section of the body. It's usually found in the south and southern Midwest, but has spread to other parts of the country in recent years. The brown recluse is active mostly at night, lives in dark sheltered areas such as under porches and in woodpiles, and typically bites when trapped. Hobo spiders are found chiefly in the northwestern United States and western Canada. The symptoms of a hobo spider bite are similar to those from the bite of a brown recluse, but milder.

If bitten by a black widow, you should apply ice or cold packs and go immediately to the nearest emergency room. Complications of a black widow bite may include muscle spasms, breathing difficulties and high blood pressure. The bite of a brown recluse or hobo spider typically causes a large, inflamed wound, sometimes associated with fever and chills. If bitten, apply ice and see a physician.

Glossary

For a hilarious and informative look at Boston dialect, browse Adam Gaffin's site at www.boston-online.com/wickedv.html.

Abenaki – a New England Native American tribe
alpine slide – a curvy chute navigated for fun on a simple wheeled cart or, if it's a water slide, on an inflatable cushion
AMC – Appalachian Mountain Club
ayuh – locution pronounced by some people in Maine during pauses in conversation; perhaps a distant variant of 'yes'; vaguely positive in meaning

Back Bay – a Boston neighborhood developed during the 19th century by filling in a bay in the Charles River
batholith – a mass of rock formed deep in the earth, later perhaps thrust to the surface; customarily of large-crystalled rock (such as granite) and appears as mountainous domes of rock above surrounding terrain of softer material (as Mt Monadnock in southern New Hampshire)
boondocks or **boonies** – a city-dweller's derogatory term for the countryside, especially a remote rural place, as in 'The inn is nice, but it's way out in the boonies'
Brahmin – member of Boston's wealthy, well-educated, 19th-century class; now, any wealthy, cultured Bostonian
BYO or **BYOB** – 'bring your own' or 'bring your own bottle'; designates a restaurant that allows patrons to bring their own wine or beer; see *dry town*

cabinet – milkshake with ice-cream (Rhode Island)
Cape, the – Cape Cod
CCC – Civilian Conservation Corps, the Depression-era federal program established in 1933 to employ unskilled young workers, mainly on projects aimed at the conservation of US wildlands
CCNS – Cape Cod National Seashore
chamber of commerce – a co-operative of local businesses that operates a center offering information on member businesses, including hotels, restaurants and tourist attractions
chandlery – retail shop specializing in yachting equipment
cobble – a high rocky knoll of limestone, marble or quartzite that is found in western Massachusetts
cod cheeks – soft oyster-like bits of meat found on the sides of a codfish's 'face'; a delicacy, along with cod tongues, in some parts of New England and Atlantic Canada
common – see *green*

DAR – Daughters of the American Revolution, a patriotic service organization for women

gimcrack – a small item of uncertain use, perhaps frivolous; a gizmo
glacial pond – a deep, round freshwater pond formed by glacial gouging action during the ice age; a common feature of the New England terrain (such as Walden Pond in Concord, Massachusetts)
green – the grass-covered open space typically found at the center of a traditional New England village or town, originally used as common pastureland ('the common'), but now serving as a central park; often surrounded by community service buildings such as the town hall
grinder – a large sandwich of meat, cheese, lettuce, tomato, dressing etc in a long bread roll; in other parts of the US often called a 'submarine,' 'po' boy,' 'Cuban' or 'hoagie'

hidden drive – a driveway entering a road in such a way that visibility for approaching drivers is impaired; signs warn of them
hookup – a facility at an RV camping site for connecting (hooking up) a vehicle to electricity, water, sewer or even cable TV
housekeeping cabin/unit – a hotel or motel room or detached housing unit equipped with kitchen facilities, rented by the day, week or month; see *efficiency*
hybrid bike – cross between a road bike and a mountain bike with medium-thickness tires

Indian summer – a brief warm period, usually in late autumn, before the cold weather sets in for the winter
ironclad – a 19th-century wooden warship with iron sheathing
Islands, the – Martha's Vineyard and Nantucket islands

leaf-peeping – recreational touring (by 'leaf-peepers') to enjoy autumn foliage colors; see also *foliage season*
lean-to – a simple shelter for camping, usually without walls, windows or doors, with a steeply slanting roof touching the ground on one side
lobster roll – a hot-dog bun or other bread roll filled with lobster meat in a mayonnaise sauce and sometimes dressed with celery and lettuce
Lower (or Outer) Cape – the long, narrow extension of Cape Cod north and east from Orleans to Provincetown

maple – a tree of the genus *Acer* having lobed leaves, winged seeds borne in pairs and close-grained wood, well suited to making furniture and flooring; the sap of the sugar maple (*Acer saccharum*) is gathered, boiled and reduced to make maple syrup; see *sugar bush, sugaring off*

Mid-Cape – region of Cape Cod roughly from Barnstable and Hyannis eastward to Orleans

minuteman – a colonial militiaman pledged to be ready at a moment's notice to defend his home and village; originally organized against Native American attacks, the minutemen provided the first organized American military force in the Revolutionary War against British troops

mud season – springtime in New England when the snow melts and the earth thaws

NPS – National Park Service, a division of the Department of the Interior that administers US national parks and monuments

Nutmeggers – nickname for residents of Connecticut

OSV – Old Sturbridge Village, Massachusetts

P-Town – Provincetown, on Cape Cod, Massachusetts

package store – liquor store

pie – another name for pizza

raw bar – a counter where fresh uncooked shellfish (clams, oysters, etc) are served

redcoat – a soldier from the British side during the American Revolution

RISD – Rhode Island School of Design

rush tickets – sometimes called 'student rush' or 'rush seats,' these are discounted tickets bought at a theater or concert hall box office usually no more than an hour or two before a performance

sachem – Native American chieftain; Massasoit was sachem of the Wampanoag tribe

sagamon – similar to *sachem*

shire town – county seat, town holding county government buildings

soaring – term for glider (sailplane) rides

Southie – South Boston, a neighborhood inhabited largely by Bostonians of Irish descent with a strong sense of Irish identity

sugar bush – a grove of sugar-maple trees; see *maple*

sugaring off – the springtime (March) harvest of sap

from maple trees, which is collected and boiled to reduce it to maple syrup

T, the – official nickname for the Massachusetts Bay Transportation Authority (MBTA) Rapid Transit System

tall ships – tall-masted sailing vessels

taqueria – a casual Mexican food joint

tin ceiling – late-19th- to early-20th-century decorative feature consisting of thin steel sheets ('tinplates') embossed with decorative patterns, painted and used to cover ceilings

tuck-in – a substantial, sandwich-like meal

UMass – University of Massachusetts

Upper Cape – Cape Cod region near the Cape Cod Canal and the mainland

USFS – United States Forest Service, a division of the Department of Agriculture that implements policies on federal forest lands on the principles of 'multiple use,' including timber cutting, wildlife management, camping and recreation

USGS – United States Geological Survey, an agency of the Department of the Interior responsible for, among other things, detailed topographic maps of the entire country (particularly popular with hikers and backpackers)

UMass – University of Massachusetts

UVM – University of Vermont

Vineyard, the – (pronounced 'vin-yerd'), the island of Martha's Vineyard

weir – fishnet of string, bark strips, twigs etc placed in a river current to catch fish; using weirs is the oldest-known method of fishing in the world

windjammer – a tall-masted sailing ship

WPA – Works Progress Administration; established under President Roosevelt to put artists to work during the Great Depression

Yankee – perhaps from *Jan Kees* (John Cheese), a derogatory term for English settlers in Connecticut used by 17th-century Dutch colonists in New York; an inhabitant or native of New England; one from northeastern USA; a person or soldier from the northern states during the Civil War; an American

Behind the Scenes

THIS BOOK

This 4th edition of *New England* was written by five tried-and-true New Englanders. Kim Grant coordinated the book, and wrote the front and rear chapters plus the Vermont and Maine chapters. Mara Vorhees wrote the Boston, Around Boston and New Hampshire chapters. Alex Hershey wrote the Connecticut and Central Massachusetts & the Berkshires chapters. Andrew Bender covered Cape Cod, Nantucket & Martha's Vineyard, and John Spelman covered Rhode Island. Gerald Easter contributed the History chapter. The 3rd edition was written by Randall Peffer, Andrew Rebold, Kim Grant and John Spelman. Earlier editions of New England were written by Tom Brosnahan and Steve Jermanok.

THANKS from the Authors

Kim Grant On so many levels, it takes a New England-style village to pull together these books. I'm grateful beyond compare that my village is overflowing with the kindness and good grace of others. Colby Cedar Smith pulled yeoman's duty during my marathon disappearances; Kim Bolger amazed me with her laser-like observations, humor and professionalism ('she's one of us'); Clare Innes jumped in where others might have feared to tread; Martha Maude came through again; Sylvia Zareva rose to the occasion; Lynette Molnar provided virtual and tangible support. And the wise and serious Catherine Direen provided a sense of timelessness, a project plan, a commute to Starbucks to 'work' and a steady stream of Balance Bars. Whatever the question is, the answer is yes. (Unless it has to do with Red Bull after dark.)

To the great crew of co-authors: job well done. Thanks for making my job as CA a delight. To Jay Cooke, thanks for putting up with me hitting a wall and taking such an interest in New England.

Andrew Bender First thanks go to Ginny and Bill Gallagher, Ginger Bushell and Chris Barnes, and Bill de Souza. There's no way to do the rest of you justice so I hope a list will suffice: Barry Behm, Todd Bidwell, Candace Boden, Bob DuBois, Patricia Fitzpatrick, Laurel Guadazno, Kyle Hinkle, Kristen McMenamy, Michael and Sara O'Reilly, Lynne Poyant, Rob Pyles, Lisa Reefe, David Sanford, Maureen Strout and Carol Ward. In-house, thanks to Jay Cooke, Holly Alexander and Joanne Newell.

Alex Hershey First, I have Jay 'tap tap' Cooke to thank for letting me jump aboard. My father, Robert D Hershey Jr, shared with me his home, car, computer, cell phone, and journalistic savvy. Coordinating author Kim Grant steered this schooner with panache. Ingrid Edstrom & Co poured on the hospitality and poured out the dirt on the Pioneer Valley. Thanks to David in Worcester for the scoop on the city's dining scene. Krist Muroya kept the home fires burning and the roaches squashed. To TGOS, just because. Finally, I dedicate my chapters of this book to my mother, Joyce Nelson Hershey.

John Spelman Many thanks go to my Rhode Island based family, without whom I would know nothing about Benny's or ice-cream; to Devin for the Worcester help; to Dell Upton for a much needed extension; to Forest and his very accommodating roommate; to Robert for once again joining me on the road; and to my kick-ass teammates, Jay, Holly and Kim for their superb work and kindness. Thanks especially to Lisa for setting up shop in a hot, lonely city while I slept on countless beaches conducting my 'research.'

Mara Vorhees Thank you to Jay Cooke for this wonderful opportunity to be a traveler in my own backyard. Back in New England, Gordon and Helene Moodie welcomed me into their beautiful home in true Moodie style. I am grateful to Chris Saccardi, for many tips on diners (and other things) in Hanover, and to Colin Maclay, my man on the ground in Salem. Scotty B, thanks for too many things to mention, but especially your limitless supply of Boston trivia and your sheer enthusiasm for your hometown. Most of all, thank you Jerzy for bringing me to Boston and sharing my happy home.

CREDITS

New England 4 was commissioned and developed in Lonely Planet's Oakland office by Jay Cooke. Cartography for this guide was developed by Alison Lyall. Production was coordinated by Holly Alexander (editorial) and Emma McNicol (cartography). Overseeing production were Ray Thomson and Celia Wood (project managers).

Editorial assistance was provided by Joanne Newell, Kristin Odijk, Brooke Lyons, Suzannah Shwer, Fionnuala Twomey, Simon Williamson, Katie Lynch, Piers Kelly and Andrea Dobbin. Cartographic assistance was provided by Piotr Czajkowski, Anthony Phelan, Daniel Fennessey, Corey Hutchinson and Owen Eszeki. Technical support for maps was provided by Lachlan Ross and Chris LeeAck.

The book was laid out by Jacqui Saunders, with assistance from Jacqueline Mcleod and Laura Jane. The cover was designed by Candice Jacobus. Special thanks go to Vivek Wagle for his awesome work on the Highlights chapter. Huge thanks to Melanie Dankel and Kerryn Burgess for their support.

SEND US YOUR FEEDBACK

We love to hear from travelers – your comments keep us on our toes and help make our books better. Our well-travelled team reads every word on what you loved or loathed about this book. Although we cannot reply individually to postal submissions, we always guarantee that your feedback goes straight to the appropriate authors, in time for the next edition. Each person who sends us information is thanked in the next edition – and the most useful submissions are rewarded with a free book.

To send us your updates – and find out about Lonely Planet events, newsletters and travel news – visit our award-winning website: **www.lonelyplanet.com/feedback**

Note: We may edit, reproduce and incorporate your comments in Lonely Planet products such as guidebooks, websites and digital products, so let us know if you don't want your comments reproduced or your name acknowledged. For a copy of our privacy policy visit www.lonelyplanet.com/privacy

THANKS from Lonely Planet

Many thanks to the following travelers who used the last edition and wrote to us with helpful hints, useful advice and interesting anecdotes.

Hilmir Asgeirsson, Rutger Beekelaar, Avi Beigelman, Rosemarie Brickley, Cletus Coble, Jenny Cooper, John Deacon, Louise Dillon, Mark Firmstone, Jessica Gregory, James Jordan, Michael Kent, Stephan Klink, Susan Lavender, Renny Loisel, Elke Moritz, Sonia Ortiz, Linda Paisley, Pamela Paull, M Rehorst, Sara Robinson, Gloria Ser, Priya Shah, Nadine Spitz, Kerry Strayer, Eric Thomsen, Karine Verquin, Vicki Wilhite

ACKNOWLEDGMENTS

Many thanks to the following for the use of their content:

Globe on back cover © Mountain High Maps 1993 Digital Wisdom, Inc.

Massachusetts Bay Transportation Authority subway map © MBTA 2004.

BEHIND THE SCENES

Index

000 Map pages
000 Location of colour photographs

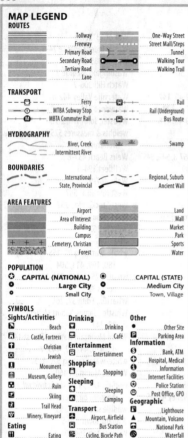

LONELY PLANET OFFICES

Australia
Head Office
Locked Bag 1, Footscray, Victoria 3011
☎ 03 8379 8000, fax 03 8379 8111
talk2us@lonelyplanet.com.au

USA
150 Linden St, Oakland, CA 94607
☎ 510 893 8555, toll free 800 275 8555
fax 510 893 8572, info@lonelyplanet.com

UK
72-82 Rosebery Ave,
Clerkenwell, London EC1R 4RW
☎ 020 7841 9000, fax 020 7841 9001
go@lonelyplanet.co.uk

Published by Lonely Planet Publications Pty Ltd
ABN 36 005 607 983

© Lonely Planet 2005

© photographers as indicated 2005

Cover photographs by Lonely Planet Images: the New Hampshire Covered Bridge #39, also known as the Flume Bridge, built in 1871, Mark Newman (front); Wet weather wooden carvings in wellies for sale in Maine, Kim Grant (back). Many of the images in this guide are available for licensing from Lonely Planet Images: www.lonelyplanetimages.com

Printed through Colorcraft Ltd, Hong Kong.
Printed in China